THE ART OF
COMPUTER PROGRAMMING

DONALD E. KNUTH *Stanford University*

ADDISON–WESLEY

Volume 4B / **Combinatorial Algorithms, Part 2**

THE ART OF
COMPUTER PROGRAMMING

Boston · Columbus · New York · San Francisco · Amsterdam · Cape Town
Dubai · London · Madrid · Milan · Munich · Paris · Montréal · Toronto · Delhi · Mexico City
São Paulo · Sydney · Hong Kong · Seoul · Singapore · Taipei · Tokyo

Lyrics have been quoted on page 65 from the songs "Mississippi Mud," written by Harry Barris and James Cavanaugh, and "Pick Yourself Up," written by Dorothy Fields and Jerome Kern. Used by permission of Shapiro, Bernstein & Co, Inc.

For government sales inquiries, please contact governmentsales@pearsoned.com
For questions about sales outside the U.S., please contact intlcs@pearson.com

Visit us on the Web: informit.com/aw

Library of Congress Cataloging-in-Publication Data
Knuth, Donald Ervin, 1938-
  The art of computer programming / Donald Ervin Knuth.
  xviii,714 p. 24 cm.
  Includes bibliographical references and index.
  Contents: v. 1. Fundamental algorithms. -- v. 2. Seminumerical
algorithms. -- v. 3. Sorting and searching. -- v. 4a. Combinatorial
algorithms, part 1. -- v. 4b. Combinatorial algorithms, part 2.
  Contents: v. 4b. Combinatorial algorithms, part 2.
  ISBN 978-0-201-89683-1 (v. 1, 3rd ed.)
  ISBN 978-0-201-89684-8 (v. 2, 3rd ed.)
  ISBN 978-0-201-89685-5 (v. 3, 2nd ed.)
  ISBN 978-0-201-03804-0 (v. 4a)
  ISBN 978-0-201-03806-4 (v. 4b)
  1. Electronic digital computers--Programming. 2. Computer
algorithms.   I. Title.
QA76.6.K64 1997
005.1--DC21   97-2147

Internet page http://www-cs-faculty.stanford.edu/~knuth/taocp.html contains current information about this book and related books.

See also http://www-cs-faculty.stanford.edu/~knuth/sgb.html for information about *The Stanford GraphBase*, including downloadable software for dealing with the graphs used in many of the examples.

And see http://www-cs-faculty.stanford.edu/~knuth/mmix.html for basic information about the MMIX computer.

ISBN-13 978-0-201-03806-4
ISBN-10   0-201-03806-4

First printing, October 2022

2 2022

PREFACE

Begin at the beginning, and do not allow yourself to gratify
a mere idle curiosity by dipping into the book, here and there.
This would very likely lead to your throwing it aside,
with the remark "This is much too hard for me!",
and thus losing the chance of adding a very large item
to your stock of mental delights.

— LEWIS CARROLL, in *Symbolic Logic* (1896)

COMBINATORIAL ALGORITHMS are the methods that allow us to cope with problems that involve zillions of cases. The explosive growth in the knowledge of such techniques has meant that several volumes are needed to describe them. Thus my original plan to devote Volume 4 of *The Art of Computer Programming* to combinatorial algorithms has morphed into a plan to prepare Volumes 4A, 4B, and so on. This book is the second of that series, a sequel to Volume 4A.

In the preface to Volume 4A I explained why I was captivated by combinatorial algorithms soon after I fell in love with computers. "The art of writing such programs is especially important and appealing because a single good idea can save years or even centuries of computer time."

Chapter 7 began in Volume 4A with a short review of graph theory and a longer discussion of "Zeros and Ones" (Section 7.1). That volume concluded with Section 7.2.1, "Generating Basic Combinatorial Patterns," which was the first part of Section 7.2, "Generating All Possibilities." Now the story continues, with the opening parts of Section 7.2.2, "Backtrack Programming."

Backtracking is the name for an important body of techniques that have been a mainstay of combinatorial algorithms since the beginning. More than a third of this book is devoted to Section 7.2.2.1, which explores data structures whose links perform delightful dances. Such structures are ideally suited to backtrack programming in general, and to the "exact cover problem" (XC) in particular. The XC problem, also known as "set partitioning," essentially asks for all ways to cover a set of *items*, by choosing appropriate subsets of items called *options*. Dozens of important applications turn out to be special cases of XC, and the method of choice for such problems is often to use dancing links.

While writing this material I learned to my surprise that an apparently innocuous extension of the classical XC problem leads to an enormous increase in the number of significant special cases. This extended problem, called XCC (for "exact covering with colors"), allows some of the items to receive various colors. Colored items are allowed to be covered by many different options, as long as the colors are compatible.

v

Spoiler alert: With dancing links, we can solve XCC problems almost as easily as XC problems! Therefore I believe that the study of XCC solvers, now in its infancy, is destined to become quite important, and I've done my best to introduce the subject here. There also are related methods for an even more general class of problems called MCC ("multiple covering with colors"), and for finding XCC solutions of *minimum cost*.

If you turn to a random page of Section 7.2.2.1, chances are good that you'll find some sort of *puzzle* being discussed. The reason is that puzzles are by far the best means I know to illustrate the algorithms and techniques that are being introduced here. The point of a puzzle is easily grasped; and the fact that an extraordinary number of quite different puzzles all turn out to be special cases of XCC and MCC is significant in itself. Indeed, it becomes clear that the same ideas will solve many complex and harder-to-explain problems of the "real world."

The new tools provided by dancing links allow me to emphasize the process of creating *new* puzzles, rather than simply to explain how to resolve puzzles that have already been posed. I've also tried my best to discuss the history of each puzzle type, and to give credit to the brilliant innovators who created them. As a result, I'm pleased that this book now contains, as a side-product of my attempts to teach computer methods, a treasure trove of information about recreational mathematics — from popular classics like edge-matching puzzles, or queen placement, or polyominoes, or the Soma cube, or rectangle dissections, or intriguing patterns of interlocking words, to more recent crazes like sudoku, slitherlink, masyu, and hitori.

I've had loads of fun writing other parts of these volumes, but without doubt Section 7.2.2.1 has been the funnest. And I know that my delight in good puzzles is shared by a significant number of leading computer scientists and mathematicians, who have told me that they chose their careers after having been inspired by such intellectual challenges.

> *Knuth likes to include in those books* [The Art of Computer Programming]
> *as much recreational material as he can cram in.*
> — MARTIN GARDNER, *Undiluted Hocus-Pocus* (2013)

The second half of this book is devoted to Section 7.2.2.2, "Satisfiability," which addresses one of the most fundamental problems in all of computer science: Given a Boolean function, can its variables be set to at least one pattern of 0s and 1s that will make the function true? This problem arises so often, people have given it a nickname, 'SAT'.

Satisfiability might seem like an abstract exercise in understanding formal systems, but the truth is far different: Revolutionary methods for solving SAT problems emerged at the beginning of the twenty-first century, and they've led to game-changing applications in industry. These so-called "SAT solvers" can now routinely find solutions to practical problems that involve millions of variables and were thought until very recently to be hopelessly difficult.

Satisfiability is important chiefly because Boolean algebra is so versatile. Almost any problem can be formulated in terms of basic logical operations, and the formulation is particularly simple in a great many cases. Section 7.2.2.2 therefore begins with ten typical examples of widely different applications, and closes with detailed empirical results for a hundred different benchmarks. The great variety of these problems — all of which are special cases of SAT — is illustrated on pages 300 and 301 (which are my favorite pages in this book).

The story of satisfiability is the tale of a triumph of software engineering, blended with rich doses of beautiful mathematics. Section 7.2.2.2 explains how such a miracle occurred, by presenting complete details of seven SAT solvers, ranging from the small-footprint methods of Algorithms A and B to the industrial strength, state-of-the-art methods of Algorithms W, L, and C. (Well I have to hedge a little: New techniques are continually being discovered; hence SAT technology is ever-growing and the story is ongoing. But I do think that Algorithms W, L, and C compare reasonably well with the best algorithms of their class that were known in 2010. They're no longer at the cutting edge, but they still are amazingly good.)

Wow — Sections 7.2.2.1 and 7.2.2.2 have turned out to be the longest sections, by far, in *The Art of Computer Programming* — especially Section 7.2.2.2. The SAT problem is evidently a killer app, because it is key to the solution of so many other problems. Consequently I can only hope that my lengthy treatment does not also kill off my faithful readers! As I wrote this material, one topic always seemed to flow naturally into another, so there was no neat way to break either section up into separate subsections. (And anyway the format of TAOCP doesn't allow for a Section 7.2.2.1.3 or a Section 7.2.2.2.6.)

I've tried to ameliorate the reader's navigation problem by adding subheadings at the top of each right-hand page. Furthermore, as always, the exercises appear in an order that roughly parallels the order in which corresponding topics are taken up in the text. Numerous cross-references are provided between text, exercises, and illustrations, so that you have a fairly good chance of keeping in sync. I've also tried to make the index as comprehensive as possible.

Look, for example, at a "random" page — say page 264, which is part of the subsection about Monte Carlo algorithms. On that page you'll see that exercises 302, 303, 299, and 306 are mentioned. So you can guess that the main exercises about Monte Carlo algorithms are numbered in the early 300s. (Indeed, exercise 306 deals with the important special case of "Las Vegas algorithms"; and the next exercises explore a fascinating concept called "reluctant doubling.") This entire book is full of surprises and tie-ins to other aspects of computer science.

As in previous volumes, sections and subsections of the text are occasionally preceded by an asterisk ($*$), meaning that the topics discussed there are "advanced" and skippable on a first reading.

You might think that a 700-page book has probably been padded with peripheral material. But I constantly had to "cut, cut, cut" while writing it, because a great deal more is known! I found that new and potentially interesting-yet-unexplored topics kept popping up, more than enough to fill a lifetime; yet I knew that I must move on. So I hope that I've selected for treatment here a significant fraction of the concepts that will be the most important as time passes.

Every week I've been coming across fascinating new things
that simply cry out to be part of The Art.
— DONALD E. KNUTH (2008)

Most of this book is self-contained, although there are frequent tie-ins with the topics discussed in previous volumes. Low-level details of machine language programming have already been covered extensively; so the algorithms in the present book are usually specified only at an abstract level, independent of any machine. However, some aspects of combinatorial programming are heavily dependent on low-level details that didn't arise before; in such cases, all examples in this book are based on the MMIX computer, which supersedes the MIX machine that was defined in early editions of Volume 1. Details about MMIX appear in a paperback supplement to that volume called *The Art of Computer Programming*, Volume 1, Fascicle 1, containing Sections 1.3.1′, 1.3.2′, etc.; they're also available on the Internet, together with downloadable assemblers and simulators.

Another downloadable resource, a collection of programs and data called *The Stanford GraphBase*, is cited extensively in the examples of this book. Readers are encouraged to play with it, in order to learn about combinatorial algorithms in what I think will be the most efficient and most enjoyable way.

I wrote nearly a thousand computer programs while preparing this material, because I find that I don't understand things unless I try to program them. Most of those programs were quite short, of course; but several of them are rather substantial, and possibly of interest to others. Therefore I've made a selection available by listing some of them on the following webpage:

http://www-cs-faculty.stanford.edu/~knuth/programs.html

In particular you can download the programs DLX1, DLX2, DLX3, DLX5, DLX6, and DLX-PRE, which are the experimental versions of Algorithms X, C, M, C$, Z, and P, respectively, that were my constant companions while writing Section 7.2.2.1. Similarly, SAT0, SAT0W, SAT8, SAT9, SAT10, SAT11, SAT11K, SAT13 are the equivalents of Algorithms A, B, W, S, D, L, L′, C, respectively, in Section 7.2.2.2. Such programs will be useful for solving many of the exercises, if you don't have access to other XCC solvers or SAT solvers. You can also download SATexamples.tgz from that page; it's a collection of programs that generate data for all 100 of the benchmark examples discussed in the text, and many more.

Several exercises involve the lists of English words that I've used in preparing examples. You'll need the data from

http://www-cs-faculty.stanford.edu/~knuth/wordlists.tgz

if you have the courage to work the exercises that use such lists.

Special Note: During the years that I've been preparing Volume 4, I've often run across basic techniques of probability theory that I would have put into Section 1.2 of Volume 1 if I'd been clairvoyant enough to anticipate them in the 1960s. Finally I realized that I ought to collect most of them together in one place, because the story of those developments is too interesting to be broken up into little pieces scattered here and there.

Therefore this book begins with a special tutorial and review of probability theory, in an unnumbered section entitled "Mathematical Preliminaries Redux." References to its equations and exercises use the abbreviation 'MPR'. (Think of the word "improvement.")

Incidentally, just after the special MPR section, Section 7.2.2 begins intentionally on a left-hand page; and its illustrations are numbered beginning with Fig. 68. The reason is that Section 7.2.1 ended in Volume 4A on a right-hand page, and its final illustration was Fig. 67. My editor has decided to treat Chapter 7 as a single unit, even though it is being split into several physical volumes.

Special thanks are due to Nikolai Beluhov, Armin Biere, Niklas Eén, Marijn Heule, Holger Hoos, Wei-Hwa Huang, Svante Janson, Ernst Schulte-Geers, George Sicherman, Filip Stappers, and Udo Wermuth, for their detailed comments on my early attempts at exposition, as well as to dozens and dozens of other correspondents who have contributed crucial corrections. My editor at Addison–Wesley, Mark Taub, has expertly shepherded this series of books into the 21st century; and Julie Nahil, as senior content producer, has meticulously ensured that the highest publication standards have continued to be maintained. Thanks also to Tomas Rokicki for keeping my Dell workstation in shipshape order, as well as to Stanford's InfoLab for providing extra computer power when that machine had reached its limits.

I happily offer a "finder's fee" of $2.56 for each error in this book when it is first reported to me, whether that error be typographical, technical, or historical. The same reward holds for items that I forgot to put in the index. And valuable suggestions for improvements to the text are worth 32¢ each. (Furthermore, if you find a better solution to an exercise, I'll actually do my best to give you immortal glory, by publishing your name in subsequent printings:–)

Happy reading!

Stanford, California   D. E. K.
June 2022

A note on references. Several oft-cited journals and conference proceedings have special code names, which appear in the Index and Glossary at the close of this book. But the various kinds of *IEEE Transactions* are cited by including a letter code for the type of transactions, in boldface preceding the volume number. For example, '*IEEE Trans.* **C-35**' means the *IEEE Transactions on Computers*, volume 35. The IEEE no longer uses these convenient letter codes, but the codes aren't too hard to decipher: '**EC**' once stood for "Electronic Computers," '**IT**' for "Information Theory," '**PAMI**' for "Pattern Analysis and Machine Intelligence," and '**SE**' for "Software Engineering," etc.; '**CAD**' meant "Computer-Aided Design of Integrated Circuits and Systems."

A cross-reference such as 'exercise 7.10–00' points to a future exercise in Section 7.10 whose number is not yet known.

A note on notations. Simple and intuitive conventions for the algebraic representation of mathematical concepts have always been a boon to progress, especially when most of the world's researchers share a common symbolic language. The current state of affairs in combinatorial mathematics is unfortunately a bit of a mess in this regard, because the same symbols are occasionally used with completely different meanings by different groups of people; some specialists who work in comparatively narrow subfields have unintentionally spawned conflicting symbolisms. Computer science — which interacts with large swaths of mathematics — needs to steer clear of this danger by adopting internally consistent notations whenever possible. Therefore I've often had to choose among a number of competing schemes, knowing that it will be impossible to please everyone. I have tried my best to come up with notations that I believe will be best for the future, often after many years of experimentation and discussion with colleagues, often flip-flopping between alternatives until finding something that works well. Usually it has been possible to find convenient conventions that other people have not already coopted in contradictory ways.

Appendix B is a comprehensive index to all of the principal notations that are used in the present book, inevitably including several that are not (yet?) standard. If you run across a formula that looks weird and/or incomprehensible, chances are fairly good that Appendix B will direct you to a page where my intentions are clarified. But I might as well list here a few instances that you might wish to watch for when you read this book for the first time:

- Hexadecimal constants are preceded by a number sign or hash mark. For example, $^\#123$ means $(123)_{16}$.
- The "monus" operation $x \mathbin{\dot-} y$, sometimes called dot-minus or saturating subtraction, yields $\max(0, x - y)$.
- The median of three numbers $\{x, y, z\}$ is denoted by $\langle xyz \rangle$.
- The "two dots" notations $(x \mathinner{.\,.} y)$, $(x \mathinner{.\,.} y]$, $[x \mathinner{.\,.} y)$, and $[x \mathinner{.\,.} y]$ are used to denote intervals.
- A set such as $\{x\}$, which consists of a single element, is often denoted simply by x in contexts such as $X \cup x$ or $X \setminus x$.
- If n is a nonnegative integer, the number of 1-bits in n's binary representation is νn. Furthermore, if $n > 0$, the leftmost and rightmost 1-bits of n are respectively $2^{\lambda n}$ and $2^{\rho n}$. For example, $\nu 10 = 2$, $\lambda 10 = 3$, $\rho 10 = 1$.
- The Cartesian product of graphs G and H is denoted by $G \square H$. For example, $C_m \square C_n$ denotes an $m \times n$ torus, because C_n denotes a cycle of n vertices.

NOTES ON THE EXERCISES

THE EXERCISES in this set of books have been designed for self-study as well as for classroom study. It is difficult, if not impossible, for anyone to learn a subject purely by reading about it, without applying the information to specific problems and thereby being encouraged to think about what has been read. Furthermore, we all learn best the things that we have discovered for ourselves. Therefore the exercises form a major part of this work; a definite attempt has been made to keep them as informative as possible and to select problems that are enjoyable as well as instructive.

In many books, easy exercises are found mixed randomly among extremely difficult ones. A motley mixture is, however, often unfortunate because readers like to know in advance how long a problem ought to take — otherwise they may just skip over all the problems. A classic example of such a situation is the book *Dynamic Programming* by Richard Bellman; this is an important, pioneering work in which a group of problems is collected together at the end of some chapters under the heading "Exercises and Research Problems," with extremely trivial questions appearing in the midst of deep, unsolved problems. It is rumored that someone once asked Dr. Bellman how to tell the exercises apart from the research problems, and he replied, "If you can solve it, it is an exercise; otherwise it's a research problem."

Good arguments can be made for including both research problems and very easy exercises in a book of this kind; therefore, to save the reader from the possible dilemma of determining which are which, *rating numbers* have been provided to indicate the level of difficulty. These numbers have the following general significance:

Rating   Interpretation

00   An extremely easy exercise that can be answered immediately if the material of the text has been understood; such an exercise can almost always be worked "in your head," unless you're multitasking.

10   A simple problem that makes you think over the material just read, but is by no means difficult. You should be able to do this in one minute at most; pencil and paper may be useful in obtaining the solution.

20   An average problem that tests basic understanding of the text material, but you may need about fifteen or twenty minutes to answer it completely. Maybe even twenty-five.

30 A problem of moderate difficulty and/or complexity; this one may involve more than two hours' work to solve satisfactorily, or even more if the TV is on.

40 Quite a difficult or lengthy problem that would be suitable for a term project in classroom situations. A student should be able to solve the problem in a reasonable amount of time, but the solution is not trivial.

50 A research problem that has not yet been solved satisfactorily, as far as the author knew at the time of writing, although many people have tried. If you have found an answer to such a problem, you ought to write it up for publication; furthermore, the author of this book would appreciate hearing about the solution as soon as possible (provided that it is correct).

By interpolation in this "logarithmic" scale, the significance of other rating numbers becomes clear. For example, a rating of *17* would indicate an exercise that is a bit simpler than average. Problems with a rating of *50* that are subsequently solved by some reader may appear with a *40* rating in later editions of the book, and in the errata posted on the Internet (see page iv).

The remainder of the rating number divided by 5 indicates the amount of detailed work required. Thus, an exercise rated *24* may take longer to solve than an exercise that is rated *25*, but the latter will require more creativity. All exercises with ratings of *46* or more are open problems for future research, rated according to the number of different attacks that they've resisted so far.

The author has tried earnestly to assign accurate rating numbers, but it is difficult for the person who makes up a problem to know just how formidable it will be for someone else to find a solution; and everyone has more aptitude for certain types of problems than for others. It is hoped that the rating numbers represent a good guess at the level of difficulty, but they should be taken as general guidelines, not as absolute indicators.

This book has been written for readers with varying degrees of mathematical training and sophistication; as a result, some of the exercises are intended only for the use of more mathematically inclined readers. The rating is preceded by an *M* if the exercise involves mathematical concepts or motivation to a greater extent than necessary for someone who is primarily interested only in programming the algorithms themselves. An exercise is marked with the letters "*HM*" if its solution necessarily involves a knowledge of calculus or other higher mathematics not developed in this book. An "*HM*" designation does *not* necessarily imply difficulty.

Some exercises are preceded by an arrowhead, "▶"; this designates problems that are especially instructive and especially recommended. Of course, no reader/student is expected to work *all* of the exercises, so those that seem to be the most valuable have been singled out. (This distinction is not meant to detract from the other exercises!) Each reader should at least make an attempt to solve all of the problems whose rating is *10* or less; and the arrows may help to indicate which of the problems with a higher rating should be given priority.

Several sections have more than 100 exercises. How can you find your way among so many? In general the sequence of exercises tends to follow the sequence of ideas in the main text. Adjacent exercises build on each other, as in the pioneering problem books of Pólya and Szegő. The final exercises of a section often involve the section as a whole, or introduce supplementary topics.

Solutions to most of the exercises appear in the answer section. Please use them wisely; do not turn to the answer until you have made a genuine effort to solve the problem by yourself, or unless you absolutely do not have time to work this particular problem. *After* getting your own solution or giving the problem a decent try, you may find the answer instructive and helpful. The solution given will often be quite short, and it will sketch the details under the assumption that you have earnestly tried to solve it by your own means first. Sometimes the solution gives less information than was asked; often it gives more. It is quite possible that you may have a better answer than the one published here, or you may have found an error in the published solution; in such a case, the author will be pleased to know the details. Later printings of this book will give the improved solutions together with the solver's name where appropriate.

When working an exercise you may generally use the answers to previous exercises, unless specifically forbidden from doing so. The rating numbers have been assigned with this in mind; thus it is possible for exercise $n + 1$ to have a lower rating than exercise n, even though it includes the result of exercise n as a special case.

Summary of codes:		00	Immediate
		10	Simple (one minute)
		20	Medium (quarter hour)
▶	Recommended	30	Moderately hard
M	Mathematically oriented	40	Term project
HM	Requiring "higher math"	50	Research problem

EXERCISES

▶ **1.** [*00*] What does the rating "*M15*" mean?

2. [*10*] Of what value can the exercises in a textbook be to the reader?

3. [*HM45*] Prove that every simply connected, closed 3-dimensional manifold is topologically equivalent to a 3-dimensional sphere.

The men that stood for office, noted for acknowledged worth,
And for manly deeds of honour, and for honourable birth;
Train'd in exercise and art, in sacred dances and in song,
All are ousted and supplanted by a base ignoble throng.
— ARISTOPHANES, *The Frogs* (405 B.C.)

> *Here mine aduice, shall be to those Artificers that will profite in this,*
> *or any of my bookes nowe published, or that hereafter shall be,*
> *firste confusely to reade them thorow; then with more iudgement,*
> *and at the thirde readinge wittely to practise. So fewe thinges shall be vnknowen.*
>
> — LEONARDE DIGGES, *A Boke named Tectonicon* (1556)

> *Now I saw, tho' too late, the Folly of*
> *beginning a Work before we count the Cost,*
> *and before we judge rightly of our own Strength to go through with it.*
>
> — DANIEL DEFOE, *Robinson Crusoe* (1719)

CONTENTS

> *We — or the Black Chamber — have a little agreement with [Knuth];*
> *he doesn't publish the real Volume 4 of* The Art of Computer Programming,
> *and they don't render him metabolically challenged.*
>
> — CHARLES STROSS, *The Atrocity Archive* (2001)

> *In books of this nature I can only suggest you keep it*
> *as simple as the subject will allow.*
>
> — KODE VICIOUS (2012)

MATHEMATICAL PRELIMINARIES REDUX

MANY PARTS of this book deal with *discrete probabilities*, namely with a finite or countably infinite set Ω of atomic events ω, each of which has a given probability $\Pr(\omega)$, where

$$0 \leq \Pr(\omega) \leq 1 \qquad \text{and} \qquad \sum_{\omega \in \Omega} \Pr(\omega) = 1. \qquad (1)$$

This set Ω, together with the function Pr, is called a "probability space." For example, Ω might be the set of all ways to shuffle a pack of 52 playing cards, with $\Pr(\omega) = 1/52!$ for every such arrangement.

An *event* is, intuitively, a proposition that can be either true or false with certain probability. It might, for instance, be the statement "the top card is an ace," with probability $1/13$. Formally, an event A is a subset of Ω, namely the set of all atomic events for which the corresponding proposition A is true; and

$$\Pr(A) \;=\; \sum_{\omega \in A} \Pr(\omega) \;=\; \sum_{\omega \in \Omega} \Pr(\omega)[\omega \in A]. \qquad (2)$$

A *random variable* is a function that assigns a value to every atomic event. We typically use uppercase letters for random variables, and lowercase letters for the values that they might assume; thus, we might say that the probability of the event $X = x$ is $\Pr(X = x) = \sum_{\omega \in \Omega} \Pr(\omega)[X(\omega) = x]$. In our playing card example, the top card T is a random variable, and we have $\Pr(T = \text{Q}\spadesuit) = 1/52$. (Sometimes, as here, the lowercase-letter convention is ignored.)

The random variables $X_1, \ldots, X_k$ are said to be *independent* if

$$\Pr(X_1 = x_1 \text{ and } \cdots \text{ and } X_k = x_k) \;=\; \Pr(X_1 = x_1) \ldots \Pr(X_k = x_k) \qquad (3)$$

for all $(x_1, \ldots, x_k)$. For example, if F and S denote the face value and suit of the top card T, clearly F and S are independent. Hence in particular we have $\Pr(T = \text{Q}\spadesuit) = \Pr(F = \text{Q}) \Pr(S = \spadesuit)$. But T is *not* independent of the bottom card, B; indeed, we have $\Pr(T = t \text{ and } B = b) \neq 1/52^2$ for *any* cards t and b.

A system of n random variables is called k-wise independent if no k of its variables are dependent. With pairwise (2-wise) independence, for example, we could have variable X independent of Y, variable Y independent of Z, and variable Z independent of X; yet all three variables needn't be independent (see exercise 6). Similarly, k-wise independence does not imply $(k+1)$-wise independence. But $(k+1)$-wise independence does imply k-wise independence.

The *conditional probability* of an event A, given an event B, is

$$\Pr(A \mid B) \;=\; \frac{\Pr(A \cap B)}{\Pr(B)} \;=\; \frac{\Pr(A \text{ and } B)}{\Pr(B)}, \qquad (4)$$

when $\Pr(B) > 0$, otherwise it's $\Pr(A)$. Imagine breaking the whole space Ω into two parts, $\Omega' = B$ and $\Omega'' = \overline{B} = \Omega \setminus B$, with $\Pr(\Omega') = \Pr(B)$ and $\Pr(\Omega'') = 1 - \Pr(B)$. If $0 < \Pr(B) < 1$, and if we assign new probabilities by the rules

$$\Pr{}'(\omega) = \Pr(\omega | \Omega') = \frac{\Pr(\omega)[\omega \in \Omega']}{\Pr(\Omega')}, \quad \Pr{}''(\omega) = \Pr(\omega | \Omega'') = \frac{\Pr(\omega)[\omega \in \Omega'']}{\Pr(\Omega'')},$$

we obtain new probability spaces Ω' and Ω'', allowing us to contemplate a world where B is always true and another world where B is always false. It's like taking two branches in a tree, each of which has its own logic. Conditional probability is important for the analysis of algorithms because algorithms often get into different states where different probabilities are relevant. Notice that we always have

$$\Pr(A) = \Pr(A|B) \cdot \Pr(B) + \Pr(A|\overline{B}) \cdot \Pr(\overline{B}). \tag{5}$$

The events $A_1, \ldots, A_k$ are said to be independent if the random variables $[A_1], \ldots, [A_k]$ are independent. (Bracket notation applies in the usual way to events-as-statements, not just to events-as-subsets: $[A] = 1$ if A is true, otherwise $[A] = 0$.) Exercise 20 proves that this happens if and only if

$$\Pr\left(\bigcap_{j \in J} A_j\right) = \prod_{j \in J} \Pr(A_j), \quad \text{for all } J \subseteq \{1, \ldots, k\}. \tag{6}$$

In particular, events A and B are independent if and only if $\Pr(A|B) = \Pr(A)$.

When the values of a random variable X are real numbers or complex numbers, we've defined its *expected value* $\mathrm{E}\,X$ in Section 1.2.10: We said that

$$\mathrm{E}\,X = \sum_{\omega \in \Omega} X(\omega)\Pr(\omega) = \sum_x x\Pr(X = x), \tag{7}$$

provided that this definition makes sense when the sums are taken over infinitely many nonzero values. (The sum should be absolutely convergent.) A simple but extremely important case arises when A is any event, and when $X = [A]$ is a binary random variable representing the truth of that event; then

$$\mathrm{E}[A] = \sum_{\omega \in \Omega} [A](\omega)\Pr(\omega) = \sum_{\omega \in \Omega} [\omega \in A]\Pr(\omega) = \sum_{\omega \in A} \Pr(\omega) = \Pr(A). \tag{8}$$

We've also noted that the expectation of a sum, $\mathrm{E}(X_1 + \cdots + X_k)$, always equals the sum of the expectations, $(\mathrm{E}\,X_1) + \cdots + (\mathrm{E}\,X_k)$, whether or not the random variables X_j are independent. Furthermore the expectation of a product, $\mathrm{E}\,X_1 \ldots X_k$, is the product of the expectations, $(\mathrm{E}\,X_1) \ldots (\mathrm{E}\,X_k)$, if those variables do happen to be independent. In Section 3.3.2 we defined the covariance,

$$\mathrm{covar}(X, Y) = \mathrm{E}\big((X - \mathrm{E}\,X)(Y - \mathrm{E}\,Y)\big) = (\mathrm{E}\,XY) - (\mathrm{E}\,X)(\mathrm{E}\,Y), \tag{9}$$

which tends to measure the way X and Y depend on each other. The variance, $\mathrm{var}(X)$, is $\mathrm{covar}(X, X)$; the middle formula in (9) shows why it is nonnegative whenever the random variable X takes on only real values.

All of these notions of expected value carry over to *conditional expectation*,

$$\mathrm{E}(X \,|\, A) = \sum_{\omega \in A} X(\omega)\frac{\Pr(\omega)}{\Pr(A)} = \sum_x x\frac{\Pr(X = x \text{ and } A)}{\Pr(A)}, \tag{10}$$

conditioned on any event A, when we want to work in the probability space for which A is true. (If $\Pr(A) = 0$, we define $\mathrm{E}(X \mid A) = \mathrm{E}X$.) One of the most important formulas, analogous to (5), is

$$\mathrm{E}X = \sum_y \mathrm{E}(X \mid Y=y) \Pr(Y=y)$$

$$= \sum_y \sum_x x \Pr(X=x \mid Y=y) \Pr(Y=y). \tag{11}$$

Furthermore there's also another important kind of conditional expectation: When X and Y are random variables, it's often helpful to write '$\mathrm{E}(X \mid Y)$' for "the expectation of X given Y." Using that notation, Eq. (11) becomes simply

$$\mathrm{E}X = \mathrm{E}\big(\mathrm{E}(X \mid Y)\big). \tag{12}$$

This is a truly marvelous identity, great for hand-waving and for impressing outsiders — except that it can be confusing until you understand what it means.

In the first place, if Y is a Boolean variable, '$\mathrm{E}(X \mid Y)$' might look as if it means '$\mathrm{E}(X \mid Y=1)$', thus asserting that Y is true, just as '$\mathrm{E}(X \mid A)$' asserts the truth of A in (10). No; that interpretation is wrong, quite wrong. Be warned.

In the second place, you might think of $\mathrm{E}(X \mid Y)$ as a function of Y. Well, yes; but the best way to understand $\mathrm{E}(X \mid Y)$ is to regard it as a *random variable*. That's why we're allowed to compute its expected value in (12).

All random variables are functions of the atomic events ω. The value of $\mathrm{E}(X \mid Y)$ at ω is the average of $X(\omega')$ over all events ω' such that $Y(\omega') = Y(\omega)$:

$$\mathrm{E}(X \mid Y)(\omega) = \sum_{\omega' \in \Omega} X(\omega') \Pr(\omega')[Y(\omega') = Y(\omega)] / \Pr(Y = Y(\omega)). \tag{13}$$

Similarly, $\mathrm{E}(X \mid Y_1, \ldots, Y_r)$ averages over events with $Y_j(\omega') = Y_j(\omega)$ for $1 \le j \le r$.

For example, suppose X_1 through X_n are binary random variables constrained by the condition that $\nu(X_1 \ldots X_n) = X_1 + \cdots + X_n = m$, where m and n are constants with $0 \le m \le n$; all $\binom{n}{m}$ such bit vectors $X_1 \ldots X_n$ are assumed to be equally likely. Clearly $\mathrm{E}X_1 = m/n$. But what is $\mathrm{E}(X_2 \mid X_1)$? If $X_1 = 0$, the expectation of X_2 is $m/(n-1)$; otherwise that expectation is $(m-1)/(n-1)$; consequently $\mathrm{E}(X_2 \mid X_1) = (m - X_1)/(n-1)$. And what is $\mathrm{E}(X_k \mid X_1, \ldots, X_{k-1})$? The answer is easy, once you get used to the notation: If $\nu(X_1 \ldots X_{k-1}) = r$, then $X_k \ldots X_n$ is a random bit vector with $\nu(X_k \ldots X_n) = m - r$; hence the average value of X_k will be $(m-r)/(n+1-k)$ in that case. We conclude that

$$\mathrm{E}(X_k \mid X_1, \ldots, X_{k-1}) = \frac{m - \nu(X_1 \ldots X_{k-1})}{n + 1 - k}, \quad \text{for } 1 \le k \le n. \tag{14}$$

The random variables on both sides of these equations are the same.

Inequalities. In practice we often want to prove that certain events are rare, in the sense that they occur with very small probability. Conversely, our goal is sometimes to show that an event is *not* rare. And we're in luck, because mathematicians have devised several fairly easy ways to derive upper bounds or lower bounds on probabilities, even when the exact values are unknown.

We've already discussed the most important technique of this kind in Section 1.2.10. Stated in highly general terms, the basic idea can be formulated as follows: *Let f be any nonnegative function such that $f(x) \geq s > 0$ when $x \in S$. Then*

$$\Pr(X \in S) \leq \mathrm{E}\,f(X)/s, \tag{15}$$

provided that $\Pr(X \in S)$ and $\mathrm{E}\,f(X)$ both exist. For example, $f(x) = |x|$ yields

$$\Pr(|X| \geq m) \leq \mathrm{E}|X|/m \tag{16}$$

whenever $m > 0$. The proof is amazingly simple, because we obviously have

$$\mathrm{E}\,f(X) \geq \Pr(X \in S) \cdot s + \Pr(X \notin S) \cdot 0. \tag{17}$$

Formula (15) is often called *Markov's inequality*, because A. A. Markov discussed the special case $f(x) = |x|^a$ in *Izvîestîîā Imp. Akad. Nauk* (6) **1** (1907), 707–716. If we set $f(x) = (x - \mathrm{E}\,X)^2$, we get the famous 19th-century inequality of Bienaymé and Chebyshev:

$$\Pr\bigl(|X - \mathrm{E}\,X| \geq r\bigr) \leq \mathrm{var}(X)/r^2. \tag{18}$$

The case $f(x) = e^{ax}$ is also extremely useful.

Another fundamental estimate, known as *Jensen's inequality* [*Acta Mathematica* **30** (1906), 175–193], applies to *convex* functions f; we've seen it so far only as a "hint" to exercise 6.2.2–36(!). The real-valued function f is said to be convex in an interval I of the real line, and $-f$ is said to be concave in I, if

$$f(px + qy) \leq pf(x) + qf(y) \qquad \text{for all } x, y \in I, \tag{19}$$

whenever $p \geq 0$, $q \geq 0$, and $p+q = 1$. This condition turns out to be equivalent to saying that $f''(x) \geq 0$ for all $x \in I$, if f has a second derivative f''. For example, the functions e^{ax} and x^{2n} are convex for all constants a and all nonnegative integers n; and if we restrict consideration to positive values of x, then $f(x) = x^n$ is convex for *all* integers n (notably $f(x) = 1/x$ when $n = -1$). The functions $\ln(1/x)$ and $x \ln x$ are also convex for $x > 0$. Jensen's inequality states that

$$f(\mathrm{E}\,X) \leq \mathrm{E}\,f(X) \tag{20}$$

when f is convex in the interval I and the random variable X takes values only in I. (See exercise 42 for a proof.) For example, we have $1/\mathrm{E}\,X \leq \mathrm{E}(1/X)$ and $\ln \mathrm{E}\,X \geq \mathrm{E}\ln X$ and $(\mathrm{E}\,X)\ln \mathrm{E}\,X \leq \mathrm{E}(X \ln X)$, when X is positive, since the function $\ln x$ is concave for $x > 0$. Notice that (20) actually reduces to the very definition of convexity, (19), in the special case when $X = x$ with probability p and $X = y$ with probability $q = 1 - p$.

Next on our list of remarkably useful inequalities are two classical results that apply to any random variable X whose values are nonnegative integers:

$$\Pr(X > 0) \leq \mathrm{E}\,X; \qquad \text{("the first moment principle")} \tag{21}$$

$$\Pr(X > 0) \geq (\mathrm{E}\,X)^2 / (\mathrm{E}\,X^2). \qquad \text{("the second moment principle")} \tag{22}$$

Formula (21) is obvious, because the left side is $p_1 + p_2 + p_3 + \cdots$ when p_k is the probability that $X = k$, while the right side is $p_1 + 2p_2 + 3p_3 + \cdots$.

Formula (22) isn't quite so obvious; it is $p_1 + p_2 + p_3 + \cdots$ on the left and $(p_1 + 2p_2 + 3p_3 + \cdots)^2/(p_1 + 4p_2 + 9p_3 + \cdots)$ on the right. However, as we saw with Markov's inequality, there is a remarkably simple proof, once we happen to discover it: If X is nonnegative but not always zero, we have

$$\begin{aligned}
\mathrm{E}\,X^2 &= \mathrm{E}(X^2 \mid X > 0)\Pr(X > 0) + \mathrm{E}(X^2 \mid X = 0)\Pr(X = 0) \\
&= \mathrm{E}(X^2 \mid X > 0)\Pr(X > 0) \\
&\geq \left(\mathrm{E}(X \mid X > 0)\right)^2 \Pr(X > 0) = (\mathrm{E}\,X)^2/\Pr(X > 0).
\end{aligned} \tag{23}$$

In fact this proof shows that the second moment principle is valid even when X is not restricted to integer values (see exercise 46). Furthermore the argument can be strengthened to show that (22) holds even when X can take arbitrary *negative* values, provided only that $\mathrm{E}\,X \geq 0$ (see exercise 47). See also exercise 118.

Exercise 54 applies (21) and (22) to the study of random graphs.

Another important inequality, which applies in the special case where $X = X_1 + \cdots + X_m$ is the sum of *binary* random variables X_j, was introduced more recently by S. M. Ross [*Probability, Statistics, and Optimization* (New York: Wiley, 1994), 185–190], who calls it the "conditional expectation inequality":

$$\Pr(X > 0) \geq \sum_{j=1}^{m} \frac{\mathrm{E}\,X_j}{\mathrm{E}(X \mid X_j{=}1)}. \tag{24}$$

Ross showed that the right-hand side of this inequality is always at least as big as the bound $(\mathrm{E}\,X)^2/(\mathrm{E}\,X^2)$ that we get from the second moment principle (see exercise 50). Furthermore, (24) is often easier to compute, even though it may look more complicated at first glance.

For example, his method applies nicely to the problem of estimating a reliability polynomial, $f(p_1, \ldots, p_n)$, when f is a monotone Boolean function; here p_j represents the probability that component j of a system is "up." We observed in Section 7.1.4 that reliability polynomials can be evaluated exactly, using BDD methods, when n is reasonably small; but approximations are necessary when f gets complicated. The simple example $f(x_1, \ldots, x_5) = x_1 x_2 x_3 \vee x_2 x_3 x_4 \vee x_4 x_5$ illustrates Ross's general method: Let $(Y_1, \ldots, Y_5)$ be independent binary random variables, with $\mathrm{E}\,Y_j = p_j$; and let $X = X_1 + X_2 + X_3$, where $X_1 = Y_1 Y_2 Y_3$, $X_2 = Y_2 Y_3 Y_4$, and $X_3 = Y_4 Y_5$ correspond to the prime implicants of f. Then $\Pr(X > 0) = \Pr(f(Y_1, \ldots, Y_5) = 1) = \mathrm{E}\,f(Y_1, \ldots, Y_5) = f(p_1, \ldots, p_5)$, because the Y's are independent. And we can evaluate the bound in (24) easily:

$$\Pr(X > 0) \geq \frac{p_1 p_2 p_3}{1 + p_4 + p_4 p_5} + \frac{p_2 p_3 p_4}{p_1 + 1 + p_5} + \frac{p_4 p_5}{p_1 p_2 p_3 + p_2 p_3 + 1}. \tag{25}$$

If, for example, each p_j is 0.9, this formula gives ≈ 0.848, while $(\mathrm{E}\,X)^2/(\mathrm{E}\,X^2) \approx 0.847$; the true value, $p_1 p_2 p_3 + p_2 p_3 p_4 + p_4 p_5 - p_1 p_2 p_3 p_4 - p_2 p_3 p_4 p_5$, is 0.9558.

Many other important inequalities relating to expected values have been discovered, of which the most significant for our purposes in this book is the *FKG inequality* discussed in exercise 61. It yields easy proofs that certain events are correlated, as illustrated in exercise 62.

Martingales. A sequence of dependent random variables can be difficult to analyze, but if those variables obey invariant constraints we can often exploit their structure. In particular, the "martingale" property, named after a classic betting strategy (see exercise 67), proves to be amazingly useful when it applies. Joseph L. Doob featured martingales in his pioneering book *Stochastic Processes* (New York: Wiley, 1953), and developed their extensive theory.

The sequence $\langle Z_n \rangle = Z_0, Z_1, Z_2, \ldots$ of real-valued random variables is called a *martingale* if it satisfies the condition

$$\mathrm{E}(Z_{n+1} \mid Z_0, \ldots, Z_n) = Z_n \qquad \text{for all } n \geq 0. \tag{26}$$

(We also implicitly assume, as usual, that the expectations $\mathrm{E}\, Z_n$ are well defined.) For example, when $n = 0$, the random variable $\mathrm{E}(Z_1 \mid Z_0)$ must be the same as the random variable Z_0 (see exercise 63).

Figure P illustrates George Pólya's famous "urn model" [F. Eggenberger and G. Pólya, *Zeitschrift für angewandte Math. und Mech.* **3** (1923), 279–289], which is associated with a particularly interesting martingale. Imagine an urn that initially contains two balls, one red and one black. Repeatedly remove a randomly chosen ball from the urn, then replace it and contribute a new ball of the same color. The numbers (r, b) of red and black balls will follow a path in the diagram, with the respective local probabilities indicated on each branch.

One can show without difficulty that all $n + 1$ nodes on level n of Fig. P will be reached with the same probability, $1/(n + 1)$. Furthermore, the probability that a red ball is chosen when going from any level to the next is always $1/2$. Thus the urn scheme might seem at first glance to be rather tame and uniform. But in fact the process turns out to be full of surprises, because any inequity between red and black tends to perpetuate itself. For example, if the first ball chosen is black, so that we go from $(1, 1)$ to $(1, 2)$, the probability is only $2 \ln 2 - 1 \approx .386$ that the red balls will ever overtake the black ones in the future (see exercise 88).

One good way to analyze Pólya's process is to use the fact that the ratios $r/(r + b)$ form a martingale. Each visit to the urn changes this ratio either to $(r+1)/(r+b+1)$ (with probability $r/(r+b)$) or to $r/(r+b+1)$ (with probability $b/(r+b)$); so the expected new ratio is $(rb+r^2+r)/((r+b)(r+b+1)) = r/(r+b)$, no different from what it was before. More formally, let $X_0 = 1$, and for $n > 0$ let X_n be the random variable '[the nth ball chosen is red]'. Then there are $X_0 + \cdots + X_n$ red balls and $\overline{X}_0 + \cdots + \overline{X}_n + 1$ black balls at level n of Fig. P; and the sequence $\langle Z_n \rangle$ is a martingale if we define

$$Z_n = (X_0 + \cdots + X_n)/(n + 2). \tag{27}$$

In practice it's usually most convenient to define martingales $Z_0, Z_1, \ldots$ in terms of auxiliary random variables $X_0, X_1, \ldots$, as we've just done. The sequence $\langle Z_n \rangle$ is said to be a *martingale with respect to the sequence* $\langle X_n \rangle$ if Z_n is a function of $(X_0, \ldots, X_n)$ that satisfies

$$\mathrm{E}(Z_{n+1} \mid X_0, \ldots, X_n) = Z_n \qquad \text{for all } n \geq 0. \tag{28}$$

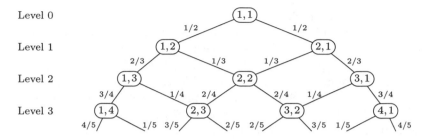

Level 0

Level 1

Level 2

Level 3

Fig. P. Pólya's urn model. The probability of taking any downward path from $(1,1)$ to (r, b) is the product of the probabilities shown on the branches.

Furthermore we say that a sequence $\langle Y_n \rangle$ is *fair with respect to the sequence* $\langle X_n \rangle$ if Y_n is a function of $(X_0, \ldots, X_n)$ that satisfies the simpler condition

$$\mathrm{E}(Y_{n+1} \,|\, X_0, \ldots, X_n) \;=\; 0 \qquad \text{for all } n \geq 0; \tag{29}$$

and we call $\langle Y_n \rangle$ *fair* whenever

$$\mathrm{E}(Y_{n+1} \,|\, Y_0, \ldots, Y_n) \;=\; 0 \qquad \text{for all } n \geq 0. \tag{30}$$

Exercise 77 proves that (28) implies (26) and that (29) implies (30); thus an auxiliary sequence $\langle X_n \rangle$ is sufficient but not necessary for defining martingales and fair sequences.

Whenever $\langle Z_n \rangle$ is a martingale, we obtain a fair sequence $\langle Y_n \rangle$ by letting $Y_0 = Z_0$ and $Y_n = Z_n - Z_{n-1}$ for $n > 0$, because the identity $\mathrm{E}(Y_{n+1} \,|\, Z_0, \ldots, Z_n) = \mathrm{E}(Z_{n+1} - Z_n \,|\, Z_0, \ldots, Z_n) = Z_n - Z_n$ shows that $\langle Y_n \rangle$ is fair with respect to $\langle Z_n \rangle$. Conversely, whenever $\langle Y_n \rangle$ is fair, we obtain a martingale $\langle Z_n \rangle$ by letting $Z_n = Y_0 + \cdots + Y_n$, because the identity $\mathrm{E}(Z_{n+1} \,|\, Y_0, \ldots, Y_n) = \mathrm{E}(Z_n + Y_{n+1} \,|\, Y_0, \ldots, Y_n) = Z_n$ shows that $\langle Z_n \rangle$ is a martingale with respect to $\langle Y_n \rangle$. In other words, fairness and martingaleness are essentially equivalent. The Y's represent unbiased "tweaks" that change one Z to its successor.

It's easy to construct fair sequences. For example, every sequence of *independent* random variables with mean 0 is fair. And if $\langle Y_n \rangle$ is fair with respect to $\langle X_n \rangle$, so is the sequence $\langle Y'_n \rangle$ defined by $Y'_n = f_n(X_0, \ldots, X_{n-1})Y_n$ when $f_n(X_0, \ldots, X_{n-1})$ is almost *any* function whatsoever! (We need only keep f_n small enough that $\mathrm{E}\,Y'_n$ is well defined.) In particular, we can let $f_n(X_0, \ldots, X_{n-1}) = 0$ for all large n, thereby making $\langle Z_n \rangle$ eventually fixed.

A sequence of functions $N_n(x_0, \ldots, x_{n-1})$ is called a *stopping rule* if each value is either 0 or 1 and if $N_n(x_0, \ldots, x_{n-1}) = 0$ implies $N_{n+1}(x_0, \ldots, x_n) = 0$. We can assume that $N_0 = 1$. The number of steps before stopping, with respect to a sequence of random variables $\langle X_n \rangle$, is then the random variable

$$N \;=\; N_1(X_0) + N_2(X_0, X_1) + N_3(X_0, X_1, X_2) + \cdots. \tag{31}$$

(Intuitively, $N_n(x_0, \ldots, x_{n-1})$ means [the values $X_0 = x_0$, $\ldots$, $X_{n-1} = x_{n-1}$ do *not* stop the process]; hence it's really more about "going" than "stopping.") Any martingale $Z_n = Y_0 + \cdots + Y_n$ with respect to $\langle X_n \rangle$ can be adapted to stop with this strategy if we change it to $Z'_n = Y'_0 + \cdots + Y'_n$, where $Y'_n = N_n(X_0, \ldots, X_{n-1})Y_n$. Gamblers who wish to "quit when ahead" are using the stopping rule $N_{n+1}(X_0, \ldots, X_n) = [Z'_n \leq 0]$, when Z'_n is their current balance.

Notice that if the stopping rule always stops after at most m steps — in other words, if the function $N_m(x_0, \ldots, x_{m-1})$ is identically zero — then we have $Z'_m = Z'_N$, because Z'_n doesn't change after the process has stopped. Therefore $\mathrm{E}\, Z'_N = \mathrm{E}\, Z'_m = \mathrm{E}\, Z'_0 = \mathrm{E}\, Z_0$: *No stopping rule can change the expected outcome of a martingale when the number of steps is bounded.*

An amusing game of chance called Ace Now illustrates this optional stopping principle. Take a deck of cards, shuffle it and place the cards face down; then turn them face up one at a time as follows: Just before seeing the nth card, you are supposed to say either "Stop" or "Deal," based on the cards you've already observed. (If $n = 52$ you *must* say "Stop.") After you've decided to stop, you win \$12 if the next card is an ace; otherwise you lose \$1. What is the best strategy for playing this game? Should you hold back until you have a pretty good chance at the \$12? What is the worst strategy? Exercise 82 has the answer.

Tail inequalities from martingales. The essence of martingales is *equality* of expectations. Yet martingales turn out to be important in the analysis of algorithms because we can use them to derive *inequalities*, namely to show that certain events occur with very small probability.

To begin our study, let's introduce inequality into Eq. (26): A sequence $\langle Z_n \rangle$ is called a *submartingale* if it satisfies

$$\mathrm{E}(Z_{n+1} \mid Z_0, \ldots, Z_n) \geq Z_n \qquad \text{for all } n \geq 0. \tag{32}$$

Similarly, it's called a *supermartingale* if '$\geq$' is changed to '$\leq$' in the left-hand part of this definition. (Thus a martingale is both sub- and super-.) In a submartingale we have $\mathrm{E}\, Z_0 \leq \mathrm{E}\, Z_1 \leq \mathrm{E}\, Z_2 \leq \cdots$, by taking expectations in (32). A supermartingale, similarly, has ever *smaller* expectations as n grows. One way to remember the difference between submartingales and supermartingales is to observe that their names are the reverse of what you might expect.

Submartingales are significant largely because of the fact that they're quite common. Indeed, if $\langle Z_n \rangle$ is any martingale and if f is any convex function, then $\langle f(Z_n) \rangle$ is a submartingale (see exercise 84). For example, the sequences $\langle |Z_n| \rangle$ and $\langle \max(Z_n, c) \rangle$ and $\langle Z_n^2 \rangle$ and $\langle e^{Z_n} \rangle$ all are submartingales whenever $\langle Z_n \rangle$ is known to be a martingale. If, furthermore, Z_n is always positive, then $\langle Z_n^3 \rangle$ and $\langle 1/Z_n \rangle$ and $\langle \ln(1/Z_n) \rangle$ and $\langle Z_n \ln Z_n \rangle$, etc., are submartingales.

If we modify a submartingale by applying a stopping rule, it's easy to see that we get another submartingale. Furthermore, if that stopping rule is guaranteed to quit within m steps, we'll have $\mathrm{E}\, Z_m \geq \mathrm{E}\, Z_N = \mathrm{E}\, Z'_N = \mathrm{E}\, Z'_m$. Therefore *no stopping rule can increase the expected outcome of a submartingale, when the number of steps is bounded.*

That comparatively simple observation has many important consequences. For example, exercise 86 uses it to give a simple proof of the so-called "maximal inequality": If $\langle Z_n \rangle$ is a nonnegative submartingale then

$$\Pr\big(\max(Z_0, Z_1, \ldots, Z_n) \geq x\big) \leq \mathrm{E}\, Z_n/x, \qquad \text{for all } x > 0. \tag{33}$$

Special cases of this inequality are legion. For instance, martingales $\langle Z_n \rangle$ satisfy

$$\Pr\big(\max(|Z_0|, |Z_1|, \ldots, |Z_n|) \geq x\big) \leq \mathrm{E}\, |Z_n|/x, \qquad \text{for all } x > 0; \tag{34}$$

$$\Pr\big(\max(Z_0^2, Z_1^2, \ldots, Z_n^2) \geq x\big) \leq \mathrm{E}\, Z_n^2/x, \qquad \text{for all } x > 0. \tag{35}$$

Relation (35) is known as *Kolmogorov's inequality*, because A. N. Kolmogorov proved it when $Z_n = X_1 + \cdots + X_n$ is the sum of independent random variables with $\mathrm{E}\, X_k = 0$ and $\mathrm{var}\, X_k = \sigma_k^2$ for $1 \leq k \leq n$ [*Math. Annalen* **99** (1928), 309–311]. In that case $\mathrm{var}\, Z_n = \sigma_1^2 + \cdots + \sigma_n^2 = \sigma^2$, and the inequality can be written

$$\Pr\big(|X_1| < t\sigma, \ |X_1 + X_2| < t\sigma, \ \ldots, \ |X_1 + \cdots + X_n| < t\sigma\big) \geq 1 - 1/t^2. \tag{36}$$

Chebyshev's inequality gives only $\Pr\big(|X_1 + \cdots + X_n| < t\sigma\big) \geq 1 - 1/t^2$, which is a considerably weaker result.

Another important inequality applies in the common case where we have good bounds on the terms $Y_1, \ldots, Y_n$ that enter into the standard representation $Z_n = Y_0 + Y_1 + \cdots + Y_n$ of a martingale. This one is called the *Hoeffding–Azuma inequality*, after papers by W. Hoeffding [*J. Amer. Statistical Association* **58** (1963), 13–30] and K. Azuma [*Tôhoku Math. Journal* (2) **19** (1967), 357–367]. It reads as follows: If $\langle Y_n \rangle$ is any fair sequence with $a_n \leq Y_n \leq b_n$ when $Y_0, Y_1, \ldots, Y_{n-1}$ are given, then

$$\Pr(Y_1 + \cdots + Y_n \geq x) \leq e^{-2x^2/((b_1 - a_1)^2 + \cdots + (b_n - a_n)^2)}. \tag{37}$$

The same bound applies to $\Pr(Y_1 + \cdots + Y_n \leq -x)$, since $-b_n \leq -Y_n \leq -a_n$; so

$$\Pr(|Y_1 + \cdots + Y_n| \geq x) \leq 2e^{-2x^2/((b_1 - a_1)^2 + \cdots + (b_n - a_n)^2)}. \tag{38}$$

Exercise 90 breaks the proof of this result into small steps. In fact, the proof even shows that a_n and b_n may be functions of $\{Y_0, \ldots, Y_{n-1}\}$.

Applications. The Hoeffding–Azuma inequality is useful in the analysis of many algorithms because it applies to "Doob martingales," a very general class of martingales that J. L. Doob featured as Example 1 in his *Stochastic Processes* (1953), page 92. (In fact, he had already considered them many years earlier, in *Trans. Amer. Math. Soc.* **47** (1940), 486.) Doob martingales arise from *any* sequence of random variables $\langle X_n \rangle$, independent or not, and from any *other* random variable Q: We simply define

$$Z_n = \mathrm{E}(Q \mid X_0, \ldots, X_n). \tag{39}$$

Then, as Doob pointed out, the resulting sequence is a martingale (see exercise 91). In our applications, Q is an aspect of some algorithm that we wish to study, and the variables $X_0, X_1, \ldots$ reflect the inputs to the algorithm. For example, in an algorithm that uses random bits, the X's are those bits.

Consider a hashing algorithm in which t objects are placed into m random lists, where the nth object goes into list X_n; thus $1 \leq X_n \leq m$ for $1 \leq n \leq t$, and we assume that each of the m^t possibilities is equally likely. Let $Q(x_1, \ldots, x_t)$ be the number of lists that remain empty after the objects have been placed into lists $x_1, \ldots, x_t$, and let $Z_n = \mathrm{E}(Q \mid X_1, \ldots, X_n)$ be the associated Doob martingale. Then $Z_0 = \mathrm{E}\, Q$ is the *average* number of empty lists; and $Z_t = Q(X_1, \ldots, X_t)$ is the *actual* number, in any particular run of the algorithm.

What fair sequence corresponds to this martingale? If $1 \leq n \leq t$, the random variable $Y_n = Z_n - Z_{n-1}$ is $f_n(X_1, \ldots, X_n)$, where $f_n(x_1, \ldots, x_n)$ is the average of

$$\Delta(x_1, \ldots, x_t) = \sum_{x=1}^{m} \Pr(X_n = x)\big(Q(x_1, \ldots, x_{n-1}, x_n, x_{n+1}, \ldots, x_t)$$
$$- Q(x_1, \ldots, x_{n-1}, x, x_{n+1}, \ldots, x_t)\big) \quad (40)$$

taken over all m^{t-n} values of $(x_{n+1}, \ldots, x_t)$.

In our application the function $Q(x_1, \ldots, x_t)$ has the property that

$$\big|Q(x_1, \ldots, x_{n-1}, x', x_{n+1}, \ldots, x_t) - Q(x_1, \ldots, x_{n-1}, x, x_{n+1}, \ldots, x_t)\big| \leq 1 \quad (41)$$

for all x and x', because a change to any one hash address always changes the number of empty lists by either 1, 0, or -1. Consequently, for any fixed setting of the variables $(x_1, \ldots, x_{n-1}, x_{n+1}, \ldots, x_t)$, we have

$$\max_{x_n} \Delta(x_1, \ldots, x_t) \; \leq \; \min_{x_n} \Delta(x_1, \ldots, x_t) + 1. \quad (42)$$

The Hoeffding–Azuma inequality (37) therefore allows us to conclude that

$$\Pr(Z_t - Z_0 \geq x) \; = \; \Pr(Y_1 + \cdots + Y_t \geq x) \; \leq \; e^{-2x^2/t}. \quad (43)$$

Furthermore, Z_0 in this example is $m(m-1)^t/m^t$, because exactly $(m-1)^t$ of the m^t possible hash sequences leave any particular list empty. And the random variable Z_t is the actual number of empty lists when the algorithm is run. Hence we can, for example, set $x = \sqrt{t\ln f(t)}$ in (43), thereby proving that

$$\Pr\big(Z_t \geq (m-1)^t/m^{t-1} + \sqrt{t\ln f(t)}\,\big) \; \leq \; 1/f(t)^2. \quad (44)$$

The same upper bound applies to $\Pr\big(Z_t \leq (m-1)^t/m^{t-1} - \sqrt{t\ln f(t)}\,\big)$.

Notice that the inequality (41) was crucial in this analysis. Therefore the strategy we've used to prove (43) is often called the "method of bounded differences." In general, a function $Q(x_1, \ldots, x_t)$ is said to satisfy a *Lipschitz condition* in coordinate n if we have

$$\big|Q(x_1, \ldots, x_{n-1}, x, x_{n+1}, \ldots, x_t) - Q(x_1, \ldots, x_{n-1}, x', x_{n+1}, \ldots, x_t)\big| \leq c_n \quad (45)$$

for all x and x'. (This terminology mimics a well-known but only slightly similar constraint that was introduced long ago into functional analysis by Rudolf Lipschitz [*Crelle* **63** (1864), 296–308].) Whenever condition (45) holds, for a function Q associated with a Doob martingale for *independent* random variables $X_1, \ldots, X_t$, we can prove that $\Pr(Y_1 + \cdots + Y_t \geq x) \leq \exp(-2x^2/(c_1^2 + \cdots + c_t^2))$.

Let's work out one more example, due to Colin McDiarmid [*London Math. Soc. Lecture Notes* **141** (1989), 148–188, §8(a)]: Again we consider independent integer-valued random variables $X_1, \ldots, X_t$ with $1 \leq X_n \leq m$ for $1 \leq n \leq t$;

but this time we allow each X_n to have a different probability distribution. Furthermore we define $Q(x_1, \ldots, x_t)$ to be the *minimum number of bins* into which objects of sizes x_1, ..., x_t can be packed, where each bin has capacity m.

This bin-packing problem sounds a lot harder than the hashing problem that we just solved. Indeed, the task of evaluating $Q(x_1, \ldots, x_t)$ is well known to be NP-complete [see M. R. Garey and D. S. Johnson, *SICOMP* **4** (1975), 397–411]. Yet Q obviously satisfies the condition (45) with $c_n = 1$ for $1 \le n \le t$. Therefore the method of bounded differences tells us that inequality (43) is true, in spite of the apparent difficulty of this problem!

The only difference between this bin-packing problem and the hashing problem is that we're clueless about the value of Z_0. Nobody knows how to compute $E\,Q(X_1, \ldots, X_t)$, except for very special distributions of the random variables. However — and this is the magic of martingales — we do know that, whatever the value is, the actual numbers Z_t will be tightly concentrated around that average.

If all the X's have the same distribution, the values $\beta_t = E\,Q(X_1, \ldots, X_t)$ satisfy $\beta_{t+t'} \le \beta_t + \beta_{t'}$, because we could always pack the t and t' items separately. Therefore, by the subadditive law (see the answer to exercise 2.5–39), β_t/t approaches a limit β as $t \to \infty$. Still, however, random trials won't give us decent bounds on that limit, because we have no good way to compute the Q function.

> *If only he could have enjoyed Martingale for its beauty and its peace*
> *without being chained to it by this band of responsibility and guilt!*
> — P. D. JAMES, *Cover Her Face* (1962)

Statements that are almost sure, or even quite sure. Probabilities that depend on an integer n often have the property that they approach 0 or 1 as $n \to \infty$, and special terminology simplifies the discussion of such phenomena. If, say, A_n is an event for which $\lim_{n \to \infty} \Pr(A_n) = 1$, it's convenient to express this fact in words by saying, "A_n occurs almost surely, when n is large." (Indeed, we usually don't bother to state that n is large, if we already understand that n is approaching infinity in the context of the current discussion.)

For example, if we toss a fair coin n times, we'll find that the coin almost surely comes up heads more than $.49n$ times, but fewer than $.51n$ times.

Furthermore, we'll occasionally want to express this concept tersely in formulas, by writing just 'a.s.' instead of spelling out the words "almost surely." For instance, the statement just made about n coin tosses can be formulated as

$$.49n < X_1 + \cdots + X_n < .51n \text{ a.s.,} \tag{46}$$

if X_1, ..., X_n are independent binary random variables, each with $E\,X_j = 1/2$. In general a statement such as "A_n a.s." means that $\lim_{n \to \infty} \Pr(A_n) = 1$; or, equivalently, that $\lim_{n \to \infty} \Pr(\overline{A}_n) = 0$. It's asymptotically almost sure.

If A_n and B_n are both a.s., then the combined event $C_n = A_n \cap B_n$ is also a.s., regardless of whether those events are independent. The reason is that $\Pr(\overline{C}_n) = \Pr(\overline{A}_n \cup \overline{B}_n) \le \Pr(\overline{A}_n) + \Pr(\overline{B}_n)$, which approaches 0 as $n \to \infty$.

Thus, to prove (46) we need only show that $X_1 + \cdots + X_n > .49n$ a.s. and that $X_1 + \cdots + X_n < .51n$ a.s., or in other words that $\Pr(X_1 + \cdots + X_n \le .49n)$

and $\Pr(X_1 + \cdots + X_n \geq .51n)$ both approach 0. Those probabilities are actually equal, by symmetry between heads and tails; so we need only show that $p_n = \Pr(X_1 + \cdots + X_n \leq .49n)$ approaches 0. And that's no sweat, because we know from exercise 1.2.10–21 that $p_n \leq e^{-.0001n}$.

In fact, we've proved more: We've shown that p_n is *superpolynomially small*, namely that

$$p_n = O(n^{-K}) \qquad \text{for all fixed numbers } K. \tag{47}$$

When the probability of an event $\overline{A}_n$ is superpolynomially small, we say that A_n holds "quite surely," and abbreviate that by 'q.s.'. In other words, we've proved

$$.49n < X_1 + \cdots + X_n < .51n \quad \text{q.s.} \tag{48}$$

We've seen that the combination of any two a.s. events is a.s.; hence the combination of any finite number of a.s. events is also a.s. That's nice, but q.s. events are even nicer: *The combination of any polynomial number of q.s. events is also q.s.* For example, if n^4 different people each toss n coins, it is quite sure that *every one of them*, without exception, will obtain between $.49n$ and $.51n$ heads!

(When making such asymptotic statements we ignore the inconvenient truth that our bound on the failure of the assertion, $2n^4 e^{-.0001n}$ in this case, becomes negligible only when n is greater than 700,000 or so.)

EXERCISES

1. [*M21*] (*Nontransitive dice.*) Suppose three biased dice with the respective faces

$$A = \boxed{\cdots} , \qquad B = \boxed{\cdots} , \qquad C = \boxed{\cdots}$$

are rolled independently at random.
   a) Show that $\Pr(A > B) = \Pr(B > C) = \Pr(C > A) = 5/9$.
   b) Find dice with $\Pr(A > B)$, $\Pr(B > C)$, $\Pr(C > A)$ all *greater* than 5/9.
   c) If Fibonacci dice have F_m faces instead of just six, show that we could have

$$\Pr(A > B) = \Pr(B > C) = F_{m-1}/F_m \quad \text{and} \quad \Pr(C > A) = F_{m-1}/F_m \pm 1/F_m^2.$$

2. [*M32*] Prove that the previous exercise is asymptotically *optimum*, in the sense that $\min(\Pr(A > B), \Pr(B > C), \Pr(C > A)) < 1/\phi$, regardless of the number of faces.

3. [*22*] (*Lake Wobegon dice.*) Continuing the previous exercises, find three dice such that $\Pr(A > \frac{1}{3}(A+B+C)) \geq \Pr(B > \frac{1}{3}(A+B+C)) \geq \Pr(C > \frac{1}{3}(A+B+C)) \geq 16/27$. Each face of each die should be $\boxed{\cdot}$ or $\boxed{\because}$ or $\boxed{\therefore}$ or $\boxed{::}$ or $\boxed{\because\cdot}$ or $\boxed{:::}$.

4. [*22*] (*Nontransitive Bingo.*) Each player in the game of NanoBingo has a card containing four numbers from the set $S = \{1, 2, 3, 4, 5, 6\}$, arranged in two rows. An announcer calls out the elements of S, in random order; the first player whose card has a horizontal row with both numbers called shouts "Bingo!" and wins. (Or victory is shared when there are multiple Bingoes.) For example, consider the four cards

$$A = \begin{array}{|c|c|} \hline 1 & 2 \\ \hline 3 & 5 \\ \hline \end{array}, \qquad B = \begin{array}{|c|c|} \hline 2 & 3 \\ \hline 4 & 6 \\ \hline \end{array}, \qquad C = \begin{array}{|c|c|} \hline 3 & 4 \\ \hline 1 & 5 \\ \hline \end{array}, \qquad D = \begin{array}{|c|c|} \hline 1 & 4 \\ \hline 2 & 6 \\ \hline \end{array}.$$

If the announcer calls "6, 2, 5, 1" when A plays against B, then A wins; but the sequence "1, 3, 2" would yield a tie. One can show that $\Pr(A \text{ beats } B) = \frac{336}{720}$, $\Pr(B \text{ beats } A) = \frac{312}{720}$, and $\Pr(A \text{ and } B \text{ tie}) = \frac{72}{720}$. Determine the probabilities of all possible outcomes when there are (a) two (b) three (c) four different players using those cards.

▶ **5.** [*HM22*] (T. M. Cover, 1989.) Common wisdom asserts that longer games favor the stronger player, because they provide more evidence of the relative skills.

However, consider an n-round game in which Alice scores $A_1 + \cdots + A_n$ points while Bob scores $B_1 + \cdots + B_n$ points. Here each of $A_1, \ldots, A_n$ are independent random variables with the same distribution, all representing Alice's strength; similarly, each of $B_1, \ldots, B_n$ independently represent Bob's strength (and are independent of the A's). Suppose Alice wins with probability P_n.

a) Show that it's possible to have $P_1 = .99$ but $P_{1000} < .0001$.

b) Let $m_k = 2^{k^3}$, $n_k = 2^{k^2 + k}$, and $q_k = 2^{-k^2}/D$, where $D = 2^{-0} + 2^{-1} + 2^{-4} + 2^{-9} + \cdots \approx 1.56447$. Suppose the random variable A takes the values $(m_0, m_2, m_4, \ldots)$ with probabilities $(q_0, q_2, q_4, \ldots)$; otherwise $A = 0$. Independently, the random variable B takes the values $(m_1, m_3, m_5, \ldots)$ with probabilities $(q_1, q_3, q_5, \ldots)$; otherwise $B = 0$. What are $\Pr(A > B)$, $\Pr(A < B)$, and $\Pr(A = B)$?

c) With the distributions in (b), prove that $P_{n_k} \to [k \text{ even}]$ as $k \to \infty$.

▶ **6.** [*M22*] Consider random Boolean (or binary) vectors $X_1 \ldots X_n$, where $n \geq 2$, with the following distribution: The vector $x_1 \ldots x_n$ occurs with probability $1/(n-1)^2$ if $x_1 + \cdots + x_n = 2$, with probability $(n-2)/(2n-2)$ if $x_1 + \cdots + x_n = 0$, and with probability 0 otherwise. Show that the components are pairwise independent (that is, X_i is independent of X_j when $i \neq j$); but they are not k-wise independent for $k > 2$.

Also find a joint distribution, depending only on $\nu x = x_1 + \cdots + x_n$, that is k-wise independent for $k = 2$ and $k = 3$ but not $k = 4$.

7. [*M30*] (Ernst Schulte-Geers, 2012.) Generalizing exercise 6, construct a νx-based distribution that has k-wise but not $(k+1)$-wise independence, given $k \geq 1$.

▶ **8.** [*M20*] Suppose the Boolean vector $x_1 \ldots x_n$ occurs with probability $(2 + (-1)^{\nu x})/2^{n+1}$, where $\nu x = x_1 + \cdots + x_n$. For what k is this distribution k-wise independent?

9. [*M20*] Find a distribution of Boolean vectors $x_1 \ldots x_n$ such that any two components are dependent; yet if we know the value of any x_j, the remaining components are $(n-1)$-wise independent. *Hint:* The answer is so simple, you might feel hornswoggled.

▶ **10.** [*M21*] Let $Y_1, \ldots, Y_m$ be independent and uniformly distributed elements of $\{0, 1, \ldots, p-1\}$, where p is prime. Also let $X_j = (j^m + Y_1 j^{m-1} + \cdots + Y_m) \bmod p$, for $1 \leq j \leq n$. For what k are the X's k-wise independent?

11. [*M20*] If $X_1, \ldots, X_{2n}$ are independent random variables with the same discrete distribution, and if α is any real number whatsoever, prove that

$$\Pr\left(\left| \frac{X_1 + \cdots + X_{2n}}{2n} - \alpha \right| \leq \left| \frac{X_1 + \cdots + X_n}{n} - \alpha \right| \right) > \frac{1}{2}.$$

12. [*21*] Which of the following four statements are equivalent to the statement that $\Pr(A \mid B) > \Pr(A)$? (i) $\Pr(B \mid A) > \Pr(B)$; (ii) $\Pr(A \mid B) > \Pr(A \mid \bar{B})$; (iii) $\Pr(B \mid A) > \Pr(B \mid \bar{A})$; (iv) $\Pr(\bar{A} \mid \bar{B}) > \Pr(\bar{A} \mid B)$.

13. [*15*] True or false: $\Pr(A \mid C) > \Pr(A)$ if $\Pr(A \mid B) > \Pr(A)$ and $\Pr(B \mid C) > \Pr(B)$.

14. *[10]* (Thomas Bayes, 1763.) Prove the "chain rule" for conditional probability:
$$\Pr(A_1 \cap \cdots \cap A_n) = \Pr(A_1)\Pr(A_2 \,|\, A_1) \ldots \Pr(A_n \,|\, A_1 \cap \cdots \cap A_{n-1}).$$

15. *[12]* True or false: $\Pr(A \,|\, B \cap C)\Pr(B \,|\, C) = \Pr(A \cap B \,|\, C)$.

16. *[M15]* Under what circumstances is $\Pr(A \,|\, B) = \Pr(A \cup C \,|\, B)$?

▸ **17.** *[15]* Evaluate the conditional probability $\Pr(T$ is an ace $\,|\, B = \mathsf{Q}\spadesuit)$ in the playing card example of the text, where T and B denote the top and bottom cards.

18. *[20]* Let M and m be the maximum and minimum values of the random variable X. Prove that $\operatorname{var} X \le (M - \mathrm{E}\,X)(\mathrm{E}\,X - m)$.

▸ **19.** *[HM28]* Let X be a random nonnegative integer, with $\Pr(X = x) = 1/2^{x+1}$, and suppose that $X = (\ldots X_2 X_1 X_0)_2$ and $X + 1 = (\ldots Y_2 Y_1 Y_0)_2$ in binary notation.
  a) What is $\mathrm{E}\,X_n$? *Hint:* Express this number in the binary number system.
  b) Prove that the random variables $\{X_0, X_1, \ldots, X_{n-1}\}$ are independent.
  c) Find the mean and variance of $S = X_0 + X_1 + X_2 + \cdots$.
  d) Find the mean and variance of $R = X_0 \oplus X_1 \oplus X_2 \oplus \cdots$.
  e) Let $\pi = (11.p_0 p_1 p_2 \ldots)_2$. What is the probability that $X_n = p_n$ for all $n \ge 0$?
  f) What is $\mathrm{E}\,Y_n$? Show that Y_0 and Y_1 are *not* independent.
  g) Find the mean and variance of $T = Y_0 + Y_1 + Y_2 + \cdots$.

20. *[M18]* Let $X_1, \ldots, X_k$ be binary random variables for which we know that $\mathrm{E}(\prod_{j \in J} X_j) = \prod_{j \in J} \mathrm{E}\,X_j$ for all $J \subseteq \{1, \ldots, k\}$. Prove that the X's are independent.

21. *[M20]* Find a small-as-possible example of random variables X and Y that satisfy $\operatorname{covar}(X, Y) = 0$, that is, $\mathrm{E}\,XY = (\mathrm{E}\,X)(\mathrm{E}\,Y)$, although they aren't independent.

▸ **22.** *[M20]* Use Eq. (8) to prove the "union inequality"
$$\Pr(A_1 \cup \cdots \cup A_n) \le \Pr(A_1) + \cdots + \Pr(A_n).$$

▸ **23.** *[M21]* If each X_k is an independent binary random variable with $\mathrm{E}\,X_k = p$, the *cumulative binomial distribution* $B_{m,n}(p)$ is the probability that $X_1 + \cdots + X_n \le m$. Thus it's easy to see that $B_{m,n}(p) = \sum_{k=0}^{m} \binom{n}{k} p^k (1-p)^{n-k}$.
  Show that $B_{m,n}(p)$ is *also* equal to $\sum_{k=0}^{m} \binom{n-m-1+k}{k} p^k (1-p)^{n-m}$, for $0 \le m \le n$. *Hint:* Consider the random variables $J_1, J_2, \ldots,$ and T defined by the rule that $X_j = 0$ if and only if j has one of the T values $\{J_1, J_2, \ldots, J_T\}$, where $1 \le J_1 < J_2 < \cdots < J_T \le n$. What is $\Pr(T \ge r$ and $J_r = s)$?

▸ **24.** *[HM28]* The cumulative binomial distribution also has many other properties.
  a) Prove that $B_{m,n}(p) = (n - m)\binom{n}{m} \int_p^1 x^m (1-x)^{n-1-m} dx$, for $0 \le m < n$.
  b) Use that formula to prove that $B_{m,n}(m/n) > \frac{1}{2}$, for $0 \le m < n/2$. *Hint:* Show that $\int_0^{m/n} x^m (1-x)^{n-1-m} dx < \int_{m/n}^1 x^m (1-x)^{n-1-m} dx$.
  c) Show furthermore that $B_{m,n}(m/n) > \frac{1}{2}$ when $n/2 \le m \le n$. [Thus m is the *median* value of $X_1 + \cdots + X_n$, when $p = m/n$ and m is an integer.]

25. *[M25]* Suppose $X_1, X_2, \ldots$ are independent random binary variables, with means $\mathrm{E}\,X_k = p_k$. Let $\left(\!\binom{n}{k}\!\right)$ be the probability that $X_1 + \cdots + X_n = k$; thus $\left(\!\binom{n}{k}\!\right) = p_n \left(\!\binom{n-1}{k-1}\!\right) + q_n \left(\!\binom{n-1}{k}\!\right) = [z^k] \, (q_1 + p_1 z) \ldots (q_n + p_n z)$, where $q_k = 1 - p_k$.
  a) Prove that $\left(\!\binom{n}{k}\!\right) \ge \left(\!\binom{n}{k+1}\!\right)$, if $p_j \le (k+1)/(n+1)$ for $1 \le j \le n$.
  b) Furthermore $\left(\!\binom{n}{k}\!\right) \le \binom{n}{k} p^k q^{n-k}$, if $p_j \le p \le k/n$ for $1 \le j \le n$.

26. *[M27]* Continuing exercise 25, prove that $\left(\!\binom{n}{k}\!\right)^2 \ge \left(\!\binom{n}{k-1}\!\right)\left(\!\binom{n}{k+1}\!\right)\left(1 + \frac{1}{k}\right)\left(1 + \frac{1}{n-k}\right)$ for $0 < k < n$. *Hint:* Consider $r_{n,k} = \left(\!\binom{n}{k}\!\right) / \binom{n}{k}$.

27. [*M22*] Find an expression for the generalized cumulative binomial distribution $\sum_{k=0}^{m} \left(\binom{n}{k}\right)$ that is analogous to the alternative formula in exercise 23.

28. [*HM28*] (W. Hoeffding, 1956.) Let $X = X_1 + \cdots + X_n$ and $p_1 + \cdots + p_n = np$ in exercise 25, and suppose that $\mathrm{E}\,g(X) = \sum_{k=0}^{n} g(k)\left(\binom{n}{k}\right)$ for some function g.

  a) Prove that $\mathrm{E}\,g(X) \leq \sum_{k=0}^{n} g(k)\binom{n}{k}p^k(1-p)^{n-k}$ if g is convex in $[0 \mathinner{\ldotp\ldotp} n]$.

  b) If g isn't convex, show that the maximum of $\mathrm{E}\,g(X)$, over all choices of $\{p_1, \ldots, p_n\}$ with $p_1 + \cdots + p_n = np$ can always be attained by a set of probabilities for which at most three distinct values $\{0, a, 1\}$ occur among the p_j.

  c) Furthermore $\sum_{k=0}^{m} \left(\binom{n}{k}\right) \leq B_{m,n}(p)$, whenever $p_1 + \cdots + p_n = np \geq m+1$.

29. [*HM29*] (S. M. Samuels, 1965.) Continuing exercise 28, prove that we have $B_{m,n}(p) \geq \left((1-p)(m+1)/((1-p)m+1)\right)^{n-m}$ whenever $np \leq m+1$.

30. [*HM34*] Let $X_1, \ldots, X_n$ be independent random variables whose values are non-negative integers, where $\mathrm{E}X_k = 1$ for all k, and let $p = \Pr(X_1 + \cdots + X_n \leq n)$.

  a) What is p, if each X_k takes only the values 0 and $n+1$?

  b) Show that, in any set of distributions that minimize p, each X_k assumes only two integer values, 0 and m_k, where $1 \leq m_k \leq n+1$.

  c) Furthermore we have $p > 1/e$, if each X_k has the same two-valued distribution.

▶ **31.** [*M20*] Assume that $A_1, \ldots, A_n$ are random events such that, for every subset $I \subseteq \{1, \ldots, n\}$, the probability $\Pr(\bigcap_{i \in I} A_i)$ that all A_i for $i \in I$ occur simultaneously is π_I; here π_I is a number with $0 \leq \pi_I \leq 1$, and $\pi_\emptyset = 1$. Show that the probability of any combination of the events, $\Pr(f([A_1], \ldots, [A_n]))$ for any Boolean function f, can be found by expanding f's multilinear reliability polynomial $f([A_1], \ldots, [A_n])$ and replacing each term $\prod_{i \in I}[A_i]$ by π_I. For example, the reliability polynomial of $x_1 \oplus x_2 \oplus x_3$ is $x_1 + x_2 + x_3 - 2x_1x_2 - 2x_1x_3 - 2x_2x_3 + 4x_1x_2x_3$; hence $\Pr([A_1] \oplus [A_2] \oplus [A_3]) = \pi_1 + \pi_2 + \pi_3 - 2\pi_{12} - 2\pi_{13} - 2\pi_{23} + 4\pi_{123}$. (Here '$\pi_{12}$' is short for $\pi_{\{1,2\}}$, etc.)

32. [*M21*] Not all sets of numbers π_I in the preceding exercise can arise in an actual probability distribution. For example, if $I \subseteq J$ we must have $\pi_I \geq \pi_J$. What is a necessary and sufficient condition for the 2^n values of π_I to be legitimate?

33. [*M20*] Suppose X and Y are binary random variables whose joint distribution is defined by the probability generating function $G(w, z) = \mathrm{E}(w^X z^Y) = pw + qz + rwz$, where $p, q, r > 0$ and $p + q + r = 1$. Use the definitions in the text to compute the probability generating function $\mathrm{E}(z^{\mathrm{E}(X|Y)})$ for the conditional expectation $\mathrm{E}(X\,|\,Y)$.

34. [*M17*] Write out an algebraic proof of (12), using the definitions (7) and (13).

▶ **35.** [*M22*] True or false: (a) $\mathrm{E}(\mathrm{E}(X\,|\,Y)\,|\,Y) = \mathrm{E}(X\,|\,Y)$; (b) $\mathrm{E}(\mathrm{E}(X\,|\,Y)\,|\,Z) = \mathrm{E}(X\,|\,Z)$.

36. [*M21*] Simplify the formulas (a) $\mathrm{E}(f(X)\,|\,X)$; (b) $\mathrm{E}(f(Y)\,\mathrm{E}(g(X)\,|\,Y))$.

▶ **37.** [*M20*] Suppose $X_1 \ldots X_n$ is a random permutation of $\{1, \ldots, n\}$, with every permutation occurring with probability $1/n!$. What is $\mathrm{E}(X_k\,|\,X_1, \ldots, X_{k-1})$?

38. [*M26*] Let $X_1 \ldots X_n$ be a random restricted growth string of length n, each with probability $1/\varpi_n$ (see Section 7.2.1.5). What is $\mathrm{E}(X_k\,|\,X_1, \ldots, X_{k-1})$?

▶ **39.** [*HM21*] A hen lays N eggs, where $\Pr(N = n) = e^{-\mu}\mu^n/n!$ obeys the Poisson distribution. Each egg hatches with probability p, independent of all other eggs. Let K be the resulting number of chicks. Express (a) $\mathrm{E}(K\,|\,N)$, (b) $\mathrm{E}\,K$, and (c) $\mathrm{E}(N\,|\,K)$ in terms of N, K, μ, and p.

40. [*M16*] Suppose X is a random variable with $X \leq M$, and let m be any value with $m < M$. Show that $\Pr(X > m) \geq (\mathrm{E}\,X - m)/(M - m)$.

41. [*HM21*] Which of the following functions are convex in the set of all real numbers x? (a) $|x|^a$, where a is a constant; (b) $\sum_{k\geq n} x^k/k!$, where $n \geq 0$ is an integer; (c) $e^{e^{|x|}}$; (d) $f(x)[x \in I] + \infty[x \notin I]$, where f is convex in the interval I.

42. [*HM21*] Prove Jensen's inequality (20).

▶ **43.** [*M18*] Use (12) and (20) to strengthen (20): *If f is convex in I and if the random variable X takes values in I, then $f(E\,X) \leq E(f(E(X\,|\,Y))) \leq E\,f(X)$.*

▶ **44.** [*M25*] If f is convex on the real line and if $E\,X = 0$, prove that $E\,f(aX) \leq E\,f(bX)$ whenever $0 \leq a \leq b$.

45. [*M18*] Derive the first moment principle (21) from Markov's inequality (15).

46. [*M15*] Explain why $E(X^2\,|\,X > 0) \geq (E(X\,|\,X > 0))^2$ in (23).

47. [*M15*] If X is random and $Y = \max(0, X)$, show that $E\,Y \geq E\,X$ and $E\,Y^2 \leq E\,X^2$.

▶ **48.** [*M20*] Suppose $X_1, \ldots, X_n$ are independent random variables with $E\,X_k = 0$ and $E\,X_k^2 = \sigma_k^2$ for $1 \leq k \leq n$. Chebyshev's inequality tells us that $\Pr(|X_1 + \cdots + X_n| \geq a) \leq (\sigma_1^2 + \cdots + \sigma_n^2)/a^2$; show that the second moment principle gives a somewhat better one-sided estimate, $\Pr(X_1 + \cdots + X_n \geq a) \leq (\sigma_1^2 + \cdots + \sigma_n^2)/(a^2 + \sigma_1^2 + \cdots + \sigma_n^2)$, if $a \geq 0$.

49. [*M20*] If X is random and ≥ 0, prove that $\Pr(X = 0) \leq (E\,X^2)/(E\,X)^2 - 1$.

▶ **50.** [*M27*] Let $X = X_1 + \cdots + X_m$ be the sum of binary random variables, with $E\,X_j = p_j$. Let J be independent of the X's, and uniformly distributed in $\{1, \ldots, m\}$.
  a) Prove that $\Pr(X > 0) = \sum_{j=1}^m E(X_j/X \mid X_j > 0) \cdot \Pr(X_j > 0)$.
  b) Therefore (24) holds. *Hint:* Use Jensen's inequality with $f(x) = 1/x$.
  c) What are $\Pr(X_J = 1)$ and $\Pr(J = j \mid X_J = 1)$?
  d) Let $t_j = E(X \mid J = j$ and $X_J = 1)$. Prove that $E\,X^2 = \sum_{j=1}^m p_j t_j$.
  e) Jensen's inequality now implies that the right side of (24) is $\geq (E\,X)^2/(E\,X^2)$.

▶ **51.** [*M21*] Show how to use the conditional expectation inequality (24) to obtain also an *upper* bound on the value of a reliability polynomial, and apply your method to the case illustrated in (25).

52. [*M21*] What lower bound does inequality (24) give for the reliability polynomial of the symmetric function $S_{\geq k}(x_1, \ldots, x_n)$, when $p_1 = \cdots = p_n = p$?

53. [*M20*] Use (24) to obtain a lower bound for the reliability polynomial of the *non-monotonic* Boolean function $f(x_1, \ldots, x_6) = x_1 x_2 \bar{x}_3 \vee x_2 x_3 \bar{x}_4 \vee \cdots \vee x_5 x_6 \bar{x}_1 \vee x_6 x_1 \bar{x}_2$.

▶ **54.** [*M22*] Suppose each edge of a random graph on the vertices $\{1, \ldots, n\}$ is present with probability p, independent of every other edge. If u, v, w are distinct vertices, let X_{uvw} be the binary random variable $[\{u, v, w\}$ is a 3-clique]; thus $X_{uvw} = [u\!-\!v][u\!-\!w][v\!-\!w]$, and $E\,X_{uvw} = p^3$. Also let $X = \sum_{1 \leq u < v < w \leq n} X_{uvw}$ be the total number of 3-cliques. Use the (a) first and (b) second moment principle to derive bounds on the probability that the graph contains at least one 3-clique.

55. [*23*] Evaluate the upper and lower bounds in the previous exercise numerically in the case $n = 10$, and compare them to the true probability, when (a) $p = 1/2$; (b) $p = 1/10$.

56. [*HM20*] Evaluate the upper and lower bounds of exercise 54 asymptotically when $p = \lambda/n$ and $n \to \infty$.

▶ **57.** [*M21*] Obtain a lower bound for the probability in exercise 54(b) by using the conditional expectation inequality (24) instead of the second moment principle (22).

58. [*M22*] Generalizing exercise 54, find bounds on the probability that a random graph on n vertices has a k-clique, when each edge has probability p.

▶ **59.** [*HM30*] (*The four functions theorem.*) The purpose of this exercise is to prove an inequality that applies to four sequences $\langle a_n \rangle$, $\langle b_n \rangle$, $\langle c_n \rangle$, $\langle d_n \rangle$ of nonnegative numbers:

$$a_j b_k \le c_{j|k} d_{j\&k} \quad \text{for } 0 \le j, k < \infty \quad \text{implies} \quad \sum_{j=0}^{\infty}\sum_{k=0}^{\infty} a_j b_k \le \sum_{j=0}^{\infty}\sum_{k=0}^{\infty} c_j d_k. \quad (*)$$

(The sums will be ∞ if they don't converge.) Although the inequality might appear at first to be merely a curiosity, of interest only to a few lovers of esoteric formulas, we shall see that it's a fundamental result with many applications of great importance.

a) Prove the special case where $a_j = b_j = c_j = d_j = 0$ for $j \ge 2$, namely that

$$a_0 b_0 \le c_0 d_0, \quad a_0 b_1 \le c_1 d_0, \quad a_1 b_0 \le c_1 d_0, \quad \text{and} \quad a_1 b_1 \le c_1 d_1$$
$$\text{implies} \quad (a_0 + a_1)(b_0 + b_1) \le (c_0 + c_1)(d_0 + d_1).$$

Can equality hold in the first four relations but not in the last one? Can equality hold in the last relation but not in the first four?

b) Use that result to prove $(*)$ when $a_j = b_j = c_j = d_j = 0$ for all $j \ge 2^n$, given $n > 0$.

c) Conclude that $(*)$ is true in general.

▶ **60.** [*M21*] If $\mathcal{F}$ is a family of sets, and if α is a function that maps sets into real numbers, let $\alpha(\mathcal{F}) = \sum_{S \in \mathcal{F}} \alpha(S)$. Suppose $\mathcal{F}$ and $\mathcal{G}$ are finite families of sets for which nonnegative set functions α, β, γ, and δ have been defined with the property that

$$\alpha(S)\beta(T) \le \gamma(S \cup T)\delta(S \cap T) \quad \text{for all } S \in \mathcal{F} \text{ and } T \in \mathcal{G}.$$

a) Use exercise 59 to prove that $\alpha(\mathcal{F})\beta(\mathcal{G}) \le \gamma(\mathcal{F} \sqcup \mathcal{G})\delta(\mathcal{F} \sqcap \mathcal{G})$.

b) In particular, $|\mathcal{F}||\mathcal{G}| \le |\mathcal{F} \sqcup \mathcal{G}||\mathcal{F} \sqcap \mathcal{G}|$ for all families $\mathcal{F}$ and $\mathcal{G}$.

▶ **61.** [*M28*] Consider random sets in which S occurs with probability $\mu(S)$, where

$$\mu(S) \ge 0 \quad \text{and} \quad \mu(S)\mu(T) \le \mu(S \cup T)\mu(S \cap T) \quad \text{for all sets } S \text{ and } T. \quad (**)$$

Assume also that $U = \bigcup_{\mu(S)>0} S$ is a finite set.

a) Prove the *FKG inequality* (which is named for C. M. Fortuin, P. W. Kasteleyn, and J. Ginibre): If f and g are real-valued set functions, then

$$f(S) \le f(T) \text{ and } g(S) \le g(T) \text{ for all } S \subseteq T \quad \text{implies} \quad E(fg) \ge (E\,f)(E\,g).$$

Here, as usual, $E\,f$ stands for $\sum_S \mu(S)f(S)$. The conclusion can also be written 'covar$(f, g) \ge 0$', using the notation of (9); we say that f and g are "positively correlated" when this is true. (The awkward term "nonnegatively correlated" would be more accurate, because f and g might actually be independent.) *Hint:* Prove the result first in the special case that both f and g are nonnegative.

b) Furthermore,

$$f(S) \ge f(T) \text{ and } g(S) \ge g(T) \text{ for all } S \subseteq T \quad \text{implies} \quad E(fg) \ge (E\,f)(E\,g);$$
$$f(S) \le f(T) \text{ and } g(S) \ge g(T) \text{ for all } S \subseteq T \quad \text{implies} \quad E(fg) \le (E\,f)(E\,g).$$

c) It isn't necessary to verify condition $(**)$ for all sets, if $(**)$ is known to hold for sufficiently many pairs of "neighboring" sets. Given μ, let's say that set S is *supported* if $\mu(S) \ne 0$. Prove that $(**)$ holds for all S and T whenever the following three conditions are satisfied: (i) If S and T are supported, so are $S \cup T$ and $S \cap T$.

(ii) If S and T are supported and $S \subseteq T$, the elements of $T \setminus S$ can be labeled $t_1, \ldots, t_k$ such that each of the intermediate sets $S \cup \{t_1, \ldots, t_j\}$ is supported, for $1 \leq j \leq k$. (iii) Condition $(**)$ holds whenever $S = R \cup s$ and $T = R \cup t$ and $s, t \notin R$.

d) The *multivariate Bernoulli distribution* $B(p_1, \ldots, p_m)$ on subsets of $\{1, \ldots, m\}$ is

$$\mu(S) = \left(\prod_{j=1}^{m} p_j^{[j \in S]} \right) \left(\prod_{j=1}^{m} (1 - p_j)^{[j \notin S]} \right),$$

given $0 \leq p_1, \ldots, p_m \leq 1$. (Thus each element j is included independently with probability p_j, as in exercise 25.) Show that this distribution satisfies $(**)$.

e) Describe other simple distributions for which $(**)$ holds.

▶ **62.** [*M20*] Suppose the $m = \binom{n}{2}$ edges E of a random graph G on n vertices are chosen with the Bernoulli distribution $B(p_1, \ldots, p_m)$. Let $f(E) = [G$ is connected] and $g(E) = [G$ is 4-colorable]. Prove that f is negatively correlated with g.

63. [*M17*] Suppose Z_0 and Z_1 are random ternary variables with $\Pr(Z_0 = a$ and $Z_1 = b) = p_{ab}$ for $0 \leq a, b \leq 2$, where $p_{00} + p_{01} + \cdots + p_{22} = 1$. What can you say about those nine probabilities p_{ab} when $E(Z_1 | Z_0) = Z_0$?

▶ **64.** [*M22*] (a) If $E(Z_{n+1} | Z_n) = Z_n$ for all $n \geq 0$, is $\langle Z_n \rangle$ a martingale? (b) If $\langle Z_n \rangle$ is a martingale, is $E(Z_{n+1} | Z_n) = Z_n$ for all $n \geq 0$?

65. [*M21*] If $\langle Z_n \rangle$ is any martingale, show that any subsequence $\langle Z_{m(n)} \rangle$ is also a martingale, where the nonnegative integers $\langle m(n) \rangle$ satisfy $m(0) < m(1) < m(2) < \cdots$.

▶ **66.** [*M22*] Find all martingales $Z_0, Z_1, \ldots$ such that each random variable Z_n assumes only the values $\pm n$.

67. [*M20*] The Equitable Bank of El Dorado features a money machine such that, if you insert k dollars, you receive $2k$ dollars back with probability exactly $1/2$; otherwise you get nothing. Thus you either gain $\$k$ or lose $\$k$, and your expected profit is $\$0$. (Of course these transactions are all done electronically.)

a) Consider, however, the following scheme: Insert $\$1$; if that loses, insert $\$2$; if that also loses, insert $\$4$; then $\$8$, etc. If you first succeed after inserting 2^n dollars, stop (and take the 2^{n+1} dollars). What's your expected net profit at the end?

b) Continuing (a), what's the expected total amount that you put into the machine?

c) If Z_n is your net profit after n trials, show that $\langle Z_n \rangle$ is a martingale.

68. [*HM23*] When J. H. Quick (a student) visited El Dorado, he decided to proceed by making repeated bets of $\$1$ each, and to stop when he first came out ahead. (He was in no hurry, and was well aware of the perils of the high-stakes strategy in exercise 67.)

a) What martingale $\langle Z_n \rangle$ corresponds to this more conservative strategy?

b) Let N be the number of bets that Quick made before stopping. What is the probability that $N = n$?

c) What is the probability that $N \geq n$?

d) What is $E N$?

e) What is the probability that $\min(Z_0, Z_1, \ldots) = -m$? (Possible "gambler's ruin.")

f) What is the expected number of indices n such that $Z_n = -m$, given $m \geq 0$?

69. [*M20*] Section 1.2.5 discusses two basic ways by which we can go from permutations of $\{1, \ldots, n-1\}$ to permutations of $\{1, \ldots, n\}$: "Method 1" inserts n among the previous elements in all possible ways; "Method 2" puts a number k from 1 to n in the final position, and adds 1 to each previous number that was $\geq k$.

Show that, using either method, every permutation can be associated with a node of Fig. P, using a rule that obeys the probability assumptions of Pólya's urn model.

70. [*M25*] If Pólya's urn model is generalized so that we start with c balls of *different* colors, is there a martingale that generalizes Fig. P?

71. [*M21*] (G. Pólya.) What is the probability of going from node (r, b) to node (r', b') in Fig. P, given r, r', b, and b' with $r' \geq r$ and $b' \geq b$?

72. [*M23*] Let X_n be the red-ball indicator for Pólya's urn, as discussed in the text. What is $E(X_{n_1} X_{n_2} \ldots X_{n_m})$ when $0 < n_1 < n_2 < \cdots < n_m$?

73. [*M24*] The ratio $Z_n = r/(n+2)$ at node $(r, n+2-r)$ of Fig. P is not the only martingale definable on Pólya's urn. For example, $r[n = r - 1]$ is another; so is $r\binom{n+1}{r}/2^n$.

Find the most general martingale $\langle Z_n \rangle$ for this model: Given any sequence $a_0, a_1, \ldots$, show that there's exactly one suitable function $Z_n = f(r, n)$ such that $f(1, k) = a_k$.

74. [*M20*] (*Bernard Friedman's urn.*) Instead of contributing a ball of the same color, as in Fig. P, suppose we use the *opposite* color. Then the process changes to

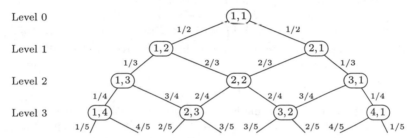

and the probabilities of reaching each node become quite different. What are they?

75. [*M25*] Find an interesting martingale for Bernard Friedman's urn.

76. [*M20*] If $\langle Z_n \rangle$ and $\langle Z'_n \rangle$ are martingales, is $\langle Z_n + Z'_n \rangle$ a martingale?

77. [*M21*] Prove or disprove: If $\langle Z_n \rangle$ is a martingale with respect to $\langle X_n \rangle$, then $\langle Z_n \rangle$ is a martingale with respect to itself (that is, a martingale).

78. [*M20*] A sequence of random variables $\langle V_n \rangle$ for which $E(V_{n+1} \mid V_0, \ldots, V_n) = 1$ is called "multiplicatively fair." Show that $Z_n = V_0 V_1 \ldots V_n$ is a martingale in such a case. Conversely, does every martingale lead to a multiplicatively fair sequence?

79. [*M20*] (*De Moivre's martingale.*) Let X_1, X_2, $\ldots$ be a sequence of independent coin tosses, with $\Pr([\text{"heads" occurred on the } n\text{th toss}]) = \Pr(X_n = 1) = p$ for each n. Show that $Z_n = (q/p)^{2(X_1+\cdots+X_n)-n}$ defines a martingale, where $q = 1 - p$.

80. [*M20*] Are the following statements true or false for every fair sequence $\langle Y_n \rangle$? (a) $E(Y_3^2 Y_5) = 0$. (b) $E(Y_3 Y_5^2) = 0$. (c) $E(Y_{n_1} Y_{n_2} \ldots Y_{n_m}) = 0$ if $n_1 < n_2 < \cdots < n_m$.

81. [*M21*] Suppose $E(X_{n+1} \mid X_0, \ldots, X_n) = X_n + X_{n-1}$ for $n \geq 0$, where $X_{-1} = 0$. Find sequences a_n and b_n of coefficients so that $Z_n = a_n X_n + b_n X_{n-1}$ is a martingale, where $Z_0 = X_0$ and $Z_1 = 2X_0 - X_1$. (We might call this a "Fibonacci martingale.")

▶ **82.** [*M20*] In the game of Ace Now, let $X_n = [\text{the } n\text{th card is an ace}]$, with $X_0 = 0$.
  a) Show that $Z_n = (4 - X_1 - \cdots - X_n)/(52 - n)$ satisfies (28) for $0 \leq n < 52$.
  b) Consequently $E Z_N = 1/13$, regardless of the stopping rule employed.
  c) Hence all strategies are equally good (or bad); you win $0 on average.

▶ **83.** [*HM22*] Given a sequence $\langle X_n \rangle$ of independent and nonnegative random variables, let $S_n = X_1 + \cdots + X_n$. If $N_n(x_0, \ldots, x_{n-1})$ is any stopping rule and if N is defined by (31), prove that $\mathrm{E}\, S_N = \mathrm{E} \sum_{k=1}^{N} \mathrm{E}\, X_k$. (In particular, if $\mathrm{E}\, X_n = \mathrm{E}\, X_1$ for all $n > 0$ we have "Wald's equation," which states that $\mathrm{E}\, S_N = (\mathrm{E}\, N)(\mathrm{E}\, X_1)$.)

84. [*HM21*] Let $f(x)$ be a convex function for $a \leq x \leq b$, and assume that $\langle Z_n \rangle$ is a martingale such that $a \leq Z_n \leq b$ for all $n \geq 0$. (Possibly $a = -\infty$ and/or $b = +\infty$.)
   a) Prove that $\langle f(Z_n) \rangle$ is a submartingale.
   b) What can you say if the sequence $\langle Z_n \rangle$ is assumed only to be a submartingale?

85. [*M20*] Suppose there are R_n red balls and B_n black balls at level n of Pólya's urn (Fig. P). Prove that the sequence $\langle R_n/B_n \rangle$ is a submartingale.

▶ **86.** [*M22*] Prove (33) by inventing a suitable stopping rule $N_{n+1}(Z_0, \ldots, Z_n)$.

87. [*M18*] What does the maximal inequality (33) reveal about the chances that Pólya's urn will hold thrice as many red balls as black balls at some point?

▶ **88.** [*HM30*] Let $S = \sup Z_n$ be the least upper bound of Z_n as $n \to \infty$ in Fig. P.
   a) Prove that $S > 1/2$ with probability $\ln 2 \approx .693$.
   b) Similarly, show that $\Pr(S > 2/3) = \ln 3 - \pi/\sqrt{27} \approx .494$.
   c) Generalize to $\Pr(S > (t-1)/t)$, for all $t \geq 2$. *Hint:* See exercise 7.2.1.6–36.

89. [*M17*] Let $(X_1, \ldots, X_n)$ be random variables that have the Bernoulli distribution $B(p_1, \ldots, p_n)$, and suppose $c_1, \ldots, c_n$ are nonnegative. Use (37) to show that

$$\Pr(c_1 X_1 + \cdots + c_n X_n \geq c_1 p_1 + \cdots + c_n p_n + x) \leq e^{-2x^2/(c_1^2 + \cdots + c_n^2)}.$$

90. [*HM25*] The Hoeffding–Azuma inequality (37) can be derived as follows:
   a) Show first that $\Pr(Y_1 + \cdots + Y_n \geq x) \leq \mathrm{E}(e^{(Y_1 + \cdots + Y_n)t})/e^{tx}$ for all $t > 0$.
   b) If $0 \leq p \leq 1$ and $q = 1 - p$, show that $e^{yt} \leq e^{f(t)} + y e^{g(t)}$ when $-p \leq y \leq q$ and $t > 0$, where $f(t) = -pt + \ln(q + pe^t)$ and $g(t) = -pt + \ln(e^t - 1)$.
   c) Prove that $f(t) \leq t^2/8$. *Hint:* Use Taylor's formula, Eq. 1.2.11.3–(5).
   d) Consequently $a \leq Y \leq b$ implies $e^{Yt} \leq e^{(b-a)^2 t^2/8} + Y h(t)$, for some function $h(t)$.
   e) Let $c = (c_1^2 + \cdots + c_n^2)/2$, where $c_k = b_k - a_k$. Prove that $\mathrm{E}(e^{(Y_1 + \cdots + Y_n)t}) \leq e^{ct^2/4}$.
   f) We obtain (37) by choosing the best value of t.

91. [*M20*] Prove that Doob's general formula (39) always defines a martingale.

▶ **92.** [*M20*] Let $\langle Q_n \rangle$ be the Doob martingale that corresponds to Pólya's urn (27) when $Q = X_m$, for some fixed $m > 0$. Calculate Q_0, Q_1, Q_2, etc.

93. [*M20*] Solve the text's hashing problem under the more general model considered in the bin-packing problem: Each variable X_n has probability p_{nk} of being equal to k, for $1 \leq n \leq t$ and $1 \leq k \leq m$. What formula do you get instead of (44)?

▶ **94.** [*M22*] Where is the fact that the variables $\{X_1, \ldots, X_t\}$ are independent used in the previous exercise?

95. [*M20*] True or false: "Pólya's urn q.s. accumulates more than 100 red balls."

96. [*HM22*] Let X be the number of heads seen in n flips of an unbiased coin. Decide whether each of the following statements about X is a.s., q.s., or neither, as $n \to \infty$:
   (i) $|X - n/2| < \sqrt{n} \ln n$;   (ii) $|X - n/2| < \sqrt{n \ln n}$;
   (iii) $|X - n/2| < \sqrt{n \ln \ln n}$;   (iv) $|X - n/2| < \sqrt{n}$.

▶ **97.** [*HM21*] Suppose $\lfloor n^{1+\delta} \rfloor$ items are hashed into n bins, where δ is a positive constant. Prove that every bin q.s. gets between $\frac{1}{2}n^\delta$ and $2n^\delta$ of them.

▶ **98.** [*M21*] Many algorithms are governed by a loop of the form

$$X \leftarrow n; \text{ while } X > 0, \text{ set } X \leftarrow X - F(X)$$

where $F(X)$ is a random integer in the range $[1 .. X]$. We assume that each integer $F(X)$ is completely independent of any previously generated values, subject only to the requirement that $\mathrm{E}\,F(j) \geq g_j$, where $0 < g_1 \leq g_2 \leq \cdots \leq g_n$.

Prove that the loop sets $X \leftarrow X - F(X)$ at most $1/g_1 + 1/g_2 + \cdots + 1/g_n$ times, on the average. ("If one step reduces by g_n, then perhaps $(1/g_n)$th of a step reduces by 1.")

99. [*HM30*] Show that the result in the previous exercise holds even when the range of $F(X)$ is $(-\infty .. X]$, given $0 < g_1 \leq \cdots \leq g_n \leq g_{n+1} \leq \cdots$. (Thus X might *increase*.)

100. [*HM17*] A certain randomized algorithm takes T steps, where $\Pr(T = t) = p_t$ for $1 \leq t \leq \infty$. Prove that (a) $\lim_{m \to \infty} \mathrm{E}\min(m, T) = \mathrm{E}\,T$; (b) $\mathrm{E}\,T < \infty$ implies $p_\infty = 0$.

101. [*HM22*] Suppose $X = X_1 + \cdots + X_m$ is the sum of independent geometrically distributed random integers, with $\Pr(X_k = n) = p_k(1 - p_k)^{n-1}$ for $n \geq 1$. Prove that $\Pr(X \geq r\mu) \leq re^{1-r}$ for all $r \geq 1$, where $\mu = \mathrm{E}\,X = \sum_{k=1}^{m} 1/p_k$.

102. [*M20*] Cora collects coupons, using a random process. After already owning $k - 1$ of them, her chance of success when trying for the kth is at least one chance in s_k, independent of any previous successes or failures. Prove that she will a.s. own m coupons before making $(s_1 + \cdots + s_m) \ln n$ trials. And she will q.s. need at most $s_k \ln n \ln \ln n$ trials to obtain the kth coupon, for each $k \leq m$, if $m = O(n^{1000})$.

▶ **103.** [*M30*] This exercise is based on two functions of the ternary digits $\{0, 1, 2\}$:

$$f_0(x) = \max(0, x - 1); \qquad f_1(x) = \min(2, x + 1).$$

a) What is $\Pr(f_{X_1}(f_{X_2}(\ldots(f_{X_n}(i))\ldots)) = j)$, for each $i, j \in \{0, 1, 2\}$, assuming that $X_1, X_2, \ldots, X_n$ are independent, uniformly random bits?

b) Here's an algorithm that computes $f_{X_1}(f_{X_2}(\ldots(f_{X_n}(i))\ldots))$ for $i \in \{0, 1, 2\}$, and stops when all three values have coalesced to a common value:

  Set $a_0 a_1 a_2 \leftarrow 012$ and $n \leftarrow 0$. Then while $a_0 \neq a_2$, set $n \leftarrow n + 1$, $t_0 t_1 t_2 \leftarrow (X_n? 122: 001)$, and $a_0 a_1 a_2 \leftarrow a_{t_0} a_{t_1} a_{t_2}$. Output a_0.

  (Notice that $a_0 \leq a_1 \leq a_2$ always holds.) What is the probability that this algorithm outputs j? What are the mean and variance of N, the final value of n?

c) A similar algorithm computes $f_{X_n}(\ldots(f_{X_2}(f_{X_1}(i)))\ldots)$, if we change '$a_{t_0} a_{t_1} a_{t_2}$' to '$t_{a_0} t_{a_1} t_{a_2}$'. What's the probability of output j in *this* algorithm?

d) Why on earth are the results of (b) and (c) so different?

e) The algorithm in (c) doesn't really use a_1. Therefore we might try to speed up process (b) by cleverly evaluating the functions in the opposite direction. Consider the following subroutine, called sub(T):

  Set $a_0 a_2 \leftarrow 02$ and $n \leftarrow 0$. Then while $n < T$ set $n \leftarrow n + 1$, $X \leftarrow$ random bit, and $a_0 a_2 \leftarrow (X_n? f_1(a_0) f_1(a_2): f_0(a_0) f_0(a_2))$. If $a_0 = a_2$ output a_0, otherwise output -1.

  Then the algorithm of (b) would seem to be equivalent to

  Set $T \leftarrow 1$, $a \leftarrow -1$; while $a < 0$ set $T \leftarrow 2T$ and $a \leftarrow$ sub(T); output a.

  Prove, however, that this fails. (Randomized algorithms can be quite delicate!)

f) Patch the algorithm of (e) and obtain a correct alternative to (b).

104. [*M21*] Solve exercise 103(b) and 103(c) when each X_k is 1 with probability p.

▶ **105.** [*M30*] (*Random walk on an n-cycle.*) Given integers a and n, with $0 \leq a \leq n$, let N be minimum such that $(a + (-1)^{X_1} + (-1)^{X_2} + \cdots + (-1)^{X_N})$ mod $n = 0$, where $X_1, X_2, \ldots$ is a sequence of independent random bits. Find the generating function $g_a = \sum_{k=0}^{\infty} \Pr(N = k) z^k$. What are the mean and variance of N?

106. [*M25*] Consider the algorithm of exercise 103(b) when the digits are d-ary instead of ternary; thus $f_0(x) = \max(0, x - 1)$ and $f_1(x) = \min(d - 1, x + 1)$. Find the generating function, mean, and variance of the number N of steps required before $a_0 = a_1 = \cdots = a_{d-1}$ is first reached in this more general situation.

▶ **107.** [*M22*] (*Coupling.*) If X is a random variable on the probability space Ω' and Y is another random variable on another probability space Ω'', we can study them together by redefining them on a common probability space Ω. All conclusions about X or Y are valid with respect to Ω, provided that we have $\Pr(X = x) = \Pr'(X = x)$ and $\Pr(Y = y) = \Pr''(Y = y)$ for all x and y.

Such "coupling" is obviously possible if we let Ω be the set $\Omega' \times \Omega''$ of pairs $\{\omega'\omega'' \mid \omega' \in \Omega' \text{ and } \omega'' \in \Omega''\}$, and if we define $\Pr(\omega'\omega'') = \Pr'(\omega') \Pr''(\omega'')$ for each pair of events. But coupling can also be achieved in many other ways.

For example, suppose Ω' and Ω'' each contain only two events, $\{Q, K\}$ and $\{♣, ♠\}$, with $\Pr'(Q) = p$, $\Pr'(K) = 1 - p$, $\Pr''(♣) = q$, $\Pr''(♠) = 1 - q$. We could couple them with a four-event space $\Omega = \{Q♣, Q♠, K♣, K♠\}$, having $\Pr(Q♣) = pq$, $\Pr(Q♠) = p(1-q)$, $\Pr(K♣) = (1-p)q$, $\Pr(K♠) = (1-p)(1-q)$. But if $p < q$ we could also get by with just three events, letting $\Pr(Q♣) = p$, $\Pr(K♣) = q - p$, $\Pr(K♠) = 1 - q$. A similar scheme works when $p > q$, omitting K♣. And if $p = q$ we need only two events, Q♣ and K♠.

a) Show that if Ω' and Ω'' each have just three events, with respective probabilities $\{p_1, p_2, p_3\}$ and $\{q_1, q_2, q_3\}$, they can always be coupled in a five-event space Ω.

b) Also, four events suffice if $\{p_1, p_2, p_3\} = \{\frac{1}{12}, \frac{5}{12}, \frac{6}{12}\}$, $\{q_1, q_2, q_3\} = \{\frac{2}{12}, \frac{3}{12}, \frac{7}{12}\}$.

c) But some three-event distributions cannot be coupled with fewer than five.

108. [*HM21*] If X and Y are integer-valued random variables such that $\Pr'(X \geq n) \leq \Pr''(Y \geq n)$ for all integers n, find a way to couple them so that $X \leq Y$ always holds.

109. [*M27*] Suppose X and Y have values in a finite partially ordered set P, and that

$$\Pr'(X \succeq a \text{ for some } a \in A) \leq \Pr''(Y \succeq a \text{ for some } a \in A), \qquad \text{for all } A \subseteq P.$$

We will show that there's a coupling in which $X \preceq Y$ always holds.

a) Write out exactly what needs to be proved, in the simple case where $P = \{1, 2, 3\}$ and the partial order has $1 \prec 3$, $2 \prec 3$. (Let $p_k = \Pr'(X = k)$ and $q_k = \Pr''(Y = k)$ for $k \in P$. When $P = \{1, \ldots, n\}$, a coupling is an $n \times n$ matrix (p_{ij}) of nonnegative probabilities whose row sums are $\sum_j p_{ij} = p_i$ and column sums are $\sum_i p_{ij} = q_j$.) Compare this to the result proved in the preceding exercise.

b) Prove that $\Pr'(X \preceq b \text{ for some } b \in B) \geq \Pr''(Y \preceq b \text{ for some } b \in B)$, for all $B \subseteq P$.

c) A coupling between n pairs of events can be viewed as a flow in a network that has $2n + 2$ vertices $\{s, x_1, \ldots, x_n, y_1, \ldots, y_n, t\}$, where there are p_i units of flow from s to x_i, p_{ij} units of flow from x_i to y_j, and q_j units of flow from y_j to t. The "max-flow min-cut theorem" [see Section 7.5.3] states that such a flow is possible if and only if there are no subsets $I, J \subseteq \{1, \ldots, n\}$ such that (i) every path from s to t goes through some arc $s \longrightarrow x_i$ for $i \in I$ or some arc $y_j \longrightarrow t$ for $j \in J$, and (ii) $\sum_{i \in I} p_i + \sum_{j \in J} q_j < 1$. Use that theorem to prove the desired result.

110. [*M25*] If X and Y take values in $\{1, \ldots, n\}$, let $p_k = \Pr'(X = k)$, $q_k = \Pr''(Y = k)$, and $r_k = \min(p_k, q_k)$ for $1 \leq k \leq n$. The probability that $X = Y$ in any coupling is obviously at most $r = \sum_{k=1}^{n} r_k$.

a) Show that there always is a coupling with $\Pr(X = Y) = r$.

b) Can the result of the previous exercise be extended, so that we have not only $\Pr(X \preceq Y) = 1$ but also $\Pr(X = Y) = r$?

▶ **111.** [*M20*] A family of N permutations of the numbers $\{1, \ldots, n\}$ is called *minwise independent* if, whenever $1 \le j \le k \le n$ and $\{a_1, \ldots, a_k\} \subseteq \{1, \ldots, n\}$, exactly N/k of the permutations π have $\min(a_1\pi, \ldots, a_k\pi) = a_j\pi$.

For example, the family F of $N = 60$ permutations obtained by cyclic shifts of

$$123456, 126345, 152346, 152634, 164235, 154263, 165324, 164523, 156342, 165432$$

can be shown to be minwise independent permutations of $\{1, 2, 3, 4, 5, 6\}$.

a) Verify the independence condition for F in the case $k = 3$, $a_1 = 1$, $a_2 = 3$, $a_3 = 4$.

b) Suppose we choose a random π from a minwise independent family, and assign the "sketch" $S_A = \min_{a \in A} a\pi$ to every $A \subseteq \{1, \ldots, n\}$. Prove that, if A and B are arbitrary subsets, $\Pr(S_A = S_B) = |A \cap B| / |A \cup B|$.

c) Given three subsets A, B, C, what is $\Pr(S_A = S_B = S_C)$?

112. [*M25*] The size of a family F of minwise independent permutations must be a multiple of k for each $k \le n$, by definition. In this exercise we'll see how to construct such a family with the minimum possible size, namely $N = \text{lcm}(1, 2, \ldots, n)$.

The basic idea is that, if all elements of the permutations in F that exceed m are replaced by ∞, the "truncated" family is still minwise independent in the sense that, if $\min_{a \in A} a\pi = \infty$, we can imagine that the minimum occurs at a random element of A. (This can happen only if π takes *all* elements of A to ∞.)

a) Conversely, show that an m-truncated family can be lifted to an $(m+1)$-truncated family if, for each subset B of size $n - m$, we insert $m + 1$ equally often into each of B's $n - m$ positions, within the permutations whose ∞'s are in B.

b) Use this principle to construct minimum-size families F.

113. [*M25*] Although minwise permutations are defined only in terms of the minimum operation, a minwise independent family actually turns out to be also maxwise independent — and even more is true!

a) Let E be the event that $a_i\pi < k$, $b\pi = k$, and $c_j\pi > k$, for any disjoint sets $\{a_1, \ldots, a_l\}$, $\{b\}$, $\{c_1, \ldots, c_r\} \subseteq \{1, \ldots, n\}$. Prove that, if π is chosen randomly from a minwise independent set, $\Pr(E)$ is the same as the probability that E occurs when π is chosen randomly from the set of all permutations. (For example, $\Pr(5\pi < 7, 2\pi = 7, 1\pi > 7, 8\pi > 7) = 6(n - 7)(n - 8)(n - 4)!/n!$, whenever $n \ge 8$.)

b) Furthermore, if $\{a_1, \ldots, a_k\} \subseteq \{1, \ldots, n\}$, the probability that $a_j\pi$ is the rth largest element of $\{a_1\pi, \ldots, a_k\pi\}$ is $1/k$, whenever $1 \le j, r \le k$.

▶ **114.** [*M28*] (*The "combinatorial nullstellensatz."*) Let $f(x_1, \ldots, x_n)$ be a polynomial in which the coefficient of $x_1^{d_1} \ldots x_n^{d_n}$ is nonzero and each term has degree $\le d_1 + \cdots + d_n$. Given subsets $S_1, \ldots, S_n$ of the field of coefficients, with $|S_j| > d_j$ for $1 \le j \le n$, choose $X_1, \ldots, X_n$ independently and uniformly, with each $X_j \in S_j$. Prove that

$$\Pr(f(X_1, \ldots, X_n) \ne 0) \ge \frac{|S_1| + \cdots + |S_n| - (d_1 + \cdots + d_n + n) + 1}{|S_1| \ldots |S_n|}.$$

Hint: See exercise 4.6.1–16.

115. [*M21*] Prove that an $m \times n$ grid cannot be fully covered by p horizontal lines, q vertical lines, r diagonal lines of slope $+1$, and r diagonal lines of slope -1, if $m = p + 2\lfloor r/2 \rfloor + 1$ and $n = q + 2\lceil r/2 \rceil + 1$. *Hint:* Apply exercise 114 to a suitable polynomial $f(x, y)$.

116. [*HM25*] Use exercise 114 to prove that, if p is prime, any multigraph G on n vertices with more than $(p-1)n$ edges contains a nonempty subgraph in which the degree of every vertex is a multiple of p. (In particular, if each vertex of G has fewer than $2p$ neighbors, G contains a p-regular subgraph. A loop from v to itself adds two to v's degree.) *Hint:* Let the polynomial contain a variable x_e for each edge e of G.

▶ **117.** [*HM25*] Let X have the binomial distribution $B_n(p)$, so that $\Pr(X = k) = \binom{n}{k}p^k(1-p)^{n-k}$ for $0 \le k \le n$. Prove that $X \bmod m$ is approximately uniform:

$$\left| \Pr(X \bmod m = r) - \frac{1}{m} \right| < \frac{2}{m} \sum_{j=1}^{\infty} e^{-8p(1-p)j^2 n/m^2}, \quad \text{for } 0 \le r < m.$$

118. [*M20*] Use the second moment principle to prove the *Paley–Zygmund inequality*

$$\Pr(X \ge x) \ge \frac{(\mathrm{E}\,X - x)^2}{\mathrm{E}\,X^2}, \quad \text{if } 0 \le x \le \mathrm{E}\,X.$$

119. [*HM24*] Let x be a fixed value in $[0..1]$. Prove that, if we independently and uniformly choose $U \in [0..x]$, $V \in [x..1]$, $W \in [0..1]$, then the median $\langle UVW \rangle$ is uniformly distributed in $[\min(U,V,W)..\max(U,V,W)]$.

120. [*M20*] Consider random binary search trees T_n obtained by successively inserting independent uniform deviates U_1, U_2, ... into an initially empty tree. Let T_{nk} be the number of external nodes on level k, and define $T_n(z) = \sum_{k=0}^{\infty} T_{nk}z^k/(n+1)$. Prove that $Z_n = T_n(z)/g_{n+1}(z)$ is a martingale, where $g_n(z) = (2z+n-2)(2z+n-3)\dots(2z)/n!$ is the generating function for the cost of the nth insertion (exercise 6.2.2–6).

▶ **121.** [*M26*] Let X and Y be random variables with the distributions $\Pr(X = t) = x(t)$ and $\Pr(Y = t) = y(t)$. The ratio $\rho(t) = y(t)/x(t)$, which may be infinity, is called the *probability density* of Y with respect to X. We define the *relative entropy of X with respect to Y*, also called the *Kullback–Leibler divergence of X from Y*, by the formulas

$$D(y\|x) = \mathrm{E}(\rho(X)\lg\rho(X)) = \mathrm{E}\lg\rho(Y) = \sum_t y(t)\lg\frac{y(t)}{x(t)},$$

with $0\lg 0$ and $0\lg(0/0)$ understood to mean 0. It can be viewed intuitively as the number of bits of information that are lost when X is used to approximate Y.

a) Suppose X is a random six-sided die with the uniform distribution, but Y is a "loaded" die in which $\Pr(Y = \boxed{\cdot}) = \frac{1}{5}$ and $\Pr(Y = \boxed{::}) = \frac{2}{15}$, instead of $\frac{1}{6}$. Compute $D(y\|x)$ and $D(x\|y)$.

b) Prove that $D(y\|x) \ge 0$. When is it zero?

c) If $p = \Pr(X \in T)$ and $q = \Pr(Y \in T)$, show that $\mathrm{E}(\lg\rho(Y)\,|\,Y \in T) \ge \lg(q/p)$.

d) Suppose $x(t) = 1/m$ for all t in an m-element set S, and $y(t) \ne 0$ only when $t \in S$. Express $D(y\|x)$ in terms of the *entropy* $H_Y = \mathrm{E}\lg(1/Y)$ (see Eq. 6.2.2–(18)).

e) Let $Z(u,v) = \Pr(X = u \text{ and } Y = v)$ when X and Y have any joint distribution, and let $W(u,v)$ be that same probability under the assumption that X and Y are independent. The *joint entropy* $H_{X,Y}$ is defined to be H_Z, and the *mutual information* $I_{X,Y}$ is defined to be $D(z\|w)$. Prove that $H_W = H_X + H_Y$ and $I_{X,Y} = H_W - H_Z$. (Consequently $H_{X,Y} \le H_X + H_Y$, and $I_{X,Y}$ measures the difference.)

f) Let $H_{X|Y} = H_X - I_{X,Y} = H_{X,Y} - H_Y = \sum_t y(t)H_{X|t}$ be the average uncertainty of X, in bits, after Y has been revealed. Prove that $H_{X|(Y,Z)} \le H_{X|Y}$.

122. [*HM24*] Continuing exercise 121, compute $D(y\|x)$ and $D(x\|y)$ when

a) $x(t) = 1/2^{t+1}$ and $y(t) = 3^t/4^{t+1}$ for $t = 0, 1, 2, \ldots$;

b) $x(t) = e^{-np}(np)^t/t!$ and $y(t) = \binom{n}{t}p^t(1-p)^{n-t}$, for $t \ge 0$ and $0 < p < 1$. (Give asymptotic answers with absolute error $O(1/n)$, for fixed p as $n \to \infty$.)

▶ **123.** [*M20*] Let X and Y be as in exercise 121. The random variable $Z = A?\ Y\colon X$ either has the distribution $x(t)$ or $y(t)$, but we don't know whether A is true or false. If we believe that the hypothesis $Z = Y$ holds with the *a priori* probability $\Pr(A) = p_k$, we assume that $z_k(t) = \Pr_k(Z = t) = p_k x(t) + (1 - p_k)y(t)$. But after seeing a new value of Z, say $Z = Z_k$, we will believe the hypothesis with the *a posteriori* probability $p_{k+1} = \Pr(A \mid Z_k)$. Show that $D(y\|x)$ is the expected "information gained," $\lg(p_{k+1}/(1 - p_{k+1})) - \lg(p_k/(1 - p_k))$, averaged with respect to the distribution of Y.

124. [*HM22*] (*Importance sampling.*) In the setting of exercise 121, we have $\mathrm{E}\,f(Y) = \mathrm{E}(\rho(X)f(X))$ for any function f; thus $\rho(t)$ measures the "importance" of the X-value t with respect to the Y-value t. Many situations arise when it's easy to generate random variables with an approximate distribution $x(t)$, but difficult to generate them with the exact distribution $y(t)$. In such cases we can estimate the average value $E(f) = \mathrm{E}\,f(Y)$ by calculating $E_n(f) = (\rho(X_1)f(X_1) + \cdots + \rho(X_n)f(X_n))/n$, where the X_j are independent random variables, each distributed as $x(t)$.

Let $n = c^4 2^{D(y\|x)}$. Prove that if $c > 1$, this estimate E_n is relatively accurate:

$$|E(f) - E_n(f)| \le \|f\|\,(1/c + 2\sqrt{\Delta_c}), \qquad \text{where } \Delta_c = \Pr(\rho(Y) > c^2 2^{D(y\|x)}).$$

(Here $\|f\|$ denotes $(\mathrm{E}\,f(Y)^2)^{1/2}$.) On the other hand if $c < 1$ the estimate is poor:

$$\Pr(E_n(1) \ge a) \le c^2 + (1 - \Delta_c)/a. \qquad \text{for } 0 < a < 1,$$

Here '1' denotes the constant function $f(y) = 1$ (hence $E(1) = 1$).

▶ **125.** [*M28*] Let $\langle a_n \rangle = a_0, a_1, a_2, \ldots$ be a sequence of nonnegative numbers with no "internal zeros" (no indices $i < j < k$ such that $a_i > 0$, $a_j = 0$, $a_k > 0$). We call it *log-convex* if $a_n^2 \le a_{n-1}a_{n+1}$ for all $n \ge 1$, and *log-concave* if $a_n^2 \ge a_{n-1}a_{n+1}$ for all $n \ge 1$.

    a) What sequences are both log-convex and log-concave?

    b) If $\langle a_n \rangle$ is log-convex or log-concave, so is its "left shift" $\langle a_{n+1} \rangle = a_1, a_2, a_3, \ldots$. What can be said about the "right shift" $\langle a_{n-1} \rangle = c, a_0, a_1, \ldots$, given c?

    c) Show that a log-concave sequence has $a_m a_n \ge a_{m-1}a_{n+1}$ whenever $1 \le m \le n$.

    d) If $\langle a_n \rangle$ and $\langle b_n \rangle$ are log-convex, show that $\langle a_n + b_n \rangle$ is also log-convex.

    e) If $\langle a_n \rangle$ and $\langle b_n \rangle$ are log-convex, show that $\langle \sum_k \binom{n}{k} a_k b_{n-k} \rangle$ is also log-convex.

    f) If $\langle a_n \rangle$ and $\langle b_n \rangle$ are log-concave, is $\langle \sum_k a_k b_{n-k} \rangle$ also log-concave?

    g) If $\langle a_n \rangle$ and $\langle b_n \rangle$ are log-concave, is $\langle \sum_k \binom{n}{k} a_k b_{n-k} \rangle$ also log-concave?

126. [*HM22*] Suppose $X_1, \ldots, X_n$ are independent binary random variables with $\mathrm{E}\,X_k = m/n$ for all k, where $0 \le m \le n$. Prove that $\Pr(X_1 + \cdots + X_n = m) = \Omega(n^{-1/2})$.

127. [*HM30*] Say that a binary vector $x = x_1 \ldots x_n$ is *sparse* if $\nu x \le \theta n$, where θ is a given threshold parameter, $0 < \theta < \frac{1}{2}$. Let $S(n, \theta)$ be the number of sparse vectors.

    a) Show that $S(n, \theta) \le 2^{H(\theta)n}$, where H denotes entropy.

    b) On the other hand, $S(n, \theta)$ is also $\Omega(2^{H(\theta)n}/\sqrt{n})$.

    c) Let X' and X'' be independent and uniformly distributed sparse vectors, and let x be any binary vector, all of length n. Prove that $x \oplus X' \oplus X''$ is q.s. not sparse. [*Hint:* Both X' and X'' q.s. have nearly θn 1s. Furthermore exercise 126 can be used to pretend that the individual bits of $x \oplus X' \oplus X''$ are independent.]

▶ **128.** [*HM26*] Consider n independent processors that are competing for access to a shared database. They're totally unable to communicate with each other, so they agree to adopt the following protocol: During each unit of time, called a "round," each processor independently generates a random uniform deviate U and "pings" the database (attempts an access) if $U < 1/n$. If exactly one processor pings, its attempt succeeds; otherwise *nobody* gets access during that round.

a) What is the probability that some processor pings successfully, in a given round?

b) How many rounds does a particular processor have to wait, on average, before being successful? (Give an asymptotic answer, correct to $O(1/n)$.)

c) Let ϵ be any positive constant. Prove that the processors a.s. will all have at least one success during the first $(1 + \epsilon)en \ln n$ rounds. *Hint:* See exercise 3.3.2–10.

d) But prove also that they a.s. will *not* all succeed during $(1 - \epsilon)en \ln n$ rounds.

129. [*HM28*] (*General rational summation.*) Let $r(x) = p(x)/q(x)$, where p and q are polynomials, $\deg(q) \geq \deg(p) + 2$, and q has no integer roots. Prove that

$$\sum_{k=-\infty}^{\infty} \frac{p(k)}{q(k)} = -\pi \sum_{j=1}^{t} (\text{Residue of } r(z) \cot \pi z \text{ at } z_j),$$

where $z_1, \ldots, z_t$ are the roots of q. *Hint:* Show that $\frac{1}{2\pi i} \oint r(z) \cot \pi z \, dz = O(1/M)$, when the integral is taken along the square path for which $\max(|\Re z|, |\Im z|) = M + \frac{1}{2}$.

Use this method to evaluate the following sums in "closed form":

$$\sum_{k=-\infty}^{\infty} \frac{1}{(2k-1)^2}; \quad \sum_{k=-\infty}^{\infty} \frac{1}{k^2+1}; \quad \sum_{k=-\infty}^{\infty} \frac{1}{k^2+k+1}; \quad \sum_{k=-\infty}^{\infty} \frac{1}{(k^2+k+1)(2k-1)}.$$

130. [*HM30*] Many of the probability distributions that arise in modern computer applications have "heavy tails," in contrast to bell-shaped curves that are concentrated near the mean. The simplest and most useful example — although it also is somewhat paradoxical — is the *Cauchy distribution*, defined by

$$\Pr(X \leq x) = \frac{1}{\pi} \int_{-\infty}^{x} \frac{dt}{1+t^2}.$$

a) If X is a Cauchy deviate, what are $E X$ and $E X^2$?

b) What are $\Pr(|X| \leq 1)$, $\Pr(|X| \leq \sqrt{3})$, and $\Pr(|X| \leq 2 + \sqrt{3})$?

c) If U is a uniform deviate, show that $\tan(\pi(U - 1/2))$ is a Cauchy deviate.

d) Suggest other ways to generate Cauchy deviates.

e) Let $Z = pX + qY$ where X and Y are independent Cauchy deviates and $p + q = 1$, $p, q > 0$. Prove that Z has the Cauchy distribution.

f) Let $X = (X_1, \ldots, X_n)$ be a vector of n independent Cauchy deviates, and let $c = (c_1, \ldots, c_n)$ be any vector of real numbers. What is the distribution of the dot product $c \cdot X = (c_1 X_1 + \cdots + c_n X_n)$?

g) What is the "characteristic function" $E e^{itX}$, when X is a Cauchy deviate?

131. [*HM30*] An integer-valued analog of Cauchy deviates, which we shall call the "iCauchy distribution" for convenience, has $\Pr(X = n) = c/(1 + n^2)$ for $-\infty < n < \infty$.

a) What constant c makes this a valid probability distribution?

b) Compare the distribution of $X + Y$ to the distribution of $2Z$, when X, Y, and Z are independent iCauchy deviates.

▶ **132.** [*HM26*] Choose n balls from an urn that contains N balls, K of which are green.

a) What's the probability p_k that exactly k green balls are chosen?

b) What are the mean, modes, and variance? (A *mode* in a probability distribution is a value of k that's a local maximum: $p_{k-1} \leq p_k \geq p_{k+1}$ and $p_k > 0$.)

c) Let $X_j = $ [the jth ball is green], so that $p_k = \Pr(X_1 + \cdots + X_n = k)$. Use a Doob martingale to establish an exponentially small upper bound on the tail probability $\Pr(X_1 + \cdots + X_n \geq nK/N + x)$.

133. [*M25*] Call t rows of a binary matrix *shattered* if all 2^t possible columns occur.
   a) Prove that any binary matrix with m rows and more than $f(m, t) = \binom{m}{0} + \binom{m}{1} + \cdots + \binom{m}{t-1}$ distinct columns contains t shattered rows.
   b) Construct a matrix with m rows and $f(m, t)$ distinct columns, no t shattered.

134. [*HM28*] (V. N. Vapnik and A. Ya. Chervonenkis, 1971.) Many different events $\mathcal{A} = \{A_1, \ldots, A_n\}$, which depend on each other in complicated ways, might be of interest simultaneously, and we often want to learn their probabilities $p_j = \Pr(A_j)$ by observing a sufficiently large sample. If $\mathcal{X} = \{X_1, \ldots, X_m\}$ is a subset of the probability space Ω, the probability of sampling $\mathcal{X}$ (with replacement) is $\Pr(X_1) \ldots \Pr(X_m)$.

Consider the random $m \times n$ binary matrix whose entries are $X_{ij} = [X_i \in A_j] = $ [the atomic event X_i is an instance of A_j]. The empirical probability $\widehat{P}_j(\mathcal{X})$ based on sample $\mathcal{X}$ is then $M_j(\mathcal{X})/m$, where $M_j(\mathcal{X}) = X_{1j} + \cdots + X_{mj}$, for $1 \leq j \leq n$.

Let $E_j(\mathcal{X}) = |\widehat{P}_j(\mathcal{X}) - p_j|$ be the difference between the empirical and actual probabilities. We hope that the *uniform sampling error* $E(\mathcal{X}) = \max_{1 \leq j \leq n} E_j(\mathcal{X})$ is small.
   a) For all $\epsilon > 0$ and $1 \leq j \leq n$, prove that $\Pr(E_j(\mathcal{X}) > \epsilon) \leq 1/(4\epsilon^2 m)$.
   b) Given independent m-samples $\mathcal{X}$ and $\mathcal{X}'$, let $\widehat{E}_j(\mathcal{X}, \mathcal{X}') = |\widehat{P}_j(\mathcal{X}) - \widehat{P}_j(\mathcal{X}')|$. Show that $\Pr(\widehat{E}_j(\mathcal{X}, \mathcal{X}') > \epsilon) < 2e^{-2\epsilon^2 m}$. *Hint:* See exercise 132.
   c) Let $\Delta_m(\mathcal{A})$ be the maximum number of distinct columns that can appear in any of the $m \times n$ binary matrices obtainable from samples $\mathcal{X}$ of size m. If $m \geq 2/\epsilon^2$, use (a) and (b) to prove that $\Pr(E(\mathcal{X}) > \epsilon) \leq 4\Delta_{2m}(\mathcal{A}) e^{-\epsilon^2 m/8}$.

[*Note:* The maximum d such that d atomic events of Ω can be shattered by the events of $\mathcal{A}$ is called the Vapnik–Chervonenkis dimension of $\mathcal{A}$. Exercise 133 shows that $\Delta_m(\mathcal{A})$ has polynomial growth of degree d.]

135. [*HM30*] (*Baxter permutations.*) Let $P = p_1 \ldots p_n$ be a permutation of $\{1, \ldots, n\}$, and let $P^- = q_1 \ldots q_n$ be its inverse. These permutations are called Baxter permutations if and only if there are no indices k and l with $0 < k, l < n$ such that either ($p_k < l$ and $p_{k+1} > l$ and $q_l > k$ and $q_{l+1} < k$) or ($q_k < l$ and $q_{k+1} > l$ and $p_l > k$ and $p_{l+1} < k$).
What's a good way to count the number b_n of n-element Baxter permutations?

136. [*HM20*] Let $f(x) = [x > 0] x \ln x$ be the fundamental convex function that underlies formulas for entropy. Prove or disprove: If $0 \leq x \leq y \leq 1$ then $|f(y) - f(x)| \leq |f(y - x)|$.

137. [*HM31*] The *median* of a real-valued random variable X is a value m for which $\Pr(X \leq m) \geq \frac{1}{2}$ and $\Pr(X \geq m) \geq \frac{1}{2}$. For example, if X is a binary random variable with $E X = p$, then 1 is a median $\iff p \geq \frac{1}{2}$; 0 is a median $\iff p \leq \frac{1}{2}$; and a value m between 0 and 1 is a median $\iff p = \frac{1}{2}$. Let med X be the set of all X's medians.
   a) Show that med X is always a closed interval $[\underline{m} .. \overline{m}]$, for some real $\underline{m} \leq \overline{m}$.
   b) If $\underline{m} < \overline{m}$, then $\Pr(X \leq \underline{m}) = \Pr(X \geq \overline{m}) = \frac{1}{2}$. (Discretely, X is never actually *equal* to any value of med X except for the two extreme elements $\underline{m}$ and $\overline{m}$.)
   c) True or false: If $\Pr(X \in [x .. y]) \geq \frac{1}{2}$ then $[x .. y] \supseteq$ med X.
   d) Assuming that $E |X - c|$ exists for all c, show that $E |X - m| = \min_c E |X - c|$ if and only if $m \in$ med X.
   e) True or false: If $\mu = E X$ and $\sigma^2 = \text{var } X$ and $m \in$ med X then $|\mu - m| \leq \sigma$.
   f) Prove an analog of Jensen's inequality: If f is convex for all real values of x, then $f(\text{med } X) \leq \text{med } f(X)$, assuming that we interpret this formula properly in cases when med X and/or med $f(X)$ aren't unique.

▶ **138.** [*M21*] (*Law of total variance.*) The "truly marvelous identity" (12), which is often called the law of total expectation, has an even more marvelous counterpart:

$$\text{var}(X) = \text{var}(E(X\,|\,Y)) + E(\text{var}(X\,|\,Y)).$$

"The overall variance of a random variable X is the variance of its average plus the average of its variance, with respect to any other random variable Y." Prove it.

▶ **139.** [*HM33*] (Frank Spitzer, 1956.) A random walk is defined by $S_0 = 0$ and $S_n = S_{n-1} + X_n$ for $n > 0$, where the integer-valued random variables X_1, X_2, $\ldots$ are independent and have the same distribution. Let $S_n^+ = \max(S_n, 0)$, $S_n^- = \max(-S_n, 0)$, $R_n = \max(S_0, S_1, \ldots, S_n)$, $R_n^+ = R_n - S_n$, and define the generating functions

$$r_n(w, z) = \sum_{j,k} \Pr(R_n{=}j, R_n^+{=}k)w^j z^k, \quad s_n^+(z) = \sum_k \Pr(S_n^+{=}k)z^k, \quad s_n^-(z) = \sum_k \Pr(S_n^-{=}k)z^k.$$

Prove that these three basic quantities are related by the remarkable formula

$$\sum_{n=0}^{\infty} r_n(w, z)t^n = \exp\left(\sum_{n=1}^{\infty} (s_n^+(w) + s_n^-(z) - 1)\frac{t^n}{n}\right).$$

▶ **140.** [*HM34*] (*Smoothed analysis.*) Algorithms are traditionally analyzed by either studying their worst case or an "average" case. A nice compromise between these extremes was introduced by D. A. Spielman and S.-H. Teng in *JACM* **51** (2004), 385–463: An adversary sets up the data for some particular case, and this data is *perturbed* by some random process. Then we analyze the expected running time when the algorithm is applied to the perturbed data, maximizing over all cases.

The purpose of this exercise is to carry out a smoothed analysis of Algorithm 1.2.10M, the very first algorithm that was analyzed in TAOCP: Given a sequence $X = x_1 \ldots x_n$ of distinct numbers, let $\lambda(X)$ be the number of left-to-right maxima, namely the number of indices k with $x_k > x_j$ for $1 \le j < k$. When X is a random permutation, we showed in Section 1.2.10 that $E\,\lambda(X) = H_n \approx \ln n$ and $\text{var}\,\lambda(X) = H_n - H_n^{(2)}$. On the other hand, $\lambda(X)$ can be as large as n.

Several natural models will give a smooth transition between $\ln n$ and n, when we suppose that an arbitrary sequence $\bar{X} = \bar{x}_1 \ldots \bar{x}_n$ is perturbed to get $X = x_1 \ldots x_n$.

a) Given a permutation $\bar{X}$ of $\{1, \ldots, n\}$, mark each $\bar{x}_k$ with probability p (independently); then permute the marked elements uniformly to get X. What is $E\,\lambda(X)$ when $\bar{X} = 12 \ldots n$ (the only case for which $\lambda(\bar{X}) = n$), and $0 < p < 1$ is fixed?

b) Continuing (a), explore $E\,\lambda(X)$ when $\bar{X} = (n - m + 1) \ldots n 1 \ldots (n - m)$, $p = \frac{1}{2}$.

c) Continuing (a) and (b), show that $E\,\lambda(X) = O(\sqrt{(n \log n)/p})$ for all $\bar{X}$.

d) A single swap in model (a) can reduce $\lambda(X)$ from n to 1! So the following model is better: Let $0 \le \bar{x}_k \le 1$ for $1 \le k \le n$, and set $x_k \leftarrow \bar{x}_k + \delta_k$, where δ_k is uniformly random in $[-\epsilon .. \epsilon]$. Show that $E\,\lambda(X)$ is greatest when $\bar{x}_1 \le \cdots \le \bar{x}_n$.

e) Continuing (d), show that in this model we have $E\,\lambda(X) = O(\sqrt{n/\epsilon} + \log n)$.

141. [*M20*] (*Arithmetic and geometric mean inequality*). When $x_k, p_k > 0$, prove that

$$\frac{p_1 x_1 + p_2 x_2 + \cdots + p_n x_n}{p_1 + p_2 + \cdots + p_n} \ge (x_1^{p_1} x_2^{p_2} \ldots x_n^{p_n})^{1/(p_1 + p_2 + \cdots + p_n)}.$$

(For integer p_k, these are the means of the multiset $\{p_1 \cdot x_1, p_2 \cdot x_2, \ldots, p_n \cdot x_n\}$.)

▶ **142.** [*M30*] (L. J. Rogers, 1887.) Let $M_r = \mathrm{E}\,|X|^r$ be the rth absolute "moment" of the random variable X. (In particular, $M_r = \infty$ if $r < 0$ and $\mathrm{Pr}(X{=}0) > 0$.)

    a) Suppose $q \le r \le s \le t$ and $q{+}t = r{+}s$. Set the values of (a_j, b_j, x_j, y_j) in Binet's identity, exercise 1.2.3–30, to $(p_j, p_j x_j^{s-q}, x_j^q, x_j^r)$, where $p_1, p_2, \ldots$ are probabilities that sum to 1. What inequality involving M_q, M_r, M_s, M_t do you get?

    b) Deduce from exercise 141 that $M_q^{s-r} M_r^{q-s} M_s^{r-q} \ge 1$ when $q < r < s$ and $M_r < \infty$. *Hint:* What happens when p_j and x_j are replaced respectively by $p_j x_j^r$ and x_j^{s-r}?

    c) Let $p > 1$. Use the fact that $M_{1/p} \le M_1^{1/p}$ to prove *Hölder's inequality*:

$$\sum_{k=1}^{n} a_k b_k \le \left(\sum_{k=1}^{n} a_k^p\right)^{\frac{1}{p}} \left(\sum_{k=1}^{n} b_k^q\right)^{\frac{1}{q}}, \quad \text{if } \tfrac{1}{p} + \tfrac{1}{q} = 1 \text{ and } a_k, b_k \ge 0.$$

    d) Consequently $|\mathrm{E}\,XY| \le (\mathrm{E}\,|X|^p)^{1/p} (\mathrm{E}\,|Y|^q)^{1/q}$.

143. [*M22*] For $p > 1$, use Hölder's inequality to prove *Minkowski's inequality*:

$$(\mathrm{E}\,|X + Y|^p)^{1/p} \le (\mathrm{E}\,|X|^p)^{1/p} + (\mathrm{E}\,|Y|^p)^{1/p}.$$

144. [*HM26*] If $\mathrm{E}\,X$ exists and is finite, clearly $\mathrm{E}(X - \mathrm{E}\,X) = 0$.

    a) If $p \ge 1$ and $\mathrm{E}\,Y = 0$, then $\mathrm{E}\,|X|^p \le \mathrm{E}\,|X + Y|^p$ when X and Y are independent.

    b) The *symmetrization* of a random variable X is $X^{\mathrm{sym}} = X^+ - X^-$, where X^+ and X^- are independent random variables, each with the same distribution as X. Prove that $p \ge 1$ and $\mathrm{E}\,X = 0$ implies $\mathrm{E}\,|X|^p \le \mathrm{E}\,|X^{\mathrm{sym}}|^p$.

    c) Suppose $X_1, \ldots, X_n$ are independent random variables that are symmetric about 0, in the sense that $\mathrm{Pr}(X_j = x) = \mathrm{Pr}(X_j = -x)$ for $1 \le j \le n$ and all x. Prove that $\mathrm{E}\,|X_1|^p + \cdots + \mathrm{E}\,|X_n|^p \le \mathrm{E}\,|X_1 + \cdots + X_n|^p$, when $p \ge 2$. *Hint:* $|x|^p + |y|^p \le \tfrac{1}{2}(|x + y|^p + |x - y|^p)$.

    d) Now suppose only that $X_1, \ldots, X_n$ are independent with $\mathrm{E}\,X_1 = \cdots = \mathrm{E}\,X_n = 0$. Prove that $\mathrm{E}\,|X_1|^p + \cdots + \mathrm{E}\,|X_n|^p \le 2^p\,\mathrm{E}\,|X_1 + \cdots + X_n|^p$ for $p \ge 2$.

▶ **145.** [*M20*] (*Khinchin's inequality*.) Let $a_1, \ldots, a_n$ be real numbers and let $X_1, \ldots, X_n$ be random signs: Independently, each X_k is equally likely to be $+1$ or -1. Prove that

$$(a_1^2 + \cdots + a_n^2)^m \le \mathrm{E}\big((a_1 X_1 + \cdots + a_n X_n)^{2m}\big) \le (2m - 1)!!\,(a_1^2 + \cdots + a_n^2)^m$$

for all integers $m \ge 0$, where $(2m - 1)!! = \prod_{k=1}^{m}(2k - 1)$ is a "semifactorial."

146. [*M25*] (*Marcinkiewicz and Zygmund's inequality*.) Let $X_1, \ldots, X_n$ be independent random variables, each with mean 0 but possibly with different distributions. Then

$$\frac{1}{2^{2m}}\,\mathrm{E}\left(\left(\sum_{k=1}^{n} X_k^2\right)^m\right) \le \mathrm{E}\left(\left(\sum_{k=1}^{n} X_k\right)^{2m}\right) \le 2^{2m}(2m - 1)!!\,\mathrm{E}\left(\left(\sum_{k=1}^{n} X_k^2\right)^m\right).$$

147. [*M34*] (*Rosenthal's inequality*.) Under the assumptions of exercise 146,

$$\frac{1}{2^{2m}}\,B \le \mathrm{E}\left(\left(\sum_{k=1}^{n} X_k\right)^{2m}\right) \le 2^{m^2+2m}(2m - 1)!!\,B, \quad B = \max\left(\sum_{k=1}^{n} \mathrm{E}\,X_k^{2m}, \left(\sum_{k=1}^{n} \mathrm{E}\,X_k^2\right)^m\right).$$

Every man must judge for himself between conflicting vague probabilities.
— CHARLES DARWIN, letter to N. A. von Mengden (5 June 1879)

> *Nowhere to go but out,*
> *Nowhere to come but back.*
> — BEN KING, in *The Sum of Life* (c. 1893)

> *Lewis back-tracked the original route up the Missouri.*
> — LEWIS R. FREEMAN, in *National Geographic Magazine* (1928)

> *When you come to one legal road that's blocked,*
> *you back up and try another.*
> — PERRY MASON, in *The Case of the Black-Eyed Blonde* (1944)

7.2.2. Backtrack Programming

Now that we know how to generate simple combinatorial patterns such as tuples, permutations, combinations, partitions, and trees, we're ready to tackle more exotic patterns that have subtler and less uniform structure. Instances of almost *any* desired pattern can be generated systematically, at least in principle, if we organize the search carefully. Such a method was christened "backtrack" by R. J. Walker in the 1950s, because it is basically a way to examine all fruitful possibilities while exiting gracefully from situations that have been fully explored.

Most of the patterns we shall deal with can be cast in a simple, general framework: We seek all sequences $x_1 x_2 \ldots x_n$ for which some property $P_n(x_1, x_2, \ldots, x_n)$ holds, where each item x_k belongs to some given domain D_k of integers. The backtrack method, in its most elementary form, involves the invention of intermediate "cutoff" properties $P_l(x_1, \ldots, x_l)$ for $1 \le l < n$, such that

$$P_l(x_1, \ldots, x_l) \text{ is true whenever } P_{l+1}(x_1, \ldots, x_{l+1}) \text{ is true;} \tag{1}$$

$$P_l(x_1, \ldots, x_l) \text{ is fairly easy to test, if } P_{l-1}(x_1, \ldots, x_{l-1}) \text{ holds.} \tag{2}$$

(We assume that $P_0()$ is always true. Exercise 1 shows that all of the basic patterns studied in Section 7.2.1 can easily be formulated in terms of domains D_k and cutoff properties P_l.) Then we can proceed lexicographically as follows:

Algorithm B (*Basic backtrack*). Given domains D_k and properties P_l as above, this algorithm visits all sequences $x_1 x_2 \ldots x_n$ that satisfy $P_n(x_1, x_2, \ldots, x_n)$.

B1. [Initialize.] Set $l \leftarrow 1$, and initialize the data structures needed later.

B2. [Enter level l.] (Now $P_{l-1}(x_1, \ldots, x_{l-1})$ holds.) If $l > n$, visit $x_1 x_2 \ldots x_n$ and go to B5. Otherwise set $x_l \leftarrow \min D_l$, the smallest element of D_l.

B3. [Try x_l.] If $P_l(x_1, \ldots, x_l)$ holds, update the data structures to facilitate testing P_{l+1}, set $l \leftarrow l + 1$, and go to B2.

B4. [Try again.] If $x_l \ne \max D_l$, set x_l to the next larger element of D_l and return to B3.

B5. [Backtrack.] Set $l \leftarrow l - 1$. If $l > 0$, downdate the data structures by undoing the changes recently made in step B3, and return to B4. (Otherwise stop.) ∎

The main point is that if $P_l(x_1, \ldots, x_l)$ is false in step B3, we needn't waste time trying to append any further values $x_{l+1} \ldots x_n$. Thus we can often rule out huge regions of the space of all potential solutions. A second important point is that very little memory is needed, although there may be many, many solutions.

For example, let's consider the classic *problem of n queens*: In how many ways can n queens be placed on an $n \times n$ board so that no two are in the same row, column, or diagonal? We can suppose that one queen is in each row, and that the queen in row k is in column x_k, for $1 \le k \le n$. Then each domain D_k is $\{1, 2, \ldots, n\}$; and $P_n(x_1, \ldots, x_n)$ is the condition that

$$x_j \ne x_k \quad \text{and} \quad |x_k - x_j| \ne k - j, \qquad \text{for } 1 \le j < k \le n. \tag{3}$$

(If $x_j = x_k$ and $j < k$, two queens are in the same column; if $|x_k - x_j| = k - j$, they're in the same diagonal.)

This problem is easy to set up for Algorithm B, because we can let property $P_l(x_1, \ldots, x_l)$ be the same as (3) but restricted to $1 \le j < k \le l$. Condition (1) is clear; and so is condition (2), because P_l requires testing (3) only for $k = l$ when P_{l-1} is known. Notice that $P_1(x_1)$ is always true in this example.

One of the best ways to learn about backtracking is to execute Algorithm B by hand in the special case $n = 4$ of the n queens problem: First we set $x_1 \leftarrow 1$. Then when $l = 2$ we find $P_2(1, 1)$ and $P_2(1, 2)$ false; hence we don't get to $l = 3$ until trying $x_2 \leftarrow 3$. Then, however, we're stuck, because $P_3(1, 3, x)$ is false for $1 \le x \le 4$. Backtracking to level 2, we now try $x_2 \leftarrow 4$; and this allows us to set $x_3 \leftarrow 2$. However, we're stuck again, at level 4; and this time we must back up all the way to level 1, because there are no further valid choices at levels 3 and 2. The next choice $x_1 \leftarrow 2$ does, happily, lead to a solution without much further ado, namely $x_1 x_2 x_3 x_4 = 2413$. And one more solution (3142) turns up before the algorithm terminates.

The behavior of Algorithm B is nicely visualized as a tree structure, called a search tree or *backtrack tree*. For example, the backtrack tree for the four queens problem has just 17 nodes,

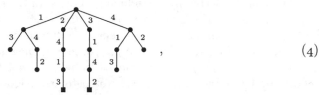

$$\tag{4}$$

corresponding to the 17 times step B2 is performed. Here x_l is shown as the label of an edge from level $l - 1$ to level l of the tree. (Level l of the algorithm actually corresponds to the tree's level $l - 1$, because we've chosen to represent patterns using subscripts from 1 to n instead of from 0 to $n-1$ in this discussion.) The *profile* $(p_0, p_1, \ldots, p_n)$ of this particular tree — the number of nodes at each level — is $(1, 4, 6, 4, 2)$; and we see that the number of solutions, $p_n = p_4$, is 2.

Figure 68 shows the corresponding tree when $n = 8$. This tree has 2057 nodes, distributed according to the profile $(1, 8, 42, 140, 344, 568, 550, 312, 92)$. Thus the early cutoffs facilitated by backtracking have allowed us to find all 92 solutions by examining only 0.01% of the $8^8 = 16{,}777{,}216$ possible sequences $x_1 \ldots x_8$. (And 8^8 is only 0.38% of the $\binom{64}{8} = 4{,}426{,}165{,}368$ ways to put eight queens on the board.)

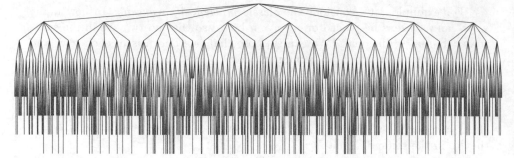

Fig. 68. The problem of placing eight nonattacking queens has this backtrack tree.

Notice that, in this case, Algorithm B spends most of its time in the vicinity of level 5 below the root. Such behavior is typical: The tree for $n = 16$ queens has 1,141,190,303 nodes, and its profile is (1, 16, 210, 2236, 19688, 141812, 838816, 3998456, 15324708, 46358876, 108478966, 193892860, 260303408, 253897632, 171158018, 72002088, 14772512), concentrated near level 12.

Data structures. Backtrack programming is often used when a *huge* tree of possibilities needs to be examined. Thus we want to be able to test property P_l as quickly as possible in step B3.

One way to implement Algorithm B for the n queens problem is to avoid auxiliary data structures and simply to make a bunch of sequential comparisons in that step: "Is $x_l - x_j \in \{j-l, 0, l-j\}$ for some $j < l$?" Assuming that we must access memory whenever referring to x_j, given a trial value x_l in a register, such an implementation performs approximately 112 billion memory accesses when $n = 16$; that's about 98 mems per node.

We can do better by introducing three simple arrays. Property P_l in (3) says essentially that the numbers x_k are distinct, and so are the numbers $x_k + k$, and so are the numbers $x_k - k$. Therefore we can use auxiliary Boolean arrays $a_1 \ldots a_n$, $b_1 \ldots b_{2n-1}$, and $c_1 \ldots c_{2n-1}$, where a_j means 'some $x_k = j$', b_j means 'some $x_k + k - 1 = j$', and c_j means 'some $x_k - k + n = j$'. Those arrays are readily updated and downdated if we customize Algorithm B as follows:

B1*. [Initialize.] Set $a_1 \ldots a_n \leftarrow 0 \ldots 0$, $b_1 \ldots b_{2n-1} \leftarrow 0 \ldots 0$, $c_1 \ldots c_{2n-1} \leftarrow 0 \ldots 0$, and $l \leftarrow 1$.

B2*. [Enter level l.] (Now $P_{l-1}(x_1, \ldots, x_{l-1})$ holds.) If $l > n$, visit $x_1 x_2 \ldots x_n$ and go to B5*. Otherwise set $t \leftarrow 1$.

B3*. [Try t.] If $a_t = 1$ or $b_{t+l-1} = 1$ or $c_{t-l+n} = 1$, go to B4*. Otherwise set $a_t \leftarrow 1$, $b_{t+l-1} \leftarrow 1$, $c_{t-l+n} \leftarrow 1$, $x_l \leftarrow t$, $l \leftarrow l + 1$, and go to B2*.

B4*. [Try again.] If $t < n$, set $t \leftarrow t + 1$ and return to B3*.

B5*. [Backtrack.] Set $l \leftarrow l - 1$. If $l > 0$, set $t \leftarrow x_l$, $c_{t-l+n} \leftarrow 0$, $b_{t+l-1} \leftarrow 0$, $a_t \leftarrow 0$, and return to B4*. (Otherwise stop.) ▮

Notice how step B5* neatly undoes the updates that step B3* had made, in the reverse order. Reverse order for downdating is typical of backtrack algorithms, although there is some flexibility; we could, for example, have restored a_t before b_{t+l-1} and c_{t-l+n}, because those arrays are independent.

The auxiliary arrays a, b, c make it easy to test property P_l at the beginning of step B3*, but we must also access memory when we update them and downdate them. Does that cost us more than it saves? Fortunately, no: The running time for $n = 16$ goes down to about 34 billion mems, roughly 30 mems per node.

Furthermore we could keep the bit vectors a, b, c entirely in registers, on a machine with 64-bit registers, assuming that $n \leq 32$. Then there would be just two memory accesses per node, namely to store $x_l \leftarrow t$ and later to fetch $t \leftarrow x_l$. However, quite a lot of in-register computation would become necessary.

Walker's method. The 1950s-era programs of R. J. Walker organized backtracking in a somewhat different way. Instead of letting x_l run through all elements of D_l, he calculated and stored the set

$$S_l \leftarrow \{x \in D_l \mid P_l(x_1, \ldots, x_{l-1}, x) \text{ holds}\} \tag{5}$$

upon entry to each node at level l. This computation can often be done efficiently all at once, instead of piecemeal, because some cutoff properties make it possible to combine steps that would otherwise have to be repeated for each $x \in D_l$. In essence, he used the following variant of Algorithm B:

Algorithm W (*Walker's backtrack*). Given domains D_k and cutoffs P_l as above, this algorithm visits all sequences $x_1 x_2 \ldots x_n$ that satisfy $P_n(x_1, x_2, \ldots, x_n)$.

W1. [Initialize.] Set $l \leftarrow 1$, and initialize the data structures needed later.

W2. [Enter level l.] (Now $P_{l-1}(x_1, \ldots, x_{l-1})$ holds.) If $l > n$, visit $x_1 x_2 \ldots x_n$ and go to W4. Otherwise determine the set S_l as in (5).

W3. [Try to advance.] If S_l is nonempty, set $x_l \leftarrow \min S_l$, update the data structures to facilitate computing S_{l+1}, set $l \leftarrow l+1$, and go to W2.

W4. [Backtrack.] Set $l \leftarrow l - 1$. If $l > 0$, downdate the data structures by undoing changes made in step W3, set $S_l \leftarrow S_l \setminus x_l$, and retreat to W3. ∎

Walker applied this method to the n queens problem by computing $S_l = U \setminus A_l \setminus B_l \setminus C_l$, where $U = D_l = \{1, \ldots, n\}$ and

$$A_l = \{x_j \mid 1 \leq j < l\}, \; B_l = \{x_j + j - l \mid 1 \leq j < l\}, \; C_l = \{x_j - j + l \mid 1 \leq j < l\}. \tag{6}$$

He represented these auxiliary sets by bit vectors a, b, c, analogous to (but different from) the bit vectors of Algorithm B* above. Exercise 10 shows that the updating in step W3 is easy, using bitwise operations on n-bit numbers; furthermore, no downdating is needed in step W4. The corresponding run time when $n = 16$ turns out to be just 9.1 gigamems, or 8 mems per node.

Let $Q(n)$ be the number of solutions to the n queens problem. Then we have

$n =$	0	1	2	3	4	5	6	7	8	9	10	11	12	13	14	15	16
$Q(n) =$	1	1	0	0	2	10	4	40	92	352	724	2680	14200	73712	365596	2279184	14772512

and the values for $n \leq 11$ were computed independently by several people during the nineteenth century. Small cases were relatively easy; but when T. B. Sprague had finished computing $Q(11)$ he remarked that "This was a very heavy piece of work, and occupied most of my leisure time for several months. ... It will, I imagine, be scarcely possible to obtain results for larger boards, unless a number of persons co-operate in the work." [See *Proc. Edinburgh Math. Soc.* **17** (1899), 43–68; Sprague was the leading actuary of his day.] Nevertheless, H. Onnen went on to evaluate $Q(12) = 14,200$—an astonishing feat of hand calculation—in 1910. [See W. Ahrens, *Math. Unterhaltungen und Spiele* **2**, second edition (1918), 344.]

All of these hard-won results were confirmed in 1960 by R. J. Walker, using the SWAC computer at UCLA and the method of exercise 10. Walker also computed $Q(13)$; but he couldn't go any further with the machine available to him at the time. The next step, $Q(14)$, was computed by Michael D. Kennedy at the University of Tennessee in 1963, commandeering an IBM 1620 for 120 hours. S. R. Bunch evaluated $Q(15)$ in 1974 at the University of Illinois, using about two hours on an IBM System 360-75; then J. R. Bitner found $Q(16)$ after about three hours on the same computer, but with an improved method.

Computers and algorithms have continued to get better, of course, and such results are now obtained almost instantly. Hence larger and larger values of n lie at the frontier. The whopping value $Q(27) = 234,907,967,154,122,528$, found in 2016 by Thomas B. Preußer and Matthias R. Engelhardt, probably won't be exceeded for awhile! [See *J. Signal Processing Systems* **88** (2017), 185–201. This distributed computation occupied a dynamic cluster of diverse FPGA devices for 383 days; those devices provided a total peak of more than 7000 custom-designed hardware solvers to handle 2,024,110,796 independent subproblems.]

Permutations and Langford pairs. Every solution $x_1 \ldots x_n$ to the n queens problem is a permutation of $\{1, \ldots, n\}$, and many other problems are permutation-based. Indeed, we've already seen Algorithm 7.2.1.2X, which is an elegant backtrack procedure specifically designed for special kinds of permutations. When that algorithm begins to choose the value of x_l, it makes all of the appropriate elements $\{1, 2, \ldots, n\} \setminus \{x_1, \ldots, x_{l-1}\}$ conveniently accessible in a linked list.

We can get further insight into such data structures by returning to the problem of Langford pairs, which was discussed at the very beginning of Chapter 7. That problem can be reformulated as the task of finding all permutations of $\{1, 2, \ldots, n\} \cup \{-1, -2, \ldots, -n\}$ with the property that

$$x_j = k \quad \text{implies} \quad x_{j+k+1} = -k, \quad \text{for } 1 \leq j \leq 2n \text{ and } 1 \leq k \leq n. \quad (7)$$

For example, when $n = 4$ there are two solutions, namely $234\bar{2}1\bar{3}1\bar{4}$ and $41\bar{3}1\bar{2}4\bar{3}\bar{2}$. (As usual we find it convenient to write $\bar{1}$ for -1, $\bar{2}$ for -2, etc.) Notice that if $x = x_1 x_2 \ldots x_{2n}$ is a solution, so is its "dual" $-x^R = (-x_{2n}) \ldots (-x_2)(-x_1)$.

Here's a Langford-inspired adaptation of Algorithm 7.2.1.2X, with the former notation modified slightly to match Algorithms B and W: We want to maintain pointers $p_0 p_1 \ldots p_n$ such that, if the positive integers not already present in $x_1 \ldots x_{l-1}$ are $k_1 < k_2 < \cdots < k_t$ when we're choosing x_l, we have the linked list

$$p_0 = k_1, \; p_{k_1} = k_2, \; \ldots, \; p_{k_{t-1}} = k_t, \; p_{k_t} = 0. \quad (8)$$

Such a condition turns out to be easy to maintain.

Algorithm L (*Langford pairs*). This algorithm visits all solutions $x_1 \ldots x_{2n}$ to (7) in lexicographic order, using pointers $p_0 p_1 \ldots p_n$ that satisfy (8), and also using an auxiliary array $y_1 \ldots y_{2n}$ for backtracking.

L1. [Initialize.] Set $x_1 \ldots x_{2n} \leftarrow 0 \ldots 0$, $p_k \leftarrow k+1$ for $0 \le k < n$, $p_n \leftarrow 0$, $l \leftarrow 1$.

L2. [Enter level l.] Set $k \leftarrow p_0$. If $k = 0$, visit $x_1 x_2 \ldots x_{2n}$ and go to L5. Otherwise set $j \leftarrow 0$, and while $x_l < 0$ set $l \leftarrow l+1$.

L3. [Try $x_l = k$.] (At this point we have $k = p_j$.) If $l + k + 1 > 2n$, go to L5. Otherwise, if $x_{l+k+1} = 0$, set $x_l \leftarrow k$, $x_{l+k+1} \leftarrow -k$, $y_l \leftarrow j$, $p_j \leftarrow p_k$, $l \leftarrow l+1$, and return to L2.

L4. [Try again.] (We've found all solutions that begin with $x_1 \ldots x_{l-1}k$ or something smaller.) Set $j \leftarrow k$ and $k \leftarrow p_j$, then go to L3 if $k \ne 0$.

L5. [Backtrack.] Set $l \leftarrow l - 1$. If $l > 0$ do the following: While $x_l < 0$, set $l \leftarrow l - 1$. Then set $k \leftarrow x_l$, $x_l \leftarrow 0$, $x_{l+k+1} \leftarrow 0$, $j \leftarrow y_l$, $p_j \leftarrow k$, and go back to L4. Otherwise terminate the algorithm. ∎

Careful study of these steps will reveal how everything fits together nicely. Notice that, for example, step L3 removes k from the linked list (8) by simply setting $p_j \leftarrow p_k$. That step also sets $x_{l+k+1} \leftarrow -k$, in accordance with (7), so that we can skip over position $l + k + 1$ when we encounter it later in step L2.

The main point of Algorithm L is the somewhat subtle way in which step L5 undoes the deletion operation by setting $p_j \leftarrow k$. The pointer p_k still retains the appropriate link to the next element in the list, *because p_k has not been changed by any of the intervening updates.* (Think about it.) This is the germ of an idea called "dancing links" that we will explore in Section 7.2.2.1.

To draw the search tree corresponding to a run of Algorithm L, we can label the edges with the positive choices of x_l as we did in (4), while labeling the nodes with any previously set negative values that are passed over in step L2. For instance the tree for $n = 4$ is

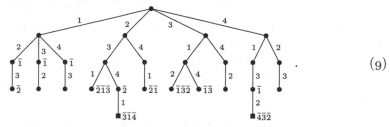

$$(9)$$

Solutions appear at depth n in this tree, even though they involve $2n$ values $x_1 x_2 \ldots x_{2n}$.

Algorithm L sometimes makes false starts and doesn't realize the problem until probing further than necessary. Notice that the value $x_l = k$ can appear only when $l + k + 1 \le 2n$; hence if we haven't seen k by the time l reaches $2n - k - 1$, we're *forced* to choose $x_l = k$. For example, the branch $12\bar{1}$ in (9) needn't be pursued, because 4 must appear in $\{x_1, x_2, x_3\}$. Exercise 20 explains how to incorporate this cutoff principle into Algorithm L. When $n = 17$, it reduces the number of nodes in the search tree from 1.29 trillion to 330 billion, and reduces the running time from 25.0 teramems to 8.1 teramems. (The amount of work has gone up from 19.4 mems per node to 24.4 mems per node, because of the extra tests for cutoffs, yet there's a significant overall reduction.)

Furthermore, we can "break the symmetry" by ensuring that we don't consider both a solution and its dual. This idea, exploited in exercise 21, reduces the search tree to just 160 billion nodes and costs just 3.94 teramems — that's 24.6 mems per node.

Word rectangles. Let's look next at a problem where the search domains D_l are much larger. An $m \times n$ *word rectangle* is an array of n-letter words* whose columns are m-letter words. For example,

$$
\begin{array}{cccccc}
\text{S} & \text{T} & \text{A} & \text{T} & \text{U} & \text{S} \\
\text{L} & \text{O} & \text{W} & \text{E} & \text{S} & \text{T} \\
\text{U} & \text{T} & \text{O} & \text{P} & \text{I} & \text{A} \\
\text{M} & \text{A} & \text{K} & \text{I} & \text{N} & \text{G} \\
\text{S} & \text{L} & \text{E} & \text{D} & \text{G} & \text{E}
\end{array}
\tag{10}
$$

is a 5×6 word rectangle whose columns all belong to WORDS(5757), the collection of 5-letter words in the Stanford GraphBase. To find such patterns, we can suppose that column l contains the x_lth most common 5-letter word, where $1 \le x_l \le 5757$ for $1 \le l \le 6$; hence there are $5757^6 = 36{,}406{,}369{,}848{,}837{,}732{,}146{,}649$ ways to choose the columns. In (10) we have $x_1 \ldots x_6 = 1446\ 185\ 1021\ 2537\ 66\ 255$. Of course very few of those choices will yield suitable rows; but backtracking will hopefully help us to find all solutions in a reasonable amount of time.

We can set this problem up for Algorithm B by storing the n-letter words in a trie (see Section 6.3), with one trie node of size 26 for each l-letter prefix of a legitimate word, $0 \le l \le n$.

For example, such a trie for $n = 6$ represents 15727 words with 23667 nodes. The prefix ST corresponds to node number 260, whose 26 entries are

$$(484, 0, 0, 0, 1589, 0, 0, 0, 2609, 0, 0, 0, 0, 0, 1280, 0, 0, 251, 0, 0, 563, 0, 0, 0, 1621, 0); \tag{11}$$

this means that STA is node 484, STE is node 1589, ..., STY is node 1621, and there are no 6-letter words beginning with STB, STC, ..., STX, STZ. A slightly different convention is used for prefixes of length $n - 1$; for example, the entries for node 580, 'CORNE', are

$$(3879, 0, 0, 3878, 0, 0, 0, 0, 0, 0, 0, 0, 9602, 0, 0, 0, 0, 0, 171, 0, 5013, 0, 0, 0, 0, 0, 0); \tag{12}$$

meaning that CORNEA, CORNED, CORNEL, CORNER, and CORNET are ranked 3879, 3878, 9602, 171, and 5013 in the list of 6-letter words.

---

* Whenever five-letter words are used in the examples of this book, they're taken from the 5757 Stanford GraphBase words as explained at the beginning of Chapter 7. Words of other lengths are taken from *The Official SCRABBLE® Players Dictionary*, fourth edition (Hasbro, 2005), because those words have been incorporated into many widely available computer games. Such words have been ranked according to the British National Corpus of 2007 — where 'the' occurs 5,405,633 times and the next-most common word, 'of', occurs roughly half as often (3,021,525). The OSPD4 list includes respectively (101, 1004, 4002, 8887, 15727, 23958, 29718, 29130, 22314, 16161, 11412) words of lengths (2, 3, ..., 12), of which (97, 771, 2451, 4474, 6910, 8852, 9205, 8225, 6626, 4642, 3061) occur at least six times in the British National Corpus.

Suppose x_1 and x_2 specify the 5-letter column-words SLUMS and TOTAL as in (10). Then the trie tells us that the next column-word x_3 must have the form $c_1c_2c_3c_4c_5$ where $c_1 \in \{A, E, I, O, R, U, Y\}$, $c_2 \notin \{E, H, J, K, Y, Z\}$, $c_3 \in \{E, M, O, T\}$, $c_4 \notin \{A, B, O\}$, and $c_5 \in \{A, E, I, O, U, Y\}$. (There are 221 such words.)

Let $a_{l1} \ldots a_{lm}$ be the trie nodes corresponding to the prefixes of the first l columns of a partial solution to the word rectangle problem. This auxiliary array enables Algorithm B to find all solutions, as explained in exercise 24. It turns out that there are exactly 625,415 valid 5×6 word rectangles, according to our conventions; and the method of exercise 24 needs about 19 teramems of computation to find them all. In fact, the profile of the search tree is

$$(1,\ 5757,\ 2458830,\ 360728099,\ 579940198,\ 29621728,\ 625415), \qquad (13)$$

indicating for example that just 360,728,099 of the $5757^3 = 190,804,533,093$ choices for $x_1x_2x_3$ will lead to valid prefixes of 6-letter words.

With care, exercise 24's running time can be significantly decreased, once we realize that every node of the search tree for $1 \le l \le n$ requires testing 5757 possibilities for x_l in step B3. If we build a more elaborate data structure for the 5-letter words, so that it becomes easy to run though all words that have a specific letter in a specific position, we can refine the algorithm so that the average number of possibilities per level that need to be investigated becomes only

$$(5757.0,\ 1697.9,\ 844.1,\ 273.5,\ 153.5,\ 100.8); \qquad (14)$$

the total running time then drops to 1.15 teramems. Exercise 25 has the details. And exercise 28 discusses a method that's faster yet.

Commafree codes. Our next example deals entirely with *four*-letter words. But it's not obscene; it's an intriguing question of coding theory. The problem is to find a set of four-letter codewords that can be decoded even if we don't put spaces or other delimiters between them. If we take any message that's formed from strings of the set by simply concatenating them together, likethis, and if we look at any seven consecutive letters $\ldots x_1x_2x_3x_4x_5x_6x_7 \ldots$, exactly one of the four-letter substrings $x_1x_2x_3x_4$, $x_2x_3x_4x_5$, $x_3x_4x_5x_6$, $x_4x_5x_6x_7$ will be a codeword. Equivalently, if $x_1x_2x_3x_4$ and $x_5x_6x_7x_8$ are codewords, then $x_2x_3x_4x_5$ and $x_3x_4x_5x_6$ and $x_4x_5x_6x_7$ aren't. (For example, iket isn't.) Such a set is called a "commafree code" or a "self-synchronizing block code" of length four.

Commafree codes were introduced by F. H. C. Crick, J. S. Griffith, and L. E. Orgel [*Proc. National Acad. Sci.* **43** (1957), 416–421], and studied further by S. W. Golomb, B. Gordon, and L. R. Welch [*Canadian Journal of Mathematics* **10** (1958), 202–209], who considered the general case of m-letter alphabets and n-letter words. They constructed optimum commafree codes for all m when $n = 2$, 3, 5, 7, 9, 11, 13, and 15; and optimum codes for all m were subsequently found also for $n = 17, 19, 21, \ldots$ (see exercise 37). We will focus our attention on the four-letter case here ($n = 4$), partly because that case is still very far from being resolved, but mostly because the task of finding such codes is especially instructive. Indeed, our discussion will lead us naturally to an understanding of several significant techniques that are important for backtrack programming in general.

To begin, we can see immediately that a commafree codeword cannot be "periodic," like dodo or gaga. Such a string already appears within two adjacent copies of itself. Thus we're restricted to *aperiodic* strings like item, of which there are $m^4 - m^2$. Notice further that if item has been chosen, we aren't allowed to include any of its cyclic shifts temi, emit, or mite, because they all appear within itemitem. Hence the maximum number of codewords in our commafree code cannot exceed $(m^4 - m^2)/4$.

For example, consider the binary case, $m = 2$, when this maximum is 3. Can we choose three four-bit "words," one from each of the cyclic classes

$$\begin{aligned}
[0001] &= \{0001, 0010, 0100, 1000\}, \\
[0011] &= \{0011, 0110, 1100, 1001\}, \\
[0111] &= \{0111, 1110, 1101, 1011\},
\end{aligned} \tag{15}$$

so that the resulting code is commafree? Yes: One solution in this case is simply to choose the smallest word in each class, namely 0001, 0011, and 0111. (Alert readers will recall that we studied the smallest word in the cyclic class of *any* aperiodic string in Section 7.2.1.1, where such words were called *prime strings* and where some of the remarkable properties of prime strings were proved.)

That trick doesn't work when $m = 3$, however, when there are $(81 - 9)/4 = 18$ cyclic classes. Then we cannot include 1112 after we've chosen 0001 and 0011. Indeed, a code that contains 0001 and 1112 can't contain either 0011 or 0111.

We could systematically backtrack through 18 levels, choosing x_1 in [0001] and x_2 in [0011], etc., and rejecting each x_l as in Algorithm B whenever we discover that $\{x_1, x_2, \ldots, x_l\}$ isn't commafree. For example, if $x_1 = 0010$ and we try $x_2 = 1001$, this approach would backtrack because x_1 occurs inside $x_2 x_1$.

But a naïve strategy of that kind, which recognizes failure only after a bad choice has been made, can be vastly improved. If we had been clever enough, we could have looked a little bit ahead, and never even considered the choice $x_2 = 1001$ in the first place. Indeed, after choosing $x_1 = 0010$, we can automatically exclude *all* further words of the form ∗001, such as 2001 when $m \geq 3$ and 3001 when $m \geq 4$.

Even better pruning occurs if, for example, we've chosen $x_1 = 0001$ and $x_2 = 0011$. Then we can immediately rule out all words of the forms 1∗∗∗ or ∗∗∗0, because $x_1 1∗∗∗$ includes x_2 and ∗∗∗$0x_2$ includes x_1. Already we could then deduce, in the case $m \geq 3$, that classes [0002], [0021], [0111], [0211], and [1112] *must* be represented by 0002, 0021, 0111, 0211, and 2111, respectively; each of the other three possibilities in those classes has been wiped out!

Thus we see the desirability of a lookahead mechanism.

Dynamic ordering of choices. Furthermore, we can see from this example that it's not always good to choose x_1, then x_2, then x_3, and so on when trying to satisfy a general property $P_n(x_1, x_2, \ldots, x_n)$ in the setting of Algorithm B. Maybe the search tree will be much smaller if we first choose x_5, say, and then turn next to some other x_j, depending on the particular value of x_5 that was selected. Some orderings might have much better cutoff properties than others, and every branch of the tree is free to choose its variables in any desired order.

Indeed, our commafree coding problem for ternary 4-tuples doesn't dictate any particular ordering of the 18 classes that would be likely to keep the search tree small. Therefore, instead of calling those choices x_1, x_2, ..., x_{18}, it's better to identify them by the various class names, namely x_{0001}, x_{0002}, x_{0011}, x_{0012}, x_{0021}, x_{0022}, x_{0102}, x_{0111}, x_{0112}, x_{0121}, x_{0122}, x_{0211}, x_{0212}, x_{0221}, x_{0222}, x_{1112}, x_{1122}, x_{1222}. (Algorithm 7.2.1.1F is a good way to generate those names.) At every node of the search tree we then can choose a convenient variable on which to branch, based on previous choices. After beginning with $x_{0001} \leftarrow 0001$ at level 1 we might decide to try $x_{0011} \leftarrow 0011$ at level 2; and then, as we've seen, the choices $x_{0002} \leftarrow 0002$, $x_{0021} \leftarrow 0021$, $x_{0111} \leftarrow 0111$, $x_{0211} \leftarrow 0211$, and $x_{1112} \leftarrow 2111$ are forced, so we should make them at levels 3 through 7.

Furthermore, after those forced moves are made, it turns out that they don't force any others. But only two choices for x_{0012} will remain, while x_{0122} will have three. Therefore it will probably be wiser to branch on x_{0012} rather than on x_{0122} at level 8. (Incidentally, it also turns out that there *is* no commafree code of length $(m^4 - m^2)/4$ with $x_{0001} = 0001$ and $x_{0011} = 0011$, *except* when $m = 2$.)

It's easy to adapt Algorithms B and W to allow dynamic ordering. Every node of the search tree can be given a "frame" in which we record the variable being set and the choice that was made. This choice of variable and value can be called a "move" made by the backtrack procedure.

Dynamic ordering can be helpful also after backtracking has taken place. If we continue the example above, where $x_{0001} = 0001$ and we've explored all cases in which $x_{0011} = 0011$, we aren't obliged to continue by trying another value for x_{0011}. We do want to remember that 0011 should no longer be considered legal, until x_{0001} changes; but we could decide to explore next a case such as $x_{0002} \leftarrow 2000$ at level 2. In fact, $x_{0002} = 2000$ is quickly seen to be impossible in the presence of 0001 (see exercise 39). An even more efficient choice at level 2 turns out to be $x_{0012} \leftarrow 0012$, because that branch immediately forces $x_{0002} \leftarrow 0002$, $x_{0022} \leftarrow 0022$, $x_{0122} \leftarrow 0122$, $x_{0222} \leftarrow 0222$, $x_{1222} \leftarrow 1222$, and $x_{0011} \leftarrow 1001$.

Sequential allocation redux. The choice of a variable and value on which to branch is a delicate tradeoff. We don't want to devote more time to planning than we'll save by having a good plan.

If we're going to benefit from dynamic ordering, we'll need efficient data structures that will lead to good decisions without much deliberation. On the other hand, elaborate data structures need to be updated whenever we branch to a new level, and they need to be downdated whenever we return from that level. Algorithm L illustrates an efficient mechanism based on linked lists; but sequentially allocated lists are often even more appealing, because they are cache-friendly and they involve fewer accesses to memory.

Assume then that we wish to represent a set of items as an unordered sequential list. The list begins in a cell of memory pointed to by HEAD, and TAIL points just beyond the end of the list. For example,

$$(16)$$

is one way to represent the set $\{1, 3, 4, 9\}$. The number of items currently in the set is $\texttt{TAIL} - \texttt{HEAD}$; thus $\texttt{TAIL} = \texttt{HEAD}$ if and only if the list is empty. If we wish to insert a new item x, knowing that x isn't already present, we simply set

$$\texttt{MEM[TAIL]} \leftarrow x, \quad \texttt{TAIL} \leftarrow \texttt{TAIL} + 1. \qquad (17)$$

Conversely, if $\texttt{HEAD} \leq \texttt{P} < \texttt{TAIL}$, we can easily delete $\texttt{MEM[P]}$:

$$\texttt{TAIL} \leftarrow \texttt{TAIL} - 1; \quad \text{if } \texttt{P} \neq \texttt{TAIL}, \text{ set } \texttt{MEM[P]} \leftarrow \texttt{MEM[TAIL]}. \qquad (18)$$

(We've tacitly assumed in (17) that $\texttt{MEM[TAIL]}$ is available for use whenever a new item is inserted. Otherwise we would have had to test for memory overflow.)

We can't delete an item from a list without knowing its $\texttt{MEM}$ location. Thus we will often want to maintain an "inverse list," assuming that all items x lie in the range $0 \leq x < M$. For example, (16) becomes the following, if $M = 10$:

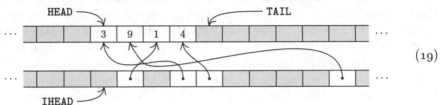

$$(19)$$

(Shaded cells have undefined contents.) With this setup, insertion (17) becomes

$$\texttt{MEM[TAIL]} \leftarrow x, \quad \texttt{MEM[IHEAD} + x] \leftarrow \texttt{TAIL}, \quad \texttt{TAIL} \leftarrow \texttt{TAIL} + 1, \qquad (20)$$

and $\texttt{TAIL}$ will never exceed $\texttt{HEAD} + M$. Similarly, deletion of x becomes

$$\texttt{P} \leftarrow \texttt{MEM[IHEAD} + x], \quad \texttt{TAIL} \leftarrow \texttt{TAIL} - 1;$$
$$\text{if } \texttt{P} \neq \texttt{TAIL}, \text{ set } y \leftarrow \texttt{MEM[TAIL]}, \texttt{MEM[P]} \leftarrow y, \texttt{MEM[IHEAD} + y] \leftarrow \texttt{P}. \quad (21)$$

For example, after deleting '9' from (19) we would obtain this:

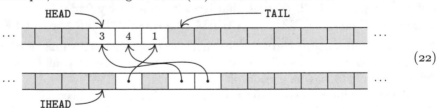

$$(22)$$

In more elaborate situations we also want to test whether or not a given item x is present. If so, we can keep more information in the inverse list. A particularly useful variation arises when the list that begins at $\texttt{IHEAD}$ contains a *complete* permutation of the values $\{\texttt{HEAD}, \texttt{HEAD} + 1, \ldots, \texttt{HEAD} + M - 1\}$, and the memory cells beginning at $\texttt{HEAD}$ contain the inverse permutation — although only the first $\texttt{TAIL} - \texttt{HEAD}$ elements of that list are considered to be "active."

For example, in our commafree code problem with $m = 3$, we can begin by putting items representing the $M = 18$ cycle classes $[0001]$, $[0002]$, $\ldots$, $[1222]$ into memory cells $\texttt{HEAD}$ through $\texttt{HEAD} + 17$. Initially they're all active, with $\texttt{TAIL} = \texttt{HEAD} + 18$ and $\texttt{MEM[IHEAD} + c] = \texttt{HEAD} + c$ for $0 \leq c < 18$. Then whenever we decide to choose a codeword for class c, we delete c from the active list by using a souped-up version of (21) that maintains full permutations:

$$\texttt{P} \leftarrow \texttt{MEM[IHEAD} + c\texttt{]}, \quad \texttt{TAIL} \leftarrow \texttt{TAIL} - 1;$$
$$\text{if P} \neq \texttt{TAIL, set } y \leftarrow \texttt{MEM[TAIL]}, \quad \texttt{MEM[TAIL]} \leftarrow c, \quad \texttt{MEM[P]} \leftarrow y,$$
$$\texttt{MEM[IHEAD} + c\texttt{]} \leftarrow \texttt{TAIL}, \quad \texttt{MEM[IHEAD} + y\texttt{]} \leftarrow \texttt{P}. \quad (23)$$

Later on, after backtracking to a state where we once again want c to be considered active, we simply set $\texttt{TAIL} \leftarrow \texttt{TAIL} + 1$, because c will already be in place! (This data-structuring technique has been called a *sparse-set representation*; see P. Briggs and L. Torczon, *ACM Letters Prog. Lang. and Syst.* **2** (1993), 59–69.)

Lists for the commafree problem. The task of finding all four-letter commafree codes of maximum length is not difficult when $m = 3$ and only 18 cycle classes are involved. But it already becomes challenging when $m = 4$, because we must then deal with $(4^4 - 4^2)/4 = 60$ classes. Therefore we'll want to give it some careful thought as we try to set it up for backtracking.

The example scenarios for $m = 3$ considered above suggest that we'll repeatedly want to know the answers to questions such as, "How many words of the form 02** are still available for selection as codewords?" Redundant data structures, oriented to queries of that kind, appear to be needed. Fortunately, we shall see that there's a nice way to provide them, using sequential lists as in (19)–(23).

In Algorithm C below, each of the m^4 four-letter words is given one of three possible states during the search for commafree codes. A word is *green* if it's part of the current set of tentative codewords. It is *red* if it's not currently a candidate for such status, either because it is incompatible with the existing green words or because the algorithm has already examined all scenarios in which it is green in their presence. Every other word is *blue*, and sort of in limbo; the algorithm might or might not decide to make it red or green. All words are initially blue — except for the m^2 periodic words, which are permanently red.

We'll use the Greek letter α to stand for the integer value of a four-letter word x in radix m. For example, if $m = 3$ and if x is the word 0102, then $\alpha = (0102)_3 = 11$. The current state of word x is kept in $\texttt{MEM}[\alpha]$, using one of the arbitrary internal codes 2 (GREEN), 0 (RED), or 1 (BLUE).

The most important feature of the algorithm is that *every blue word* $x = x_1x_2x_3x_4$ *is potentially present in seven different lists*, called $\texttt{P1}(x)$, $\texttt{P2}(x)$, $\texttt{P3}(x)$, $\texttt{S1}(x)$, $\texttt{S2}(x)$, $\texttt{S3}(x)$, and $\texttt{CL}(x)$, where

- $\texttt{P1}(x)$, $\texttt{P2}(x)$, $\texttt{P3}(x)$ are the blue words matching x_1***, x_1x_2**, $x_1x_2x_3$*;
- $\texttt{S1}(x)$, $\texttt{S2}(x)$, $\texttt{S3}(x)$ are the blue words matching ***x_4, **x_3x_4, *$x_2x_3x_4$;
- $\texttt{CL}(x)$ hosts the blue words in $\{x_1x_2x_3x_4, x_2x_3x_4x_1, x_3x_4x_1x_2, x_4x_1x_2x_3\}$.

These seven lists begin respectively in $\texttt{MEM}$ locations $\texttt{P1OFF} + p_1(\alpha)$, $\texttt{P2OFF} + p_2(\alpha)$, $\texttt{P3OFF} + p_3(\alpha)$, $\texttt{S1OFF} + s_1(\alpha)$, $\texttt{S2OFF} + s_2(\alpha)$, $\texttt{S3OFF} + s_3(\alpha)$, and $\texttt{CLOFF} + 4cl(\alpha)$; here ($\texttt{P1OFF}$, $\texttt{P2OFF}$, $\texttt{P3OFF}$, $\texttt{S1OFF}$, $\texttt{S2OFF}$, $\texttt{S3OFF}$, $\texttt{CLOFF}$) are respectively $(2m^4, 5m^4, 8m^4, 11m^4, 14m^4, 17m^4, 20m^4)$. We define $p_1((x_1x_2x_3x_4)_m) = (x_1000)_m$, $p_2((x_1x_2x_3x_4)_m) = (x_1x_200)_m$, $p_3((x_1x_2x_3x_4)_m) = (x_1x_2x_30)_m$; and $s_1((x_1x_2x_3x_4)_m) = (x_4000)_m$, $s_2((x_1x_2x_3x_4)_m) = (x_3x_400)_m$, $s_3((x_1x_2x_3x_4)_m) = (x_2x_3x_40)_m$; and finally $cl((x_1x_2x_3x_4)_m)$ is an internal number, between 0 and

Table 1

LISTS USED BY ALGORITHM C ($m = 2$), ENTERING LEVEL 1

	0	1	2	3	4	5	6	7	8	9	a	b	c	d	e	f	
0	RED	BLUE	BLUE	BLUE	RED	RED	BLUE	BLUE	RED	BLUE	RED	BLUE	BLUE	BLUE	BLUE	RED	
10		20	21	22			23	24		29		2c	28	2b	2a		
20	0001	0010	0011	0110	0111				1100	1001	1110	1101	1011				P1
30	25								2d								
40		50	51	52			54	55		58		59	5c	5e	5d		
50	0001	0010	0011		0110	0111				1001	1011		1100	1110	1101		P2
60	53				56				5a				5f				
70		80	82	83			86	87		88		8a	8c	8d	8e		
80	0001		0010	0011			0110	0111	1001		1011		1100	1101	1110		P3
90	81		84		84		88		89		8b		8e		8f		
a0		b8	b0	b9			b1	bb		ba		bd	b2	bc	b3		
b0	0010	0110	1100	1110					0001	0011	1001	0111	1101	1011			S1
c0	b4								be								
d0		e4	e8	ec			e9	ed		e5		ee	e0	e6	ea		
e0	1100				0001	1001	1101		0010	0110	1110		0011	0111	1011		S2
f0	e1				e7				eb				ef				
100		112	114	116			11c	11e		113		117	118	11a	11d		
110		0001	1001	0010			0011	1011	1100		1101		0110	1110	0111		S3
120	110		114		115		118		119		11b		11e		11f		
130		140	141	144			145	148		147		14b	146	14a	149		
140	0001	0010			0011	0110	1100	1001	0111	1110	1101	1011					CL
150	142				148				14c								

This table shows MEM locations 0000 through 150f, using hexadecimal notation. (For example, MEM[40d]=5e; see exercise 41.) Blank entries are unused by the algorithm.

$(m^4 - m^2)/4 - 1$, assigned to each class. The seven MEM locations where x appears in these seven lists are respectively kept in inverse lists that begin in MEM locations P1OFF $- m^4 + \alpha$, P2OFF $- m^4 + \alpha$, ..., CLOFF $- m^4 + \alpha$. And the TAIL pointers, which indicate the current list sizes as in (19)–(23), are respectively kept in MEM locations P1OFF $+ m^4 + p_1(\alpha)$, P2OFF $+ m^4 + p_2(\alpha)$, ..., S3OFF $+ m^4 + s_3(\alpha)$, CLOFF $+ m^4 + 4cl(\alpha)$. (Whew; got that?)

This vast apparatus, which occupies $22m^4$ cells of MEM, is illustrated in Table 1, at the beginning of the computation for the case $m = 2$. Fortunately it's not really as complicated as it may seem at first. Nor is it especially vast: After all, $22m^4$ is only 13,750 when $m = 5$.

(A close inspection of Table 1 reveals incidentally that the words 0100 and 1000 have been colored red, not blue. That's because we can assume without loss of generality that class [0001] is represented either by 0001 or by 0010. The other two cases are covered by left-right reflection of all codewords.)

Algorithm C finds these lists invaluable when it is deciding where next to branch. But it has no further use for a list in which one of the items has become green. Therefore it declares such lists "closed"; and it saves most of the work of list maintenance by updating only the lists that remain open. A closed list is represented internally by setting its TAIL pointer to HEAD $- 1$.

For example, Table 2 shows how the lists in MEM will have changed just after $x = 0010$ has been chosen to be a tentative codeword. The elements $\{0001, 0010, 0011, 0110, 0111\}$ of P1(x) are effectively hidden, because the tail

Table 2

LISTS USED BY ALGORITHM C ($m = 2$), ENTERING LEVEL 2

	0	1	2	3	4	5	6	7	8	9	a	b	c	d	e	f	
0	RED	RED	GREEN	BLUE	RED	RED	BLUE	BLUE	RED	RED	RED	BLUE	BLUE	BLUE	BLUE	RED	
10												29	28	2b	2a		
20									1100	1011	1110	1101					P1
30	1f								2c								
40							54	55				58	5c	5e	5d		
50					0110	0111			1011				1100	1110	1101		P2
60	4f				56								5f				
70							86	87				8a	8c	8d	8e		
80							0110	0111			1011		1100	1101	1110		P3
90	80		81		84		88		88		8b		8e		8f		
a0			b9				bb					b8		ba			
b0									1011	0011	1101	0111					S1
c0	af								bc								
d0			ec				ed					ee	e0	e4			
e0		1100			1101								0011	0111	1011		S2
f0	e1				e5				e7				ef				
100			116				11c	11e				117	118	11a	11d		
110							0011	1011	1100		1101		0110	1110	0111		S3
120	110		112		113		118		119		11b		11e		11f		
130			144				145	148				14b	146	14a	149		
140							0011	0110	1100		0111	1110	1101	1011			CL
150	13f				147				14c								

The word 0010 has become green, thus closing its seven lists and making 0001 red. The logic of Algorithm C has also made 1001 red. Hence 0001 and 1001 have been deleted from the open lists in which they formerly appeared (see exercise 42).

pointer MEM[30] = 1f = 20 − 1 marks that list as closed. (Those list elements actually do still appear in MEM locations 200 through 204, just as they did in Table 1. But there's no need to look at that list while any word of the form 0∗∗∗ is green.)

A general mechanism for doing and undoing. We're almost ready to finalize the details of Algorithm C and to get on with the search for commafree codes, but a big problem still remains: The state of computation at every level of the search involves all of the marvelous lists that we've just specified, and those lists aren't tiny. They occupy more than 5000 cells of MEM when $m = 4$, and they can change substantially from level to level.

We could make a new copy of the entire state, whenever we advance to a new node of the search tree. But that's a bad idea, because we don't want to perform thousands of memory accesses per node. A much better strategy would be to stick with a single instance of MEM, and to update and downdate the lists as the search progresses, if we could only think of a simple way to do that.

And we're in luck: There *is* such a way, first formulated by R. W. Floyd in his classic paper "Nondeterministic algorithms" [*JACM* **14** (1967), 636–644]. Floyd's original idea, which required a special compiler to generate forward and backward versions of every program step, can in fact be greatly simplified when all of the changes in state are confined to a single MEM array. All we need to do is to replace every assignment operation of the form 'MEM[a] ← v' by the slightly more cumbersome operation

$\text{store}(a, v):$ Set $\text{UNDO}[u] \leftarrow (a, \text{MEM}[a])$, $\text{MEM}[a] \leftarrow v$, and $u \leftarrow u + 1$.   (24)

Here UNDO is a sequential stack that holds (address, value) pairs; in our application we could say '$\text{UNDO}[u] \leftarrow (a \ll 16) + \text{MEM}[a]$', because the cell addresses and values never exceed 16 bits. Of course we'll also need to check that the stack pointer u doesn't get too large, if the number of assignments has no a priori limit.

Later on, when we want to undo all changes to MEM that were made after the time when u had reached a particular value u_0, we simply do this:

$\text{unstore}(u_0):$ While $u > u_0$, set $u \leftarrow u - 1$,
$$(a, v) \leftarrow \text{UNDO}[u], \text{ and } \text{MEM}[a] \leftarrow v. \qquad (25)$$

In our application the unstacking operation '$(a, v) \leftarrow \text{UNDO}[u]$' here could be implemented by saying '$a \leftarrow \text{UNDO}[u] \gg 16$, $v \leftarrow \text{UNDO}[u] \mathbin{\&} {}^{\#}\text{ffff}$'.

A useful refinement of this reversible-memory technique is often advantageous, based on the idea of "stamping" that is part of the folklore of programming. It puts only one item on the UNDO stack when the same memory address is updated more than once in the same round.

$\text{store}(a, v):$ If $\text{STAMP}[a] \neq \sigma$, set $\text{STAMP}[a] \leftarrow \sigma$,
$\qquad\qquad \text{UNDO}[u] \leftarrow (a, \text{MEM}[a])$, and $u \leftarrow u + 1$.
$\qquad$ Then set $\text{MEM}[a] \leftarrow v$.   (26)

Here STAMP is an array with one entry for each address in MEM. It's initially all zero, and σ is initially 1. Whenever we come to a fallback point, where the current stack pointer will be remembered as the value u_0 for some future undoing, we "bump" the current stamp by setting $\sigma \leftarrow \sigma + 1$. Then (26) will continue to do the right thing. (In programs that run for a long time, we must be careful when integer overflow causes σ to be bumped to zero; see exercise 43.)

Notice that the combination of (24) and (25) will perform five memory accesses for each assignment and its undoing. The combination of (26) and (25) will cost seven mems for the first assignment to $\text{MEM}[a]$, but only two mems for every subsequent assignment to the same address. So (26) wins, if multiple assignments exceed one-time-only assignments.

Backtracking through commafree codes.   OK, we're now equipped with enough basic knowhow to write a pretty good backtrack program for the problem of generating all commafree four-letter codes.

Algorithm C below incorporates one more key idea, which is a lookahead mechanism that is specific to commafree backtracking; we'll call it the "poison list." Every item on the poison list is a pair, consisting of a suffix and a prefix that the commafree rule forbids from occurring together. Every green word $x_1x_2x_3x_4$ — that is, every word that will be a final codeword in the current branch of our backtrack search — contributes three items to the poison list, namely

$$(*x_1x_2x_3, x_4{*}{*}{*}), \quad (**x_1x_2, x_3x_4{*}{*}), \quad \text{and} \quad (***x_1, x_2x_3x_4{*}). \qquad (27)$$

If there's a green word on both sides of a poison list entry, we're dead: The commafree condition fails, and we mustn't proceed. If there's a green word on one side but not the other, we can kill off all blue words on the other side by making them red. And if either side of a poison list entry corresponds to an *empty* list, we can remove this entry from the poison list because it will never affect the outcome. (Blue words become red or green, but red words stay red.)

For example, consider the transition from Table 1 to Table 2. When word 0010 becomes green, the poison list receives its first three items:

$$(*001, 0***), \quad (**00, 10**), \quad (***0, 010*).$$

The first of these kills off the *001 list, because 0*** contains the green word 0010. That makes 1001 red. The last of these, similarly, kills off the 010* list; but that list is empty when $m = 2$. The poison list now reduces to a single item, $(**00, 10**)$, which remains poisonous because list **00 contains the blue word 1100 and 10** contains the blue word 1011.

We'll maintain the poison list at the end of MEM, following the CL lists. It obviously will contain at most $3(m^4 - m^2)/4$ entries, and in fact it usually turns out to be quite small. No inverse list is required; so we shall adopt the simple method of (17) and (18), but with two cells per entry so that TAIL will change by ± 2 instead of by ± 1. The value of TAIL will be stored in MEM at key times so that temporary changes to it can be undone.

The case $m = 4$, in which each codeword consists of four *quaternary* digits $\{0, 1, 2, 3\}$, is particularly interesting, because an early backtrack program by Lee Laxdal found that no such commafree code can make use of all 60 of the cycle classes [0001], [0002], ..., [2333]. [See B. H. Jiggs, *Canadian Journal of Math.* **15** (1963), 178–187.] Laxdal's program also reportedly showed that at least three of those classes must be omitted; and it found several valid 57-word sets. Further details were never published, because the proof that 58 codewords are impossible depended on what Jiggs called a "quite time-consuming" computation.

Because size 60 is impossible, our algorithm cannot simply assume that a move such as 1001 is forced when the other words 0011, 0110, 1100 of its class have been ruled out. We must also consider the possibility that class [0011] is entirely absent from the code. Such considerations add an interesting further twist to the problem, and Algorithm C describes one way to cope with it.

Algorithm C (*Four-letter commafree codes*). Given an alphabet size $m \le 7$ and a goal g in the range $L - m(m-1) \le g \le L$, where $L = (m^4 - m^2)/4$, this algorithm finds all sets of g four-letter words that are commafree and include either 0001 or 0010. It uses an array MEM of $M = \lfloor 23.5m^4 \rfloor$ 16-bit numbers, as well as several more auxiliary arrays: ALF of size $16^3 m$; STAMP of size M; X, C, S, and U of size $L + 1$; FREE and IFREE of size L; and a sufficiently large array called UNDO whose maximum size is difficult to guess.

C1. [Initialize.] Set $\text{ALF}[(abcd)_{16}] \leftarrow (abcd)_m$ for $0 \le a, b, c, d < m$. Set $\text{STAMP}[k] \leftarrow 0$ for $0 \le k < M$ and $\sigma \leftarrow 0$. Put the initial prefix, suffix, and class lists into MEM, as in Table 1. Also create an empty poison list by setting MEM[PP] ← POISON, where POISON $= 22m^4$ and PP = POISON -1. Set FREE[k] ← IFREE[k] ← k for $0 \le k < L$. Then set $l \leftarrow 1$, $x \leftarrow$ #0001, $c \leftarrow 0$, $s \leftarrow L - g$, $f \leftarrow L$, $u \leftarrow 0$, and go to step C3. (Variable l is the level, x is a trial word, c is its class, s is the "slack," f is the number of free classes, and u is the size of the UNDO stack.)

C2. [Enter level l.] If $l > L$, visit the solution $x_1 \ldots x_L$ and go to C6. Otherwise choose a candidate word x and class c as described in exercise 44.

C3. [Try the candidate.] Set U[l] ← u and $\sigma \leftarrow \sigma + 1$. If $x < 0$, go to C6 if $s = 0$ or $l = 1$, otherwise set $s \leftarrow s - 1$. If $x \ge 0$, update the data structures to make x green, as described in exercise 45, escaping to C5 if trouble arises.

C4. [Make the move.] Set X[l] ← x, C[l] ← c, S[l] ← s, $p \leftarrow$ IFREE[c], $f \leftarrow f - 1$. If $p \ne f$, set $y \leftarrow$ FREE[f], FREE[p] ← y, IFREE[y] ← p, FREE[f] ← c, IFREE[c] ← f. (This is (23).) Then set $l \leftarrow l + 1$ and go to C2.

C5. [Try again.] While $u > $ U[l], set $u \leftarrow u - 1$ and MEM[UNDO[u] $\gg 16$] ← UNDO[u] & #ffff. (Those operations restore the previous state, as in (25).) Then $\sigma \leftarrow \sigma + 1$ and redden x (see exercise 45). Go to C2.

C6. [Backtrack.] Set $l \leftarrow l - 1$, and terminate if $l = 0$. Otherwise set $x \leftarrow$ X[l], $c \leftarrow$ C[l], $f \leftarrow f + 1$. If $x < 0$, repeat this step (class c was omitted from the code). Otherwise set $s \leftarrow$ S[l] and go back to C5. ∎

Exercises 44 and 45 provide the instructive details that flesh out this skeleton.

Algorithm C needs just 13, 177, and 2380 megamems to prove that no solutions exist for $m = 4$ when g is 60, 59, and 58. It needs about 22800 megamems to find the 1152 solutions for $g = 57$; see exercise 47. There are roughly (14, 240, 3700, 38000) thousand nodes in the respective search trees, with most of the activity taking place on levels 30 ± 10. The height of the UNDO stack never exceeds 2804, and the poison list never contains more than 12 entries at a time.

Running time estimates. Backtrack programs are full of surprises. Sometimes they produce instant answers to a supposedly difficult problem. But sometimes they spin their wheels endlessly, trying to traverse an astronomically large search tree. And sometimes they deliver results just about as fast as we might expect.

Fortunately, we needn't sit in the dark. There's a simple Monte Carlo algorithm by which we can often tell in advance whether or not a given backtrack strategy will be feasible. This method, based on random sampling, can actually be worked out by hand *before* writing a program, in order to help decide whether to invest further time while following a particular approach. In fact, the very act of carrying out this pleasant pencil-and-paper method often suggests useful cutoff strategies and/or data structures that will be valuable later when a program is being written. For example, the author developed Algorithm C above after first doing some armchair experiments with random choices of potential commafree codewords; these dry runs revealed that a family of lists such as those in Tables 1 and 2 would be quite helpful when making further choices.

To illustrate the method, let's consider the n queens problem again, as represented in Algorithm B* above. When $n = 8$, we can obtain a decent "ballpark

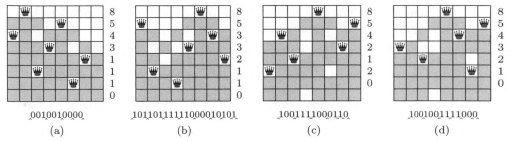

Fig. 69. Four random attempts to solve the 8 queens problem. Such experiments help to estimate the size of the backtrack tree in Fig. 68. The branching degrees are shown at the right of each diagram, while the random bits used for sampling appear below. Cells have been shaded in gray if they are attacked by one or more queens in earlier rows.

estimate" of the size of Fig. 68 by examining only a few random paths in that search tree. We start by writing down the number $D_1 \leftarrow 8$, because there are eight ways to place the queen in row 1. (In other words, the root node of the search tree has degree 8.) Then we use a source of random numbers — say the binary digits of $\pi \bmod 1 = (.001001000011\ldots)_2$ — to select one of those placements. Eight choices are possible, so we look at three of those bits; we shall set $X_1 \leftarrow 2$, because 001 is the second of the eight possibilities $(000, 001, \ldots, 111)$.

Given $X_1 = 2$, the queen in row 2 can't go into columns 1, 2, or 3. Hence five possibilities remain for X_2, and we write down $D_2 \leftarrow 5$. The next three bits of π lead us to set $X_2 \leftarrow 5$, since 5 is the second of the available columns (4, 5, 6, 7, 8) and 001 is the second value of $(000, 001, \ldots, 100)$. Incidentally, if π had continued with 101 or 110 or 111 instead of 001, we would have used the "rejection method" of Section 3.4.1 and moved to the next three bits; see exercise 49.

Continuing in this way leads to $D_3 \leftarrow 4$, $X_3 \leftarrow 1$; then $D_4 \leftarrow 3$, $X_4 \leftarrow 4$. (Here we used the two bits 00 to select X_3, and the next two bits 00 to select X_4.) The remaining branches are forced: $D_5 \leftarrow 1$, $X_5 \leftarrow 7$; $D_6 \leftarrow 1$, $X_6 \leftarrow 3$; $D_7 \leftarrow 1$, $X_7 \leftarrow 6$; and we're stuck when we reach level 8 and find $D_8 \leftarrow 0$.

These sequential random choices are depicted in Fig. 69(a), where we've used them to place each queen successively into an unshaded cell. Parts (b), (c), and (d) of Fig. 69 correspond in the same way to choices based on the binary digits of $e \bmod 1$, $\phi \bmod 1$, and $\gamma \bmod 1$. Exactly 10 bits of π, 20 bits of e, 13 bits of ϕ, and 13 bits of γ were used to generate these examples.

In this discussion the notation D_k stands for a branching degree, not for a domain of values. We've used uppercase letters for the numbers D_1, X_1, D_2, etc., because those quantities are random variables. Once we've reached $D_l = 0$ at some level, we're ready to estimate the overall cost, by implicitly assuming that the path we've taken is representative of *all* root-to-leaf paths in the tree.

The cost of a backtrack program can be assessed by summing the individual amounts of time spent at each node of the search tree. Notice that every node on level l of that tree can be labeled uniquely by a sequence $x_1 \ldots x_{l-1}$, which defines the path from the root to that node. Thus our goal is to estimate the sum of all $c(x_1 \ldots x_{l-1})$, where $c(x_1 \ldots x_{l-1})$ is the cost associated with node $x_1 \ldots x_{l-1}$.

For example, the four queens problem is represented by the search tree (4), and its cost is the sum of 17 individual costs

$$c() + c(1) + c(13) + c(14) + c(142) + c(2) + c(24) + \cdots + c(413) + c(42). \quad (28)$$

If $C(x_1 \ldots x_l)$ denotes the total cost of the subtree rooted at $x_1 \ldots x_l$, then

$$C(x_1 \ldots x_l) = c(x_1 \ldots x_l) + C(x_1 \ldots x_l x_{l+1}^{(1)}) + \cdots + C(x_1 \ldots x_l x_{l+1}^{(d)}) \quad (29)$$

when the choices for x_{l+1} at node $x_1 \ldots x_l$ are $\{x_{l+1}^{(1)}, \ldots, x_{l+1}^{(d)}\}$. For instance in (4) we have $C(1) = c(1) + C(13) + C(14)$; $C(13) = c(13)$; and $C() = c() + C(1) + C(2) + C(3) + C(4)$ is the overall cost (28).

In these terms a Monte Carlo estimate for $C()$ is extremely easy to compute:

Theorem E. *Given D_1, X_1, D_2, X_2, $\ldots$ as above, the cost of backtracking is*

$$C() = \mathrm{E}\big(c() + D_1(c(X_1) + D_2(c(X_1 X_2) + D_3(c(X_1 X_2 X_3) + \cdots)))\big). \quad (30)$$

Proof. Node $x_1 \ldots x_l$, with branch degrees $d_1, \ldots, d_l$ above it, is reached with probability $1/d_1 \ldots d_l$; so it contributes $d_1 \ldots d_l c(x_1 \ldots x_l)/d_1 \ldots d_l = c(x_1 \ldots x_l)$ to the expected value in this formula. ∎

For example, the tree (4) has six root-to-leaf paths, and they occur with respective probabilities $1/8$, $1/8$, $1/4$, $1/4$, $1/8$, $1/8$. The first one contributes $1/8$ times $c() + 4(c(1) + 2(c(13)))$, namely $c()/8 + c(1)/2 + c(13)$, to the expected value. The second contributes $c()/8 + c(1)/2 + c(14) + c(142)$; and so on.

A special case of Theorem E, with all $c(x_1 \ldots x_l) = 1$, tells us how to estimate the total size of the tree, which is often a crucial quantity:

Corollary E. *The number of nodes in the search tree, given D_1, D_2, $\ldots$, is*

$$\mathrm{E}(1 + D_1 + D_1 D_2 + \cdots) = \mathrm{E}\big(1 + D_1(1 + D_2(1 + D_3(1 + \cdots)))\big). \quad (31)$$

For example, Fig. 69 gives us four estimates for the size of the tree in Fig. 68, using the numbers D_j at the right of each 8×8 diagram. The estimate from Fig. 69(a) is $1 + 8(1 + 5(1 + 4(1 + 3(1 + 1(1 + 1(1 + 1)))))) = 2129$; and the other three are respectively 2689, 1489, 2609. None of them is extremely far from the true number, 2057, although we can't expect to be so lucky all the time.

The detailed study in exercise 53 shows that the estimate (31) in the case of 8 queens turns out to be quite well behaved:

$$\big(\text{min } 489, \quad \text{ave } 2057, \quad \text{max } 7409, \quad \text{dev } \sqrt{1146640} \approx 1071\big). \quad (32)$$

The analogous problem for 16 queens has a much less homogeneous search tree:

$$\big(\text{min } 2597105, \quad \text{ave } 1141190303, \quad \text{max } 131048318769, \quad \text{dev} \approx 1234000000\big). \quad (33)$$

Still, this standard deviation is roughly the same as the mean, so we'll usually guess the correct order of magnitude. (For example, ten independent experiments predicted .632, .866, .237, 1.027, 4.006, .982, .143, .140, 3.402, and .510 billion nodes, respectively. The mean of these is 1.195.) A thousand trials with $n = 64$ suggest that the problem of 64 queens will have about 3×10^{65} nodes in its tree.

Let's formulate this estimation procedure precisely, so that it can be performed conveniently by machine as well as by hand:

Algorithm E (*Estimated cost of backtrack*). Given domains D_k and properties P_l as in Algorithm B, together with node costs $c(x_1 \ldots x_l)$ as above, this algorithm computes the quantity S whose expected value is the total cost $C()$ in (30). It uses an auxiliary array $y_0 y_1 \ldots$ whose size should be $\geq \max(|D_1|, \ldots, |D_n|)$.

E1. [Initialize.] Set $l \leftarrow D \leftarrow 1$, $S \leftarrow 0$, and initialize any data structures needed.

E2. [Enter level l.] (At this point $P_{l-1}(X_1, \ldots, X_{l-1})$ holds.) Set $S \leftarrow S + D \cdot c(X_1 \ldots X_{l-1})$. If $l > n$, terminate the algorithm. Otherwise set $d \leftarrow 0$ and set $x \leftarrow \min D_l$, the smallest element of D_l.

E3. [Test x.] If $P_l(X_1, \ldots, X_{l-1}, x)$ holds, set $y_d \leftarrow x$ and $d \leftarrow d + 1$.

E4. [Try again.] If $x \neq \max D_l$, set x to the next larger element of D_l and return to step E3.

E5. [Choose and try.] If $d = 0$, terminate. Otherwise set $D \leftarrow D \cdot d$ and $X_l \leftarrow y_I$, where I is a uniformly random integer in $\{0, \ldots, d-1\}$. Update the data structures to facilitate testing P_{l+1}, set $l \leftarrow l + 1$, and go back to E2. ∎

Although Algorithm E looks rather like Algorithm B, it never backtracks.

Of course we can't expect this algorithm to give decent estimates in cases where the backtrack tree is wildly erratic. The *expected* value of S, namely $\mathrm{E}\,S$, is indeed the true cost; but the *probable* values of S might be quite different.

An extreme example of bad behavior occurs if property P_l is the simple condition '$x_1 > \cdots > x_l$', and all domains are $\{1, \ldots, n\}$. Then there's only one solution, $x_1 \ldots x_n = n \ldots 1$; and backtracking is a particularly stupid way to find it!

The search tree for this somewhat ridiculous problem is, nevertheless, quite interesting. It is none other than the binomial tree T_n of Eq. 7.2.1.3–(21), which has $\binom{n}{l}$ nodes on level $l + 1$ and 2^n nodes in total. If we set all costs to 1, the expected value of S is therefore $2^n = e^{n \ln 2}$. But exercise 52 proves that S will almost always be much smaller, less than $e^{(\ln n)^2 \ln \ln n}$. Furthermore the average value of l when Algorithm E terminates with respect to T_n is only $H_n + 1$. When $n = 100$, for example, the probability that $l \geq 20$ on termination is only 0.0000000027, while the vast majority of the nodes are near level 51.

Many refinements of Algorithm E are possible. For example, exercise 54 shows that the choices in step E5 need not be uniform. We shall discuss improved estimation techniques in Section 7.2.2.9, after having seen numerous examples of backtracking in practice.

*Estimating the number of solutions. Sometimes we know that a problem has more solutions than we could ever hope to generate, yet we still want to know roughly how many there are. Algorithm E will tell us the approximate number, in cases where the backtrack process never reaches a dead end — that is, if it never terminates with $d = 0$ in step E5. There may be another criterion for successful termination in step E2 even though l might still be $\leq n$. The expected final value of D is exactly the total number of solutions, because every solution $\cdot X_1 \ldots X_l$ constructed by the algorithm is obtained with probability $1/D$.

For example, suppose we want to know the number of different paths by which a king can go from one corner of a chessboard to the opposite corner, without revisiting any square. One such path, chosen at random using the bits of π for guidance as we did in Fig. 69(a), is shown here. Starting in the upper left corner, we have 3 choices for the first move. Then, after moving to the right, there are 4 choices for the second move. And so on. We never make a move that would disconnect us from the goal; in particular, two of the moves are actually forced. (Exercise 58 explains one way to avoid fatal mistakes.)

The probability of obtaining this particular path is exactly $\frac{1}{3}\frac{1}{4}\frac{1}{6}\frac{1}{6}\frac{1}{2}\frac{1}{6}\frac{1}{7}\cdots\frac{1}{2} = 1/D$, where $D = 3\times4\times6\times6\times2\times6\times7\times\cdots\times2 = 1^2\cdot2^4\cdot3^4\cdot4^{10}\cdot5^9\cdot6^6\cdot7^1 \approx 8.7\times10^{20}$. Thus we can reasonably guess, at least tentatively, that there are 10^{21} such paths, more or less.

Of course that guess, based on a single random sample, rests on very shaky ground. But we know that the average value $M_N = (D^{(1)} + \cdots + D^{(N)})/N$ of N guesses, in N independent experiments, will almost surely approach the correct number.

How large should N be, before we can have any confidence in the results? The actual values of D obtained from random king paths tend to vary all over the map. Figure 70 plots typical results, as N varies from 1 to 10000. For each value of N we can follow the advice of statistics textbooks and calculate the sample variance $V_N = S_N/(N-1)$ as in Eq. 4.2.2–(16); then $M_N \pm \sqrt{V_N/N}$ is the textbook estimate. The top diagram in Fig. 70 shows these "error bars" in gray, surrounding black dots for M_N. This sequence M_N does appear to settle down after N reaches 3000 or so, and to approach a value near 5×10^{25}. That's much higher than our first guess, but it has lots of evidence to back it up.

On the other hand, the bottom chart in Fig. 70 shows the distribution of the *logarithms* of the 10000 values of D that were used to make the top chart. Almost half of those values were totally negligible — less than 10^{20}. About 75% of them were less than 10^{24}. But some of them* exceeded 10^{28}. Can we really rely on a result that's based on such chaotic behavior? Is it really right to throw away most of our data and to trust almost entirely on observations that were obtained from comparatively few rare events?

Yes, we're okay! Some of the justification appears in exercise MPR–124, which is based on theoretical work by S. Chatterjee and P. Diaconis. In the paper cited with that exercise, they defend a simple measure of quality,

$$\widehat{\chi}_N = \max(D^{(1)},\ldots,D^{(N)})/(NM_N) = \frac{\max(D^{(1)},\ldots,D^{(N)})}{D^{(1)} + \cdots + D^{(N)}}, \qquad (34)$$

---

* Four of the actual values that led to Fig. 70 were larger than 10^{28}; the largest, $\approx 2.1\times10^{28}$, came from a path of length 57. The smallest estimate, 19361664, came from a path of length 10.

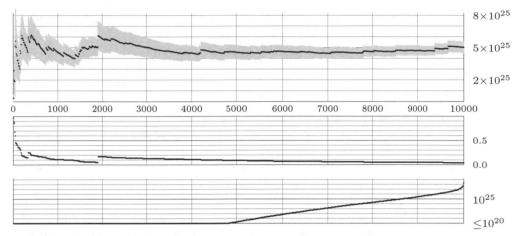

Fig. 70. Estimates of the number of king paths, based on up to 10000 random trials. The middle graph shows the corresponding quality measures of Eq. (34). The lower graph shows the *logarithms* of the individual estimates $D^{(k)}$, after they've been sorted.

arguing that a reasonable policy in most experiments such as these is to stop sampling when $\widehat{\chi}_N$ gets small. (Values of this statistic $\widehat{\chi}_N$ have been plotted in the middle of Fig. 70.)

Furthermore we can estimate other properties of the solutions to a backtrack problem, instead of merely counting those solutions. For example, the expected value of lD on termination of the random king's path algorithm is the total *length* of such paths. The data underlying Fig. 70 suggests that this total is $(2.66 \pm .14) \times 10^{27}$; hence the average path length appears to be about 53. The samples also indicate that about 34% of the paths pass through the center; about 46% touch the upper right corner; about 22% touch both corners; and about 7% pass through the center and both corners.

For this particular problem we don't actually need to rely on estimates, because the ZDD technology of Section 7.1.4 allows us to compute the *true* values. (See exercise 59.) The total number of simple corner-to-corner king paths on a chessboard is exactly 50,819,542,770,311,581,606,906,543; this value lies almost within the error bars of Fig. 70 for all $N \geq 250$, except for a brief interval near $N = 1400$. And the total length of all these paths turns out to be exactly 2,700,911,171,651,251,701,712,099,831, which is a little higher than our estimate. The true average length is therefore ≈ 53.15. The true probabilities of hitting the center, a given corner, both corners, and all three of those spots are respectively about 38.96%, 50.32%, 25.32%, and 9.86%.

The total number of corner-to-corner king paths of the maximum length, 63, is 2,811,002,302,704,446,996,926. This is a number that can *not* be estimated well by a method such as Algorithm E without additional heuristics.

The analogous problem for corner-to-corner *knight* paths, of any length, lies a bit beyond ZDD technology because many more ZDD nodes are needed. Using Algorithm E we can estimate that there are about $(8.6 \pm 1.2) \times 10^{19}$ such paths.

Factoring the problem. Imagine an instance of backtracking that is equivalent to solving two *independent* subproblems. For example, we might be looking for all sequences $x = x_1 x_2 \ldots x_n$ that satisfy $P_n(x_1, x_2, \ldots, x_n) = F(x_1, x_2, \ldots, x_n)$, where

$$F(x_1, x_2, \ldots, x_n) \;=\; G(x_1, \ldots, x_k) \wedge H(x_{k+1}, \ldots, x_n). \tag{35}$$

Then the size of the backtrack tree is essentially the *product* of the tree sizes for G and for H, even if we use dynamic ordering. Hence it's obviously foolish to apply the general setup of (1) and (2). We can do much better by finding all solutions to G first, then finding all solutions to H, thereby reducing the amount of computation to the *sum* of the tree sizes. Again we've divided and conquered, by factoring the compound problem (35) into separate subproblems.

We discussed a less obvious application of problem factorization near the beginning of Chapter 7, in connection with latin squares: Recall that E. T. Parker sped up the solution of 7–(6) by more than a dozen orders of magnitude, when he discovered 7–(7) by essentially factoring 7–(6) into ten subproblems whose solutions could readily be combined.

In general, each solution x to some problem F often implies the existence of solutions $x^{(p)} = \phi_p(x)$ to various simpler problems F_p that are "homomorphic images" of F. And if we're lucky, the solutions to those simpler problems can be combined and "lifted" to a solution of the overall problem. Thus it pays to be on the lookout for such simplifications.

Let's look at another example. F. A. Schossow invented a tantalizing puzzle [*U.S. Patent 646463* (3 April 1900)] that went viral in 1967 when a marketing genius decided to rename it "Instant Insanity." The problem is to take four cubes such as

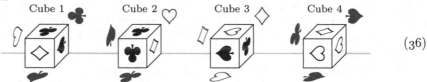

$$\tag{36}$$

where each face has been marked in one of four ways, and to arrange them in a row so that all four markings appear on the top, bottom, front, and back sides. The placement in (36) is incorrect, because there are two ♣s (and no ♠) on top. But we get a solution if we rotate each cube by 90°.

There are 24 ways to place each cube, because any of the six faces can be on top and we can rotate four ways while keeping the top unchanged. So the total number of placements is $24^4 = 331776$. But this problem can be factored in an ingenious way, so that all solutions can be found quickly by hand! [See F. de Carteblanche, *Eureka* **9** (1947), 9–11.] The idea is that any solution to the puzzle gives us two each of $\{\clubsuit, \diamondsuit, \heartsuit, \spadesuit\}$, if we look only at the top and bottom or only at the front and back. That's a much easier problem to solve.

For this purpose a cube can be characterized by its three pairs of markings on opposite faces; in (36) these face-pairs are respectively

$$\{\clubsuit\spadesuit, \clubsuit\diamondsuit, \spadesuit\heartsuit\}, \quad \{\clubsuit\clubsuit, \clubsuit\heartsuit, \spadesuit\diamondsuit\}, \quad \{\heartsuit\heartsuit, \spadesuit\diamondsuit, \clubsuit\diamondsuit\}, \quad \{\spadesuit\diamondsuit, \spadesuit\heartsuit, \clubsuit\heartsuit\}. \tag{37}$$

Which of the $3^4 = 81$ ways to choose one face-pair from each cube will give us $\{\clubsuit,\clubsuit,\diamondsuit,\diamondsuit,\heartsuit,\heartsuit,\spadesuit,\spadesuit\}$? They can all be discovered in a minute or two, by listing the nine possibilities for cubes $(1,2)$ and the nine for $(3,4)$. We get just three,

$$(\clubsuit\diamondsuit,\clubsuit\heartsuit,\spadesuit\diamondsuit,\spadesuit\heartsuit), \quad (\spadesuit\heartsuit,\clubsuit\heartsuit,\clubsuit\diamondsuit,\spadesuit\diamondsuit), \quad (\spadesuit\heartsuit,\spadesuit\diamondsuit,\clubsuit\diamondsuit,\clubsuit\heartsuit). \tag{38}$$

Notice furthermore that each solution can be "halved" so that one each of $\{\clubsuit,\diamondsuit,\heartsuit,\spadesuit\}$ appears on both sides, by swapping face-pairs; we can change (38) to

$$(\diamondsuit\clubsuit,\clubsuit\heartsuit,\spadesuit\diamondsuit,\heartsuit\spadesuit), \quad (\heartsuit\spadesuit,\clubsuit\heartsuit,\diamondsuit\clubsuit,\spadesuit\diamondsuit), \quad (\heartsuit\spadesuit,\spadesuit\diamondsuit,\diamondsuit\clubsuit,\clubsuit\heartsuit). \tag{39}$$

Each of these solutions to the opposite-face subproblem can be regarded as a 2-regular graph, because every vertex of the multigraph whose edges are (say) $\diamondsuit$—$\clubsuit$, $\clubsuit$—$\heartsuit$, $\spadesuit$—$\diamondsuit$, $\heartsuit$—$\spadesuit$ has exactly two neighbors.

A solution to "Instant Insanity" will give us *two* such 2-regular factors, one for top-and-bottom and one for front-and-back. Furthermore those two factors will have disjoint edges: We can't use the same face-pair in both. Therefore problem (36) can be solved only by using the first and third factor in (39).

Conversely, whenever we have two disjoint 2-regular graphs, we can always use them to position the cubes as desired, thus "lifting" the factors to a solution of the full problem.

Exercise 67 illustrates another kind of problem factorization. We can conveniently think of each subproblem as a "relaxation" of constraints.

Historical notes. The origins of backtrack programming are obscure. Equivalent ideas must have occurred to many people, yet there was hardly any reason to write them down until computers existed. We can be reasonably sure that James Bernoulli used such principles in the 17th century, when he successfully solved the "Tot tibi sunt dotes" problem that had eluded so many others (see Section 7.2.1.7), because traces of the method exist in his exhaustive list of solutions.

Backtrack programs typically traverse the tree of possibilities by using what is now called depth-first search, a general graph exploration procedure that Édouard Lucas credited to a telegraph engineer named Trémaux [*Récréations Mathématiques* **1** (Paris: Gauthier-Villars, 1882), 47–50].

The eight queens problem was first proposed by Max Bezzel [*Schachzeitung* **3** (1848), 363; **4** (1849), 40] and by Franz Nauck [*Illustrirte Zeitung* **14**, 361 (1 June 1850), 352; **15**, 377 (21 September 1850), 182], perhaps independently. C. F. Gauss saw the latter publication, and wrote several letters about it to his friend H. C. Schumacher. Gauss's letter of 27 September 1850 is especially interesting, because it explained how to find all the solutions by backtracking — which he called 'Tatonniren', from a French term meaning "to feel one's way." He also listed the lexicographically first solutions of each equivalence class under reflection and rotation: 15863724, 16837425, 24683175, 25713864, 25741863, 26174835, 26831475, 27368514, 27581463, 35281746, 35841726, and 36258174.

Computers arrived a hundred years later, and people began to use them for combinatorial problems. The time was therefore ripe for backtracking to be described as a general technique, and Robert J. Walker rose to the occasion [*Proc. Symposia in Applied Math.* **10** (1960), 91–94]. His brief note introduced

Algorithm W in machine-oriented form, and mentioned that the procedure could readily be extended to find variable-length patterns $x_1 \ldots x_n$ where n is not fixed.

The next milestone was a paper by Solomon W. Golomb and Leonard D. Baumert [*JACM* **12** (1965), 516–524], who formulated the general problem carefully and presented a variety of examples. In particular, they discussed the search for maximum commafree codes, and noted that backtracking can be used to find successively better and better solutions to combinatorial optimization problems. They introduced certain kinds of lookahead, as well as the important idea of dynamic ordering by branching on variables with the fewest remaining choices.

Backtrack methods allow special cutoffs when applied to integer programming problems [see E. Balas, *Operations Research* **13** (1965), 517–546]. A. M. Geoffrion simplified and extended that work, calling it "implicit enumeration" because many cases aren't enumerated explicitly [*SIAM Rev.* **9** (1967), 178–190].

Other noteworthy early discussions of backtrack programming appear in Mark Wells's book *Elements of Combinatorial Computing* (1971), Chapter 4; in a survey by J. R. Bitner and E. M. Reingold, *CACM* **18** (1975), 651–656; and in the Ph.D. thesis of John Gaschnig [Report CMU-CS-79-124 (Carnegie Mellon University, 1979), Chapter 4]. Gaschnig introduced techniques of "backmarking" and "backjumping" that we shall discuss later.

Monte Carlo estimates of the cost of backtracking were first described briefly by M. Hall, Jr., and D. E. Knuth in *Computers and Computing, AMM* **72**, 2, part 2, Slaught Memorial Papers No. 10 (February 1965), 21–28. Knuth gave a much more detailed exposition a decade later, in *Math. Comp.* **29** (1975), 121–136. Such methods can be considered as special cases of so-called "importance sampling"; see J. M. Hammersley and D. C. Handscomb, *Monte Carlo Methods* (London: Methuen, 1964), 57–59. Studies of random self-avoiding walks such as the king paths discussed above were inaugurated by M. N. Rosenbluth and A. W. Rosenbluth, *J. Chemical Physics* **23** (1955), 356–359.

Backtrack applications are nicely adaptable to parallel programming, because different parts of the search tree are often completely independent of each other; thus disjoint subtrees can be explored on different machines, with a minimum of interprocess communication. Already in 1964, D. H. Lehmer explained how to subdivide a problem so that two computers of different speeds could work on it simultaneously and finish at the same time. The problem that he considered had a search tree of known shape (see Theorem 7.2.1.3L); but we can do essentially similar load balancing even in much more complicated situations, by using Monte Carlo estimates of the subtree sizes. Although many ideas for parallelizing combinatorial searches have been developed over the years, such techniques are beyond the scope of this book. Readers can find a nice introduction to a fairly general approach in the paper by R. Finkel and U. Manber, *ACM Transactions on Programming Languages and Systems* **9** (1987), 235–256.

M. Alekhnovich, A. Borodin, J. Buresh-Oppenheim, R. Impagliazzo, A. Magen, and T. Pitassi have defined *priority branching trees*, a general model of computation with which they were able to prove rigorous bounds on what backtrack programs can do, in *Computational Complexity* **20** (2011), 679–740.

EXERCISES

▶ **1.** [*22*] Explain how the tasks of generating (i) n-tuples, (ii) permutations of distinct items, (iii) combinations, (iv) integer partitions, (v) set partitions, and (vi) nested parentheses can all be regarded as special cases of backtrack programming, by presenting suitable domains D_k and cutoff properties $P_l(x_1, \dots, x_l)$ that satisfy (1) and (2).

2. [*10*] True or false: We can choose D_1 so that $P_1(x_1)$ is always true.

3. [*20*] Let T be any tree. Is it possible to define domains D_k and cutoff properties $P_l(x_1, \dots, x_l)$ so that T is the backtrack tree traversed by Algorithm B?

4. [*16*] Using a chessboard and eight coins to represent queens, one can follow the steps of Algorithm B and essentially traverse the tree of Fig. 68 by hand in about three hours. Invent a trick to save half of the work.

▶ **5.** [*20*] Reformulate Algorithm B as a *recursive* procedure called $try(l)$, having global variables n and $x_1 \dots x_n$, to be invoked by saying '$try(1)$'. Can you imagine why the author of this book decided *not* to present the algorithm in such a recursive form?

6. [*20*] Given r, with $1 \le r \le 8$, in how many ways can 7 nonattacking queens be placed on an 8×8 chessboard, if no queen is placed in row r?

7. [*20*] (T. B. Sprague, 1890.) Are there any values $n > 5$ for which the n queens problem has a "framed" solution with $x_1 = 2$, $x_2 = n$, $x_{n-1} = 1$, and $x_n = n - 1$?

8. [*20*] Are there two 8-queen placements with the same $x_1 x_2 x_3 x_4 x_5 x_6$?

9. [*21*] Can a $4m$-queen placement have $3m$ queens on "white" squares?

▶ **10.** [*22*] Adapt Algorithm W to the n queens problem, using bitwise operations on n-bit numbers as suggested in the text.

11. [*M25*] (W. Ahrens, 1910.) Both solutions of the n queens problem when $n = 4$ have *quarterturn symmetry*: Rotation by $90°$ leaves them unchanged, but reflection doesn't.

a) Can the n queens problem have a solution with reflection symmetry?

b) Show that quarterturn symmetry is impossible if $n \bmod 4 \in \{2, 3\}$.

c) Sometimes the solution to an n queens problem contains four queens that form the corners of a tilted square, as shown here. Prove that we can always get another solution by tilting the square the other way (but leaving the other $n - 4$ queens in place).

d) Let C_n be the number of solutions with $90°$ symmetry, and suppose c_n of them have $x_k > k$ for $1 \le k \le n/2$. Prove that $C_n = 2^{\lfloor n/4 \rfloor} c_n$.

12. [*M28*] (*Wraparound queens.*) Replace (3) by the stronger conditions '$x_j \ne x_k$, $(x_k - x_j) \bmod n \ne k - j$, $(x_j - x_k) \bmod n \ne k - j$'. (The $n \times n$ grid becomes a torus.) Prove that the resulting problem is solvable if and only if n is not divisible by 2 or 3.

13. [*M30*] For which $n \ge 0$ does the n queens problem have at least one solution?

14. [*M25*] If exercise 12 has $T(n)$ toroidal solutions, show that $Q(mn) \ge Q(m)^n T(n)$.

15. [*HM42*] (M. Simkin, 2021.) Show that $Q(n) \approx \sigma^n n!$ as $n \to \infty$, where $\sigma \approx 0.389068$.

16. [*21*] Let $H(n)$ be the number of ways that n queen bees can occupy an $n \times n$ honeycomb so that no two are in the same line. (For example, one of the $H(4) = 7$ ways is shown here.) Compute $H(n)$ for small n.

17. [*15*] J. H. Quick (a student) noticed that the loop in step L2 of Algorithm L can be changed from 'while $x_l < 0$' to 'while $x_l \ne 0$', because x_l cannot be positive at that point of the algorithm. So he decided to eliminate the minus signs and just set $x_{l+k+1} \leftarrow k$ in step L3. Was it a good idea?

18. [*17*] Suppose that $n = 4$ and Algorithm L has reached step L2 with $l = 4$ and $x_1 x_2 x_3 = 241$. What are the current values of $x_4 x_5 x_6 x_7 x_8$, $p_0 p_1 p_2 p_3 p_4$, and $y_1 y_2 y_3$?

19. [*M10*] What are the domains D_l in Langford's problem (7)?

▶ **20.** [*21*] Extend Algorithm L so that it forces $x_l \leftarrow k$ whenever $k \notin \{x_1, \ldots, x_{l-1}\}$ and $l \geq 2n - k - 1$.

▶ **21.** [*M25*] If $x = x_1 x_2 \ldots x_{2n}$, let $x^D = (-x_{2n}) \ldots (-x_2)(-x_1) = -x^R$ be its dual.

a) Show that if n is odd and x solves Langford's problem (7), we have $x_k = n$ for some $k \leq \lfloor n/2 \rfloor$ if and only if $x_k^D = n$ for some $k > \lfloor n/2 \rfloor$.

b) Find a similar rule that distinguishes x from x^D when n is even.

c) Consequently the algorithm of exercise 20 can be modified so that exactly one of each dual pair of solutions $\{x, x^D\}$ is visited.

22. [*M26*] Explore "loose Langford pairs": Replace '$j + k + 1$' in (7) by '$j + \lfloor 3k/2 \rfloor$'.

23. [*17*] We can often obtain one word rectangle from another by changing only a letter or two. Can you think of any 5×6 word rectangles that almost match (10)?

24. [*20*] Customize Algorithm B so that it will find all 5×6 word rectangles.

▶ **25.** [*25*] Explain how to use *orthogonal lists*, as in Fig. 13 of Section 2.2.6, so that it's easy to visit all 5-letter words whose kth character is c, given $1 \leq k \leq 5$ and $\mathtt{a} \leq c \leq \mathtt{z}$. Use those sublists to speed up the algorithm of exercise 24.

26. [*21*] Can you find nice word rectangles of sizes 5×7, 5×8, 5×9, 5×10?

27. [*22*] What profile and average node costs replace (13) and (14) when we ask the algorithm of exercise 25 for 6×5 word rectangles instead of 5×6?

▶ **28.** [*23*] The method of exercises 24 and 25 does n levels of backtracking to fill the cells of an $m \times n$ rectangle one column at a time, using a trie to detect illegal prefixes in the rows. Devise a method that does mn levels of backtracking and fills just *one* cell per level, using tries for *both* rows and columns.

29. [*20*] Do any 5×6 word rectangles contain fewer than 11 different words?

30. [*22*] *Symmetric* word squares, whose columns are the same as their rows, were popular in England during the 1850s. For example, A. De Morgan praised the square

```
L E A V E
E L L E N
A L O N E
V E N O M
E N E M Y
```

because it actually is "meaningful"! Determine the total number of symmetric 5×5 word squares, by adapting the method of exercise 28. How many belong to $\mathtt{WORDS}(500)$?

31. [*20*] (Charles Babbage, 1864.) Do any of the symmetric 5×5 word squares also have valid words on both diagonals?

32. [*22*] How many symmetric word squares of sizes 2×2, 3×3, $\ldots$, are supported by *The Official SCRABBLE® Players Dictionary*, fourth edition (Hasbro, 2005)?

33. [*21*] Puzzlers who tried to construct word squares by hand found long ago that it was easiest to work from bottom to top. Therefore they used "reverse dictionaries," whose words appear in colex order. Does this idea speed up computer experiments?

34. [*15*] What's the largest commafree subset of the following words?

    `aced babe bade bead beef cafe cede dada dead deaf face fade feed`

▶ **35.** [*22*] Let w_1, w_2, ..., w_n be four-letter words on an m-letter alphabet. Design an algorithm that accepts or rejects each w_j, according as w_j is commafree or not with respect to the accepted words of $\{w_1, \ldots, w_{j-1}\}$.

36. [*M22*] A two-letter block code on an m-letter alphabet can be represented as a digraph D on m vertices, with $a \to b$ if and only if ab is a codeword.

    a) Prove that the code is commafree $\iff$ D has no oriented paths of length 3.

    b) How many arcs can be in an m-vertex digraph with no oriented paths of length r?

▶ **37.** [*M30*] (W. L. Eastman, 1965.) The following elegant construction yields a commafree code of maximum size for any *odd* block length n, over any alphabet. Given a sequence $x = x_0 x_1 \ldots x_{n-1}$ of nonnegative integers, where x differs from each of its other cyclic shifts $x_k \ldots x_{n-1} x_0 \ldots x_{k-1}$ for $0 < k < n$, the procedure outputs a cyclic shift σx with the property that the set of all such σx is commafree.

We regard x as an infinite periodic sequence $\langle x_n \rangle$ with $x_k = x_{k-n}$ for all $k \geq n$. Each cyclic shift then has the form $x_k x_{k+1} \ldots x_{k+n-1}$. The simplest nontrivial example occurs when $n = 3$, where $x = x_0 x_1 x_2 x_0 x_1 x_2 x_0 \ldots$ and we don't have $x_0 = x_1 = x_2$. In this case the algorithm outputs $x_k x_{k+1} x_{k+2}$ where $x_k \geq x_{k+1} < x_{k+2}$; and the set of all such triples clearly satisfies the commafree condition.

One key idea is to think of x as partitioned into t substrings by boundary markers b_j, where $0 \leq b_0 < b_1 < \cdots < b_{t-1} < n$ and $b_j = b_{j-t} + n$ for $j \geq t$. Then substring y_j is $x_{b_j} x_{b_j+1} \ldots x_{b_{j+1}-1}$. The number t of substrings is always odd. Initially $t = n$ and $b_j = j$ for all j; ultimately $t = 1$, and $\sigma x = y_0$ is the desired output.

Eastman's algorithm is based on comparison of adjacent substrings y_{j-1} and y_j. If those substrings have the same length, we use lexicographic comparison; otherwise we declare that the longer substring is bigger.

The second key idea is the notion of "dips," which are substrings of the form $z = z_1 \ldots z_k$ where $k \geq 2$ and $z_1 \geq \cdots \geq z_{k-1} < z_k$. It's easy to see that any string $y = y_0 y_1 \ldots$ in which we have $y_i < y_{i+1}$ for infinitely many i can be factored into a sequence of dips, $y = z^{(0)} z^{(1)} \ldots$, and this factorization is unique. For example,

    $31415926535897932384626433383\ldots = 314\ 15\ 926\ 535\ 89\ 79\ 323\ 846\ 26\ 4338\ 3\ldots$.

Furthermore, if y is a periodic sequence, its factorization into dips is also ultimately periodic, although some of the initial factors may not occur in the period. For example,

    $1234435501234435501234435550\ldots = 12\ 34\ 435\ 501\ 23\ 4435\ 501\ 23\ 4435\ \ldots$.

Given a periodic, nonconstant sequence y described by boundary markers as above, where the period length t is odd, its periodic factorization will contain an odd number of odd-length dips. Each round of Eastman's algorithm simply retains the boundary points at the left of those odd-length dips. Then t is reset to the number of retained boundary points, and another round begins if $t > 1$.

    a) Play through the algorithm by hand when $n = 19$ and $x = 3141592653589793238$.

    b) Show that the number of rounds is at most $\lfloor \log_3 n \rfloor$.

    c) Exhibit a binary x that achieves this worst-case bound when $n = 3^e$.

    d) Implement the algorithm with full details. (It's surprisingly short!)

    e) Explain why the algorithm yields a commafree code.

38. [*HM28*] What is the probability that Eastman's algorithm finishes in one round? (Assume that x is a random m-ary string of odd length $n > 1$, unequal to any of its other cyclic shifts. Use a generating function to express the answer.)

39. [*18*] Why can't a commafree code of length $(m^4 - m^2)/4$ contain 0001 and 2000?

▶ **40.** [*15*] Why do you think sequential data structures such as (16)–(23) weren't featured in Section 2.2.2 of this series of books (entitled "Sequential Allocation")?

41. [*17*] What's the significance of (a) MEM[40d]=5e and (b) MEM[904]=84 in Table 1?

42. [*18*] Why does Table 2 have (a) MEM[f8] = e7 and (b) MEM[a0d] = ba?

43. [*20*] Suppose you're using the undoing scheme (26) and the operation $\sigma \leftarrow \sigma + 1$ has just bumped the current stamp σ to zero. What should you do?

▶ **44.** [*25*] Spell out the low-level implementation details of the candidate selection process in step C2 of Algorithm C. Use the routine store(a, v) of (26) whenever changing the contents of MEM, and use the following selection strategy:
   a) Find a class c with the least number r of blue words.
   b) If $r = 0$, set $x \leftarrow -1$; otherwise set x to a word in class c.
   c) If $r > 1$, use the poison list to find an x that maximizes the number of blue words that could be killed on the other side of the prefix or suffix list that contains x.

▶ **45.** [*28*] Continuing exercise 44, spell out the details of step C3 when $x \geq 0$.
   a) What updates should be done to MEM when a blue word x becomes red?
   b) What updates should be done to MEM when a blue word x becomes green?
   c) Step C3 begins its job by making x green as in part (b). Explain how it should finish its job by updating the poison list.

46. [*M35*] Is there a *binary* ($m = 2$) commafree code with one codeword in each of the $(\sum_{d\backslash n} \mu(d) 2^{n/d})/n$ cycle classes, for every word length n?

47. [*HM29*] A commafree code on m letters is equivalent to at most $2m!$ such codes if we permute the letters and/or replace each codeword by its left-right reflection.
   Determine all of the nonisomorphic commafree codes of length 4 on m letters when m is (a) 2 (b) 3 (c) 4 and there are (a) 3 (b) 18 (c) 57 codewords.

48. [*M42*] Find a maximum-size commafree code of length 4 on $m = 5$ letters.

49. [*20*] Explain how the choices in Fig. 69 were determined from the "random" bits that are displayed. For instance, why was X_2 set to 1 in Fig. 69(b)?

50. [*M15*] Interpret the value $E(D_1 \ldots D_l)$, in the text's Monte Carlo algorithm.

51. [*M22*] What's a simple martingale that corresponds to Theorem E?

▶ **52.** [*HM25*] Elmo uses Algorithm E with $D_k = \{1, \ldots, n\}$, $P_l = [x_1 > \cdots > x_l]$, $c = 1$.
   a) Alice flips n coins independently, where coin k yields "heads" with probability $1/k$. True or false: She obtains exactly l heads with probability $\begin{bmatrix} n \\ l \end{bmatrix}/n!$.
   b) Let $Y_1, Y_2, \ldots, Y_l$ be the numbers on the coins that come up heads. (Thus $Y_1 = 1$, and $Y_2 = 2$ with probability $1/2$.) Show that $\Pr(\text{Alice obtains } Y_1, Y_2, \ldots, Y_l) = \Pr(\text{Elmo obtains } X_1 = Y_l, X_2 = Y_{l-1}, \ldots, X_l = Y_1)$.
   c) Prove that Alice q.s. obtains at most $(\ln n)(\ln \ln n)$ heads.
   d) Consequently Elmo's S is q.s. less than $\exp((\ln n)^2 (\ln \ln n))$.

▶ **53.** [*M30*] Extend Algorithm B so that it also computes the minimum, maximum, mean, and variance of the Monte Carlo estimates S produced by Algorithm E.

54. [*M21*] Instead of choosing each y_i in step E5 with probability $1/d$, we could use a biased distribution where $\Pr(I = i \mid X_1, \ldots, X_{l-1}) = p_{X_1 \ldots X_{l-1}}(y_i) > 0$. How should the estimate S be modified so that its expected value in this general scheme is still $C()$?

55. [*M20*] If all costs $c(x_1, \ldots, x_l)$ are positive, show that the biased probabilities of exercise 54 can be chosen in such a way that the estimate S is always exact.

▶ **56.** [*M25*] The commafree code search procedure in Algorithm C doesn't actually fit the mold of Algorithm E, because it incorporates lookahead, dynamic ordering, reversible memory, and other enhancements to the basic backtrack paradigms. How could its running time be reliably estimated with Monte Carlo methods?

57. [*HM21*] Algorithm E can potentially follow M different paths $X_1 \ldots X_{l-1}$ before it terminates, where M is the number of leaves of the backtrack tree. Suppose the final values of D at those leaves are $D^{(1)}, \ldots, D^{(M)}$. Prove that $\left(D^{(1)} \ldots D^{(M)}\right)^{1/M} \geq M$.

58. [*27*] The text's king path problem is a special case of the general problem of counting simple paths from vertex s to vertex t in a given graph.

We can generate such paths by random walks from s that don't get stuck, if we maintain a table of values DIST(v) for all vertices v not yet in the path, representing the shortest distance from v to t through unused vertices. For with such a table we can simply move at each step to a vertex for which DIST(v) $< \infty$.

Devise a way to update the DIST table dynamically without unnecessary work.

59. [*26*] A ZDD with 3,174,197 nodes can be constructed for the family of all simple corner-to-corner king paths on a chessboard, using the method of exercise 7.1.4–225. Explain how to use this ZDD to compute (a) the total length of all paths; (b) the number of paths that touch any given subset of the center and/or corner points.

▶ **60.** [*20*] Experiment with biased random walks (see exercise 54), weighting each non-dead-end king move to a new vertex v by $1 + \text{DIST}(v)^2$ instead of choosing every such move with the same probability. Does this strategy improve on Fig. 70?

61. [*HM26*] Let P_n be the number of integer sequences $x_1 \ldots x_n$ such that $x_1 = 1$ and $1 \leq x_{k+1} \leq 2x_k$ for $1 \leq k < n$. (The first few values are 1, 2, 6, 26, 166, 1626, $\ldots$; this sequence was introduced by A. Cayley in *Philosophical Magazine* (4) **13** (1857), 245–248, who showed that P_n enumerates the partitions of $2^n - 1$ into powers of 2.)

a) Show that P_n is the number of different profiles that are possible for a binary tree of height n.

b) Find an efficient way to compute P_n for large n. *Hint:* Consider the more general sequence $P_n^{(m)}$, defined similarly but with $x_1 = m$.

c) Use the estimation procedure of Theorem E to prove that $P_n \geq 2^{\binom{n}{2}}/(n-1)!$.

▶ **62.** [*22*] When the faces of four cubes are colored randomly with four colors, estimate the probability that the corresponding "Instant Insanity" puzzle has a unique solution. How many 2-regular graphs tend to appear during the "factored" solution process?

63. [*20*] Find *five* cubes, each of whose faces has one of *five* colors, and where every color occurs at least five times, such that the corresponding puzzle has a unique solution.

64. [*24*] Assemble five cubes with uppercase letters on each face, using the patterns

By extending the principles of "Instant Insanity," show that these cubes can be placed in a row so that four 5-letter words are visible. (Each word's letters should have a consistent orientation. The letters C and U, H and I, N and Z are related by 90° rotation.)

65. [*25*] Show that the generalized "Instant Insanity" problem, with n cubes and n colors on their faces, is NP-complete, even though cases with small n are fairly easy.

▶ **66.** [*23*] (*The Fool's Disk.*) "Rotate the four disks of the left-hand illustration below so that the four numbers on each ray sum to 12." (The current sums are $4+3+2+4 = 13$, etc.) Show that this problem factors nicely, so that it can be solved readily by hand.

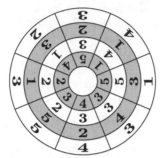
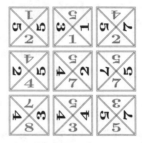

The Fool's Disk   The Royal Aquarium Thirteen Puzzle

▶ **67.** [*26*] (*The Royal Aquarium Thirteen Puzzle.*) "Rearrange the nine cards of the right-hand illustration above, optionally rotating some of them by $180°$, so that the six horizontal sums of gray letters and the six vertical sums of black letters all equal 13." (The current sums are $1 + 5 + 4 = 10, \ldots, 7 + 5 + 7 = 19$.) The author of *Hoffmann's Puzzles Old and New* (1893) stated that "There is no royal road to the solution. The proper order must be arrived at by successive transpositions until the conditions are fulfilled." Prove that he was wrong: "Factor" this problem and solve it by hand.

▶ **68.** [*28*] (Johan de Ruiter, 14 March 2018.) Put a digit into each empty box, in such a way that every box names the exact number of distinct digits that it points to.

69. [*41*] Is there a puzzle like exercise 68 whose clues contain *more* than 32 digits of π?

70. [*HM40*] (M. Bousquet-Mélou.) Consider self-avoiding paths from the upper left corner of an $m \times n$ grid to the lower right, where each step is either up, down, or to the right. If we generate such paths at random, making either 1 or 2 or 3 choices at each step as in Algorithm E, the expected value $\mathrm{E}\,D_{mn}$ is the total number of such paths, m^{n-1}. But the variance is considerably larger: Construct polynomials $P_m(z)$ and $Q_m(z)$ such that we have $G_m(z) = \sum_{n=1}^{\infty}(\mathrm{E}\,D_{mn}^2)z^n = zP_m(z)/Q_m(z)$ for $m \geq 2$. For example, $G_3(z) = (z+z^2)/(1-9z-6z^2) = z + 10z^2 + 96z^3 + 924z^4 + 8892z^5 + \cdots$. Prove furthermore that $\mathrm{E}\,D_{mn}^2 = \Theta(\rho_m^n)$, where $\rho_m = 2^m + O(1)$.

Table 666

TWENTY QUESTIONS (SEE EXERCISE 71)

---

1. The first question whose answer is A is:
(A) 1   (B) 2   (C) 3   (D) 4   (E) 5

2. The next question with the same answer as this one is:
(A) 4   (B) 6   (C) 8   (D) 10   (E) 12

3. The only two consecutive questions with identical answers are questions:
(A) 15 and 16   (B) 16 and 17   (C) 17 and 18   (D) 18 and 19   (E) 19 and 20

4. The answer to this question is the same as the answers to questions:
(A) 10 and 13   (B) 14 and 16   (C) 7 and 20   (D) 1 and 15   (E) 8 and 12

5. The answer to question 14 is:
(A) B   (B) E   (C) C   (D) A   (E) D

6. The answer to this question is:
(A) A   (B) B   (C) C   (D) D   (E) none of those

7. An answer that appears most often is:
(A) A   (B) B   (C) C   (D) D   (E) E

8. Ignoring answers that appear equally often, the least common answer is:
(A) A   (B) B   (C) C   (D) D   (E) E

9. The sum of all question numbers whose answers are correct and the same as this one is:
(A) ∈ [59..62]   (B) ∈ [52..55] (C) ∈ [44..49]   (D) ∈ [59..67]   (E) ∈ [44..53]

10. The answer to question 17 is:
(A) D   (B) B   (C) A   (D) E   (E) wrong

11. The number of questions whose answer is D is:
(A) 2   (B) 3   (C) 4   (D) 5   (E) 6

12. The number of *other* questions with the same answer as this one is the same as the number of questions with answer:
(A) B   (B) C   (C) D   (D) E   (E) none of those

13. The number of questions whose answer is E is:
(A) 5   (B) 4   (C) 3   (D) 2   (E) 1

14. No answer appears exactly this many times:
(A) 2   (B) 3   (C) 4   (D) 5   (E) none of those

15. The set of odd-numbered questions with answer A is:
(A) {7}   (B) {9}   (C) not {11}   (D) {13}   (E) {15}

16. The answer to question 8 is the same as the answer to question:
(A) 3   (B) 2   (C) 13   (D) 18   (E) 20

17. The answer to question 10 is:
(A) C   (B) D   (C) B   (D) A   (E) correct

18. The number of prime-numbered questions whose answers are vowels is:
(A) prime   (B) square   (C) odd   (D) even   (E) zero

19. The last question whose answer is B is:
(A) 14   (B) 15   (C) 16   (D) 17   (E) 18

20. The maximum score that can be achieved on this test is:
(A) 18   (B) 19   (C) 20   (D) indeterminate
                                                   (E) achievable only by getting this question wrong

---

▶ **71.** [*M29*] (Donald R. Woods, 2000.) Find all ways to maximize the number of correct answers to the questionnaire in Table 666. Each question must be answered with a letter from A to E. *Hint:* Begin by clarifying the exact meaning of this exercise. What answers are best for the following two-question, two-letter "warmup problem"?

1. (A) Answer 2 is B.   (B) Answer 1 is A.

2. (A) Answer 1 is correct.   (B) Either answer 2 is wrong or answer 1 is A, but not both.

72. [*HM28*] Show that exercise 71 has a surprising, somewhat paradoxical answer if two changes are made to Table 666: 9(E) becomes '∈ [39..43]'; 15(C) becomes '{11}'.

▶ **73.** [*30*] (*A clueless anacrostic.*) The letters of 29 five-letter words

$$\overline{1\ \ 2\ \ 3\ \ 4\ \ 5}, \quad \overline{6\ \ 7\ \ 8\ \ 9\ \ 10}, \quad \overline{11\ \ 12\ \ 13\ \ 14\ \ 15}, \quad \overline{16\ \ 17\ \ 18\ \ 19\ \ 20}, \quad \dots, \quad \overline{141\ 142\ 143\ 144\ 145},$$

all belonging to WORDS(1000), have been shuffled to form the following mystery text:

$$\overline{30\ \ 29\ \ 9} \quad \overline{140\ 12\ \ 13\ 145\ 90\ \ 45\ \ 99} \quad \overline{26\ 107} \quad \overline{47\ \ 84\ \ 53\ \ 51\ \ 27\ 133\ 39} \quad \overline{137\,139} \quad \overline{66\ 112\ 69\ \ 14\ \ \ 8\ \ 20\ \ 91\ 129\ 70}$$

$$\overline{16\ \ \ 7\ \ 93\ \ 19\ \ 85} \quad \overline{101\ 76\ \ 78\ \ 44\ \ 10\ 106\ 60} \quad \overline{118\,119} \quad \overline{24\ \ 25\ 100} \quad \overline{1\ \ \ 5\ \ 64\ \ 11\ \ 71} \quad \overline{42\ 122\,123}$$

$$\overline{103\,104\ 63\ \ 49\ \ 31\ 121\ 98\ \ 79\ \ 80} \quad \overline{46\ \ 48} \quad \overline{134\,135\,131} \quad \overline{143\ 96\ 142\,120\ 50\ 132\ 33\ \ 43\ \ 34\ \ 40}.\quad\dots$$

$$\overline{111\ 97\ 113\,105\ 38\ 102\ 62\ \ 65\ 114} \quad \overline{74\ \ 82\ \ 81\ \ 83\ 136\ 37\ \ 21\ \ 61\ \ 88\ \ 86\ \ 55} \bigg(\overline{32\ \ 35} \quad \overline{117\,116\ 23\ \ 52}$$

$$\overline{56\ \ 17\ \ 18\ \ 94\ \ 67} \quad \overline{128\ 15\ \ 57\ \ 58\ \ 89} \quad \overline{87\ 109} \quad \overline{2\ \ \ 4\ \ \ 6\ \ 28\ \ 95} \quad \overline{3\ 126\ 77\ 144\ 54\ 41}\bigg) \quad \overline{68\ 115}$$

$$\overline{75\ 138\ 73\ 124\ 36\ 130\,127\,141} \quad \overline{22\ \ 92} \quad \overline{72\ \ 59} \quad \overline{108\,125\,110}.$$

Furthermore, their initial letters $\underline{\ \ \ }_{1}, \underline{\ \ \ }_{6}, \underline{\ \ \ }_{11}, \underline{\ \ \ }_{16}, \dots, \underline{\ \ \ }_{141}$ identify the source of that quotation, which consists entirely of common English words. What does it say?

74. [*21*] The fifteenth mystery word in exercise 73 is '$\underline{\ \ \ }_{134\,135\,131}$'. Why does its special form lead to a partial *factorization* of that problem?

▶ **75.** [*30*] (*Connected subsets.*) Let v be a vertex of some graph G, and let H be a connected subset of G that contains v. The vertices of H can be listed in a canonical way by starting with $v_0 \leftarrow v$ and then letting $v_1, v_2, \dots$ be the neighbors of v_0 that lie in H, followed by the neighbors of v_1 that haven't yet been listed, and so on. (We assume that the neighbors of each vertex are listed in some fixed order.)

For example, if G is the 3×3 grid $P_3 \,\square\, P_3$, exactly 21 of its connected five-element subsets contain the upper left corner element v. Their canonical orderings are

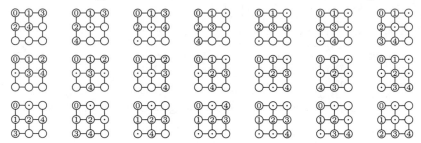

if we order the vertices top-to-bottom, left-to-right when listing their neighbors. (Vertices labeled ⓪, ①, ②, ③, ④ indicate v_0, v_1, v_2, v_3, v_4. Other vertices are not in H.)

Design a backtrack algorithm to generate all of the n-element connected subsets that contain a specified vertex v, given a graph that is represented in SGB format (which has ARCS, TIP, and NEXT fields, as described near the beginning of Chapter 7).

76. [*23*] Use the algorithm of exercise 75 to generate *all* of the connected n-element subsets of a given graph G. How many such subsets does $P_n \,\square\, P_n$ have, for $1 \le n \le 9$?

77. [*M22*] A v-reachable subset of a directed graph G is a nonempty set of vertices H with the property that every $u \in H$ can be reached from v by at least one oriented path in $G \,|\, H$. (In particular, v itself must be in H.)

    a) The digraph $P_3^{\rightarrow} \,\square\, P_3^{\rightarrow}$ is like $P_3 \,\square\, P_3$, except that all arcs between vertices are directed downward or to the right. Which of the 21 connected subsets in exercise 75 are also v-reachable from the upper left corner element v of $P_3^{\rightarrow} \,\square\, P_3^{\rightarrow}$?

b) True or false: H is v-reachable if and only if $G\,|\,H$ contains a dual oriented spanning tree rooted at v. (An oriented tree has arcs $u \longrightarrow p_u$, where p_u is the parent of the nonroot node u; in a *dual* oriented tree, the arcs are reversed: $p_u \longrightarrow u$.)

c) True or false: If G is undirected, so that $w \longrightarrow u$ whenever $u \longrightarrow w$, its v-reachable subsets are the same as the connected subsets that contain v.

d) Modify the algorithm of exercise 75 so that it generates all of the n-element v-reachable subsets of a digraph G, given n, v, and G.

78. [*22*] Extend the algorithm of exercise 77 to weighted graphs, in which every vertex has a nonnegative weight: Generate all of the connected induced subgraphs whose total weight w satisfies $L \le w < U$.

▶ **79.** [*M30*] The author and his wife own a pipe organ that contains 812 pipes, each of which is either playing or silent. Therefore 2^{812} different sounds (including silence) can potentially be created. However, the pipes are controlled by a conventional organ console, which has only $56+56+32 = 144$ keys and pedals that can be played by hands and feet, together with 20 on-off switches to define the connections between keys and pipes. Therefore at most 2^{164} different sounds are actually playable! The purpose of this exercise is to determine the exact number of n-pipe playable sounds, for small n.

The keys are binary vectors $s = s_0 s_1 \ldots s_{55}$ and $g = g_0 g_1 \ldots g_{55}$; the pedals are $p = p_0 p_1 \ldots p_{31}$; the console control switches are $c = c_0 c_1 \ldots c_{19}$; and the pipes are $r_{i,j}$ for $0 \le i < 16$ and $0 \le j < 56$. Here are the precise rules that define the pipe activity $r_{i,j}$ in terms of the input vectors s, g, p, and c that are governed by the organist:

$$r_{i,j} = \begin{cases} c_i p_j \vee c_{i+15} p_{j-12}, & i \in \{0,1\}; \\ c_i p_j, & i \in \{2\}; \end{cases}$$

$$r_{i,j} = \begin{cases} (c_i \vee c_{i+1}[j<12]) s_j^*, & i \in \{3\}; \\ c_i[j \ge 12] s_j^*, & i \in \{4,8\}; \\ c_i s_j^*, & i \in \{5,6,7\}; \end{cases}$$

$$r_{i,j} = \begin{cases} (c_i \vee c_{i+1}[j<12]) g_j^*, & i \in \{9\}; \\ c_i[j \ge 12] g_j^*, & i \in \{10\}; \\ c_i g_j^*, & i \in \{11,12\}; \\ (c_{13} \vee c_{14}) g_j^*, & i \in \{13\}; \\ c_{14} g_j^*. & i \in \{14,15\}. \end{cases}$$

Here $p_j = 0$ if $j < 0$ or $j \ge 32$; $s_j^* = s_j \vee c_{17} g_j \vee c_{18} p_j$; $g_j^* = g_j \vee c_{19} p_j$. [In organ jargon, the array of pipes has 16 "ranks"; ranks $\{0,1,2\}$, $\{3,\ldots,8\}$, $\{9,\ldots,15\}$ constitute the Pedal, Swell, and Great divisions. Ranks 3 and 4 share their lower 12 pipes, as do ranks 9 and 10. Ranks 13, 14, and 15 form a "mixture," c_{14}. Unit ranks c_{15} and c_{16} extend ranks 0 and 1, twelve notes higher. Console switches c_{17}, c_{18}, c_{19} are "couplers" Swell → Great, Swell → Pedal, Great → Pedal, which explain the formulas for s_j^* and g_j^*.]

A *playable sound* S is a set of pairs (i,j) such that we have $r_{i,j} = [(i,j) \in S]$ for at least one choice of the input vectors s, g, p, c. For example, the first chord of Bach's *Toccata in D minor* is the 8-pipe sound $\{(3,33),(3,45),(4,33),(4,45),(5,33),(5,45),$ $(6,33),(6,45)\}$, which is achievable when $s_{33} = s_{45} = c_3 = c_4 = c_5 = c_6 = 1$ and all other inputs are 0. We want to find the number Q_n of playable sounds with $\|S\| = n$.

a) There are 16×56 variables $r_{i,j}$ but only 812 actual pipes, because some of the ranks are incomplete. For which pairs (i,j) is $r_{i,j}$ always false?

b) True or false: If $s \subseteq s'$, $g \subseteq g'$, $p \subseteq p'$, and $c \subseteq c'$, then $r \subseteq r'$.

c) Show that every playable sound is achievable with $c_{17} = c_{18} = c_{19} = 0$.

d) Find a 5-pipe playable sound in which just five of the s_j, g_j, p_j, c_j are nonzero.

e) For which i and i' are the 2-pipe sounds $\{(i,40),(i',50)\}$ playable?

f) Determine Q_1 by hand, and explain why it is less than 812.

g) Determine Q_{811} by hand.

h) Determine $Q_2, \ldots, Q_{10}$ by computer, and compare them to $\binom{812}{2}, \ldots, \binom{812}{10}$.

We hold several threads in our hands,
and the odds are that one or other of them guides us to the truth.
We may waste time in following the wrong one,
but sooner or later we must come upon the right.

— SHERLOCK HOLMES, in *The Hound of the Baskervilles* (1901)

The following Receipts are not a mere marrow-less collection of
shreds, and patches, and cuttings, and pastings, from obsolete works,
but a bona fide register of practical facts . . .
the author submitting to a labour no preceding cookery-book-maker, perhaps,
ever attempted to encounter; and having not only dressed, but eaten
each Receipt before he set it down in his book.

— WILLIAM KITCHINER, *Apicius Redivivus; Or, The Cook's Oracle* (1817)

Just as we hope you will learn from us, we have learned from you,
from the recipes and short cuts and tips and traditions
you have been kind enough to tell us about.
Without your help, truly, this book could not have been written.

— *McCall's Cook Book* (1963)

> *What a dance*
> *do they do*
> *Lordy, how I'm tellin' you!*
> — HARRY BARRIS, *Mississippi Mud* (1927)

> *Don't lose your confidence if you slip,*
> *Be grateful for a pleasant trip,*
> *And pick yourself up, dust yourself off, start all over again.*
> — DOROTHY FIELDS, *Pick Yourself Up* (1936)

7.2.2.1. Dancing links. One of the chief characteristics of backtrack algorithms is the fact that they usually need to *undo* everything that they *do* to their data structures. In this section we'll study some extremely simple link-manipulation techniques that modify and unmodify the structures with ease. We'll also see that these ideas have many, many practical applications.

Suppose we have a doubly linked list, in which each node X has a predecessor and successor denoted respectively by LLINK(X) and RLINK(X). Then we know that it's easy to delete X from the list, by setting

$$\text{RLINK(LLINK(X))} \leftarrow \text{RLINK(X)}, \qquad \text{LLINK(RLINK(X))} \leftarrow \text{LLINK(X)}. \qquad (1)$$

At this point the conventional wisdom is to recycle node X, making it available for reuse in another list. We might also want to tidy things up by clearing LLINK(X) and RLINK(X) to Λ, so that stray pointers to nodes that are still active cannot lead to trouble. (See, for example, Eq. 2.2.5–(4), which is the same as (1) except that it also says 'AVAIL $\Leftarrow$ X'.) By contrast, the dancing-links trick resists any urge to do garbage collection. *In a backtrack application, we're better off leaving* LLINK(X) *and* RLINK(X) *unchanged.* Then we can undo operation (1) by simply setting

$$\text{RLINK(LLINK(X))} \leftarrow \text{X}, \qquad \text{LLINK(RLINK(X))} \leftarrow \text{X}. \qquad (2)$$

For example, we might have a 4-element list, as in 2.2.5–(2):

List head

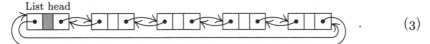
(3)

If we use (1) to delete the third element, (3) becomes

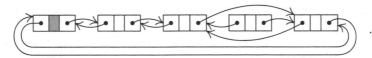
.

And if we now decide to delete the second element also, we get

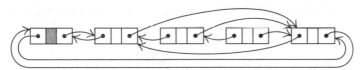
.

Subsequent deletion of the final element, then the first, will leave us with this:

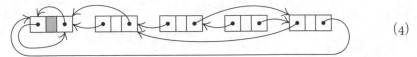

$$(4)$$

The list is now empty, and its links have become rather tangled. (See exercise 1.)
But we know that if we proceed to backtrack at this point, using (2) to undelete
elements 1, 4, 2, and 3 in that order, we will magically restore the initial state (3).
The choreography that underlies the motions of these pointers is fun to watch,
and it explains the name "dancing links."

Exact cover problems. We will be seeing many examples where links dance
happily and efficiently, as we study more and more examples of backtracking.
The beauty of the idea can perhaps be seen most naturally in an important
class of problems known as *exact covering*: We're given an $M \times N$ matrix A of
0s and 1s, and the problem is to find all subsets of rows whose sum is exactly 1
in every column. For example, consider the 6×7 matrix

$$A = \begin{pmatrix} 0 & 0 & 1 & 0 & 1 & 0 & 0 \\ 1 & 0 & 0 & 1 & 0 & 0 & 1 \\ 0 & 1 & 1 & 0 & 0 & 1 & 0 \\ 1 & 0 & 0 & 1 & 0 & 1 & 0 \\ 0 & 1 & 0 & 0 & 0 & 0 & 1 \\ 0 & 0 & 0 & 1 & 1 & 0 & 1 \end{pmatrix}. \tag{5}$$

Each row of A corresponds to a subset of a 7-element universe. A moment's
thought shows that there's only one way to cover all seven of these columns with
disjoint rows, namely by choosing rows 1, 4, and 5. We want to teach a computer
how to solve such problems, when there are many, many rows and many columns.

Matrices of 0s and 1s appear frequently in combinatorial problems, and
they help us to understand the relations between problems that are essentially
the same although they appear to be different (see exercise 5). But inside a
computer, we rarely want to represent an exact cover problem explicitly as a two-
dimensional array of bits, because the matrix tends to be extremely sparse: There
normally are very few 1s. Thus we'll use a different representation, essentially
with one node in our data structure for each 1 in the matrix.

Furthermore, we won't even talk about rows and columns! Some of the exact
cover problems we deal with already involve concepts that are called "rows" and
"columns" in their own areas of application. Instead we will speak of *options*
and *items*: Each option is a set of items; and *the goal of an exact cover problem
is to find disjoint options that cover all the items.*

For example, we shall regard (5) as the specification of six options involving
seven items. Let's name the items a, b, c, d, e, f, g; then the options are

$$\text{`}c\ e\text{'};\qquad \text{`}a\ d\ g\text{'};\qquad \text{`}b\ c\ f\text{'};\qquad \text{`}a\ d\ f\text{'};\qquad \text{`}b\ g\text{'};\qquad \text{`}d\ e\ g\text{'}. \tag{6}$$

The first, fourth, and fifth options give us each item exactly once.

One of the nicest things about exact cover problems is that every tentative choice we make leaves us with a residual exact cover problem that is smaller — often substantially smaller. For example, suppose we try to cover item a in (6) by choosing the option '$a\ d\ g$': The residual problem has only two options,

$$\text{'}c\ e\text{'} \qquad \text{and} \qquad \text{'}b\ c\ f\text{'}, \tag{7}$$

because the other four involve the already-covered items. Now it's easy to see that (7) has no solution; therefore we can *remove* option '$a\ d\ g$' from (6). That leaves us with only one option for item a, namely '$a\ d\ f$'. And its residual,

$$\text{'}c\ e\text{'} \qquad \text{and} \qquad \text{'}b\ g\text{'}, \tag{8}$$

gives us the solution we were looking for.

Thus we're led naturally to a recursive algorithm that's based on the primitive operation of "covering an item": *To cover item i, we delete all of the options that involve i, from our database of currently active options, and we also delete i from the list of items that need to be covered.* The algorithm is then quite simple.

- Select an item i that needs to be covered; but terminate
    successfully if none are left (we've found a solution).
- If no active options involve i, terminate unsuccessfully
    (there's no solution). Otherwise cover item i.   (9)
- For each just-deleted option O that involves i, one at a time, do this:
    for each item $j \neq i$ in O, cover item j; then
    recursively append O to each solution of the residual problem.

(Everything that's covered must later be uncovered, of course, as we'll see.)

Interesting details arise when we flesh out this algorithm and look at appropriate low-level mechanisms. There's a doubly linked "horizontal" list of all items that need to be covered; and each item also has its own "vertical" list of all the active options that involve it. For example, the data structures for (6) are:

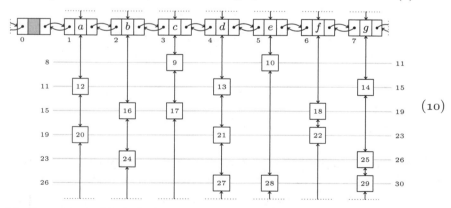

$$(10)$$

(In this diagram, doubly linked pointers "wrap around" at the dotted lines.) The horizontal list has LLINK and RLINK pointers; the vertical lists have ULINK and DLINK. Nodes of each vertical list also point to their list header via TOP fields.

The top row of diagram (10) shows the initial state of the horizontal item list and its associated vertical headers. The other rows illustrate the six options of (6), which are represented by sixteen nodes within the vertical lists. Those options implicitly form horizontal lists, indicated by light gray lines; but their nodes *don't* need to be linked together with pointers, because the option lists don't change. We can therefore save time and space by allocating them sequentially. On the other hand, our algorithm does require an ability to traverse each option cyclically, in both directions. Therefore we insert *spacer nodes* between options. A spacer node x is identified by the condition $\texttt{TOP}(x) \leq 0$; it also has

$$\begin{aligned}\texttt{ULINK}(x) &= \text{address of the first node in the option before } x; \\ \texttt{DLINK}(x) &= \text{address of the last node in the option after } x.\end{aligned} \quad (11)$$

These conventions lead to the internal memory layout shown in Table 1. First come the records for individual items; those records have $\texttt{NAME}$, $\texttt{LLINK}$, and $\texttt{RLINK}$ fields, where $\texttt{NAME}$ is used in printouts. Then come the nodes, which have $\texttt{TOP}$, $\texttt{ULINK}$, and $\texttt{DLINK}$ fields. The $\texttt{TOP}$ field is, however, called $\texttt{LEN}$ in the nodes that serve as item headers, because Algorithm X below uses those fields to store the lengths of the item lists. Nodes 8, 11, 15, 19, 23, 26, and 30 in this example are the spacers. Fields marked '—' are unused and can contain anything.

Table 1
THE INITIAL CONTENTS OF MEMORY CORRESPONDING TO (6) AND (10)

i:	0	1	2	3	4	5	6	7
$\texttt{NAME}(i)$:	—	a	b	c	d	e	f	g
$\texttt{LLINK}(i)$:	7	0	1	2	3	4	5	6
$\texttt{RLINK}(i)$:	1	2	3	4	5	6	7	0

x:	0	1	2	3	4	5	6	7
$\texttt{LEN}(x)$:	—	2	2	2	3	2	2	3
$\texttt{ULINK}(x)$:	—	20	24	17	27	28	22	29
$\texttt{DLINK}(x)$:	—	12	16	9	13	10	18	14

x:	8	9	10	11	12	13	14	15
$\texttt{TOP}(x)$:	0	3	5	−1	1	4	7	−2
$\texttt{ULINK}(x)$:	—	3	5	9	1	4	7	12
$\texttt{DLINK}(x)$:	10	17	28	14	20	21	25	18

x:	16	17	18	19	20	21	22	23
$\texttt{TOP}(x)$:	2	3	6	−3	1	4	6	−4
$\texttt{ULINK}(x)$:	2	9	6	16	12	13	18	20
$\texttt{DLINK}(x)$:	24	3	22	22	1	27	6	25

x:	24	25	26	27	28	29	30	
$\texttt{TOP}(x)$:	2	7	−5	4	5	7	−6	
$\texttt{ULINK}(x)$:	16	14	24	21	10	25	27	
$\texttt{DLINK}(x)$:	2	29	29	4	5	7	—	

OK, we're ready now to spell out precisely what happens inside the computer's memory when Algorithm X wants to cover a given item i:

$$\text{cover}(i) = \begin{cases} \text{Set } p \leftarrow \texttt{DLINK}(i). \text{ (Undeclared variables like } p, l, r \text{ are local.)} \\ \text{While } p \neq i, \text{ hide}(p), \text{ then set } p \leftarrow \texttt{DLINK}(p) \text{ and repeat.} \\ \text{Set } l \leftarrow \texttt{LLINK}(i), \ r \leftarrow \texttt{RLINK}(i), \\ \quad \texttt{RLINK}(l) \leftarrow r, \ \texttt{LLINK}(r) \leftarrow l. \end{cases} \quad (12)$$

$$\text{hide}(p) = \begin{cases} \text{Set } q \leftarrow p + 1, \text{ and repeat the following while } q \neq p: \\ \quad \text{Set } x \leftarrow \text{TOP}(q), \, u \leftarrow \text{ULINK}(q), \, d \leftarrow \text{DLINK}(q); \\ \quad \text{if } x \leq 0, \text{ set } q \leftarrow u \text{ (q was a spacer)}; \\ \quad \text{otherwise set } \text{DLINK}(u) \leftarrow d, \text{ ULINK}(d) \leftarrow u, \\ \quad \quad \text{LEN}(x) \leftarrow \text{LEN}(x) - 1, \, q \leftarrow q + 1. \end{cases} \quad (13)$$

And — here's the point — those operations can readily be undone:

$$\text{uncover}(i) = \begin{cases} \text{Set } l \leftarrow \text{LLINK}(i), \, r \leftarrow \text{RLINK}(i), \\ \quad \text{RLINK}(l) \leftarrow i, \text{ LLINK}(r) \leftarrow i. \\ \text{Set } p \leftarrow \text{ULINK}(i). \\ \text{While } p \neq i, \text{ unhide}(p), \text{ then set } p \leftarrow \text{ULINK}(p) \text{ and repeat.} \end{cases} \quad (14)$$

$$\text{unhide}(p) = \begin{cases} \text{Set } q \leftarrow p - 1, \text{ and repeat the following while } q \neq p: \\ \quad \text{Set } x \leftarrow \text{TOP}(q), \, u \leftarrow \text{ULINK}(q), \, d \leftarrow \text{DLINK}(q); \\ \quad \text{if } x \leq 0, \text{ set } q \leftarrow d \text{ (q was a spacer)}; \\ \quad \text{otherwise set } \text{DLINK}(u) \leftarrow q, \text{ ULINK}(d) \leftarrow q, \\ \quad \quad \text{LEN}(x) \leftarrow \text{LEN}(x) + 1, \, q \leftarrow q - 1. \end{cases} \quad (15)$$

We're careful here to do everything backwards, using operation (2) inside (14) and (15) to undelete in precisely the reverse order of the way that we'd previously used operation (1) inside (12) and (13) to delete. Furthermore, we're able to do this in place, without copying, by waltzing through the data structure at the same time as we're modifying it.

Algorithm X (*Exact cover via dancing links*). This algorithm visits all solutions to a given exact cover problem, using the data structures just described. It also maintains a list $x_0, x_1, \ldots, x_T$ of node pointers for backtracking, where T is large enough to accommodate one entry for each option in a partial solution.

X1. [Initialize.] Set the problem up in memory, as in Table 1. (See exercise 8.) Also set N to the number of items, Z to the last spacer address, and $l \leftarrow 0$.

X2. [Enter level l.] If $\text{RLINK}(0) = 0$ (hence all items have been covered), visit the solution that is specified by $x_0 x_1 \ldots x_{l-1}$ and go to X8. (See exercise 13.)

X3. [Choose i.] At this point the items $i_1, \ldots, i_t$ still need to be covered, where $i_1 = \text{RLINK}(0)$, $i_{j+1} = \text{RLINK}(i_j)$, $\text{RLINK}(i_t) = 0$. Choose one of them, and call it i. (The MRV heuristic of exercise 9 often works well in practice.)

X4. [Cover i.] Cover item i using (12), and set $x_l \leftarrow \text{DLINK}(i)$.

X5. [Try x_l.] If $x_l = i$, go to X7 (we've tried all options for i). Otherwise set $p \leftarrow x_l + 1$, and do the following while $p \neq x_l$: Set $j \leftarrow \text{TOP}(p)$; if $j \leq 0$, set $p \leftarrow \text{ULINK}(p)$; otherwise cover$(j)$ and set $p \leftarrow p + 1$. (This covers the items $\neq i$ in the option that contains x_l.) Set $l \leftarrow l + 1$ and return to X2.

X6. [Try again.] Set $p \leftarrow x_l - 1$, and do the following while $p \neq x_l$: Set $j \leftarrow \text{TOP}(p)$; if $j \leq 0$, set $p \leftarrow \text{DLINK}(p)$; otherwise uncover$(j)$ and set $p \leftarrow p - 1$. (This uncovers the items $\neq i$ in the option that contains x_l, using the reverse of the order in X5.) Set $i \leftarrow \text{TOP}(x_l)$, $x_l \leftarrow \text{DLINK}(x_l)$, and return to X5.

X7. [Backtrack.] Uncover item i using (14).

X8. [Leave level l.] Terminate if $l = 0$. Otherwise set $l \leftarrow l - 1$ and go to X6. ∎

The reader is strongly advised to work exercise 11 now — yes, now, really! — in order to experience the dance steps of this instructive algorithm. When the procedure terminates, all of the links will be restored to their original settings.

We're going to see lots of applications of Algorithm X, and similar algorithms, in this section. Let's begin by fulfilling a promise that was made on page 2 of Chapter 7, namely to solve the problem of *Langford pairs* efficiently by means of dancing links.

The task is to put $2n$ numbers $\{1, 1, 2, 2, \ldots, n, n\}$ into $2n$ slots $s_1 s_2 \ldots s_{2n}$, in such a way that exactly i numbers fall between the two occurrences of i. It illustrates exact covering nicely, because we can regard the n values of i and the $2n$ slots s_j as items to be covered. The allowable options for placing the i's are then

$$\text{`$i\ s_j\ s_k$'}, \qquad \text{for } 1 \le j < k \le 2n, \quad k = i + j + 1, \quad 1 \le i \le n; \qquad (16)$$

for example, when $n = 3$ they're

$$\text{`$1\ s_1\ s_3$', `$1\ s_2\ s_4$', `$1\ s_3\ s_5$', `$1\ s_4\ s_6$', `$2\ s_1\ s_4$', `$2\ s_2\ s_5$', `$2\ s_3\ s_6$', `$3\ s_1\ s_5$', `$3\ s_2\ s_6$'.} \qquad (17)$$

An exact covering of all items is equivalent to placing each pair and filling each slot. Algorithm X quickly determines that (17) has just two solutions,

$$\text{`$3\ s_1\ s_5$', `$2\ s_3\ s_6$', `$1\ s_2\ s_4$'} \qquad \text{and} \qquad \text{`$3\ s_2\ s_6$', `$2\ s_1\ s_4$', `$1\ s_3\ s_5$',}$$

corresponding to the placements $3\,1\,2\,1\,3\,2$ and $2\,3\,1\,2\,1\,3$. Notice that those placements are mirror images of each other; exercise 15 shows how to save a factor of 2 and eliminate such symmetry, by omitting some of the options in (16).

With that change, there are exactly 326,721,800 solutions when $n = 16$, and Algorithm X needs about 1.13 trillion memory accesses to visit them all. That's pretty good — it amounts to roughly 3460 mems per solution, as the links whirl.

Of course, we've already looked at a backtrack procedure that's specifically tuned to the Langford problem, namely Algorithm 7.2.2L near the beginning of Section 7.2.2. With the enhancement of exercise 7.2.2–21, that one handles the case $n = 16$ somewhat faster, finishing after about 400 billion mems. But Algorithm X can be pleased that its general-purpose machinery isn't way behind the best custom-tailored method.

Secondary items. Can the classical problem of n queens also be formulated as an exact cover problem? Yes, of course! But the construction isn't quite so obvious. Instead of setting the problem up as we did in 7.2.2–(3), where we chose a queen placement for each row of the board, we shall now allow both rows and columns to participate equally when making the necessary choices.

There are n^2 options for placing queens, and we want exactly one queen in every row and exactly one in every column. Furthermore, we want *at most* one queen in every diagonal. More precisely, if x_{ij} is the binary variable that signifies a queen in row i and column j, we want

$$\sum_{i=1}^{n} x_{ij} = 1 \quad \text{for } 1 \le j \le n; \qquad \sum_{j=1}^{n} x_{ij} = 1 \quad \text{for } 1 \le i \le n; \qquad (18)$$

$$\sum \{x_{ij} \mid 1 \le i, j \le n, \ i + j = s\} \le 1 \quad \text{for } 1 < s \le 2n; \tag{19}$$

$$\sum \{x_{ij} \mid 1 \le i, j \le n, \ i - j = d\} \le 1 \quad \text{for } -n < d < n. \tag{20}$$

The inequalities in (19) and (20) can be changed to equalities by introducing "slack variables" $u_2, \ldots, u_{2n}, v_{-n+1}, \ldots, v_{n-1}$, each of which is 0 or 1:

$$\sum \{x_{ij} \mid 1 \le i, j \le n, \ i + j = s\} + u_s = 1 \quad \text{for } 1 < s \le 2n; \tag{21}$$

$$\sum \{x_{ij} \mid 1 \le i, j \le n, \ i - j = d\} + v_d = 1 \quad \text{for } -n < d < n. \tag{22}$$

Thus we've shown that the problem of n nonattacking queens is equivalent to the problem of finding $n^2 + 4n - 2$ binary variables x_{ij}, u_s, v_d for which certain subsets of the variables sum to 1, as specified in (18), (21), and (22).

And that is essentially an exact cover problem, whose options correspond to the binary variables and whose items correspond to the subsets. The items are r_i, c_j, a_s, and b_d, representing respectively row i, column j, upward diagonal s, and downward diagonal d. The options are '$r_i\,c_j\,a_{i+j}\,b_{i-j}$' for queen placements, together with trivial options 'a_s' and 'b_d' to take up any slack.

For example, when $n = 4$ the n^2 placement options are

$$
\begin{array}{llll}
\text{‘}r_1\,c_1\,a_2\,b_0\text{’;} & \text{‘}r_2\,c_1\,a_3\,b_1\text{’;} & \text{‘}r_3\,c_1\,a_4\,b_2\text{’;} & \text{‘}r_4\,c_1\,a_5\,b_3\text{’;} \\
\text{‘}r_1\,c_2\,a_3\,b_{-1}\text{’;} & \text{‘}r_2\,c_2\,a_4\,b_0\text{’;} & \text{‘}r_3\,c_2\,a_5\,b_1\text{’;} & \text{‘}r_4\,c_2\,a_6\,b_2\text{’;} \\
\text{‘}r_1\,c_3\,a_4\,b_{-2}\text{’;} & \text{‘}r_2\,c_3\,a_5\,b_{-1}\text{’;} & \text{‘}r_3\,c_3\,a_6\,b_0\text{’;} & \text{‘}r_4\,c_3\,a_7\,b_1\text{’;} \\
\text{‘}r_1\,c_4\,a_5\,b_{-3}\text{’;} & \text{‘}r_2\,c_4\,a_6\,b_{-2}\text{’;} & \text{‘}r_3\,c_4\,a_7\,b_{-1}\text{’;} & \text{‘}r_4\,c_4\,a_8\,b_0\text{’;}
\end{array}
\tag{23}
$$

and the $4n - 2$ slack options (which contain just one item each) are

$$\text{‘}a_2\text{’; ‘}a_3\text{’; ‘}a_4\text{’; ‘}a_5\text{’; ‘}a_6\text{’; ‘}a_7\text{’; ‘}a_8\text{’; ‘}b_{-3}\text{’; ‘}b_{-2}\text{’; ‘}b_{-1}\text{’; ‘}b_0\text{’; ‘}b_1\text{’; ‘}b_2\text{’; ‘}b_3\text{’.} \tag{24}$$

Algorithm X will solve this small problem easily, although its treatment of the slacks is somewhat awkward (see exercise 16).

A closer look shows, however, that a slight change to Algorithm X will allow us to avoid slack options entirely! Let's divide the items of an exact cover problem into two groups: *primary* items, which must be covered *exactly* once, and *secondary* items, which must be covered *at most* once. If we simply modify step X1 so that only the primary items appear in the active list, everything will work like a charm. (Think about it.) In fact, the necessary changes to step X1 already appear in the answer to exercise 8.

Secondary items turn out to be extremely useful in applications. So let's redefine the exact cover problem, taking them into account: Henceforth we shall assume that an exact cover problem involves N distinct items, of which N_1 are primary and $N_2 = N - N_1$ are secondary. It is defined by a family of options, each of which is a subset of the items. *Every option must include at least one primary item.* The task is to find all subsets of the options that (i) contain every primary item exactly once, and (ii) contain every secondary item at most once.

(Options that are purely secondary are excluded from this new definition, because they will never be chosen by Algorithm X as we've refined it. If for some reason you don't like that rule, you can always go back to the idea of slack options. Exercise 19 discusses another interesting alternative.)

The order in which primary items appear in Algorithm X's active list can have a significant effect on the running time, because the implementation of step X3 in exercise 9 selects the *first* item of minimum length. For example, if we consider the primary items of the n queens problem in the natural order $r_1, c_1,$ $r_2, c_2, \ldots, r_n, c_n$, queens tend to be placed at the top and left before we try to place them at the bottom and right. By contrast, if we use the "organ-pipe order" $r_{\lfloor n/2 \rfloor+1}, c_{\lfloor n/2 \rfloor+1}, r_{\lfloor n/2 \rfloor}, c_{\lfloor n/2 \rfloor}, r_{\lfloor n/2 \rfloor+2}, c_{\lfloor n/2 \rfloor+2}, r_{\lfloor n/2 \rfloor-1}, c_{\lfloor n/2 \rfloor-1},$ $\ldots, (r_1 \text{ or } r_n), (c_1 \text{ or } c_n)$, the queens are placed first in the center, where they prune the remaining possibilities more effectively. For example, the time needed to find all 14772512 ways to place 16 queens is 76 Gμ (gigamems) with the natural order, but only 40 Gμ with the organ-pipe order.

These running times can be compared with 9 Gμ, which we obtained using efficient bitwise operations with Algorithm 7.2.2W. Although that algorithm was specially tuned, the general-purpose dancing links technique runs only five times slower. Furthermore, the setup we've used here allows us to solve other problems that wouldn't be anywhere near as easy with ordinary backtrack. For example, we can limit the solutions to those that contain queens on each of the $2 + 4l$ longest diagonals, simply by regarding a_s and b_d as primary items instead of secondary, for $|n + 1 - s| \le l$ and $|d| \le l$. (There are 18048 such solutions when $n = 16$ and $l = 4$, found with organ-pipe order in 2.7 Gμ.)

We can also use secondary items to remove symmetry, so that most of the solutions are found only once instead of eight times (see exercises 22 and 23). The central idea is to use a *pairwise ordering* trick that works also in many other situations. Consider the following family of $2m$ options:

$$\alpha_j = `a \; x_0 \; \ldots \; x_{j-1}' \quad \text{and} \quad \beta_j = `b \; x_j' \qquad \text{for } 0 \le j < m, \tag{25}$$

where a and b are primary while $x_0, x_1, \ldots, x_{m-1}$ are secondary. For example, when $m = 4$ the options are

$$
\begin{aligned}
\alpha_0 &= `a'; & \beta_0 &= `b \; x_0'; \\
\alpha_1 &= `a \; x_0'; & \beta_1 &= `b \; x_1'; \\
\alpha_2 &= `a \; x_0 \; x_1'; & \beta_2 &= `b \; x_2'; \\
\alpha_3 &= `a \; x_0 \; x_1 \; x_2'; & \beta_3 &= `b \; x_3'.
\end{aligned}
$$

It's not hard to see that there are exactly $\binom{m+1}{2}$ ways to cover both a and b, namely to choose α_j and β_k with $0 \le j \le k < m$. For if we choose α_j, the secondary items x_0 through x_{j-1} knock out the options $\beta_0, \ldots, \beta_{j-1}$.

This construction involves a total of $\binom{m+1}{2}$ entries in the α options and $2m$ entries in the β options. But exercise 20 shows that it's possible to achieve pairwise ordering with only $O(m \log m)$ entries in both α's and β's. For example, when $m = 4$ it produces the following elegant pattern:

$$
\begin{aligned}
\alpha_0 &= `a'; & \beta_0 &= `b \; y_1 \; y_2'; \\
\alpha_1 &= `a \; y_1'; & \beta_1 &= `b \; y_2'; \\
\alpha_2 &= `a \; y_2'; & \beta_2 &= `b \; y_3'; \\
\alpha_3 &= `a \; y_3 \; y_2'; & \beta_3 &= `b'.
\end{aligned}
\tag{26}
$$

Progress reports. Many of the applications of Algorithm X take a long time, especially when we're using it to solve a tough problem that is breaking new ground. So we don't want to just start it up and wait with our fingers crossed, hoping that it will finish soon. We really want to watch it in action and see how it's doing. How many more hours will it probably run? Is it almost half done?

A simple amendment to step X2 will alleviate such worries. At the beginning of that step, as we enter a new node of the search tree, we can test whether the accumulated running time T has passed a certain threshold Θ, which is initially set to Δ. If $T \geq \Theta$, we print a progress report and set $\Theta \leftarrow \Theta + \Delta$. (Thus if $\Delta = \infty$, we get no reports; if $\Delta = 0$, we see a report at each node.)

The author's experimental program measures time in mems, so that he can obtain machine-independent results; and he usually takes $\Delta = 10\,\mathrm{G}\mu$. His program has two main ways to show progress, namely a long form and a short form. The long form gives full details about the current state of the search, based on exercise 12. For example, here's the first progress report that it displays when finding all solutions to the 16 queens problem as described above:

```
Current state (level 15):
   r8 c3 ab ba (4 of 16)
   c8 a8 bn r0 (1 of 13)
   r7 cb ai bj (7 of 10)
   r6 c4 aa bd (2 of 7)
        .   .   .
   3480159 solutions, 10000000071 mems, and max level 16 so far.
```

(The computer's internal encoding for items is different from the conventions we have used; for example, 'r8 c3 ab ba' stands for what we called 'r_9 c_4 a_{13} b_5'. The first choice at level 0 was to cover item r8, meaning to put a queen into row 9. The fourth of 16 options for that item has placed it in column 4. Then at level 1 we tried the first of 13 ways to cover item c8, meaning to put a queen into column 9. And so on. At each level, the leftmost item shown for the option being tried is the one that was chosen in step X3 for branching.)

That's the long form. The short form, which is the default, produces just one line for each state report:

```
10000000071mu: 3480159 sols, 4g 1d 7a 27 36 24 23 13 12 12 22 12 ... .19048
20000000111mu: 6604373 sols, 7g cd 6a 88 36 35 44 44 24 11 12 22 .43074
30000000052mu: 9487419 sols, bg cd 9a 68 37 35 24 13 12 12 .68205
40000000586mu: 12890124 sols, fg 6d aa 68 46 35 23 33 23 .90370
Altogether 14772512 solutions, 62296+45565990457 mems, 193032021 nodes.
```

Two-character codes are used to indicate the current position in the tree; for example, '4g' means branch 4 of 16, then '1d' means branch 1 of 13, etc. By watching these steadily increasing codes — it's fun! — we can monitor the action.

Each line in the short form ends with an estimate of how much of the tree has been examined, assuming that the search tree structure is fairly consistent. For instance, '.19048' means that we're roughly 19% done. If we're currently working at level l on choice c_l of t_l, this number is computed by the formula

$$\frac{c_0 - 1}{t_0} + \frac{c_1 - 1}{t_0 t_1} + \cdots + \frac{c_l - 1}{t_0 t_1 \ldots t_l} + \frac{1}{2 t_0 t_1 \ldots t_l}. \qquad (27)$$

Sudoku. A "sudoku square" is a 9×9 array that has been divided into 3×3 boxes and filled with the digits $\{1,2,3,4,5,6,7,8,9\}$ in such a way that

- every row contains each of the digits $\{1,2,3,4,5,6,7,8,9\}$ exactly once;
- every column contains each of the digits $\{1,2,3,4,5,6,7,8,9\}$ exactly once;
- every box contains each of the digits $\{1,2,3,4,5,6,7,8,9\}$ exactly once.

(Since there are nine cells in each row, each column, and each box, the words 'exactly once' can be replaced by 'at least once' or 'at most once', anywhere in this definition.) Here, for example, are three highly symmetrical sudoku squares:

(a)
```
1 2 3 4 5 6 7 8 9
4 5 6 7 8 9 1 2 3
7 8 9 1 2 3 4 5 6
2 3 4 5 6 7 8 9 1
5 6 7 8 9 1 2 3 4
8 9 1 2 3 4 5 6 7
3 4 5 6 7 8 9 1 2
6 7 8 9 1 2 3 4 5
9 1 2 3 4 5 6 7 8
```
(b)
```
1 2 3 4 5 6 7 8 9
4 5 6 7 8 9 1 2 3
7 8 9 1 2 3 4 5 6
2 3 1 5 6 4 8 9 7
5 6 4 8 9 7 2 3 1
8 9 7 2 3 1 5 6 4
3 1 2 6 4 5 9 7 8
6 4 5 9 7 8 3 1 2
9 7 8 3 1 2 6 4 5
```
(c)
```
1 2 3 4 5 6 7 8 9
5 6 4 8 9 7 2 3 1
9 7 8 3 1 2 6 4 5
6 4 5 9 7 8 3 1 2
7 8 9 1 2 3 4 5 6
2 3 1 5 6 4 8 9 7
8 9 7 2 3 1 5 6 4
3 1 2 6 4 5 9 7 8
4 5 6 7 8 9 1 2 3
```
. (28)

When the square has been only partially specified, the task of completing it — by filling in the blank cells — often turns out to be a fascinating challenge. Howard Garns used this idea as the basis for a series of puzzles that he called Number Place, first published in *Dell Pencil Puzzles & Word Games* #16 (May 1979), 6. The concept soon spread to Japan, where Nikoli Inc. gave it the name Su Doku (数独, "Unmarried Numbers") in 1984; and eventually it went viral. By the beginning of 2005, major newspapers had begun to feature daily sudoku puzzles. Today, sudoku ranks among the most popular recreations of all time.

Every sudoku puzzle corresponds to an exact cover problem that has a particularly nice form. Consider, for example, the following three instances:

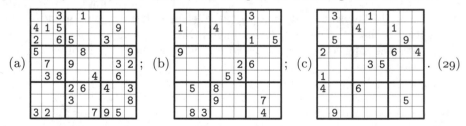

(The clues in (29a) match the first 32 digits of π; but the clues in (29b) and (29c) disagree with π after awhile.) For convenience, let's number the rows, columns, and boxes from 0 to 8. Then every sudoku square $S = (s_{ij})$ corresponds naturally to the solution of a master exact cover problem whose $9 \cdot 9 \cdot 9 = 729$ options are

$$`p_{ij}\ r_{ik}\ c_{jk}\ b_{xk}' \quad \text{for } 0 \le i,j < 9,\ 1 \le k \le 9,\ \text{and } x = 3\lfloor i/3 \rfloor + \lfloor j/3 \rfloor, \quad (30)$$

and whose $4 \cdot 9 \cdot 9 = 324$ items are p_{ij}, r_{ik}, c_{jk}, b_{xk}. The reason is that option (30) is chosen with parameters (i,j,k) if and only if $s_{ij} = k$. Item p_{ij} must be covered by exactly one of the nine options that fill cell (i,j); item r_{ik} must be covered by exactly one of the nine options that put k in row i; ...; item b_{xk} must be covered by exactly one of the nine options that put k in box x. Got it?

*My own motive for writing on the subject is partly to justify
the appalling number of hours I have squandered solving Sudoku.*
— BRIAN HAYES, in *American Scientist* (2006)

To find all sudoku squares that contain a given *partial* specification, we simply remove all of the items p_{ij}, r_{ik}, c_{jk}, b_{xk} that are already covered, as well as all of the options that involve any of those items. For example, (29a) leads to an exact cover problem with $4 \cdot (81 - 32) = 196$ items p_{00}, p_{01}, p_{03}, ..., r_{02}, r_{04}, r_{05}, ..., c_{01}, c_{06}, c_{07}, ..., b_{07}, b_{08}, b_{09}, ...; it has 146 options, beginning with '$p_{00}\ r_{07}\ c_{07}\ b_{07}$' and ending with '$p_{88}\ r_{86}\ c_{86}\ b_{86}$'. These options can be visualized by making a chart that shows every value that hasn't been ruled out:

	0	1	2	3	4	5	6	7	8
0	789	89	**3**	4 6 / 78	**1**	2 6 89	2 56 78	2 4 78	456 7
1	**4**	**1**	**5**	6 / 78 7	23	23 6 8	2 6 78	**9**	6 7
2	**2**	89	**6**	**5**	4 7 9	89	**3**	1 4 78	1 4 7
3	**5**	4 6 / 12 4	12 4	1 7 / 6	**8**	123 6	1 7	1 4 7	**9**
4	1 6	**7**	1 4	**9**	5	1 56	1 5 8	**3**	**2**
5	1 9	**3**	**8**	1 7	2 5 7	**4**	1 5 7	**6**	1 5 7
6	1 789	5 89 / 7 9	1 7 9	**2**	**6**	1 5 89	**4**	1 7	**3**
7	1 6 7 9	456 9	1 4 7 9	**3**	45 9	1 5 9	12 6 7	12 7	**8**
8	**3**	**2**	1 4	1 4 8	4	**7**	**9**	**5**	1 6

$$(31)$$

The active list for item p_{00}, say, has options for values $\{7, 8, 9\}$; the active list for item r_{02} has options for columns $\{5, 6, 7\}$; the active list for item c_{01} has options for rows $\{4, 5, 6, 7\}$; and so on. (Indeed, sudoku experts tend to have charts like this in mind, implicitly or explicitly, as they work.)

Aha! Look at the lonely '5' in the middle! There's only one option for p_{44}; so we can promote that '5' to '**5**'. Hence we can also erase the other '5's that appear in row 4, column 4, or box 4. This operation is called "forcing a naked single."

And there's *another* naked single in cell $(8, 4)$. Promoting this one from '4' to '**4**' produces others in cells $(7, 4)$ and $(8, 2)$. Indeed, if the items p_{ij} have been placed first in step X1, Algorithm X will follow a merry path of forced moves that lead immediately to a complete solution of (29a), *entirely* via naked singles.

Of course sudoku puzzles aren't always this easy. For example, (29b) has only 17 clues, not 32; that makes naked singles less likely. (Puzzle (29b) comes from Gordon Royle's online collection of approximately 50,000 17-clue sudokus — all of which are essentially different, and all of which have a unique completion despite the paucity of clues. Royle's collection appears to be nearly complete: Whenever a sudoku fanatic encounters a 17-clue puzzle nowadays, that puzzle almost invariably turns out to be equivalent to one in Royle's list.)

A massive computer calculation, supervised by Gary McGuire and completed in 2012, has shown that *every uniquely solvable sudoku puzzle must contain at least 17 clues.* We will see in Section 7.2.3 that exactly 5,472,730,538 nonisomorphic sudoku squares exist. McGuire's program examined each of them, and showed that comparatively few 16-clue subsets could possibly characterize it. About 16,000 subsets typically survived this initial screening; but they too were shown to fail. All this was determined in roughly 3.6 seconds per sudoku square, thanks to nontrivial and highly optimized bitwise algorithms. [See G. McGuire, B. Tugemann, and G. Civario, *Experimental Mathematics* **23** (2014), 190–217.]

The 17 clues of puzzle (29b) produce the following chart analogous to (31):

$$(32)$$

	0	1	2	3	4	5	6	7	8
0	{2,4,5,6,7,8}	{2,4,6,7,9}	{2,4,5,6,7,8,9}	{1,2,5,6,7}	{1,2,6,7,8,9}	{1,5,6,7,8,9}	**3**	{2,6,8,9}	{2,4,6,7,8,9}
1	**1**	{2,3,6,7,9}	{2,5,6,7,8,9}	**4**	{2,3,6,7,8,9}	{5,6,7,8,9}	{2,7,8,9}	{2,6,8,9}	{2,6,7,8,9}
2	{2,3,4,6,7,8}	{2,3,4,6,7,9}	{2,4,6,7,8,9}	{2,3,6,7}	{2,3,6,7,8,9}	{6,7,8,9}	**1**	{2,6,8,9}	**5**
3	**9**	{1,2,3,4,6,7}	{1,2,4,5,6,7,8}	{1,6,7}	{1,4,6,7,8}	{1,4,6,7,8}	{2,4,5,7,8}	{1,2,3,5,8}	{1,2,3,4,7,8}
4	{3,4,5,7,8}	{1,4,7}	{1,3,4,5,7,8}	{1,7}	{1,4,7,8,9}	**2**	**6**	{1,3,5,8,9}	{1,3,4,7,8,9}
5	{2,4,6,7,8}	{1,2,4,6,7}	{1,2,4,6,7,8}	{1,6,7}	**5**	**3**	{2,4,7,8,9}	{1,2,8,9}	{1,2,4,7,8,9}
6	{2,4,6,7}	**5**	{1,2,4,6,7,9}	**8**	{1,2,3,4,6,7}	{1,4,6,7}	{2,9}	{1,2,3,6,9}	{1,2,3,6,9}
7	{2,4,6}	{1,2,4,6}	{1,2,4,6}	**9**	{1,2,3,4,6}	{1,4,5,6}	{2,5,8}	**7**	{1,2,3,6,8}
8	{2,6,7}	**8**	**3**	{1,2,5,6,7}	{1,2,6,7}	{1,5,6,7}	{2,5,9}	**4**	{1,2,6,9}

This one has 307 options remaining — more than twice as many as before. Also, as we might have guessed, it has no naked singles. But it still reveals forced moves, if we look more closely! For example, column 3 contains only one instance of '3'; we can promote it to '3', and kill all of the other '3's in row 2 and box 1. This operation is called "forcing a hidden single."

Similarly, box 2 in (32) contains only one instance of '4'; and two other hidden singles are also present (see exercise 47). These forced moves cause other hidden singles to appear, and naked singles also arise soon. But after 16 forced promotions have been made, the low-hanging fruit is all gone:

$$(33)$$

	0	1	2	3	4	5	6	7	8
0	**5**	{6,7,8,9}	**2**	{1,6,7,8}	{1,6,7,8,9}	**3**	{6,8,9}	**4**	{6,8,9}
1	**1**	**3**	{2,6,7,8}	**4**	{6,7,8}	**5**	{7,8}	{2,6,8,9}	{2,6,7,9}
2	{2,4,6,7,8}	{2,4,6,7,9}	{2,4,6,7,8}	**3**	{6,7,8}	{6,7,8,9}	**1**	{2,6,8,9}	**5**
3	**9**	{1,2,4,6,7}	{1,2,4,5,6,7,8}	{1,6,7}	{1,4,6,7,8}	{1,4,6,7,8}	{4,7,8}	{1,2,3,5,8}	{1,2,3,7}
4	**3**	{1,4,7}	{1,4,5,7,8}	{1,7}	**9**	**2**	**6**	{1,5,7,8}	{1,7}
5	{2,4,6,7,8}	{1,2,4,6,7}	{1,2,4,6,7,8}	{1,7}	**5**	**3**	{4,7,8}	{1,2,8,9}	{1,2,7,9}
6	{4,6,7}	**5**	**9**	**8**	{1,4,6,7}	{1,4,6,7}	**2**	{1,3,6}	{1,3,6}
7	{2,4,6}	{1,2,4,6}	{1,2,4,6}	**9**	**3**	{1,4,6}	**5**	**7**	**8**
8	{6,7}	**8**	**3**	**5**	**2**	{1,6,7}	**9**	**4**	{1,6}

Algorithm X readily deduces (33) from (32), because it sees naked singles and hidden singles whenever an item p_{ij} or r_{ik} or c_{jk} or b_{xk} has only one remaining option, and because its data structures change easily as the links dance. But when state (33) is reached, the algorithm resorts to two-way branching, in this case looking first at case '7' of p_{16}, then backtracking later to consider case '8'.

A human sudoku expert would actually glance at (33) and notice that there's a more intelligent way to proceed, because (33) contains a "naked pair": Cells $(4, 3)$ and $(4, 8)$ both contain the same two choices; hence we're allowed to delete '1' and '7' wherever they appear elsewhere in row 4; and this will produce a naked '4' in column 1. Exercise 49 explores such higher-order deductions in detail.

Fancy logic that involves pairs and triples might well be preferable for earthlings, but simple backtracking works just fine for machines. In fact, Algorithm X finds the solution to (29b) after exploring a search tree with just 89 nodes, the first 16 of which led it directly to (33). (It spends about 250 kilomems initializing the data structures in step X1, then 50 more kilomems to complete the task. Much more time would have been needed if it had tried to look for complicated patterns in step X3.) Here's the solution that it discovers:

```
c33 b13 p23 r23 (1 of 1)
r13 c13 b03 p11 (1 of 1)
      .   .   .
c42 b72 p84 r82 (1 of 1)
p16 r18 c68 b28 (2 of 2)
b27 p18 r17 c87 (1 of 1)
      .   .   .
p85 r81 c51 b71 (1 of 1)
```

After it selects the correct value for column 6 of row 1, the rest is forced.

The dancing links method actually cruises to victory with amazing speed, on almost every known sudoku puzzle. Among several dozen typical specimens — seen by the author since 2005 in newspapers, magazines, books, and webpages worldwide, and subsequently presented to Algorithm X — roughly 70% were found to be solvable entirely by forced moves, based on naked or hidden singles, even though many of those puzzles had been rated 'diabolical' or 'fiendish' or 'torturous'! Only 10% of them led to a search tree exceeding 100 nodes, and none of the trees had more than 282 nodes. (See, however, exercise 52.)

It's interesting to consider what happens when the algorithm is weakened, so that its forced moves come only from naked singles, which are the easiest deductions for people to make. Suppose we classify the items r_{ik}, c_{jk}, and b_{xk} as *secondary*, leaving only p_{ij} as primary. (In other words, the specification will require *at most* one occurrence of each value k, in every row, every column, and every box, but it won't explicitly insist that every k should be covered.) The search tree for puzzle (29b) then grows to a whopping 41,877 nodes.

Finally, what about puzzle (29c)? That one has only 16 clues, so we know that it cannot have a unique solution. But those 16 clues specify only seven of the nine digits; they give us no way to distinguish 7 from 8. Algorithm X deduces, with a 129-node search tree, that only two solutions exist. (Of course those two are essentially the same; they're obtainable from each other by swapping 7 ↔ 8.)

Puzzlists have invented many intriguing variations on the traditional sudoku challenge, several of which are discussed in the exercises below. Among the best are "jigsaw sudoku puzzles" (also known as "geometric sudoku," "polyomino sudoku," "squiggly sudoku," etc.), where the boxes have different shapes instead of simply being 3×3 subsquares. Consider, for example,

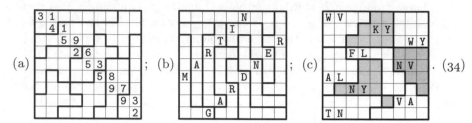

In puzzle (34a), which the author designed in 2017 with the help of Bob Harris, one can see for instance that there are only two places to put a '4' in the top row, because of the '4' in the next row. This puzzle is an exact cover problem just like (30), except that x is now a more complicated function of i and j. Similarly, Harris's classic puzzle (34b) [*Mathematical Wizardry for a Gardner* (2009), 55–57] asks us to put the letters $\{G, R, A, N, D, T, I, M, E\}$ into each row, column, and irregularly shaped box. Again we use (30), but with the values of k running through letters instead of digits. [*Hint:* Cell $(0, 2)$ must contain 'A', because column 2 needs an 'A' somewhere.] Puzzle (34c), The United States Jigsaw Sudoku, is a masterpiece designed and posted online by Thomas Snyder in 2006. It brilliantly uses boxes in the shapes of West Virginia, Kentucky, Wyoming, Alabama, Florida, Nevada, Tennessee, New York (including Long Island), and Virginia — and its clues are postal codes! (See exercise 59.)

Jigsaw sudoku was invented by J. Mark Thompson, who began to publish such puzzles in 1996 [*GAMES World of Puzzles*, #14 (July 1996), 51, 67] under the name Latin Squares. At that time he had not yet heard about sudoku; one of the advantages of his puzzles over normal sudoku was the fact that they can be of any size, not necessarily 9×9. Thompson's first examples were 6×6.

The *solutions* to puzzles of this kind actually have an interesting prehistory: Walter Behrens, a pioneer in the applications of mathematics to agriculture, wrote an influential paper in 1956 that proposed using such patterns in empirical studies of crops that have been treated with various fertilizers [*Zeitschrift für landwirtschaftliches Versuchs- und Untersuchungswesen* **2** (1956), 176–193]. He presented dozens of designs, ranging from 4×4 to 10×10, including

(a)
1	5	4	2	3
2	4	3	5	1
3	1	2	4	5
4	3	5	1	2
5	2	1	3	4

; (b)
1	3	8	7	9	5	2
2	6	9	5	3	8	4
3	8	2	4	6	7	1
4	7	6	9	1	3	8
5	1	3	8	7	6	9
6	9	7	1	4	2	6
7	5	4	2	8	9	6
8	2	1	3	5	4	7
9	4	5	6	2	1	3

; (c)
1	5	8	6	4	3	9	7	2
2	6	9	5	7	8	1	3	4
3	7	4	1	9	2	5	6	8
4	9	2	8	6	7	3	1	5
5	3	7	4	2	1	6	8	9
6	8	1	3	5	9	2	4	7
7	2	6	9	1	4	8	5	3
8	4	5	2	3	6	7	9	1
9	1	3	7	8	5	4	2	6

.   (35)

Notice that Behrens's (35b) is actually 9×7, so its rows don't exhibit all 9 possibilities. He required only that no treatment number be repeated in any row or column. Notice also that his (35c) is actually a normal sudoku arrangement; this is the earliest known publication of what is now called a sudoku solution. Following a suggestion of F. Ragaller, Behrens called these designs "gerechte" ("equitable") latin squares or latin rectangles, because they assign neighborhood groupings to tracts of land that have been subjected to all n treatments.

All of his designs were partitions of rectangles into connected regions, each with n square cells. We'll see next that *that* idea actually turns out to have its own distinguished history of fascinating combinatorial patterns and recreations.

Polyominoes. A rookwise-connected region of n square cells is often called an *n-omino*, following a suggestion by S. W. Golomb [*AMM* **61** (1954), 675–682]. When $n = 1, 2, 3, \ldots$, Golomb's definition gives us monominoes, dominoes, trominoes, tetrominoes, pentominoes, hexominoes, and so on. In general, when n is unspecified, Golomb called such regions *polyominoes.*

We've already encountered small polyominoes, together with their relation to exact covering, in 7.1.4–(130). It's clear that a domino has only one possible shape. But there are two distinct species of trominoes, one of which is "straight" (1×3) and the other is "bent," occupying three cells of a 2×2 square. Similarly, the tetrominoes can be classified into five distinct types. (Can you draw all five, before looking at exercise 274? Tetris® players will have no trouble doing this.)

The most piquant polyominoes, however, are almost certainly the *pentom-inoes*, of which there are twelve. These twelve shapes have become the personal friends of millions of people, because they can be put together in so many elegant ways. Sets of pentominoes, made from finely crafted hardwoods or from brilliantly colored plastic, are readily available at reasonable cost. Every home really ought to have at least one such set — even though "virtual" pentominoes can easily be manipulated in computer apps — because there's no substitute for the strangely fascinating tactile experience of arranging these delightful physical objects by hand. Furthermore, we'll see that pentominoes have much to teach us about combinatorial computing.

> *If mounted on cardboard, [these pieces]*
> *will form a source of perpetual amusement in the home.*
> — HENRY E. DUDENEY, *The Canterbury Puzzles* (1907)

> *Which English nouns ending in -o pluralize with -s and which with -es?*
> *If the word is still felt as somewhat alien, it takes -s,*
> *while if it has been fully naturalized into English, it takes -es.*
> *Thus,* echoes, potatoes, tomatoes, dingoes, embargoes, *etc.,*
> *whereas Italian musical terms are* altos, bassos, cantos, pianos, solos, *etc.,*
> *and there are Spanish words like* tangos, armadillos, *etc.*
> *I once held a trademark on 'Pentomino(-es)', but I now prefer*
> *to let these words be my contribution to the language as public domain.*
> — SOLOMON W. GOLOMB, letter to Donald Knuth (16 February 1994)

One of the first things we might try to do with twelve pieces of 5 cells each is to pack them into a rectangular box, either 6×10 or 5×12 or 4×15 or 3×20. The first three tasks are fairly easy; but a 3×20 box presents more of a challenge. Golomb posed this question in his article of 1954, without providing any answer. At that time he was unaware that Frans Hansson had already given a solution many years earlier, in an obscure publication called *The Problemist: Fairy Chess Supplement* **2**, 12 and 13 (June and August, 1935), problem 1844:

$$(36)$$

Hansson had in fact observed that the bracketed pieces "may also be rotated through two right angles, to give the only other possible solution."

This problem, and many others of a similar kind, can be formulated nicely in terms of exact covering. But before we do this, we need *names* for the individual pentomino shapes. Everybody agrees that seven of the pentominoes should be named after seven consecutive letters of the alphabet:

T   U   V   W   X   Y   Z

But two different systems of nomenclature have been proposed for the other five:

F   I   L   P   N   or   O   P   Q   R   S

(S. W. Golomb)   (J. H. Conway)

where Golomb liked to think of the word 'Filipino' while Conway preferred to map the twelve pentominoes onto twelve consecutive letters from O to Z. Conway's scheme tends to work better in computer programs, so we'll use it here.

The task of 3×20 pentomino packing is to arrange pentominoes in such a way that every piece name $\{\mathtt{O}, \mathtt{P}, \ldots, \mathtt{Z}\}$ is covered exactly once, and so is every cell ij for $0 \le i < 3$ and $0 \le j < 20$. Thus there are $12 + 3 \cdot 20 = 72$ items; and there's an option for each way to place an individual pentomino, namely

'O 00 01 02 03 04'

$\cdots$

'O 2f 2g 2h 2i 2j'
'P 00 01 02 10 11'

$$(37)$$

$\cdots$

'Z 0j 1h 1i 1j 2h'

if we extend hexadecimal notation so that the "digits" $(\mathtt{a}, \mathtt{b}, \ldots, \mathtt{j})$ represent $(10, 11, \ldots, 19)$. In this list, pieces $(\mathtt{O}, \mathtt{P}, \ldots, \mathtt{Z})$ contribute respectively $(48, 220,$

136, 144, 136, 72, 110, 72, 72, 18, 136, 72) options, making 1236 altogether. Exercise 266 explains how to generate all of the options for problems like this.

When Algorithm X is applied to (37), it finds eight solutions, because each of Hansson's arrangements is obtained with horizontal and/or vertical reflection. We can remove that symmetry by insisting that the V pentomino must appear in its 'Γ-like' orientation, as it does in (36), namely by removing all but 18 of its 72 options. (Do you see why? Think about it.) Without that simplification, a 32,644-node search tree finds 8 solutions in 146 megamems; with it, a 21,805-node search tree finds 2 solutions in 103 megamems.

A closer look shows that we can actually do much better. For example, one of the Γ-like options for V is 'V 09 0a 0b 19 29', representing

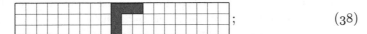

$$;\qquad\qquad (38)$$

but this placement could never be used, because it asks us to pack pentominoes into the 27 cells at V's left. Many of the options for other pieces are similarly unusable, because (like (38)) they isolate a region whose area isn't a multiple of 5.

In fact, if we remove all such options, only 728 of the original 1236 potential placements remain; they include respectively (48, 156, 132, 28, 128, 16, 44, 16, 12, 4, 128, 16) placements of (O, P, ..., Z). That gives us 716 options, when we remove also the 12 surviving placements for V that make it non-'Γ'. When Algorithm X is applied to this reduced set, the search tree for finding all solutions goes down to 1243 nodes, and the running time is only 4.5 megamems.

(There's also a slightly better way to remove the symmetry: Instead of insisting that piece V looks like 'Γ' we can insist that piece X lies in the left half, and that piece Z hasn't been "flipped over." This implies that there are (16, 2, 8) potential placements for (V, X, Z), instead of (4, 4, 16). The resulting search tree has just 1128 nodes, and the running time is 4.0 Mμ.)

Notice that we could have begun with a weaker formulation of this problem: We could merely have asked for pentomino arrangements that use each piece *at most* once, while covering each cell ij exactly once. That would be essentially the same as saying that the piece names $\{O, P, ..., Z\}$ are *secondary* items instead of primary. Then the original set of 1236 options in (37) would have led to a search tree with 61,851 nodes, and a runtime of 291 Mμ. Dually, we could have kept the piece names primary but made the cell names secondary; that would have yielded a 1,086,521,921-node tree, with a runtime of 2.94 Tμ! These statistics are curiously *reversed*, however, with respect to the reduced set of 716 options obtained by discarding cases like (38): Then piece names secondary yields 19306 nodes (68 Mμ); cell names secondary yields 11656 nodes (37 Mμ).

In the early days of computing, pentomino problems served as useful benchmarks for combinatorial calculations. Programmers didn't have the luxury of large random-access memory until much later; therefore techniques such as dancing links, in which more than a thousand options are explicitly listed and manipulated, were unthinkable at the time. Instead, the options for each piece were implicitly generated on-the-fly as needed, and there was no incentive to use fancy heuristics while backtracking. Each branch of the search was essentially based on the available ways to cover the first cell ij that hadn't yet been occupied.

We can simulate the behavior of those historic methods by running Algorithm X without the MRV heuristic and simply setting $i \leftarrow$ RLINK(0) in step X3. An interesting phenomenon now arises: If the cells ij are considered in their natural order — first 00, then 01, ..., then 0j, then 10, ..., finally 2j — the search tree has 1.5 billion nodes. (There are 29 ways to cover 00; if we choose '00 01 02 03 04 0' there are 49 ways to cover 05; and so on.) But if we consider the 20×3 problem instead of 3×20, so that the cells ij for $0 \leq i < 20$ and $0 \leq j < 3$ are processed in order 00, 01, 02, 10, ..., 2j, the search tree has just 71191 nodes, and all eight solutions are found very quickly. (This speedup is mostly due to having a better "focus," which we'll discuss later.) Again we see that a small change in problem setup can have enormous ramifications.

The best of these early programs were highly tuned, written in assembly language with ingenious uses of macro instructions. Memwise, they were therefore superior to Algorithm X on smallish problems. [See J. G. Fletcher, *CACM* **8**, 10 (October 1965), cover and 621–623; N. G. de Bruijn, *FGbook* pages 465–466.] But the MRV heuristic eventually wins, as problems get larger.

Exercises 268–323 discuss some of the many intriguing and instructive problems that arise when we explore the patterns that can be made with pentominoes and similar families of planar shapes. Several of these problems are indeed large — beyond the capabilities of today's machines.

Polycubes. And if you think two-dimensional shapes are fun, you'll probably enjoy three dimensions even more! A *polycube* is a solid object formed by taking one or more $1 \times 1 \times 1$ cubes and joining them face-to-face. We call them monocubes, dicubes, tricubes, tetracubes, pentacubes, etc.; but we *don't* call them "n-cubes" when they're made from n unit cubies, because mathematicians have reserved that term for n-dimensional objects.

A new situation arises when $n = 4$. In two dimensions we found it natural to regard the tetromino '⌐⌐' as identical to its mirror image '⌐', because we could simply flip it over. But the tetracube '⬚' is noticeably different from its mirror reflection '⬚', because we can't change one into the other without going into the fourth dimension. Polycubes that differ from their mirror images are called *chiral*, a word coined by Lord Kelvin in 1893 when he studied chiral molecules.

The simplest polycubes are *cuboids* — also called "rectangular parallelepipeds" by people who like long names — which are like bricks of size $l \times m \times n$. But things get particularly interesting when we consider noncuboidal shapes. Piet Hein noticed in 1933 that the seven smallest shapes of that kind, namely

         ,   (39)

1: bent   2: ell   3: tee   4: skew   5: L-twist   6: R-twist   7: claw

can be put together to form a $3 \times 3 \times 3$ cube, and he liked the pieces so much that he called them *Soma*. Notice that the first four pieces are essentially planar, while the other three are inherently three-dimensional. The twists are chiral.

Martin Gardner wrote about the joys of Soma in *Scientific American* **199**, 3 (September 1958), 182–188, and it soon became wildly popular: More than two million SOMA® cubes were sold in America alone, after Parker Brothers began to market a well-made set together with an instruction booklet written by Hein.

> *A minimum number of blocks of simple form are employed.* ...
> *Experiments and calculations have shown that from the set of seven blocks*
> *it is possible to construct approximately the same number of geometrical*
> *figures as could be constructed from twenty-seven separate cubes.*
> — PIET HEIN, *United Kingdom Patent Specification 420,349* (1934)

The task of packing these seven pieces into a cube is easy to formulate as an exact cover problem, just as we did when packing pentominoes. But this time we have 24 3D-rotations of the pieces to consider, instead of 8 2D-rotations and/or 3D-reflections; so exercise 324 is used instead of exercise 266 to generate the options of the problem. It turns out that there are 688 options, involving 34 items that we can call 1, 2, ..., 7, 000, 001, ..., 222. For example, the first option

$$\text{`1}\quad 000\quad 001\quad 010\text{'} \tag{40}$$

characterizes one of the 144 potential ways to place the "bent" piece 1.

Algorithm X needs just 407 megamems to find all 11,520 solutions to this problem. Furthermore, we can save most of that time by taking advantage of symmetry: Every solution can be rotated into a unique "canonical" solution in which the "ell" piece 2 has not been rotated; hence we can restrict that piece to only six placements, namely $(000, 010, 020, 100)$, $(001, 011, 021, 101)$, ..., $(102, 112, 122, 202)$ — all shifts of each other. This restriction removes $138 = \frac{23}{24} \cdot 144$ options, and the algorithm now finds the 480 canonical solutions in just 20 megamems. (These canonical solutions form 240 mirror-image pairs.)

Factoring an exact cover problem. In fact, we can simplify the Soma cube problem much further, so that all of its solutions can actually be found by hand in a reasonable time, by *factoring* the problem in a clever way.

Let's observe first that any solution to an exact cover problem automatically solves infinitely many *other* problems. Going back to our original formulation in terms of an $m \times n$ matrix $A = (a_{ij})$, the task is to find all sets of rows whose sum is 1 in every column, namely to find all binary vectors $x_1 \ldots x_m$ such that $\sum_{i=1}^{m} x_i a_{ij} = 1$ for $1 \leq j \leq n$. Therefore if we set $b_i = \alpha_1 a_{i1} + \cdots + \alpha_n a_{in}$ for $1 \leq i \leq m$, where $(\alpha_1, \ldots, \alpha_n)$ is any n-tuple of coefficients, the vectors $x_1 \ldots x_m$ will also satisfy $\sum_{i=1}^{m} x_i b_i = \alpha_1 + \cdots + \alpha_n$. By choosing the α's intelligently we may be able to learn a lot about the possibilities for $x_1 \ldots x_m$.

For example, consider again the 6×7 matrix A in (5), and let $\alpha_1 = \cdots = \alpha_7 = 1$. The sum of the entries in each row of A is either 2 or 3; thus we're supposed to cover 7 things, by burying either 2 or 3 at a time. Without knowing anything more about the detailed structure of A, we can conclude immediately that there's only one way to obtain a total of 7, namely by selecting $2 + 2 + 3$! Furthermore, only rows 1 and 5 have 2 as their sum; we *must* choose them.

Now here's a more interesting challenge: "Cover the 64 cells of a chessboard with 21 straight trominoes and one monomino." This problem corresponds to a big matrix that has $96 + 64$ rows and $1 + 64$ columns,

$$
\begin{pmatrix}
0 & 1 & 1 & 1 & 0 & 0 & 0 & 0 & 0 & 0 & 0 & 0 & 0 & 0 & 0 & 0 & 0 & 0 & 0 & 0 & 0 & 0 & 0 & 0 & \ldots & 0 & 0 & 0 & 0 \\
0 & 1 & 0 & 0 & 0 & 0 & 0 & 0 & 1 & 0 & 0 & 0 & 0 & 0 & 0 & 0 & 1 & 0 & 0 & 0 & 0 & 0 & 0 & 0 & \ldots & 0 & 0 & 0 & 0 \\
0 & 0 & 1 & 1 & 1 & 0 & 0 & 0 & 0 & 0 & 0 & 0 & 0 & 0 & 0 & 0 & 0 & 0 & 0 & 0 & 0 & 0 & 0 & 0 & \ldots & 0 & 0 & 0 & 0 \\
0 & 0 & 1 & 0 & 0 & 0 & 0 & 0 & 0 & 0 & 1 & 0 & 0 & 0 & 0 & 0 & 0 & 0 & 1 & 0 & 0 & 0 & 0 & 0 & \ldots & 0 & 0 & 0 & 0 \\
 & & & & & & & & & \cdot & \cdot & \cdot & \cdot & \cdot & & & & & & & & & & & & & & & \\
0 & 0 & 0 & 0 & 0 & 0 & 0 & 0 & 0 & 0 & 0 & 0 & 0 & 0 & 0 & 0 & 0 & 0 & 0 & 0 & 0 & 0 & 0 & 0 & \ldots & 0 & 1 & 1 & 1 \\
1 & 1 & 0 & 0 & 0 & 0 & 0 & 0 & 0 & 0 & 0 & 0 & 0 & 0 & 0 & 0 & 0 & 0 & 0 & 0 & 0 & 0 & 0 & 0 & \ldots & 0 & 0 & 0 & 0 \\
1 & 0 & 1 & 0 & 0 & 0 & 0 & 0 & 0 & 0 & 0 & 0 & 0 & 0 & 0 & 0 & 0 & 0 & 0 & 0 & 0 & 0 & 0 & 0 & \ldots & 0 & 0 & 0 & 0 \\
 & & & & & & & & & \cdot & \cdot & \cdot & \cdot & \cdot & & & & & & & & & & & & & & & \\
1 & 0 & 0 & 0 & 0 & 0 & 0 & 0 & 0 & 0 & 0 & 0 & 0 & 0 & 0 & 0 & 0 & 0 & 0 & 0 & 0 & 0 & 0 & 0 & \ldots & 0 & 0 & 0 & 1 \\
\end{pmatrix}, \qquad (41)
$$

with column headers M 00 01 02 03 04 05 06 07 10 11 12 13 14 15 16 17 20 21 22 23 24 ... 74 75 76 77

where the first 96 rows specify all possible ways to place a tromino and the other 64 rows specify the possibilities for the monomino. Column ij represents cell (i, j); column 'M' means "monomino."

The three cells (i, j) covered by a straight tromino always lead to distinct values of $(i - j) \bmod 3$. Therefore, if we add up the 22 columns of (41) for which $(i - j) \bmod 3 = 0$, we get 1 in each of the first 96 rows, and 0 or 1 in the other 64 rows. We're supposed to get a total of 22 in the chosen rows; hence the monomino has to go into a cell (i, j) with $i \equiv j$ (modulo 3).

A similar argument, using $i + j$ instead of $i - j$, shows that the monomino must also go into a cell with $i + j \equiv 1$ (modulo 3). Therefore $i \equiv j \equiv 2$. We've *proved that there are only four possibilities for* (i, j), namely $(2, 2)$, $(2, 5)$, $(5, 2)$, $(5, 5)$. [Golomb made this observation in his 1954 paper that introduced polyominoes, after "coloring" the cells of a chessboard with three colors. The general notion of factoring includes all such coloring arguments as special cases.]

Our proof that (38) is an impossible pentomino placement can also be regarded as an instance of factorization. The residual problem, if (38) is chosen, has a total of either 0 or 5 in the first 27 columns of each remaining row of the associated matrix. Therefore we can't achieve a total of 27 from those rows.

Consider now a three-dimensional problem [J. Slothouber and W. Graatsma, *Cubics* (1970), 108–109]: Can six $1 \times 2 \times 2$ cuboids be packed into a $3 \times 3 \times 3$ box? This is the problem of choosing six rows of the 36×27 matrix

column headers: 000 001 002 010 011 012 020 021 022 100 101 102 110 111 112 120 121 122 200 201 202 210 211 212 220 221 222

$$
\begin{pmatrix}
1 & 1 & 0 & 1 & 1 & 0 & 0 & 0 & 0 & 0 & 0 & 0 & 0 & 0 & 0 & 0 & 0 & 0 & 0 & 0 & 0 & 0 & 0 & 0 & 0 & 0 & 0 \\
1 & 1 & 0 & 0 & 0 & 0 & 0 & 0 & 0 & 1 & 1 & 0 & 0 & 0 & 0 & 0 & 0 & 0 & 0 & 0 & 0 & 0 & 0 & 0 & 0 & 0 & 0 \\
1 & 0 & 0 & 1 & 0 & 0 & 0 & 0 & 0 & 1 & 0 & 0 & 1 & 0 & 0 & 0 & 0 & 0 & 0 & 0 & 0 & 0 & 0 & 0 & 0 & 0 & 0 \\
0 & 1 & 1 & 0 & 1 & 1 & 0 & 0 & 0 & 0 & 0 & 0 & 0 & 0 & 0 & 0 & 0 & 0 & 0 & 0 & 0 & 0 & 0 & 0 & 0 & 0 & 0 \\
0 & 1 & 1 & 0 & 0 & 0 & 0 & 0 & 0 & 0 & 1 & 1 & 0 & 0 & 0 & 0 & 0 & 0 & 0 & 0 & 0 & 0 & 0 & 0 & 0 & 0 & 0 \\
0 & 1 & 0 & 0 & 1 & 0 & 0 & 0 & 0 & 0 & 1 & 0 & 0 & 1 & 0 & 0 & 0 & 0 & 0 & 0 & 0 & 0 & 0 & 0 & 0 & 0 & 0 \\
0 & 0 & 1 & 0 & 0 & 1 & 0 & 0 & 0 & 0 & 0 & 1 & 0 & 0 & 1 & 0 & 0 & 0 & 0 & 0 & 0 & 0 & 0 & 0 & 0 & 0 & 0 \\
 & & & & & & & & & \cdot & \cdot & \cdot & \cdot & \cdot & & & & & & & & & & & & & \\
0 & 0 & 0 & 0 & 0 & 0 & 0 & 0 & 0 & 0 & 0 & 0 & 0 & 0 & 0 & 0 & 0 & 0 & 0 & 0 & 0 & 0 & 1 & 1 & 0 & 1 & 1 \\
\end{pmatrix}, \qquad (42)
$$

in such a way that all of the column sums are ≤ 1.

The 27 cubies (i, j, k) of a $3 \times 3 \times 3$ cube fall into four classes, depending on how many of its coordinates have the middle value 1:

A vertex cubie has no 1s. $(\binom{3}{0}2^3 = 8$ cases.)

An edge cubie has one 1. $(\binom{3}{1}2^2 = 12$ cases.)

A face cubie has two 1s. $(\binom{3}{2}2^1 = 6$ cases.)   (43)

A central cubie has three 1s. $(\binom{3}{3}2^0 = 1$ case.)

Every symmetry of the cube preserves these classes.

Imagine placing four new columns v, e, f, c at the right of (42), representing the number of vertex, edge, face, and central cubies of a placement. Then 24 of the rows will have $(v, e, f, c) = (1, 2, 1, 0)$, and the other 12 rows will have $(v, e, f, c) = (0, 1, 2, 1)$. If we choose a rows of the first kind and b rows of the second kind, this factorization tells us that we must have

$$a \geq 0, \quad b \geq 0, \quad a + b = 6, \quad a \leq 8, \quad 2a + b \leq 12, \quad a + 2b \leq 6, \quad b \leq 1. \quad (44)$$

That's more than enough to prove that $b = 0$ and $a = 6$, and thus to find the essentially unique way to pack those six cuboids.

(We could paraphrase this argument as follows, making it more impressive by concealing the low-level algebra that inspired it: "Each $1 \times 2 \times 2$ cuboid occupies at least one face cubie. So each of them must be placed on a different face.")

With these examples in mind, we're ready now to apply factorization to the Soma cube. The possible (v, e, f, c) values for pieces 1 through 7 in (39) are:

Piece 1: $(0, 1, 1, 1)$, $(0, 0, 2, 1)$, $(0, 1, 2, 0)$, $(0, 2, 1, 0)$, $(1, 1, 1, 0)$, $(1, 2, 0, 0)$.
Piece 2: $(0, 1, 2, 1)$, $(0, 2, 2, 0)$, $(1, 2, 1, 0)$, $(2, 2, 0, 0)$.
Piece 3: $(0, 0, 3, 1)$, $(0, 2, 1, 1)$, $(0, 3, 1, 0)$, $(2, 1, 1, 0)$.
Piece 4: $(0, 1, 2, 1)$, $(1, 2, 1, 0)$.   (45)
Piece 5: $(0, 1, 2, 1)$, $(0, 2, 2, 0)$, $(1, 1, 1, 1)$, $(1, 2, 1, 0)$.
Piece 6: $(0, 1, 2, 1)$, $(0, 2, 2, 0)$, $(1, 1, 1, 1)$, $(1, 2, 1, 0)$.
Piece 7: $(0, 2, 1, 1)$, $(0, 0, 3, 1)$, $(1, 1, 2, 0)$, $(1, 3, 0, 0)$.

(This is actually much more information than we need, but it doesn't hurt.)

Looking only at the totals for v, we see that we must have

$$(0 \text{ or } 1) + (0, 1, \text{ or } 2) + (0 \text{ or } 2) + (0 \text{ or } 1) + (0 \text{ or } 1) + (0 \text{ or } 1) + (0 \text{ or } 1) = 8;$$

and the *only* way to achieve this is via

$$(0 \text{ or } 1) + (1 \text{ or } 2) + 2 + (0 \text{ or } 1) + (0 \text{ or } 1) + (0 \text{ or } 1) + (0 \text{ or } 1) = 8,$$

thus eliminating several options for pieces 2 and 3. More precisely, *piece 2 must touch at least one vertex; piece 3 must be placed along an edge.*

Looking next at the totals for $v + f$, which are the "black" cubies if we color them alternately black and white with black in the corners, we must also have

$$(1 \text{ or } 2) + 2 + 3 + 2 + 2 + 2 + (1 \text{ or } 3) = 14;$$

and the only way to achieve this is with two from piece 1 and one from piece 7: *Piece 1 must occupy two black cubies, and piece 7 must occupy just one.*

We have therefore eliminated 200 of the 688 options in the list that begins with (40). And we also know that exactly five of the pieces 1, 2, 4, 5, 6, 7 occupy as many of the corner vertices as they individually can. This extra information can be encoded by introducing 13 new primary items

$$*, \quad 1+, \quad 1-, \quad 2+, \quad 2-, \quad 4+, \quad 4-, \quad 5+, \quad 5-, \quad 6+, \quad 6-, \quad 7+, \quad 7- \qquad (46)$$

and six new options

$$\begin{array}{l} \text{`* 1+ 2- 4- 5- 6- 7-'} \\ \text{`* 1- 2+ 4- 5- 6- 7-'} \\ \text{`* 1- 2- 4+ 5- 6- 7-'} \\ \text{`* 1- 2- 4- 5+ 6- 7-'} \\ \text{`* 1- 2- 4- 5- 6+ 7-'} \\ \text{`* 1- 2- 4- 5- 6- 7+'} \end{array} \qquad (47)$$

and by appending $p+$ or $p-$ to each of piece p's options that do or don't touch the most corners. For example, this new set of $6 + 488$ options for the Soma cube problem includes the following typical ways to place various pieces:

$$\begin{array}{l} \text{`1 000 001 011 1+'} \\ \text{`1 001 011 101 1-'} \\ \text{`2 000 001 002 010 2+'} \\ \text{`2 000 001 011 021 2-'} \\ \text{`3 000 001 002 011'} \\ \text{`4 000 001 011 012 4+'} \\ \text{`4 001 011 111 121 4-'} \\ \text{`5 000 001 010 110 5+'} \\ \text{`5 001 010 011 101 5-'} \\ \text{`6 000 001 010 101 6+'} \\ \text{`6 001 010 011 110 6-'} \\ \text{`7 000 001 010 100 7+'} \\ \text{`7 001 010 011 111 7-'} \end{array}$$

As before, Algorithm X finds 11,520 solutions; but now it needs only 108 megamems to do so. Each of the new options is used in at least 21 of the solutions, hence we've removed all of the "fat" in the original set. [This instructive analysis of Soma is due to M. J. T. Guy, R. K. Guy, and J. H. Conway in 1961. See Berlekamp, Conway, and Guy, *Winning Ways*, second edition (2004), 845–847.]

To reduce the number of solutions, using symmetry, we can force piece 3 to occupy the cells $\{000, 001, 002, 011\}$ (thus saving a factor of 24), and we can remove all options for piece 7 that use a cell ijk with $k = 2$ (saving an additional factor of 2). From the remaining 455 options, Algorithm X needs just 2 megamems to generate all 240 of the essentially distinct solutions.

The seven Soma pieces are amazingly versatile, and so are the other polycubes of small sizes. Exercises 324–350 explore some of their remarkable properties, together with historical references.

Color-controlled covering. *Take a break!* Before reading any further, please spend a minute or two solving the "word search" puzzle in Fig. 71. Comparatively mindless puzzles like this one provide a low-stress way to sharpen your word-recognition skills. It can be solved easily — for instance, by making eight passes over the array — and the solution can be found in Fig. 72 on the next page.

Fig. 71. Find the mathematicians*:

Put ovals around the following names where they appear in the 15×15 array shown here, reading either forward or backward or upward or downward, or diagonally in any direction. After you've finished, the leftover letters will form a hidden message. (The solution appears on the next page.)

O	T	H	E	S	C	A	T	A	L	A	N	D	A	U
T	S	E	A	P	U	S	T	H	O	R	S	R	O	F
T	L	S	E	E	A	Y	R	R	L	Y	H	A	P	A
E	P	E	A	R	E	L	R	G	O	U	E	M	S	I
N	N	A	R	R	C	V	L	T	R	T	A	A	M	A
I	T	H	U	O	T	E	K	W	I	A	N	D	E	M
L	A	N	T	N	B	S	I	M	I	C	M	A	A	W
L	G	D	N	A	R	T	R	E	B	L	I	H	C	E
E	R	E	C	I	Z	E	C	E	P	T	N	E	D	Y
M	E	A	R	S	H	R	H	L	I	P	K	A	T	H
E	J	E	N	S	E	N	H	R	I	E	O	N	E	T
H	S	U	I	N	E	B	O	R	F	E	W	N	A	R
T	M	A	R	K	O	F	F	O	F	C	S	O	K	M
P	L	U	T	E	R	P	F	R	O	E	K	G	R	A
G	M	M	I	N	S	E	J	T	L	E	I	T	S	G

ABEL	HENSEL	MELLIN
BERTRAND	HERMITE	MINKOWSKI
BOREL	HILDERT	NETTO
CANTOR	HURWITZ	PERRON
CATALAN	JENSEN	RUNGE
FROBENIUS	KIRCHHOFF	STERN
GLAISHER	KNOPP	STIELTJES
GRAM	LANDAU	SYLVESTER
HADAMARD	MARKOFF	WEIERSTRASS

Our goal in this section is not to discuss how to *solve* such puzzles; instead, we shall consider how to *create* them. It's by no means easy to pack those 27 names into the box in such a way that their 184 characters occupy only 135 cells, with eight directions well mixed. How can that be done with reasonable efficiency?

For this purpose we shall extend the idea of exact covering by introducing *color codes*. Let's imagine that each cell ij of the array is to be "colored" with one of the letters $\{A, \ldots, Z\}$. Then the task of creating such a puzzle is essentially to choose from among a vast set of options

'ABEL 00:A 01:B 02:E 03:L'
'ABEL 00:A 10:B 20:E 30:L'
'ABEL 00:A 11:B 22:E 33:L'
'ABEL 00:L 01:E 02:B 03:A'
$\cdot \quad \cdot \quad \cdot \quad \cdot$
'WEIERSTRASS e4:S e5:S e6:A e7:R e8:T e9:S ea:R eb:E ec:I ed:E ee:W'

$$(48)$$

in such a way that the following conditions are satisfied:

i) Exactly one option must be chosen for each of the 27 mathematicians' names.

ii) The chosen options must give consistent colors to each of the 15×15 cells ij.

---

* The journal *Acta Mathematica* celebrated its 21st birthday by publishing a special *Table Générale des Tomes 1–35*, edited by Marcel Riesz (Uppsala: 1913), 179 pp. It contained a complete list of all papers published so far in that journal, together with portraits and brief biographies of all the authors. The 27 mathematicians mentioned in Fig. 71 are those who were subsequently mentioned in Volumes 1, 2, or 3 of *The Art of Computer Programming* — except for people like MITTAG-LEFFLER or POINCARÉ, whose names contain special characters.

Fig. 72. Solution to the puzzle of the hidden mathematicians (Fig. 71). Notice that the central letter R actually participates in six different names:

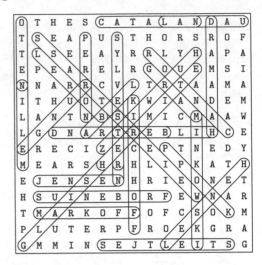

BERTRAND
GLAISHER
HERMITE
HILBERT
KIRCHHOFF
WEIERSTRASS

The T to its left participates in five.

Here's what the leftover letters say:

These authors of early papers in *Acta Mathematica* were cited years later in *The Art of Computer Programming*.

There also are informal constraints: It's desirable to have many shared letters between names, and to intermix the various directions, so that the puzzle has plenty of variety and perhaps a few surprises. But conditions (i) and (ii) are the important criteria for a computer to consider; the auxiliary informalities are best handled interactively, with human guidance.

Notice that the color constraints (ii) are significantly different from the name constraints (i). Several *distinct* options are allowed to specify the color of the *same* cell, as long as those specifications don't conflict with each other.

Let us therefore define a new problem, *exact covering with colors*, or XCC for short. As before, we're given a set of items, of which N_1 are primary and $N - N_1$ are secondary. We're also given a family of M options, each of which includes at least one primary item. The new rule is that a *color* is assigned to the secondary items of each option. The new task is to find all choices of options such that

   i) every primary item occurs exactly once; and
   ii) every secondary item has been assigned at most one color.

The primary items are required; the secondary items are elective.

Color assignments are denoted by a colon; for example, '00:A' in (48) means that color A is assigned to the secondary item 00. When a secondary item of an option is *not* followed by a colon, it is implicitly assigned a *unique* color, which doesn't match the color of any other option. Therefore the ordinary exact cover problems that we've been studying so far, in which secondary items don't explicitly receive colors but cannot be chosen in more than one option, are just special cases of the XCC problem, even though nothing about color was mentioned.

A tremendous variety of combinatorial problems can be expressed readily in the XCC framework. And there's good news: The dancing links technique works beautifully with such problems! Indeed, we will see that this considerably more general problem can be solved with only a few small extensions to Algorithm X.

The nodes of Algorithm X have just three fields: TOP, ULINK, and DLINK. We now add a fourth field, COLOR; this field is set to the positive value c when the node represents an item that has explicitly been assigned color c. Consider, for example, the following toy problem with three primary items $\{p, q, r\}$ and two secondary items $\{x, y\}$, where the options are

$$
\begin{array}{l}
\text{`p\quad q\quad x\quad y:A' ;} \\
\text{`p\quad r\quad x:A\quad y' ;} \\
\text{`p\quad x:B' ;} \\
\text{`q\quad x:A' ;} \\
\text{`r\quad y:B' .}
\end{array} \qquad (49)
$$

Table 2 shows how it would be represented in memory, extending the conventions of Table 1. Notice that COLOR $= 0$ when no color has been specified. The COLOR fields of the header nodes (nodes 1–5 in this example) need not be initialized because they're never examined except in printouts (see the answer to exercise 12). The COLOR fields of the spacer nodes (nodes 6, 11, 16, 19, 22, 25) are unimportant, except that they must be nonnegative.

Table 2

THE INITIAL CONTENTS OF MEMORY CORRESPONDING TO (49)

i:	0	1	2	3	4	5	6
NAME(i):	—	p	q	r	x	y	—
LLINK(i):	3	0	1	2	6	4	5
RLINK(i):	1	2	3	0	5	6	4

x:	0	1	2	3	4	5	6
LEN(x), TOP(x):	—	3	2	2	4	3	0
ULINK(x):	—	17	20	23	21	24	—
DLINK(x):	—	7	8	13	9	10	10
COLOR(x):	—	—	—	—	—	—	0

x:	7	8	9	10	11	12	13
TOP(x):	1	2	4	5	−1	1	3
ULINK(x):	1	2	4	5	7	7	3
DLINK(x):	12	20	14	15	15	17	23
COLOR(x):	0	0	0	A	0	0	0

x:	14	15	16	17	18	19	20
TOP(x):	4	5	−2	1	4	−3	2
ULINK(x):	9	10	12	12	14	17	8
DLINK(x):	18	24	18	1	21	21	2
COLOR(x):	A	0	0	0	B	0	0

x:	21	22	23	24	25		
TOP(x):	4	−4	3	5	−5		
ULINK(x):	18	20	13	15	23		
DLINK(x):	4	24	3	5	—		
COLOR(x):	A	0	0	B	0		

It's easy to see how these COLOR fields can be used to get the desired effect: When an option is chosen, we "purify" any secondary items that it names, by effectively removing all options that have conflicting colors. One slightly subtle point arises, because we don't want to waste time purifying a list that has already been culled. The trick is to set COLOR$(x) \leftarrow -1$ in every node x that's already known to have the correct color, except in nodes that have already been hidden.

Thus we want to upgrade the original operations cover(i) and hide(p) in (12) and (13), as well as their counterparts uncover(i) and unhide(p) in (14) and (15), in order to incorporate color controls. The changes are simple:

$\text{cover}'(i)$ is like $\text{cover}(i)$, but it calls $\text{hide}'(p)$ instead of $\text{hide}(p)$; (50)

$\text{hide}'(p)$ is like $\text{hide}(p)$, but it ignores node q when $\text{COLOR}(q) < 0$; (51)

$\text{uncover}'(i)$ is like $\text{uncover}(i)$, but it calls $\text{unhide}'(p)$ instead of $\text{unhide}(p)$; (52)

$\text{unhide}'(p)$ is like $\text{unhide}(p)$, but it ignores node q when $\text{COLOR}(q) < 0$. (53)

Our colorful algorithm also introduces two new operations and their inverses:

$$\text{commit}(p, j) = \begin{cases} \text{If } \text{COLOR}(p) = 0, \text{ cover}'(j); \\ \text{if } \text{COLOR}(p) > 0, \text{ purify}(p). \end{cases} \qquad (54)$$

$$\text{purify}(p) = \begin{cases} \text{Set } c \leftarrow \text{COLOR}(p), \ i \leftarrow \text{TOP}(p), \ \text{COLOR}(i) \leftarrow c, \ q \leftarrow \text{DLINK}(i). \\ \text{While } q \neq i, \text{ do the following and set } q \leftarrow \text{DLINK}(q): \\ \qquad \text{if } \text{COLOR}(q) = c, \text{ set } \text{COLOR}(q) \leftarrow -1; \\ \qquad \text{otherwise } \text{hide}'(q). \end{cases} \qquad (55)$$

$$\text{uncommit}(p, j) = \begin{cases} \text{If } \text{COLOR}(p) = 0, \text{ uncover}'(j); \\ \text{if } \text{COLOR}(p) > 0, \text{ unpurify}(p). \end{cases} \qquad (56)$$

$$\text{unpurify}(p) = \begin{cases} \text{Set } c \leftarrow \text{COLOR}(p), \ i \leftarrow \text{TOP}(p), \ q \leftarrow \text{ULINK}(i). \\ \text{While } q \neq i, \text{ do the following and set } q \leftarrow \text{ULINK}(q): \\ \qquad \text{if } \text{COLOR}(q) < 0, \text{ set } \text{COLOR}(q) \leftarrow c; \\ \qquad \text{otherwise } \text{unhide}'(q). \end{cases} \qquad (57)$$

Otherwise Algorithm C is almost word-for-word identical to Algorithm X.

Algorithm C (*Exact covering with colors*). This algorithm visits all solutions to a given XCC problem, using the same conventions as Algorithm X.

C1. [Initialize.] Set the problem up in memory, as in Table 2. (See exercise 8.) Also set N to the number of items, Z to the last spacer address, and $l \leftarrow 0$.

C2. [Enter level l.] If $\text{RLINK}(0) = 0$ (hence all items have been covered), visit the solution that is specified by $x_0 x_1 \ldots x_{l-1}$ and go to C8. (See exercise 13.)

C3. [Choose i.] At this point the items $i_1, \ldots, i_t$ still need to be covered, where $i_1 = \text{RLINK}(0)$, $i_{j+1} = \text{RLINK}(i_j)$, $\text{RLINK}(i_t) = 0$. Choose one of them, and call it i. (The MRV heuristic of exercise 9 often works well in practice.)

C4. [Cover i.] Cover item i using (50), and set $x_l \leftarrow \text{DLINK}(i)$.

C5. [Try x_l.] If $x_l = i$, go to C7 (we've tried all options for i). Otherwise set $p \leftarrow x_l + 1$, and do the following while $p \neq x_l$: Set $j \leftarrow \text{TOP}(p)$; if $j \leq 0$, set $p \leftarrow \text{ULINK}(p)$; otherwise $\text{commit}(p, j)$ and set $p \leftarrow p + 1$. (This commits the items $\neq i$ in the option that contains x_l.) Set $l \leftarrow l+1$ and return to C2.

C6. [Try again.] Set $p \leftarrow x_l - 1$, and do the following while $p \neq x_l$: Set $j \leftarrow \text{TOP}(p)$; if $j \leq 0$, set $p \leftarrow \text{DLINK}(p)$; otherwise $\text{uncommit}(p, j)$ and set $p \leftarrow p - 1$. (This uncommits the items $\neq i$ in the option that contains x_l, using the reverse order.) Set $i \leftarrow \text{TOP}(x_l)$, $x_l \leftarrow \text{DLINK}(x_l)$, and return to C5.

C7. [Backtrack.] Uncover item i using (52).

C8. [Leave level l.] Terminate if $l = 0$. Otherwise set $l \leftarrow l - 1$ and go to C6. ∎

Algorithm C applies directly to several problems that we've already discussed in previous sections. For example, it readily generates word rectangles, as well as intriguing patterns of words that have more intricate structure (see exercises 87–93). We can use it to find all de Bruijn cycles, and their two-dimensional counterparts (see exercises 94–97). The extra generality of exact covering options also invites us to impose additional constraints for special applications. Furthermore, Algorithm C facilitates experiments with the tetrad tiles that we studied in Section 2.3.4.3 (see exercises 120 and 121).

The great combinatorialist P. A. MacMahon introduced several families of colorful geometric patterns that continued to fascinate him throughout his life. For example, in U.K. Patent 3927 of 1892, written with J. R. J. Jocelyn, he considered the 24 different triangles that can be made with four colors on their edges,

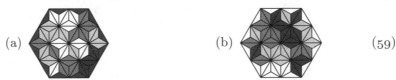

$$(58)$$

and showed two ways in which they could be arranged to form a hexagon with matching colors at adjacent edges and with solid colors on the outer boundary:

$$(59)$$

(Notice that chiral pairs, like △ and △ in (58), are considered to be distinct; MacMahon's tiles can be rotated, but they can't be "flipped over.")

> *Four suitable colours are black, white, red, and blue,*
> *as they are readily distinguishable at night.*
> — P. A. MACMAHON, *New Mathematical Pastimes* (1921)

Let's assume that the boundary is supposed to be all white, as in pattern (59b). There are millions of ways to satisfy this condition; but every really distinct solution is counted 72 times, because the hexagon has 12 symmetries under rotation and reflection, and because the three nonwhite colors can be permuted in $3! = 6$ ways. We can remove the hexagon symmetries by fixing the position of the all-white triangle (see exercise 119). And the color symmetries can be removed by using an interesting extension of Algorithm C, which reduces the number of solutions by a factor of $d!$ when the options are symmetrical with respect to d colors (see exercise 122). In this way all of the solutions — can you guess how many? — can actually be found with only 5.2 Gμ of computation (see exercise 126).

MacMahon went on to study many other matching problems with these triangles, as well as with similar sets of tiles that are based on squares, hexagons, and other shapes. He also considered three-dimensional arrangements of colored cubes, which are supposed to match where they touch. Exercises 127–148 are devoted to some of the captivating questions that have arisen from this work.

Introducing multiplicity. We've now seen from numerous examples that Algorithm C — which extends Algorithm X and solves arbitrary XCC problems — is enormously versatile. In fact, there's a sense in which *every* constraint satisfaction problem is a special case of an XCC problem (see exercise 100).

But we can extend Algorithm C even further, again without substantial changes, so that it goes well beyond the original notion of exact covering. For example, let's consider Robert Wainwright's "partridge puzzle" (1981), which was inspired by the well-known fact that the sum of the first n cubes is a perfect square:

$$1^3 + 2^3 + \cdots + n^3 = N^2, \quad \text{where } N = 1 + 2 + \cdots + n. \tag{60}$$

Wainwright wondered if this relation could be verified geometrically, by taking one square of size 1×1, two squares of size 2×2, ..., n squares of size $n \times n$, and packing them all into a big square of size $N \times N$. (We know from exercise 1.2.1–8 that $4k$ squares of each size $k \times k$ can be packed into a $2N \times 2N$ square. But Wainwright hoped for a more direct corroboration of (60).) He proved the task impossible for $2 \le n \le 5$, but found a perfect packing when $n = 12$; so he thought of the 12 days of Christmas, and named his puzzle accordingly (see exercise 154).

This partridge puzzle is easily expressed in terms of options that involve n items #k for $1 \le k \le n$, as well as N^2 items ij for $0 \le i, j < N$. By analogy with what we did with pentominoes in (37), the options are

$$\text{`#}k\ ij\ i(j{+}1)\ \ldots\ i(j{+}k{-}1)\ (i{+}1)j\ (i{+}1)(j{+}1)\ \ldots\ (i{+}k{-}1)(j{+}k{-}1)\text{'} \tag{61}$$

for $1 \le k \le n$ and $0 \le i, j \le N - k$. (Exactly $(N + 1 - k)^2$ options involve #k, and each of them names $1 + k^2$ items.) For example, the options when $n = 2$ are

'#1 00', '#1 01', '#1 02', '#1 10', '#1 11', '#1 12', '#1 20', '#1 21', '#1 22',

'#2 00 01 10 11', '#2 01 02 11 12', '#2 10 11 20 21', '#2 11 12 21 22'.

As before, we want to cover each of the N^2 cells ij exactly once. But there's a difference: We now want to cover primary item #k exactly k times, not just once.

That's a rather big difference. But in Algorithm M below, we'll see that the dancing links approach can handle it. For example, that algorithm can show that the partridge puzzle has no perfect packings for $n = 6$ or $n = 7$; but it finds thousands of surprising solutions when $n = 8$, such as

$$\tag{62}$$

When we first defined exact cover problems, near the beginning of this section, we considered $M \times N$ matrices of 0s and 1s, such as (5). In matrix terms, the task was to find all subsets of the rows whose sum is $11\ldots1$. Algorithm M is going to do much more: It will find all subsets of rows whose sum is $v_1 v_2 \ldots v_N$, where $v_1 v_2 \ldots v_N$ is *any* desired vector of multiplicities.

In fact, Algorithm M will go further yet, by allowing *intervals* $[u_j \mathinner{\ldotp\ldotp} v_j]$ to be prescribed for each multiplicity. It will actually solve the general *MCC problem*, "multiple covering with colors," which is defined as follows: There are N items, of which N_1 are primary and $N - N_1$ are secondary. Each primary item j for $1 \le j \le N_1$ is assigned an interval $[u_j \mathinner{\ldotp\ldotp} v_j]$ of permissible values, where $0 \le u_j \le v_j$ and $v_j > 0$. There also are M options, each of which includes at least one primary item. A color is assigned to the secondary items of each option; a "blank" color is understood to represent a unique color that appears nowhere else. The task is to find all subsets of options such that

  i) each primary item j occurs at least u_j times and at most v_j times;

  ii) every secondary item has been assigned at most one color.

Thus every XCC problem is the special case $u_j = v_j = 1$ of an MCC problem.

Indeed, the MCC problem is *extremely* general! For example, its special case $u_j = 1$ and $v_j = M$, without secondary items, is the classical not-necessarily-exact *cover problem*, in which we simply require each item to appear in *at least* one option. Section 7.2.2.6 will be entirely devoted to the cover problem.

Let's confine our attention here to a few more examples of the MCC problem, in preparation for Algorithm M. In the first place, we can tackle a refined version of Wainwright's partridge puzzle: "Pack at most k squares of size $k \times k$, for $1 \le k \le n$, into an $N \times N$ square, without overlapping, so that as many as possible of the N^2 cells are covered." (As before, $N = 1 + 2 + \cdots + n$.) We know from (62) that the entire square can be covered when $n = 8$; but smaller cases are another story. Solutions for $2 \le n \le 5$ are readily found by hand:

$$(63)$$

And to prove that every packing for $n = 5$ must leave at least 13 cells vacant, Algorithm M will show that the MCC problem (61) has no solutions when items #1, #2, #3 are respectively given the multiplicities $[0\mathinner{\ldotp\ldotp}13]$, $[0\mathinner{\ldotp\ldotp}2]$, $[0\mathinner{\ldotp\ldotp}3]$ instead of 1, 2, 3. Exercise 157 constructs optimum packings when $n = 6$ and $n = 7$, thereby settling all small cases of the partridge puzzle.

Next, let's consider an MCC problem of quite a different kind: "Place m queens so that they control all cells of an $n \times n$ chessboard." (The classic 5-queens problem — which should be distinguished from the '5 queens problem' considered earlier — is the special case $m = 5$, $n = 8$.) Exercise 7.1.4–241 discusses the history of this problem, which goes back to a remarkable book by de Jaenisch (1863).

We can solve it, MCC-wise, by introducing $n^2 + 1$ primary items, namely the pairs ij for $0 \le i, j < n$ and the special item #, together with n^2 options:

$$\text{`\# } ij \; i_1 j_1 \; i_2 j_2 \; \ldots \; i_t j_t \text{'} \quad \text{for } 0 \le i, j < n, \tag{64}$$

where $i_1 j_1, i_2 j_2, \ldots, i_t j_t$ are the cells attacked by a queen on ij. Each cell ij is assigned the multiplicity $[1 \mathinner{.\,.} m]$; item # gets multiplicity m.

From this specification Algorithm M will readily find all 4860 solutions to the 5-queens problem, after 13 gigamems of computation. For example, it begins with 22 ways to cover the corner cell 00. If it puts a queen there, it has 22 ways to cover cell 17; and so on. The branching factor at each step tends to decrease rapidly after three queens have been placed.

The beauty of the MCC setup in (64) is that we can solve many related problems by making simple changes to the specifications. For example, by retaining only the 36 options for $1 \le i, j \le 6$, we could find the 284 solutions that place no queens at the edges of the board. Or by removing the 16 options for $2 \le i, j \le 5$, we would discover that exactly 880 of the solutions place no queens near the middle. Exactly 88 solutions avoid the central two rows and the central two columns. Exactly 200 solutions put all five queens on "black" cells (with $i + j$ even). Exactly 90 avoid the upper left and lower right quadrants. Exactly 2 solutions (can you find them?) place all five queens in the top half of the board.

By changing the multiplicities in the bottom row from $[1 \mathinner{.\,.} 5]$ to 1, we get 18 solutions for which every cell in that row is attacked just once. Or, changing the central 16 multiplicities to $[2 \mathinner{.\,.} 5]$ yields 48 solutions for which every cell near the center is attacked at least twice. Changing all the cell multiplicities to $[1 \mathinner{.\,.} 4]$ reduces the number of solutions from 4860 to 3248; changing them all to $[1 \mathinner{.\,.} 3]$ reduces it to 96. Exercise 161 illustrates several of the less obvious possibilities.

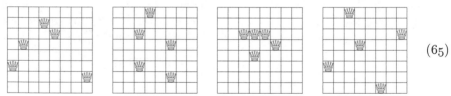

$$(65)$$

The examples of MCC problems that we've seen so far have involved primary items only. Secondary items, and their color controls, add new dimensions and extend the range of applications enormously. Consider, for example, the *word rectangles* that we investigated briefly in Section 7.2.2. Here's a 4×5 word rectangle that uses only nine distinct letters of the alphabet:

$$\begin{matrix} \text{L} & \text{A} & \text{B} & \text{E} & \text{L} \\ \text{A} & \text{B} & \text{I} & \text{D} & \text{E} \\ \text{S} & \text{L} & \text{A} & \text{I} & \text{N} \\ \text{T} & \text{E} & \text{S} & \text{T} & \text{S} \end{matrix}$$

Can we find one that uses only *eight* distinct letters, while sticking to common words? (More precisely, is there such a rectangle whose columns are chosen from the most common 1000 four-letter words of English, and whose rows belong to WORDS(2000), the curated collection from the Stanford GraphBase?)

The answer is yes, and in fact there are six solutions:

```
S T R U T    E A S E D    W A D E D    R A D A R    L L A M A    S C A R S
T E A S E    A G I L E    A R E N A    A R E N A    E A G E R    C O C O A
E A T E N    S E N S E    S E E D S    S E A T S    S T E A M    A R R A Y
P R E S S    E D G E D    H A R S H    H A R S H    T E S T S    R E E D S
```
$$(66)$$

One way to find them is to set up an MCC problem in which the primary items are A_0, A_1, A_2, A_3, D_0, D_1, D_2, D_3, D_4, #A, #B, ..., #Z, #; they all have multiplicity 1 except that # has multiplicity 8. There also are secondary items A, B, ..., Z, and ij for $0 \le i < 4$, $0 \le j < 5$. The letter-counting is handled by $2 \cdot 26$ short options:

$$\text{'#A A:0', '#A A:1 #'; '#B B:0', '#B B:1 #'; ...; '#Z Z:0', '#Z Z:1 #'.} \qquad (67)$$

Then each legal 5-letter word $c_1 c_2 c_3 c_4 c_5$ yields four options, 'A_i $i0{:}c_1$ $i1{:}c_2$ $i2{:}c_3$ $i3{:}c_4$ $i4{:}c_5$ $c_1{:}1$ $c_2{:}1$ $c_3{:}1$ $c_4{:}1$ $c_5{:}1$', for $0 \le i < 4$; each legal 4-letter word $c_1 c_2 c_3 c_4$ yields five options, 'D_j $0j{:}c_1$ $1j{:}c_2$ $2j{:}c_3$ $3j{:}c_4$ $c_1{:}1$ $c_2{:}1$ $c_3{:}1$ $c_4{:}1$', for $0 \le j < 5$. (Letters that occur more than once in a word are listed only once.)

For example, one of the options chosen for the first solution in (66) is 'A_3 30:P 31:R 32:E 33:S 34:S P:1 R:1 E:1 S:1'; it forces the options '#P P:1 #', '#R R:1 #', '#E E:1 #', '#S S:1 #' to be chosen too, thus contributing four to the number of chosen options that contain #.

By the way, when Algorithm M is applied to these options, it's important to use the "nonsharp preference heuristic" discussed in exercise 10 and its answer. Otherwise the algorithm will foolishly make binary branches on the items #A, ..., #Z, before trying out actual words. A 1000-way branch on D_0 is much better than a 2-way branch on #Q, in this situation.

*A new dance step. In order to implement multiplicity, we need to update the data structures in a new way. Suppose, for example, that there are five options available for some primary item p, and suppose they are represented in nodes a, b, c, d, and e. Then p's vertical list of active options has the following links:

x:	p	a	b	c	d	e	
ULINK(x):	e	p	a	b	c	d	(68)
DLINK(x):	a	b	c	d	e	p	

If the multiplicity of p is 3, there are $\binom{5}{3} = 10$ ways to choose three of the five options; but we do *not* want to make a 10-way branch! Instead, each branch of Algorithm M below chooses only the *first* of the options that will appear in the solution. Then it reduces the problem recursively; the reduced problem will have a shorter list for p, from which two further options should be selected. Since we must choose either a, b, or c as the first option, the algorithm will therefore begin with a 3-way branch. For example, if b is chosen to be first, the reduced problem will ask for two of options $\{c, d, e\}$ to be chosen eventually.

The algorithm will recursively find all solutions to that reduced problem. But it won't necessarily begin by branching again on the *same* item, p; some other item, q, might well have become more significant. For instance, the choice of b might have assigned color values that make $\texttt{LEN}(q) \leq 1$. (The choice of b might also have made c, d, and/or e illegal.)

The main point is that, after we've chosen the first of three options for p in the original problem, we have *not* "covered" p as we did in Algorithms X and C. Item p remains on an equal footing with all other active items of the reduced problem, so we need to modify (68) accordingly.

The operation of reducing the problem by removing an option from an item list, in the presence of multiplicity, is called "tweaking" that option. For example, just after the algorithm has chosen b as the first option for p, it will have tweaked both a and b. This operation is deceptively simple:

$$\text{tweak}(x, p) = \begin{cases} \text{hide}'(x) \text{ and set } d \leftarrow \texttt{DLINK}(x), \texttt{DLINK}(p) \leftarrow d, \\ \texttt{ULINK}(d) \leftarrow p, \texttt{LEN}(p) \leftarrow \texttt{LEN}(p) - 1. \end{cases} \quad (69)$$

(See (51). We will tweak(x,p) only when $x = \texttt{DLINK}(p)$ and $p = \texttt{ULINK}(x)$.) Notice that tweaking x does more than hiding x, but it does less than covering p.

Eventually the algorithm will have tried each of a, b, and c as p's first option, and it will want to backtrack and undo the tweaking. The actions tweak(a,p), tweak(b,p), tweak(c,p) will have clobbered most of the original uplinks in (68):

x:	p	a	b	c	d	e	
$\texttt{ULINK}(x)$:	e	p	p	p	p	d	(70)
$\texttt{DLINK}(x)$:	d	b	c	d	e	p	

Unfortunately, this residual data isn't sufficient for us to restore the original state, because we've lost track of node a. But if we had recorded the value of a when we began, we would be in good shape, because a pointer to node a together with the DLINKs in (70) would now lead us to node b, then to c, and then to d.

Therefore the algorithm maintains an array $\texttt{FT}[l]$, to remember the locations of the "first tweaks" that were made at every level l. And it adds a new dance step, "untweaking," to its repertoire of link manipulations:

$$\text{untweak}(l) = \begin{cases} \text{Set } a \leftarrow \texttt{FT}[l], p \leftarrow (a \leq N? \ a: \texttt{TOP}(a)), x \leftarrow a, y \leftarrow p; \\ \text{set } z \leftarrow \texttt{DLINK}(p), \texttt{DLINK}(p) \leftarrow x, k \leftarrow 0; \\ \text{while } x \neq z, \text{ set } \texttt{ULINK}(x) \leftarrow y \text{ and } k \leftarrow k+1, \\ \quad \text{unhide}'(x), \text{ and set } y \leftarrow x, x \leftarrow \texttt{DLINK}(x); \\ \text{finally set } \texttt{ULINK}(z) \leftarrow y \text{ and } \texttt{LEN}(p) \leftarrow \texttt{LEN}(p) + k. \end{cases} \quad (71)$$

(See exercise 163. This computation relies on a surprising fact proved in exercise 2(a), namely that unhiding can safely be done in the same order as hiding.)

The same mechanism can be used when the specified multiplicity is an *interval* instead of a single number. For example, suppose item p in the example above is required to occur in either 2, 3, or 4 options, not exactly 3. Then the first option chosen must be a, b, c, or d; and the reduced problem will ask p to occur in either 1, 2, or 3 of the options that remain. Eventually the algorithm will resort to untweaking, after a, b, c, and d have all been tweaked and explored.

Similarly, if p's multiplicity has been specified to be either 0, 1, or 2, the algorithm below will tweak each of a through e in turn. It will also run though all solutions that omit *all* of p's options, before finally untweaking and backtracking.

A special case arises, however, when p's multiplicity has been specified to be either 0 or 1. In such cases we're not allowed to choose options b, c, d, or e after option a has been chosen. Therefore it's important to invoke cover$'(p)$, as in Algorithm C, instead of hiding one option at a time. (See (50).) The individual options of p are then tweaked, to remove them one by one from the active list; this tweaking uses the special operation tweak$'(x, p)$, which is like tweak(x, p) in (69) except that it omits the operation hide$'(x)$, because hiding was already done when p was covered. Finally, the case of 0-or-1 multiplicity eventually concludes by invoking the routine untweak$'(l)$, which is like untweak(l) in (71) except that (i) it omits unhide$'(x)$, and (ii) it calls uncover$'(p)$ after restoring LEN(p).

We're ready now to write Algorithm M, except that we need a way to represent the multiplicities in the data structures. For this purpose every primary item has two new fields, SLACK and BOUND. Suppose the desired multiplicity of p is in the interval $[u..v]$, where $0 \leq u \leq v$ and $v \neq 0$; Algorithms X and C correspond to the case $u = v = 1$. Then we set

$$\text{SLACK}(p) \leftarrow v - u, \qquad \text{BOUND}(p) \leftarrow v \qquad (72)$$

when the algorithm begins. The value of SLACK(p) will never be changed. But BOUND(p) will decrease dynamically, as we reduce the problem, so that we will never choose more options for p than its current bound.

Algorithm M (*Covering with multiplicities and colors*). This algorithm visits all solutions to a given MCC problem, extending Algorithms X and C.

M1. [Initialize.] Set the problem up in memory as in step C1 of Algorithm C, with the addition of multiplicity specifications (72). Also set N to the number of items, N_1 to the number of primary items, Z to the last spacer address, and $l \leftarrow 0$.

M2. [Enter level l.] If RLINK$(0) = 0$ (hence all items have been covered), visit the solution that is specified by $x_0 x_1 \ldots x_{l-1}$ and go to M9. (See exercise 164.)

M3. [Choose i.] At this point the items $i_1, \ldots, i_t$ still need to be covered, where $i_1 = \text{RLINK}(0)$, $i_{j+1} = \text{RLINK}(i_j)$, RLINK$(i_t) = 0$. Choose one of them, and call it i. (The MRV heuristic of exercise 166 often works well in practice.) If the branching degree θ_i is zero (see exercise 166), go to M9.

M4. [Prepare to branch on i.] Set $x_l \leftarrow \text{DLINK}(i)$ and BOUND$(i) \leftarrow \text{BOUND}(i) - 1$. If BOUND$(i)$ is now zero, cover item i using (50). If BOUND$(i) \neq 0$ or SLACK$(i) \neq 0$, set FT$[l] \leftarrow x_l$.

M5. [Possibly tweak x_l.] If BOUND$(i) = \text{SLACK}(i) = 0$, go to M6 if $x_l \neq i$, to M8 if $x_l = i$. (That case is like Algorithm C.) Otherwise if LEN$(i) \leq \text{BOUND}(i) - \text{SLACK}(i)$, go to M8 (list i is too short). Otherwise if $x_l \neq i$, call tweak(x_l, i) (see (69)), or tweak$'(x_l, i)$ if BOUND$(i) = 0$. Otherwise if BOUND$(i) \neq 0$, set $p \leftarrow \text{LLINK}(i)$, $q \leftarrow \text{RLINK}(i)$, RLINK$(p) \leftarrow q$, LLINK$(q) \leftarrow p$.

M6. [Try x_l.] If $x_l \neq i$, set $p \leftarrow x_l + 1$, and do the following while $p \neq x_l$: Set $j \leftarrow \text{TOP}(p)$; if $j \leq 0$, set $p \leftarrow \text{ULINK}(p)$; otherwise if $j \leq N_1$, set BOUND$(j) \leftarrow \text{BOUND}(j) - 1$, $p \leftarrow p + 1$, and cover$'(j)$ if BOUND(j) is now 0;

otherwise commit(p, j) and set $p \leftarrow p+1$. (This loop covers or commits the items $\neq i$ in the option that contains x_l.) Set $l \leftarrow l+1$ and return to M2.

M7. [Try again.] Set $p \leftarrow x_l - 1$, and do the following steps while $p \neq x_l$: Set $j \leftarrow$ TOP(p); if $j \leq 0$, set $p \leftarrow$ DLINK(p); otherwise if $j \leq N_1$, set BOUND$(j) \leftarrow$ BOUND$(j) + 1$, $p \leftarrow p - 1$, and uncover$'(j)$ if BOUND(j) is now 1; otherwise uncommit(p, j) and set $p \leftarrow p - 1$. (This loop uncovers or uncommits the items $\neq i$ in the option that contains x_l, using the reverse order.) Set $x_l \leftarrow$ DLINK(x_l) and return to M5.

M8. [Restore i.] If BOUND(i) = SLACK(i) = 0, uncover item i using (52). Otherwise call untweak(l) (see (71)), or untweak$'(l)$ if BOUND(i) = 0. Set BOUND$(i) \leftarrow$ BOUND$(i) + 1$.

M9. [Leave level l.] Terminate if $l = 0$. Otherwise set $l \leftarrow l - 1$. If $x_l \leq N$, set $i \leftarrow x_l$, $p \leftarrow$ LLINK(i), $q \leftarrow$ RLINK(i), RLINK$(p) \leftarrow$ LLINK$(q) \leftarrow i$, and go to M8. (That reactivates i.) Otherwise set $i \leftarrow$ TOP(x_l) and go to M7. ∎

*Analysis of Algorithm X. Now let's get quantitative, and see what we can actually *prove* about the running time of these algorithms.

For simplicity, we'll ignore color constraints and look only at Algorithm X, as it finds all solutions to an exact cover problem, where the problem is specified in terms of an $M \times N$ matrix A of 0s and 1s such as (5).

We'll assume that the problem is *strict*, in the sense that no two rows of the matrix are identical, and no two columns of the matrix are identical. For if two or more rows or columns are equal, we need keep only one of them; it's easy to relate all solutions of the original problem A to the solutions of this reduced problem A'. (See exercise 179.)

Our first goal will be to find an upper bound on the number of nodes in the search tree, as a function of the number of rows of A (the number of options). This upper bound grows exponentially, because the exact cover problem can have lots of solutions; but we'll see that it can't actually be extremely large.

For this purpose we'll define the *doomsday function* $D(n)$, which will have the property that the search tree for every strict exact cover problem with n options has at most $D(n)$ nodes, when Algorithm X uses the MRV heuristic in step X3.

The search tree has a root node labeled with the original matrix A, and its other nodes are defined recursively: When a node at level l is labeled with a subproblem for which step X3 makes a t-way branch, that node has t subtrees, whose roots are labeled by the reduced problem that remains after step X4 has covered item i and after step X5 has optionally covered one or more other items j, for t different choices of x_l.

Here, for example, is the complete search tree when A is the matrix of (5):

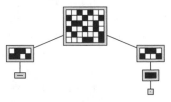

(Each matrix and submatrix in this diagram has been framed with a light-gray border. The node at bottom left illustrates a 0×1 submatrix, where the algorithm had to backtrack because it had no way to cover the remaining column. The node at bottom right illustrates a 0×0 submatrix, which happens to be a solution to the 1×2 problem above it.) We can, if we like, *reduce* all of the submatrices by eliminating repeated columns, although Algorithm X doesn't do this; then we get *strict* exact cover problems at every node of the search tree:

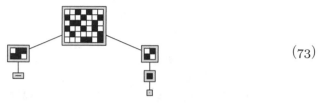

$$(73)$$

A t-way branch implies that the matrix A has a certain structure. We know that there's some column, say $i_1 = i$, that has 1 in exactly t rows, say $o_1, \ldots, o_t$, and that *every* column contains at least t 1s. When we branch on row o_p, for $1 \le p \le t$, the reduced problem that defines the pth subtree will retain all but s_p of the rows of A, where s_p is the number of rows that intersect o_p. We can order the rows so that $s_1 \le \cdots \le s_t$. For example, in (73) we have $t = 2$ and $s_1 = s_2 = 4$.

A nice thing now happens: There's always a unique index $0 \le t' \le t$ such that

$$s_p = t + p - 1, \qquad \text{for } 1 \le p \le t'. \qquad (74)$$

That is, either $s_1 > t$ and $t' = 0$; or $s_1 = t$ and $t' = 1$ and either ($t = 1$ or $s_2 > t + 1$); or $s_1 = t$ and $s_2 = t + 1$ and $t' = 2$ and either ($t = 2$ or $s_3 > t + 2$); or $\ldots$; or $s_1 = t$ and $s_2 = t + 1$ and $\ldots$ and $s_t = 2t - 1$ and $t' = t$.

Suppose, for example, that $t = 4$ and $s_1 = 4$; we must prove that $s_2 \ge 5$. Since $s_1 = 4$, row o_1 doesn't intersect any rows except $\{o_1, \ldots, o_t\}$; consequently option o_1 consists of the *single* item 'i_1'. Hence option o_2 must contain at least two items, '$i_1 \ i_2 \ldots$', otherwise the problem wouldn't be strict. This new item appears in at least 4 options, however, one of which is different from o_1. Option o_2 therefore intersects 5 or more options (including itself). QED.

Similarly, if $t = 4$ and $s_1 = 4$ and $s_2 = 5$, exercise 180 proves that $s_3 \ge 6$, and indeed it proves that even more is true. For example, if $t = t' = 4$, so that $(s_1, s_2, s_3, s_4) = (4, 5, 6, 7)$ as demanded by (74), exercise 180 proves the existence of options o_5, o_6, o_7 that have a particularly simple form:

$$o_1 = \text{'}i_1\text{'}; \quad o_2 = \text{'}i_1 \ i_2\text{'}; \quad o_3 = \text{'}i_1 \ i_2 \ i_3\text{'}; \quad o_4 = \text{'}i_1 \ i_2 \ i_3 \ i_4\text{'};$$
$$o_5 = \text{'}i_2 \ i_3 \ i_4 \ldots\text{'}; \quad o_6 = \text{'}i_3 \ i_4 \ldots\text{'}; \quad o_7 = \text{'}i_4 \ldots\text{'}. \qquad (75)$$

Okay, we're ready now to construct the promised "doomsday function" $D(n)$. It starts out very tame,

$$D(0) = D(1) = 1; \qquad (76)$$

and for convenience we set $D(n) = -\infty$ if $n < 0$. When $n \ge 2$ the definition is

$$D(n) = \max\{d(n, t, t') \mid 1 \le t < n \text{ and } 0 \le t' \le t\}, \qquad (77)$$

where $d(n, t, t')$ is an upper bound for the size of the search tree over all n-option strict exact cover problems whose parameters (74) are t and t'. One such bound,

$$d(n, t, 0) = 1 + t \cdot D(n - t - 1), \tag{78}$$

handles the case $t' = 0$, because the search tree in that case is a t-way branch

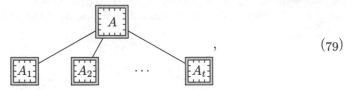
$$\tag{79}$$

and each subproblem A_p has at most $n - t - 1$ options.

The formula for $t' > 0$ is more intricate, and less obvious:

$$d(n, t, t') = t' + t' \cdot D(n - t - t' + 1) + (t - t') \cdot D(n - t - t' - 1), \quad \text{if } 1 \le t' \le t. \tag{80}$$

It can be justified by the structure theory of exercise 180, using the fact that each of the first $t' - 1$ branches is immediately followed by a 1-way branch. For example, the search tree looks like this when $t = 5$ and $t' = 3$:

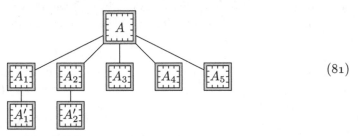
$$\tag{81}$$

Here A'_1 is the only way to cover i_2 in A_1, and A'_2 is the only way to cover i_3 in A_2. The strict problems A'_1, A'_2, and A_3 have at most $n - 7$ options; A_4 and A_5 have at most $n - 9$. Therefore (81) has at most $3 + 3D(n - 7) + 2D(n - 9)$ nodes.

With an easy computer program, (76), (78), and (80) lead to the values

$$n = 0\ 1\ 2\ 3\ 4\ 5\ 6\ 7\ 8\ 9\ 10\ 11\ 12\ 13\ 14\ 15\ 16\ 17\ 18\ 19\ 20\ 21$$
$$D(n) = 1\ 1\ 2\ 4\ 5\ 6\ 10\ 13\ 17\ 22\ 31\ 41\ 53\ 69\ 94\ 125\ 165\ 213\ 283\ 377\ 501\ 661$$

and it turns out that the maximum is attained *uniquely* when $t = 4$ and $t' = 0$, for all $n \ge 19$. Hence we have $D(n) = 1 + 4D(n - 5)$ for all sufficiently large n; and in fact exercise 181 exhibits a simple formula that expresses $D(n)$ exactly.

Theorem E. *The search tree of a strict exact cover problem with n options has $O(4^{n/5}) = O(1.31951^n)$ nodes; it might have as many as $\Omega(7^{n/8}) = \Omega(1.27537^n)$.*

Proof. The upper bound follows from exercise 181; the lower bound follows from the family of problems in exercise 182. ∎

[David Eppstein presented this theorem to the author as a birthday greeting(!); see `11011110.github.io/blog/2008/01/10/analyzing-algorithm-x.html`.]

So far we've simply been analyzing the number of nodes in Algorithm X's search tree. But some nodes might cost much more than others, because they might remove unusually many options from the currently active lists.

Therefore let's probe deeper, by studying the number of *updates* that Algorithm X makes to its data structures, namely the number of times that it uses operation (1) to remove an element from a doubly linked list. (This is also the number of times that it will eventually use operation (2) to *restore* an element.) More precisely, the number of updates is the number of times cover(i) is called, plus the number of times that hide(p) sets LEN(x) $\leftarrow$ LEN(x) $-$ 1. (See (12) and (13).) The total running time of Algorithm X, measured in mems, usually turns out to be roughly 13 times the total number of updates that it makes.

It's instructive to analyze the number of updates that are made when solving the "extreme" exact cover problems, which arise when there are n items and $2^n - 1$ options: Such problems have the most solutions and the most data, because *every* nonempty subset of the items is an option. The solutions to these extreme problems are precisely the *set partitions* — the ϖ_n possible ways to partition the items into disjoint blocks, which we studied in Section 7.2.1.5. For example, when $n = 3$ the options are '1', '2', '1 2', '3', '1 3', '2 3', '1 2 3', and there are $\varpi_3 = 5$ solutions: '1', '2', '3'; '1', '2 3'; '1 2', '3'; '1 3', '2'; '1 2 3'.

Any given item can be covered in 2^{n-1} ways; and if we cover it with an option of size k, we're left with the extreme problem on the remaining $n - k$ items. Algorithm X therefore advances 2^{n-1} times from level 0 to level 1, after which it essentially calls itself recursively. And at level 0 it performs a certain number of updates, say v_n, regardless of what strategy is used in step X3 to choose an item for branching. Therefore it makes a total of x_n updates, where

$$x_n = v_n + \binom{n-1}{0}x_{n-1} + \binom{n-1}{1}x_{n-2} + \cdots + \binom{n-1}{n-1}x_0. \qquad (82)$$

The solution to this recurrence is $x_0 = v_0$, $x_1 = v_0 + v_1$, $x_2 = 2v_0 + v_1 + v_2$, and in general $x_n = \sum_{k=0}^{n} a_{nk}v_k$, where the matrix (a_{nk}) is

$$
\begin{pmatrix}
1 & 0 & 0 & 0 & 0 & 0 & 0 & \cdots \\
1 & 1 & 0 & 0 & 0 & 0 & 0 & \cdots \\
2 & 1 & 1 & 0 & 0 & 0 & 0 & \cdots \\
5 & 3 & 1 & 1 & 0 & 0 & 0 & \cdots \\
15 & 9 & 4 & 1 & 1 & 0 & 0 & \cdots \\
52 & 31 & 14 & 5 & 1 & 1 & 0 & \cdots \\
203 & 121 & 54 & 20 & 6 & 1 & 1 & \cdots \\
 & \cdot & \cdot & \cdot & \cdot & \cdot & \cdot &
\end{pmatrix}
=
\begin{pmatrix}
1 & 0 & 0 & 0 & 0 & 0 & 0 & \cdots \\
-1 & 1 & 0 & 0 & 0 & 0 & 0 & \cdots \\
-1 & -1 & 1 & 0 & 0 & 0 & 0 & \cdots \\
-1 & -2 & -1 & 1 & 0 & 0 & 0 & \cdots \\
-1 & -3 & -3 & -1 & 1 & 0 & 0 & \cdots \\
-1 & -4 & -6 & -4 & -1 & 1 & 0 & \cdots \\
-1 & -5 & -10 & -10 & -5 & -1 & 1 & \cdots \\
 & \cdot & \cdot & \cdot & \cdot & \cdot & \cdot &
\end{pmatrix}^{-1}, \qquad (83)
$$

with rows and columns numbered from 0. The numbers a_{n0} in the left column, which solve (82) when $v_n = \delta_{n0}$, are the familiar Bell numbers ϖ_n; they enumerate the leaves in the search tree. The numbers a_{n1} in the next column, which solve (82) when $v_n = \delta_{n1}$, are the Gould numbers $\hat{\varpi}_n$; they enumerate set partitions whose last block or "tail" is a singleton, when the blocks of the partition are ordered by their least elements. In general, a_{nk} for $k > 0$ is the number of set partitions whose tail has size k. [See H. W. Gould and J. Quaintance, *Applicable Analysis and Discrete Mathematics* **1** (2007), 371–385.]

Exercise 186 proves that the actual number of updates at level 0 is

$$v_n = \big((9n - 27)4^n - (8n - 32)3^n + (36n - 36)2^n + 72 - 41\delta_{n0}\big)/72; \quad (84)$$

and exercise 187 exploits relationships between the sequences $\langle a_{nk} \rangle$ to show that

$$x_n = 22\varpi_n + 12\widehat{\varpi}_n - (\tfrac{2}{3}n - 1)3^n - \tfrac{5}{2}n2^n - 12n - 5 - 12\delta_{n1} - 18\delta_{n0}. \quad (85)$$

Asymptotically, $\widehat{\varpi}_n/\varpi_n$ converges rapidly to the "Euler–Gompertz constant"

$$\hat{g} = \int_0^\infty \frac{e^{-x}dx}{1 + x} = 0.59634\,73623\,23194\,07434\,10784\,99369\,27937\,60741+ \quad (86)$$

(see exercise 189). Thus $x_n \approx (22 + 12\hat{g})\varpi_n \approx 29.156\varpi_n$, and we've proved that *Algorithm X performs approximately 29.156 updates per solution to the extreme exact cover problem, on average.* That's encouraging: One might suspect that the list manipulations needed to deal with 2^n options of average length n would cost substantially more, but the dancing-links approach turns out to be within a constant factor of Section 7.2.1.5's highly tuned methods for set partitions.

*Analysis of matching problems.
Among the simplest exact cover problems are the ones whose options don't contain many items. For example, a so-called X2C problem ("exact cover with 2-sets") is the special case where every option has exactly 2 items; an X3C problem has 3 items per option; and so on. We've seen in (30) that sudoku is an X4C problem.

Let's take a close look at the simplest case, the X2C problems. Despite their simplicity, we'll see that such problems actually include many cases of interest. Every X2C problem corresponds in an obvious way to a graph G, whose vertices v are the items and whose edges $u - v$ are the pairs of items that occur together in an option '$u\ v$'. In these terms the X2C problem is the classical task of finding a perfect matching, namely a set of edges that contains each vertex exactly once.

We shall study efficient algorithms for perfect matching in Section 7.5.5 below. But an interesting question faces us now, in the present section: How well does our general-purpose Algorithm X compare to the highly tuned special-purpose algorithms that have been developed especially for matching in graphs?

Suppose, for example, that G is the complete graph K_{2q+1}. In other words, suppose that there are $n = 2q + 1$ items $\{0, 1, \ldots, 2q\}$, and that there are $m = \binom{2q+1}{2} = (2q + 1)q$ options '$i\ j$' for $0 \le i < j \le 2q$. This problem clearly has no solution, because we can't cover an odd number of points with 2-element sets! But Algorithm X won't know this (unless we give it a hint by factoring the problem appropriately). Thus it's interesting to see how long Algorithm X will spin its wheels before giving up on this problem.

In fact the analysis is easy: No matter what item i is chosen in step X3, the algorithm will split nicely into $2q$ branches, one for each option '$i\ j$' with $j \ne i$. And each of those branches will be equivalent to the matching problem on the remaining $2q - 1$ items; the remaining options will, in fact, be equivalent to the complete graph K_{2q-1}. Thus the search tree will have $2q$ nodes at depth 1,

$(2q)(2q-2)$ nodes at depth 2, ..., and $(2q)(2q-2)\ldots(2) = 2^q q!$ nodes at depth q. Backtracking will occur at the latter nodes, which are leaves because they correspond to impossible matching in the graph K_1.

How long does this process take? A closer look (see exercise 193) shows that the total number of updates to the data structure will satisfy the recurrence

$$U(2q+1) = 1 + 2q + 4q^2 + 2qU(2q-1), \quad \text{for } q > 0; \qquad U(1) = 1. \qquad (87)$$

Consequently (see exercise 194) the number of updates needed by Algorithm X to discover that K_{2q+1} has no perfect matching turns out to be less than 8.244 times the number of leaves.

There's better news when Algorithm X is presented with the complete graph K_{2q}, because this problem has solutions — lots of them. Indeed, it's easy to see that K_{2q} has exactly $(2q-1)(2q-3)\ldots(3)(1) = (2q)!/(2^q q!)$ perfect matchings. For example, K_8 has $7 \cdot 5 \cdot 3 \cdot 1 = 105$ of them. The total number of updates in this case satisfies a recurrence similar to (87):

$$U(2q) = 1 - 2q + 4q^2 + (2q-1)U(2q-2), \quad \text{for } q > 0; \qquad U(0) = 0. \qquad (88)$$

And exercise 194 proves that this is less than 10.054 updates per matching found.

Armed with these facts, we can work out what happens when the graph

$$(89)$$

is presented to Algorithm X. (This graph has $2q + 2r + 2$ vertices.) The result, which is revealed in exercise 195, is both instructive and bizarre.

A 2D matching problem — also called bipartite matching, and 2DM for short — is the special case of an X2C problem in which every option has the form '$X_j\ Y_k$', where the items $\{X_1, \ldots, X_n\}$ and $\{Y_1, \ldots, Y_n\}$ are disjoint sets. Higher-dimensional matching is defined similarly; sudoku is actually a case of 4DM.

Let's round out our analyses of matching by considering the *bounded permutation problem*: "Given a sequence of positive integers $a_1 \ldots a_n$, find all permutations $p_1 \ldots p_n$ of $\{1, \ldots, n\}$ such that $p_j \leq a_j$ for $1 \leq j \leq n$." We can assume that $a_1 \leq \cdots \leq a_n$, because $p_1 \ldots p_n$ is a permutation; we can also assume that $a_j \geq j$, otherwise there are no solutions; and we can assume without loss of generality that $a_n \leq n$. This is easily seen to be a 2DM problem, having exactly $a_1 + \cdots + a_n$ options, namely '$X_j\ Y_k$' for $1 \leq j \leq n$ and $1 \leq k \leq a_j$.

Suppose we branch first on X_1. Then each of the a_1 subproblems is easily seen to be essentially a bounded permutation problem with n decreased by 1, and with $a_1 \ldots a_n$ replaced by $(a_2 - 1) \ldots (a_n - 1)$. Thus a recursive analysis applies, and again we find that the dancing links algorithm does rather well. For example, if $a_j = \min(j+1, n)$ for $1 \leq j \leq n$, there are 2^{n-1} solutions, and Algorithm X performs only about 12 updates per solution. If $a_j = \min(2j, n)$ for $1 \leq j \leq n$, there are $\lfloor \frac{n+1}{2} \rfloor! \lfloor \frac{n+2}{2} \rfloor!$ solutions, and Algorithm X needs only about $4e - 1 \approx 9.87$ updates per solution. Exercise 196 has the details.

Maintaining a decent focus. Some backtrack algorithms waste time by trying to solve two or more loosely related problems at once. Consider, for example, the 2DM problem with 7 items $\{0, 1, \ldots, 6\}$ and the following 13 options:

$$\text{`0 1', `0 2', `1 4', `1 5', `1 6', `2 4', `2 5', `2 6', `3 4', `3 5', `3 6', `4 5', `4 6'.} \quad (90)$$

Algorithm X, using its MRV heuristic, will branch on item 0, choosing either '0 1' or '0 2'; then it will be faced with a three-way branch; and it will eventually conclude that there's no solution, after implicitly traversing a 19-node search tree,

$$(91)$$

We get an extreme example of bad focus if we take n independent copies of problem (90), with $7n$ items $\{k0, k1, \ldots, k6\}$ and $13n$ options '$k0\ k1$', '$k0\ k2$', $\ldots$, '$k4\ k6$', for $0 \leq k < n$: The algorithm will begin with 2-way branches on each of 00, 10, $\ldots$, $(n{-}1)0$; then it will show that each of the 2^n resulting subproblems is unsolvable, making 3-way branches as it begins to study each one. Its search tree, before giving up, will have $10 \cdot 2^n - 1$ nodes. By contrast, if we had somehow forced the algorithm to keep its attention on the very first copy of (90) (the case $k = 0$), instead of using the MRV heuristic, it would have concluded that there are no solutions after backtracking through only 19 nodes.

Similarly, the simple exact cover problem on items $\{0, 1, \ldots, 5\}$ with options

$$\text{`0 1', `0 2', `1 3 4', `1 3 5', `1 4 5', `2 3 4', `2 3 4 5', `2 4 5', `3 4', `3 5', `4 5',} \quad (92)$$

has a search tree with 9 nodes, one of which is a solution:

$$(93)$$

Taking n independent copies of (92) gives us an exact cover problem with a unique solution, whose search tree via Algorithm X and MRV has $8 \cdot 2^n - 7$ nodes. But if the algorithm had been able to focus on one problem at a time, it would have discovered the solution with a search tree of only $8n + 1$ nodes.

From a practical standpoint, it must be admitted that the exponential behavior of these badly focused toy examples is worrisome only when n is larger than 30 or so, because 2^n is not scary for modern computers when n is small. Still, we can see that a well-focused approach can give significant advantages. So it will be useful to understand how Algorithm X and its cousins behave in general, when the input actually consists of two independent problems.

Let's pause a minute to define the search tree precisely. Given an $m \times n$ matrix A of 0s and 1s, the search tree T of its associated exact cover problem is simply a solution node '∎' when $n = 0$; otherwise T is

$$T_1 \quad T_2 \quad \ldots \quad T_d, \qquad d \geq 0, \quad (94)$$

where the item chosen for branching in step X3 has d options, and T_k is the search tree for the reduced problem after the items of the kth option have been removed. (With the MRV heuristic, d is the minimum length of all active item lists, and we choose the leftmost item having this value of d.)

The exact cover problem that we get when trying to solve two independent problems given by matrices A and A' is the problem that corresponds to the direct sum $A \oplus A'$ (see Eq. 7–(40)). Therefore if T and T' are the corresponding search trees, we will write $T \oplus T'$ for the search tree of $A \oplus A'$, under the MRV heuristic. (That tree depends only on T and T', not on any other aspects of A or A'.) If either T or T' is simply a solution node, the rule is simple:

$$T \oplus \blacksquare = T; \qquad \blacksquare \oplus T' = T'. \tag{95}$$

Otherwise T and T' have the form (94), and we have

$$T \oplus T' = \begin{cases} \overbrace{T_1 \oplus T' \quad T_2 \oplus T' \quad \cdots \quad T_d \oplus T'} & \text{if } d \leq d'; \\[2em] \overbrace{T \oplus T'_1 \quad T \oplus T'_2 \quad \cdots \quad T \oplus T'_{d'}} & \text{if } d > d'. \end{cases} \tag{96}$$

Dear reader, please work exercise 202 — which is very easy! — before reading further. That exercise will help you to understand the definition of $T \oplus T'$; and you'll also see that every node of $T \oplus T'$ is associated with an ordered pair $\alpha\alpha'$, where α and α' are nodes of T and T', respectively. These ordered pairs are the key to the structure of $T \oplus T'$: If α and α' appear at levels $l > 0$ and $l' > 0$ of their trees, so that they are reached from the roots by the respective paths $\alpha_0 - \alpha_1 - \cdots - \alpha_l = \alpha$ and $\alpha'_0 - \alpha'_1 - \cdots - \alpha'_{l'} = \alpha'$, then the parent of $\alpha\alpha'$ in $T \oplus T'$ is either $\alpha_{l-1}\alpha'$ or $\alpha\alpha'_{l'-1}$. Consequently every ancestor α_k of α in T, for $0 \leq k \leq l$, occurs in an ancestor $\alpha_k\alpha'_{k'}$ of $\alpha\alpha'$ in $T \oplus T'$, for some $0 \leq k' \leq l'$.

Let $\deg(\alpha)$ be the number of children that node α has in a search tree, except that we define $\deg(\alpha) = \infty$ when α is a solution node. (Equivalently, $\deg(\alpha)$ is the minimum length of an item list, taken over all active items in the subproblem that corresponds to node α. If α is a solution, there are no active items, hence the minimum is infinite.) Let's call α a *dominant node* if its degree exceeds the degree of all its proper ancestors. The root node is always dominant, and so is every solution node. For example, (91) has three dominant nodes, and (93) has four.

In these terms, exercise 205 proves a significant fact about direct sums:

Lemma D. *Every node of $T \oplus T'$ corresponds to an ordered pair $\alpha\alpha'$ of nodes belonging to T and T'. Either α or α' is dominant in its tree, or both are.* ∎

Lemma D is good news, focuswise, because the search trees that arise in practice tend to have comparatively few dominant nodes. In such cases the MRV heuristic manages to keep the search reasonably well focused, because $T \oplus T'$ isn't too large. For example, the search trees for Langford pairs, or for the n queens problem, are "minimally dominant": Only their root nodes and their solutions dominate; elsewhere the branching degrees don't reach new heights.

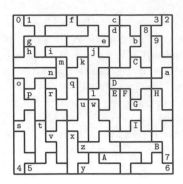

Fig. 73. A 15 × 15 square can be tiled with Y pentominoes, by setting up an exact cover problem with one item for each cell and one option for each placement of a Y. (To eliminate the 8-fold symmetry, only 5 of the 40 options for occupying the center cell were permitted.) Algorithm X's first solution, shown here, was found by branching successively on the possible ways to fill the cells marked 0, 1, ..., 9, a, ..., z, A, ..., I.

Let's look now at a non-contrived example. Figure 73 illustrates a somewhat surprising way to pack 45 Y pentominoes into a 15 × 15 square. [Such tilings were first found in 1973 by J. Haselgrove, at a time when perfect Y-packings were known only for rectangles whose area was even. Her program first ruled out all rectangles of odd area less than 225, as well as the case 9 × 25, before discovering a 15 × 15 solution. See *JRM* **7** (1974), 229.] Notice that the first eight pentominoes in Fig. 73, those marked 0 through 7, were placed in or next to the four corners — thus flirting dangerously with the possibility that the algorithm might be trying to solve four independent problems at once! Luckily, the subsequent choices were able to gain and retain focus, because hard-to-fill cells almost always kept popping up near the recent activity. A five-way branch was needed only when placing the pentominoes marked 8, b, e, g, h, and C in the solution shown.

Focus can sometimes be improved by explicitly preferring some items to others, based on their names; see the "sharp preference" heuristic of exercise 10.

Exercise 207 discusses another approach, an experimental modification of Algorithm X, which attempts to improve focus in situations like Fig. 73 by allowing a user to specify the importance of recent activity. The ideas are interesting, but so far they haven't led to any spectacular successes.

Exploiting local equivalence. A close look at Fig. 73 reveals another phenomenon that is often present in exact cover problems: The tiles marked 8 and b, near the upper right corner, form an 'H' shape, which could be reflected left-right to yield another valid tiling. In fact there are three other such H's in the picture; therefore Fig. 73 actually represents $2^4 = 16$ different solutions to the problem, although those solutions are "locally" equivalent.

It turns out that the 15 × 15 tiling problem in Fig. 73 has exactly 212 mutually incongruent solutions, each of which can be rotated and/or reflected to make a set of eight that are congruent to each other; and each of those solutions contains at least two H's. Algorithm X needs just 92 Gμ to find them all. But we can do even better, because of H-equivalence: A slight extension to the options of the exact cover problem will produce only the solutions for which every 'H' has just one of its two forms — and so does every 'Ⱶ', namely every 90° rotation of an 'H'. (See exercise 208.) This modified problem has just 16 solutions, which are obtained with only 26 Gμ of computation and compactly represent all 212.

In general, an exact cover might contain four distinct options α, β, α', β' for which α and β are disjoint, α' and β' are disjoint, and

$$\alpha + \beta = \alpha' + \beta'. \tag{97}$$

(The '+' sign here is like '$\cup$'; it stands for addition of binary vectors, when options are rows of a 0–1 matrix.) In such cases we say that $(\alpha, \beta; \alpha', \beta')$ is a *bipair*. Whenever $(\alpha, \beta; \alpha', \beta')$ is a bipair, every solution that contains both α and β leads to another solution that contains both α' and β', and vice versa. Thus we can avoid considering half of all such solutions if we exclude one of those alternatives. And it's easy to do that: For example, to exclude all cases that contain both α' and β', we simply introduce a new secondary item, and append it to options α' and β'.

To illustrate this idea, let's apply it to the unsolvable toy problem (90). That problem has many bipairs, but we'll consider only two of them,

$$(\text{'0 1', '2 4'; '0 2', '1 4'})   \text{and}   (\text{'0 1', '2 5'; '0 2', '1 5'}). \tag{98}$$

To avoid solutions that contain both '0 1' and '2 4', as well as those that contain both '0 2' and '1 5', we introduce secondary items A and B, and we extend four of the options (90) to

$$\text{'0 1 A',   '0 2 B',   '1 5 B',   '2 4 A'.} \tag{99}$$

Then the search tree (91) reduces to

$$\tag{100}$$

and the former focusing problems disappear.

But wait, you say. Both of the bipairs in (98) involve the options '0 1' and '0 2'. Why is it legal to prefer different halves of those overlapping bipairs? Isn't it possible that we might "paint ourselves into a corner," if we allow ourselves to make arbitrary decisions about each of several interrelated bipairs?

That's a good question. Indeed, bad decisions *can* lead to trouble. Consider, for example, the problem of perfect matching on the complete bipartite graph $K_{3,3}$, which can be coded as an X2C with the nine options 'x X' for $x \in \{\mathsf{x}, \mathsf{y}, \mathsf{z}\}$ and $X \in \{\mathsf{X}, \mathsf{Y}, \mathsf{Z}\}$. (The problem of perfect matching on $K_{n,n}$ is equivalent to finding the permutations of n elements; thus $K_{3,3}$ has $3! = 6$ perfect matchings.)

Every bipair ('t u', 'v w'; 't w', 'u v') in a perfect matching problem is equivalent to a 4-cycle $t - u - v - w - t$ in the given graph. And if we disallow the right halves of the six bipairs

$$\begin{array}{ll} (\text{'x Y', 'y X'; 'x X', 'y Y'}) & (\text{'x Y', 'y Z'; 'x Z', 'y Y'}) \\ (\text{'y Y', 'z X'; 'y X', 'z Y'}) & (\text{'y Y', 'z Z'; 'y Z', 'z Y'}) \\ (\text{'z Y', 'x X'; 'z X', 'x Y'}) & (\text{'z Y', 'x Z'; 'z Z', 'x Y'}) \end{array}$$

we obtain nine options that have no solution:

$$\begin{array}{lll} \text{'x X A',} & \text{'y X B',} & \text{'z X C',} \\ \text{'x Y C D',} & \text{'y Y A E',} & \text{'z Y B F',} \\ \text{'x Z E',} & \text{'y Z F',} & \text{'z Z D'.} \end{array} \tag{101}$$

Fortunately, however, there's always a safe and easy way to proceed. We can assign an arbitrary (but fixed) ordering to the set of all options. Then, if for every bipair $(\alpha, \beta; \alpha', \beta')$ we always choose the half that contains $\min(\alpha, \beta, \alpha', \beta')$, the choices will be consistent.

More precisely, we can express every bipair in the canonical form

$$(\alpha, \beta; \alpha', \beta') \qquad \alpha < \beta,\ \alpha < \alpha',\ \text{and } \alpha' < \beta', \tag{102}$$

with respect to any fixed ordering of the options. An exact covering is called *strong*, with respect to a set of such canonical bipairs, if its options don't include both α' and β' for any bipair in that set.

Theorem S. *If an exact cover problem has a solution, it has a strong solution.*

Proof. Every solution Σ corresponds to a binary vector $x = x_1 \ldots x_M$, where $x_j = [\text{option } j \text{ is in } \Sigma]$. If Σ isn't strong, with respect to a given set of canonical bipairs, it violates at least one of those bipairs, say $(\alpha, \beta; \alpha', \beta')$. Thus there are indices j, k, j', k' with $j < k$, $j < j'$, and $j' < k'$ such that α, β, α', β' are respectively the jth, kth, j'th, k'th options, and such that $x_{j'} = x_{k'} = 1$. By (97), $x_j = x_k = 0$; and we obtain another solution Σ' by setting $x'_j \leftarrow x'_k \leftarrow 1$, $x'_{j'} \leftarrow x'_{k'} \leftarrow 0$, otherwise $x'_i = x_i$. This vector x' is lexicographically greater than x; so we'll eventually obtain a strong solution by repeating the process. ∎

In particular, we're allowed to exclude both '0 1' and '2 4', as well as both '0 2' and '1 5', with respect to the bipairs (98), because we can choose an ordering in which options '1 4' and '2 5' precede the other options '0 1', '0 2', '1 5', '2 4'.

Another convenient way to make consistent choices among related bipairs is based on ordering the primary items, instead of the options. (See exercise 212).

It's interesting to apply this theory to the problem of perfect matching in the complete graph K_{2q+1}. We showed in (87) above that Algorithm X needs a *long* time — $\Omega(2^q q!)$ mems — to discover that this problem has no solution. But bipairs come to the rescue.

Indeed, K_{2q+1} has lots of bipairs, $\Theta(q^4)$ of them. A straightforward application of Theorem S, using the natural order '0 1' < '0 2' < $\cdots$ < '$(2q-1)$ $2q$' on the $\binom{2q+1}{2}$ options, solves the problem in $\Theta(q^4)$ mems, by using just $\Theta(q^3)$ of the bipairs. And a more clever way to order the options allows us to solve it in only $\Theta(q^2)$ mems, using just $\Theta(q^2)$ well-chosen bipairs. The search tree can in fact be reduced to just $2q + 1$ nodes — which is optimum! Exercise 215 explains all.

***Preprocessing the options.** Sometimes the input to an XCC problem can be greatly simplified, because we can eliminate many of its options and/or items. The general idea of "preprocessing," which transforms one combinatorial problem into an equivalent but hopefully simpler one, is an important paradigm, which is often called *kernelization* for reasons that we shall discuss later.

Algorithm P below is a case in point. It takes any sequence of items and options that would be acceptable to Algorithm X or to Algorithm C, and produces another such sequence with the same number of solutions. Any solution of the new problem can in fact be converted to a solution of the original one, if desired.

The algorithm is based entirely on two general principles, used repeatedly until they no longer apply:

- An option can be removed if it blocks all uses of some primary item.
- An item can be removed if some primary item always forces it to appear.

More precisely, let o be a generic option 'i_1 $i_2[:c_2]$ ... $i_t[:c_t]$', where i_1 is primary and the other $t - 1$ items might have color controls. When Algorithm C deals with option o, it covers i_1 in step C4 and commits the other items in step C5, thereby removing all options that aren't compatible with o. If this process causes some primary item p to lose its last remaining option, we say that p is "blocked" by o. In such a case o is useless, and we can remove it. For example, 'd e g' can be removed from (6), because it blocks a; '1 s_4 s_6' can be removed from (17), because it blocks s_3; then '1 s_1 s_3' and '2 s_2 s_5' also go away, because they block s_4.

That was the first principle mentioned above, the one that removes options. The item-removing principle is similar, but more dramatic when it applies: Let p be a primary item, and suppose that p's options all contain an uncolored instance of some other item, i. In such a case we say that p "forces" i; and we can remove item i, because p must be covered in every solution and it carries i along. For example, a forces d in (6). Hence we can remove item d, shortening the second and fourth options to just 'a g' and 'a f'.

These two principles, blocking and forcing, are by no means a complete catalog of transformations that could be used to preprocess exact cover problems. For example, they are incapable of discovering the fact that (38) is a useless option in the pentomino problem, nor do they discover the simplifications that we deduced by factoring the Soma cube problem. (See the discussion before (46).) Exercise 219 discusses yet another way to discard superfluous options.

A "perfect" and "complete" preprocessor would in fact be able to recognize *any* problem that has at most one solution. We can't hope to achieve that, so we've got to stop somewhere. We shall limit ourselves to the removal of blocking and forcing, because those transformations can be done in polynomial time, and because no other easily recognizable simplifications are apparent.

Algorithm P discovers all such simplifications by systematically traversing the given items and options, using the same data structures that were enjoyed by Algorithm C. It cycles through all items i, trying first to remove i by studying what happens when i is covered. If that fails, it studies what happens when the items of options that begin with i are committed. It needs some small variations of the former 'cover' and 'hide' operations (compare with (12)–(15), (50)–(53)):

$$\text{cover}''(i) = \begin{cases} \text{Set } p \leftarrow \text{DLINK}(i). \text{ While } p \neq i, \\ \quad \text{hide}''(i) \text{ unless COLOR}(p) \neq 0, \\ \quad \text{then set } p \leftarrow \text{DLINK}(p) \text{ and repeat.} \end{cases} \qquad (103)$$

$$\text{hide}''(p) = \begin{cases} \text{Do operation hide}(p); \text{ but also set } S \leftarrow x, \\ \quad \text{whenever LEN}(x) \text{ has been set to 0 and } x \leq N_1. \end{cases} \qquad (104)$$

$$\text{uncover}''(i) = \begin{cases} \text{Set } p \leftarrow \text{ULINK}(i). \text{ While } p \neq i, \\ \quad \text{unhide}(i) \text{ unless COLOR}(p) \neq 0, \\ \quad \text{then set } p \leftarrow \text{ULINK}(p) \text{ and repeat.} \end{cases} \qquad (105)$$

Algorithm P (*Preprocessing for exact covering*). This algorithm reduces a given XCC problem until no instances of blocking or forcing are present. It uses the data structures of Algorithm C, together with new global variables C and S.

P1. [Initialize.] Set the problem up in memory, as in step C1 of Algorithm C. (Again there are N items, of which N_1 are primary.) Also set $C \leftarrow 1$. If there's an item $i \le N_1$ with LEN$(i) = 0$, go to P9.

P2. [Begin a round.] If $C = 0$, go to P10. Otherwise set $C \leftarrow 0$, $i \leftarrow 1$.

P3. [Is item i active?] If $i = N$, return to P2. Otherwise if LEN$(i) = 0$, go to P8.

P4. [Cover i.] Set $S \leftarrow 0$. Use (103) to cover item i. Then go to P7 if $S \neq 0$; otherwise set $x \leftarrow$ DLINK(i).

P5. [Try x.] If x isn't the leftmost remaining node of its option, go to P6. Otherwise use the method of exercise 220 to test whether this option blocks some primary item. If so, set $C \leftarrow 1$, TOP$(x) \leftarrow S$, and $S \leftarrow x$.

P6. [Try again.] Set $x \leftarrow$ DLINK(x), and return to P5 if $x \neq i$. Otherwise uncover item i using (105); use the method of exercise 221 to delete all options that were stacked in step P5; and go to P8.

P7. [Remove item i.] Uncover item i (which is forced by the primary item S). Then use the method of exercise 222 to delete or shorten every option that uses item i. Finally, set $C \leftarrow 1$, DLINK$(i) \leftarrow$ ULINK$(i) \leftarrow i$, LEN$(i) \leftarrow 0$.

P8. [Loop on i.] Set $i \leftarrow i + 1$ and return to P3.

P9. [Collapse.] Set $N \leftarrow 1$ and delete all options. (The problem is unsolvable.)

P10. [Finish.] Output the reduced problem, whose items are those for which LEN$(i) > 0$ or $i = N = 1$, and terminate. (See exercise 223.) ∎

How effective is Algorithm P? Well, sometimes it spins its wheels and finds absolutely nothing to simplify. For example, the options (16) for n Langford pairs contain no instances of blocking or forcing when $n > 5$. Neither do the options for the n queens problem when $n > 3$. There's no "excess fat" in those specifications. In MacMahon's triangle problem (exercise 126), Algorithm P needs just 20 megamems to remove 576 of the 1537 options; but the options that it removes don't really matter, because Algorithm C traverses exactly the same search tree, with or without them.

We do gain 10% when we try to pack pentominoes into a 6×10 box (exercise 271): Without preprocessing, Algorithm X needs 4.11 Gμ to discover all 2339 solutions to that classic task. But Algorithm P needs just 0.19 Gμ to remove 235 of the 2032 options, after which Algorithm X finds the same 2339 solutions in 3.52 Gμ; so the total time has been reduced to 3.71 Gμ. The similar problem of packing the *one-sided* pentominoes into a 6×15 box has an even bigger payoff: It has 3308 options without preprocessing, and 15.5 Tμ are needed to process them. But after preprocessing — which costs a mere 260 Mμ — there are 3157 options, and the running time has decreased to 13.1 Tμ.

The simplifications discovered by Algorithm P for those pentomino problems involve only blocking (see exercise 225). But more subtle reductions occur in the

Y pentomino problem of Fig. 73. For example, cell 20 is forced by cell 10, in that problem; and in round 2, cell 00 is forced by cell 22. In round 4, cell 61 is blocked by the option '50 51 52 53 62' — a surprising discovery! Unfortunately, however, those clever reductions have little effect on the overall running time.

Preprocessing really shines on the problem of exercise 114, which asks for all sudoku solutions that are self-equivalent when reflected about their main diagonal. In this case Algorithm P is presented with 5410 options that involve intricate color controls, on 585 primary items and 90 secondary items. It rapidly reduces them to just 2426 options, on 506 primaries and 90 secondaries; and Algorithm C needs only 287 $G\mu$ to process the reduced options and to discover the 30,286,432 solutions. That's 7.5 times faster than the 2162 $G\mu$ it would have needed without reduction.

Thus, preprocessing is a mixed bag. It might win big, or it might be a waste of time. We can hedge our bets by allocating a fixed budget — for instance by deciding that Algorithm P will be allowed to run at most a minute or so. Its data structures are in a "safe" state at the beginning of step P3; therefore we can jump from there directly to step P10 if we don't want to run to completion.

Of course, preprocessing can also be applied to the subproblems that arise in the midst of a longer computation. A careful balancing of different strategies might be the key to solving problems that are especially tough.

Minimum-cost solutions. Many of the exact cover problems that we've been studying have few solutions, if any. In such cases our joy is to discover the rare gems. But in many other cases the problems have solutions galore; and for such problems we've focused our attention so far on the task of minimizing the amount of time per solution, assuming that all of the solutions are interesting.

A new perspective arises when each option of our problem has been assigned a nonnegative *cost*. Then it becomes natural to seek solutions of minimum cost. And ideally we'd like to do this without examining very many of the high-cost solutions at all; they're basically useless, but a low-cost solution might be priceless.

Fortunately there's a reasonably simple way to modify our algorithms, so that they will indeed find minimum-cost solutions rather quickly. But before we look at the details of those modifications, it will be helpful to look at several examples of what is possible.

Consider, for instance, the problem of Langford pairs from this point of view. We observed near the very beginning of Chapter 7 that there are $2L_{16} = 653,443,600$ ways to place the 32 numbers $\{1, 1, 2, 2, \ldots, 16, 16\}$ into an array $a_1 a_2 \ldots a_{32}$ so that exactly i entries lie between the two occurrences of i, for $1 \le i \le 16$. And we claimed that the pairing displayed in 7–(3), namely

$$2\ 3\ 4\ 2\ 1\ 3\ 1\ 4\ 16\ 13\ 15\ 5\ 14\ 7\ 9\ 6\ 11\ 5\ 12\ 10\ 8\ 7\ 6\ 13\ 9\ 16\ 15\ 14\ 11\ 8\ 10\ 12, \quad (106)$$

is one of 12,016 solutions that maximize the sum $\Sigma_1 = \sum_{k=1}^{32} k a_k$. Consequently the *reverse* of that pairing, namely

$$12\ 10\ 8\ 11\ 14\ 15\ 16\ 9\ 13\ 6\ 7\ 8\ 10\ 12\ 5\ 11\ 6\ 9\ 7\ 14\ 5\ 15\ 13\ 16\ 4\ 1\ 3\ 1\ 2\ 4\ 3\ 2, \quad (107)$$

is one of 12,016 solutions that *minimize* Σ_1. We noted in (16) above that Langford pairs are the solutions to a simple exact cover problem, whose options '$i\ s_j\ s_k$' represent the assignments $a_j = i$ and $a_k = i$. Therefore, if we associate the cost $\$(ji + ki)$ with option '$i\ s_j\ s_k$', the minimum-cost solutions will be precisely the Langford pairings that minimize Σ_1. (See exercise 226.)

One way to minimize the total cost is, of course, to visit all solutions and to compute the individual sums. But there's a better way: The min-cost variant of Algorithm X below, which we shall call Algorithm X$, finds a solution of cost \$3708 and proves its minimality after only 60 gigamems of computation. That's more than 36 times faster than the use of plain vanilla Algorithm X, which needs 2.2 *teramems* to run through the full set of solutions.

Moreover, Algorithm X$ doesn't stop there. It actually will compute the K solutions of least cost, for any given value of K. For example, if we take $K = 12500$, it needs just 70 gigamems to discover the 12,016 solutions of cost \$3708, together with 484 solutions of the next-lowest cost (which happens to be \$3720).

The news is even better when we try to minimize $\Sigma_2 = \sum_{k=1}^{32} k^2 a_k$ instead of Σ_1. Algorithm X$ needs just 28 Gμ to prove that the minimum Σ_2 is \$68880. And better yet is the fact, obtained in only 10 Gμ, that the minimum of $\sum_{k=1}^{32} k a_k^2$ is \$37552, obtainable *uniquely* by the remarkable pairing

$$16\ 14\ 15\ 9\ 6\ 13\ 5\ 7\ 12\ 10\ 11\ 6\ 5\ 9\ 8\ 7\ 14\ 16\ 15\ 13\ 10\ 12\ 11\ 8\ 4\ 1\ 3\ 1\ 2\ 4\ 3\ 2, \quad (108)$$

which also happens to minimize both Σ_1 and Σ_2! (See exercise 229.)

Another classic combinatorial task, the 16 queens problem, provides another instructive example. We know from previous discussions that there are exactly 14,772,512 ways to place 16 nonattacking queens on a 16×16 board. We also know that Algorithm X needs about 40 Gμ of computation to visit them all, when we give it options like (23).

Let's suppose that the cost of placing a queen in cell (i, j) is the *distance* from that cell to the center of the board. (If we number the rows and columns from 1 to 16, that distance $d(i, j)$ is $\sqrt{(i - 17/2)^2 + (j - 17/2)^2}$; it varies from $d(8, 8) = 1/\sqrt{2}$ to $d(1, 1) = 15/\sqrt{2}$.) Thus we want to concentrate the queens near the center as much as possible, although many of them must lie at or near the edges because there must be one queen in each row and one queen in each column.

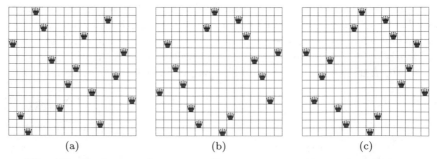

(a)   (b)   (c)

Fig. 74. Optimum solutions to the 16 queens problem, placing them (a) as close as possible to the center, or (b, c) as far as possible from it.

Figure 74(a) shows how to minimize the total cost — and this answer actually turns out to be unique, except for rotation and reflection. Similarly, Figs. 74(b) and 74(c) show the placements that *maximize* the cost. (Curiously, those solutions are obtainable from each other by reflecting the middle eight rows, without changing the top four or the bottom four.) Algorithm X$, with $K = 9$, discovers and proves the optimality of those placements in just (a) 3.7 Gμ; (b,c) 0.8 Gμ.

The modifications that convert Algorithm X to Algorithm X$ also convert Algorithm C into Algorithm C$. Therefore we can find minimum-cost solutions to XCC problems, which go well beyond ordinary exact cover problems.

For example, here's a toy problem that now becomes tractable: *Put ten different 5-digit prime numbers into the rows and columns of a 5×5 array, in such a way that their product is as small as possible.* (A 5-digit prime number is one of the 8363 primes between 10007 and 99991, inclusive.) One such "prime square," made up entirely of primes that are less than 30000, is

$$\begin{bmatrix} 2 & 1 & 2 & 1 & 1 \\ 2 & 0 & 1 & 0 & 1 \\ 1 & 1 & 0 & 0 & 3 \\ 1 & 1 & 0 & 6 & 9 \\ 1 & 1 & 1 & 1 & 3 \end{bmatrix}. \tag{109}$$

To set this up as an XCC problem, introduce ten primary items $\{a_1, a_2, a_3, a_4, a_5\}$ and $\{d_1, d_2, d_3, d_4, d_5\}$ that represent "across" and "down," together with 25 secondary items ij for $1 \le i, j \le 5$ that represent cells of the array, together with 8363 additional secondary items $p_1p_2p_3p_4p_5$, one for eligible prime $p = p_1p_2p_3p_4p_5$. The options for placing p in row i or column j are then

$$\begin{array}{llllll} \text{`}a_i & i1{:}p_1 & i2{:}p_2 & i3{:}p_3 & i4{:}p_4 & i5{:}p_5 & p_1p_2p_3p_4p_5\text{'}; \\ \text{`}d_j & 1j{:}p_1 & 2j{:}p_2 & 3j{:}p_3 & 4j{:}p_4 & 5j{:}p_5 & p_1p_2p_3p_4p_5\text{'}. \end{array} \tag{110}$$

For example, 'a_4 41:1 42:1 43:0 44:6 45:9 11069' enables the prime 11069 in (109).

This is a good example where preprocessing is helpful, because the primes that are usable in a_1 and d_1 must not contain a 0; furthermore, the primes that are usable in a_5 and d_5 must contain only the digits $\{1, 3, 7, 9\}$. Algorithm P discovers those facts on its own, without being told anything special about number theory. It reduces the 83630 options of (110) to only 62900; and those reductions provide useful clues for the choices of items on which to branch.

The Monte Carlo estimate of exercise 86 tells us that there are roughly 6×10^{14} different ways to fit ten primes into a 5×5 array — a vast number. We probably don't need to look at too many of those possibilities, yet it isn't easy to decide which of them can safely be left unexamined.

To minimize the product of the primes, we assign the cost $\$(\ln p)$ to each of the options in (110). (This works because the logarithm of a product is the sum of the logarithms of the factors.) More precisely, we use the cost $\$\lfloor C \ln p \rfloor$, where C is large enough to make truncation errors negligible, but not large enough to cause arithmetic overflow, because Algorithm C$ wants all costs to be integers.

Every solution has the same cost as its transpose. Thus we can get the best five prime squares by asking Algorithm C$ to compute the $K = 10$ least-cost solutions, each of which occurs twice. Here they are, with the best at the left:

$$\begin{bmatrix} 1&1&1&1&3 \\ 1&0&1&0&3 \\ 1&1&0&0&3 \\ 3&1&7&6&9 \\ 1&1&1&7&1 \end{bmatrix} \begin{bmatrix} 1&1&1&1&3 \\ 1&0&1&0&3 \\ 1&1&0&0&3 \\ 3&1&7&7&1 \\ 1&1&1&9&7 \end{bmatrix} \begin{bmatrix} 1&1&1&1&3 \\ 1&0&0&0&7 \\ 1&1&0&0&3 \\ 3&1&6&9&9 \\ 1&1&1&1&7 \end{bmatrix} \begin{bmatrix} 1&1&1&1&3 \\ 1&0&0&0&7 \\ 1&1&0&0&3 \\ 3&1&6&6&3 \\ 1&1&1&7&7 \end{bmatrix} \begin{bmatrix} 1&1&1&1&3 \\ 1&0&0&0&7 \\ 1&1&0&0&3 \\ 3&1&6&6&3 \\ 1&1&1&9&7 \end{bmatrix}. \quad (111)$$

The running time, 440 Gμ, would have been 1270 Gμ without preprocessing; so the 280 Gμ spent in preprocessing paid off. But the five greatest-cost solutions,

$$\begin{bmatrix} 9&9&9&8&9 \\ 8&8&9&9&7 \\ 9&8&6&8&9 \\ 9&9&7&9&3 \\ 9&9&9&9&1 \end{bmatrix} \begin{bmatrix} 9&9&9&8&9 \\ 8&9&8&9&9 \\ 9&6&7&9&9 \\ 9&8&7&3&7 \\ 9&9&9&9&1 \end{bmatrix} \begin{bmatrix} 9&9&9&8&9 \\ 8&8&9&9&7 \\ 9&8&8&9&7 \\ 9&9&5&7&1 \\ 9&9&9&7&1 \end{bmatrix} \begin{bmatrix} 9&9&9&8&9 \\ 8&8&9&9&7 \\ 9&8&8&9&7 \\ 9&9&5&8&1 \\ 9&9&9&9&1 \end{bmatrix} \begin{bmatrix} 9&9&9&8&9 \\ 8&8&9&9&7 \\ 9&8&8&9&7 \\ 9&9&5&7&7 \\ 9&9&9&7&1 \end{bmatrix} \quad (112)$$

(greatest at the right), can be found in just 22 Gμ, without preprocessing.

Let's turn now from purely mathematical problems to some "organic" scenarios that are more typical of the real world. The USA's 48 contiguous states

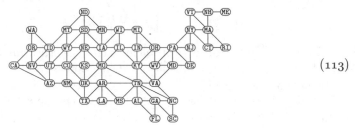

define an interesting planar graph that has already supplied us with a variety of instructive examples. This graph G has 48 vertices and 105 edges. Suppose we want to partition it into eight connected subgraphs of six vertices each. What's the minimum number of edges whose removal will do that?

Well, exercise 7.2.2–76 has told us how to list all of the connected subsets of six states, and there happen to be 11505 of them. That gives us 11505 options for an exact cover problem on 48 items, whose solutions are precisely the potential partitions of interest. The total number of solutions turns out to be 4,536,539; and Algorithm X is able to visit them all, at a cost of 807 gigamems.

But let's try to do better, using Algorithm X$. Every induced subgraph $G|U$ has an *exterior cost*, which is the number of edges from U to vertices not in U. When we partition a graph by removing edges, every such edge contributes to the exterior cost of two of the components that remain; hence the number of removed edges is exactly half the sum of the exterior costs. The best partition therefore corresponds to the minimum-cost solution to our exact cover problem, if we assign the exterior costs to each option. For example, one of the 11505 options is

$$\text{`ND SD NE KS OK TX'}, \quad (114)$$

and we assign a cost of \$19 to that option.

Algorithm X$ now obligingly finds, in just 3.2 gigamems, that the optimum solution costs \$72. Hence we get the desired partition by removing only 36 edges.

Before we look at the answer, let's stare at the problem a bit longer, because we still haven't discovered the best way to solve it! A closer examination shows that option (114) is useless, because it could never actually appear in any solution: It cuts the graph into two pieces, with 11 states to the left and 31 states to the right. (We encountered a similar situation earlier in (38).) In fact, 4961 of the 11505 options turn out to be unusable, for essentially the same reason. The state of Maine (ME), for example, belongs to 25 connected subgraphs of order 6; but we can easily see that the only way to get ME into the final partition is to group it with the other five states of New England (NH, VT, MA, CT, RI). Exercise 242 explains how to detect and reject the useless options quickly.

The remaining problem, which has 6544 options, is solved by Algorithm X in 327 Gμ and by Algorithm X$^\$$ in just 1046 Mμ.

Essentially the same methods will partition the graph nicely into six connected clusters of order eight. This time the exact cover problem has 40520 options after reduction, and a total of 4,177,616 solutions. But Algorithm X$^\$$ needs less than 2 Gμ to determine the minimum cost, which is \$54.

Here are examples of the optimum partitions found, 8×6 and 6×8:

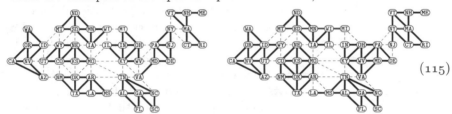

(115)

In each case the optimum can actually be achieved in two ways: On the left, one could swap the affiliations of VA and WV; on the right, a more complicated cyclic shuffle (MI NE LA VA) could be used.

It's also instructive to solve a different kind of problem, namely to use census data and to partition G based on the *population* of each state. For example, let's try to find eight connected clusters that each contain nearly the same number of people. The total population, P, of the 48 states was officially 306084180 in 2010. We want each cluster to represent $P/8$ people, or as close to $P/8$ as we can get. That's about 38 million people per cluster.

The algorithm of exercise 242 will find and reduce all connected subgraphs whose total population x satisfies $L \le x < U$, for any given bounds L and U. If we take $L > \lfloor P/9 \rfloor$ (which is about 34 million) and $U \le \lceil P/7 \rceil$ (which is about 44 million), those candidate subgraphs will define an exact cover problem for which every solution uses exactly eight options, because $9x > P$ and $7x < P$.

That algorithm proves that G contains 1,926,811 connected sets of states whose population lies in $[34009354 .. 43726312)$; and it prunes away 1,571,057 of them, leaving 355,754. But that's overkill. This problem has enough flexibility that its final solution can be expected to contain only sets whose population is quite close to 38 million. Therefore we might as well restrict ourselves to the range $[37000000 .. 39000000)$ instead. There are 34,111 such options; surely they should be enough to solve our problem.

Well, that's very plausible, but unfortunately it doesn't work: Those 34,111 options have no solution, because Algorithm X can't use them to cover NY (New York)! Notice that NY is an articulation point of G. The population of New York is about 19.4 million, and the combined population of the six New England states is about 14.3 million. Whatever option covers New York had better cover all of New England too, otherwise New England is stranded. So that makes $19.4 + 14.3 = 33.7$ million people. New York's only other neighbors are New Jersey (8.8 million) and Pennsylvania (12.7 million); adding either of them will put us over 42 million.

So we're clearly not going to be able to cover New York with a cluster that's close to the desired 38 million. We'll either need a lightweight one (New York plus New England) or a heavyweight one (with New Jersey too). Let's throw those two options in with the other 34,111.

Notice that this problem is quite different from the others we've been discussing, because its options vary greatly in size. One of the options contains just one state, CA (California), whose population is the largest (37.3 million); others contain up to fifteen states, almost spanning the continent from DE to NV.

Now we assign the cost $\$(x^2)$ to each option with population x, because the minimum-cost solutions will then minimize the squared deviations $(x_1 - P/8)^2 + \cdots + (x_8 - P/8)^2$. (See exercise 243.) This works well; and Algorithm X$^\$$ needs only 3.3 gigamems to find the optimum solution below. The seven options not involving New York all contain between 37.3 and 38.1 million people.

A similar analysis, partitioning into six equipopulated clusters instead of eight, gives in 1.1 Gμ a minimum-cost solution whose six populations are all in the range $[50650000 . . 51150000]$. Both solutions are illustrated here, with the area of each vertex proportional to its population:

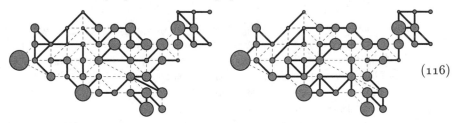

(116)

In both cases the solution is unique. (And in both cases, let's face it, the solution is also pretty weird. Partitions like this could only be concocted by a computer. Exercise 246 discusses approximate solutions that are less eccentric.)

*Implementing the min-cost cutoffs. OK, we've now seen lots of reasons why Algorithms X$^\$$ and C$^\$$ are desirable. But how exactly can we obtain those algorithms by extending Algorithm X and C? It will suffice to describe Algorithm C$^\$$.

The mission of Algorithm C$^\$$ is to find the K min-cost solutions. More precisely, it should discover K solutions whose total cost is as small as possible, with the understanding that different solutions might have the same cost. Let's imagine, for example, a problem that has exactly ten solutions, and that their costs are \$3, \$1, \$4, \$1, \$5, \$9, \$2, \$6, \$5, \$3, in the order that Algorithm C would discover them. Algorithm C$ won't differ from Algorithm C until it has found K solutions, because those K might turn out to be the best. After K are known, however, it will be harder to please: It will accept a new solution only if that solution is better than one of the best K it knows. Thus if $K = 3$, say, the accepted solutions will have costs $3, $1, $4, $1, $2; Algorithm C$ won't find the other five.

To implement that behavior, we maintain a BEST table, which contains the K least costs known so far. That table is "heap ordered," with

$$\text{BEST}[\lfloor j/2 \rfloor] \geq \text{BEST}[j] \qquad \text{for } 1 \leq \lfloor j/2 \rfloor < j \leq K \qquad (117)$$

(see Eq. 5.2.3–(3)). In particular, BEST[1] will be the greatest of the least K costs, and we call it the *cutoff value*, T. Algorithm C$ will reject any solution whose cost is T or more. Initially, BEST[j] $= \infty$ for $1 \leq j \leq K$; then every new solution of cost $c < T$ will be "sifted" into the BEST table as in Algorithm 5.2.3H. The successive cutoff values in the example above, if $K = 3$, would therefore be $\infty, \infty, 4, 3, 3, 3, 2, 2, 2, 2$. If $K = 4$ they'd be $\infty, \infty, \infty, 4, 4, 4, 3, 3, 3, 3$.

Algorithm C$ adds a COST field to every node, thereby making each node 64 bits larger than before. Step C1$ stores the cost of every option, assumed to be a nonnegative integer, in each node belonging to that option.

The costs in every list of options created by step C1$ are *ordered*, so that

$$\text{COST}(x) \leq \text{COST}(y) \qquad \text{if } y = \text{DLINK}(x), \qquad (118)$$

whenever neither x nor y is a header node. Therefore, if p is primary and belongs to t options, we have $\text{COST}(x_1) \leq \text{COST}(x_2) \leq \cdots \leq \text{COST}(x_t)$, where $x_1 = \text{DLINK}(p)$, $x_{j+1} = \text{DLINK}(x_j)$ for $1 \leq j < t$, and $p = \text{DLINK}(x_t)$. This fact will allow us to ignore options that are too expensive to be part of a min-cost solution.

For this purpose we generalize the basic operations of covering, purifying, uncovering, and unpurifying (see (50)–(57)), by including a *threshold* parameter ϑ: Their loops in Algorithm C$ now say 'While $q \neq i$ and $\text{COST}(q) < \vartheta$' instead of simply 'While $q \neq i$'. We also change the uncovering and unpurifying operations, so that they now go downward using DLINKs instead of upward using ULINKs. Furthermore, we make the unhiding operation of (15) go from left to right, with q increasing, just as hiding does in (13). (These conventions clearly flout the rules by which we established the validity of dancing links in the first place! But we're lucky, because they're justified by the theory in exercise 2.)

At level l of the search, Algorithm C$ has constructed a partial solution, consisting of l options represented by nodes $x_0 \dots x_{l-1}$. Let C_l be their total cost. In step C4$ we set $x_l \leftarrow \text{DLINK}(i)$, then cover item i using the threshold value $\vartheta_0 = T - C_l - \text{COST}(x_l)$. (Item i will have been chosen so that $\vartheta_0 > 0$.) The covering process will now proceed faster than before, if ϑ_0 is fairly low, because it won't bother to hide options that could not be in an accepted solution. We need to remember the value of ϑ_0, so that exactly the same threshold will be used when backtracking; therefore step C4$ sets THO[l] $\leftarrow \vartheta_0$, and step C7$ uses THO[l] as the threshold for uncovering item i, where THO is an auxiliary array.

The cutoff value T decreases as computation proceeds. Therefore the threshold $\vartheta = T - C_l - \text{COST}(x_l)$ used in step C5$ for covering and purification might be different each time. Step C5$ should go directly to C7$ if $\vartheta \leq 0$. Otherwise it sets $TH[l] \leftarrow \vartheta$ in that step, and uses $TH[l]$ for undoing in step C6$, where TH is another auxiliary array.

Step C3$, which chooses the item on which to branch at level l, is of course crucially important. If some primary item i has no options, or if the cost of its least expensive option is so high that it can't lead to a solution better than we've already found, step C3$ should jump immediately to step C8$. Otherwise, many strategies are worthy of investigation, and there's room here to discuss only the method that was used in the author's experiments: Good results were obtained by choosing an i with the fewest not-too-costly options, as in the MRV heuristic. In case of ties, the author's implementation chose an i whose least expensive option cost the *most*. (That item must be covered sooner or later, so there's no way to avoid paying that much. We probably have a better chance of reaching a cutoff quickly if we maximize our chances of failure.) Exercise 248 has full details.

Many applications of Algorithm C$ have special features that allow us to prune unproductive branches from the search tree long before they would be cut off by the methods discussed so far. For example, every option in our "square of primes" problem has exactly one primary item (see (110)). In such cases, we know that every solution obtained by extending $x_0 \ldots x_{l-1}$ must cost at least

$$C_l + \text{COST}(\text{DLINK}(i_1)) + \cdots + \text{COST}(\text{DLINK}(i_t)), \tag{119}$$

because of (118), where $i_1, \ldots, i_t$ are the primary items still active. If this total is T or more, step C3$ can proceed immediately to step C8$.

Similarly, in the n queens problem, every option has exactly two primary items, one of the form R_i and one of the form C_j. The active items $i_1, \ldots, i_t$ must therefore contain $t/2$ of each. Let C_R and C_C be $\sum \text{COST}(\text{DLINK}(i_j))$, summed over those types. If *either* $C_l + C_R$ *or* $C_l + C_C$ is $\geq T$, step C3$ can jump to C8$.

In our first problem for the contiguous USA, every option has exactly 6 items. (See (114).) Hence the number of active items, t, is always a multiple of 6. Exercise 249 presents a nice algorithm to find the least possible cost of $t/6$ future options; step C3$ of Algorithm C$ uses that method to find early cutoffs.

The Langford pair problem has options with three items, one of which is a digit. The pentomino problems have options with six items, one of which is a piece name. In both cases, Algorithm C$ can obtain suitable lower bounds for early cutoffs by *combining* the strategies already mentioned. (See exercise 250.)

Finally, Algorithm C$ uses one other important technique: It gains traction by *preprocessing the costs*. Notice that *if p is a primary item, and if the cost of every option that includes p is c or more, we could decrease the cost of all those options by c, without changing the set of min-cost solutions.* That's true because p is going to appear exactly once in every solution. We can think of c as an unavoidable *tax* or "cover charge," which must be paid "up front."

In general there are many ways to preprocess the costs without changing the underlying problem. Properly transformed costs can help the algorithm's heuristics to make much more intelligent choices. Exercise 247 discusses the simple method that was used for step C1$ in the author's experiments discussed earlier.

*Dancing with ZDDs. The solutions visited by Algorithm X in step X2 can be represented naturally in the form of a decision tree, as we discussed in Section 7.1.4. For example, here's a decision tree for the solutions to the problem of covering the eight cells of a 3×3 board with four dominoes, after the corner cell 22 has been removed:

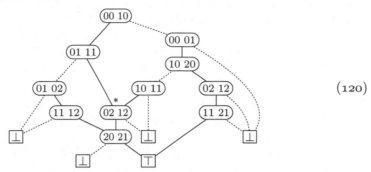

$$(120)$$

This diagram uses the standard ZDD conventions: Every branch node names an option. A solid line means that the option is taken, while a broken line means that it is not. The terminal nodes $\perp$ and $\top$ represent failure and success. This problem has four solutions, corresponding to the four paths from the root to $\top$.

We learned in Section 7.1.4 that ZDDs can readily be manipulated, and that a small ZDD can sometimes characterize a large family of solutions. If we're lucky, we can save a huge amount of time and energy by simply generating an appropriate ZDD instead of visiting the solutions one by one.

Such economies arise when the same subproblem occurs repeatedly. For example, two branches come together in (120) at the node marked '*'; this happens because the problem that remains after placing two dominoes '00 10' and '01 11' is the same as the residual problem after placing '00 01' and '10 11'. "We've been there and done that." Hence we needn't recapitulate our former actions, if we've already built a subZDD to remember what we did. (Those two pairs of domino placements form a "bipair," as discussed earlier; but the ZDD idea is considerably more general and powerful.)

Let's look more closely at the underlying details. The exact cover problem solved by (120) has eight items 00, 01, 10, 02, 11, 20, 12, 21, representing cells to be covered; and it has the following ten options, representing domino placements:

$$\begin{array}{lllll} 1\colon 00\ 01 & 3\colon 01\ 02 & 5\colon 02\ 12 & 7\colon 10\ 20 & 9\colon 11\ 21 \\ 2\colon 00\ 10 & 4\colon 01\ 11 & 6\colon 10\ 11 & 8\colon 11\ 12 & 10\colon 20\ 21 \end{array} \quad (121)$$

The ZDD (120) is internally represented as a sequence of branching instructions,

$$\begin{array}{lll} I_{12} = (\bar{2}?\,8\colon 11), & I_9 = (\bar{8}?\,0\colon 2), & I_6 = (\bar{5}?\,0\colon 5), \\ I_{11} = (\bar{4}?\,10\colon 3), & I_8 = (\bar{1}?\,0\colon 7), & I_5 = (\bar{9}?\,0\colon 1), & I_3 = (\bar{5}?\,0\colon 2), \\ I_{10} = (\bar{3}?\,0\colon 9), & I_7 = (\bar{7}?\,4\colon 6), & I_4 = (\bar{6}?\,0\colon 3), & I_2 = (\overline{10}?\,0\colon 1), \end{array} \quad (122)$$

where 0 and 1 stand for $\perp$ and $\top$. (See, for instance, 7.1.4–(8).) "If we don't take option 2, go to instruction 8; but if we do take it, continue with instruction 11."

A few modifications to Algorithm X will transform it from a solution-visiting method into a constructor of ZDDs. In fact, color controls can be handled too:

Algorithm Z (*Dancing with ZDDs*). Given an XCC problem as in Algorithm C, this algorithm outputs a free ZDD for the sets of options that satisfy it. The ZDD instructions $\{I_2, \ldots, I_s\}$ have the form $(\bar{o}_j? \; l_j: h_j)$ illustrated in (122), and I_s is the root. (But if the problem has no solutions, the algorithm terminates with $s = 1$, and the root is 0.) The data structures of Algorithm C are extended by a "memo cache" consisting of signatures $S[j]$ and ZDD pointers $Z[j]$. Algorithm C's table of choices $x_0 x_1 \ldots$ is joined by two new auxiliary tables $m_0 m_1 \ldots$ and $z_0 z_1 \ldots$, indexed by the current level l.

Z1. [Initialize.] Set the problem up in memory, as in step C1 of Algorithm C. Also set N to the number of items, Z to the last spacer address, $l \leftarrow 0$, $S[0] \leftarrow 0$, $Z[0] \leftarrow 1$, $m \leftarrow 1$, $s \leftarrow 1$.

Z2. [Enter level l.] Form a "signature" σ that characterizes the current subproblem (see below). If $\sigma = S[t]$ for some t (this is a "cache hit"), set $\zeta \leftarrow Z[t]$ and go to Z8. Otherwise set $S[m] \leftarrow \sigma$, $m_l \leftarrow m$, $z_l \leftarrow 0$, and $m \leftarrow m + 1$.

Z3. [Choose i.] At this point items i_1, ..., i_t still need to be covered, as in step C3 of Algorithm C. Choose one of them, and call it i.

Z4. [Cover i.] Cover item i using (12), and set $x_l \leftarrow \text{DLINK}(i)$.

Z5. [Try x_l.] If $x_l = i$, go to Z7. Otherwise set $p \leftarrow x_l + 1$, and do the following while $p \neq x_l$: Set $j \leftarrow \text{TOP}(p)$; if $j \leq 0$, set $p \leftarrow \text{ULINK}(p)$; otherwise commit$(p, j)$ and set $p \leftarrow p + 1$. Set $l \leftarrow l + 1$ and return to Z2.

Z6. [Try again.] Set $p \leftarrow x_l - 1$, and do the following while $p \neq x_l$: Set $j \leftarrow \text{TOP}(p)$; if $j \leq 0$, set $o \leftarrow 1 - j$ and $p \leftarrow \text{DLINK}(p)$; otherwise uncommit$(p, j)$ and set $p \leftarrow p - 1$. If $\zeta \neq 0$, set $s \leftarrow s + 1$, output $I_s = (\bar{o}? \; z_l: \zeta)$, and set $z_l \leftarrow s$. Set $i \leftarrow \text{TOP}(x_l)$, $x_l \leftarrow \text{DLINK}(x_l)$, and return to Z5.

Z7. [Backtrack.] Uncover item i using (14). Then set $Z[m_l] \leftarrow z_l$ and $\zeta \leftarrow z_l$.

Z8. [Leave level l.] Terminate if $l = 0$. Otherwise set $l \leftarrow l - 1$ and go to Z6. ∎

Important: The 'commit' and 'uncommit' operations in steps Z5 and Z6 should modify (54)–(57), by calling cover(j), hide(q), uncover(j), and unhide(q) instead of cover$'(j)$, hide$'(q)$, uncover$'(j)$, and unhide$'(q)$. These changes cause every step of Algorithm Z to be slightly different from the corresponding step of Algorithm C. (Yet only step Z2 has changed substantially.)

Exercise 253 shows that a few more changes will make Algorithm Z compute the total number of solutions, instead of (or in addition to) outputting a ZDD.

The keys to Algorithm Z's success are the *signatures* computed in step Z2. This computation is easy if there are no secondary items: The signature σ is then simply a bit vector of length N, containing 1 in every position i where item i is still active. The computation is, however, somewhat subtler in the presence of secondary items; exercise 254 has the details.

It's instructive to analyze some special cases. For example, suppose Algorithm Z is asked to find the perfect matchings of the complete graph K_N. This problem has N primary items $\{1, \ldots, N\}$, and $\binom{N}{2}$ options 'j k' for $1 \leq j < k \leq N$. We noted earlier, in the discussion preceding (87), that every item list on level l has exactly $N - 1 - 2l$ options, regardless of the choices made in step Z3. If we always choose the smallest uncovered item, step Z2 will compute exactly $\binom{N-l}{l}$ different signatures on level l, namely the signatures in which items $\{1, \ldots, l\}$ are covered and so are l of the other items $\{l + 1, \ldots, N\}$. Hence the total number of cache entries is $\sum_{l=0}^{N} \binom{N-l}{l} = F_{N+1}$, a Fibonacci number(!). (See exercise 1.2.8–16.) Moreover, the main loops in steps Z5 and Z6 are executed $(N-1-2l)\binom{N-l}{l}$ times at level l, since steps Z3 and Z4 are executed $\binom{N-l}{l}$ times.

In fact, when N is even, the ZDD that is output for all perfect matchings of K_N turns out to have exactly $\sum_{l=0}^{N}(N-1-2l)\binom{N-l}{l} + 2$ nodes, which is approximately $\frac{N}{5}F_{N+1}$. Exercise 255 shows that the total running time to compute this ZDD is $\Theta(N^2 F_N) = \Theta(N^2 \phi^N)$; and the same estimate holds also when N is odd and the ZDD has only one node '$\bot$'. This is much smaller than the time needed by Algorithm X, which is $\Theta\big((N/e)^{N/2}\big)$.

More concretely, Algorithm X computes the 2,027,025 perfect matchings of K_{16} in about 360 megamems, using about 6 kilobytes of memory. Algorithm Z needs only about 2 megamems to characterize those matchings with a 10,228-node ZDD; but it uses 2.5 megabytes of memory. For K_{32} there are 191,898, 783,962,510,625 perfect matchings, and the difference is even more dramatic: Algorithm X costs about 34 thousand petamems and 25 kilobytes; Algorithm Z costs about 16 gigamems and 85 megabytes, for a ZDD with 48 meganodes.

This example illustrates several important points: (1) Algorithm Z can greatly reduce the running time of Algorithm X (or Algorithm C), trading time for space. (2) These improvements can also be achieved for problems that have no solutions, like matchings of K_{2q+1}. (3) The number of nodes in the ZDD that is output might greatly exceed the number of memos in Algorithm Z's cache.

Let's take a closer look at the ZDDs. The output for $N = 8$ is, schematically,

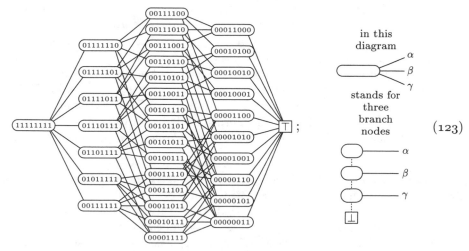

where, for example, '00101101' represents nodes for the signature 00101101.

A signature represents a subproblem. If that subproblem has at least one solution, the ZDD for the full problem will have a subZDD that specifies all solutions of the subproblem. And if the signature is in cache location $S[t]$, the root of the corresponding subZDD will be stored in $Z[t]$, at the end of step Z7.

This subZDD has a very special structure, illustrated in (123). Suppose we branch on item i when working on signature σ; and suppose solutions are found for options $o_1, o_2, \ldots, o_k$ in the list for item i. Then there will be subZDDs rooted at $\zeta_1, \zeta_2, \ldots, \zeta_k$, associated with the subproblems whose signatures are $\sigma \setminus o_1, \sigma \setminus o_2, \ldots, \sigma \setminus o_k$. The net effect of steps Z3–Z6 is to construct a subZDD for σ that essentially begins with k conditional instructions:

$$o_k? \; \zeta_k: \; \ldots \; o_2? \; \zeta_2: o_1? \; \zeta_1: \perp. \tag{124}$$

(The ZDD is constructed from bottom to top, so it tests o_k first.)

For example, '$\boxed{00101101}$' in (123) is the root of the subZDD for the subproblem that needs to cover $\{3, 5, 6, 8\}$. We branch on item 3, whose list has the three options '3 5', '3 6', '3 8'. Three branch instructions are output,

$$I_\theta = (\overline{3\ 5}? \; 0: \gamma), \quad I_\eta = (\overline{3\ 6}? \; \theta: \beta), \quad I_\zeta = (\overline{3\ 8}? \; \eta: \alpha);$$

here γ, β, α are the subZDDs for signatures 00000101, 00001001, 00001100, respectively. The subZDD for 00101101 begins at ζ.

Thus (123) illustrates a ZDD with $1 \cdot 7 + 7 \cdot 5 + 15 \cdot 3 + 10 \cdot 1 + 2 = 99$ nodes. Notice that the dotted links always go either to $\perp$ or to an "invisible" node, which is one of the $k - 1$ subsidiary nodes in a chain of branches such as (124). Every invisible node has a single parent. But there is one visible node for each successful signature, and a visible node may have many parents.

Exercises 256–262 discuss a number of examples where Algorithm Z gives spectacular improvements over Algorithm X (and over Algorithm C when colors are involved). Many additional examples could also be given. But most of the exact cover problems we've been considering in our examples do *not* have an abundance of common subproblems, so they reap little benefit from the memo cache.

For example, consider our old standby, the problem of Langford pairs. Algorithm X needs 15 Gμ to show that there are no solutions when $n = 14$; Algorithm Z reduces this slightly, to 11 Gμ. Algorithm X needs 1153 Gμ to list the 326,721,800 solutions for $n = 16$; Algorithm Z computes that number in 450 Gμ; but it needs 20 *gigabytes* of memory, and produces a ZDD of 500 million nodes!

Similarly, Algorithm Z is not the method of choice for the n queens problem, or for word-packing problems, although it does yield modest speedups more often than one might suspect. Exercise 263 surveys some typical examples.

Summary. We began this section by observing that simple properties of linked lists can enhance the efficiency of backtracking, especially when applied to exact cover problems (XC). Then we noticed that a wide variety of combinatorial tasks, going well beyond matching, turn out to be special cases of exact covering.

The most important "takeaway," however, has been the fact that *color codes* lead to a significant generalization of the classical exact cover problem.

Indeed, the general XCC problem, "exact covering with colors," has a truly extraordinary number of applications. The exercises below exhibit dozens and dozens of instructive problems that are quite naturally describable in terms of "options," which involve "items" that may or may not be colored in certain ways. We've discussed Algorithm X (for XC problems) and Algorithm C (for XCC problems); and the good news is that those algorithms are almost identical.

Furthermore, we've seen how to extend Algorithm C in several directions: Algorithm M handles the general MCC problem, which allows items to be covered with different ranges of multiplicities. Algorithm C$ associates a cost with each option, and finds XCC solutions of minimum total cost. Algorithm Z produces XCC solutions as ZDDs, which can be manipulated and optimized in other ways.

Historical notes. The basic idea of (2) was introduced by H. Hitotumatu and K. Noshita [*Information Processing Letters* **8** (1979), 174–175], who applied it to the n queens problem. Algorithm 7.2.1.2X, which was published by J. S. Rohl in 1983, can be regarded as a simplified version of dancing links, for cases when singly linked lists suffice. (Indeed, as Rohl observed, the n queens problem is such a case.) Its extension to exact cover problems in general, as in Algorithm X above, was the subject of the author's tribute to C. A. R. Hoare in *Millennial Perspectives in Computer Science* (2000), 187–214, where numerous examples were given. [That paper was subsequently reprinted with additions and corrections as Chapter 38 of *FGbook*.] His original implementation, called DLX, used a more complex data structure than (10), involving nodes with four-way links.

Knuth extended Algorithm X to Algorithm C in November 2000, while thinking about two-dimensional de Bruijn sequences. A special case of Algorithm M, in which all multiplicities are fixed, followed in August 2004, when he was thinking about packing various sizes of bricks into boxes. The current form of Algorithm M was developed in January 2017, after he'd studied an independent generalization of Algorithm X that Wei-Hwa Huang had written in 2007.

The first computer programs for exact cover problems were developed independently by J. F. Pierce [*Management Science* **15** (1968), 191–209] and by R. S. Garfinkel and G. L. Nemhauser [*Operations Research* **17** (1969), 848–856]. In both cases the given options each had an associated cost, and the goal was to obtain minimum-cost solutions instead of arbitrary solutions. Both algorithms were similar, although they used different ways to prune nonoptimum choices: Items were chosen for branching according to a fixed, precomputed order, and options were represented as bit vectors. An option was never removed from its item list; it would repeatedly be rejected if its bits intersected with previously chosen items. (*Caution:* Literature from the operations research community traditionally reverses the roles of rows and columns in matrices like (5). For them, items are rows and options are columns, even though bit vectors look like rows.)

The concept of "dancing with ZDDs" was introduced by M. Nishino, N. Yasuda, S. Minato, and M. Nagata, in the *AAAI Conference on Artificial Intelligence* **31** (2017), 868–874, where they presented the special case of Algorithm Z in which all items are primary.

The history of XCC solving is clearly still in its infancy, and much more work needs to be done. For example, many applications will benefit from improved ways to choose an item for branching — especially in step M3 of Algorithm M, where only a few strategies have been explored so far. It's important to maintain a good "focus"; furthermore, techniques of "factoring" can dramatically prune away unproductive branches, as shown for example in exercise 343.

Algorithm M deserves to be extended to Algorithm M$, and perhaps also to produce ZDD output. A further generalization would be to allow each item of each option to have an associated weight. (Thus the associated matrix, analogous to (5), would not consist merely of 0s and 1s.)

Hence we can expect to see many continued advances in XCC solving.

EXERCISES — First Set

▶ **1.** [*M25*] A doubly linked list of n elements, with a list head at 0, begins with $\mathtt{LLINK}(k) = k - 1$ and $\mathtt{RLINK}(k - 1) = k$ for $1 \le k \le n$; furthermore $\mathtt{LLINK}(0) = n$ and $\mathtt{RLINK}(n) = 0$, as in (3). But after we use operation (1) to delete elements a_1, a_2, ..., a_n, where $a_1 a_2 \ldots a_n$ is a permutation of $\{1, 2, \ldots, n\}$, the list will be empty and the links will be entangled as in (4).

a) Show that the final settings of $\mathtt{LLINK}$ and $\mathtt{RLINK}$ can be described in terms of the binary search tree that is obtained when the keys a_n, ..., a_2, a_1 (in reverse order) are inserted by Algorithm 6.2.2T into an initially empty tree.

b) Say that permutations $a_1 a_2 \ldots a_n$ and $b_1 b_2 \ldots b_n$ are equivalent if they both yield the same $\mathtt{LLINK}$ and $\mathtt{RLINK}$ values after deletion. How many distinct equivalence classes arise, for a given value of n?

c) How many of those equivalence classes contain just one permutation?

2. [*M30*] Continuing exercise 1, we know that the original list will be restored if we use (2) to undelete the elements a_n, ..., a_2, a_1, reversing the order of deletion.

a) Prove that it's restored *also* if we use the unreversed order a_1, a_2, ..., a_n (!).

b) Is the original list restored if we undelete the elements in *any* order whatsoever?

c) What if we delete only k of the elements, say a_1, ..., a_k, then undelete them in exactly the same order a_1, ..., a_k. Is the list always restored?

3. [*20*] An $m \times n$ matrix that's supposed to be exactly covered can be regarded as a set of n simultaneous equations in m unknowns. For example, (5) is equivalent to

$$x_2 + x_4 = x_3 + x_5 = x_1 + x_3 = x_2 + x_4 + x_6 = x_1 + x_6 = x_3 + x_4 = x_2 + x_5 + x_6 = 1,$$

where each $x_k = [\text{choose row } k]$ is either 0 or 1.

a) What is the general solution to those seven equations?

b) Why is this approach to exact cover problems almost never useful in practice?

4. [*M20*] Given a graph G, construct a matrix with one row for each vertex v and one column for each edge e, putting the value $[e \text{ touches } v]$ into column e of row v. What do the exact covers of this "incidence matrix" represent?

5. [*18*] Among the many combinatorial problems that can be formulated in terms of 0–1 matrices, some of the most important deal with *families of sets*: The columns of the matrix represent elements of a given universe, and the rows represent subsets of that universe. The exact cover problem is then to partition the universe into such subsets. In geometric contexts, an exact cover is often called a *tiling*.

Equivalently, we can use the terminology of hypergraphs, speaking of hyperedges (rows) that consist of vertices (columns); then the exact cover problem is to find a perfect matching, also called a perfect packing, namely a set of nonoverlapping hyperedges that hit every vertex.

Such problems generally have *duals*, which arise when we transpose the rows and columns of the input matrix. What is the dual of the exact cover problem, in hypergraph terminology?

6. [*15*] If an exact cover problem has N items and M options, and if the total length of all options is L, how many nodes are in the data structures used by Algorithm X?

7. [*16*] Why is TOP(23) = −4 in Table 1? Why is DLINK(23) = 25?

8. [*22*] Design an algorithm to set up the initial memory contents of an exact cover problem, as needed by Algorithm X and illustrated in Table 1. The input to your algorithm should consist of a sequence of lines with the following format:
- The very first line lists the names of all items.
- Each remaining line specifies the items of a particular option, one option per line.

9. [*18*] Explain how to branch in step X3 on an item i for which LEN(i) is minimum. If several items have that minimum length, i itself should also be minimum. (This choice is often called the "minimum remaining values" (MRV) heuristic.)

10. [*20*] In some applications the MRV heuristic of exercise 9 leads the search astray, because certain primary items have short lists yet convey little information about desirable choices. Modify answer 9 so that an item p whose name does not begin with the character '#' will be chosen only if LEN(p) ≤ 1 or no other choices exist. (This tactic is called the "sharp preference" heuristic.)

▶ **11.** [*19*] Play through Algorithm X by hand, using exercise 9 in step X3 and the input in Table 1, until first reaching step X7. What are the contents of memory at that time?

▶ **12.** [*21*] Design an algorithm that prints the option associated with a given node x, cyclically ordering the option so that TOP(x) is its first item. Also print the position of that option in the vertical list for that item. (For example, if $x = 21$ in Table 1, your algorithm should print '$d\ f\ a$' and state that it's option 2 of 3 in the list for item d.)

13. [*16*] When Algorithm X finds a solution in step X2, how can we use the values of $x_0 x_1 \ldots x_{l-1}$ to figure out what that solution is?

▶ **14.** [*20*] (*Problème des ménages.*) "In how many ways can n male-female couples sit at a circular table, with men and women alternating, and with no couples adjacent?"
  a) Suppose the women have already been seated, and let the vacant seats be $(S_0, S_1, \ldots, S_{n-1})$. Let M_j be the spouse of the woman between seats S_j and $S_{(j+1) \bmod n}$. Formulate the ménage problem as an exact cover problem with items S_j and M_j.
  b) Apply Algorithm X to find the solutions for $n \le 10$. Approximately how many mems are needed per solution, with and without the MRV heuristic?

15. [*20*] The options in (16) give us every solution to the Langford pair problem twice, because the left-right reversal of any solution is also a solution. Show that, if a few of those options are removed, we'll get only half as many solutions; the others will be the reversals of the solutions found.

16. [*16*] What are the solutions to the four queens problem, as formulated in (23) and (24)? What branches are taken at the top four levels of Algorithm X's search tree?

17. [*16*] Repeat exercise 16, but consider a_j and b_j to be secondary items and omit the slack options (24). Consider the primary items in order $r_3, c_3, r_2, c_2, r_4, c_4, r_1, c_1$.

18. [*10*] What are the solutions to (6) if items e, f, and g are *secondary*?

▶ **19.** [*21*] Modify Algorithm X so that it doesn't require the presence of any primary items in the options. A valid solution should not contain any purely secondary options; but it must intersect every such option. (For example, if only items a and b of (6) were primary, the only valid solution would be to choose options 'a d g' and 'b c f'.)

▶ **20.** [*25*] Generalize (26) to a pairwise ordering of options $(\alpha_0, \ldots, \alpha_{m-1}; \beta_0, \ldots, \beta_{m-1})$ that uses at most $\lceil \lg m \rceil$ of the secondary items y_1, $\ldots$, y_{m-1} in each option. *Hint:* Think of binary notation, and use y_j at most $2^{\rho j}$ times within each of the α's and β's.

21. [*22*] Extend exercise 20 to k-wise ordering of km options α_j^i, for $1 \le i \le k$ and $0 \le j < m$. The solutions should be $(\alpha_{j_1}^1, \ldots, \alpha_{j_k}^k)$ with $0 \le j_1 \le \cdots \le j_k < m$. Again there should be at most $\lceil \lg m \rceil$ secondary items in each option.

▶ **22.** [*28*] Most of the solutions to the n queens problem are unsymmetrical, hence they lead to seven other solutions when rotated and/or reflected. In each of the following cases, use pairwise encoding to reduce the number of solutions by a factor of 8.

a) No queen is in either diagonal, and n is odd.
b) Only one of the two diagonals contains a queen.   (a)   (b)   (c)
c) There are two queens in the two diagonals.

23. [*28*] Use pairwise encoding to reduce the number of solutions by *nearly* a factor of 8 in the remaining cases not covered by exercise 22:

a) No queen is in either diagonal, and n is even.
b) A queen is in the center of the board, and n is odd.

24. [*20*] With Algorithm X, find all solutions to the n queens problem that are unchanged when they're rotated by (a) 180°; (b) 90°.

25. [*20*] By setting up an exact cover problem and solving it with Algorithm X, show that the queen graph Q_8 (exercise 7.1.4–241) cannot be colored with eight colors.

26. [*21*] In how many ways can the queen graph Q_8 be colored in a "balanced" fashion, using eight queens of color 0 and seven each of colors 1 to 8?

27. [*22*] Introduce secondary items cleverly into the options (16), so that only *planar* solutions to Langford's problem are obtained. (See exercise 7–8.)

28. [*M22*] For what integers c_0, t_0, c_1, t_1, $\ldots$, c_l, t_l with $1 \le c_j \le t_j$ does the text's formula (27) for estimated completion ratio give the value (a) 1/2? (b) 1/3?

▶ **29.** [*26*] Let T be any tree. Construct the 0–1 matrix of an unsolvable exact cover problem for which T is the backtrack tree traversed by Algorithm X with the MRV heuristic. (A *unique* item should have the minimum LEN value whenever step X3 is encountered.) Illustrate your construction when $T = \bigwedge\!\bigwedge$.

30. [*25*] Continuing exercise 29, let T be a tree in which certain leaves have been distinguished from the others and designated as "solutions." Can all such trees arise as backtrack trees in Algorithm X?

31. [*M21*] The running time of Algorithm X depends on the order of primary items in the active list, as well as on the order of options in the individual item lists. Explain how to *randomize* the algorithm so that (a) every item list is in random order after step X1; (b) step X3 chooses randomly among items with the minimum LEN.

32. [*M21*] The solution to an exact cover problem with M options can be regarded as a binary vector $x = x_1 \ldots x_M$, with $x_k = [\text{choose option } k]$. The *distance* between two solutions x and x' can then be defined as the Hamming distance $d(x, x') = \nu(x \oplus x')$, the number of places where x and x' differ. The *diversity* of the problem is the minimum distance between two of its solutions. (If there's at most one solution, the diversity is ∞.)

a) Is it possible to have diversity 1?

b) Is it possible to have diversity 2?

c) Is it possible to have diversity 3?

d) Prove that the distance between solutions of a *uniform* exact cover problem — that is, a problem having the same number of items in each option — is always even.

e) Most of the exact cover problems that arise in applications are at least *quasi-uniform*, in the sense that they have a nonempty subset of primary items such that the problem is uniform when restricted to only those items. (For example, every polyomino or polycube packing problem is quasi-uniform, because every option specifies exactly one piece name.) Can such problems have odd distances?

33. [*M16*] Given an exact cover problem, specified by a 0–1 matrix A, construct an exact cover problem A' that has exactly one more solution than A does. [Consequently it is NP-hard to determine whether an exact cover problem with at least one solution has more than one solution.] Assume that A contains no all-zero rows.

34. [*M25*] Given an exact cover problem A as in exercise 33, construct an exact cover problem A' such that (i) A' has at most three 1s in every column; (ii) A' and A have exactly the same number of solutions.

35. [*M21*] Continuing exercise 34, construct A' having *exactly* three 1s per column.

▶ **36.** [25] Let $i_k = \mathtt{TOP}(x_k)$ be the item on which branching occurs at level k in Algorithm X. Modify that algorithm so that it finds the solution for which $i_0 x_0 i_1 x_1 i_2 x_2 \ldots$ is *smallest* in lexicographic order. (It's easy to do this by simply setting $i \leftarrow \mathtt{RLINK}(0)$ in step X3. But there's a much faster way, by using the MRV heuristic most of the time.)

What is the lexicographically first solution to the 32 queens problem?

37. [*M46*] (N. J. A. Sloane, 2016.) Let $\langle q_n \rangle$ be the lexicographically smallest solution to the ∞ queens problem. (This sequence begins

$$1, 3, 5, 2, 4, 9, 11, 13, 15, 6, 8, 19, 7, 22, 10, 25, 27, 29, 31, 12, 14, 35, 37, 39, 41, 16, 18, 45, \ldots,$$

and it clearly has strange regularities and irregularities.)

a) Prove that every positive integer occurs in the sequence.

b) Prove that q_n is either $n\phi + O(1)$ or $n/\phi + O(1)$.

▶ **38.** [*M25*] Devise an efficient way to compute the sequence $\langle q_n \rangle$ of exercise 37.

▶ **39.** [*M21*] Experiment with exact cover problems that are defined by m *random* options on n items. (Each option is generated independently, with repetitions permitted.)

a) Use a fixed probability p that item i is included in any given option.

b) Let every option be a random sample of r distinct items.

▶ **40.** [21] If we merely want to count the number of solutions to an exact cover problem, without actually constructing them, a completely different approach based on bitwise manipulation instead of list processing is sometimes useful.

The following naïve algorithm illustrates the idea: We're given an $m \times n$ matrix of 0s and 1s, represented as n-bit vectors $r_1, \ldots, r_m$. The algorithm works with a (potentially huge) database of pairs (s_j, c_j), where s_j is an n-bit number representing a set of items, and c_j is a positive integer representing the number of ways to cover that set exactly. Let p be the n-bit mask that represents the primary items.

N1. [Initialize.] Set $N \leftarrow 1$, $s_1 \leftarrow 0$, $c_1 \leftarrow 1$, $k \leftarrow 1$.

N2. [Done?] If $k > m$, terminate; the answer is $\sum_{j=1}^{N} c_j [s_j \& p = p]$.

N3. [Append r_k where possible.] Set $t \leftarrow r_k$. For $N \geq j \geq 1$, if $s_j \& t = 0$, insert $(s_j + t, c_j)$ into the database (see below).

N4. [Loop on k.] Set $k \leftarrow k + 1$ and return to N2. ∎

To insert (s, c) there are two cases: If $s = s_i$ for some (s_i, c_i) already present, we simply set $c_i \leftarrow c_i + c$. Otherwise we set $N \leftarrow N + 1$, $s_N \leftarrow s$, $c_N \leftarrow c$.

Show that this algorithm can be significantly improved by using the following trick: Set $u_k \leftarrow r_k \& \bar{f}_k$, where $f_k = r_{k+1} | \cdots | r_m$ is the bitwise OR of all future rows. If $u_k \neq 0$, we can remove any entry from the database for which s_j does not contain $u_k \& p$. We can also exploit the nonprimary items of u_k to compress the database further.

41. [*25*] Implement the improved algorithm of the previous exercise, and compare its running time to that of Algorithm X when applied to the n queens problem.

42. [*M21*] Explain how the method of exercise 40 could be extended to give representations of all solutions, instead of simply counting them.

43. [*M20*] Give formulas for the entries a_{ij}, b_{ij}, c_{ij} of the sudoku squares in (28).

44. [*M04*] Could the clues of a sudoku puzzle be the first 33 digits of π? (See (29a).)

45. [*14*] List the sequence of naked single moves by which Algorithm X cruises to the solution of (29a). (If several such p_{ij} are possible, choose the smallest ij at each step.)

46. [*19*] List all of the *hidden* single sudoku moves that are present in chart (31).

47. [*19*] What hidden singles are present in (32), after '3' is placed in cell $(2,3)$?

▶ **48.** [*24*] Chart (33) essentially plots rows versus columns. Show that the same data could be plotted as either (a) rows versus values; or (b) values versus columns.

▶ **49.** [*24*] Any solution to an exact cover problem will also solve the "relaxed" subproblems that are obtained by removing some of the items. For example, we might relax a sudoku problem (30) by removing all items c_{jk} and b_{xk}, as well as r_{ik} with $i \neq i_0$. Then we're left with a subproblem in which every option contains just two items, '$p_{i_0 j}\ r_{i_0 k}$', for certain pairs (j, k). In other words, we're left with a 2D matching problem.

Consider the bipartite graph with u_j — v_k whenever a sudoku option contains '$p_{i_0 j}\ r_{i_0 k}$'. For example, the graph for $i_0 = 4$ in (33) is illustrated below. A perfect matching of this graph must take u_3 and u_8 to either v_7 or v_1, hence the edges from other u's to those v's can be deleted; that's called a "naked pair" in row i_0. Dually, v_5 and v_8 must be matched to either u_2 or u_7, hence the edges from other v's to those u's can be deleted; that's called a "hidden pair" in row i_0.

In general, q of the u's form a *naked q-tuple* if their neighbors include only q of the v's; and q of the v's form a *hidden q-tuple* if their neighbors include only q of the u's.

a) These definitions have been given for rows. Show that naked and hidden q-tuples can be defined analogously for (i) columns, (ii) boxes.

b) Prove that if the bipartite graph has r vertices in each part, it has a hidden q-tuple if and only if it has a naked $(r - q)$-tuple.

c) Find all the naked and hidden q-tuples of (33). What options do they rule out?

d) Consider deleting items p_{ij} and b_{xk}, as well as all r_{ik} and c_{jk} for $k \neq k_0$. Does this lead to further reductions of (33)?

50. [*20*] How many uniquely solvable 17-clue puzzles contain the 16 clues of (29c)?

51. [*22*] In how many ways can (29c) be completed so that every row, every column, and every box contains a permutation of the multiset $\{1, 2, 3, 4, 5, 6, 7, 7, 9\}$?

52. [*40*] Try to find a sudoku puzzle that's as difficult as possible for Algorithm X.

53. [*M26*] Beginners to sudoku might want to cut their teeth on a miniature variant called *shidoku*, which features 4×4 squares divided into four 2×2 boxes.
  a) Prove that every uniquely solvable shidoku problem has at least four clues.
  b) Two shidoku problems are equivalent if we can get from one to the other by permuting rows and columns in such a way that boxes are preserved, and/or by 90° rotation, and/or by permuting the numbers. Show that exactly 13 essentially different 4-clue shidoku problems have a unique solution.

▶ **54.** [*35*] (*Minimal clues.*) Puzzle (29a) contains more clues than necessary to make the sudoku solution unique. (For example, the final '95' could be omitted.) Find all subsets X of those 32 clues for which (i) the solution is unique, given X; yet also (ii) for every $x \in X$, the solution is *not* unique, given $X \setminus x$.

55. [*34*] (G. McGuire.) Prove that at least 18 clues are necessary, in any sudoku puzzle whose unique answer is (28a). Also find 18 clues that suffice. *Hint:* At least two of the nine appearances of $\{1, 4, 7\}$ in the top three rows must be among the clues.
   Similarly, find a smallest-possible set of clues whose unique answer is (28b).

56. [*47*] What is the largest number of clues in a minimal sudoku puzzle?

57. [*22*] Every sudoku solution has at most 27 horizontal trios and 27 vertical trios, namely the 3-digit sets that appear within a single row or column of a box. For example, (28a) has nine horizontal trios $\{1, 2, 3\}$, $\{2, 3, 4\}$, ..., $\{9, 1, 2\}$ and three vertical trios $\{1, 4, 7\}$, $\{2, 5, 8\}$, $\{3, 6, 9\}$; (28b) has just three of each. The solution to (29a) has 26 horizontal trios and 23 vertical trios; $\{3, 6, 8\}$ occurs once horizontally, twice vertically.
   Let T be the 27 trios $\{\{A, B, C\} \mid A \in \{1, 2, 3\}, B \in \{4, 5, 6\}, C \in \{7, 8, 9\}\}$. Find all sudoku solutions whose horizontal trios and vertical trios are both equal to T.

▶ **58.** [*22*] (A. Thoen and A. van de Wetering, 2019.) Find all sudoku solutions for which the 1s, 2s, ..., 7s also solve the nine queens problem.

59. [*20*] Solve the jigsaw sudokus in (34). How large is Algorithm X's search tree?

60. [*20*] (*The Puzzlium Sudoku ABC.*) Complete these hexomino-shaped boxes:

(a) 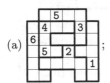 ; (b) 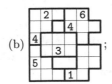 ; (c) 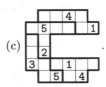 .

61. [*21*] Turn Behrens's 5×5 gerechte design (35a) into a jigsaw sudoku puzzle, by erasing all but five of its 25 entries.

▶ **62.** [*34*] For $n \leq 7$, generate all of the ways in which an $n \times n$ square can be packed with n nonstraight n-ominoes. (These are the possible arrangements of boxes in a square jigsaw sudoku.) How many of them are symmetric? *Hint:* See exercise 7.2.2–76.

63. [*29*] In how many different ways can Behrens's 9×9 array (35c) be regarded as a gerechte latin square? (In other words, how many decompositions of that square into nine boxes of size 9 have a complete "rainbow" $\{1, 2, 3, 4, 5, 6, 7, 8, 9\}$ in each box? None of the boxes should simply be an entire row or an entire column.)

64. [23] (*Clueless jigsaw sudoku.*) A jigsaw sudoku puzzle can be called "clueless" if its solution is uniquely determined by the entries in a single row or column, because such clues merely assign names to the n individual symbols that appear. For example, the first such puzzle to be published, discovered in 2000 by Oriel Maxime, is shown here.

   a) Find all clueless sudoku jigsaw puzzles of order $n \le 6$.
   b) Prove that such puzzles exist of all orders $n \ge 4$.

65. [24] Find the unique solutions to the following examples of jigsaw sudoku:

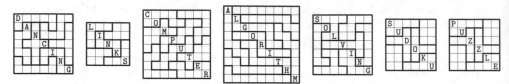

▶ **66.** [30] Arrange the following sets of nine cards in a 3×3 array so that they define a sudoku problem with a unique solution. (Don't rotate them.)

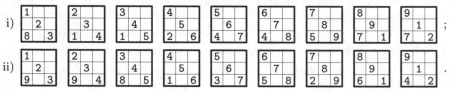

▶ **67.** [22] *Hypersudoku* extends normal sudoku by adding four more (shaded) boxes in which a complete "rainbow" $\{1,2,3,4,5,6,7,8,9\}$ is required to appear:

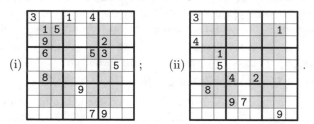

(Such puzzles, introduced by P. Ritmeester in 2005, are featured by many newspapers.)
   a) Show that a hypersudoku solution actually has 18 rainbow boxes, not only 13.
   b) Use that observation to solve hypersudoku puzzles efficiently by extending (30).
   c) How much does that observation help when solving (i) and (ii)?
   d) True or false: A hypersudoku solution remains a hypersudoku solution if the four 4×4 blocks that touch its four corners are simultaneously rotated 180°, while also flipping the middle half-rows and middle half-columns (keeping the center fixed).

68. [28] A polyomino is called *convex* if it contains all of the cells between any two of its cells that lie in the same row or the same column. (This happens if and only if it has the same perimeter as its minimum bounding box does, because each row and column contribute 2.) For example, all of the pentominoes (36) are convex, except for 'U'.
   a) Generate all ways to pack n convex n-ominoes into an $n \times n$ box, for $n \le 7$.
   b) In how many ways can nine convex nonominoes be packed into a 9×9 box, when each of them is small enough to fit into a 4×4? (Consider also the symmetries.)

▶ **69.** [*30*] Diagram (i) below shows the 81 communities of Bitland, and their nine elec-
toral districts. The voters in each community are either Big-Endian (B) or Little-Endian
(L). Each district has a representative in Bitland's parliament, based on a majority vote.

Notice that there are five Ls and four Bs in every district, hence the parliament is
100% Little-Endian. Everybody agrees that this is unfair. So you have been hired as
a computer consultant, to engineer the redistricting.

A rich bigwig secretly offers to pay you a truckload of money if you get the best
possible deal for his side. You could gerrymander the districts as in diagram (ii),
thereby obtaining seven Big-Endian seats. But that would be too blatantly biased.

(i)
B	B	L	B	L	L	L	L	B
L	L	L	B	L	L	L	B	L
B	B	L	B	L	B	B	L	B
L	L	L	L	L	L	L	L	L
B	B	B	L	L	B	L	L	B
L	B	L	B	B	B	B	B	B
B	B	L	B	B	B	B	B	L
L	B	L	L	L	L	B	L	L
L	L	B	L	L	B	B	L	L

;

(ii)
B	B	L	B	L	L	L	L	B
L	L	L	B	L	L	L	B	L
B	B	L	B	L	B	B	L	B
L	L	L	L	L	L	L	L	L
B	B	B	L	L	B	L	L	B
L	B	L	B	B	B	B	B	B
B	B	L	B	B	B	B	B	L
L	B	L	L	L	L	B	L	L
L	L	B	L	L	B	B	L	L

.

Show that seven wins for B are actually obtainable with nine districts that do
respect the local neighborhoods of Bitland quite decently, because each of them is a
convex nonomino that fits in a 4 × 4 square (see exercise 68).

70. [*21*] *Dominosa* is a solitaire game in which you "shuffle" the 28 pieces ▰,
▰, ..., ▦ of double-six dominoes and place them at random into a 7 × 8 frame.
Then you write down the number of spots in each cell, put the dominoes away, and try
to reconstruct their positions based only on that 7 × 8 array of numbers. For example,

yields the array

$$
\begin{pmatrix}
0 & 6 & 5 & 2 & 1 & 4 & 1 & 2 \\
1 & 4 & 5 & 3 & 5 & 3 & 3 & 6 \\
1 & 1 & 5 & 6 & 0 & 0 & 4 & 4 \\
4 & 4 & 5 & 6 & 2 & 2 & 2 & 3 \\
0 & 0 & 5 & 6 & 1 & 3 & 3 & 6 \\
6 & 6 & 2 & 0 & 3 & 2 & 5 & 1 \\
1 & 5 & 0 & 4 & 4 & 0 & 3 & 2
\end{pmatrix}.
$$

a) Show that *another* placement of dominoes also yields the same matrix of numbers.
b) What domino placement yields the array

$$
\begin{pmatrix}
3 & 3 & 6 & 5 & 1 & 5 & 1 & 5 \\
6 & 5 & 6 & 1 & 2 & 3 & 2 & 4 \\
2 & 4 & 3 & 3 & 3 & 6 & 2 & 0 \\
4 & 1 & 6 & 1 & 4 & 4 & 6 & 0 \\
3 & 0 & 3 & 0 & 1 & 1 & 4 & 4 \\
2 & 6 & 2 & 5 & 0 & 5 & 0 & 0 \\
2 & 5 & 0 & 5 & 4 & 2 & 1 & 6
\end{pmatrix} ?
$$

▶ **71.** [*20*] Show that Dominosa reconstruction is a special case of 3DM (3D matching).

72. [*M22*] Generate random instances of Dominosa, and estimate the probability of
obtaining a 7×8 matrix with a unique solution. Use two models of randomness: (i) Each
matrix whose elements are permutations of the multiset $\{8 \times 0, 8 \times 1, \ldots, 8 \times 6\}$ is equally
likely; (ii) each matrix obtained from a random shuffle of the dominoes is equally likely.

73. [*46*] What's the maximum number of solutions to an instance of Dominosa?

74. [*22*] (M. Keller, 1987.) Is there a uniquely solvable Dominosa array for which every domino matches two adjacent cells of the array in either three or four places?

▶ **75.** [*M24*] A *grope* is a set G together with a binary operation ∘, in which the identity $x \circ (y \circ x) = y$ is satisfied for all $x \in G$ and $y \in G$.

a) Prove that the identity $(x \circ y) \circ x = y$ also holds, in every grope.

b) Which of the following "multiplication tables" define a grope on $\{0, 1, 2, 3\}$?

$$\begin{matrix} 0123 \\ 1032 \\ 2301 \\ 3210 \end{matrix} , \quad \begin{matrix} 0321 \\ 3210 \\ 2103 \\ 1032 \end{matrix} , \quad \begin{matrix} 0132 \\ 1023 \\ 3210 \\ 2301 \end{matrix} , \quad \begin{matrix} 0231 \\ 3102 \\ 1320 \\ 2013 \end{matrix} , \quad \begin{matrix} 0312 \\ 2130 \\ 3021 \\ 1203 \end{matrix} .$$

(In the first example, $x \circ y = x \oplus y$; in the second, $x \circ y = (-x - y) \bmod 4$. The last two have $x \circ y = x \oplus f(x \oplus y)$ for certain functions f.)

c) For all n, construct a grope whose elements are $\{0, 1, \ldots, n - 1\}$.

d) Consider the exact cover problem that has n^2 items xy for $0 \le x, y < n$ and the following $n + (n^3 - n)/3$ options:

   i) 'xx', for $0 \le x < n$;

   ii) '$xx\ xy\ yx$', for $0 \le x < y < n$;

   iii) '$xy\ yz\ zx$', for $0 \le x < y, z < n$.

Show that its solutions are in one-to-one correspondence with the multiplication tables of gropes on the elements $\{0, 1, \ldots, n - 1\}$.

e) Element x of a grope is *idempotent* if $x \circ x = x$. If k elements are idempotent and $n - k$ are not, prove that $k \equiv n^2$ (modulo 3).

76. [*21*] Modify the exact cover problem of exercise 75(d) in order to find the multiplication tables of (a) all idempotent gropes — gropes such that $x \circ x = x$ for all x; (b) all commutative gropes — gropes such that $x \circ y = y \circ x$ for all x and y; (c) all gropes with the identity element 0 — gropes such that $x \circ 0 = 0 \circ x = x$ for all x.

77. [*M21*] Given graphs G and H, each with n vertices, use Algorithm X to decide whether or not G is isomorphic to a subgraph of H. (In such a case we say that G is *embedded* in H.)

78. [*16*] Show that it's quite easy to pack the 27 mathematicians' names of Fig. 71 into a 12×15 array, with all names reading correctly from left to right. (Of course that would be a *terrible* word search puzzle.)

79. [*M20*] How many options are in (48), when they are completely listed?

80. [*19*] Play through Algorithm C by hand, using exercise 9 in step C3 and the input in Table 2, until first reaching a solution. What are the contents of memory then?

81. [*21*] True or false: An exact cover problem that has no color assignments has exactly the same running time on Algorithms X and C.

82. [*21*] True or false: It's possible to save memory references in Algorithms X and C by not updating the LEN fields in the hide/unhide operations when $x > N_1$.

▶ **83.** [*20*] Algorithm C can be extended in the following curious way: Let p be the primary item that is covered first, and suppose that there are k ways to cover it. Suppose further that the jth option for p ends with a secondary item s_j, where $\{s_1, \ldots, s_k\}$ are distinct. Modify the algorithm so that, whenever a solution contains the jth option for p, it leaves items $\{s_1, \ldots, s_{j-1}\}$ uncovered. (In other words, the modified algorithm will emulate the behavior of the unmodified algorithm on a much larger instance, in which the jth option for p contains all of $s_1, s_2, \ldots, s_j$.)

▶ **84.** [*25*] Number the options of an XCC problem from 1 to M. A *minimax solution* is one whose maximum option number is as small as possible. Explain how to modify Algorithm C so that it determines all of the minimax solutions (omitting any that are known to be worse than a solution already found).

85. [*22*] Sharpen the algorithm of exercise 84 so that it produces *exactly one* minimax solution — unless, of course, there are no solutions at all.

▶ **86.** [*M25*] Modify Algorithm C so that, instead of finding all solutions to a given XCC problem, it gives a *Monte Carlo estimate* of the number of solutions and the time needed to find them, using Theorem 7.2.2E. (Thus the modified algorithm is to Algorithm C as Algorithm 7.2.2E is to Algorithm 7.2.2B.)

87. [*20*] A *double word square* is an $n \times n$ array whose rows and columns contain $2n$ different words. Encode this problem as an XCC problem. Can you save a factor of 2 by not generating the transpose of previous solutions? Does Algorithm C compete with the algorithm of exercise 7.2.2–28 (which was designed explicitly to handle such problems)?

88. [*21*] Instead of finding *all* of the double word squares, we usually are more interested in finding the *best* one, in the sense of using only words that are quite common. For example, it turns out that a double word square can be made from the words of WORDS(1720) but not from those of WORDS(1719). Show that it's rather easy to find the smallest W such that WORDS(W) supports a double word square, via dancing links.

89. [*24*] What are the best double word squares of sizes 2×2, 3×3, ..., 7×7, in the sense of exercise 88, with respect to *The Official SCRABBLE® Players Dictionary*? [Exercise 7.2.2–32 considered the analogous problem for *symmetric* word squares.]

▶ **90.** [*22*] A *word stair* of period p is a cyclic arrangement of words, offset stepwise, that contains $2p$ distinct words across and down. They exist in two varieties, left and right:

```
. . .                            . . .
        S T A I R                        S T A I R
        S H A R P                        S L O O P
        S T E M S                        S T O O D
        S C R A P                        S T E E R
        S T A I R                        S T A I R
        S H A R P                        S L O O P
        S T E M S        p = 4           S T O O D
        S C R A P                        S T E E R
        S T A I R                        S T A I R
. . .                                       . . .
```

What are the best five-letter word stairs, in the sense of exercise 88, for $1 \le p \le 10$? *Hint:* You can save a factor of $2p$ by assuming that the first word is the most common.

91. [*40*] For given W, find the largest p such that WORDS(W) supports a word stair of period p. (There are two questions for each W, examining stairs to the {left, right}.)

92. [*24*] Some p-word cycles define *two-way* word stairs that have $3p$ distinct words:

```
      . . .                          . . .
        R A P I D                        R A P I D
        R A T E D                        R A T E D
        L A C E S                        L A C E S
        R O B E S                        R O B E S
        R A P I D                        R A P I D
        R A T E D                        R A T E D
        L A C E S        p = 4           L A C E S
        R O B E S                        R O B E S
        R A P I D                        R A P I D
      . . .                                 . . .
```

What are the best five-letter examples of this variety, for $1 \le p \le 10$?

93. [22] Another periodic arrangement of $3p$ words, perhaps even nicer than that of exercise 92 and illustrated here for $p = 3$, lets us read them *diagonally* up or down, as well as across. What are the best five-letter examples of *this* variety, for $1 \le p \le 10$? (Notice that there is $2p$-way symmetry.)

```
          · · · ·
S L A N T   (F L I N T)
F L U N K   (B L A N K)
B L I N K   (S L U N K)
S K A N T   (F L I N T)
F L U N K   (S L I N K)
B L I N K   (F L A N K)
S L A N T   (B L U N T)
F L U N K   (S L I N K)
          · · · ·
```

94. [20] (É. Lucas.) Find a binary cycle $(x_0 x_1 \ldots x_{15})$ for which the 16 quadruples $x_k x_{(k+1) \bmod 16} x_{(k+3) \bmod 16} x_{(k+4) \bmod 16}$ for $0 \le k < 16$ are distinct.

▸ **95.** [20] Given $0 \le p < q \le n$, explain how to use color controls and Algorithm C to find all cycles $(x_0 x_1 \ldots x_{m-1})$ of 0s and 1s, where $m = \sum_{k=p}^{q} \binom{n}{k}$, with the property that the m binary vectors $\{x_0 x_1 \ldots x_{n-1}, x_1 x_2 \ldots x_n, \ldots, x_{m-1} x_0 \ldots x_{n-2}\}$ are distinct and have weight between p and q. (In other words, all n-bit binary vectors $y = y_1 \ldots y_n$ with $p \le \nu y \le q$ occur exactly once in the cycle. We studied the special case of *de Bruijn cycles*, for which $p = 0$ and $q = n$, in Section 7.2.1.1.)

For example, when $n = 7$, $p = 0$, and $q = 3$, the cycle

$$(0000000100000110000101000101100010010101001001100100011010000111)$$

exhibits all binary 7-tuples with a majority of 0s. When $n = 7$, $p = 3$, $q = 4$, the cycle

$$(0000111000101100011010010101011010100110011011001011100100111010001111)$$

shows all 7-tuples obtainable by removing the first bit of an 8-tuple with four 0s, four 1s.

Exactly how many cycles exist, when $(n, p, q) = (7, 0, 3)$ or $(7, 3, 4)$? How long does it take for Algorithm C to find them?

96. [M20] Find an 8×8 binary torus whose sixty-four 2×3 subrectangles are distinct.

97. [M21] Find all 9×9 ternary ourotoruses $D = (d_{i,j})$ that are symmetrical, in the sense that $d_{(i+3) \bmod 9, (j+3) \bmod 9} = (d_{i,j} + 1) \bmod 3$. (See exercise 7.2.1.1–109.)

98. [25] Prove that the exact cover problem with color controls is NP-complete, even if every option consists of only two items.

99. [20] True or false: Every XCC problem can be reformulated as an *ordinary* exact cover problem with the same solutions and the same number of options.

▸ **100.** [20] The general *constraint satisfaction problem* (CSP) is the task of finding all n-tuples $x_1 \ldots x_n$ that satisfy a given system of constraints $C_1, \ldots, C_m$, where each constraint is defined by a relation on a nonempty subset of the variables $\{x_1, \ldots, x_n\}$.

For example, a unary constraint is a relation of the form $x_k \in D_k$; a binary constraint is a relation of the form $(x_j, x_k) \in D_{jk}$; a ternary constraint is a relation of the form $(x_i, x_j, x_k) \in D_{ijk}$; and so on.

a) Find all $x_1 x_2 x_3 x_4 x_5$ for which $0 \le x_1 \le x_2 \le x_3 \le x_4 \le x_5 \le 2$ and $x_1 + x_3 + x_5 = 3$.
b) Formulate the problem of part (a) as an XCC problem.
c) Explain how to formulate *any* CSP as an XCC problem.

▸ **101.** [25] (*The zebra puzzle.*) Formulate the following query as an XCC problem: "Five people, from five different countries, have five different occupations, own five different pets, drink five different beverages, and live in a row of five differently colored houses.

- The Englishman lives in a red house.
- The yellow house hosts a diplomat.
- The Norwegian's house is the leftmost.
- The milk drinker lives in the middle house.

- The painter comes from Japan.
- The coffee-lover's house is green.
- The dog's owner is from Spain.
- The violinist drinks orange juice.

- The white house is just left of the green one.   • The Ukrainian drinks tea.
- The Norwegian lives next to the blue house.   • The sculptor breeds snails.
- The horse lives next to the diplomat.   • The nurse lives next to the fox.

Who trains the zebra, and who prefers to drink just plain water?"

▶ **102.** [*25*] Explain how to find all solutions to a *Japanese arrow puzzle* with Algorithm C. (See exercise 7.2.2–68.)

▶ **103.** [*M28*] Musical pitches in the Western system of "equal temperament" are the notes whose frequency is $440 \cdot 2^{n/12}$ cycles per second, for some integer n. The *pitch class* of such a note is $n \bmod 12$, and seven of the twelve possible pitch classes are conventionally designated by letters:

$$0 = \text{A}, \quad 2 = \text{B}, \quad 3 = \text{C}, \quad 5 = \text{D}, \quad 7 = \text{E}, \quad 8 = \text{F}, \quad 10 = \text{G}.$$

The other classes are named by appending sharp ($\sharp$) or flat ($\flat$) signs, to go up or down by 1; thus $1 = \text{A}\sharp = \text{B}\flat$, $4 = \text{C}\sharp = \text{D}\flat$, ..., $11 = \text{G}\sharp = \text{A}\flat$.

Arnold Schoenberg popularized a composition technique that he called a twelve-tone row, which is simply a permutation of the twelve pitch classes. For example, his student Alban Berg featured the motif

which is the twelve-tone row 8 7 3 0 10 5 11 4 6 9 1 2, in the first movement of his Lyric Suite (1926), and in another composition he had written in 1925.

In general we can say that an n-tone row $x = x_0 x_1 \ldots x_{n-1}$ is a permutation of $\{0, 1, \ldots, n-1\}$. Two n-tone rows x and x' are considered to be *equivalent* if they differ only by a transposition — that is, if $x'_k = (x_k + d) \bmod n$ for some d and for $0 \le k < n$. Thus, the number of inequivalent n-tone rows is exactly $(n-1)!$.

- a) Berg's 12-tone row above has the additional property that the intervals between adjacent notes, $(x_k - x_{k-1}) \bmod n$, are $\{1, \ldots, n-1\}$. Prove that an n-tone row can have this all-interval property only if n is even and $x_{n-1} = (x_0 + n/2) \bmod n$.
- b) Use Algorithm C to find n-tone rows with the all-interval property. How many inequivalent solutions arise, when $2 \le n \le 12$?
- c) Any all-interval n-tone row leads easily to several others. For example, if $x = x_0 x_1 \ldots x_{n-1}$ is a solution, so is its reversal $x^R = x_{n-1} \ldots x_1 x_0$; and so is $cx = (cx_0 \bmod n)(cx_1 \bmod n) \ldots (cx_{n-1} \bmod n)$ whenever $c \perp n$. Prove that the cyclic shift $x^Q = x_k \ldots x_{n-1} x_0 \ldots x_{k-1}$ is also a solution, when $x_k - x_{k-1} = \pm n/2$.
- d) True or false: In part (c) we always have $x^{RQ} = x^{QR}$.
- e) The 12-tone row of Alban Berg shown above is symmetrical, because it is equivalent to x^R. Other kinds of symmetry are also possible; for example, the row $x = 0\,1\,3\,7\,2\,5\,11\,10\,8\,4\,9\,6$ is equivalent to $-x^Q$. How many symmetrical all-interval n-tone rows exist, for $n \le 12$?

104. [*M28*] Assume that $n + 1 = p$ is prime. Given an n-tone row $x = x_0 x_1 \ldots x_{n-1}$, define $y_k = x_{(k-1) \bmod p}$ whenever k is not a multiple of p, and let $x^{(r)} = y_r y_{2r} \ldots y_{nr}$ be the n-tone row consisting of "every rth element of x" (if x_n is blank). For example, when $n = 12$, every 5th element of x is the sequence $x^{(5)} = x_4 x_9 x_1 x_6 x_{11} x_3 x_8 x_0 x_5 x_{10} x_2 x_7$.

An n-tone row is called *perfect* if it is equivalent to $x^{(r)}$ for $1 \le r \le n$. For example, the amazing 12-tone row $0\,1\,4\,2\,9\,5\,11\,3\,8\,10\,7\,6$ is perfect.

- a) Prove that a perfect n-tone row has the all-interval property.
- b) Prove that a perfect n-tone row also satisfies $x \equiv x^R$.

105. [22] Using the "word search puzzle" conventions of Figs. 71 and 72, show that the words ONE, TWO, THREE, FOUR, FIVE, SIX, SEVEN, EIGHT, NINE, TEN, ELEVEN, and TWELVE can all be packed into a 6 × 6 square, leaving one cell untouched.

106. [22] Also pack *two* copies of ONE, TWO, THREE, FOUR, FIVE into a 5 × 5 square.

▶ **107.** [25] Pack as many of the following words as possible into a 9 × 9 array, simultaneously satisfying the rules of *both* word search *and* sudoku:

ACRE	COMPARE	CORPORATE	MACRO	MOTET	ROAM
ART	COMPUTER	CROP	META	PARAMETER	TAME

▶ **108.** [32] The first 44 presidents of the U.S.A. had 38 distinct surnames: ADAMS, ARTHUR, BUCHANAN, BUSH, CARTER, CLEVELAND, CLINTON, COOLIDGE, EISENHOWER, FILLMORE, FORD, GARFIELD, GRANT, HARDING, HARRISON, HAYES, HOOVER, JACKSON, JEFFERSON, JOHNSON, KENNEDY, LINCOLN, MADISON, MCKINLEY, MONROE, NIXON, OBAMA, PIERCE, POLK, REAGAN, ROOSEVELT, TAFT, TAYLOR, TRUMAN, TYLER, VANBUREN, WASHINGTON, WILSON.

    a) What's the smallest square into which all of these names can be packed, using word search conventions, and requiring all words to be *connected* via overlaps?

    b) What's the smallest *rectangle*, under the same conditions?

▶ **109.** [28] A "wordcross puzzle" is the challenge of packing a given set of words into a rectangle under the following conditions: (i) All words must read either across or down, as in a crossword puzzle. (ii) No letters are adjacent unless they belong to one of the given words. (iii) The words are rookwise connected. (iv) Words overlap only when one is vertical and the other is horizontal. For example, the eleven words ZERO, ONE, ..., TEN can be placed into an 8 × 8 square under constraints (i) and (ii) as shown; but (iii) is violated, because there are three different components.

```
T H R E E   F
W         S I X
O N E       V
          S E V E N
Z             I
  E I G H T   N
R         E   E
F O U R   N
```

    Explain how to encode a wordcross puzzle as an XCC problem. Use your encoding to find a correct solution to the problem above. Do those eleven words fit into a *smaller* rectangle, under conditions (i), (ii), and (iii)?

110. [30] What's the smallest wordcross square that contains the surnames of the first 44 U.S. presidents? (Use the names in exercise 108, but change VANBUREN to VAN BUREN.)

111. [21] Find all 8 × 8 crossword puzzle diagrams that contain exactly (a) 12 3-letter words, 12 4-letter words, and 4 5-letter words; (b) 12 5-letter words, 8 2-letter words, and 4 8-letter words. They should have no words of other lengths.

▶ **112.** [28] A popular word puzzle in Brazil, called 'Torto' ('bent'), asks solvers to find as many words as possible that can be traced by a noncrossing king path in a given 6 × 3 array of letters. For example, each of the words THE, MATURE, ART, OF, COMPUTER, and PROGRAMMING can be found in the array shown here.

```
O C G
F M N
M I P
A U R
T R O
E H G
```

    a) Does that array contain other common words of eight or more letters?

    b) Create a 6 × 3 array that contains TORTO, WORDS, SOLVER, and many other interesting English words of five or more letters. (Let your imagination fly.)

    c) Is it possible to pack ONE, TWO, THREE, ..., EIGHT, NINE, TEN into a Torto array?

▶ **113.** [21] An 'alphabet block' is a cube whose six faces are marked with letters. Is there a set of five alphabet blocks that are able to spell the 25 words TREES, NODES, STACK, AVAIL, FIRST, RIGHT, ORDER, LISTS, GIVEN, LINKS, QUEUE, GRAPH, TIMES, BLOCK, VALUE, TABLE, FIELD, EMPTY, ABOVE, POINT, THREE, UNTIL, HENCE, QUITE, DEQUE? (Each of these words appears more than 50 times in Chapter 2.)

114. [*M25*] Let α be a permutation of the cells of a 9×9 array that takes any sudoku solution into another sudoku solution. We say that α is an *automorphism* of the sudoku solution $S = (s_{ij})$ if there's a permutation π of $\{1, 2, \ldots, 9\}$ such that $s_{(ij)\alpha} = s_{ij}\pi$ for $0 \le i, j < 9$. For example, the permutation that takes ij into $(ij)\alpha = ji$, commonly called *transposition*, is an automorphism of (28b), with respect to the permutation $\pi = (24)(37)(68)$; but it is *not* an automorphism of (28a) or (28c).

Show that Algorithm C can be used to find all sudoku solutions that have a given automorphism α, by defining an appropriate XCC problem.

How many sudoku solutions have transposition as an automorphism?

115. [*M25*] Continuing exercise 114, how many *hypersudoku* solutions have automorphisms of the following types? (a) transposition; (b) the transformation of exercise 67(d); (c) 90° rotation; (d) both (b) and (c).

▶ **116.** [*M25*] Given a graph G on vertices V, let $\mu(G)$ be obtained by (i) adding new vertices $V' = \{v' \mid v \in V\}$, with $u' \!-\! v$ when $u \!-\! v$; and also (ii) adding another vertex w, with $w \!-\! v'$ for all $v' \in V'$. (If G has m edges and n vertices, $\mu(G)$ has $3m+n$ edges and $2n+1$ vertices.) The *Mycielski graphs* M_c are defined for all $c \ge 2$ by setting $M_2 = K_2$ and $M_{c+1} = \mu(M_c)$; they have $\frac{7}{18}3^c - \frac{3}{4}2^c + \frac{1}{2}$ edges and $\frac{3}{2}2^c - 1$ vertices:

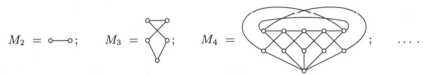

$$M_2 = \circ\!-\!\!-\!\circ; \qquad M_3 = \qquad ; \qquad M_4 = \qquad ; \qquad \cdots .$$

a) Prove that each M_c is triangle-free (contains no subgraph K_3).
b) Prove that the chromatic number $\chi(M_c) = c$.
c) Prove that each M_c is in fact "χ-critical": Removing any edge decreases χ.

▶ **117.** [*24*] (*Graph coloring.*) Suppose we want to find all possible ways to label the vertices of graph G with d colors; adjacent vertices should have different colors.
a) Formulate this as an exact cover problem, with one primary item for each vertex and with d secondary items for each edge.
b) Sometimes G's edges are conveniently specified by giving a family $\{C_1, \ldots, C_r\}$ of cliques, where each C_j is a subset of vertices; then $u \!-\! v$ if and only if $u \in C_j$ and $v \in C_j$ for some j. (For example, the 728 edges of the queen graph Q_8 can be specified by just $8+8+13+13 = 42$ cliques — one clique for each row, column, and diagonal.) Modify the construction of (a) so that there are only rd secondary items.
c) In how many ways can Q_8 be 9-colored? (Compare method (a) to method (b).)
d) Each solution to the coloring problem that uses k different colors is obtained $d^{\underline{k}} = d(d-1)\ldots(d-k+1)$ times, because of the symmetry between colors. Modify (a) and (b) so that each essentially different solution is obtained just once, when the symmetry-breaking technique of exercise 122 is used.
e) In how many ways can the Mycielski graph M_c be c-colored, for $2 \le c \le 5$?
f) Use Algorithm C to verify that M_c can't be $(c-1)$-colored, for $2 \le c \le 5$.
g) Try $(c-1)$-coloring M_c when a random edge is removed, for $2 \le c \le 5$.

118. [*21*] (*Hypergraph coloring.*) Color the 64 cells of a chessboard with four colors, so that no three cells of the same color lie in a straight line of any slope.

119. [*21*] Show that all solutions to the problem of placing MacMahon's 24 triangles (58) into a hexagon with all-white border can be rotated and reflected so that the all-white triangle has the position that it occupies in (59b). *Hint:* Factorize.

120. [*M29*] Section 2.3.4.3 discussed Hao Wang's "tetrad tiles," which are squares that have specified colors on each side. Find all ways in which the entire plane can be filled with tiles from the following families of tetrad types, always matching colors at the edges where adjacent tiles meet [see *Scientific American* **231**, 5 (Nov. 1965), 103, 106]:

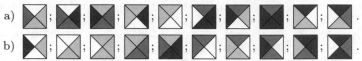

(The tetrad tiles must *not* be rotated or flipped.) *Hint:* Algorithm C will help.

▸ **121.** [*M29*] Exercise 2.3.4.3–5 discusses 92 types of tetrads that are able to tile the plane, and proves that no such tiling is toroidal (periodic).

  a) Show that the tile called βUS in that exercise can't be part of any infinite tiling. In fact, it can appear in only $n + 1$ cells of an $m \times n$ array, when $m, n \geq 4$.

  b) Show that, for all $k \geq 1$, there's a unique $(2^k - 1) \times (2^k - 1)$ tiling for which the middle tile is δRD. (Consequently, by the infinity lemma, there's a unique tiling of the entire plane in which δRD is placed at the origin.)

  c) Similarly, show that there are exactly $(2, 3, 3, 57)$ tilings of size $(2^k - 1) \times (2^k - 1)$ whose middle tile is respectively $(\delta RU, \delta LD, \delta LU, \delta SU)$, for all $k \geq 3$.

  d) How many tilings of the infinite plane have $(\delta RU, \delta LD, \delta LU, \delta SU)$ at the origin?

▸ **122.** [*28*] Extend Algorithm C so that it finds only $1/d!$ of the solutions, in cases where the input options are totally symmetric with respect to d of the color values, and where every solution contains each of those color values at least once. Assume that those values are $\{v, v+1, \ldots, v+d-1\}$, and that all other colors have values $< v$. *Hint:* Modify the algorithm so that the first such color it assigns is always v, then $v + 1$, etc.

123. [*M20*] Apply the algorithm of exercise 122 to the following toy problem with parameters m and n: There are n primary items p_k and n secondary items q_k, for $1 \leq k \leq n$; and there are mn options, '$p_k\ q_k{:}j$' for $1 \leq j \leq m$ and $1 \leq k \leq n$. (The solutions to this problem are the mappings of $\{1, \ldots, n\}$ into $\{1, \ldots, m\}$, which may also be regarded as the partitions of $\{1, \ldots, n\}$ into parts labeled $\{1, \ldots, m\}$.) Algorithm C will obviously find $m^n = \{{n \atop 1}\}m^{\underline{1}} + \{{n \atop 2}\}m^{\underline{2}} + \cdots + \{{n \atop m}\}m^{\underline{m}}$ solutions. But the modified algorithm finds only the "unlabeled" partitions, of which there are $\{{n \atop 1}\} + \{{n \atop 2}\} + \cdots + \{{n \atop m}\}$.

▸ **124.** [*M22*] Devise a system of coordinates for representing the positions of equilateral triangles in patterns such as (59). Represent also the edges between them.

125. [*M20*] When a set of s triangles is magnified by an integer k, we obtain sk^2 triangles. Describe the coordinates of those triangles, in term of the coordinates of the originals, using the system of exercise 124.

126. [*23*] Find all solutions of MacMahon's problem (59), by applying Algorithm C to a suitable set of items and options based on the coordinate system in exercise 124. How much time is saved by using the improved algorithm of exercise 122?

127. [*M28*] There are 4^{12} ways to prescribe the border colors of a hexagon like those in (59). Which of them can be completed to a color-matched placement of all 24 triangles?

▸ **128.** [*25*] Eleven of MacMahon's triangles (58) involve only the first three colors (not black). Arrange them into a pleasant pattern that tiles the entire plane when replicated.

▸ **129.** [*M34*] The most beautiful patterns that can be made with MacMahon's triangles are those with attractive symmetries, which can be of two kinds: *strong symmetry* (a rotation or reflection that doesn't change the pattern, except for permutation of colors) or *weak symmetry* (a rotation or reflection that preserves the "color patches," the set of boundaries between different colors).

strong symmetry: 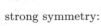 ;   weak symmetry: .

Exactly how many essentially different symmetrical patterns are possible, in a hexagon?

130. [*21*] Partition MacMahon's triangles (58) into three sets of eight, each of which can be placed on the faces of an octahedron, with matching edge colors.

131. [*28*] (P. A. MacMahon, 1921.) Instead of using the colored tiles of (58), which yield (59), we can form hexagons from 24 different triangles in two other ways:

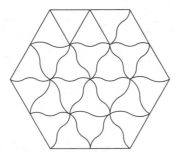 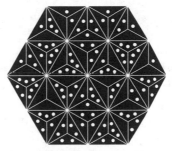

The left diagram shows a "jigsaw puzzle" whose pieces have four kinds of edges. The right diagram shows "triple three triominoes," which have zero, one, two, or three spots at each edge; adjacent triominoes should have a total of three spots where they meet.

    a) In how many ways can that jigsaw puzzle make a hexagon? (All pieces are white.)

    b) How many triomino arrangements have that pattern of dots at the edges?

132. [*40*] (W. E. Philpott, 1971.) There are $4624 = 68^2$ tiles in a set that's like (58), but it uses 24 different colors instead of 4. Can they be assembled into an equilateral triangle of size 68, with constant color on the boundary and with matching edges inside?

133. [*21*] (P. A. MacMahon, 1921.) A set of 24 *square* tiles can be constructed, analogous to the triangular tiles of (58), if we restrict ourselves to just three colors. For example, they can be arranged in a 4×6 rectangle as shown, with all-white border. In how many ways can this be done?

134. [*23*] The nonwhite areas of the pattern in exercise 133 form polyominoes (rotated 45°); in fact, the lighter color has an S pentomino, while the darker color has both P and V. How often do each of the twelve pentominoes occur, among all of the solutions?

135. [*23*] (H. L. Nelson, 1970.) Show that MacMahon's squares of exercise 133 can be used to wrap around the faces of a $2 \times 2 \times 2$ cube, matching colors wherever adjacent.

▶ **136.** [*HM28*] (J. H. Conway, 1958.) There are twelve ways to label the edges of a pentagon with $\{0, 1, 2, 3, 4\}$, if we don't consider rotations and reflections to be different:

Cover a *dodecahedron* with these tiles, matching edge numbers. (Reflections are OK.)

137. [*22*] A popular puzzle called Drive Ya Nuts consists of seven "hex nuts" that have been decorated with permutations of the numbers $\{1, 2, 3, 4, 5, 6\}$. The object is to arrange them as shown, with numbers matching at the edges.

a) Show that this puzzle has a unique solution, with that particular set of seven. (Reflections of the nuts are *not* OK!)

b) Can those seven nuts form the same shape, but with the label numbers summing to 7 where they meet ($\{1, 6\}$, $\{2, 5\}$, or $\{3, 4\}$)?

c) Hex nuts can be decorated with $\{1, 2, 3, 4, 5, 6\}$ in $5! = 120$ different ways. If seven of them are chosen at random, what's the approximate probability that they define a puzzle with a unique solution, under matching condition (a)?

d) Find seven hex nuts that have a unique solution under both conditions (a) and (b).

138. [*25*] (*Heads and tails.*) Here's a set of 24 square tiles that MacMahon missed(!):

They each show two "heads" and two "tails" of triangles, in four colors that exhibit all possible permutations, with heads pointing to tails. The tiles can be rotated, but not flipped over. We can match them properly in many ways, such as

or

,

where the 4×6 arrangement will tile the plane; the 5×5 arrangement has a special "joker" tile in the middle, containing all four heads.

a) How many 4×6 arrangements will tile the plane? (Consider symmetries.)

b) Notice that the half-objects at the top, bottom, left, and right of the 5×5 arrangement match the heads in the middle. How many such arrangements are possible?

c) Devise a 5×5 arrangement that will tile the plane, in conjunction with the 5×5 pattern shown above. *Hint:* Use an "anti-joker" tile, which contains all four tails.

139. [*M25*] Excellent human-scale puzzles have been made by choosing nine of the 24 tiles in exercise 138, redrawing them with whimsical illustrations in place of the triangles, and asking for a 3×3 arrangement in which heads properly match tails.

a) How many of the $\binom{24}{9}$ choices of 9 tiles lead to essentially different puzzles?

b) How many of those puzzles have exactly k solutions, for $k = 0, 1, 2, \ldots$?

140. [*29*] (C. D. Langford, 1959.) MacMahon colored the *edges* of his tiles, but we can color the *vertices* instead. For example, we can make two parallelograms, or a truncated triangle, by assembling the 24 vertex-colored analogs of (58):

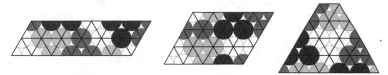

Such arrangements are much rarer than those based on edge matching, because edges are common to only two tiles but vertices might involve up to six.

   a) In how many essentially distinct ways can those shapes be formed?
   b) The first parallelogram is a scaled-up version of the "straight hexiamond" ▰▰, with dimensions doubled. How many of the other eleven scaled-up hexiamond shapes can be assembled from Langford's tiles? (See exercises 125 and 309.)
   c) Each of the seven *tetrahexes* also yields an interesting shape that consists of 24 triangles. (See exercise 316.) How do Langford's tiles behave in those shapes?

141. [*24*] Combining exercises 133 and 140, we can also adapt MacMahon's 24 tri-colored squares to vertex matching instead of edge matching. Noteworthy solutions are

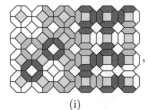 ; 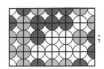 ; 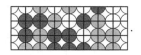 .

   a) In how many essentially different ways can those 24 tiles be properly packed into rectangles of these sizes, leaving a hole in the middle of the 5×5?
   b) Discuss tiling the plane with such solutions.

▶ **142.** [*23*] (Zdravko Zivkovic, 2008.) Edge and vertex matching can be combined into a single design if we replace MacMahon's 24 squares by 24 octagons. For example,

  , 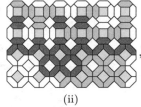 ,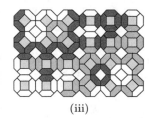

         (i)   (ii)   (iii)

illustrate 4×6 arrangements in which there's vertex matching in the (i) left half, (ii) bottom half, or (iii) northwest and southeast quadrants, while edge matching occurs elsewhere. (We get vertex matching when an octagon's center is '◇', edge matching when it's '▢'.) How many 4×6 arrangements satisfy (i), (ii), and (iii), respectively?

▶ **143.** [*M25*] The graph *simplex*$(n, a, b, c, 0, 0, 0)$ in the Stanford GraphBase is the trun-cated triangular grid consisting of all vertices xyz such that $x + y + z = n$, $0 \le x \le a$, $0 \le y \le b$, and $0 \le z \le c$. Two vertices are adjacent if their coordinates all differ by at most 1. The boundary edges always define a convex polygon. For example, *simplex*$(7, 7, 5, 3, 0, 0, 0)$ is illustrated here.

   a) What *simplex* graphs correspond to the three shapes in exercise 140?

b) The examples in (a) have 24 interior triangles, but $simplex(7, 7, 5, 3, 0, 0, 0)$ has 29. Can any other convex polygons be made from 24 triangles, connected edgewise?

c) Design an efficient algorithm that lists all possible convex polygons that can be formed from exactly N triangles, given N. *Hint:* Every convex polygon in a triangular grid can be characterized by the six numbers in its boundary path $x_0 x_1 x_2 x_3 x_4 x_5$, which moves x_k steps in direction $(60k)°$ for $k = 0, 1, \ldots, 5$. For example, the boundary of $simplex(7, 7, 5, 3, 0, 0, 0)$ is 503412.

d) Can every convex polygon in a triangular grid be described by a *simplex* graph?

144. [*24*] The idea of exercise 142 applies also to triangles and hexagons, allowing us to do both vertex and edge matching with yet another set of 24 tiles:

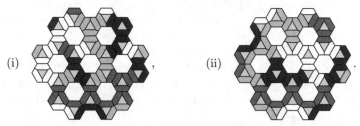

Here there's vertex matching in the bottom five tiles of (i), and in the upper left five and bottom five of (ii), with edge matching elsewhere. In how many ways can the big hexagon be made from these 24 little hexagons, under constraints (i) and (ii)?

▸ **145.** [*M20*] Many problems that involve an $l \times m \times n$ cuboid require a good internal representation of its $(l+1)(m+1)(n+1)$ vertices, its $l(m+1)(n+1) + (l+1)m(n+1) + (l+1)(m+1)n$ edges, and its $lm(n+1)+l(m+1)n+(l+1)mn$ faces, in addition to its lmn individual cells. Show that there's a convenient way to do this with integer coordinates (x, y, z) whose ranges are $0 \le x \le 2l$, $0 \le y \le 2m$, $0 \le z \le 2n$.

▸ **146.** [*M30*] There are 30 ways to paint the colors $\{a, b, c, d, e, f\}$ on the faces of a cube:

(If **a** is on top, there are five choices for the bottom color, then six cyclic permutations of the remaining four.) Here's one way to arrange six differently painted cubes in a row, with distinct colors on top, bottom, front, and back (as in "Instant Insanity"), and with the further proviso that adjacent cubes have matching colors where they share a face:

$$(*)$$

a) Explain why any such arrangement also has the same color at the left and right.

b) Invent a way to name each cube, distinguishing it from the other 29.

c) How many essentially different arrangements like (∗) are possible?

d) Can all 30 cubes be used to make five such arrangements simultaneously?

147. [*30*] The 30 cubes of exercise 146 can be used to make "bricks" of various sizes $l \times m \times n$, by assembling $l \cdot m \cdot n$ of them into a cuboid that has solid colors on each exterior face, as well as matching colors on each interior face. For example, each cube naturally joins with its mirror image to form a $1 \times 1 \times 2$ brick. Two such bricks can then join up to make a $1 \times 2 \times 2$; the one illustrated here has **a** in front, **b** in the back, **c** at the left and right, **d** at the top, and **e** at the bottom.

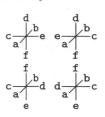

a) Assemble all 30 cubes into a magnificent brick of size $2 \times 3 \times 5$.

b) Compile a catalog of all the essentially different bricks that can be made.

148. [*24*] Find all the distinct cubes whose faces are colored **a**, **b**, or **c**, when opposite faces are required to have different colors. Then arrange them into a symmetric shape (with matching colors wherever they are in contact).

149. [*M22*] (*Vertex-colored tetrahedra.*) The graph $simplex(3,3,3,3,3,0,0)$ is a tetrahedron of side 3 with 20 vertices. It has 60 edges, which come from 10 unit tetrahedra.

There are ten ways to color the vertices of a unit tetrahedron with four of the five colors $\{a, b, c, d, e\}$, because mirror reflections are distinct. Can those ten colored tetrahedra be packed into $simplex(3,3,3,3,3,0,0)$, with matching colors at every vertex?

150. [*23*] Here's a classic 19th century puzzle that was the first of its kind: "Arrange all the pieces to fill the square ... so that all the links of the Chain join together, forming an Endless Chain. The Chain may be any shape, so long as all the links join together, and all the pieces are used. This Puzzle can be done several different ways."

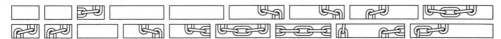

(The desired square is 8×8.) In exactly how many different ways *can* it be solved?

▶ **151.** [*30*] (*Path dominoes.*) A domino has six natural attachment points on its boundary, where we could draw part of a path that connects to neighboring dominoes. Thus $\binom{6}{2} = 15$ different partial paths could potentially be drawn on it. However, only 9 distinct domino patterns with one subpath actually arise, because the 15 possibilities are reduced under 180° rotation to six pairs, plus three patterns that have central symmetry. Similarly, there are 27 distinct domino patterns that contain *two* partial paths (where the paths might cross each other). An 8×9 arrangement, which nicely illustrates all 36 of the possibilities, is shown; notice that its path is a Hamiltonian cycle, consisting of a *single loop*.

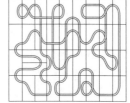

a) Only two of the dominoes in the arrangement above are in horizontal position. Find a single-loop 8×9 arrangement that has 18 horizontals and 18 verticals.

b) Similarly, find an arrangement that has the *maximum* number of horizontals.

152. [*30*] The *complete* set of path dominoes includes also twelve more patterns:

Arrange all 48 of them in an 8×12 array, forming a single loop.

153. [*25*] Here are six of the path dominoes, plus a "start" piece and a "stop" piece:

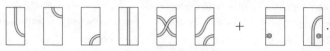

a) Place them within a 4×5 array so that they define a path from "start" to "stop."
b) How many distinct "start" or "stop" pieces are possible, if they're each supposed to contain a single subpath together with a single terminal point?
c) Design an eight-piece puzzle that's like (a), but it involves *four* of the two-subpath dominoes instead of only two. (Your puzzle should have a unique solution.)

154. [*M30*] (C. R. J. Singleton, 1996.) After twelve days of Christmas, the person who sings a popular carol has received twelve partridges in pear trees, plus eleven pairs of humming birds, ..., plus one set of twelve drummers drumming, from his or her true love. Therefore an "authentic" partridge puzzle should try to pack $(n+1-k)$ squares of size $k \times k$, for $1 \le k \le n$, into a box that contains $P(n) = n \cdot 1^2 + (n-1) \cdot 2^2 + \cdots + 1 \cdot n^2$ cells. For which values of n is $P(n)$ a perfect square?

155. [*20*] That "authentic" partridge puzzle has a square solution when $n = 6$.
a) Exactly how many different solutions does it have in that case?
b) The *affinity score* of a partridge packing is the number of internal edges that lie on the boundary between two squares of the same size. (In (62) the scores are 165 and 67.) What solutions to (a) have the maximum and minimum affinity scores?

▶ **156.** [*30*] Straightforward backtracking will solve the partridge puzzle for $n = 8$, using bitwise techniques to represent a partially filled 36×36 square in just 36 octabytes, instead of by treating it as the huge MCC problem (61) and applying a highly general solver such as Algorithm M. Compare these two approaches, by implementing them both. How many essentially different solutions does that partridge puzzle have?

157. [*22*] Complete the study of small partridges by extending (63) to $n = 6$ and 7.

158. [*23*] Another variation of the partridge puzzle when $2 \le n \le 7$ asks for the *smallest rectangular area* that will contain k nonoverlapping squares of size $k \times k$ for $1 \le k \le n$. For example, here are solutions for $n = 2$, 3, and 4:

(To show optimality for $n = 4$ one must prove that rectangles of sizes 6×17, 8×13, 5×21, and 7×15 are too small.) Solve this puzzle for $n = 5$, 6, and 7.

▶ **159.** [*21*] Suggest a way to speed up the text's solution to the 5-queens problem, by using the symmetries of a square to modify the items and options of (64).

160. [*21*] The 5-queens problem leads to an interesting graph, whose vertices are the 4860 solutions, with $u \,\text{---}\, v$ when we can get from u to v by moving one queen. How many connected components does this graph have? Is one of them a "giant"?

▶ **161.** [*23*] Three restricted queen-domination problems are prominent in the literature:
i) No two queens of a solution attack each other.
ii) Each queen of a solution is attacked by at least one of the others.
iii) The queens of a solution form a clique.
(The third and fourth examples in (65) are instances of types (ii) and (i).)
   Explain how to formulate each of these variants as an MCC problem, analogous to (64). How many solutions of each type are present in the 5-queens problem?

162. [*24*] Say that a $\mathcal{Q}_n$ is an $n \times n$ array of n nonattacking queens. Sometimes a $\mathcal{Q}_n$ contains a $\mathcal{Q}_m$ for $m < n$; for example, eight of the possible $\mathcal{Q}_5$'s contain a $\mathcal{Q}_4$, and the $\mathcal{Q}_{17}$ illustrated here contains both a $\mathcal{Q}_4$ and a $\mathcal{Q}_5$.

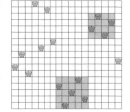

What is the smallest n such that at least one $\mathcal{Q}_n$ contains (a) two $\mathcal{Q}_4$'s? (b) three $\mathcal{Q}_4$'s? (c) four $\mathcal{Q}_4$'s? (d) five $\mathcal{Q}_4$'s? (e) two $\mathcal{Q}_5$'s? (f) three $\mathcal{Q}_5$'s? (g) four $\mathcal{Q}_5$'s? (h) two $\mathcal{Q}_6$'s? (i) three $\mathcal{Q}_6$'s?

163. [*20*] Explain the peculiar rule for setting p in (71).

164. [*17*] When Algorithm M finds a solution $x_0 x_1 \ldots x_{l-1}$ in step M2, some of the nodes x_j might represent the fact that some primary item will appear in no further options. Explain how to handle this "null" case, by modifying answer 13.

165. [*M30*] Consider an MCC problem in which we must choose 2 of 4 options to cover item 1, and 5 of 7 options to cover item 2; the options don't interact.
- a) What's the size of the search tree if we branch first on item 1, then on item 2? Would it better to branch first on item 2, then on item 1?
- b) Generalize part (a) to the case when item 1 needs p of $p+d$ options, while item 2 needs q of $q+d$ options, where $q > p$ and $d > 0$.

166. [*21*] Extend answer 9 to the more general situation that arises in Algorithm M:
- a) Let θ_p be the number of different choices that will be explored at the current position of the search tree if primary item p is selected for branching. Express θ_p as a function of $\text{LEN}(p)$, $\text{SLACK}(p)$, and $\text{BOUND}(p)$.
- b) Suppose $\theta_p = \theta_{p'}$ and $\text{SLACK}(p) = \text{SLACK}(p') = 0$, but $\text{LEN}(p) < \text{LEN}(p')$. Should we prefer to branch on p or on p', based on exercise 165?

167. [*24*] Let M_p be the number of options that involve the primary item p in a given MCC problem, and suppose that the upper bound v_p for p's multiplicity is $\geq M_p$. Does the precise value of this upper bound affect the behavior of Algorithm M? (In other words, does $v_p = \infty$ lead to the same running time as $v_p = M_p$?)

▶ **168.** [*15*] An MCC problem might have two *identical* options α, whose items are allowed to occur more than once. In such cases we might want the second copy of α to be in the solution only if the first copy is also present. How can that be achieved?

▶ **169.** [*22*] Let G be a graph with n vertices. Formulate the problem of finding all of its t-element independent sets as an MCC problem with $1 + n$ items and n options.

170. [*22*] Continuing exercise 169, generate all of G's t-element *kernels* — its *maximal* independent sets. (Your formulation will now need additional items and options.)

171. [*25*] Label the vertices of the Petersen graph with ten 5-letter words, in such a way that vertices are adjacent if and only if their labels have a common letter.

▶ **172.** [*29*] A *snake-in-the-box* path in a graph G is a set U of vertices for which the induced graph $G|U$ is a path. (Thus there are start/stop vertices $s \in U$ and $t \in U$ that each have exactly one neighbor in U; every other vertex of U has exactly two neighbors in U; and $G|U$ is connected.)

For example, let $G = P_4 \boxtimes P_4$ be the graph of king moves on a 4×4 board. The set of kings illustrated at the right is *not* a snake-in-the-box path in G; but it becomes one if we remove the king in the corner.
- a) Use Algorithm M to discover all of the longest snake-in-the-box paths that are possible on an 8×8 chessboard, when G is the graph of all (i) king moves; (ii) knight moves; (iii) bishop moves; (iv) rook moves; (v) queen moves.

b) Similarly, a *snake-in-the-box cycle* is a set for which $G \mid U$ is a cycle. (In other words, that induced graph is connected and 2-regular.) What are the longest possible snake-in-the-box cycles for those five chess pieces?

▶ **173.** [*30*] (*Knight and bishop sudoku.*) Diagram (i) shows 27 knights, arranged with three in each row, three in each column, and three in each 3×3 box. Each of them has been labeled with the number of others that are a knight's move away. Diagram (ii) shows 8 of them, from which the positions of the other 19 can be deduced. Diagrams (iii) and (iv) are analogous, but for bishops instead of knights: (iii) solves puzzle (iv).

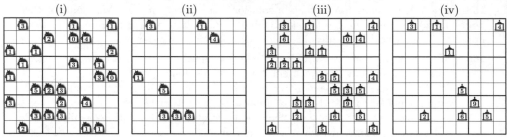

a) Explain how to find all completions of such diagrams using Algorithm M.
b) Find the unique completions of the following puzzles:

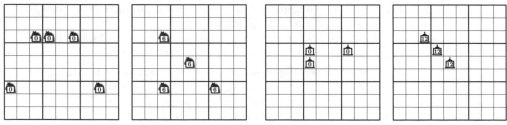

c) Compose additional puzzles like those of (b), in which all clues have the same numerical labels. Try to use as few clues as possible.
d) Construct a uniquely solvable knight sudoku puzzle that has only three clues.

174. [*35*] (Nikolai Beluhov, 2019.) Find a uniquely solvable sudoku puzzle with nine labeled knights that remains uniquely solvable when the knights are changed to bishops.

▶ **175.** [*M21*] Given an $M \times N$ matrix $A = (a_{ij})$ of 0s and 1s, explain how to find all vectors $x = (x_1 \ldots x_M)$ with $0 \le x_i \le a_i$ for $1 \le i \le M$ such that $xA = (y_1 \ldots y_N)$, where $u_j \le y_j \le v_j$ for $1 \le j \le N$. (This generalizes the MCC problem by allowing the ith option to be repeated up to a_i times.)

▶ **176.** [*M25*] Given an $M \times N$ matrix $A = (a_{ij})$ of 0s, 1s, and 2s, explain how to find all subsets of its rows that sum to exactly (a) 2 (b) 3 (c) 4 (d) 11 in each column, by formulating those tasks as MCC problems.

177. [*M21*] Algorithm 7.2.1.5M generates the $p(n_1, \ldots, n_m)$ partitions of the multiset $\{n_1 \cdot x_1, \ldots, n_m \cdot x_m\}$ into submultisets. Consider the special cases where $n_1 = \cdots = n_s = 1$ and $n_{s+1} = \cdots = n_{s+t} = 2$ and $s + t = m$.

a) Generate those partitions with Algorithm M, using the previous two exercises.
b) Also generate the $q(n_1, \ldots, n_m)$ multipartitions into *distinct* multisets.

178. [*M22*] (*Factorizations of an integer.*) Use Algorithm M to find all representations of 360 as a product $n_1 \cdot n_2 \cdot \ldots \cdot n_t$, where (a) $1 < n_1 < \cdots < n_t$; (b) $2 \le n_1 \le \cdots \le n_t$.

179. [*15*] By removing duplicate rows and columns, matrix A reduces to A':

$$A = \begin{pmatrix} 1 & 0 & 0 & 0 & 0 & 0 \\ 0 & 1 & 1 & 1 & 0 & 0 \\ 1 & 1 & 0 & 1 & 1 & 1 \\ 0 & 1 & 1 & 1 & 0 & 0 \\ 0 & 0 & 0 & 0 & 1 & 1 \\ 0 & 0 & 0 & 0 & 1 & 1 \\ 1 & 0 & 1 & 0 & 0 & 0 \\ 0 & 1 & 0 & 1 & 1 & 1 \\ 1 & 1 & 1 & 1 & 0 & 0 \end{pmatrix}; \qquad A' = \begin{pmatrix} 1 & 0 & 0 & 0 \\ 0 & 1 & 1 & 0 \\ 1 & 1 & 0 & 1 \\ 0 & 0 & 0 & 1 \\ 1 & 0 & 1 & 0 \\ 0 & 1 & 0 & 1 \\ 1 & 1 & 1 & 0 \end{pmatrix}.$$

Derive the exact covers of A from the exact covers of A'.

▶ **180.** [*M28*] (D. Eppstein, 2008.) Prove that every strict exact cover problem with parameters $1 \le t' \le t$, as defined in (74), contains t' items $i_1, \ldots, i_{t'}$ and $t+t'-1$ options

$$O_p = `i_1 \ldots i_p\text{'}, \text{ for } 1 \le p \le t'; \qquad O_{p+q} = ` \ldots i_{t'} \ldots \text{'}, \text{ for } 1 \le q < t.$$

Furthermore, $i_r \in O_{p+q}$ if and only if $1 \le q < t - r - t'$, for $1 \le r \le t'$.

181. [*M20*] Find constants c_r such that $D(5n+r) = 4^n c_r - \frac{1}{3}$ for $n \ge 3$ and $0 \le r < 5$.

182. [*21*] (D. Eppstein, 2008.) Find a strict exact cover problem with 8 options, whose search tree contains 16 nodes and 7 solutions.

183. [*46*] Let $\widehat{D}(n)$ be the maximum number of nodes in Algorithm X's search tree, taken over all strict exact cover problems with n options. What is $\limsup_{n\to\infty} \widehat{D}(n)^{1/n}$?

▶ **184.** [*M22*] Suppose $0 \le t \le \varpi_n$. Is there a strict exact cover problem with n items that has exactly t solutions? (For example, consider the case $n = 9$, $t = 10000$.)

185. [*M23*] What is the largest number of solutions to a strict exact cover problem that has N_1 primary items and N_2 secondary items?

186. [*M24*] Consider $l = 0$ when Algorithm X is given the extreme problem of order n.
a) How many updates, u_n, does it perform when covering i in step X4?
b) How many does it perform in step X5, when the option containing x_0 has size k?
c) Therefore derive (84).

187. [*HM29*] Let $X(z) = \sum_n x_n z^n/n!$ generate the sequence $\langle x_n \rangle$ of (82).
a) Use (84) to prove that $X(z) = e^{e^z} \int_0^z ((2t - 1)e^{4t} - (t - 1)e^{3t} + 2te^{2t} + e^t) e^{-e^t}\, dt$.
b) Let $T_{r,s}(z) = e^{e^z} \int_0^z t^r e^{st} e^{-e^t}\, dt$. Prove that $T_{r,0}(z)/r!$ generates $\langle a_{n,r+1} \rangle$ in (83).
c) Show that $T_{r,0}(z) = (T_{r+1,1}(z) + z^{r+1})/(r + 1)$; furthermore, when $s > 0$,

$$T_{r,s}(z) = \left(\sum_{k=0}^{r} \frac{(-1)^k r^{\underline{k}}}{s^{k+1}} \left(T_{r-k,s+1}(z) + z^{r-k} e^{sz}\right) \right) - \frac{(-1)^r r!}{s^{r+1}} e^{e^z - 1}.$$

d) Therefore $X(z) = 22e^{e^z - 1} + 12T_{0,0}(z) - (2z - 1)e^{3z} - 5ze^{2z} - (12z+5)e^z - 12z - 18$.

▶ **188.** [*M21*] Prove that the Gould numbers $\langle \widehat{\varpi}_n \rangle = \langle 0, 1, 1, 3, 9, 31, 121, 523, 2469, \ldots \rangle$ can be calculated rapidly by forming a triangle of numbers analogous to Peirce's triangle 7.2.1.5–(12):

$$
\begin{array}{cccccc}
0 \\
1 & 1 \\
3 & 2 & 1 \\
9 & 6 & 4 & 3 \\
31 & 22 & 16 & 12 & 9 \\
121 & 90 & 68 & 52 & 40 & 31
\end{array}
$$

Here the entries $\widehat{w}_{n1}, \widehat{w}_{n2}, \ldots, \widehat{w}_{nn}$ of the nth row obey the simple recurrence

$$\widehat{w}_{nk} = \widehat{w}_{(n-1)k} + \widehat{w}_{n(k+1)}, \text{ if } 1 \leq k < n; \qquad \widehat{w}_{nn} = \widehat{w}_{(n-1)1}, \text{ if } n > 2;$$

and initially $\widehat{w}_{11} = 0$, $\widehat{w}_{22} = 1$. *Hint:* Give a combinatorial interpretation of $\widehat{w}_{nk}$.

189. [*HM34*] Let $\rho_n = \widehat{w}_n - \hat{g}\varpi_n$ (see (86)). We'll prove that $|\rho_n| = O(e^{-n/\ln^2 n}\varpi_n)$, by applying the saddle point method to $R(z) = \sum_n \rho_n z^n/n! = e^{e^z}\int_z^\infty e^{-e^t}dt$. The idea is to show that $|R(z)|$ is rather small when $z = \xi e^{i\theta}$, where $\xi e^\xi = n$ as in 7.2.1.5–(24).
   a) Express $|e^{e^z}|$ and $|e^{-e^z}|$ in terms of x and y when $z = x + iy$.
   b) If $0 \leq \theta \leq \frac{\pi}{2}$, $y = \xi \sin\theta \leq \frac{3}{2}$, $0 < c_1 < \cos\frac{3}{2}$, prove $|R(\xi e^{i\theta})| = O(\exp(e^\xi - c_1 e^\xi))$.
   c) If $0 \leq \theta \leq \frac{\pi}{2}$, $y = \xi \sin\theta \geq \frac{3}{2}$, $0 < c_2 < \frac{9}{8}$, prove $|R(\xi e^{i\theta})| = O(\exp(e^\xi - c_2 e^\xi/\xi))$.
   d) Consequently $\rho_{n-1}/\varpi_{n-1} = O(e^{-n/\ln^2 n})$, as desired.

190. [*HM46*] Study the *signs* of the residual quantities $\rho_n = \widehat{w}_n - \hat{g}\varpi_n$ in exercise 189.

191. [*HM22*] The length of the tail of a random set permutation is known to have a probability distribution whose generating function is $G(z) = \int_0^\infty e^{-x}(1+x)^z dx - 1 = \sum_{k=1}^\infty \hat{g}_k z^k$. (The first few probabilities in this distribution are

$$(\hat{g}_1, \hat{g}_2, \ldots, \hat{g}_9) \approx (.59635, .26597, .09678, .03009, .00823, .00202, .00045, .00009, .00002);$$

see answer 189.) What is the average length? What is the variance?

192. [*HM29*] What's the asymptotic value of $\hat{g}_n$ when n is large?

193. [*M21*] Why do (87) and (88) count updates when matching in complete graphs?

194. [*HM23*] Consider recurrences of the form $X(t+1) = a_t + tX(t-1)$. For example, $a_t = 1$ yields the total number of nodes in the search tree for matching K_{t+1}.
   a) Prove that $1 + 2q + (2q)(2q - 2) + \cdots + (2q)(2q - 2)\ldots(2) = \lfloor e^{1/2}2^q q! \rfloor$.
   b) Find a similar "closed formula" for $1 + (2q - 1) + (2q - 1)(2q - 3) + \cdots + (2q - 1) \cdot (2q - 3)\ldots(3)(1)$. *Hint:* Use the fact that $e^x \operatorname{erf}(\sqrt{x}) = \sum_{n \geq 0} x^{n+1/2}/(n+1/2)!$.
   c) Estimate the solution $U(2q + 1)$ of (87) to within $O(1)$.
   d) Similarly, give a good approximation to the solution $U(2q)$ of (88).

▶ **195.** [*M22*] Approximately how many updates does Algorithm X perform, when it is asked to find all of the perfect matchings of the graph (89)?

▶ **196.** [*M29*] Given a bounded permutation problem defined by $a_1 \ldots a_n$, consider the "dual" problem defined by $b_1 \ldots b_n$, where b_k is the number of j such that $1 \leq j \leq n$ and $a_j \geq n + 1 - k$. [Equivalently, $b_n \ldots b_1$ is the *conjugate* of the integer partition $a_n \ldots a_1$, in the sense of Section 7.2.1.4.]
   a) What is the dual problem when $n = 9$ and $a_1 \ldots a_9 = 246677889$?
   b) Prove that the solutions to the dual problem are essentially the *inverses* of the permutations that solve the original problem.
   c) If Algorithm X begins with an a_1-way branch on item X_1, how many updates does it perform while preparing for the subproblems at depth 1 of its search tree?
   d) How many solutions does a bounded permutation problem have, given $a_1 \ldots a_n$?
   e) Give a formula for the total number of updates, assuming that the algorithm always branches on X_j at depth $j - 1$ of the search tree.
   f) Evaluate the formula of (e) when $a_j = n$ for $1 \leq j \leq n$ (that is, *all* permutations).
   g) Evaluate the formula of (e) when $a_j = \min(j+1, n)$ for $1 \leq j \leq n$.
   h) Evaluate the formula of (e) when $a_j = \min(2j, n)$ for $1 \leq j \leq n$.
   i) Show, however, that the assumption in (e) is not always correct. How can the total updates be calculated correctly in general?

197. [*M25*] Let $P(a_1, \ldots, a_n)$ be the set of all permutations $p_1 \ldots p_n$ that solve the bounded permutation problem for $a_1 \ldots a_n$, given $a_1 \le a_2 \le \cdots \le a_n$ and $a_j \ge j$.
   a) Prove that $P(a_1, \ldots, a_n) = \{(nt_n) \ldots (2t_2)(1t_1) \mid j \le t_j \le a_n \text{ for } 1 \le j \le n\}$.
   b) Also prove that $P(a_1, \ldots, a_n) = \{\sigma_{nt_n} \ldots \sigma_{2t_2} \sigma_{1t_1} \mid j \le t_j \le a_n \text{ for } 1 \le j \le n\}$, where σ_{st} is the $(t+1-s)$-cycle $(t\ t-1\ \ldots s+1\ s)$.
   c) Let $C(p)$ be the number of cycles in the permutation p, and let $I(p)$ be the number of inversions. Find the generating functions

$$C(a_1, \ldots, a_n) = \sum_{p \in P(a_1, \ldots, a_n)} z^{C(p)} \quad \text{and} \quad I(a_1, \ldots, a_n) = \sum_{p \in P(a_1, \ldots, a_n)} z^{I(p)}.$$

198. [*M25*] Let $\pi_{rs} = \Pr(p_r = s)$, when p is a random element of $P(a_1, \ldots, a_n)$.
   a) Compute these probabilities when $n = 9$ and $a_1 a_2 \ldots a_9 = 255667999$.
   b) If $r < r'$ and $s < s'$, show that $\pi_{rs}/\pi_{rs'} = \pi_{r's}/\pi_{r's'}$, when $\pi_{rs'}\pi_{r's'} \ne 0$.

199. [*M25*] Analyze the behavior of Algorithm X on the 3D matching problem whose options are '$a_i\ b_j\ c_k$' for $1 \le i, j \le n$ and $1 \le k \le (i \le m? \ m-1: n)$.

▶ **200.** [*HM25*] (A. Björklund, 2010.) We can use polynomial algebra, instead of backtracking, to decide whether or not a given 3D matching problem is solvable. Let the items be $\{a_1, \ldots, a_n\}$, $\{b_1, \ldots, b_n\}$, $\{c_1, \ldots, c_n\}$, and assign a symbolic variable to each option. If X is any subset of C, let $Q(X)$ be the $n \times n$ matrix whose entry in row i and column j is the sum of the variables for all options '$a_i\ b_j\ c_k$' with $c_k \notin X$.

For example, suppose $n = 3$. The seven options t: '$a_1\ b_1\ c_2$', u: '$a_1\ b_2\ c_1$', v: '$a_2\ b_3\ c_2$', w: '$a_2\ b_3\ c_3$', x: '$a_3\ b_1\ c_3$', y: '$a_3\ b_2\ c_1$', z: '$a_3\ b_2\ c_2$' yield the matrices

$$
\begin{array}{cccccccc}
X = & \emptyset & \{c_3\} & \{c_2\} & \{c_2, c_3\} & \{c_1\} & \{c_1, c_3\} & \{c_1, c_2\}
\end{array}
$$

$$
Q(X) = \begin{pmatrix} t & u & 0 \\ 0 & 0 & v+w \\ x & y+z & 0 \end{pmatrix} \begin{pmatrix} t & u & 0 \\ 0 & 0 & v \\ 0 & y+z & 0 \end{pmatrix} \begin{pmatrix} 0 & u & 0 \\ 0 & 0 & w \\ x & y & 0 \end{pmatrix} \begin{pmatrix} 0 & u & 0 \\ 0 & 0 & 0 \\ 0 & y & 0 \end{pmatrix} \begin{pmatrix} t & 0 & 0 \\ 0 & 0 & v+w \\ x & z & 0 \end{pmatrix} \begin{pmatrix} t & 0 & 0 \\ 0 & 0 & v \\ 0 & z & 0 \end{pmatrix} \begin{pmatrix} 0 & 0 & 0 \\ 0 & 0 & w \\ x & 0 & 0 \end{pmatrix}
$$

(and $Q(C)$ is always zero). The determinant of $Q(\emptyset)$ is $u(v+w)x - t(v+w)(y+z)$.
   a) If the given problem has r solutions, prove that the polynomial

$$S = \sum_{X \subseteq C} (-1)^{|X|} \det Q(X)$$

is the sum of r monomials, each with coefficient ± 1. (In the given example it is $uvx - twy$.) *Hint:* Consider the case where all possible options are present.
   b) Use this fact to design a randomized algorithm that decides q.s. whether or not a matching exists, in $O(2^n n^4)$ steps.

▶ **201.** [*M30*] Consider the bipartite matching problem that has $3n$ options, '$X_j\ Y_k$' for $1 \le j, k \le n$ and $(j - k) \bmod n \in \{0, 1, n-1\}$. (Assume that $n \ge 3$.)
   a) What "natural, intuitively obvious" problem is equivalent to this one?
   b) How many solutions does this problem have?
   c) How many updates does Algorithm X make when finding all solutions, if the items are ordered $X_1, Y_1, \ldots, X_n, Y_n$, and if exercise 9 is used in step X3?

202. [*13*] What is

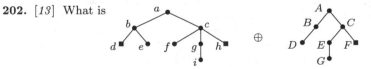

203. [*M15*] Equation (95) shows that the binary operation $T \oplus T'$ on search trees has an identity element, '■'. Is that operation (a) associative? (b) commutative?

204. [*M25*] True or false: Node $\alpha\alpha'$ is dominant in $T \oplus T'$ if and only if α is dominant in T and α' is dominant in T'. *Hint:* Express $\deg(\alpha\alpha')$ in terms of $\deg(\alpha)$ and $\deg(\alpha')$.

205. [*M28*] Prove Lemma D, about the structure of $T \oplus T'$.

206. [*20*] If T is minimally dominant and $\deg(\text{root}(T)) \le \deg(\text{root}(T'))$, show that it's easy to describe the tree $T \oplus T'$.

207. [*35*] The principal SAT solver that we shall discuss later, Algorithm 7.2.2.2C, maintains focus by computing "activity scores," which measure recent changes to the data structures. A similar idea can be applied to Algorithm X, by computing the score

$$\alpha_i = \rho^{t_1} + \rho^{t_2} + \cdots, \quad \text{for each item } i,$$

where ρ (typically 0.9) is a user-specified damping factor, and where i's list of active options was modified at times $t - t_1$, $t - t_2$, $\ldots$; here t denotes the current "time," as measured by some convenient clock. When step X3 chooses an item for branching, the MRV heuristic of exercise 9 rates i by its degree $\lambda_i = \text{LEN}(i)$; the new heuristic replaces this by

$$\lambda_i' = \begin{cases} \lambda_i, & \text{if } \lambda_i \le 1; \\ 1 + \lambda_i/(1 + \mu\alpha_i), & \text{if } \lambda_i \ge 2. \end{cases}$$

Here μ is another user-specified parameter. If $\mu = 0$, decisions are made as before; but larger and larger values of μ cause greater and greater attention to be given to the recently active items, even if they have a somewhat large degree of branching.

a) For example, suppose $\alpha_i = 1$, $\alpha_j = 1/2$, and $\mu = 1$. Which item will be preferable, i or j, if $\text{LEN}(i) = \text{LEN}(j) + 1$ and $0 \le \text{LEN}(j) \le 4$?

b) What modifications to Algorithm X will implement this scheme?

c) What values of ρ and μ will avoid exponential growth, when applied to n independent copies of the toy problems (90) and (92)?

d) Does this method save time in the Y pentomino problem of Fig. 73?

▶ **208.** [*21*] Modify the exact cover problem of Fig. 73 so that none of the Y pentominoes that occur in an 'H' or '⊞' have been flipped over. *Hint:* To prevent the flipped-over Y's marked 8 and b from occurring simultaneously, use the options '1c 2c 3c 4c 3b V_{1b}' and '1a 2a 3a 4a 2b V_{1b}', where V_{1b} is a secondary item.

209. [*20*] Improve the search tree (93) in the same way that (100) improves on (91), by considering two bipairs of (92).

210. [*21*] A "bitriple" $(\alpha, \beta, \gamma; \alpha', \beta', \gamma')$ is analogous to a bipair, but with (97) replaced by $\alpha + \beta + \gamma = \alpha' + \beta' + \gamma'$. How can we modify an exact cover problem so that it excludes all solutions in which options α', β', and γ' are simultaneously present?

211. [*20*] Do the options of the text's formulation of the Langford pair problem have any bipairs? How about the n queens problem? And sudoku?

▶ **212.** [*M21*] If the primary items of an exact cover problem have been linearly ordered, we can say that the bipair $(\alpha, \beta; \alpha', \beta')$ is canonical if (i) the smallest item in all four options appears in α and α'; and (ii) option α is lexicographically smaller than option α', when their items have been listed in ascending order.

a) Prove that Theorem S applies to exact coverings that are strong according to this definition of canonicity. *Hint:* Show that it's a special case of the text's definition.

b) Does such an ordering justify the choices made in (99)?

213. [*M21*] If π and π' are two partitions of the same set, say that $\pi < \pi'$ if the restricted growth string of π is lexicographically less than the restricted growth string of π'. Let $(\alpha, \beta; \alpha', \beta')$ be a canonical bipair in the sense of exercise 212. Also let π be a partition of the items such that α and β are two of its parts, and let π' be the same partition but with α' and β' substituted. Is $\pi < \pi'$?

▶ **214.** [*21*] Under the assumptions of Theorem S, how can the set of all solutions to an exact cover problem be found from the set of all strong solutions?

▶ **215.** [*M30*] The perfect matching problem on the complete graph K_{2q+1} is the X2C problem with $2q+1$ primary items $\{0, \ldots, 2q\}$ and $\binom{2q+1}{2}$ options '$i\,j$' for $0 \le i < j \le 2q$.

    a) How many bipairs are present in this problem?

    b) Say that (i, j, k, l) is *excluded* if there's a canonical bipair $(\alpha, \beta; \alpha', \beta')$ for which $\alpha' = $ '$i\,j$' and $\beta' = $ '$k\,l$'. Prove that, regardless of the ordering of the options, the number of excluded quadruples is 2/3 of the number of bipairs.

    c) What quadruples are excluded when the options are ordered lexicographically?

    d) We reduce the amount of search by introducing a secondary item (i, j, k, l) for each excluded quadruple, and appending it to the options for '$i\,j$' and '$k\,l$'. Describe the search tree when this has been done for the quadruples of (c).

    e) Show that only $\Theta(q^3)$ excluded quadruples suffice to obtain that search tree.

    f) Order the options cleverly so that the search tree has only $2q + 1$ nodes.

    g) How many excluded quadruples suffice to obtain *that* search tree?

216. [*25*] Continuing exercise 215, experiment with the search trees that are obtained by (i) choosing a *random* ordering of the options, and (ii) using only m of the quadruples that are excluded by that ordering (again chosen at random).

217. [*M32*] A *bipair of pentominoes* $(\alpha, \beta; \alpha', \beta')$ is a configuration such as

where two pentominoes occupy a 10-cell region in two different ways. In this example we may write $\alpha = S + 00 + 01 + 11 + 12 + 13$, $\beta = Y + 02 + 03 + 04 + 05 + 14$, $\alpha' = S + 04 + 05 + 12 + 13 + 14$, $\beta' = Y + 00 + 01 + 02 + 03 + 11$; hence $\alpha + \beta = \alpha' + \beta'$ as in (97).

    Compile a complete catalog of all bipairs that are possible with distinct pentominoes. In particular, show that each of the twelve pentominoes participates in at least one such bipair. (It's difficult to do this by hand without missing anything. One good approach is to exploit the equation $\alpha - \alpha' = -(\beta - \beta')$: First find all the delta values $\pm(\alpha - \alpha')$ for each of the twelve pentominoes individually; then study all deltas that are shared by two or more of them. For example, the S and Y pentominoes both have $00 + 01 - 04 - 05 + 11 - 14$ among their deltas.)

▶ **218.** [*20*] Why must i be uncolored, in the definition of "forcing" for Algorithm P?

219. [*20*] Suppose p and q are primary items of an XCC problem, and that every option containing p or q includes an uncolored instance of either i or j (or both), where i and j are other items; yet p and q never occur in the same option. Prove that every option that contains i or j, but neither p nor q, can be removed without changing the problem.

220. [*28*] Step P5 of Algorithm P needs to emulate step C5 of Algorithm C, to see if some primary item will lose all of its options. Describe in detail what needs to be done.

221. [*23*] After all options that begin with item i have been examined in step P5, those that were found to be blocked appear on a stack, starting at S. Explain how to delete them. *Caution:* The problem might become unsolvable when an option goes away.

222. [*22*] Before item i is deleted in step P7, it should be removed from every option that contains S, by changing the corresponding node into a spacer. All options that involve i but not S should also be deleted. Spell out the low-level details of this process.

223. [20] Implement the output phase of Algorithm P (step P10).

▸ **224.** [M21] Construct an exact cover problem with $O(n)$ options that causes Algorithm P to perform n rounds of reduction (that is, it executes step P2 n times).

225. [21] Why does Algorithm P remove 235 options in the 6×10 pentomino problem, but only 151 options in the "one-sided" 6×15 case?

226. [M20] Assume that $a_1 \ldots a_{2n}$ is a Langford pairing, and let $a'_k = a_{2n+1-k}$ so that $a'_1 \ldots a'_{2n}$ is the reverse of $a_1 \ldots a_{2n}$. Are there any obvious relations between the sums

$$\Sigma_1 = \sum_{k=1}^{2n} ka_k, \quad \Sigma'_1 = \sum_{k=1}^{2n} ka'_k, \quad \Sigma_2 = \sum_{k=1}^{2n} k^2 a_k, \quad \Sigma'_2 = \sum_{k=1}^{2n} k^2 a'_k?$$

What about the analogous sums $S = \sum_{k=1}^{2n} ka_k^2$ and $S' = \sum_{k=1}^{2n} k(a'_k)^2$?

227. [10] What cost should be assigned to option (16), to minimize (a) Σ_2? (b) S?

228. [M30] The Langford pairings for $n = 16$ that minimize Σ_2 turn out to be precisely the 12,016 pairings that minimize Σ_1; and their reversals turn out to be precisely the 12,016 pairings that *maximize* both Σ_2 and Σ_1. Is this surprising, or what?

▸ **229.** [25] What Langford pairings for $n = 16$ are lexicographically smallest and largest?

230. [20] Explain how Algorithm X$^\$$, which *minimizes* the sum of option costs, can also be used to *maximize* that sum, in problems like that of Fig. 74.

231. [21] What's the maximum SCRABBLE®-like score you can achieve by filling the grid below with 4-letter and 5-letter words that all are among the (a) 1000 (b) 2000 (c) 3000 most common words of English having that many letters?

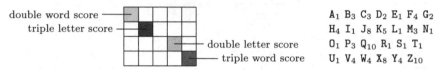

double word score

triple letter score

double letter score

triple word score

A₁ B₃ C₃ D₂ E₁ F₄ G₂
H₄ I₁ J₈ K₅ L₁ M₃ N₁
O₁ P₃ Q₁₀ R₁ S₁ T₁
U₁ V₄ W₄ X₈ Y₄ Z₁₀

For example, WATCH|AGILE|RADAR|TREND scores $26+10+7+18+14+9+5+7+24$ points.

232. [20] The costs supplied to Algorithm X$^\$$ must be nonnegative integers; but $d(i, j)$ in the 16 queens problem of Fig. 74 is never an integer. Is it OK to use $\$\lfloor d(i,j) \rfloor$ instead of $\$d(i, j)$ for the cost of placing a queen in cell (i, j)?

233. [20] Minimize and maximize the *product* of the 16 queen distances, not the sum.

234. [M20] What is the minimum-cost placement of n nonattacking queens when the cost of a queen in cell (i, j) is $\$d(i, j)^2$, the *square* of its distance from the center?

▸ **235.** [21] Solve the problem of Fig. 74 using the (integer) costs $\$4d(i, j)^4$.

▸ **236.** [M41] When the cost of a queen in cell (i, j) is $\$d(i, j)^N$, for larger and larger values of N, the minimum-cost solutions to the n queens problem eventually converge to a fixed pattern. And those "ultimate" solutions turn out to be quite attractive — indeed, this family of solutions is arguably the most beautiful of all! For example, the case $n = 16$, illustrated here, can actually be discovered by hand, with a few moments of concentrated thought. Notice that it is doubly symmetric and nicely "rounded."

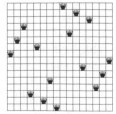

    Discover such optimum placements for as many n as you can (*not* by hand).

▸ **237.** [M21] True or false: Two solutions to the text's prime square problem cannot have the same product unless they are transposes of each other.

238. [*24*] Find $3 \times n$ arrays filled with distinct 3-digit and n-digit primes, for $3 \leq n \leq 7$, having the minimum and maximum possible product.

▶ **239.** [*M27*] Given a family $\{S_1, \ldots, S_m\}$ of subsets of $\{1, \ldots, n\}$, together with positive weights $(w_1, \ldots, w_m)$, the *optimum set cover* problem asks for a minimum-weight way to cover $\{1, \ldots, n\}$ with a union of S_j's. Formulate this problem as an *optimum exact cover* problem, suitable for solution by Algorithm X$. *Hint:* Maximize the weight of all sets that do *not* participate in the cover.

240. [*16*] What usable 6-state options include MT and TX in the USA-partition problem?

241. [*21*] Does preprocessing by Algorithm P remove the useless option (114)?

▶ **242.** [*M23*] Extend the algorithm of exercise 7.2.2–78 so that it visits only subgraphs that don't cut off connected regions whose size isn't a sum of integers in $[L \mathbin{..} U]$.

243. [*M20*] Assume that every item i of an XCC problem has been given a *weight* w_i, and that every solution to the problem involves exactly d options. If the cost of every option is $\$(x^2)$, where x is the sum of the option's weights, prove that every minimum-cost solution also minimizes $\sum_{k=1}^d (x_k - r)^2$, for any given real number r.

244. [*M21*] The induced subgraphs $G \mid U$ of a graph or digraph G have an *interior cost*, defined to be the number of ordered pairs of vertices in U that are *not* adjacent. For example, the interior cost of option (114) is 20, which is the maximum possible for six connected vertices of an undirected graph.

Consider any exact cover problem whose items are the vertices of G, and whose options all contain exactly t items. True or false: A solution that minimizes the sum of the interior costs also minimizes the sum of the exterior costs, as defined in the text.

245. [*23*] Augment the USA graph by adding a 49th vertex, DC, adjacent to MD and VA. Partition this graph into seven connected components, (a) all of size 7, removing as few edges as possible; (b) of any size, equalizing their populations as much as possible.

246. [*22*] The left-hand graph partition in (116) has a bizarre component that connects AZ with ND and OK, without going through NM, CO, or UT. Would we obtain more reasonable-looking solutions if we kept the same options, but minimized the exterior costs instead of the squared populations? (That is, on the left we'd consider the 34,111 options with population in $[37 \mathbin{..} 39]$ million, plus two options that include New York, New England, and possibly New Jersey. The options of the right-hand example would again be the connected subsets with population in $[50.5 \mathbin{..} 51.5]$ million.)

Consider also minimizing the *interior* costs, as defined in exercise 244.

247. [*23*] Specify step C1$, which takes the place of step C1 when Algorithm C is extended to Algorithm C$. Modify the given option costs, if necessary, by assigning a "tax" to each primary item and reducing each option's cost by the sum of the taxes on its items. These new costs should be nonnegative; and every primary item should belong to at least one option whose cost is now zero. Be sure to obey condition (118).

248. [*22*] Let $\vartheta = T - C_l$ in step C3$, where T is the current cutoff threshold and C_l is the cost of the current partial solution on levels less than l. Explain how to choose an active item i that probably belongs to the fewest options of cost $< \vartheta$. Instead of taking the time to make a complete search, assume conservatively that there are LEN(i) such items, after verifying that item i has at least L of them, where L is a parameter.

249. [*21*] A set of dk costs, with $0 \leq c_1 \leq c_2 \leq \cdots \leq c_{dk}$, is said to be bad if $c_k + c_{2k} + \cdots + c_{dk} \geq \theta$. Design an "online algorithm" that identifies a bad set as quickly as possible, when the costs are learned one by one in arbitrary order.

For example, suppose $d = 6$, $k = 2$, and $\theta = 16$. If costs appear in the order $(3, 1, 4, 1, 5, 9, 2, 6, 5, 3, 5, 8)$, your algorithm should stop after seeing the 2.

250. [*21*] Users of Algorithm C$ are allowed to supply hints that speed up the computation, by specifying (i) a set Z of characters, such that every element of Z is the first character of exactly one primary item in every option; also (ii) a number $z > 0$, meaning that every option contains exactly z primary items whose names *don't* begin with a character in Z. (For example, $Z = \{p, r, c, b\}$ in the sudoku options (30); $z = 1$ in options (110). In the options (16) for Langford pairs, we could change the name of each numeric item i to '!i', then let $Z = \{!\}$ and $z = 2$.) Explain how to use these hints to supply an early-cutoff test at the beginning of step C3$, as explained in the text.

251. [*18*] If a given problem is solvable, when does Algorithm Z first discover that fact?

▸ **252.** [*20*] Algorithm Z produces the ZDD (120) from the options (121) if step Z3 simply chooses the leftmost item $i_1 = \mathtt{RLINK(0)}$ instead of using the MRV heuristic. What ZDD would have been obtained if the method of exercise 9 had been used instead?

▸ **253.** [*21*] Extend Algorithm Z so that it reports the total number of solutions.

▸ **254.** [*28*] The signature σ computed by Algorithm Z in step Z2 is supposed to characterize the current subproblem completely. It contains one bit for each primary item, indicating whether or not that item still needs to be covered.

a) Explain why one bit isn't sufficient for secondary items with colors.

b) Suggest a good way to implement the computation of σ.

c) Algorithm C uses the operations hide$'$ and unhide$'$ in (50)–(57), in order to avoid unnecessary accesses to memory in nodes for secondary items. Explain why Algorithm Z does not want to use those optimizations. *Hint:* Algorithm Z needs to know whether the option list for a secondary item is empty.

d) When the list for item i is purified, its options of the wrong color are removed from other lists. But they *remain* on list i, in order to be unpurified later. How then can Algorithm Z know when list i is no longer relevant to the current subproblem?

255. [*HM29*] Express the exact number of updates made by Algorithm Z when it finds the perfect matchings of K_N, as well as the exact number of ZDD nodes produced, in terms of Fibonacci numbers. *Hint:* See exercise 193.

▸ **256.** [*M23*] What is the behavior of Algorithm Z when it is asked to find all perfect matchings of the "bizarre" graph (89)?

▸ **257.** [*21*] How does Algorithm Z do on the "extreme" exact cover problem, with n items and $2^n - 1$ options? (See the discussion preceding (82).)

a) What signatures are formed in step Z2?

b) Draw the schematic ZDD, analogous to (123), when $n = 4$.

258. [*HM21*] How many updates does Algorithm Z perform, in that extreme problem?

259. [*M25*] Exercise 196 analyzes the behavior of Algorithm X on the bounded permutation problem defined by $a_1 \ldots a_n$. Show that Algorithm Z is considerably faster, by determining the number of memos, ZDD nodes, and updates when $a_1 a_2 \ldots a_{n-1} a_n$ is (a) $n\,n \ldots n\,n$ [with $n!$ solutions]; (b) $2\,3 \ldots n\,n$ [with 2^{n-1} solutions]. Assume that the items are X_1, X_2, $\ldots$, X_n, Y_1, Y_2, $\ldots$, Y_n, in that order.

260. [*M21*] Exercises 14 and 201 are bipartite matching problems related to choosing seats at a circular table. Test Algorithm Z empirically on those problems, and show that it solves the latter in linear time (despite exponentially many solutions).

▶ **261.** [*23*] Let G be a directed acyclic graph, with source vertices S and sink vertices T.
  a) Use Algorithm C (or Z) to find all sets of m vertex-disjoint paths from S to T.
  b) Also find all such sets of paths from s_k to t_k for $1 \le k \le m$, given s_k and t_k.
  c) Apply (a) to find all sets of $n - 1$ disjoint paths that enter an $n \times n$ square at the
     north or east edge, proceed by south and/or west steps, and exit at the south or
     west edge, avoiding the corners. (A random 16×16 example is shown.)

  d) Apply (b) to find all vertex-disjoint, downward paths of eight knights that start
     on the top row of a chessboard and end on the bottom row in reverse order.

▶ **262.** [*M23*] One of the advantages of Algorithm Z is that a ZDD allows us to generate
  uniformly random solutions. (See the remarks following 7.1.4–(13).)
  a) Determine the number of ZDD nodes output by Algorithm Z for the set of all
     domino tilings of S_n, where S_n is the shape obtained after right triangles of side 7
     have been removed from each corner of a $16 \times n$ rectangle:

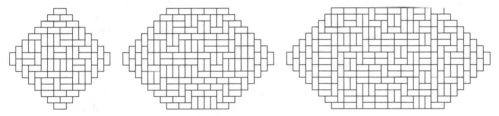

  How many tilings are possible for S_{16} (the Aztec diamond of order 8)? For S_{32}?
  b) Similarly, determine the ZDD size for the family of all diamond tilings of T_n —
     the grid $simplex(n + 16, n + 8, 16, n + 8, 0, 0, 0)$, a hexagon of sides $(8, 8, n, 8, 8, n)$:

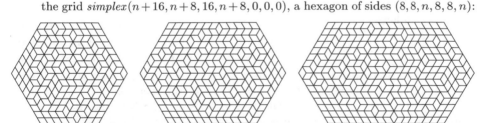

263. [*24*] Compare the time and space requirements of Algorithms C and Z when they
are applied to (a) the 16 queens problem; (b) pentominoes, as in exercises 271 and 274;
(c) MacMahon's triangle problem, as in exercise 126; (d) the generalized de Bruijn
sequences of exercise 95; (e) the "right word stair" problem of exercise 90; (f) the 6×6
"word search" problem of exercise 105; (g) the kakuro problem in exercise 431.

264. [*M21*] Suppose step Z3 always chooses the first active item $i = \text{RLINK}(0)$, instead
of using the MRV heuristic, unless some other active item has $\text{LEN}(i) = 0$. Prove that
Algorithm Z will then output an *ordered* ZDD.

▶ **265.** [*22*] Prove that Algorithm Z will never produce identical ZDD nodes $(\bar{o}_i?\, l_i\!:\! h_i) = (\bar{o}_j?\, l_j\!:\! h_j)$ for $i \ne j$, if all items are primary. But secondary items *can* cause duplicates.

EXERCISES — Second Set

Thousands of fascinating recreational problems have been based on polyominoes and their polyform cousins (the polycubes, polyiamonds, polyhexes, polysticks, ...). The following exercises explore "the cream of the crop" of such classic puzzles, as well as a few gems that were not discovered until recently.

In most cases the point of the exercise is to find a good way to discover all solutions, usually by setting up an appropriate exact cover problem that can be solved without taking an enormous amount of time.

▶ **266.** [*25*] Sketch the design of a utility program that will create sets of options by which an exact cover solver will fill a given shape with a given set of polyominoes.

267. [*18*] Using Conway's piece names, pack five pentominoes into the shape  so that they spell a common English word when read from left to right.

▶ **268.** [*21*] There are 1010 ways to pack the twelve pentominoes into a 5×12 box, not counting reflections. What's a good way to find them all, using Algorithm X?

269. [*21*] How many of those 1010 packings decompose into $5 \times k$ and $5 \times (12-k)$?

270. [*21*] In how many ways can the eleven nonstraight pentominoes be packed into a 5×11 box, not counting reflections as different? (Reduce symmetry cleverly.)

271. [*20*] There are 2339 ways to pack the twelve pentominoes into a 6×10 box, not counting reflections. What's a good way to find them all, using Algorithm X?

272. [*23*] Continuing exercise 271, explain how to find special kinds of packings:
  a) Those that decompose into $6 \times k$ and $6 \times (10-k)$.
  b) Those that have all twelve pentominoes touching the outer boundary.
  c) Those with all pentominoes touching that boundary *except* for V, which doesn't.
  d) Same as (c), with each of the other eleven pentominoes in place of V.
  e) Those with the *minimum* number of pentominoes touching the outer boundary.
  f) Those that are characterized by Arthur C. Clarke's description, as quoted below.
That is, the X pentomino should touch only the F (aka R), the N (aka S), the U, and the V — no others.

> *Very gently, he replaced the titanite cross*
> *in its setting between the F, N, U, and V pentominoes.*
> — ARTHUR C. CLARKE, *Imperial Earth* (1976)

273. [*25*] All twelve pentominoes fit into a 3×20 box only in two ways, shown in (36).
  a) How many ways are there to fit *eleven* of them into that box?
  b) In how many solutions to (a) are the five holes *nonadjacent*, kingwise?
  c) In how many ways can eleven pentominoes be packed into a 3×19 box?

274. [*21*] There are five different *tetrominoes*, namely

☐ ;   ▭ ;   ⬓ ;   ⌐ ;   ⊤ .

square   straight   skew   ell   tee

In how many essentially different ways can each of them be packed into an 8×8 square together with the twelve pentominoes?

275. [*21*] If an 8×8 checkerboard is cut up into thirteen pieces, representing the twelve pentominoes together with one of the tetrominoes, some of the pentominoes will have more black cells than white. Is it possible to do this in such a way that U, V, W, X, Y, Z have a black majority while the others do not?

276. [*18*] Design a nice, simple tiling pattern that's based on the five tetrominoes.

277. [*25*] How many of the 6×10 pentomino packings are *strongly three-colorable*, in the sense that each individual piece could be colored red, white, or blue in such a way that no pentominoes of the same color touch each other—not even at corner points?

▸ **278.** [*32*] Use the catalog of bipairs in exercise 217 to reduce the number of 6×10 pentomino packings, listing strong solutions only (see Theorem S). How much time is saved?

279. [*40*] (H. D. Benjamin, 1948.) Show that the twelve pentominoes can be wrapped around a cube of size $\sqrt{10} \times \sqrt{10} \times \sqrt{10}$. For example, here are front and back views of such a cube, made from twelve colorful fabrics by the author's wife in 1993:

(Photos by
Héctor García)

What is the best way to do this, minimizing undesirable distortions at the corners?

▸ **280.** [*M26*] Arrange the twelve pentominoes into a Möbius strip of width 4. The pattern should be "faultfree": Every straight line must intersect some piece.

▸ **281.** [*20*] The white cells of a $(2n+1) \times (2n+1)$ checkerboard, with black corners, form an interesting graph called the *Aztec diamond* of order n; and the black cells form the Aztec diamond of order $n+1/2$. For example, the diamonds of orders $11/2$ and $13/2$ are

(i) 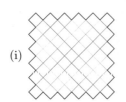   and   (ii) 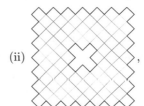 ,

except that (ii) has a "hole" of order $3/2$. Thus (i) has 61 cells, and (ii) has 80.
    a) Find all ways to pack (i) with the twelve pentominoes and one monomino.
    b) Find all ways to pack (ii) with the 12 pentominoes and 5 tetrominoes.
Speed up the process by not producing solutions that are symmetric to each other.

▸ **282.** [*22*] (Craig S. Kaplan.) A polyomino can sometimes be surrounded by nonoverlapping copies of itself that form a *fence*: Every cell that touches the polyomino—even at a corner—is part of the fence; conversely, every piece of the fence touches the inner polyomino. Furthermore, the pieces must not enclose any unoccupied "holes."
    Find the (a) smallest and (b) largest fences for each of the twelve pentominoes. (Some of these patterns are unique, and quite pretty.)

283. [*22*] Solve exercise 282 for fences that satisfy the *tatami* condition of exercise 7.1.4–215: No four edges of the tiles should come together at any "crossroads."

▸ **284.** [*27*] Solomon Golomb discovered in 1965 that there's only one placement of two pentominoes in a 5×5 square that blocks the placement of all the others.
    Place (a) $\{O, P, U, V\}$ and (b) $\{P, R, T, U\}$ into a 7×7 square in such a way that none of the other eight will fit in the remaining spaces.

285. [21] (T. H. O'Beirne, 1961.) The *one-sided pentominoes* are the eighteen distinct 5-cell pieces that can arise if we aren't allowed to flip pieces over:

Notice that there now are two versions of P, Q, R, S, Y, and Z.

In how many ways can all eighteen of them be packed into rectangles?

286. [21] If you want to pack the twelve pentominoes into a 6×10 box *without* turning any pieces over, 2^6 different problems arise, depending on the orientations of the one-sided pieces. Which of those 64 problems has (a) the fewest (b) the most solutions?

▶ **287.** [23] A princess asks you to pack an $m \times n$ box with pentominoes, rewarding you with $\$c \cdot (ni + j)$ if you've covered cell (i, j) with piece c, where $c = (1, 2, \ldots, 12)$ for pieces $(\mathrm{O}, \mathrm{P}, \ldots, \mathrm{Z})$. (The most valuable packing will be "closest to alphabetical order.")

Use Algorithm X$ to maximize your bounty when packing boxes of sizes 4×15, 5×12, 6×10, 10×6, 12×5, and 15×4. Consider also the princess's circle-shaped subset of a 9×9 box, where you are to cover only the 60 cells whose distances from the center are between 1 and $\sqrt{18}$. How do the running times of Algorithm X$ compare to the amounts of time that Algorithm X would take to find *all* solutions?

288. [21] Similarly, pack the one-sided pentominoes optimally into 9×10 and 10×9.

▶ **289.** [29] (*Pentominoes of pentominoes.*) Magnify the 3×20 pentomino packing (36) by replacing each of its unit cells by (a) 3×4 rectangles; (b) 4×3 rectangles. In how many ways can the resulting 720-cell shape be packed with twelve complete sets of twelve pentominoes, using one set for each of the original pentomino regions?

(c) Also partition the 720-cell shape below into 3×20 approximately *square* 12-cell regions, by assigning each gray cell to an adjacent region. (This shape has been superimposed on a grid whose $\sqrt{12} \times \sqrt{12}$ regions are *perfectly* square.) Minimize the total perimeter of the 60 resulting regions, and try for a pleasantly symmetrical solution.

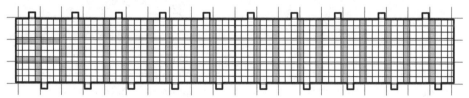

Use your partition to present a scaled-up version of (36), again with 12 complete sets.

290. [21] When tetrominoes are both checkered and one-sided (see exercises 275 and 285), ten possible pieces arise. In how many ways can all ten of them fill a rectangle?

291. [24] (*A puzzle a day.*) Using the two trominoes, the five tetrominoes, and three of the pentominoes, one can cover up 11 of the 12 "months" and 30 of the 31 "days" in the following pair of diagrams, thereby revealing the current month and day:

I	II	III	IV
V	VI	VII	VIII
IX	X	XI	XII

1	2	3	4	5	6	7
8	9	10	11	12	13	14
15	16	17	18	19	20	21
22	23	24	25	26	27	28
29	30	31				

Which of the $\binom{12}{3}$ sets of three pentominoes always allow this to be done?

292. [*20*] There are 35 *hexominoes*, first enumerated in 1934 by the master puzzlist H. D. Benjamin. At Christmastime that year, he offered ten shillings to the first person who could pack them into a 14×15 rectangle — although he wasn't sure whether or not it could be done. The prize was won by F. Kadner, but not as expected: Kadner proved that the hexominoes actually *can't* be packed into *any* rectangle! Nevertheless, Benjamin continued to play with them, eventually discovering that they fit nicely into the triangle shown here.

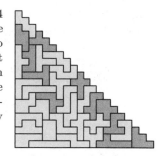

    Prove Kadner's theorem. *Hint:* See exercise 275.

293. [*24*] (Frans Hansson, 1947.) The fact that $35 = 1^2 + 3^2 + 5^2$ suggests that we might be able to pack the hexominoes into three boxes that represent a *single* hexomino shape at three levels of magnification, such as

For which hexominoes can this be done?

▶ **294.** [*30*] Show that the 35 hexominoes can be packed into five "castles":

In how many ways can this be done?

295. [*41*] For which values of m can the hexominoes be packed into a box like this?

296. [*41*] Perhaps the nicest hexomino packing uses a 5×45 rectangle with 15 holes

proposed by W. Stead in 1954. In how many ways can the 35 hexominoes fill it?

297. [*24*] (P. Torbijn, 1989.) Can the 35 hexominoes be packed into six 6×6 squares?

▶ **298.** [*22*] In how many ways can the twelve pentominoes be placed into an 8×10 rectangle, leaving holes in the shapes of the five tetrominoes? (The holes should not touch the boundary, nor should they touch each other, even at corners; one example is shown at the right.) Explain how to encode this puzzle as an XCC problem.

299. [*39*] If possible, solve the analog of exercise 298 for the case of 35 *hexominoes* in a 5×54 rectangle, leaving holes in the shapes of the twelve *pentominoes*.

▶ **300.** [*23*] In how many ways can the twelve pentominoes be arranged in a 10×10 square, filling exactly six of the cells in every row and exactly six of the cells in every column, if we also require that (a) the cells on both diagonals are completely empty? (b) the cells on both diagonals are completely filled? (c) the design is really interesting?

301. [*25*] Here's one way to place the twelve pentominoes into a 5×5 square, covering the cells of rows $(1, 2, 3, 4, 5)$ exactly $(2, 3, 2, 3, 2)$ times:

QY	SX	ST	ST	RT
QXY	XYZ	RXZ	RST	RSV
QY	XZ	UW	RT	UV
QYZ	QWZ	UVW	PUV	PUV
OW	OW	OP	OP	OP

a) How many such placements are possible?
b) Suppose we've placed O first, P next, Q next, ..., Z last, when making the arrangement above. Then Z is above W is above V is above U is above P is above O; hence the pentominoes have been stacked up on six levels. Show that a different order of placement would require only four levels.
c) Find a solution to (a) that needs only three levels.
d) Find a solution to (a) that can't be achieved with only four levels.

302. [*26*] Say that an n-omino is "small" if it fits in a $(\sqrt{n} + 1) \times (\sqrt{n} + 1)$ box, and "slim" if it contains no 2×2 tetromino. Thus, for example, pentominoes O, Q, S, Y aren't small; P isn't slim.

a) How many nonominoes are both small and slim?
b) Fit nine different small-and-slim nonominoes into a 9×9 box.
c) Use a solution to (b) as the basis of a jigsaw sudoku puzzle with a unique solution. The clues of your puzzle should be the initial digits of π.

▶ **303.** [*HM35*] A *parallelogram polyomino*, or "parallomino" for short, is a polyomino whose boundary consists of two paths that each travel only north and/or east. (Equivalently, it is a "staircase polygon," "skew Young tableau," or a "skew Ferrers board," the difference between the diagrams of two tableaux or partitions; see Sections 5.1.4 and 7.2.1.4.) For example, there are five parallominoes whose boundary paths have length 4:

NNNE / ENNN ; NNEE / ENEN ; NNEE / EENN ; NENE / EENN ; NEEE / EEEN .

a) Find a one-to-one correspondence that maps the set of ordered trees with m leaves and n nodes into the set of parallominoes with width m and height $n - m$. The area of each parallomino should be the path length of its corresponding tree.
b) Study the generating function $G(w, x, y) = \sum_{\text{parallominoes}} w^{\text{area}} x^{\text{width}} y^{\text{height}}$.
c) Prove that the parallominoes whose width-plus-height is n have total area 4^{n-2}.
d) Part (c) suggests that we might be able to pack all of those parallominoes into a $2^{n-2} \times 2^{n-2}$ square, *without* rotating them or flipping them over. Such a packing is clearly impossible when $n = 3$ or $n = 4$; but is it possible when $n = 5$ or $n = 6$?

304. [*M25*] Prove that it's NP-complete to decide whether or not n given polyominoes, each of which fits in a $\Theta(\log n) \times \Theta(\log n)$ square, can be exactly packed into a square.

305. [*25*] When a square grid is scaled by $1/\sqrt{2}$ and rotated $45°$, we can place half of its vertices on top of the original ones; the other "odd-parity" vertices then correspond to the centers of the original square cells.

Using this idea we can glue a small domino of area 1 over portions of an ordinary domino of area 2, thereby obtaining ten distinct two-layer pieces called the *windmill dominoes*:

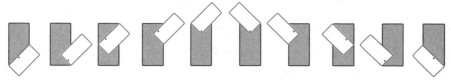

a) Arrange four windmill dominoes so that the upper layer resembles a windmill.
b) Place all ten windmill dominoes inside a 4×5 box, without overlapping.
c) Similarly, pack them all into a 2×10 box.
d) Place them so that the upper layer fills a $(4/\sqrt{2}) \times (5/\sqrt{2})$ rectangle.
e) Similarly, fit the upper layer into a $(2/\sqrt{2}) \times (10/\sqrt{2})$ rectangle.

In each case (a)–(e), use Algorithm X to count the total number of possible placements. Also look at the output and choose arrangements that are especially pleasing.

▶ **306.** [*30*] (S. Grabarchuk, 1996.) In how many ways can the ten windmill dominoes be arranged so that the 20 large squares define a snake-in-the-box cycle, in the sense of exercise 172(b), and so do the 20 small squares? (For example, arrangements like

 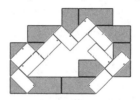

satisfy one snake-in-the-box condition but not the other.)

307. [*M21*] If a $(3m+1) \times (3n+2)$ box is packed with $3mn+2m+n$ straight trominoes and one domino, where must the domino be placed?

308. [*22*] A *polyiamond* is a connected set of triangles in a triangular grid, inspired by the diamond ◇ — just as a polyomino is a connected set of squares in a square grid, inspired by the domino ▯. Thus we can speak of moniamonds, diamonds, triamonds, etc.
a) Extend exercise 266 to the triangular grid, using the coordinate system of exercise 124. How many base placements do each of the tetriamonds have?
b) Find all ways to pack the pentiamonds into a convex polygon (see exercise 143).
c) Similarly, find all such ways to pack the *one-sided* pentiamonds.

309. [*24*] The *hexiamonds* are particularly appealing, because — like pentominoes — there are 12 of them. Here they are, with letter names suggested by J. H. Conway:

A   B   C   D   E   F   G   H   I   J   K   L

a) How many base placements do *they* have?
b) In how many ways can *they* be packed into convex polygons, as in exercise 308?

310. [*23*] What's the smallest m for which the 12 hexiamonds fit without overlap in

Find a pleasant way to place them inside of that smallest box.

▶ **311.** [*30*] (*Hexiamond wallpaper.*) Place the twelve hexiamonds into a region of N triangles, so that (i) shifted copies of the region fill the plane; (ii) the hexiamonds of the resulting infinite pattern do not touch each other, even at vertices; (iii) N is minimum.

312. [*22*] The following shape can be folded, to cover the faces of an octahedron:

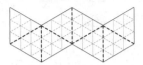

Fill it with hexiamonds so that they cross the folded edges as little as possible.

▶ **313.** [*29*] (*Hexiamonds of hexiamonds.*) A "whirl," shown here, is an inter- esting dodeciamond that tiles the plane in a remarkably beautiful way.

If each triangle '△' of a hexiamond is replaced by a whirl, in how many ways can the resulting 72-triangle shape be packed with the full set of hexiamonds? (Exercise 289 discusses the analogous problem for pentominoes.)

Consider also using "flipped whirls," the left-right reflections of each whirl.

▶ **314.** [*28*] (G. Sicherman, 2008.) Can the four pentiamonds be used to make two 10-iamonds of the same shape? Formulate this question as an exact cover problem.

315. [*20*] A *polyhex* is a connected shape formed by pasting hexagons together at their edges, just as polyominoes are made from squares and polyiamonds are made from triangles. For example, there's one monohex and one dihex, but there are three trihexes. Chemists have studied polyhexes since the 19th century, and named the small ones:

$$\text{benzene} = \hexagon \; ; \qquad \text{naphthalene} = \hexagonhexagon \; ;$$

$$\text{anthracene} = \text{\includegraphics{anthracene}} \, , \quad \text{phenanthrene} = \text{\includegraphics{phenanthrene}} \, , \quad \text{phenalene} = \text{\includegraphics{phenalene}} \; ; \qquad \text{etc.}$$

(Groups of six carbon atoms can bond together in a nearly planar fashion, forming long chains of hexagons, with hydrogen atoms attached. But the correspondence between polyhexes and polycyclic aromatic hydrocarbons is not exact.)

Represent the individual hexagons of an infinite grid by Cartesian-like coordinates

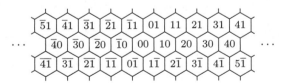

where $\bar{1} = -1, \bar{2} = -2$, etc. Extending exercises 266 and 308(a), explain how to find the base placements of a polyhex, given the coordinates of its cells when placed on this grid.

316. [*20*] Show that the complete set of trihexes and tetrahexes can be packed nicely into a rosette that consists of 37 concentric hexagons. In how many ways can it be done?

317. [*22*] (*Tetrahexes of tetrahexes.*) If we replace each hexagon of a tetrahex by a rosette of seven hexagons, we get a 28-hex. In how many ways can that scaled-up shape be packed with the seven distinct tetrahexes? (See exercises 289 and 313.)

▶ **318.** [*20*] Let's say that the *T-grid* is the set of all hexagons xy with $x \not\equiv y$ (modulo 3):

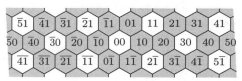

Show that there's a one-to-one correspondence between the hexagons of the T-grid and the triangles of the infinite triangular grid, in which every polyiamond corresponds to a polyhex. (Therefore the study of polyiamonds is a special case of the study of polyhexes!) *Hint:* Exercise 124 discusses a coordinate system for representing triangles.

319. [*21*] After polyominoes, polyiamonds, and polyhexes, the next most popular polyforms are the *polyaboloes*, originally proposed by S. J. Collins in 1961. These are the shapes obtainable by attaching isosceles right triangles at their edges; for example, there are three diaboloes: $\{\square, \diagup, \triangle\}$. Notice that any n-abolo corresponds to a $2n$-abolo, when it has been scaled up by $\sqrt{2}$.

The 14 tetraboloes can be named by using rough resemblances to hexiamonds:

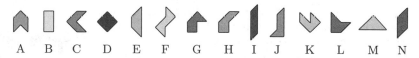

A   B   C   D   E   F   G   H   I   J   K   L   M   N

Show that the study of polyaboloes can be reduced to the study of (slightly generalized) polyominoes, just as exercise 318 reduces polyiamonds to polyhexes.

▶ **320.** [*M28*] Explain how to enumerate all of the N-aboloes that are *convex*. How many of the convex 56-aboloes can be packed by the fourteen tetraboloes?

321. [*24*] (T. H. O'Beirne, 1962.) In how many ways can a square be formed from the eight *one-sided tetraboloes* and their mirror images?

322. [*23*] The *polysticks* provide us with another intriguing family of shapes that can be combined in interesting ways. An "*n*-stick" is formed by joining n horizontal and/or vertical unit line segments together near grid points. For example, there are two disticks and five tristicks; and of course there's only one monostick. They're shown here in white, surrounded by the sixteen tetrasticks in black.

Polysticks introduce yet another twist into polyform puzzles, because we must not allow different pieces to cross each other when we pack them into a container. Extend exercise 266 to polysticks, so that Algorithm X can deal with them conveniently.

323. [*M25*] We've now seen polyominoes, polyiamonds, polyhexes, ..., polysticks, each of which have contributed new insights; and many other families of "polyforms" have in fact been studied. Let's close our survey with *polyskews*, a relatively new family that seems worthy of further exploration. Polyskews are the shapes that arise when we join squares alternately with rhombuses, in checkerboard fashion. For example, here are the ten tetraskews:

There are two monoskews, one diskew, and five triskews.

a) Explain how to draw such skewed pixel diagrams.

b) Show that polyskews, like polyaboloes, can be reduced to polyominoes.

c) In how many ways do the tetraskews make a skewed rectangle?

▶ **324.** [*20*] Extend exercise 266 to three dimensions. How many base placements do each of the seven Soma pieces have?

325. [*27*] The *Somap* is the graph whose vertices are the 240 distinct solutions to the Soma cube problem, with u —— v if and only if u can be obtained from an equivalent of v by changing the positions of at most three pieces. The *strong* Somap is similar, but it has u —— v only when a change of just *two* pieces gets from one to the other.

a) What are the degree sequences of the Somap graphs?

b) How many connected components do they have? How many bicomponents?

▶ **326.** [*M25*] Use factorization to prove that Fig. 75's W-wall cannot be built.

327. [*24*] Figure 75(a) shows some of the many "low-rise" (2-level) shapes that can be built from the seven Soma pieces. Which of them is hardest (has the fewest solutions)? Which is easiest? Answer those questions also for the 3-level prism shapes in Fig. 75(b).

▶ **328.** [*M23*] Generalizing the first four examples of Fig. 75, study the set of *all* shapes obtainable by deleting three cubies from a $3 \times 5 \times 2$ box. (Two examples are shown here.) How many essentially different shapes are possible? Which shape is easiest? Which shape is hardest?

329. [*22*] Similarly, consider (a) all shapes that consist of a $3 \times 4 \times 3$ box with just three cubies in the top level; (b) all 3-level prisms that fit into a $3 \times 4 \times 3$ box.

330. [*25*] How many of the 1285 *nonominoes* define a prism that can be realized by the Soma pieces? Do any of those packing problems have a unique solution?

331. [*M40*] Make empirical tests of Piet Hein's belief that the number of shapes achievable with seven Soma pieces is approximately the number of 27-cubie polycubes.

332. [*20*] (B. L. Schwartz, 1969.) Show that the Soma pieces can make shapes that appear to have more than 27 cubies, because of holes hidden inside or at the bottom:

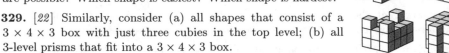

staircase   penthouse   pyramid

In how many ways can each of these three trick shapes be constructed?

333. [*22*] Show that the seven Soma pieces can also make structures such as

casserole   cot   vulture   mushroom   cantilever
,

which are "self-supporting" via gravity. (You may need to place a small book on top.)

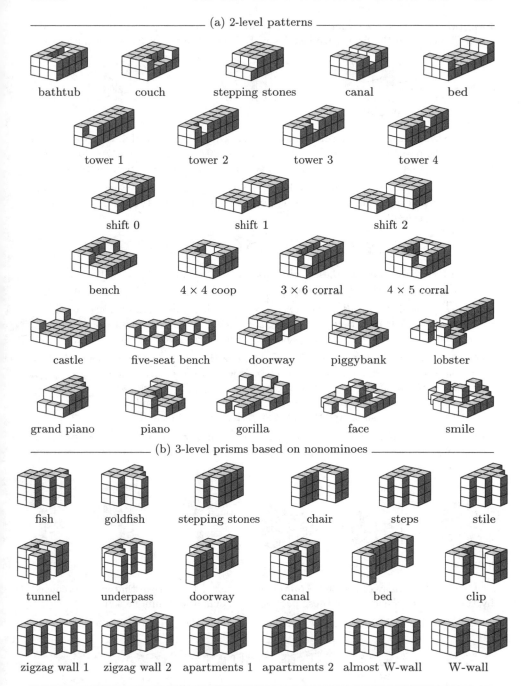

——————— (a) 2-level patterns ———————

bathtub   couch   stepping stones   canal   bed

tower 1   tower 2   tower 3   tower 4

shift 0   shift 1   shift 2

bench 4×4 coop 3×6 corral 4×5 corral

castle   five-seat bench   doorway   piggybank   lobster

grand piano   piano   gorilla   face   smile

——————— (b) 3-level prisms based on nonominoes ———————

fish   goldfish   stepping stones   chair   steps   stile

tunnel   underpass   doorway   canal   bed   clip

zigzag wall 1   zigzag wall 2   apartments 1   apartments 2   almost W-wall   W-wall

Fig. 75. Gallery of noteworthy polycubes that contain 27 cubies. All of them can be built from the seven Soma pieces, except for the W-wall. Many constructions are also stable when tipped on edge and/or when turned upside down. (See exercises 326–334.)

▶ **334.** [*M32*] Impossible structures *can* be built, if we insist only that they look genuine when viewed from the front (like façades in Hollywood movies)! Find all solutions to

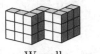

W-wall

X-wall

cube

that are visually correct. (To solve this exercise, you need to know that the illustrations here use the non-isometric projection $(x, y, z) \mapsto (30x - 42y, 14x + 10y + 45z)u$ from three dimensions to two, where u is a scale factor.) All seven Soma pieces must be used.

335. [*30*] The earliest known example of a polycube puzzle is the "Cube Diabolique," manufactured in late nineteenth century France by Charles Watilliaux; it contains six flat pieces of sizes 2, 3, ..., 7:

  a) In how many ways do these pieces make a $3 \times 3 \times 3$ cube?
  b) Are there six polycubes, of sizes 2, 3, ..., 7, that make a cube in just *one* way?

336. [*21*] (*The L-bert Hall.*) Take two cubies and drill three holes through each of them; then glue them together and attach a solid cubie and dowel, as shown. Prove that there's only one way to pack nine such pieces into a $3 \times 3 \times 3$ box.

337. [*29*] (Angus Lavery, 1989.) Design a puzzle that consists of nine bent tricubes, whose face squares are either blank or colored with a red or green spot. red   green The goal is to assemble the pieces into a $3 \times 3 \times 3$ cube in two ways: (i) No green spots are visible, and the red spots match a left-handed die. (ii) No red spots are visible, and the green spots match a right-handed die.

338. [*22*] Show that there are exactly eight different *tetracubes*—polycubes of size 4. Which of the following shapes can they make, respecting gravity? How many solutions are possible?

                         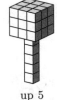

twin towers   double claw   cannon   up 3   up 4   up 5

339. [*25*] How many of the 369 *octominoes* define a 4-level prism that can be realized by the tetracubes? Do any of those packing problems have a unique solution?

340. [*30*] There are 29 *pentacubes*, conveniently identified with one-letter codes:

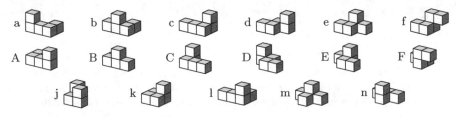

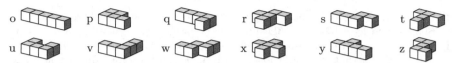

Pieces o through z are called, not surprisingly, the *solid pentominoes* or *flat pentacubes*.

    a) What are the mirror images of a, b, c, d, e, f, A, B, C, D, E, F, j, k, l, ..., z?

    b) In how many ways can the solid pentominoes be packed into an $a \times b \times c$ cuboid?

    c) What "natural" set of 25 pentacubes is able to fill the $5 \times 5 \times 5$ cube?

▶ **341.** [*25*] The full set of 29 pentacubes can build an enormous variety of elegant structures, including a particularly stunning example
called "Dowler's Box." This $7 \times 7 \times 5$ container, first considered by
R. W. M. Dowler in 1979, is constructed from five flat slabs. Yet
only 12 of the pentacubes lie flat; the other 17 must somehow be
worked into the edges and corners.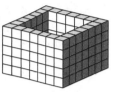

    Despite these difficulties, Dowler's Box has so many solutions that we can actually
impose many further conditions on its construction:

    a) Build Dowler's Box in such a way that the chiral pieces a, b, c, d, e, f and their
images A, B, C, D, E, F all appear in horizontally mirror-symmetric positions.

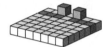 

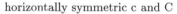

        horizontally symmetric c and C   diagonally symmetric c and C

    b) Alternatively, build it so that those pairs are *diagonally* mirror-symmetric.

    c) Alternatively, place piece x in the center, and build the remaining structure from
four congruent pieces that have seven pentacubes each.

342. [*25*] The 29 pentacubes can also be used to make the shape
shown here, exploiting the curious fact that $3^4 + 4^3 = 29 \cdot 5$. But
Algorithm X will take a long, long time before telling us how to
construct it, unless we're lucky, because the space of possibilities is
huge. How can we find a solution quickly?

343. [*40*] (T. Sillke, 1995.) For each of the twelve pentomino shapes, build the tallest
possible tower whose walls are vertical and whose floors all have the given shape, using
distinct pentacubes. *Hint:* Judicious factorization will give tremendous speedup.

344. [*20*] In how many distinct ways can a $5 \times 5 \times 5$ cube by packed with 25 solid
Y pentominoes? (See Fig. 73.) Discuss how to remove the 48 symmetries of this
problem.

345. [*20*] Pack twelve U-shaped dodecacubes into a $4 \times 6 \times 6$ box
without letting any two of them form a "cross."

346. [*M30*] An (l, m, n)-*tripod* is a cluster of $l + m + n + 1$ cubies in which
three "legs" of lengths l, m, and n are attached to a corner cubie, as in the
(1,2,3)-tripod shown here. A "pod" is the special case where the tripod is

$$(l, m, n) \cup \{(l', m, n) \mid 0 \le l' < l\} \cup \{(l, m', n) \mid 0 \le m' < m\} \cup \{(l, m, n') \mid 0 \le n' < n\}.$$

    a) Prove that, for all $m, n \ge 0$, shifted copies of nonoverlapping $(1, m, n)$-tripods are
able to fill all of 3-dimensional space, without rotation or reflection. *Hint:* Pack
N^2 of them into an $N \times N \times N$ torus, where $N = m + n + 2$.

b) Show that 7/9 of 3-dimensional space can be packed with shifted $(2, 2, 2)$-tripods.

c) Similarly, at least 65/108 of 3D space can be packed with shifted $(3, 3, 3)$-tripods.

d) Let $r(l, m, n)$ be the maximum number of pods that can be packed in an $l \times m \times n$ cuboid. Prove that at least $(1+l+m+n)r(l, m, n)/(4lmn)$ of 3-dimensional space can be packed with shifted (l, m, n)-tripods.

e) Use Algorithm M to evaluate $r(l, m, n)$ for $4 \leq l \leq m \leq n \leq 6$.

▶ **347.** [*M21*] (N. G. de Bruijn, 1961.) Prove that an $l \times m \times n$ box can be completely filled with $1 \times 1 \times k$ bricks only if k is a divisor of l, m, or n. (Consequently, it can be completely filled with $a \times b \times c$ bricks only if a, b, and c all satisfy this condition.)

348. [*M41*] Find the maximum number of "canonical bricks" $(1 \times 2 \times 4)$ that can be packed into an $l \times m \times n$ box, leaving as few empty cells as possible.

▶ **349.** [*M27*] (D. Hoffman.) Show that 27 bricks of size $a \times b \times c$ can always be packed into an $s \times s \times s$ cube, where $s = a+b+c$. But if $s/4 < a < b < c$, 28 bricks won't fit.

350. [*22*] Can 28 bricks of size $3 \times 4 \times 5$ be packed into a $12 \times 12 \times 12$ cube?

351. [*M46*] Can 5^5 hypercuboids of size $a \times b \times c \times d \times e$ always be packed into a 5-dimensional hypercube of size $(a + b + c + d + e) \times \cdots \times (a + b + c + d + e)$?

352. [*21*] In how many ways can the 12 pentominoes be packed into a $2 \times 2 \times 3 \times 5$ box?

353. [*20*] A *weak polycube* is a set of cubies that are loosely connected via common edges, not necessarily via common faces. In other words, we consider cubies to be adjacent when their centers are at most $\sqrt{2}$ units apart; up to 18 neighbors are possible. Find all the weak polycubes of size 3, and pack them into a symmetrical container.

▶ **354.** [*M30*] A *polysphere* is a connected set of spherical cells that belong to the "face-centered cubic lattice," which is one of the two principal ways to pack cannonballs (or oranges) with maximum efficiency. That lattice is conveniently regarded as the set S of all quadruples (w, x, y, z) of integers for which $w + x + y + z = 0$. Each cell of S has 12 neighbors, obtained by adding 1 to one coordinate and subtracting 1 from another.

It's instructive to view S in two different ways, by slicing it into plane layers that either have constant $x+y+z$ (hence constant w) or constant $y+z$ (hence constant $w+x$):

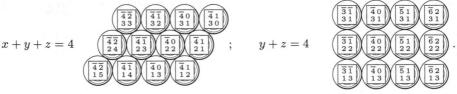

$$x + y + z = 4 \qquad ; \qquad y + z = 4 \qquad .$$

(Here $\boxed{\substack{w\,x \\ y\,z}}$ stands for (w, x, y, z).) If we include the layers above and below, we get

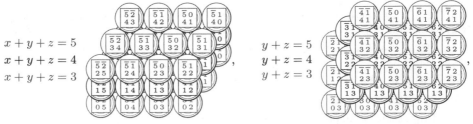

$$x + y + z = 5$$
$$x + y + z = 4 \qquad , \qquad y + z = 5$$
$$x + y + z = 3 \qquad\qquad y + z = 4 \qquad ,$$
$$\qquad\qquad\qquad\qquad y + z = 3$$

with each sphere nestling in the gap between the three or four spheres below it. In the "hex layers" on the left, (w, x, y, z) lies directly above $(w + 3, x - 1, y - 1, z - 1)$, but doesn't touch it; in the "quad layers" on the right, (w, x, y, z) lies directly above $(w+1, x+1, y-1, z-1)$, but doesn't touch it.

a) Show that every polyomino, and every polyhex, may be regarded as a polysphere:

b) Conversely, every *planar* polysphere looks like either a polyomino or a polyhex.

c) Every polysphere $\{(w_1, x_1, y_1, z_1), \ldots, (w_n, x_n, y_n, z_n)\}$ has a unique *base place-ment* $\{(w'_1, x'_1, y'_1, z'_1), \ldots, (w'_n, x'_n, y'_n, z'_n)\}$ obtained by subtracting (w', x', y', z') from each (w_k, x_k, y_k, z_k), where $x' = \min\{x_1, \ldots, x_n\}$, $y' = \min\{y_1, \ldots, y_n\}$, $z' = \min\{z_1, \ldots, z_n\}$, and $w' + x' + y' + z' = 0$. Prove that $x'_k + y'_k + z'_k < n$.

d) As with polycubes, we say that polyspheres v and v' are *equivalent* if the base placement of v is also a base placement of some rotation of v' in three dimensions. (Reflections of "chiral" polyspheres are not considered to be equivalent.) Formally speaking, a rotation of S about a line through the origin is an orthogonal 4×4 matrix that has determinant 1 and preserves $w + x + y + z$. Find such matrices for (i) rotation of the hex layers by $120°$; (ii) rotation of the quad layers by $90°$.

e) A planar polysphere is equivalent to its reflection, because we can rotate by $180°$ around a line in its plane. Find suitable 4×4 matrices by which we can legally reflect polyspheres that are equivalent to (i) polyominoes; (ii) polyhexes.

f) Prove that every rotation that takes a polysphere into another polysphere is obtainable as a product of the matrices exhibited in (d) and (e).

355. [*25*] The theory in exercise 354 allows us to represent polysphere cells with three integer coordinates xyz, because x, y, and z are nonnegative in base placements. The other variable, w, is redundant (but worth keeping in mind); it always equals $-x-y-z$.

a) What's a good way to find all the base placements of a given polysphere $\{x_1 y_1 z_1, x_2 y_2 z_2, \ldots, x_n y_n z_n\}$? *Hint:* Use exercise 354 to tweak the method of exercise 324.

b) Any three points of three-dimensional space lie in a plane. So exercise 354(b) tells us that there are just four trispheres: a tromino, two trihexes, and one that's both:

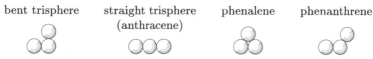

bent trisphere straight trisphere phenalene phenanthrene
        (anthracene)

What are their base placements?

c) According to exercise 354(c), every base placement of a tetrasphere occurs in the SGB graph $simplex(3, 3, 3, 3, 3, 0, 0)$. Use exercise 7.2.2–75 to find all of the four-element connected subsets of that graph, and identify all of the distinct tetraspheres. How many times does each tetrasphere occur in the graph?

356. [*23*] Polysphere puzzles often involve the construction of three kinds of shapes:

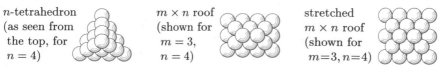

n-tetrahedron (as seen from the top, for $n = 4$) $m \times n$ roof (shown for $m = 3$, $n = 4$) stretched $m \times n$ roof (shown for $m=3, n=4$)

(An $n \times n$ roof or stretched roof is called an "n-pyramid" or a "stretched n-pyramid.")

a) Define each of these configurations by specifying a suitable base placement.

b) Each of the shapes illustrated is made from 20 spheres, and so is the stretched 4×3 roof. Find all multisets of five *tetraspheres* that suffice to make these shapes.

   c) The 4-pyramid and the stretched 4-pyramid involve 30 spheres. What multisets
of ten *trispheres* are able to make them?

   d) The *truncated octahedron*, which represents all permutations of $\{1, 2, 3, 4\}$, is a
noteworthy 24-cell subset of S (see exercise 5.1.1–10). What multisets of six
tetraspheres can build it?

357. [*M40*] Investigate "polysplatts," which are the sets of truncated octahedra that
can be built by pasting adjacent faces together (either square or hexagonal).

358. [*HM41*] Investigate "polyhexaspheres," which are the connected sets of spheres in
the *hexagonal close packing*. (This packing differs from that of exercise 354 because each
sphere of a hexagonal layer is directly above a sphere that's 2, not 3, layers below it.)

359. [*29*] Nick Baxter devised an innocuous-looking but maddeningly difficult "Square
Dissection" puzzle for the International Puzzle Party in 2014, asking that the nine pieces

be placed flat into a 65×65 square. One quickly checks that $17 \times 20 + 18 \times 20 + \cdots + 24 \times 25 = 65^2$; yet nothing seems to work! Solve his puzzle with the help of Algorithm X.

▶ **360.** [*20*] The next group of exercises is devoted to the decomposition of
rectangles into rectangles, as in the Mondrianesque pattern shown here.
The *reduction* of such a pattern is obtained by distorting it, if necessary,
so that it fits into an $m \times n$ grid, with each of the vertical coordinates
$\{0, 1, \ldots, m\}$ used in at least one horizontal boundary and each of the horizontal coordinates $\{0, 1, \ldots, n\}$ used in at least one vertical boundary. For
example, the illustrated pattern reduces to ▦, where $m = 3$ and $n = 5$.
(Notice that the original rectangles needn't have rational width or height.)
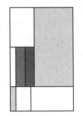
    A pattern is called *reduced* if it is equal to its own reduction. Design an exact cover
problem by which Algorithm M will discover all of the reduced decompositions of an
$m \times n$ rectangle, given m and n. How many of them are possible when $(m, n) = (3, 5)$?

361. [*M25*] The maximum number of subrectangles in a reduced $m \times n$ pattern is
obviously mn. What is the *minimum* number?

362. [*10*] A reduced pattern is called *strictly reduced* if each of its subrectangles
$[a \mathbin{..} b) \times [c \mathbin{..} d)$ has $(a, b) \neq (0, m)$ and $(c, d) \neq (0, n)$ — in other words, if no subrectangle
"cuts all the way across." Modify the construction of exercise 360 so that it produces
only strictly reduced solutions. How many 3×5 patterns are strictly reduced?

363. [*20*] A rectangle decomposition is called *faultfree* if it cannot be split into two or
more rectangles. For example, ▦ is *not* faultfree, because it has a fault line between
rows 2 and 3. (It's easy to see that every reduced faultfree pattern is *strictly* reduced,
unless $m = n = 1$.) Modify the construction of exercise 360 so that it produces only
faultfree solutions. How many reduced 3×5 patterns are faultfree?

364. [*23*] True or false: Every faultfree packing of an $m \times n$ rectangle by 1×3 trominoes
is reduced, except in the trivial cases $(m, n) = (1, 3)$ or $(3, 1)$.

365. [*22*] (*Motley dissections.*) Many of the most interesting decompositions of an
$m \times n$ rectangle involve strictly reduced patterns whose subrectangles $[a_i \mathbin{..} b_i) \times [c_i \mathbin{..} d_i)$
satisfy the extra condition

$$(a_i, b_i) \neq (a_j, b_j) \quad \text{and} \quad (c_i, d_i) \neq (c_j, d_j) \quad \text{when } i \neq j.$$

Thus no two subrectangles are cut off by the same pair of horizontal or vertical lines. The smallest such "motley dissections" are the 3×3 pinwheels, ⊞ and ⊟, which are considered to be essentially the same because they are mirror images of each other. There are eight essentially distinct motley rectangles of size $4 \times n$, namely

The two 4×4s can each be drawn in 8 different ways, under rotations and reflections. Similarly, most of the 4×5s can be drawn in 4 different ways. But the last two have only two forms, because they're symmetric under $180°$ rotation. (And the last two are actually equivalent, if we swap the two x coordinates in the middle.)

Design an exact cover problem by which Algorithm M will discover all of the motley dissections of an $m \times n$ rectangle, given m and n. (When $m = n = 4$ the algorithm should find $8 + 8$ solutions; when $m = 4$ and $n = 5$ it should find $4 + 4 + 4 + 4 + 2 + 2$.)

▶ **366.** [*25*] Improve the construction of the previous exercise by taking advantage of symmetry to cut the number of solutions in half. (When $m = 4$ there will now be $4 + 4$ solutions when $n = 4$, and $2 + 2 + 2 + 2 + 1 + 1$ when $n = 5$.) *Hint:* A motley dissection is never identical to its left-right reflection, so we needn't visit both.

367. [*20*] The *order* of a motley dissection is the number of subrectangles it has. There are no motley dissections of order six. Show, however, that there are $m \times m$ motley dissections of order $2m - 1$ and $m \times (m+1)$ motley dissections of order $2m$, for all $m > 3$.

368. [*M21*] (H. Postl, 2017.) Show that an $m \times n$ motley dissection of order t can exist only if $n < 2t/3$. *Hint:* Consider adjacent subrectangles.

369. [*21*] An $m \times n$ motley dissection must have order less than $\binom{m+1}{2}$, because only $\binom{m+1}{2} - 1$ intervals $[a_i .. b_i]$ are permitted. What is the maximum order that's actually achievable by an $m \times n$ motley dissection, for $m = 5$, 6, and 7?

▶ **370.** [*23*] Explain how to generate all of the $m \times n$ motley dissections that have $180°$-rotational symmetry, as in the last two examples of exercise 365, by modifying the construction of exercise 366. (In other words, if $[a .. b) \times [c .. d)$ is a subrectangle of the dissection, its complement $[m - b .. m - a) \times [n - d .. n - c)$ must also be one of the subrectangles, possibly the same one.) How many such dissections have size 8×16?

371. [*24*] Further symmetry is possible when $m = n$ (as in exercise 365's pinwheel).
    a) Explain how to generate all of the $n \times n$ motley dissections that have $90°$-rotational symmetry. This means that $[a .. b) \times [c .. d)$ implies $[c .. d) \times [n - b .. n - a)$.
    b) Explain how to generate all of the $n \times n$ motley dissections that are symmetric under reflection about both diagonals. This means that $[a .. b) \times [c .. d)$ implies $[c .. d) \times [a .. b)$ and $[n - d .. n - c) \times [n - b .. n - a)$, hence $[n - b .. n - a) \times [n - d .. n - c)$.
    c) What's the smallest n for which symmetric solutions of type (b) exist?

▶ **372.** [*M35*] (*Floorplans.*) If a rectangle decomposition satisfies the tatami condition — "no four rectangles meet" — it's often called a *floorplan*, and its subrectangles are called *rooms*. The line segments that delimit rooms are called *bounds*. Four possibilities arise when room r is adjacent to bound s: Either $s \downarrow r$, $r \rightarrow s$, $r \downarrow s$, or $s \rightarrow r$, meaning respectively that the top, right, bottom, or left boundary of r is part of s.

    For example, the floorplans shown on the next page have 10 rooms $\{A, B, \ldots, J\}$, $7 + 6$ bounds $\{h_0, \ldots, h_6, v_0, \ldots, v_5\}$, and the following adjacencies: $h_0 \downarrow A \downarrow h_3 \downarrow D \downarrow$ $h_5 \downarrow E \downarrow h_6$, $h_0 \downarrow B \downarrow h_1 \downarrow C \downarrow h_3 \downarrow F \downarrow h_6$, $h_1 \downarrow G \downarrow h_2 \downarrow H \downarrow h_4 \downarrow I \downarrow h_6$, $h_2 \downarrow J \downarrow h_6$; $v_0 \rightarrow A \rightarrow v_1 \rightarrow B \rightarrow v_5$, $v_1 \rightarrow C \rightarrow v_3 \rightarrow H \rightarrow v_4$, $v_0 \rightarrow D \rightarrow v_2 \rightarrow F \rightarrow v_3 \rightarrow G \rightarrow v_5$, $v_0 \rightarrow E \rightarrow v_2$, $v_3 \rightarrow I \rightarrow v_4 \rightarrow J \rightarrow v_5$.

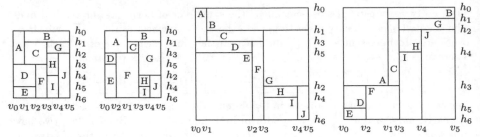

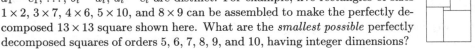

Two floorplans with the same adjacencies are considered to be equivalent. Thus, all four of the floorplans above are essentially the same, even though they look rather different: In particular, room C needn't overlap room D; we require only C $\downarrow h_3 \downarrow$ D.

a) Let $r \Downarrow r'$ mean that $r = r_0 \downarrow s_0 \downarrow r_1 \downarrow \cdots \downarrow s_{k-1} \downarrow r_k = r'$ for some $k > 0$; define $r \Rightarrow r'$ similarly. Prove that $[r \Downarrow r'] + [r \Rightarrow r'] + [r' \Downarrow r] + [r' \Rightarrow r] = 1$, when $r \ne r'$. *Hint:* Every floorplan has unique diagonal and antidiagonal equivalents, as shown.

b) A *twin tree* is a data structure whose nodes v have four pointer fields, $\text{LO}(v)$, $\text{RO}(v)$, $\text{L1}(v)$, $\text{R1}(v)$. It defines two binary trees T_0 and T_1 on the nodes, where T_θ is rooted at $\text{ROOT}\theta$ and has child links $(\text{L}\theta, \text{R}\theta)$. These two trees satisfy $\text{inorder}(T_0) = \text{inorder}(T_1) = v_1 \ldots v_n$; $\text{RO}(v_k) = \Lambda \iff \text{R1}(v_k) \ne \Lambda$, for $1 \le k < n$.

For each room r, if r's top left corner is a $\top$ junction, set $\text{LO}(r) \leftarrow \Lambda$ and $\text{L1}(r) \leftarrow r'$, where r' is the room opposite r in that corner; otherwise reverse the roles of LO and L1. Similarly, set $\text{RO}(r) \leftarrow \Lambda$ and $\text{R1}(r) \leftarrow r'$ if the bottom right corner of r is a $\dashv$ junction, or vice versa otherwise. (Use $r' = \Lambda$ at extreme corners.) Also set ROOT0 and ROOT1 to the bottom-left and top-right rooms. Show that a twin tree is created, convenient for representing this floorplan.

373. [*26*] A "perfectly decomposed rectangle" of order t is a faultfree dissection of a rectangle into t subrectangles $[a_i .. b_i) \times [c_i .. d_i)$ such that the $2t$ dimensions $b_1 - a_1$, $d_1 - c_1$, $\ldots$, $b_t - a_t$, $d_t - c_t$ are distinct. For example, five rectangles of sizes 1×2, 3×7, 4×6, 5×10, and 8×9 can be assembled to make the perfectly decomposed 13×13 square shown here. What are the *smallest possible* perfectly decomposed squares of orders 5, 6, 7, 8, 9, and 10, having integer dimensions?

374. [*M28*] An "incomparable dissection" of order t is a decomposition of a rectangle into t subrectangles, none of which will fit inside another. In other words, if the heights and widths of the subrectangles are respectively $h_1 \times w_1$, $\ldots$, $h_t \times w_t$, we have neither $(h_i \le h_j$ and $w_i \le w_j)$ nor $(h_i \le w_j$ and $w_i \le h_j)$ when $i \ne j$.

a) True or false: An incomparable dissection is perfectly decomposed.

b) True or false: The reduction of an incomparable dissection is motley.

c) True or false: The reduction of an incomparable dissection can't be a pinwheel.

d) Prove that every incomparable dissection of order ≤ 7 reduces to the first 4×4 motley dissection in exercise 365; and its seven regions can be labeled as shown, with $h_7 < h_6 < \cdots < h_2 < h_1$ and $w_1 < w_2 < \cdots < w_6 < w_7$.

e) Suppose the reduction of an incomparable dissection is $m \times n$, and suppose its regions have been labeled $\{1, \ldots, t\}$. Then there are numbers $x_1, \ldots, x_n, y_1, \ldots, y_m$ such that the widths are sums of the x's and the heights are sums of the y's. (For example, in (d) we have $w_2 = x_1$, $h_2 = y_1 + y_2 + y_3$, $w_7 = x_2 + x_3 + x_4$, $h_7 = y_1$, etc.) Prove that such a dissection exists with $w_1 < w_2 < \cdots < w_t$ if and only if the linear inequalities $w_1 < w_2 < \cdots < w_t$ have a positive solution $(x_1, \ldots, x_n)$ and the linear inequalities $h_1 > h_2 > \cdots > h_t$ have a positive solution $(y_1, \ldots, y_m)$.

375. [*M29*] Among all the incomparable dissections of order (a) seven and (b) eight, restricted to integer sizes, find the rectangles with the smallest possible semiperimeter (height plus width). Also find the smallest possible *squares* that have incomparable dissections in integers. *Hint:* Show that there are 2^t potential ways to mix the h's with the w's, preserving their order; and find the smallest semiperimeter for each of those cases.

▶ **376.** [*M25*] Find seven *different* rectangles of area 1/7 that can be assembled into a square of area 1, and prove that the answer is unique.

377. [*M28*] Two rectangles of shapes $h \times w$ and $h' \times w'$ can be *concatenated* to form a larger rectangle of size $(h + h') \times w$ if $w = w'$, or of size $h \times (w + w')$ if $h = h'$.
   a) Given a set S of rectangle shapes, let $\Lambda(S)$ be the set of all shapes that can be made from the elements of S by repeated concatenation. Describe $\Lambda(\{1{\times}2, 3{\times}1\})$.
   b) Find the smallest $S \subseteq T$ such that $T \subseteq \Lambda(S)$, where $T = \{h{\times}w \mid 1 < h < w\}$.
   c) What's the smallest S with $\Lambda(S) = \{h{\times}w \mid h, w > 1$ and $hw \bmod 8 = 0\}$?
   d) Given m and n, solve (c) with $\Lambda(S) = \{h{\times}w \mid h, w > m$ and $hw \bmod n = 0\}$.

▶ **378.** [*M30*] (*A finite basis theorem.*) Continuing exercise 377, prove that *any* set T of rectangular shapes contains a finite subset S such that $T \subseteq \Lambda(S)$.

▶ **379.** [*23*] What $h \times w$ rectangles can be packed with copies of the Q pentomino? *Hint:* It suffices to find a finite basis for all such rectangles, using the previous exercise.

380. [*35*] Solve exercise 379 for the Y pentomino.

381. [*20*] Show that $3n$ copies of the *disconnected* shape '☐ ☐☐ ☐' can pack a $12 \times n$ rectangle for all sufficiently large values of n.

▶ **382.** [*18*] There's a natural way to extend the idea of motley dissection to three dimensions, by subdividing an $l \times m \times n$ cuboid into subcuboids $[a_i \mathinner{\ldotp\ldotp} b_i) \times [c_i \mathinner{\ldotp\ldotp} d_i) \times [e_i \mathinner{\ldotp\ldotp} f_i)$ that have no repeated intervals $[a_i \mathinner{\ldotp\ldotp} b_i)$ or $[c_i \mathinner{\ldotp\ldotp} d_i)$ or $[e_i \mathinner{\ldotp\ldotp} f_i)$.

For example, Scott Kim has discovered a remarkable motley $7 \times 7 \times 7$ cube consisting of 23 individual blocks, 11 of which are illustrated here. (Two of them are hidden behind the others.) The full cube is obtained by suitably placing a mirror image of these pieces in front, together with a $1 \times 1 \times 1$ cubie in the center.

By studying this picture, show that Kim's construction can be defined by coordinate intervals $[a_i \mathinner{\ldotp\ldotp} b_i) \times [c_i \mathinner{\ldotp\ldotp} d_i) \times [e_i \mathinner{\ldotp\ldotp} f_i)$, with $0 \le a_i, b_i, c_i, d_i, e_i, f_i \le 7$ for $1 \le i \le 23$, in such a way that the pattern is symmetrical under the transformation $xyz \mapsto \bar{y}\bar{z}\bar{x}$. In other words, if $[a \mathinner{\ldotp\ldotp} b) \times [c \mathinner{\ldotp\ldotp} d) \times [e \mathinner{\ldotp\ldotp} f)$ is one of the subcuboids, so is $[7 - d \mathinner{\ldotp\ldotp} 7 - c) \times [7 - f \mathinner{\ldotp\ldotp} 7 - e) \times [7 - b \mathinner{\ldotp\ldotp} 7 - a)$.

383. [*29*] Use exercise 382 to construct a perfectly decomposed $92 \times 92 \times 92$ cube, consisting of 23 subcuboids that have 69 distinct integer dimensions. (See exercise 373.)

384. [*24*] By generalizing exercises 365 and 366, explain how to find *every* motley dissection of an $l \times m \times n$ cuboid, using Algorithm M. *Note:* In three dimensions, the strictness condition '$(a_i, b_i) \ne (0, m)$ and $(c_i, d_i) \ne (0, n)$' of exercise 362 should become

$$[(a_i, b_i) = (0, l)] + [(c_i, d_i) = (0, m)] + [(e_i, f_i) = (0, n)] \le 1.$$

What are the results when $l = m = n = 7$?

385. [*M36*] (H. Postl, 2017.) Arbitrarily large motley cuboids can be constructed by repeatedly nesting one motley cuboid within another (see answer 367). Say that a motley cuboid is *primitive* if it doesn't contain a nested motley subcuboid.

Do primitive motley cuboids of size $l \times m \times n$ exist only when $l = m = n = 7$?

▶ **386.** [*M34*] A polyomino can have eight different types of symmetry:

(i)	(ii)	(iii)	(iv)	(v)	(vi)	(vii)	(viii)
full	90°	180°	biaxial	bidiagonal	axial	diagonal	none

(Case (i) is often called 8-fold symmetry; case (iii) is often called central symmetry; case (vi) is often called left-right symmetry. Cases (ii), (iv), (v) are 4-fold symmetries; cases (ii) and (iii) are rotation symmetries; cases (iv)–(vii) are reflection symmetries.) In each case an n-omino of that symmetry type has been shown, where n is minimum.

How many symmetry types can a polyiamond or polyhex have? Give example n-iamonds and n-hexes of each type, where n is minimum.

▶ **387.** [*M36*] Continuing exercise 386, how many symmetry types can a polycube have? Give an example of each type, using the minimum number of cubies. (Note that mirror reflection is *not* a legal symmetry for a polycube; L-twist $\neq$ R-twist!)

EXERCISES — Third Set

The following exercises are based on several intriguing logic puzzles that have recently become popular: futoshiki, kenken, masyu, slitherlink, kakuro, etc. Like sudoku, these puzzles typically involve a hidden pattern, for which only partial information has been revealed. The point of each exercise is usually to set up an appropriate exact cover problem, and to use it either to solve such a puzzle or to create new ones.

▶ **388.** [*21*] The goal of a *futoshiki* puzzle is to deduce the entries of a secret latin square, given only two kinds of hints: A "strong clue" is an explicit entry; a "weak clue" is a greater-than relation between neighboring entries. The entries are the numbers 1 to n, where n is usually 5 as in the following examples:

a)   b)   c)

Solve these puzzles by hand, using sudoku-like principles.

389. [*20*] Sketch a simple algorithm that finds simple lower and upper bounds for each entry that is part of a weak clue in a futoshiki puzzle, by repeatedly using the rule that $a \leq x < y \leq b$ implies $x \leq b - 1$ and $y \geq a + 1$. (Your algorithm shouldn't attempt to give the best possible bounds; that would solve the puzzle! But it should deduce the values of five entries in puzzle (a) of exercise 388, as well as entry $(4, 2)$ of puzzle (b).)

▶ **390.** [*21*] Show that every futoshiki puzzle is a special case of an exact cover problem. In fact, show that every such puzzle can be formulated in at least two different ways:

   a) Use a *pairwise ordering trick* analogous to (25) or (26), to encode the weak clues.
   b) Use *color controls* to formulate an XCC problem suitable for Algorithm C.

391. [*20*] A futoshiki puzzle is said to be *valid* if it has exactly one solution. Use Algorithm X to generate all possible 5×5 latin squares. Explain why many of them can't be the solution to a valid futoshiki puzzle unless it has at least one strong clue.

▶ **392.** [*25*] There are $2^6 \binom{40}{6} = 245656320$ ways to construct a 5×5 futoshiki puzzle that has six weak clues and no strong ones. How many of them (a) are valid? (b) have no solutions? (c) have more than one solution? Also refine those counts, by considering how many such puzzles of types (a), (b), and (c) have at least one "long path" $p < q < r < s < t$ (like the path that's present in exercise 388(a)). Give an example of each case.

393. [*25*] There are $5^6 \binom{25}{6} = 2767187500$ ways to construct a 5×5 futoshiki puzzle that has six strong clues and no weak ones. How many of them (a) are valid? (b) have no solutions? (c) have more than one solution? Give an example of each case.

394. [*29*] Show that every 5×5 futoshiki puzzle that has only five clues — strong, weak, or a mixture of both — has at least four solutions. Which puzzles attain this minimum?

395. [*25*] Continuing exercise 391, find a 5×5 latin square that cannot be the solution to a valid futoshiki puzzle unless at least *three* strong clues have been given.

▶ **396.** [*25*] Inspired by exercise 388(c), construct a valid 9×9 futoshiki puzzle whose diagonal contains the strong clues $(3, 1, 4, 1, 5, 9, 2, 6, 5)$ in that order. Every *other* clue should be a weak '<' — not a '>', not a '∧', not a '∨'.

▶ **397.** [*30*] (*Save the sheep.*) Given a grid in which some of the cells are occupied by sheep, the object of this puzzle is to construct a fence that keeps all the sheep on one side. The fence must begin and end at the edge of the grid, and it must follow the grid lines without visiting any point twice. Furthermore, *exactly two edges of each sheep's square should be part of the fence.* For example, consider the following 5×5 grids:

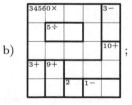

The four sheep on the left can be "saved" only with the fence shown in the middle. Once you understand why, you'll be ready to save the four sheep on the right.

    a) Explain how Algorithm C can help to solve puzzles like this, by showing that every solution satisfies a certain XCC problem. *Hint:* Imagine "coloring" each square with 0 or 1, with 1 indicating the cells on the sheep's side of the fence.

    b) Devise an interesting 8×8 puzzle that has a unique solution and at most 10 sheep.

398. [*23*] (*KenKen®.*) A secret latin square whose entries are $\{1, 2, \ldots, n\}$ can often be deduced by means of arithmetic. A kenken puzzle specifies the sum, difference, product, or quotient of the entries in each of its "cages," which are groups of cells indicated by heavy lines, as in the following examples:

a) ; b) ; c) .

(When the operation is '−' or '÷', the cage must have just two cells. A one-cell cage simply states its contents, without any operation; hence its solution is a no-brainer.)

    Cages look rather like the boxes of jigsaw sudoku (see (34)); but in fact the rules are quite different: Two entries of the same cage can be equal, if they belong to different rows and different columns. For example, the '9×' in (a) can be achieved only by multiplying the three entries $\{1,3,3\}$; hence there's exactly one way to fill that cage.

Solve (a), (b), (c) by hand. Show that one of them is actually *not* a valid puzzle.

▶ **399.** [*22*] How can all solutions to a kenken puzzle be obtained with Algorithm C?

400. [*21*] Many clues of a kenken puzzle often turn out to be redundant, in the sense that the contents of one cage might be fully determined by the clues from other cages. For example, it turns out that any one of the clues in puzzle 398(a) could actually be omitted, without permitting a new solution.

Find all subsets of those 11 clues that suffice to determine a unique latin square.

401. [*22*] Find all 4×4 kenken puzzles whose unique solution is the latin square shown at the right, and whose cages all have two cells. Furthermore, there should be exactly two cages for each of the four operations $+, -, \times, \div$.

1234
2143
4312
3421

402. [*24*] Solve this 12×12 kenken puzzle, using hexadecimal digits from 1 to C:

The five-cell cages of this puzzle have multiplicative clues, associated with the names of the twelve pentominoes:

O, 9240×
P, 5184×
Q, 3168×
R, 720×
S, 15840×
T, 19800×
U, 10560×
V, 4032×
W, 1620×
X, 5040×
Y, 576×
Z, 17248×

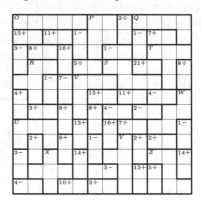

▶ **403.** [*31*] Inspired by exercises 398(a) and 398(c), construct a valid 9×9 kenken puzzle whose clues exactly match the decimal digits of π, for as many places as you can.

▶ **404.** [*25*] (*Hidato*®.) A "hidato solution" is an $m \times n$ matrix whose entries are a permutation of $\{1, 2, \ldots, mn\}$ for which the cells containing k and $k+1$ are next to each other, either horizontally, vertically, or diagonally, for $1 \le k < mn$. (In other words, it specifies a Hamiltonian path of king moves on an $m \times n$ board.) A "hidato puzzle" is a subset of those numbers, which uniquely determines the others; the solver is supposed to recreate the entire path from the given clues.

	3	14	1
5	9		
		8	

(i)

	3	14	1
	4		2
5	9		
		8	

(ii)

	3	14	1
4			2
5	9		
6		8	

(iii)

16	3	14	1
4	15	2	13
5	9	10	12
6	7	8	11

(iv)

For example, consider the 4×4 puzzle (i). There's only one place to put '2'. Then there are two choices for '4'; but one of them blocks the upper left corner (see (ii)), so we must choose the other. Similarly, '6' must not block any corner. Therefore (iii) is forced; and it's easy to fill in all of the remaining blanks, thereby obtaining solution (iv). Explain how to encode such puzzles for solution by Algorithm C.

405. [*21*] The preceding exercise needs a subroutine to determine the endpoints of all simple paths of lengths 1, 2, ..., L from a given vertex v in a given graph. That problem is NP-hard; but sketch an algorithm that works well for small L in small graphs.

406. [*16*] Show that the following hidato puzzle isn't as hard as it might look at first:

19	52	53	54	4	62	63	64
20							1
21							60
41							59
31							58
32							9
33							10
35	34	37	28	27	26	11	12

▶ **407.** [*20*] Here's a curious 4 × 8 array that is consistent with 52 hidato solutions:

22						12	
	29		26	16	8	3	

Change it to a valid hidato puzzle, by adding one more clue.

408. [*28*] (N. Beluhov.) Construct 6 × 6 hidato puzzles that have (a) only five clues; (b) at least eighteen clues, all of which are necessary.

▶ **409.** [*30*] Can the first 10 clues of a 10 × 10 hidato puzzle be the first 20 digits of π?

410. [*22*] (*Slitherlink.*) Another addictive class of puzzles is based on finding closed paths or "loops" in a given graph, when the allowable cycles must satisfy certain constraints. For instance, a slitherlink puzzle prescribes the *number of loop edges* that surround particular cells of a rectangular grid, as in diagram (i) below.

The first step in solving puzzle (i) is to note where the secret edges are definitely absent or definitely present. The 0s prohibit not only the edges immediately next to them but also a few more, because the path can't enter a dead end. Conversely, the 3 forces the path to go through the upper left corner; we arrive at situation (ii):

```
 3  1         3  1          3 1         3  1 □       3 1
 2 2          2 2           2 2         2 2          2 2
   1 0          1·0·          1 0          1 0          1 0
 2   0        2  ·0·        2   0        2   0        2   0
  (i)           (ii)          (iii)        (iv)         (v)
```

Some experimentation now tells us which edge must go with the lower 1. We must not form two loops, as in (iii) or (iv). And hurrah: There's a unique solution, (v).

Which of the following 5 × 5 slitherlink diagrams are valid puzzles? Solve them.

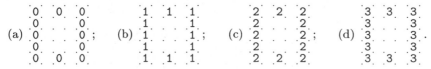

411. [*20*] True or false: A slitherlink diagram with a numeric clue given in every cell always has at most one solution. *Hint:* Consider the 2 × 2 case.

▶ **412.** [*22*] A "weak solution" to a slitherlink diagram is a set of edges that obeys the numeric constraints, and touches every vertex of the grid either twice or not at all; but it may form arbitrarily many loops. For example, the diagram of exercise 410(i) has six weak solutions, three of which are shown in 410(iii), (iv), and (v).

Show that there's a nice way to obtain all the weak solutions of a given diagram, by formulating a suitable XCC problem. *Hint:* Think of the edges as constructed from tiles centered at the vertices, and use even/odd coordinates as in answer 133.

▶ **413.** [*30*] Explain how to modify Algorithm C so that the construction of exercise 412 will produce only the true "single-loop" solutions. Your modified algorithm shouldn't be specific to slitherlink; it should apply also to masyu and other loop-discovery puzzles.

414. [*25*] The "strongest possible" answer to exercise 413 would cause the modified Algorithm C to backtrack as soon as the current choice of edge colors is incompatible with any single loop. Show that the algorithm in that answer is *not* as strong as possible, by examining its behavior on the puzzle at the right.

```
· · · · · ·
 1 0
 2   3
     3 0
· · · · ·
```

▶ **415.** [*M33*] Exactly $5 \cdot (2^{25} - 1)$ nonempty slitherlink diagrams of size 5×5 are "homogeneous," in the sense that all of their clues involve the same digit $d \in \{0, 1, 2, 3, 4\}$. (See exercise 410(a)–(d).) How many of them are valid puzzles? What are the minimum and maximum number of clues, for each d, in puzzles that contain no redundant clues?

416. [*M30*] For each $d \in \{0, 1, 2, 3, 4\}$, construct valid $n \times n$ slitherlink diagrams whose nonblank clues are all equal to d, for infinitely many n.

417. [*M46*] (N. Beluhov, 2018.) Exercise 410(a, b, d) illustrates three homogeneous slitherlink puzzles that are valid for exactly the same pattern of nonblank clues. Do infinitely many such square puzzles exist?

418. [*M29*] An $m \times n$ slitherlink diagram is said to be *symmetrical* if cells (i, j) and $(m - 1 - i, n - 1 - j)$ are both blank or both nonblank, for $0 \le i < m$ and $0 \le j < n$. (Many grid-based puzzles obey this oft-unwritten rule.)

a) There are exactly $6^{25} \approx 2.8 \times 10^{19}$ slitherlink diagrams of size 5×5, since each of the 25 cells can contain either '0', '1', '2', '3', '4', or ' '. How many of those diagrams are symmetrical?

b) How many of the symmetric diagrams in (a) are valid puzzles?

c) How many of those valid puzzles are *minimal*, in the sense that the deletion of nonblank clues in (i, j) and $(4 - i, 4 - j)$ would make the solution nonunique?

d) What is the minimum number of clues in a valid 5×5 symmetrical puzzle?

e) What is the maximum number of clues in a minimal 5×5 symmetrical puzzle?

419. [*30*] What surprise is concealed in the following symmetrical slitherlink puzzle?

```
  · · 2· 1 1 1 · · 1· 1· 1· · ·
  · · 2· · · 0 1 · · 0 1· · 1 2·
  · · ·2 1· · ·2 1· 2· 1 1· 1·
  2· 2· · 2 2 1· 1· 2· · · · ·
  3· 0· 0· · 2· · 1 2· 0 0 0· 0·
  · · · 1· · 1· 0· · 1· 0· · ·
  · · · · ·2 0· 1· 1 1 0· · · ·

      · · ·2 1 1· 0· 1 1· · ·
      · · 1· · 1· · 0· 1· · 0·
  0· · 0 2 1· 1 0· · 1· · 0· 0· 0·
      · · · 2· 0· 1 1 1· · 0· 0·
  0· · 2 1· 1· 0· 1· · 1 0· · ·
  0 1· · 1 1· · 1 1· · · 0· · ·
      · · 1· 1· 0· · 1 2 1· 0· · ·
```

420. [*M22*] Consider an $m \times n$ slitherlink with m and n odd, having 2s in the pattern

$$2 \quad 2 \quad 2 \quad 2 \quad 2 \quad 2 \quad 2$$
$$2 \quad 2 \quad 2 \quad 2 \quad 2 \quad 2 \quad 2$$
$$2 \quad 2 \quad 2 \quad 2 \quad 2 \quad 2 \quad 2$$

(and possibly other clues). Show that there's no solution if $m \bmod 4 = n \bmod 4 = 1$.

▶ **421.** [*20*] (*Masyu.*) A masyu ("evil influence") puzzle, like slitherlink, conceals a hidden loop of straight segments. But there are two important differences. First, the loop passes through the *centers* of grid cells, instead of following the edges. Second, no numerical quantities are involved; the clues are entirely visual and geometrical.

Clues appear in *circles* through which the loop must pass: (i) The path must *turn* 90° at every black circle; but it must travel *straight* through the two neighboring cells just before and after turning. (ii) The path must *not* turn 90° when it goes through a white circle; and it must *not* travel straight through the two neighboring cells just before and after not turning. (Thus it must actually turn, at one or both of those cells. We get at least one turn per clue, and at least one straight segment.)

Consider, for example, a 5 × 5 puzzle with a black clue in cell 02, and with white clues in cells 13, 30, 32, and 43 as shown. The loop clearly will have to include the subpaths 20 — 30 — 40 — 41 and 42 — 43 — 44 — 34 in some order. It also must include either 00 — 01 — 02 — 12 — 22 or 04 — 03 — 02 — 12 — 22, because of the black clue. But the latter alternative is impossible, because it leaves no way to go straight through the white clue in 13. Thus 10 — 00 — 01 — 02 — 12 — 22 is forced; and also 23 — 13 — 03 — 04 — 14 — 24 — 34. (We couldn't go 24 — 23, because that would close the loop prematurely.) The rest of the path now sort of falls into place.

Show that one of the clues in this example puzzle is actually redundant. But if any of the other four clues are absent, show that alternative solutions are possible.

422. [*21*] Show that the "weak solutions" to any given masyu puzzle are the solutions to an easily constructed XCC problem, by adapting the solution of exercise 412.

▶ **423.** [*M25*] For each of the $(m-1)n + m(n-1)$ potential edges e in the solution of an $m \times n$ masyu puzzle, let x_e be the Boolean variable '[e is present]'. The XCC problem constructed in exercise 422 is essentially a set of constraints on those variables.

Explain how to improve that construction dramatically, by exploiting the following special property that is enjoyed by masyu puzzles: Let N, S, E, and W be the edges leading out of a cell that holds a clue. If the clue is black, we have $N = {\sim}S$ and $E = {\sim}W$; if the clue is white, we have $N = S$, $E = W$, and $E = {\sim}N$. (Thus every clue reduces the number of independent variables by at least 2.)

▶ **424.** [*36*] Make an exhaustive study of 6 × 6 masyu, and gather whatever statistics you think are particularly interesting. For example, how many of the $3^{36} \approx 1.5 \times 10^{17}$ ways to place white or black clues lead to a valid puzzle? Which of the valid puzzles have the fewest clues? the most clues? the shortest loops? the longest loops? only white clues? only black clues? How many of those puzzles are *minimal*, in the sense that none of their clues can be removed without allowing a new solution?

How many of the $2^{36} \approx 6.9 \times 10^{10}$ ways to occupy cells occur as the pattern of white clues in a valid puzzle? How many of them occur as the pattern of black clues? How many puzzles remain valid when white and black are interchanged? Which 6 × 6 masyu puzzle do you think is most difficult to solve?

425. [*28*] The solution to a masyu puzzle is composed of five kinds of "tiles": '⊖', '◖●◗', '⊟', '⊡', and blank. For example, the 3 × 3 solution shown here contains two tiles of each nonblank type.

Find 4 × 4, 5 × 5, and 6 × 6 puzzles whose unique solutions have exactly k tiles of each nonblank type, for every possible k.

▶ **426.** [*31*] Obtain a valid masyu puzzle from diagram (i) below by changing each '●' clue into either '○' or '●'.

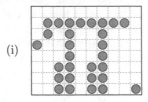

(i)

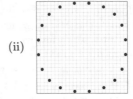

(ii)

▶ **427.** [*25*] Design a 25 × 25 masyu puzzle by adding white clues (only) to diagram (ii) above. All of your clues should preserve the 8-fold symmetry of this pattern.

428. [*M28*] For infinitely many n, construct a valid $n \times n$ masyu puzzle with $O(n)$ clues whose loop goes through all four corner cells, where all clues are (a) black; (b) white.

429. [*21*] A closed path on a triangular grid may have "sharp turns," which change the direction by 120°, or "slack turns," which change the direction by 60°, or both. Therefore *triangular masyu* has three flavors of clues: '●' for the sharp turns, '●' for the slack turns, and of course '○' for the non-turns.

   a) Solve the following homogeneous triangular masyu puzzles:

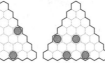

   b) The following patterns for triangular masyu are clearly impossible to solve. But show that each of them *is* solvable if the colors $\{\bigcirc, \bullet, \bullet\}$ are suitably permuted:

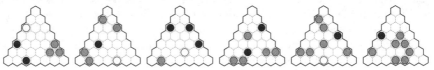

▶ **430.** [*26*] (*Kakuro.*) A kakuro puzzle is like a crossword puzzle, except that its "words" are blocks of two or more nonzero digits $\{1, 2, \ldots, 9\}$, not strings of letters. The digits of each block must be distinct, and their *sum* is given as a clue. Every cell to be filled belongs to exactly one horizontal block and one vertical block.

For example, the mini-kakuro shown here has just three horizontal blocks and three vertical blocks. Notice that the desired sums are indicated to the immediate left or above each block; thus the first horizontal block is supposed to be filled with two digits that sum to 5, so there are four possibilities: 14, 23, 32, 41. The first vertical block should sum to 6; again there are four possibilities, this time 15, 24, 42, 51 (because 33 is forbidden). The second horizontal block has three digits that should sum to 19; it is considerably less constrained. Indeed, there are thirty ways to obtain 19-in-three, namely the permutations of $\{2, 8, 9\}$ or $\{3, 7, 9\}$ or $\{4, 6, 9\}$ or $\{4, 7, 8\}$ or $\{5, 6, 8\}$.

a) Solve the puzzle. *Hint:* There's only one possibility for the lower right corner.

b) Sketch a simple way to build a table of all suitable combinations of n-in-k, for $2 \leq k \leq 9$ and $2 \leq n \leq 45$. Which n and k have the most? *Hint:* Use bitmaps.

c) *Generalized kakuro* is a related puzzle, for which each block of length k has a specified set of combinations, chosen from among the $\binom{9}{k}$ possibilities (regardless of their sum). For example, suppose the three horizontal blocks of mini-kakuro must be filled respectively with permutations of $\{1,3\}$, $\{3,5\}$, or $\{5,7\}$; $\{1,3,5\}$, $\{1,7,9\}$, $\{2,4,6\}$, $\{6,8,9\}$, or $\{7,8,9\}$; $\{2,4\}$, $\{4,6\}$, or $\{6,8\}$; and require the same for the three vertical blocks. Find the unique solution to that puzzle.

d) It would be easy to formulate kakuro as an XCC problem, as we did word squares in exercise 87, by simply giving one option for each possible placement of a block. But the resulting problem might be gigantic: For example, long blocks are not uncommon in kakuro, and each 9-digit block would have $9! = 362{,}880$ options(!). Show that generalized kakuro *can* be formulated efficiently as an XCC problem.

▶ **431.** [*30*] The inventor of kakuro, Jacob E. Funk of Manitoba (who always called his puzzles "Cross Sums"), published the following challenge on pages 50 and 66 of the August/September 1950 issue of *Dell Official Crossword Puzzles:*

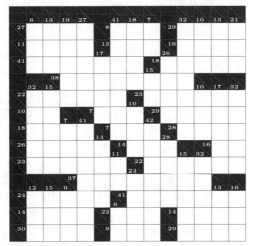

Many ingenious constructions are present here; but unfortunately, he failed to realize that there is more than one solution. Find all solutions, and obtain a valid puzzle by repairing some of his original clues.

▶ **432.** [*M25*] We can't simply design new kakuro puzzles by randomly filling the blanks and using the resulting sums as the constraints, because the vast majority of feasible sums yield nonunique solutions. Verify this experimentally for the generic diagrams

a)  ;   b)  .

In each case determine the exact number of ways to fill the blanks, without repeated digits in any row or column, as well as exactly how many of those filled-in diagrams are uniquely reconstructible from their block sums. Consider also symmetry.

433. [*26*] Six of the sum-clues in this little kakuro diagram are unspecified:

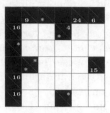

In how many ways can you obtain valid puzzles by specifying them?

434. [*30*] Exactly how many kakuro diagrams are possible in a 9×9 grid? (Every row and every column should contain at least one block of empty cells, except that the topmost row and leftmost column are completely black. All blocks must have length ≥ 2. Empty cells needn't be rookwise connected.) What is the maximum number of blocks?

435. [*31*] Design a rectangular kakuro puzzle for which the blocks at the top of the solution are 31, 41, 59, 26, 53, 58, 97 (the first fourteen digits of π).

▶ **436.** [*20*] (*Hitori.*) Let's wind up this potpourri of examples by considering a completely different combinatorial challenge. A hitori puzzle ("alone") is an $m \times n$ array in which we're supposed to cross elements out until three conditions are achieved:

  i) No row or column contains repeated elements.
  ii) Adjacent elements cannot be crossed out.
  iii) The remaining elements are rookwise connected.

For example, consider the 4×5 word rectangle (α). Conditions (i) and (ii) can be satisfied in sixteen ways, such as (β) and (γ). But only (δ) satisfies also (iii).

(α)	(β)	(γ)	(δ)
S K I F F	S K I F F	S K I F F	S K I F F
I N N E R	I N N E R	I N N E R	I N N E R
T I T L E	T I T L E	T I T L E	T I T L E
S T O L E	S T O L E	S T O L E	S T O L E

A crossed-out cell is said to be black; the other cells are white. While solving a hitori, it's helpful to *circle* an entry that is certain to become white. We can initially circle all the "seeds" — the entries that don't match any others in their row or column.

For example, puzzle (α) has eight seeds. If we decide to blacken a cell, we immediately circle its neighbors (because they cannot also be black). Thus, for instance, we shouldn't cross out the E in cell $(2,4)$: That would circle the L in $(2,3)$, forcing the other L to be black and cutting off the corner E as in (β).

The precise value of a seed is immaterial to the puzzle; it can be replaced by any other symbol that differs from everything else in its row or column.

We say as usual that a hitori puzzle is *valid* if it has exactly one solution. Explain why (a) a valid hitori puzzle has exactly one solution with all seeds white; (b) a hitori puzzle that has a unique solution with all seeds white is valid if and only if all the seed cells *not* adjacent to black in that solution are "articulation points" for the set of white cells — that is, their removal would disconnect the whites. (See $(3,1)$ and $(3,2)$ in (δ).)

▶ **437.** [*21*] A *weak solution* to a hitori puzzle is a solution for which all seeds are white, and for which properties (i) and (ii) of exercise 436 hold. Given a hitori puzzle, define an XCC problem whose solutions are precisely its weak solutions.

438. [*30*] Explain how to modify Algorithm C so that, when given an XCC problem from the construction in answer 437, it will produce only solutions that satisfy also the connectivity condition (iii). *Hint:* See exercise 413; also consider reachability.

439. [*M20*] Let G be a graph on the vertices V. A *hitori cover* of G is a set $U \subseteq V$ such that (i) $G|U$ is connected; (ii) if $v \notin U$ and $u \!-\! v$ then $u \in U$; (iii) if $u \in U$ and if $v \in U$ for all $u \!-\! v$, then $G|(U \setminus u)$ is not connected.
   a) Describe a hitori cover in terms of standard graph theory terminology.
   b) Show that the solution of a valid hitori puzzle is a hitori cover of $P_m \,\square\, P_n$.

440. [*21*] True or false: If the letter A occurs exactly twice in the top row of a valid hitori puzzle, exactly one of those occurrences will survive in the solution.

441. [*18*] Describe every valid hitori puzzle of size $1 \times n$ on a d-letter alphabet.

▶ **442.** [*M33*] Enumerate all hitori covers of $P_m \,\square\, P_n$, for $1 \le m \le n \le 9$.

▶ **443.** [*M30*] Prove that an $m \times n$ hitori cover has at most $(mn + 2)/3$ black cells.

444. [*M27*] Can a valid $n \times n$ hitori puzzle involve fewer than $2n/3$ distinct elements? Construct a valid puzzle of size $3k \times 3k$, using only the elements $\{0, 1, \ldots, 2k\}$.

▶ **445.** [*M22*] It's surprisingly difficult to construct a valid hitori puzzle that has no seeds. In fact, there are no $n \times n$ examples for $n \le 9$ except when $n = 6$. But it turns out that quite a few seedless 6×6 hitori puzzles do exist.

    Consider the five hitori covers below. Determine, for each of them, the exact number of valid hitori puzzles with no seeds, having that pattern of white and black cells as the solution. *Hint:* In some cases the answer is zero.

(i)   (ii)   (iii)   (iv)   (v)

▶ **446.** [*24*] The digits of e, 2.718281828459045..., are well known to have a curious repeating pattern. In fact, the first 25 digits actually define a valid 5×5 hitori puzzle! What is the probability that a random 5×5 array of decimal digits will have that property? And what about octal digits? Hexadecimal digits?

447. [*22*] (Johan de Ruiter.) Are there any values of $m > 1$ and $n > 1$ for which the first mn digits of π define a valid $m \times n$ hitori puzzle?

448. [*22*] Do any of the 31344 double word squares formed from WORDS(3000) make valid hitori puzzles? (See exercise 87.)

▶ **449.** [*40*] (*Hidden nuggets.*) Johan de Ruiter noticed in 2017 that George Orwell had included a valid hitori puzzle in his novel *Nineteen Eighty-Four* (part 2, chapter 9):

B	E	I	N	G	I	N	A	M	I
N	O	R	I	T	Y	E	V	E	N
A	M	I	N	O	R	I	T	Y	O
F	O	N	E	D	I	D	N	O	T
M	A	K	E	Y	O	U	M	A	D

Did Homer, Shakespeare, Tolstoy, and others also create hitori puzzles accidentally?

450. [*22*] Use Algorithm X to solve the "tot tibi sunt dotes" problem of Section 7.2.1.7.

We should "play up" the role of play.
— FRANCIS EDWARD SU, "Mathematics for Human Flourishing" (2017)

He reaps no satisfaction but from low and sensual objects,
or from the indulgence of malignant passions.
— DAVID HUME, *The Sceptic* (1742)

I can't get no . . .
— MICK JAGGER and KEITH RICHARDS, *Satisfaction* (1965)

7.2.2.2. Satisfiability. We turn now to one of the most fundamental problems of computer science: Given a Boolean formula $F(x_1, \ldots, x_n)$, expressed in so-called "conjunctive normal form" as an AND of ORs, can we "satisfy" F by assigning values to its variables in such a way that $F(x_1, \ldots, x_n) = 1$? For example, the formula

$$F(x_1, x_2, x_3) = (x_1 \vee \bar{x}_2) \wedge (x_2 \vee x_3) \wedge (\bar{x}_1 \vee \bar{x}_3) \wedge (\bar{x}_1 \vee \bar{x}_2 \vee x_3) \qquad (1)$$

is satisfied when $x_1 x_2 x_3 = 001$. But if we rule that solution out, by defining

$$G(x_1, x_2, x_3) = F(x_1, x_2, x_3) \wedge (x_1 \vee x_2 \vee \bar{x}_3), \qquad (2)$$

then G is unsatisfiable: It has no satisfying assignment.

Section 7.1.1 discussed the embarrassing fact that nobody has ever been able to come up with an efficient algorithm to solve the general satisfiability problem, in the sense that the satisfiability of any given formula of size N could be decided in $N^{O(1)}$ steps. Indeed, the famous unsolved question "does P = NP?" is equivalent to asking whether such an algorithm exists. We will see in Section 7.9 that satisfiability is a natural progenitor of every NP-complete problem.*

On the other hand enormous technical breakthroughs in recent years have led to amazingly good ways to approach the satisfiability problem. We now have algorithms that are much more efficient than anyone had dared to believe possible before the year 2000. These so-called "SAT solvers" are able to handle industrial-strength problems, involving millions of variables, with relative ease, and they've had a profound impact on many areas of research and development such as computer-aided verification. In this section we shall study the principles that underlie modern SAT-solving procedures.

---

* At the present time very few people believe that P = NP [see *SIGACT News* **43**, 2 (June 2012), 53–77]. In other words, almost everybody who has studied the subject thinks that satisfiability cannot be decided in polynomial time. The author of this book, however, suspects that $N^{O(1)}$-step algorithms do exist, yet that they're unknowable. Almost all polynomial time algorithms are so complicated that they lie beyond human comprehension, and could never be programmed for an actual computer in the real world. Existence is different from embodiment.

To begin, let's define the problem carefully and simplify the notation, so that our discussion will be as efficient as the algorithms that we'll be considering. Throughout this section we shall deal with *variables*, which are elements of any convenient set. Variables are often denoted by $x_1, x_2, x_3, \ldots$, as in (1); but any other symbols can also be used, like a, b, c, or even d_{74}'''. We will in fact often use the numerals 1, 2, 3, ... to stand for variables; and in many cases we'll find it convenient to write just j instead of x_j, because it takes less time and less space if we don't have to write so many x's. Thus '2' and 'x_2' will mean the same thing in many of the discussions below.

A *literal* is either a variable or the complement of a variable. In other words, if v is a variable, both v and $\bar{v}$ are literals. If there are n possible variables in some problem, there are $2n$ possible literals. If l is the literal $\bar{x}_2$, which is also written $\bar{2}$, then the complement of l, denoted by $\bar{l}$, is x_2, which is also written 2.

The variable that corresponds to a literal l is denoted by $|l|$; thus we have $|v| = |\bar{v}| = v$ for every variable v. Sometimes we write $\pm v$ for a literal that is either v or $\bar{v}$. We might also denote such a literal by σv, where σ is ± 1. The literal l is called *positive* if $|l| = l$; otherwise $|l| = \bar{l}$, and l is said to be *negative*.

Two literals l and l' are *distinct* if $l \neq l'$. They are *strictly distinct* if $|l| \neq |l'|$. A set of literals $\{l_1, \ldots, l_k\}$ is strictly distinct if $|l_i| \neq |l_j|$ for $1 \le i < j \le k$.

The satisfiability problem, like all good problems, can be understood in many equivalent ways, and we will find it convenient to switch from one viewpoint to another as we deal with different aspects of the problem. Example (1) is an AND of clauses, where every clause is an OR of literals; but we might as well regard every clause as simply a *set* of literals, and a formula as a set of clauses. With that simplification, and with 'x_j' identical to 'j', Eq. (1) becomes

$$F = \{\{1, \bar{2}\}, \{2, 3\}, \{\bar{1}, \bar{3}\}, \{\bar{1}, \bar{2}, 3\}\}.$$

And we needn't bother to represent the clauses with braces and commas either; we can simply write out the literals of each clause. With that shorthand we're able to perceive the real essence of (1) and (2):

$$F = \{1\bar{2}, 23, \bar{1}\bar{3}, \bar{1}\bar{2}3\}, \qquad G = F \cup \{12\bar{3}\}. \tag{3}$$

Here F is a set of four clauses, and G is a set of five.

In this guise, the satisfiability problem is equivalent to a *covering problem*, analogous to the exact cover problems that we considered in Section 7.2.2.1: Let

$$T_n = \{\{x_1, \bar{x}_1\}, \{x_2, \bar{x}_2\}, \ldots, \{x_n, \bar{x}_n\}\} = \{1\bar{1}, 2\bar{2}, \ldots, n\bar{n}\}. \tag{4}$$

"Given a set $F = \{C_1, \ldots, C_m\}$, where each C_i is a clause and each clause consists of literals based on the variables $\{x_1, \ldots, x_n\}$, find a set L of n literals that 'covers' $F \cup T_n$, in the sense that every clause contains at least one element of L." For example, the set F in (3) is covered by $L = \{\bar{1}, \bar{2}, 3\}$, and so is the set T_3; hence F is satisfiable. The set G is covered by $\{1, \bar{1}, 2\}$ or $\{1, \bar{1}, 3\}$ or $\cdots$ or $\{\bar{2}, 3, \bar{3}\}$, but not by any three literals that also cover T_3; so G is unsatisfiable.

Similarly, a family F of clauses is satisfiable if and only if it can be covered by a set L of *strictly distinct* literals.

If F' is any formula obtained from F by complementing one or more variables, it's clear that F' is satisfiable if and only if F is satisfiable. For example, if we replace 1 by $\bar{1}$ and 2 by $\bar{2}$ in (3) we obtain

$$F' = \{\bar{1}2, \bar{2}3, 1\bar{3}, 123\}, \qquad G' = F' \cup \{\bar{1}\bar{2}\bar{3}\}.$$

In this case F' is *trivially* satisfiable, because each of its clauses contains a positive literal: Every such formula is satisfied by simply letting L be the set of positive literals. Thus the satisfiability problem is the same as the problem of switching signs (or "polarities") so that no all-negative clauses remain.

Another problem equivalent to satisfiability is obtained by going back to the Boolean interpretation in (1) and complementing both sides of the equation. By De Morgan's laws 7.1.1–(11) and (12) we have

$$\overline{F}(x_1, x_2, x_3) = (\bar{x}_1 \wedge x_2) \vee (\bar{x}_2 \wedge \bar{x}_3) \vee (x_1 \wedge x_3) \vee (x_1 \wedge x_2 \wedge \bar{x}_3); \qquad (5)$$

and F is unsatisfiable $\Longleftrightarrow F = 0 \Longleftrightarrow \overline{F} = 1 \Longleftrightarrow \overline{F}$ is a tautology. Consequently F is satisfiable if and only if $\overline{F}$ is not a tautology: The tautology problem and the satisfiability problem are essentially the same.*

Since the satisfiability problem is so important, we simply call it SAT. And instances of the problem such as (1), in which there are no clauses of length greater than 3, are called 3SAT. In general, kSAT is the satisfiability problem restricted to instances where no clause has more than k literals.

Clauses of length 1 are called *unit clauses*, or unary clauses. Binary clauses, similarly, have length 2; then come ternary clauses, quaternary clauses, and so forth. Going the other way, the *empty clause*, or nullary clause, has length 0 and is denoted by ϵ; it is always unsatisfiable. Short clauses are very important in algorithms for SAT, because they are easier to deal with than long clauses. But long clauses aren't necessarily bad; they're much easier to satisfy than the short ones.

A slight technicality arises when we consider clause length: The binary clause $(x_1 \vee \bar{x}_2)$ in (1) is equivalent to the ternary clause $(x_1 \vee x_1 \vee \bar{x}_2)$ as well as to $(x_1 \vee \bar{x}_2 \vee \bar{x}_2)$ and to longer clauses such as $(x_1 \vee x_1 \vee x_1 \vee \bar{x}_2)$; so we can regard it as a clause of *any* length ≥ 2. But when we think of clauses as *sets* of literals rather than ORs of literals, we usually rule out multisets such as $11\bar{2}$ or $1\bar{2}\bar{2}$ that aren't sets; in that sense a binary clause is *not* a special case of a ternary clause. On the other hand, every binary clause $(x \vee y)$ can be replaced by *two* ternary clauses, $(x \vee y \vee z) \wedge (x \vee y \vee \bar{z})$, if z is another variable; and every k-ary clause is equivalent to the AND of two $(k+1)$-ary clauses. Therefore we can assume, if we like, that kSAT deals only with clauses whose length is exactly k.

A clause is tautological (always satisfied) if it contains both v and $\bar{v}$ for some variable v. Tautological clauses can be denoted by $\wp$ (see exercise 7.1.4–222). They never affect a satisfiability problem; so we usually assume that the clauses input to a SAT-solving algorithm consist of strictly distinct literals.

When we discussed the 3SAT problem briefly in Section 7.1.1, we took a look at formula 7.1.1–(32), "the shortest interesting formula in 3CNF." In our new

---

* Strictly speaking, TAUT is coNP-complete, while SAT is NP-complete; see Section 7.9.

shorthand, it consists of the following eight unsatisfiable clauses:

$$R = \{12\bar{3}, 23\bar{4}, 341, 4\bar{1}2, \bar{1}23, \bar{2}34, \bar{3}4\bar{1}, \bar{4}1\bar{2}\}. \tag{6}$$

This set makes an excellent little test case, so we will refer to it frequently below. (The letter R reminds us that it is based on R. L. Rivest's associative block design 6.5–(13).) The first seven clauses of R, namely

$$R' = \{12\bar{3}, 23\bar{4}, 341, 4\bar{1}2, \bar{1}23, \bar{2}34, \bar{3}4\bar{1}\}, \tag{7}$$

also make nice test data; they are satisfied only by choosing the complements of the literals in the omitted clause, namely $\{4, \bar{1}, 2\}$. More precisely, the literals 4, $\bar{1}$, and 2 are necessary and sufficient to cover R'; we can also include either 3 or $\bar{3}$ in the solution. Notice that (6) is symmetric under the cyclic permutation $1 \to 2 \to 3 \to 4 \to \bar{1} \to \bar{2} \to \bar{3} \to \bar{4} \to 1$ of literals; thus, omitting *any* clause of (6) gives a satisfiability problem equivalent to (7).

A simple example. SAT solvers are important because an enormous variety of problems can readily be formulated Booleanwise as ANDs of ORs. Let's begin with a little puzzle that leads to an instructive family of example problems: *Find a binary sequence $x_1 \ldots x_8$ that has no three equally spaced 0s and no three equally spaced 1s.* For example, the sequence 01001011 almost works; but it doesn't qualify, because x_2, x_5, and x_8 are equally spaced 1s.

If we try to solve this puzzle by backtracking manually through all 8-bit sequences in lexicographic order, we see that $x_1 x_2 = 00$ forces $x_3 = 1$. Then $x_1 x_2 x_3 x_4 x_5 x_6 x_7 = 0010011$ leaves us with no choice for x_8. A minute or two of further hand calculation reveals that the puzzle has just six solutions, namely

$$00110011, 01011010, 01100110, 10011001, 10100101, 11001100. \tag{8}$$

Furthermore it's easy to see that none of these solutions can be extended to a suitable binary sequence of length 9. We conclude that *every binary sequence $x_1 \ldots x_9$ contains three equally spaced 0s or three equally spaced 1s*.

Notice now that the condition $x_2 x_5 x_8 \neq 111$ is the same as the Boolean clause $(\bar{x}_2 \vee \bar{x}_5 \vee \bar{x}_8)$, namely $\bar{2}\bar{5}\bar{8}$. Similarly $x_2 x_5 x_8 \neq 000$ is the same as 258. So we have just verified that the following 32 clauses are unsatisfiable:

$$123, 234, \ldots, 789, 135, 246, \ldots, 579, 147, 258, 369, 159,$$
$$\bar{1}\bar{2}\bar{3}, \bar{2}\bar{3}\bar{4}, \ldots, \bar{7}\bar{8}\bar{9}, \bar{1}\bar{3}\bar{5}, \bar{2}\bar{4}\bar{6}, \ldots, \bar{5}\bar{7}\bar{9}, \bar{1}\bar{4}\bar{7}, \bar{2}\bar{5}\bar{8}, \bar{3}\bar{6}\bar{9}, \bar{1}\bar{5}\bar{9}. \tag{9}$$

This result is a special case of a general fact that holds for any given positive integers j and k: *If n is sufficiently large, every binary sequence $x_1 \ldots x_n$ contains either j equally spaced 0s or k equally spaced 1s* (or both). The smallest such n is denoted by $W(j, k)$ in honor of B. L. van der Waerden, who proved an even more general result (see exercise 2.3.4.3–6): *If n is sufficiently large, and if k_0, ..., k_{b-1} are positive integers, every b-ary sequence $x_1 \ldots x_n$ contains k_a equally spaced a's for some digit a, $0 \le a < b$.* The least such n is $W(k_0, \ldots, k_{b-1})$.

Let us accordingly define the following set of clauses when $j, k, n > 0$:

$$waerden(j, k; n) = \{(x_i \vee x_{i+d} \vee \cdots \vee x_{i+(j-1)d}) \mid 1 \le i \le n - (j{-}1)d, d \ge 1\}$$
$$\cup \{(\bar{x}_i \vee \bar{x}_{i+d} \vee \cdots \vee \bar{x}_{i+(k-1)d}) \mid 1 \le i \le n - (k{-}1)d, d \ge 1\}. \tag{10}$$

The 32 clauses in (9) are $waerden(3, 3; 9)$; and in general $waerden(j, k; n)$ is an appealing instance of SAT, satisfiable if and only if $n < W(j, k)$.

It's obvious that $W(1, k) = k$ and $W(2, k) = 2k - [k \text{ even}]$; but when j and k exceed 2 the numbers $W(j, k)$ are quite mysterious. We've seen that $W(3, 3) = 9$, and the following nontrivial values are currently known:

$k =$	3	4	5	6	7	8	9	10	11	12	13	14	15	16	17	18	19
$W(3, k) =$	9	18	22	32	46	58	77	97	114	135	160	186	218	238	279	312	349
$W(4, k) =$	18	35	55	73	109	146	309	?	?	?	?	?	?	?	?	?	?
$W(5, k) =$	22	55	178	206	260	?	?	?	?	?	?	?	?	?	?	?	?
$W(6, k) =$	32	73	206	1132	?	?	?	?	?	?	?	?	?	?	?	?	?

V. Chvátal inaugurated the study of $W(j, k)$ by computing the values for $j+k \leq 9$ as well as $W(3, 7)$ [*Combinatorial Structures and Their Applications* (1970), 31–33]. Most of the large values in this table have been calculated by state-of-the-art SAT solvers [see M. Kouril and J. L. Paul, *Experimental Math.* **17** (2008), 53–61; M. Kouril, *Integers* **12** (2012), A46:1–A46:13]. The table entries for $j = 3$ suggest that we might have $W(3, k) < k^2$ when $k > 4$, but that isn't true: SAT solvers have also been used to establish the lower bounds

$k =$	20	21	22	23	24	25	26	27	28	29	30
$W(3, k) \geq$	389	416	464	516	593	656	727	770	827	868	903

(which might in fact be the true values for this range of k); see T. Ahmed, O. Kullmann, and H. Snevily [*Discrete Applied Math.* **174** (2014), 27–51].

Notice that the literals in every clause of $waerden(j, k; n)$ have the same sign: They're either all positive or all negative. Does this "monotonic" property make the SAT problem any easier? Unfortunately, no: Exercise 10 proves that *any* set of clauses can be converted to an equivalent set of monotonic clauses.

Exact covering. The exact cover problems that we solved with "dancing links" in Section 7.2.2.1 can easily be reformulated as instances of SAT and handed off to SAT solvers. For example, let's look again at Langford pairs, the task of placing two 1s, two 2s, ..., two n's into $2n$ slots so that exactly k slots intervene between the two appearances of k, for each k. The corresponding exact cover problem when $n = 3$ has nine items and eight options (see 7.2.2.1–(17)):

$$`d_1 \, s_1 \, s_3`, `d_1 \, s_2 \, s_4`, `d_1 \, s_3 \, s_5`, `d_1 \, s_4 \, s_6`, `d_2 \, s_1 \, s_4`, `d_2 \, s_2 \, s_5`, `d_2 \, s_3 \, s_6`, `d_3 \, s_1 \, s_5`. \qquad (11)$$

The items are d_i for $1 \leq i \leq 3$ and s_j for $1 \leq j \leq 6$; the option '$d_i \, s_j \, s_k$' means that digit i is placed in slots j and k. Left-right symmetry allows us to omit the option '$d_3 \, s_2 \, s_6$' from this specification.

We want to select options of (11) so that each item appears just once. Let the Boolean variable x_j mean 'select option j', for $1 \leq j \leq 8$; the problem is then to satisfy the nine constraints

$$S_1(x_1, x_2, x_3, x_4) \wedge S_1(x_5, x_6, x_7) \wedge S_1(x_8)$$
$$\wedge S_1(x_1, x_5, x_8) \wedge S_1(x_2, x_6) \wedge S_1(x_1, x_3, x_7)$$
$$\wedge S_1(x_2, x_4, x_5) \wedge S_1(x_3, x_6, x_8) \wedge S_1(x_4, x_7), \qquad (12)$$

one for each item. (Here, as usual, $S_1(y_1, \ldots, y_p)$ denotes the symmetric function $[y_1 + \cdots + y_p = 1]$.) For example, we must have $x_5 + x_6 + x_7 = 1$, because item d_2 appears in options 5, 6, and 7 of (11).

One of the simplest ways to express the symmetric Boolean function S_1 as an AND of ORs is to use $1 + \binom{p}{2}$ clauses:

$$S_1(y_1, \ldots, y_p) = (y_1 \vee \cdots \vee y_p) \wedge \bigwedge_{1 \leq j < k \leq p} (\bar{y}_j \vee \bar{y}_k). \tag{13}$$

"At least one of the y's is true, but not two." Then (12) becomes, in shorthand,

$$\{1234, \bar{1}\bar{2}, \bar{1}\bar{3}, \bar{1}\bar{4}, \bar{2}\bar{3}, \bar{2}\bar{4}, \bar{3}\bar{4}, 567, \bar{5}\bar{6}, \bar{5}\bar{7}, \bar{6}\bar{7}, 8,$$
$$158, \bar{1}\bar{5}, \bar{1}\bar{8}, \bar{5}\bar{8}, 26, \bar{2}\bar{6}, 137, \bar{1}\bar{3}, \bar{1}\bar{7}, \bar{3}\bar{7},$$
$$245, \bar{2}\bar{4}, \bar{2}\bar{5}, \bar{4}\bar{5}, 368, \bar{3}\bar{6}, \bar{3}\bar{8}, \bar{6}\bar{8}, 47, \bar{4}\bar{7}\}; \tag{14}$$

we shall call these clauses *langford*(3). (Notice that only 30 of them are actually distinct, because $\bar{1}\bar{3}$ and $\bar{2}\bar{4}$ appear twice.) Exercise 13 defines *langford*(n); we know from exercise 7–1 that *langford*(n) is satisfiable $\iff$ $n \bmod 4 = 0$ or 3.

The unary clause 8 in (14) tells us immediately that $x_8 = 1$. Then from the binary clauses $\bar{1}\bar{8}$, $\bar{5}\bar{8}$, $\bar{3}\bar{8}$, $\bar{6}\bar{8}$ we have $x_1 = x_5 = x_3 = x_6 = 0$. The ternary clause 137 then implies $x_7 = 1$; finally $x_4 = 0$ (from $\bar{4}\bar{7}$) and $x_2 = 1$ (from 1234). Options 8, 7, and 2 of (11) now give us the desired Langford pairing 3 1 2 1 3 2.

Incidentally, the function $S_1(y_1, y_2, y_3, y_4, y_5)$ can also be expressed as

$$(y_1 \vee y_2 \vee y_3 \vee y_4 \vee y_5) \wedge (\bar{y}_1 \vee \bar{y}_2) \wedge (\bar{y}_1 \vee \bar{y}_3) \wedge (\bar{y}_1 \vee \bar{t})$$
$$\wedge (\bar{y}_2 \vee \bar{y}_3) \wedge (\bar{y}_2 \vee \bar{t}) \wedge (\bar{y}_3 \vee \bar{t}) \wedge (t \vee \bar{y}_4) \wedge (t \vee \bar{y}_5) \wedge (\bar{y}_4 \vee \bar{y}_5),$$

where t is a new variable. In general, if p gets big, it's possible to express $S_1(y_1, \ldots, y_p)$ with only $3p - 5$ clauses instead of $\binom{p}{2} + 1$, by using $\lfloor (p-3)/2 \rfloor$ new variables as explained in exercise 12. When this alternative encoding is used to represent Langford pairs of order n, we'll call the resulting clauses *langford'*(n).

Do SAT solvers do a better job with the clauses *langford*(n) or *langford'*(n)? Stay tuned: We'll find out later.

Coloring a graph. The classical problem of coloring a graph with at most d colors is another rich source of benchmark examples for SAT solvers. If the graph has n vertices V, we can introduce nd variables v_j, for $v \in V$ and $1 \leq j \leq d$, signifying that v has color j; the resulting clauses are quite simple:

$$(v_1 \vee v_2 \vee \cdots \vee v_d) \text{ for } v \in V \text{ ("every vertex has at least one color");} \tag{15}$$
$$(\bar{u}_j \vee \bar{v}_j) \text{ for } u \!-\! v, 1 \leq j \leq d \text{ ("adjacent vertices have different colors"). } \tag{16}$$

We could also add $n\binom{d}{2}$ additional so-called *exclusion clauses*

$$(\bar{v}_i \vee \bar{v}_j) \text{ for } v \in V, 1 \leq i < j \leq d \text{ ("every vertex has at most one color");} \tag{17}$$

but they're optional, because vertices with more than one color are harmless. Indeed, if we find a solution with $v_1 = v_2 = 1$, we'll be extra happy, because it gives us *two* legal ways to color vertex v. (See exercise 14.)

```
 00 | 01 | 02 | 03 | 04 | 05 | 06 | 07 | 08 | 09
    | 11 | 12 | 13 | 14 | 15 | 16 | 17 | 18 | 19
         | 22 | 23 | 24 | 25 | 26 | 27 | 28 | 29
              | 33 | 34 | 35 | 36 | 37 | 38 | 39
                   | 44 | 45 | 46 | 47 | 48 | 49
                        | 55 | 56 | 57 | 58 | 59
                             | 66 | 67 | 68 | 69
                                  | 77 | 78 | 79
                                       | 88 | 89
                                            | 99
                                       | 20 | 21
                                  | 30 | 31 | 32
                             | 40 | 41 | 42 | 43
                        | 50 | 51 | 52 | 53 | 54
                   | 60 | 61 | 62 | 63 | 64 | 65
              | 70 | 71 | 72 | 73 | 74 | 75 | 76
         | 80 | 81 | 82 | 83 | 84 | 85 | 86 | 87
    | 90 | 91 | 92 | 93 | 94 | 95 | 96 | 97 | 98
 a0 | a1 | a2 | a3 | a4 | a5 | a6 | a7 | a8 | a9
                                            10
```

Fig. 76. The McGregor graph of order 10. Each region of this "map" is identified by a two-digit hexadecimal code. Can you color the regions with four colors, never using the same color for two adjacent regions?

Martin Gardner astonished the world in 1975 when he reported [*Scientific American* **232**, 4 (April 1975), 126–130] that a proper coloring of the planar map in Fig. 76 requires *five* distinct colors, thereby disproving the longstanding four-color conjecture. (In that same column he also cited several other "facts" supposedly discovered in 1974: (i) $e^{\pi\sqrt{163}}$ is an integer; (ii) pawn-to-king-rook-4 ('h4') is a winning first move in chess; (iii) the theory of special relativity is fatally flawed; (iv) Leonardo da Vinci invented the flush toilet; and (v) Robert Ripoff devised a motor that is powered entirely by psychic energy. Thousands of readers failed to notice that they had been April Fooled!)

The map in Fig. 76 actually *can* be 4-colored; you are hereby challenged to discover a suitable way to do this, before turning to the answer of exercise 18. Indeed, the four-color conjecture became the Four Color Theorem in 1976, as mentioned in Section 7. Fortunately that result was still unknown in April of 1975; otherwise this interesting graph would probably never have appeared in print. McGregor's graph has 110 vertices (regions) and 324 edges (adjacencies between regions); hence (15) and (16) yield $110 + 1296 = 1406$ clauses on 440 variables, which a modern SAT solver can polish off quickly.

We can also go much further and solve problems that would be extremely difficult by hand. For example, we can add constraints to limit the number of regions that receive a particular color. Randal Bryant exploited this idea in 2010 to discover that there's a four-coloring of Fig. 76 that uses one of the colors only 7 times (see exercise 17). His coloring is, in fact, unique, and it leads to an explicit way to 4-color the McGregor graphs of all orders $n \geq 3$ (exercise 18).

Such additional constraints can be generated in many ways. We could, for instance, append $\binom{110}{8}$ clauses, one for every choice of 8 regions, specifying that those 8 regions aren't all colored 1. But no, we'd better scratch that idea: $\binom{110}{8} = 409{,}705{,}619{,}895$. Even if we restricted ourselves to the 74,792,876,790 sets of 8 regions that are *independent*, we'd be dealing with far too many clauses.

An interesting SAT-oriented way to ensure that $x_1 + \cdots + x_n$ is at most r, which works well when n and r are rather large, was found by C. Sinz [*LNCS* **3709** (2005), 827–831]. His method introduces $(n - r)r$ new variables s_j^k for $1 \leq j \leq n - r$ and $1 \leq k \leq r$. If F is any satisfiability problem and if we add the $(n - r - 1)r + (n - r)(r + 1)$ clauses

$$(\bar{s}_j^k \vee s_{j+1}^k), \qquad \text{for } 1 \leq j < n - r \text{ and } 1 \leq k \leq r, \tag{18}$$

$$(\bar{x}_{j+k} \vee \bar{s}_j^k \vee s_j^{k+1}), \qquad \text{for } 1 \leq j \leq n - r \text{ and } 0 \leq k \leq r, \tag{19}$$

where $\bar{s}_j^k$ is omitted when $k = 0$ and s_j^{k+1} is omitted when $k = r$, then the new set of clauses is satisfiable if and only if F is satisfiable with $x_1 + \cdots + x_n \leq r$. (See exercise 26.) With this scheme we can limit the number of red-colored regions of McGregor's graph to at most 7 by appending 1538 clauses in 721 new variables.

Another way to achieve the same goal, which turns out to be even better, has been proposed by O. Bailleux and Y. Boufkhad [*LNCS* **2833** (2003), 108–122]. Their method is a bit more difficult to describe, but still easy to implement: Consider a complete binary tree that has $n-1$ internal nodes numbered 1 through $n - 1$, and n leaves numbered n through $2n - 1$; the children of node k, for $1 \leq k < n$, are nodes $2k$ and $2k+1$ (see 2.3.4.5–(5)). We form new variables b_j^k for $1 < k < n$ and $1 \leq j \leq t_k$, where t_k is the minimum of r and the number of leaves below node k. Then the following clauses, explained in exercise 27, do the job:

$$(\bar{b}_i^{2k} \vee \bar{b}_j^{2k+1} \vee b_{i+j}^k), \quad \text{for } 0 \leq i \leq t_{2k}, \, 0 \leq j \leq t_{2k+1}, \, 1 \leq i+j \leq t_k+1, \, 1 < k < n; \tag{20}$$

$$(\bar{b}_i^2 \vee \bar{b}_j^3), \qquad \text{for } 0 \leq i \leq t_2, \, 0 \leq j \leq t_3, \, i + j = r + 1. \tag{21}$$

In these formulas we let $t_k = 1$ and $b_1^k = x_{k-n+1}$ for $n \leq k < 2n$; all literals $\bar{b}_0^k$ and b_{r+1}^k are to be omitted. Applying (20) and (21) to McGregor's graph, with $n = 110$ and $r = 7$, yields just 1216 new clauses in 399 new variables.

The same ideas apply when we want to ensure that $x_1 + \cdots + x_n$ is *at least* r, because of the identity $S_{\geq r}(x_1, \ldots, x_n) = S_{\leq n-r}(\bar{x}_1, \ldots, \bar{x}_n)$. And exercise 30 considers the case of equality, when our goal is to make $x_1 + \cdots + x_n = r$. We'll discuss other encodings of such cardinality constraints below.

Factoring integers. Next on our agenda is a family of SAT instances with quite a different flavor. *Given an $(m + n)$-bit binary integer $z = (z_{m+n} \ldots z_2 z_1)_2$, do there exist integers $x = (x_m \ldots x_1)_2$ and $y = (y_n \ldots y_1)_2$ such that $z = x \times y$?* For example, if $m = 2$ and $n = 3$, we want to invert the binary multiplication

$$
\begin{array}{r}
y_3\, y_2\, y_1 \\
\times \quad x_2\, x_1 \\
\hline
a_3\, a_2\, a_1 \\
b_3\, b_2\, b_1 \\
\hline
c_3\, c_2\, c_1 \\
\hline
z_5\, z_4\, z_3\, z_2\, z_1
\end{array}
$$

$$(a_3 a_2 a_1)_2 = (y_3 y_2 y_1)_2 \times x_1$$
$$(b_3 b_2 b_1)_2 = (y_3 y_2 y_1)_2 \times x_2$$

$$
\begin{aligned}
z_1 &= a_1 \\
(c_1 z_2)_2 &= a_2 + b_1 \\
(c_2 z_3)_2 &= a_3 + b_2 + c_1 \qquad (22) \\
(c_3 z_4)_2 &= b_3 + c_2 \\
z_5 &= c_3
\end{aligned}
$$

when the z bits are given. This problem is satisfiable when $z = 21 = (10101)_2$, in the sense that suitable binary values x_1, x_2, y_1, y_2, y_3, a_1, a_2, a_3, b_1, b_2, b_3, c_1, c_2, c_3 do satisfy these equations. But it's unsatisfiable when $z = 19 = (10011)_2$.

Arithmetical calculations like (22) are easily expressed in terms of clauses that can be fed to a SAT solver: We first specify the computation by constructing a Boolean chain, then we encode each step of the chain in terms of a few clauses. One such chain, if we identify a_1 with z_1 and c_3 with z_5, is

$$z_1 \leftarrow x_1 \wedge y_1, \quad b_1 \leftarrow x_2 \wedge y_1, \quad z_2 \leftarrow a_2 \oplus b_1, \quad s \leftarrow a_3 \oplus b_2, \quad z_3 \leftarrow s \oplus c_1, \quad z_4 \leftarrow b_3 \oplus c_2,$$
$$a_2 \leftarrow x_1 \wedge y_2, \quad b_2 \leftarrow x_2 \wedge y_2, \quad c_1 \leftarrow a_2 \wedge b_1, \quad p \leftarrow a_3 \wedge b_2, \quad q \leftarrow s \wedge c_1, \quad z_5 \leftarrow b_3 \wedge c_2,$$
$$a_3 \leftarrow x_1 \wedge y_3, \quad b_3 \leftarrow x_2 \wedge y_3, \qquad\qquad\qquad\qquad\qquad\qquad c_2 \leftarrow p \vee q, \qquad\qquad (23)$$

using a "full adder" to compute $c_2 z_3$ and "half adders" to compute $c_1 z_2$ and $c_3 z_4$ (see 7.1.2–(23) and (24)). And that chain is equivalent to the 49 clauses

$$(x_1 \vee \bar{z}_1) \wedge (y_1 \vee \bar{z}_1) \wedge (\bar{x}_1 \vee \bar{y}_1 \vee z_1) \wedge \cdots \wedge (\bar{b}_3 \vee \bar{c}_2 \vee \bar{z}_4) \wedge (b_3 \vee \bar{z}_5) \wedge (c_2 \vee \bar{z}_5) \wedge (\bar{b}_3 \vee \bar{c}_2 \vee z_5)$$

obtained by expanding the elementary computations according to simple rules:

$$t \leftarrow u \wedge v \text{ becomes } (u \vee \bar{t}) \wedge (v \vee \bar{t}) \wedge (\bar{u} \vee \bar{v} \vee t);$$
$$t \leftarrow u \vee v \text{ becomes } (\bar{u} \vee t) \wedge (\bar{v} \vee t) \wedge (u \vee v \vee \bar{t}); \qquad\qquad (24)$$
$$t \leftarrow u \oplus v \text{ becomes } (\bar{u} \vee v \vee t) \wedge (u \vee \bar{v} \vee t) \wedge (u \vee v \vee \bar{t}) \wedge (\bar{u} \vee \bar{v} \vee \bar{t}).$$

To complete the specification of this factoring problem when, say, $z = (10101)_2$, we simply append the unary clauses $(z_5) \wedge (\bar{z}_4) \wedge (z_3) \wedge (\bar{z}_2) \wedge (z_1)$.

Logicians have known for a long time that computational steps can readily be expressed as conjunctions of clauses. Rules such as (24) are now called *Tseytin encoding*, after Gregory Tseytin (1966). Our representation of a small five-bit factorization problem in 49+5 clauses may not seem very efficient; but we will see shortly that m-bit by n-bit factorization corresponds to a satisfiability problem with fewer than $6mn$ variables, and fewer than $20mn$ clauses of length 3 or less.

> *Even if the system has hundreds or thousands of formulas,*
> *it can be put into the conjunctive normal form "piece by piece",*
> *without any "multiplying out."*
> — MARTIN DAVIS and HILARY PUTNAM (1958)

Suppose $m \leq n$. The easiest way to set up Boolean chains for multiplication is probably to use a scheme that goes back to John Napier's *Rabdologiæ* (Edinburgh, 1617), pages 137–143, as modernized by Luigi Dadda [*Alta Frequenza* **34** (1964), 349–356]: First we form all mn products $x_i \wedge y_j$, putting every such bit into $bin[i + j]$, which is one of $m + n$ "bins" that hold bits to be added for a particular power of 2 in the binary number system. The bins will contain respectively $(0, 1, 2, \ldots, m, m, \ldots, m, \ldots, 2, 1)$ bits at this point, with $n - m + 1$ occurrences of "m" in the middle. Now we look at $bin[k]$ for $k = 2, 3, \ldots$. If $bin[k]$ contains a single bit b, we simply set $z_{k-1} \leftarrow b$. If it contains two bits $\{b, b'\}$, we use a half adder to compute $z_{k-1} \leftarrow b \oplus b'$, $c \leftarrow b \wedge b'$, and we put the carry bit c into $bin[k + 1]$. Otherwise $bin[k]$ contains $t \geq 3$ bits; we choose any three of them, say $\{b, b', b''\}$, and remove them from the bin. With a full adder we then compute $r \leftarrow b \oplus b' \oplus b''$ and $c \leftarrow \langle bb'b'' \rangle$, so that $b + b' + b'' = r + 2c$; and we put r into $bin[k]$, c into $bin[k+1]$. This decreases t by 2, so eventually we will have computed z_{k-1}. Exercise 41 quantifies the exact amount of calculation involved.

This method of encoding multiplication into clauses is quite flexible, since we're allowed to choose *any* three bits from $bin[k]$ whenever four or more bits are present. We could use a first-in-first-out strategy, always selecting bits from the "rear" and placing their sum at the "front"; or we could work last-in-first-out, essentially treating $bin[k]$ as a stack instead of a queue. We could also select the bits randomly, to see if this makes our SAT solver any happier. Later in this section we'll refer to the clauses that represent the factoring problem by calling them *factor_fifo*(m, n, z), *factor_lifo*(m, n, z), or *factor_rand*(m, n, z, s), respectively, where s is a seed for the random number generator used to generate them.

It's somewhat mind-boggling to realize that numbers can be factored without using any number theory! No greatest common divisors, no applications of Fermat's theorems, etc., are anywhere in sight. We're providing no hints to the solver except for a bunch of Boolean formulas that operate almost blindly at the bit level. Yet factors are found.

Of course we can't expect this method to compete with the sophisticated factorization algorithms of Section 4.5.4. But the problem of factoring does demonstrate the great versatility of clauses. And its clauses can be combined with *other* constraints that go well beyond any of the problems we've studied before.

Fault testing. Lots of things can go wrong when computer chips are manufactured in the "real world," so engineers have long been interested in constructing test patterns to check the validity of a particular circuit. For example, suppose that all but one of the logical elements are functioning properly in some chip; the bad one, however, is stuck: Its output is constant, always the same regardless of the inputs that it is given. Such a failure is called a *single-stuck-at fault*.

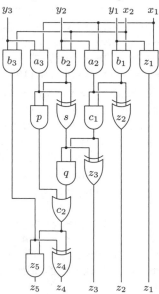

Fig. 77. A circuit that corresponds to (23).

Figure 77 illustrates a typical digital circuit in detail: It implements the 15 Boolean operations of (23) as a network that produces five output signals $z_5 z_4 z_3 z_2 z_1$ from the five inputs $y_3 y_2 y_1 x_2 x_1$. In addition to having 15 AND, OR, and XOR gates, each of which transforms two inputs into one output, it has 15 "fanout" gates (indicated by dots at junction points), each of which splits one input into two outputs. As a result it comprises 50 potentially distinct logical signals, one for each internal "wire." Exercise 47 shows that a circuit with m outputs, n inputs, and g conventional 2-to-1 gates will have $g + m - n$ fanout gates and $3g + 2m - n$ wires. A circuit with w wires has $2w$ possible single-stuck-at faults, namely w faults in which the signal on a wire is stuck at 0 and w more on which it is stuck at 1.

Table 1 shows 101 scenarios that are possible when the 50 wires of Fig. 77 are activated by one particular sequence of inputs, assuming that at

Table 1

SINGLE-STUCK-AT FAULTS IN FIGURE 77 WHEN $x_2x_1 = 11$, $y_3y_2y_1 = 110$

$$\scriptsize
\begin{array}{l}
\text{OK } x_1\,x_1^1\,x_1^2\,x_1^3\,x_1^4\,x_2\,x_2^1\,x_2^2\,x_2^3\,x_2^4\,y_1\,y_1^1\,y_1^2\,y_2\,y_2^1\,y_2^2\,y_3\,y_3^1\,y_3^2\,z_1\,a_2\,a_2^1\,a_2^2\,a_3\,a_3^1\,a_3^2\,b_1\,b_1^1\,b_1^2\,b_2\,b_2^1\,b_2^2\,b_3\,b_3^1\,b_3^2\,z_2\,c_1\,c_1^1\,c_1^2\,s\,s^1\,s^2\,p\,z_3\,q\,c_2\,c_2^1\,c_2^2\,z_4\,z_5
\end{array}
$$

label	OK	bits
$x_1 \leftarrow$ input	1	01111111111111111111111111111111111111111111111111111111111111111111111111111111111111111111111111111
$x_1^1 \leftarrow x_1$	1	01011111111111111111111111111111111111111111111111111111111111111111111111111111111111111111111111111
$x_1^2 \leftarrow x_1$	1	01011011111111111111111111111111111111111111111111111111111111111111111111111111111111111111111111111
$x_1^3 \leftarrow x_1$	1	01011101111111111111111111111111111111111111111111111111111111111111111111111111111111111111111111111
$x_1^4 \leftarrow x_1$	1	01011111011111111111111111111111111111111111111111111111111111111111111111111111111111111111111111111
$x_2 \leftarrow$ input	1	11111111110111111111111111111111111111111111111111111111111111111111111111111111111111111111111111111
$x_2^1 \leftarrow x_2$	1	11111111110101111111111111111111111111111111111111111111111111111111111111111111111111111111111111111
$x_2^2 \leftarrow x_2$	1	11111111110110111111111111111111111111111111111111111111111111111111111111111111111111111111111111111
$x_2^3 \leftarrow x_2$	1	11111111110101101111111111111111111111111111111111111111111111111111111111111111111111111111111111111
$x_2^4 \leftarrow x_2$	1	11111111110101111011111111111111111111111111111111111111111111111111111111111111111111111111111111111
$y_1 \leftarrow$ input	0	00000000000000000001000000000000000000000000000000000000000000000000000000000000000000000000000000000
$y_1^1 \leftarrow y_1$	0	00000000000000000001010000000000000000000000000000000000000000000000000000000000000000000000000000000
$y_1^2 \leftarrow y_1$	0	00000000000000000001000100000000000000000000000000000000000000000000000000000000000000000000000000000
$y_2 \leftarrow$ input	1	11111111111111111111011111111111111111111111111111111111111111111111111111111111111111111111111111111
$y_2^1 \leftarrow y_2$	1	11111111111111111111010110111111111111111111111111111111111111111111111111111111111111111111111111111
$y_2^2 \leftarrow y_2$	1	11111111111111111111011101111111111111111111111111111111111111111111111111111111111111111111111111111
$y_3 \leftarrow$ input	1	11111111111111111111111111011111111111111111111111111111111111111111111111111111111111111111111111111
$y_3^1 \leftarrow y_3$	1	11111111111111111111111111010111111111111111111111111111111111111111111111111111111111111111111111111
$y_3^2 \leftarrow y_3$	1	11111111111111111111111111011011111111111111111111111111111111111111111111111111111111111111111111111
$z_1 \leftarrow x_1^2 \wedge y_1^1$	0	00000000000000000010100000000001000000000000000000000000000000000000000000000000000000000000000000000
$a_2 \leftarrow x_1^3 \wedge y_1^2$	1	01011011111111111111111111110101111111111011111111111111111111111111111111111111111111111111111111111
$a_2^1 \leftarrow a_2$	1	01011011111111111111111111110101111111111010111111111111111111111111111111111111111111111111111111111
$a_2^2 \leftarrow a_2$	1	01011011111111111111111111110101111111111011011111111111111111111111111111111111111111111111111111111
$a_3 \leftarrow x_1^4 \wedge y_3^1$	1	01011101011111111111111111110101111111111010101111111111101111111111111111111111111111111111111111111
$a_3^1 \leftarrow a_3$	1	01011101011111111111111111111111111010101111111111101011111111111111111111111111111111111111111111111
$a_3^2 \leftarrow a_3$	1	01011101011111111111111111110101011111111101101111111111111111111111111111111111111111111111111111111
$b_1 \leftarrow x_2^2 \wedge y_1^2$	0	00000000000000000001000100000000000000000000010000000000000000000000000000000000000000000000000000000
$b_1^1 \leftarrow b_1$	0	00000000000000000001000100000000000000000000101000000000000000000000000000000000000000000000000000000
$b_1^2 \leftarrow b_1$	0	00000000000000000001000100000000000000000000100010000000000000000000000000000000000000000000000000000
$b_2 \leftarrow x_2^3 \wedge y_2^2$	1	11111111110101101111111111011111111111111111111010111111111111111111111111111111111111111111111111111
$b_2^1 \leftarrow b_2$	1	11111111110101101111111111011111111111111111111010101111111111111111111111111111111111111111111111111
$b_2^2 \leftarrow b_2$	1	11111111110101101111111111011111111111111111111011011111111111111111111111111111111111111111111111111
$b_3 \leftarrow x_2^4 \wedge y_3^2$	1	11111111110101111011111111011111111111011011111111111111011111111111111111111111111111111111111111111
$b_3^1 \leftarrow b_3$	1	11111111110101111011111111011111111111011011111111111111010111111111111111111111111111111111111111111
$b_3^2 \leftarrow b_3$	1	11111111110101111011111111011111111111011011111111111111011011111111111111111111111111111111111111111
$z_2 \leftarrow a_2 \oplus b_1^1$	1	01011011111111111110111001011111111101011111111101011111111111011111111111111111111111111111111111111
$c_1 \leftarrow a_2^1 \wedge b_1^2$	0	00000000000000000001000100000000000000000100010000000000000010000000000000000000000000000000000000000
$c_1^1 \leftarrow c_1$	0	00000000000000000001000100000000000000000100010000000000000010100000000000000000000000000000000000000
$c_1^2 \leftarrow c_1$	0	00000000000000000001000100000000000000000100010000000000000010001000000000000000000000000000000000000
$s \leftarrow a_3^1 \oplus b_2^1$	0	10100000101010001000000001000101010000000010100000001010000000000000010000000000000000000000000000000
$s^1 \leftarrow s$	0	10100010101000100000000010001010100000000101000000001010000000000000101000000000000000000000000000000
$s^2 \leftarrow s$	0	10100000101010001000000001000101010000000101000000001010000000000000010000000000000000000000000000000
$p \leftarrow a_3^2 \wedge b_2^2$	1	01011110101011011011111111011101010101111111111011011011111111110111111111111111111101111111111111111
$z_3 \leftarrow s^1 \oplus c_1^1$	0	10100000101010001000100011000101010000000101000100011010000000010100101000100000010000000000000000000
$q \leftarrow s^2 \wedge c_1^2$	0	00000000000000000000000000000000000000000000000000000000000000000000000001000000000000000000000000000
$c_2 \leftarrow p \vee q$	1	01011110101010110111111110110101010101111011011111111011011111111111111111111111101111011111111111111
$c_2^1 \leftarrow c_2$	1	01011110101010110111111110110101010101111011011111111011011111111111111111111111101011101011111111111
$c_2^2 \leftarrow c_2$	1	01011110101011011011111111011011011101011111011011111111011011111111111111111111101110110111011111111
$z_4 \leftarrow b_3^1 \oplus c_2^1$	0	10100000100000010100000001000100101000000010010000001001010100000000000010101000001000000010100000100
$z_5 \leftarrow b_3^2 \wedge c_2^2$	1	01011110101010110110101111011010101010111111111011011010101111111111101110110111101101111011011011101

most one stuck-at fault is present. The column headed OK shows the correct
behavior of the Boolean chain (which nicely multiplies $x = 3$ by $y = 6$ and
obtains $z = 18$). We can call these the "default" values, because, well, they have
no faults. The other 100 columns show what happens if all but one of the 50
wires have error-free signals; the two columns under b_2^1, for example, illustrate
the results when the rightmost wire that fans out from gate b_2 is stuck at 0
or 1. Each row is obtained bitwise from previous rows or inputs, except that the
boldface digits are forced. When a boldface value agrees with the default, its
entire column is correct; otherwise errors might propagate. All values above the
bold diagonal match the defaults.

     If we want to test a chip that has n inputs and m outputs, we're allowed
to apply test patterns to the inputs and see what outputs are produced. Close

inspection shows, for instance, that the pattern considered in Table 1 doesn't detect an error when q is stuck at 1, even though q should be 0, because all five output bits $z_5 z_4 z_3 z_2 z_1$ are correct in spite of that error. In fact, the value of $c_2 \leftarrow p \lor q$ is unaffected by a bad q, because $p = 1$ in this example. Similarly, the fault "x_1^2 stuck at 0" doesn't propagate into $z_1 \leftarrow x_1^2 \land y_1^1$ because $y_1^1 = 0$. Altogether 44 faults, not 50, are discovered by this particular test pattern.

All of the relevant repeatable faults, whether they're single-stuck-at or wildly complicated, could obviously be discovered by testing all 2^n possible patterns. But that's out of the question unless n is quite small. Fortunately, testing isn't hopeless, because satisfactory results are usually obtained in practice if we do have enough test patterns to detect all of the detectable single-stuck-at faults. Exercise 49 shows that just five patterns suffice to certify Fig. 77 by this criterion.

The detailed analysis in exercise 49 also shows, surprisingly, that one of the faults, namely "s^2 stuck at 1," cannot be detected! Indeed, an erroneous s^2 can propagate to an erroneous q only if $c_1^2 = 1$, and that forces $x_1 = x_2 = y_1 = y_2 = 1$; only two possibilities remain, and neither $y_3 = 0$ nor $y_3 = 1$ reveals the fault. Consequently we can simplify the circuit by removing gate q; the chain (23) becomes shorter, with "$q \leftarrow s \land c_1$, $c_2 \leftarrow p \lor q$" replaced by "$c_2 \leftarrow p \lor c_1$."

Of course Fig. 77 is just a tiny little circuit, intended only to introduce the concept of stuck-at faults. Test patterns are needed for the much larger circuits that arise in real computers; and we will see that SAT solvers can help us to find them. Consider, for example, the generic multiplier circuit $prod(m, n)$, which is part of the Stanford GraphBase. It multiplies an m-bit number x by an n-bit number y, producing an $(m + n)$-bit product z. Furthermore, it's a so-called "parallel multiplier," with delay time $O(\log(m + n))$; thus it's much more suited to hardware design than methods like the *factor_fifo* schemes that we considered above, because those circuits need $\Omega(m + n)$ time for carries to propagate.

Let's try to find test patterns that will smoke out all of the single-stuck-at faults in $prod(32, 32)$, which is a circuit of depth 33 that has 64 inputs, 64 outputs, 3660 AND gates, 1203 OR gates, 2145 XOR gates, and (therefore) 7008 fanout gates and 21,088 wires. How can we guard it against 42,176 different faults?

Before we construct clauses to facilitate that task, we should realize that most of the single-stuck-at faults are easily detected by choosing patterns at random, since faults usually cause big trouble and are hard to miss. Indeed, choosing $x = $ #3243F6A8 and $y = $ #885A308D more-or-less at random already eliminates 14,733 cases; and $(x, y) = ($#2B7E1516, #28AED2A6$)$ eliminates 6,918 more. We might as well keep doing this, because bitwise operations such as those in Table 1 are fast. Experience with the smaller multiplier in Fig. 77 suggests that we get more effective tests if we bias the inputs, choosing each bit to be 1 with probability .9 instead of .5 (see exercise 49). A million such random inputs will then generate, say, 243 patterns that detect all but 140 of the faults.

Our remaining job, then, is essentially to find 140 needles in a haystack of size 2^{64}, after having picked $42{,}176 - 140 = 42{,}036$ pieces of low-hanging fruit. And that's where a SAT solver is useful. Consider, for example, the analogous but simpler problem of finding a test pattern for "q stuck at 0" in Fig. 77.

We can use the 49 clauses F derived from (23) to represent the well-behaved circuit; and we can imagine corresponding clauses F' that represent the faulty computation, using "primed" variables z_1', a_2', $\ldots$, z_5'. Thus F' begins with $(x_1 \vee \bar{z}_1') \wedge (y_1 \vee \bar{z}_1')$ and ends with $(\bar{b}_3' \vee \bar{c}_2' \vee z_5')$; it's like F except that the clauses representing $q' \leftarrow s' \wedge c_1'$ in (23) are changed to simply $\bar{q}'$ (meaning that q' is stuck at 0). Then the clauses of F and F', together with a few more clauses to state that $z_1 \neq z_1'$ or $\cdots$ or $z_5 \neq z_5'$, will be satisfiable only by variables for which $(y_3 y_2 y_1)_2 \times (x_2 x_1)_2$ is a suitable test pattern for the given fault.

This construction of F' can obviously be simplified, because z_1' is identical to z_1; any signal that differs from the correct value must be located "downstream" from the one-and-only fault. Let's say that a wire is *tarnished* if it is the faulty wire or if at least one of its input wires is tarnished. We introduce new variables g' only for wires g that are tarnished. Thus, in our example, the only clauses F' that are needed to extend F to a faulty companion circuit are $\bar{q}'$ and the clauses that correspond to $c_2' \leftarrow p \vee q'$, $z_4' \leftarrow b_3 \oplus c_2'$, $z_5' \leftarrow b_3 \wedge c_2'$.

Moreover, any fault that is revealed by a test pattern must have an *active path* of wires, leading from the fault to an output; all wires on this path must carry a faulty signal. Therefore Tracy Larrabee [*IEEE Trans.* **CAD-11** (1992), 4–15] decided to introduce additional "sharped" variables $g^\sharp$ for each tarnished wire, meaning that g lies on the active path. The two clauses

$$(\bar{g}^\sharp \vee g \vee g') \wedge (\bar{g}^\sharp \vee \bar{g} \vee \bar{g}') \tag{25}$$

ensure that $g \neq g'$ whenever g is part of that path. Furthermore we have $(\bar{v}^\sharp \vee g^\sharp)$ whenever g is an AND, OR, or XOR gate with tarnished input v. Fanout gates are slightly tricky in this regard: When wires g^1 and g^2 fan out from a tarnished wire g, we need variables $g^{1\sharp}$ and $g^{2\sharp}$ as well as $g^\sharp$; and we introduce the clause

$$(\bar{g}^\sharp \vee g^{1\sharp} \vee g^{2\sharp}) \tag{26}$$

to specify that the active path takes at least one of the two branches.

According to these rules, our example acquires the new variables $q^\sharp$, $c_2^\sharp$, $c_2^{1\sharp}$, $c_2^{2\sharp}$, $z_4^\sharp$, $z_5^\sharp$, and the new clauses

$$(\bar{q}^\sharp \vee q \vee q') \wedge (\bar{q}^\sharp \vee \bar{q} \vee \bar{q}') \wedge (\bar{q}^\sharp \vee c_2^\sharp) \wedge (\bar{c}_2^\sharp \vee c_2 \vee c_2') \wedge (\bar{c}_2^\sharp \vee \bar{c}_2 \vee \bar{c}_2') \wedge (\bar{c}_2^\sharp \vee c_2^{1\sharp} \vee c_2^{2\sharp}) \wedge$$
$$(\bar{c}_2^{1\sharp} \vee z_4^\sharp) \wedge (\bar{z}_4^\sharp \vee z_4 \vee z_4') \wedge (\bar{z}_4^\sharp \vee \bar{z}_4 \vee \bar{z}_4') \wedge (\bar{c}_2^{2\sharp} \vee z_5^\sharp) \wedge (\bar{z}_5^\sharp \vee z_5 \vee z_5') \wedge (\bar{z}_5^\sharp \vee \bar{z}_5 \vee \bar{z}_5').$$

The active path begins at q, so we assert the unit clause $(q^\sharp)$; it ends at a tarnished output, so we also assert $(z_4^\sharp \vee z_5^\sharp)$. The resulting set of clauses will find a test pattern for this fault if and only if the fault is detectable. Larrabee found that such active-path variables provide important clues to a SAT solver and significantly speed up the solution process.

Returning to the large circuit $prod(32, 32)$, one of the 140 hard-to-test faults is "W_{21}^{26} stuck at 1," where W_{21}^{26} denotes the 26th extra wire that fans out from the OR gate called W_{21} in §75 of the Stanford GraphBase program GB_GATES; W_{21}^{26} is an input to gate $b_{40}^{40} \leftarrow d_{40}^{19} \wedge W_{21}^{26}$ in §80 of that program. Test patterns for that fault can be characterized by a set of 23,194 clauses in 7,082 variables (of which only 4 variables are "primed" and 4 are "sharped").

Fortunately the solution $(x, y) = (\texttt{\#7F13FEDD}, \texttt{\#5FE57FFE})$ was found rather quickly in the author's experiments; and this pattern also killed off 13 of the other cases, so the score was now "14 down and 126 to go"!

The next fault sought was "$A_5^{36,2}$ stuck at 1," where $A_5^{36,2}$ is the second extra wire to fan out from the AND gate A_5^{36} in §72 of GB_GATES (an input to $R_{11}^{36} \leftarrow A_5^{36,2} \wedge R_1^{35,2}$). This fault corresponds to 26,131 clauses on 8,342 variables; but the SAT solver took a quick look at those clauses and decided almost instantly that they are *unsatisfiable*. Therefore the fault is undetectable, and the circuit $prod(32, 32)$ can be simplified by setting $R_{11}^{36} \leftarrow R_1^{35,2}$. A closer look showed, in fact, that clauses corresponding to the Boolean equations

$$x = y \wedge z, \quad y = v \wedge w, \quad z = t \wedge u, \quad u = v \oplus w$$

were present (where $t = R_{13}^{44}$, $u = A_{58}^{45}$, $v = R_4^{44}$, $w = A_{14}^{45}$, $x = R_{23}^{46}$, $y = R_{13}^{45}$, $z = R_{19}^{45}$); these clauses *force* $x = 0$. Therefore it was not surprising to find that the list of unresolved faults also included R_{23}^{46}, $R_{23}^{46,1}$, and $R_{23}^{46,2}$ stuck at 0. Altogether 26 of the 140 faults undetected by random inputs turned out to be *absolutely* undetectable; and only one of these, namely "Q_{26}^{46} stuck at 0," required a nontrivial proof of undetectability.

Some of the $126 - 26 = 100$ faults remaining on the to-do list turned out to be significant challenges for the SAT solver. While waiting, the author therefore had time to take a look at a few of the previously found solutions, and noticed that those patterns themselves were forming a pattern! Sure enough, the extreme portions of this large and complicated circuit actually have a fairly simple structure, stuck-at-fault-wise. Hence number theory came to the rescue: The factorization $\texttt{\#87FBC059} \times \texttt{\#F0F87817} = 2^{63} - 1$ solved many of the toughest challenges, some of which occur with probability less than 2^{-34} when 32-bit numbers are multiplied; and the "Aurifeuillian" factorization $(2^{31} - 2^{16} + 1)(2^{31} + 2^{16} + 1) = 2^{62} + 1$, which the author had known for more than forty years (see Eq. 4.5.4–(15)), polished off most of the others.

The bottom line (see exercise 51) is that all 42,150 of the detectable single-stuck-at faults of the parallel multiplication circuit $prod(32, 32)$ can actually be detected with at most 196 well-chosen test patterns.

Learning a Boolean function. Sometimes we're given a "black box" that evaluates a Boolean function $f(x_1, \ldots, x_N)$. We have no way to open the box, but we suspect that the function is actually quite simple. By plugging in various values for $x = x_1 \ldots x_N$, we can observe the box's behavior and possibly learn the hidden rule that lies inside. For example, a secret function of $N = 20$ Boolean variables might take on the values shown in Table 2, which lists 16 cases where $f(x) = 1$ and 16 cases where $f(x) = 0$.

Suppose we assume that the function has a DNF (disjunctive normal form) with only a few terms. We'll see in a moment that it's easy to express such an assumption as a satisfiability problem. And when the author constructed clauses corresponding to Table 2 and presented them to a SAT solver, he did in fact learn almost immediately that a very simple formula is consistent with all of the data:

$$f(x_1, \ldots, x_{20}) = \bar{x}_2 \bar{x}_3 \bar{x}_{10} \vee \bar{x}_6 \bar{x}_{10} x_{12} \vee x_8 \bar{x}_{13} \bar{x}_{15} \vee \bar{x}_8 x_{10} \bar{x}_{12}. \tag{27}$$

Table 2
VALUES TAKEN ON BY AN UNKNOWN FUNCTION

Cases where $f(x) = 1$

$x_1 x_2 x_3 x_4 x_5 x_6 x_7 x_8 x_9 \quad \cdots \quad x_{20}$

```
11001001000011111101
10101010001000100001
01101000110000100011
01001100010011000110
01100010100010111000
00001101110000011100
11010001001010010000
00100100111000010000
10001010010011111100
11000111010000000010
00001011101111010100
01100011101100010011
10011011001000100101
00010100101000001000
01111001100011100011
01000000010011011101
```

Cases where $f(x) = 0$

$x_1 x_2 x_3 x_4 x_5 x_6 x_7 x_8 x_9 \quad \cdots \quad x_{20}$

```
10101101111110000101
01000101100010100010
10111011010010101001
10101010111110111100
01010110001000000010
01110011110100111100
11110001110110001011
10011100010110000011
11001110001011010011
01101001010110101001
11100001001101100100
00010001010001100100
00110011111101011100
11001001001110011101
11001110001001001001
10110011111011111001
```

This formula was discovered by constructing clauses in $2MN$ variables $p_{i,j}$ and $q_{i,j}$ for $1 \leq i \leq M$ and $1 \leq j \leq N$, where M is the maximum number of terms allowed in the DNF (here $M = 4$) and where

$$p_{i,j} = [\text{term } i \text{ contains } x_j], \qquad q_{i,j} = [\text{term } i \text{ contains } \bar{x}_j]. \qquad (28)$$

If the function is constrained to equal 1 at P specified points, we also use auxiliary variables $z_{i,k}$ for $1 \leq i \leq M$ and $1 \leq k \leq P$, one for each term at every such point.

Table 2 says that $f(1, 1, 0, 0, \ldots, 1) = 1$, and we can capture this specification by constructing the clause

$$(z_{1,1} \vee z_{2,1} \vee \cdots \vee z_{M,1}) \qquad (29)$$

together with the clauses

$$(\bar{z}_{i,1} \vee \bar{q}_{i,1}) \wedge (\bar{z}_{i,1} \vee \bar{q}_{i,2}) \wedge (\bar{z}_{i,1} \vee \bar{p}_{i,3}) \wedge (\bar{z}_{i,1} \vee \bar{p}_{i,4}) \wedge \cdots \wedge (\bar{z}_{i,1} \vee \bar{q}_{i,20}) \qquad (30)$$

for $1 \leq i \leq M$. Translation: (29) says that at least one of the terms in the DNF must evaluate to true; and (30) says that, if term i is true at the point $1100\ldots1$, it cannot contain $\bar{x}_1$ or $\bar{x}_2$ or x_3 or x_4 or $\cdots$ or $\bar{x}_{20}$.

Table 2 also tells us that $f(1, 0, 1, 0, \ldots, 1) = 0$. This specification corresponds to the clauses

$$(q_{i,1} \vee p_{i,2} \vee q_{i,3} \vee p_{i,4} \vee \cdots \vee q_{i,20}) \qquad (31)$$

for $1 \leq i \leq M$. (Each term of the DNF must be zero at the given point; thus either $\bar{x}_1$ or x_2 or $\bar{x}_3$ or x_4 or $\cdots$ or $\bar{x}_{20}$ must be present for each value of i.)

In general, every case where $f(x) = 1$ yields one clause like (29) of length M, plus MN clauses like (30) of length 2. Every case where $f(x) = 0$ yields M clauses like (31) of length N. We use $q_{i,j}$ when $x_j = 1$ at the point in question, and $p_{i,j}$ when $x_j = 0$, for both (30) and (31). This construction is due to A. P. Kamath, N. K. Karmarkar, K. G. Ramakrishnan, and M. G. C. Resende [*Mathematical Programming* **57** (1992), 215–238], who presented numerous examples.

From Table 2, with $M = 4$, $N = 20$, and $P = 16$, it generates 1360 clauses of total length 3904 in 224 variables; a SAT solver then finds a solution with $p_{1,1} = q_{1,1} = p_{1,2} = 0$, $q_{1,2} = 1$, ..., leading to (27).

The simplicity of (27) makes it plausible that the SAT solver has indeed psyched out the true nature of the hidden function $f(x)$. The chance of agreeing with the correct value 32 times out of 32 is only 1 in 2^{32}, so we seem to have overwhelming evidence in favor of that equation.

But no: Such reasoning is fallacious. The numbers in Table 2 actually arose in a completely different way, and Eq. (27) has essentially *no* credibility as a predictor of $f(x)$ for any other values of x! (See exercise 53.) The fallacy comes from the fact that short-DNF Boolean functions of 20 variables are not at all rare; there are many more than 2^{32} of them.

D. Morgenstern has found a much simpler formula that also matches Table 2:

$$f(x_1, \ldots, x_{20}) = \bar{x}_4 x_{10} \bar{x}_{12} \vee \bar{x}_6 \bar{x}_{10} \bar{x}_{12} \vee x_9 \bar{x}_{10} x_{11}.$$

But it's actually further than (27) from the "true" f that's revealed in exercise 53.

On the other hand, when we *do* know that the hidden function $f(x)$ has a DNF with at most M terms (although we know nothing else about it), the clauses (29)–(31) give us a nice way to discover those terms, provided that we also have a sufficiently large and unbiased "training set" of observed values.

For example, let's assume that (27) actually *is* the function in the box. If we examine $f(x)$ at 32 random points x, we don't have enough data to make any deductions. But 100 random training points will almost always home in on the correct solution (27). This calculation typically involves 3942 clauses in 344 variables; yet it goes quickly, needing only about 100 million accesses to memory.

One of the author's experiments with a 100-element training set yielded

$$\hat{f}(x_1, \ldots, x_{20}) = \bar{x}_2 \bar{x}_3 \bar{x}_{10} \vee x_3 \bar{x}_6 \bar{x}_{10} \bar{x}_{12} \vee x_8 \bar{x}_{13} \bar{x}_{15} \vee \bar{x}_8 x_{10} \bar{x}_{12}, \qquad (32)$$

which is close to the truth but not quite exact. (Exercise 59 proves that $\hat{f}(x)$ is equal to $f(x)$ more than 97% of the time.) Further study of this example showed that another nine training points were enough to deduce $f(x)$ uniquely, thus obtaining 100% confidence (see exercise 61).

Bounded model checking. Some of the most important applications of SAT solvers in practice are related to the verification of hardware or software, because designers generally want some kind of assurance that particular implementations correctly meet their specifications.

A typical design can usually be modeled as a *transition relation* between Boolean vectors $X = x_1 \ldots x_n$ that represent the possible states of a system. We write $X \to X'$ if state X at time t can be followed by state X' at time $t + 1$. The task in general is to study sequences of state transitions

$$X_0 \to X_1 \to X_2 \to \cdots \to X_r, \qquad (33)$$

and to decide whether or not there are sequences that have special properties. For example, we hope that there's no such sequence for which X_0 is an "initial state" and X_r is an "error state"; otherwise there'd be a bug in the design.

Fig. 78. Conway's rule (35) defines these three successive transitions.

Questions like this are readily expressed as satisfiability problems: Each state X_t is a vector of Boolean variables $x_{t1} \ldots x_{tn}$, and each transition relation can be represented by a set of m clauses $T(X_t, X_{t+1})$ that must be satisfied. These clauses $T(X, X')$ involve $2n$ variables $\{x_1, \ldots, x_n, x'_1, \ldots, x'_n\}$, together with q auxiliary variables $\{y_1, \ldots, y_q\}$ that might be needed to express Boolean formulas in clause form as we did with the Tseytin encodings in (24). Then the existence of sequence (33) is equivalent to the satisfiability of mr clauses

$$T(X_0, X_1) \wedge T(X_1, X_2) \wedge \cdots \wedge T(X_{r-1}, X_r) \qquad (34)$$

in the $n(r+1)+qr$ variables $\{x_{tj} \mid 0 \le t \le r,\ 1 \le j \le n\} \cup \{y_{tk} \mid 0 \le t < r,\ 1 \le k \le q\}$. We've essentially "unrolled" the sequence (33) into r copies of the transition relation, using variables x_{tj} for state X_t and y_{tk} for the auxiliary quantities in $T(X_t, X_{t+1})$. Additional clauses can now be added to specify constraints on the initial state X_0 and/or the final state X_r, as well as any other conditions that we want to impose on the sequence.

This general setup is called "bounded model checking," because we're using it to check properties of a model (a transition relation), and because we're considering only sequences that have a bounded number of transitions, r.

John Conway's fascinating *Game of Life* provides a particularly instructive set of examples that illustrate basic principles of bounded model checking. The states X of this game are two-dimensional bitmaps, corresponding to arrays of square cells that are either alive (1) or dead (0). Every bitmap X has a unique successor X', determined by the action of a simple 3×3 cellular automaton: Suppose cell x has the eight neighbors $\{x_{\text{NW}}, x_{\text{N}}, x_{\text{NE}}, x_{\text{W}}, x_{\text{E}}, x_{\text{SW}}, x_{\text{S}}, x_{\text{SE}}\}$, and let $\nu = x_{\text{NW}} + x_{\text{N}} + x_{\text{NE}} + x_{\text{W}} + x_{\text{E}} + x_{\text{SW}} + x_{\text{S}} + x_{\text{SE}}$ be the number of neighbors that are alive at time t. Then x is alive at time $t + 1$ if and only if either (a) $\nu = 3$, or (b) $\nu = 2$ and x is alive at time t. Equivalently, the transition rule

$$x' = [2 < x_{\text{NW}} + x_{\text{N}} + x_{\text{NE}} + x_{\text{W}} + \tfrac{1}{2}x + x_{\text{E}} + x_{\text{SW}} + x_{\text{S}} + x_{\text{SE}} < 4] \qquad (35)$$

holds at every cell x. (See, for example, Fig. 78, where the live cells are black.)

Conway called Life a "no-player game," because it involves no strategy: Once an initial state X_0 has been set up, all subsequent states X_1, X_2, ... are completely determined. Yet, in spite of the simple rules, he also proved that Life is inherently complicated and unpredictable, indeed beyond human comprehension, in the sense that it is universal: *Every finite, discrete, deterministic system, however complex, can be simulated faithfully by some finite initial state X_0 of Life.* [See Berlekamp, Conway, and Guy, *Winning Ways* (2004), Chapter 25.]

In exercises 7.1.4–160 through 162, we've already seen some of the amazing Life histories that are possible, using BDD methods. And many further aspects of Life can be explored with SAT methods, because SAT solvers can often deal with many more variables. For example, Fig. 78 was discovered by using $7 \times 15 = 105$ variables for each state X_0, X_1, X_2, X_3. The values of X_3 were obviously predetermined; but the other $105 \times 3 = 315$ variables had to be computed, and BDDs can't handle that many. Moreover, additional variables were introduced to ensure that the initial state X_0 would have as few live cells as possible.

Here's the story behind Fig. 78, in more detail: Since Life is two-dimensional, we use variables x_{ij} instead of x_j to indicate the states of individual cells, and x_{tij} instead of x_{tj} to indicate the states of cells at time t. We generally assume that $x_{tij} = 0$ for all cells outside of a given finite region, although the transition rule (35) can allow cells that are arbitrarily far away to become alive as Life goes on. In Fig. 78 the region was specified to be a 7×15 rectangle at each unit of time. Furthermore, configurations with three consecutive live cells on a boundary edge were forbidden, so that cells "outside the box" wouldn't be activated.

The transitions $T(X_t, X_{t+1})$ can be encoded without introducing additional variables, but only if we introduce 190 rather long clauses for each cell not on the boundary. There's a better way, based on the binary tree approach underlying (20) and (21) above, which requires only about 63 clauses of size ≤ 3, together with about 14 auxiliary variables per cell. This approach (see exercise 65) takes advantage of the fact that many intermediate calculations can be shared. For example, cells x and $x_{\rm W}$ have four neighbors $\{x_{\rm NW}, x_{\rm N}, x_{\rm SW}, x_{\rm S}\}$ in common; so we need to compute $x_{\rm NW} + x_{\rm N} + x_{\rm SW} + x_{\rm S}$ only once, not twice.

The clauses that correspond to a four-step sequence $X_0 \to X_1 \to X_2 \to X_3 \to X_4$ leading to $X_4 = $ **LIFE** turn out to be unsatisfiable without going outside of the 7×15 frame. (Only 10 gigamems of calculation were needed to establish this fact, using Algorithm C below, even though roughly 34000 clauses in 9000 variables needed to be examined!) So the next step in the preparation of Fig. 78 was to try $X_3 = $ **LIFE**; and this trial succeeded. Additional clauses, which permitted X_0 to have at most 39 live cells, led to the solution shown, at a cost of about 17 gigamems; and that solution is optimum, because a further run (costing 12 gigamems) proved that there's no solution with at most 38.

Let's look for a moment at some of the patterns that can occur on a chessboard, an 8×8 grid. Human beings will never be able to contemplate more than a tiny fraction of the 2^{64} states that are possible; so we can be fairly sure that "Lifenthusiasts" haven't already explored every tantalizing configuration that exists, even on such a small playing field.

One nice way to look for a sequence of interesting Life transitions is to assert that no cell stays alive more than four steps in a row. Let us therefore say that a *mobile* Life path is a sequence of transitions $X_0 \to X_1 \to \cdots \to X_r$ with the additional property that we have

$$(\bar{x}_{tij} \vee \bar{x}_{(t+1)ij} \vee \bar{x}_{(t+2)ij} \vee \bar{x}_{(t+3)ij} \vee \bar{x}_{(t+4)ij}), \qquad \text{for } 0 \leq t \leq r - 4. \quad (36)$$

To avoid trivial solutions we also insist that X_r is not entirely dead. For example, if we impose rule (36) on a chessboard, with x_{tij} permitted to be alive only if $1 \leq i, j \leq 8$, and with the further condition that at most five cells are alive in each generation, a SAT solver can quickly discover interesting mobile paths such as

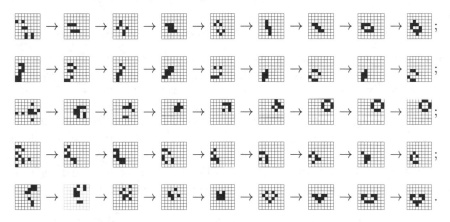

$$\cdots , \quad (37)$$

which last quite awhile before leaving the board. And indeed, the five-celled object that moves so gracefully in this path is R. K. Guy's famous *glider* (1970), which is surely the most interesting small creature in Life's universe. The glider moves diagonally, recreating a shifted copy of itself after every four steps.

Interesting mobile paths appear also if we restrict the population at each time to $\{6, 7, 8, 9, 10\}$ instead of $\{1, 2, 3, 4, 5\}$. For example, here are some of the first such paths that the author's solver came up with, having length $r = 8$:

These paths illustrate the fact that symmetry can be gained, but never lost, as Life evolves deterministically. Marvelous designs are spawned in the process. In each of these sequences the next bitmap, X_9, would break our ground rules: The population immediately after X_8 grows to 12 in the first and last examples, but shrinks to 5 in the second-from-last; and the path becomes immobile in the other two. Indeed, we have $X_5 = X_7$ in the second example, hence $X_6 = X_8$ and $X_7 = X_9$, etc. Such a repeating pattern is called an *oscillator* of period 2. The third example ends with an oscillator of period 1, known as a "still life."

What are the ultimate destinations of these paths? The first one becomes still, with $X_{69} = X_{70}$; and the fourth becomes *very* still, with $X_{12} = 0$! The fifth is the most fascinating of the group, because it continues to produce ever more elaborate valentine shapes, then proceeds to dance and sparkle, until finally beginning to twinkle with period 2 starting at time 177. Thus its members X_2 through X_7 qualify as "Methuselahs," defined by Martin Gardner as "Life patterns of population less than 10 that do not become stable within 50 generations." (A repetitive pattern, like the glider or an oscillator, is called *stable*.)

SAT solvers are basically useless for the study of Methuselahs, because the state space becomes too large. But they are quite helpful when we want to illuminate many other aspects of Life, and exercises 66–85 discuss some notable instances. We will consider one more instructive example before moving on, namely an application to "eaters." Consider a Life path of the form

$$X_0 = \blacksquare \rightarrow \blacksquare \rightarrow \blacksquare \rightarrow \blacksquare \rightarrow \blacksquare \rightarrow \blacksquare = X_5, \qquad (38)$$

where the gray cells form a still life and the cells of X_1, X_2, X_3 are unknown. Thus $X_4 = X_5$ and $X_0 = X_5 +$ glider. Furthermore we require that the still life X_5 does not interact with the glider's parent, $\blacksquare$; see exercise 77. The idea is that a glider will be gobbled up if it happens to glide into this particular still life, and the still life will rapidly reconstitute itself as if nothing had happened.

Algorithm C almost instantaneously (well, after about 100 megamems) finds

$$\blacksquare \rightarrow \blacksquare \rightarrow \blacksquare \rightarrow \blacksquare \rightarrow \blacksquare \rightarrow \blacksquare, \qquad (39)$$

the four-step eater that was first observed in action by R. W. Gosper in 1971.

Applications to mutual exclusion. Let's look now at how bounded model checking can help us to prove that algorithms are correct. (Or incorrect.) Some of the most challenging issues of verification arise when we consider parallel processes that need to synchronize their concurrent behavior. To simplify our discussion it will be convenient to tell a little story about Alice and Bob.

Alice and Bob are casual friends who share an apartment. One of their joint rooms is special: When they're in that critical room, which has two doors, they don't want the other person to be present. Furthermore, being busy people, they don't want to interrupt each other needlessly. So they agree to control access to the room by using an indicator light, which can be switched on or off.

The first protocol they tried can be characterized by symmetrical algorithms:

A0. Maybe go to A1.	B0. Maybe go to B1.	
A1. If l go to A1, else to A2.	B1. If l go to B1, else to B2.	
A2. Set $l \leftarrow 1$, go to A3.	B2. Set $l \leftarrow 1$, go to B3.	(40)
A3. Critical, go to A4.	B3. Critical, go to B4.	
A4. Set $l \leftarrow 0$, go to A0.	B4. Set $l \leftarrow 0$, go to B0.	

At any instant of time, Alice is in one of five states, $\{A0, A1, A2, A3, A4\}$, and the rules of her program show how that state might change. In state A0 she isn't interested in the critical room; but she goes to A1 when she does wish to use it. She reaches that objective in state A3. Similar remarks apply to Bob. When the indicator light is on ($l = 1$), they wait until the other person has exited the room and switched the light back off ($l = 0$).

Alice and Bob don't necessarily operate at the same speed. But they're allowed to dawdle only when in the "maybe" state A0 or B0. More precisely, we model the situation by converting every relevant scenario into a discrete sequence of state transitions. At every time $t = 0, 1, 2, \ldots$, either Alice or Bob (but not both) will perform the command associated with their current state, thereby perhaps changing to a different state at time $t + 1$. This choice is nondeterministic.

Only four kinds of primitive commands are permitted in the procedures we shall study, all of which are illustrated in (40): (1) "Maybe go to s"; (2) "Critical, go to s"; (3) "Set $v \leftarrow b$, go to s"; and (4) "If v go to s_1, else to s_0". Here s denotes a state name, v denotes a shared Boolean variable, and b is 0 or 1.

Unfortunately, Alice and Bob soon learned that protocol (40) is unreliable: One day she went from A1 to A2 and he went from B1 to B2, before either of them had switched the indicator on. Embarrassment (A3 and B3) followed.

They could have discovered this problem in advance, if they'd converted the state transitions of (40) into clauses for bounded model checking, as in (33), then applied a SAT solver. In this case the vector X_t that corresponds to time t consists of Boolean variables that encode each of their current states, as well as the current value of l. We can, for example, have eleven variables $A0_t$, $A1_t$, $A2_t$, $A3_t$, $A4_t$, $B0_t$, $B1_t$, $B2_t$, $B3_t$, $B4_t$, l_t, together with ten binary exclusion clauses $(\overline{A0_t} \vee \overline{A1_t})$, $(\overline{A0_t} \vee \overline{A2_t})$, ..., $(\overline{A3_t} \vee \overline{A4_t})$ to ensure that Alice is in at most one state, and with ten similar clauses for Bob. There's also a variable $@_t$, which is true or false depending on whether Alice or Bob executes their program step at time t. (We say that Alice was "bumped" if $@_t = 1$, and Bob was bumped if $@_t = 0$.)

If we start with the initial state X_0 defined by unit clauses

$$A0_0 \wedge \overline{A1_0} \wedge \overline{A2_0} \wedge \overline{A3_0} \wedge \overline{A4_0} \wedge B0_0 \wedge \overline{B1_0} \wedge \overline{B2_0} \wedge \overline{B3_0} \wedge \overline{B4_0} \wedge \bar{l}_0, \quad (41)$$

the following clauses for $0 \leq t < r$ (discussed in exercise 87) will emulate the first r steps of every legitimate scenario defined by (40):

$$
\begin{array}{lll}
(@_t \vee \overline{A0_t} \vee A0_{t+1}) & (\overline{@_t} \vee \overline{A0_t} \vee A0_{t+1} \vee A1_{t+1}) & (@_t \vee \overline{B0_t} \vee B0_{t+1} \vee B1_{t+1}) \\
(@_t \vee \overline{A1_t} \vee A1_{t+1}) & (\overline{@_t} \vee \overline{A1_t} \vee \bar{l}_t \vee A1_{t+1}) & (@_t \vee \overline{B1_t} \vee \bar{l}_t \vee B1_{t+1}) \\
(@_t \vee \overline{A2_t} \vee A2_{t+1}) & (\overline{@_t} \vee \overline{A1_t} \vee l_t \vee A2_{t+1}) & (@_t \vee \overline{B1_t} \vee l_t \vee B2_{t+1}) \\
(@_t \vee \overline{A3_t} \vee A3_{t+1}) & (\overline{@_t} \vee \overline{A2_t} \vee A3_{t+1}) & (@_t \vee \overline{B2_t} \vee B3_{t+1}) \\
(@_t \vee \overline{A4_t} \vee A4_{t+1}) & (\overline{@_t} \vee \overline{A2_t} \vee l_{t+1}) & (@_t \vee \overline{B2_t} \vee l_{t+1}) \\
(@_t \vee \overline{B0_t} \vee B0_{t+1}) & (\overline{@_t} \vee \overline{A3_t} \vee A4_{t+1}) & (@_t \vee \overline{B3_t} \vee B4_{t+1}) \\
(@_t \vee \overline{B1_t} \vee B1_{t+1}) & (\overline{@_t} \vee \overline{A4_t} \vee A0_{t+1}) & (@_t \vee \overline{B4_t} \vee B0_{t+1}) \\
(@_t \vee \overline{B2_t} \vee B2_{t+1}) & (\overline{@_t} \vee \overline{A4_t} \vee \bar{l}_{t+1}) & (@_t \vee \overline{B4_t} \vee \bar{l}_{t+1}) \\
(@_t \vee \overline{B3_t} \vee B3_{t+1}) & (\overline{@_t} \vee l_t \vee A2_t \vee A4_t \vee \bar{l}_{t+1}) & (@_t \vee l_t \vee B2_t \vee B4_t \vee \bar{l}_{t+1}) \\
(@_t \vee \overline{B4_t} \vee B4_{t+1}) & (\overline{@_t} \vee \bar{l}_t \vee A2_t \vee A4_t \vee l_{t+1}) & (@_t \vee \bar{l}_t \vee B2_t \vee B4_t \vee l_{t+1})
\end{array}
\quad (42)
$$

If we now add the unit clauses $(A3_r)$ and $(B3_r)$, the resulting set of $13 + 50r$ clauses in $11 + 12r$ variables is readily satisfiable when $r = 6$, thereby proving that the critical room might indeed be jointly occupied. (Incidentally, standard terminology for mutual exclusion protocols would say that "two threads concurrently execute a *critical section*"; but we shall continue with our roommate metaphor.)

Back at the drawing board, one idea is to modify (40) by letting Alice use the room only when $l = 1$, but letting Bob in when $l = 0$:

A0. Maybe go to A1.	B0. Maybe go to B1.
A1. If l go to A2, else to A1.	B1. If l go to B1, else to B2.
A2. Critical, go to A3.	B2. Critical, go to B3.
A3. Set $l \leftarrow 0$, go to A0.	B3. Set $l \leftarrow 1$, go to B0.

$$(43)$$

Computer tests with $r = 100$ show that the corresponding clauses are unsatisfiable; thus mutual exclusion is apparently guaranteed by (43).

But (43) is a nonstarter, because it imposes an intolerable cost: Alice can't use the room k times until Bob has already done so! Scrap that.

How about installing another light, so that each person controls one of them?

A0. Maybe go to A1.	B0. Maybe go to B1.
A1. If b go to A1, else to A2.	B1. If a go to B1, else to B2.
A2. Set $a \leftarrow 1$, go to A3.	B2. Set $b \leftarrow 1$, go to B3. (44)
A3. Critical, go to A4.	B3. Critical, go to B4.
A4. Set $a \leftarrow 0$, go to A0.	B4. Set $b \leftarrow 0$, go to B0.

No; this suffers from the same defect as (40). But maybe we can cleverly switch the order of steps 1 and 2:

A0. Maybe go to A1.	B0. Maybe go to B1.
A1. Set $a \leftarrow 1$, go to A2.	B1. Set $b \leftarrow 1$, go to B2.
A2. If b go to A2, else to A3.	B2. If a go to B2, else to B3. (45)
A3. Critical, go to A4.	B3. Critical, go to B4.
A4. Set $a \leftarrow 0$, go to A0.	B4. Set $b \leftarrow 0$, go to B0.

Yes! Exercise 95 proves easily that this protocol does achieve mutual exclusion.

Alas, however, a new problem now arises, namely the problem known as "deadlock" or "livelock." Alice and Bob can get into states A2 and B2, after which they're stuck — each waiting for the other to go critical.

In such cases they could agree to "reboot" somehow. But that would be a cop-out; they really seek a better solution. And they aren't alone: Many people have struggled with this surprisingly delicate problem over the years, and several solutions (both good and bad) appear in the exercises below. Edsger Dijkstra, in some pioneering lecture notes entitled *Cooperating Sequential Processes* [Technological University Eindhoven (September 1965), §2.1], thought of an instructive way to improve on (45):

A0. Maybe go to A1.	B0. Maybe go to B1.
A1. Set $a \leftarrow 1$, go to A2.	B1. Set $b \leftarrow 1$, go to B2.
A2. If b go to A3, else to A4.	B2. If a go to B3, else to B4.
A3. Set $a \leftarrow 0$, go to A1.	B3. Set $b \leftarrow 0$, go to B1. (46)
A4. Critical, go to A5.	B4. Critical, go to B5.
A5. Set $a \leftarrow 0$, go to A0.	B5. Set $b \leftarrow 0$, go to B0.

But he realized that this too is unsatisfactory, because it permits scenarios in which Alice, say, might wait forever while Bob repeatedly uses the critical room. (Indeed, if Alice and Bob are in states A1 and B2, she might go to A2, A3, then A1, thereby letting him run to B4, B5, B0, B1, and B2; they're back where they started, yet she's made no progress.)

The existence of this problem, called *starvation*, can also be detected via bounded model checking. The basic idea (see exercise 91) is that starvation occurs if and only if there is a loop of transitions

$$X_0 \rightarrow X_1 \rightarrow \cdots \rightarrow X_p \rightarrow X_{p+1} \rightarrow \cdots \rightarrow X_r = X_p \qquad (47)$$

such that (i) Alice and Bob each are bumped at least once during the loop; and (ii) at least one of them is never in a "maybe" or "critical" state during the loop.

And those conditions are easily encoded into clauses, because we can identify the variables for time r with the variables for time p, and we can append the clauses

$$(\overline{@_p} \vee \overline{@_{p+1}} \vee \cdots \vee \overline{@_{r-1}}) \wedge (@_p \vee @_{p+1} \vee \cdots \vee @_{r-1}) \qquad (48)$$

to guarantee (i). Condition (ii) is simply a matter of appending unit clauses; for example, to test whether Alice can be starved by (46), the relevant clauses are $\overline{A0_p} \wedge \overline{A0_{p+1}} \wedge \cdots \wedge \overline{A0_{r-1}} \wedge \overline{A4_p} \wedge \overline{A4_{p+1}} \wedge \cdots \wedge \overline{A4_{r-1}}$.

The deficiencies of (43), (45), and (46) can all be viewed as instances of starvation, because (47) and (48) are satisfiable (see exercise 90). Thus we can use bounded model checking to find counterexamples to *any* unsatisfactory protocol for mutual exclusion, either by exhibiting a scenario in which Alice and Bob are both in the critical room or by exhibiting a feasible starvation cycle (47).

Of course we'd like to go the other way, too: If a protocol has no counterexamples for, say, $r = 100$, we still might not know that it is really reliable; a counterexample might exist only when r is extremely large. Fortunately there are ways to obtain decent upper bounds on r, so that bounded model checking can be used to prove correctness as well as to demonstrate incorrectness. For example, we can verify the simplest known correct solution to Alice and Bob's problem, a protocol by G. L. Peterson [*Information Proc. Letters* **12** (1981), 115–116], who noticed that a careful combination of (43) and (45) actually suffices:

A0. Maybe go to A1.	B0. Maybe go to B1.	
A1. Set $a \leftarrow 1$, go to A2.	B1. Set $b \leftarrow 1$, go to B2.	
A2. Set $l \leftarrow 0$, go to A3.	B2. Set $l \leftarrow 1$, go to B3.	
A3. If b go to A4, else to A5.	B3. If a go to B4, else to B5.	(49)
A4. If l go to A5, else to A3.	B4. If l go to B3, else to B5.	
A5. Critical, go to A6.	B5. Critical, go to B6.	
A6. Set $a \leftarrow 0$, go to A0.	B6. Set $b \leftarrow 0$, go to B0.	

Now there are *three* signal lights, a, b, and l—one controlled by Alice, one controlled by Bob, and one switchable by both.

To show that states A5 and B5 can't be concurrent, we can observe that the shortest counterexample will not repeat any state twice; in other words, it will be a *simple* path of transitions (33). Thus we can assume that r is at most the total number of states. However, (49) has $7 \times 7 \times 2 \times 2 \times 2 = 392$ states; that's a finite bound, not really out of reach for a good SAT solver on this particular problem, but we can do much better. For example, it's not hard to devise clauses that are satisfiable if and only if there's a simple path of length $\leq r$ (see exercise 92), and in this particular case the longest simple path turns out to have only 54 steps.

We can in fact do better yet by using the important notion of *invariants*, which we encountered in Section 1.2.1 and have seen repeatedly throughout this series of books. Invariant assertions are the key to most proofs of correctness, so it's not surprising that they also give a significant boost to bounded model checking. Formally speaking, if $\Phi(X)$ is a Boolean function of the state vector X, we say that Φ is invariant if $\Phi(X)$ implies $\Phi(X')$ whenever $X \to X'$. For example, it's not hard to see that the following clauses are invariant with respect to (49):

$$\Phi(X) = (A0 \lor A1 \lor A2 \lor A3 \lor A4 \lor A5 \lor A6) \land (B0 \lor B1 \lor B2 \lor B3 \lor B4 \lor B5 \lor B6)$$
$$\land (\overline{A0} \lor \bar{a}) \land (\overline{A1} \lor \bar{a}) \land (\overline{A2} \lor a) \land (\overline{A3} \lor a) \land (\overline{A4} \lor a) \land (\overline{A5} \lor a) \land (\overline{A6} \lor a)$$
$$\land (\overline{B0} \lor \bar{b}) \land (\overline{B1} \lor \bar{b}) \land (\overline{B2} \lor b) \land (\overline{B3} \lor b) \land (\overline{B4} \lor b) \land (\overline{B5} \lor b) \land (\overline{B6} \lor b). \quad (50)$$

(The clause $\overline{A0} \lor \bar{a}$ says that $a = 0$ when Alice is in state A0, etc.) And we can use a SAT solver to *prove* that Φ is invariant, by showing that the clauses

$$\Phi(X) \land (X \to X') \land \neg\Phi(X') \quad (51)$$

are *unsatisfiable*. Furthermore $\Phi(X_0)$ holds for the initial state X_0, because $\neg\Phi(X_0)$ is unsatisfiable. (See exercise 93.) Therefore $\Phi(X_t)$ is true for all $t \geq 0$, by induction, and we may add these helpful clauses to all of our formulas.

The invariant (50) reduces the total number of states by a factor of 4. And the real clincher is the fact that the clauses

$$(X_0 \to X_1 \to \cdots \to X_r) \land \Phi(X_0) \land \Phi(X_1) \land \cdots \land \Phi(X_r) \land A5_r \land B5_r, \quad (52)$$

where X_0 is *not* required to be the initial state, turn out to be unsatisfiable when $r = 3$. In other words, there's no way to go back more than two steps from a bad state, without violating the invariant. We can conclude that mutual exclusion needs to be verified for (49) only by considering paths of length 2(!). Furthermore, similar ideas (exercise 98) show that (49) is starvation-free.

Caveat: Although (49) is a correct protocol for mutual exclusion according to Alice and Bob's ground rules, it *cannot* be used safely on most modern computers unless special care is taken to synchronize cache memories and write buffers. The reason is that hardware designers use all sorts of trickery to gain speed, and those tricks might allow one process to see $a = 0$ at time $t + 1$ even though another process has set $a \leftarrow 1$ at time t. We have developed the algorithms above by assuming a model of parallel computation that Leslie Lamport has called *sequential consistency* [*IEEE Trans.* **C-28** (1979), 690–691].

Digital tomography. Another set of appealing questions amenable to SAT solving comes from the study of binary images for which partial information is given. Consider, for example, Fig. 79, which shows the "Cheshire cat" of Section 7.1.3 in a new light. This image is an $m \times n$ array of Boolean variables $(x_{i,j})$, with $m = 25$ rows and $n = 30$ columns: The upper left corner element, $x_{1,1}$, is 0, representing white; and $x_{1,24} = 1$ corresponds to the lone black pixel in the top row. We are given the row sums $r_i = \sum_{j=1}^{n} x_{i,j}$ for $1 \leq i \leq m$ and the column sums $c_j = \sum_{i=1}^{m} x_{i,j}$ for $1 \leq j \leq n$, as well as both sets of sums in the 45° diagonal directions, namely

$$a_d = \sum_{i+j=d+1} x_{i,j} \quad \text{and} \quad b_d = \sum_{i-j=d-n} x_{i,j} \quad \text{for } 0 < d < m+n. \quad (53)$$

To what extent can such an image be reconstructed from its sums r_i, c_j, a_d, and b_d? Small examples are often uniquely determined by these Xray-like projections (see exercise 103). But the discrete nature of pixel images makes the reconstruction problem considerably more difficult than the corresponding

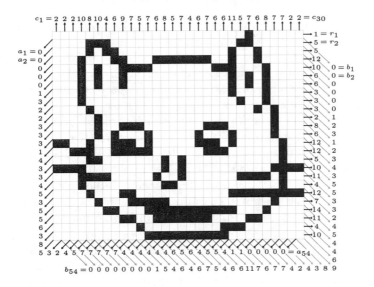

Fig. 79. An array of black and white pixels together with its row sums r_i, column sums c_j, and diagonal sums a_d, b_d.

continuous problem, in which projections from many different angles are available. Notice, for example, that the classical "8 queens problem" — to place eight nonattacking queens on a chessboard — is equivalent to solving an 8×8 digital tomography problem with the constraints $r_i = 1$, $c_j = 1$, $a_d \leq 1$, and $b_d \leq 1$.

The constraints of Fig. 79 appear to be quite strict, so we might expect that most of the pixels $x_{i,j}$ are determined uniquely by the given sums. For instance, the fact that $a_1 = \cdots = a_5 = 0$ tells us that $x_{i,j} = 0$ whenever $i + j \leq 6$; and similar deductions are possible at all four corners of the image. A crude "ballpark estimate" suggests that we're given a few more than 150 sums, most of which occupy 5 bits each; hence we have roughly $150 \times 5 = 750$ bits of data, from which we wish to reconstruct $25 \times 30 = 750$ pixels $x_{i,j}$. Actually, however, this problem turns out to have many billions of solutions (see Fig. 80), most of which aren't catlike! Exercise 106 provides a less crude estimate, which shows that this abundance of solutions isn't really surprising.

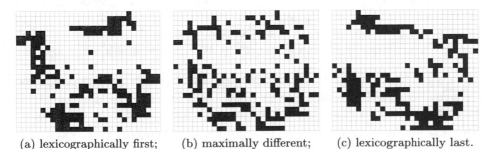

(a) lexicographically first;　　(b) maximally different;　　(c) lexicographically last.

Fig. 80. Extreme solutions to the constraints of Fig. 79.

A digital tomography problem such as Fig. 79 is readily represented as a sequence of clauses to be satisfied, because each of the individual requirements is just a special case of the cardinality constraints that we've already considered in the clauses of (18)–(21). This problem differs from the other instances of SAT that we've been discussing, primarily because it consists *entirely* of cardinality constraints: It is a question of solving $25 + 30 + 54 + 54 = 163$ simultaneous linear equations in 750 variables $x_{i,j}$, where each variable must be either 0 or 1. So it's essentially an instance of *integer programming* (IP), not an instance of satisfiability (SAT). On the other hand, Bailleux and Boufkhad devised clauses (20) and (21) precisely because they wanted to apply SAT solvers, not IP solvers, to digital tomography. In the case of Fig. 79, their method yields approximately 40,000 clauses in 9,000 variables, containing about 100,000 literals altogether.

Figure 80(b) illustrates a solution that differs as much as possible from Fig. 79. Thus it minimizes the sum $x_{1,24} + x_{2,5} + x_{2,6} + \cdots + x_{25,21}$ of the 182 variables that correspond to black pixels, over all 0-or-1-valued solutions to the linear equations. If we use linear programming to minimize that sum over $0 \le x_{i,j} \le 1$, *without* requiring the variables to be integers, we find almost instantly that the minimum value is ≈ 31.38 under these relaxed conditions; hence every black-and-white image must have at least 32 black pixels in common with Fig. 79. Furthermore, Fig. 80(b) — which can be computed in a few seconds by widely available IP solvers such as CPLEX — actually achieves this minimum. By contrast, state-of-the-art SAT solvers as of 2013 had great difficulty finding such an image, even when told that a 32-in-common solution is possible.

Parts (a) and (c) of Fig. 80 are, similarly, quite relevant to the current state of the SAT-solving art: They represent hundreds of individual SAT instances, where the first k variables are set to particular known values and we try to find a solution with the next variable either 0 or 1, respectively. Several of the subproblems that arose while computing rows 6 and 7 of Fig. 80(c) turned out to be quite challenging, although resolvable in a few hours; and similar problems, which correspond to different kinds of lexicographic order, apparently still lie beyond the reach of contemporary SAT-oriented methods. Yet IP solvers polish these problems off with ease. (See exercises 109 and 111.)

If we provide more information about an image, our chances of being able to reconstruct it uniquely are naturally enhanced. For example, suppose we also compute the numbers r'_i, c'_j, a'_d, and b'_d, which count the *runs of 1s* that occur in each row, column, and diagonal. (We have $r'_1 = 1$, $r'_2 = 2$, $r'_3 = 4$, and so on.) Given this additional data, we can show that Fig. 79 is the only solution, because a suitable set of clauses turns out to be unsatisfiable. Exercise 117 explains one way by which (20) and (21) can be modified so that they provide constraints based on the run counts. Furthermore, it isn't difficult to express even more detailed constraints, such as the assertion that "column 4 contains runs of respective lengths $(6, 1, 3)$," as a sequence of clauses; see exercise 438.

SAT examples — summary. We've now seen convincing evidence that simple Boolean clauses — ANDs of ORs of literals — are enormously versatile. Among other things, we've used them to encode problems of graph coloring, integer factorization, hardware fault testing, machine learning, model checking, and tomography. And indeed, Section 7.9 will demonstrate that 3SAT is the "poster child" for NP-complete problems in general: *Any* problem in NP — which is a huge class, essentially comprising all yes-or-no questions of size N whose affirmative answers are verifiable in $N^{O(1)}$ steps — can be formulated as an equivalent instance of 3SAT, without greatly increasing the problem size.

Backtracking for SAT. OK, we've seen a dizzying variety of intriguing and important examples of SAT that are begging to be solved. How shall we solve them?

Any instance of SAT that involves at least one variable can be solved systematically by choosing a variable and setting it to 0 or 1. Either of those choices gives us a smaller instance of SAT; so we can continue until reaching either an empty instance — which is trivially satisfiable, because no clauses need to be satisfied — or an instance that contains an empty clause. In the latter case we must back up and reconsider one of our earlier choices, proceeding in the same fashion until we either succeed or exhaust all the possibilities.

For example, consider again the formula F in (1). If we set $x_1 = 0$, F reduces to $\bar{x}_2 \wedge (x_2 \vee x_3)$, because the first clause $(x_1 \vee \bar{x}_2)$ loses its x_1, while the last two clauses contain $\bar{x}_1$ and are satisfied. It will be convenient to have a notation for this reduced problem; so let's write

$$F \,|\, \bar{x}_1 \;=\; \bar{x}_2 \wedge (x_2 \vee x_3). \tag{54}$$

Similarly, if we set $x_1 = 1$, we obtain the reduced problem

$$F \,|\, x_1 \;=\; (x_2 \vee x_3) \wedge \bar{x}_3 \wedge (\bar{x}_2 \vee x_3). \tag{55}$$

F is satisfiable if and only if we can satisfy either (54) or (55).

In general if F is any set of clauses and if l is any literal, then $F \,|\, l$ (read "F given l" or "F conditioned on l") is the set of clauses obtained from F by

- removing every clause that contains l; and
- removing $\bar{l}$ from every clause that contains $\bar{l}$.

This conditioning operation is commutative, in the sense that $F \,|\, l \,|\, l' = F \,|\, l' \,|\, l$ when $l' \neq \bar{l}$. If $L = \{l_1, \dots, l_k\}$ is any set of strictly distinct literals, we can also write $F \,|\, L = F \,|\, l_1 \,|\, \cdots \,|\, l_k$. In these terms, F is satisfiable if and only if $F \,|\, L = \emptyset$ for some such L, because the literals of L satisfy every clause of F when $F \,|\, L = \emptyset$.

The systematic strategy for SAT that was sketched above can therefore be formulated as the following recursive procedure $B(F)$, which returns the special value $\perp$ when F is unsatisfiable, otherwise it returns a set L that satisfies F:

$$B(F) = \begin{cases} \text{If } F = \emptyset, \text{ return } \emptyset. \text{ (}F \text{ is trivially satisfiable.)} \\ \text{Otherwise if } \epsilon \in F, \text{ return } \perp. \text{ (}F \text{ is unsatisfiable.)} \\ \text{Otherwise let } l \text{ be a literal in } F \text{ and set } L \leftarrow B(F \,|\, l). \\ \text{If } L \neq \perp, \text{ return } L \cup l. \text{ Otherwise set } L \leftarrow B(F \,|\, \bar{l}). \\ \text{If } L \neq \perp, \text{ return } L \cup \bar{l}. \text{ Otherwise return } \perp. \end{cases} \tag{56}$$

Let's try to flesh out this abstract algorithm by converting it to efficient code at a lower level. From our previous experience with backtracking, we know that it will be crucial to have data structures that allow us to go quickly from

F to $F \mid l$, then back again to F if necessary, when F is a set of clauses and l is a literal. In particular, we'll want a good way to find all of the clauses that contain a given literal.

A combination of sequential and linked structures suggests itself for this purpose, based on our experience with exact cover problems: We can represent each clause as a set of *cells*, where each cell p contains a literal $l = \mathtt{L}(p)$ together with pointers $\mathtt{F}(p)$ and $\mathtt{B}(p)$ to other cells that contain l, in a doubly linked list. We'll also need $\mathtt{C}(p)$, the number of the clause to which p belongs. The cells of clause C_i will be in consecutive locations $\mathtt{START}(i) + j$, for $0 \le j < \mathtt{SIZE}(i)$.

We will find it convenient to represent the literals x_k and $\bar{x}_k$, which involve variable x_k, by using the integers $2k$ and $2k + 1$. With this convention we have

$$\bar{l} = l \oplus 1 \qquad \text{and} \qquad |l| = x_{l \gg 1}. \tag{57}$$

Our implementation of (56) will assume that the variables are $x_1, x_2, \ldots, x_n$; thus the $2n$ possible literals will be in the range $2 \le l \le 2n + 1$.

Cells 0 through $2n + 1$ are reserved for special purposes: Cell l is the head of the list for the occurrences of l in other cells. Furthermore, if l is a literal whose value has not yet been fixed, $\mathtt{C}(l)$ will be the length of that list, namely the number of currently active clauses in which l appears.

For example, the $m = 7$ ternary clauses R' of (7) might be represented internally in $2n + 2 + 3m = 31$ cells as follows, using these conventions:

```
p = 0 1 2  3  4  5  6  7  8  9 10 11 12 13 14 15 16 17 18 19 20 21 22 23 24 25 26 27 28 29 30
L(p) = - - -  -  -  -  -  -  -  -  -  -  9  7  3  8  7  5  6  5  3  8  4  3  8  6  2  9  6  4  7  4  2
F(p) = - - 30 21 29 17 26 28 22 25  9  7  3  8 11  5  6 15 12 13  4 18 19 16  2 10 23 20 14 27 24
B(p) = - - 24 12 20 15 16 11 13 10 25 14 18 19 28 17 23  5 21 22 27  3  8 26 30  9  6 29  7  4  2
C(p) = - - 2  3  3  2  3  3  3  2  7  7  7  6  6  6  5  5  5  4  4  4  3  3  3  2  2  2  1  1  1
```

The literals of each clause appear in decreasing order here; for example, the literals $\mathtt{L}(p) = (8, 4, 3)$ in cells 19 through 21 represent the clause $x_4 \vee x_2 \vee \bar{x}_1$, which appears as the fourth clause, '$4\bar{1}2$' in (7). This ordering turns out to be quite useful, because we'll always choose the smallest unset variable as the l or $\bar{l}$ in (56); then l or $\bar{l}$ will always appear at the right of its clauses, and we can remove it or put it back by simply changing the relevant $\mathtt{SIZE}$ fields.

The clauses in this example have $\mathtt{START}(i) = 31 - 3i$ for $1 \le i \le 7$, and $\mathtt{SIZE}(i) = 3$ when computation begins.

Algorithm A (*Satisfiability by backtracking*). Given nonempty clauses $C_1 \wedge \cdots \wedge C_m$ on $n > 0$ Boolean variables $x_1 \ldots x_n$, represented as above, this algorithm finds a solution if and only if the clauses are satisfiable. It records its current progress in an array $m_1 \ldots m_n$ of "moves," whose significance is explained below.

A1. [Initialize.] Set $a \leftarrow m$ and $d \leftarrow 1$. (Here a represents the number of active clauses, and d represents the depth-plus-one in an implicit search tree.)

A2. [Choose.] Set $l \leftarrow 2d$. If $\mathtt{C}(l) \le \mathtt{C}(l + 1)$, set $l \leftarrow l + 1$. Then set $m_d \leftarrow (l \,\&\, 1) + 4[\mathtt{C}(l \oplus 1) = 0]$. (See below.) Terminate successfully if $\mathtt{C}(l) = a$.

A3. [Remove $\bar{l}$.] Delete $\bar{l}$ from all active clauses; but go to A5 if that would make a clause empty. (We want to ignore $\bar{l}$, because we're making l true.)

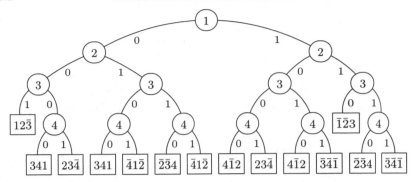

Fig. 81. The search tree that is implicitly traversed by Algorithm A, when that algorithm is applied to the eight unsatisfiable clauses R defined in (6). Branch nodes are labeled with the variable being tested; leaf nodes are labeled with a clause that is found to be contradicted.

A4. [Deactivate l's clauses.] Suppress all clauses that contain l. (Those clauses are now satisfied.) Then set $a \leftarrow a - C(l)$, $d \leftarrow d + 1$, and return to A2.

A5. [Try again.] If $m_d < 2$, set $m_d \leftarrow 3 - m_d$, $l \leftarrow 2d + (m_d \ \& \ 1)$, and go to A3.

A6. [Backtrack.] Terminate unsuccessfully if $d = 1$ (the clauses are unsatisfiable). Otherwise set $d \leftarrow d - 1$ and $l \leftarrow 2d + (m_d \ \& \ 1)$.

A7. [Reactivate l's clauses.] Set $a \leftarrow a + C(l)$, and unsuppress all clauses that contain l. (Those clauses are now unsatisfied, because l is no longer true.)

A8. [Unremove $\bar{l}$.] Reinstate $\bar{l}$ in all the active clauses that contain it. Then go back to A5. ▮

(See exercise 121 for details of the low-level list processing operations that are needed to update the data structures in steps A3 and A4, and to downdate them in A7 and A8.)

The move codes m_j of Algorithm A are integers between 0 and 5 that encode the state of the algorithm's progress as follows:

- $m_j = 0$ means we're trying $x_j = 1$ and haven't yet tried $x_j = 0$.
- $m_j = 1$ means we're trying $x_j = 0$ and haven't yet tried $x_j = 1$.
- $m_j = 2$ means we're trying $x_j = 1$ after $x_j = 0$ has failed.
- $m_j = 3$ means we're trying $x_j = 0$ after $x_j = 1$ has failed.
- $m_j = 4$ means we're trying $x_j = 1$ when $\bar{x}_j$ doesn't appear.
- $m_j = 5$ means we're trying $x_j = 0$ when x_j doesn't appear.

Codes 4 and 5 refer to so-called "pure literals": If no clause contains the literal $\bar{l}$, we can't go wrong by assuming that l is true.

For example, when Algorithm A is presented with the clauses (7), it cruises directly to a solution by setting $m_1 m_2 m_3 m_4 = 1014$; the solution is $x_1 x_2 x_3 x_4 = 0101$. But when the unsatisfiable clauses (6) are given, the successive code strings $m_1 \ldots m_d$ in step A2 are

$$1, 11, 110, 1131, 121, 1211, 1221, 21, 211, 2111, 2121, 221, 2221, \qquad (58)$$

before the algorithm gives up. (See Fig. 81.)

It's helpful to display the current string $m_1 \ldots m_d$ now and then, as a convenient indication of progress; this string increases lexicographically. Indeed, fascinating patterns appear as the 2s and 3s gradually move to the left. (Try it!)

When the algorithm terminates successfully in step A2, a satisfying assignment can be read off from the move table by setting $x_j \leftarrow 1 \oplus (m_j \;\&\; 1)$ for $1 \leq j \leq d$. Algorithm A stops after finding a single solution; see exercise 122 if you want them all.

Lazy data structures. Instead of using the elaborate doubly linked machinery that underlies Algorithm A, we can actually get by with a much simpler scheme discovered by Cynthia A. Brown and Paul W. Purdom, Jr. [*IEEE Trans.* **PAMI-4** (1982), 309–316], who introduced the notion of *watched literals*. They observed that we don't really need to know all of the clauses that contain a given literal, because only one literal per clause is actually relevant at any particular time.

Here's the idea: When we work on clauses $F \mid L$, the variables that occur in L have known values, but the other variables do not. For example, in Algorithm A, variable x_j is implicitly known to be either true or false when $j \leq d$, but its value is unknown when $j > d$. Such a situation is called a *partial assignment*. A partial assignment is *consistent* with a set of clauses if no clause consists entirely of false literals. Algorithms for SAT usually deal exclusively with consistent partial assignments; the goal is to convert them to consistent *total* assignments, by gradually eliminating the unknown values.

Thus every clause in a consistent partial assignment has at least one nonfalse literal; and we can adjust the data so that such a literal appears first, when the clause is represented in memory. Many nonfalse literals might be present, but only one of them is designated as the clause's "watchee." When a watched literal becomes false, we can find another nonfalse literal to swap into its place — unless the clause has been reduced to a unit, a clause of size 1.

With such a scheme we need only maintain a relatively short list for every literal l, namely a list W_l of all clauses that currently watch l. This list can be singly linked. Hence we need only one link per clause; and we have a total of only $2n + m$ links altogether, instead of the two links for each *cell* that are required by Algorithm A.

Furthermore — and this is the best part! — *no updates need to be made to the watch lists when backtracking.* The backtrack operations never falsify a nonfalse literal, because they only change values from known to unknown. Perhaps for this reason, data structures based on watched literals are called *lazy*, in contrast with the "eager" data structures of Algorithm A.

Let us therefore redesign Algorithm A and make it more laid-back. Our new data structure for each cell p has only one field, $\mathtt{L}(p)$; the other fields $\mathtt{F}(p)$, $\mathtt{B}(p)$, $\mathtt{C}(p)$ are no longer necessary, nor do we need $2n + 2$ special cells. As before we will represent clauses sequentially, with the literals of C_j beginning at $\mathtt{START}(j)$ for $1 \leq j \leq m$. The watched literal will be the one in $\mathtt{START}(j)$; and a new field, $\mathtt{LINK}(j)$, will be the number of another clause with the same watched literal (or 0, if C_j is the last such clause). Moreover, our new algorithm won't need $\texttt{SIZE}(j)$. Instead, we can assume that the final literal of C_j is in location $\texttt{START}(j-1)-1$, provided that we define $\texttt{START}(0)$ appropriately.

The resulting procedure is almost unbelievably short and sweet. It's surely the simplest SAT solver that can claim to be efficient on problems of modest size:

Algorithm B (*Satisfiability by watching*). Given nonempty clauses $C_1 \wedge \cdots \wedge C_m$ on $n > 0$ Boolean variables $x_1 \ldots x_n$, represented as above, this algorithm finds a solution if and only if the clauses are satisfiable. It records its current progress in an array $m_1 \ldots m_n$ of "moves," whose significance was explained above.

B1. [Initialize.] Set $d \leftarrow 1$.

B2. [Rejoice or choose.] If $d > n$, terminate successfully. Otherwise set $m_d \leftarrow [W_{2d} = 0 \text{ or } W_{2d+1} \neq 0]$ and $l \leftarrow 2d + m_d$.

B3. [Remove $\bar{l}$ if possible.] For all j such that $\bar{l}$ is watched in C_j, watch another literal of C_j. But go to B5 if that can't be done. (See exercise 124.)

B4. [Advance.] Set $W_{\bar{l}} \leftarrow 0$, $d \leftarrow d + 1$, and return to B2.

B5. [Try again.] If $m_d < 2$, set $m_d \leftarrow 3 - m_d$, $l \leftarrow 2d + (m_d \,\&\, 1)$, and go to B3.

B6. [Backtrack.] Terminate unsuccessfully if $d = 1$ (the clauses are unsatisfiable). Otherwise set $d \leftarrow d - 1$ and go back to B5. ∎

Readers are strongly encouraged to work exercise 124, which spells out the low-level operations that are needed in step B3. Those operations accomplish essentially everything that Algorithm B needs to do.

This algorithm doesn't use move codes 4 or 5, because lazy data structures don't have enough information to identify pure literals. Fortunately pure literals are comparatively unimportant in practice; problems that are helped by the pure literal shortcut can usually also be solved quickly without it.

Notice that steps A2 and B2 use different criteria for deciding whether to try $x_d = 1$ or $x_d = 0$ first at each branch of the search tree. Algorithm A chooses the alternative that satisfies the most clauses; Algorithm B chooses to make l true instead of $\bar{l}$ if the watch list for $\bar{l}$ is empty but the watch list for l is not. (All clauses in which $\bar{l}$ is watched will have to change, but those containing l are satisfied and in good shape.) In case of a tie, both algorithms set $m_d \leftarrow 1$, which corresponds to $x_d = 0$. The reason is that human-designed instances of SAT tend to have solutions made up of mostly false literals.

Forced moves from unit clauses. The simple logic of Algorithm B works well on many problems that aren't too large. But its insistence on setting x_1 first, then x_2, etc., makes it quite inefficient on many other problems, because it fails to take advantage of unit clauses. A unit clause (l) forces l to be true; therefore two-way branching is unnecessary whenever a unit clause is present. Furthermore, unit clauses aren't rare: Far from it. Experience shows that they're almost ubiquitous in practice, so that the actual search trees often involve only dozens of branch nodes instead of thousands or millions.

The importance of unit clauses was recognized already in the first computer implementation of a SAT solver, designed by Martin Davis, George Logemann, and Donald Loveland [*CACM* **5** (1962), 394–397] and based on ideas that Davis had developed earlier with Hilary Putnam [*JACM* **7** (1960), 201–215]. They extended Algorithm A by introducing mechanisms that recognize when the size of a clause decreases to 1, or when the number of unsatisfied clauses containing a literal drops to 0. In such cases, they put variables onto a "ready list," and assigned those variables to fixed values before doing any further two-way branching. The resulting program was fairly complex; indeed, computer memory was so limited in those days, they implemented branching by writing all the data for the current node of the search tree onto magnetic tape, then backtracking when necessary by restoring the data from the most recently written tape records! The names of these four authors are now enshrined in the term "DPLL algorithm," which refers generally to SAT solving via partial assignment and backtracking.

Brown and Purdom, in the paper cited earlier, showed that unit clauses can be detected more simply by using watched literals as in Algorithm B. We can supplement the data structures of that algorithm by introducing indices $h_1 \ldots h_n$ so that the variable whose value is being set at depth d is x_{h_d} instead of x_d. Furthermore we can arrange the not-yet-set variables whose watch lists aren't empty into a circular list called the "active ring"; the idea is to proceed through the active ring, checking to see whether any of its variables are currently in a unit clause. We resort to two-way branching only if we go all around the ring without finding any such units.

For example, let's consider the 32 unsatisfiable clauses of $waerden(3,3;9)$ in (9). The active ring is initially (1 2 3 4 5 6 7), because 8, $\bar{8}$, 9, and $\bar{9}$ aren't being watched anywhere. There are no unit clauses yet. The algorithm below will decide to try $\bar{1}$ first; then it will change the clauses 123, 135, 147, and 159 to 213, 315, 417, and 519, respectively, so that nobody watches the false literal 1. The active ring becomes (2 3 4 5 6 7) and the next choice is $\bar{2}$; so 213, 234, 246, and 258 morph respectively into 312, 324, 426, 528. Now, with active ring (3 4 5 6 7), the unit clause '3' is detected (because 1 and 2 are false in '312'). This precipitates further changes, and the first steps of the computation can be summarized thus:

Active ring	$x_1 x_2 x_3 x_4 x_5 x_6 x_7 x_8 x_9$	Units	Choice	Changed clauses
(1 2 3 4 5 6 7)	– – – – – – – – –		$\bar{1}$	$213, 315, 417, 519$
(2 3 4 5 6 7)	0 – – – – – – – –		$\bar{2}$	$312, 324, 426, 528$
(3 4 5 6 7)	0 0 – – – – – – –	3	3	$\overline{435}, \overline{537}, \overline{639}$
(4 5 6 7)	0 0 1 – – – – – –		$\bar{4}$	$624, 714, 546, 648$
(5 6 7)	0 0 1 0 – – – – –	6	6	$\overline{936}, \overline{768}$
(9 7 5)	0 0 1 0 – 1 – – –	$\bar{9}$	$\bar{9}$	
(7 5)	0 0 1 0 – 1 – – 0	7	7	$867, \overline{879}$
(8 5)	0 0 1 0 – 1 1 – 0	$\bar{8}$	$\bar{8}$	
(5)	0 0 1 0 – 1 1 0 0	5, $\bar{5}$	Backtrack	
(6 9 7 8 5)	0 0 1 – – – – – –		4	$\overline{534}, \overline{546}, \overline{648}$
(6 9 7 8 5)	0 0 1 1 – – – – –	$\bar{5}$	$\bar{5}$	$456, 825, 915, 657, 759$

(59)

When 6 is found, 7 is also a unit clause; but the algorithm doesn't see it yet, because variable x_6 is tested first. The active ring changes first to (7 5) after 6

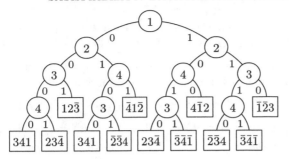

Fig. 82. The search tree that is implicitly traversed by Algorithm D, when that algorithm is applied to the eight unsatisfiable clauses R defined in (6). Branch nodes are labeled with the variable being tested; leaf nodes are labeled with a clause that is found to be contradicted. When the right child of a branch node is a leaf, the left branch was forced by a conditional unary clause.

is found, because 5 is cyclically after 6; we want to look at 7 before 5, instead of revisiting more-or-less the same clauses. After 6 has been chosen, 9 is inserted at the left, because the watch list for $\bar{9}$ becomes nonempty. After backtracking, vari- ables 8, 7, 9, 6 are successively inserted at the left as they lose their forced values.

The following algorithm represents the active ring by giving a NEXT field to each variable, with $x_{\text{NEXT}(k)}$ the successor of x_k. The ring is accessed via "head" and "tail" pointers h and t at the left and right, with $h = \text{NEXT}(t)$. If the ring is empty, however, $t = 0$, and h is undefined.

Algorithm D (*Satisfiability by cyclic DPLL*). Given nonempty clauses $C_1 \wedge \cdots \wedge C_m$ on $n > 0$ Boolean variables $x_1 \ldots x_n$, represented with lazy data structures and an active ring as explained above, this algorithm finds a solution if and only if the clauses are satisfiable. It records its current progress in an array $h_1 \ldots h_n$ of indices and an array $m_0 \ldots m_n$ of "moves," whose significance is explained below.

D1. [Initialize.] Set $m_0 \leftarrow d \leftarrow h \leftarrow t \leftarrow 0$, and do the following for $k = n, n-1$, $\ldots$, 1: Set $x_k \leftarrow -1$ (denoting an unset value); if $W_{2k} \neq 0$ or $W_{2k+1} \neq 0$, set $\text{NEXT}(k) \leftarrow h$, $h \leftarrow k$, and if $t = 0$ also set $t \leftarrow k$. Finally, if $t \neq 0$, complete the active ring by setting $\text{NEXT}(t) \leftarrow h$.

D2. [Success?] Terminate if $t = 0$ (all clauses are satisfied). Otherwise set $k \leftarrow t$.

D3. [Look for unit clauses.] Set $h \leftarrow \text{NEXT}(k)$ and use the subroutine in exer- cise 129 to compute $f \leftarrow [2h$ is a unit$] + 2[2h+1$ is a unit$]$. If $f = 3$, go to D7. If $f = 1$ or 2, set $m_{d+1} \leftarrow f + 3$, $t \leftarrow k$, and go to D5. Otherwise, if $h \neq t$, set $k \leftarrow h$ and repeat this step.

D4. [Two-way branch.] Set $h \leftarrow \text{NEXT}(t)$ and $m_{d+1} \leftarrow [W_{2h} = 0$ or $W_{2h+1} \neq 0]$.

D5. [Move on.] Set $d \leftarrow d+1$, $h_d \leftarrow k \leftarrow h$. If $t = k$, set $t \leftarrow 0$; otherwise delete variable k from the ring by setting $\text{NEXT}(t) \leftarrow h \leftarrow \text{NEXT}(k)$.

D6. [Update watches.] Set $b \leftarrow (m_d+1) \bmod 2$, $x_k \leftarrow b$, and clear the watch list for $\bar{x}_k$ (see exercise 130). Return to D2.

D7. [Backtrack.] Set $t \leftarrow k$. While $m_d \geq 2$, set $k \leftarrow h_d$, $x_k \leftarrow -1$; if $W_{2k} \neq 0$ or $W_{2k+1} \neq 0$, set $\text{NEXT}(k) \leftarrow h$, $h \leftarrow k$, $\text{NEXT}(t) \leftarrow h$; and set $d \leftarrow d - 1$.

D8. [Failure?] If $d > 0$, set $m_d \leftarrow 3 - m_d$, $k \leftarrow h_d$, and return to D6. Otherwise terminate the algorithm (because the clauses aren't satisfiable). ∎

The move codes of this algorithm are slightly different from the earlier ones:

- $m_j = 0$ means we're trying $x_{h_j} = 1$ and haven't yet tried $x_{h_j} = 0$.
- $m_j = 1$ means we're trying $x_{h_j} = 0$ and haven't yet tried $x_{h_j} = 1$.
- $m_j = 2$ means we're trying $x_{h_j} = 1$ after $x_{h_j} = 0$ has failed.
- $m_j = 3$ means we're trying $x_{h_j} = 0$ after $x_{h_j} = 1$ has failed.
- $m_j = 4$ means we're trying $x_{h_j} = 1$ because it's forced by a unit clause.
- $m_j = 5$ means we're trying $x_{h_j} = 0$ because it's forced by a unit clause.

As before, the number of two-way branch nodes in the implicit search tree is the number of times that m_j is set to 0 or 1.

Comparison of the algorithms. OK, we've just seen three rudimentary SAT solvers. How well do they actually do? Detailed performance statistics will be given later in this section, after we've studied several more algorithms. But a brief quantitative study of Algorithms A, B, and D now will give us some concrete facts with which we can calibrate our expectations before moving on.

Consider, for example, $langford(n)$, the problem of Langford pairs. This problem is typical of SAT instances where many unit clauses arise during the computation. For example, when Algorithm D is applied to $langford(5)$, it reaches a stage where the move codes are

$$m_1 m_2 \ldots m_d = 125555555555555555114545545, \tag{60}$$

indicating only four two-way branches (the 1s and the 2) amongst a sea of forced moves (the 4s and the 5s). We therefore expect Algorithm D to outperform Algorithms A and B, which don't capitalize on unit clauses.

Sure enough, Algorithm D wins (slightly), even on a small example such as $langford(5)$, which has 213 clauses, 480 cells, 28 variables. The detailed stats are

Algorithm A: $5379 + 108952$ mems, 10552 bytes, 705 nodes.
Algorithm B: $1206 + 30789$ mems, 4320 bytes, 771 nodes.
Algorithm D: $1417 + 28372$ mems, 4589 bytes, 11 nodes.

(Here "$5379 + 108952$ mems" means that 5379 memory accesses were made while initializing the data structures before the algorithm began; then the algorithm itself accessed octabytes of memory 108,952 times.) Notice that Algorithm B is more than thrice as fast as Algorithm A in this example, although it makes 771 two-way branches instead of 705. Algorithm A needs fewer nodes, because it recognizes pure literals; but Algorithm B does much less work per node. Algorithm D, on the other hand, works very hard at each node, yet comes out ahead because its decision-making choices reduce the search to only a few nodes.

These differences become more dramatic when we consider larger problems. For instance, $langford(9)$ has 1722 clauses, 3702 cells, 104 variables, and we find

Algorithm A: 332.0 megamems, 77216 bytes, 1,405,230 nodes.
Algorithm B: 53.4 megamems, 31104 bytes, 1,654,352 nodes.
Algorithm D: 23.4 megamems, 32057 bytes, 6093 nodes.

And with $langford(13)$'s 5875 clauses, 12356 cells, 228 variables, the results are

Algorithm A: 2699.1 gigamems, 253.9 kilobytes, 8.7 giganodes.
Algorithm B: 305.2 gigamems, 101.9 kilobytes, 10.6 giganodes.
Algorithm D: 71.7 gigamems, 104.0 kilobytes, 14.0 meganodes.

Mathematicians will recall that, at the beginning of Chapter 7, we used elementary reasoning to prove the unsatisfiability of $langford(4k + 1)$ for all k. Evidently SAT solvers have great difficulty discovering this fact, even when k is fairly small. We are using that problem here as a benchmark test, not because we recommend replacing mathematics by brute force! Its unsatisfiability actually enhances its utility as a benchmark, because algorithms for satisfiability are more easily compared with respect to unsatisfiable instances: Extreme variations in performance occur when clauses are satisfiable, because solutions can be found purely by luck. Still, we might as well see what happens when our three algorithms are set loose on the satisfiable problem $langford(16)$, which turns out to be "no sweat." Its 11494 clauses, 23948 cells, and 352 variables lead to the statistics

Algorithm A: 11262.6 megamems, 489.2 kilobytes, 28.8 meganodes.
Algorithm B: 932.1 megamems, 196.2 kilobytes, 40.9 meganodes.
Algorithm D: 4.9 megamems, 199.4 kilobytes, 167 nodes.

Algorithm D is certainly our favorite so far, based on the $langford$ data. But it is far from a panacea, because it loses badly to the lightweight Algorithm B on other problems. For example, the 2779 unsatisfiable clauses, 11662 cells, and 97 variables of $waerden(3, 10; 97)$ yield

Algorithm A: 150.9 gigamems, 212.8 kilobytes, 106.7114 meganodes.
Algorithm B: 6.2 gigamems, 71.2 kilobytes, 106.7116 meganodes.
Algorithm D: 1430.4 gigamems, 72.1 kilobytes, 102.7 meganodes.

And $waerden(3, 10; 96)$'s 2721 satisfiable clauses, 11418 cells, 96 variables give us

Algorithm A: 96.9 megamems, 208.3 kilobytes, 72.9 kilonodes.
Algorithm B: 12.4 megamems, 69.8 kilobytes, 207.7 kilonodes.
Algorithm D: 57962.8 megamems, 70.6 kilobytes, 4447.7 kilonodes.

In such cases unit clauses don't reduce the search tree size by very much, so we aren't justified in spending so much time per node.

*Speeding up by working harder. Algorithms A, B, and D are OK on smallish problems, but they cannot really cope with the larger instances of SAT that have arisen in our examples. Significant enhancements are possible if we are willing to do more work and to develop more elaborate algorithms.

Mathematicians generally strive for nice, short, elegant proofs of theorems; and computer scientists generally aim for nice, short, elegant sequences of steps with which a problem can quickly be solved. But some theorems have no short proofs, and some problems cannot be solved efficiently with short programs.

Let us therefore adopt a new attitude, at least temporarily, by fearlessly deciding to throw lots of code at SAT: Let's look at the bottlenecks that hinder Algorithm D on large problems, and let's try to devise new methods that will streamline the calculations even though the resulting program might be ten times larger. In this subsection we shall examine an advanced SAT solver, Algorithm L, which is able to outperform Algorithm D by many orders of magnitude on many important problems. This algorithm cannot be described in just a few lines; but it does consist of cooperating procedures that are individually nice, short, elegant, and understandable by themselves.

The first important ingredient of Algorithm L is an improved mechanism for unit propagation. Algorithm D needs only a few lines of code in step D3 to discover whether or not the value of an unknown variable has been forced by previous assignments; but that mechanism isn't particularly fast, because it is based on indirect inferences from a lazy data structure. We can do better by using "eager" data structures that are specifically designed to recognize forced values quickly, because high-speed propagation of the consequences of a newly asserted value turns out to be extremely important in practice.

A literal l is forced true when it appears in a clause C whose other literals have become false, namely when the set of currently assigned literals L has reduced C to the unit clause $C \mid L = (l)$. Such unit clauses arise from the reduction of binary clauses. Algorithm L therefore keeps track of the binary clauses $(u \vee v)$ that are relevant to the current subproblem $F \mid L$. This information is kept in a so-called "bimp table" $\text{BIMP}(l)$ for every literal l, which is a list of other literals l' whose truth is implied by the truth of l. Indeed, instead of simply including binary clauses within the whole list of given clauses, as Algorithms A, B, and D do, Algorithm L stores the relevant facts about $(u \vee v)$ directly, in a ready-to-use way, by listing u in $\text{BIMP}(\bar{v})$ and v in $\text{BIMP}(\bar{u})$. Each of the $2n$ tables $\text{BIMP}(l)$ is represented internally as a sequential list of length $\text{BSIZE}(l)$, with memory allocated dynamically via the buddy system (see exercise 134).

Binary clauses, in turn, are spawned by ternary clauses. For simplicity, Algorithm L assumes that all clauses have length 3 or less, because every instance of general SAT can readily be converted to 3SAT form (see exercise 28). And for speed, Algorithm L represents the ternary clauses by means of "timp tables," which are analogous to the bimp tables: Every literal l has a sequential list $\text{TIMP}(l)$ of length $\text{TSIZE}(l)$, consisting of pairs $p_1 = (u_1, v_1)$, $p_2 = (u_2, v_2)$, $\ldots$, such that the truth of l implies that each $(u_i \vee v_i)$ becomes a relevant binary clause. If $(u \vee v \vee w)$ is a ternary clause, there will be three pairs $p = (v, w)$, $p' = (w, u)$, and $p'' = (u, v)$, appearing in the respective lists $\text{TIMP}(\bar{u})$, $\text{TIMP}(\bar{v})$, and $\text{TIMP}(\bar{w})$. Moreover, these three pairs are linked together cyclically, with

$$\text{LINK}(p) = p', \qquad \text{LINK}(p') = p'', \qquad \text{LINK}(p'') = p. \qquad (61)$$

Memory is allocated for the timp tables once and for all, as the clauses are input, because Algorithm L does not generate new ternaries during its computations.

Individual pairs p are, however, swapped around within these sequential tables, so that the currently active ternary clauses containing u always appear in the first $\mathtt{TSIZE}(\bar{u})$ positions that have been allocated to $\mathtt{TIMP}(\bar{u})$.

For example, let's consider again the ternary clauses (9) of $waerden(3,3;9)$. Initially there are no binary clauses, so all $\mathtt{BIMP}$ tables are empty. Each of the ternary clauses appears in three of the $\mathtt{TIMP}$ tables. At level 0 of the search tree we might decide that $x_5 = 0$; then $\mathtt{TIMP}(\bar{5})$ tells us that we gain eight binary clauses, namely $\{13, 19, 28, 34, 37, 46, 67, 79\}$. These new binary clauses are represented by sixteen entries in $\mathtt{BIMP}$ tables; $\mathtt{BIMP}(\bar{3})$, for instance, will now be $\{1, 4, 7\}$. Furthermore, we'll want all of the $\mathtt{TIMP}$ pairs that involve either 5 or $\bar{5}$ to become inactive, because the ternary clauses that contain 5 are weaker than the new binary clauses, and the ternary clauses that contain $\bar{5}$ are now satisfied. (See exercise 136.)

As in (57) above, we shall assume that the variables of a given formula are numbered from 1 to n, and we represent the literals k and $\bar{k}$ internally by the numbers $2k$ and $2k+1$. Algorithm L introduces a new twist, however, by allowing variables to have many different *degrees of truth* [see M. Heule, M. Dufour, J. van Zwieten, and H. van Maaren, *LNCS* **3542** (2005), 345–359]: We say that x_k is true with degree D if $\mathtt{VAL}[k] = D$, and false with degree D if $\mathtt{VAL}[k] = D + 1$, where D is any even number.

The highest possible degree, typically $2^{32} - 2$ inside a computer, is called $\mathtt{RT}$ for "real truth." The next highest degree, typically $2^{32} - 4$, is called $\mathtt{NT}$ for "near truth"; and then comes $\mathtt{PT} = 2^{32} - 6$, "proto truth." Lower degrees $\mathtt{PT} - 2$, $\mathtt{PT} - 4$, ..., 2 also turn out to be useful. A literal l is said to be *fixed in context* T if and only if $\mathtt{VAL}[|l|] \geq T$; it is *fixed true* if we also have $\mathtt{VAL}[|l|] \mathbin{\&} 1 = l \mathbin{\&} 1$, and it is *fixed false* if its complement $\bar{l}$ is fixed true.

Suppose, for example, that $\mathtt{VAL}[2] = \mathtt{RT} + 1$ and $\mathtt{VAL}[7] = \mathtt{PT}$; hence x_2 is "really false" while x_7 is "proto true." Then the literal '7', represented internally by $l = 14$, is fixed true in context $\mathtt{PT}$, but l is not fixed in contexts $\mathtt{NT}$ or $\mathtt{RT}$. The literal '$\bar{2}$', represented internally by $l = 5$, is fixed true in *every* context.

Algorithm L uses a sequential stack R_0, R_1, ..., to record the names of literals that have received values. The current stack size, E, satisfies $0 \leq E \leq n$. With those data structures we can use a simple breadth-first search procedure to propagate the binary consequences of a literal l in context T at high speed:

$$\begin{aligned}
&\text{Set } H \leftarrow E; \text{ take account of } l; \\
&\text{while } H < E, \text{ set } l \leftarrow R_H, H \leftarrow H + 1, \text{ and} \\
&\qquad \text{take account of } l' \text{ for all } l' \text{ in } \mathtt{BIMP}(l).
\end{aligned} \qquad (62)$$

Here "take account of l" means "if l is fixed true in context T, do nothing; if l is fixed false in context T, go to step $\mathtt{CONFLICT}$; otherwise set $\mathtt{VAL}[|l|] \leftarrow T + (l \mathbin{\&} 1)$, $R_E \leftarrow l$, and $E \leftarrow E + 1$." The step called $\mathtt{CONFLICT}$ is changeable.

A literal's $\mathtt{BIMP}$ table might grow repeatedly as computation proceeds. But we can undo the consequences of bad decisions by simply resetting $\mathtt{BSIZE}(l)$ to the value that it had before those decisions were made. A special variable $\mathtt{ISTAMP}$ is increased whenever we begin a new round of decision-making, and each literal l has its private stamp $\text{IST}(l)$. Whenever $\text{BSIZE}(l)$ is about to increase, we check if $\text{IST}(l) = \text{ISTAMP}$. If not, we set

$$\text{IST}(l) \leftarrow \text{ISTAMP}, \quad \text{ISTACK}[I] \leftarrow (l, \text{BSIZE}(l)), \quad I \leftarrow I + 1. \qquad (63)$$

Then the entries on ISTACK make it easy to downdate the BIMP tables when we backtrack. (See step L13 in the algorithm below.)

We're ready now to look at the detailed steps of Algorithm L, except that one more member of its arsenal of data structures needs to be introduced: There's an array VAR, which contains a permutation of $\{1, \ldots, n\}$, with $\text{VAR}[k] = x$ if and only if $\text{INX}[x] = k$. Furthermore $\text{VAR}[k]$ is a "free variable" — not fixed in context RT — if and only if $0 \leq k < N$. This setup makes it convenient to keep track of the variables that are currently free: A variable becomes fixed by swapping it to the end of the free list and decreasing N (see exercise 137); then we can free it later by simply increasing N, without swapping.

Algorithm L (*Satisfiability by DPLL with lookahead*). Given nonempty clauses $C_1 \wedge \cdots \wedge C_m$ of size ≤ 3, on $n > 0$ Boolean variables $x_1 \ldots x_n$, this algorithm finds a solution if and only if the clauses are satisfiable. Its family of cooperating data structures is discussed in the text.

L1. [Initialize.] Record all binary clauses in the BIMP array and all ternary clauses in the TIMP array. Let U be the number of distinct variables in unit clauses; terminate unsuccessfully if two unit clauses contradict each other, otherwise record all distinct unit literals in $\text{FORCE}[k]$ for $0 \leq k < U$. Set $\text{VAR}[k] \leftarrow k+1$ and $\text{INX}[k+1] \leftarrow k$ for $0 \leq k < n$; and $d \leftarrow F \leftarrow I \leftarrow \text{ISTAMP} \leftarrow 0$. (Think $d =$ depth, $F =$ fixed variables, $I = \text{ISTACK}$ size.)

L2. [New node.] Set $\text{BRANCH}[d] \leftarrow -1$. If $U = 0$, invoke Algorithm X below (which looks ahead for simplifications and also gathers data about how to make the next branch). Terminate happily if Algorithm X finds all clauses satisfied; go to L15 if Algorithm X discovers a conflict; go to L5 if $U > 0$.

L3. [Choose l.] Select a literal l that's desirable for branching (see exercise 168). If $l = 0$, set $d \leftarrow d + 1$ and return to L2. Otherwise set $\text{DEC}[d] \leftarrow l$, $\text{BACKF}[d] \leftarrow F$, $\text{BACKI}[d] \leftarrow I$, and $\text{BRANCH}[d] \leftarrow 0$.

L4. [Try l.] Set $U \leftarrow 1$, $\text{FORCE}[0] \leftarrow l$.

L5. [Accept near truths.] Set $T \leftarrow \text{NT}$, $G \leftarrow E \leftarrow F$, $\text{ISTAMP} \leftarrow \text{ISTAMP} + 1$, and $\text{CONFLICT} \leftarrow \text{L11}$. Perform the binary propagation routine (62) for $l \leftarrow \text{FORCE}[0], \ldots, l \leftarrow \text{FORCE}[U-1]$; then set $U \leftarrow 0$.

L6. [Choose a nearly true L.] (At this point the stacked literals R_k are "really true" for $0 \leq k < G$, and "nearly true" for $G \leq k < E$. We want them all to be really true.) If $G = E$, go to L10. Otherwise set $L \leftarrow R_G$, $G \leftarrow G+1$.

L7. [Promote L to real truth.] Set $X \leftarrow |L|$ and $\text{VAL}[X] \leftarrow \text{RT} + L \& 1$. Remove variable X from the free list and from all TIMP pairs (see exercise 137). Do step L8 for all pairs (u, v) in $\text{TIMP}(L)$, then return to L6.

L8. [Consider $u \vee v$.] (We have deduced that u or v must be true; five cases arise.) If either u or v is fixed true (in context T, which equals NT), do nothing. If both u and v are fixed false, go to CONFLICT. If u is fixed false but v isn't fixed, perform (62) with $l \leftarrow v$. If v is fixed false but u isn't fixed, perform (62) with $l \leftarrow u$. If neither u nor v is fixed, do step L9.

L9. [Exploit $u \lor v$.] If $\bar{v} \in$ BIMP$(\bar{u})$, perform (62) with $l \leftarrow u$ (because $\bar{u}$ implies both v and $\bar{v}$). Otherwise if $v \in$ BIMP$(\bar{u})$, do nothing (because we already have the clause $u \lor v$). Otherwise if $\bar{u} \in$ BIMP$(\bar{v})$, perform (62) with $l \leftarrow v$. Otherwise append v to BIMP$(\bar{u})$ and u to BIMP$(\bar{v})$. (Each change to BIMP means that (63) might be invoked. Exercise 139 explains how to improve this step by deducing further implications called "compensation resolvents.")

L10. [Accept real truths.] Set $F \leftarrow E$. If BRANCH$[d] \geq 0$, set $d \leftarrow d + 1$ and go to L2. Otherwise go to L3 if $d > 0$, to L2 if $d = 0$.

L11. [Unfix near truths.] While $E > G$, set $E \leftarrow E - 1$ and VAL$[|R_E|] \leftarrow 0$.

L12. [Unfix real truths.] While $E > F$, do the following: Set $E \leftarrow E - 1$ and $X \leftarrow |R_E|$; reactivate the TIMP pairs that involve X and restore X to the free list (see exercise 137); set VAL$[X] \leftarrow 0$.

L13. [Downdate BIMPs.] If BRANCH$[d] \geq 0$, do the following while $I >$ BACKI$[d]$: Set $I \leftarrow I - 1$ and BSIZE$(l) \leftarrow s$, where ISTACK$[I] = (l, s)$.

L14. [Try again?] (We've discovered that DEC$[d]$ doesn't work.) If BRANCH$[d] = 0$, set $l \leftarrow$ DEC$[d]$, DEC$[d] \leftarrow l \leftarrow \bar{l}$, BRANCH$[d] \leftarrow 1$, and go back to L4.

L15. [Backtrack.] Terminate unsuccessfully if $d = 0$. Otherwise set $d \leftarrow d - 1$, $E \leftarrow F$, $F \leftarrow$ BACKF$[d]$, and return to L12. ∎

Exercise 143 extends this algorithm so that it will handle clauses of arbitrary size.

*Speeding up by looking ahead. Algorithm L as it stands is incomplete, because step L2 relies on an as-yet-unspecified "Algorithm X" before it chooses a literal for branching. If we use the simplest possible Algorithm X, by branching on whatever literal happens to be first in the current list of free variables, the streamlined methods for propagating forced moves in (62) and (63) will tend to make Algorithm L run roughly three times as fast as Algorithm D, and that isn't a negligible improvement. But with a sophisticated Algorithm X we can often gain another factor of 10 or more in speed, on significant problems.

For example, here are some typical empirical statistics:

Problem	Algorithm D	Algorithm L^0	Algorithm L$^+$
$waerden(3, 10; 97)$	1430 gigamems,	391 gigamems,	772 megamems,
	103 meganodes	31 meganodes	4672 nodes
$langford(13)$	71.7 gigamems,	21.5 gigamems,	45.7 gigamems,
	14.0 meganodes	10.9 meganodes	944 kilonodes
$rand(3, 420, 100, 0)$	184 megamems,	34 megamems,	626 kilomems,
	34 kilonodes	7489 nodes	19 nodes

Here Algorithm L^0 stands for Algorithm L with the simplest Algorithm X, while Algorithm L$^+$ uses all of the lookahead heuristics that we are about to discuss. The first two problems involve rather large clauses, so they use the extended

Algorithm L of exercise 143. The third problem consists of 420 random ternary clauses on 100 variables. (Algorithm B, incidentally, needs 80.1 teramems, and a search tree of 4.50 teranodes, to show that those clauses are unsatisfiable.)

The moral of this story is that it's wise to do 100 times as much computation at every node of a large search tree, if we can thereby decrease the size of the tree by a factor of 1000.

How then can we distinguish a variable that's good for branching from a variable that isn't? We shall consider a three-step approach:

- Preselecting, to identify free variables that appear to be good candidates;
- Nesting, to allow candidate literals to share implied computations;
- Exploring, to examine the immediate consequences of hypothetical decisions.

While carrying out these steps, Algorithm X might discover a contradiction (in which case Algorithm L will take charge again at step L15); or the lookahead process might discover that several of the free literals are forced to be true (in which case it places them in the first U positions of the FORCE array). The explorations might even discover a way to satisfy all of the clauses (in which case Algorithm L will terminate and everybody will be happy). Thus, Algorithm X might do much more than simply choose a good variable on which to branch.

The following recommendations for Algorithm X are based on Marijn Heule's lookahead solver called march, one of the world's best, as it existed in 2013.

The first stage, preselection, is conceptually simplest, although it also involves some "handwaving" because it depends on necessarily shaky assumptions. Suppose there are N free variables. Experience has shown that we tend to get a good heuristic score $h(l)$ for each literal l, representing the relative amount by which asserting l will reduce the current problem, if these scores approximately satisfy the simultaneous nonlinear equations

$$h(l) = 0.1 + \alpha \sum_{\substack{u \in \text{BIMP}(l) \\ u \text{ not fixed}}} \hat{h}(u) + \sum_{(u,v) \in \text{TIMP}(l)} \hat{h}(u)\hat{h}(v). \tag{64}$$

Here α is a magic constant, typically 3.5; and $\hat{h}(l)$ is a multiple of $h(l)$ chosen so that $\sum_l \hat{h}(l) = 2N$ is the total number of free literals. (In other words, the h scores on the right are "normalized" so that their average is 1.)

Any given set of scores $h(l)$ can be used to derive a refined set $h'(l)$ by letting

$$h'(l) = 0.1 + \alpha \sum_{\substack{u \in \text{BIMP}(l) \\ u \text{ not fixed}}} \frac{h(u)}{h_{\text{ave}}} + \sum_{(u,v) \in \text{TIMP}(l)} \frac{h(u)}{h_{\text{ave}}} \frac{h(v)}{h_{\text{ave}}}, \quad h_{\text{ave}} = \frac{1}{2N} \sum_l h(l). \tag{65}$$

Near the root of the search tree, when $d \leq 1$, we start with $h(l) = 1$ for all l and then refine it five times (say). At deeper levels we start with the $h(l)$ values from the parent node and refine it once. Exercise 145 contains an example.

We've computed $h(l)$ for all of the free literals l, but we won't have time to explore them all. The next step is to select free variables CAND[j] for $0 \leq j < C$, where C isn't too large; we will insist that the number of candidates does not exceed

$$C_{\text{max}} = \max(C_0, C_1/d), \tag{66}$$

using cutoff parameters that are typically $C_0 = 30$, $C_1 = 600$. (See exercise 148.)

We start by dividing the free variables into "participants" and "newbies": A *participant* is a variable such that either x or $\bar{x}$ has played the role of u or v in step L8, at some node above us in the search tree; a *newbie* is a nonparticipant. When $d = 0$ every variable is a newbie, because we're at the root of the tree. But usually there is at least one participant, and we want to branch only on participants whenever possible, in order to maintain focus while backtracking.

If we've got too many potential candidates, even after restricting consideration to participants, we can winnow the list down by preferring the variables x that have the largest combined score $h(x)h(\bar{x})$. Step X3 below describes a fairly fast way to come up with the desired selection of $C \leq C_{\max}$ candidates.

A simple lookahead algorithm can now proceed to compute a more accurate heuristic score $H(l)$, for each of the $2C$ literals $l = \text{CAND}[j]$ or $l = \neg\text{CAND}[j]$ that we've selected for further scrutiny. The idea is to simulate what would happen if l were used for branching, by mimicking steps L4–L9 (at least to a first approximation): Unit literals are propagated as in the exact algorithm, but whenever we get to the part of step L9 that changes the BIMP tables, we don't actually make such a change; we simply note that a branch on l would imply $u \vee v$, and we consider the value of that potential new clause to be $h(u)h(v)$. The heuristic score $H(l)$ is then defined to be the sum of all such clause weights:

$$H(l) = \sum \{h(u)h(v) \mid \text{asserting } l \text{ in L4 leads to asserting } u \vee v \text{ in L9}\}. \quad (67)$$

For example, the problem $waerden(3, 3; 9)$ of (9) has nine candidate variables $\{1, 2, \ldots, 9\}$ at the root of the search tree, and exercise 145 finds their rough heuristic scores $h(l)$. The more discriminating scores $H(l)$ turn out to be

$$H(1) = h(\bar{2})h(\bar{3}) + h(\bar{3})h(\bar{5}) + h(\bar{4})h(\bar{7}) + h(\bar{5})h(\bar{9}) \approx 168.6;$$
$$H(2) = h(\bar{1})h(\bar{3}) + h(\bar{3})h(\bar{4}) + h(\bar{4})h(\bar{6}) + h(\bar{5})h(\bar{8}) \approx 157.3;$$
$$H(3) = h(\bar{1})h(\bar{2}) + h(\bar{2})h(\bar{4}) + h(\bar{4})h(\bar{5}) + \cdots + h(\bar{6})h(\bar{9}) \approx 233.4;$$
$$H(4) = h(\bar{2})h(\bar{3}) + h(\bar{3})h(\bar{5}) + h(\bar{5})h(\bar{6}) + \cdots + h(\bar{1})h(\bar{7}) \approx 231.8;$$
$$H(5) = h(\bar{3})h(\bar{4}) + h(\bar{4})h(\bar{6}) + h(\bar{6})h(\bar{7}) + \cdots + h(\bar{1})h(\bar{9}) \approx 284.0.$$

This problem is symmetrical, so we also have $H(6) = H(\bar{6}) = H(4) = H(\bar{4})$, etc. The best literal for branching, according to this estimate, is 5 or $\bar{5}$.

Suppose we set x_5 false and proceed to look ahead at the reduced problem, with $d = 1$. At this point there are eight candidates, $\{1, 2, 3, 4, 6, 7, 8, 9\}$; and they're now related also by binary implications, because the original clause '357' has, for instance, been reduced to '37'. In fact, the BIMP tables now define the dependency digraph

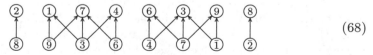

$$(68)$$

because $\bar{3} \longrightarrow 7$, etc.; and in general the $2C$ candidate literals will define a dependency digraph whose structure yields important clues about the current subproblem. We can, for example, use Tarjan's algorithm to find the strong

components of that digraph, as mentioned after Theorem 7.1.1K. If some strong
component includes both l and $\bar{l}$, the current subproblem is unsatisfiable. Otherwise two literals of the same component are constrained to have the same value;
so we shall choose one literal from each of the $S \leq 2C$ strong components, and
use those choices as the actual candidates for lookahead.

Continuing our example, at this point we can use a nice trick to save
redundant computation, by extracting a *subforest* of the dependency digraph:

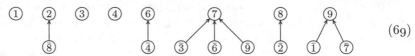

$$(69)$$

The relation $\bar{8} \longrightarrow 2$ means that whatever happens after asserting the literal
'2' will also happen after asserting '$\bar{8}$'; hence we need not repeat the steps for
'2' while studying '$\bar{8}$'. And similarly, each of the other subordinate literals '$\bar{1}$',
..., '$\bar{9}$' inherits the assertions of its parent in this hierarchy. Tarjan's algorithm
actually produces such a subforest with comparatively little extra work.

The nested structure of a forest also fits beautifully with "degrees of truth"
in our data structure, if we visit the S candidate literals in *preorder* of the
subforest, and if we successively assert each literal l at the truth degree that
corresponds to twice its position in *postorder*. For instance, (69) becomes the
following arrangement, which we shall call the "lookahead forest":

$$
\begin{array}{lcccccccccccccc}
\text{preorder} & 1 & 2 & \bar{8} & 3 & 4 & 6 & \bar{4} & 7 & \bar{3} & \bar{6} & \bar{9} & 8 & \bar{2} & 9 & \bar{1} & \bar{7} \\
2\cdot\text{postorder} & 2 & 6 & 4 & 8 & 10 & 14 & 12 & 22 & 16 & 18 & 20 & 26 & 24 & 32 & 28 & 30
\end{array}
\tag{70}
$$

A simulation of steps L4–L9 with $l \leftarrow 1$ and $T \leftarrow 2$ makes x_1 true at degree 2 (we
say that it's "2fixed" or "2true"); it also computes the score $H(1) \leftarrow h(\bar{2})h(\bar{3}) +
h(\bar{4})h(\bar{7})$, but spawns no other activity if Algorithm Y below isn't active. Sim-
ulation with $l \leftarrow 2$ and $T \leftarrow 6$ then 6fixes 2 and computes $H(2) \leftarrow h(\bar{1})h(\bar{3}) +
h(\bar{3})h(\bar{4}) + h(\bar{4})h(\bar{6})$; during this process x_1's value isn't seen, because it is less
than T. Things get interesting when $l \leftarrow \bar{8}$ and $T \leftarrow 4$: Now we 4fix $\bar{8}$, and we're
still able to see that x_2 is true because $6 > T$. So we save a little computation
by inheriting $H(2)$ and setting $H(\bar{8}) \leftarrow H(2) + h(4)h(6) + h(6)h(7) + h(7)h(9)$.

The real action begins to break through a few steps later, when we set $l \leftarrow \bar{4}$
and $T \leftarrow 12$. Then (62) will 12fix not only $\bar{4}$ but also 3, since $\bar{4} \longrightarrow 3$; and the
12truth of 3 will soon take us to the simulated step L8 with $u = \bar{6}$ and $v = \bar{9}$.
Aha: We 12fix $\bar{9}$, because 6 is 14true. Then we also 12fix the literals 7, 1, ..., and
reach a contradiction. *This contradiction shows that branching on $\bar{4}$ will lead to
a conflict*; hence the literal 4 must be true, if the current clauses are satisfiable.

Whenever the lookahead simulation of Algorithm X learns that some literal l
must be true, as in this example, it places l on the FORCE list and makes l *proto
true* (that is, true in context PT). A proto true literal will remain fixed true
throughout this round of lookahead, because all relevant values of T will be
less than PT. Later, Algorithm L will promote proto truth to near truth, and
ultimately to real truth — unless a contradiction arises. (And in the case of
waerden$(3, 3; 9)$, such a contradiction does in fact arise; see exercise 150.)

Why does the combination of preorder and postorder work so magically in (70)? It's because of a basic property of forests in general, which we noted for example in exercise 2.3.2–20: *If u and v are nodes of a forest, u is a proper ancestor of v if and only if u precedes v in preorder and u follows v in postorder.* Moreover, when we look ahead at candidate literals in this way, an important invariant relation is maintained on the R stack, namely that truth degrees never increase as we move from the bottom to the top:

$$\text{VAL}[|R_{j-1}|] \mid 1 \;\ge\; \text{VAL}[|R_j|], \qquad \text{for } 1 \le j < E. \tag{71}$$

Real truths appear at the bottom, then near truths, then proto truths, etc. For example, the stack at one point in the problem above contains seven literals,

$$
\begin{array}{ccccccccc}
j &=& 0 & 1 & 2 & 3 & 4 & 5 & 6 \\
R_j &=& \bar{5} & 6 & \bar{4} & 3 & \bar{9} & 7 & 1 \\
\text{VAL}[|R_j|] &=& \text{RT}{+}1 & 14 & 13 & 12 & 13 & 12 & 12
\end{array}
$$

One consequence is that the current visibility of truth values matches the recursive structure by which false literals are purged from ternary clauses.

The second phase of Algorithm X, after preselection of candidates, is called "nesting," because it constructs a lookahead forest analogous to (70). More precisely, it constructs a sequence of literals LL[j] and corresponding truth offsets LO[j], for $0 \le j < S$. It also sets up PARENT pointers to indicate the forest structure more directly; for example, with (69) we would have PARENT($\bar{8}$) $= 2$ and PARENT(2) $= \Lambda$.

The third phase, "exploration," now does the real work. It uses the lookahead forest to evaluate heuristics $H(l)$ for the candidate literals — and also (if it's lucky) to discover literals whose values are forced.

The heart of the exploration phase is a breadth-first search based on steps L5, L6, and L8. This routine propagates truth values of degree T and also computes w, the weight of new binary clauses that would be spawned by branching on l:

> Set $l_0 \leftarrow l$, $i \leftarrow w \leftarrow 0$, and $G \leftarrow E \leftarrow F$; perform (62);
> while $G < E$, set $L \leftarrow R_G$, $G \leftarrow G+1$, and
>   take account of (u,v) for all (u,v) in TIMP(L);
> generate new binary clauses $(\bar{l}_0 \vee W_k)$ for $0 \le k < i$.   (72)

Here "take account of (u,v)" means "if either u or v is fixed true (in context T), do nothing; if both u and v are fixed false, go to CONFLICT; if u is fixed false but v isn't fixed, set $W_i \leftarrow v$, $i \leftarrow i+1$, and perform (62) with $l \leftarrow v$; if v is fixed false but u isn't fixed, set $W_i \leftarrow u$, $i \leftarrow i+1$, and perform (62) with $l \leftarrow u$; if neither u nor v is fixed, set $w \leftarrow w + h(u)h(v)$."

Explanation: A ternary clause of the form $\bar{L} \vee u \vee v$, where L is fixed true and u is fixed false as a consequence of l_0 being fixed true, is called a "windfall." Such clauses are good news, because they imply that the *binary* clause $\bar{l}_0 \vee v$ must be satisfied in the current subproblem. Windfalls are recorded on a stack called W, and appended to the BIMP database at the end of (72).

The exploration phase also exploits an important fact called the *autarky principle*, which generalizes the notion of "pure literal" that we discussed above in connection with Algorithm A. An "autarky" for a SAT problem F is a set of strictly distinct literals $A = \{a_1, \ldots, a_t\}$ with the property that every clause of F either contains at least one literal of A or contains none of the literals of $\overline{A} = \{\bar{a}_1, \ldots, \bar{a}_t\}$. In other words, A satisfies every clause that A or $\overline{A}$ "touches."

An autarky is a self-sufficient system. Whenever A is an autarky, we can assume without loss of generality that all of its literals are actually true; for if F is satisfiable, the untouched clauses are satisfiable, and A tells us how to satisfy the touched ones. Step X9 of the following algorithm shows that we can detect certain autarkies easily while we're looking ahead.

Algorithm X (*Lookahead for Algorithm L*). This algorithm, which is invoked in step L2 of Algorithm L, uses the data structures of that algorithm together with additional arrays of its own to explore properties of the current subproblem. It discovers $U \geq 0$ literals whose values are forced, and puts them in the FORCE array. It terminates either by (i) satisfying all clauses; (ii) finding a contradiction; or (iii) computing heuristic scores $H(l)$ that will allow step L3 to choose a good literal for branching. In case (iii) it might also discover new binary clauses.

X1. [Satisfied?] If $F = n$, terminate happily (no variables are free).

X2. [Compile rough heuristics.] Set $N = n - F$. For each free literal l, set VAL$[l] \leftarrow 0$, and use (65) to compute a rough score $h(l)$.

X3. [Preselect candidates.] Let C be the current number of free variables that are "participants," and put them into the CAND array. If $C = 0$, set $C \leftarrow N$ and put *all* free variables into CAND; terminate happily, however, if all clauses are satisfied (see exercise 152). Give each variable x in CAND the rating $r(x) = h(x)h(\bar{x})$. Then while $C > 2C_{\max}$ (see (66)), delete all elements of CAND whose rating is less than the mean rating; but terminate this loop if no elements are actually deleted. Finally, if $C > C_{\max}$, reduce C to $C_{\max}$ by retaining only top-ranked candidates. (See exercise 153.)

X4. [Nest the candidates.] Construct a lookahead forest, represented in LL$[j]$ and LO$[j]$ for $0 \leq j < S$ and by PARENT pointers (see exercise 155).

X5. [Prepare to explore.] Set $U' \leftarrow j' \leftarrow$ BASE $\leftarrow j \leftarrow 0$ and CONFLICT $\leftarrow$ X13.

X6. [Choose l for lookahead.] Set $l \leftarrow$ LL$[j]$ and $T \leftarrow$ BASE + LO$[j]$. Set $H(l) \leftarrow H(\text{PARENT}(l))$, where $H(\Lambda) = 0$. If l is not fixed in context T, go to X8. Otherwise, if l is fixed false but not proto false, do step X12 with $l \leftarrow \bar{l}$.

X7. [Move to next.] If $U > U'$, set $U' \leftarrow U$ and $j' \leftarrow j$. Then set $j \leftarrow j + 1$. If $j = S$, set $j \leftarrow 0$ and BASE $\leftarrow$ BASE + $2S$. Terminate normally if $j = j'$, or if $j = 0$ and BASE + $2S \geq$ PT (beware of overflow). Otherwise return to X6.

X8. [Compute sharper heuristic.] Perform (72). Then if $w > 0$, set $H(l_0) \leftarrow H(l_0) + w$ and go to X10.

X9. [Exploit an autarky.] If $H(l_0) = 0$, do step X12 with $l \leftarrow l_0$. Otherwise generate the new binary clause $l_0 \vee \neg\text{PARENT}(l_0)$. (Exercise 166 explains why.)

X10. [Optionally look deeper.] Perform Algorithm Y below.

X11. [Exploit necessary assignments.] Do step X12 for all literals $l \in \text{BIMP}(\bar{l}_0)$ that are fixed true but not proto true. Then go to X7. (See exercise 167.)

X12. [Force l.] Set $\text{FORCE}[U] \leftarrow l$, $U \leftarrow U + 1$, $T' \leftarrow T$, and perform (72) with $T \leftarrow \text{PT}$. Then set $T \leftarrow T'$. (This step is a subroutine, used by other steps.)

X13. [Recover from conflict.] If $T < \text{PT}$, do step X12 with $l \leftarrow \bar{l}_0$ and go to X7. Otherwise terminate with a contradiction. ∎

Notice that, in steps X5–X7, this algorithm proceeds cyclically through the forest, continuing to look ahead until completing a pass in which no new forced literals are found. The **BASE** address of truth values continues to grow, if necessary, but it isn't allowed to become too close to **PT**.

*__Looking even further ahead.__ If it's a good idea to look one step ahead, maybe it's a better idea to look *two* steps ahead. Of course that's a somewhat scary proposition, because our data structures are already pretty stretched; and besides, double lookahead might take way too much time. Nevertheless, there's a way to pull it off, and to make Algorithm L run even faster on many problems.

Algorithm X looks at the immediate consequences of assuming that some literal l_0 is true. Algorithm Y, which is launched in step X10, goes further out on that limb, and investigates what would happen if *another* literal, $\hat{l}_0$, were also true. The goal is to detect branches that die off early, allowing us to discover new implications of l_0 or even to conclude that l_0 must be false.

For this purpose Algorithm Y stakes out an area of truth space between the current context T and a degree of truth called "double truth" or **DT**, which is defined in step Y2. The size of this area is determined by a parameter Y, which is typically less than 10. The same lookahead forest is used to give relative truth degrees below **DT**. Double truth is less trustworthy than proto truth, **PT**; but literals that are fixed at level **DT** are known to be conditionally true ("Dtrue") or conditionally false ("Dfalse") under the hypothesis that l_0 is true.

Going back to our example of $waerden(3, 3; 9)$, the scenario described above was based on the assumption that double lookahead was not done. Actually, however, further activity by Algorithm Y will usually take place after $H(1)$ has been set to $h(\bar{2})h(\bar{3}) + h(\bar{4})h(\bar{7})$. The value of **DT** will be set to 130, assuming that $Y = 8$, because $S = 8$. Literal 1 will become Dtrue. Looking then at 2 will 6fix 2; and that will 6fix $\bar{3}$ because of the clause $\bar{1}2\bar{3}$. Then $\bar{3}$ will 6fix 4 and 7, contradicting $\bar{1}4\bar{7}$ and causing 2 to become Dfalse. Other literals also will soon become Dtrue or Dfalse, leading to a contradiction; and that contradiction will allow Algorithm Y to make literal 1 proto false before Algorithm X has even begun to look ahead at literal 2.

The main loop of double lookahead is analogous to (72), but it's simpler, because we're further removed from reality:

$$\begin{aligned}
&\text{Set } \hat{l}_0 \leftarrow l \text{ and } G \leftarrow E \leftarrow F; \text{ perform (62);} \\
&\text{while } G < E, \text{ set } L \leftarrow R_G, \, G \leftarrow G + 1, \text{ and} \\
&\quad \text{take account of } (u, v) \text{ for all } (u, v) \text{ in } \text{TIMP}(L).
\end{aligned} \qquad (73)$$

Now "take account of (u, v)" means "if either u or v is fixed true (in context T), or if neither u nor v is fixed, do nothing; if both u and v are fixed false, go to CONFLICT; if u is fixed false but v isn't fixed, perform (62) with $l \leftarrow v$; if v is fixed false but u isn't fixed, perform (62) with $l \leftarrow u$."

Since double-looking is costly, we want to try it only when there's a fairly good chance that it will be helpful, namely when $H(l_0)$ is large. But how large is large enough? The proper threshold depends on the problem being solved: Some sets of clauses are handled more quickly by double-looking, while others are immune to such insights. Marijn Heule and Hans van Maaren [LNCS 4501 (2007), 258–271] have developed an elegant feedback mechanism that automatically tunes itself to the characteristics of the problem at hand: Let τ be a "trigger," initially 0. Step Y1 allows double-look only if $H(l_0) > \tau$; otherwise τ is decreased to $\beta\tau$, where β is a damping factor (typically 0.999), so that double-looking will become more attractive. On the other hand if double-look doesn't find a contradiction that makes l_0 proto false, the trigger is raised to $H(l_0)$ in step Y6.

Algorithm Y (*Double lookahead for Algorithm X*). This algorithm, invoked in step X10, uses the same data structures (and a few more) to look ahead more deeply. Parameters β and Y are explained above. Initially DFAIL$(l) = 0$ for all l.

Y1. [Filter.] Terminate if DFAIL(l_0) = ISTAMP, or if $T + 2S(Y + 1) >$ PT. Otherwise, if $H(l_0) \leq \tau$, set $\tau \leftarrow \beta\tau$ and terminate.

Y2. [Initialize.] Set BASE $\leftarrow T - 2$, LBASE $\leftarrow$ BASE $+ 2S \cdot Y$, DT $\leftarrow$ LBASE $+$ LO$[j]$, $i \leftarrow \hat{j}' \leftarrow \hat{j} \leftarrow 0$, $E \leftarrow F$, and CONFLICT $\leftarrow$ Y8. Perform (62) with $l \leftarrow l_0$ and $T \leftarrow$ DT.

Y3. [Choose l for double look.] Set $l \leftarrow$ LL$[\hat{j}]$ and $T \leftarrow$ BASE $+$ LO$[\hat{j}]$. If l is not fixed in context T, go to Y5. Otherwise, if l is fixed false but not Dfalse, do step Y7 with $l \leftarrow \bar{l}$.

Y4. [Move to next.] Set $\hat{j} \leftarrow \hat{j} + 1$. If $\hat{j} = S$, set $\hat{j} \leftarrow 0$ and BASE $\leftarrow$ BASE $+ 2S$. Go to Y6 if $\hat{j}' = \hat{j}$, or if $\hat{j} = 0$ and BASE = LBASE. Otherwise return to Y3.

Y5. [Look ahead.] Perform (73), and return to Y4 (if no conflict arises).

Y6. [Finish.] Generate new binary clauses $(\bar{l}_0 \lor W_k)$ for $0 \leq k < i$. Then set BASE $\leftarrow$ LBASE, $T \leftarrow$ DT, $\tau \leftarrow H(l_0)$, DFAIL$(l_0) \leftarrow$ ISTAMP, CONFLICT $\leftarrow$ X13, and terminate.

Y7. [Assume also l.] Set $\hat{j}' \leftarrow \hat{j}$, $T' \leftarrow T$, and perform (73) with $T \leftarrow$ DT. Then set $T \leftarrow T'$, $W_i \leftarrow \bar{l}_0$, $i \leftarrow i + 1$. (This step is a subroutine.)

Y8. [Recover from conflict.] If $T <$ DT, do step Y7 with $l \leftarrow \neg$LL$[\hat{j}]$ and go to Y4. Otherwise set BASE $\leftarrow$ LBASE, CONFLICT $\leftarrow$ X13, and exit to X13. ∎

Some quantitative statistics will help to ground these algorithms in reality: When Algorithm L was let loose on $rand(3, 2062, 500, 314)$, a problem with 500 variables and 2062 random ternary clauses, it proved unsatisfiability after making 684,433,234,661 memory accesses and constructing a search tree of 9,530,489 nodes. Exercise 173 explains what would have happened if various parts of the algorithm had been disabled. None of the other SAT solvers we shall discuss are able to handle such large random problems in a reasonable amount of time.

Random satisfiability. There seems to be no easy way to analyze the satisfiability problem under random conditions. In fact, the basic question "How many random clauses of 3SAT on n variables do we need to consider, on the average, before they can't all be satisfied?" is a famous unsolved research problem.

From a practical standpoint this question isn't as relevant as the analogous questions were when we studied algorithms for sorting or searching, because real-world instances of 3SAT tend to have highly *non*random clauses. Deviations from randomness in combinatorial algorithms often have a dramatic effect on running time, while methods of sorting and searching generally stay reasonably close to their expected behavior. Thus a focus on randomness can be misleading. On the other hand, random SAT clauses do serve as a nice, clean model, so they give us insights into what goes on in Boolean territory. Furthermore the mathematical issues are of great interest in their own right. And fortunately, much of the basic theory is in fact elementary and easy to understand. So let's take a look at it.

Exercise 180 shows that random satisfiability can be analyzed *exactly*, when there are at most five variables. We might as well start there, because the "tiny" 5-variable case is still large enough to shed some light on the bigger picture. When there are n variables and k literals per clause, the number N of possible clauses that involve k different variables is clearly $2^k \binom{n}{k}$: There are $\binom{n}{k}$ ways to choose the variables, and 2^k ways to either complement or not. So we have, for example, $N = 2^3 \binom{5}{3} = 80$ possible clauses in a 3SAT problem on 5 variables.

Let q_m be the probability that m of those clauses, distinct but otherwise selected at random, are satisfiable. Thus $q_m = Q_m / \binom{N}{m}$, where Q_m is the number of ways to choose m of the N clauses so that at least one Boolean vector $x = x_1 \ldots x_n$ satisfies them all. Figure 83 illustrates these probabilities when $k = 3$ and $n = 5$. Suppose we're being given distinct random clauses one by one. According to Fig. 83, the chances are better than 77% that we'll still be able to satisfy them after 20 different clauses have been received, because $q_{20} \approx 0.776$. But by the time we've accumulated 30 of the 80 clauses, the chance of satisfiability has dropped to $q_{30} \approx 0.179$; and after ten more we reach $q_{40} \approx 0.016$.

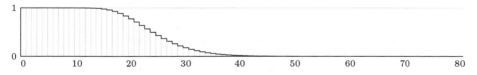

Fig. 83. The probability q_m that m distinct clauses of 3SAT on 5 variables are simultaneously satisfiable, for $0 \leq m \leq 80$.

The illustration makes it appear as if $q_m = 1$ for $m < 15$, say, and as if $q_m = 0$ for $m > 55$. But q_8 is actually *less* than 1, because of (6); exercise 179 gives the exact value. And q_{70} is *greater* than 0, because $Q_{70} = 32$; indeed, every Boolean vector x satisfies exactly $(2^k - 1)\binom{n}{k} = (1 - 2^{-k})N$ of the N possible k-clauses, so it's no surprise that 70 noncontradictory 3-clauses on 5 variables can be found. Of course those clauses will hardly ever be the first 70 received, in a random situation. The actual value of q_{70} is $32/1646492110120 \approx 2 \times 10^{-11}$.

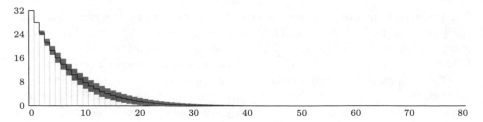

Fig. 84. The total number T_m of different Boolean vectors $x = x_1 \ldots x_5$ that simultaneously satisfy m distinct clauses of 3SAT on 5 variables, for $0 \le m \le 80$.

Figure 84 portrays the same process from another standpoint: It shows *in how many ways* a random set of m clauses can be satisfied. This value, T_m, is a random variable whose mean is indicated in black, surrounded by a gray region that shows the mean plus-or-minus the standard deviation. For example, T_0 is always 32, and T_1 is always 28; but T_2 is either 24, 25, or 26, and it takes these values with the respective probabilities $(2200, 480, 480)/3160$. Thus the mean for $m = 2$ is ≈ 24.5, and the standard deviation is ≈ 0.743.

When $m = 20$, we know from Fig. 83 that T_{20} is nonzero more than 77% of the time; yet Fig. 84 shows that $T_{20} \approx 1.47 \pm 1.17$. (Here the notation $\mu \pm \sigma$ stands for the mean value μ with standard deviation σ.) It turns out, in fact, that 20 random clauses are *uniquely satisfiable*, with $T_{20} = 1$, more than 33% of the time; and the probability that $T_{20} > 4$ is only 0.013. With 30 clauses, satisfiability gets dicier and dicier: $T_{30} \approx 0.20 \pm 0.45$; indeed, T_{30} is less than 2, more than 98% of the time — although it can be as high as 11 if the clause-provider is being nice to us. By the time 40 clauses are reached, the odds that T_{40} exceeds 1 are less than 1 in 4700. Figure 85 shows the probability that $T_m = 1$ as m varies.

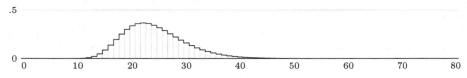

Fig. 85. $\Pr(T_m = 1)$, the probability that m distinct clauses of 3SAT on 5 variables are uniquely satisfiable, for $0 \le m \le 80$.

Let P be the number of clauses that have been received when we're first unable to satisfy them all. Thus we have $P = m$ with probability p_m, where $p_m = q_{m-1} - q_m$ is the probability that $m - 1$ random clauses are satisfiable but m are not. These probabilities are illustrated in Fig. 86. Is it surprising that Figs. 85 and 86 look roughly the same? (See exercise 183.)

The expected "stopping time," $\mathrm{E}\,P$, is by definition equal to $\sum_m m p_m$; and it's not difficult to see, for example by using the technique of summation by parts (exercise 1.2.7–10), that we can compute it by summing the probabilities in Fig. 83:

$$\mathrm{E}\,P = \sum_m q_m. \tag{74}$$

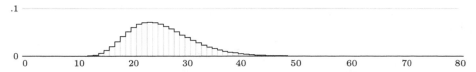

Fig. 86. The stopping time probabilities, p_m, that m distinct clauses of 3SAT on 5 variables have just become unsatisfiable, for $0 \le m \le 80$.

The variance of P, namely $\mathrm{E}(P - \mathrm{E}\,P)^2 = (\mathrm{E}\,P^2) - (\mathrm{E}\,P)^2$, also has a simple expression in terms of the q's, because

$$\mathrm{E}\,P^2 \;=\; \sum_m (2m+1)q_m. \tag{75}$$

In Figs. 83 and 86 we have $\mathrm{E}\,P \approx 25.22$, with variance ≈ 35.73.

So far we've been focusing our attention on 3SAT problems, but the same ideas apply also to kSAT for other clause sizes k. Figure 87 shows exact results for the probabilities when $n = 5$ and $1 \le k \le 4$. Larger values of k give clauses that are easier to satisfy, so they increase the stopping time. With five variables the typical stopping times for random 1SAT, 2SAT, 3SAT, and 4SAT turn out to be respectively $4.06 + 1.19$, $11.60 + 3.04$, 25.22 ± 5.98, and 43.39 ± 7.62. In general if $P_{k,n}$ is the stopping time for kSAT on n variables, we let

$$S_{k,n} \;=\; \mathrm{E}\,P_{k,n} \tag{76}$$

be its expected value.

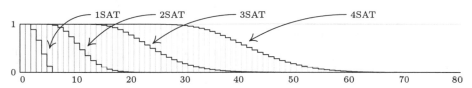

Fig. 87. Extension of Fig. 83 to clauses of other sizes.

Our discussions so far have been limited in another way too: We've been assuming that m *distinct* clauses are being presented to a SAT solver for solution. In practice, however, it's much easier to generate clauses by allowing repetitions, so that every clause is chosen without any dependence on the past history. In other words, there's a more natural way to approach random satisfiability, by assuming that N^m possible *ordered sequences* of clauses are equally likely after m steps, not that we have $\binom{N}{m}$ equally likely *sets* of clauses.

Let $\hat{q}_m$ be the probability that m random clauses $C_1 \wedge \cdots \wedge C_m$ are satisfiable, where each C_j is randomly chosen from among the $N = 2^k \binom{n}{k}$ possibilities in a kSAT problem on n variables. Figure 88 illustrates these probabilities in the case $k = 3$, $n = 5$; notice that we always have $\hat{q}_m \ge q_m$. If N is large while m is small, it's clear that $\hat{q}_m$ will be very close to q_m, because repeated clauses are unlikely in such a case. Still, we must keep in mind that q_N is always zero, while $\hat{q}_m$ is *never* zero. Furthermore, the "birthday paradox" discussed in Section 6.4 warns

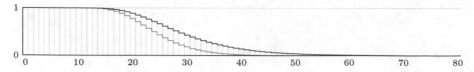

Fig. 88. Random 3SAT on 5 variables when the clauses are sampled with replacement. The probabilities $\hat{q}_m$ are shown with a black line; the smaller probabilities q_m of Fig. 83 are shown in gray.

us that repetitions aren't as rare as we might expect. The deviations of $\hat{q}_m$ from q_m are particularly noticeable in small cases such as the scenario of Fig. 88.

In any event, there's a direct way to compute $\hat{q}_m$ from the probabilities q_t and the value of N (see exercise 184):

$$\hat{q}_m = \sum_{t=0}^{N} \left\{ {m \atop t} \right\} t!\, q_t \binom{N}{t} \Big/ N^m. \tag{77}$$

And there are surprisingly simple formulas analogous to (74) and (75) for the stopping time $\widehat{P}$, where $\hat{p}_m = \hat{q}_{m-1} - \hat{q}_m$, as shown in exercise 186:

$$\mathrm{E}\,\widehat{P} = \sum_{m=0}^{N-1} \frac{N}{N-m}\, q_m; \tag{78}$$

$$\mathrm{E}\,\widehat{P}^2 = \sum_{m=0}^{N-1} \frac{N}{N-m}\, q_m \left(1 + 2\left(\frac{N}{N-1} + \cdots + \frac{N}{N-m}\right)\right). \tag{79}$$

These formulas prove that the expected behavior of $\widehat{P}$ is very much like that of P, if q_m is small whenever m/N isn't small. In the case $k = 3$ and $n = 5$, the typical stopping times $\widehat{P} = 30.58 \pm 9.56$ are significantly larger than those of P; but we are mostly interested in cases where n is large and where $\hat{q}_m$ is essentially indistinguishable from q_m. In order to indicate plainly that the probability $\hat{q}_m$ depends on k and n as well as on m, we shall denote it henceforth by $S_k(m, n)$:

$$S_k(m, n) = \Pr(m \text{ random clauses of } k\mathrm{SAT} \text{ are satisfiable}), \tag{80}$$

where the m clauses are "sampled with replacement" (they needn't be distinct). Suitable pseudorandom clauses $rand(k, m, n, seed)$ can easily be generated.

Exact formulas appear to be out of reach when $n > 5$, but we can make empirical tests. For example, extensive experiments on random 3SAT problems by B. Selman, D. G. Mitchell, and H. J. Levesque [*Artificial Intelligence* **81** (1996), 17–29] showed a dramatic drop in the chances of satisfiability when the number of clauses exceeds about $4.27n$. This "phase transition" becomes much sharper as n grows (see Fig. 89).

Similar behavior occurs for random kSAT, and this phenomenon has spawned an enormous amount of research aimed at evaluating the so-called *satisfiability thresholds*

$$\alpha_k = \lim_{n\to\infty} S_{k,n}/n. \tag{81}$$

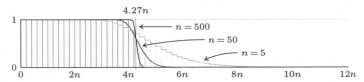

Fig. 89. Empirical probability data shows that random 3SAT problems rapidly become unsatisfiable when there are more than $\alpha_3 n$ clauses, if n is large enough.

Indeed, we can obtain quite difficult kSAT problems by generating approximately $\alpha_k n$ random k-clauses, using empirically observed estimates of α_k. If n is large, the running time for random 3SAT with $4.3n$ clauses is typically orders of magnitude larger than it is when the number of clauses is $4n$ or $4.6n$. (And still tougher problems arise in rare instances when we have, say, $3.9n$ clauses that happen to be *un*satisfiable.)

Strictly speaking, however, nobody has been able to prove that the so-called constants α_k actually exist, for all k! The empirical evidence is overwhelming; but rigorous proofs for $k = 3$ have so far only established the bounds

$$\liminf_{n\to\infty} S_{3,n}/n \geq 3.52; \qquad \limsup_{n\to\infty} S_{3,n}/n \leq 4.49. \qquad (82)$$

[See M. Hajiaghayi and G. B. Sorkin, arXiv:math/0310193 [math.CO] (2003), 8 pages; A. C. Kaporis, L. M. Kirousis, and E. G. Lalas, *Random Struct. & Alg.* **28** (2006), 444–480; J. Díaz, L. Kirousis, D. Mitsche, and X. Pérez-Giménez, *Theoretical Comp. Sci.* **410** (2009), 2920–2934.] A "sharp threshold" result has been established by E. Friedgut [*J. American Math. Soc.* **12** (1999), 1017–1045, 1053–1054], who proved the existence for $k \geq 2$ of functions $\alpha_k(n)$ with

$$\lim_{n\to\infty} S_k\big(\lfloor(\alpha_k(n) - \epsilon)n\rfloor, n\big) = 1, \qquad \lim_{n\to\infty} S_k\big(\lfloor(\alpha_k(n) + \epsilon)n\rfloor, n\big) = 0, \qquad (83)$$

when ϵ is any positive number. But those functions might not approach a limit. They might, for example, fluctuate periodically, like the "wobble function" that we encountered in Eq. 5.2.2–(47).

The current best guess for α_3, based on heuristics of the "survey propagation" technique to be discussed below, is that $\alpha_3 = 4.26675\pm0.00015$ [S. Mertens, M. Mézard, and R. Zecchina, *Random Structures & Algorithms* **28** (2006), 340–373]. Similarly, it appears reasonable to believe that $\alpha_4 \approx 9.931$, $\alpha_5 \approx 21.12$, $\alpha_6 \approx 43.37$, $\alpha_7 \approx 87.79$. The α's grow as $\Theta(2^k)$ (see exercise 195); and they *are* known to be constant when k is sufficiently large [see J. Ding, A. Sly, and N. Sun, *STOC* **47** (2015), 59–68].

Analysis of random 2SAT. Although nobody knows how to prove that random 3SAT problems almost always become unsatisfiable when the number of clauses reaches $\approx 4.27n$, the corresponding question for 2SAT does have a nice answer: *The satisfiability threshold α_2 equals* 1. For example, when the author first tried 1000 random 2SAT problems with a million variables, 999 of them turned out to be satisfiable when there were 960,000 clauses, while all were unsatisfiable when the number of clauses rose to 1,040,000. Figure 90 shows how this transition becomes sharper as n increases.

Fig. 90. Empirical satisfaction probabilities for 2SAT with approximately n random clauses. (When $n = 100$, the probability doesn't become negligible until more than roughly 180 clauses have been generated.)

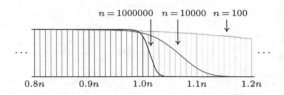

The fact that $S_{2,n} \approx n$ was discovered in 1991 by V. Chvátal and B. Reed [*FOCS* **33** (1992), 620–627], and the same result was obtained independently at about the same time by A. Goerdt and by W. Fernandez de la Vega [see *J. Comp. Syst. Sci.* **53** (1996), 469–486; *Theor. Comp. Sci.* **265** (2001), 131–146].

The study of this phenomenon is instructive, because it relies on properties of the digraph that characterizes all instances of 2SAT. Furthermore, the proof below provides an excellent illustration of the "first and second moment principles," equations MPR–(21) and MPR–(22). Armed with those principles, we're ready to derive the 2SAT threshold:

Theorem C. *Let c be a fixed constant. Then*

$$\lim_{n \to \infty} S_2\big(\lfloor cn \rfloor, n\big) = \begin{cases} 1, & \text{if } c < 1; \\ 0, & \text{if } c > 1. \end{cases} \tag{84}$$

Proof. Every 2SAT problem corresponds to an *implication digraph* on the literals, with arcs $\bar{l} \longrightarrow l'$ and $\bar{l}' \longrightarrow l$ for each clause $l \vee l'$. We know from Theorem 7.1.1K that a set of 2SAT clauses is satisfiable if and only if no strong component of its implication digraph contains both x and $\bar{x}$ for some variable x. That digraph has $2m = 2\lfloor cn \rfloor$ arcs and $2n$ vertices. If it were a random digraph, well-known theorems of Karp (which we shall study in Section 7.4.4) would imply that only $O(\log n)$ vertices are reachable from any given vertex when $c < 1$, but that there is a unique "giant strong component" of size $\Omega(n)$ when $c > 1$.

The digraph that arises from random 2SAT isn't truly random, because its arcs come in pairs, $u \longrightarrow v$ and $\bar{v} \longrightarrow \bar{u}$. But intuitively we can expect that similar behavior will apply to digraphs that are just halfway random. For example, when the author generated a random 2SAT problem with $n = 1000000$ and $m = .99n$, the resulting digraph had only two complementary pairs of strong components with more than one vertex, and their sizes were only 2, 2 and 7, 7; so the clauses were easily satisfiable. Adding another $.01n$ clauses didn't increase the number of nontrivial strong components, and the problem remained satisfiable. But another experiment with $m = n = 1000000$ yielded a strong component of size 420, containing 210 variables and their complements; that problem was unsatisfiable.

Based on a similar intuition into the underlying structure, Chvátal and Reed introduced the following "snares and snakes" approach to the proof of Theorem C: Let's say that an *s-chain* is any sequence of s strictly distinct literals; thus there are $2^s n^{\underline{s}}$ possible s-chains. Every s-chain C corresponds to clauses

$$(\bar{l}_1 \vee l_2), \ (\bar{l}_2 \vee l_3), \ \ldots, \ (\bar{l}_{s-1} \vee l_s), \tag{85}$$

which in turn correspond to two paths

$$l_1 \longrightarrow l_2 \longrightarrow l_3 \longrightarrow \cdots \longrightarrow l_s \quad \text{and} \quad \bar{l}_s \longrightarrow \cdots \longrightarrow \bar{l}_3 \longrightarrow \bar{l}_2 \longrightarrow \bar{l}_1 \qquad (86)$$

in the digraph. An s-*snare* $(C; t, u)$ consists of an s-chain C and two indices t and u, where $1 < t \le s$ and $1 \le |u| < s$; it specifies the clauses (85) together with

$$(l_t \vee l_1) \quad \text{and} \quad (\bar{l}_s \vee l_u) \text{ if } u > 0, \ (\bar{l}_s \vee \bar{l}_{-u}) \text{ if } u < 0, \qquad (87)$$

representing $\bar{l}_t \longrightarrow l_1$ and either $l_s \longrightarrow l_{|u|}$ or $l_s \longrightarrow \bar{l}_{|u|}$. The number of possible s-snares is $2^{s+1}(s-1)^2 n^{\underline{s}}$. Their clauses are rarely all present when m is small.

Exercise 200 explains how to use these definitions to prove Theorem C in the case $c < 1$. First we show that *every unsatisfiable 2SAT formula contains all the clauses of at least one snare.* Then, if we define the binary random variable

$$X(C; t, u) = [\text{all clauses of } (C; t, u) \text{ are present}], \qquad (88)$$

it isn't difficult to prove that the snares of every s-chain C are unlikely:

$$\mathrm{E}\,X(C; t, u) \le m^{s+1}/\big(2n(n-1)\big)^{s+1}. \qquad (89)$$

Finally, letting X be the sum of $X(C; t, u)$ over all snares, we obtain

$$\mathrm{E}\,X = \sum \mathrm{E}\,X(C; t, u) \le \sum_{s \ge 0} 2^{s+1} s(s-1) n^{\underline{s}} \left(\frac{m}{2n(n-1)}\right)^{s+1} = \frac{2}{n}\left(\frac{m}{n-1-m}\right)^3$$

by Eq. 1.2.9–(20). This formula actually establishes a stronger form of (84), because it shows that $\mathrm{E}\,X$ is only $O(n^{-1/4})$ when $m = n - n^{3/4} > cn$. Thus

$$S_2\big(\lfloor n - n^{3/4}\rfloor, n\big) \ge \Pr(X = 0) = 1 - \Pr(X > 0) \ge 1 - O(n^{-1/4}) \qquad (90)$$

by the first moment principle.

The other half of Theorem C can be proved by using the concept of a t-*snake*, which is the special case $(C; t, -t)$ of a $(2t-1)$-snare. In other words, given any chain $(l_1, \ldots, l_t, \ldots, l_{2t-1})$, with $s = 2t - 1$ and l_t in the middle, a t-snake generates the clauses (85) together with $(l_t \vee l_1)$ and $(\bar{l}_s \vee \bar{l}_t)$. When $t = 5$, for example, and $(l_1, \ldots, l_{2t-1}) = (x_1, \ldots, x_9)$, the $2t = 10$ clauses are

$$5\bar{1}, \ \bar{1}2, \ \bar{2}3, \ \bar{3}4, \ \bar{4}5, \ \bar{5}6, \ \bar{6}7, \ \bar{7}8, \ \bar{8}9, \ \bar{9}\bar{5},$$

and they correspond to 20 arcs that loop around to form a strong component as shown here. We will prove that, when $c > 1$ in (84), the digraph almost always contains such impediments to satisfiability.

Given a $(2t-1)$-chain C, where the parameter t will be chosen later, let

$$X_C = [\text{each clause of } (C; t, -t) \text{ occurs exactly once}]. \qquad (91)$$

The expected value $\mathrm{E}\,X_C$ is clearly $f(2t)$, where

$$f(r) = m^{\underline{r}}\big(2n(n-1) - r\big)^{m-r}/\big(2n(n-1)\big)^m \qquad (92)$$

is the probability that r specific clauses occur once each. Notice that

$$f(r) = \left(\frac{m}{2n(n-1)}\right)^r \left(1 + O\left(\frac{r^2}{m}\right) + O\left(\frac{rm}{n^2}\right)\right); \qquad (93)$$

thus the relative error will be $O(t^2/n)$ if $m = \Theta(n)$ as $n \to \infty$.

Now let $X = \sum X_C$, summed over all $R = 2^{2t-1}n^{2t-1}$ possible t-snakes C; thus $E X = Rf(2t)$. We want to show that $\Pr(X > 0)$ is very nearly 1, using the second moment principle; so we want to show that the expectation $E X^2 = E\left(\sum_C X_C\right)\left(\sum_D X_D\right) = \sum_C \sum_D E X_C X_D$ is small. The key observation is that

$$E X_C X_D = f(4t - r) \qquad \text{if } C \text{ and } D \text{ have exactly } r \text{ clauses in common.} \quad (94)$$

Let p_r be the probability that a randomly chosen t-snake has exactly r clauses in common with the fixed snake $(x_1, \ldots, x_{2t-1})$. Then

$$\frac{E X^2}{(E X)^2} = \frac{R^2 \sum_{r=0}^{2t} p_r f(4t - r)}{R^2 f(2t)^2}$$

$$= \sum_{r=0}^{2t} p_r \frac{f(4t - r)}{f(2t)^2} = \sum_{r=0}^{2t} p_r \left(\frac{2n(n-1)}{m}\right)^r \left(1 + O\left(\frac{t^2}{n}\right)\right). \quad (95)$$

By studying the interaction of snakes (see exercise 201) one can prove that

$$(2n)^r p_r = O(t^4/n) + O(t)[r \ge t] + O(n)[r = 2t], \qquad \text{for } 1 \le r \le 2t. \quad (96)$$

Finally then, as explained in exercise 202, we can choose $t = \lfloor n^{1/5} \rfloor$ and $m = \lfloor n + n^{5/6} \rfloor$, to deduce a sharper form of (84) when $c > 1$:

$$S_2\left(\lfloor n + n^{5/6} \rfloor, n\right) = O(n^{-1/30}). \quad (97)$$

(Deep breath.) Theorem C is proved. ∎

Much more precise results have been derived by B. Bollobás, C. Borgs, J. T. Chayes, J. H. Kim, and D. B. Wilson, in *Random Structures & Algorithms* **18** (2001), 201–256. For example, they showed that

$$S_2\left(\lfloor n - n^{3/4} \rfloor, n\right) = \exp\left(-\Theta(n^{-1/4})\right); \quad S_2\left(\lfloor n + n^{3/4} \rfloor, n\right) = \exp\left(-\Theta(n^{1/4})\right). \quad (98)$$

Resolution. The backtracking process of Algorithms A, B, D, and L is closely connected to a logical proof procedure called *resolution*. Starting with a family of clauses called "axioms," there's a simple rule by which new clauses can be derived from this given set: Whenever both $x \vee A'$ and $\bar{x} \vee A''$ are in our repertoire of clauses, we're allowed to derive the "resolvent" clause $A = A' \vee A''$, denoted by $(x \vee A') \diamond (\bar{x} \vee A'')$. (See exercises 218 and 219.)

A *proof by resolution* consists of a directed acyclic graph (dag) whose vertices are labeled with clauses in the following way: (i) Every source vertex is labeled with an axiom. (ii) Every other vertex has in-degree 2. (iii) If the predecessors of vertex v are v' and v'', the label of v is $C(v) = C(v') \diamond C(v'')$.

When such a dag has a sink vertex labeled A, we call it a "resolution proof of A"; and if A is the empty clause, the dag is also called a "resolution refutation."

The dag of a proof by resolution can be expanded to a binary tree, by replicating any vertex that has out-degree greater than 1. Such a tree is said to be *regular* if no path from the root to a leaf uses the same variable twice to form a resolvent. For example, Fig. 91 is a regular resolution tree that refutes Rivest's unsatisfiable axioms (6). All arcs in this tree are directed upwards.

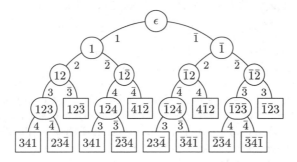

Fig. 91. One way to derive ϵ by resolving the inconsistent clauses (6).

Notice that Fig. 91 is essentially identical to Fig. 82 on page 217, the backtrack tree by which Algorithm D discovers that the clauses of (6) are unsatisfiable. In fact this similarity is no coincidence: *Every backtrack tree that records the behavior of Algorithm D on a set of unsatisfiable clauses corresponds to a regular resolution tree that refutes those axioms,* unless Algorithm D makes an unnecessary branch. (An unnecessary branch occurs if the algorithm tries $x \leftarrow 0$ and $x \leftarrow 1$ without using their consequences to discover an unsatisfiable subset of axioms.) Conversely, every regular refutation tree corresponds to a sequence of choices by which a backtrack-based SAT solver could prove unsatisfiability.

The reason behind this correspondence isn't hard to see. Suppose both values of x need to be tried in order to prove unsatisfiability. When we set $x \leftarrow 0$ in one branch of the backtrack tree, we replace the original clauses F by $F \mid \bar{x}$, as in (54). The key point is that *we can prove the empty clause by resolution from $F \mid \bar{x}$ if and only if we can prove x by resolution from F without resolving on x.* (See exercise 224.) Similarly, setting $x \leftarrow 1$ corresponds to changing the clauses from F to $F \mid x$.

Consequently, if F is an inconsistent set of clauses that has no short refutation tree, Algorithm D cannot conclude that those clauses are unsatisfiable unless it runs for a long time. Neither can Algorithm L, in spite of enhanced lookahead.

R. Impagliazzo and P. Pudlák [*SODA* **11** (2000), 128–136] have introduced an appealing *Prover–Delayer game,* with which it's relatively easy to demonstrate that certain sets of unsatisfiable clauses require large refutation trees. The Prover names a variable x, and the Delayer responds by saying either $x \leftarrow 0$ or $x \leftarrow 1$ or $x \leftarrow *$. In the latter case the Prover gets to decide the value of x; but the Delayer scores one point. The game ends when the current assignments have falsified at least one clause. If the Delayer has a strategy that guarantees a score of at least m points, exercise 226 shows that every refutation tree has at least 2^m

leaves; hence at least $2^m - 1$ resolutions must be done, and every backtrack-based solver needs $\Omega(2^m)$ operations to declare the clauses unsatisfiable.

We can apply their game, for example, to the following interesting clauses:

$$(\bar{x}_{jj}), \qquad\qquad \text{for } 1 \le j \le m; \qquad\qquad\qquad (99)$$

$$(\bar{x}_{ij} \vee \bar{x}_{jk} \vee x_{ik}), \qquad \text{for } 1 \le i,j,k \le m; \qquad\qquad (100)$$

$$(x_{j1} \vee x_{j2} \vee \cdots \vee x_{jm}), \qquad \text{for } 1 \le j \le m. \qquad\qquad (101)$$

There are m^2 variables x_{jk}, for $1 \le j,k \le m$, which we can regard as the incidence matrix for a binary relation '$j \prec k$'. With this formulation, (99) says that the relation is irreflexive, and (100) says that it's transitive; thus, (99) and (100) amount to saying that $j \prec k$ is a *partial ordering*. Finally, (101) says that, for every j, there's a k with $j \prec k$. So these clauses state that there's a partial ordering on $\{1, \ldots, m\}$ in which no element is maximal; and they can't all be satisfied.

We can, however, always score $m - 1$ points if we're playing Delayer in that game, by using the following strategy suggested by Massimo Lauria: At every step we know an ordered set S of elements, regarded as "small"; initially $S = \emptyset$, and we'll have $S = \{j_1, \ldots, j_s\}$ when our score is s. Suppose the Prover queries x_{jk}, and $s < m-2$. If $j = k$, we naturally reply that $x_{jk} \leftarrow 0$. Otherwise, if $j \notin S$ and $k \notin S$, we respond $x_{jk} \leftarrow *$; then $s \leftarrow s+1$, and $j_s \leftarrow j$ or k according as the Prover specifies $x_{jk} \leftarrow 1$ or $x_{jk} \leftarrow 0$. Otherwise, if $j \in S$ and $k \notin S$, we respond $x_{jk} \leftarrow 1$; if $j \notin S$ and $k \in S$, we respond $x_{jk} \leftarrow 0$. Finally, if $j = j_a \in S$ and $k = j_b \in S$, we respond $x_{jk} \leftarrow [a < b]$. These responses always satisfy (99) and (100). And no clause of (101) becomes false until the Delayer is finally asked a question with $s = m - 2$. Then the response $x_{jk} \leftarrow *$ gains another point. We've proved

Theorem R. *Every refutation tree for the clauses* (99), (100), (101) *represents at least $2^{m-1} - 1$ resolution steps.* ∎

On the other hand, those clauses do have a refutation *dag* of size $O(m^3)$. Let I_j and T_{ijk} stand for the irreflexivity and transitivity axioms (99) and (100); and let $M_{jk} = x_{j1} \vee \cdots \vee x_{jk}$, so that (101) is M_{jm}. Then we have

$$M_{im} \diamond T_{imk} \;=\; M_{i(m-1)} \vee \bar{x}_{mk}, \qquad \text{for } 1 \le i,k < m. \qquad (102)$$

Calling this new clause M'_{imk}, we can now derive

$$M_{j(m-1)} \;=\; \big((\cdots((M_{mm} \diamond M'_{jm1}) \diamond M'_{jm2}) \diamond \cdots) \diamond M'_{jm(m-1)}\big) \diamond I_m,$$

for $1 \le j < m$. Hence $(m - 1)^2 + (m - 1)m$ resolutions have essentially reduced m to $m - 1$. Eventually we can therefore derive M_{11}; then $M_{11} \diamond I_1 = \epsilon$. [This elegant refutation is due to G. Stålmarck, *Acta Informatica* **33** (1996), 277–280.]

The method we've just used to obtain $M_{j(m-1)}$ from M_{mm} is, incidentally, a special case of a useful general formula called *hyperresolution* that is easily proved by induction on r:

$$\big(\cdots((C_0 \vee x_1 \vee \cdots \vee x_r) \diamond (C_1 \vee \bar{x}_1)) \diamond \cdots\big) \diamond (C_r \vee \bar{x}_r)$$
$$= C_0 \vee C_1 \vee \cdots \vee C_r. \qquad (103)$$

*Lower bounds for general resolution. Let's change our perspective slightly: Instead of visualizing a proof by resolution as a directed graph, we can think of it as a "straight line" *resolution chain*, analogous to the addition chains of Section 4.6.3 and the Boolean chains of Section 7.1.2. A resolution chain based on m axioms $C_1, \ldots, C_m$ appends additional clauses $C_{m+1}, \ldots, C_{m+r}$, each of which is obtained by resolving two previous clauses of the chain. Formally, we have

$$C_i = C_{j(i)} \diamond C_{k(i)}, \qquad \text{for } m+1 \le i \le m+r, \qquad (104)$$

where $1 \le j(i) < i$ and $1 \le k(i) < i$. It's a *refutation chain* for $C_1, \ldots, C_m$ if $C_{m+r} = \epsilon$. The tree in Fig. 91, for example, yields the refutation chain

$$12\bar{3}, 23\bar{4}, 341, 4\bar{1}\bar{2}, \bar{1}23, \bar{2}34, \bar{3}4\bar{1}, \bar{4}1\bar{2}, 123, 12\bar{4}, \bar{1}2\bar{4}, \bar{1}2\bar{3}, 12, 1\bar{2}, \bar{1}\bar{2}, \bar{1}2, 1, \bar{1}, \epsilon$$

for the axioms (6); and there are many other ways to refute those axioms, such as

$$12\bar{3}, 23\bar{4}, 341, 4\bar{1}\bar{2}, \bar{1}23, \bar{2}34, \bar{3}4\bar{1}, \bar{4}1\bar{2}, 1\bar{2}\bar{3}, 1\bar{3}, 14, \bar{3}\bar{4}, 24, 2\bar{4}, 2, \bar{1}3, \bar{3}4, 1\bar{4}, \bar{3}, 1, \bar{1}, \epsilon. \quad (105)$$

This chain is quite different from Fig. 91, and perhaps nicer: It has three more steps, but after forming '$12\bar{3}$' it constructs only very short clauses.

We'll see in a moment that short clauses are crucial if we want short chains. That fact turns out to be important when we try to prove that certain easily understood families of axioms are inherently more difficult than (99), (100), and (101), in the sense that they can't be refuted with a chain of polynomial size.

Consider, for example, the well known "pigeonhole principle," which states that $m+1$ pigeons don't fit in m pigeon-sized holes. If x_{jk} means that pigeon j occupies hole k, for $0 \le j \le m$ and $1 \le k \le m$, the relevant unsatisfiable clauses are

$$(x_{j1} \vee x_{j2} \vee \cdots \vee x_{jm}), \qquad \text{for } 0 \le j \le m; \qquad (106)$$
$$(\bar{x}_{ik} \vee \bar{x}_{jk}), \qquad \text{for } 0 \le i < j \le m \text{ and } 1 \le k \le m. \qquad (107)$$

("Every pigeon has a hole, but no hole hosts more than one pigeon.") These clauses increased the pigeonhole principle's fame during the 1980s, when Armin Haken [*Theoretical Computer Science* **39** (1985), 297–308] proved that they have no short refutation chain. His result marked the first time that *any* set of clauses had been shown to be intractable for resolution in general.

> *It is absolutely necessary that two people have equally many hairs.*
> — JEAN APPIER HANZELET, *Recreation Mathematicque* (1624)

Haken's original proof was rather complicated. But simpler approaches were eventually found, culminating in a method by E. Ben-Sasson and A. Wigderson [*JACM* **48** (2001), 149–169], which is based on clause length and applies to many other sets of axioms. If α is any sequence of clauses, let us say that its *width*, written $w(\alpha)$, is the length of its longest clause or clauses. Furthermore, if $\alpha_0 = (C_1, \ldots, C_m)$, we write $w(\alpha_0 \vdash \epsilon)$ for the minimum of $w(\alpha)$ over all refutation chains $\alpha = (C_1, \ldots, C_{m+r})$ for α_0, and $\|\alpha_0 \vdash \epsilon\|$ for the minimum length r of all such chains. The following lemma is the key to proving lower bounds with Ben-Sasson and Wigderson's strategy:

Lemma B. $\|\alpha_0 \vdash \epsilon\| \geq e^{(w(\alpha_0 \vdash \epsilon)-1)^2/(8n)} - 2$, *for clauses in* $n \geq w(\alpha_0)^2$ *variables.*
Thus there's exponential growth if we have $w(\alpha_0) = O(1)$ and $w(\alpha_0 \vdash \epsilon) = \Omega(n)$.

Proof. Let $\alpha = (C_1, \dots, C_{m+r})$ be a refutation of α_0 with $r = \|\alpha_0 \vdash \epsilon\|$. We will say that a clause is "fat" if its length is W or more, where $W \geq w(\alpha_0)$ is a parameter to be set later. If $\alpha \setminus \alpha_0$ contains f fat clauses, those clauses contain at least Wf literals; hence some literal l appears in at least $Wf/(2n)$ of them.

Now $\alpha \mid l$, the chain obtained by replacing each clause C_j by $C_j \mid l$, is a refutation of $\alpha_0 \mid l$ that contains at most $\lfloor \rho f \rfloor$ fat clauses, where $\rho = 1 - W/(2n)$. (The clause $C_j \mid l$ will be $\wp$ if $l \in C_j$, thus tautological and effectively absent.)

Suppose $f < \rho^{-b}$ for some integer b. We will prove, by induction on b and secondarily on the total length of all clauses, that there's a refutation β of α_0 such that $w(\beta) \leq W + b$. This assertion holds when $b = 0$, since $W \geq w(\alpha_0)$. If $b > 0$, there's a refutation β_0 of $\alpha_0 \mid l$ with $w(\beta_0) \leq W + b - 1$, when we choose l as above, because $\rho f < \rho^{1-b}$ and $\alpha \mid l$ refutes $\alpha_0 \mid l$. Then we can form a resolution chain β_1 that derives $\bar{l}$ from α_0, by inserting $\bar{l}$ appropriately into clauses of β_0. And there's a simple chain β_2 that derives the clauses of $\alpha_0 \mid \bar{l}$ from α_0 and $\bar{l}$. There's also a refutation β_3 of $\alpha_0 \mid \bar{l}$ with $w(\beta_3) \leq W + b$, by induction, because $\alpha \mid \bar{l}$ refutes $\alpha_0 \mid \bar{l}$. Thus the combination $\beta = \{\beta_1, \beta_2, \beta_3\}$ refutes α_0, with

$$w(\beta) = \max(w(\beta_0)+1, w(\beta_2), w(\beta_3)) \leq \max(W+b, w(\alpha_0), W+b) = W+b.$$

Finally, exercise 238 chooses W so that we get the claimed bound. ∎

The pigeon axioms are too wide to be inserted directly into Lemma B. But Ben-Sasson and Wigderson observed that a simplified version of those axioms, involving only clauses of 5SAT, is already intractable.

Notice that we can regard the variable x_{jk} as indicating the presence of an edge between a_j and b_k in a bipartite graph on the vertices $A = \{a_0, \dots, a_m\}$ and $B = \{b_1, \dots, b_m\}$. Condition (106) says that each a_j has degree ≥ 1, while condition (107) says that each b_k has degree ≤ 1. There is, however, a bipartite graph G_0 on those vertices for which each a_j has degree ≤ 5 and such that the following strong "expansion" condition is satisfied:

Every subset $A' \subseteq A$ *with* $|A'| \leq m/3000$ *has* $|\partial A'| \geq |A'|$ *in* G_0.   (108)

Here $\partial A'$ denotes the bipartite boundary of A', namely the set of all b_k that have exactly one neighbor in A'.

Given such a graph G_0, whose existence is proved (nonconstructively) in exercise 240, we can formulate a *restricted pigeonhole principle*, by which the pigeonhole clauses are unsatisfiable if we also require $\bar{x}_{jk}$ whenever $a_j \not\!-\!\!\!-\; b_k$ in G_0.

Let $\alpha(G_0)$ denote the resulting clauses, which are obtained when axioms (106) and (107) are conditioned on all such literals $\bar{x}_{jk}$. Then $w(\alpha(G_0)) \leq 5$, and at most $5m + 5$ unspecified variables x_{jk} remain. Lemma B tells us that all refutation chains for $\alpha(G_0)$ have length $\exp \Omega(m)$ if we can prove that they all have width $\Omega(m)$. Haken's theorem, which asserts that all refutation chains for (106) and (107) also have length $\exp \Omega(m)$, will follow, because any short refutation would yield a short refutation of $\alpha(G_0)$ after conditioning on the $\bar{x}_{jk}$.

Thus the following result gives our story a happy ending:

Theorem B. *The restricted pigeonhole axioms $\alpha(G_0)$ have refutation width*

$$w(\alpha(G_0) \vdash \epsilon) \geq m/6000. \tag{109}$$

Proof. We can assign a complexity measure to every clause C by defining

$$\mu(C) = \min\{|A'| \mid A' \subseteq A \text{ and } \alpha(A') \vdash C\}. \tag{110}$$

Here $\alpha(A')$ is the set of "pigeon axioms" (106) for $a_j \in A'$, together with all of the "hole axioms" (107); and $\alpha(A') \vdash C$ means that clause C can be proved by resolution when starting with only those axioms. If C is one of the pigeon axioms, this definition makes $\mu(C) = 1$, because we can let $A' = \{a_j\}$. And if C is a hole axiom, clearly $\mu(C) = 0$. The subadditive law

$$\mu(C' \diamond C'') \leq \mu(C') + \mu(C'') \tag{111}$$

also holds, because a proof of $C' \diamond C''$ needs at most the axioms of $\alpha(A') \cup \alpha(A'')$ if C' follows from $\alpha(A')$ and C'' follows from $\alpha(A'')$.

We can assume that $m \geq 6000$. And we must have $\mu(\epsilon) > m/3000$, because of the strong expansion condition (108). (See exercise 241.) Therefore every refutation of $\alpha(G_0)$ must contain a clause C with $m/6000 \leq \mu(C) < m/3000$; indeed, the first clause C_j with $\mu(C_j) \geq m/6000$ will satisfy this condition, by (111).

Let A' be a set of vertices with $|A'| = \mu(C)$ and $\alpha(A') \vdash C$. Also let b_k be any element of $\partial A'$, with a_j its unique neighbor in A'. Since $|A' \setminus a_j| < \mu(C)$, there must be an assignment of variables that satisfies all axioms of $\alpha(A' \setminus a_j)$, but falsifies C and the pigeon axiom for j. That assignment puts no two pigeons into the same hole, and it places every pigeon of $A' \setminus a_j$.

Now suppose C contains no literal of the form $x_{j'k}$ or $\bar{x}_{j'k}$, for any $a_{j'} \in A$. Then we could set $x_{j'k} \leftarrow 0$ for all j', without falsifying any axiom of $\alpha(A' \setminus a_j)$; and we could then make the axioms of $\alpha(\{a_j\})$ true by setting $x_{jk} \leftarrow 1$. But that change to the assignment would leave C false, contradicting our assumption that $\alpha(A') \vdash C$. Thus C contains some $\pm x_{j'k}$ for each $b_k \in \partial A'$; and we must have $w(C) \geq |\partial A'| \geq m/6000$. ∎

A similar proof establishes a linear lower bound on the refutation width, hence an exponential lower bound on the refutation length, of almost all random 3SAT instances with n variables and $\lfloor \alpha n \rfloor$ clauses, for fixed α as $n \to \infty$ (see exercise 243), a theorem of V. Chvátal and E. Szemerédi [*JACM* **35** (1988), 759–768].

Historical notes: Proofs by resolution, in the more general setting of first-order logic, were introduced by J. A. Robinson in *JACM* **12** (1965), 23–41. [They're also equivalent to G. Gentzen's "cut rule for sequents," *Mathematische Zeitschrift* **39** (1935), 176–210, III.1.21.] Inspired by Robinson's paper, Gregory Tseytin developed the first nontrivial techniques to prove lower bounds on the length of resolution proofs, based on unsatisfiable graph axioms that are considered in exercise 245. His lectures of 1966 were published in Volume 8 of the Steklov Mathematical Institute Seminars in Mathematics (1968); see A. O. Slisenko's English translation, *Studies in Constructive Mathematics and Mathematical Logic*, part 2 (1970), 115–125.

Tseytin pointed out that there's a simple way to get around the lower bounds he had proved for his graph-oriented problems, by allowing new kinds of proof steps: Given any set of axioms F, we can introduce a new variable z that doesn't appear anywhere in F, and add three new clauses $G = \{xz, yz, \bar{x}\bar{y}\bar{z}\}$; here x and y are arbitrary literals of F. It's clear that F is satisfiable if and only if $F \cup G$ is satisfiable, because G essentially says that $z = \text{NAND}(x, y)$. Adding new variables in this way is somewhat analogous to using lemmas when proving a theorem, or to introducing a memo cache in a computer program.

His method, which is called *extended resolution*, can be much faster than pure resolution. For example, it allows the pigeonhole clauses (106) and (107) to be refuted in only $O(m^4)$ steps (see exercise 237). It doesn't appear to help much with certain other classes of problems such as random 3SAT; but who knows?

SAT solving via resolution. The concept of resolution also suggests alternative ways to solve satisfiability problems. In the first place we can use it to eliminate variables: If F is any set of clauses on n variables, and if x is one of those variables, we can construct a set F' of clauses on the other $n - 1$ variables in such a way that F is satisfiable if and only if F' is satisfiable. The idea is simply to resolve every clause of the form $x \lor A'$ with every clause of the form $\bar{x} \lor A''$, and then to discard those clauses.

For example, consider the following six clauses in four variables:

$$1234, \ 1\bar{2}, \ \bar{1}2\bar{3}, \ \bar{1}3, \ 2\bar{3}, \ 3\bar{4}. \tag{112}$$

We can eliminate the variable x_4 by forming $1234 \diamond 3\bar{4} = 123$. Then we can eliminate x_3 by resolving 123 and $\bar{1}3$ with $\bar{1}2\bar{3}$ and $2\bar{3}$:

$$123 \diamond \bar{1}2\bar{3} = \wp, \quad 123 \diamond 2\bar{3} = 12, \quad \bar{1}3 \diamond \bar{1}2\bar{3} = \bar{1}2, \quad \bar{1}3 \diamond 2\bar{3} = \bar{1}2.$$

Now we're left with $\{12, 1\bar{2}, \bar{1}2, \bar{1}\bar{2}\}$, because the tautology $\wp$ goes away. Eliminating x_2 gives $\{1, \bar{1}\}$, and eliminating x_1 gives $\{\epsilon\}$; hence (112) is unsatisfiable.

This method, which was originally proposed for hand calculation by E. W. Samson and R. K. Mueller in 1955, works beautifully on small problems. But why is it valid? There are (at least) two good ways to understand the reason. First, it's easy to see that F' is satisfiable whenever F is satisfiable, because $C' \diamond C''$ is true whenever C' and C'' are both true. Conversely, if F' is satisfied by some setting of the other $n - 1$ variables, that setting must either satisfy A' for all clauses of the form $x \lor A'$, or else it must satisfy A'' for all clauses of the form $\bar{x} \lor A''$. (Otherwise neither A' nor A'' would be satisfied, for some A' and some A'', and the clause $A' \lor A''$ in F' would be false.) Thus at least one of the settings $x \leftarrow 0$ or $x \leftarrow 1$ will satisfy F.

Another good way to understand variable elimination is to notice that it corresponds to the elimination of an existential quantifier (see exercise 248).

Suppose p clauses of F contain x and q clauses contain $\bar{x}$. Then the elimination of x will give us at most pq new clauses, in the worst case; so F' will have no more clauses than F did, whenever $pq \leq p + q$, namely when $(p-1)(q-1) \leq 1$. This condition clearly holds whenever $p = 0$ or $q = 0$; indeed, we called x a "pure literal" when such cases arose in Algorithm A. The condition also holds whenever $p = 1$ or $q = 1$, and even when $p = q = 2$.

Furthermore we don't always get pq new clauses. Some of the resolvents might turn out to be tautologous, as above; others might be subsumed by existing clauses. (The clause C is said to *subsume* another clause C' if $C \subseteq C'$, in the sense that every literal of C appears also in C'. In such cases we can safely discard C'.) And some of the resolvents might also subsume existing clauses.

Therefore repeated elimination of variables doesn't always cause the set of clauses to explode. In the worst case, however, it can be quite inefficient.

In January of 1972, Stephen Cook showed his students at the University of Toronto a rather different way to employ resolution in SAT-solving. His elegant procedure, which he called "Method I," essentially learns new clauses by doing resolution on demand:

Algorithm I (*Satisfiability by clause learning*). Given m nonempty clauses $C_1 \wedge \cdots \wedge C_m$ on n Boolean variables $x_1 \ldots x_n$, this algorithm either proves them unsatisfiable or finds strictly distinct literals $l_1 \ldots l_n$ that satisfy them all. In the process, new clauses may be generated by resolution (and m will then increase).

I1. [Initialize.] Set $d \leftarrow 0$.

I2. [Advance.] If $d = n$, terminate successfully (the literals $\{l_1, \ldots, l_d\}$ satisfy $\{C_1, \ldots, C_m\}$). Otherwise set $d \leftarrow d+1$, and let l_d be a literal strictly distinct from $l_1, \ldots, l_{d-1}$.

I3. [Find falsified C_i.] If none of $C_1, \ldots, C_m$ are falsified by $\{l_1, \ldots, l_d\}$, go back to I2. Otherwise let C_i be a falsified clause.

I4. [Find falsified C_j.] (At this point we have $\bar{l}_d \in C_i \subseteq \{\bar{l}_1, \ldots, \bar{l}_d\}$, but no clause is contained in $\{\bar{l}_1, \ldots, \bar{l}_{d-1}\}$.) Set $l_d \leftarrow \bar{l}_d$. If none of $C_1, \ldots, C_m$ are falsified by $\{l_1, \ldots, l_d\}$, go back to I2. Otherwise let $\bar{l}_d \in C_j \subseteq \{\bar{l}_1, \ldots, \bar{l}_d\}$.

I5. [Resolve.] Set $m \leftarrow m+1$, $C_m \leftarrow C_i \diamond C_j$. Terminate unsuccessfully if C_m is empty. Otherwise set $d \leftarrow \max\{t \mid \bar{l}_t \in C_m\}$, $i \leftarrow m$, and return to I4. ∎

In step I5 the new clause C_m cannot be subsumed by any previous clause C_k for $k < m$, because $C_i \diamond C_j \subseteq \{\bar{l}_1, \ldots, \bar{l}_{d-1}\}$. Therefore, in particular, no clause is generated twice, and the algorithm must terminate.

This description is intentionally vague when it uses the word "let" in steps I2, I3, and I4: *Any* available literal l_d can be selected in step I2, and *any* falsified clauses C_i and C_j can be selected in steps I3 and I4, without making the method fail. Thus Algorithm I really represents a family of algorithms, depending on what heuristics are used to make those selections.

For example, Cook proposed the following way ("Method IA") to select l_d in step I2: Choose a literal that occurs most frequently in the set of currently unsatisfied clauses that have the fewest unspecified literals. When applied to the six clauses (112), this rule would set $l_1 \leftarrow 3$ and $l_2 \leftarrow 2$ and $l_3 \leftarrow 1$; then step I3 would find $C_i = \bar{1}2\bar{3}$ false. So step I4 would set $l_3 \leftarrow \bar{1}$ and find $C_j = 1\bar{2}$ false, and step I5 would learn $C_7 = 2\bar{3}$. (See exercise 249 for the sequel.)

Cook's main interest when introducing Algorithm I was to minimize the number of resolution steps; he wasn't particularly concerned with minimizing the running time. Subsequent experiments by R. A. Reckhow [Ph.D. thesis

(Univ. Toronto, 1976), 81–84] showed that, indeed, relatively short resolution refutations are found with this approach. Furthermore, exercise 251 demonstrates that Algorithm I can handle the anti-maximal-element clauses (99)–(101) in polynomial time; thus it trounces the exponential behavior exhibited by all backtrack-based algorithms for this problem (see Theorem R).

On the other hand, Algorithm I does tend to fill memory with a great many new clauses when it is applied to large problems, and there's no obvious way to deal with those clauses efficiently. Therefore Cook's method did not appear to be of practical importance, and it remained unpublished for more than forty years.

Conflict driven clause learning. Algorithm I demonstrates the fact that unsuccessful choices of literals can lead us to discover valuable new clauses, thereby increasing our knowledge about the characteristics of a problem. When that idea was rediscovered from another point of view in the 1990s, it proved to be revolutionary: Significant industrial instances of SAT with many thousands or even millions of variables suddenly became feasible for the first time.

The name CDCL solver is often given to these new methods, because they are based on "conflict driven clause learning" rather than on classical backtracking. A CDCL solver shares many concepts with the DPLL algorithms that we've already seen; yet it is sufficiently different that we can understand it best by developing the ideas from scratch. Instead of implicitly exploring a search tree such as Fig. 82, a CDCL solver is built on the notion of a *trail*, which is a sequence $L_0 L_1 \ldots L_{F-1}$ of strictly distinct literals that do not falsify any clause. We can start with $F = 0$ (the empty trail). As computation proceeds, our task is to extend the current trail until $F = n$, thus solving the problem, or to prove that no solution exists, by essentially learning that the empty clause is true.

Suppose there's a clause c of the form $l \vee \bar{a}_1 \vee \cdots \vee \bar{a}_k$, where a_1 through a_k are in the trail but l isn't. Literals in the trail are tentatively assumed to be true, and c must be satisfied; so we're forced to make l true. In such cases we therefore append l to the current trail and say that c is its "reason." (This operation is equivalent to what we called "unit propagation" in previous algorithms; those algorithms effectively removed the literals $\bar{a}_1, \ldots, \bar{a}_k$ when they became false, thereby leaving l as a "unit" all by itself. But our new viewpoint keeps each clause c intact, and knows all of its literals.) A *conflict* occurs if the complementary literal $\bar{l}$ is already in the trail, because l can't be both true and false; but let's assume for now that no conflicts arise, so that l can legally be appended by setting $L_F \leftarrow l$ and $F \leftarrow F + 1$.

If no such forcing clause exists, and if $F < n$, we choose a new distinct literal in some heuristic way, and we append it to the current trail with a "reason" of Λ. Such literals are called *decisions*. They partition the trail into a sequence of decision *levels*, whose boundaries can be indicated by a sequence of indices with $0 = i_0 \leq i_1 < i_2 < i_3 < \cdots$; literal L_t belongs to level d if and only if $i_d \leq t < i_{d+1}$. Level 0, at the beginning of the trail, is special: It contains literals that are forced by clauses of length 1, if such clauses exist. Any such literals are unconditionally true. Every other level begins with exactly one decision.

Consider, for example, the problem $waerden(3, 3; 9)$ of (9). The first items placed on the trail might be

t	L_t	level	reason	
0	$\bar{6}$	1	Λ	(a decision)
1	$\bar{9}$	2	Λ	(a decision)
2	3	2	396	(rearrangement of the clause 369)
3	$\bar{4}$	3	Λ	(a decision)
4	5	3	546	(rearrangement of the clause 456)
5	8	3	846	(rearrangement of the clause 468)
6	2	3	246	
7	$\bar{7}$	3	$\bar{7}5\bar{3}$	(rearrangement of the clause $3\bar{5}\bar{7}$)
8	$\bar{2}$	3	$\bar{2}5\bar{8}$	(a conflict!)

$$(113)$$

Three decisions were made, and they started levels at $i_1 = 0$, $i_2 = 1$, $i_3 = 3$. Several clauses have been rearranged; we'll soon see why. And propagations have led to a conflict, because both 2 and $\bar{2}$ have been forced. (We don't actually consider the final entry L_8 to be part of the trail, because it contradicts L_6.)

If the reason for l includes the literal $\bar{l}'$, we say "l depends directly on l'." And if there's a chain of one or more direct dependencies, from l to l_1 to $\cdots$ to $l_k = l'$, we say simply that "l depends on l'." For example, 5 depends directly on $\bar{4}$ and $\bar{6}$ in (113), and $\bar{2}$ depends directly on 5 and 8; hence $\bar{2}$ depends on $\bar{6}$.

Notice that a literal can depend only on literals that precede it in the trail. Furthermore, every literal l that's forced at level $d > 0$ depends directly on some *other* literal on that same level d; otherwise l would already have been forced at a previous level. Consequently l must necessarily depend on the dth decision.

The reason for reasons is that we need to deal with conflicts. We will see that every conflict allows us to construct a new clause c that must be true whenever the existing clauses are satisfiable, although c itself does not contain any existing clause. Therefore we can "learn" c by adding it to the existing clauses, and we can try again. This learning process can't go on forever, because only finitely many clauses are possible. Sooner or later we will therefore either find a solution or learn the empty clause. That will be nice, especially if it happens sooner.

A conflict clause c on decision level d has the form $\bar{l} \vee \bar{a}_1 \vee \cdots \vee \bar{a}_k$, where l and all the a's belong to the trail; furthermore l and at least one a_i belong to level d. We can assume that l is rightmost in the trail, of all the literals in c. Hence l cannot be the dth decision; and it has a reason, say $l \vee \bar{a}'_1 \vee \cdots \vee \bar{a}'_{k'}$. Resolving c with this reason gives the clause $c' = \bar{a}_1 \vee \cdots \vee \bar{a}_k \vee \bar{a}'_1 \vee \cdots \vee \bar{a}'_{k'}$, which includes at least one literal belonging to level d. If more than one such literal is present, then c' is itself a conflict clause; we can set $c \leftarrow c'$ and repeat the process. Eventually we are bound to obtain a new clause c' of the form $\bar{l}' \vee \bar{b}_1 \vee \cdots \vee \bar{b}_r$, where l' is on level d and where b_1 through b_r are on lower levels.

Such a c' is learnable, as desired, because it can't contain any existing clauses. (Every subclause of c', including c' itself, would otherwise have given us something to force at a lower level.) We can now *discard* levels $> d'$ of the trail, where d' is the maximum level of b_1 through b_r; and—this is the punch line—

we can append $\bar{l}'$ to the end of level d', with c' as its reason. The forcing process now resumes at level d', as if the learned clause had been present all along.

For example, after the conflict in (113), the initial conflict clause is $c = \bar{2}5\bar{8}$, our shorthand notation for $\bar{x}_2 \vee \bar{x}_5 \vee \bar{x}_8$; and its rightmost complemented literal in the trail is 2, because 5 and 8 came earlier. So we resolve c with 246, the reason for 2, and get $c' = 4\bar{5}6\bar{8}$. This new clause contains complements of three literals from level 3, namely $\bar{4}$, 5, and 8; so it's still a conflict clause. We resolve it with the reason for 8 and get $c' = 4\bar{5}6$. Again c' is a conflict clause. But the result of resolving this conflict with the reason for 5 is $c' = 46$, a clause that is falsified by the literals currently on the trail but has only $\bar{4}$ at level 3. Good — we have learned '46': In every solution to $waerden(3, 3; 9)$, either x_4 or x_6 must be true.

Thus the sequel to (113) is

$$
\begin{array}{cclll}
t & L_t & \text{level} & \text{reason} & \\
0 & \bar{6} & 1 & \Lambda & \text{(a decision)} \\
1 & 4 & 1 & 46 & \text{(the newly learned clause)}
\end{array}
\qquad (114)
$$

and the next step will be to begin a new level 2, because nothing more is forced.

Notice that the former level 2 has gone away. We've learned that there was no need to branch on the decision variable x_9, because $\bar{6}$ already forces 4. This improvement to the usual backtrack regimen is sometimes called "backjumping," because we've jumped back to a level that can be regarded as the root cause of the conflict that was just discovered.

Exercise 253 explores a possible continuation of (114); dear reader, please jump to it now. Incidentally, the clause '46' that we learned in this example involves the complements of former decisions $\bar{4}$ and $\bar{6}$; but exercise 255 shows that newly learned clauses might not contain any decision variables whatsoever.

The process of constructing the learned clause from a conflict is not as difficult as it may seem, because there's an efficient way to perform all of the necessary resolution steps. Suppose, as above, that the initial conflict clause is $\bar{l} \vee \bar{a}_1 \vee \cdots \vee \bar{a}_k$. Then we "stamp" each of the literals a_i with a unique number s; and we also insert $\bar{a}_i$ into an auxiliary array, which will eventually hold the literals $\bar{b}_1, \ldots, \bar{b}_r$, whenever a_i is a literal that received its value on a level d' with $0 < d' < d$. We stamp l too; and we count how many literals of level d have thereby been stamped. Then we repeatedly go back through the trail until coming to a literal L_t whose stamp equals s. If the counter is bigger than 1 at this point, and if L_t's reason is $L_t \vee \bar{a}'_1 \vee \cdots \vee \bar{a}'_{k'}$, we look at each a'_i, stamping it and possibly putting it into the b array if it had not already been stamped with s. Eventually the count of unresolved literals will decrease to 1; the learned clause is then $\bar{L}_t \vee \bar{b}_1 \vee \cdots \vee \bar{b}_r$.

These new clauses might turn out to be quite large, even when we're solving a problem whose clauses were rather small to start with. For example, Table 3 gives a glimpse of typical behavior in a medium-size problem. It shows the beginning of the trail generated when a CDCL solver was applied to the 2779 clauses of $waerden(3, 10; 97)$, after about 10,000 clauses had been learned. (Recall that this problem tries to find a binary vector $x_1 x_2 \ldots x_{97}$ that has no three equally spaced 0s and no ten equally spaced 1s.) Level 18 in the table has just been

Table 3
THE FIRST LEVELS OF A MODERATE-SIZE TRAIL

t	L_t	level	reason	t	L_t	level	reason	t	L_t	level	reason
0	$\overline{53}$	1	Λ	15	70	11	70 36 53	30	08	15	08 46 27
1	55	2	Λ	16	35	12	Λ	31	65	15	65 46 27
2	44	3	Λ	17	39	13	Λ	32	60	15	60 46 53
3	54	4	Λ	18	$\overline{37}$	14	Λ	33	$\overline{50}$	15	**
4	43	5	Λ	19	38	14	38 37 36	34	64	15	64 50 36
5	30	6	Λ	20	47	14	47 37 27	35	22	15	22 50 36
6	34	7	Λ	21	17	14	17 37 27	36	24	15	24 50 37
7	45	8	Λ	22	32	14	32 37 27	37	42	15	42 50 46
8	40	9	Λ	23	69	14	69 37 53	38	48	15	48 50 46
9	$\overline{27}$	10	Λ	24	$\overline{21}$	14	21 37 53	39	73	15	73 50 27
10	79	10	79 53 27	25	$\overline{46}$	15	Λ	40	04	15	04 50 27
11	01	10	01 27 53	26	28	15	28 46 37	41	63	15	63 50 37
12	$\overline{36}$	11	Λ	27	41	15	41 46 36	42	33	16	Λ
13	18	11	18 36 27	28	$\overline{26}$	15	26 46 36	43	51	17	Λ
14	19	11	19 36 53	29	56	15	56 46 36	44	$\overline{57}$	18	Λ

(Here ** denotes the previously learned clause $\overline{50}\ \overline{26}\ 27\ \overline{30}\ \overline{32}\ \overline{35}\ \overline{38}\ \overline{40}\ \overline{41}\ \overline{44}\ \overline{45}\ \overline{47}\ \overline{50}\ 55\ \overline{60}\ 65\ 70$.)

launched with the decision $L_{44} = \overline{57}$; and that decision will trigger the setting of many more literals 15, 49, 61, 68, 77, 78, 87, $\overline{96}$, ..., eventually leading to a conflict when trying to set L_{67}. The conflict clause turns out to have length 22:

$$53\ 27\ 36\ \overline{70}\ \overline{35}\ 37\ \overline{69}\ \overline{21}\ 46\ \overline{28}\ 56\ 65\ \overline{60}\ 50\ \overline{64}\ 24\ 42\ 73\ 63\ \overline{33}\ \overline{51}\ 57\ . \tag{115}$$

(Its literals are shown here in order of the appearance of their complements in the trail.) When we see such a monster clause, we might well question whether we really want to "learn" such an obscure fact!

A closer look, however, reveals that many of the literals in (115) are redundant. For example, $\overline{70}$ can safely be deleted, because its reason is '70 36 53'; both 36 and 53 already appear in (115), hence (115) $\diamond$ (70 36 53) gets rid of $\overline{70}$. Indeed, more than half of the literals in this example are redundant, and (115) can be simplified to the much shorter and more memorable clause

$$53\ 27\ 36\ \overline{35}\ 37\ 46\ 50\ \overline{33}\ \overline{51}\ 57\ . \tag{116}$$

Exercise 257 explains how to discover such simplifications, which turn out to be quite important in practice. For example, the clauses learned while proving $waerden\,(3, 10; 97)$ unsatisfiable had an average length of 19.9 before simplification, but only 11.2 after; simplification made the algorithm run about 33% faster.

Most of the computation time of a CDCL solver is devoted to unit propagation. Thus we need to know when the value of a literal has been forced by previous assignments, and we hope to know it quickly. The idea of "lazy data structures," used above in Algorithm D, works nicely for this purpose, in the presence of long clauses, provided that we extend it so that every clause now has *two* watched literals instead of one. If we know that the first two literals of a clause are not false, then we needn't look at this clause until one of them becomes false, even though other literals in the clause might be repeatedly veering between transient states of true, false, and undefined. And when a watchee does become false, we'll try to swap it with a nonfalse partner that can be watched instead. Propagations or conflicts will arise only when all of the remaining literals are false.

Algorithm C below therefore represents clauses with the following data structures: A monolithic array called MEM is assumed to be large enough to hold all of the literals in all of the clauses, interspersed with control information. Each clause $c = l_0 \vee l_1 \vee \cdots \vee l_{k-1}$ with $k > 1$ is represented by its starting position in MEM, with MEM$[c + j] = l_j$ for $0 \leq j < k$. Its two watched literals are l_0 and l_1, and its size k is stored in MEM$[c - 1]$. Unit clauses, for which $k = 1$, are treated differently; they appear in level 0 of the trail, not in MEM.

A learned clause c can be distinguished from an initial clause because it has a relatively high number, with MINL $\leq c <$ MAXL. Initially MAXL is set equal to MINL, the smallest cell in MEM that is available for learned clauses; then MAXL grows as new clauses are added to the repertoire. The set of learned clauses is periodically culled, so that the less desirable ones don't clutter up memory and slow things down. Additional information about a learned clause c is kept in MEM$[c - 4]$ and MEM$[c - 5]$, to help with this recycling process (see below).

Individual literals x_k and $\bar{x}_k$, for $1 \leq k \leq n$, are represented internally by the numbers $2k$ and $2k + 1$ as in (57) above. And each of these $2n$ literals l has a list pointer W_l, which begins a linked list of the clauses in which l is watched. We have $W_l = 0$ if there is no such clause; but if $W_l = c > 0$, the next link in this "watch list" is in MEM$[c - 2]$ if $l = l_0$, in MEM$[c - 3]$ if $l = l_1$. [See Armin Biere, *Journal on Satisfiability, Boolean Modeling and Comp.* **4** (2008), 75–97.]

For example, the first few cells of MEM might contain the following data when we are representing the clauses (9) of *waerden*(3, 3; 9):

$$i = \ 0 \ \ 1 \ \ 2 \ \ 3 \ \ 4 \ \ 5 \ \ 6 \ \ 7 \ \ 8 \ \ 9 \ \ 10 \ 11 \ 12 \ 13 \ 14 \ 15 \ 16 \ 17 \ \ldots$$
$$\text{MEM}[i] = \ 9 \ 45 \ 3 \ \ 2 \ \ 4 \ \ 6 \ \ 15 \ 51 \ 3 \ \ 4 \ \ 6 \ \ 8 \ \ 21 \ 45 \ 3 \ \ 6 \ \ 8 \ \ 10 \ \ldots$$

(Clause 3 is '123', clause 9 is '234', clause 15 is '345', …, clause 45 is '135', clause 51 is '246', …; the watch lists for literals x_1, x_2, x_3, x_4 begin respectively at $W_2 = 3$, $W_4 = 3$, $W_6 = 9$, $W_8 = 15$.)

The other major data structures of Algorithm C are focused on variables, not clauses. Each variable x_k for $1 \leq k \leq n$ has six current attributes S(k), VAL(k), OVAL(k), TLOC(k), HLOC(k), and ACT(k), which interact as follows: S(k) is the "stamp" that's used during clause formation. If neither x_k nor $\bar{x}_k$ appears in the current trail, then VAL$(k) = -1$, and we say that x_k and its two literals are "free." But if $L_t = l$ is a literal of the trail, belonging to level d, we have

$$\text{VAL}(|l|) = 2d + (l \ \& \ 1) \quad \text{and} \quad \text{TLOC}(|l|) = t, \qquad \text{where } |l| = l \gg 1, \qquad (117)$$

and we say that l is "true" and $\bar{l}$ is "false." Thus a given literal l is false if and only if VAL$(|l|)$ is nonnegative and VAL$(|l|) + l$ is odd. In most cases a watched literal is not false; but there are exceptions to this rule (see exercise 265). The "reason" for literal l's current value is kept in variable R_l.

The attributes ACT(k) and HLOC(k) tell the algorithm how to select the next decision variable. Each variable x_k has an *activity* score ACT(k), which heuristically estimates its desirability for branching. All of the free variables, and possibly others, are kept in an array called HEAP, which is arranged so that

$$\text{ACT(HEAP}[j]) \leq \text{ACT(HEAP}[(j-1) \gg 1]) \qquad \text{for } 0 < j < h \qquad (118)$$

when it contains h elements (see Section 5.2.3). Thus HEAP[0] will always be a free variable of maximum activity, if it is free; so it's the variable that will be chosen to govern the decision when the trail starts to acquire a new level.

Activity scores help the algorithm to focus on recent conflicts. Suppose, for example, that $M = 100$ conflicts have been resolved, hence 100 clauses have been learned. Suppose further that x_j or $\bar{x}_j$ was stamped while resolving the conflicts numbered 3, 47, 95, 99, and 100; but x_k or $\bar{x}_k$ was stamped during conflicts 41, 87, 94, 95, 96, and 97. We could express their recent activity by computing

$$\text{ACT}(j) = \rho^0 + \rho^1 + \rho^5 + \rho^{53} + \rho^{97}, \quad \text{ACT}(k) = \rho^3 + \rho^4 + \rho^5 + \rho^6 + \rho^{13} + \rho^{59},$$

where ρ is a damping factor (say $\rho = .95$), because $100 - 100 = 0$, $100 - 99 = 1$, $100 - 95 = 5$, ..., $100 - 41 = 59$. In this particular case j would be considered to be less active than k unless ρ is less than about .8744.

In order to update the activity scores according to this measure, we would have to do quite a bit of recomputation whenever a new conflict occurs: The new scores would require us to multiply all n of the old scores by ρ, then to increase the activity of every newly stamped variable by 1. But there's a much better way, namely to compute $\rho^{-M} = \rho^{-100}$ times the scores shown above:

$$\text{ACT}(j) = \rho^{-3} + \rho^{-47} + \rho^{-95} + \rho^{-99} + \rho^{-100}, \quad \text{ACT}(k) = \rho^{-41} + \cdots + \rho^{-96} + \rho^{-97}.$$

These newly scaled scores, suggested by Niklas Eén, give us the same information about the relative activity of each variable; and they're updated easily, because we need to do only one addition per stamped variable when resolving conflicts.

The only problem is that the new scores can become really huge, because ρ^{-M} can cause floating point overflow after the number M of conflicts becomes large. The remedy is to *divide* them all by 10^{100}, say, whenever any variable gets a score that exceeds 10^{100}. The HEAP needn't change, since (118) still holds.

During the algorithm the variable DEL holds the current scaling factor ρ^{-M}, divided by 10^{100} each time all of the activities have been rescaled.

Finally, the parity of OVAL(k) is used to control the polarity of each new decision in step C6. Algorithm C starts by simply making each OVAL(k) odd, although other initialization schemes are possible. Afterwards it sets OVAL(k) ← VAL(k) whenever x_k leaves the trail and becomes free, as recommended by D. Frost and R. Dechter [*AAAI Conf.* **12** (1994), 301–306] and independently by K. Pipatsrisawat and A. Darwiche [*LNCS* **4501** (2007), 294–299], because experience has shown that the recently forced polarities tend to remain good. This technique is called "sticking" or "progress saving" or "phase saving."

Algorithm C is based on the framework of a pioneering CDCL solver called Chaff, and on an early descendant of Chaff called MiniSAT that was developed by N. Eén and N. Sörensson [*LNCS* **2919** (2004), 502–518].

Algorithm C (*Satisfiability by CDCL*). Given a set of clauses on n Boolean variables, this algorithm finds a solution $L_0 L_1 \ldots L_{n-1}$ if and only if the clauses are satisfiable, meanwhile discovering M new ones that are consequences of the originals. After discovering M_p new clauses, it will purge some of them from its memory and reset M_p; after discovering M_f of them, it will flush part of its trail, reset M_f, and start over. (Details of purging and flushing will be discussed later.)

C1. [Initialize.] Set $\text{VAL}(k) \leftarrow \text{OVAL}(k) \leftarrow \text{TLOC}(k) \leftarrow -1$, $\text{ACT}(k) \leftarrow \text{S}(k) \leftarrow 0$, $R_{2k} \leftarrow R_{2k+1} \leftarrow \Lambda$, $\text{HLOC}(k) \leftarrow p_k - 1$, and $\text{HEAP}[p_k - 1] \leftarrow k$, for $1 \le k \le n$, where $p_1 \ldots p_n$ is a random permutation of $\{1, \ldots, n\}$. Then input the clauses into MEM and the watch lists, as described above. Put the distinct unit clauses into $L_0 L_1 \ldots L_{F-1}$; but terminate unsuccessfully if there are contradictory clauses (l) and $(\bar{l})$. Set MINL and MAXL to the first available position in MEM. (See exercise 260.) Set $i_0 \leftarrow d \leftarrow s \leftarrow M \leftarrow G \leftarrow 0$, $h \leftarrow n$, $\text{DEL} \leftarrow 1$.

C2. [Level complete?] (The trail $L_0 \ldots L_{F-1}$ now contains all of the literals that are forced by $L_0 \ldots L_{G-1}$.) Go to C5 if $G = F$.

C3. [Advance G.] Set $l \leftarrow L_G$ and $G \leftarrow G + 1$. Then do step C4 for all c in the watch list of $\bar{l}$, unless that step detects a conflict and jumps to C7. If there is no conflict, return to C2. (See exercise 261.)

C4. [Does c force a unit?] Let $l_0 l_1 \ldots l_{k-1}$ be the literals of clause c, where $l_1 = \bar{l}$. (Swap $l_0 \leftrightarrow l_1$ if necessary.) If l_0 is true, do nothing. Otherwise look for a literal l_j with $1 < j < k$ that is not false. If such a literal is found, move c to the watch list of l_j. But if $l_2, \ldots, l_{k-1}$ are all false, jump to C7 if l_0 is also false. On the other hand if l_0 is free, make it true by setting $L_F \leftarrow l_0$, $\text{TLOC}(|l_0|) \leftarrow F$, $\text{VAL}(|l_0|) \leftarrow 2d + (l_0 \,\&\, 1)$, $R_{l_0} \leftarrow c$, and $F \leftarrow F + 1$.

C5. [New level?] If $F = n$, terminate successfully. Otherwise if $M \ge M_p$, prepare to purge excess clauses (see below). Otherwise if $M \ge M_f$, flush literals as explained below and return to C2. Otherwise set $d \leftarrow d + 1$ and $i_d \leftarrow F$.

C6. [Make a decision.] Set $k \leftarrow \text{HEAP}[0]$ and delete k from the heap (see exercises 262 and 266). If $\text{VAL}(k) \ge 0$, repeat this step. Otherwise set $l \leftarrow 2k + (\text{OVAL}(k) \,\&\, 1)$, $\text{VAL}(k) \leftarrow 2d + (\text{OVAL}(k) \,\&\, 1)$, $L_F \leftarrow l$, $\text{TLOC}(|l|) \leftarrow F$, $R_l \leftarrow \Lambda$, and $F \leftarrow F + 1$. (At this point $F = G + 1$.) Go to C3.

C7. [Resolve a conflict.] Terminate unsuccessfully if $d = 0$. Otherwise use the conflict clause c to construct a new clause $\bar{l}' \vee \bar{b}_1 \vee \cdots \vee \bar{b}_r$ as described above. Set $\text{ACT}(|l|) \leftarrow \text{ACT}(|l|) + \text{DEL}$ for all literals l stamped during this process; also set d' to the maximum level occupied by $\{b_1, \ldots, b_r\}$ in the trail. (See exercise 263. Increasing $\text{ACT}(|l|)$ may also change HEAP.)

C8. [Backjump.] While $F > i_{d'+1}$, do the following: Set $F \leftarrow F - 1$, $l \leftarrow L_F$, $k \leftarrow |l|$, $\text{OVAL}(k) \leftarrow \text{VAL}(k)$, $\text{VAL}(k) \leftarrow -1$, $R_l \leftarrow \Lambda$; and if $\text{HLOC}(|l|) < 0$ insert k into HEAP (see exercise 262). Then set $G \leftarrow F$ and $d \leftarrow d'$.

C9. [Learn.] If $d > 0$, set $c \leftarrow \text{MAXL}$, store the new clause in MEM at position c, and advance MAXL to the next available position in MEM. (Exercise 263 gives full details.) Set $M \leftarrow M + 1$, $L_F \leftarrow \bar{l}'$, $\text{VAL}(|l'|) \leftarrow 2d + (\bar{l}' \,\&\, 1)$, $\text{TLOC}(|l'|) \leftarrow F$, $R_{l'} \leftarrow c$, $F \leftarrow F + 1$, $\text{DEL} \leftarrow \text{DEL}/\rho$, and return to C3. ∎

The high-level operations on data structures in this algorithm are spelled out in terms of elementary low-level steps in exercises 260–263. Exercises 266–271 discuss simple enhancements that were made in the experiments reported below.

Reality check: Although detailed statistics about the performance of Algorithm C on a wide variety of problems will be presented later, a few examples of typical behavior will help now to clarify how the method actually works in practice. Random choices make the running time of this algorithm more variable than it was in Algorithms A, B, D, or L; sometimes we're lucky, sometimes we're not.

In the case of *waerden*$(3, 10; 97)$, the modest 97-variable-and-2779-clause problem that was considered in Table 3, nine test runs of Algorithm C established unsatisfiability after making between 250 and 300 million memory accesses; the median was 272 Mμ. (This is more than twice as fast as our best previous time, which was obtained with Algorithm L.) The average number of decisions made — namely the number of times $L_F \leftarrow l$ was done in step C6 — was about 63 thousand; this compares to 1701 "nodes" in Algorithm L, step L3, and 100 million nodes in Algorithms A, B, D. About 53 thousand clauses were learned, having an average size of 11.5 literals (after averaging about 19.9 before simplification).

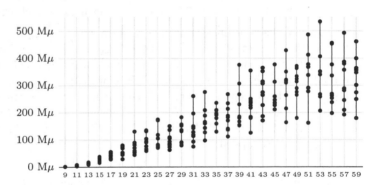

Fig. 92. It is not possible to color the edges of the flower snark graph J_q with three colors, when q is odd. Algorithm C is able to prove this with amazing speed: Computation times (in megamems) are shown for nine trials at each value of q.

Algorithm C often speeds things up much more dramatically, in fact. For example, Fig. 92 shows how it whips through a sequence of three-coloring problems that are based on "flower snarks." Exercise 176 defines *fsnark*(q), an interesting set of $42q + 3$ unsatisfiable clauses on $18q$ variables. The running time of Algorithms A, B, D, and L on *fsnark*(q) is proportional to 2^q, so it's way off the chart — well over a gigamem already when $q = 19$. But Algorithm C polishes off the case $q = 99$ in that same amount of time (thus winning by 24 orders of magnitude)! On the other hand, no satisfactory theoretical explanation for the apparently linear behavior in Fig. 92 is presently known.

Certificates of unsatisfiability. When a SAT solver reports that a given instance is satisfiable, it also produces a set of distinct literals from which we can easily check that every clause is satisfied. But if its report is *negative* — UNSAT — how confident can we be that such a claim is true? Maybe the implementation contains a subtle error; after all, large and complicated programs are notoriously buggy, and computer hardware isn't perfect either. A negative answer can therefore leave both programmers and users unsatisfied, as well as the problem.

We've seen that unsatisfiability can be proved rigorously by constructing a resolution refutation, namely a chain of resolution steps that ends with the empty clause ϵ, as in Fig. 91. But such refutations amount to the construction of a huge directed acyclic graph.

A much more compact characterization of unsatisfiability is possible. Let's say that the sequence of clauses $(C_1, C_2, \ldots, C_t)$ is a *certificate of unsatisfiability* for a family of clauses F if $C_t = \epsilon$, and if we have

$$F \wedge C_1 \wedge \cdots \wedge C_{i-1} \wedge \overline{C}_i \vdash_1 \epsilon \qquad \text{for } 1 \leq i \leq t. \tag{119}$$

Here the subscript 1 in '$G \vdash_1 \epsilon$' means that the clauses G lead to a contradiction by *unit propagation*; and if C_i is the clause $(a_1 \vee \cdots \vee a_k)$, then $\overline{C}_i$ is an abbreviation for the conjunction of unit clauses $(\bar{a}_1) \wedge \cdots \wedge (\bar{a}_k)$.

For example, let $F = R$ be Rivest's clauses (6), which were proved unsatisfiable in Fig. 91. Then $(12, 1, 2, \epsilon)$ is a certificate of unsatisfiability, because

$$\begin{aligned}
R \wedge \bar{1} \wedge \bar{2} &\vdash_1 3 \vdash_1 \bar{4} \vdash_1 \epsilon &&\text{(using } 12\bar{3},\ 23\bar{4},\text{ and } 341\text{);}\\
R \wedge 12 \wedge \bar{1} &\vdash_1 2 \vdash_1 \bar{4} \vdash_1 \bar{3} \vdash_1 \epsilon &&\text{(using } 12,\ \bar{4}1\bar{2},\ \bar{2}\bar{3}4,\text{ and } 341\text{);}\\
R \wedge 12 \wedge 1 \wedge \bar{2} &\vdash_1 4 \vdash_1 3 \vdash_1 \epsilon &&\text{(using } 4\bar{1}2,\ 23\bar{4},\text{ and } \bar{3}4\bar{1}\text{);}\\
R \wedge 12 \wedge 1 \wedge 2 &\vdash_1 3 \vdash_1 4 \vdash_1 \epsilon &&\text{(using } \bar{1}23,\ \bar{2}\bar{3}4,\text{ and } \bar{3}4\bar{1}\text{).}
\end{aligned}$$

A certificate of unsatisfiability gives a convincing proof, since (119) implies that each C_i must be true whenever F, C_1, ..., C_{i-1} are true. And it's easy to check whether or not $G \vdash_1 \epsilon$, for any given set of clauses G, because everything is forced and no choices are involved. Unit propagation is analogous to water flowing downhill; we can be pretty sure that it has been implemented correctly, even if we don't trust the CDCL solver that generated the certificate being checked.

E. Goldberg and Y. Novikov [*Proceedings of DATE: Design, Automation and Test in Europe* **6**,1 (2003), 886–891] have pointed out that CDCL solvers actually produce such certificates as a natural byproduct of their operation:

Theorem G. *If Algorithm C terminates unsuccessfully, the sequence $(C_1, C_2, \ldots, C_t)$ of clauses that it has learned is a certificate of unsatisfiability.*

Proof. It suffices to show that, whenever Algorithm C has learned the clause $C' = \bar{l}' \vee \bar{b}_1 \vee \cdots \vee \bar{b}_r$, unit propagation will deduce ϵ if we append the unit clauses $(l') \wedge (b_1) \wedge \cdots \wedge (b_r)$ to the clauses that the algorithm already knows. The key point is that C' has essentially been obtained by repeated resolution steps,

$$C' = \left(\ldots ((C \diamond R_{l_1}) \diamond R_{l_2}) \diamond \cdots \right) \diamond R_{l_s}, \tag{120}$$

where C is the original conflict clause and R_{l_1}, R_{l_2}, ..., R_{l_s} are the reasons for each literal that was removed while C' was constructed in step C7. More precisely, we have $C = A_0$ and $R_{l_i} = l_i \vee A_i$, where all literals of $A_0 \cup A_1 \cup \cdots \cup A_s$ are false (their complements appear in the trail); and

$$\begin{aligned}
&\bar{l}_i \in A_0 \cup \cdots \cup A_{i-1}, \text{ for } 1 \leq i \leq s;\\
&A_0 \cup A_1 \cup \cdots \cup A_s = \{\bar{l}', \bar{l}_1, \ldots, \bar{l}_s, \bar{b}_1, \ldots, \bar{b}_r\}.
\end{aligned} \tag{121}$$

Thus the known clauses, plus b_1, ..., b_r, and l', will force l_s using clause R_{l_s}. And l_{s-1} will then be forced, using $R_{l_{s-1}}$. And so on. ∎

Since the unit literals in this proof are propagated in reverse order l_s, l_{s-1}, ..., l_1 from the resolution steps in (120), this certificate-checking procedure has become known as "reverse unit propagation" [see A. Van Gelder, *Proc. Int. Symp. on Artificial Intelligence and Math.* **10** (2008), 9 pages, online as ISAIM2008].

Notice that the proof of Theorem G doesn't claim that reverse unit propagation will reconstruct the precise reasoning by which Algorithm C learned a clause. Many different downhill paths to ϵ, built from $\vdash_1$ steps, usually exist in a typical situation. We merely have shown that every clause learnable from a single conflict does imply the existence of at least one such downhill path.

Many of the clauses learned during a typical run of Algorithm C will be "shots in the dark," which turn out to have been aimed in unfruitful directions. Thus the certificates in Theorem G will usually be longer than actually necessary to demonstrate unsatisfiability. For example, Algorithm C learns about 53,000 clauses when refuting $waerden(3, 10; 97)$, and about 135,000 when refuting $fsnark(99)$; but fewer than 50,000 of the former, and fewer than 47,000 of the latter, were actually used in subsequent steps. Exercise 284 explains how to shorten a certificate of unsatisfiability while checking its validity.

An unexpected difficulty arises, however: We might spend more time verifying a certificate than we needed to generate it! For example, a certificate for $waerden(3, 10; 97)$ was found in 272 megamems, but the time needed to check it with straightforward unit-propagations was actually 2.2 *giga*mems. Indeed, this discrepancy becomes significantly worse in larger problems, because a simple program for checking must keep all of the clauses active in its memory. If there are a million active clauses, there are two million literals being watched; hence every change to a literal will require many updates to the data structures.

The solution to this problem is to provide extra hints to the certificate checker. As we are about to see, Algorithm C does *not* keep all of the learned clauses in its memory; it systematically purges its collection, so that the total number stays reasonable. At such times it can also inform the certificate checker that the purged clauses will no longer be relevant to the proof.

Further improvements also allow annotated certificates to accommodate stronger proof rules, such as Tseytin's extended resolution and techniques based on generalized autarkies; see N. Wetzler, M. J. H. Heule, and W. A. Hunt, Jr., *LNCS* **8561** (2014), 422–429.

Whenever a family of clauses has a certificate of unsatisfiability, a variant of Algorithm C will actually find one that isn't too much longer. (See exercise 386.)

*Purging unhelpful clauses. After thousands of conflicts have occurred, Algorithm C has learned thousands of new clauses. New clauses guide the search by steering us away from unproductive paths; but they also slow down the propagation process, because we have to watch them.

We've seen that certificates can usually be shortened; therefore we know that many of the learned clauses will probably never be needed again. For this reason Algorithm C periodically attempts to weed out the ones that appear to be more harmful than helpful, by ranking the clauses that have accumulated.

I consider that a man's brain originally is like a little empty attic, and
you have to stock it with such furniture as you choose. . . . the skilled workman
is very careful indeed as to what he takes into his brain-attic.
. . . It is a mistake to think that that little room has elastic walls
and can distend to any extent. . . . It is of the highest importance, therefore,
not to have useless facts elbowing out the useful ones.

— SHERLOCK HOLMES, in *A Study in Scarlet* (1887)

Algorithm C initiates a special clause-refinement process as soon as it has learned $M \geq M_p$ clauses and arrived at a reasonably stable state (step C5). Let's continue our running example, *waerden*$(3, 10; 97)$, in order to make the issues concrete. If M_p is so huge that no clauses are ever thrown away, a typical run will learn roughly 48 thousand clauses, and do roughly 800 megamems of computation, before proving unsatisfiability. But if $M_p = 10000$, it will learn roughly 50 thousand clauses, and the computation time will go down to about 500 megamems. In the latter case the total number of learned clauses in memory will rarely exceed 10 thousand.

Indeed, let's set $M_p = 10000$ and take a close look at exactly what happened during the author's first experiments. Algorithm C paused to reconnoiter the situation after having learned 10002 clauses. At that point only 6252 of those 10002 clauses were actually present in memory, however, because of the clause-discarding mechanism discussed in exercise 271. Some clauses had length 2, while the maximum size was 24 and the median was 11; here's a complete histogram:

2 9 49 126 216 371 542 719 882 1094 661 540 414 269 176 111 35 20 10 3 1 1 1.

Short clauses tend to be more useful, because they reduce more quickly to units.

A learned clause cannot be purged if it is the reason for one of the literals on the trail. In our example, 12 of the 6252 fell into this category; for instance, $\overline{30}$ appeared on level 10 of the trail because '$\overline{30}\ \overline{33}\ \overline{39}\ 41\ \overline{42}\ \overline{45}\ 46\ \overline{48}\ \overline{54}\ \overline{57}$' had been learned, and we may need to know that clause in a future resolution step.

The purging process will try to remove at least half of the existing learned clauses, so that at most 3126 remain. We aren't allowed to touch the 12 reason-bound ones; hence we want to forget 3114 of the other 6240. Which of them should we expel?

Among many heuristics that have been tried, the most successful in practice are based on what Gilles Audemard and Laurent Simon have called "literal block distance" [see *Proc. Int. Joint Conference on Artificial Intelligence* **21** (2009), 399–404]. They observed that each level of the trail can be considered to be a block of more-or-less related variables; hence a long clause might turn out to be more useful than a short clause, if the literals of the long one all lie on just one or two levels while the literals of the short one belong to three or more.

Suppose all the literals of a clause $C = l_1 \vee \cdots \vee l_r$ appear in the trail, either positively as l_j or negatively as $\bar{l}_j$. We can group them by level so that exactly $p + q$ levels are represented, where p of the levels contain at least one positive l_j and the other q contain nothing but $\bar{l}_j$'s. Then (p, q) is the *signature* of C with respect to the trail, and $p + q$ is the literal block distance. For example, the very first clause learned from $waerden(3, 10; 97)$ in the author's test run was

$$\overline{11}\ \overline{16}\ \overline{21}\ \overline{26}\ \overline{36}\ \overline{46}\ \overline{51}\ 61\ 66\ 91; \qquad\qquad (122)$$

later, when it was time to rank clauses for purging, the values and trail levels of those literals were specified by $\text{VAL}(11), \text{VAL}(16), \ldots, \text{VAL}(91)$, which were

$$20\ 21\ 21\ 21\ 20\ 15\ 16\ 8\ 14\ 20.$$

Thus 61 was true on level $8 \gg 1 = 4$; $\overline{46}$ and 66 were true on level $15 \gg 1 = 14 \gg 1 = 7$; $\overline{51}$ was false on level 8; the others were a mixture of true and false on level 10; hence (122) had $p = 3$ and $q = 1$ with respect to the current trail.

If C has signature (p, q) and C' has signature (p', q'), where $p \le p'$ and $q \le q'$ and $(p, q) \ne (p', q')$, we can expect that C is more likely than C' to be useful in future propagations. The same conclusion is plausible also when $p + q = p' + q'$ and $p < p'$, because C' won't force anything until literals from at least $p + 1$ different levels change sign. These intuitive expectations are borne out by the following detailed data obtained from $waerden(3, 10; 97)$:

$$
\begin{pmatrix}
0 & 4 & 17 & 22 & 30 & 54 & 67 & 99 & 17 \\
17 & 81 & 191 & 395 & 360 & 404 & 438 & 66 & 6 \\
63 & 232 & 463 & 536 & 521 & 386 & 117 & 6 & 0 \\
52 & 243 & 291 & 298 & 308 & 112 & 22 & 0 & 0 \\
18 & 59 & 86 & 77 & 53 & 7 & 0 & 0 & 0 \\
0 & 8 & 3 & 10 & 0 & 0 & 0 & 0 & 0 \\
0 & 0 & 1 & 0 & 0 & 0 & 0 & 0 & 0
\end{pmatrix}
\quad
\begin{pmatrix}
0 & 1 & 9 & 15 & 21 & 16 & 15 & 3 & 0 \\
7 & 26 & 74 & 107 & 82 & 57 & 16 & 1 & 0 \\
20 & 74 & 104 & 86 & 61 & 21 & 9 & 0 & 0 \\
13 & 40 & 37 & 16 & 14 & 4 & 0 & 0 & 0 \\
6 & 10 & 9 & 4 & 1 & 1 & 0 & 0 & 0 \\
0 & 1 & 1 & 0 & 0 & 0 & 0 & 0 & 0 \\
0 & 0 & 0 & 0 & 0 & 0 & 0 & 0 & 0
\end{pmatrix}
$$

The matrix on the left shows how many of the 6240 eligible clauses had a given signature (p, q), for $1 \le p \le 7$ and $0 \le q \le 8$; the matrix on the right shows how many would have been used to resolve future conflicts, if none of them had been removed. There were, for example, 536 learned clauses with $p = q = 3$, of which only 86 actually turned out to be useful. This data is illustrated graphically in Fig. 93, which shows gray rectangles whose areas correspond to the left matrix, overlaid by black rectangles whose areas correspond to the right matrix. We can't predict the future, but small (p, q) tends to increase the ratio of black to gray.

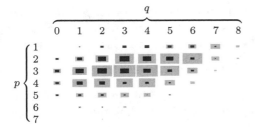

Fig. 93. Learned clauses that have p positive and q all-negative levels. The gray ones will never be used again. Unfortunately, there's no easy way to distinguish gray from black without being clairvoyant.

An alert reader will be wondering, however, how such signatures were found, because we can't compute them for all clauses until all variables appear in the trail—and that doesn't happen until all clauses are satisfied! The answer [see A. Goultiaeva and F. Bacchus, *LNCS* **7317** (2012), 30–43] is that it's quite possible to carry out a "full run" in which *every* variable is assigned a value, by making only a slight change to the normal behavior of Algorithm C: Instead of resolving conflicts immediately and backjumping, we can carry on after each conflict until all propagations cease, and we can continue to build the trail in the same way until every variable is present on some level. Conflicts may have occurred on several different levels; but we can safely resolve them later, learning new clauses at that time. Meanwhile, a full trail allows us to compute signatures based on VAL fields. And those VAL fields go into the OVAL fields after backjumping, so the variables in each block will tend to maintain their relationships.

The author's implementation of Algorithm C assigns an eight-bit value

$$\text{RANGE}(c) \;\leftarrow\; \min\big(\lfloor 16(p+\alpha q)\rfloor,\,255\big) \tag{123}$$

to each clause c; here α is a parameter, $0 \le \alpha \le 1$. We also set $\text{RANGE}(c) \leftarrow 0$ if c is the reason for some literal in the trail; $\text{RANGE}(c) \leftarrow 256$ if c is satisfied at level 0. If there are m_j clauses of range j, and if we want to keep at most T clauses in memory, we find the largest $j \le 256$ such that

$$s_j \;=\; m_0 + m_1 + \cdots + m_{j-1} \;\le\; T. \tag{124}$$

Then we retain all clauses for which $\text{RANGE}(c) < j$, together with $T - s_j$ "tie-breakers" that have $\text{RANGE}(c) = j$ (unless $j = 256$). When α has the relatively high value $\frac{15}{16} = .9375$, this rule essentially preserves as many clauses of small literal block distance as it can; and for constant $p+q$ it favors those with small p.

For example, with $\alpha = \frac{15}{16}$ and the data from Fig. 93, we save clauses that have $p = (1,2,3,4,5)$ when $q \le (5,4,3,2,0)$, respectively. This gives us $s_{95} = 12 + 3069$ clauses, just 45 shy of our target $T = 3126$. So we also choose 45 tie-breakers from among the 59 clauses that have $\text{RANGE}(c) = 95$, $(p,q) = (5,1)$.

Tie-breaking can be done by using a secondary heuristic $\text{ACT}(c)$, "clause activity," which is analogous to the activity score of a variable but it is more easily maintained. If clause c has been used to resolve the conflicts numbered 3, 47, 95, 99, and 100, say, then

$$\text{ACT}(c) \;=\; \varrho^{-3} + \varrho^{-47} + \varrho^{-95} + \varrho^{-99} + \varrho^{-100}. \tag{125}$$

This damping factor ϱ (normally .999) is independent of the factor ρ that is used for variable activities. In the case of Fig. 93, if the 59 clauses with $(p,q) = (5,1)$ are arranged in order of increasing ACT scores, the gray-and-black pattern is

■■■■■■■□■□■■■□■■■■■□■■□□■■■■□■■■■■■■■■■■■■■■■■■■■■■■□■■■■■□■■■■■■■■■.

So if we retain the 45 with highest activity, we pick up 8 of the 10 that turn out to be useful. (Clause activities are imperfect predictors, but they are usually somewhat better than this example implies.)

Exercises 287 and 288 present full details of clause purging in accordance with these ideas. One question remains: After we've completed a purge, when should we schedule the next one? Successful results are obtained by having two parameters, Δ_p and δ_p. Initially $M_p = \Delta_p$; then after each purge, we set $\Delta_p \leftarrow \Delta_p + \delta_p$ and $M_p \leftarrow M_p + \Delta_p$. For example, if $\Delta_p = 10000$ and $\delta_p = 100$, purging will occur after approximately 10000, 20100, 30300, 40600, $\ldots$, $k\Delta_p + \binom{k}{2}\delta_p$,

... clauses have been learned; and the number of clauses at the beginning of the kth round will be approximately $20000 + 200k = 2\Delta_p + 2k\delta_p$. (See exercise 289.)

We've based this discussion on $waerden(3, 10; 97)$, which is quite a simple problem. Algorithm C's gain from clause-purging on larger problems is naturally much more substantial. For example, $waerden(3, 13; 160)$ is only a bit larger than $waerden(3, 10; 97)$. With $\Delta_p = 10000$ and $\delta_p = 100$, it finishes in 132 gigamems, after learning 9.5 million clauses and occupying only 503 thousand MEM cells. Without purging, it proves unsatisfiability after learning only 7.1 million clauses, yet at well over ten times the cost: 4307 gigamems, and 102 million cells of MEM.

*Flushing literals and restarting. Algorithm C interrupts itself in step C5 not only to purge clauses but also to "flush literals" that may not have been the best choices for decisions in the trail. The task of solving a tough satisfiability problem is a delicate balancing act: We don't want to get bogged down in the wrong part of the search space; but we also don't want to lose the fruits of hard work by "throwing out the baby with the bath water." A nice compromise has been found by Peter van der Tak, Antonio Ramos, and Marijn Heule [*J. Satisfiability, Bool. Modeling and Comp.* **7** (2011), 133–138], who devised a useful way to rejuvenate the trail periodically by following trends in the activity scores $\mathtt{ACT}(k)$.

Let's go back to Table 3, to illustrate their method. After learning the clause (116), Algorithm C will update the trail by setting $L_{44} \leftarrow 57$ on level 17; that will force $L_{45} \leftarrow \overline{66}$, because 39, 42, ..., 63 have all become true; and further positive literals 6, 58, 82, 86, 95, 96 will also join the trail in some order. Step C5 might then intervene to suggest that we should contemplate flushing some or all of the $F = 52$ literals whose values are currently assigned.

The decision literals $\overline{53}$, 55, 44, ..., 51 on levels 1, 2, 3, ..., 17 each were selected because they had the greatest current activity scores when their level began. But activity scores are continually being updated, so the old ones might be considerably out of touch with present realities. For example, we've just boosted $\mathtt{ACT}(53)$, $\mathtt{ACT}(27)$, $\mathtt{ACT}(36)$, $\mathtt{ACT}(70)$, ..., in the process of learning (116) — see (115). Thus it's quite possible that several of the first 17 decisions no longer seem wise, because those literals haven't participated in any recent conflicts.

Let x_k be a variable with maximum $\mathtt{ACT}(k)$, among all of the variables not in the current trail. It's easy to find such a k (see exercise 290). Now consider, as a thought experiment, what would happen if we were to jump back all the way to level 0 at this point and start over. Recall that our phase-saving strategy dictates that we would set $\mathtt{OVAL}(j) \leftarrow \mathtt{VAL}(j)$ just before setting $\mathtt{VAL}(j) \leftarrow -1$, as the variables become unassigned.

If we now restart at step C6 with $d \leftarrow 1$, all variables whose activity exceeds $\mathtt{ACT}(k)$ will receive their former values (although not necessarily in the same order), because the corresponding literals will enter the trail either as decisions or as forced propagations. History will more-or-less repeat itself, because the old assignments did not cause any conflicts, and because phases were saved.

Therefore we might as well avoid most of this back-and-forth unsetting and resetting, by reusing the trail and jumping back only partway, to the first level where the current activity scores significantly change the picture:

Set $d' \leftarrow 0$. While $\texttt{ACT}(|L_{i_{d'+1}}|) \geq \texttt{ACT}(k)$, set $d' \leftarrow d' + 1$.
Then if $d' < d$, jump back to level d'. $\qquad\qquad(126)$

This is the technique called "literal flushing," because it removes the literals on levels $d' + 1$ through d and leaves the others assigned. It effectively redirects the search into new territory, without being as drastic as a full restart.

In Table 3, for example, $\texttt{ACT}(49)$ might exceed the activity score of every other unassigned variable; and it might also exceed $\texttt{ACT}(46)$, the activity of the decision literal $\overline{46}$ on level 15. If the previous 14 decision-oriented activities $\texttt{ACT}(53), \texttt{ACT}(55), \ldots, \texttt{ACT}(37)$ are all $\geq \texttt{ACT}(49)$, we would flush all the literals $L_{25}, L_{26}, \ldots$ above level $d' = 14$, and commence a new level 15.

Notice that some of the flushed literals other than $\overline{46}$ might actually have the largest activities of all. In such cases they will re-insert themselves, before 49 ever enters the scene. Eventually, though, the literal 49 will inaugurate a new level before a new conflict arises. (See exercise 291.)

Experience shows that flushing can indeed be extremely helpful. On the other hand, it can be harmful if it causes us to abandon a fruitful line of attack. When the solver is perking along and learning useful clauses by the dozen, we don't want to upset the applecart by rocking the boat. Armin Biere has therefore introduced a useful statistic called *agility*, which tends to be correlated with the desirability of flushing at any given moment. His idea [*LNCS* **4996** (2008), 28–33] is beautifully simple: We maintain a 32-bit integer variable called $\texttt{AGILITY}$, initially zero. Whenever a literal l is placed on the trail in steps C4, C6, or C9, we update the agility by setting

$$\texttt{AGILITY} \leftarrow \texttt{AGILITY} - (\texttt{AGILITY} \gg 13) + \bigl(\bigl((\texttt{OVAL}(|l|) - \texttt{VAL}(|l|)) \& 1\bigr) \ll 19\bigr). \quad(127)$$

In other words, the fraction $\texttt{AGILITY}/2^{32}$ is essentially multiplied by $1 - \delta$, then increased by δ if the new polarity of l differs from its previous polarity, where $\delta = 2^{-13} \approx .0001$. High agility means that lots of the recent propagations are flipping the values of variables and trying new possibilities; low agility means that the algorithm is basically in a rut, spinning its wheels and getting nowhere.

Table 4
TO FLUSH OR NOT TO FLUSH?

Let $a = \texttt{AGILITY}/2^{32}$ when setting $M_{\mathrm{f}} \leftarrow M + \Delta_{\mathrm{f}}$, and let $\psi = 1/6$, $\theta = 17/16$.

If Δ_{f} is	then flush if	If Δ_{f} is	then flush if	If Δ_{f} is	then flush if
1	$a \leq \psi \approx .17$	32	$a \leq \theta^5\psi \approx .23$	1024	$a \leq \theta^{10}\psi \approx .31$
2	$a \leq \theta\psi \approx .18$	64	$a \leq \theta^6\psi \approx .24$	2048	$a \leq \theta^{11}\psi \approx .32$
4	$a \leq \theta^2\psi \approx .19$	128	$a \leq \theta^7\psi \approx .25$	4096	$a \leq \theta^{12}\psi \approx .34$
8	$a \leq \theta^3\psi \approx .20$	256	$a \leq \theta^8\psi \approx .27$	8192	$a \leq \theta^{13}\psi \approx .37$
16	$a \leq \theta^4\psi \approx .21$	512	$a \leq \theta^9\psi \approx .29$	16384	$a \leq \theta^{14}\psi \approx .39$

Armed with the notion of agility, we can finally state what Algorithm C does when step C5 finds $M \geq M_{\mathrm{f}}$: First M_{f} is reset to $M + \Delta_{\mathrm{f}}$, where Δ_{f} is

a power of two determined by the "reluctant doubling" sequence $\langle 1, 1, 2, 1, 1,$
$2, 4, 1, \ldots \rangle$; that sequence is discussed below and in exercise 293. Then the
agility is compared to a threshold, depending on Δ_{f}, according to the schedule
in Table 4. (The parameter ψ in that table can be raised or lowered, if you want
to increase or decrease the amount of flushing.) If the agility is sufficiently small,
x_k is found and (126) is performed. Nothing changes if the agility is large or if
$d' = d$; otherwise (126) has flushed some literals, using the operations of step C8.

Monte Carlo algorithms. Let's turn now to a completely different way to
approach satisfiability problems, based on finding solutions by totally heuristic
and randomized methods, often called *stochastic local search*. We often use such
methods in our daily lives, even though there's no guarantee of success. The
simplest satisfiability-oriented technique of this kind was introduced by Jun Gu
[see *SIGART Bulletin* **3**, 1 (January 1992), 8–12] and by Christos Papadimitriou
[*FOCS* **32** (1991), 163–169] as a byproduct of more general studies:

> "Start with any truth assignment. While there are unsatisfied
> clauses, pick any one, and flip a random literal in it."

Some programmers are known to debug their code in a haphazard manner,
somewhat like this approach; and we know that such "blind" changes are foolish
because they usually introduce new bugs. Yet this idea does have merit when it
is applied to satisfiability, so we shall formulate it as an algorithm:

Algorithm P (*Satisfiability by random walk*). Given m nonempty clauses
$C_1 \wedge \cdots \wedge C_m$ on n Boolean variables $x_1 \ldots x_n$, this algorithm either finds a
solution or terminates unsuccessfully after making N trials.

P1. [Initialize.] Assign random Boolean values to $x_1 \ldots x_n$. Set $j \leftarrow 0$, $s \leftarrow 0$,
and $t \leftarrow 0$. (We know that s clauses are satisfied after having made t flips.)

P2. [Success?] If $s = m$, terminate successfully with solution $x_1 \ldots x_n$. Otherwise set $j \leftarrow (j \bmod m)+1$. If clause C_j is satisfied by $x_1 \ldots x_n$, set $s \leftarrow s+1$
and repeat this step.

P3. [Done?] If $t = N$, terminate unsuccessfully.

P4. [Flip one bit.] Let clause C_j be $(l_1 \vee \cdots \vee l_k)$. Choose a random index
$i \in \{1, \ldots, k\}$, and change variable $|l_i|$ so that literal l_i becomes true. Set
$s \leftarrow 1$, $t \leftarrow t+1$, and return to P2. ∎

Suppose, for example, that we're given the seven clauses R' of (7). Thus
$m = 7$, $n = 4$; and there are two solutions, 01*1. In this case every nonsolution
violates a unique clause; for example, 1100 violates the clause $\bar{1}23$, so step P4 is
equally likely to change 1100 to 0100, 1000, or 1110, only one of which is closer
to a solution. An exact analysis (see exercise 294) shows that Algorithm P will
find a solution after making 8.25 flips, on the average. That's no improvement
over a brute-force search through all $2^n = 16$ possibilities; but a small example
like this doesn't tell us much about what happens when n is large.

Papadimitriou observed that Algorithm P is reasonably effective when it's
applied to 2SAT problems, because each flip has roughly a 50-50 chance of making

progress in that case. Several years later, Uwe Schöning [*Algorithmica* **32** (2002), 615–623] discovered that the algorithm also does surprisingly well on instances of 3SAT, even though the flips when $k > 2$ in step P4 tend to go "the wrong way":

Theorem U. *If the given clauses are satisfiable, and if each clause has at most three literals, Algorithm P will succeed with probability* $\Omega((3/4)^n/n)$ *after making at most n flips.*

Proof. By complementing variables, if necessary, we can assume that $0\ldots0$ is a solution; under this assumption, every clause has at least one negative literal. Let $X_t = x_1 + \cdots + x_n$ be the number of 1s after t flips have been made. Each flip changes X_t by ± 1, and we want to show that there's a nontrivial chance that X_t will become 0. After step P1, the random variable X_0 will be equal to q with probability $\binom{n}{q}/2^n$.

A clause that contains three negative literals is good news for Algorithm P, because it is violated only when all three variables are 1; a flip will *always* decrease X_t in such a case. Similarly, a violated clause with two negatives and one positive will invoke a flip that makes progress 2/3 of the time. The worst case occurs only when a problematic clause has only one negative literal. Unfortunately, every clause might belong to this worst case, for all we know.

Instead of studying X_t, which depends on the pattern of clauses, it's much easier to study another random variable Y_t defined as follows: Initially $Y_0 = X_0$; but $Y_{t+1} = Y_t - 1$ only when step P4 flips the negative literal that has the smallest subscript; otherwise $Y_{t+1} = Y_t + 1$. For example, after taking care of a violated clause such as $x_3 \vee \bar{x}_5 \vee \bar{x}_8$, we have $X_{t+1} = X_t+(+1,-1,-1)$ but $Y_{t+1} = Y_t + (+1,-1,+1)$ in the three possible cases. Furthermore, if the clause contains fewer than three literals, we penalize Y_{t+1} even more, by allowing it to be $Y_t - 1$ only with probability 1/3. (After a clause such as $x_4 \vee \bar{x}_6$, for instance, we put $Y_{t+1} = Y_t-1$ in only 2/3 of the cases when x_6 is flipped; otherwise $Y_{t+1} = Y_t+1$.)

We clearly have $X_t \le Y_t$ for all t. Therefore $\Pr(X_t = 0) \ge \Pr(Y_t = 0)$, after t flips have been made; and we've defined things so that it's quite easy to calculate $\Pr(Y_t = 0)$, because Y_t doesn't depend on the current clause j:

$$\Pr(Y_{t+1} = Y_t - 1) = 1/3 \quad \text{and} \quad \Pr(Y_{t+1} = Y_t + 1) = 2/3 \quad \text{when} \quad Y_t > 0.$$

Indeed, the theory of random walks developed in Section 7.2.1.6 tells us how to count the number of scenarios that begin with $Y_0 = q$ and end with $Y_t = 0$, after Y_t has increased p times and decreased $p + q$ times while remaining positive for $0 \le t < 2p + q$. It is the "ballot number" of Eq. 7.2.1.6–(23),

$$C_{p,p+q-1} = \frac{q}{2p+q}\binom{2p+q}{p}. \tag{128}$$

The probability that $Y_0 = q$ and that $Y_t = 0$ for the first time when $t = 2p + q$ is therefore exactly

$$f(p,q) = \frac{1}{2^n}\binom{n}{q}\frac{q}{2p+q}\binom{2p+q}{p}\left(\frac{1}{3}\right)^{p+q}\left(\frac{2}{3}\right)^p. \tag{129}$$

Every value of p and q gives a lower bound for the probability that Algorithm P succeeds; and exercise 296 shows that we get the result claimed in Theorem U by choosing $p = q \approx n/3$. ∎

Theorem U might seem pointless, because it predicts success only with exponentially small probability when $N = n$. But if at first we don't succeed, we can try and try again, by repeating Algorithm P with different random choices. And if we repeat it $Kn(4/3)^n$ times, for large enough K, we're almost certain to find a solution unless the clauses can't all be satisfied.

In fact, even more is true, because the proof of Theorem U doesn't exploit the full power of Eq. (129). Exercise 297 carries the analysis further, in a particularly instructive way, and proves a much sharper result:

Corollary W. *When Algorithm P is applied $K(4/3)^n$ times with $N = 2n$ to a set of satisfiable ternary clauses, its success probability exceeds $1 - e^{-K/2}$.* ∎

If the clauses $C_1 \wedge \cdots \wedge C_m$ are unsatisfiable, Algorithm P will never demonstrate that fact conclusively. But if we repeat it $100(4/3)^n$ times and get no solution, Corollary W tells us that the chances of satisfiability are incredibly small (less than 10^{-21}). So it's a safe bet that no solution exists in such a case.

Thus Algorithm P has a surprisingly good chance of finding solutions "with its eyes closed," while walking at random in the gigantic space of all 2^n binary vectors; and we can well imagine that even better results are possible if we devise randomized walking methods that proceed with eyes wide open. Therefore many people have experimented with strategies that try to make intelligent choices about which direction to take at each flip-step. One of the simplest and best of these improvements, popularly known as WalkSAT, was devised by B. Selman, H. A. Kautz, and B. Cohen [*Nat. Conf. Artificial Intelligence* **12** (1994), 337–343]:

Algorithm W (*WalkSAT*). Given m nonempty clauses $C_1 \wedge \cdots \wedge C_m$ on n Boolean variables $x_1 \ldots x_n$, and a "greed-avoidance" parameter p, this algorithm either finds a solution or terminates unsuccessfully after making N trials. It uses auxiliary arrays $c_1 \ldots c_n$, $f_0 \ldots f_{m-1}$, $k_1 \ldots k_m$, and $w_1 \ldots w_m$.

W1. [Initialize.] Assign random Boolean values to $x_1 \ldots x_n$. Also set $r \leftarrow t \leftarrow 0$ and $c_1 \ldots c_n \leftarrow 0 \ldots 0$. Then, for $1 \leq j \leq m$, set k_j to the number of true literals in C_j; and if $k_j = 0$, set $f_r \leftarrow j$, $w_j \leftarrow r$, and $r \leftarrow r + 1$; or if $k_j = 1$ and the only true literal of C_j is x_i or $\bar{x}_i$, set $c_i \leftarrow c_i + 1$. (Now r is the number of unsatisfied clauses, and the f array lists them. The number c_i is the "cost" or "break count" for variable x_i, namely the number of additional clauses that will become false if x_i is flipped.)

W2. [Done?] If $r = 0$, terminate successfully with solution $x_1 \ldots x_n$. Otherwise, if $t = N$, terminate unsuccessfully.

W3. [Choose j.] Set $j \leftarrow f_q$, where q is uniformly random in $\{0, 1, \ldots, r - 1\}$. (In other words, choose an unsatisfied clause C_j at random, considering every such clause to be equally likely; exercise 3.4.1–3 discusses the best way to compute q.) Let clause C_j be $(l_1 \vee \cdots \vee l_k)$.

W4. [Choose l.] Let c be the smallest cost among the literals $\{l_1, \ldots, l_k\}$. If $c = 0$, or if $c \geq 1$ and $U \geq p$ where U is uniform in $[0 \mathinner{\ldotp\ldotp} 1)$, choose l randomly from among the literals of cost c. (We call this a "greedy" choice, because flipping l will minimize the number of newly false clauses.) Otherwise choose l randomly in $\{l_1, \ldots, l_k\}$.

W5. [Flip l.] Change the value of variable $|l|$, and update r, $c_1 \ldots c_n$, $f_0 \ldots f_{r-1}$, $k_1 \ldots k_m$, $w_1 \ldots w_m$ to agree with this new value. (Exercise 302 explains how to implement steps W4 and W5 efficiently, with computer-friendly changes to the data structures.) Set $t \leftarrow t + 1$ and return to W2. ∎

If, for example, we try to satisfy the seven clauses of (7) with Algorithm W, as we did earlier with Algorithm P, the choice $x_1 x_2 x_3 x_4 = 0110$ violates $\bar{2}\bar{3}4$; and $c_1 c_2 c_3 c_4$ turns out to be 0110 in this situation. So step W4 will choose to flip x_4, and we'll have the solution 0111. (See exercise 303.)

Notice that step W3 focuses attention on clauses whose variables need to change. Furthermore, a literal that appears in the most unsatisfied clauses is most likely to appear in the chosen clause C_j.

If no cost-free flip is available, step W4 makes nongreedy choices with probability p. This policy keeps the algorithm from getting stuck in an unsatisfiable region from which there's no greedy exit. Extensive experiments by S. Seitz, M. Alava, and P. Orponen [*J. Statistical Mechanics* (June 2005), P06006:1–27] indicate that the best choice of p is .57 when large random 3SAT problems are being tackled and when $N = \infty$. For example, with this setting of p, and with $m = 4.2n$ random 3-literal clauses, Algorithm W works fantastically well: It tends to find solutions after making fewer than $10,000n$ flips when $n = 10^4$, and fewer than $2500n$ flips when $10^5 \leq n \leq 10^6$.

What about the parameter N? Should we set it equal to $2n$ (as recommended for 3SAT problems with respect to Algorithm P), or perhaps to n^2 (as recommended for 2SAT in exercise 299), or to $2500n$ (as just mentioned for 3SAT in Algorithm W), or to something else? When we use an algorithm like WalkSAT, whose behavior can vary wildly depending on random choices and on unknown characteristics of the data, it's often wise to "cut our losses" and to start afresh with a brand new pattern of random numbers.

Exercise 306 proves that such an algorithm always has an optimum cutoff value $N = N^*$, which minimizes the expected time to success when the algorithm is restarted after each failure. Sometimes $N^* = \infty$ is the best choice, meaning that we should always keep plowing ahead; in other cases N^* is quite small.

But N^* exists only in theory, and the theory requires perfect knowledge of the algorithm's behavior. In practice we usually have little or no information about how N should best be specified. Fortunately there's still an effective way to proceed, by using the notion of *reluctant doubling* introduced by M. Luby, A. Sinclair, and D. Zuckerman [*Information Proc. Letters* **47** (1993), 173–180], who defined the interesting sequence

$$S_1, S_2, \ldots = 1, 1, 2, 1, 1, 2, 4, 1, 1, 2, 1, 1, 2, 4, 8, 1, 1, 2, 1, 1, 2, 4, 1, 1, 2, \ldots. \tag{130}$$

The elements of this sequence are all powers of 2. Furthermore we have $S_{n+1} = 2S_n$ if the number S_n has already occurred an even number of times, otherwise $S_{n+1} = 1$. A convenient way to generate this sequence is to work with two integers (u, v), and to start with $(u_1, v_1) = (1, 1)$; then

$$(u_{n+1}, v_{n+1}) = (u_n \mathbin{\&} -u_n = v_n? \; (u_n + 1, 1): (u_n, 2v_n)). \qquad (131)$$

The successive pairs are $(1, 1)$, $(2, 1)$, $(2, 2)$, $(3, 1)$, $(4, 1)$, $(4, 2)$, $(4, 4)$, $(5, 1)$, $\ldots$, and we have $S_n = v_n$ for all $n \geq 1$.

The reluctant doubling strategy is to run Algorithm W repeatedly with $N = cS_1$, cS_2, cS_3, $\ldots$, until success is achieved, where c is some constant. Exercise 308 proves that the expected running time X obtained in this way exceeds the optimum by at most a factor of $O(\log X)$. Other sequences besides $\langle S_n \rangle$ also have this property, and they're sometimes better (see exercise 311). The best policy is probably to use $\langle cS_n \rangle$, where c represents our best guess about the value of N^*; in this way we hedge our bets in case c is too small.

The Local Lemma. The existence of particular combinatorial patterns is often established by using a nonconstructive proof technique called the "probabilistic method," pioneered by Paul Erdős. If we can show that $\Pr(X) > 0$, in some probability space, then X must be true in at least one case. For example [*Bull. Amer. Math. Soc.* **53** (1947), 292–294], Erdős famously observed that there is a graph G on n vertices such that neither G nor $\overline{G}$ contains a k-clique, whenever

$$\binom{n}{k} < 2^{k(k-1)/2-1}. \qquad (132)$$

For if we consider a random graph G, each of whose $\binom{n}{2}$ edges is present with probability $1/2$, and if U is any particular subset of k vertices in G, the probability that either $G \,|\, U$ or $\overline{G} \,|\, U$ is a complete graph is clearly $2/2^{k(k-1)/2}$. Hence the probability that this doesn't happen for any of the $\binom{n}{k}$ subsets U is at least $1 - \binom{n}{k}2^{1-k(k-1)/2}$. This probability is positive; so such a graph must exist.

The proof just given does not provide any explicit construction. But it does show that we can find such a graph by making at most $1 / \big(1 - \binom{n}{k}2^{1-k(k-1)/2}\big)$ random trials, on the average, provided that n and k are small enough that we are able to test all $\binom{n}{k}$ subgraphs in a reasonable amount of time.

Probability calculations of this kind are often complicated by dependencies between the random events being considered. For example, the presence of a clique in one part of a graph affects the likelihood of many other cliques that share some of the same vertices. But the interdependencies are often highly localized, so that "remote" events are essentially independent of each other. László Lovász introduced an important way to deal with such situations early in the 1970s, and his approach has become known as the "Local Lemma" because it has been used to establish many theorems. First published as a lemma on pages 616–617 of a longer paper [Erdős and Lovász, *Infinite and Finite Sets, Colloquia Math. Soc. János Bolyai* **10** (1975), 609–627], and subsequently extended to a "lopsided" form [P. Erdős and J. Spencer, *Discrete Applied Math.* **30** (1991), 151–154], it can be stated as follows:

Lemma L. *Let $A_1, \ldots, A_m$ be events in some probability space. Let G be a graph on vertices $\{1, \ldots, m\}$, and let $(p_1, \ldots, p_m)$ be numbers such that*

$$\Pr(A_i \mid \overline{A}_{j_1} \cap \cdots \cap \overline{A}_{j_k}) \;\leq\; p_i \text{ whenever } k \geq 0 \text{ and } i \not\!\!-\! j_1, \ldots, i \not\!\!-\! j_k. \quad (133)$$

Then $\Pr(\overline{A}_1 \cap \cdots \cap \overline{A}_m) > 0$ whenever $(p_1, \ldots, p_m)$ lies in a certain set $\mathcal{R}(G)$. ∎

In applications we think of the A_j as "bad" events, which are undesirable conditions that interfere with whatever we're trying to find. The graph G is called a "lopsidependency graph" for our application; this name was coined as an extension of Lovász's original term "dependency graph," for which the strict condition '$= p_i$' was assumed in place of '$\leq p_i$' in (133).

The set $\mathcal{R}(G)$ of probability bounds for which we can guarantee that all bad events can simultaneously be avoided, given (133), will be discussed further below. If G is the complete graph K_m, so that (133) simply states that $\Pr(A_i) \leq p_i$, $\mathcal{R}(G)$ is clearly $\{(p_1, \ldots, p_m) \mid (p_1, \ldots, p_m) \geq (0, \ldots, 0) \text{ and } p_1 + \cdots + p_m < 1\}$; this is the smallest possible $\mathcal{R}(G)$. At the other extreme, if G is the empty graph $\overline{K_m}$, we get $\{(p_1, \ldots, p_m) \mid 0 \leq p_j < 1 \text{ for } 1 \leq j \leq m\}$, the largest possible $\mathcal{R}(G)$. Adding an edge to G makes $\mathcal{R}(G)$ smaller. Notice that, if $(p_1, \ldots, p_m)$ is in $\mathcal{R}(G)$ and $0 \leq p'_j \leq p_j$ for $1 \leq j \leq m$, then also $(p'_1, \ldots, p'_m) \in \mathcal{R}(G)$.

Lovász discovered an elegant local condition that suffices to make Lemma L widely applicable [see J. Spencer, *Discrete Math.* **20** (1977), 69–76]:

Theorem L. *The probability vector $(p_1, \ldots, p_m)$ is in $\mathcal{R}(G)$ when there are numbers $0 \leq \theta_1, \ldots, \theta_m < 1$ such that*

$$p_i = \theta_i \prod_{i - j \text{ in } G} (1 - \theta_j). \quad (134)$$

Proof. Exercise 344(e) proves that $\Pr(\overline{A}_1 \cap \cdots \cap \overline{A}_m) \geq (1 - \theta_1) \ldots (1 - \theta_m)$. ∎

James B. Shearer [*Combinatorica* **5** (1985), 241–245] went on to determine the exact maximum extent of $\mathcal{R}(G)$ for all graphs G, as we'll see later; and he also established the following important special case:

Theorem J. *Suppose every vertex of G has degree $\leq d$, where $d > 1$. Then $(p, \ldots, p) \in \mathcal{R}(G)$ when $p \leq (d-1)^{d-1}/d^d$.*

Proof. See the interesting inductive argument in exercise 317. ∎

This condition on p holds whenever $p \leq 1/(ed)$ (see exercise 319).

Further study led to a big surprise: The Local Lemma proves only that desirable combinatorial patterns *exist*, although they might be rare. But Robin Moser and Gábor Tardos discovered [*JACM* **57** (2010), 11:1–11:15] that we can efficiently *compute* a pattern that avoids all of the bad A_j, using an almost unbelievably simple algorithm analogous to WalkSAT!

Algorithm M (*Local resampling*). Given m events $\{A_1, \ldots, A_m\}$ that depend on n Boolean variables $\{x_1, \ldots, x_n\}$, this algorithm either finds a vector $x_1 \ldots x_n$ for which none of the events is true, or loops forever. We assume that A_j is a function of the variables $\{x_k \mid k \in \Xi_j\}$ for some given subset $\Xi_j \subseteq \{1, \ldots, n\}$.

Whenever the algorithm assigns a value to x_k, it sets $x_k \leftarrow 1$ with probability ξ_k and $x_k \leftarrow 0$ with probability $1 - \xi_k$, where ξ_k is another given parameter.

M1. [Initialize.] For $1 \leq k \leq n$, set $x_k \leftarrow [U < \xi_k]$, where U is uniform in $[0 .. 1)$.

M2. [Choose j.] Set j to the index of any event such that A_j is true. If no such j exists, terminate successfully, having found a solution $x_1 \ldots x_n$.

M3. [Resample for A_j.] For each $k \in \Xi_j$, set $x_k \leftarrow [U < \xi_k]$, where U is uniform in $[0 .. 1)$. Return to M2. ∎

(We have stated Algorithm M in terms of binary variables x_k purely for convenience. The same ideas apply when each x_k has a discrete probability distribution on *any* set of values, possibly different for each k.)

To tie this algorithm to the Local Lemma, we assume that event A_i holds with probability $\leq p_i$ whenever the variables it depends on have the given distribution. For example, if A_i is the event "$x_3 \neq x_5$" then p_i must be at least $\xi_3(1 - \xi_5) + (1 - \xi_3)\xi_5$.

We also assume that there's a graph G on vertices $\{1, \ldots, m\}$ such that condition (133) is true, and that $i - j$ whenever $i \neq j$ and $\Xi_i \cap \Xi_j \neq \emptyset$. Then G is a suitable dependency graph for $\{A_1, \ldots, A_m\}$, because the events A_{j_1}, ..., A_{j_k} can't possibly influence A_i when $i \not\!\!-\, j_1$, ..., $i \not\!\!-\, j_k$. (Those events share no common variables with A_i.) We can also sometimes get by with fewer edges by making G a *lopsidependency* graph; see exercise 351.

Algorithm M might succeed with *any* given events, purely by chance. But if the conditions of the Local Lemma are satisfied, success can be guaranteed:

Theorem M. *If* (133) *holds with probabilities that satisfy condition* (134) *of Theorem L, step M3 is performed for A_j at most $\theta_j/(1 - \theta_j)$ times, on average.*

Proof. Exercise 352 shows that this result is a corollary of the more general analysis that is carried out below. The stated upper bound is good news, because θ_j is usually quite small. ∎

Traces and pieces. The best way to understand why Algorithm M is so efficient is to view it algebraically in terms of "traces." The theory of traces is a beautiful area of mathematics in which amazingly simple proofs of profound results have been discovered. Its basic ideas were first formulated by P. Cartier and D. Foata [*Lecture Notes in Math.* **85** (1969)], then independently developed from another point of view by R. M. Keller [*JACM* **20** (1973), 514–537, 696–710] and A. Mazurkiewicz ["Concurrent program schemes and their interpretations," DAIMI Report PB 78 (Aarhus University, July 1977)]. Significant advances were made by G. X. Viennot [*Lecture Notes in Math.* **1234** (1985), 321–350], who presented many wide-ranging applications and explained how the theory could readily be visualized in terms of what he called "heaps of pieces."

Trace theory is the study of algebraic products whose variables are not necessarily commutative. Thus it forms a bridge between the study of strings (in which, for example, *acbbaca* is quite distinct from *baccaab*) and the study of ordinary commutative algebra (in which both of those examples are equal to

$aaabbcc = a^3b^2c^2$). Each adjacent pair of letters $\{a, b\}$ either *commutes*, meaning that $ab = ba$, or *clashes*, meaning that ab is different from ba. If, for instance, we specify that a commutes with c but that b clashes with both a and c, then *acbbaca* is equal to *cabbaac*, and it has six variants altogether; similarly, there are ten equally good ways to write *baccaab*.

Formally speaking, a *trace* is an equivalence class of strings that can be converted to each other by repeatedly interchanging pairs of adjacent letters that don't clash. But we don't need to fuss about the fact that equivalence classes are present; we can simply represent a trace by any one of its equivalent strings, just as we don't distinguish between equivalent fractions such as $1/2$ and $3/6$.

Every graph whose vertices represent distinct letters defines a family of traces on those letters, when we stipulate that two letters clash if and only if they are adjacent in the graph. For example, the path graph a — b — c corresponds to the rules stated above. The distinct traces for this graph are

$$\epsilon, a, b, c, aa, ab, ac, ba, bb, bc, cb, cc, aaa, aab, \ldots, ccb, ccc, aaaa, \ldots \qquad (135)$$

if we list them first by size and then in lexicographic order. (Notice that *ca* is absent, because *ac* has already appeared.) The complete graph K_n defines traces that are the same as strings, when *nothing* commutes; the empty graph $\overline{K_n}$ defines traces that are the same as monomials, when *everything* commutes. If we use the path a — b — c — d — e — f to define clashes, the traces *bcebafdc* and *efbcdbca* turn out to be the same.

Viennot observed that partial commutativity is actually a familiar concept, if we regard the letters as "pieces" that occupy "territory." Pieces clash if and only if their territories overlap; pieces commute if and only if their territories are disjoint. A trace corresponds to stacking the pieces on top of one another, from left to right, letting each new piece "fall" until it either rests on the ground or on another piece. In the latter case, it must rest on the most recent piece with which it clashes. He called this configuration an *empilement* — a nice French word.

More precisely, each piece a is assigned a nonempty subset $T(a)$ of some universe, and we say that a clashes with b if and only if $T(a) \cap T(b) \neq \emptyset$. For example, the constraints of the graph a — b — c — d — e — f arise when we let

$$T(a) = \{1, 2\}, \quad T(b) = \{2, 3\}, \quad T(c) = \{3, 4\}, \quad \ldots, \quad T(f) = \{6, 7\};$$

then the traces *bcebafdc* and *efbcdbca* both have

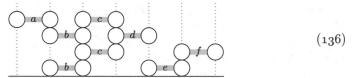

$$(136)$$

as their empilement. (Readers who have played the game of Tetris® will immediately understand how such diagrams are formed, although the pieces in trace theory differ from those of Tetris because they occupy only a single horizontal level. Furthermore, each type of piece always falls in exactly the same place; and a piece's territory $T(a)$ might have "holes" — it needn't be connected.)

Two traces are the same if and only if they have the same *empilement*. In fact, the diagram implicitly defines a partial ordering on the pieces that appear; and the number of different strings that represent any given trace is the number of ways to sort that ordering topologically (see exercise 324).

Every trace α has a *length*, denoted by $|\alpha|$, which is the number of letters in any of its equivalent strings. It also has a *height*, written $h(\alpha)$, which is the number of levels in its empilement. For example, $|bcebafdc| = 8$ and $h(bcebafdc) = 4$.

Arithmetic on traces. To multiply traces, we simply concatenate them. If, for example, $\alpha = bcebafdc$ is the trace corresponding to (136), then $\alpha\alpha^R = bcebafdccdfabecb$ has the following empilement:

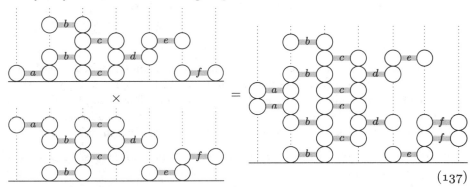

$$(137)$$

The algorithm in exercise 327 formulates this procedure precisely. A moment's thought shows that $|\alpha\beta| = |\alpha| + |\beta|$, $h(\alpha\beta) \le h(\alpha) + h(\beta)$, and $h(\alpha\alpha^R) = 2h(\alpha)$.

Traces can also be *divided*, in the sense that $\alpha = (\alpha\beta)/\beta$ can be determined uniquely when $\alpha\beta$ and β are given. All we have to do is remove the pieces of β from the pieces of $\alpha\beta$, one by one, working our way down from the top of the empilements. Similarly, the value of $\beta = \alpha \setminus (\alpha\beta)$ can be computed from the traces α and $\alpha\beta$. (See exercises 328 and 329.)

Notice that we could rotate diagrams like (136) and (137) by 90 degrees, thereby letting the pieces "fall" to the *left* instead of downwards. (We've used a left-to-right approach for similar purposes in Section 5.3.4, Fig. 50.) Or we could let them fall upwards, or to the right. Different orientations are sometimes more natural, depending on what we're trying to do.

We can also add and subtract traces, thereby obtaining polynomials in variables that are only partially commutative. Such polynomials can be multiplied in the normal way; for example, $(\alpha + \beta)(\gamma - \delta) = \alpha\gamma - \alpha\delta + \beta\gamma - \beta\delta$. Indeed, we can even work with *infinite* sums, at least formally: The generating function for all traces that belong to the graph $a - b - c$ is

$$1 + a + b + c + aa + ab + ac + ba + bb + bc + cb + cc + aaa + \cdots + ccc + aaaa + \cdots. \quad (138)$$

(Compare with (135); we now use 1, not ϵ, to stand for the empty string.)

The infinite sum (138) can actually be expressed in closed form: It equals

$$\frac{1}{1 - a - b - c + ac} = 1 + (a + b + c - ac) + (a + b + c - ac)^2 + \cdots, \quad (139)$$

an identity that is correct not only when the variables are commutative, but also in the algebra of traces, when variables commute only when they don't clash.

In their original monograph of 1969, Cartier and Foata showed that the sum of all traces with respect to *any* graph can be expressed in a remarkably simple way that generalizes (139). Let's define the *Möbius function* of a trace α with respect to a graph G by the rule

$$\mu_G(\alpha) = \begin{cases} 0, & \text{if } h_G(\alpha) > 1; \\ (-1)^{|\alpha|}, & \text{otherwise.} \end{cases} \tag{140}$$

(The classical Möbius function $\mu(n)$ for integers, defined in exercise 4.5.2–10, is analogous.) Then the *Möbius series* for G is defined to be

$$M_G = \sum_\alpha \mu_G(\alpha)\alpha, \tag{141}$$

where the sum is over all traces. This sum is a polynomial, when G is finite, because it contains exactly one nonzero term for every independent set of vertices in G; therefore we might call it the *Möbius polynomial*. For example, when G is the path $a - b - c$, we have $M_G = 1 - a - b - c + ac$, the denominator in (139). Cartier and Foata's generalization of (139) has a remarkably simple proof:

Theorem F. *The generating function T_G for the sum of all traces, with respect to any graph G, is $1/M_G$.*

Proof. We want to show that $M_G T_G = 1$, in the (partially commutative) algebra of traces. This infinite product is $\sum_{\alpha,\beta} \mu_G(\alpha)\alpha\beta = \sum_\gamma \sum_{\alpha,\beta} \mu_G(\alpha)\gamma[\gamma = \alpha\beta]$.

Hence we want to show that the sum of $\mu_G(\alpha)$, over all ways to factorize $\gamma = \alpha\beta$ as the product of two traces α and β, is zero whenever γ is nonempty.

But that's easy. We can assume that the letters are ordered in some arbitrary fashion. Let a be the smallest letter in the bottom level of γ's empilement. We can restrict attention to cases where α consists of independent (commuting) letters (pieces), because $\mu_G(\alpha) = 0$ otherwise. Now if $\alpha = a\alpha'$ for some trace α', let $\beta' = a\beta$; otherwise we must have $\beta = a\beta'$ for some trace β', and we let $\alpha' = a\alpha$. In both cases $\alpha\beta = \alpha'\beta'$, $(\alpha')' = \alpha$, $(\beta')' = \beta$, and $\mu_G(\alpha) + \mu_G(\alpha') = 0$. So we've grouped all possible factorizations of γ into pairs that cancel out in the sum. ∎

The Möbius series for any graph can be computed recursively via the formula

$$M_G = M_{G\setminus a} - aM_{G\setminus a^*}, \qquad a^* = \{a\} \cup \{b \mid a - b\}, \tag{142}$$

where a is any letter (vertex) of G, because we have $a \notin I$ or $a \in I$ whenever I is independent. For example, if G is the path $a - b - c - d - e - f$, then $G \setminus a^* = G \mid \{c, d, e, f\}$ is the path $c - d - e - f$; repeated use of (142) yields

$$\begin{aligned} M_G = {} & 1 - a - b - c - d - e - f + ac + ad + ae + af \\ & + bd + be + bf + ce + cf + df - ace - acf - adf - bdf \end{aligned} \tag{143}$$

in this case. Since M_G is a polynomial, we can indicate its dependence on the variables by writing $M_G(a, b, c, d, e, f)$. Notice that M_G is always multilinear (that is, linear in each variable); and $M_{G\setminus a}(b, c, d, e, f) = M_G(0, b, c, d, e, f)$.

In applications we often want to replace each letter in the polynomial by a single variable, such as z, and write $M_G(z)$. The polynomial in (143) then becomes $M_G(z) = 1 - 6z + 10z^2 - 4z^3$; and we can conclude from Theorem F that the number of traces of length n with respect to G is $[z^n]\, 1/(1 - 6z + 10z^2 - 4z^3) = \frac{1}{4}(2 + \sqrt{2})^{n+2} + \frac{1}{4}(2 - \sqrt{2})^{n+2} - 2^{n+1}$.

Although (142) is a simple recurrence for M_G, we can't conclude that M_G is easy to compute when G is a large and complicated graph. Indeed, the degree of M_G is the size of a maximum independent set in G; and it's NP-hard to determine that number! On the other hand, there are many classes of graphs, such as interval graphs and forests, for which M_G can be computed in linear time.

If α is any trace, the letters that can occur first in a string that represents it are called the *sources* of α; these are the pieces on the bottom level of α's empilement, also called its minimal pieces. Dually, the letters that can occur last are the *sinks* of α, its maximal pieces. A trace that has only one source is called a *cone*; in this case all pieces are ultimately supported by a single piece at the bottom. A trace that has only one sink is, similarly, called a *pyramid*. Viennot proved a nice generalization of Theorem F in his lecture notes:

$$M_{G\backslash A}/M_G \text{ is the sum of all traces whose sources are contained in } A. \quad (144)$$

(See exercise 338; Theorem F is the special case where A is the set of all vertices.) In particular, the cones for which a is the only source are generated by

$$M_{G\backslash a}/M_G - 1 = a M_{G\backslash a^*}/M_G. \quad (145)$$

*Traces and the Local Lemma. Now we're ready to see why the theory of traces is intimately connected with the Local Lemma. If G is any graph on the vertices $\{1, \ldots, m\}$, we say that $\mathcal{R}(G)$ is the set of all nonnegative vectors $(p_1, \ldots, p_m)$ such that $M_G(p'_1, \ldots, p'_m) > 0$ whenever $0 \le p'_j \le p_j$ for $1 \le j \le m$. This definition of $\mathcal{R}(G)$ is consistent with the implicit definition already given in Lemma L, because of the following characterization found by J. B. Shearer:

Theorem S. *Under condition* (133) *of Lemma L,* $(p_1, \ldots, p_m) \in \mathcal{R}(G)$ *implies*

$$\Pr(\overline{A}_1 \cap \cdots \cap \overline{A}_m) \ge M_G(p_1, \ldots, p_m) > 0. \quad (146)$$

Conversely, if $(p_1, \ldots, p_m) \notin \mathcal{R}(G)$, *there are events* $B_1, \ldots, B_m$ *such that*

$$\Pr(B_i \mid \overline{B}_{j_1} \cap \cdots \cap \overline{B}_{j_k}) = p_i \text{ whenever } k \ge 0 \text{ and } i \not\!-\!\!- j_1, \ldots, i \not\!-\!\!- j_k, \quad (147)$$

and $\Pr(\overline{B}_1 \cap \cdots \cap \overline{B}_m) = 0$.

Proof. When $(p_1, \ldots, p_m) \in \mathcal{R}(G)$, exercise 344 proves that there's a unique distribution for events $B_1, \ldots, B_m$ such that they satisfy (147) and also

$$\Pr\left(\bigcap_{j \in J} \overline{A}_j\right) \ge \Pr\left(\bigcap_{j \in J} \overline{B}_j\right) = M_G\left(p_1[1 \in J], \ldots, p_m[m \in J]\right) \quad (148)$$

for every subset $J \subseteq \{1, \ldots, m\}$. In this "extreme" worst-possible distribution, $\Pr(B_i \cap B_j) = 0$ whenever $i \!-\!\!- j$ in G. Exercise 345 proves the converse. ∎

Given a probability vector $(p_1, \ldots, p_m)$, let

$$M_G^*(z) = M_G(p_1 z, \ldots, p_m z). \tag{149}$$

Theorem F tells us that the coefficient of z^n in the power series $1/M_G^*(z)$ is the sum of all traces of length n for G. Since this coefficient is nonnegative, we know by Pringsheim's theorem (see exercise 348) that the power series converges for all $z < 1 + \delta$, where $1 + \delta$ is the smallest real root of the polynomial equation $M_G^*(z) = 0$; this number δ is called the *slack* of $(p_1, \ldots, p_m)$ with respect to G.

It's easy to see that $(p_1, \ldots, p_m) \in \mathcal{R}(G)$ if and only if the slack is positive. For if $\delta \leq 0$, the probabilities $(p_1', \ldots, p_m')$ with $p_j' = (1 + \delta)p_j$ make $M_G = 0$. But if $\delta > 0$, the power series converges when $z = 1$. And (since it represents the sum of all traces) it also converges to the positive number $1/M_G$ if any p_j is decreased; hence $(p_1, \ldots, p_m)$ lies in $\mathcal{R}(G)$ by definition. Indeed, this argument shows that, when $(p_1, \ldots, p_m) \in \mathcal{R}(G)$, we can actually *increase* the probabilities to $((1 + \epsilon)p_1, \ldots, (1 + \epsilon)p_m)$, and they will still lie in $\mathcal{R}(G)$ whenever $\epsilon < \delta$.

Let's return now to Algorithm M. Suppose the successive bad events A_j that step M3 tries to quench are $X_1, X_2, \ldots, X_N$, where N is the total number of times step M3 is performed (possibly $N = \infty$). To prove that Algorithm M is efficient, we shall show that this random variable N has a small expected value, in the probability space of the independent uniform deviates U that appear in steps M1 and M3. The main idea is that $X_1 X_2 \ldots X_N$ is essentially a trace for the underlying graph; hence we can consider it as an empilement of pieces.

Some simple and concrete examples will help to develop our intuition; we shall consider two case studies. In both cases there are $m = 6$ events A, B, C, D, E, F, and there are $n = 7$ variables $x_1 \ldots x_7$. Each variable is a random bit; thus $\xi_1 = \cdots = \xi_7 = 1/2$ in the algorithm. Event A depends on $x_1 x_2$, while B depends on $x_2 x_3$, $\ldots$, and F depends on $x_6 x_7$. Furthermore, each event occurs with probability $1/4$. In Case 1, each event is true when its substring is '10'; thus all events are false if and only if $x_1 \ldots x_7$ is sorted — that is, $x_1 \leq x_2 \leq \cdots \leq x_7$. In Case 2, each event is true when its substring is '11'; thus all events are false if and only if $x_1 \ldots x_7$ has no two consecutive 1s.

What happens when we apply Algorithm M to those two cases? One possible scenario is that step M3 is applied $N = 8$ times, with $X_1 X_2 \ldots X_8 = BCEBAFDC$. The actual changes to the bits $x_1 \ldots x_7$ might then be

Case 1   Case 2

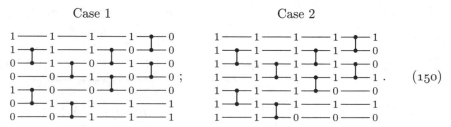

(150)

(Read $x_1 \ldots x_7$ from top to bottom in these diagrams, and scan from left to right. Each module '$\mathbf{I}$' means "replace the two bad bits at the left by two random bits at the right." In examples such as this, any valid solution $x_1 \ldots x_7$ can be placed at the far right; all values to the left of the modules are then forced.)

Notice that these diagrams are like the empilement (136), except that they've been rotated 90°. We know from (136) that the same diagram applies to the scenario $EFBCDBCA$ as well as to $BCEBAFDC$, because they're the same, as traces. Well ..., not quite! In truth, $EFBCDBCA$ doesn't give exactly the same result as $BCEBAFDC$ in Algorithm M, if we execute that algorithm as presently written. But the results *would* be identical if we used *separate* streams of independent random numbers U_k for each variable x_k. Thus we can legitimately *equate* equivalent traces, in the probability space of our random events.

The algorithm runs much faster in practice when it's applied to Case 1 than when it's applied to Case 2. How can that be? Both of the diagrams in (150) occur with the same probability, namely $(1/2)^7 (1/4)^8$, as far as the random numbers are concerned. And every diagram for Case 1 has a corresponding diagram for Case 2; so we can't distinguish the cases by the number of different diagrams. The real difference comes from the fact that, in Case 1, we never have two events to choose from in step M2, unless they are disjoint and can be handled in either order. In Case 2, by contrast, we are deluged at almost every step with events that need to be snuffed out. Therefore the scenario at the right of (150) is actually quite unlikely; why should the algorithm pick B as the first event to correct, and then C, rather than A? Whatever method is used in step M2, we'll find that the diagrams for Case 2 will occur less frequently than dictated by the strict probabilities, because of the decreasing likelihood that any particular event will be worked on next, in the presence of competing choices. (See also exercise 353.)

Worst-case upper bounds on the running time of Algorithm M therefore come from situations like Case 1. In general, the empilement $BCEBAFDC$ in (150) will occur in a run of Algorithm M with probability at most *bcebafdc*, if we write 'a' for the probabilistic upper bound for event A that is denoted by 'p_i' in (133) when A is A_i, and if 'b', ..., 'f' are similar for B, ..., F. The reason is that *bcebafdc* is clearly the probability that those events are produced by the independent random variables x_k set by the algorithm, if the layers of the corresponding empilement are defined by dependencies between the variable sets Ξ_j. And even if events in the same layer are dependent (by shared variables) yet not lopsidependent (in the sense of exercise 351), such events are positively correlated; so the FKG inequality of exercise MPR–61, which holds for the Bernoulli-distributed variables of Algorithm M, shows that *bcebafdc* is an upper bound. Furthermore the probability that step M2 actually chooses B, C, E, B, A, F, D, and C to work on is at most 1.

Therefore, when $(p_1, \ldots, p_m) \in \mathcal{R}(G)$, Algorithm M's running time is maximized when it is applied to events B_1, ..., B_m that have the extreme distribution (148) of exercise 344. And we can actually write down the *generating function* for the running time with respect to those extreme events: We have

$$\sum_{N \geq 0} \Pr(\text{Algorithm M on } B_1, \ldots, B_m \text{ does } N \text{ resamplings}) z^N = \frac{M_G^*(1)}{M_G^*(z)}, \quad (151)$$

where $M_G^*(z)$ is defined in (149), because the coefficient of z^N in $1/M_G^*(z)$ is the sum of the probabilities of all the traces of length N. Theorem F describes the meaning of $1/M_G^*(1)$ as a "formal" power series in the variables p_i; we proved it without considering whether or not the infinite sum converges when those variables receive numerical values. But when $(p_1, \ldots, p_m) \in \mathcal{R}(G)$, this series is indeed convergent (it even has a positive "slack").

This reasoning leads to the following theorem of K. Kolipaka and M. Szegedy [*STOC* **43** (2011), 235–243]:

Theorem K. *If* $(p_1, \ldots, p_m) \in \mathcal{R}(G)$, *Algorithm M resamples* Ξ_j *at most*

$$E_j = p_j M_{G \setminus A_j^*}(p_1, \ldots, p_m)/M_G(p_1, \ldots, p_m) \tag{152}$$

times, on the average. In particular, the expected number of iterations of step M3 is at most $E_1 + \cdots + E_m \le m/\delta$, *where* δ *is the slack of* $(p_1, \ldots, p_m)$.

Proof. The extreme distribution $B_1, \ldots, B_m$ maximizes the number of times Ξ_j is resampled, and the generating function for that number in the extreme case is

$$\frac{M_G(p_1, \ldots, p_{j-1}, p_j, p_{j+1}, \ldots, p_m)}{M_G(p_1, \ldots, p_{j-1}, p_j z, p_{j+1}, \ldots, p_m)}. \tag{153}$$

Differentiating with respect to z, then setting $z \leftarrow 1$, gives (152), because the derivative of the denominator is $-p_j M_{G \setminus A_j^*}(p_1, \ldots, p_m)$ by (141).

The stated upper bound on $E_1 + \cdots + E_m$ is proved in exercise 355. ∎

*Message passing. Physicists who study statistical mechanics have developed a significantly different way to apply randomization to satisfiability problems, based on their experience with the behavior of large systems of interacting particles. From their perspective, a set of Boolean variables whose values are 0 or 1 is best viewed as an ensemble of particles that have positive or negative "spin"; these particles affect each other and change their spins according to local attractions and repulsions, analogous to laws of magnetism. A satisfiability problem can be formulated as a joint probability distribution on spins for which the states of minimum "energy" are achieved precisely when the spins satisfy as many clauses as possible.

In essence, their approach amounts to considering a bipartite structure in which each variable is connected to one or more clauses, and each clause is connected to one or more variables. We can regard both variables and clauses as active agents, who continually tweet to their neighbors in this social network. A variable might inform its clauses that "I think I should probably be true"; but several of those clauses might reply, "I really wish you were false." By carefully balancing these messages against each other, such local interactions can propagate and build up more and more knowledge of distant connections, often converging to a state where the whole network is reasonably happy.

A particular message-passing strategy called *survey propagation* [A. Braunstein, M. Mézard, and R. Zecchina, *Random Structures & Algorithms* **27** (2005),

201–226] has proved to be astonishingly good at solving random satisfiability problems in the "hard" region just before the threshold of unsatisfiability.

Let C be a clause and let l be one of its literals. A "survey message" $\eta_{C \to l}$ is a fraction between 0 and 1 that represents how urgently C wants l to be true. If $\eta_{C \to l} = 1$, the truth of l is desperately needed, lest C be false; but if $\eta_{C \to l} = 0$, clause C isn't the least bit worried about the value of variable $|l|$. Initially we set each $\eta_{C \to l}$ to a completely random fraction.

We shall consider an extension of the original survey propagation method [see J. Chavas, C. Furtlehner, M. Mézard, and R. Zecchina, *J. Statistical Mechanics* (November 2005), P11016:1–25; A. Braunstein and R. Zecchina, *Physical Review Letters* **96** (27 January 2006), 030201:1–4], which introduces additional "reinforcement messages" η_l for each literal l. These new messages, which are initially all zero, represent an external force that acts on l. They help to focus the network activity by reinforcing decisions that have turned out to be fruitful.

Suppose v is a variable that appears in just three clauses: positively in A and B, negatively in C. This variable will respond to its incoming messages $\eta_{A \to v}$, $\eta_{B \to v}$, $\eta_{C \to \bar{v}}$, η_v, and $\eta_{\bar{v}}$ by computing two "flexibility coefficients," π_v and $\pi_{\bar{v}}$, using the following formulas:

$$\pi_v = (1 - \eta_v)(1 - \eta_{A \to v})(1 - \eta_{B \to v}), \qquad \pi_{\bar{v}} = (1 - \eta_{\bar{v}})(1 - \eta_{C \to \bar{v}}).$$

If, for instance, $\eta_v = \eta_{\bar{v}} = 0$ while $\eta_{A \to v} = \eta_{B \to v} = \eta_{C \to \bar{v}} = 2/3$, then $\pi_v = 1/9$, $\pi_{\bar{v}} = 1/3$. The π's are essentially dual to the η's, because high urgency corresponds to low flexibility and vice versa. The general formula for each literal l is

$$\pi_l = (1 - \eta_l) \prod_{l \in C} (1 - \eta_{C \to l}). \tag{154}$$

Survey propagation uses these coefficients to estimate variable v's tendency to be either 1 (true), 0 (false), or $*$ (wild), by computing three numbers

$$p = \frac{(1 - \pi_v)\pi_{\bar{v}}}{\pi_v + \pi_{\bar{v}} - \pi_v \pi_{\bar{v}}}, \qquad q = \frac{(1 - \pi_{\bar{v}})\pi_v}{\pi_v + \pi_{\bar{v}} - \pi_v \pi_{\bar{v}}}, \qquad r = \frac{\pi_v \pi_{\bar{v}}}{\pi_v + \pi_{\bar{v}} - \pi_v \pi_{\bar{v}}}; \tag{155}$$

then $p + q + r = 1$, and (p, q, r) is called the "field" of v, representing respectively (truth, falsity, wildness). The field turns out to be $(8/11, 2/11, 1/11)$ in our example above, indicating that v should probably be assigned the value 1. But if $\eta_{A \to v}$ and $\eta_{B \to v}$ had been only $1/3$ instead of $2/3$, the field would have been $(5/17, 8/17, 4/17)$, and we would probably want $v = 0$ in order to satisfy clause C. Figure 94 shows lines of constant $p - q$ as a function of π_v and $\pi_{\bar{v}}$; the most decisive cases ($|p - q| \approx 1$) occur at the lower right and upper left.

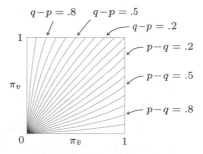

Fig. 94. Lines of constant bias in a variable's "field."

If $\pi_v = \pi_{\bar{v}} = 0$, there's no flexibility at all: Variable v is being asked to be both true and false. The field is undefined in such cases, and the survey propagation method hopes that this doesn't happen.

After each literal l has computed its flexibility, the clauses that involve l or $\bar{l}$ can use π_l and $\pi_{\bar{l}}$ to refine their survey messages. Suppose, for example, that C is the clause $u \vee \bar{v} \vee w$. It will replace the former messages $\eta_{C\to u}$, $\eta_{C\to\bar{v}}$, $\eta_{C\to w}$ by

$$\eta'_{C\to u} = \gamma_{\bar{v}\to C}\gamma_{w\to C}, \qquad \eta'_{C\to\bar{v}} = \gamma_{u\to C}\gamma_{w\to C}, \qquad \eta'_{C\to w} = \gamma_{u\to C}\gamma_{\bar{v}\to C},$$

where each $\gamma_{l\to C}$ is a "bias message" received from literal l,

$$\gamma_{l\to C} = \frac{(1 - \pi_{\bar{l}})\pi_l/(1 - \eta_{C\to l})}{\pi_{\bar{l}} + (1 - \pi_{\bar{l}})\pi_l/(1 - \eta_{C\to l})}, \tag{156}$$

reflecting l's propensity to be false in clauses other than C. In general we have

$$\eta'_{C\to l} = \left(\prod_{l'\in C} \gamma_{l'\to C}\right) \bigg/ \gamma_{l\to C}. \tag{157}$$

(Appropriate conventions must be used to avoid division by zero in formulas (156) and (157); see exercise 359.)

New reinforcement messages η'_l can also be computed periodically, using the formula

$$\eta'_l = \frac{\kappa(\pi_{\bar{l}} \doteq \pi_l)}{\pi_l + \pi_{\bar{l}} - \pi_l\pi_{\bar{l}}} \tag{158}$$

for each literal l; here $x \doteq y$ denotes $\max(x - y, 0)$, and κ is a reinforcement parameter specified by the algorithm. Notice that $\eta'_l > 0$ only if $\eta'_{\bar{l}} = 0$.

For example, here are messages that might be passed when we want to satisfy the seven clauses of (7):

l_1 l_2 l_3	$\eta_{C\to l_1}$	$\eta_{C\to l_2}$	$\eta_{C\to l_3}$	$\gamma_{l_1\to C}$	$\gamma_{l_2\to C}$	$\gamma_{l_3\to C}$	l	π_l	η_l	
1 2 $\bar{3}$	0	0	0	3/5	0	0	1	1	0	
$\bar{1}$ $\bar{2}$ 3	1/5	0	0	0	3/5	1/3	$\bar{1}$	2/5	1/2	
2 3 $\bar{4}$	1/5	0	0	0	1/3	3/5	2	2/5	1/2	
$\bar{2}$ $\bar{3}$ 4	0	0	0	3/5	0	0	$\bar{2}$	1	0	
1 3 4	0	0	1/5	3/5	1/3	0	3	1	0	(159)
$\bar{1}$ 3 $\bar{4}$	0	0	0	0	0	3/5	$\bar{3}$	2/3	1/3	
$\bar{1}$ 2 4	0	0	0	0	0	0	4	2/5	1/2	
							$\bar{4}$	1	0	

(Recall that the only solutions to these clauses are $\bar{1}\,2\,3\,4$ and $\bar{1}\,2\,\bar{3}\,4$.) In this case the reader may verify that the messages of (159) constitute a "fixed point": The η messages determine the π's; conversely, we also have $\eta'_{C\to l} = \eta_{C\to l}$ for all clauses C and all literals l, if the reinforcement messages η_l remain constant.

Exercise 361 proves that every solution to a satisfiable set of clauses yields a fixed point of the simultaneous equations (154), (156), (157), with the property that $\eta_l = [l$ is true in the solution$]$.

Experiments with this message-passing strategy have shown, however, that the best results are obtained by using it only for preliminary screening, with the goal of discovering variables whose settings are most critical; we needn't continue to transmit messages until every clause is fully satisfied. Once we've assigned suitable values to the most delicate variables, we're usually left with a residual problem that can readily be solved by other algorithms such as WalkSAT.

The survey, reinforcement, and bias messages can be exchanged using a wide variety of different protocols. The following procedure incorporates two ideas from an implementation prepared by C. Baldassi in 2012: (1) The reinforcement strength κ begins at zero, but approaches 1 exponentially. (2) Variables are rated 1, 0, or $*$ after each reinforcement, according as $\max(p, q, r)$ in their current field is p, q, or r. If every clause then has at least one literal that is true or $*$, message passing will cease even though some surveys might still be fluctuating.

Algorithm S (*Survey propagation*). Given m nonempty clauses on n variables, this algorithm tries to assign values to most of the variables in such a way that the still-unsatisfied clauses will be relatively easy to satisfy. It maintains arrays π_l and η_l of floating point numbers for each literal l, as well as $\eta_{C \to l}$ for each clause C and each $l \in C$. It has a variety of parameters: ρ (the damping factor for reinforcement), N_0 and N (the minimum and maximum iteration limits), ϵ (the tolerance for convergence), and ψ (the confidence level).

S1. [Initialize.] Set $\eta_l \leftarrow \pi_l \leftarrow 0$ for all literals l, and $\eta_{C \to l} \leftarrow U$ for all clauses C and $l \in C$, where U is uniformly random in $[0 .. 1)$. Also set $i \leftarrow 0$, $\phi \leftarrow 1$.

S2. [Done?] Terminate unsuccessfully if $i \geq N$. If i is even or $i < N_0$, go to S5.

S3. [Reinforce.] Set $\phi \leftarrow \rho\phi$ and $\kappa \leftarrow 1 - \phi$. Replace η_l by η'_l for all literals l, using (158); but terminate unsuccessfully if $\pi_l = \pi_{\bar{l}} = 0$.

S4. [Test pseudo-satisfiability.] Go to S5 if there is at least one clause whose literals l all appear to be false, in the sense that $\pi_{\bar{l}} < \pi_l$ and $\pi_{\bar{l}} < \frac{1}{2}$ (see exercise 358). Otherwise go happily to S8.

S5. [Compute the π's.] Compute each π_l, using (154); see also exercise 359.

S6. [Update the surveys.] Set $\delta \leftarrow 0$. For all clauses C and literals $l \in C$, compute $\eta'_{C \to l}$ using (157), and set $\delta \leftarrow \max(\delta, |\eta'_{C \to l} - \eta_{C \to l}|)$, $\eta_{C \to l} \leftarrow \eta'_{C \to l}$.

S7. [Loop on i.] If $\delta \geq \epsilon$, set $i \leftarrow i + 1$ and return to S2.

S8. [Reduce the problem.] Assign a value to each variable whose field satisfies $|p - q| \geq \psi$. (Exercise 362 has further details.) ∎

Computational experience — otherwise known as trial and error — suggests suitable parameter values. The defaults $\rho = .995$, $N_0 = 5$, $N = 1000$, $\epsilon = .01$, and $\psi = .50$ seem to provide a decent starting point for problems of modest size. They worked well, for instance, when the author first tried a random 3SAT problem with 42,000 clauses and 10,000 variables: These clauses were pseudo-satisfiable when $i = 143$ (although $\delta \approx .43$ was still rather large); then step S8 fixed the values of 8,282 variables with highly biased fields, and unit propagation gave values to 57 variables more. This process needed only about 218 megamems of calculation. The reduced problem had 1526 2-clauses and 196 3-clauses on

1464 variables (because many other variables were no longer needed); 626 steps of WalkSAT polished it off after an additional 42 kilomems. By contrast, when WalkSAT was presented with the original problem (using $p = .57$), it needed more than 31 million steps to find a solution after 3.4 gigamems of computation.

Similarly, the author's first experience applying survey propagation to a random 3SAT problem on $n = 10^6$ variables with $m = 4.2n$ clauses was a smashing success: More than 800,000 variables were eliminated after only 32.8 gigamems of computation, and WalkSAT solved the residual clauses after 8.5 megamems more. By contrast, pure WalkSAT needed 237 gigamems to perform 2.1 billion steps.

A million-variable problem with 4,250,000 clauses proved to be more challenging. These additional 50,000 clauses put the problem well beyond WalkSAT's capability; and Algorithm S failed too, with its default parameters. However, the settings $\rho = .9999$ and $N_0 = 9$ slowed the reinforcement down satisfactorily, and produced some instructive behavior. Consider the matrix

$$
\begin{pmatrix}
3988 & 3651 & 3071 & 2339 & 1741 & 1338 & 946 & 702 & 508 & 329 \\
5649 & 5408 & 4304 & 3349 & 2541 & 2052 & 1448 & 1050 & 666 & 510 \\
8497 & 7965 & 6386 & 4918 & 3897 & 3012 & 2248 & 1508 & 1075 & 718 \\
11807 & 11005 & 8812 & 7019 & 5328 & 4135 & 3117 & 2171 & 1475 & 1063 \\
15814 & 14789 & 11726 & 9134 & 7188 & 5425 & 4121 & 3024 & 2039 & 1372 \\
20437 & 19342 & 15604 & 12183 & 9397 & 7263 & 5165 & 3791 & 2603 & 1781 \\
26455 & 24545 & 19917 & 15807 & 12043 & 9161 & 6820 & 5019 & 3381 & 2263 \\
33203 & 31153 & 25052 & 19644 & 15587 & 11802 & 8865 & 6309 & 4417 & 2919 \\
39962 & 38097 & 31060 & 24826 & 18943 & 14707 & 10993 & 7924 & 5225 & 3637 \\
40731 & 40426 & 32716 & 26561 & 20557 & 15739 & 11634 & 8327 & 5591 & 4035
\end{pmatrix},
$$

which shows the distribution of $\pi_{\bar{v}}$ versus π_v (see Fig. 94); for example, '3988' at the upper left means that 3988 of the million variables had $\pi_{\bar{v}}$ between 0.0 and 0.1 and π_v between 0.9 and 1.0. This distribution, which appeared after δ had been reduced to ≈ 0.0098 by 110 iterations, is terrible — very few variables are biased in a meaningful way. Therefore another run was made with ϵ reduced to .001; but that failed to converge after 1000 iterations. Finally, with $\epsilon = .001$ and $N = 2000$, pseudo-satisfaction occurred at $i = 1373$, with the nice distribution

$$
\begin{pmatrix}
406678 & 1946 & 1045 & 979 & 842 & 714 & 687 & 803 & 1298 & 167649 \\
338 & 2 & 2 & 3 & 0 & 3 & 1 & 4 & 2 & 1289 \\
156 & 1 & 0 & 0 & 0 & 1 & 0 & 2 & 1 & 875 \\
118 & 4 & 0 & 0 & 0 & 0 & 0 & 0 & 1 & 743 \\
99 & 0 & 0 & 0 & 0 & 0 & 0 & 1 & 0 & 663 \\
62 & 0 & 0 & 0 & 0 & 0 & 1 & 0 & 3 & 810 \\
41 & 0 & 0 & 0 & 0 & 0 & 0 & 0 & 0 & 1015 \\
55 & 0 & 0 & 0 & 1 & 0 & 1 & 1 & 0 & 1139 \\
63 & 0 & 0 & 1 & 0 & 0 & 0 & 1 & 2 & 1949 \\
116 & 61 & 72 & 41 & 61 & 103 & 120 & 162 & 327 & 406839
\end{pmatrix}
$$

(although δ was now $\approx 1!$). The biases were now pronounced, yet not entirely reliable; the ψ parameter had to be raised, in order to avoid a contradiction when propagating unit literals in the reduced problem. Finally, with $\psi = .99$, more than 800,000 variables could be set successfully. A solution was obtained after 210 gigamems (including 21 megamems for WalkSAT to finish the job).

Even better results occur when step S8 is allowed to backtrack, resetting less-biased variables when problems arise. See R. Marino, G. Parisi, and F. Ricci-Tersenghi, *Nature Communications* **7**, 12996 (2016), 1–8.

Success with survey propagation isn't guaranteed. But hey, when it works, it's sometimes the only known way to solve a particularly tough problem.

Algorithm S may be viewed as an extension of the "belief propagation" messages used in the study of Bayesian networks [see J. Pearl, *Probabilistic Reasoning in Intelligent Systems* (1988), Chapter 4]; it essentially goes beyond Boolean logic on $\{0, 1\}$ to a three-valued logic on $\{0, 1, *\}$. Analogous message-passing heuristics had actually been considered much earlier by H. A. Bethe and R. E. Peierls [*Proc. Royal Society of London* **A150** (1935), 552–575], and independently by R. G. Gallager [*IRE Transactions* **IT-8** (1962), 21–28]. For further information see M. Mézard and A. Montanari, *Information, Physics, and Computation* (2009), Chapters 14–22.

*Preprocessing of clauses. A SAT-solving algorithm will often run considerably faster if its input has been transformed into an equivalent but simpler set of clauses. Such transformations and simplifications typically require data structures that would be inappropriate for the main work of a solver, so they are best considered separately.

Of course we can combine a preprocessor and a solver into a single program; and "preprocessing" techniques can be applied again after new clauses have been learned, if we reach a stage where we want to clean up and start afresh. In the latter case the simplifications are called *inprocessing*. But the basic ideas are most easily explained by assuming that we just want to preprocess a given family of clauses F. Our goal is to produce nicer clauses F', which are satisfiable if and only if F is satisfiable.

We shall view preprocessing as a sequence of elementary transformations

$$F = F_0 \to F_1 \to \cdots \to F_r = F', \qquad (160)$$

where each step $F_j \to F_{j+1}$ "flows downhill" in the sense that it either (i) eliminates a variable without increasing the number of clauses, or (ii) retains all the variables but decreases the number of literals in clauses. Many different downhill transformations are known; and we can try to apply each of the gimmicks in our repertoire, in some order, until none of them lead to any further progress.

Sometimes we'll actually *solve* the given problem, by reaching an F' that is either trivially satisfiable ($\emptyset$) or trivially unsatisfiable (contains ϵ). But we probably won't be so lucky unless F was pretty easy to start with, because we're going to consider only downhill transformations that are quite simple.

Before discussing particular transformations, however, let's think about the endgame: Suppose F has n variables but F' has $n' < n$. After we've fed the clauses F' into a SAT solver and received back a solution, $x'_1 \ldots x'_{n'}$, how can we convert it to a full solution $x_1 \ldots x_n$ of the original problem F? Here's how: For every transformation $F_j \to F_{j+1}$ that eliminates a variable x_k, we shall specify an *erp rule* (so called because it reverses the effect of *preprocessing*). An erp rule for elimination is simply an assignment '$l \leftarrow E$', where l is x_k or $\bar{x}_k$, and E is a Boolean expression that involves only variables that have not been eliminated. We undo the effect of elimination by assigning to x_k the value that makes l true if and only if E is true.

For example, suppose two transformations remove x and y with the erp rules

$$\bar{x} \leftarrow \bar{y} \vee z, \qquad y \leftarrow 1.$$

To reverse these eliminations, right to left, we would set y true, then $x \leftarrow \bar{z}$.

As the preprocessor discovers how to eliminate variables, it can immediately write the corresponding erp rules to a file, so that those rules don't consume memory space. Afterwards, given a reduced solution $x_1' \ldots x_{n'}'$, a postprocessor can read that file *in reverse order* and provide the unreduced solution $x_1 \ldots x_n$.

Transformation 1. Unit conditioning. If a unit clause '(l)' is present, we can replace F by $F \mid l$ and use the erp rule $l \leftarrow 1$. This elementary simplification will be carried out naturally by most solvers; but it is perhaps even more important in a preprocessor, since it often enables further transformations that the solver would not readily see. Conversely, other transformations in the preprocessor might enable unit conditionings that will continue to ripple down.

One consequence of unit conditioning is that all clauses of F' will have length two or more, unless F' is trivially unsatisfiable.

Transformation 2. Subsumption. If every literal in clause C appears also in another clause C', we can remove C'. In particular, duplicate clauses will be discarded. No erp rule is needed, because no variable goes away.

Transformation 3. Self-subsumption. If every literal in C except $\bar{x}$ appears also in another clause C', where C' contains x, we can delete x from C' because $C' \setminus x = C \diamond C'$. In other words, the fact that C *almost* subsumes C' allows us at least to *strengthen* C', without actually removing it. Again there's no erp rule. [Self-subsumption was called "the replacement principle" by J. A. Robinson in *JACM* **12** (1965), 39.]

Exercise 374 discusses data structures and algorithms by which subsumptions and self-subsumptions can be discovered with reasonable efficiency.

Transformation 4. Downhill resolution. Suppose x appears only in clauses $C_1, \ldots, C_p$ and $\bar{x}$ appears only in $C_1', \ldots, C_q'$. We've observed (see (112)) that variable x can be eliminated if we replace those $p + q$ clauses by the pq clauses $\{C_i \diamond C_j' \mid 1 \le i \le p, 1 \le j \le q\}$. The corresponding erp rule (see exercise 367) is

$$\text{either} \quad \bar{x} \leftarrow \bigwedge_{i=1}^{p}(C_i \setminus x) \qquad \text{or} \quad x \leftarrow \bigwedge_{j=1}^{q}(C_j' \setminus \bar{x}). \tag{161}$$

Every variable can be eliminated in this way, but we might be flooded with too many clauses. We can prevent this by limiting ourselves to "downhill" cases, in which the new clauses don't outnumber the old ones. The condition $pq \le p+q$ is equivalent to $(p-1)(q-1) \le 1$, as noted above following (112); the variable is always removed in such cases. But the number of new clauses might be small even when pq is large, because of tautologies or subsumption. Furthermore, N. Eén and A. Biere wrote a fundamental paper on preprocessing [*LNCS* **3569** (2005), 61–75], which introduced important special cases that allow many of the pq potential clauses to be omitted; see exercise 369. Therefore a preprocessor typically tries to eliminate via resolution whenever $\min(p, q) \leq 10$, say, and abandons the attempt only when more than $p+q$ resolvents have been generated.

Many other transformations are possible, although the four listed above have proved to be the most effective in practice. We could, for instance, look for *failed literals*: If unit propagation leads to a contradiction when we assume that some literal l is true (namely when $F \wedge (l) \vdash_1 \epsilon$), then we're allowed to assume that l is false (because the unit clause $(\bar{l})$ is certifiable). This observation and several others related to it were exploited in the lookahead mechanisms of Algorithm Y above. But Algorithm C generally has no trouble finding failed literals all by itself, as a natural byproduct of its mechanism for resolving conflicts. Exercises 378–384 discuss other techniques that have been proposed for preprocessing.

Sometimes preprocessing turns out to be dramatically successful. For example, the anti-maximal-element clauses of exercise 228 can be proved unsatisfiable via transformations 1–4 after only about 400 megamems of work when $m = 50$. Yet Algorithm C spends 3 gigamems on that untransformed problem when m is only 14; and it needs 11 Gμ when $m = 15$, ..., failing utterly before $m = 20$.

A more typical example arises in connection with Fig. 78 above: The problem of showing that there's no 4-step path to **LIFE** involves 8725 variables, 33769 clauses, and 84041 literals, and Algorithm C requires about 6 gigamems to demonstrate that those clauses are unsatisfiable. Preprocessing needs less than 10 *mega*mems to reduce that problem to just 3263 variables, 19778 clauses, and 56552 literals; then Algorithm C can handle those with 5 Gμ of further work.

On the other hand, preprocessing might take too long, or it might produce clauses that are more difficult to deal with than the originals. It's totally useless on the *waerden* or *langford* problems. (Further examples are discussed below.)

Encoding constraints into clauses. Some problems, like $waerden(j, k; n)$, are inherently Boolean, and they're essentially given to us as native-born ANDs of ORs. But in most cases we can represent a combinatorial problem via clauses in many different ways, not immediately obvious, and the particular encoding that we choose can have an enormous effect on the speed with which a SAT solver is able to crank out an answer. Thus the art of problem encoding turns out to be just as important as the art of devising algorithms for satisfiability.

Our study of SAT instances has already introduced us to dozens of interesting encodings; and new applications often lead to further ideas, because Boolean algebra is so versatile. Each problem may seem at first to need its own special tricks. But we'll see that several general principles are available for guidance.

In the first place, different solvers tend to like different encodings: An encoding that's good for one algorithm might be bad for another.

Consider, for example, the *at-most-one* constraint, $y_1 + \cdots + y_p \leq 1$, which arises in a great many applications. The obvious way to enforce this condition is to assert $\binom{p}{2}$ binary clauses $(\bar{y}_i \vee \bar{y}_j)$, for $1 \leq i < j \leq p$, so that $y_i = y_j = 1$ is forbidden; but those clauses become unwieldy when p is large. The alternative encoding in exercise 12, due to Marijn Heule, does the same job with only $3p - 6$ binary constraints when $p \geq 3$, by introducing a few auxiliary variables

$a_1, \ldots, a_{\lfloor (p-3)/2 \rfloor}$. When we formulated Langford's problem in terms of clauses, via (12), (13), and (14) above, we therefore considered two variants called *langford*(*n*) and *langford'*(*n*), where the former uses the obvious encoding of at-most-one constraints and the latter uses Heule's method. Furthermore, exercise 7.1.1–55(b) encoded at-most-one constraints in yet another way, having the same number of binary clauses but about twice as many auxiliary variables; let's give the name *langford''*(*n*) to the clauses that we get from that scheme.

We weren't ready to discuss which of the encodings works better in practice, when we introduced *langford*(*n*) and *langford'*(*n*) above, because we hadn't yet examined any SAT-solving algorithms. But now we're ready to reveal the answer; and the answer is: "It depends." Sometimes *langford'*(*n*) wins over *langford*(*n*); sometimes it loses. It always seems to beat *langford''*(*n*). Here, for example, are typical statistics, with runtimes rounded to megamems (Mμ) or kilomems (Kμ):

	variables	clauses	Algorithm D	Algorithm L	Algorithm C	
langford(9)	104	1722	23 Mμ	16 Mμ	15 Mμ	(UNSAT)
langford'(9)	213	801	82 Mμ	16 Mμ	21 Mμ	(UNSAT)
langford''(9)	335	801	139 Mμ	20 Mμ	24 Mμ	(UNSAT)
langford(13)	228	5875	71685 Mμ	45744 Mμ	295571 Mμ	(UNSAT)
langford'(13)	502	1857	492992 Mμ	38589 Mμ	677815 Mμ	(UNSAT)
langford''(13)	795	1857	950719 Mμ	46398 Mμ	792757 Mμ	(UNSAT)
langford(16)	352	11494	5 Mμ	52 Mμ	301 Kμ	(SAT)
langford'(16)	796	2928	12 Mμ	31 Mμ	418 Kμ	(SAT)
langford''(16)	1264	2928	20 Mμ	38 Mμ	510 Kμ	(SAT)
langford(64)	6016	869650	(huge)	(bigger)	35 Mμ	(SAT)
langford'(64)	14704	53184	(huger)	(big)	73 Mμ	(SAT)
langford''(64)	23488	53184	(hugest)	(biggest)	304 Mμ	(SAT)

Algorithm D prefers *langford* to *langford'*, because it doesn't perform unit propagations very efficiently. Algorithm L, which excels at unit propagation, likes *langford'* better. Algorithm C also excels at unit propagation, but it exhibits peculiar behavior: It prefers *langford*, and on satisfiable instances it zooms in quickly to find a solution; but for some reason it runs *very* slowly on unsatisfiable instances when $n \geq 10$.

Another general principle is that short encodings — encodings with few variables and/or few clauses — are *not* necessarily better than longer encodings. For example, we often need to use Boolean variables to encode the value of a variable x that actually ranges over $d > 2$ different values, say $0 \leq x < d$. In such cases it's natural to use the binary representation $x = (x_{l-1} \ldots x_0)_2$, where $l = \lceil \lg d \rceil$, and to construct clauses based on the independent bits x_j; but that representation, known as the *log encoding*, surprisingly turns out to be a bad idea in many cases unless d is large. A *direct encoding* with d binary variables $x_0, x_1, \ldots, x_{d-1}$, where $x_j = [x = j]$, is often much better. And the *order encoding* with $d - 1$ binary variables $x^1, \ldots, x^{d-1}$, where $x^j = [x \geq j]$, is often better yet; this encoding was introduced in 1994 by J. M. Crawford and A. B. Baker [*AAAI Conf.* **12** (1994), 1092–1097]. In fact, exercise 408 presents an important application where the order encoding is the method of choice even when d is 1000 or more! The order encoding is exponentially larger than the log encoding, yet it wins in this application because it allows the SAT solver to deduce consequences rapidly via unit propagation.

Graph coloring problems illustrate this principle nicely. When we tried early in this section to color a graph with d colors, we encoded the color of each vertex with a direct representation, (15); but we could have used binary notation for those colors. And we could also have used the order encoding, even though the numerical ordering of colors is irrelevant in the problem itself. With a log encoding, exercise 391 exhibits three distinct ways to enforce the constraint that adjacent vertices have different colors. With the order encoding, exercise 395 explains that it's easy to handle graph coloring. And there also are four ways to work with the direct encoding, namely (a) to insist on one color per vertex by including the at-most-one exclusion clauses (17); or (b) to allow multivalued (multicolored) vertices by omitting those clauses; or (c) to actually *welcome* multicolored vertices, by omitting (17) and forcing each color class to be a kernel, as suggested in answer 14; or (d) to include (17) but to replace the "preclusion" clauses (16) by so-called "support" clauses as explained in exercise 399.

These eight options can be compared empirically by trying to arrange 64 colored queens on a chessboard so that no queens of the same color appear in the same row, column, or diagonal. That task is possible with 9 colors, but not with 8. By symmetry we can prespecify the colors of all queens in the top row.

encoding	colors	variables	clauses	Algorithm L	Algorithm C	
univalued	8	512	7688	$3333\,M\mu$	$9813\,M\mu$	(UNSAT)
multivalued	8	512	5896	$1330\,M\mu$	$11997\,M\mu$	(UNSAT)
kernel	8	512	6408	$4196\,M\mu$	$12601\,M\mu$	(UNSAT)
support	8	512	13512	$16796\,M\mu$	$20990\,M\mu$	(UNSAT)
log(a)	8	2376	5120	(immense)	$20577\,M\mu$	(UNSAT)
log(b)	8	192	5848	(enormous)	$15033\,M\mu$	(UNSAT)
log(c)	8	192	5848	(enormous)	$15033\,M\mu$	(UNSAT)
order	8	448	6215	$43615\,M\mu$	$5122\,M\mu$	(UNSAT)
univalued	9	576	8928	$2907\,M\mu$	$464\,M\mu$	(SAT)
multivalued	9	576	6624	$104\,M\mu$	$401\,M\mu$	(SAT)
kernel	9	576	7200	$93\,M\mu$	$87\,M\mu$	(SAT)
support	9	576	15480	$2103\,M\mu$	$613\,M\mu$	(SAT)
log(a)	9	3168	6776	(gigantic)	$1761\,M\mu$	(SAT)
log(b)	9	256	6776	(colossal)	$1107\,M\mu$	(SAT)
log(c)	9	256	6584	(mammoth)	$555\,M\mu$	(SAT)
order	9	512	7008	(monstrous)	$213\,M\mu$	(SAT)

(Each running time shown here is the median of nine runs, made with different random seeds.) It's clear from this data that the log encodings are completely unsuitable for Algorithm L; and even the order encoding confuses that algorithm's heuristics. But Algorithm L shines over Algorithm C with respect to most of the direct encodings. On the other hand, Algorithm C loves the order encoding, especially in the difficult unsatisfiable case.

And that's not the end of the story. H. Tajima [M.S. thesis, Kobe University (2008)] and N. Tamura noticed that order encoding has another property, which beats all other encodings with respect to graph coloring: Every k-clique of vertices $\{v_1, \ldots, v_k\}$ in a graph allows us to append two additional "hint clauses"

$$(\bar{v}_1^{d-k+1} \vee \cdots \vee \bar{v}_k^{d-k+1}) \wedge (v_1^{k-1} \vee \cdots \vee v_k^{k-1}) \tag{162}$$

to the clauses for d-coloring — because some vertex of the clique must have a color $\leq d - k$, and some vertex must have a color $\geq k - 1$. With these additional clauses, the running time to prove unsatisfiability of the 8-coloring problem drops drastically to just $60\,M\mu$ with Algorithm L, and to only $13\,M\mu$ with Algorithm C. We can even reduce it to just $2\,M\mu(!)$ by using that idea *twice* (see exercise 396).

The order encoding has several other nice properties, so it deserves a closer look. When we represent a value x in the range $0 \leq x < d$ by the binary variables $x^j = [x \geq j]$ for $1 \leq j < d$, we always have

$$x = x^1 + x^2 + \cdots + x^{d-1}; \tag{163}$$

hence order encoding is often known as *unary representation*. The axiom clauses

$$(\bar{x}^{j+1} \vee x^j) \qquad \text{for } 1 \leq j < d - 1 \tag{164}$$

are always included, representing the fact that $x \geq j+1$ implies $x \geq j$ for each j; these clauses force all the 1s to the left and all the 0s to the right. When $d = 2$ the unary representation reduces to a one-bit encoding equal to x itself; when $d = 3$ it's a two-bit encoding with 00, 10, and 11 representing 0, 1, and 2.

We might not know all of the bits x^j of x's unary encoding while a problem is in the course of being solved. But if we do know that, say, $x^3 = 1$ and $x^7 = 0$, then we know that x belongs to the interval $[3 .. 7]$.

Suppose we know the unary representation of x. Then no calculation is necessary if we want to know the unary representation of $y = x + a$, when a is a constant, because $y^j = x^{j-a}$. Similarly, $z = a - x$ is equivalent to $z^j = \bar{x}^{a+1-j}$; and $w = \lfloor x/a \rfloor$ is equivalent to $w^j = x^{aj}$. Out-of-bounds superscripts are easy to handle in formulas such as this, because $x^i = 1$ when $i \leq 0$ and $x^i = 0$ when $i \geq d$. The special case $\bar{x} = d - 1 - x$ is obtained by left-right reflection of $\bar{x}^1 \ldots \bar{x}^{j-1}$:

$$(d - 1 - x)^j = (\bar{x})^j = \overline{x^{d-j}}. \tag{165}$$

If we are using the order encoding for two independent variables x and y, with $0 \leq x, y < d$, it's similarly easy to encode the additional relation $x \leq y + a$:

$$x - y \leq a \iff x \leq y + a \iff \bigwedge_{j=\max(0,a+1)}^{\min(d-1,d+a)} (\bar{x}^j \vee y^{j-a}). \tag{166}$$

And there are analogous ways to place bounds on the sum, $x + y$:

$$x + y \leq a \iff x \leq \bar{y} + a + 1 - d \iff \bigwedge_{j=\max(0,a+2-d)}^{\min(d-1,a+1)} (\bar{x}^j \vee \bar{y}^{a+1-j}); \tag{167}$$

$$x + y \geq a \iff \bar{x} \leq y - a - 1 + d \iff \bigwedge_{j=\max(1,a+1-d)}^{\min(d,a)} (x^j \vee y^{a+1-j}). \quad (168)$$

In fact, exercise 405 shows that the general condition $ax + by \leq c$ can be enforced with at most d binary clauses, when a, b, and c are constant. Any set of such relations, involving at most two variables per constraint, is therefore a 2SAT problem.

Relations between three or more order-encoded variables can also be handled without difficulty, as long as d isn't too large. For example, conditions such as $x + y \leq z$ and $x + y \geq z$ can be expressed with $O(d \log d)$ clauses of length ≤ 3 (see exercise 407). Arbitrary linear inequalities can also be represented, in principle. But of course we shouldn't expect SAT solvers to compete with algebraic methods on problems that are inherently numerical.

Another constraint of great importance in the encoding of combinatorial problems is the relation of *lexicographic order*: Given two bit vectors $x_1 \ldots x_n$ and $y_1 \ldots y_n$, we want to encode the condition $(x_1 \ldots x_n)_2 \leq (y_1 \ldots y_n)_2$ as a conjunction of clauses. Fortunately there's a nice way to do this with just $3n - 2$ ternary clauses involving $n - 1$ auxiliary variables $a_1, \ldots, a_{n-1}$, namely

$$\bigwedge_{k=1}^{n-1} \left((\bar{x}_k \vee y_k \vee \bar{a}_{k-1}) \wedge (\bar{x}_k \vee a_k \vee \bar{a}_{k-1}) \wedge (y_k \vee a_k \vee \bar{a}_{k-1}) \right) \wedge (\bar{x}_n \vee y_n \vee \bar{a}_{n-1}), \quad (169)$$

where '$\bar{a}_0$' is omitted. For example, the clauses

$$(\bar{x}_1 \vee y_1) \wedge (\bar{x}_1 \vee a_1) \wedge (y_1 \vee a_1) \wedge (\bar{x}_2 \vee y_2 \vee \bar{a}_1) \wedge (\bar{x}_2 \vee a_2 \vee \bar{a}_1) \wedge (y_2 \vee a_2 \vee \bar{a}_1) \wedge (\bar{x}_3 \vee y_3 \vee \bar{a}_2)$$

assert that $x_1 x_2 x_3 \leq y_1 y_2 y_3$. And the same formula, but with the final term $(\bar{x}_n \vee y_n \vee \bar{a}_{n-1})$ replaced by $(\bar{x}_n \vee \bar{a}_{n-1}) \wedge (y_n \vee \bar{a}_{n-1})$, works for the *strict* comparison $x_1 \ldots x_n < y_1 \ldots y_n$. These formulas arise by considering the carries that occur when $(\bar{x}_1 \ldots \bar{x}_n)_2 + (1 \text{ or } 0)$ is added to $(y_1 \ldots y_n)_2$. (See exercise 415.)

The *general* problem of encoding a constraint on the Boolean variables $x_1, \ldots, x_n$ is the question of finding a family of clauses F that are satisfiable if and only if $f(x_1, \ldots, x_n)$ is true, where f is a given Boolean function. We usually introduce auxiliary variables $a_1, \ldots, a_m$ into the clauses of F, unless f can be expressed directly with a short CNF formula; thus the encoding problem is to find a "good" family F such that we have

$$f(x_1, \ldots, x_n) = 1 \iff \exists a_1 \ldots \exists a_m \bigwedge_{C \in F} C, \quad (170)$$

where each C is a clause on the variables $\{a_1, \ldots, a_m, x_1, \ldots, x_n\}$. The variables $a_1, \ldots, a_m$ can be eliminated by resolution as in (112), at least in principle, leaving us with a CNF for f — although that CNF might be huge. (See exercise 248.)

If there's a simple circuit that computes f, we know from (24) and exercise 42 that there's an equally simple "Tseytin encoding" F, with one auxiliary variable for each gate in the circuit. For example, suppose we want to encode the condition $x_1 \ldots x_n \neq y_1 \ldots y_n$. The shortest CNF expression for this function $f(x_1, \ldots, x_n, y_1, \ldots, y_n)$ has 2^n clauses (see exercise 413); but there's a simple circuit (Boolean chain) with just $n + 1$ gates:

$$a_1 \leftarrow x_1 \oplus y_1, \quad \ldots, \quad a_n \leftarrow x_n \oplus y_n, \quad f \leftarrow a_1 \vee \cdots \vee a_n.$$

Using (24) we get the $4n$ clauses

$$\bigwedge_{j=1}^{n} \left((\bar{x}_j \vee y_j \vee a_j) \wedge (x_j \vee \bar{y}_j \vee a_j) \wedge (x_j \vee y_j \vee \bar{a}_j) \wedge (\bar{x}_j \vee \bar{y}_j \vee \bar{a}_j) \right), \qquad (171)$$

together with $(a_1 \vee \cdots \vee a_n)$, as a representation of '$x_1 \ldots x_n \neq y_1 \ldots y_n$'.

But this is overkill; D. A. Plaisted and S. Greenbaum have pointed out [*Journal of Symbolic Computation* **2** (1986), 293–304] that we can often avoid about half of the clauses in such situations. Indeed, only $2n$ of the clauses (171) are necessary (and sufficient), namely the ones involving $\bar{a}_j$:

$$\bigwedge_{j=1}^{n} \left((x_j \vee y_j \vee \bar{a}_j) \wedge (\bar{x}_j \vee \bar{y}_j \vee \bar{a}_j) \right). \qquad (172)$$

The other clauses are "blocked" (see exercise 378) and unhelpful. Thus it's a good idea to examine whether all of the clauses in a Tseytin encoding are really needed. Exercise 416 illustrates another interesting case.

An efficient encoding is possible also when f has a small BDD, and in general whenever f can be computed by a short branching program. Recall the example "Pi function" introduced in 7.1.1–(22); we observed in 7.1.2–(6) that it can be written $\left(((x_2 \wedge \bar{x}_4) \oplus \bar{x}_3) \wedge \bar{x}_1 \right) \oplus x_2$. Thus it has a 12-clause Tseytin encoding

$$(x_2 \vee \bar{a}_1) \wedge (\bar{x}_4 \vee \bar{a}_1) \wedge (\bar{x}_2 \vee x_4 \vee a_1) \wedge (x_3 \vee a_1 \vee a_2) \wedge (\bar{x}_3 \vee \bar{a}_1 \vee a_2) \wedge (\bar{x}_3 \vee a_1 \vee \bar{a}_2)$$
$$\wedge (x_3 \vee \bar{a}_1 \vee \bar{a}_2) \wedge (\bar{x}_1 \vee \bar{a}_3) \wedge (a_2 \vee \bar{a}_3) \wedge (x_1 \vee \bar{a}_2 \vee a_3) \wedge (x_2 \vee a_3) \wedge (\bar{x}_2 \vee \bar{a}_3).$$

The Pi function also has a short branching program, 7.1.4–(8), namely

$$I_8 = (\bar{1}?\, 7{:}6), I_7 = (\bar{2}?\, 5{:}4), I_6 = (\bar{2}?\, 0{:}1), I_5 = (\bar{3}?\, 1{:}0),$$
$$I_4 = (\bar{3}?\, 3{:}2), I_3 = (\bar{4}?\, 1{:}0), I_2 = (\bar{4}?\, 0{:}1),$$

where the instruction '$(\bar{v}?\, l{:}h)$' means "If $x_v = 0$, go to I_l, otherwise go to I_h," except that I_0 and I_1 unconditionally produce the values 0 and 1. We can convert any such branching program into a sequence of clauses, by translating '$I_j = (\bar{v}?\, l{:}h)$' into

$$(\bar{a}_j \vee x_v \vee a_l) \wedge (\bar{a}_j \vee \bar{x}_v \vee a_h), \qquad (173)$$

where a_0 is omitted, and where any clauses containing a_1 are dropped. We also omit $\bar{a}_t$, where I_t is the first instruction; in this example $t = 8$. (These simplifications correspond to asserting the unit clauses $(\bar{a}_0) \wedge (a_1) \wedge (a_t)$.) The branching program above therefore yields ten clauses,

$$(x_1 \vee a_7) \wedge (\bar{x}_1 \vee a_6) \wedge (\bar{a}_7 \vee x_2 \vee a_5) \wedge (\bar{a}_7 \vee \bar{x}_2 \vee a_4) \wedge (\bar{a}_6 \vee x_2)$$
$$\wedge (\bar{a}_5 \vee \bar{x}_3) \wedge (\bar{a}_4 \vee x_3 \vee a_3) \wedge (\bar{a}_4 \vee \bar{x}_3 \vee a_2) \wedge (\bar{a}_3 \vee \bar{x}_4) \wedge (\bar{a}_2 \vee x_4).$$

We can readily eliminate a_6, a_5, a_3, a_2, thereby getting a six-clause equivalent

$$(x_1 \vee a_7) \wedge (\bar{x}_1 \vee x_2) \wedge (\bar{a}_7 \vee x_2 \vee \bar{x}_3) \wedge (\bar{a}_7 \vee \bar{x}_2 \vee a_4) \wedge (\bar{a}_4 \vee x_3 \vee \bar{x}_4) \wedge (\bar{a}_4 \vee \bar{x}_3 \vee x_4);$$

and a preprocessor will simplify this to the four-clause CNF

$$(\bar{x}_1 \vee x_2) \wedge (x_2 \vee \bar{x}_3) \wedge (x_1 \vee \bar{x}_2 \vee x_3 \vee \bar{x}_4) \wedge (x_1 \vee \bar{x}_3 \vee x_4), \qquad (174)$$

which appeared in exercise 7.1.1–19.

Exercise 417 explains why this translation scheme is valid. The method applies to *any* branching program whatsoever: The x variables can be tested in any order — that is, the v's need not be decreasing as in a BDD; moreover, a variable may be tested more than once.

Unit propagation and forcing. The effectiveness of an encoding depends largely on how well that encoding avoids bad partial assignments to the variables. If we're trying to encode a Boolean condition $f(x_1, x_2, \ldots, x_n)$, and if the tentative assignments $x_1 \leftarrow 1$ and $x_2 \leftarrow 0$ cause f to be false regardless of the values of x_3 through x_n, we'd like the solver to deduce this fact without further ado, ideally by unit propagation once x_1 and $\bar{x}_2$ have been asserted. With a CDCL solver like Algorithm C, a quickly recognized conflict means a relatively short learned clause — and that's a hallmark of progress. Even better would be a situation in which unit propagation, after asserting x_1, would already force x_2 to be true; and furthermore if unit propagation after $\bar{x}_2$ would also force $\bar{x}_1$.

Such scenarios aren't equivalent to each other. For example, consider the clauses $F = (\bar{x}_1 \vee x_3) \wedge (\bar{x}_1 \vee x_2 \vee \bar{x}_3)$. Then, using the notation '$F \vdash_1 l$' to signify that F leads to l via unit propagation, we have $F \mid x_1 \vdash_1 x_2$, but $F \mid \bar{x}_2 \nvdash_1 \bar{x}_1$. And with the clauses $G = (\bar{x}_1 \vee x_2 \vee x_3) \wedge (\bar{x}_1 \vee x_2 \vee \bar{x}_3)$ we have $G \mid x_1 \mid \bar{x}_2 \vdash_1 \epsilon$ (see Eq. (119)), but $G \mid x_1 \nvdash_1 x_2$ and $G \mid \bar{x}_2 \nvdash_1 \bar{x}_1$.

Consider now the simple at-most-one constraint on just three variables: $f(x_1, x_2, x_3) = [x_1 + x_2 + x_3 \leq 1]$. We can try to represent f by proceeding methodically using the methods suggested above, either by constructing a circuit for f or by constructing f's BDD. The first alternative (see exercise 420) yields

$$F = (x_1 \vee \bar{x}_2 \vee a_1) \wedge (\bar{x}_1 \vee x_2 \vee a_1) \wedge (x_1 \vee x_2 \vee \bar{a}_1) \wedge (\bar{x}_1 \vee \bar{x}_2) \wedge (\bar{x}_3 \vee \bar{a}_1); \qquad (175)$$

the second approach (see exercise 421) leads to a somewhat different solution,

$$G = (x_1 \vee a_4) \wedge (\bar{x}_1 \vee a_3) \wedge (\bar{a}_4 \vee \bar{x}_2 \vee a_2) \wedge (\bar{a}_3 \vee x_2 \vee a_2) \wedge (\bar{a}_3 \vee \bar{x}_2) \wedge (\bar{a}_2 \vee \bar{x}_3). \qquad (176)$$

But neither of these encodings is actually very good, because $F \mid x_3 \nvdash_1 \bar{x}_1$ and $G \mid x_3 \nvdash_1 \bar{x}_1$. Much better is the encoding that we get from the general scheme of (18) and (19) in the case $n = 3$, $r = 1$, namely

$$S = (\bar{a}_1 \vee a_2) \wedge (\bar{x}_1 \vee a_1) \wedge (\bar{x}_2 \vee a_2) \wedge (\bar{x}_2 \vee \bar{a}_1) \wedge (\bar{x}_3 \vee \bar{a}_2), \qquad (177)$$

where a_1 and a_2 stand for s_1^1 and s_2^1; or the one obtained from (20) and (21),

$$B = (\bar{x}_3 \vee a_1) \wedge (\bar{x}_2 \vee a_1) \wedge (\bar{x}_2 \vee \bar{x}_3) \wedge (\bar{a}_1 \vee \bar{x}_1), \qquad (178)$$

where a_1 stands for b_1^2. With either (177) or (178) we have $S \mid x_i \vdash_1 \bar{x}_j$ and $B \mid x_i \vdash_1 \bar{x}_j$ by unit propagation whenever $i \neq j$. And of course the obvious encoding for this particular f is best of all, because n is so small:

$$O = (\bar{x}_1 \vee \bar{x}_2) \wedge (\bar{x}_1 \vee \bar{x}_3) \wedge (\bar{x}_2 \vee \bar{x}_3). \qquad (179)$$

Suppose $f(x_1, \ldots, x_n)$ is a Boolean function that's represented by a family of clauses F, possibly involving auxiliary variables $\{a_1, \ldots, a_m\}$, as in (170). We say that F is a *forcing* representation if we have

$$F \mid L \vdash l \qquad \text{implies} \qquad F \mid L \vdash_1 l \qquad\qquad (180)$$

whenever $L \cup l$ is a set of strictly distinct literals contained in $\{x_1, \ldots, x_n, \bar{x}_1, \ldots, \bar{x}_n\}$. In other words, if the partial assignment represented by L logically implies the truth of some other literal l, we insist that unit propagation alone should be able to deduce l from $F \mid L$. The auxiliary variables $\{a_1, \ldots, a_m\}$ are exempt from this requirement; only the potential forcings between *primary* variables $\{x_1, \ldots, x_n\}$ are supposed to be recognized easily when they occur.

(*Technical point:* If $F \mid L \vdash \epsilon$, meaning that $F \mid L$ is unsatisfiable, we implicitly have $F \mid L \vdash l$ for *all* literals l. In such a case (180) tells us that $F \mid L \vdash_1 l$ and $F \mid L \vdash_1 \bar{l}$ both hold; hence $F \mid L$ can then be proved unsatisfiable by unit propagation alone.)

We've seen that the clauses S and B in (177) and (178) are forcing for the constraint $[x_1 + x_2 + x_3 \leq 1]$, but the clauses F and G in (175) and (176) are not. In fact, the clauses of (18) and (19) that led to (177) are *always* forcing, for the general cardinality constraint $[x_1 + \cdots + x_n \leq r]$; and so are the clauses of (20) and (21) that led to (178). (See exercises 429 and 430.) Moreover, the general at-most-one constraint $[x_1 + \cdots + x_n \leq 1]$ can be represented more efficiently by Heule's $3(n-2)$ binary clauses and $\lfloor (n-3)/2 \rfloor$ auxiliary variables (exercise 12), or with about $n \lg n$ binary clauses and only $\lceil \lg n \rceil$ auxiliary variables (exercise 394); both of those representations are forcing.

In general, we're glad to know as soon as possible when a variable's value has been forced by other values, because the variables of a large problem typically participate in many constraints simultaneously. If we know that x can't be 0 in constraint f, then we can often conclude that some other variable y can't be 1 in some other constraint g, if x appears in both f and g. There's lots of feedback.

On the other hand it might be worse to use a large representation F that is forcing than to use a small representation G that isn't, because additional clauses can make a SAT solver work harder. The tradeoffs are delicate, and they're difficult to predict in advance.

Every Boolean constraint $f(x_1, \ldots, x_n)$ has at least one forcing representation that involves no auxiliary variables. Indeed, it's easy to see that the *conjunctive prime form* F of f — the AND of all f's prime clauses — is forcing.

Smaller representations are also often forcing, even without auxiliaries. For example, the simple constraint $[x_1 \geq x_2 \geq \cdots \geq x_n]$ has $\binom{n}{2}$ prime clauses, namely $(x_j \vee \bar{x}_k)$ for $1 \leq j < k \leq n$; but only $n-1$ of those clauses, the cases when $k = j+1$ as in (164), are necessary and sufficient for forcing. Exercise 424 presents another, more-or-less random example.

In the worst case, all forcing representations of certain constraints are known to be huge, even when auxiliary variables are introduced (see exercise 428). But exercises 431–441 discuss many examples of useful and instructive forcing representations that require relatively few clauses.

We've glossed over an interesting technicality in definition (180), however: A sneaky person might actually construct a representation F that is absolutely useless in practice, even though it meets all of those criteria for forcing. For example, let $G(a_1, \ldots, a_m)$ be a family of clauses that are satisfiable — but only when the auxiliary variables a_j are set to extremely hard-to-find values. Then we might have $f(x_1) = x_1$ and $F = (x_1) \wedge G(a_1, \ldots, a_m)$(!). This defect in definition (180) was first pointed out by M. Gwynne and O. Kullmann [arXiv:1406.7398 [cs.CC] (2014), 67 pages], who have also traced the history of the subject.

To avoid such a glitch, we implicitly assume that F is an *honest* representation of f, in the following sense: Whenever L is a set of n literals that fully characterizes a solution $x_1 \ldots x_n$ to the constraint $f(x_1, \ldots, x_n) = 1$, *the clauses $F \mid L$ must be easy to satisfy*, using the SLUR algorithm of exercise 444. That algorithm is efficient because it does not backtrack. All of the examples in exercises 439–444 meet this test of honesty; indeed, the test is automatically passed whenever every clause of F contains at most one negated auxiliary variable.

Some authors have suggested that a SAT solver should branch only on primary variables x_i, rather than on auxiliary variables a_j, whenever possible. But an extensive study by M. Järvisalo and I. Niemelä [*LNCS* **4741** (2007), 348–363; *J. Algorithms* **63** (2008), 90–113] has shown that such a restriction is not advisable with Algorithm C, and it might lead to a severe slowdown.

Symmetry breaking. Sometimes we can achieve enormous speedup by exploiting symmetries. Consider, for example, the clauses for placing $m+1$ pigeons into m holes, (106)–(107). We've seen in Lemma B and Theorem B that Algorithm C and other resolution-related methods cannot demonstrate the unsatisfiability of those clauses without performing exponentially many steps as m grows. However, the clauses are symmetrical with respect to pigeons; independently, they're also symmetrical with respect to holes: If π is any permutation of $\{0, 1, \ldots, m\}$ and if ρ is any permutation of $\{1, 2, \ldots, m\}$, the transformation $x_{jk} \mapsto x_{(j\pi)(k\rho)}$ for $0 \le j \le m$ and $1 \le k \le m$ leaves the set of clauses (106)–(107) unchanged. Thus the pigeonhole problem has $(m+1)! \, m!$ symmetries.

We'll prove below that the symmetries on the holes allow us to assume safely that the hole-occupancy vectors are lexicographically ordered, namely that

$$x_{0k}x_{1k} \ldots x_{mk} \le x_{0(k+1)}x_{1(k+1)} \cdots x_{m(k+1)}, \quad \text{for } 1 \le k < m. \tag{181}$$

These constraints preserve satisfiability; and we know from (169) that they are readily expressed as clauses. Without the help of such additional clauses the running time of Algorithm C rises from 19 megamems for $m = 7$ to 177 Mμ for $m = 8$, and then to 3.5 gigamems and 86 Gμ for $m = 9$ and 10. But with (181), the same algorithm shows unsatisfiability for $m = 10$ after only 1 megamem; and for $m = 20$ and $m = 30$ after only 284 Mμ and 3.6 Gμ, respectively.

Even better results occur when we order the *pigeon*-occupancy vectors:

$$x_{j1}x_{j2} \ldots x_{jm} \le x_{(j+1)1}x_{(j+1)2} \cdots x_{(j+1)m}, \quad \text{for } 0 \le j < m. \tag{182}$$

With these constraints added to (106) and (107), Algorithm C polishes off the case $m = 10$ in just 69 *kilo*mems. It can even handle $m = 100$ in 133 Mμ. This remarkable improvement was achieved by adding only $m^2 - m$ new variables and $3m^2 - 2m$ new clauses to the original $m^2 + m$ variables and $(m+1) + (m^3 + m^2)/2$ clauses of (106) and (107). (Moreover, the reasoning that justifies (182) doesn't "cheat" by invoking the mathematical pigeonhole principle behind the scenes.)

Actually that's not all. The theory of columnwise symmetry (see exercise 498) also tells us that we're allowed to add the $\binom{m}{2}$ simple binary clauses

$$(x_{(j-1)j} \vee \bar{x}_{(j-1)k}) \quad \text{for } 1 \le j < k \le m \tag{183}$$

to (106) and (107), instead of (182). This principle is rather weak in general; but it turns out to be ideally suited to pigeons: It reduces the running time for $m = 100$ to just 21 megamems, although it needs no auxiliary variables whatsoever!

Of course the status of (106)–(107) has never been in doubt. Those clauses serve merely as training wheels because of their simplicity; they illustrate the fact that many symmetry-breaking strategies exist. Let's turn now to a more interesting problem, which has essentially the same symmetries, but with the roles of pigeons and holes played by "points" and "lines" instead. Consider a set of m points and n lines, where each line is a subset of points; we will require that no two points appear together in more than one line. (Equivalently, no two lines may intersect in more than one point.) Such a configuration may be called *quad-free*, because it is equivalent to an $m \times n$ binary matrix (x_{ij}) that contains no "quad," namely no 2×2 submatrix of 1s; element x_{ij} means that point i belongs to line j. Quad-free matrices are obviously characterized by $\binom{m}{2}\binom{n}{2}$ clauses,

$$(\bar{x}_{ij} \vee \bar{x}_{ij'} \vee \bar{x}_{i'j} \vee \bar{x}_{i'j'}), \quad \text{for } 1 \le i < i' \le m \text{ and } 1 \le j < j' \le n. \tag{184}$$

What is the maximum number of 1s in an $m \times n$ quad-free matrix? [This question, when $m = n$, was posed by K. Zarankiewicz, *Colloquium Mathematicæ* **2** (1951), 301, who also considered how to avoid more general submatrices of 1s.] Let's call that value $Z(m, n) - 1$; then $Z(m, n)$ is the smallest r such that every $m \times n$ matrix with r nonzero entries contains a quad.

We've actually encountered examples of this problem before, but in a disguised form. For example (see exercise 448), a Steiner triple system on v objects exists if and only if v is odd and there is a quad-free matrix with $m = v$, $n = v(v-1)/6$, and $r = v(v-1)/2$. Other combinatorial block designs have similar characterizations.

Table 5 shows the values of $Z(m, n)$ for small cases. These values were discovered by delicate combinatorial reasoning, without computer assistance; so it's instructive to see how well a SAT solver can compete against real intelligence.

The first interesting case occurs when $m = n = 8$: One can place 24 markers on a chessboard without forming a quad, but $Z(8, 8) = 25$ markers is too many. If we simply add the cardinality constraints $\sum_{i=1}^{m} \sum_{j=1}^{n} x_{ij} \ge r$ to (184), Algorithm C will quickly find a solution when $m = n = 8$ and $r = 24$. But it bogs down when $r = 25$, requiring about 10 teramems to show unsatisfiability.

Fortunately we can take advantage of $m! \, n!$ symmetries, which permute rows and columns without affecting quads. Exercise 495 shows that those symmetries

Table 5

$Z(m,n)$, THE MINIMUM NUMBER OF 1S WITH (184) UNSATISFIABLE

n =	2	3	4	5	6	7	8	9	10	11	12	13	14	15	16	17	18	19	20	21	22	23	24	25	26	27
m = 2:	4	5	6	7	8	9	10	11	12	13	14	15	16	17	18	19	20	21	22	23	24	25	26	27	28	29
m = 3:	5	7	8	9	10	11	12	13	14	15	16	17	18	19	20	21	22	23	24	25	26	27	28	29	30	31
m = 4:	6	8	10	11	13	14	15	16	17	18	19	20	21	22	23	24	25	26	27	28	29	30	31	32	33	34
m = 5:	7	9	11	13	15	16	18	19	21	22	23	24	25	26	27	28	29	30	31	32	33	34	35	36	37	38
m = 6:	8	10	13	15	17	19	20	22	23	25	26	28	29	31	32	33	34	35	36	37	38	39	40	41	42	43
m = 7:	9	11	14	16	19	22	23	25	26	28	29	31	32	34	35	37	38	40	41	43	44	45	46	47	48	49
m = 8:	10	12	15	18	20	23	25	27	29	31	33	34	36	37	39	40	42	43	45	46	48	49	51	52	54	55
m = 9:	11	13	16	19	22	25	27	30	32	34	37	38	40	41	43	44	46	47	49	50	52	53	55	56	58	59
m = 10:	12	14	17	21	23	26	29	32	35	37	40	41	43	45	47	48	50	52	53	55	56	58	59	61	62	64
m = 11:	13	15	18	22	25	28	31	34	37	40	43	45	46	48	51	52	54	56	58	60	61	63	64	66	67	69
m = 12:	14	16	19	23	26	29	33	37	40	43	46	49	50	52	54	56	58	61	62	64	66	67	69	71	73	74
m = 13:	15	17	20	24	28	31	34	38	41	45	49	53	54	56	58	60	62	65	67	68	80	72	74	76	79	80
m = 14:	16	18	21	25	29	32	36	40	43	46	50	54	57	59	61	64	66	69	71	73	74	76	79	81	83	85
m = 15:	17	19	22	26	31	34	37	41	45	48	52	56	59	62	65	68	70	73	76	78	79	81	83	86	87	89
m = 16:	18	20	23	27	32	35	39	43	47	51	54	58	61	65	68	71	74	77	81	82	84	86	88	91	92	94

[*References:* R. K. Guy, in *Theory of Graphs*, Tihany 1966, edited by Erdős and Katona (Academic Press, 1968), 119–150; R. J. Nowakowski, Ph.D. thesis (Univ. of Calgary, 1978), 202.]

allow us to add the lexicographic constraints

$$x_{i1}x_{i2}\ldots x_{in} \geq x_{(i+1)1}x_{(i+1)2}\cdots x_{(i+1)n}, \quad \text{for } 1 \leq i < m; \qquad (185)$$

$$x_{1j}x_{2j}\ldots x_{mj} \geq x_{1(j+1)}x_{2(j+1)}\cdots x_{m(j+1)}, \quad \text{for } 1 \leq j < n. \qquad (186)$$

(Increasing order, with '$\leq$' in place of '$\geq$', could also have been used, but decreasing order turns out to be better; see exercise 497.) The running time to prove unsatisfiability when $r = 25$ now decreases dramatically, to only about 50 megamems. And it falls to 48 Mμ if the lexicographic constraints are shortened to consider only the leading 4 elements of a row or column, instead of testing all 8.

The constraints of (185) and (186) are useful in satisfiable problems too — not in the easy case $m = n = 8$, when they aren't necessary, but for example in the case $m = n = 13$ when $r = 52$: Then they lead Algorithm C to a solution after about 200 gigamems, while it needs more than 18 teramems to find a solution without such help. (See exercise 449.)

Satisfiability-preserving maps. Let's proceed now to the promised theory of symmetry breaking. In fact, we will do more: Symmetry is about *permutations* that preserve structural properties, but we will consider arbitrary *mappings* instead. Mappings are more general than permutations, because they needn't be invertible. If $x = x_1 \ldots x_n$ is any potential solution to a satisfiability problem, our theory is based on transformations τ that map $x \mapsto x\tau = x'_1 \ldots x'_n$, where $x\tau$ is required to be a solution whenever x is a solution.

In other words, if F is a family of clauses on n variables and if $f(x) = [x$ satisfies $F]$, then we are interested in all mappings τ for which $f(x) \leq f(x\tau)$. Such a mapping is conventionally called an *endomorphism* of the solutions.* If an

---

* This word is a bit of a mouthful. But it's easier to say "endomorphism" than to say "satisfiability-preserving transformation," and you can use it to impress your friends. The term "conditional symmetry" has also been used by several authors in special cases.

endomorphism τ is actually a permutation, it's called an *automorphism*. Thus, if there are K solutions to the problem, out of $N = 2^n$ possibilities, the total number of mappings is N^N; the total number of endomorphisms is $K^K N^{N-K}$; and the total number of automorphisms is $K!\,(N - K)!$.

Notice that we don't require $f(x)$ to be exactly equal to $f(x\tau)$. An endomorphism is allowed to map a nonsolution into a solution, and only $K^K (N - K)^{N-K}$ mappings satisfy that stronger property. On the other hand, automorphisms always *do* satisfy $f(x) = f(x\tau)$; see exercise 454.

Here, for instance, is a more-or-less random mapping when $n = 4$:

$$
\begin{array}{l}
1100 \to 0011 \quad 1011 \to 1010 \to 0101 \to 0110 \quad 0111 \to 1000 \quad 1110 \\
0001 \to 0010 \to 0100 \to 1111 \to 1101 \to 0000 \qquad\qquad\qquad 1001 \to 1000
\end{array}
\tag{187}
$$

Exercises 455 and 456 discuss potential endomorphisms of this mapping.

In general there will be one or more *cycles*, and every element of a cycle is the root of an oriented tree that leads to it. For example, the cycles of (187) are (0011), (1010 0101 0110), and (1000).

Several different endomorphisms $\tau_1, \tau_2, \ldots, \tau_p$ are often known. In such cases it's helpful to imagine the digraph with 2^n vertices that has arcs from each vertex x to its successors $x\tau_1, x\tau_2, \ldots, x\tau_p$. This digraph will have one or more *sink components*, which are strongly connected components Y from which there is no escape: If $x \in Y$ then $x\tau_k \in Y$ for $1 \le k \le p$. (In the special case where each τ_k is an automorphism, the sink components are traditionally called *orbits* of the automorphism group.) When $p = 1$, a sink component is the same as a cycle.

The clauses F are satisfiable if and only if $f(x) = 1$ for at least one x. Such an x will lead to at least one sink component Y, all of whose elements will satisfy $f(y) = 1$. Thus it suffices to test satisfiability by checking just one element y in every sink component Y, to see if $f(y) = 1$.

Let's consider a simple problem based on the "sweep" of an $m \times n$ matrix $X = (x_{ij})$, which is the largest diagonal sum of any $t \times t$ submatrix:

$$
\operatorname{sweep}(X) = \max_{\substack{1 \le i_1 < i_2 < \cdots < i_t \le m \\ 1 \le j_1 < j_2 < \cdots < j_t \le n}} (x_{i_1 j_1} + x_{i_2 j_2} + \cdots + x_{i_t j_t}).
\tag{188}
$$

When X is binary, $\operatorname{sweep}(X)$ is the length of the longest downward-and-rightward path that passes through its 1s. We can use satisfiability to decide whether such a matrix exists having $\operatorname{sweep}(X) \le k$ and $\sum_{i=1}^{m} \sum_{j=1}^{n} x_{ij} \ge r$, given m, n, k, and r; suitable clauses are exhibited in exercise 460. A solution with $m = n = 10$, $k = 3$, and $r = 51$ appears at the right: It has 51 1s, but no four of them lie in a monotonic southeasterly path.

```
0000111111
0000100011
0000100011
0001101101
0111111001
1111100001
1010000011
1010000010
1110111110
1111100000
```

This problem has 2^{mn} candidate matrices X, and experiments with small m and n suggest several endomorphisms that can be applied to such candidates without increasing the sweep.

- τ_1: If $x_{ij} = 1$ and $x_{i(j+1)} = 0$, and if $x_{i'j} = 0$ for $1 \le i' < i$, we can set $x_{ij} \leftarrow 0$ and $x_{i(j+1)} \leftarrow 1$.
- τ_2: If $x_{ij} = 1$ and $x_{(i+1)j} = 0$, and if $x_{ij'} = 0$ for $1 \le j' < j$, we can set $x_{ij} \leftarrow 0$ and $x_{(i+1)j} \leftarrow 1$.

- τ_3: If the 2×2 submatrix in rows $\{i, i+1\}$ and columns $\{j, j+1\}$ is $\begin{smallmatrix} 11 \\ 10 \end{smallmatrix}$, we can change it to $\begin{smallmatrix} 01 \\ 11 \end{smallmatrix}$.

These transformations are justified in exercise 462. They're sometimes applicable for several different i and j; for instance, τ_3 could be used to change any of eight different 2×2 submatrices in the example solution. In such cases we make an arbitrary decision, by choosing (say) the lexicographically smallest possible i and j.

The clauses that encode this problem have auxiliary variables besides x_{ij}; but we can ignore the auxiliary variables when reasoning about endomorphisms.

Each of these endomorphisms either leaves X unchanged or replaces it by a lexicographically *smaller* matrix. *Therefore the sink components of $\{\tau_1, \tau_2, \tau_3\}$ consist of the matrices X that are fixed points of all three transformations.* Hence we're allowed to append additional clauses, stating that neither τ_1 nor τ_2 nor τ_3 is applicable. For instance, transformation τ_3 is ruled out by the clauses

$$\bigwedge_{i=1}^{m-1} \bigwedge_{j=1}^{n-1} \left(\bar{x}_{ij} \vee \bar{x}_{i(j+1)} \vee \bar{x}_{(i+1)j} \vee x_{(i+1)(j+1)} \right), \tag{189}$$

which state that the submatrix $\begin{smallmatrix} 11 \\ 10 \end{smallmatrix}$ doesn't appear. The clauses for τ_1 and τ_2 are only a bit more complicated (see exercise 461).

These additional clauses give interesting answers in satisfiable instances, although they aren't really helpful running-time-wise. On the other hand, they're spectacularly successful when the problem is *unsatisfiable*.

For example, we can show, without endomorphisms, that the case $m = n = 10$, $k = 3$, $r = 52$ is impossible, and hence that any solution for $r = 51$ is optimum; Algorithm C proves this after about 16 gigamems of work. Adding the clauses for τ_1 and τ_2, but not τ_3, increases the running time to 23 Gμ; on the other hand the clauses for τ_3 without τ_1 or τ_2 reduce it to 6 Gμ. When we use all three endomorphisms simultaneously, however, the running time to prove unsatisfiability goes down to just 3.5 *mega*mems, a speedup of more than 4500.

Even better is the fact that the fixed points of $\{\tau_1, \tau_2, \tau_3\}$ actually have an extremely simple form — see exercise 463 — from which we can readily determine the answer by hand, without running the machine at all! Computer experiments have helped us to guess this result; but once we've proved it, we've solved infinitely many cases in one fell swoop. Theory and practice are synergistic.

Another interesting example arises when we want to test whether or not a given graph has a *perfect matching*, which is a set of nonoverlapping edges that exactly touch each vertex. We'll discuss beautiful, efficient algorithms for this problem in Sections 7.5.1 and 7.5.5; but it's interesting to see how well a simple-minded SAT solver can compete with those methods.

Perfect matching is readily expressible as a SAT problem whose variables are called 'uv', one for each edge $u - v$. Variables 'uv' and 'vu' are identical. Whenever the graph contains a 4-cycle $v_0 - v_1 - v_2 - v_3 - v_0$, we might include two of its edges $\{v_0 v_1, v_2 v_3\}$ in the matching; but we could equally well have included $\{v_1 v_2, v_3 v_0\}$ instead. Thus there's an endomorphism that says, "If $v_0 v_1 = v_2 v_3 = 1$ (hence $v_1 v_2 = v_3 v_0 = 0$), set $v_0 v_1 \leftarrow v_2 v_3 \leftarrow 0$ and $v_1 v_2 \leftarrow v_3 v_0 \leftarrow 1$."

And we can carry this idea further: Let the edges be totally ordered in some arbitrary fashion, and for each edge uv consider all 4-cycles in which uv is the largest edge. In other words, we consider all cycles of the form $u - v - u' - v' - u$ in which vu', $u'v'$, $v'u$ all precede uv in the ordering. If any such cycles exist, choose one of them arbitrarily, and let τ_{uv} be one of two endomorphisms:

$$\tau_{uv}^{-}: \text{ "If } uv = u'v' = 1, \text{ set } uv \leftarrow u'v' \leftarrow 0 \text{ and } vu' \leftarrow v'u \leftarrow 1\text{."}$$
$$\tau_{uv}^{+}: \text{ "If } vu' = v'u = 1, \text{ set } uv \leftarrow u'v' \leftarrow 1 \text{ and } vu' \leftarrow v'u \leftarrow 0\text{."}$$

Either τ_{uv}^{-} or τ_{uv}^{+} is stipulated, for each uv. Exercise 465 proves that a perfect matching is in the sink component of any such family of endomorphisms if and only if it is fixed by all of them. Therefore we need only search for fixed points.

For example, consider the problem of covering an $m \times n$ board with dominoes. This is the problem of finding a perfect matching on the grid graph $P_m \square P_n$. The graph has mn vertices (i, j), with $m(n - 1)$ "horizontal" edges h_{ij} from (i, j) to $(i, j+1)$ and $(m - 1)n$ "vertical" edges v_{ij} from (i, j) to $(i+1, j)$. It has exactly $(m - 1)(n - 1)$ 4-cycles; and if we number the edges from left to right, no two 4-cycles have the same largest edge. Therefore we can construct $(m - 1)(n - 1)$ endomorphisms, in each of which we're free to decide whether to allow a particular cycle to be filled by two horizontal dominoes or by two vertical ones.

Let's stipulate that h_{ij} and $h_{(i+1)j}$ are allowed together only when $i + j$ is odd; v_{ij} and $v_{i(j+1)}$ are allowed together only when $i + j$ is even. The nine endomorphisms when $m = n = 4$ are then

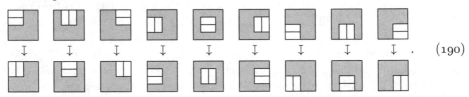

$$(190)$$

And it's not difficult to see that only *one* 4×4 domino covering is fixed by all nine. Indeed (exercise 466), the solution turns out to be unique for *all* m and n.

The famous problem of the "mutilated chessboard" asks for a domino covering when two opposite corner cells have been removed. This problem is unsatisfiable when m and n are both even, by exercise 7.1.4–213. But a SAT solver can't discover this fact quickly from the clauses alone, because there are many ways to get quite close to a solution; see the discussion following 7.1.4–(130). [S. Dantchev and S. Riis, in *FOCS* **42** (2001), 220–229, have proved in fact that every resolution refutation of these clauses requires $2^{\Omega(n)}$ steps.]

When Algorithm C is presented with mutilated boards of sizes 6×6, 8×8, 10×10, ..., 16×16, it needs respectively about $55\,\mathrm{K}\mu$, $1.4\,\mathrm{M}\mu$, $31\,\mathrm{M}\mu$, $668\,\mathrm{M}\mu$, $16.5\,\mathrm{G}\mu$, and $.91\,\mathrm{T}\mu$ (that's *tera*mems) to prove unsatisfiability. The even-odd endomorphisms typified by (190) come to our rescue, however: They narrow the search space spectacularly, reducing the respective running times to only $15\,\mathrm{K}\mu$, $60\,\mathrm{K}\mu$, $135\,\mathrm{K}\mu$, $250\,\mathrm{K}\mu$, $470\,\mathrm{K}\mu$ (that's *kilo*mems). They even can verify the unsatisfiability of a mutilated 256×256 domino cover after fewer than $4.2\,\mathrm{G}\mu$ of calculation, exhibiting a growth rate of roughly $O(n^3)$.

Endomorphisms can also speed up SAT solving in another important way:

Theorem E. *Let $p_1p_2 \ldots p_n$ be any permutation of $\{1, 2, \ldots, n\}$. If the Boolean function $f(x_1, x_2, \ldots, x_n)$ is satisfiable, then it has a solution such that $x_{p_1} x_{p_2} \ldots x_{p_n}$ is lexicographically less than or equal to $x'_{p_1} x'_{p_2} \ldots x'_{p_n}$ for every endomorphism of f that takes $x_1 x_2 \ldots x_n \mapsto x'_1 x'_2 \ldots x'_n$.*

Proof. The lexicographically smallest solution of f has this property. ∎

Maybe we shouldn't call this a "theorem"; it's an obvious consequence of the fact that endomorphisms always map solutions into solutions. But it deserves to be remembered and placed on some sort of pedestal, because we will see that it has many useful applications.

Theorem E is extremely good news, at least potentially, because every Boolean function has a *huge* number of endomorphisms. (See exercise 457.) On the other hand, there's a catch: We almost never *know* any of those endomorphisms until after we've solved the problem! Still, whenever we *do* happen to know one of the zillions of nontrivial endomorphisms that exist, we're allowed to add clauses that narrow the search. There's always a "lex-leader" solution that satisfies $x_1 x_2 \ldots x_n \leq x'_1 x'_2 \ldots x'_n$, if there's any solution at all.

A second difficulty that takes some of the shine away from Theorem E is the fact that most endomorphisms are too complicated to express neatly as clauses. What we really want is an endomorphism that's nice and simple, so that lexicographic ordering is equally simple.

Fortunately, such endomorphisms are often available; in fact, they're usually *automorphisms* — symmetries of the problem — defined by *signed permutations* of the variables. A signed permutation represents the operation of permuting variables and/or complementing them; for example, the signed permutation '$\bar{4}13\bar{2}$' stands for the mapping $(x_1, x_2, x_3, x_4) \mapsto (x_{\bar{4}}, x_1, x_3, x_{\bar{2}}) = (\bar{x}_4, x_1, x_3, \bar{x}_2)$. This operation transforms the states in a much more regular way than (187):

$$(191)$$

If σ takes the literal u into v, we write $u\sigma = v$; and in such cases σ also takes $\bar{u}$ into $\bar{v}$. Thus we always have $\bar{u}\sigma = \overline{u\sigma}$. We also write $x\sigma$ for the result of applying σ to a sequence x of literals; for example, $(x_1, x_2, x_3, x_4)\sigma = (\bar{x}_4, x_1, x_3, \bar{x}_2)$. This mapping is a symmetry or automorphism of $f(x)$ if and only if $f(x) = f(x\sigma)$ for all x. Exercises 474 and 475 discuss basic properties of such symmetries; see also exercise 7.2.1.2–20.

Notice that a signed permutation can be regarded as an unsigned permutation of the $2n$ literals $\{x_1, \ldots, x_n, \bar{x}_1, \ldots, \bar{x}_n\}$, and as such it can be written as a product of cycles. For instance, the symmetry $\bar{4}13\bar{2}$ corresponds to the cycles $(1\bar{4}2)(\bar{1}4\bar{2})(3)(\bar{3})$. We can multiply signed permutations by multiplying these cycles in the normal way, just as in Section 1.3.3.

The product $\sigma\tau$ of two symmetries σ and τ is always a symmetry. Thus in particular, if σ is any symmetry, so are its powers σ^2, σ^3, etc. We say that σ has order r if σ, σ^2, $\ldots$, σ^r are distinct and σ^r is the identity. A signed permutation of order 1 or 2 is called a *signed involution*; this important special case arises if and only if σ is its own inverse ($\sigma^2 = 1$).

It's clearly easier to work with permutations of $2n$ literals than to work with permutations of 2^n states $x_1 \ldots x_n$. The main advantage of a signed permutation σ is that we can test whether or not σ preserves the family F of clauses in a satisfiability problem. If it does, we can be sure that σ also is an automorphism when it acts on all 2^n states. (See exercise 492.)

Let's go back to the example $waerden(3, 10; 97)$ that we've often discussed above. These clauses have an obvious symmetry, which takes $x_1 x_2 \ldots x_{97} \mapsto x_{97} x_{96} \ldots x_1$. If we don't break this symmetry, Algorithm C typically verifies unsatisfiability after about 530 Mμ of computation. Now Theorem E tells us that we can also assert that $x_1 x_2 x_3 \leq x_{97} x_{96} x_{95}$, say; but that symmetry-breaker doesn't really help at all, because x_1 has very little influence on x_{97}. Fortunately, however, Theorem E allows us to choose *any* permutation $p_1 p_2 \ldots p_n$ on which to base lexicographic comparisons. For example, we can assert that $x_{48} x_{47} x_{46} \ldots \leq x_{50} x_{51} x_{52} \ldots$ — provided that we don't *also* require $x_1 x_2 x_3 \ldots \leq x_{97} x_{96} x_{95} \ldots$. (One fixed global ordering must be used, but the endomorphs can be arbitrary.)

Even the simple assertion that $x_{48} \leq x_{50}$, which is the clause '$\overline{48}\,50$', cuts the running time down to about 410 Mμ, because this new clause combines nicely with the existing clauses 46 48 50, 48 49 50, 48 50 52 to yield the helpful binary clauses 46 50, 49 50, 50 52. If we go further and assert that $x_{48} x_{47} \leq x_{50} x_{51}$, the running time improves to 345 Mμ. And the next steps $x_{48} x_{47} x_{46} \leq x_{50} x_{51} x_{52}$, $\ldots$, $x_{48} x_{47} x_{46} x_{45} x_{44} x_{43} \leq x_{50} x_{51} x_{52} x_{53} x_{54} x_{55}$ take us down to 290 Mμ, then 260 Mμ, 235 Mμ, 220 Mμ; we've saved more than half of the running time by exploiting a single reflection symmetry! Only 16 simple additional clauses, namely

$$\overline{48}\,50, \quad \overline{48}\,a_1, \quad 50\,a_1, \quad \overline{47}\,51\,\bar{a}_1, \quad \overline{47}\,a_2\,\bar{a}_1, \quad 51\,a_2\,\bar{a}_1, \quad \overline{46}\,52\,\bar{a}_2, \quad \ldots, \overline{43}\,55\,\bar{a}_5$$

are needed to get this speedup, using the efficient encoding of lex order in (169).

Of course all good things come to an end, and we've now reached the point of diminishing returns: Further clauses to assert that $x_{48} x_{47} \ldots x_{42} \leq x_{50} x_{51} \ldots x_{56}$ in the $waerden(3, 10; 97)$ problem turn out to be counterproductive.

A wonderful simplification occurs when a symmetry σ is a signed involution that has comparatively few 2-cycles. Suppose, for example, that $\sigma = 5\overline{3}\overline{2}41\overline{6}9\overline{8}\overline{7}$; in cycle form this is $(15)(\overline{1}\overline{5})(2\overline{3})(\overline{2}3)(4)(\overline{4})(6\overline{6})(7\overline{9})(\overline{7}9)(8\overline{8})$. Then the lexicographic relation $x = x_1 \ldots x_9 \leq x_1' \ldots x_9' = x\sigma$ holds if and only if $x_1 x_2 x_6 \leq x_5 \bar{x}_3 \bar{x}_6$. The reason is clear, once we look closer (see F. A. Aloul, A. Ramani, I. L. Markov, and K. A. Sakallah, *IEEE Trans.* **CAD-22** (2003), 1117–1137, §III.C): The relation $x_1 \ldots x_9 \leq x_1' \ldots x_9'$ means, in this case, "$x_1 \leq x_5$; if $x_1 = x_5$ then $x_2 \leq \bar{x}_3$; if $x_1 = x_5$ and $x_2 = \bar{x}_3$ then $x_3 \leq \bar{x}_2$; if $x_1 = x_5$, $x_2 = \bar{x}_3$, and $x_3 = \bar{x}_2$ then $x_4 \leq x_4$; if $x_1 = x_5$, $x_2 = \bar{x}_3$, $x_3 = \bar{x}_2$, and $x_4 = x_4$ then $x_5 \leq x_1$; if $x_1 = x_5$, $x_2 = \bar{x}_3$, $x_3 = \bar{x}_2$, $x_4 = x_4$, and $x_5 = x_1$ then $x_6 \leq \bar{x}_6$; if $x_1 = x_5$, $x_2 = \bar{x}_3$, $x_3 = \bar{x}_2$, $x_4 = x_4$, $x_5 = x_1$, and $x_6 = \bar{x}_6$ then we're done for." With this expanded description the simplifications are obvious.

In general this reasoning allows us to improve Theorem E as follows:

Corollary E. *Let* $p_1p_2 \ldots p_n$ *be any permutation of* $\{1, 2, \ldots, n\}$. *For every signed involution* σ *that is a symmetry of clauses* F, *we can write* σ *in cycle form*

$$(p_{i_1} \pm p_{j_1})(\bar{p}_{i_1} \mp p_{j_1})(p_{i_2} \pm p_{j_2})(\bar{p}_{i_2} \mp p_{j_2}) \ldots (p_{i_t} \pm p_{j_t})(\bar{p}_{i_t} \mp p_{j_t}) \qquad (192)$$

with $i_1 \leq j_1$, $i_2 \leq j_2$, $\ldots$, $i_t \leq j_t$, $i_1 < i_2 < \cdots < i_t$, *and with* $(\bar{p}_{i_k} \mp p_{j_k})$ *omitted when* $i_k = j_k$; *and we're allowed to append clauses to* F *that assert the lexicographic relation* $x_{p_{i_1}} x_{p_{i_2}} \ldots x_{p_{i_q}} \leq x_{\pm p_{j_1}} x_{\pm p_{j_2}} \ldots x_{\pm p_{j_q}}$, *where* $q = t$ *or* q *is the smallest* k *with* $i_k = j_k$. ∎

In the common case when σ is an ordinary signless involution, all of the signs can be eliminated here; we simply assert that $x_{p_{i_1}} \ldots x_{p_{i_t}} \leq x_{p_{j_1}} \ldots x_{p_{j_t}}$.

This involution principle justifies all of the symmetry-breaking techniques that we used above in the pigeonhole and quad-free matrix problems. See, for example, the details discussed in exercise 495.

The idea of breaking symmetry by appending clauses was pioneered by J.-F. Puget [*LNCS* **689** (1993), 350–361], then by J. Crawford, M. Ginsberg, E. Luks, and A. Roy [*Int. Conf. Knowledge Representation and Reasoning* **5** (1998), 148–159], who considered unsigned permutations only. They also attempted to discover symmetries algorithmically from the clauses that were given as input. Experience has shown, however, that useful symmetries can almost always be better supplied by a person who understands the structure of the underlying problem.

Indeed, symmetries are often "semantic" rather than "syntactic." That is, they are symmetries of the underlying Boolean function, but not of the clauses themselves. In the Zarankiewicz problem about quad-free matrices, for example, we appended efficient cardinality clauses to ensure that $\sum x_{ij} \geq r$; that condition is symmetric under row and column swaps, but the clauses are not.

In this connection it may also be helpful to mention the *monkey wrench principle*: All of the techniques by which we've proved quickly that the pigeonhole clauses are unsatisfiable would have been useless if there had been one more clause such as $(x_{01} \vee x_{11} \vee \bar{x}_{22})$; that clause would have destroyed the symmetry!

We conclude that we're allowed to *remove* clauses from F until reaching a subset of clauses F_0 for which symmetry-breakers S can be added. If $F = F_0 \cup F_1$, and if F_0 is satisfiable $\iff F_0 \cup S$ is satisfiable, then $F_0 \cup S \vdash \epsilon \implies F \vdash \epsilon$.

One hundred test cases. And now — ta da! — let's get to the climax of this long story, by looking at how our SAT solvers perform when presented with 100 moderately challenging instances of the satisfiability problem. The 100 sets of clauses summarized on the next two pages come from a cornucopia of different applications, many of which were discussed near the beginning of this section, while others appear in the exercises below.

Every test case has a code name, consisting of a letter and a digit. Table 6 characterizes each problem and also shows exactly how many variables, clauses, and total literals are involved. For example, the description of problem A1 ends with '2043|24772|55195|U'; this means that A1 consists of 24772 clauses on 2043 variables, having 55195 literals altogether, and those clauses are unsatisfiable. Furthermore, since '24772' is underlined, all of A1's clauses have length 3 or less.

Table 6

CAPSULE SUMMARIES OF THE HUNDRED TEST CASES

A1. Find $x = x_1 x_2 \ldots x_{99}$ with $\nu x = 27$ and no three equally spaced 1s. (See exercise 31.)
2043|24772|55195|U

A2. Like A1, but $x_1 x_2 \ldots x_{100}$.
2071|25197|56147|S

B1. Cover a mutilated 10×10 board with 49 dominoes, *without* using extra clauses to break symmetry.
176|572|1300|U

B2. Like B1, but a 12×12 board with 71 dominoes.
260|856|1948|U

C1. Find an 8-step Boolean chain that computes $(z_2 z_1 z_0)_2 = x_1 + x_2 + x_3 + x_4$. (See exercise 479(a).)
384|16944|66336|U

C2. Find a 7-step Boolean chain that computes the modified full adder functions z_1, z_2, z_3 in exercise 481(b).
469|26637|100063|U

C3. Like C2, but with 8 steps.
572|33675|134868|S

C4. Find a 9-step Boolean chain that computes z_l and z_r in the mod-3 addition problem of exercise 480(b).
678|45098|183834|S

C5. Connect A to A, . . . , J to J in Dudeney's puzzle of exercise 392, (*iv*).
1980|22518|70356|S

C6. Like C5, but move the J in row 8 from column 4 to column 5.
1980|22518|70356|U

C7. Given binary strings $s_1, \ldots, s_{50}$ of length 200, randomly generated at distances $\le r_j$ from some string x, find x (see exercise 502).
65719|577368|1659623|S

C8. Given binary strings $s_1, \ldots, s_{40}$ of length 500, inspired by biological data, find a string at distance ≤ 42 from each of them.
123540|909120|2569360|U

C9. Like C8, but at distance ≤ 43.
124100|926200|2620160|S

D1. Satisfy *factor_fifo*$(18, 19, 111111111111)$. (See exercise 41.)
1940|6374|16498|U

D2. Like D1, but *factor_lifo*.
1940|6374|16498|U

D3. Like D1, but $(19, 19, 111111111111)$.
2052|6745|17461|S

D4. Like D2, but $(19, 19, 111111111111)$.
2052|6745|17461|S

D5. Solve $(x_1 \ldots x_9)_2 \times (y_1 \ldots y_9)_2 \ne (x_1 \ldots x_9)_2 \times (y_1 \ldots y_9)_2$, with two copies of the *same* Dadda multiplication circuit.
864|2791|7236|U

E0. Find an Erdős discrepancy pattern $x_1 \ldots x_{500}$ (see exercise 482).
1603|9157|27469|S

E1. Like E0, but $x_1 \ldots x_{750}$.
2556|14949|44845|S

E2. Like E0, but $x_1 \ldots x_{1000}$.
3546|21035|63103|S

F1. Satisfy *fsnark*(99). (See exercise 176.)
1782|4161|8913|U

F2. Like F1, but without the clauses $(\bar{e}_{1,3} \vee \bar{f}_{99,3}) \wedge (\bar{f}_{1,1} \vee \bar{e}_{2,1})$.
1782|4159|8909|S

G1. Win Late Binding Solitaire with the "most difficult winnable deal" in answer 486.
1242|22617|65593|S

G2. Like G1, but with the most difficult *unwinnable* deal.
1242|22612|65588|U

G3. Find a test pattern for the fault "B_{43}^{43} stuck at 0" in *prod*$(16, 32)$.
3498|11337|29097|S

G4. Like G3, but for the fault "$D_{34}^{13,9}$ stuck at 0."
3502|11349|29127|S

G5. Find a 7×15 array X_0 leading to $X_3 =$ **LIFE** as in Fig. 78, having at most 38 live cells.
7150|28508|71873|U

G6. Like G5, but at most 39 live cells.
7152|28536|71956|S

G7. Like G5, but $X_4 =$ **LIFE** and X_0 can be arbitrary.
8725|33769|84041|U

G8. Find a configuration in the Game of Life that proves $f^*(7,7) = 28$ (see exercise 83).
97909|401836|1020174|S

K0. Color the 8×8 queen graph with 8 colors, using the direct encoding (15) and (16), also forcing the colors of all vertices in the top row.
512|5896|12168|U

K1. Like K0, but with the exclusion clauses (17) also.
512|7688|15752|U

K2. Like K1, but with kernel clauses instead of (17) (see answer 14).
512|6408|24328|U

K3. Like K1, but with support clauses instead of (16) (see exercise 399).
512|13512|97288|U

K4. Like K1, but using the order encoding for colors.
448|6215|21159|U

K5. Like K4, but with the hint clauses (162) appended.
448|6299|21663|U

K6. Like K5, but with double clique hints (exercise 396).
896|8559|27927|U

K7. Like K1, but with the log encoding of exercise 391(a).
2376|5120|15312|U

K8. Like K1, but with the log encoding of exercise 391(b).
192|5848|34968|U

L1. Satisfy *langford*(10).
130|2437|5204|U

L2. Satisfy *langford'*(10).
273|1020|2370|U

L3. Satisfy *langford*(13).
228|5875|12356|U

L4. Satisfy *langford'*(13).
502|1857|4320|U

L5. Satisfy *langford*(32).
1472|102922|210068|S

L6. Satisfy *langford'*(32).
3512|12768|29760|U

L7. Satisfy *langford*(64).
6016|869650|1756964|S

L8. Satisfy *langford'*(64).
14704|53184|124032|U

M1. Color the McGregor graph of order 10 (Fig. 76) with 4 colors, using one color at most 6 times, via the cardinality constraints (18) and (19).
1064|2752|6244|U

M2. Like M1, but via (20) and (21).
814|2502|5744|U

M3. Like M1, but at most 7 times.
1161|2944|6726|S

M4. Like M2, but at most 7 times.
864|2647|6226|S

M5. Like M4, but order 16 and at most
11 times.   2256|7801|18756|S

M6. Like M5, but at most 12 times.
2288|8080|19564|S

M7. Color the McGregor graph of order 9
with 4 colors, and with at least 18 regions
doubly colored (see exercise 19).
952|4539|13875|S

M8. Like M7, but with at least 19 regions.
952|4540|13877|U

N1. Place 100 nonattacking queens on
a 100×100 board.   10000|1151800|2313400|S

O1. Solve a random open shop scheduling
problem with 8 machines and 8 jobs, in
1058 units of time.   50846|557823|1621693|U

O2. Like O1, but in 1059 units.
50901|558534|1623771|U

P0. Satisfy (99), (100), and (101) for
$m = 20$, thereby exhibiting a poset of size
20 with no maximal element.   400|7260|22080|U

P1. Like P0, but with $m = 14$ and using
only the clauses of exercise 228.   196|847|2667|U

P2. Like P0, but with $m = 12$ and using
only the clauses of exercise 229.   144|530|1674|U

P3. Like P2, but omitting the clause
$(\bar{x}_{31} \vee \bar{x}_{16} \vee x_{36})$.   144|529|1671|S

P4. Like P3, but with $m = 20$.   400|2509|7827|S

Q0. Like K0, but with 9 colors.
576|6624|13688|S

Q1. Like K1, but with 9 colors.
576|8928|18296|S

Q2. Like K2, but with 9 colors.
576|7200|27368|S

Q3. Like K3, but with 9 colors.
576|15480|123128|S

Q4. Like K4, but with 9 colors.
512|7008|24200|S

Q5. Like K5, but with 9 colors.
512|7092|24704|S

Q6. Like K6, but with 9 colors.
1024|9672|31864|S

Q7. Like K7, but with 9 colors.
3168|6776|20800|S

Q8. Like K8, but with 9 colors.
256|6776|52832|S

Q9. Like Q8, but with the log encoding
of exercise 391(c).   256|6584|42256|S

R1. Satisfy $rand(3, 1061, 250, 314159)$.
250|1061|3183|S

R2. Satisfy $rand(3, 1062, 250, 314159)$.
250|1062|3186|U

S1. Find a 4-term disjunctive normal form
on $\{x_1, \ldots, x_{20}\}$ that differs from (27) but
agrees with it at 108 random training points.
356|4229|16596|S

S2. Like S1, but at 109 points.
360|4310|16760|U

S3. Find a sorting network on nine
elements that begins with the comparators
[1:6][2:7][3:8][4:9] and finishes in five more
parallel rounds. (See exercise 64.)
5175|85768|255421|U

S4. Like S3, but in six more rounds.
6444|107800|326164|S

T1. Find a 24×100 tatami tiling that spells
'TATAMI' as in exercise 118.   2874|10527|26112|S

T2. Like T1, but 24×106 and the 'I' should
have serifs.   3048|11177|27724|U

T3. Solve the TAOCP problem of exercise
389 with only 4 knight moves.
3752|12069|27548|U

T4. Like T3, but with 5 knight moves.
3756|12086|27598|S

T5. Find the pixel in row 5, column
18 of Fig. 80(c), the lexicographically
last solution to the Cheshire Tom problem.
8837|39954|100314|S

T6. Like T5, but column 19.
8837|39955|100315|U

T7. Solve the run-count extension of the
Cheshire Tom problem (see exercise 117).
25734|65670|167263|S

T8. Like T7, but find a solution that differs
from Fig. 79.   25734|65671|167749|U

W1. Satisfy $waerden(3, 10; 97)$.
97|2779|11662|U

W2. Satisfy $waerden(3, 13; 159)$.
159|7216|31398|S

W3. Satisfy $waerden(5, 5; 177)$.
177|7656|38280|S

W4. Satisfy $waerden(5, 5; 178)$.
178|7744|38720|U

X1. Prove that the "taking turns"
protocol (43) gives mutual exclusion for
at least 100 steps.   1010|3612|10614|U

X2. Prove that assertions Φ for the four-bit
protocol of exercise 101, analogous to (50),
are invariant.   129|354|926|U

X3. Prove that Bob won't starve in 36 steps,
assuming the Φ of X2.   1652|10552|28971|U

X4. Prove that there's a simple 36-step
path with the four-bit protocol, assuming
the Φ of X2.   22199|50264|130404|S

X5. Like X4, but 37 steps. 23388|52822|137034|U

X6. Like X1, but with Peterson's proto-
col (49) instead of (43).   2218|8020|23222|U

X7. Prove that there's a simple 54-step
path with protocol (49).   26450|56312|147572|S

X8. Like X7, but 55 steps.
27407|58317|152807|U

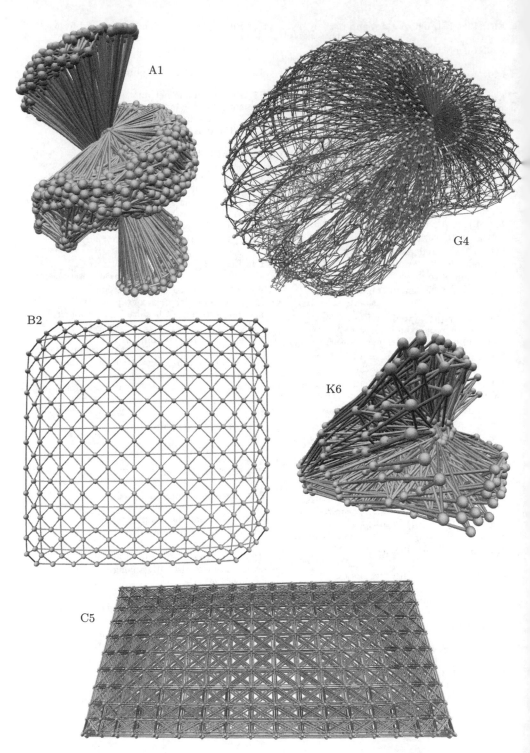

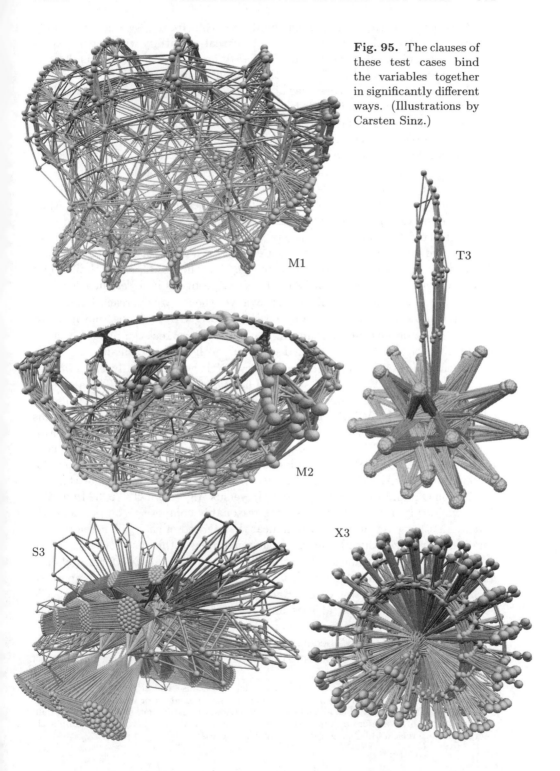

Fig. 95. The clauses of these test cases bind the variables together in significantly different ways. (Illustrations by Carsten Sinz.)

Of course we can't distinguish hard problems from easy ones by simply counting variables, clauses, and literals. The great versatility with which clauses can capture logical relationships means that different sets of clauses can lead to wildly different phenomena. Some of this immense variety is indicated in Fig. 95, which depicts ten instructive "variable interaction graphs." Each variable is represented by a ball, and two variables are linked when they appear together in at least one clause. (Some edges are darker than others; see exercise 506. For further examples of such 3D visualizations, presented also in color, see Carsten Sinz, *Journal of Automated Reasoning* **39** (2007), 219–243.)

A single SAT solver cannot be expected to excel on all of the many species of problems. Furthermore, nearly all of the 100 instances in Table 6 are well beyond the capabilities of the simple algorithms that we began with: Algorithms A, B, and D are unable to crack *any* of those test cases without needing more than fifty gigamems of computation, except for the simplest examples — L1, L2, L5, P3, P4, and X2. Algorithm L, the souped-up refinement of Algorithm D, also has a lot of difficulty with most of them. On the other hand, Algorithm C does remarkably well. It polishes off 79 of the given problems in fewer than *ten* Gμ.

Thus the test cases of Table 6 are tough, yet they're within reach. Almost all of them can be solved in say two minutes, at most, with methods known today.

Complete details can be found in the file `SATexamples.tgz` on the author's website, together with many related problems both large and small.

Exactly 50 of these 100 cases are satisfiable. So we're naturally led to wonder whether Algorithm W ("WalkSAT") will handle such cases well. The answer is that Algorithm W sometimes succeeds brilliantly — especially on problems C7, C9, L5, L7, M3, M4, M6, P3, P4, Q0, Q1, R1, S1, where it typically outperforms all the other methods we've discussed. In particular it solved S1 in just 1 Mμ, in the author's tests with $N = 50n$ and $p = .4$, compared to 25 Mμ by the next best method, Algorithm C; it won by 15 Mμ versus Algorithm C's 83 Mμ on M3, by 83 Mμ versus Algorithm L's 104 Mμ on Q0, by 95 Mμ versus Algorithm C's 464 Mμ on Q1, and by a whopping 104 Mμ versus Algorithm C's 7036 Mμ on C7. That was a surprise. WalkSAT also was reasonably competitive on problem N1. But in all other cases it was nowhere near the method of choice. Therefore we'll consider only Algorithms L and C in the remainder of this discussion.*

When does a lookahead algorithm like Algorithm L outperform a clause-learning algorithm like Algorithm C? Figure 96 shows how they compare to each other on our 100 test cases: Each problem is plotted with Algorithm C's running time on the vertical axis and Algorithm L's on the horizontal axis. Thus Algorithm L is the winner for problems that appear above the dotted line. (This dotted line is "wavy" because times aren't drawn to scale: The kth fastest running time is shown as k units from the left of the page or from the bottom.)

---

* There actually are *two* variants of Algorithm L, because the alternative heuristics of exercise 143 must be used for looking ahead when clauses of length 4 or more are present. We could use exercise 143 even when given all-ternary clauses; but experience shows that we'd tend to lose a factor of 2 or more by doing so. Our references to Algorithm L therefore implicitly assume that exercise 143 is being applied only when necessary.

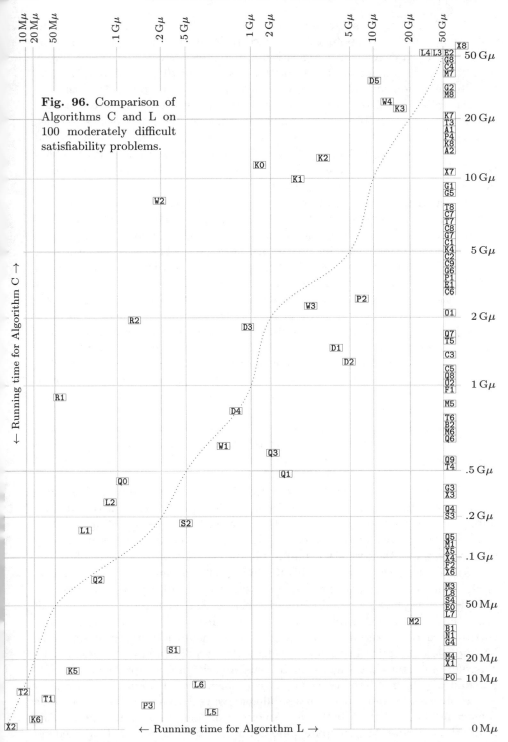

Fig. 96. Comparison of Algorithms C and L on 100 moderately difficult satisfiability problems.

All of these experiments were aborted after $50\,\mathrm{G}\mu$, if necessary, since many of these problems could potentially take centuries before running to completion. Thus the test cases for which Algorithm L timed out appear at the right edge of Fig. 96, and the tough cases for Algorithm C appear at the top. Only E2 and X8 were too hard for both algorithms to handle within the specified cutoff time.

Algorithm L is deterministic: It uses no random variables. However, a slight change (see exercise 505) will randomize it, because the inputs can be shuffled as they are in Algorithm C; and we might as well assume that this change has been made. Then both Algorithms L and C have variable running times. They will find solutions or prove unsatisfiability more quickly on some runs than on others, as we've already seen for Algorithm C in Fig. 92.

To compensate for this variability, each of the runtimes reported in Fig. 96 is the *median* of nine independent trials. Figure 97 shows all 9×100 of the empirical running times obtained with Algorithm C, sorted by their median values. We can see that many of the problems have near-constant behavior; indeed, the ratio max/min was less than 2 in 38 of the cases. But 10 cases turned out to be highly erratic in these experiments, with max/min > 100; problem P4 was actually solved once after only 323 *kilo*mems, while another run lasted 339 *giga*mems!

One might expect satisfiable problems, such as P4, to benefit more from lucky guesses than unsatisfiable problems do; and these experiments strongly support that hypothesis: Of the 21 problems with max/min > 30, all but P0 are satisfiable, and all 32 of the problems with max/min < 1.7 are unsatisfiable. One might also expect the mean running time (the arithmetic average) to exceed the median running time, in problems like this — because bad luck can be significantly bad, though hopefully rare. Yet the mean is actually *smaller* than the median in 30 cases, about equally distributed between satisfiable and unsatisfiable.

The median is a nice measure because it is meaningful even in the presence of occasional timeouts. It's also fair, because we are able to achieve the median time, or better, more often than not.

We should point out that input/output has been excluded from these time comparisons. Each satisfiability problem is supposed to appear within a computer's memory as a simple list of clauses, after which the counting of mems actually begins. We include the cost of initializing the data structures and solving the problem, but then we stop counting before actually outputting a solution.

Some of the test cases in Table 6 and Fig. 96 represent different encodings of the same problem. For example, problems K0–K8 all demonstrate that the 8×8 queen graph can't be colored with 8 colors. Similarly, problems Q0–Q9 all show that 9 colors will suffice. We've already discussed these examples above when considering alternative encodings; and we noted that the best solutions, K6 and Q5, are obtained with an extended order encoding and with Algorithm C. Therefore the fact that Algorithm L beats Algorithm C on problems K0, K1, K2, and K3 is somewhat irrelevant; those problems won't occur in practice.

Problems L5 and L6 compare different ways to handle the at-most-one constraint. L6 is slightly better for Algorithm L, but Algorithm C prefers L5. Similarly, M1 and M2 compare different ways to deal with a more general

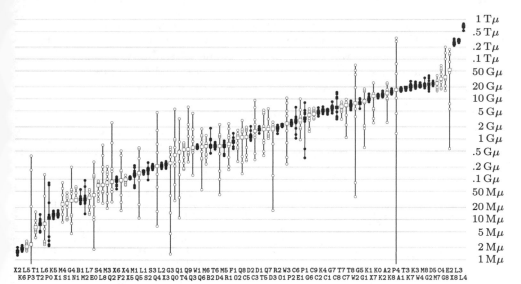

X2 L5 T1 L6 K5 M4 G4 B1 L7 S4 M3 X6 X4 M1 L1 S3 L2 G3 Q1 Q9 W1 M6 T6 M5 F1 Q8 D2 D1 Q7 R2 W3 C6 P1 C9 K4 G7 T7 T8 G5 K1 K0 A2 P4 T3 K3 M8 D5 C4 E2 L3
K6 P3 T2 P0 X1 S1 N1 M2 E0 L8 Q2 F2 X5 Q5 S2 Q4 X3 Q0 T4 Q3 Q6 B2 D4 R1 O2 C5 C3 T5 D3 O1 P2 E1 G6 C2 C1 C8 C7 W2 G1 X7 K2 K8 A1 K7 W4 G2 M7 G8 X8 L4

Fig. 97. Nine random running times of Algorithm C, sorted by their medians. (Unsatisfiable cases have solid dots or squares; satisfiable cases are hollow.)

cardinality constraint. Here M2 turns out to be better, although both are quite easy for Algorithm C and difficult for Algorithm L.

We've already noted that Algorithm L shines with respect to random problems such as R1 and R2, and it dominates all competitors even more when unsatisfiable random 3SAT problems get even bigger. Lookahead methods are also successful in *waerden* problems like W1–W4.

Unsatisfiable Langford problems such as L3 and L4 are definitely *bêtes noires* for Algorithm C, although not so bad for Algorithm L. Even the world's fastest CDCL solver, "Treengeling," was unable to refute the clauses of *langford*(17) in 2013 until it had learned 26.7 billion clauses; this process took more than a week, using a cluster of 24 computers working together. By contrast, the backtrack method of exercise 7.2.2–21 was able to prove unsatisfiability after fewer than $4\,\mathrm{T}\mu$ of computation — that's about 50 minutes on a single vintage-2013 CPU.

We've now discussed every case where Algorithm L trounces Algorithm C, *except* for D5; and D5 is actually somewhat scandalous! It's an inherently simple problem that hardware designers call a "miter": Imagine two *identical* circuits that compute some function $f(x_1, \ldots, x_n)$, one with gates $g_1, \ldots, g_m$ and another with corresponding gates $g'_1, \ldots, g'_m$, all represented as in (24). The problem is to find $x_1 \ldots x_n$ for which the final results g_m and g'_m aren't equal. It's obviously unsatisfiable. Furthermore, there's an obvious way to refute it, by successively learning the clauses $(\bar{g}_1 \vee g'_1)$, $(\bar{g}'_1 \vee g_1)$, $(\bar{g}_2 \vee g'_2)$, $(\bar{g}'_2 \vee g_2)$, etc. In theory, therefore, Algorithm C will almost surely finish in polynomial time (see exercise 386). But in practice, the algorithm won't discover those clauses without quite a lot of flailing around, unless special-purpose techniques are introduced to help it discover isomorphic gates.

Thus Algorithm C does have an Achilles heel or two. On the other hand, it is the clear method of choice in the vast majority of our test cases, and we can expect it to be the major workhorse for most of the satisfiability problems that we encounter in daily work. Therefore it behooves us to understand its behavior in some detail, not just to look at its total cost as measured in mems.

Table 7
ALGORITHM C'S EMPIRICAL BEHAVIOR ON THE HUNDRED TEST CASES

name	runtime	bytes	cells	nodes	learned	of size	triv	disc	sub	flushes	sat?
X2	0+2 Mμ	57 K	9 K	2 K	1 K	32.0 → 12.0	50%	6%	1%	30	U
K6	0+2 Mμ	314 K	46 K	1 K	0 K	15.8 → 11.8	22%	4%	3%	6	U
L5	1+1 Mμ	1841 K	210 K	0 K	0 K	146.1 → 38.4	51%	23%	0%	0	S
P3	0+2 Mμ	96 K	19 K	2 K	1 K	18.4 → 12.6	4%	11%	1%	45	S
T1	0+6 Mμ	541 K	35 K	3 K	1 K	7.4 → 6.8	3%	2%	6%	9	S
T2	0+7 Mμ	574 K	37 K	4 K	1 K	7.2 → 6.8	1%	2%	4%	6	U
L6	0+8 Mμ	672 K	39 K	1 K	0 K	195.9 → 67.8	86%	0%	0%	0	S
P0	0+11 Mμ	376 K	81 K	8 K	4 K	17.8 → 14.7	3%	10%	10%	28	U
K5	0+13 Mμ	294 K	55 K	3 K	2 K	18.6 → 12.4	33%	1%	1%	14	U
X1	0+13 Mμ	284 K	38 K	29 K	4 K	6.3 → 5.8	0%	3%	8%	53	U
M4	0+24 Mμ	308 K	47 K	6 K	4 K	20.5 → 16.3	14%	2%	1%	3	S
S1	0+25 Mμ	366 K	72 K	9 K	4 K	34.0 → 26.7	22%	4%	1%	14	S
G4	0+29 Mμ	759 K	76 K	3 K	2 K	37.1 → 24.2	26%	0%	0%	1	S
N1	16+14 Mμ	19644 K	2314 K	41 K	0 K	629.3 → 291.7	44%	6%	0%	15	S
B1	0+31 Mμ	251 K	55 K	10 K	7 K	13.5 → 11.3	3%	5%	4%	14	U
M2	0+32 Mμ	326 K	53 K	7 K	5 K	18.2 → 12.8	20%	1%	1%	6	U
L7	12+23 Mμ	14695 K	1758 K	2 K	1 K	411.2 → 107.6	66%	4%	0%	0	S
E0	0+40 Mμ	571 K	95 K	5 K	3 K	30.2 → 19.3	14%	11%	0%	6	S
S4	1+69 Mμ	3291 K	600 K	6 K	2 K	17.2 → 12.6	19%	1%	1%	8	S
L8	1+72 Mμ	3047 K	224 K	3 K	2 K	547.9 → 169.1	87%	0%	0%	0	S
M3	0+83 Mμ	493 K	84 K	13 K	9 K	28.4 → 19.2	31%	0%	1%	1	S
Q2	0+87 Mμ	885 K	190 K	11 K	8 K	61.7 → 45.8	36%	0%	0%	11	S
X6	0+93 Mμ	775 K	122 K	86 K	17 K	13.5 → 11.4	0%	3%	3%	32	U
F2	0+95 Mμ	714 K	118 K	42 K	22 K	14.3 → 13.1	0%	2%	4%	5	S
X4	1+98 Mμ	3560 K	158 K	24 K	3 K	16.2 → 11.4	9%	2%	3%	623	S
X5	1+106 Mμ	3747 K	166 K	23 K	3 K	16.5 → 11.0	11%	3%	3%	726	U
M1	0+131 Mμ	483 K	84 K	16 K	12 K	23.2 → 13.4	33%	1%	0%	1	U
Q5	0+143 Mμ	708 K	157 K	13 K	11 K	28.8 → 23.6	21%	2%	2%	6	S
L1	0+157 Mμ	597 K	139 K	21 K	18 K	36.7 → 19.0	60%	3%	0%	30	U
S2	0+176 Mμ	722 K	161 K	29 K	17 K	37.5 → 27.5	33%	3%	1%	8	U
S3	1+201 Mμ	2624 K	471 K	12 K	6 K	14.5 → 9.8	21%	1%	2%	1	U
Q4	0+213 Mμ	781 K	175 K	19 K	16 K	29.2 → 23.3	25%	3%	1%	6	S
L2	0+216 Mμ	588 K	136 K	23 K	20 K	36.2 → 17.4	75%	1%	0%	6	U
X3	0+235 Mμ	1000 K	191 K	61 K	25 K	37.7 → 19.3	34%	1%	2%	14	U
G3	0+251 Mμ	1035 K	145 K	12 K	9 K	57.9 → 28.1	42%	1%	0%	0	S
Q0	0+401 Mμ	1493 K	342 K	37 K	28 K	63.3 → 40.0	50%	0%	0%	14	S
Q1	0+464 Mμ	1516 K	343 K	41 K	33 K	63.0 → 41.0	45%	0%	0%	14	S
T4	0+546 Mμ	2716 K	544 K	202 K	18 K	218.3 → 61.5	83%	1%	0%	3018	S
Q9	0+555 Mμ	1409 K	343 K	152 K	71 K	26.7 → 20.6	3%	5%	2%	99	S
Q3	0+613 Mμ	1883 K	448 K	27 K	22 K	60.1 → 40.3	41%	1%	1%	7	S
W1	0+626 Mμ	848 K	208 K	71 K	63 K	20.8 → 13.4	5%	14%	1%	28	S
Q6	0+646 Mμ	1211 K	266 K	40 K	35 K	30.4 → 23.2	30%	1%	1%	2	S
M6	0+660 Mμ	1378 K	266 K	80 K	52 K	34.0 → 22.2	33%	1%	1%	59	S
B2	0+668 Mμ	906 K	216 K	96 K	75 K	17.1 → 13.2	4%	5%	2%	16	U
T6	1+668 Mμ	2355 K	291 K	34 K	25 K	41.4 → 19.1	57%	0%	1%	11	U
D4	0+669 Mμ	1009 K	186 K	35 K	28 K	55.7 → 15.9	70%	0%	0%	2	S
M5	0+677 Mμ	1183 K	219 K	73 K	48 K	32.6 → 20.2	37%	1%	1%	139	U
R1	0+756 Mμ	913 K	220 K	87 K	74 K	17.3 → 12.4	3%	8%	0%	9	U
F1	0+859 Mμ	1485 K	311 K	218 K	135 K	17.6 → 15.1	1%	3%	3%	6	U
O2	7+1069 Mμ	18951 K	3144 K	3 K	2 K	17.0 → 9.5	35%	0%	0%	1	S
Q8	0+1107 Mμ	1786 K	437 K	184 K	109 K	29.4 → 20.2	6%	6%	1%	109	S

name	runtime	bytes	cells	nodes	learned	of size	triv	disc	sub	flushes	sat?
C5	0+1127 Mμ	1987 K	419 K	159 K	104 K	24.4 → 16.5	12%	2%	1%	776	S
D2	0+1159 Mμ	962 K	177 K	54 K	45 K	51.8 → 11.5	73%	0%	0%	2	U
C3	0+1578 Mμ	2375 K	571 K	190 K	96 K	49.7 → 23.4	39%	3%	2%	11	S
D1	0+1707 Mμ	1172 K	230 K	76 K	62 K	45.1 → 11.6	73%	0%	0%	2	U
T5	1+1735 Mμ	3658 K	617 K	80 K	59 K	72.5 → 40.9	50%	0%	0%	43	S
Q7	0+1761 Mμ	2055 K	419 K	515 K	118 K	33.9 → 20.3	9%	7%	0%	12	S
D3	0+1807 Mμ	1283 K	254 K	77 K	64 K	57.3 → 14.0	80%	0%	0%	1	S
R2	0+1886 Mμ	1220 K	296 K	173 K	149 K	17.0 → 11.8	3%	9%	0%	14	U
O1	7+2212 Mμ	18928 K	3140 K	5 K	3 K	17.3 → 8.9	39%	0%	0%	4	U
W3	0+2422 Mμ	1819 K	448 K	191 K	174 K	19.3 → 15.5	2%	12%	1%	18	S
P2	0+2435 Mμ	2039 K	504 K	378 K	301 K	20.9 → 13.7	3%	11%	1%	45	U
C6	0+2792 Mμ	2551 K	560 K	305 K	217 K	27.0 → 17.0	20%	2%	1%	492	U
E1	0+2902 Mμ	2116 K	453 K	180 K	144 K	38.0 → 20.5	21%	18%	0%	2	S
P1	0+3280 Mμ	2726 K	674 K	819 K	549 K	18.2 → 14.4	0%	9%	3%	45	U
G6	1+3941 Mμ	3523 K	647 K	380 K	253 K	31.0 → 17.8	31%	0%	0%	0	S
C9	13+4220 Mμ	35486 K	4923 K	116 K	32 K	11.8 → 9.9	5%	1%	1%	4986	S
C2	0+4625 Mμ	2942 K	712 K	442 K	255 K	46.1 → 18.8	42%	4%	1%	15	U
K4	0+5122 Mμ	1858 K	446 K	267 K	241 K	19.6 → 13.7	19%	2%	1%	5	U
C1	0+5178 Mμ	2532 K	613 K	510 K	311 K	48.9 → 17.0	48%	6%	1%	20	U
G7	1+6070 Mμ	4227 K	771 K	546 K	369 K	32.5 → 17.6	35%	0%	0%	0	U
C8	13+6081 Mμ	35014 K	4823 K	151 K	58 K	15.3 → 10.7	15%	1%	1%	8067	U
T7	1+6467 Mμ	5428 K	544 K	333 K	108 K	26.8 → 15.3	32%	1%	1%	14565	S
C7	8+7029 Mμ	20971 K	3174 K	908 K	32 K	9.5 → 8.4	0%	3%	0%	4965	S
T8	1+7046 Mμ	5322 K	517 K	356 K	117 K	26.9 → 15.0	33%	0%	1%	15026	U
W2	0+7785 Mμ	3561 K	884 K	501 K	432 K	34.7 → 21.3	13%	17%	1%	28	S
G5	1+7799 Mμ	4312 K	844 K	642 K	446 K	33.4 → 17.4	39%	0%	0%	0	U
G1	0+8681 Mμ	5052 K	1221 K	631 K	350 K	61.1 → 34.1	38%	1%	2%	55	S
K1	0+9813 Mμ	2864 K	685 K	405 K	360 K	36.2 → 18.4	53%	2%	0%	13	U
X7	1+11857 Mμ	6235 K	697 K	1955 K	224 K	40.6 → 23.7	35%	0%	1%	31174	S
K0	0+11997 Mμ	3034 K	731 K	493 K	421 K	35.6 → 19.4	45%	2%	0%	14	U
K2	0+12601 Mμ	3028 K	729 K	500 K	427 K	34.8 → 18.0	46%	2%	0%	12	U
A2	0+13947 Mμ	3766 K	843 K	645 K	585 K	34.4 → 15.9	32%	1%	0%	0	S
K8	0+15033 Mμ	2748 K	680 K	821 K	699 K	21.2 → 13.1	8%	15%	1%	93	U
P4	0+16907 Mμ	6936 K	1721 K	1676 K	1314 K	36.5 → 24.0	5%	11%	1%	33	S
A1	0+17073 Mμ	3647 K	815 K	763 K	701 K	30.7 → 14.7	29%	2%	0%	0	U
T3	0+19266 Mμ	10034 K	2373 K	2663 K	323 K	291.8 → 72.9	86%	1%	0%	34265	U
K7	0+20577 Mμ	3168 K	721 K	1286 K	828 K	23.3 → 13.5	9%	15%	0%	9	U
K3	0+20990 Mμ	3593 K	878 K	453 K	407 K	36.7 → 19.0	55%	2%	0%	6	U
W4	0+21295 Mμ	3362 K	834 K	977 K	899 K	19.0 → 14.1	4%	15%	0%	21	U
M8	0+22281 Mμ	4105 K	994 K	992 K	785 K	37.3 → 20.5	43%	1%	1%	6	U
G2	0+23424 Mμ	6910 K	1685 K	1198 K	701 K	68.8 → 34.3	47%	1%	1%	120	U
D5	0+24141 Mμ	3232 K	779 K	787 K	654 K	63.5 → 13.4	78%	0%	0%	2	U
M7	0+24435 Mμ	4438 K	1077 K	1047 K	819 K	40.6 → 23.3	42%	1%	1%	6	S
C4	1+31898 Mμ	8541 K	2108 K	1883 K	1148 K	60.6 → 25.7	42%	4%	1%	12	S
G8	7+35174 Mμ	24854 K	2992 K	4350 K	1101 K	48.0 → 34.7	9%	0%	0%	1523	S
E2	0+53739 Mμ	5454 K	1258 K	2020 K	1658 K	41.5 → 20.8	25%	21%	0%	3	S
X8	2+248789 Mμ	12814 K	2311 K	17005 K	3145 K	56.4 → 22.5	63%	0%	0%	330557	U
L3	0+295571 Mμ	19653 K	4894 K	7402 K	6886 K	70.7 → 31.0	63%	8%	0%	30	U
L4	0+677815 Mμ	22733 K	5664 K	8545 K	7931 K	78.6 → 35.4	86%	0%	0%	5	U

Table 7 summarizes the salient statistics, again listing all cases in order of their median running time (exclusive of input and output). Each running time is actually broken into two parts, '$x+y$', where x is the time to initialize the data structures in step C1 and y is the time for the other steps, both rounded to megamems. For example, the exact median processing time for case L5 was $1,484,489\mu$ to initialize, then $655,728\mu$ to find a solution; this is shown as '$1+1\,\mathrm{M}\mu$' in the third line of the table. The time for initialization is usually negligible except when there are many clauses, as in problem N1.

The median run of problem L5 also allocated 1,841,372 bytes of memory for data; this total includes the space needed for 210,361 cells in the MEM array, at 4 bytes per cell, together with other arrays such as VAL, OVAL, HEAP, etc. The implementation considered here keeps unlearned binary clauses in a separate BIMP table, as explained in the answer to exercise 267.

This run of L5 found a solution after implicitly traversing a search tree with 138 "nodes." The number of nodes, or "decisions," is the number of times step C6 of the algorithm goes to step C3. It is shown as '0 K' in Table 7, because the node counts, byte counts, and cell counts are rounded to the nearest thousand.

The number of nodes always exceeds or equals the number of learned clauses, which is the number of conflicts detected at levels $d > 0$. (See step C7.) In the case of problem L5, only 84 clauses were learned; so again the table reports '0 K'. These 84 clauses had average length $r+1 = 146.1$; then the simplification process of exercise 257 reduced this average to just 38.4. Nevertheless, the resulting simplified clauses were still sufficiently long that the "trivial" clauses discussed in exercise 269 were sometimes used instead; this substitution happened 43 times (51%). Furthermore 19 of the learned clauses (23%) were immediately discarded, using the method of exercise 271. These percentages show up in the 'triv' and 'disc' columns of the table.

Sometimes, as in problems D1–D5, a large majority of the learned clauses were replaced by trivial ones; on the other hand, 27 of the 100 cases turned out to be less than 10% trivial in this sense. Table 7 also shows that the discard rate was 5% or more in 26 cases. The 'sub' column refers to learned clauses that were "subsumed on the fly" by the technique of exercise 270; this optimization is less common, yet it occurs often enough to be worthwhile.

The great variety in our examples is reflected in the variety of behaviors exhibited in Table 7, although several interesting trends can also be perceived. For example, the number of nodes is naturally correlated with the number of learned clauses, and both statistics tend to grow as the total running time increases. But there are significant exceptions: Two outliers, O1 and O2, have a remarkably high ratio of mems per learned clause, because of their voluminous data.

The penultimate column of Table 7 counts how often Algorithm C decided to restart itself after flushing unproductive literals from its current trail. This quantity does not simply represent the number of times step C5 discovers that $M \geq M_f$; it depends also on the current agility level (see (127)) and on the parameter ψ in Table 4. Some problems, like A1 and A2, had such high agility that they were solved satisfactorily with no restarts whatsoever; but another one, T4, finished in about 500 megamems after restarting more than 3000 times.

The number of "purges" (recycling phases) is not shown, but it can be estimated from the number of learned clauses (see exercise 508). An aggressive purging policy has kept the total number of memory cells comfortably small.

Tuning up the parameters. Table 7 shows that the hardest problem of all for Algorithm C in these experiments, L4, found itself substituting trivial clauses 86% of the time but making only 5 restarts. That test case would probably have been solved much more quickly if the algorithm's parameters had been specially adjusted for instances of the Langford problem.

Algorithm C, as implemented in the experiments above, has ten major parameters that can be modified by the user on each run:

α, tradeoff between p and q in clause RANGE scores (see Eq. (123));

ρ, damping factor in variable ACT scores (see after (118));

ϱ, damping factor in clause ACT scores (see Eq. (125));

Δ_p, initial value of the purging threshold M_p (see after (125));

δ_p, amount of gradual increase in M_p (see after (125));

τ, threshold used to prefer trivial clauses (see answer to exercise 269);

w, full "warmup" runs done after a restart (see answer to exercise 287);

p, probability of choosing a decision variable at random (see exercise 266);

P, probability that OVAL(k) is initially even;

ψ, agility threshold for flushing (see Table 4).

The values for these parameters initially came from seat-of-the-pants guesses

$$\alpha = 0.2, \quad \rho = 0.95, \quad \varrho = 0.999, \quad \Delta_\mathrm{p} = 20000, \quad \delta_\mathrm{p} - 500,$$
$$\tau = 1, \quad w = 0, \quad p = 0.02, \quad P = 0, \quad \psi = 0.166667; \qquad (193)$$

and those defaults gave reasonably good results, so they were used happily for many months (although there was no good reason to believe that they couldn't be improved). Then finally, after the author had assembled the set of 100 test cases in Table 6, it was time to decide whether to recommend the default values (193) or to come up with a better set of numbers.

Parameter optimization for general broad-spectrum use is a daunting task, not only because of significant differences between species of SAT instances but also because of the variability due to random choices when solving any specific instance. It's hard to know whether a change of parameter will be beneficial or harmful, when running times are so highly erratic. Ouch — Fig. 97 illustrates dramatic variations even when all ten parameters are held fixed, and only the seed for random numbers is changed! Furthermore the ten parameters are not at all independent: An increase in ρ, say, might be a good thing, but only if the other nine parameters are also modified appropriately. How then could *any* set of defaults be recommended, without an enormous expense of time and money?

Fortunately there's a way out of this dilemma, thanks to advances in the theory of learning. F. Hutter, H. H. Hoos, K. Leyton-Brown, and T. Stützle have developed a tool called ParamILS intended specifically for making such tuneups [*J. Artificial Intelligence Research* **36** (2009), 267–306]; the 'ILS' in this name stands for "iterated local search." The basic idea is to start with a representative training set of not-too-hard problems, and to carry out random walks in the 10-dimensional parameter space using sophisticated refinements of WalkSAT-like principles. The best parameters discovered during this training session are then evaluated on more difficult problems outside the training set.

In March 2015, Holger Hoos helped the author to tune Algorithm C using ParamILS. The resulting parameters then yielded Fig. 97, and Table 7, and many other runtime values discussed above and below. Our training set consisted of 17 problems that usually cost less than $200\,\mathrm{M}\mu$ with the original parameters (193), namely $\{K5, K6, M2, M4, N1, S1, S4, X4, X6\}$ together with stripped-down versions of $\{A1, C2, C3, D1, D2, D3, D4, K0\}$. For example, instead of the vector $x_1 \ldots x_{100}$ required by problem A1, we looked only for a shorter vector $x = x_1 \ldots x_{62}$, now with $\nu x = 20$; instead of D1 and D2 we sought 13-bit factors of 31415926; instead of K0 we tried to 9-color the SGB graph jean.

Ten independent training runs with ParamILS gave ten potential parameter settings $(\alpha_i, \rho_i, \ldots, \psi_i)$. We evaluated them on our original 17 benchmarks, together with 25 others that were a bit more difficult: $\{F1, F2, S2, S3, T4, X5\}$, plus less-stripped-down variants of $\{A1, A2, A2, C7, C7, D3, D4, F1, F2, G1, G1,$ $G2, G2, G8, K0, O1, O2, Q0, Q2\}$. For each of the ten shortlisted parameter settings, we ran each of these $17 + 25$ problems with each of the random seeds $\{1, 2, \ldots, 25\}$. Finally, hurrah, we had a winner: The parameters $(\alpha, \rho, \ldots, \psi)$ with minimum total running time in this experiment were

$$\alpha = 0.4, \quad \rho = 0.9, \quad \varrho = 0.9995, \quad \Delta_\mathrm{p} = 1000, \quad \delta_\mathrm{p} = 500,$$
$$\tau = 10, \quad w = 0, \quad p = 0.02, \quad P = 0.5, \quad \psi = 0.05. \qquad (194)$$

And these are now the recommended defaults for general-purpose use.

How much have we thereby gained? Figure 98 compares the running times of our 100 examples, before and after tuning. It shows that the vast majority — 77 of them — now run faster; these are the cases to the right of the dotted line from $(1\,\mathrm{M}\mu, 1\,\mathrm{M}\mu)$ to $(1\,\mathrm{T}\mu, 1\,\mathrm{T}\mu)$. Half of the cases experience a speedup exceeding 1.455; 27 of them now run more than twice as fast as they previously did.

Of course every rule has exceptions. The behavior of case P4 has gotten spectacularly worse, almost three orders of magnitude slower! Indeed, we saw earlier in Fig. 97 that this case has an amazingly unstable running time; further peculiarities of P4 are discussed in exercise 511.

Our other major SAT solver, Algorithm L, also has parameters, notably

α, magic tradeoff coefficient in heuristic scores (see Eq. (64));

β, damping factor for double-look triggering (see step Y1);

γ, clause weight per literal in heuristic scores (see exercise 175);

ε, offset in heuristic scores (see answer to exercise 146);

Θ, maximum heuristic score threshold (see answer to exercise 145);

Y, maximum depth of double-lookahead (see step Y1).

ParamILS suggests the following default values, which have been used in Fig. 96:

$$\alpha = 3.5, \quad \beta = 0.9998, \quad \gamma = 0.2, \quad \varepsilon = 0.001, \quad \Theta = 20.0, \quad Y = 1. \qquad (195)$$

Returning to Fig. 98, notice that the change from (193) to (194) has substantially hindered cases G3 and G4, which are examples of test pattern generation. Evidently such clauses have special characteristics that make them prefer special

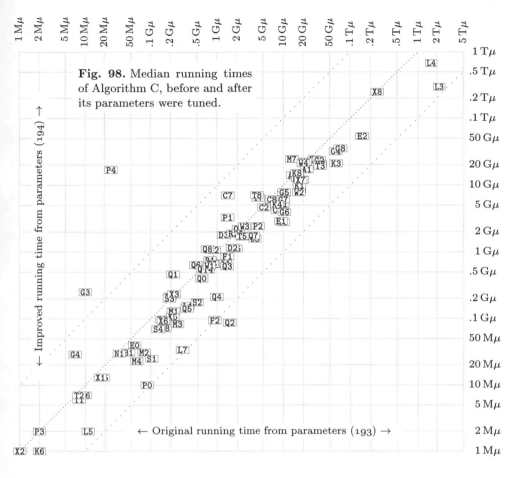

Fig. 98. Median running times of Algorithm C, before and after its parameters were tuned.

← Improved running time from parameters (194) →

← Original running time from parameters (193) →

settings of the parameters. Our main reason for introducing parameters in the first place was, of course, to allow tweaking for different families of clauses.

Instead of finding values of $(\alpha, \rho, \dots, \psi)$ that give good results in a broad spectrum of applications, we can clearly use a system like ParamILS to find values that are specifically tailored to a particular class of problems. In fact, this task is easier. For example, Hoos and the author asked for settings of the ten parameters that will tend to make Algorithm C do its best on problems of the form $waerden(3, k; n)$. A pair of ParamILS runs, based solely on the easy training cases $waerden(3, 9; 77)$ and $waerden(3, 10; 95)$, suggested the parameters

$$\alpha = 0.5, \quad \rho = 0.9995, \quad \varrho = 0.99, \quad \Delta_{\mathrm{p}} = 100, \quad \delta_{\mathrm{p}} = 10,$$
$$\tau = 10, \quad w = 8, \quad p = 0.01, \quad P = 0.5, \quad \psi = 0.15, \qquad (196)$$

and this set indeed works very well. Figure 99 shows typical details, with $7 \le k \le 14$ and with nine independent sample runs for every choice of k and n. Each unsatisfiable instance has $n = W(3, k)$, as given in the table following (10) above; each satisfiable instance has $n = W(3, k) - 1$. The fastest run using default

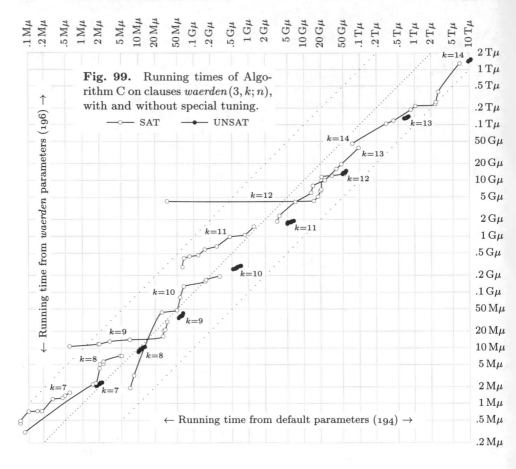

Fig. 99. Running times of Algorithm C on clauses $waerden(3, k; n)$, with and without special tuning.

—o— SAT   —•— UNSAT

↑ Running time from *waerden* parameters (196) ↓

← Running time from default parameters (194) →

parameters (194) has been paired in Fig. 99 with the fastest run using *waerden*-tuned parameters (196); similarly, the second-fastest, ..., second-slowest, and slowest runs have also been paired. Notice that satisfiable instances tend to take an unpredictable amount of time, as in Fig. 97. In spite of the fact that the new parameters (196) were found by a careful study of just two simple instances, they clearly yield substantial savings when applied to much, much harder problems of a similar nature. (See exercise 512 for another instructive example.)

Exploiting parallelism. Our focus in the present book is almost entirely on sequential algorithms, but we should be aware that the really tough instances of SAT are best solved by parallel methods.

Problems that are amenable to backtracking can readily be decomposed into subproblems that partition the space of solutions. For example, if we have 16 processors available, we can start them off on independent SAT instances in which variables $x_1 x_2 x_3 x_4$ have been forced to equal 0000, 0001, ..., 1111.

A naïve decomposition of that kind is rarely the best strategy, however. Perhaps only one of those sixteen cases is really challenging. Perhaps some of the processors are slower than others. Perhaps several processors will learn new clauses that the other processors ought to know. Furthermore, the splitting into subproblems need not occur only at the root of the search tree. Careful load-balancing and sharing of information will do much better. These challenges were addressed by a pioneering system called PSATO [H. Zhang, M. P. Bonacina, and J. Hsiang, *Journal of Symbolic Computation* **21** (1996), 543–560].

A much simpler approach should also be mentioned: We can start up many different solvers, or many copies of the same solver, with different sources of random numbers. As soon as one has finished, we can then terminate the others.

The best parallelized SAT solvers currently available are based on the "cube and conquer" paradigm, which combines conflict driven clause learning with lookahead techniques that choose branch variables for partitioning; see M. J. H. Heule, O. Kullmann, S. Wieringa, and A. Biere, *LNCS* **7261** (2012), 50–65. In particular, this approach is excellent for the *waerden* problems.

> *Today has proved to be an epoch in my Logical work.*
> *... I think of calling it the 'Genealogical Method.'*
> — CHARLES L. DODGSON, *Diary* (16 July 1894)

> *The method of showing a statement to be tautologous*
> *consists merely of constructing a table under it in the usual way*
> *and observing that the column under the main connective*
> *is composed entirely of 'T's.*
> — W. V. O. QUINE, *Mathematical Logic* (1940)

A brief history. The classic syllogism "All men are mortal; Socrates is a man; hence Socrates is mortal" shows that the notion of *resolution* is quite ancient:

$$\neg \text{Man} \lor \text{Mortal}; \quad \neg \text{Socrates} \lor \text{Man}; \quad \therefore \ \neg \text{Socrates} \lor \text{Mortal}.$$

Of course, algebraic demonstrations that $(\neg x \lor y) \land (\neg z \lor x)$ implies $(\neg z \lor y)$, when x, y, and z are arbitrary Boolean expressions, had to wait until Boole and his 19th-century followers brought mathematics to bear on the subject. The most notable contributor, resolutionwise, was perhaps C. L. Dodgson, who spent the last years of his life working out theories of inference by which complex chains of reasoning could be analyzed by hand. He published *Symbolic Logic*, Part I, in 1896, addressing it to children and to the young-in-heart by using his famous pen name Lewis Carroll. Section VII.II.§3 of that book explains and illustrates how to eliminate variables by resolution, which he called the Method of Underscoring.

When Dodgson died unexpectedly at the beginning of 1898, his nearly com-plete manuscript for *Symbolic Logic*, Part II, vanished until W. W. Bartley III was able to resurrect it in 1977. Part II was found to contain surprisingly novel ideas — especially its Method of Trees, which would have completely changed the history of mechanical theorem proving if it had come to light earlier. In this method, which Carroll documented at length in a remarkably clear and enter-taining way, he constructed search trees essentially like Fig. 82, then converted them into proofs by resolution. Instead of backtracking as in Algorithm D,

which is a recursive depth-first method, he worked breadth-first: Starting at the
root, he exploited unit clauses when possible, and branched on binary (or even
ternary) clauses when necessary, successively filling out all unfinished branches
level-by-level in hopes of being able to reuse computations.

Logicians of the 20th century took a different tack. They basically dealt with
the satisfiability problem in its equivalent dual form as the tautology problem,
namely to decide when a Boolean formula is always true. But they dismissed
tautology-checking as a triviality, because it could always be solved in a finite
number of steps by just looking at the truth table. Logicians were far more
interested in problems that were provably *unsolvable* in finite time, such as
the halting problem — the question of whether or not an algorithm terminates.
Nobody was bothered by the fact that an n-variable function has a truth table
of length 2^n, which exceeds the size of the universe even when n is rather small.

Practical computations with disjunctive normal forms were pioneered by
Archie Blake in 1937, who introduced the "consensus" of two implicants, which
is dual to the resolvent of two clauses. Blake's work was, however, soon forgotten;
E. W. Samson, B. E. Mills, and (independently) W. V. O. Quine rediscovered
the consensus operation in the 1950s, as discussed in exercise 7.1.1–31.

The next important step was taken by E. W. Samson and R. K. Mueller
[Report AFCRC-TR-55-118 (Cambridge, Mass.: Air Force Cambridge Research
Center, 1955), 16 pages], who presented an algorithm for the tautology problem
that uses consensus to eliminate variables one by one. Their algorithm therefore
was equivalent to SAT solving by successively eliminating variables via resolution. Samson and Mueller demonstrated their algorithm by applying it to the
unsatisfiable clauses that we considered in (112) above.

Independently, Martin Davis and Hilary Putnam had begun to work on the
satisfiability problem, motivated by the search for algorithms to deduce formulas
in first-order logic — unlike Samson, Mills, and Mueller, who were chiefly interested in synthesizing efficient circuits. Davis and Putnam wrote an unpublished
62-page report "Feasible computational methods in the propositional calculus"
(Rensselaer Polytechnic Institute, October 1958) in which a variety of different
approaches were considered, such as the removal of unit clauses and pure literals,
as well as "case analysis," that is, backtracking with respect to the subproblems
$F \mid x$ and $F \mid \bar{x}$. As an alternative to case analysis, they also discussed eliminating
the variable x by resolution. The account of this work that was eventually published [*JACM* **7** (1960), 201–215] concentrated on hand calculation, and omitted
case analysis in favor of resolution; but when the process was later implemented
on a computer, jointly with George Logemann and Donald Loveland [*CACM* **5**
(1962), 394–397], the method of backtracking through different cases was found
to work better with respect to memory requirements. (See Davis's account of
these developments in *Handbook of Automated Reasoning* (2001), 3–15.)

This early work didn't actually cause the satisfiability problem to appear
on many people's mental radar screens, however. Far from it; ten years went
by before SAT became an important buzzword. The picture changed in 1971,
when Stephen A. Cook showed that satisfiability is the key to solving NP-

complete problems: He proved that any algorithm to solve a decision problem in nondeterministic polynomial time can be represented efficiently as a conjunction of ternary clauses to be satisfied. (See *STOC* **3** (1971), 151–158. We'll study NP-completeness in Section 7.9.) Thus, a great multitude of hugely important problems could all be solved rather quickly, if we could only devise a decent algorithm for a *single* problem, 3SAT; and 3SAT seemed almost absurdly simple to solve.

A year of heady optimism following the publication of Cook's paper soon gave way to the realization that, alas, 3SAT might not be so easy after all. Ideas that looked promising in small cases didn't scale well, as the problem size was increased. Hence the central focus of work on satisfiability largely retreated into theoretical realms, unrelated to programming practice, except for occasional studies that used SAT as a simple model for the behavior of backtracking algorithms in general. Examples of such investigations, pioneered by A. T. Goldberg, P. W. Purdom, Jr., C. A. Brown, J. V. Franco, and others, appear in exercises 213–216. See P. W. Purdom, Jr., and G. N. Haven, *SICOMP* **26** (1997), 456–483, for a survey of subsequent progress on questions of that kind.

The state of SAT art in the early 90s was well represented by an international programming competition held in 1992 [see M. Buro and H. Kleine Büning, *Bulletin EATCS* **49** (February 1993), 143–151]. The winning programs in that contest can be regarded as the first successful lookahead solvers on the path from Algorithm A to Algorithm L. Max Böhm "took the gold" by choosing the next branch variable based on lexicographically maximal $(H_1(x), \ldots, H_n(x))$, where

$$H_k(x) = h_k(x) + h_k(\bar{x}) + \min(h_k(x), h_k(\bar{x})), \quad h_k(x) = |\{C \in F \mid x \in C, |C| = k\}|.$$

[See M. Böhm and E. Speckenmeyer, *Ann. Math. Artif. Intelligence* **17** (1996), 381–400. A. Rauzy had independently proposed a somewhat similar branching criterion in 1988; see *Revue d'intelligence artificielle* **2** (1988), 41–60.] The silver medal went to Hermann Stamm, who used strong components of the dependency digraph to narrow the search at each branch node.

Advances in practical algorithms for satisfiability now began to take off. The benchmark problems of 1992 had been chosen at random, but the DIMACS Implementation Challenge of 1993 featured also a large number of structured instances of SAT. The main purpose of this "challenge" was not to crown a winner, but to bring more than 100 researchers together for a three-day workshop, at which they could compare and share results. In retrospect, the best overall performance at that time was arguably achieved by an elaborate lookahead solver called C-SAT, which introduced techniques for detailed exploration of the first-order effects of candidate literals [see O. Dubois, P. Andre, Y. Boufkhad, and J. Carlier, *DIMACS* **26** (1996), 415–436]. Further refinements leading towards the ideas in Algorithm L appeared in a Ph.D. thesis by Jon W. Freeman (Univ. of Pennsylvania, 1995), and in the work of Chu Min Li, who introduced double lookahead [see *Information Processing Letters* **71** (1999), 75–80]. The weighted binary heuristic (67) was proposed by O. Dubois and G. Dequen, *Proc. International Joint Conference on Artificial Intelligence* **17** (2001), 248–253.

Meanwhile the ideas underlying Algorithm C began to emerge. Matthew L. Ginsberg [*J. Artificial Intelligence Research* **1** (1993), 25–46] showed that efficient backjumping was possible while remembering only at most two learned clauses for each variable. João P. Marques-Silva, in his 1995 thesis directed by Karem A. Sakallah, discovered how to turn unit-propagation conflicts into one or more clauses learned at "unique implication points," thus enhancing the potential for backjumping past decisions that didn't affect the conflict. [See *IEEE Trans.* **C48** (1999), 506–521.] Similar methods were developed independently by Roberto J. Bayardo, Jr., and Robert C. Schrag [*AAAI Conf.* **14** (1997), 203–208], who considered only the special case of new clauses that include the current decision literal, but introduced techniques for purging a learned clause when one of its literals was forced to flip its value. These new methods gave significant speedups on benchmark problems related to industrial applications.

The existence of fast SAT solvers, coupled with Gunnar Stålmarck's new ideas about applying logic to computer design [see Swedish patent 467076 (1992)], led to the introduction of bounded model checking techniques by Armin Biere, Alessandro Cimatti, Edmund Clarke, and Yunshan Zhu [*LNCS* **1579** (1999), 193–207]. Satisfiability techniques had also been introduced to solve classical planning problems in artificial intelligence [Henry Kautz and Bart Selman, *Proc. European Conf. Artificial Intelligence* **10** (1992), 359–363]. Designers could now verify much larger models than had been possible with BDD methods.

The major breakthroughs appeared in a solver called Chaff [M. W. Moskewicz, C. F. Madigan, Y. Zhao, L. Zhang, and S. Malik, *ACM/IEEE Design Automation Conf.* **38** (2001), 530–535], which had two especially noteworthy innovations: (i) "VSIDS" (the Variable State Independent Decaying Sum heuristic), a surprisingly effective way to select decision literals, which also worked well with restarts, and which suggested the even better `ACT` heuristic of Algorithm C that soon replaced it; also (ii) lazy data structures with two watched literals per clause, which made unit propagation much faster with respect to large learned clauses. (A somewhat similar watching scheme, introduced earlier by H. Zhang and M. Stickel [*J. Automated Reasoning* **24** (2000), 277–296], had the disadvantage that it needed to be downdated while backtracking.)

These exciting developments sparked a revival of international SAT competitions, which have been held annually since 2002. The winner in 2002, BerkMin by E. Goldberg and Y. Novikov, has been described well in *Discrete Applied Mathematics* **155** (2007), 1549–1561. And year after year, these challenging contests have continued to spawn further progress. By 2010, more than twice as many benchmarks could be solved in a given period of time as in 2002, using the programs of 2002 and 2010 on the computers of 2010 [see M. Järvisalo, D. Le Berre, O. Roussel, and L. Simon, *AI Magazine* **33**,1 (Spring 2012), 89–94].

The overall champion in 2007 was `SATzilla`, which was actually not a separate SAT solver but rather a program that knew how to choose intelligently between *other* solvers on any given instance. `SATzilla` would first take a few seconds to compute basic features of a problem: the distribution of literals per clause and clauses per literal, the balance between positive and negative occurrences of variables, the proximity to Horn clauses, etc. Samples could quickly be taken to estimate how many unit propagations occur at levels 1, 4, 16, 64, 256, and how many decisions are needed before reaching a conflict. Based on these numbers, and experience with the performance of the other solvers on the previous year's benchmarks, SATzilla was trained to select the algorithm that appeared most likely to succeed. This "portfolio" approach, which tunes itself nicely to the characteristics of vastly different sets of clauses, has continued to dominate the international competitions ever since. Of course portfolio solvers rely on the existence of "real" solvers, invented independently and bug-free, which shine with respect to particular classes of problems. And of course the winner of competitions may not be the best actual system for practical use. [See L. Xu, F. Hutter, H. H. Hoos, and K. Leyton-Brown, *J. Artificial Intelligence Research* **32** (2008), 565–606; *LNCS* **7317** (2012), 228–241; *CACM* **57**, 5 (May 2014), 98–107.]

Historical notes about details of the algorithms, and about important related techniques such as preprocessing and encoding, have already been discussed above as the algorithms and techniques were described.

One recurring theme appears to be that the behavior of SAT solvers is full of surprises: Some of the most important improvements have been introduced for what has turned out to be the wrong reasons, and a theoretical understanding is still far from adequate.

[The next future breakthrough might come from "variable learning," as suggested by Tseytin's idea of extended resolution: Just as clause learning increases the number of clauses, m, we might find good ways to increase the number of variables, n. The subject seems to be far from fully explored.]

EXERCISES

1. [*10*] What are the shortest (a) satisfiable (b) unsatisfiable sets of clauses?

2. [*20*] Travelers to the remote planet Pincus have reported that all the healthy natives like to dance, unless they're lazy. The lazy nondancers are happy, and so are the healthy dancers. The happy nondancers are healthy; but natives who are lazy and healthy aren't happy. Although the unhappy, unhealthy ones are always lazy, the lazy dancers are healthy. What can we conclude about Pincusians, based on these reports?

3. [*M21*] Exactly how many clauses are in $waerden(j, k; n)$?

4. [*22*] Show that the 32 constraints of $waerden(3, 3; 9)$ in (9) remain unsatisfiable even if up to four of them are removed.

5. [*M46*] Is $W(3, k) = \Theta(k^2)$?

▶ **6.** [*HM37*] Use the Local Lemma to show that $W(3, k) = \Omega(k^2/(\log k)^3)$.

7. [*21*] Can one satisfy the clauses $\{(x_i \vee x_{i+2^d} \vee x_{i+2^{d+1}}) \mid 1 \le i \le n - 2^{d+1}, d \ge 0\} \cup \{(\bar{x}_i \vee \bar{x}_{i+2^d} \vee \bar{x}_{i+2^{d+1}}) \mid 1 \le i \le n - 2^{d+1}, d \ge 0\}$?

▶ **8.** [*20*] Define clauses $waerden(k_0, k_1, \dots, k_{b-1}; n)$ that are satisfiable if and only if $n < W(k_0, k_1, \dots, k_{b-1})$.

9. [*24*] Determine the value of $W(2, 2, k)$ for all $k \ge 0$. *Hint:* Consider $k \bmod 6$.

▶ **10.** [*21*] Show that every satisfiability problem with m clauses and n variables can be transformed into an equivalent monotonic problem with $m+n$ clauses and $2n$ variables, in which the first m clauses have only negative literals, and the last n clauses are binary with two positive literals.

11. [*27*] (M. Tsimelzon, 1994.) Show that a general 3SAT problem with clauses $\{C_1, \ldots, C_m\}$ and variables $\{1, \ldots, n\}$ can be reduced to a 3D matching problem of size $10m$ that involves the following cleverly designed triples:

Each clause C_j corresponds to 3×10 vertices, namely lj, $\bar{l}j$, $|l|j'$, and $|l|j''$ for each $l \in C_j$, together with wj, xj, yj, and zj, and also $j'k$ and $j''k$ for $1 \le k \le 7$. If i or $\bar{i}$ occurs in t clauses $C_{j_1}, \ldots, C_{j_t}$, there are t "true" triples $\{ij_k, ij_k', ij_k''\}$ and t "false" triples $\{\bar{i}j_k, ij_k', ij_{1+(k \bmod t)}''\}$, for $1 \le k \le t$. Each clause $C_j = (l_1 \vee l_2 \vee l_3)$ also spawns three "satisfiability" triples $\{\bar{l}_1j, j'1, j''1\}$, $\{\bar{l}_2j, j'1, j''2\}$, $\{\bar{l}_3j, j'1, j''3\}$; six "filler" triples $\{l_1j, j'2, j''1\}$, $\{\bar{l}_1j, j'3, j''1\}$, $\{l_2j, j'4, j''2\}$, $\{\bar{l}_2j, j'5, j''2\}$, $\{l_3j, j'6, j''3\}$, $\{\bar{l}_3j, j'7, j''3\}$; and twelve "gadget" triples $\{wj, j'2, j''4\}$, $\{wj, j'4, j''4\}$, $\{wj, j'6, j''4\}$, $\{xj, j'2, j''5\}$, $\{xj, j'5, j''5\}$, $\{xj, j'7, j''5\}$, $\{yj, j'3, j''6\}$, $\{yj, j'4, j''6\}$, $\{yj, j'7, j''6\}$, $\{zj, j'3, j''7\}$, $\{zj, j'5, j''7\}$, $\{zj, j'6, j''7\}$. Thus there are $27m$ triples altogether.

For example, Rivest's satisfiability problem (6) leads to a 3D matching problem with 216 triples on 240 vertices; the triples that involve vertices 18 and $\bar{1}8$ are $\{18, 18', 18''\}$, $\{\bar{1}8, 18', 11''\}$, $\{\bar{1}8, 8'1, 8''2\}$, $\{18, 8'4, 8''2\}$, $\{\bar{1}8, 8'5, 8''2\}$.

12. [*21*] (M. J. H. Heule.) Simplify (13) by exploiting the identity

$$S_{\le 1}(y_1, \ldots, y_p) = \exists t \, (S_{\le 1}(y_1, \ldots, y_j, t) \wedge S_{\le 1}(\bar{t}, y_{j+1}, \ldots, y_p)).$$

13. [*24*] Exercise 7.2.2.1–15 defines an exact cover problem that corresponds to Langford pairs of order n.

a) What are the constraints analogous to (12) when $n = 4$?

b) Show that there's a simple way to avoid duplicate binary clauses such as those in (14), whenever an exact cover problem is converted to clauses using (13).

c) Describe the corresponding clauses $langford(4)$ and $langford'(4)$.

14. [*22*] Explain why the clauses (17) might help a SAT solver to color a graph.

15. [*24*] By comparing the McGregor graph of order 10 in Fig. 76 with the McGregor graph of order 3 shown here, give a precise definition of the vertices and edges of the McGregor graph whose order is a given number $n \ge 3$. Exactly how many vertices and edges are present in this graph, as a function of n?

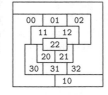

16. [*21*] Do McGregor graphs have cliques of size 4?

17. [*26*] Let $f(n)$ and $g(n)$ be the smallest and largest values of r such that McGregor's graph of order n can be 4-colored, and such that some color appears exactly r times. Use a SAT solver to find as many values of $f(n)$ and $g(n)$ as you can.

▶ **18.** [*28*] By examining the colorings found in exercise 17, define an explicit way to 4-color a McGregor graph of *arbitrary* order n, in such a way that one of the colors is used at most $\frac{5}{6}n$ times. *Hint:* The construction depends on the value of $n \bmod 6$.

▶ **19.** [*29*] Continuing exercise 17, let $h(n)$ be the largest number of regions that can be given two colors simultaneously (without using the clauses (17)). Investigate $h(n)$.

20. [*40*] In exactly how many ways can McGregor's map (Fig. 76) be four-colored?

21. [*22*] Use a SAT solver to find a minimum-size *kernel* in the graph of Fig. 76.

22. [*20*] Color the graph $\overline{C_5 \boxtimes C_5}$ with the fewest colors. (Two vertices of this graph can receive the same color if and only if they are a king move apart in a 5×5 torus.)

23. [*20*] Compare the clauses (18) and (19) to (20) and (21) in the case $n = 7$, $r = 4$.

▶ **24.** [*M34*] The clauses obtained from (20) and (21) in the previous exercise can be simplified, because we can remove the two that contain the pure literal b_1^2.

a) Prove that the literal b_1^2 is *always* pure in (20) and (21), when $r > n/2$.

b) Show that b_1^2 might also be pure in some cases when $r < n/2$.

c) The clauses obtained from (20) and (21) have *many* pure literals b_j^k when r has its maximum value $n - 1$. Furthermore, their removal makes other literals pure. How many clauses will remain in this case after all pure literals have been eliminated?

d) Show that the complete binary tree with $n \geq 2$ leaves is obtained from complete binary trees with n' and $n'' = n - n'$ leaves, where either n' or n'' is a power of 2.

e) Let $a(n, r)$ and $c(n, r)$ be respectively the number of auxiliary variables b_j^k and the total number of clauses that remain after all of the pure auxiliary literals have been removed from (20) and (21). What are $a(2^k, 2^{k-1})$ and $c(2^k, 2^{k-1})$?

f) Prove that $a(n, r) = a(n, n'') = a(n, n')$ for $n'' \leq r \leq n'$, and this common value is $\max_{1 \leq r < n} a(n, r)$. Also $a(n, r) = a(n, n - r)$; and $c(n, r) \geq c(n, n - r)$ if $r \leq n/2$.

25. [*21*] Show that (18)–(19) and (20)–(21) are equally effective when $r = 2$.

26. [*22*] Prove that Sinz's clauses (18) and (19) enforce the cardinality constraint $x_1 + \cdots + x_n \leq r$. *Hint:* Show that they imply $s_j^k = 1$ whenever $x_1 + \cdots + x_{j+k-1} \geq k$.

27. [*20*] Similarly, prove the correctness of Bailleux and Boufkhad's (20) and (21). *Hint:* They imply $b_j^k = 1$ whenever the leaves below node k contain j or more 1s.

▶ **28.** [*20*] What clauses result from (18) and (19) when we want to ensure that $x_1 + \cdots + x_n \geq 1$? (This special case converts arbitrary clauses into 3SAT clauses.)

▶ **29.** [*20*] Instead of the single constraint $x_1 + \cdots + x_n \leq r$, suppose we wish to impose a sequence of constraints $x_1 + \cdots + x_i \leq r_i$ for $1 \leq i \leq n$. Can this be done nicely with additional clauses and auxiliary variables?

▶ **30.** [*22*] If auxiliary variables s_j^k are used as in (18) and (19) to make $x_1 + \cdots + x_n \leq r$, while $s_j'^k$ are used to make $\bar{x}_1 + \cdots + \bar{x}_n \leq n - r$, show that we may unify them by taking $s_k'^j = \overline{s_j^k}$, for $1 \leq j \leq n - r$, $1 \leq k \leq r$. Can (20) and (21) be similarly unified?

▶ **31.** [*28*] Let $F_t(r)$ be the smallest n for which there is a bit vector $x_1 \ldots x_n$ with $x_1 + \cdots + x_n = r$ and with no t equally spaced 1s. For example, $F_3(12) = 30$ because of the unique solution 101100011010000000010110001101. Discuss how $F_t(r)$ might be computed efficiently with the help of a SAT solver.

32. [*15*] A *list coloring* is a graph coloring in which v's color belongs to a given set $L(v)$, for each vertex v. Represent list coloring as a SAT problem.

33. [*21*] A *double coloring* of a graph is an assignment of two distinct colors to every vertex in such a way that neighboring vertices share no common colors. Similarly, a q-tuple coloring assigns q distinct colors to each vertex. Find double and triple colorings of the cycle graphs C_5, C_7, C_9, ..., using as few colors as possible.

34. [*HM26*] The *fractional coloring number* $\chi^*(G)$ of a graph G is defined to be the minimum ratio p/q for which G has a q-tuple coloring that uses p colors.

a) Prove that $\chi^*(G) \leq \chi(G)$, and show that equality holds in McGregor's graphs.

b) Let $S_1, \ldots, S_N$ be all the independent subsets of G's vertices. Show that

$$\chi^*(G) = \min_{\lambda_1, \ldots, \lambda_N \geq 0} \{\lambda_1 + \cdots + \lambda_N \mid \textstyle\sum_{j=1}^N \lambda_j [v \in S_j] = 1 \text{ for all vertices } v\}.$$

(This is a fractional exact cover problem.)

c) What is the fractional coloring number $\chi^*(C_n)$ of the cycle graph C_n?

d) Consider the following greedy algorithm for coloring G: Set $k \leftarrow 0$ and $G_0 \leftarrow G$; while G_k is nonempty, set $k \leftarrow k+1$ and $G_k \leftarrow G_{k-1} \setminus C_k$, where C_k is a maximum independent set of G_{k-1}. Prove that $k \leq H_{\alpha(G)}\chi^*(G)$, where $\alpha(G)$ is the size of G's largest independent set; hence $\chi(G)/\chi^*(G) \leq H_{\alpha(G)} = O(\log n)$. *Hint:* Let $t_v = 1/|C_i|$ if $v \in C_i$, and show that $\sum_{v \in S} t_v \leq H_{|S|}$ whenever S is an independent set.

35. [22] Determine $\chi^*(G)$ when G is (a) the graph of the contiguous United States (see 7.2.2.1–(113)); (b) the graph of exercise 22.

▶ **36.** [22] A *radio coloring* of a graph, also known as an $L(2,1)$ labeling, is an assignment of integer colors to vertices so that the colors of u and v differ by at least 2 when $u \!-\! v$, and by at least 1 when u and v have a common neighbor. (This notion, introduced by Fred Roberts in 1988, was motivated by the problem of assigning channels to radio transmitters, without interference from "close" transmitters and without strong interference from "very close" transmitters.) Find a radio coloring of McGregor's graph, Fig. 76, that uses only 16 consecutive colors.

37. [20] Find an optimum radio coloring of the contiguous USA graph, 7.2.2.1–(113).

38. [M25] How many consecutive colors are needed for a radio coloring of (a) the $n \times n$ square grid $P_n \mathbin{\square} P_n$? (b) the vertices $\{(x,y,z) \mid x,y,z \geq 0, x+y+z = n\}$, which form a triangular grid with $n + 1$ vertices on each side?

39. [M46] Find an optimum radio coloring of the n-cube, for some value of $n > 6$.

40. [01] Is the factorization problem (22) unsatisfiable whenever z is a prime number?

41. [M21] Determine the number of Boolean operations $\wedge$, $\vee$, $\oplus$ needed to multiply m-bit numbers by n-bit numbers with Dadda's scheme, when $2 \leq m \leq n$.

42. [21] Tseytin encoding analogous to (24) can be devised also for ternary operations, without introducing any additional variables besides those of the function being encoded. Illustrate this principle by encoding the basic operations $x \leftarrow t \oplus u \oplus v$ and $y \leftarrow \langle tuv \rangle$ of a full adder directly, instead of composing them from $\oplus$, $\wedge$, and $\vee$.

▶ **43.** [21] For which integers $n \geq 2$ do there exist odd palindromic binary numbers $x = (x_n \ldots x_1)_2 = (x_1 \ldots x_n)_2$ and $y = (y_n \ldots y_1)_2 = (y_1 \ldots y_n)_2$ such that their product $xy = (z_{2n} \ldots z_1)_2 = (z_1 \ldots z_{2n})_2$ is also palindromic?

▶ **44.** [30] (Maximum ones.) Find the largest possible value of $\nu x + \nu y + \nu(xy)$, namely the greatest total number of 1 bits, over all multiplications of 32-bit binary x and y.

45. [20] Specify clauses that constrain $(z_t \ldots z_1)_2$ to be a perfect square.

46. [30] Find the largest perfect square less than 2^{100} that is a binary palindrome.

▶ **47.** [20] Suppose a circuit such as Fig. 77 has m outputs and n inputs, with g gates that transform two signals into one and h gates that transform one signal into two. Find a relation between g and h, by expressing the total number of wires in two ways.

48. [20] The small circuit shown here has three inputs, three XOR gates, one fanout gate, eight wires, and one output. Which single-stuck-at faults are detected by each of the eight test patterns pqr?

49. [24] Write a program that determines exactly which of the 100 single-stuck-at faults of the circuit in Fig. 77 are detected by each of the 32 possible input patterns. Also find all the minimum sets of test patterns that will discover every such fault (unless it's not detectable).

50. [24] Demonstrate Larrabee's method of representing stuck-at faults by describing the clauses that characterize test patterns for the fault "x_2^1 stuck at 1" in Fig. 77. (This is the wire that splits off of x_2 and feeds into x_2^3 and x_2^4, then to b_2 and b_3; see Table 1.)

51. [40] Study the behavior of SAT solvers on the problem of finding a small number of test patterns for all of the detectable single-stuck-at faults of the circuit $prod(32, 32)$. Can a complete set of patterns for this large circuit be discovered "automatically" (without relying on number theory)?

52. [15] What clauses correspond to (29) and (30) when the *second* case on the left of Table 2, $f(1, 0, 1, 0, \ldots, 1) = 1$, is taken into account?

▶ **53.** [M20] The numbers in Table 2 are definitely nonrandom. Can you see why?

▶ **54.** [23] Extend Table 2 using the rule in the previous exercise. How many rows are needed before $f(x)$ has no M-term representation in DNF, when $M = 3, 4$, and 5?

55. [21] Find an equation analogous to (27) that is consistent with Table 2 and has every variable complemented. (Thus the resulting function is monotone decreasing.)

▶ **56.** [22] Equation (27) exhibits a function matching Table 2 that depends on only 8 of the 20 variables. Use a SAT solver to show that we can actually find a suitable f that depends on only *five* of the x_j.

▶ **57.** [29] Combining the previous exercise with the methods of Section 7.1.2, exhibit a function f for Table 2 that can be evaluated with only six Boolean operations(!).

▶ **58.** [20] Discuss adding the clauses $\bar{p}_{i,j} \lor \bar{q}_{i,j}$ to (29), (30), and (31).

59. [M20] Compute the exact probability that $\hat{f}(x)$ in (32) differs from $f(x)$ in (27).

60. [24] Experiment with the problem of learning $f(x)$ in (27) from training sets of sizes 32 and 64. Use a SAT solver to find a conjectured function, $\hat{f}(x)$; then use BDD methods to determine the probability that this $\hat{f}(x)$ differs from $f(x)$ for random x.

61. [20] Explain how to test when a set of clauses generated from a training set via (29)–(31) is satisfiable only by the function $f(x)$ in (27).

62. [23] Try to learn a secret small-DNF function with N-bit training sets $x^{(0)}$, $x^{(1)}$, $x^{(2)}$, $\ldots$, where $x^{(0)}$ is random but each bit of $x^{(k)} \oplus x^{(k-1)}$ for $k > 0$ is 1 with probability p. (Thus, if p is small, successive data points will tend to be near each other.) Do such sets turn out to be more efficient in practice than the purely random ones that arise for $p = 1/2$?

▶ **63.** [20] Given an n-network $\alpha = [i_1 : j_1][i_2 : j_2] \ldots [i_r : j_r]$, as defined in the exercises for Section 5.3.4, explain how to use a SAT solver to test whether or not α is a sorting network. *Hint:* Use Theorem 5.3.4Z.

64. [26] The exact minimum time $\hat{T}(n)$ of a sorting network for n elements is a famous unsolved problem, and the fact that $\hat{T}(9) = 7$ was first established in 1987 by running a highly optimized program for many hours on a Cray 2 supercomputer.

Show that this result can now be proved with a SAT solver in less than a second(!).

▶ **65.** [28] Describe encodings of the Life transition function (35) into clauses.
   a) Use only the variables x'_{ij} and x_{ij}.
   b) Use auxiliary variables as in the Bailleux and Boufkhad encoding (20)–(21), sharing intermediate results between neighboring cells as discussed in the text.

66. [24] Use a SAT solver to find short counterparts to Fig. 78 in which (a) $X_1 = $ **LIFE**; (b) $X_2 = $ **LIFE**. In each case X_0 should have the smallest possible number of live cells.

67. [*24*] Find a mobile chessboard path $X_0 \to X_1 \to \ldots \to X_{21}$ with no more than five cells alive in each X_t. (The glider in (37) leaves the board after X_{20}.) How about X_{22}?

68. [*39*] Find a maximum-length mobile path in which 6 to 10 cells are always alive.

69. [*23*] Find all (a) still lifes and (b) oscillators of period > 1 that live in a 4×4 board.

70. [*21*] The live cells of an oscillator are divided into a *rotor* (those that change) and a *stator* (those that stay alive).
   a) Show that the rotor cannot be just a single cell.
   b) Find the smallest example of an oscillator whose rotor is ▫ ↔ ■.
   c) Similarly, find the smallest oscillators of period 3 whose rotors have the following forms: ▫ → ■ → ▫ → ▫; ▫ → ■ → ■ → ▫; ■ → ▫ → ■ → ■.

▸ **71.** [*22*] When looking for sequences of Life transition on a square grid, an asymmetrical solution will appear in eight different forms, because the grid has eight different symmetries. Furthermore, an asymmetrical periodic solution will appear in $8r$ different forms, if r is the length of the period.
   Explain how to add further clauses so that essentially equivalent solutions will occur only once: Only "canonical forms" will satisfy the conditions.

72. [*28*] Oscillators of period 3 are particularly intriguing, because Life seems so inherently binary.
   a) What are the smallest such oscillators (in terms of bounding box)?
   b) Find period-3 oscillators of sizes $9 \times n$ and $10 \times n$, with n odd, that have "fourfold symmetry": The patterns are unchanged after left-right and/or up-down reflection. (Such patterns are not only pleasant to look at, they also are much easier to find, because we need only consider about one-fourth as many variables.)
   c) What period-3 oscillators with fourfold symmetry have the most possible live cells, on grids of sizes 15×15, 15×16, and 16×16?
   d) The period-3 oscillator shown here has another kind of four-way symmetry, because it's unchanged after 90° rotation. (It was discovered in 1972 by Robert Wainwright, who called it "snake dance" because its stator involves four snakes.) What period-3 oscillators with 90° symmetry have the most possible live cells, on grids of sizes 15×15 and 16×16?

▸ **73.** [*21*] (*Mobile flipflops.*) An oscillator of period 2 is called a *flipflop*, and the Life patterns of mobile flipflops are particularly appealing: Each cell is either blank (dead at every time t) or type A (alive when t is even) or type B (alive when t is odd). Every nonblank cell (i) has exactly three neighbors of the other type, and (ii) doesn't have exactly two or three neighbors of the same type.
   a) The blank cells of a mobile flipflop also satisfy a special condition. What is it?
   b) Find a mobile flipflop on an 8×8 grid, with top row `BA ABAB`.
   c) Find patterns that are mobile flipflops on $m \times n$ toruses for various m and n. (Thus, if replicated indefinitely, each one will tile the plane with an infinite mobile flipflop.) *Hint:* One solution has no blank cells whatsoever; another has blank cells like a checkerboard.

74. [*M28*] Continuing the previous exercise, prove that no nonblank cell of a finite mobile flipflop has more than one neighbor of its own type. (This fact greatly speeds up the search for finite mobile flipflops.) Can two type A cells be diagonally adjacent?

75. [*M22*] (Stephen Silver, 2000.) Show that a finite, mobile oscillator of period $p \geq 3$ must have some cell that is alive more than once during the cycle.

76. [*41*] Construct a mobile Life oscillator of period 3.

77. [*20*] "Step X_{-1}," which precedes X_0 in (38), has the glider configuration ▟ instead of ▛. What conditions on the still life X_5 will ensure that state X_0 is indeed reached? (We don't want digestion to begin prematurely.)

78. [*21*] Find a solution to the four-step eater problem in (38) that works on a $7 \times n$ grid, for some n, instead of 8×8.

79. [*23*] What happens if the glider meets the eater of (39) in its opposite phase (namely ▞ instead of ▛)?

80. [*21*] To counteract the problem in the previous exercise, find an eater that is symmetrical when reflected about a diagonal, so that it eats both ▞ and ▛. (You'll have to go larger than 8×8, and you'll have to wait longer for digestion.)

81. [*21*] Conway discovered a remarkable "spaceship," where X_4 is X_0 shifted up 2:

$$X_0 = \boxed{} \rightarrow \boxed{} \rightarrow \boxed{} \rightarrow \boxed{} \rightarrow \boxed{} = X_4.$$

Is there a left-right symmetrical still life that will eat such spaceships?

▶ **82.** [*22*] (*Light speed.*) Imagine Life on an infinite plane, with all cells dead at time 0 except in the lower left quadrant. More precisely, suppose $X_t = (x_{tij})$ is defined for all $t \geq 0$ and all integers $-\infty < i, j < +\infty$, and that $x_{0ij} = 0$ whenever $i > 0$ or $j > 0$.

a) Prove that $x_{tij} = 0$ whenever $0 \leq t < \max(i, j)$.

b) Furthermore $x_{tij} = 0$ when $0 \leq -i \leq j$ and $0 \leq t < i + 2j$.

c) And $x_{tij} = 0$ for $0 \leq t < 2i + 2j$, if $i \geq 0$ and $j \geq 0$. *Hint:* If $x_{tij} = 0$ whenever $i \geq -j$, prove that $x_{tij} = 0$ whenever $i > -j$.

83. [*21*] According to the previous exercise, the earliest possible time that cell (i, j) can become alive, if all initial life is confined to the lower left quadrant of the plane, is at least

$$f(i, j) = i[i \geq 0] + j[j \geq 0] + (i + j)[i + j \geq 0].$$

For example, when $|i| \leq 5$ and $|j| \leq 5$ the values of $f(i, j)$ are shown at the right.

5	6	7	8	9	10	12	14	16	18	20
4	4	5	6	7	8	10	12	14	16	18
3	3	3	4	5	6	8	10	12	14	16
2	2	2	2	3	4	6	8	10	12	14
1	1	1	1	1	2	4	6	8	10	12
0	0	0	0	0	0	2	4	6	8	10
0	0	0	0	0	0	1	3	5	7	9
0	0	0	0	0	0	1	2	4	6	8
0	0	0	0	0	0	1	2	3	5	7
0	0	0	0	0	0	1	2	3	4	6
0	0	0	0	0	0	1	2	3	4	5

Let $f^*(i, j)$ be the actual minimum time at which cell (i, j) can be alive, for some such initial state. Devise a set of clauses by which a SAT solver can test whether or not $f^*(i_0, j_0) = f(i_0, j_0)$, given i_0 and j_0. (Such clauses make interesting benchmark tests.)

84. [*33*] Prove that $f^*(i, j) = f(i, j)$ in the following cases when $j > 0$: (a) $i = j$, $i = j + 1$, and $i = j - 1$. (b) $i = 0$ and $i = -1$. (c) $i = 1 - j$. (d) $i = j - 2$. (e) $i = -2$.

▶ **85.** [*39*] A *Garden of Eden* is a state of Life that has no predecessor.

a) If the pattern of 92 cells illustrated here occurs anywhere within a bitmap X, verify that X is a Garden of Eden. (The gray cells can be either dead or alive.)

b) This "orphan" pattern, found with a SAT solver's help, is the smallest that is currently known. Can you imagine how it was discovered?

86. [*M23*] How many Life predecessors does a random 10×10 bitmap have, on average?

87. [*21*] Explain why the clauses (42) represent Alice and Bob's programs (40), and give a general recipe for converting such programs into equivalent sets of clauses.

88. [*18*] Satisfy (41) and (42) for $0 \le t < 6$, and the 20×6 additional binary clauses that exclude multiple states, along with the "embarrassing" unit clauses $(A3_6) \wedge (B3_6)$.

89. [*21*] Here's a mutual-exclusion protocol once recommended in 1966. Does it work?

A0. Maybe go to A1.
A1. Set $a \leftarrow 1$, go to A2.
A2. If l go to A3, else to A5.
A3. If b go to A3, else to A4.
A4. Set $l \leftarrow 0$, go to A2.
A5. Critical, go to A6.
A6. Set $a \leftarrow 0$, go to A0.

B0. Maybe go to B1.
B1. Set $b \leftarrow 1$, go to B2.
B2. If l go to B5, else to B3.
B3. If a go to B3, else to B4.
B4. Set $l \leftarrow 1$, go to B2.
B5. Critical, go to B6.
B6. Set $b \leftarrow 0$, go to B0.

90. [*20*] Show that (43), (45), and (46) permit starvation, by satisfying (47) and (48).

91. [*M21*] Formally speaking, Alice is said to "starve" if there is (i) an infinite sequence of transitions $X_0 \to X_1 \to \cdots$ starting from the initial state X_0, and (ii) an infinite sequence @$_0$, @$_1$, ... of Boolean "bumps" that changes infinitely often, such that (iii) Alice is in a "maybe" or "critical" state only a finite number of times. Prove that this can happen if and only if there is a starvation cycle (47) as discussed in the text.

92. [*20*] Suggest $O(r^2)$ clauses with which we can determine whether or not a mutual exclusion protocol permits a path $X_0 \to X_1 \to \cdots \to X_r$ of *distinct* states.

93. [*20*] What clauses correspond to the term $\neg\Phi(X')$ in (51)?

▶ **94.** [*21*] Suppose we know that $(X_0 \to X_1 \to \cdots \to X_r) \wedge \neg\Phi(X_r)$ is unsatisfiable for $0 \le r \le k$. What clauses will guarantee that Φ is invariant? (The case $k = 1$ is (51).)

95. [*20*] Using invariants like (50), prove that (45) and (46) provide mutual exclusion.

96. [*22*] Find all solutions to (52) when $r = 2$. Also illustrate the fact that invariants are extremely helpful, by finding a solution with distinct states X_0, X_1, ..., X_r and with r substantially greater than 2, if the clauses involving Φ are removed.

97. [*20*] Can states A6 and B6 occur simultaneously in Peterson's protocol (49)?

▶ **98.** [*M23*] This exercise is about proving the nonexistence of starvation cycles (47).
   a) A cycle of states is called "pure" if one of the players is never bumped, and "simple" if no state is repeated. Prove that the shortest impure cycle, if any, is either simple or consists of two simple pure cycles that share a common state.
   b) If Alice is starved by some cycle with protocol (49), we know that she is never in states A0 or A5 within the cycle. Show that she can't be in A1, A2, or A6 either.
   c) Construct clauses to test whether there exist states $X_0 \to X_1 \to \cdots \to X_r$, with X_0 arbitrary, such that $(X_0 X_1 \ldots X_{k-1})$ is a starvation cycle for some $k \le r$.
   d) Therefore we can conclude that (49) is starvation-free without much extra work.

99. [*25*] Th. Dekker devised the first correct mutual-exclusion protocol in 1965:

A0. Maybe go to A1.
A1. Set $a \leftarrow 1$, go to A2.
A2. If b go to A3, else to A6.
A3. If l go to A4, else to A2.
A4. Set $a \leftarrow 0$, go to A5.
A5. If l go to A5, else to A1.
A6. Critical, go to A7.
A7. Set $l \leftarrow 1$, go to A8.
A8. Set $a \leftarrow 0$, go to A0.

B0. Maybe go to B1.
B1. Set $b \leftarrow 1$, go to B2.
B2. If a go to B3, else to B6.
B3. If l go to B2, else to B4.
B4. Set $b \leftarrow 0$, go to B5.
B5. If l go to B1, else to B5.
B6. Critical, go to B7.
B7. Set $l \leftarrow 0$, go to B8.
B8. Set $b \leftarrow 0$, go to B0.

Use bounded model checking to verify its correctness.

100. [*22*] Show that the following protocol can starve one player but not the other:

B0. Maybe go to B1.

A0. Maybe go to A1.

A1. Set $a \leftarrow 1$, go to A2.

A2. If b go to A2, else to A3.

A3. Critical, go to A4.

A4. Set $a \leftarrow 0$, go to A0.

B0. Maybe go to B1.

B1. Set $b \leftarrow 1$, go to B2.

B2. If a go to B3, else to B5.

B3. Set $b \leftarrow 0$, go to B4.

B4. If a go to B4, else to B1.

B5. Critical, go to B6.

B6. Set $b \leftarrow 0$, go to B0.

▶ **101.** [*31*] Protocol (49) has the potential defect that Alice and Bob might both be trying to set the value of l at the same time. Design a mutual-exclusion protocol in which each of them controls two binary signals, visible to the other. *Hint:* The method of the previous exercise can be enclosed in another protocol.

102. [*22*] If Alice is setting a variable at the same time that Bob is trying to read it, we might want to consider a more stringent model under which he sees either 0 or 1, nondeterministically. (And if he looks k times before she moves to the next step, he might see 2^k possible sequences of bits.) Explain how to handle this model of "flickering" variables by modifying the clauses of exercise 87.

103. [*18*] (Do this exercise *by hand*, it's fun!) Find the 7×21 image whose tomographic sums are $(r_1, \ldots, r_7) = (1, 0, 13, 6, 12, 7, 19)$; $(c_1, \ldots, c_{21}) = (4, 3, 3, 4, 1, 6, 1, 3, 3, 3, 5, 1,$ $1, 5, 1, 5, 1, 5, 1, 1, 1)$; $(a_1, \ldots, a_{27}) = (0, 0, 1, 2, 2, 3, 2, 3, 3, 2, 3, 3, 4, 3, 2, 3, 3, 3, 4, 3, 2, 2, 1,$ $1, 1, 1, 1)$; $(b_1, \ldots, b_{27}) = (0, 0, 0, 0, 0, 1, 3, 3, 4, 3, 2, 2, 2, 3, 3, 4, 2, 3, 3, 3, 3, 3, 4, 3, 2, 1, 1)$.

104. [*M21*] For which m and n is it possible to satisfy the digital tomography problem with $a_d = b_d = 1$ for $0 < d < m + n$? (Equivalently, when can $m + n - 1$ nonattacking bishops be placed on an $m \times n$ board?)

▶ **105.** [*M28*] A matrix whose entries are $\{-1, 0, +1\}$ is *tomographically balanced* if its row, column, and diagonal sums are all zero. Two binary images $X = (x_{ij})$ and $X' = (x'_{ij})$ clearly have the same row, column, and diagonal sums if and only if $X - X'$ is tomographically balanced.

   a) Suppose Y is tomographically balanced and has m rows, n columns, and t occurrences of $+1$. How many $m \times n$ binary matrices X and X' satisfy $X - X' = Y$?

   b) Express the condition "Y is tomographically balanced" in terms of clauses, with the values $\{-1, 0, +1\}$ represented respectively by the 2-bit codes $\{10, 00, 01\}$.

   c) Count the number $T(m, n)$ of tomographically balanced matrices, for $m, n \leq 8$.

   d) How many such matrices have exactly four occurrences of $+1$?

   e) At most how many $+1$s can a $2n \times 2n$ tomographically balanced matrix have?

   f) True or false: The positions of the $+1$s determine the positions of the -1s.

106. [*M20*] Determine a generous upper bound on the possible number of different sets of input data $\{r_i, c_j, a_d, b_d\}$ that might be given to a 25 × 30 digital tomography problem, by assuming that each of those sums independently has any of its possible values. How does this bound compare to 2^{750}?

▶ **107.** [*22*] Basket weavers from the Tonga culture of Inhambane, Mozambique, have developed appealing periodic designs called "gipatsi patterns" such as this:

(Notice that an ordinary pixel grid has been rotated by 45°.) Formally speaking, a gipatsi pattern of period p and width n is a $p \times n$ binary matrix $(x_{i,j})$ in which we have

$x_{i,1} = x_{i,n} = 1$ for $1 \le i \le p$. Row i of the matrix is to be shifted right by $i - 1$ places in the actual pattern. The example above has $p = 6$, $n = 13$, and the first row of its matrix is 1111101111101. Such a pattern has row sums $r_i = \sum_{j=1}^{n} x_{i,j}$ for $1 \le i \le p$ and column sums $c_j = \sum_{i=1}^{p} x_{i,j}$ for $1 \le j \le n$, as usual. By analogy with (53), it also has

$$a_d = \sum_{i+j \equiv d \,(\text{modulo } p)} x_{i,j}, \quad 1 \le d \le p; \qquad b_d = \sum_{2i+j \equiv d \,(\text{modulo } 2p)} x_{i,j}, \quad 1 \le d \le 2p.$$

    a) What are the tomographic parameters r_i, c_j, a_d, and b_d in the example pattern?

    b) Do any other gipatsi patterns have the same parameters?

108. [*23*] The column sums c_j in the previous exercise are somewhat artificial, because they count black pixels in only a small part of an infinite line. If we rotate the grid at a different angle, however, we can obtain infinite periodic patterns for which each of Fig. 79's four directions encounters only a finite number of pixels.

    Design a pattern of period 6 in which parallel lines always have equal tomographic projections, by changing each of the gray pixels in the following diagram to either white or black:

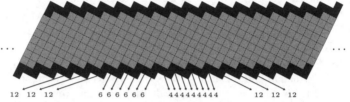

▶ 109. [*20*] Explain how to find the lexicographically smallest solution $x_1 \ldots x_n$ to a satisfiability problem, using a SAT solver repeatedly. (See Fig. 80(a).)

110. [*19*] What are the lexicographically (first, last) solutions to *waerden*(3, 10; 96)?

111. [*40*] The lexicographically first and last solutions to the "Cheshire Tom" problem in Fig. 80 are based on the top-to-bottom-and-left-to-right ordering of pixels. Experiment with other pixel orderings — for example, try bottom-to-top-and-right-to-left.

112. [*46*] Exactly how many solutions does the tomography problem of Fig. 79 have?

▶ 113. [*30*] Prove that the digital tomography problem is NP-complete, even if the marginal sums r, c, a, b are binary: Show that an efficient algorithm to decide whether or not an $n \times n$ pixel image (x_{ij}) exists, having given 0–1 values of $r_i = \sum_j x_{ij}$, $c_j = \sum_i x_{ij}$, $a_d = \sum_{i+j=d+1} x_{ij}$, and $b_d = \sum_{i-j=d-n} x_{ij}$, could be used to solve the binary tensor contingency problem of exercise 212(a).

114. [*27*] Each cell (i, j) of a given rectangular grid either contains a land mine $(x_{i,j} = 1)$ or is safe $(x_{i,j} = 0)$. In the game of *Minesweeper*, you are supposed to identify all of the hidden mines, by probing locations that you hope are safe: If you decide to probe a cell with $x_{i,j} = 1$, the mine explodes and you die (at least virtually). But if $x_{i,j} = 0$ you're told the number $n_{i,j}$ of neighboring cells that contain mines, $0 \le n_{i,j} \le 8$, and you live to make another probe. By carefully considering these numeric clues, you can often continue with completely safe probes, eventually touching every mine-free cell.

    For example, suppose the hidden mines happen to match the 25×30 pattern of the Cheshire cat (Fig. 79), and you start by probing the upper right corner. That cell turns out to be safe, and you learn that $n_{1,30} = 0$; hence it's safe to probe all three neighbors of $(1, 30)$. Continuing in this vein soon leads to illustration (α) below, which depicts information about cells (i, j) for $1 \le i \le 9$ and $21 \le j \le 30$; unprobed cells are shown in gray, otherwise the value of $n_{i,j}$ appears. From this data it's easy to deduce that $x_{1,24} = x_{2,24} = x_{3,25} = x_{4,25} = \cdots = x_{9,26} = 1$; you'll never want to probe in those places, so you can mark such cells with X, arriving at state (β) since $n_{3,24} = n_{5,25} = 4$. Further progress downward to row 17, then leftward and up, leads without difficulty to state (γ). (Notice that this process is analogous to digital tomography, because you're trying to reconstruct a binary array from information about partial sums.)

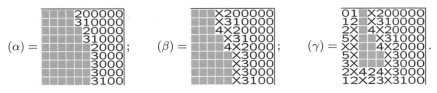

a) Now find safe probes for all thirteen of the cells that remain gray in (γ).

b) Exactly how much of the Cheshire cat can be revealed without making any unsafe guesses, if you're told in advance that (i) $x_{1,1} = 0$? (ii) $x_{1,30} = 0$? (iii) $x_{25,1} = 0$? (iv) $x_{25,30} = 0$? (v) all four corners are safe? *Hint:* A SAT solver can help.

115. [*25*] Empirically estimate the probability that a 9×9 game of Minesweeper, with 10 randomly placed mines, can be won with entirely safe probes after the first guess.

116. [*22*] Find examples of Life flipflops for which X and X' are tomographically equal.

117. [*23*] Given a sequence $x = x_1 \ldots x_n$, let $\nu^{(2)}x = x_1 x_2 + x_2 x_3 + \cdots + x_{n-1} x_n$. (A similar sum appears in the serial correlation coefficient, 3.3.2–(23).)

a) Show that, when x is a binary sequence, the number of runs of 1s in x can be expressed in terms of νx and $\nu^{(2)}x$.

b) Explain how to encode the condition $\nu^{(2)}x \le r$ as a set of clauses, by modifying the cardinality constraints (20)–(21) of Bailleux and Boufkhad.

c) Similarly, encode the condition $\nu^{(2)}x \ge r$.

118. [*20*] A *tatami tiling* is a covering by dominoes in which no three share a corner:

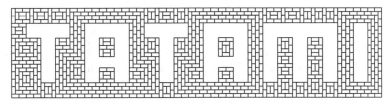

(Notice that ⊞ is disallowed, but ⊟ would be fine.) Explain how to use a SAT solver to find a tatami tiling that covers a given set of pixels, unless no such tiling exists.

119. [*18*] Let $F = \textit{waerden}(3, 3; 9)$ be the 32 clauses in (9). For which literal l is the reduced formula $F \mid l$ smallest? Exhibit the resulting clauses.

120. [*M20*] True or false: $F \mid L = \{C \setminus \overline{L} \mid C \in F \text{ and } C \cap L = \emptyset\}$, if $\overline{L} = \{\overline{l} \mid l \in L\}$.

121. [*21*] Spell out the changes to the link fields in the data structures, by expanding the higher-level descriptions that appear in steps A3, A4, A7, and A8 of Algorithm A.

▶ **122.** [*21*] Modify Algorithm A so that it finds *all* satisfying assignments of the clauses.

123. [*17*] Show the contents of the internal data structures L, START, and LINK when Algorithm B or Algorithm D begins to process the seven clauses R' of (7).

▶ **124.** [*21*] Spell out the low-level link field operations that are sketched in step B3.

▶ **125.** [*20*] Modify Algorithm B so that it finds *all* satisfying assignments of the clauses.

126. [*20*] Extend the computation in (59) by one more step.

127. [*17*] What move codes $m_1 \ldots m_d$ correspond to the computation sketched in (59), just before and after backtracking occurs?

128. [*19*] Describe the entire computation by which Algorithm D proves that Rivest's clauses (6) are unsatisfiable, using a format like (59). (See Fig. 82.)

129. [*20*] In the context of Algorithm D, design a subroutine that, given a literal l, returns 1 or 0 according as l is or is not being watched in some clause whose other literals are entirely false.

130. [*22*] What low-level list processing operations are needed to "clear the watch list for $\bar{x}_k$" in step D6?

▶ **131.** [*30*] After Algorithm D exits step D3 without finding any unit clauses, it has examined the watch lists of every free variable. Therefore it could have computed the lengths of those watch lists, with little additional cost; and information about those lengths could be used to make a more informed decision about the variable that's chosen for branching in step D4. Experiment with different branching heuristics of this kind.

▶ **132.** [*22*] Theorem 7.1.1K tells us that every 2SAT problem can be solved in linear time. Is there a sequence of 2SAT clauses for which Algorithm D takes exponential time?

▶ **133.** [*25*] The size of a backtrack tree such as Fig. 82 can depend greatly on the choice of branching variable that is made at every node.
  a) Find a backtrack tree for *waerden*(3, 3; 9) that has the fewest possible nodes.
  b) What's the *largest* backtrack tree for that problem?

134. [*22*] The `BIMP` tables used by Algorithm L are sequential lists of dynamically varying size. One attractive way to implement them is to begin with every list having capacity 4 (say); then when a list needs to become larger, its capacity can be doubled.

   Adapt the buddy system (Algorithm 2.5R) to this situation. (Lists that shrink when backtracking needn't free their memory, since they're likely to grow again later.)

▶ **135.** [*16*] The literals l' in `BIMP`(l) are those for which $l \longrightarrow l'$ in the "implication digraph" of a given satisfiability problem. How can we easily find all of the literals l'' such that $l'' \longrightarrow l$, given l?

136. [*15*] What pairs will be in `TIMP`$(\bar{3})$, before and after x_5 is set to zero with respect to the clauses (9) of *waerden*(3, 3; 9), assuming that we are on decision level $d = 0$?

137. [*24*] Spell out in detail the processes of (a) removing a variable X from the free list and from all pairs in `TIMP` lists (step L7 of Algorithm L), and of (b) restoring it again later (step L12). Exactly how do the data structures change?

▶ **138.** [*20*] Discuss what happens in step L9 of Algorithm L if we happen to have both $\bar{v} \in$ `BIMP`$(\bar{u})$ and $\bar{u} \in$ `BIMP`$(\bar{v})$.

139. [*25*] (*Compensation resolvents.*) If $w \in$ `BIMP`(v), the binary clause $u \vee v$ implies the binary clause $u \vee w$, because we can resolve $u \vee v$ with $\bar{v} \vee w$. Thus step L9 could exploit each new binary clause further, by appending w as well as v to `BIMP`$(\bar{u})$, for all such w. Discuss how to do this efficiently.

140. [*21*] The `FORCE`, `BRANCH`, `BACKF`, and `BACKI` arrays in Algorithm L will obviously never contain more than n items each. Is there a fairly small upper bound on the maximum possible size of `ISTACK`?

141. [*18*] Algorithm L might increase `ISTAMP` so often that it overflows the size of the `IST`(l) fields. How can the mechanism of (63) avoid bugs in such a case?

142. [*24*] Algorithms A, B, and D can display their current progress by exhibiting a sequence of move codes $m_1 \ldots m_d$ such as (58) and (60); but Algorithm L has no such codes. Show that an analogous sequence $m_1 \ldots m_F$ could be printed in step L2, if desired. Use the codes of Algorithm D; but extend them to show $m_j = 6$ (or 7) if R_{j-1} is a true (or false) literal whose value was found to be forced by Algorithm X, or forced by being a unit clause in the input.

▶ **143.** [*30*] Modify Algorithm L so that it will apply to nonempty clauses of any size. Call a clause *big* if its size is greater than 2. Instead of `TIMP` tables, represent every big clause by '`KINX`' and '`CINX`' tables: Every literal l has a sequential list `KINX`(l) of big clause numbers; every big clause c has a sequential list `CINX`(c) of literals; c is in `KINX`(l) if and only if l is in `CINX`(c). The current number of active clauses containing l is indicated by `KSIZE`(l); the current number of active literals in c is indicated by `CSIZE`(c).

144. [*15*] True or false: If l doesn't appear in any clause, $h'(l) = 0.1$ in (65).

145. [*23*] Starting with $h(l) = 1$ for each of the 18 literals l in *waerden*(3, 3; 9), find successively refined estimates $h'(l)$, $h''(l)$, ..., using (65) with respect to the 32 ternary clauses (9). Then, assuming that x_5 has been set false as in exercise 136, and that the resulting binary clauses 13, 19, 28, 34, 37, 46, 67, 79 have been included in the `BIMP` tables, do the same for the 16 literals that remain at depth $d = 1$.

146. [*25*] Suggest an alternative to (64) and (65) for use when Algorithm L has been extended to nonternary clauses as in exercise 143. (Strive for simplicity.)

147. [*05*] Evaluate $C_{\max}$ in (66) for $d = 0$, 1, 10, 20, 30, using the default C_0 and C_1.

148. [*21*] Equation (66) bounds the maximum number of candidates using a formula that depends on the current depth d, but not on the total number of free variables. The same cutoffs are used in problems with any number of variables. Why is that a reasonable strategy?

▶ **149.** [*26*] Devise a data structure that makes it convenient to tell whether a given variable x is a "participant" in Algorithm L.

150. [*24*] Continue the text's story of lookahead in *waerden*(3, 3; 9): What happens at depth $d = 1$ when $l \leftarrow 7$ and $T \leftarrow 22$ (see (70)), after literal 4 has become proto true? (Assume that no double-lookahead is done.)

▶ **151.** [*26*] The dependency digraph (68) has 16 arcs, only 8 of which are captured in the subforest (69). Show that, instead of (70), we could actually list the literals l and give them offsets $o(l)$ in such a way that u appears before v in the list and has $o(u) > o(v)$ if and only if $v \longrightarrow u$ in (68). Thus we could capture all 16 dependencies via levels of truth.

152. [*22*] Give an instance of 3SAT for which no free "participants" are found in step X3, yet all clauses are satisfied. Also describe an efficient way to verify satisfaction.

153. [*17*] What's a good way to weed out unwanted candidates in step X3, if $C > C_{\max}$?

154. [*20*] Suppose we're looking ahead with just four candidate variables, $\{a, b, c, d\}$, and that they're related by three binary clauses $(a \vee \bar{b}) \wedge (a \vee \bar{c}) \wedge (c \vee \bar{d})$. Find a subforest and a sequence of truth levels to facilitate lookaheads, analogous to (69) and (70).

155. [*32*] Sketch an efficient way to construct the lookahead forest in step X4.

156. [*05*] Why is a pure literal a special case of an autarky?

157. [*10*] Give an example of an autarky that is not a pure literal.

158. [*15*] If l is a pure literal, will Algorithm X discover it?

159. [*M17*] True or false: (a) A is an autarky for F if and only if $F \mid A \subseteq F$. (b) If A is an autarky for F and $A' \subseteq A$, then $A \setminus A'$ is an autarky for $F \mid A'$.

160. [*18*] (*Black and white principle.*) Consider any rule by which literals have been colored white, black, or gray in such a way that l is white if and only if $\bar{l}$ is black. (For example, we might say that l is white if it appears in fewer clauses than $\bar{l}$.)

    a) Suppose every clause of F that contains a white literal also contains a black literal. Prove that F is satisfiable if and only if its all-gray clauses are satisfiable.

    b) Explain why this metaphor is another way to describe the notion of an autarky.

▶ **161.** [*21*] (*Black and blue principle.*) Now consider coloring literals either white, black, orange, blue, or gray, in such a way that l is white if and only if $\bar{l}$ is black, and l is orange if and only if $\bar{l}$ is blue. (Hence l is gray if and only if $\bar{l}$ is gray.) Suppose further that F is a set of clauses in which every clause containing a white literal also contains either a black literal or a blue literal (or both). Let $A = \{a_1, \ldots, a_p\}$ be the black literals and let $L = \{l_1, \ldots, l_q\}$ be the blue literals. Also let F' be the set of clauses obtained by adding p additional clauses $(\bar{l}_1 \vee \cdots \vee \bar{l}_q \vee a_j)$ to F, for $1 \le j \le p$.

    a) Prove that F is satisfiable if and only if F' is satisfiable.

    b) Restate and simplify that result in the case that $p = 1$.

    c) Restate and simplify that result in the case that $q = 1$.

    d) Restate and simplify that result in the case that $p = q = 1$. (In this special case, $(\bar{l} \vee a)$ is called a *blocked binary clause*.)

162. [*21*] Devise an efficient way to discover all of the (a) blocked binary clauses $(\bar{l} \vee a)$ and (b) size-two autarkies $A = \{a, a'\}$ of a given kSAT problem F.

▶ **163.** [*M25*] Prove that the following recursive procedure $R(F)$ will solve any n-variable 3SAT problem F with at most $O(\phi^n)$ executions of steps R1, R2, or R3:

R1. [Check easy cases.] If $F = \emptyset$, return true. If $\emptyset \in F$, return false. Otherwise let $\{l_1, \ldots, l_s\} \in F$ be a clause of minimum size s.

R2. [Check autarkies.] If $s = 1$ or if $\{l_s\}$ is an autarky, set $F \leftarrow F \mid l_s$ and return to R1. Otherwise if $\{\bar{l}_s, l_{s-1}\}$ is an autarky, set $F \leftarrow F \mid \bar{l}_s, l_{s-1}$ and return to R1.

R3. [Recurse.] If $R(F \mid l_s)$ is true, return true. Otherwise set $F \leftarrow F \mid \bar{l}_s$, $s \leftarrow s - 1$, and go back to R2. ∎

164. [*M30*] Continuing exercise 163, bound the running time when F is kSAT.

▶ **165.** [*26*] Design an algorithm to find the largest positive autarky A for a given F, namely an autarky that contains only positive literals. *Hint:* Warm up by finding the largest positive autarky for the clauses $\{12\bar{3}, 12\bar{5}, \bar{1}34, 13\bar{6}, 1\bar{4}5, 156, \bar{2}35, 2\bar{4}6, 345, \bar{3}56\}$.

166. [*30*] Justify the operations of step X9. *Hint:* Prove that an autarky can be constructed, if $w = 0$ after (72) has been performed.

▶ **167.** [*21*] Justify step X11 and the similar use of X12 in step X6.

168. [*26*] Suggest a way to choose the branch literal l in step L3, based on the heuristic scores $H(l)$ that were compiled by Algorithm X in step L2. *Hint:* Experience shows that it's good to have both $H(l)$ and $H(\bar{l})$ large.

▶ **169.** [*HM30*] (T. Ahmed, O. Kullmann.) Excellent results have been obtained in some problems when the branch variable in step L3 is chosen to minimize the quantity $\tau(H(l), H(\bar{l}))$, where $\tau(a, b)$ is the positive solution to $\tau^{-a} + \tau^{-b} = 1$. (For example, $\tau(1, 2) = \phi \approx 1.62$ and $\tau(\sqrt{2}, \sqrt{2}) = 2^{1/\sqrt{2}} \approx 1.63$, so we prefer $(1, 2)$ to $(\sqrt{2}, \sqrt{2})$.) Given a list of pairs of positive numbers $(a_1, b_1), \ldots, (a_s, b_s)$, what's an efficient way to determine an index j that minimizes $\tau(a_j, b_j)$, without computing logarithms?

170. [*25*] (Marijn Heule, 2013.) Show that Algorithm L solves 2SAT in linear time.

171. [*20*] What is the purpose of DFAIL in Algorithm Y?

172. [*21*] Explain why '+LO[j]' appears in step Y2's formula for DT.

173. [*40*] Use an implementation of Algorithm L to experiment with random 3SAT problems such as *rand*(3, 2062, 500, 314). Examine the effects of such things as (i) disabling double lookahead; (ii) disabling "wraparound," by changing the cases $j = S$ and $\hat{j} = S$ in X7 and Y4 so that they simply go to X6 and Y3; (iii) disabling the lookahead forest, by letting all candidate literals have null PARENT; (iv) disabling compensation resolvents in step L9; (v) disabling "windfalls" in (72); (vi) branching on a *random* free candidate l in L3, instead of using the H scores as in exercise 168; or (vii) disabling all lookahead entirely as in "Algorithm L^0."

174. [*15*] What's an easy way to accomplish (i) in the previous exercise?

175. [*32*] When Algorithm L is extended to nonternary clauses as in exercise 143, how should Algorithms X and Y also change? (Instead of using (64) and (65) to compute a heuristic for preselection, use the much simpler formula in answer 146. And instead of using $h(u)h(v)$ in (67) to estimate the weight of a ternary clause that will be reduced to binary, consider a simulated reduced clause of size $s \geq 2$ to have weight $K_s \approx \gamma^{s-2}$, where γ is a constant (typically 0.2).)

176. [*M25*] The "flower snark" J_q is a cubic graph with $4q$ vertices t_j, u_j, v_j, w_j, and $6q$ edges $t_j \!-\! t_{j+1}$, $t_j \!-\! u_j$, $u_j \!-\! v_j$, $u_j \!-\! w_j$, $v_j \!-\! w_{j+1}$, $w_j \!-\! v_{j+1}$, for $1 \leq j \leq q$, with subscripts treated modulo q. Here, for example, are J_5 and its line graph $L(J_5)$:

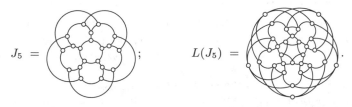

$$J_5 = \qquad ; \qquad L(J_5) = \qquad .$$

a) Give labels a_j, b_j, c_j, d_j, e_j, and f_j to the edges of J_q, for $1 \leq j \leq q$. (Thus a_j denotes $t_j \!-\! t_{j+1}$ and b_j denotes $t_j \!-\! u_j$, etc.) What are the edges of $L(J_q)$?
b) Show that $\chi(J_q) = 2$ and $\chi(L(J_q)) = 3$ when q is even.
c) Show that $\chi(J_q) = 3$ and $\chi(L(J_q)) = 4$ when q is odd. *Note:* Let *fsnark*(q) denote the clauses (15) and (16) that correspond to 3-coloring $L(J_q)$, together with $(b_{1,1}) \wedge (c_{1,2}) \wedge (d_{1,3})$ to set the colors of (b_1, c_1, d_1) to $(1, 2, 3)$. These clauses make excellent benchmark tests for SAT solvers.

177. [*HM26*] Let I_q be the number of independent sets of the flower snark line graph $L(J_q)$. Compute I_q for $1 \leq q \leq 8$, and determine the asymptotic growth rate.

▶ **178.** [*M23*] When Algorithm B is presented with the unsatisfiable clauses *fsnark*(q) of exercise 176, with q odd, its speed depends critically on the ordering of the variables.

Show that the running time is $\Theta(2^q)$ when the variables are considered in the order

$$a_{1,1}a_{1,2}a_{1,3}b_{1,1}b_{1,2}b_{1,3}c_{1,1}c_{1,2}c_{1,3}d_{1,1}d_{1,2}d_{1,3}e_{1,1}e_{1,2}e_{1,3}f_{1,1}f_{1,2}f_{1,3}\,a_{2,1}a_{2,2}a_{2,3}\ldots;$$

but much, much more time is needed when the order is

$$a_{1,1}b_{1,1}c_{1,1}d_{1,1}e_{1,1}f_{1,1}a_{2,1}b_{2,1}c_{2,1}d_{2,1}e_{2,1}f_{2,1}\ldots a_{q,1}b_{q,1}c_{q,1}d_{q,1}e_{q,1}f_{q,1}a_{1,2}b_{1,2}c_{1,2}\ldots.$$

179. [*25*] Show that there are exactly 4380 ways to fill the 32 cells of the 5-cube with eight 4-element subcubes. For example, one such way is to use the subcubes 000∗∗, 001∗∗, ..., 111∗∗, in the notation of 7.1.1–(29); a more interesting way is to use

$$0{*}0{*}0, \quad 1{*}0{*}0, \quad {*}{*}001, \quad {*}{*}110, \quad {*}010{*}, \quad {*}110{*}, \quad 0{*}{*}11, \quad 1{*}{*}11.$$

What does this fact tell you about the value of q_8 in Fig. 83?

▶ **180.** [*25*] Explain how to use BDDs to compute the numbers Q_m that underlie Fig. 83. What is $\max_{0 \le m \le 80} Q_m$?

▶ **181.** [*25*] Extend the idea of the previous exercise so that it is possible to determine the probability distributions T_m of Fig. 84.

182. [*M16*] For which values of m in Fig. 84 does T_m have a constant value?

183. [*M30*] Discuss the relation between Figs. 85 and 86.

184. [*M20*] Why does (77) characterize the relation between $\hat{q}_m$ and q_m?

185. [*M20*] Use (77) to prove the intuitively obvious fact that $\hat{q}_m \ge q_m$.

186. [*M21*] Use (77) to reduce $\sum_m \hat{q}_m$ and $\sum_m (2m+1)\hat{q}_m$ to (78) and (79).

187. [*M20*] Analyze random satisfiability in the case $k = n$: What are $S_{n,n}$ and $\widehat{S}_{n,n}$?

▶ **188.** [*HM25*] Analyze random 1SAT, the case $k = 1$: What are $S_{1,n}$ and $\widehat{S}_{1,n}$?

189. [*27*] Apply BDD methods to random 3SAT problems on 50 variables. What is the approximate BDD size after m distinct clauses have been ANDed together, as m grows?

190. [*M20*] Exhibit a Boolean function of 4 variables that can't be expressed in 3CNF. (No auxiliary variables are allowed: Only x_1, x_2, x_3, and x_4 may appear.)

191. [*M25*] How many Boolean functions of 4 variables *can* be expressed in 3CNF?

▶ **192.** [*HM21*] Another way to model satisfiability when there are N equally likely clauses is to study $S(p)$, the probability of satisfiability when each clause is independently present with probability p.
   a) Express $S(p)$ in terms of the numbers $Q_m = \binom{N}{m}q_m$.
   b) Assign uniform random numbers in $[0\mathinner{\ldotp\ldotp}1)$ to each clause; then at time t, for $0 \le t \le N$, consider all clauses that have been assigned a number less than t/N. (Approximately t clauses will therefore be selected, when N is large.) Show that $\overline{S}_{k,n} = \int_0^N S_{k,n}(t/N)\,dt$, the expected amount of time during which the chosen clauses remain satisfiable, is very similar to the satisfiability threshold $S_{k,n}$ of (76).

193. [*HM48*] Determine the satisfiability threshold (81) of random 3SAT. Is it true that $\liminf_{n\to\infty} S_{3,n}/n = \limsup_{n\to\infty} S_{3,n}/n$? If so, is the limit ≈ 4.2667?

194. [*HM49*] If $\alpha < \liminf_{n\to\infty} S_{3,n}/n$, is there a polynomial-time algorithm that is able to satisfy $\lfloor \alpha n \rfloor$ random 3SAT clauses with probability $\ge \delta$, for some $\delta > 0$?

195. [*HM21*] (J. Franco and M. Paull, 1983.) Use the first moment principle MPR–(21) to prove that $\lfloor (2^k \ln 2)n \rfloor$ random kSAT clauses are almost always unsatisfiable. *Hint:* Let $X = \sum_x [x$ satisfies all clauses$]$, summed over all 2^n binary vectors $x = x_1 \ldots x_n$.

▶ **196.** [*HM25*] (D. B. Wilson.) A clause of a satisfiability problem is "easy" if it contains one or more variables that don't appear in any other clauses. Prove that, with probability $1 - O(n^{-2\epsilon})$, a kSAT problem that has $m = \lfloor \alpha n \rfloor$ random clauses contains $(1 - (1 - e^{-k\alpha})^k) m + O(n^{1/2+\epsilon})$ easy ones. (For example, about $0.000035n$ of the $4.27n$ clauses in a random 3SAT problem near the threshold will be easy.)

197. [*HM21*] Prove that the quotient $q(a, b, A, B, n) = \binom{(a+b)n}{an}\binom{(A+B)n}{An} / \binom{(a+b+A+B)n}{(a+A)n}$ is $O(n^{-1/2})$ as $n \to \infty$, if $a, b, A, B > 0$.

▶ **198.** [*HM30*] Use exercises 196 and 197 to show that the phase transition in Fig. 89 is not extremely abrupt: If $S_3(m, n) > \frac{2}{3}$ and $S_3(m', n) < \frac{1}{3}$, prove that $m' = m + \Omega(\sqrt{n})$.

199. [*M21*] Let $p(t, m, N)$ be the probability that t specified letters each occur at least once within a random m-letter word on an N-letter alphabet.

a) Prove that $p(t, m, N) \le m^{\underline{t}}/N^t$.

b) Derive the exact formula $p(t, m, N) = \sum_k \binom{t}{k}(-1)^k (N - k)^m / N^m$.

c) And $p(t, m, N)/t! = \{\begin{smallmatrix}t\\t\end{smallmatrix}\}\binom{m}{t}/N^t - \{\begin{smallmatrix}t+1\\t\end{smallmatrix}\}\binom{m}{t+1}/N^{t+1} + \{\begin{smallmatrix}t+2\\t\end{smallmatrix}\}\binom{m}{t+2}/N^{t+2} - \cdots$.

▶ **200.** [*M21*] Complete the text's proof of (84) when $c < 1$:

a) Show that every unsatisfiable 2SAT formula contains clauses of a snare.

b) Conversely, are the clauses of a snare always unsatisfiable?

c) Verify the inequality (89). *Hint:* See exercise 199.

201. [*HM29*] The t-snake clauses specified by a chain $(l_1, \ldots, l_{2t-1})$ can be written $(\bar{l}_i \lor l_{i+1})$ for $0 \le i < 2t$, where $l_0 = \bar{l}_t$ and subscripts are treated mod $2t$.

a) Describe all ways to set two of the l's so that $(\bar{x}_1 \lor x_2)$ is one of those $2t$ clauses.

b) Similarly, set three l's in order to obtain $(\bar{x}_1 \lor x_2)$ and $(\bar{x}_2 \lor x_3)$.

c) Also set three to obtain both $(\bar{x}_0 \lor x_1)$ and $(\bar{x}_{t-1} \lor x_t)$; here $\bar{x}_0 \equiv x_t$ and $t > 2$.

d) How can the clauses $(\bar{x}_i \lor x_{i+1})$ for $0 \le i < t$ all be obtained by setting t of the l's?

e) In general, let $N(q, r)$ be the number of ways to choose r of the standard clauses $(\bar{x}_i \lor x_{i+1})$, which involve exactly q of the variables $\{x_1, \ldots, x_{2t-1}\}$, and to set q values of $\{l_1, \ldots, l_{2t-1}\}$ in order to obtain the r chosen clauses. Evaluate $N(2, 1)$.

f) Similarly, evaluate $N(3, 2)$, $N(t, t)$, and $N(2t - 1, 2t)$.

g) Show that the probability p_r in (95) is $\le \sum_q N(q, r)/(2^q n^q)$.

h) Therefore the upper bound (96) is valid.

202. [*HM21*] This exercise amplifies the text's proof of Theorem C when $c > 1$.

a) Explain the right-hand side of Eq. (93).

b) Why does (97) follow from (95), (96), and the stated choices of t and m?

▶ **203.** [*HM33*] (K. Xu and W. Li, 2000.) Beginning with the n graph-coloring clauses (15), and optionally the $n\binom{d}{2}$ exclusion clauses (17), consider using randomly generated binary clauses instead of (16). There are mq random binary clauses, obtained as m independent sets of q clauses each, where every such set is selected by choosing distinct vertices u and v, then choosing q distinct binary clauses $(\bar{u}_i \lor \bar{v}_j)$ for $1 \le i, j \le d$. (The number of different possible sequences of random clauses is therefore exactly $(\binom{n}{2}\binom{d^2}{q})^m$ and each sequence is equally likely.) This method of clause generation is known as "Model RB"; it generalizes random 2SAT, which is the case $d = 2$ and $q = 1$.

Suppose $d = n^\alpha$ and $q = pd^2$, where we require $\frac{1}{2} < \alpha < 1$ and $0 \le p \le \frac{1}{2}$. Also let $m = rn \ln d$. For this range of the parameters, we will prove that there is a sharp threshold of satisfiability: The clauses are unsatisfiable q.s., as $n \to \infty$, if $r \ln(1 - p) + 1 < 0$; but they are satisfiable a.s. if $r \ln(1 - p) + 1 > 0$.

Let $X(j_1, \ldots, j_n) = $ [all clauses are satisfied when each ith variable v has $v_{j_i} = 1$]; here $1 \le j_1, \ldots, j_n \le d$. Also let $X = \sum_{1 \le j_1, \ldots, j_n \le d} X(j_1, \ldots, j_n)$. Then $X = 0$ if and only if the clauses are unsatisfiable.

a) Use the first moment principle to prove that $X = 0$ q.s. when $r \ln(1-p) + 1 < 0$.

b) Find a formula for $p_s = \Pr(X(j_1, \ldots, j_n) = 1 \mid X(1, \ldots, 1) = 1)$, given that exactly s of the colors $\{j_1, \ldots, j_n\}$ are equal to 1.

c) Use (b) and the conditional expectation inequality MPR–(24) to prove that $X > 0$ a.s. if

$$\sum_{s=0}^{n} \binom{n}{s} \left(\frac{1}{d}\right)^s \left(1 - \frac{1}{d}\right)^{n-s} \left(1 + \frac{p}{1-p} \frac{s^2}{n^2}\right)^m \to 1 \qquad \text{as } n \to \infty.$$

d) Letting t_s denote the term for s in that sum, prove that $\sum_{s=0}^{3n/d} t_s \approx 1$.

e) Suppose $r \ln(1-p) + 1 = \epsilon > 0$, where ϵ is small. Show that the terms t_s first increase, then decrease, then increase, then decrease again, as s grows from 0 to n. *Hint:* Consider the ratio $x_s = t_{s+1}/t_s$.

f) Finally, prove that t_s is exponentially small for $3n/d \le s \le n$.

▶ **204.** [*28*] Figure 89 might suggest that 3SAT problems on n variables are always easy when there are fewer than $2n$ clauses. We shall prove, however, that *any* set of m ternary clauses on n variables can be transformed mechanically into another set of ternary clauses on $N = O(m)$ variables in which no variable occurs more than four times. The transformed problem has the same number of solutions as the original one; thus it isn't any simpler, although (with at most $4N$ literals) it has at most $\frac{4}{3}N$ clauses.

a) First replace the original m clauses by m new clauses $(X_1 \lor X_2 \lor X_3), \ldots, (X_{3m-2} \lor X_{3m-1} \lor X_{3m})$, on $3m$ new variables, and show how to add $3m$ clauses of size 2 so that the resulting $4m$ clauses have exactly as many solutions as the original.

b) Construct ternary clauses that have a unique solution, yet no variable occurs more than four times.

c) Use (a) and (b) to prove the N-variable result claimed above.

205. [*26*] If F and F' are sets of clauses, let $F \sqcup F'$ stand for any other set obtained from $F \cup F'$ by replacing one or more clauses C of F by $x \lor C$ and one or more clauses C' of F' by $\bar{x} \lor C'$, where x is a new variable. Then $F \sqcup F'$ is unsatisfiable whenever F and F' are both unsatisfiable. For example, if $F = \{\epsilon\}$ and $F' = \{1, \bar{1}\}$, then $F \sqcup F'$ is either $\{2, 1\bar{2}, \bar{1}\bar{2}\}$ or $\{2, 1, \bar{1}\bar{2}\}$ or $\{2, 1\bar{2}, \bar{1}\}$.

a) Construct 16 unsatisfiable ternary clauses on 15 variables, where each variable occurs at most four times.

b) Construct an unsatisfiable 4SAT problem in which every variable occurs at most five times.

206. [*M22*] A set of clauses is *minimally unsatisfiable* if it is unsatisfiable, yet becomes satisfiable if any clause is deleted. Show that, if F and F' have no variables in common, then $F \sqcup F'$ is minimally unsatisfiable if and only if F and F' are minimally unsatisfiable.

207. [*25*] Each of the literals $\{1, \bar{1}, 2, \bar{2}, 3, \bar{3}, 4, \bar{4}\}$ occurs exactly thrice in the eight unsatisfiable clauses (6). Construct an unsatisfiable 3SAT problem with 15 variables in which each of the 30 literals occurs exactly *twice*. *Hint:* Consider $\{\bar{1}2, \bar{2}3, \bar{3}1, 123, \bar{1}\bar{2}\bar{3}\}$.

208. [*25*] Via exercises 204(a) and 207, show that any 3SAT problem can be transformed into an equivalent set of ternary clauses where every literal occurs just twice.

209. [*25*] (C. A. Tovey.) Prove that every kSAT formula in which no variable occurs more than k times is satisfiable. (Thus the limits on occurrences in exercises 204–208 cannot be lowered, when $k = 3$ and $k = 4$.) *Hint:* Use the theory of bipartite matching.

210. [*M36*] But the result in the previous exercise can be improved when k is large. Use the Local Lemma to show that every 7SAT problem with at most 13 occurrences of each variable is satisfiable.

211. [*30*] (R. W. Irving and M. Jerrum, 1994.) Use exercise 208 to reduce 3SAT to the problem of list coloring a grid graph of the form $K_N \square K_3$. (Hence the latter problem, which is also called *latin rectangle construction*, is NP-complete.)

212. [*32*] Continuing the previous exercise, we shall reduce grid list coloring to another interesting problem called *partial latin square construction*. Given three $n \times n$ binary matrices (r_{ik}), (c_{jk}), (p_{ij}), the task is to construct an $n \times n$ array (X_{ij}) such that X_{ij} is blank when $p_{ij} = 0$, otherwise $X_{ij} = k$ for some k with $r_{ik} = c_{jk} = 1$; furthermore the nonblank entries must be distinct in each row and column.

  a) Show that this problem is symmetrical in all three coordinates: It's equivalent to constructing a binary $n \times n \times n$ tensor (x_{ijk}) such that $x_{*jk} = c_{jk}$, $x_{i*k} = r_{ik}$, and $x_{ij*} = p_{ij}$, for $1 \le i,j,k \le n$, where '$*$' denotes summing an index from 1 to n. (Therefore it is also known as the *binary $n \times n \times n$ contingency problem*, given n^2 row sums, n^2 column sums, and n^2 pile sums.)

  b) A necessary condition for solution is that $c_{*k} = r_{*k}$, $c_{j*} = p_{*j}$, and $r_{i*} = p_{i*}$. Exhibit a small example where this condition is not sufficient.

  c) If $M < N$, reduce $K_M \square K_N$ list coloring to the problem of $K_N \square K_N$ list coloring.

  d) Finally, explain how to reduce $K_N \square K_N$ list coloring to the problem of constructing an $n \times n$ partial latin square, where $n = N + \sum_{I,J} |L(I,J)|$. *Hint:* Instead of considering integers $1 \le i,j,k \le n$, let i, j, k range over a *set* of n elements. Define $p_{ij} = 0$ for most values of i and j; also make $r_{ik} = c_{ik}$ for all i and k.

▶ **213.** [*M20*] Experience with the analyses of sorting algorithms in Chapter 5 suggests that random satisfiability problems might be modeled nicely if we assume that, in each of m independent clauses, the literals x_j and $\bar{x}_j$ occur with respective probabilities p and q, independently for $1 \le j \le n$, where $p + q \le 1$. Why is this *not* an interesting model as $n \to \infty$, when p and q are constant? *Hint:* What is the probability that $x_1 \ldots x_n = b_1 \ldots b_n$ satisfies all of the clauses, when $b_1 \ldots b_n$ is a given binary vector?

214. [*HM38*] Although the random model in the preceding exercise doesn't teach us how to solve SAT problems, it does lead to interesting mathematics: Let $0 < p < 1$ and consider the recurrence

$$T_0 = 0; \qquad T_n = n + 2 \sum_{k=0}^{n-1} \binom{n}{k} p^k (1-p)^{n-k} T_k, \qquad \text{for } n > 0.$$

  a) Find a functional relation satisfied by $T(z) = \sum_{n=0}^{\infty} T_n z^n / n!$.

  b) Deduce that we have $T(z) = ze^z \sum_{m=0}^{\infty} (2p)^m \prod_{k=0}^{m-1} (1 - e^{-p^k(1-p)z})$.

  c) Hence, if $p \ne 1/2$, we can use Mellin transforms (as in the derivation of 5.2.2–(50)) to show that $T_n = C_p n^\alpha (1 + \delta(n) + O(1/n)) + n/(1 - 2p)$, where $\alpha = 1/\lg(1/p)$, C_p is a constant, and δ is a small "wobble" with $\delta(n) = \delta(pn)$.

▶ **215.** [*HM28*] What is the expected profile of the search tree when a simple backtrack procedure is used to find all solutions to a random 3SAT problem with m independent clauses on n variables? (There is a node on level l for every partial solution $x_1 \ldots x_l$ that doesn't contradict any of the clauses.) Compute these values when $m = 200$ and $n = 50$. Also estimate the total tree size when $m = \alpha n$, for fixed α as $n \to \infty$.

216. [*HM38*] (P. W. Purdom, Jr., and C. A. Brown.) Extend the previous exercise to a more sophisticated kind of backtracking, where all choices forced by unit clauses are pursued before two-way branching is done. (The "pure literal rule" is not exploited, however, because it doesn't find all solutions.) Prove that the expected tree size is greatly reduced when $m = 200$ and $n = 50$. (An upper bound is sufficient.)

217. [20] True or false: If A and B are arbitrary clauses that are simultaneously satisfiable, and if l is any literal, then the clause $C = (A \cup B) \setminus \{l, \bar{l}\}$ is also satisfiable. (We're thinking here of A, B, and C as *sets* of literals, not as disjunctions of literals.)

218. [20] Express the formula $(x \vee A) \wedge (\bar{x} \vee B)$ in terms of the ternary operator $u? v: w$.

▸ **219.** [M20] Formulate a general definition of the resolution operator $C = C' \diamond C''$ that (i) agrees with the text's definition when $C' = x \vee A'$ and $C'' = \bar{x} \vee A''$; (ii) applies to *arbitrary* clauses C' and C''; (iii) has the property that $C' \wedge C''$ implies $C' \diamond C''$.

220. [M24] We say that clause C *subsumes* clause C', written $C \subseteq C'$, if $C' = \wp$ or if $C' \neq \wp$ and every literal of C appears in C'.
 a) True or false: $C \subseteq C'$ and $C' \subseteq C''$ implies $C \subseteq C''$.
 b) True or false: $(C \vee \alpha) \diamond (C' \vee \alpha') \subseteq (C \diamond C') \vee \alpha \vee \alpha'$, with $\diamond$ as in exercise 219.
 c) True or false: $C' \subseteq C''$ implies $C \diamond C' \subseteq C \diamond C''$.
 d) The notation $C_1, \ldots, C_m \vdash C$ means that a resolution chain $C_1, \ldots, C_{m+r}$ exists with $C_{m+r} \subseteq C$, for some $r \geq 0$. Show that we might have $C_1, \ldots, C_m \vdash C$ even though C cannot be obtained from $\{C_1, \ldots, C_m\}$ by successive resolutions (104).
 e) Prove that if $C_1 \subseteq C_1', \ldots, C_m \subseteq C_m'$, and $C_1', \ldots, C_m' \vdash C$, then $C_1, \ldots, C_m \vdash C$.
 f) Furthermore $C_1, \ldots, C_m \vdash C$ implies $C_1 \vee \alpha_1, \ldots, C_m \vee \alpha_m \vdash C \vee \alpha_1 \vee \cdots \vee \alpha_m$.

221. [16] Draw the search tree analogous to Fig. 81 that is implicitly traversed when Algorithm A is applied to the unsatisfiable clauses $\{12, 2, \bar{2}\}$. Explain why it does *not* correspond to a resolution refutation that is analogous to Fig. 91.

222. [M30] (Oliver Kullmann, 2000.) Prove that, for every clause C in a satisfiability problem F, there is an autarky satisfying C if and only if C cannot be used as the label of a source vertex in any resolution refutation of F.

223. [HM40] Step X9 deduces a binary clause that cannot be derived by resolution (see exercise 166). Prove that, nevertheless, the running time of Algorithm L on unsatisfiable input will never be less than the length of a shortest treelike refutation.

224. [M20] Given a resolution tree that refutes the axioms $F \mid \bar{x}$, show how to construct a resolution tree of the same size that either refutes the axioms F or derives the clause $\{x\}$ from F without resolving on the variable x.

▸ **225.** [M31] (G. S. Tseytin, 1966.) If T is any resolution tree that refutes a set of axioms F, show how to convert it to a *regular* resolution tree T_r that refutes F, where T_r is no larger than T.

226. [M20] If α is a node in a refutation tree, let $C(\alpha)$ be its label, and let $\|\alpha\|$ denote the number of leaves in its subtree. Show that, given a refutation tree with N leaves, the Prover can find a node with $\|\alpha\| \leq N/2^s$ for which the current assignment falsifies $C(\alpha)$, whenever the Delayer has scored s points in the Prover–Delayer game.

227. [M27] Given an extended binary tree, exercise 7.2.1.6–124 explains how to label each node with its Horton–Strahler number. For example, the nodes at depth 2 in Fig. 91 are labeled 1, because their children have the labels 1 and 0; the root is labeled 3.

   Prove that the maximum score that the Delayer can guarantee, when playing the Prover–Delayer game for a set of unsatisfiable clauses F, is equal to the minimum possible Horton–Strahler root label in a tree refutation of F.

▶ **228.** [*M21*] Stålmarck's refutation of (99)–(101) actually obtains ϵ without using all of the axioms! Show that only about $1/3$ of those clauses are sufficient for unsatisfiability.

▶ **229.** [*M21*] Continuing exercise 228, prove also that the set of clauses (99), (100′), (101) is unsatisfiable, where (100′) denotes (100) restricted to the cases $i \leq k$ and $j < k$.

230. [*M22*] Show that the clauses with $i \neq j$ in the previous exercise form a *minimal* unsatisfiable set: Removing any one of them leaves a satisfiable remainder.

231. [*M30*] (Sam Buss.) Refute the clauses of exercise 229 with a resolution chain of length $O(m^3)$. *Hint:* Derive the clauses $G_{ij} = (x_{ij} \vee x_{i(j+1)} \vee \cdots \vee x_{im})$ for $1 \leq i \leq j \leq m$.

▶ **232.** [*M28*] Prove that the clauses $fsnark(q)$ of exercise 176 can be refuted by treelike resolution in $O(q^6)$ steps.

233. [*16*] Explain why (105) satisfies (104), by exhibiting $j(i)$ and $k(i)$ for $9 \leq i \leq 22$.

234. [*20*] Show that the Delayer can score at least m points against any Prover who tries to refute the pigeonhole clauses (106) and (107).

▶ **235.** [*30*] Refute those pigeonhole clauses with a chain of length $m(m+3)2^{m-2}$.

236. [*48*] Is the chain in the previous exercise as short as possible?

▶ **237.** [*28*] Show that a polynomial number of steps suffice to refute the pigeonhole clauses (106), (107), if the *extended resolution* trick is used to append new clauses.

238. [*HM21*] Complete the proof of Lemma B. *Hint:* Make $r \leq \rho^{-b}$ when $W - b$.

▶ **239.** [*M21*] What clauses α_0 on n variables make $\|\alpha_0 \vdash \epsilon\|$ as large as possible?

▶ **240.** [*HM23*] Choose integers $f_{ij} \in \{1, \ldots, m\}$ uniformly at random, for $1 \leq i \leq 5$ and $0 \leq j \leq m$, and let G_0 be the bipartite graph with edges $a_j \!-\! b_k$ if and only if $k \in \{f_{1j}, \ldots, f_{5j}\}$. Show that $\Pr(G_0$ satisfies the strong expansion condition (108)$) \geq 1/2$.

241. [*20*] Prove that any set of at most $m/3000$ pigeons can be matched to distinct holes, under the restricted pigeonhole constraints G_0 of Theorem B.

242. [*M20*] The pigeonhole axioms (106) and (107) are equivalent to the clauses (15) and (16) that arise if we try to color the complete graph K_{m+1} with m colors.

Suppose we include further axioms corresponding to (17), namely

$$(\bar{x}_{jk} \vee \bar{x}_{jk'}), \qquad \text{for } 0 \leq j \leq m \text{ and } 1 \leq k < k' \leq m.$$

Does Theorem B still hold, or do these additional axioms decrease the refutation width?

243. [*HM31*] (E. Ben-Sasson and A. Wigderson.) Let F be a set of $\lfloor \alpha n \rfloor$ random 3SAT clauses on n variables, where $\alpha > 1/e$ is a given constant. For any clause C on those variables, define $\mu(C) = \min\{ |F'| \mid F' \subseteq F \text{ and } F' \vdash C \}$. Also let $V(F')$ denote the variables that occur in a given family of clauses F'.
   a) Prove that $|V(F')| \geq |F'|$ a.s., when $F' \subseteq F$ and $|F'| \leq n/(2\alpha e^2)$.
   b) Therefore either F is satisfiable or $\mu(\epsilon) > n/(2\alpha e^2)$, a.s.
   c) Let $n' = n/(1000000\alpha^4)$, and assume that $n' \geq 2$. Prove that $2|V(F')| - 3|F'| \geq n'/4$ q.s., when $F' \subseteq F$ and $n'/2 \leq |F'| < n'$.
   d) Consequently either F is satisfiable or $w(F \vdash \epsilon) \geq n'/4$, a.s.

244. [*M20*] If A is a set of variables, let $[A]^0$ or $[A]^1$ stand for the set of all clauses that can be formed from A with an even or odd number of negative literals, respectively; each clause should involve all of the variables. (For example, $[\{1, 2, 3\}]^1 = \{12\bar{3}, 1\bar{2}3, \bar{1}23, \bar{1}2\bar{3}\}$.) If A and B are disjoint, express $[A \cup B]^0$ in terms of the sets $[A]^0$, $[A]^1$, $[B]^0$, $[B]^1$.

▶ **245.** [*M27*] Let G be a connected graph whose vertices $v \in V$ have each been labeled 0 or 1, where the sum of all labels is odd. We will construct clauses on the set of variables e_{uv}, one for each edge $u \text{---} v$ in G. The axioms are $\alpha(v) = [E(v)]^{l(v) \oplus 1}$ for each $v \in V$ (see exercise 244), where $E(v) = \{e_{uv} \mid u \text{---} v\}$ and $l(v)$ is the label of v.

For example, vertex 1 of the graph below is shown as a black dot in order to indicate that $l(1) = 1$, while the other vertices appear as white dots and are labeled $l(2) = \cdots = l(6) = 0$. The graph and its axioms are

$$
\begin{array}{ll}
\alpha(1) = \{af, \bar{a}\bar{f}\}, & \alpha(4) = \{c\bar{d}, \bar{c}d\}, \\
\alpha(2) = \{ab\bar{g}, a\bar{b}g, \bar{a}bg, \bar{a}\bar{b}\bar{g}\}, & \alpha(5) = \{de\bar{h}, d\bar{e}h, \bar{d}eh, \bar{d}\bar{e}\bar{h}\}, \\
\alpha(3) = \{bc\bar{h}, b\bar{c}h, \bar{b}ch, \bar{b}\bar{c}\bar{h}\}, & \alpha(6) = \{ef\bar{g}, e\bar{f}g, \bar{e}fg, \bar{e}\bar{f}\bar{g}\}.
\end{array}
$$

Notice that, when v has $d > 0$ neighbors in G, the set $\alpha(v)$ consists of 2^{d-1} clauses of size d. Furthermore, the axioms of $\alpha(v)$ are all satisfied if and only if

$$
\bigoplus_{e_{uv} \in E(v)} e_{uv} = l(v).
$$

If we sum this equation over all vertices v, mod 2, we get 0 on the left, because each edge e_{uv} occurs exactly twice (once in $E(u)$ and once in $E(v)$). But we get 1 on the right. Therefore the clauses $\alpha(G) = \bigcup_v \alpha(v)$ are unsatisfiable.

a) The axioms $\alpha(G)|b$ and $\alpha(G)|\bar{b}$ in this example turn out to be $\alpha(G')$ and $\alpha(G'')$, where $G' = $ ⬤⟨⟩▷∘ and $G'' = $ ⬤⟨⟩▷∘. Explain what happens in general.

b) Let $\mu(C) = \min\{|V'| \mid V' \subseteq V$ and $\bigcup_{v \in V'} \alpha(v) \vdash C\}$, for every clause C involving the variables e_{uv}. Show that $\mu(C) = 1$ for every axiom $C \in \alpha(G)$. What is $\mu(\epsilon)$?

c) If $V' \subseteq V$, let $\partial V' = \{e_{uv} \mid u \in V'$ and $v \notin V'\}$. Prove that, if $\bigcup_{v \in V'} \alpha(v) \vdash C$ and $|V'| = \mu(C)$, every variable of $\partial V'$ appears in C.

d) A nonbipartite cubic Ramanujan graph G on m vertices V has three edges $v \text{---} v\rho$, $v \text{---} v\sigma$, $v \text{---} v\tau$ touching each vertex, where ρ, σ, and τ are permutations with the following properties: (i) $\rho = \rho^-$ and $\tau = \sigma^-$; (ii) G is connected; (iii) If V' is any subset of s vertices, and if there are t edges between V' and $V \setminus V'$, then we have $s/(s+t) \le (s/m + 8)/9$. Prove that $w(\alpha(G) \vdash \epsilon) > m/78$.

▶ **246.** [*M28*] (G. S. Tseytin.) Given a labeled graph G with m edges, n vertices, and N unsatisfiable clauses $\alpha(G)$ as in the previous exercise, explain how to refute those clauses with $O(mn + N)$ steps of *extended* resolution.

247. [*18*] Apply variable elimination to just five of the six clauses (112), omitting '$1\bar{2}$'.

248. [*M20*] Formally speaking, SAT is the problem of evaluating the quantified formula

$$
\exists x_1 \ldots \exists x_{n-1} \exists x_n \, F(x_1, \ldots, x_{n-1}, x_n),
$$

where F is a Boolean function given in CNF as a conjunction of clauses. Explain how to transform the CNF for F into the CNF for F' in the reduced problem

$$
\exists x_1 \ldots \exists x_{n-1} F'(x_1, \ldots, x_{n-1}), \quad F'(x_1, \ldots, x_{n-1}) = F(x_1, \ldots, x_{n-1}, 0) \vee F(x_1, \ldots, x_{n-1}, 1).
$$

249. [*18*] Apply Algorithm I to (112) using Cook's Method IA.

250. [*25*] Since the clauses R' in (7) are satisfiable, Algorithm I might discover a solution without ever reaching step I4. Try, however, to make the choices in steps I2, I3, and I4 so that the algorithm takes as long as possible to discover a solution.

▶ **251.** [*30*] Show that Algorithm I can prove the unsatisfiability of the anti-maximal-element clauses (99)–(101) by making $O(m^3)$ resolutions, if suitably clairvoyant choices are made in steps I2, I3, and I4.

252. [*M26*] Can the unsatisfiability of (99)–(101) be proved in polynomial time by repeatedly performing variable elimination and subsumption?

▶ **253.** [*18*] What are the next two clauses learned if decision '5' follows next after (114)?

254. [*16*] Given the binary clauses $\{12, \bar{1}3, 2\bar{3}, \bar{2}4, \bar{3}4\}$, what clause will a CDCL solver learn first if it begins by deciding that 1 is true?

▶ **255.** [*20*] Construct a satisfiability problem with ternary clauses, for which a CDCL solver that is started with decision literals '1', '2', '3' on levels 1, 2, and 3 will learn the clause '45' after a conflict on level 3.

256. [*20*] How might the clause '**∗∗**' in Table 3 have been easily learned?

▶ **257.** [*30*] (Niklas Sörensson.) A literal $\bar{l}$ is said to be *redundant*, with respect to a given clause c and the current trail, if l is in the trail and either (i) l is defined at level 0, or (ii) l is not a decision literal and every false literal in l's reason is either in c or (recursively) redundant. (This definition is stronger than the special cases by which (115) reduces to (116), because $\bar{l}$ itself needn't belong to c.) If, for example, $c = (\bar{l}' \vee \bar{b}_1 \vee \bar{b}_2 \vee \bar{b}_3 \vee \bar{b}_4)$, let the reason for b_4 be $(b_4 \vee \bar{b}_1 \vee \bar{a}_1)$, where the reason for a_1 is $(a_1 \vee \bar{b}_2 \vee \bar{a}_2)$ and the reason for a_2 is $(a_2 \vee \bar{b}_1 \vee \bar{b}_3)$. Then $\bar{b}_4$ is redundant, because $\bar{a}_2$ and $\bar{a}_1$ are redundant.
  a) Suppose $c = (\bar{l}' \vee \bar{b}_1 \vee \cdots \vee \bar{b}_r)$ is a newly learned clause. Prove that if $\bar{b}_j \in c$ is redundant, some other $\bar{b}_i \in c$ became false on the same level of the trail as $\bar{b}_j$ did.
  b) Devise an efficient algorithm that discovers all of the redundant literals $\bar{b}_i$ in a given newly learned clause $c = (\bar{l}' \vee \bar{b}_1 \vee \cdots \vee \bar{b}_r)$. *Hint:* Use stamps.

258. [*21*] A non-decision literal l in Algorithm C's trail always has a reason $R_l = (l_0 \vee l_1 \vee \cdots \vee l_{k-1})$, where $l_0 = l$ and $\bar{l}_1, \ldots, \bar{l}_{k-1}$ precede l in the trail. Furthermore, the algorithm discovered this clause while looking at the watch list of l_1. True or false: $\bar{l}_2, \ldots, \bar{l}_{k-1}$ precede $\bar{l}_1$ in the trail. *Hint:* Consider Table 3 and its sequel.

259. [*M20*] Can $\mathrm{ACT}(j)$ exceed $\mathrm{ACT}(k)$ for values of ρ near 0 or 1, but not for *all* ρ?

260. [*18*] Describe in detail step C1's setting-up of MEM, the watch lists, and the trail.

261. [*21*] The main loop of Algorithm C is the unit-propagation process of steps C3 and C4. Describe the low-level details of link adjustment, etc., to be done in those steps.

262. [*20*] What low-level operations underlie changes to the heap in steps C6–C8?

263. [*21*] Write out the gory details by which step C7 constructs a new clause and step C9 puts it into the data structures of Algorithm C.

264. [*20*] Suggest a way by which Algorithm C could indicate progress by displaying "move codes" analogous to those of Algorithms A, B, D, and L. (See exercise 142.)

265. [*21*] Describe several circumstances in which the watched literals l_0 and/or l_1 of a clause c actually become false during the execution of Algorithm C.

266. [*20*] In order to keep from getting into a rut, CDCL solvers are often designed to make decisions at random, with a small probability p (say $p = .02$), instead of always choosing a variable of maximum activity. How would this policy change step C6?

▶ **267.** [*25*] Instances of SAT often contain numerous binary clauses, which are handled efficiently by the unit-propagation loop (62) of Algorithm L but not by the corresponding loop in step C3 of Algorithm C. (The technique of watched literals is great for long clauses, but it is comparatively cumbersome for short ones.) What additional data structures will speed up Algorithm C's inner loop, when binary clauses are abundant?

268. [*21*] When Algorithm C makes a literal false at level 0 of the trail, we can remove it from all of the clauses. Such updating might take a long time, if we did it "eagerly"; but there's a lazy way out: We can delete a permanently false literal if we happen to encounter it in step C3 while looking for a new literal to watch (see exercise 261).

Explain how to adapt the MEM data structure conventions so that such deletions can be done *in situ*, without copying clauses from one location into another.

269. [*23*] Suppose Algorithm C reaches a conflict at level d of the trail, after having chosen the decision literals $u_1, u_2, \ldots, u_d$. Then the "trivial clause" $(\bar{l}' \vee \bar{u}_1 \vee \cdots \vee \bar{u}_{d'})$ must be true if the given clauses are satisfiable, where l' and d' are defined in step C7.

   a) Show that, if we start with the clause $(\bar{l}' \vee \bar{b}_1 \vee \cdots \vee \bar{b}_r)$ that is obtained in step C7 and then resolve it somehow with zero or more known clauses, we can always reach a clause that subsumes the trivial clause.

   b) Sometimes, as in (115), the clause that is slated to be learned in step C9 is much longer than the trivial clause. Construct an example in which $d = 3$, $d' = 1$, and $r = 10$, yet none of $\bar{b}_1, \ldots, \bar{b}_r$ are redundant in the sense of exercise 257.

   c) Suggest a way to improve Algorithm C accordingly.

270. [*25*] (*On-the-fly subsumption.*) The intermediate clauses that arise in step C7, immediately after resolving with a reason R_l, occasionally turn out to be equal to the shorter clause $R_l \setminus l$. In such cases we have an opportunity to *strengthen* that clause by deleting l from it, thus making it potentially more useful in the future.

   a) Construct an example where two clauses can each be subsumed in this way while resolving a single conflict. The subsumed clauses should both contain two literals assigned at the current level in the trail, as well as one literal from a lower level.

   b) Show that it's easy to recognize such opportunities, and to strengthen such clauses efficiently, by modifying the steps of answer 263.

▶ **271.** [*25*] The sequence of learned clauses $C_1, C_2, \ldots$ often includes cases where C_i subsumes its immediate predecessor, C_{i-1}. In such cases we might as well *discard* C_{i-1}, which appears at the very end of MEM, and store C_i in its place, unless C_{i-1} is still in use as a reason for some literal on the trail. (For example, more than 8,600 of the 52,000 clauses typically learned from *waerden*(3, 10; 97) by Algorithm C can be discarded in this way. Such discards are different from the on-the-fly subsumptions considered in exercise 270, because the subsumed C_{i-1} includes only one literal from its original conflict level; furthermore, learned clauses have usually been significantly simplified by the procedure of exercise 257, unless they're trivial.)

Design an efficient way to discover when C_{i-1} can be safely discarded.

272. [*30*] Experiment with the following idea: The clauses of *waerden*(j, k; n) are symmetrical under reflection, in the sense that they remain unchanged overall if we replace x_k by $x_k^R = x_{n+1-k}$ for $1 \le k \le n$. Therefore, whenever Algorithm C learns a clause $C = (\bar{l}' \vee \bar{b}_1 \vee \cdots \vee \bar{b}_r)$, it is also entitled to learn the reflected clause $C^R = (\bar{l}'^R \vee \bar{b}_1^R \vee \cdots \vee \bar{b}_r^R)$.

273. [*27*] A clause C that is learned from *waerden*(j, k; n) is valid also with respect to *waerden*(j, k; n') when $n' > n$; and so are the clauses $C + i$ that are obtained by adding i to each literal of C, for $1 \le i \le n' - n$. For example, the fact that '35' follows from *waerden*(3, 3; 7) allows us to add the clauses 35, 46, 57 to *waerden*(3, 3; 9).

   a) Exploit this idea to speed up the calculation of van der Waerden numbers.

b) Explain how to apply it also to bounded model checking.

274. [*35*] Algorithm C sets the "reason" for a literal l as soon as it notices a clause that forces l to be true. Later on, other clauses that force l are often encountered, in practice; but Algorithm C ignores them, even though one of them might be a "better reason." (For example, another forcing clause might be significantly shorter.) Explore a modification of Algorithm C that tries to improve the reasons of non-decision literals.

▶ **275.** [*22*] Adapt Algorithm C to the problem of finding the lexicographically smallest solution to a satisfiability problem, by incorporating the ideas of exercise 109.

276. [*M15*] True or false: If F is a family of clauses and L is a set of strictly distinct literals, then $F \wedge L \vdash_1 \epsilon$ if and only if $(F|L) \vdash_1 \epsilon$.

277. [*M18*] If $(C_1, \ldots, C_t)$ is a certificate of unsatisfiability for F, and if all clauses of F have length ≥ 2, prove that some C_i is a unit clause.

278. [*22*] Find a six-step certificate of unsatisfiability for $waerden\,(3, 3; 9)$.

279. [*M20*] True or false: Every unsatisfiable 2SAT problem has a certificate '(l, ϵ)'.

▶ **280.** [*M26*] The problem $cook\,(j, k)$ consists of all $\binom{n}{j}$ positive j-clauses and all $\binom{n}{k}$ negative k-clauses on $\{1, \ldots, n\}$, where $n = j + k - 1$. For example, $cook\,(2, 3)$ is

$$\{12, 13, 14, 23, 24, 34, \overline{123}, \overline{124}, \overline{134}, \overline{234}\}.$$

a) Why are these clauses obviously unsatisfiable?

b) Find a totally positive certificate for $cook\,(j, k)$, of length $\binom{n-1}{j-1}$.

c) Prove in fact that Algorithm C always learns *exactly* $\binom{n-1}{j-1}$ clauses when it proves the unsatisfiability of $cook\,(j, k)$, if $M_p = M_f = \infty$ (no purging or flushing).

281. [*21*] Construct a certificate of unsatisfiability that refutes (99), (100), (101).

▶ **282.** [*M33*] Construct a certificate of unsatisfiability for the clauses $fsnark\,(q)$ of exercise 176 when $q \geq 3$ is odd, using $O(q)$ clauses, all having length ≤ 4. *Hint:* Include the clauses $(\bar{a}_{j,p} \vee \bar{e}_{j,p})$, $(\bar{a}_{j,p} \vee \bar{f}_{j,p})$, $(\bar{e}_{j,p} \vee \bar{f}_{j,p})$, and $(a_{j,p} \vee e_{j,p} \vee f_{j,p})$ for $1 \leq j \leq q, 1 \leq p \leq 3$.

283. [*HM46*] Does Algorithm C solve the flower snark problem in linear time? More precisely, let $p_q(M)$ be the probability that the algorithm refutes $fsnark\,(q)$ while making at most M references to MEM. Is there a constant N such that $p_q(Nq) > \frac{1}{2}$ for all q?

284. [*23*] Given F and $(C_1, \ldots, C_t)$, a certificate-checking program tests condition (119) by verifying that F and clauses $\overline{C}_1, \ldots, \overline{C}_{i-1}$ will force a conflict when they are augmented by the unit literals of $\overline{C}_i$. While doing this, it can mark each clause of $F \cup \{C_1, \ldots, C_{i-1}\}$ that was reduced to a unit during the forcing process; then the truth of C_i does not depend on the truth of any unmarked clause.

In practice, many clauses of F are never marked at all, hence F will remain unsatisfiable even if we leave them out. Furthermore, many clauses C_i are not marked during the verification of any of their successors, $\{C_{i+1}, \ldots, C_t\}$; such clauses C_i needn't be verified, nor need we mark any of the clauses on which they depend.

Therefore we can save work by checking the certificate backwards: Start by marking the final clause C_t, which is ϵ and always needs to be verified. Then, for $i = t, t-1, \ldots$, check C_i only if it has been marked.

The unit propagations can all be done without recording the "reason" R_l that has caused any literal l to be forced. In practice, however, many of the forced literals don't actually contribute to the conflicts that arise, and we don't want to mark any clauses that aren't really involved.

Explain how to use reasons, as in Algorithm C, so that clauses are marked by the verifier only if they actually participate in the proof of a marked clause C_i.

285. [*19*] Using the data in Fig. 93, the text observes that Eq. (124) gives $j = 95$, $s_j = 3081$, and $m_j = 59$ when $\alpha = \frac{15}{16}$. What are j, s_j, and m_j when (a) $\alpha = \frac{9}{16}$? (b) $\alpha = \frac{1}{2}$? (c) $\alpha = \frac{7}{16}$? Also compare the effectiveness of different α's by computing the number b_j of "black" clauses (those with $0 < \text{RANGE}(c) < j$ that proved to be useful).

286. [*M24*] What choice of signatures-to-keep in Fig. 93 is *optimum*, in the sense that it maximizes $\sum b_{pq} x_{pq}$ subject to the conditions $\sum a_{pq} x_{pq} \leq 3114$, $x_{pq} \in \{0, 1\}$, and $x_{pq} \geq x_{p'q'}$ for $1 \leq p \leq p' \leq 7$, $0 \leq q \leq q' \leq 8$? Here a_{pq} and b_{pq} are the areas of the gray and black clauses that have signature (p, q), as given by the matrices in the text. [This is a special case of the "knapsack problem with a partial ordering."]

287. [*25*] What changes to Algorithm C are necessary to make it do a "full run," and later to learn from all of the conflicts that arose during that run?

288. [*28*] Spell out the details of computing **RANGE** scores and then compressing the database of learned clauses, during a round of purging.

289. [*M20*] Assume that the kth round of purging begins with y_k clauses in memory after $k\Delta + \binom{k}{2}\delta$ clauses have been learned, and that purging removes $\frac{1}{2}y_k$ of those clauses. Find a closed formula for y_k as a function of k.

290. [*17*] Explain how to find x_k, the unassigned variable of maximum activity that is used for flushing literals. *Hint:* It's in the **HEAP** array.

291. [*20*] In the text's hypothetical scenario about flushing Table 3 back to level 15, why will 49 soon appear on the trail, instead of $\overline{49}$?

292. [*M21*] How large can **AGILITY** get after repeatedly executing (127)?

293. [*21*] Spell out the details of updating M_f to $M + \Delta_f$ when deciding whether or not to flush. Also compute the agility threshold that's specified in Table 4. *Hint:* See (131).

294. [*HM21*] For each binary vector $\alpha = x_1 x_2 x_3 x_4$, find the generating function $g_\alpha(z) = \sum_{j=0}^{\infty} p_{\alpha,j} z^j$, where $p_{\alpha,j}$ is the probability that Algorithm P will solve the seven clauses of (7) after making exactly j flips, given the initial values α in step P1. Deduce the mean and variance of the number of steps needed to find a solution.

295. [*M23*] Algorithm P often finds solutions much more quickly than predicted by Corollary W. But show that some 3SAT clauses will indeed require $\Omega((4/3)^n)$ trials.

296. [*HM20*] Complete the proof of Theorem U by (approximately) maximizing the quantity $f(p, q)$ in (129). *Hint:* Consider $f(p + 1, q)/f(p, q)$.

▶ **297.** [*HM26*] (Emo Welzl.) Let $G_q(z) = \sum_p C_{p,p+q-1} (z/3)^{p+q} (2z/3)^p$ be the generating function for stopping time $t = 2p + q$ when $Y_0 = q$ in the proof of Theorem U.
  a) Find a closed form for $G_q(z)$, using formulas from Section 7.2.1.6.
  b) Explain why $G_q(1)$ is less than 1.
  c) Evaluate and interpret the quantity $G_q'(1)/G_q(1)$.
  d) Use Markov's inequality to bound the probability that $Y_t = 0$ for some $t \leq N$.
  e) Show that Corollary W follows from this analysis.

298. [*HM22*] Generalize Theorem U and Corollary W to the case where each clause has at most k literals, where $k \geq 3$.

299. [*HM23*] Continuing the previous exercise, investigate the case $k = 2$.

▶ **300.** [*25*] Modify Algorithm P so that it can be implemented with bitwise operations, thereby running (say) 64 independent trials simultaneously.

▶ **301.** [*25*] Discuss implementing the algorithm of exercise 300 efficiently on **MMIX**.

302. [*26*] Expand the text's high-level description of steps W4 and W5, by providing low-level details about exactly what the computer should do.

303. [*HM20*] Solve exercise 294 with Algorithm W in place of Algorithm P.

304. [*HM34*] Consider the 2SAT problem with $n(n-1)$ clauses $(\bar{x}_j \vee x_k)$ for all $j \neq k$. Find the generating functions for the number of flips taken by Algorithms P and W. *Hint:* Exercises 1.2.6–68 and MPR–105 are helpful for finding the exact formulas.

▶ **305.** [*HM29*] Add one more clause, $(\bar{x}_1 \vee \bar{x}_2)$, to the previous exercise and find the resulting generating functions when $n = 4$. What happens when $p = 0$ in Algorithm W?

▶ **306.** [*HM32*] (Luby, Sinclair, and Zuckerman, 1993.) Consider a "Las Vegas algorithm" that succeeds or fails; it succeeds at step t with probability p_t, and fails with probability $p_\infty < 1$. Let $q_t = p_1 + p_2 + \cdots + p_t$ and $E_t = p_1 + 2p_2 + \cdots + tp_t$; also let $E_\infty = \infty$ if $p_\infty > 0$, otherwise $E_\infty = \sum_t tp_t$. (The latter sum might be ∞.)

    a) Suppose we abort the algorithm and restart it again, whenever the first N steps have not succeeded. Show that if $q_N > 0$, this strategy will succeed after performing an average of $l(N) < \infty$ steps. What is $l(N)$?

    b) Compute $l(N)$ when $p_m = \frac{m}{n}$, $p_\infty = \frac{n-m}{n}$, otherwise $p_t = 0$, where $1 \leq m \leq n$.

    c) Given the uniform distribution, $p_t = \frac{1}{n}$ for $1 \leq t \leq n$, what is $l(N)$?

    d) Find all probability distributions such that $l(N) = l(1)$ for all $N \geq 1$.

    e) Find all probability distributions such that $l(N) = l(n)$ for all $N \geq n$.

    f) Find all probability distributions such that $q_{n+1} = 1$ and $l(n) \leq l(n+1)$.

    g) Find all probability distributions such that $q_3 = 1$ and $l(1) < l(3) < l(2)$.

    h) Let $l = \inf_{N \geq 1} l(N)$, and let N^* be the least positive integer such that $l(N^*) = l$, or ∞ if no such integer exists. Prove that $N^* = \infty$ implies $l = E_\infty < \infty$.

    i) Find N^* for the probability distribution $p_t = [t > n]/((t-n)(t+1-n))$, given $n \geq 0$.

    j) Exhibit a simple example of a probability distribution for which $N^* = \infty$.

    k) Let $L = \min_{t \geq 1} t/q_t$. Prove that $l \leq L \leq 2l - 1$.

307. [*HM28*] Continuing exercise 306, consider a more general strategy defined by an infinite sequence of positive integers $(N_1, N_2, \dots)$: "Set $j \leftarrow 0$; then, while success has not yet been achieved, set $j \leftarrow j+1$ and run the algorithm with cutoff parameter N_j."

    a) Explain how to compute $\mathrm{E}\,X$, where X is the number of steps taken before this strategy succeeds.

    b) Let $T_j = N_1 + \cdots + N_j$. Prove that $\mathrm{E}\,X = \sum_{j=1}^{\infty} \Pr(T_{j-1} < X \leq T_j) l(N_j)$, if we have $q_{N_j} > 0$ for all j.

    c) Consequently the steady strategy $(N^*, N^*, \dots)$ is best: $\mathrm{E}\,X \geq l(N^*) = l$.

    d) Given n, exercise 306(b) defines n simple probability distributions $p^{(m)}$ that have $l(N^*) = n$, but the value of $N^* = m$ is different in each case. Prove that any sequence $(N_1, N_2, \dots)$ must have $\mathrm{E}\,X > \frac{1}{4}nH_n - \frac{1}{2}n = \frac{1}{4}lH_l - \frac{1}{2}l$ on at least one of those $p^{(m)}$. *Hint:* Consider the smallest r such that, for each m, the probability is $\geq \frac{1}{2}$ that r trial runs suffice; show that $\geq n/(2m)$ of $\{N_1, \dots, N_r\}$ are $\geq m$.

308. [*M29*] This exercise explores the "reluctant doubling" sequence (130).

    a) What is the smallest n such that $S_n = 2^a$, given $a \geq 0$?

    b) Show that $\{n \mid S_n = 1\} = \{2k + 1 - \nu k \mid k \geq 0\}$; hence the generating function $\sum_n z^n [S_n = 1]$ is the infinite product $z(1 + z)(1 + z^3)(1 + z^7)(1 + z^{15}) \dots$.

    c) Find similar expressions for $\{n \mid S_n = 2^a\}$ and $\sum_n z^n [S_n = 2^a]$.

    d) Let $\Sigma(a, b, k) = \sum_{n=1}^{r(a,b,k)} S_n$, where $S_{r(a,b,k)}$ is the $2^b k$th occurrence of 2^a in $\langle S_n \rangle$. For example, $\Sigma(1, 0, 3) = S_1 + \cdots + S_{10} = 16$. Evaluate $\Sigma(a, b, 1)$ in closed form.

    e) Show that $\Sigma(a, b, k+1) - \Sigma(a, b, k) \leq (a + b + 2k - 1)2^{a+b}$, for all $k \geq 1$.

f) Given any probability distribution as in exercise 306(k), let $a = \lceil \lg t \rceil$ and $b = \lceil \lg 1/q_t \rceil$, where $t/q_t = L$; thus $L \le 2^{a+b} < 4L$. Prove that if the strategy of exercise 307 is used with $N_j = S_j$, we have

$$\mathrm{E}\,X \le \Sigma(a, b, 1) + \sum_{k \ge 1} Q^k\big(\Sigma(a, b, k+1) - \Sigma(a, b, k)\big), \quad \text{where } Q = (1 - q_{2a})^{2^b}.$$

g) Therefore $\langle S_n \rangle$ gives $\mathrm{E}\,X < 13l \lg l + 49l$, for every probability distribution.

309. [*20*] Exercise 293 explains how to use the reluctant doubling sequence with Algorithm C. Is Algorithm C a Las Vegas algorithm?

310. [*M25*] Explain how to compute the "reluctant Fibonacci sequence"

$$1, 1, 2, 1, 2, 3, 1, 1, 2, 3, 5, 1, 1, 2, 1, 2, 3, 5, 8, 1, 1, 2, 1, 2, 3, 1, 1, 2, 3, 5, 8, 13, 1, \ldots,$$

which is somewhat like (130) and useful as in exercise 308, but its elements are Fibonacci numbers instead of powers of 2.

311. [*21*] Compute approximate values of $\mathrm{E}\,X$ for the 100 probability distributions of exercise 306(b) when $n = l = 100$, using the method of exercise 307 with the sequences $\langle S_n \rangle$ of exercise 308 and $\langle S'_n \rangle$ of exercise 310. Also consider the more easily generated "ruler doubling" sequence $\langle R_n \rangle$, where $R_n = n \mathbin{\&} -n = 2^{\rho n}$. Which sequence is best?

312. [*HM24*] Let $T(m, n) = \mathrm{E}\,X$ when the reluctant doubling method is applied to the probability distribution defined in exercise 306(b). Express $T(m, n)$ in terms of the generating functions in exercise 308(c).

▶ **313.** [*22*] Algorithm W always flips a cost-free literal if one is present in C_j, without considering its parameter p. Show that such a flip always decreases the number of unsatisfied clauses, r; but it might *increase* the distance from x to the nearest solution.

▶ **314.** [*36*] (H. H. Hoos, 1998.) If the given clauses are satisfiable, and if $p > 0$, can there be an initial x for which Algorithm W always loops forever?

315. [*M18*] What value of p is appropriate in Theorem J when $d = 1$?

316. [*HM20*] Is Theorem J a consequence of Theorem L?

▶ **317.** [*M26*] Let $\alpha(G) = \Pr(\overline{A}_1 \cap \cdots \cap \overline{A}_m)$ under the assumptions of (133), when $p_i = p = (d-1)^{d-1}/d^d$ for $1 \le i \le m$ and every vertex of G has degree at most $d > 1$. Prove, by induction on m, that $\alpha(G) > 0$ and that $\alpha(G) > \frac{d-1}{d}\alpha(G \setminus v)$ when v has degree $< d$.

318. [*HM27*] (J. B. Shearer.) Prove that Theorem J is the best possible result of its kind: If $p > (d-1)^{d-1}/d^d$ and $d > 1$, there is a graph G of maximum degree d for which $(p, \ldots, p) \notin \mathcal{R}(G)$. *Hint:* Consider complete t-ary trees, where $t = d - 1$.

319. [*HM20*] Show that $pde < 1$ implies $p \le (d-1)^{d-1}/d^d$.

320. [*M24*] Given a lopsidependency graph G, the *occurrence threshold* $\rho(G)$ is the smallest value p such that it's sometimes impossible to avoid all events when each event occurs with probability p. For example, the Möbius polynomial for the path P_3 is $1 - p_1 - p_2 - p_3 + p_1 p_3$; so the occurrence threshold is ϕ^{-2}, the least p with $1 - 3p + p^2 \le 0$.

a) Prove that the occurrence threshold for P_m is $1/(4\cos^2 \frac{\pi}{m+2})$.

b) What is the occurrence threshold for the cycle graph C_m?

321. [*M24*] Suppose each of four random events A, B, C, D occurs with probability p, where $\{A, C\}$ and $\{B, D\}$ are independent. According to exercise 320(b) with $m = 4$, there's a joint distribution of (A, B, C, D) such that at least one of the events always occurs, whenever $p \ge (2 - \sqrt{2})/2 \approx 0.293$. Exhibit such a distribution when $p = 3/10$.

▸ **322.** [*HM35*] (K. Kolipaka and M. Szegedy, 2011.) Surprisingly, the previous exercise *cannot* be solved in the setting of Algorithm M! Suppose we have independent random variables (W, X, Y, Z) such that A depends on W and X, B depends on X and Y, C depends on Y and Z, D depends on Z and W. Here W equals j with probability w_j for all integers j; X, Y, and Z are similar. This exercise will prove that the constraint $\overline{A} \cap \overline{B} \cap \overline{C} \cap \overline{D}$ is always satisfiable, even when p is as large as 0.333.

    a) Express the probability $\Pr(\overline{A} \cap \overline{B} \cap \overline{C} \cap \overline{D})$ in a convenient way.

    b) Suppose there's a distribution of W, X, Y, Z with $\Pr(A) = \Pr(B) = \Pr(C) = \Pr(D) = p$ and $\Pr(\overline{A} \cap \overline{B} \cap \overline{C} \cap \overline{D}) = 0$. Show that there are ten values such that

$$0 \le a, b, c, d, a', b', c', d' \le 1, \qquad 0 < \mu, \nu < 1,$$
$$\mu a + (1 - \mu)a' \le p, \qquad \mu b + (1 - \mu)b' \le p,$$
$$\nu c + (1 - \nu)c' \le p, \qquad \nu d + (1 - \nu)d' \le p,$$
$$a + d \ge 1 \text{ or } b + c \ge 1, \qquad a + d' \ge 1 \text{ or } b + c' \ge 1,$$
$$a' + d \ge 1 \text{ or } b' + c \ge 1, \qquad a' + d' \ge 1 \text{ or } b' + c' \ge 1.$$

    c) Find all solutions to those constraints when $p = 1/3$.

    d) Convert those solutions to distributions that have $\Pr(\overline{A} \cap \overline{B} \cap \overline{C} \cap \overline{D}) = 0$.

323. [*10*] What trace precedes *ccb* in the list (135)?

▸ **324.** [*22*] Given a trace $\alpha = x_1 x_2 \ldots x_n$ for a graph G, explain how to find all strings β that are equivalent to α, using Algorithm 7.2.1.2V. How many strings yield (136)?

▸ **325.** [*20*] An *acyclic orientation* of a graph G is an assignment of directions to each of its edges so that the resulting digraph has no oriented cycles. Show that the number of traces for G that are *permutations* of the vertices (with each vertex appearing exactly once in the trace) is the number of acyclic orientations of G.

326. [*20*] True or false: If α and β are traces with $\alpha = \beta$, then $\alpha^R = \beta^R$. (See (137).)

▸ **327.** [*22*] Design an algorithm to multiply two traces α and β, when clashing is defined by territory sets $T(a)$ in some universe U. Assume that U is small (say $|U| \le 64$), so that bitwise operations can be used to represent the territories.

328. [*20*] Continuing exercise 327, design an algorithm that computes α/β. More precisely, if β is a right factor of α, in the sense that $\alpha = \gamma\beta$ for some trace γ, your algorithm should compute γ; otherwise it should report that β is *not* a right factor.

329. [*21*] Similarly, design an algorithm that either computes $\alpha \setminus \beta$ or reports that α isn't a left factor of β.

▸ **330.** [*21*] Given any graph G, explain how to define territory sets $T(a)$ for its vertices a in such a way that we have $a = b$ or $a \!-\!\! b$ if and only if $T(a) \cap T(b) \ne \emptyset$. (Thus traces can always be modeled by empilements of pieces.) Under what circumstances is it possible to do this with $|T(a)| = 2$ for all a, as in the text's example (136)?

331. [*M20*] What happens if the right-hand side of (139) is expanded without allowing *any* of the variables to commute with each other?

332. [*20*] When a trace is represented by its lexicographically smallest string, no letter in that representative string is followed by a smaller letter with which it commutes. (For example, no c is followed by an a in (135), because we could get an equivalent smaller string by changing ca to ac.)

    Conversely, given any ordered set of letters, some of which commute, consider all strings having no letter followed by a smaller letter with which it commutes. Is every such string the lexicographically smallest of its trace?

▶ **333.** [*M20*] (Carlitz, Scoville, and Vaughan, 1976.) Let D be a digraph on $\{1, \ldots, m\}$, and let A be the set of all strings $a_{j_1} \ldots a_{j_n}$ such that $j_i \longrightarrow j_{i+1}$ in D for $1 \leq i < n$. Similarly let B be the set of all strings $a_{j_1} \ldots a_{j_n}$ such that $j_i \not\longrightarrow j_{i+1}$ for $1 \leq i < n$. Prove that

$$\sum_{\alpha \in A} \alpha = 1 \bigg/ \sum_{\beta \in B} (-1)^{|\beta|} \beta = \sum_{k \geq 0} \bigg(1 - \sum_{\beta \in B} (-1)^{|\beta|} \beta \bigg)^k$$

is an identity in the noncommutative variables $\{a_1, \ldots, a_m\}$. (For example, we have

$$1 + a + b + ab + ba + aba + bab + \cdots = \sum_{k \geq 0} (a + b - aa - bb + aaa + bbb - \cdots)^k$$

in the case $m = 2$, $1 \not\longrightarrow 1$, $1 \longrightarrow 2$, $2 \longrightarrow 1$, $2 \not\longrightarrow 2$.)

▶ **334.** [*25*] Design an algorithm to generate all traces of length n that correspond to a given graph on the alphabet $\{1, \ldots, m\}$, representing each trace by its lexicographically smallest string.

335. [*HM26*] If the vertices of G can be ordered in such a way that $x < y < z$ and $x \not\!\!-\!\!\!\!-\, y$ and $y \not\!\!-\!\!\!\!-\, z$ implies $x \not\!\!-\!\!\!\!-\, z$, show that the Möbius series M_G can be expressed as a determinant. For example,

if $G = $ then $M_G = \det \begin{pmatrix} 1-a & -b & -c & 0 & 0 & 0 \\ -a & 1-b & 0 & -d & 0 & 0 \\ -a & -b & 1-c & -d & -e & 0 \\ -a & -b & -c & 1-d & 0 & -f \\ -a & -b & -c & -d & 1-e & -f \\ -a & -b & -c & -d & -e & 1-f \end{pmatrix}$.

▶ **336.** [*M20*] If graphs G and H on distinct vertices have the Möbius series M_G and M_H, what are the Möbius series for (a) $G \oplus H$ and (b) G——H?

337. [*M20*] Suppose we obtain the graph G' from G by substituting a clique of vertices $\{a_1, \ldots, a_k\}$ for some vertex a, then including edges from a_j to each neighbor of a for $1 \leq j \leq k$. Describe the relation between $M_{G'}$ and M_G.

338. [*M21*] Prove Viennot's general identity (144) for source-constrained traces.

▶ **339.** [*HM26*] (G. Viennot.) This exercise explores factorization of traces into pyramids.

  a) Each letter x_j of a given trace $\alpha = x_1 \ldots x_n$ lies at the top of a unique pyramid β_j such that β_j is a left factor of α. For example, in the trace $bcebafdc$ of (136), the pyramids $\beta_1, \ldots, \beta_8$ are respectively b, bc, e, bcb, $bcba$, ef, $bced$, and $bcebdc$. Explain intuitively how to find these pyramidal left factors from α's empilement.

  b) A *labeled trace* is an assignment of distinct numbers to the letters of a trace; for example, $abca$ might become $a_4 b_7 c_6 a_3$. A *labeled pyramid* is the special case when the pyramid's top element is required to have the smallest label. Prove that every labeled trace is uniquely factorizable into labeled pyramids whose topmost labels are in ascending order. (For example, $b_6 c_2 e_4 b_7 a_8 f_5 d_1 c_3 = b_6 c_2 e_4 d_1 \cdot b_7 a_8 c_3 \cdot f_5$.)

  c) Suppose there are t_n traces of length n, and p_n pyramids. Then there are $T_n = n! \, t_n$ labeled traces and $P_n = (n-1)! \, p_n$ labeled pyramids (because only the relative order of the labels is significant). Letting $T(z) = \sum_{n \geq 0} T_n z^n / n!$ and $P(z) = \sum_{n \geq 1} P_n z^n / n!$, prove that the number of labeled traces of length n whose factorization in part (b) has exactly l pyramids is $n! \, [z^n] \, P(z)^l / l!$.

  d) Consequently $T(z) = e^{P(z)}$.

  e) Therefore (and this is the punch line!) $\ln M_G(z) = -\sum_{n \geq 1} p_n z^n / n$.

▶ **340.** [*M20*] If we assign a weight $w(\sigma)$ to every cyclic permutation σ, then every permutation π has a weight $w(\pi)$ that is the product of the weights of its cycles. For
example, if $\pi = \left(\begin{smallmatrix}1\,2\,3\,4\,5\,6\,7\\3\,1\,4\,2\,7\,6\,5\end{smallmatrix}\right) = (1\,3\,4\,2)(5\,7)(6)$ then $w(\pi) = w((1\,3\,4\,2))w((5\,7))w((6))$.

The *permutation polynomial* of a set S is the sum of $w(\pi)$ over all permutations
of S. Given any $n \times n$ matrix $A = (a_{ij})$, show that it's possible to define appropriate
cycle weights so that the permutation polynomial of $\{1, \ldots, n\}$ is the determinant of A.

341. [*M25*] The *involution polynomial* of a set S is the special case of the permutation polynomial when the cycle weights have the form $w_{jj}x$ for the 1-cycle (j) and
$-w_{ij}$ for the 2-cycle $(i\,j)$, otherwise $w(\sigma) = 0$. For example, the involution polyno-
mial of $\{1, 2, 3, 4\}$ is $w_{11}w_{22}w_{33}w_{44}x^4 - w_{11}w_{22}w_{34}x^2 - w_{11}w_{23}w_{44}x^2 - w_{11}w_{24}w_{33}x^2 - w_{12}w_{33}w_{44}x^2 - w_{13}w_{22}w_{44}x^2 - w_{14}w_{22}w_{33}x^2 + w_{12}w_{34} + w_{13}w_{24} + w_{14}w_{23}$.

Prove that, if $w_{ij} > 0$ for $1 \le i \le j \le n$, the involution polynomial of $\{1, \ldots, n\}$
has n distinct real roots. *Hint:* Show also that, if the roots for $\{1, \ldots, n-1\}$ are
$q_1 < \cdots < q_{n-1}$, then the roots r_k for $\{1, \ldots, n\}$ satisfy $r_1 < q_1 < r_2 < \cdots < q_{n-1} < r_n$.

342. [*HM25*] (Cartier and Foata, 1969.) Let G_n be the graph whose vertices are the
$\sum_{k=1}^n \binom{n}{k}(k-1)!$ cyclic permutations of subsets of $\{1, \ldots, n\}$, with $\sigma \,\text{---}\, \tau$ when σ and
τ intersect. For example, the vertices of G_3 are (1), (2), (3), (12), (13), (23), (123),
(132); and they're mutually adjacent except that $(1) \not\!\!\text{---} (2)$, $(1) \not\!\!\text{---} (3)$, $(1) \not\!\!\text{---} (23)$,
$(2) \not\!\!\text{---} (3)$, $(2) \not\!\!\text{---} (13)$, $(12) \not\!\!\text{---} (3)$. Find a beautiful relation between M_{G_n} and the
characteristic polynomial of an $n \times n$ matrix.

▶ **343.** [*M25*] If G is any cograph, show that $(p_1, \ldots, p_m) \in \mathcal{R}(G)$ if and only if we have
$M_G(p_1, \ldots, p_m) > 0$. Exhibit a non-cograph for which the latter statement is *not* true.

344. [*M33*] Given a graph G as in Theorem S, let $B_1, \ldots, B_m$ have the joint probability distribution of exercise MPR–31, with $\pi_I = 0$ whenever I contains distinct vertices
$\{i, j\}$ with $i \,\text{---}\, j$, otherwise $\pi_I = \prod_{i \in I} p_i$.

   a) Show that this distribution is legal (see exercise MPR–32) if $(p_1, \ldots, p_m) \in \mathcal{R}(G)$.

   b) Show that this "extreme distribution" also satisfies condition (147).

   c) Let $\beta(G) = \Pr(\overline{B}_1 \cap \cdots \cap \overline{B}_m)$. If $J \subseteq \{1, \ldots, m\}$, express $\beta(G | J)$ in terms of M_G.

   d) Defining $\alpha(G)$ as in exercise 317, with events A_j satisfying (133) and probabilities
$(p_1, \ldots, p_m) \in \mathcal{R}(G)$, show that $\alpha(G \mid J) \ge \beta(G \mid J)$ for all $J \subseteq \{1, \ldots, m\}$.

   e) If p_i satisfies (134), show that $\beta(G|J) \ge \prod_{j \in J}(1 - \theta_j)$.

345. [*M30*] Construct unavoidable events that satisfy (147) when $(p_1, \ldots, p_m) \notin \mathcal{R}(G)$.

▶ **346.** [*HM28*] Write (142) as $M_G = M_{G \backslash a}(1 - aK_{a,G})$ where $K_{a,G} = M_{G \backslash a^*}/M_{G \backslash a}$.

   a) If $(p_1, \ldots, p_m) \in \mathcal{R}(G)$, prove that $K_{a,G}$ is monotonic in all of its parameters: It
does not increase if any of $p_1, \ldots, p_m$ are decreased.

   b) Exploit this fact to design an algorithm that computes $M_G(p_1, \ldots, p_m)$ and
decides whether or not $(p_1, \ldots, p_m) \in \mathcal{R}(G)$, given a graph G and probabilities
$(p_1, \ldots, p_m)$. Illustrate your algorithm on the graph $G = P_3 \,\square\, P_2$ of exercise 335.

▶ **347.** [*M28*] A graph is called *chordal* when it has no induced cycle C_k for $k > 3$.
Equivalently (see Section 7.4.2), a graph is chordal if and only if its edges can be
defined by territory sets $T(a)$ that induce connected subgraphs of some tree. For
example, interval graphs and forests are chordal.

   a) Say that a graph is *tree-ordered* if its vertices can be arranged as nodes of a forest
in such a way that

$$a \,\text{---}\, b \text{ implies } a \succ b \text{ or } b \succ a;$$
$$a \succ b \succ c \text{ and } a \,\text{---}\, c \text{ implies } a \,\text{---}\, b. \tag{$*$}$$

(Here '$a \succ b$' means that a is a proper ancestor of b in the forest.) Prove that every tree-ordered graph is chordal.

b) Conversely, show that every chordal graph can be tree-ordered.

c) Show that the algorithm in the previous exercise becomes quite simple when it is applied to a tree-ordered graph, if a is eliminated before b whenever $a \succ b$.

d) Consequently Theorem L can be substantially strengthened when G is a chordal graph: *When G is tree-ordered by $\succ$, the probability vector $(p_1, \ldots, p_m)$ is in $\mathcal{R}(G)$ if and only if there are numbers $0 \le \theta_1, \ldots, \theta_m < 1$ such that*

$$p_i = \theta_i \prod_{i-j \text{ in } G, \ i \succ j} (1 - \theta_j).$$

348. [*HM26*] (A. Pringsheim, 1894.) Show that any power series $f(z) = \sum_{n=0}^{\infty} a_n z^n$ with $a_n \ge 0$ and radius of convergence ρ, where $0 < \rho < \infty$, has a singularity at $z = \rho$.

▶ **349.** [*M24*] Analyze Algorithm M *exactly* in the two examples considered in the text (see (150)): For each binary vector $x = x_1 \ldots x_7$, compute the generating function $g_x(z) = \sum_t p_{x,t} z^t$, where $p_{x,t}$ is the probability that step M3 will be executed exactly t times after step M1 produces x. Assume that step M2 always chooses the smallest possible value of j. (Thus the 'Case 2' scenario in (150) will never occur.)

What are the mean and variance of the running times, in (i) Case 1? (ii) Case 2?

▶ **350.** [*HM26*] (W. Pegden.) Suppose Algorithm M is applied to the $m = n + 1$ events

$$A_j = x_j \quad \text{for } 1 \le j \le n; \qquad A_m = x_1 \vee \cdots \vee x_n.$$

Thus A_m is true whenever any of the other A_j is true; so we could implement step M2 by never setting $j \leftarrow m$. Alternatively, we could decide to set $j \leftarrow m$ whenever possible. Let $(N_i, N_{ii}, N_{iii}, N_{iv}, N_v)$ be the number of resamplings performed when parameter ξ_k of the algorithm is (i) $1/2$; (ii) $1/(2n)$; (iii) $1/2^n$; (iv) $1/(n+k)$; (v) $1/(n+k)^2$.

a) Find the asymptotic mean and variance of each N, if j is never equal to m.

b) Find the asymptotic mean and variance of each N, if j is never less than m.

c) Let G be the graph on $\{1, \ldots, n+1\}$ with edges $j - (n+1)$ for $1 \le j \le n$, and let $p_j = \Pr(A_j)$. For which of the five choices of ξ_k is $(p_1, \ldots, p_{n+1}) \in \mathcal{R}(G)$?

▶ **351.** [*25*] The Local Lemma can be applied to the satisfiability problem for m clauses on n variables if we let A_j be the event "C_j is not satisfied." The dependency graph G then has $i - j$ whenever two clauses C_i and C_j share at least one common variable. If, say, C_i is $(x_3 \vee \bar{x}_5 \vee x_6)$, then (133) holds whenever $p_i \ge (1 - \xi_3)\xi_5(1 - \xi_6)$, assuming that each x_k is true with probability ξ_k, independent of the other x's.

But if, say, C_j is $(\bar{x}_2 \vee x_3 \vee x_7)$, condition (133) remains true even if we don't stipulate that $i - j$. Variable x_3 appears in both clauses, yet the cases when C_j is satisfied are never bad news for C_i. We need to require that $i - j$ in condition (133) only when C_i and C_j are "resolvable" clauses, namely when some variable occurs positively in one and negatively in the other.

Extend this reasoning to the general setting of Algorithm M, where we have arbitrary events A_j that depend on variables Ξ_j: Define a lopsidependency graph G for which (133) holds even though we might have $i \not\!\!- j$ in some cases when $\Xi_i \cap \Xi_j \ne \emptyset$.

352. [*M21*] Show that $E_j \le \theta_j/(1 - \theta_j)$ in (152), when (134) holds.

353. [*M21*] Consider Case 1 and Case 2 of Algorithm M as illustrated in (150).

a) How many solutions $x_1 \ldots x_n$ are possible? (Generalize from $n = 7$ to any n.)

b) How many solutions are predicted by Theorem S?

c) Show that in Case 2 the lopsidependency graph is much smaller than the dependency graph. How many solutions are predicted when the smaller graph is used?

354. [*HM20*] Show that the expected number $E\,N$ of resampling steps in Algorithm M is at most $-M_G^{*\prime}(1)/M_G^*(1)$.

355. [*HM21*] In (152), prove that $E_j \le 1/\delta$ when $(p_1,\ldots,p_m)$ has positive slack δ. *Hint:* Consider replacing p_j by $p_j + \delta p_j$.

▶ **356.** [*M33*] (*The Clique Local Lemma.*) Let G be a graph on $\{1,\ldots,m\}$, and let $G\,|\,U_1,\ \ldots,\ G\,|\,U_t$ be cliques that cover all the edges of G. Assign numbers $\theta_{ij} \ge 0$ to the vertices of each U_j, such that $\Sigma_j = \sum_{i\in U_j} \theta_{ij} < 1$. Assume that

$$\Pr(A_i) = p_i \le \theta_{ij} \prod_{k\ne j,\,i\in U_k} (1 + \theta_{ik} - \Sigma_k) \quad \text{whenever } 1 \le i \le m \text{ and } i \in U_j.$$

a) Prove that $(p_1,\ldots,p_m) \in \mathcal{R}(G)$. *Hint:* Letting $\overline{A}_S$ denote $\bigcap_{i\in S} \overline{A}_i$, show that

$$\Pr(A_i \mid \overline{A}_S) \le \theta_{ij} \quad \text{whenever } 1 \le i \le m \text{ and } i \in U_j \text{ and } S \cap U_j = \emptyset.$$

b) Also E_i in (152) is at most $\min_{i - j \text{ in } G} \theta_{ij}/(1 - \Sigma_j)$. (See Theorems M and S.)

c) Improve Theorem L by showing that, if $0 \le \theta_j < \frac{1}{2}$, then $(p_1,\ldots,p_m) \in \mathcal{R}(G)$ when

$$p_i = \theta_i \left(\prod_{i - j \text{ in } G} (1 - \theta_j) \right) \Big/ \max_{i - j \text{ in } G} (1 - \theta_j).$$

▶ **357.** [*M20*] Let $x = \pi_{\bar v}$ and $y = \pi_v$ in (155), and suppose the field of variable v is (p,q,r). Express x and y as functions of p, q, and r.

358. [*M20*] Continuing exercise 357, prove that $r = \max(p,q,r)$ if and only if $x, y \ge \frac{1}{2}$.

359. [*20*] Equations (156) and (157) should actually have been written

$$\gamma_{l\to C} = \frac{(1 - \pi_{\bar l})(1 - \eta_l) \prod_{l\in C'\ne C}(1 - \eta_{C\to l})}{\pi_{\bar l} + (1 - \pi_{\bar l})(1 - \eta_l) \prod_{l\in C'\ne C}(1 - \eta_{C\to l})} \quad \text{and} \quad \eta'_{C\to l} = \prod_{C\ni l'\ne l} \gamma_{l'\to C},$$

to avoid division by zero. Suggest an efficient way to implement these calculations.

360. [*M23*] Find all fixed points of the seven-clause system illustrated in (159), given that $\pi_1 = \pi_{\bar 2} = \pi_{\bar 4} = 1$. Assume also that $\eta_l \eta_{\bar l} = 0$ for all l.

▶ **361.** [*M22*] Describe all fixed points $\eta_{C\to l} = \eta'_{C\to l}$ of the equations (154), (156), (157), for which each $\eta_{C\to l}$ and each η_l is either 0 or 1.

362. [*20*] Spell out the computations needed to finish Algorithm S in step S8.

▶ **363.** [*M30*] (*Lattices of partial assignments.*) A partial assignment to the variables of a satisfiability problem is called *stable* (or "valid") if it is consistent and cannot be extended by unit propagation. In other words, it's stable if and only if no clause is entirely false, or entirely false except for at most one unassigned literal. Variable x_k of a partial assignment is called *constrained* if it appears in a clause where $\pm x_k$ is true but all the other literals are false (thus its value has a "reason").

The 3^n partial assignments of an n-variable problem can be represented either as strings $x = x_1 \ldots x_n$ on the alphabet $\{0, 1, *\}$ or as sets L of strictly distinct literals. For example, the string $x = *1*01*$ corresponds to the set $L = \{2, \bar 4, 5\}$. We write $x \prec x'$ if x' is equal to x except that $x_k = *$ and $x'_k \in \{0, 1\}$; equivalently $L \prec L'$ if $L' = L \cup k$ or $L' = L \cup \bar k$. Also $x \sqsubseteq x'$ if there are $t \ge 0$ stable partial assignments $x^{(j)}$ with

$$x = x^{(0)} \prec x^{(1)} \prec \cdots \prec x^{(t)} = x'.$$

Let $p_1, \ldots, p_n, q_1, \ldots, q_n$ be probabilities, with $p_k + q_k = 1$ for $1 \le k \le n$. Define the weight $W(x)$ of a partial assignment to be 0 if x is unstable, otherwise

$$W(x) = \prod \{p_k \mid x_k = *\} \cdot \prod \{q_k \mid x_k \ne * \text{ and } x_k \text{ is unconstrained}\}.$$

[E. Maneva, E. Mossel, and M. J. Wainwright, in *JACM* **54** (2007), 17:1–17:41, studied general message-passing algorithms on partial assignments that are distributed with probability proportional to their weights, in the case $p_1 = \cdots = p_n = p$, showing that survey propagation (Algorithm S) corresponds to the limit as $p \to 1$.]

a) True or false: The partial assignment specified by the literals currently on the trail in step C5 of Algorithm C is stable.

b) What weights $W(x)$ correspond to the clauses F in (1)?

c) Let x be a stable partial assignment with $x_k = 1$, and let x' and x'' be obtained from x by setting $x'_k \leftarrow 0$, $x''_k \leftarrow *$. True or false: x_k is unconstrained in x if and only if (i) x' is consistent; (ii) x' is stable; (iii) x'' is stable.

d) If the only clause is $123 = (x_1 \lor x_2 \lor x_3)$, find all sets L such that $L \sqsubseteq \{1, \bar{2}, \bar{3}\}$.

e) What are the weights when there's only a single clause $123 = (x_1 \lor x_2 \lor x_3)$?

f) Find clauses such that the sets L with $L \sqsubseteq \{1, 2, 3, 4, 5\}$ are $\emptyset$, $\{4\}$, $\{5\}$, $\{1, 4\}$, $\{2, 5\}$, $\{4, 5\}$, $\{1, 4, 5\}$, $\{2, 4, 5\}$, $\{3, 4, 5\}$, $\{1, 3, 4, 5\}$, $\{2, 3, 4, 5\}$, $\{1, 2, 3, 4, 5\}$.

g) Let $\mathcal{L}$ be a family of sets $\subseteq \{1, \ldots, n\}$, closed under intersection, with the property that $L \in \mathcal{L}$ implies $L = L^{(0)} \prec L^{(1)} \prec \cdots \prec L^{(t)} = \{1, \ldots, n\}$ for some $L^{(j)} \in \mathcal{L}$. (The sets in (f) form one such family, with $n = 5$.) Construct strict Horn clauses with the property that $L \in \mathcal{L}$ if and only if $L \sqsubseteq \{1, \ldots, n\}$.

h) True or false: If L, L', L'' are stable and $L' \prec L$, $L'' \prec L$, then $L' \cap L''$ is stable.

i) If $L' \sqsubseteq L$ and $L'' \sqsubseteq L$, prove that $L' \cap L'' \sqsubseteq L$.

j) Prove that $\sum_{x' \sqsubseteq x} W(x') = \prod \{p_k \mid x_k = *\}$ whenever x is stable.

▶ **364.** [*M21*] A *covering assignment* is a stable partial assignment in which every assigned variable is constrained. A *core assignment* is a covering assignment L that satisfies $L \sqsubseteq L'$ for some total assignment L'.

a) True or false: The empty partial assignment $L = \emptyset$ is always covering.

b) Find all the covering and core assignments of the clauses F in (1).

c) Find all the covering and core assignments of the clauses R' in (7).

d) Show that every satisfying assignment L' has a unique core.

e) The satisfying assignments form a graph, if two of them are adjacent when they differ by complementing just one literal. The connected components of this graph are called *clusters*. Prove that the elements of each cluster have the same core.

f) If L' and L'' have the same core, do they belong to the same cluster?

365. [*M27*] Prove that the clauses $waerden(3, 3; n)$ have a nontrivial (i.e., nonempty) covering assignment for all sufficiently large n (although they're unsatisfiable).

▶ **366.** [*18*] Preprocess the clauses R' of (7). What erp rules are generated?

▶ **367.** [*20*] Justify the erp rule (161) for elimination by resolution.

368. [*16*] Show that subsumption and downhill resolution imply unit conditioning: Any preprocessor that does transformations 2 and 4 will also do transformation 1.

▶ **369.** [*21*] (N. Eén and A. Biere.) Suppose l appears only in clauses $C_1, \ldots, C_p$ and $\bar{l}$ appears only in clauses $C'_1, \ldots, C'_q$, where we have $C_1 = (l \lor l_1 \lor \cdots \lor l_r)$ and $C'_j = (\bar{l} \lor \bar{l}_j)$ for $1 \le j \le r$. Prove that we can eliminate $|l|$ by using the erp rule $\bar{l} \leftarrow (l_1 \lor \cdots \lor l_r)$ and replacing those $p + q$ clauses by only $(p - 2)r + q$ others, namely

$$\{C_1 \diamond C'_j \mid r < j \le q\} \cup \{C_i \diamond C'_j \mid 1 < i \le p, \ 1 \le j \le r\}.$$

(The case $r = 1$ is especially important. In many applications — for example in the examples of fault testing, tomography, and the "Life in 4" problem about extending Fig. 78 — more than half of all variable eliminations admit this simplification.)

370. [20] The clauses obtained by resolution might be needlessly complex even when exercise 369 doesn't apply. For example, suppose that variable x appears only in the clauses $(x \vee a) \wedge (x \vee \bar{a} \vee c) \wedge (\bar{x} \vee b) \wedge (\bar{x} \vee \bar{b} \vee \bar{c})$. Resolution replaces those four clauses by three others: $(a \vee b) \wedge (a \vee \bar{b} \vee \bar{c}) \wedge (\bar{a} \vee b \vee c)$. Show, however, that only *two* clauses, both *binary*, would actually suffice in this particular case.

371. [24] By preprocessing repeatedly with transformations 1–4, and using exercise 369, prove that the 32 clauses (9) of $waerden(3, 3; 9)$ are unsatisfiable.

372. [30] Find a "small" set of clauses that *cannot* by solved entirely via transformations 1–4 and the use of exercise 369.

373. [25] The answer to exercise 228 defines $2m + \sum_{j=1}^{m}(j - 1)^2 \approx m^3/3$ clauses in m^2 variables that suffice to refute the anti-maximal-element axioms of (99)–(101). Algorithm L needs exponential time to handle these clauses, according to Theorem R; and experiments show that they are bad news for Algorithm C too. Show, however, that preprocessing with transformations 1–4 will rapidly prove them unsatisfiable.

▶ **374.** [32] Design data structures for the efficient representation of clauses within a SAT preprocessor. Also design algorithms that (a) resolve clauses C and C' with respect to a variable x; (b) find all clauses C' that are subsumed by a given clause C; (c) find all clauses C' that are self-subsumed by a given clause C and a literal $\bar{x} \in C$.

375. [21] Given $|l|$, how can one test efficiently whether or not the special situation in exercise 369 applies, using (and slightly extending) the data structures of exercise 374?

▶ **376.** [36] After a preprocessor has found a transformation that reduces the current set of clauses, it is supposed to try again and look for further simplifications. (See (160).) Suggest methods that will avoid unnecessary repetition of previous work, by using (and slightly extending) the data structures of exercise 374.

377. [22] (V. Vassilevska Williams.) If G is a graph with n vertices and m edges, construct a 2SAT problem F with $3n$ variables and $6m$ clauses, such that G contains a triangle (a 3-clique) if and only if F has a failed literal.

378. [20] (*Blocked clause elimination.*) Clause $C = (l \vee l_1 \vee \cdots \vee l_q)$ is said to be blocked by the literal l if every clause that contains $\bar{l}$ also contains either $\bar{l}_1$ or $\cdots$ or $\bar{l}_q$. Exercise 161(b) proves that clause C can be removed without making an unsatisfiable problem satisfiable. Show that this transformation requires an erp rule, even though it doesn't eliminate any of the variables. What erp rule works?

▶ **379.** [20] (*Blocked self-subsumption.*) Consider the clause $(a \vee b \vee c \vee d)$, and suppose that every clause containing $\bar{a}$ but not $\bar{b}$ nor $\bar{c}$ also contains d. Show that we can then shorten the clause to $(a \vee b \vee c)$ without affecting satisfiability. Is an erp rule needed?

380. [21] Sometimes we can use self-subsumption backwards, for example by weakening the clause $(l_1 \vee l_2 \vee l_3)$ to $(l_1 \vee \cdots \vee l_k)$ if each intermediate replacement of $(l_1 \vee \cdots \vee l_j)$ by $(l_1 \vee \cdots \vee l_{j-1})$ is justifiable for $3 < j \le k$. Then, if we're lucky, the clause $(l_1 \vee \cdots \vee l_k)$ is weak enough to be eliminated; in such cases we are allowed to eliminate $(l_1 \vee l_2 \vee l_3)$.

a) Show that $(a \vee b \vee c)$ can be eliminated if it is accompanied by the additional clauses $(a \vee b \vee \bar{d})$, $(a \vee d \vee e)$, $(b \vee d \vee \bar{e})$.

b) Show that $(a \vee b \vee c)$ can also be eliminated when accompanied by $(a \vee b \vee \bar{d})$, $(a \vee \bar{c} \vee \bar{d})$, $(b \vee d \vee \bar{e})$, $(b \vee \bar{c} \vee \bar{e})$, provided that no other clauses contain $\bar{c}$.

c) What erp rules, if any, are needed for those eliminations?

381. [*22*] Combining exercises 379 and 380, show that any one of the clauses in

$$(\bar{x}_1 \vee x_2) \wedge (\bar{x}_2 \vee x_3) \wedge \cdots \wedge (\bar{x}_{n-1} \vee x_n) \wedge (\bar{x}_n \vee x_1)$$

can be removed if there are no other clauses with negative literals. State the erp rules.

382. [*30*] Although the techniques in the preceding exercises are computationally difficult to apply, show that a lookahead forest based on the dependency digraph can be used to discover some of those simplifications efficiently.

▸ **383.** [*23*] (*Inprocessing.*) A SAT solver can partition its database of current clauses into two parts, the "hard" clauses Φ and the "soft" clauses Ψ. Initially Ψ is empty, while Φ is F, the set of all input clauses. Four kinds of changes are subsequently allowed:

• **Learning.** We can append a new soft clause C, provided that $\Phi \cup \Psi \cup C$ is satisfiable whenever $\Phi \cup \Psi$ is satisfiable.

• **Forgetting.** We can discard (purge) any soft clause.

• **Hardening.** We can reclassify any soft clause and call it hard.

• **Softening.** We can reclassify any hard clause C and call it soft, provided that Φ is satisfiable whenever $\Phi \setminus C$ is satisfiable. In this case we also should output any necessary erp rules, which change the settings of variables in such a way that any solution to $\Phi \setminus C$ becomes a solution to Φ.

a) Prove that, throughout any such procedure, F is satisfiable $\iff \Phi$ is satisfiable $\iff \Phi \cup \Psi$ is satisfiable.

b) Furthermore, given any solution to Φ, we obtain a solution to F by applying the erp rules in reverse order.

c) What is wrong with the following scenario? Start with one hard clause, (x), and no soft clauses. Reclassify (x) as soft, using the erp rule $x \leftarrow 1$. Then append a new soft clause $(\bar{x})$.

d) If C is certifiable for Φ (see exercise 385), can we safely learn C?

e) If C is certifiable for $\Phi \setminus C$, can we safely forget C?

f) In what cases is it legitimate to discard a clause, hard or soft, that is subsumed by another clause, hard or soft?

g) In what cases is self-subsumption permissible?

h) Explain how to eliminate all clauses that involve a particular variable x.

i) Show that, if z is a new variable, we can safely learn the three new soft clauses $(x \vee z)$, $(y \vee z)$, $(\bar{x} \vee \bar{y} \vee \bar{z})$ in Tseytin's concept of extended resolution.

384. [*25*] Continuing the previous exercise, show that we can always safely forget any clause C that contains a literal l for which $C \diamond C'$ is certifiable for $\Phi \setminus C$ whenever $C' \in \Phi$ contains $\bar{l}$. What erp rule is appropriate?

385. [*22*] Clause C is called *certifiable* for a set of clauses F if $F \wedge \overline{C} \vdash_1 \epsilon$, as in (119). It is said to be *absorbed* by F if it is nonempty and $F \wedge \overline{C \setminus l} \vdash_1 l$ for every $l \in C$, or if it is empty and $F \vdash_1 \epsilon$. (Every clause of F is obviously absorbed by F.)

a) True or false: If C is absorbed by F, it is certifiable for F.

b) Which of $\{\bar{1}, \bar{1}2, \bar{1}23\}$ are implied by, certifiable for, or absorbed by R' in (7)?

c) If C is certifiable for F and if all clauses of F are absorbed by F', prove that C is certifiable for F'.

d) If C is absorbed by F and if all clauses of F are absorbed by F', prove that C is absorbed by F'.

▶ **386.** [*M31*] Let Algorithm C_0 be a variant of Algorithm C that (i) makes all decisions at random; (ii) never forgets a learned clause; and (iii) restarts whenever a new clause has been learned. (Thus, step C5 ignores M_p and M_f; step C6 chooses l uniformly at random from among the $2(n-F)$ currently unassigned literals; step C8 backjumps while $F > i_1$, instead of while $F > i_{d'+1}$; and after step C9 has stored a new clause, with $d > 0$, it simply sets $d \leftarrow 0$ and returns to C5. The data structures HEAP, HLOC, OVAL, ACT are no longer used.) We will prove that Algorithm C_0 is, nevertheless, quite powerful.

In the remainder of this exercise, F denotes the set of clauses known by Algorithm C_0, both original and learned; in particular, the unit clauses of F will be the first literals $L_0, L_1, \ldots, L_{i_1-1}$ on the trail. If C is any clause and if $l \in C$, we define

$$\mathrm{score}(F, C, l) = \begin{cases} \infty, & \text{if } F \wedge \overline{C \setminus l} \vdash_1 l; \\ |\{l' \mid F \wedge \overline{C \setminus l} \vdash_1 l'\}|, & \text{otherwise.} \end{cases}$$

Thus $\mathrm{score}(F, C, l)$ represents the total number of literals on the trail after making all the unforced decisions of $\overline{C \setminus l}$, if no conflict arises. We say that Algorithm C_0 performs a "helpful round" for C and l if (i) every decision literal belongs to $\overline{C}$; and (ii) $\overline{l}$ is chosen as a decision literal only if the other elements of $\overline{C}$ are already in the trail.

a) Let C be certifiable for F, and suppose that $\mathrm{score}(F, C, l) < \infty$ for some $l \in C$. Prove that if F' denotes F together with a clause learned on a round that's helpful for C and l, then $\mathrm{score}(F', C, l) > \mathrm{score}(F, C, l)$.

b) Furthermore $\mathrm{score}(F', C, l) \geq \mathrm{score}(F, C, l)$ after an unhelpful round.

c) Therefore C will be absorbed by the set F' of known clauses after at most $|C|n$ helpful rounds have occurred.

d) If $|C| = k$, show that $\Pr(\text{helpful round}) \geq (k - 1)!/(2n)^k \geq 1/(4n^k)$.

e) Consequently, by exercise 385(c), if there exists a certificate of unsatisfiability $(C_1, \ldots, C_t)$ for a family of clauses F with n variables, Algorithm C_0 will prove F unsatisfiable after learning an average of $\mu \leq 4\sum_{i=1}^{t} |C_i|n^{1+|C_i|}$ clauses. (And it will q.s. need to learn at most $\mu n \ln n$ clauses, by exercise MPR–102.)

▶ **387.** [*21*] Graph G is said to be *embedded* in graph G' if every vertex v of G corresponds to a distinct vertex v' of G', where $u' \!\!-\!\! v'$ in G' whenever $u \!\!-\!\! v$ in G. Explain how to construct clauses that are satisfiable if and only if G can be embedded in G'.

388. [*20*] Show that the problems of deciding whether or not a given graph G (a) contains a k-clique, (b) can be k-colored, or (c) has a Hamiltonian cycle can all be regarded as graph embedding problems.

▶ **389.** [*22*] In this 4×4 diagram, it's possible to trace out the phrase 'THE␣ART␣OF␣COMPUTER␣PROGRAMMING' by making only king moves and knight moves, *except* for the final step from N to G.

Rearrange the letters so that the entire phrase can be traced.

N	T	E	F
H	I	R	␣
U	P	O	A
M	M	C	G

▶ **390.** [*23*] Let G be a graph with vertices V, edges E, $|E| = m$, $|V| = n$, and $s, t \in V$.

a) Construct $O(kn)$ clauses that are satisfiable if and only if there's a path of length k or less from s to t, given k.

b) Construct $O(m)$ clauses that are satisfiable if and only if there's at least one path from s to t.

c) Construct $O(n^2)$ clauses that are satisfiable if and only if G is connected.

d) Construct $O(km)$ clauses that are *unsatisfiable* if and only if there's a path of length k or less from s to t, given k.

e) Construct $O(m)$ clauses that are *unsatisfiable* if and only if there's at least one path from s to t.

f) Construct $O(m)$ clauses that are *unsatisfiable* if and only if G is connected. (This construction is much better than (c), in a sparse graph.)

391. [*M25*] The values of two integer variables satisfy $0 \le x, y < d$, and they are to be represented as l-bit quantities $x_{l-1} \ldots x_0$, $y_{l-1} \ldots y_0$, where $l = \lceil \lg d \rceil$. Specify three different ways to encode the relation $x \ne y$:

a) Let $x = (x_{l-1} \ldots x_0)_2$ and $y = (y_{l-1} \ldots y_0)_2$; and let the encoding enforce the conditions $(x_{l-1} \ldots x_0)_2 < d$, and $(y_{l-1} \ldots y_0)_2 < d$, as well as ensuring that $x \ne y$ by introducing $2l + 1$ additional clauses in l auxiliary variables.

b) Like (a), but there are d additional clauses (not $2l + 1$), and no auxiliaries.

c) All bit patterns $x_{l-1} \ldots x_0$ and $y_{l-1} \ldots y_0$ are valid, but some values might have two different patterns. The encoding has d clauses and no auxiliary variables.

392. [*22*] The blank spaces in the following diagrams can be filled with letters in such a way that all occurrences of the same letter are rookwise connected:

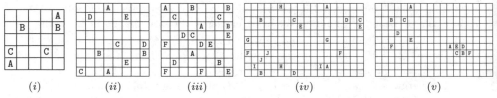

(*i*) (*ii*) (*iii*) (*iv*) (*v*)

a) Demonstrate how to do it. (Puzzle (*i*) is easy; the others less so.)

b) Similarly, solve the following puzzles — but use *kingwise* connectedness instead.

  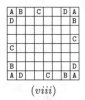

(*vi*) (*vii*) (*viii*)

c) Construct clauses with which a SAT solver can solve general puzzles of this kind: Given a graph G and disjoint sets of vertices $T_1, T_2, \ldots, T_t$, a solution should exhibit disjoint *connected* sets of vertices $S_1, S_2, \ldots, S_t$, with $T_j \subseteq S_j$ for $1 \le j \le t$.

393. [*25*] (T. R. Dawson, 1911.) Show that it's possible for each white piece in the accompanying chess diagram to capture the corresponding black piece, via a path that doesn't intersect any of the other paths. How can SAT help to solve this problem?

394. [*25*] One way to encode the at-most-one constraint $S_{\le 1}(y_1, \ldots, y_p)$ is to introduce $l = \lceil \lg p \rceil$ auxiliary variables together with the following $nl + n - 2^l$ clauses, which essentially "broadcast" the value of j when y_j becomes true:

$$(\bar{y}_j \vee (-1)^{b_t} a_t) \quad \text{for } 1 \le j \le p,\ 1 \le t \le q = \lfloor \lg(2p - j) \rfloor, \text{ where } 2p - j = (1b_1 \ldots b_q)_2.$$

For example, the clauses when $p = 3$ are $(\bar{y}_1 \vee a_1) \wedge (\bar{y}_1 \vee \bar{a}_2) \wedge (\bar{y}_2 \vee a_1) \wedge (\bar{y}_2 \vee a_2) \wedge (\bar{y}_3 \vee \bar{a}_1)$.

Experiment with this encoding by applying it to Langford's problem, using it in place of (13) whenever $p \ge 7$.

395. [*20*] What clauses should replace (15), (16), and (17) if we want to use the order encoding for a graph coloring problem?

▶ **396.** [*23*] (*Double clique hints.*) If x has one of the d values $\{0, 1, \ldots, d - 1\}$, we can represent it binarywise with respect to *two* different orderings by letting $x^j = [x \geq j]$ and $\hat{x}^j = [x\pi \geq j]$ for $1 \leq j < d$, where π is any given permutation. For example, if $d = 4$ and $(0\pi, 1\pi, 2\pi, 3\pi) = (2, 3, 0, 1)$, the representations $x^1 x^2 x^3 : \hat{x}^1 \hat{x}^2 \hat{x}^3$ of 0, 1, 2, and 3 are respectively 000:110, 100:111, 110:000, and 111:100. This double ordering allows us to encode graph coloring problems by including not only the hints (162) but also

$$(\overline{\hat{v}_1^{d-k+1}} \vee \cdots \vee \overline{\hat{v}_k^{d-k+1}}) \wedge (\hat{v}_1^{k-1} \vee \cdots \vee \hat{v}_k^{k-1}),$$

whenever the vertices $\{v_1, \ldots, v_k\}$ form a k-clique.

Explain how to construct clauses for this encoding, and experiment with coloring the $n \times n$ queens graph when $(0\pi, 1\pi, 2\pi, 3\pi, 4\pi, \ldots) = (0, d{-}1, 1, d{-}2, 2, \ldots)$ is the inverse of the organ-pipe permutation.

▶ **397.** [*22*] (N. Tamura, 2014.) Suppose $x_0, x_1, \ldots, x_{p-1}$ are integer variables with the range $0 \leq x_i < d$, represented in order encoding by Boolean variables $x_i^j = [x_i \geq j]$ for $0 \leq i < p$ and $1 \leq j < d$. Show that the *all-different* constraint, "$x_i \neq x_j$ for $0 \leq i < j < p$," can be nicely encoded by introducing auxiliary integer variables y_0, $y_1, \ldots, y_{d-1}$ with the range $0 \leq y_j < p$, represented in order encoding by Boolean variables $y_j^i = [y_j \geq i]$ for $1 \leq i < p$ and $0 \leq j < d$, and by devising clauses to enforce the condition $x_i = j \implies y_j = i$. Furthermore, hints analogous to (162) can be given.

398. [*18*] Continuing exercise 397, what's an appropriate way to enforce the all-different constraint when $x_0, \ldots, x_{p-1}$ are represented in the *direct* encoding?

▶ **399.** [*23*] If the variables u and v range over d values $\{1, \ldots, d\}$, it's natural to encode them directly as sequences $u_1 \ldots u_d$ and $v_1 \ldots v_d$, where $u_i = [u = i]$ and $v_j = [v = j]$, using the at-least-one clauses (15) and the at-most-one clauses (17). A *binary constraint* tells us which pairs (i, j) are legal; for example, the graph-coloring constraint says that $i \neq j$ when i and j are the colors of adjacent vertices in some graph.

One way to specify such a constraint is to assert the *preclusion clauses* $(\bar{u}_i \vee \bar{v}_j)$ for all *illegal* pairs (i, j), as we did for graph coloring in (16). But there's also another general way: We can assert the *support clauses*

$$\bigwedge_{i=1}^{d} \left(\bar{u}_i \vee \bigvee \{v_j \mid (i, j) \text{ is legal}\} \right) \wedge \bigwedge_{j=1}^{d} \left(\bar{v}_j \vee \bigvee \{u_i \mid (i, j) \text{ is legal}\} \right)$$

instead. Graph coloring with d colors would then be represented by clauses such as $(\bar{u}_3 \vee v_1 \vee v_2 \vee v_4 \vee \cdots \vee v_d)$, when u and v are adjacent.

a) Suppose t of the d^2 pairs (i, j) are legal. How many preclusion clauses are needed? How many support clauses?

b) Prove that the support clauses are always at least as strong as the preclusion clauses, in the sense that all consequences of the preclusion clauses under unit propagation are also consequences of the support clauses under unit propagation, given any partial assignment to the binary variables $\{u_1, \ldots, u_d, v_1, \ldots, v_d\}$.

c) Conversely, in the case of the graph-coloring constraint, the preclusion clauses are also at least as strong as the support clauses (hence equally strong).

d) However, exhibit a binary constraint for which the support clauses are strictly stronger than the preclusion clauses.

400. [*25*] Experiment with preclusion clauses versus support clauses by applying them to the n queens problem. Use Algorithms L, C, and W for comparison.

401. [*16*] If x has the unary representation $x^1 x^2 \ldots x^{d-1}$, what is the unary representation of (a) $y = \lceil x/2 \rceil$? (b) $z = \lfloor (x + 1)/3 \rfloor$?

402. [*18*] If x has the unary representation $x^1 x^2 \ldots x^{d-1}$, encode the further condition that x is (a) even; (b) odd.

403. [*20*] Suppose x, y, z have the order encoding, with $0 \le x, y, z < d$. What clauses enforce (a) $\min(x, y) \le z$? (b) $\max(x, y) \le z$? (c) $\min(x, y) \ge z$? (d) $\max(x, y) \ge z$?

▶ **404.** [*21*] Continuing exercise 403, encode the condition $|x - y| \ge a$, for a given constant $a \ge 1$, using $d + 1 - a$ clauses of length ≤ 4 and no auxiliary variables.

▶ **405.** [*M23*] The purpose of this exercise is to encode the constraint $ax + by \le c$, when a, b, c are integer constants, assuming that x, y are order-encoded with range $[0 .. d)$.
  a) Prove that it suffices to consider cases where $a, b, c > 0$.
  b) Exhibit a suitable encoding for the special case $13x - 8y \le 7$, $d = 8$.
  c) Exhibit a suitable encoding for the special case $13x - 8y \ge 1$, $d = 8$.
  d) Specify an encoding that works for general a, b, c, d.

406. [*M24*] Order-encode (a) $xy \le a$ and (b) $xy \ge a$, when a is an integer constant.

▶ **407.** [*M22*] If x, y, z are order-encoded, with $0 \le x, y < d$ and $0 \le z < 2d - 1$, the clauses

$$\bigwedge_{k=1}^{2d-2} \bigwedge_{j=\max(0, k+1-d)}^{k} (\bar{x}^j \vee \bar{y}^{k-j} \vee z^k)$$

are satisfiable if and only if $x + y \le z$; this is the basic idea underlying (20). Another way to encode the same relation is to introduce new order-encoded variables u and v, and to construct clauses for the relations $\lfloor x/2 \rfloor + \lfloor y/2 \rfloor \le u$ and $\lceil x/2 \rceil + \lceil y/2 \rceil \le v$, recursively using methods for numbers less than $\lceil d/2 \rceil$ and $\lfloor d/2 \rfloor + 1$. Then we can finish the job by letting $z^1 = v^1$, $z^{2d-2} = v^d$ (d even) or u^{d-1} (d odd), and appending the clauses

$$(\bar{u}^j \vee z^{2j}) \wedge (\bar{v}^{j+1} \vee z^{2j}) \wedge (\bar{u}^j \vee \bar{v}^{j+1} \vee z^{2j+1}), \quad \text{for } 1 \le j \le d - 2.$$

  a) Explain why the alternative method is valid.
  b) For what values of d does that method produce fewer clauses?
  c) Consider analogous methods for the relation $x + y \ge z$.

▶ **408.** [*25*] (*Open shop scheduling.*) Consider a system of m machines and n jobs, together with an $m \times n$ matrix of nonnegative integer weights $W = (w_{ij})$ that represent the amount of uninterrupted time on machine i that is needed by job j.

The open shop scheduling problem seeks a way to get all the work done in t units of time, without assigning two jobs simultaneously to the same machine and without having two machines simultaneously assigned to the same job. We want to minimize t, which is called the "makespan" of the schedule.

For example, suppose $m = n = 3$ and $W = \begin{pmatrix} 703 \\ 172 \\ 235 \end{pmatrix}$. A "greedy" algorithm, which repeatedly fills the lexicographically smallest time slot (t, i, j) such that $w_{ij} > 0$ but neither machine i nor job j have yet been scheduled at time t, achieves a makespan of 12 with the following schedule:

M1:			J1		J3		
M2:		J2			J1	J3	
M3:		J3			J2		J1

  a) Is 12 the optimum makespan for this W?
  b) Prove that the greedy algorithm always produces a schedule whose makespan is less than $(\max_{i=1}^{m} \sum_{j=1}^{n} w_{ij}) + (\max_{j=1}^{n} \sum_{i=1}^{m} w_{ij})$, unless W is entirely zero.

c) Suppose machine i begins to work on job j at time s_{ij}, when $w_{ij} > 0$. What conditions should these starting times satisfy, in order to achieve the makespan t?

d) Show that the *order encoding* of these variables s_{ij} yields SAT clauses that nicely represent any open shop scheduling problem.

e) Let $\lfloor W/k \rfloor$ be the matrix obtained by replacing each element w_{ij} of W by $\lfloor w_{ij}/k \rfloor$. Prove that if the open shop scheduling problem for $\lfloor W/k \rfloor$ and t is unsatisfiable, so is the problem for W and kt.

▶ **409.** [*M26*] Continuing exercise 408, find the best makespans in the following cases:

a) $m = 3$, $n = 3r + 1$; $w_{1j} = w_{2(r+j)} = w_{3(2r+j)} = a_j$ for $1 \le j \le r$; $w_{1n} = w_{2n} = w_{3n} = \lfloor (a_1 + \cdots + a_r)/2 \rfloor$; otherwise $w_{ij} = 0$. (The positive integers a_j are given.)

b) $m = 4$, $n = r + 2$; $w_{1j} = (r+1)a_j$ and $w_{2j} = 1$ for $1 \le j \le r$; $w_{2(n-1)} = w_{2n} = (r+1)\lfloor (a_1 + \cdots + a_r)/2 \rfloor$; $w_{3(n-1)} = w_{4n} = w_{2n} + r$; otherwise $w_{ij} = 0$.

c) $m = n$; $w_{jj} = n - 2$, $w_{jn} = w_{nj} = 1$ for $1 \le j < n$; otherwise $w_{ij} = 0$.

d) $m = 2$; $w_{1j} = a_j$ and $w_{2j} = b_j$ for $1 \le j \le n$, where $a_1 + \cdots + a_n = b_1 + \cdots + b_n = s$ and $a_j + b_j \le s$ for $1 \le j \le n$.

410. [*24*] Exhibit clauses for the constraint $13x - 8y \le 7$ when x and y are *log-encoded* as 3-bit integers $x = (x_2 x_1 x_0)_2$ and $y = (y_2 y_1 y_0)_2$. (Compare with exercise 405(b).)

▶ **411.** [*25*] If $x = (x_m \ldots x_1)_2$, $y = (y_n \ldots y_1)_2$, and $z = (z_{m+n} \ldots z_1)_2$ stand for binary numbers, the text explains how to encode the relation $xy = z$ with fewer than $20mn$ clauses, using Napier–Dadda multiplication. Explain how to encode the relations $xy \le z$ and $xy \ge z$ with fewer than $9mn$ and $11mn$ clauses, respectively.

412. [*40*] Experiment with the encoding of somewhat large numbers by using a radix-d representation in which each digit has the order encoding.

413. [*M22*] Find all CNF formulas for the function $(x_1 \oplus y_1) \vee \cdots \vee (x_n \oplus y_n)$.

414. [*M20*] How many clauses will remain after the auxiliary variables $a_1, \ldots, a_{n-1}$ of (169) have been eliminated by resolution?

▶ **415.** [*M22*] Generalize (169) to an encoding of lexicographic order on d-ary vectors, $(x_1 \ldots x_n)_d \le (y_1 \ldots y_n)_d$, where each $x_k = x_k^1 + \cdots + x_k^{d-1}$ and $y_k = y_k^1 + \cdots + y_k^{d-1}$ has the order encoding. What modifications to your construction will encode the *strict* relation $x_1 \ldots x_n < y_1 \ldots y_n$?

416. [*20*] Encode the condition 'if $x_1 \ldots x_n = y_1 \ldots y_n$ then $u_1 \ldots u_m = v_1 \ldots v_m$', using $2m + 2n + 1$ clauses and $n + 1$ auxiliary variables. *Hint:* $2n$ of the clauses are in (172).

417. [*21*] Continuing exercise 42, what is the Tseytin encoding of the ternary mux operation '$s \,?\, t : u : v$'? Use it to justify the translation of branching programs via (173).

418. [*23*] Use a branching program to construct clauses that are satisfiable if and only if (x_{ij}) is an $m \times n$ Boolean matrix whose rows satisfy the hidden weighted bit function h_n and whose columns satisfy the complementary function $\bar{h}_m$. In other words,

$$r_i = \sum_{j=1}^{n} x_{ij}, \quad c_j = \sum_{i=1}^{m} x_{ij}, \quad \text{and} \quad x_{i r_i} = 1, \ x_{c_j j} = 0, \quad \text{assuming that } x_{i0} = x_{0j} = 0.$$

419. [*M21*] If $m, n \ge 3$, find (by hand) all solutions to the problem of exercise 418 such that (a) $\sum x_{ij} = m + 1$ (the minimum); (b) $\sum x_{ij} = mn - n - 1$ (the maximum).

420. [*18*] Derive (175) mechanically (that is, "without thinking") from the Boolean chain $s \leftarrow x_1 \oplus x_2$, $c \leftarrow x_1 \wedge x_2$, $t \leftarrow s \oplus x_3$, $c' \leftarrow s \wedge x_3$, requiring $c = c' = 0$.

421. [*18*] Derive (176) mechanically from the branching program $I_5 = (\bar{1}?\,4\!:3)$, $I_4 = (\bar{2}?\,1\!:2)$, $I_3 = (\bar{2}?\,2\!:0)$, $I_2 = (\bar{3}?\,1\!:0)$, beginning at I_5.

422. [*11*] What does unit propagation deduce when the additional clause (x_1) or (x_2) is appended to (a) F in (175)? (b) G in (176)?

423. [*22*] A representation F that satisfies a condition like (180) but with l replaced by ϵ can be called "weakly forcing." Exercise 422 shows that (175) and (176) are weakly forcing. Does the BDD of *every* function define a weakly forcing encoding, via (173)?

▶ **424.** [*20*] The dual of the Pi function has the prime clauses $\{\overline{123}, \overline{134}, 2\overline{34}, 234, 12\}$ (see 7.1.1–(30)). Can any of them be omitted from a forcing representation?

425. [*18*] A clause with exactly one positive literal is called a definite Horn clause, and Algorithm 7.1.1C computes the "core" of such clauses. If F consists of definite Horn clauses, prove that x is in the core if and only if $F \vdash_1 x$, if and only if $F \wedge (\bar{x}) \vdash_1 \epsilon$.

▶ **426.** [*M20*] Suppose F is a set of clauses that represent $f(x_1, \ldots, x_n)$ using auxiliary variables $\{a_1, \ldots, a_m\}$ as in (170), where $m > 0$. Let G be the clauses that result after variable a_m has been eliminated as in (112).

   a) True or false: If F is forcing then G is forcing.

   b) True or false: If F is not forcing then G is not forcing.

427. [*M30*] Exhibit a function $f(x_1, \ldots, x_n)$ for which every set of forcing clauses that uses no auxiliary variables has size $\Omega(3^n/n^2)$, although f can actually be represented by a *polynomial* number of forcing clauses when auxiliary variables are introduced. *Hint:* See exercise 7.1.1–116.

428. [*M27*] A generic graph G on vertices $\{1, \ldots, n\}$ can be characterized by $\binom{n}{2}$ Boolean variables $X = \{x_{ij} \mid 1 \le i < j \le n\}$, where $x_{ij} = [i\!-\!j \text{ in } G]$. Properties of G can therefore be regarded as Boolean functions, $f(X)$.

   a) Let $f_{nd}(X) = [\chi(G) \le d]$; that is, f_{nd} is true if and only if G has a d-coloring. Construct clauses F_{nd} that represent the function $f_{nd}(X) \vee y$, using auxiliary variables $Z = \{z_{jk} \mid 1 \le j \le n, \ 1 \le k \le d\}$ that mean "vertex j has color k."

   b) Let G_{nd} be a forcing representation of the Boolean function $F_{nd}(X, y, Z)$, and suppose that G_{nd} has M clauses in N variables. (These N variables should include the $\binom{n}{2} + 1 + nd$ variables of F_{nd}, along with an arbitrary number of additional auxiliaries.) Explain how to construct a monotone Boolean chain of cost $O(MN^2)$ for the function $\bar{f}_{nd}$ (see exercise 7.1.2–84), given the clauses of G_{nd}.

Note: Noga Alon and Ravi B. Boppana, *Combinatorica* **7** (1987), 1–22, proved that every monotone chain for this function has length $\exp \Omega((n/\log n)^{1/3})$ when $d + 1 = \lfloor (n/\lg n)^{2/3}/4 \rfloor$. Hence M and N cannot both be of polynomial size.

429. [*22*] Prove that Bailleux and Boufkhad's clauses (20), (21) are forcing: If any r of the x's have been set to 1, then unit propagation will force all the others to 0.

430. [*25*] Similarly, Sinz's clauses (18) and (19) are forcing.

▶ **431.** [*20*] Construct efficient, forcing clauses for the relation $x_1 + \cdots + x_m \le y_1 + \cdots + y_n$.

432. [*24*] Exercise 404 gives clauses for the relation $|x - y| \ge a$. Are they forcing?

▶ **433.** [*25*] Are the lexicographic-constraint clauses in (169) forcing?

434. [*21*] Let L_l be the language defined by the regular expression $0^*1^l0^*$; in other words, the binary string $x_1 \ldots x_n$ is in L_l if and only if it consists of zero or more 0s followed by exactly l 1s followed by zero or more 0s.

   a) Explain why the following clauses are satisfiable if and only if $x_1 \ldots x_n \in L_l$: (i) $(\bar{p}_k \vee \bar{x}_k)$, $(\bar{p}_k \vee p_{k-1})$, and $(\bar{p}_{k-1} \vee x_k \vee p_k)$ for $1 \le k \le n$, also (p_0); (ii) $(\bar{q}_k \vee \bar{x}_k)$,

$(\bar{q}_k \vee q_{k+1})$, and $(\bar{q}_{k+1} \vee x_k \vee q_k)$ for $1 \le k \le n$, also (q_{n+1}); (iii) $(\bar{r}_k \vee p_{k-1}) \wedge \bigwedge_{0 \le d < l}(\bar{r}_k \vee x_{k+d}) \wedge (\bar{r}_k \vee q_{k+l})$ for $1 \le k \le n+1-l$, also $(r_1 \vee \cdots \vee r_{n+1-l})$.

　　b) Show that those clauses are forcing when $l = 1$ but not when $l = 2$.

▶ **435.** [*28*] Given $l \ge 2$, construct a set of $O(n \log l)$ clauses that characterize the language L_l of exercise 434 and are forcing.

436. [*M32*] (*Nondeterministic finite-state automata.*) A regular language L on the alphabet A can be defined in the following well-known way: Let Q be a finite set of "states," and let $I \subseteq Q$ and $O \subseteq Q$ be designated "input states" and "output states." Also let $T \subseteq Q \times A \times Q$ be a set of "transition rules." Then the string $x_1 \ldots x_n$ is in L if and only if there's a sequence of states $q_0, q_1, \ldots, q_n$ such that $q_0 \in I$, $(q_{k-1}, x_k, q_k) \in T$ for $1 \le k \le n$, and $q_n \in O$.

　　Given such a definition, where $A = \{0, 1\}$, use auxiliary variables to construct clauses that are satisfiable if and only if $x_1 \ldots x_n \in L$. The clauses should be forcing, and there should be at most $O(n|T|)$ of them.

　　As an example, write out the clauses for the language $L_2 = 0^* 1^2 0^*$ of exercise 434.

437. [*M21*] Extend exercise 436 to the general case where A has more than two letters.

438. [*21*] Construct a set of forcing clauses that are satisfiable if and only if a given binary string $x_1 \ldots x_n$ contains exactly t runs of 1s, having lengths $(l_1, l_2, \ldots, l_t)$ from left to right. (Equivalently, the string $x_1 \ldots x_n$ should belong to the language defined by the regular expression $0^* 1^{l_1} 0^+ 1^{l_2} 0^+ \ldots 0^+ 1^{l_t} 0^*$.)

▶ **439.** [*30*] Find efficient forcing clauses for the constraint that $x_1 + \cdots + x_n = t$ and that there are no two consecutive 1s. (This is the special case $l_1 = \cdots = l_t = 1$ of the previous exercise, but a much simpler construction is possible.)

440. [*M33*] Extend exercise 436 to *context free languages*, which can be defined by a set $S \subseteq N$ and by production rules U and W of the following well-known forms: $U \subseteq \{P \to a \mid P \in N, a \in A\}$ and $W \subseteq \{P \to QR \mid P, Q, R \in N\}$, where N is a set of "nonterminal symbols." A string $x_1 \ldots x_n$ with each $x_j \in A$ belongs to the language if and only if it can be produced from a nonterminal symbol $P \in S$.

441. [*M35*] Show that any threshold function $f(x_1, \ldots, x_n) = [w_1 x_1 + \cdots + w_n x_n \ge t]$ has a forcing representation whose size is polynomial in $\log|w_1| + \cdots + \log|w_n|$.

▶ **442.** [*M27*] The unit propagation relation $\vdash_1$ can be generalized to kth order propagation $\vdash_k$ as follows: Let F be a family of clauses and let l be a literal. If $(l_1, l_2, \ldots, l_p)$ is a sequence of literals, we write $L_q^- = \{l_1, \ldots, l_{q-1}, \bar{l}_q\}$ for $1 \le q \le p$. Then

$$F \vdash_0 l \iff \epsilon \in F;$$

$$F \vdash_{k+1} l \iff F | L_1^- \vdash_k \epsilon, \; F | L_2^- \vdash_k \epsilon, \; \ldots, \; \text{and } F | L_p^- \vdash_k \epsilon$$
$$\text{for some strictly distinct literals } l_1, l_2, \ldots, l_p \text{ with } l_p = l;$$

$$F \vdash_k \epsilon \iff F \vdash_k l \text{ and } F \vdash_k \bar{l} \text{ for some literal } l.$$

　　a) Verify that $\vdash_1$ corresponds to unit propagation according to this definition.

　　b) Describe $\vdash_2$ informally, using the concept of "failed literals."

　　c) Prove that $F \vdash_k \epsilon$ or $F \vdash_k \bar{l}$ implies $F | l \vdash_k \epsilon$ for all literals l, and furthermore that $F \vdash_k \epsilon$ implies $F \vdash_{k+1} \epsilon$, for all $k \ge 0$.

　　d) True or false: $F \vdash_k l$ implies $F \vdash_{k+1} l$.

　　e) Let $L_k(F) = \{l \mid F \vdash_k l\}$. What is $L_k(R')$, where R' appears in (7) and $k \ge 0$?

　　f) Given $k \ge 1$, explain how to compute $L_k(F)$ and $F | L_k(F)$ in $O(n^{2k-1}m)$ steps, when F has m clauses in n variables.

443. [*M24*] (*A hierarchy of hardness.*) Continuing the previous exercise, a family of clauses F is said to belong to class UC_k if it has the property that

$$F \,|\, L \vdash \epsilon \text{ implies } F \,|\, L \vdash_k \epsilon \qquad \text{for all sets of strictly distinct literals } L.$$

("Whenever a partial assignment yields unsatisfiable clauses, the inconsistency can be detected by kth order propagation.") And F is said to belong to class PC_k if

$$F \,|\, L \vdash l \text{ implies } F \,|\, L \vdash_k l \qquad \text{for all sets of strictly distinct literals } L \cup l.$$

a) Prove that $\mathrm{PC}_0 \subset \mathrm{UC}_0 \subset \mathrm{PC}_1 \subset \mathrm{UC}_1 \subset \mathrm{PC}_2 \subset \mathrm{UC}_2 \subset \cdots$, where the set inclusions are strict (each class is contained in but unequal to its successor).
b) Describe all families F that belong to the smallest class, PC_0.
c) Give interesting examples of families in the next smallest class, UC_0.
d) True or false: If F contains n variables, $F \in \mathrm{PC}_n$.
e) True or false: If F contains n variables, $F \in \mathrm{UC}_{n-1}$.
f) Where do the clauses R' of (7) fall in the hierarchy?

444. [*M26*] The following *single lookahead unit resolution* algorithm, called SLUR, returns either 'sat', 'unsat', or 'maybe', depending on whether a given set F of clauses is satisfiable, unsatisfiable, or beyond its ability to decide via easy propagations:

E1. [Propagate.] If $F \vdash_1 \epsilon$, terminate ('unsat'). Otherwise set $F \leftarrow F \,|\, \{l \mid F \vdash_1 l\}$.

E2. [Satisfied?] If $F = \emptyset$, terminate ('sat'). Otherwise set l to any literal within F.

E3. [Lookahead and propagate.] If $F \,|\, l \nvdash_1 \epsilon$, set $F \leftarrow F \,|\, l \,|\, \{l' \mid F \,|\, l \vdash_1 l'\}$ and return to E2. Otherwise if $F \,|\, \bar{l} \nvdash_1 \epsilon$, $F \leftarrow F \,|\, \bar{l} \,|\, \{l' \mid F \,|\, \bar{l} \vdash_1 l'\}$ and return to E2. Otherwise terminate ('maybe'). ∎

Notice that this algorithm doesn't backtrack after committing itself in E2 to either l or $\bar{l}$.

a) If F consists of Horn clauses, possibly renamed (see exercise 7.1.1–55), prove that SLUR will never return 'maybe', regardless of how it chooses l in step E2.
b) Find four clauses F on three variables such that SLUR always returns 'sat', although F is *not* a set of possibly renamed Horn clauses.
c) Prove that SLUR never returns 'maybe' if and only if $F \in \mathrm{UC}_1$ (see exercise 443).
d) Explain how to implement SLUR in linear time with respect to total clause length.

▸ **445.** [*22*] Find short certificates of unsatisfiability for the pigeonhole clauses (106)–(107), when they are supplemented by (a) (181); (b) (182); (c) (183).

446. [*M10*] What's the maximum number of edges in a subgraph of $K_{m,n}$ that has girth ≥ 6? (Express your answer in terms of $Z(m,n)$.)

▸ **447.** [*22*] Determine the maximum number of edges in a girth-8 subgraph of $K_{8,8}$.

448. [*M25*] What is $Z(m,n)$ when m is odd and $n = m(m-1)/6$? *Hint:* See 6.5–(16).

449. [*21*] Exhibit $n \times n$ quad-free matrices that contain the maximum number of 1s and obey the lexicographic constraints (185), (186), for $8 \leq n \leq 16$.

450. [*25*] Prove that there is essentially only one 10×10 quad-free system of points and lines with 34 incidences. *Hint:* First show that every line must contain either 3 points or 4 points; hence every point must belong to either 3 lines or 4 lines.

▸ **451.** [*28*] Find a way to color the squares of a 10×10 board with three colors, so that no rectangle has four corners of the same color. Prove furthermore that every such "nonchromatic rectangle" board has the color distribution $\{34, 34, 32\}$, not $\{34, 33, 33\}$. But show that if any square of the board is removed, a nonchromatic rectangle is possible with 33 squares of each color.

452. [*34*] Find a nonchromatic rectangle with *four* colors on an 18×18 board.

453. [*M23*] An $m \times n$ matrix $X = (x_{ij})$ is said to be *decomposable* if it has row indices $R \subseteq \{1, \dots, m\}$ and column indices $C \subseteq \{1, \dots, n\}$ such that $0 < |R| + |C| < m + n$, with $x_{ij} = 0$ whenever $(i \in R$ and $j \notin C)$ or $(i \notin R$ and $j \in C)$. It represents a bipartite graph on the vertices $\{u_1, \dots, u_m\}$ and $\{v_1, \dots, v_n\}$, if $[u_i\!-\!v_j] = [x_{ij} \neq 0]$.

   a) Prove that X is indecomposable if and only if its bipartite graph is connected.
   b) The *direct sum* $X' \oplus X''$ of matrices X' and X'', where X' is $m' \times n'$ and X'' is $m'' \times n''$, is the $(m' + m'') \times (n' + n'')$ "block diagonal" matrix X that has X' in its upper left corner, X'' in the lower right corner, and zeros elsewhere (see 7–(40)). True or false: If the rows and columns of X' and X'' are nonnegative and lexicographically ordered as in (185) and (186), so are the rows and columns of X.
   c) Let X be any nonnegative matrix whose rows and columns are lexicographically nonincreasing, as in (185) and (186). True or false: X is decomposable if and only if X is a direct sum of smaller matrices X' and X''.

454. [*15*] If τ is an endomorphism for the solutions of f, show that $f(x) = f(x\tau)$ for every cyclic element x (every element that's in a cycle of τ).

455. [*M20*] Suppose we know that (187) is an endomorphism of some given clauses F on the variables $\{x_1, x_2, x_3, x_4\}$. Can we be sure that F is satisfiable if and only if $F \wedge C$ is satisfiable, when (a) $C = 1\bar{2}\bar{4}$, i.e., $C = (\bar{x}_1 \vee x_2 \vee \bar{x}_4)$? (b) $C = 2\bar{3}\bar{4}$? (c) $C = 123$? (d) $C = 1\bar{3}4$?

456. [*M21*] For how many functions $f(x_1, x_2, x_3, x_4)$ is (187) an endomorphism?

457. [*HM19*] Show that every Boolean $f(x_1, x_2, x_3, x_4)$ has more than 51 quadrillion endomorphisms, and an n-variable function has more than $2^{2^n(n-1)}$.

458. [*20*] The simplification of clauses by removing an autarky can be regarded as the exploitation of an endomorphism. Explain why.

▶ **459.** [*20*] Let X_{ij} denote the submatrix of X consisting of the first i rows and the first j columns. Show that the numbers sweep(X_{ij}) satisfy a simple recurrence, from which it's easy to compute sweep$(X) = $ sweep(X_{mn}).

460. [*21*] Given m, n, k, and r, construct clauses that are satisfied by an $m \times n$ binary matrix $X = (x_{ij})$ if and only if sweep$(X) \leq k$ and $\sum_{i,j} x_{ij} \geq r$.

461. [*20*] What additional clauses will rule out non-fixed points of τ_1 and τ_2?

462. [*M22*] Explain why τ_1, τ_2, and τ_3 preserve satisfiability in the sweep problem.

▶ **463.** [*M21*] Show that X is a fixed point of τ_1, τ_2, and τ_3 if and only if its rows and columns are nondecreasing. Therefore the maximum of $\nu X = \sum_{i,j} x_{ij}$ over all binary matrices of sweep k is a simple function of m, n, and k.

▶ **464.** [*M25*] Transformations τ_1 and τ_2 don't change the text's example 10×10 matrix. Prove that they will never change *any* 10×10 matrix of sweep 3 that has $\nu X = 51$.

465. [*M21*] Justify the text's rule for simultaneous endomorphisms in the perfect matching problem: Any perfect matching must lead to one that's fixed by every τ_{uv}.

466. [*M23*] Prove that when mn is even, the text's even-odd rule (190) for endomorphisms of $m \times n$ domino coverings has exactly one fixed point.

467. [*20*] Mutilate the 7×8 and 8×7 boards by removing the upper right and lower left cells. What domino coverings are fixed by all the even-odd endomorphisms like (190)?

468. [*20*] Experiment with the mutilated chessboard problem when the even-odd endomorphisms are modified so that (a) they use the *same* rule for all i and j; or (b) they each make an independent random choice between horizontal and vertical.

▶ **469.** [*M25*] Find a certificate of unsatisfiability $(C_1, C_2, \ldots, C_t)$ for the fact that an 8×8 chessboard minus cells $(1, 8)$ and $(8, 1)$ cannot be exactly covered by dominoes h_{ij} and v_{ij} that are fixed under all of the even-odd endomorphisms. Each C_k for $1 \le k < t$ should be a single positive literal. (Therefore the clauses for this problem belong to the relatively simple class PC_2 in the hierarchy of exercise 443.)

▶ **470.** [*M22*] Another class of endomorphisms, one for *every* 4-cycle, can also be used in perfect matching problems: Let the *vertices* (instead of the edges) be totally ordered in some fashion. Every 4-cycle can be written $v_0 — v_1 — v_2 — v_3 — v_0$, with $v_0 > v_1 > v_3$ and $v_0 > v_2$; the corresponding endomorphism changes any solution for which $v_0 v_1 = v_2 v_3 = 1$ by setting $v_0 v_1 \leftarrow v_2 v_3 \leftarrow 0$ and $v_1 v_2 \leftarrow v_3 v_0 \leftarrow 1$. Prove that every perfect matching leads to a fixed point of all these transformations.

471. [*16*] Find all fixed points of the mappings in exercise 470 when the graph is K_{2n}.

472. [*M25*] Prove that even-odd endomorphisms such as (190) in the domino covering problem can be regarded as instances of the endomorphisms in exercise 470.

▶ **473.** [*M23*] Generalize exercise 470 to endomorphisms for the unsatisfiable clauses of Tseytin's graph parity problems in exercise 245.

474. [*M20*] A signed permutation σ is a *symmetry* of $f(x)$ if and only if $f(x) = f(x\sigma)$ for all x, and it is an *antisymmetry* if and only if we have $f(x) = \bar{f}(x\sigma)$ for all x.
  a) How many signed permutations of n elements are possible?
  b) Write $75\bar{1}\bar{4}\bar{2}63$ in cycle form, as an unsigned permutation of $\{1, \ldots, 7, \bar{1}, \ldots, \bar{7}\}$.
  c) For how many functions f of four variables is $\bar{4}13\bar{2}$ a symmetry?
  d) For how many functions f of four variables is $\bar{4}13\bar{2}$ an antisymmetry?
  e) For how many $f(x_1, \ldots, x_7)$ is $75\bar{1}\bar{4}\bar{2}63$ a symmetry or antisymmetry?

475. [*M22*] Continuing exercise 474, a Boolean function is called *asymmetric* if the identity is its only symmetry; it is *totally asymmetric* if it is asymmetric and has no antisymmetries.
  a) If f is totally asymmetric, how many functions are equivalent to f under the operations of permuting variables, complementing variables, and/or complementing the function?
  b) According to (a) and 7.1.1–(95), the function $(x \lor y) \land (x \oplus z)$ is not totally asymmetric. What is its nontrivial symmetry?
  c) Prove that if f is not asymmetric, it has an automorphism of prime order p.
  d) Show that if $(uvw)(\bar{u}\bar{v}\bar{w})$ is a symmetry of f, so is $(uv)(\bar{u}\bar{v})$.
  e) Make a similar statement if f has a symmetry of the form $(uvwxy)(\bar{u}\bar{v}\bar{w}\bar{x}\bar{y})$.
  f) Conclude that, if $n \le 5$, the Boolean function $f(x_1, \ldots, x_n)$ is totally asymmetric if and only if no signed involution is a symmetry or antisymmetry of f.
  g) However, exhibit a counterexample to that statement when $n = 6$.

476. [*M23*] For $n \le 5$, find Boolean functions of n variables that are (a) asymmetric but not totally asymmetric; (b) totally asymmetric. Furthermore, your functions should be the easiest to evaluate (in the sense of having a smallest possible Boolean chain), among all functions that qualify. *Hint:* Combine exercises 475 and 477.

▶ **477.** [*23*] (*Optimum Boolean evaluation.*) Construct clauses that are satisfiable if and only if there is an r-step normal Boolean chain that computes m given functions g_1,

..., g_m on n variables. (For example, if $n = 3$ and $g_1 = \langle x_1 x_2 x_3 \rangle$, $g_2 = x_1 \oplus x_2 \oplus x_3$, such clauses with $r = 4$ and 5 enable a SAT solver to discover a "full adder" of minimum cost; see 7.1.2–(1) and 7.1.2–(22).) *Hint:* Represent each bit of the truth tables.

▶ **478.** [*23*] Suggest ways to break symmetry in the clauses of exercise 477.

▶ **479.** [*25*] Use SAT technology to find optimum circuits for the following problems:

  a) Compute z_2, z_1, and z_0, when $x_1 + x_2 + x_3 + x_4 = (z_2 z_1 z_0)_2$ (see 7.1.2–(27)).

  b) Compute z_2, z_1, and z_0, when $x_1 + x_2 + x_3 + x_4 + x_5 = (z_2 z_1 z_0)_2$.

  c) Compute all four symmetric functions S_0, S_1, S_2, S_3 of $\{x_1, x_2, x_3\}$.

  d) Compute all five symmetric functions S_0, S_1, S_2, S_3, S_4 of $\{x_1, x_2, x_3, x_4\}$.

  e) Compute the symmetric function $S_3(x_1, x_2, x_3, x_4, x_5, x_6)$.

  f) Compute the symmetric function $S_{0,4}(x_1, \ldots, x_6) = [(x_1 + \cdots + x_6) \bmod 4 = 0]$.

  g) Compute all eight minterms of $\{x_1, x_2, x_3\}$ (see 7.1.2–(30)).

480. [*25*] Suppose the values 0, 1, 2 are encoded by the two-bit codes $x_l x_r = 00$, 01, and 1∗, respectively, where 10 and 11 both represent 2. (See Eq. 7.1.3–(120).)

  a) Find an optimum circuit for mod 3 addition: $z_l z_r = (x_l x_r + y_l y_r) \bmod 3$.

  b) Find an optimum circuit that computes $z_l z_r = (x_1 + x_2 + x_3 + y_l y_r) \bmod 3$.

  c) Conclude that $[x_1 + \cdots + x_n \equiv a \,(\text{modulo } 3)]$ can be computed in $< 3n$ steps.

▶ **481.** [*28*] An ordered bit pair xy can be encoded by another ordered bit pair $[\![xy]\!] = (x \oplus y)\, y$ without loss of information, because $[\![xy]\!] = uv$ implies $[\![uv]\!] = xy$.

  a) Find an optimum circuit that computes $(\|zz'\|)_2 = x_1 + x_2 + x_3$.

  b) Let $\nu[\![uv]\!] = (u \oplus v) + v$, and note that $\nu[\![00]\!] = 0$, $\nu[\![01]\!] = 2$, $\nu[\![1∗]\!] = 1$. Find an optimum circuit that, given $x_1 \ldots x_5$, computes $z_1 z_2 z_3$ such that we have $\nu[\![x_1 x_2]\!] + \nu[\![x_3 x_4]\!] + x_5 = 2\nu[\![z_1 z_2]\!] + z_3$.

  c) Use that circuit to prove by induction that the "sideways sum" $(z_{\lfloor \lg n \rfloor} \ldots z_1 z_0)_2 = x_1 + x_2 + \cdots + x_n$ can always be computed with fewer than $4.5n$ gates.

▶ **482.** [*26*] (*Erdős discrepancy patterns.*) The binary sequence $y_1 \ldots y_t$ is called *strongly balanced* if we have $|\sum_{j=1}^{k}(2y_j - 1)| \le 2$ for $1 \le k \le t$.

  a) Show that this balance condition needs to be checked only for odd $k \ge 3$.

  b) Describe clauses that efficiently characterize a strongly balanced sequence.

  c) Construct clauses that are satisfied by $x_1 x_2 \ldots x_n$ if and only if $x_d x_{2d} \ldots x_{\lfloor n/d \rfloor d}$ is strongly balanced for $1 \le d \le n$.

483. [*21*] Symmetry between colors was broken in the coloring problems of Table 6 by assigning fixed colors to a large clique in each graph. But many graphs have no large clique, so a different strategy is necessary. Explain how to encode the "restricted growth string" principle (see Section 7.2.1.5) with appropriate clauses, given an ordering $v_1 v_2 \ldots v_n$ of the vertices: The color of v_j must be at most one greater than the largest color assigned to $\{v_1, \ldots, v_{j-1}\}$. (In particular, v_1 always has color 1.)

Experiment with this scheme by applying it to the Mycielski graphs of exercise 7.2.2.1–116.

484. [*22*] (*Graph quenching.*) A graph with vertices $(v_1, \ldots, v_n)$ is called "quenchable" if either (i) $n = 1$; or (ii) there's a k such that v_k — v_{k+1} and the graph on $(v_1, \ldots, v_{k-1}, v_{k+1}, \ldots, v_n)$ can be quenched; or (iii) there's an l such that v_l — v_{l+3} and the graph on $(v_1, \ldots, v_{l-1}, v_{l+3}, v_{l+1}, v_{l+2}, v_{l+4}, \ldots, v_n)$ can be quenched.

  a) Find a 4-element graph that is quenchable although $v_3 \not\!\!- v_4$.

  b) Construct clauses that are satisfiable if and only if a given graph is quenchable. *Hint:* Use the following three kinds of variables for this model-checking problem:

$x_{t,i,j} = [v_i — v_j$ at time $t]$, for $1 \le i < j \le n-t$; $q_{t,k} = $ [a quenching move of type (ii) leads to time $t+1$]; $s_{t,l} = $ [a quenching move of type (iii) leads to time $t+1$].

▶ **485.** [*23*] Sometimes successive transitions in the previous exercise are commutative: For example, the effect of $q_{t,k}$ and $q_{t+1,k+1}$ is the same as $q_{t,k+2}$ and $q_{t+1,k}$. Explain how to break symmetry in such cases, by allowing only one of the two possibilities.

486. [*21*] (*Late Binding Solitaire.*) Shuffle a deck and deal out 18 cards; then try to reduce these 18 piles to a single pile, using a sequence of "captures" in which one pile is placed on top of another pile. A pile can capture only the pile to its immediate left, or the pile found by skipping left over two other piles. Furthermore a capture is permitted only if the top card in the capturing pile has the same suit or the same rank as the top card in the captured pile. For example, consider the following deal:

J♡ 5♡ 10♣ 8♢ J♣ A♣ K♠ A♡ 4♣ 8♠ 5♠ 5♢ 2♢ 10♠ A♠ 6♡ 3♡ 10♢

Ten captures are initially possible, including 5♡ × J♡, A♣ ××10♣, and 5♢ × 5♠. Some captures then make others possible, as in 8♠ ×× K♠ ×× 8♢.

If captures must be made "greedily" from left to right as soon as possible, this game is the same as the first 18 steps of a classic one-player game called "Idle Year," and we wind up with five piles [see *Dick's Games of Patience* (1883), 50–52]. But if we cleverly hold back until all 18 cards have been dealt, we can do much better.

Show that one can win from this position, but not if the first move is A♣ × J♣.

▶ **487.** [*27*] There are $\binom{64}{8} = 4426165368$ ways to place eight queens on a chessboard. Long ago, W. H. Turton asked which of them causes the maximum number of vacant squares to remain unattacked. [See W. W. Rouse Ball, *Mathematical Recreations and Problems*, third edition (London: Macmillan, 1896), 109–110.]

Every subset S of the vertices of a graph has three *boundary sets* defined thus:

$$\partial S = \text{the set of all edges with exactly one endpoint} \in S;$$
$$\partial_{\text{out}} S = \text{the set of all vertices} \notin S \text{ with at least one neighbor} \in S;$$
$$\partial_{\text{in}} S = \text{the set of all vertices} \in S \text{ with at least one neighbor} \notin S.$$

Find the minimum and maximum sizes of ∂S, $\partial_{\text{out}} S$, and $\partial_{\text{in}} S$, over all 8-element sets S in the queen graph Q_8 (exercise 7.1.4–241). Which set answers Turton's question?

▶ **488.** [*24*] (*Peaceable armies of queens.*) Prove that armies of nine white queens and nine black queens can coexist on a chessboard without attacking each other, but armies of size 10 cannot, by devising appropriate sets of clauses and applying Algorithm C. Also examine the effects of symmetry breaking. (This problem has sixteen symmetries, because we can swap colors and/or rotate and/or reflect the board.) How large can coexisting armies of queens be on $n \times n$ boards, for $n \le 11$?

489. [*M21*] Find a recurrence for T_n, the number of signed involutions on n elements.

▶ **490.** [*15*] Does Theorem E hold also when $p_1 p_2 \ldots p_n$ is any *signed* permutation?

▶ **491.** [*22*] The unsatisfiable clauses R in (6) have the signed permutation $234\bar{1}$ as an automorphism. How can this fact help us to verify their unsatisfiability?

492. [*M20*] Let τ be a *signed mapping* of the variables $\{x_1, \ldots, x_n\}$; for example, the signed mapping '$\bar{4}13\bar{3}$' stands for the operation $(x_1, x_2, x_3, x_4) \mapsto (x_{\bar{4}}, x_1, x_3, x_{\bar{3}}) = (\bar{x}_4, x_1, x_3, \bar{x}_3)$. When a signed mapping is applied to a clause, some of the resulting literals might coincide; or two literals might become complementary, making a tautology. When $\tau = \bar{4}13\bar{3}$, for instance, we have $(123)\tau = \bar{4}13$, $(13\bar{4})\tau = \bar{4}3$, $(1\bar{3}\bar{4})\tau = \wp$.

A family F of clauses is said to be "closed" under a signed mapping τ if $C\tau$ is subsumed by some clause of F whenever $C \in F$. Prove that τ is an endomorphism of F in such a case.

493. [20] The problem $waerden(3, 3; 9)$ has four symmetries, because we can reflect and/or complement all the variables. How can we speed up the proof of unsatisfiability by adding clauses to break those symmetries?

494. [21] Show that if $(uvw)(\bar{u}\bar{v}\bar{w})$ is a symmetry of some clauses F, we're allowed to break symmetries as if $(uv)(\bar{u}\bar{v})$, $(uw)(\bar{u}\bar{w})$, and $(vw)(\bar{v}\bar{w})$ were also symmetries. For example, if $i < j < k$ and if $(ijk)(\bar{i}\bar{j}\bar{k})$ is a symmetry, we can assert $(\bar{x}_i \vee x_j) \wedge (\bar{x}_j \vee x_k)$ with respect to the global ordering $p_1 \ldots p_n = 1 \ldots n$. What are the corresponding binary clauses when the symmetry is (i) $(ij\bar{k})(\bar{i}\bar{j}k)$? (ii) $(i\bar{j}k)(\bar{i}j\bar{k})$? (iii) $(i\bar{j}\bar{k})(\bar{i}jk)$?

495. [M22] Spell out the details of how we can justify appending clauses to assert (185) and (186), using Corollary E, whenever we have an $m \times n$ problem whose variables x_{ij} possess both row and column symmetry. (In other words we assume that $x_{ij} \mapsto x_{(i\pi)(j\rho)}$ is an automorphism for all permutations π of $\{1, \ldots, m\}$ and ρ of $\{1, \ldots, n\}$.)

▸ **496.** [M20] B. C. Dull reasoned as follows: "The pigeonhole clauses have row and column symmetry. Therefore we can assume that the rows are lexicographically increasing from top to bottom, and the columns are lexicographically increasing from right to left. Consequently the problem is easily seen to be unsatisfiable." Was he correct?

497. [22] Use BDD methods to determine the number of 8×8 binary matrices that have both rows and columns in nondecreasing lexicographic order. How many of them have exactly r 1s, for $r = 24$, $r = 25$, $r = 64 - 25 = 39$, and $r = 64 - 24 = 40$?

498. [22] Justify adding the symmetry-breakers (183) to the pigeonhole clauses.

499. [21] In the pigeonhole problem, is it legitimate to include the clauses (183) together with clauses that enforce lexicographic row and column order?

500. [16] The precocious student J. H. Quick decided to extend the monkey wrench principle, arguing that if $F_0 \cup S \vdash l$ then the original clauses F can be replaced by $F \mid l$. But he soon realized his mistake. What was it?

501. [22] Martin Gardner introduced an interesting queen placement problem in *Scientific American* **235**, 4 (October 1976), 134–137: "Place r queens on an $m \times n$ chessboard so that (i) no three are in the same row, column, or diagonal; (ii) no empty square can be occupied without breaking rule (i); and (iii) r is as small as possible." Construct clauses that are satisfiable if and only if there's a solution to conditions (i) and (ii) with at most r queens. (A similar problem was considered in exercise 7.1.4–242.)

502. [16] (*Closest strings.*) Given binary strings $s_1, \ldots, s_m$ of length n, and threshold parameters $r_1, \ldots, r_m$, construct clauses that are satisfiable by $x = x_1 \ldots x_n$ if and only if x differs from s_j in at most r_j positions, for $1 \le j \le m$.

503. [M20] (*Covering strings.*) Given s_j and r_j as in exercise 502, show that *every* string of length n is within r_j bits of *some* s_j if and only if the closest string problem has no solution with parameters $r'_j = n - 1 - r_j$.

▸ **504.** [M21] The problem in exercise 502 can be proved NP-complete as follows:

    a) Let w_j be the string of length $2n$ that is entirely 0 except for 1s in positions $2j-1$ and $2j$, and let $w_{n+j} = \bar{w}_j$, for $1 \le j \le n$. Describe all binary strings of length $2n$ that differ from each of $w_1, \ldots, w_{2n}$ in at most n bit positions.

    b) Given a clause $(l_1 \vee l_2 \vee l_3)$ with strictly distinct literals $l_1, l_2, l_3 \in \{x_1, \ldots, x_n, \bar{x}_1, \ldots, \bar{x}_n\}$, let y be the string of length $2n$ that is entirely zero except that it has

1 in position $2k - 1$ when some l_i is $\bar{x}_k$, and 1 in position $2k$ when some l_i is x_k. In how many bit positions does a string that satisfies (a) differ from y?

c) Given a 3SAT problem F with m clauses and n variables, use (a) and (b) to construct strings $s_1, \ldots, s_{m+2n}$ of length $2n$ such that F is satisfiable if and only if the closest string problem is satisfiable with $r_j = n + [j > 2n]$.

d) Illustrate your construction in (c) by exhibiting the closest string problems that correspond to the simple 3SAT problems R and R' in (6) and (7).

505. [*21*] Experiment with making Algorithm L nondeterministic, by randomizing the initial order of VAR in step L1 just as HEAP is initialized randomly in step C1. How does the modified algorithm perform on, say, problems D3, K0, and W2 of Table 6?

506. [*22*] The *weighted variable interaction graph* of a family of clauses has one vertex for each variable and the weight $\sum 2/(|c|(|c| - 1))$ between vertices u and v, where the sum is over all clauses c that contain both $\pm u$ and $\pm v$. Figure 95 indicates these weights indirectly, by making the heavier edges darker.

a) True or false: The sum of all edge weights is the total number of clauses.

b) Explain why the graph for test case B2 has exactly 6 edges of weight 2. What are the weights of the other edges in that graph?

▸ **507.** [*21*] (Marijn Heule.) Explain why "windfalls" (see (72)) help Algorithm L to deal with miter problems such as D5.

508. [*M20*] According to Table 7, Algorithm C proved problem T3 to be unsatisfiable after learning about 323 thousand clauses. About how many times did it enter a purging phase in step C7?

509. [*20*] Several of the "training set" tasks used when tuning Algorithm C's parameters were taken from the 100 test cases of Table 6. Why didn't this lead to a problem of "overfitting" (namely, of choosing parameters that are too closely associated with the trainees)?

510. [*18*] When the data points A1, A2, $\ldots$, X8 were plotted in Fig. 98, one by one, they sometimes covered parts of previously plotted points, because of overlaps. What test cases are partially hidden by (a) T2? (b) X6? (c) X7?

511. [*22*] Problem P4 in Table 6 is a strange set of clauses that lead to extreme behavior of Algorithm C in Figs. 97 and 98; and it causes Algorithm L to "time out" in Fig. 96.

a) The preprocessing algorithm of the text needs about 1.5 megamems to convert those 2509 clauses in 400 variables into just 2414 clauses in 339 variables. Show empirically that Algorithm L makes short work of the resulting 2414 clauses.

b) How efficient is Algorithm C on those preprocessed clauses?

c) What is the behavior of WalkSAT on P4, with and without preprocessing?

512. [*29*] Find parameters for Algorithm C that will find an Erdős discrepancy pattern $x_1 x_2 \ldots x_n$ rapidly when $n = 500$. (This is problem E0 in Table 6.) Then compare the running times of nine random runs with your parameters versus nine random runs with (194), when $n = 400, 500, 600, \ldots, 1100, 1160,$ and 1161.

513. [*24*] Find parameters for Algorithm L that tune it for $rand(3, m, n, seed)$.

514. [*24*] The timings quoted in the text for Algorithm W, for problems in Table 6, are based on the median of nine runs using the parameters $p = .4$ and $N = 50n$, restarting from scratch if necessary until a solution is found. Those parameters worked fine in most cases, unless Algorithm W was unsuited to the task. But problem C9 was solved more quickly with $p = .6$ and $N = 2500n$ ($943\,M\mu$ versus $9.1\,G\mu$).

Find values of p and N/n that give near-optimum performance for problem C9.

▶ **515.** [*23*] (*Hard sudoku.*) Specify SAT clauses with which a designer of sudoku puzzles can meet the following specifications: (i) If cell (i,j) of the puzzle is blank, so is cell $(10-i, 10-j)$, for $1 \le i,j \le 9$. (ii) Every row, every column, and every box contains at least one blank. (Here "box" means one of sudoku's nine special 3×3 subarrays.) (iii) No box contains an all-blank row or an all-blank column. (iv) There are at least two ways to fill every blank cell, without conflicting with nonblank entries in the same row, column, or box. (v) If a row, column, or box doesn't already contain k, there are at least two places to put k into that row, column, or box, without conflict. (vi) If the solution has a 2×2 subarray of the form $\begin{smallmatrix} k & l \\ l & k \end{smallmatrix}$, those four cells must not all be blank.

(Condition (i) is a feature of "classic" sudoku puzzles. Conditions (iv) and (v) ensure that the corresponding exact cover problem has no forced moves; see Section 7.2.2.1. Condition (vi) rules out common cases with non-unique solutions.)

516. [*M49*] Prove or disprove the *strong exponential time hypothesis*: "If $\tau < 2$, there is an integer k such that no randomized algorithm can solve every kSAT problem in fewer than τ^n steps, where n is the number of variables."

517. [*25*] Given clauses $C_1, \ldots, C_m$, the *one-per-clause* satisfiability problem asks if there is a Boolean assignment $x_1 \ldots x_n$ such that every clause is satisfied by a *unique* literal. In other words, we want to solve the simultaneous equations $\Sigma C_j = 1$ for $1 \le j \le m$, where ΣC is the sum of the literals of clause C.

a) Prove that this problem is NP-complete, by reducing 3SAT to it.

b) Prove that this problem, in turn, can be reduced to its special case "*one-in-three satisfiability*," where every given clause is required to be ternary.

518. [*M32*] Given a 3SAT problem with m clauses and n variables, we shall construct a $(6m + n) \times (6m + n)$ matrix M of integers such that the *permanent*, per M, is zero if and only if the clauses are unsatisfiable. For example, the solvable problem (7) corresponds to the 46×46 matrix indicated here; each shaded box stands for a fixed 6×6 matrix A that corresponds to a clause.

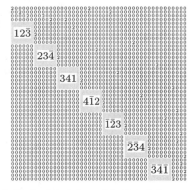

Each A has three "inputs" in columns 1, 3, 5 and three "outputs" in rows 2, 4, 6. The first n rows and the last n columns correspond to variables. Outside of the As, all entries are either 0 or 2; and the 2s link variables to clauses, according to a scheme much like the data structures in several of the algorithms in this section: Let I_{ij} and O_{ij} denote the jth input and output of clause i, for $1 \le i \le m$ and $1 \le j \le 3$. Then, if literal l appears in $t \ge 0$ clauses $i_1 < \cdots < i_t$, as element $j_1, \ldots, j_t$, we put '2' in column $I_{i_{k+1} j_{k+1}}$ of row $O_{i_k j_k}$ for $0 \le k \le t$ ($O_{i_0 j}$ is row $|l|$, $I_{i_{t+1} j}$ is column $6m+|l|$).

a) Find a 6×6 matrix $A = (a_{ij})$, whose elements are either 0, 1, or -1, such that

$$\text{per} \begin{pmatrix} a_{11} & a_{12} & a_{13} & a_{14} & a_{15} & a_{16} \\ a_{21}+2p & a_{22} & a_{23}+2q & a_{24} & a_{25}+2r & a_{26} \\ a_{31} & a_{32} & a_{33} & a_{34} & a_{35} & a_{36} \\ a_{41}+2u & a_{42} & a_{43}+2v & a_{44} & a_{45}+2w & a_{46} \\ a_{51} & a_{52} & a_{53} & a_{54} & a_{55} & a_{56} \\ a_{61}+2x & a_{62} & a_{63}+2y & a_{64} & a_{65}+2z & a_{66} \end{pmatrix} = 16 \left(\text{per} \begin{pmatrix} p+1 & q & r \\ u & v+1 & w \\ x & y & z+1 \end{pmatrix} - 1 \right).$$

Hint: There's a solution with lots of symmetry.

b) In which of the rows and columns of M does '2' occur twice? once? not at all?

c) Conclude that per $M = 2^{4m+n} s$, when the 3SAT problem has exactly s solutions.

519. [*20*] Table 7 shows inconclusive results in a race for factoring between *factor_fifo* and *factor_lifo*. What is the comparable performance of *factor_rand*$(m, n, z, 314159)$?

▸ **520.** [*24*] Every instance of SAT corresponds in a natural way to an *integer programming feasibility* problem: To find, if possible, integers $x_1, \ldots, x_n$ that satisfy the linear inequalities $0 \le x_j \le 1$ for $1 \le j \le n$ and

$$l_1 + l_2 + \cdots + l_k \ge 1 \qquad \text{for each clause } C = (l_1 \vee l_2 \vee \cdots \vee l_k).$$

For example, the inequality that corresponds to the clause $(x_1 \vee \bar{x}_3 \vee \bar{x}_4 \vee x_7)$ is $x_1 + (1 - x_3) + (1 - x_4) + x_7 \ge 1$; i.e., $x_1 - x_3 - x_4 + x_7 \ge -1$.

Sophisticated "IP solvers" have been developed by numerous researchers for solving general systems of integer linear inequalities, based on techniques of "cutting planes" in high-dimensional geometry. Thus we can solve any satisfiability problem by using such general-purpose software, as an alternative to trying a SAT solver.

Study the performance of the best available IP solvers, with respect to the 100 sets of clauses in Table 6, and compare it to the performance of Algorithm C in Table 7.

521. [*30*] Experiment with the following idea, which is much simpler than the clause-purging method described in the text: "Forget a learned clause of length k with probability p_k," where $p_1 \ge p_2 \ge p_3 \ge \cdots$ is a tunable sequence of probabilities.

▸ **522.** [*26*] (*Loopless shadows.*) A cyclic path within the cube $P_3 \mathbin{\square} P_3 \mathbin{\square} P_3$ is shown here, together with the three "shadows" that appear when it is projected onto each coordinate plane. Notice that the shadow at the bottom contains a loop, but the other two shadows do not. Does this cube contain a cycle whose three shadows are entirely *without* loops? Use SAT technology to find out.

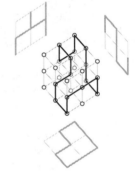

523. [*30*] Prove that, for any m or n, no cycle of the graph $P_m \mathbin{\square} P_n \mathbin{\square} P_2$ has loopless shadows.

▸ **524.** [*22*] Find all *Hamiltonian paths* of the cube $P_3 \mathbin{\square} P_3 \mathbin{\square} P_3$ that have loopless shadows.

▸ **525.** [*40*] Find the most difficult 3SAT problem you can that has at most 100 variables.

526. [*M25*] (David S. Johnson, 1974.) If F has m clauses, all of size $\ge k$, prove that some assignment leaves at most $m/2^k$ clauses unsatisfied.

Behold once more with serious labor here
Haue I refurnisht out this little frame,
Repaird some parts, defectiue here and there,
And passages new added to the same.

— SAMUEL DANIEL, *Certaine small Workes Heretofore Divulged* (1607)

ANSWERS TO EXERCISES

NOTES ON THE EXERCISES

1. A moderately easy problem for a mathematically inclined reader.

2. The author will reward you if you are first to report an error in the statement of an exercise or in its answer, assuming that he or she is suitably sagacious.

3. See H. Poincaré, *Rendiconti del Circolo Matematico di Palermo* **18** (1904), 45–110; R. H. Bing, *Annals of Math.* (2) **68** (1958), 17–37; G. Perelman, arXiv:math/0211159 [math.DG] (2002), 39 pages; 0303109 and 0307245 [math.DG] (2003), 22+7 pages.

MATHEMATICAL PRELIMINARIES REDUX

1. (a) A beats B in $5+0+5+5+0+5$ cases out of 36; B beats C in $4+2+4+4+2+4$; C beats A in $2+2+2+6+2+6$.

(b) The unique solution, without going to more than six spots per face, is

$$A = \begin{array}{c}\includegraphics\end{array}, \qquad B = \begin{array}{c}\includegraphics\end{array}, \qquad C = \begin{array}{c}\includegraphics\end{array}.$$

(c) $A = \{F_{m-2} \times 1, F_{m-1} \times 4\}$, $B = \{F_m \times 3\}$, $C = \{F_{m-1} \times 2, F_{m-2} \times 5\}$ makes $\Pr(C > A) = F_{m-2}F_{m+1}/F_m^2$; and we have $F_{m-2}F_{m+1} = F_{m-1}F_m - (-1)^m$. [Similarly, with n faces and $A = \{\lfloor n/\phi^2 \rfloor \times 1, \lceil n/\phi \rceil \times 4\}$, etc., the probabilities are $1/\phi - O(1/n)$. See R. P. Savage, Jr., *AMM* **101** (1994), 429–436. Additional properties of nontransitive dice have been explored by J. Buhler, R. Graham, and A. Hales, *AMM* **125** (2018), 387–399.]

2. Let $\Pr(A > B) = \mathcal{A}$, $\Pr(B > C) = \mathcal{B}$, $\Pr(C > A) = \mathcal{C}$. We can assume that no x appears on more than one die; if it did, we could replace it by $x + \epsilon$ in A and $x - \epsilon$ in C (for small enough ϵ) without decreasing $\mathcal{A}$, $\mathcal{B}$, or $\mathcal{C}$. So we can list the face elements in nondecreasing order and replace each one by the name of its die; for example, the previous answer (b) yields $CBBBAAAAACCCCCBBBA$. Clearly AB, BC, and CA are never consecutive in an optimal arrangement of this kind: BA is always better than AB.

Suppose the sequence is $C^{c_1}B^{b_1}A^{a_1} \ldots C^{c_k}B^{b_k}A^{a_k}$ where $c_i > 0$ for $1 \le i \le k$ and $b_i, a_i > 0$ for $1 \le i < k$. Let $\alpha_i = a_i/(a_1 + \cdots + a_k)$, $\beta_i = b_i/(b_1 + \cdots + b_k)$, $\gamma_i = c_i/(c_1 + \cdots + c_k)$; then $\mathcal{A} = \alpha_1\beta_1 + \alpha_2(\beta_1 + \beta_2) + \cdots$, $\mathcal{B} = \beta_1\gamma_1 + \beta_2(\gamma_1 + \gamma_2) + \cdots$, $\mathcal{C} = \gamma_2\alpha_1 + \gamma_3(\alpha_1 + \alpha_2) + \cdots$. We will show that $\min(\mathcal{A}, \mathcal{B}, \mathcal{C}) \le 1/\phi$ when the α's, β's, and γ's are nonnegative real numbers; then it is $< 1/\phi$ when they are rational.

The key idea is that we can assume $k \leq 2$ and $\alpha_2 = 0$. Otherwise the following transformation leads to a shorter array without decreasing $\mathcal{A}$, $\mathcal{B}$, or $\mathcal{C}$:

$$\gamma'_2 = \lambda \gamma_2, \quad \gamma'_1 = \gamma_1 + \gamma_2 - \gamma'_2, \quad \beta'_2 = \lambda \beta_2, \quad \beta'_1 = \beta_1 + \beta_2 - \beta'_2, \quad \alpha'_1 = \alpha_1/\lambda, \quad \alpha'_2 = \alpha_1 + \alpha_2 - \alpha'_1.$$

Indeed, $\mathcal{A}' = \mathcal{A}$, $\mathcal{C}' = \mathcal{C}$, and $\mathcal{B}' - \mathcal{B} = (1 - \lambda)(\beta_1 - \lambda \beta_2)\gamma_2$, and we can choose λ thus:

Case 1: $\beta_1 \geq \beta_2$. Choose $\lambda = \alpha_1/(\alpha_1 + \alpha_2)$, making $\alpha'_2 = 0$.
Case 2: $\beta_1 < \beta_2$ and $\gamma_1/\gamma_2 \leq \beta_1/\beta_2$. Choose $\lambda = 1 + \gamma_1/\gamma_2$, making $\gamma'_1 = 0$.
Case 3: $\beta_1 < \beta_2$ and $\gamma_1/\gamma_2 > \beta_1/\beta_2$. Choose $\lambda = 1 + \beta_1/\beta_2$, making $\beta'_1 = 0$.

Finally, then, $\mathcal{A} = \beta_1$, $\mathcal{B} = 1 - \beta_1 \gamma_2$, $\mathcal{C} = \gamma_2$; they can't all be greater than $1/\phi$.

[Similarly, with n dice, the asymptotic optimum probability p_n satisfies $p_n = \alpha_2^{(n)} = 1 - \alpha_1^{(n-1)} \alpha_2^{(n)} = \cdots = 1 - \alpha_1^{(2)} \alpha_2^{(3)} = \alpha_1^{(2)}$. One can show that $f_n(1 - p_n) = 0$, where $f_{n+1}(x) = f_n(x) - x f_{n-1}(x)$, $f_0(x) = 1$, $f_1(x) = 1 - x$. Then $f_n(x^2)$ is expressible as the Chebyshev polynomial $x^{n+1} U_{n+1}(\frac{1}{2x})$; and we have $p_n = 1 - 1/(4 \cos^2 \pi/(n+2))$. See Z. Usiskin, *Annals of Mathematical Statistics* **35** (1964), 857–862; S. Trybuła, *Zastosowania Matematyki* **8** (1965), 143–156; A. Komisarski, *AMM* **128** (2021), 423–434.]

3. Brute force (namely a program) finds eight solutions, of which the simplest is

$$A = \boxed{\ \text{[dice]}\ }, \qquad B = C = \boxed{\ \text{[dice]}\ },$$

all with respective probabilities $\frac{17}{27}$, $\frac{16}{27}$, $\frac{16}{27}$. [If ⚅ is also allowed, the unique solution

$$A = \boxed{\ \text{[dice]}\ }, \qquad B = \boxed{\ \text{[dice]}\ }, \qquad C = \boxed{\ \text{[dice]}\ }$$

has the property that every roll has exactly one die below the average and two above, with each of A, B, C equally likely to be below; hence all three probabilities are $2/3$. See J. Moraleda and D. G. Stork, *College Mathematics Journal* **43** (2012), 152–159.]

4. (a) The permutation $(1\,2\,3\,4)(5\,6)$ takes $A \to B \to C \to D \to A$. So B versus C is like A versus B, etc. Also $\Pr(A \text{ beats } C) = \Pr(C \text{ beats } A) = \Pr(B \text{ beats } D) = \Pr(D \text{ beats } B) = \frac{288}{720}$; $\Pr(A \text{ and } C \text{ tie}) = \Pr(B \text{ and } D \text{ tie}) = \frac{144}{720}$.

(b) Assume by symmetry the players are A, B, C. Then the bingoers are $(A, B, C, AB, AC, BC, ABC)$ with respective probabilities $(168, 216, 168, 48, 72, 36, 12)/720$.

(c) It's $(A, AB, AC, ABC, ABCD)$ with probabilities $(120, 24, 48, 12, 0)/720$.

5. (a) If $A_k = 1001$ with probability .99, otherwise $A_k = 0$, but $B_k = 1000$ always, then $P_{1000} = .99^{1000} \approx .000043$. (This example gives the smallest possible P_{1000}, because $\Pr((A_1 - B_1) + \cdots + (A_n - B_n) > 0) \geq \Pr([A_1 > B_1] \ldots [A_n > B_n]) = P_1^n$.)

(b) Let $E = q_0 + q_2 + q_4 + \cdots \approx 0.67915$ be the probability that $B = 0$. Then $\Pr(A > B) = \sum_{k=0}^{\infty} q_{2k}(E + \sum_{j=0}^{k-1} q_{2j+1}) \approx .47402$; $\Pr(A < B) = \sum_{k=0}^{\infty} q_{2k+1}(1 - E + \sum_{j=0}^{k} q_{2j}) \approx .30807$; and $\Pr(A = B) = \Pr(A = B = 0) = E(1 - E) \approx .21790$ is also the probability that $AB > 0$.

(c) During the first n_k rounds, the probability that either Alice or Bob has scored more than m_k is at most $n_k(q_{k+1} + q_{k+2} + \cdots) = O(2^{-k})$; and the probability that neither has ever scored m_k is $(1 - q_k)^{n_k} < \exp(-q_k n_k) = \exp(-2^k/D)$. Also $m_k > n_k m_{k-1}$ when $k > 1$. Thus Alice "quite surely" wins when k is even, but loses when k is odd, as $k \to \infty$. [*The American Statistician* **43** (1989), 277–278.]

6. The probability that $X_j = 1$ is clearly $p_1 = 1/(n-1)$; hence $X_j = 0$ with probability $p_0 = (n-2)/(n-1)$. And the probability that $X_i = X_j = 1$ when $i < j$ is p_1^2. Thus (see exercise 20), (X_i, X_j) will equal $(0, 1)$, $(1, 0)$, or $(0, 0)$ with the correct probabilities $p_0 p_1$, $p_1 p_0$, $p_0 p_0$. But $X_i = X_j = X_k = 1$ with probability 0 when $i < j < k$.

For 3-wise independence let $\Pr(X_1 \ldots X_n = x_1 \ldots x_n) = a_{x_1 + \cdots + x_n}/(n-2)^3$, where $a_0 = 2\binom{n-2}{3}$, $a_1 = \binom{n-2}{2}$, $a_3 = 1$, otherwise $a_j = 0$.

7. Let $f_m(n) = \sum_{j=0}^{m} \binom{n}{j}(-1)^j (n+1-m)^{m-j}$, and define probabilities via $a_j = f_{k-j}(n-j)$ as in answer 6. (In particular, we have $f_0(n) = 1$, $f_1(n) = 0$, $f_2(n) = \binom{n-1}{2}$, $f_3(n) = 2\binom{n-2}{3}$, $f_4(n) = 3\binom{n-3}{4} + \binom{n-3}{2}^2$.) This definition is valid if we can prove that $f_m(n) \geq 0$ for $n \geq m$, because of the identity $\sum_j \binom{n}{j} f_{m-j}(n-j) = (n+1-m)^m$.

To prove that inequality, Schulte-Geers notes (see *CMath* (5.19)) that $f_m(n) = \sum_{k=0}^{m} \binom{m-n}{k}(n-m)^{m-k} = \sum_{k=0}^{m} \binom{n-m-1+k}{k}(-1)^k (n-m)^{m-k}$; these terms pair up nicely to yield $\sum_{k=0}^{m-1} k\binom{n-m-1+k}{k+1}(n-m)^{m-k-1}[k \text{ even}] + \binom{n-1}{m}[m \text{ even}]$.

8. If $0 < k < n$, the probability that k of the components have any particular setting is $1/2^k$, because the remaining components have even parity as often as odd parity. So there's $(n-1)$-wise independence, but not n-wise.

9. Give probability $1/2$ to $0 \ldots 0$ and $1 \ldots 1$; all other vectors have probability 0.

10. If $n > p$ we have $X_{p+1} = X_1$, so there's no independence. Otherwise, if $m < n \leq p$, there's m-wise independence because any m vectors $(1, j, \ldots, j^{m-1})$ are linearly independent modulo p (they're columns of Vandermonde's matrix, exercise 1.2.3–37); but the X's are dependent $(m+1)$-wise, because a polynomial of degree m cannot have $m+1$ different roots. If $m \geq n$ and $n \leq p$ there is complete independence.

Instead of working mod p, we could use any finite field in this construction.

11. We can assume that $n = 1$, because $(X_1 + \cdots + X_n)/n$ and $(X_{n+1} + \cdots + X_{2n})/n$ are independent random variables with the same discrete distribution. Then $\Pr(|X_1 + X_2 - 2\alpha| \leq 2|X_1 - \alpha|) \geq \Pr(|X_1 - \alpha| + |X_2 - \alpha| \leq 2|X_1 - \alpha|) = \Pr(|X_2 - \alpha| \leq |X_1 - \alpha|) = (1 + \Pr(X_1 = X_2))/2 > 1/2$. [This exercise was suggested by T. M. Cover.]

12. Let $w = \Pr(A \text{ and } B)$, $x = \Pr(A \text{ and } \bar{B})$, $y = \Pr(\bar{A} \text{ and } B)$, $z = \Pr(\bar{A} \text{ and } \bar{B})$. All five statements are equivalent to $wz > xy$, or to $\left|\begin{smallmatrix} w & x \\ y & z \end{smallmatrix}\right| > 0$, or to "$A$ and B are strictly positively correlated" (see exercise 61). [This exercise was suggested by E. Georgiadis.]

13. False in many cases. For example, take $\Pr(\bar{A} \text{ and } \bar{B} \text{ and } \bar{C}) = \Pr(\bar{A} \text{ and } B \text{ and } \bar{C}) = 0$, $\Pr(A \text{ and } B \text{ and } C) = 2/7$, and all other joint probabilities $1/7$.

14. Induction on n. [*Philosophical Transactions* **53** (1763), 370–418, proof of Prop. 6.]

15. If $\Pr(C) > 0$, this is the chain rule, conditional on C. But if $\Pr(C) = 0$, it's false by our conventions, unless A and B are independent.

16. If and only if $\Pr(\bar{A} \cap B \cap C) = 0 \neq \Pr(B)$ or $\Pr(\bar{A} \cap C) = 0$.

17. $4/51$, because four of the cards other than Q♠ are aces.

18. Since $(M - X)(X - m) \geq 0$, we have $(M \mathbin{E} X) - (\mathbin{E} X^2) + (m \mathbin{E} X) - mM \geq 0$. [See C. Davis and R. Bhatia, *AMM* **107** (2000), 353–356, for generalizations.]

19. (a) The binary values of $\Pr(X_n = 1) = \mathbin{E} X_n$ for $n = 0, 1, 2, \ldots$, are respectively $(.0101010101010101\ldots)_2$, $(.0011001100110011\ldots)_2$, $(.0000111100001111\ldots)_2$, $\ldots$; thus they're the complemented reflections of the "magic masks" 7.1.3–(47). The answer is therefore $(2^{2^n} - 1)/(2^{2^{n+1}} - 1) = 1/(2^{2^n} + 1)$.

(b) $\Pr(X_0 X_1 \ldots X_{n-1} = x_0 x_1 \ldots x_{n-1}) = 2^{(\bar{x}_{n-1} \ldots \bar{x}_1 \bar{x}_0)_2}/(2^{2^n} - 1)$ can be "read off" from the magic masks by ANDing and complementing. [See E. Lukacs, *Characteristic Functions* (1960), 119, for related theory.]

(c) The infinite sum S is well defined because $\Pr(S = \infty) = 0$. Its expectation $\mathrm{E}\, S = \sum_{n=0}^{\infty} 1/(2^{2^n}+1) \approx 0.59606$ corresponds to the case $z = 1/2$ in answer 7.1.3–41(c). By independence, $\mathrm{var}(S) = \sum_{n=0}^{\infty} \mathrm{var}(X_n) = \sum_{n=0}^{\infty} 2^{2^n}/(2^{2^n}+1)^2 \approx 0.44148$.

(d) The *parity number* $\mathrm{E}\, R = (.0110100110010110\ldots)_2$ has the decimal value

$$0.41245\,40336\,40107\,59778\,33613\,68258\,45528\,30895-,$$

and can be shown to equal $\frac{1}{2} - \frac{1}{4}P$ where $P = \prod_{k=0}^{\infty}(1 - 1/2^{2^k})$ [R. W. Gosper and R. Schroeppel, MIT AI Laboratory Memo 239 (29 February 1972), Hack 122], which is transcendental [K. Mahler, *Mathematische Annalen* **101** (1929), 342–366; **103** (1930), 532]. (Furthermore it turns out that $1/P - 1/2 = \sum_{k=0}^{\infty} 1/\prod_{j=0}^{k-1}(2^{2^j} - 1)$.) Since R is binary, $\mathrm{var}(R) = (\mathrm{E}\, R)(1 - \mathrm{E}\, R) \approx 0.242336$.

(e) Zero (because π is irrational, hence $p_0 + p_1 + \cdots = \infty$). However, if we ask the analogous question for Euler's constant γ instead of π, nobody knows the answer.

(f) $\mathrm{E}\, Y_n = 2\,\mathrm{E}\, X_n$; in fact, $\Pr(Y_0 Y_1 Y_2 \ldots = x_0 x_1 x_2 \ldots)$, for *any* infinite string $x_0 x_1 x_2 \ldots$, is equal to $2\Pr(X_0 X_1 X_2 \ldots = x_0 x_1 x_2 \ldots) \bmod 1$, because we shift the binary representation one place to the left (and drop any carry). Thus in particular, $\mathrm{E}\, Y_m Y_n = 2\,\mathrm{E}\, X_m X_n = \frac{1}{2}\,\mathrm{E}\, Y_m\,\mathrm{E}\, Y_n$ when $m \neq n$; Y_m and Y_n are negatively correlated because $\mathrm{covar}(Y_m, Y_n) = -\frac{1}{2}\,\mathrm{E}\, Y_m\,\mathrm{E}\, Y_n$.

(g) Clearly $\mathrm{E}\, T = 2\,\mathrm{E}\, S$. Also $\mathrm{E}\, T^2 = 2\,\mathrm{E}\, S^2$, because $\mathrm{E}\, Y_m Y_n = 2\,\mathrm{E}\, X_m X_n$ for all m and n. So $\mathrm{var}(T) = 2(\mathrm{var}(S) + (\mathrm{E}\, S)^2) - (2\,\mathrm{E}\, S)^2 = 2\,\mathrm{var}(S) - 2(\mathrm{E}\, S)^2 \approx 0.17237$.

20. Let $p_j = \mathrm{E}\, X_j$. We must prove, for example, that $\mathrm{E}(X_1(1 - X_2)(1 - X_3)X_4) = p_1(1 - p_2)(1 - p_3)p_4$ when $k \geq 4$. But this is $\mathrm{E}(X_1 X_4 - X_1 X_2 X_4 - X_1 X_3 X_4 + X_1 X_2 X_3 X_4) = p_1 p_4 - p_1 p_2 p_4 - p_1 p_3 p_4 + p_1 p_2 p_3 p_4$.

21. From the previous exercise we know that they can't both be binary. Let X be binary and Y ternary, taking each of the values $(0,0)$, $(0,2)$, $(1,0)$, $(1,1)$, $(1,2)$ with probability $1/5$. Then $\mathrm{E}\, XY = \mathrm{E}\, X = 3/5$ and $\mathrm{E}\, Y = 1$; $\Pr(X = 0)\Pr(Y = 1) = 2/25 \neq 0$.

22. By (8) we have $\Pr(A_1 \cup \cdots \cup A_n) = \mathrm{E}\,[A_1 \cup \cdots \cup A_n] = \mathrm{E}\max([A_1], \ldots, [A_n]) \leq \mathrm{E}([A_1] + \cdots + [A_n]) = \mathrm{E}[A_1] + \cdots + \mathrm{E}[A_n] = \Pr(A_1) + \cdots + \Pr(A_n)$.

23. The hinted probability is $\Pr(X_s = 0$ and $X_1 + \cdots + X_{s-1} = s - r)$, so it equals $\binom{s-1}{s-r}p^{s-r}(1 - p)^r$. To get $B_{m,n}(p)$, sum it for $r = n - m$ and $n - m \leq s \leq n$. [For an algebraic rather than probabilistic/combinatorial proof, see *CMath*, exercise 8.17.]

24. (a) The derivative of $B_{m,n}(x) = \sum_{k=0}^{m} \binom{n}{k} x^k (1 - x)^{n-k}$ is

$$B_{m,n}'(x) = \sum_{k=1}^{m} \binom{n}{k} k x^{k-1}(1 - x)^{n-k} - \sum_{k=0}^{m} \binom{n}{k}(n - k)x^k(1 - x)^{n-1-k}$$

$$= n\left(\sum_{k=0}^{m-1} \binom{n-1}{k} x^k(1 - x)^{n-1-k} - \sum_{k=0}^{m} \binom{n-1}{k} x^k(1 - x)^{n-1-k}\right)$$

$$= -n\binom{n-1}{m} x^m(1 - x)^{n-1-m}.$$

[See Karl Pearson, *Biometrika* **16** (1924), 202–203.]

(b) The hint, which says that $\int_0^{a/(a+b+1)} x^a(1 - x)^b\,dx < \int_{a/(a+b+1)}^1 x^a(1 - x)^b\,dx$ when $0 \leq a \leq b$, will prove that $1 - B_{m,n}(m/n) < B_{m,n}(m/n)$. If $a > 0$ it suffices to show that $\int_0^{a/(a+b)} x^a(1-x)^b\,dx \leq \int_{a/(a+b)}^1 x^a(1-x)^b\,dx$, because we have $\int_0^{a/(a+b+1)} < \int_0^{a/(a+b)} \leq \int_{a/(a+b)}^1 < \int_{a/(a+b+1)}^1$. Let $x = (a-\epsilon)/(a+b)$, and observe that $(a-\epsilon)^a(b+\epsilon)^b$

is less than or equal to $(a + \epsilon)^a(b - \epsilon)^b$ for $0 \le \epsilon \le a$, because the quantity

$$\left(\frac{a - \epsilon}{a + \epsilon}\right)^a = e^{a(\ln(1 - \epsilon/a) - \ln(1 + \epsilon/a))} = \exp\left(-2\epsilon\left(1 + \frac{\epsilon^2}{3a^2} + \frac{\epsilon^4}{5a^4} + \cdots\right)\right)$$

is nondecreasing when a increases.

(c) Let $t_k = \binom{n}{k}m^k(n-m)^{n-k}$. When $m \ge n/2$ we can show that $1 - B_{m,n}(m/n) = \sum_{k>m} t_k/n^n < B_{m,n}(m/n) = \sum_{k=0}^{m} t_k/n^n$, because $t_{m+d} < t_{m+1-d}$ for $1 \le d \le n - m$. For if $r_d = t_{m+d}/t_{m+1-d}$, we have $r_1 = m/(m+1) < 1$; also

$$\frac{r_{d+1}}{r_d} = \frac{(n - m + d)(n - m - d)m^2}{(m + 1 + d)(m + 1 - d)(n - m)^2} < 1,$$

because $((m+1)^2 - d^2)(n-m)^2 - ((n-m)^2 - d^2)m^2 = (2m+1)(n-m)^2 + (2m-n)nd^2$.

[Peter Neumann proved in *Wissenschaftliche Zeitschrift der Technischen Universität Dresden* **15** (1966), 223–226, that m is the median. The argument in part (c) is due to Nick Lord, in *The Mathematical Gazette* **94** (2010), 331–332. See also S. Janson, *Statistics and Probability Letters* **171** (2021) 109020, 10 pages.]

25. (a) $\left(\binom{n}{k}\right) - \left(\binom{n}{k+1}\right)$ is $\sum p_I q_J(q_t/(n - k) - p_t/(k + 1))$, summed over all partitions of $\{1, \ldots, n\}$ into disjoint sets $I \cup J \cup \{t\}$, where $|I| = k$, $|J| = n - k - 1$, $p_I = \prod_{i \in I} p_i$, $q_J = \prod_{j \in J} q_j$. And $q_t/(n - k) - p_t/(k + 1) \ge 0 \iff p_t \le (k + 1)/(n + 1)$.

(b) Given $p_1, \ldots, p_{n-1}$, the quantity $\left(\binom{n}{k}\right)$ is maximized when $p_n = p$, by (a). The same argument applies symmetrically to all indices j.

26. The inequality is equivalent to $r_{n,k}^2 \ge r_{n,k-1}r_{n,k+1}$, which was stated without proof on pages 242–245 of Newton's *Arithmetica Universalis* (1707), then finally proved by Sylvester many years later [*Proc. London Math. Soc.* **1** (1865), 1–16]. We have $nr_{n,k} = kp_n r_{n-1,k-1} + (n - k)q_n r_{n-1,k}$; hence $n^2(r_{n,k}^2 - r_{n,k-1}r_{n,k+1}) = (p_n r_{n-1,k-1} - q_n r_{n-1,k})^2 + (k^2 - 1)p_n^2 A + (k - 1)(n - 1 - k)p_n q_n B + ((n - k)^2 - 1)q_n^2 C$, where $A = r_{n-1,k-1}^2 - r_{n-1,k-2}r_{n-1,k}$, $B = r_{n-1,k-1}r_{n-1,k} - r_{n-1,k-2}r_{n-1,k+1}$, and $C = r_{n-1,k}^2 - r_{n-1,k-1}r_{n-1,k+1}$ are nonnegative, by induction on n.

27. $\sum_{k=0}^{m} \left(\binom{n}{k}\right) = \sum_{k=0}^{m} \left(\binom{n-m-1+k}{k}\right)(1 - p_{n-m+k})$, by the same argument as before.

28. (a) $\left(\binom{n}{k}\right) = \left(\binom{n-2}{k}\right)A + \left(\binom{n-2}{k-1}\right)B + \left(\binom{n-2}{k-2}\right)C$ and $E g(X) = \sum_{k=0}^{n-2}\left(\binom{n-2}{k}\right)h_k$, where $A = (1 - p_{n-1})(1 - p_n)$, $C = p_{n-1}p_n$, $B = 1 - A - C$, and $h_k = Ag(k) + Bg(k + 1) + Cg(k + 2)$. If the p_j's aren't all equal, we may assume that $p_{n-1} < p < p_n$. Setting $p'_{n-1} = p_{n-1} + \epsilon$ and $p'_n = p_n - \epsilon$, where $\epsilon = \min(p_n - p, p - p_{n-1})$, changes A, B, C to $A' = A + \delta$, $B' = B - 2\delta$, $C' = C + \delta$, where $\delta = (p_n - p)(p - p_{n-1})$; hence h_k changes to $h'_k = h_k + \delta(g(k) - 2g(k + 1) + g(k + 2))$. Convex functions satisfy $g(k) - 2g(k + 1) + g(k + 2) \ge 0$, by (19) with $x = k$ and $y = k + 2$; hence we can permute the p's and repeat this transformation until $p_j = p$ for $1 \le j \le n$.

(b) Suppose $E g(X)$ is maximum, and that r of the p's are 0 and s of them are 1. Let a satisfy $(n - r - s)a + s = np$ and assume that $0 < p_{n-1} < a < p_n < 1$. As in part (a) we can write $E g(X) = \alpha A + \beta B + \gamma C$ for some coefficients α, β, γ.

If $\alpha - 2\beta + \gamma > 0$, the transformation in (a) (but with a in place of p) would increase $E g(X)$. And if $\alpha - 2\beta + \gamma < 0$, we could increase it with a similar transformation, using $\delta = -\min(p_{n-1}, 1 - p_n)$. Therefore $\alpha - 2\beta + \gamma = 0$; and we can repeat the transformation of (a) until every p_j is 0, 1, or a.

(c) Since $\sum_{k=0}^{m}\left(\binom{n}{k}\right) = 0$ when $s > m$, we may assume that $s \le m$, hence $r + s < n$. For this function $g(k) = [0 \le k \le m]$ we have $\alpha - 2\beta + \gamma = \left(\binom{n-2}{m}\right) - \left(\binom{n-2}{m-1}\right)$. This difference cannot be positive if the choice of $\{p_1, \ldots, p_n\}$ is optimum; in particular we cannot have $s = m$. If $r > 0$ we can make $p_{n-1} = 0$ and $p_n = a$, so that $\left(\!\binom{n-2}{m}\!\right) = \binom{n-r-s-1}{m-s}a^{m-s}(1-a)^{n-r-1-m}$ and $\left(\!\binom{n-2}{m-1}\!\right) = \binom{n-r-s-1}{m-1-s}a^{m-1-s}(1-a)^{n-r-m}$. But then the ratio $\left(\!\binom{n-2}{m}\!\right)/\left(\!\binom{n-2}{m-1}\!\right) = (n-r-m)a/((m-s)(1-a))$ exceeds 1; hence $r = 0$.

Similarly if $s > 0$ we can set $(p_{n-1}, p_n) = (a, 1)$, getting the ratio $\left(\!\binom{n-2}{m}\!\right)/\left(\!\binom{n-2}{m-1}\!\right) = (n-1-m)a/((m-s+1)(1-a)) \geq 1$. In this case $\left(\!\binom{n-2}{m}\!\right) = \left(\!\binom{n-2}{m-1}\!\right)$ if and only if $np = m+1$; we can transform without changing $\mathrm{E}\,g(X)$, until $s = 0$ and each $p_j = p$.

[*Reference: Annals of Mathematical Statistics* **27** (1956), 713–721. The coefficients $\left(\!\binom{n}{k}\!\right)$ also have many other important properties; see exercise 7.2.1.5–63 and the survey by J. Pitman in *J. Combinatorial Theory* **A77** (1997), 279–303.]

29. The result is obvious when $m = 0$ or n; and there's a direct proof when $m = n-1$: $B_{n-1,n}(p) = 1 - p^n \geq (1-p)n/((1-p)n + p)$ because $p - np^n + (n-1)p^{n+1} = p(1-p)(1+p+\cdots+p^{n-1} - p^{n-1}n) \geq 0$. The result is also clear when $p = 0$ or 1.

If $p = (m+1)/n$ we have $R_{m,n}(p) = ((1-p)(m+1)/((1-p)m+1))^{n-m} = ((n-m-1)/(n-m))^{n-m}$. So if $m > 0$ and $\hat{p} = m/(n-1)$, we can apply exercise 28(c) with $p_1 = \cdots = p_{n-1} = \hat{p}$ and $p_n = 1$:

$$B_{m,n}(p) \geq \textstyle\sum_{k=0}^m \left(\!\binom{n}{k}\!\right) = \sum_{k=0}^m \binom{n-1}{k-1}\hat{p}^{k-1}(1-\hat{p})^{n-k} = B_{m-1,n-1}(\hat{p}).$$

When $1 \leq m < n-1$, let $Q_{m,n}(p) = B_{m,n}(p) - R_{m,n}(p)$. The derivative

$$Q'_{m,n}(p) = (n-m)\binom{n}{m}(1-p)^{n-m-1}(A - F(p))/((1-p)m+1)^{n-m+1},$$

where $A = (m+1)^{n-m}/\binom{n}{m} > 1$ and $F(p) = p^m((1-p)m+1)^{n-m+1}$, begins positive at $p = 0$, eventually becomes negative but then is positive again at $p = 1$. (Notice that $F(0) = 0$, and $F(p)$ increases dramatically until $p = (m+1)/(n+1)$; then it decreases to $F(1) = 1$.) The facts that $Q_{m,n}(\frac{m+1}{n}) \geq 0 = Q_{m,n}(0) = Q_{m,n}(1)$ now complete the proof, because $Q'_{m,n}(p)$ changes sign only once in $[0 .. \frac{m+1}{n}]$. [*Annals of Mathematical Statistics* **36** (1965), 1272–1278.]

30. (a) $\Pr(X_k = 0) = n/(n+1)$; hence $p = n^n/(n+1)^n > 1/e \approx 0.368$.

(b) (Solution by J. H. Elton.) Let $p_{km} = \Pr(X_k = m)$. Assume that these probabilities are fixed for $1 \leq k < n$, and let $x_m = p_{nm}$. Then $x_0 = x_2 + 2x_3 + 3x_4 + \cdots$; we want to minimize $p = \sum_{m=1}^{\infty}(A_m + (m-1)A_0)x_m$ in nonnegative variables $x_1, x_2, \ldots$, where $A_m = \Pr(X_1 + \cdots + X_{n-1} \leq n-m)$, subject to the condition $\sum_{m=1}^{\infty} mx_m = 1$. Since all coefficients of p are nonnegative, the minimum is achieved when all x_m for $m \geq 1$ are zero except for one value $m = m_n$, which minimizes $(A_m + (m-1)A_0)/m$. And $m_n \leq n+1$, because $A_m = 0$ whenever $m > n$. Similarly $m_1, \ldots, m_{n-1}$ also exist.

(c) (Solution by E. Schulte-Geers.) Letting $m_1 = \cdots = m_n = t \leq n+1$, we want to minimize $B_{\lfloor n/t \rfloor, n}(1/t)$. The inequality of Samuels in exercise 29 implies that

$$B_{m,n}(p) \geq \left(1 - \frac{1}{f(m,n,p)+1}\right)^n \text{ for } p \leq \frac{m+1}{n}, \text{ where } f(m,n,p) = \frac{(m+1)(1-p)n}{(n-m)p},$$

because we can set $x = ((1-p)m+1)/((1-p)(m+1))$ in the arithmetic–geometric mean inequality $x^{n-m} \leq ((n-m)x+m)^n/n^n$. Now $1/t \leq (\lfloor n/t \rfloor + 1)/(n+1)$ and $f(\lfloor n/t \rfloor, n, 1/t) \geq n$; hence $B_{\lfloor n/t \rfloor, n}(1/t) \geq n^n/(n+1)^n$.

[Peter Winkler called this the "gumball machine problem" in *CACM* **52**, 8 (August 2009), 104–105. J. H. Elton has verified that the joint distributions in (a) are optimum when $n \leq 20$; see arXiv:0908.3528 [math.PR] (2009), 7 pages. Do those distributions in fact minimize p for all n? Uriel Feige has conjectured more generally that we have $\Pr(X_1 + \cdots + X_n < n + 1/(e-1)) \geq 1/e$ whenever $X_1, \ldots, X_n$ are independent nonnegative random variables with $\mathrm{E}\,X_k \leq 1$; see *SICOMP* **35** (2006), 964–984.]

31. This result is immediate because $\Pr(f([A_1], \ldots, [A_n])) = \mathrm{E}\, f([A_1], \ldots, [A_n])$. But a more detailed, lower-level proof will be helpful with respect to exercise 32.

Suppose, for example, that $n = 4$. The reliability polynomial is the sum of the reliability polynomials for the minterms of f; so it suffices to show that the result is true for functions like $x_1 \wedge \bar{x}_2 \wedge \bar{x}_3 \wedge x_4 = x_1(1 - x_2)(1 - x_3)x_4$. And it's clear that $\Pr(A_1 \cap \bar{A}_2 \cap \bar{A}_3 \cap A_4) = \Pr(A_1 \cap \bar{A}_2 \cap A_4) - \Pr(A_1 \cap \bar{A}_2 \cap A_3 \cap A_4) = \pi_{14} - \pi_{124} - \pi_{134} + \pi_{1234}$. (See exercise 7.1.1–12; also recall the inclusion-exclusion principle.)

32. The 2^n minterm probabilities in the previous answer must all be nonnegative, and they must sum to 1. We've already stipulated that $\pi_\emptyset = 1$, so the sum-to-1 condition is automatically satisfied. (The condition stated in the exercise when $I \subseteq J$ is necessary but not sufficient; for example, π_{12} must be $\geq \pi_1 + \pi_2 - 1$.)

33. The three events $(X, Y) = (1, 0)$, $(0, 1)$, $(1, 1)$ occur with probabilities p, q, r, respectively. The value of $\mathrm{E}(X \mid Y)$ is 1, $r/(q + r)$, $r/(q + r)$ in those cases. Hence the answer is $pz + (q + r)z^{r/(q+r)}$. (This example demonstrates why univariate generating functions are *not* used in the study of conditional random variables such as $\mathrm{E}(X \mid Y)$. But we do have the simple formula $\mathrm{E}(X \mid Y = k) = ([z^k] \frac{\partial}{\partial w} G(1, z))/([z^k] G(1, z))$.)

34. The right-hand side is

$$\sum_\omega \mathrm{E}(X \mid Y)\Pr(\omega) = \sum_\omega \Pr(\omega) \sum_{\omega'} X(\omega')\Pr(\omega')[Y(\omega') = Y(\omega)]/\Pr(Y = Y(\omega))$$

$$= \sum_\omega \Pr(\omega) \sum_{\omega'} X(\omega')\Pr(\omega')[Y(\omega') = Y(\omega)]/\Pr(Y = Y(\omega'))$$

$$= \sum_{\omega'} X(\omega')\Pr(\omega') \sum_\omega \Pr(\omega)[Y(\omega) = Y(\omega')]/\Pr(Y = Y(\omega')).$$

35. Part (b) is false. If, for instance, X and Y are independent random bits and $Z = X$, we have $\mathrm{E}(X \mid Y) = \frac{1}{2}$ and $\mathrm{E}(\frac{1}{2} \mid Z) = \frac{1}{2} \neq X = \mathrm{E}(X \mid Z)$. The correct formula instead of (b) is

$$\mathrm{E}(\mathrm{E}(X \mid Y, Z) \mid Z) = \mathrm{E}(X \mid Z). \qquad (*)$$

This is (12) in the probability spaces conditioned by Z, and it is the crucial identity that underlies exercise 91. Part (a) is true because it is the case $Y = Z$ of $(*)$.

36. (a) $f(X)$; (b) $\mathrm{E}(f(Y)g(X))$, generalizing (12). Proof: $\mathrm{E}(f(Y)\,\mathrm{E}(g(X) \mid Y)) = \sum_y f(y)\,\mathrm{E}(g(X) \mid Y = y)\Pr(Y = y) = \sum_{x,y} f(y)g(x)\Pr(X = x, Y = y) = \mathrm{E}(f(Y)g(X))$.

37. If we're given the values of $X_1, \ldots, X_{k-1}$, the value of X_k is equally likely to be any of the $n + 1 - k$ values in $\{1, \ldots, n\} \setminus \{X_1, \ldots, X_{k-1}\}$. Hence its average value is $(1 + \cdots + n - X_1 - \cdots - X_{k-1})/(n + 1 - k)$. We conclude that $\mathrm{E}(X_k \mid X_1, \ldots, X_{k-1}) = (n(n + 1)/2 - X_1 - \cdots - X_{k-1})/(n + 1 - k)$. [Incidentally, the sequence $Z_0, Z_1, \ldots$, defined by $Z_j = (n + j)X_1 + (n + j - 2)X_2 + \cdots + (n - j)X_{j+1} - (j + 1)n(n + 1)/2$ for $0 \leq j < n$ and $Z_j = Z_{n-1}$ for $j \geq n$, is therefore a martingale.]

38. Let $t_{m,n}$ be the number of restricted growth strings of length $m + n$ that begin with $01 \ldots (m-1)$. (This is the number of set partitions of $\{1, \ldots, m+n\}$ in which each of $\{1, \ldots, m\}$ appears in a different block.) The generating function $\sum_{n \geq 0} t_{m,n} z^n/n!$ turns out to be $\exp(e^z - 1 + mz)$; hence $t_{m,n} = \sum_k \varpi_k \binom{n}{k} m^{n-k}$.

Suppose $M = \max(X_1, \ldots, X_{k-1}) + 1$. Then $\Pr(X_k = j) = t_{M,n-k}/t_{M,n+1-k}$ for $0 \leq j < M$, and $t_{M+1,n-k}/t_{M,n+1-k}$ for $j = M$. Hence $\mathrm{E}(X_k \mid X_0, \ldots, X_{k-1}) = (\binom{M}{2} t_{M,n-k} + M t_{M+1,n-k})/t_{M,n+1-k}$.

39. (a) Since $E(K | N = n) = pn$ we have $E(K | N) = pN$.

(b) Hence $E K = E(E(K | N)) = E pN = p\mu$.

(c) Let $p_{nk} = \Pr(N = n, K = k) = (e^{-\mu}\mu^n/n!) \times \binom{n}{k}p^k(1-p)^{n-k} = (e^{-\mu}\mu^k p^k/k!) \times f(n-k)$, where $f(n) = (1-p)^n\mu^n/n!$. Then $E(N | K = k) = \sum_n np_{nk}/\sum_n p_{nk}$. Since $nf(n-k) = kf(n-k) + (n-k)f(n-k)$ and $nf(n) = (1-p)\mu f(n-1)$, the answer is $k + (1-p)\mu$; hence $E(N | K) = K + (1-p)\mu$. [G. Grimmett and D. Stirzaker, *Probability and Random Processes* (Oxford: 1982), §3.7.]

40. If $p = \Pr(X > m)$, clearly $E X \le (1-p)m + pM$. [We also get this result from (15), by taking $S = \{x \mid x \le m\}$, $f(x) = M - x$, $s = M - m$.]

41. (a) Convex when $a \ge 1$ or $a = 0$; otherwise neither convex nor concave. (However, x^a is concave when $0 < a < 1$ and convex when $a < 0$, if we consider only positive values of x.) (b) Convex when n is even or $n = 1$; otherwise neither convex nor concave. (This function is $\int_0^x t^{n-1}e^{x-t}dt/(n-1)!$, according to 1.2.11.3–(5); so $f''(x)/x > 0$ when $n \ge 3$ is odd.) (c) Convex. (In fact $f(|x|)$ is convex whenever $f(z)$ has a power series with nonnegative coefficients, convergent for all z.) (d) Convex, provided of course that we allow f to be infinite in the definition (19).

42. We can show by induction on n that $f(p_1x_1 + \cdots + p_nx_n) \le p_1f(x_1) + \cdots + p_nf(x_n)$, when $p_1, \ldots, p_n \ge 0$ and $p_1 + \cdots + p_n = 1$, as in exercise 6.2.2–36. The general result follows by taking limits as $n \to \infty$. [The quantity $p_1x_1 + \cdots + p_nx_n$ is called a "convex combination" of $\{x_1, \ldots, x_n\}$; similarly, $E X$ is a convex combination of X values. Jensen actually began his study by assuming only the case $p = q = \frac{1}{2}$ of (19).]

43. $f(E X) = f(E(E(X | Y))) \le E(f(E(X | Y))) \le E(E f(X) | Y) = E f(X)$. [S. M. Ross, *Probability Models for Computer Science* (2002), Lemma 3.2.1.]

44. The function $f(xy)$ is convex in y for any fixed x. Therefore $g(y) = E f(Xy)$ is convex in y: It's a convex combination of convex functions. Also $g(y) \ge f(E Xy) = f(0) = g(0)$ by (20). Hence $0 \le a \le b$ implies $g(0) \le g(a) \le g(b)$ by convexity of g. [S. Boyd and L. Vandenberghe, *Convex Optimization* (2004), exercise 3.10.]

45. $\Pr(X > 0) = \Pr(|X| \ge 1)$; set $m = 1$ in (16).

46. $E X^2 \ge (E X)^2$ in *any* probability distribution, by Jensen's inequality, because squaring is convex. We can also prove it directly, since $E X^2 - (E X)^2 = E(X - E X)^2$.

47. We always have $Y \ge X$ and $Y^2 \le X^2$. (Consequently (22) yields $\Pr(X > 0) = \Pr(Y > 0) \ge (E Y)^2/(E Y^2) \ge (E X)^2/(E X^2)$ when $E X \ge 0$.)

48. $\Pr(a - X_1 - \cdots - X_n > 0) \ge a^2/(a^2 + \sigma_1^2 + \cdots + \sigma_n^2)$, by exercise 47. [This inequality was *also* known to Chebyshev; see *J. Math. Pures et Appl.* (2) **19** (1874), 157–160. In the special case $n = 1$ it is equivalent to "Cantelli's inequality,"

$$\Pr(X \ge E X + a) \le \text{var}(X)/(\text{var}(X) + a^2), \qquad \text{for } a \ge 0;$$

see *Atti del Congresso Internazionale dei Matematici* **6** (Bologna: 1928), 47–59, §6–§7.]

49. $\Pr(X = 0) = 1 - \Pr(X > 0) \le (E X^2 - (E X)^2)/E X^2 \le (E X^2 - (E X)^2)/(E X)^2 = (E X^2)/(E X)^2 - 1$. [Some authors call *this* inequality the "second moment principle," but it is strictly weaker than (22).]

50. (a) Let $Y_j = X_j/X$ if $X_j > 0$, otherwise $Y_j = 0$. Then $Y_1 + \cdots + Y_m = [X > 0]$. Hence $\Pr(X > 0) = \sum_{j=1}^m E Y_j$; and $E Y_j = E(X_j/X | X_j > 0) \cdot \Pr(X_j > 0)$. [This identity, which requires only that $X_j \ge 0$, is elementary yet nonlinear, so it apparently lay undiscovered for many years. See D. Aldous, *Discrete Math.* **76** (1989), 168.]

(b) Since $X_j \in \{0, 1\}$, we have $\Pr(X_j > 0) = \mathrm{E}\, X_j = p_j$; and $\mathrm{E}(X_j/X \mid X_j > 0) = \mathrm{E}(X_j/X \mid X_j{=}1) = \mathrm{E}(1/X \mid X_j{=}1) \geq 1/\mathrm{E}(X \mid X_j{=}1)$.

(c) $\Pr(X_J = 1) = \sum_{j=1}^{m} \Pr(J = j \text{ and } X_j = 1) = \sum_{j=1}^{m} p_j/m = \mathrm{E}\, X/m$. Hence $\Pr(J{=}j \mid X_J{=}1) = \Pr(J{=}j \text{ and } X_j{=}1)/\Pr(X_J{=}1) = (p_j/m)/(\mathrm{E}\,X/m) = p_j/\mathrm{E}\,X$.

(d) Since J is independent we have $t_j = \mathrm{E}(X \mid J = j \text{ and } X_j = 1) = \mathrm{E}(X \mid X_j = 1)$.

(e) The right side is $(\mathrm{E}\,X)\sum_{j=1}^{m}(p_j/\mathrm{E}\,X)/t_j \geq (\mathrm{E}\,X)/\sum_{j=1}^{m}(p_j/\mathrm{E}\,X)t_j$.

51. If $g(q_1, \ldots, q_m) = 1 - f(p_1, \ldots, p_m)$ is the dual of f, where $q_j = 1 - p_j$, a lower bound on g gives an upper bound on f. For example, when f is $x_1x_2x_3 \vee x_2x_3x_4 \vee x_4x_5$, $\bar{f}$ is $\bar{x}_1\bar{x}_4 + \bar{x}_2\bar{x}_4 + \bar{x}_3\bar{x}_4 + \bar{x}_2\bar{x}_5 + \bar{x}_3\bar{x}_5$. So the inequality (24) gives $g(q_1, \ldots, q_5) \geq q_1q_4/(1 + q_2 + q_3 + q_2q_5 + q_3q_5) + q_2q_4/(q_1 + 1 + q_3 + q_5 + q_3q_5) + q_3q_4/(q_1 + q_2 + 1 + q_2q_5 + q_5) + q_2q_5/(q_1q_4 + q_4 + q_3q_4 + 1 + q_3) + q_3q_5/(q_1q_4 + q_2q_4 + q_4 + q_2 + 1)$. In particular, $g(.1, \ldots, .1) > 0.039$ and $f(.9, \ldots, .9) < 0.961$.

52. $\binom{n}{k}p^k / \sum_{j=0}^{k}\binom{k}{j}\binom{n-k}{j}p^j$.

53. $f(p_1, \ldots, p_6) \geq p_1p_2(1-p_3)/(1+p_4p_5(1-p_6)) + \cdots + p_6p_1(1-p_2)/(1+p_3p_4(1-p_5))$. Monotonicity is not required when applying this method, nor need the implicants be prime. The result is exact when the implicants are disjoint.

54. (a) $\Pr(X > 0) \leq \mathrm{E}\,X = \binom{n}{3}p^3$, because $\mathrm{E}\,X_{uvw} = p^3$ for all $u < v < w$.

(b) $\Pr(X > 0) \geq (\mathrm{E}\,X)^2/(\mathrm{E}\,X^2)$, where the numerator is the square of (a) and the denominator can be shown to be $\binom{n}{3}p^3 + 12\binom{n}{4}p^5 + 30\binom{n}{5}p^6 + 20\binom{n}{6}p^6$. For example, the expansion of X^2 contains 12 terms of the form $X_{uvw}X_{uvw'}$ with $u < v < w < w'$, and each of those terms has expected value p^5.

55. A BDD for the corresponding Boolean function of $\binom{10}{2} = 45$ variables has about 1.4 million nodes, and allows us to evaluate the true probability $(1 - p)^{45}G(p/(1 - p))$ exactly, where $G(z)$ is the corresponding generating function (see exercise 7.1.4–25). The results are: (a) $30/37 \approx .811 < 35165158461687/2^{45} \approx .999 < 15$; (b) $10/109 \approx .092 < 4180246784470862526910349589019919032987399/(4 \times 10^{43}) \approx .105 < .12$.

56. The upper bound is $\mu = \lambda^3/6$; the lower bound divides this by $1 + \mu$. [The exact asymptotic value can be obtained using the principle of inclusion and exclusion and its "bracketing" property, as in Eq. 7.2.1.4–(48); the result is $1 - e^{-\mu}$. See P. Erdős and A. Rényi, *Magyar Tudományos Akadémia Mat. Kut. Int. Közl.* **5** (1960), 17–61, §3.]

57. To compute $\mathrm{E}(X \mid X_{uvw} = 1)$ we sum $\Pr(X_{u'v'w'} \mid X_{uvw} = 1)$ over all $\binom{n}{3}$ choices of $u' < v' < w'$. If $\{u', v', w'\} \cap \{u, v, w\}$ has t elements, this probability is $p^{3-t(t-1)/2}$; and there are $\binom{3}{t}\binom{n-3}{3-t}$ such cases. Consequently we get

$$\Pr(X > 0) \geq \binom{n}{3}p^3 / \left(\binom{n-3}{3}p^3 + 3\binom{n-3}{2}p^3 + 3\binom{n-3}{1}p^2 + \binom{n-3}{0}p^0\right).$$

[In this problem the lower bound turns out to be the same using either inequality; but the derivation here was easier.]

58. $\Pr(X > 0) \leq \binom{n}{k}p^{k(k-1)/2}$. The lower bound, using the conditional expectation inequality as in the previous answer, divides this by $\sum_{t=0}^{k}\binom{k}{t}\binom{n-k}{k-t}p^{k(k-1)/2-t(t-1)/2}$.

59. (a) It suffices to prove that $a_0b_1 + a_1b_0 \leq c_0d_1 + c_1d_0$. The key observation is that $c_1d_0(c_0d_1 + c_1d_0 - a_0b_1 - a_1b_0) = (c_1d_0 - a_0b_1)(c_1d_0 - a_1b_0) + (c_0c_1d_0d_1 - a_0a_1b_0b_1)$. Thus the result holds when $c_1d_0 \neq 0$; and if $c_1d_0 = 0$ we have $a_0b_1 + a_1b_0 = 0$.

All four hypotheses hold with equality when $a_0 = b_0 = d_0 = 0$ and the other variables are 1, yet the conclusion is that $1 \leq 2$. Conversely, when $b_1 = c_1 = 2$ and the other variables are 1, we have $a_1b_0 < c_1d_0$ but conclude only that $6 \leq 6$.

(b) Let $A_l = \sum\{a_{2j+l} \mid 0 \le j < 2^{n-1}\}$ for $l = 0$ and $l = 1$, and define B_l, C_l, D_l similarly from b_{2j+l}, c_{2j+l}, d_{2j+l}. The hypotheses for $j \bmod 2 = l$ and $k \bmod 2 = m$ prove that $A_l B_m \le C_{l|m} D_{l\&m}$, by induction on n. Hence, by part (a), we have the desired inequality $(A_0 + A_1)(B_0 + B_1) \le (C_0 + C_1)(D_0 + D_1)$. [This result is due to R. Ahlswede and D. E. Daykin, *Zeitschrift für Wahrscheinlichkeitstheorie und verwandte Gebiete* **43** (1978), 183–185, who stated it in the language of the next exercise.]

(c) Now let $A_n = a_0 + \cdots + a_{2^n - 1}$, and define B_n, C_n, D_n similarly. If $A_\infty B_\infty > C_\infty D_\infty$, we'll have $A_n B_n > C_\infty D_\infty$ for some n. But $C_\infty D_\infty \ge C_n D_n$, contra (b).

[In fact much more is true: We have $\sum_{\nu j + \nu k = n} a_j b_k \le \sum_{\nu j + \nu k = n} c_j d_k$, for all n. See A. Björner, *Combinatorica* **31** (2011), 151–164; D. Christofides, arXiv:0909.5137 [math.CO] (2009), 6 pages.]

60. (a) We can consider each set to be a subset of the nonnegative integers. Let $\overline{\alpha}(S) = \alpha(S)[S \in \mathcal{F}]$, $\overline{\beta}(S) = \beta(S)[S \in \mathcal{G}]$, $\overline{\gamma}(S) = \gamma(S)[S \in \mathcal{F} \sqcup \mathcal{G}]$, $\overline{\delta}(S) = \delta(S)[S \in \mathcal{F} \sqcap \mathcal{G}]$; then $\overline{\alpha}(\wp) = \alpha(\mathcal{F})$, $\overline{\beta}(\wp) = \beta(\mathcal{G})$, $\overline{\gamma}(\wp) = \gamma(\mathcal{F} \sqcup \mathcal{G})$, and $\overline{\delta}(\wp) = \delta(\mathcal{F} \sqcap \mathcal{G})$, where $\wp$ is the family of all possible subsets. Since any set S of nonnegative integers can be encoded in the usual way as the binary number $s = \sum_{j \in S} 2^j$, the desired result follows from the four functions theorem if we let $a_s = \overline{\alpha}(S)$, $b_s = \overline{\beta}(S)$, $c_s = \overline{\gamma}(S)$, $d_s = \overline{\delta}(S)$.

(b) Let $\alpha(S) = \beta(S) = \gamma(S) = \delta(S) = 1$ for all sets S.

61. (a) In the hinted case we can let $\alpha(S) = f(S)\mu(S)$, $\beta(S) = g(S)\mu(S)$, $\gamma(S) = f(S)g(S)\mu(S)$, $\delta(S) = \mu(S)$; the four functions theorem yields the result. The general case follows because we have $\mathrm{E}(fg) - \mathrm{E}(f)\mathrm{E}(g) = \mathrm{E}(\hat{f}\hat{g}) - \mathrm{E}(\hat{f})\mathrm{E}(\hat{g})$, where $\hat{f}(S) = f(S) - f(\emptyset)$ and $\hat{g}(S) = g(S) - g(\emptyset)$. [See *Commun. Math. Physics* **22** (1971), 89–103.]

(b) Changing $f(S)$ to $\theta f(S)$ and $g(S)$ to $\phi g(S)$ changes $\mathrm{E}(fg) - \mathrm{E}(f)\mathrm{E}(g)$ to $\theta\phi(\mathrm{E}(fg) - \mathrm{E}(f)\mathrm{E}(g))$, for all real numbers θ and ϕ.

(c) If S and T are supported, then $R = S \cap T$ and $U = S \cup T$ are supported. Furthermore we can write $S = R \cup \{s_1, \ldots, s_k\}$ and $T = R \cup \{t_1, \ldots, t_l\}$ where the sets $S_i = R \cup \{s_1, \ldots, s_i\}$ and $T_j = R \cup \{t_1, \ldots, t_j\}$ are supported, as are their unions $U_{i,j} = S_i \cup T_j$, for $0 \le i \le k$ and $0 \le j \le l$. By (iii) we know that $\mu(U_{i+1,j})/\mu(U_{i,j}) \le \mu(U_{i+1,j+1})/\mu(U_{i,j+1})$ when $0 \le i < k$ and $0 \le j < l$. Multiplying these inequalities for $0 \le i < k$, we obtain $\mu(U_{k,j})/\mu(U_{0,j}) \le \mu(U_{k,j+1})/\mu(U_{0,j+1})$. Hence $\mu(S)/\mu(R) = \mu(U_{k,0})/\mu(U_{0,0}) \le \mu(U_{k,l})/\mu(U_{0,l}) = \mu(U)/\mu(T)$.

(d) In fact, equality holds, because $[j \in S] + [j \in T] = [j \in S \cup T] + [j \in S \cap T]$. [*Note:* Random variables with this distribution are often confusingly called "Poisson trials," a term that conflicts with the (quite different) Poisson distribution of exercise 39.]

(e) Choose c in the following examples so that $\sum_S \mu(S) = 1$. In each case the supported sets are subsets of $U = \{1, \ldots, m\}$. (i) Let $\mu(S) = c r_1 r_2 \ldots r_{|S|}$, where $0 < r_1 \le \cdots \le r_m$. (ii) Let $\mu(S) = c p_j$ when $S = \{1, \ldots, j\}$ and $1 \le j \le m$, otherwise $\mu(S) = 0$. (If $p_1 = \cdots = p_m$ in this case, the FKG inequality reduces to Chebyshev's monotonic inequality of exercise 1.2.3–31.) (iii) Let

$$\mu(S) = c \mu_1(S \cap U_1)\mu_2(S \cap U_2)\ldots\mu_k(S \cap U_k),$$

where each μ_j is a distribution on the subsets of $U_j \subseteq U$ that satisfies (**). The subuniverses $U_1, \ldots, U_k$ needn't be disjoint. (iv) Let $\mu(S) = c e^{-f(S)}$, where f is a submodular set function on the supported subsets of U: $f(S \cup T) + f(S \cap T) \le f(S) + f(T)$ whenever $f(S)$ and $f(T)$ are defined. (See Section 7.6.)

62. A Boolean function is essentially a set function whose values are 0 or 1. In general, under the Bernoulli distribution or any other distribution that satisfies the condition of exercise 61, the FKG inequality implies that any monotone increasing

Boolean function is positively correlated with any other monotone increasing Boolean function, but negatively correlated with any monotone *decreasing* Boolean function. In this case, f is monotone increasing but g is monotone decreasing: Adding an edge doesn't disconnect a graph; deleting an edge doesn't invalidate a 4-coloring.

(Notice that when f is a Boolean function, $\mathrm{E}\,f$ is the probability that f is true under the given distribution. The fact that $\mathrm{covar}(f,g) \leq 0$ in such a case is equivalent to saying that the conditional probability $\Pr(f \mid g)$ is $\leq \Pr(f)$.)

63. If ω is the event '$Z_0 = a$ and $Z_1 = b$', we have $Z_0(\omega) = a$ and $\mathrm{E}(Z_1 \mid Z_0)(\omega) = (p_{a1} + 2p_{a2})/(p_{a0} + p_{a1} + p_{a2})$. Hence $p_{01} = p_{02} = p_{20} = p_{21} = 0$, and $p_{10} = p_{12}$. Those conditions are necessary and sufficient for $\mathrm{E}(Z_1 \mid Z_0) = Z_0$.

64. (a) No. Consider the probability space consisting of just three events $(Z_0, Z_1, Z_2) = (0, 0, -2)$, $(1, 0, 2)$, $(1, 2, 2)$, each with probability $1/3$. Call those events a, b, c. Then $\mathrm{E}(Z_1 \mid Z_0)(a) = 0 = Z_0(a)$; $\mathrm{E}(Z_1 \mid Z_0)(b, c) = \frac{1}{2}(0 + 2) = Z_0(b, c)$; $\mathrm{E}(Z_2 \mid Z_1)(a, b) = \frac{1}{2}(-2 + 2) = Z_1(a, b)$; $\mathrm{E}(Z_2 \mid Z_1)(c) = 2 = Z_1(c)$. But $\mathrm{E}(Z_2 \mid Z_0, Z_1)(a) = -2 \neq Z_1(a)$.

(b) Yes. We have $\sum_{z_{n+1}}(z_{n+1} - z_n) \Pr(Z_0 = z_0, \ldots, Z_{n+1} = z_{n+1}) = 0$ for all fixed $(z_0, \ldots, z_n)$. Sum these to get $\sum_{z_{n+1}}(z_{n+1} - z_n) \Pr(Z_n = z_n, Z_{n+1} = z_{n+1}) = 0$.

65. Observe first that $\mathrm{E}(Z_{n+1} \mid Z_0, \ldots, Z_k) = \mathrm{E}(\mathrm{E}(Z_{n+1} \mid Z_0, \ldots, Z_n) \mid Z_0, \ldots, Z_k) = \mathrm{E}(Z_n \mid Z_0, \ldots, Z_k)$ whenever $k < n$. Thus $\mathrm{E}(Z_{m(n+1)} \mid Z_0, \ldots, Z_{m(n)}) = Z_{m(n)}$ for all $n \geq 0$. Hence $\mathrm{E}(Z_{m(n+1)} \mid Z_{m(0)}, \ldots, Z_{m(n)}) = Z_{m(n)}$, as in the previous exercise.

66. We need to specify the joint distribution of $\{Z_0, \ldots, Z_n\}$, and it's not difficult to see that there is only one solution. Let $p(\sigma_1, \ldots, \sigma_n) = \Pr(Z_1 = \sigma_1, \ldots, Z_n = \sigma_n n)$ when $\sigma_1, \ldots, \sigma_n$ are each ± 1. The martingale law $p(\sigma_1 \ldots \sigma_n 1)(n+1) - p(\sigma_1 \ldots \sigma_n \bar{1})(n+1) = \sigma_n p(\sigma_1 \ldots \sigma_n)n = \sigma_n(p(\sigma_1 \ldots \sigma_n 1) + p(\sigma_1 \ldots \sigma_n \bar{1}))n$ gives $p(\sigma_1 \ldots \sigma_{n+1})/p(\sigma_1 \ldots \sigma_n) = (1 + 2n[\sigma_n \sigma_{n+1} > 0])/(2n + 2)$. Hence we find that $\Pr(Z_1 = z_1, \ldots, Z_n = z_n) = (\prod_{k=1}^{n-1}(1 + 2k[z_k z_{k+1} > 0]))/(2^n n!)$. When $n = 3$, for example, the eight possible cases $z_1 z_2 z_3 = 123, 12\bar{3}, \ldots, \bar{1}\bar{2}\bar{3}$ occur with probabilities $(15, 3, 1, 5, 5, 1, 3, 15)/48$.

67. (a) You "always" (with probability 1) make $2^{n+1} - (1 + 2 + \cdots + 2^n) = 1$ dollar.

(b) Your total payments are $X = X_0 + X_1 + \cdots$ dollars, where $X_n = 2^n$ with probability 2^{-n}, otherwise $X_n = 0$. So $\mathrm{E}\,X_n = 1$, and $\mathrm{E}\,X = \mathrm{E}\,X_0 + \mathrm{E}\,X_1 + \cdots = \infty$.

(c) Let $\langle T_n \rangle$ be a sequence of uniformly random bits; and define the fair sequence $Y_n = (-1)^{T_n} 2^n T_0 \ldots T_{n-1}$, or $Y_n = 0$ if there is no nth bet. Then $Z_n = Y_0 + \cdots + Y_n$.

[The famous adventurer Casanova lost a fortune in 1754 using this strategy, which he called "the martingale" in his autobiography *Histoire de ma vie*. A similar betting scheme had been proposed by Nicolas Bernoulli (see P. R. de Montmort, *Essay d'Analyse sur les Jeux de Hazard*, second edition (1713), page 402); and the perplexities of (a) and (b) were studied by his cousin Daniel Bernoulli, whose important paper in *Commentarii Academiæ Scientiarum Imperialis Petropolitanæ* **5** (1731), 175–192, has caused this scenario to become known as the St. Petersburg paradox.]

68. (a) Now $Z_n = Y_1 + \cdots + Y_n$, where $Y_n = (-1)^{T_n}[N \geq n]$. Again $\Pr(Z_N = 1) = 1$.

(b) The generating function $g(z)$ equals $z(1 + g(z)^2)/2$, since he must win \$2 if the first bet loses. Hence $g(z) = (1 - \sqrt{1 - z^2})/z$; and the desired probability is $[z^n]\,g(z) = C_{(n-1)/2}[n \text{ odd}]/2^n$, where C_k is the Catalan number $\binom{2k}{k}/(k+1)$.

(c) $\Pr(N \geq n) = [z^n]\,(1 - zg(z))/(1 - z) = [z^n]\,(1 + z)/\sqrt{1 - z^2} = \binom{2\lfloor n/2 \rfloor}{\lfloor n/2 \rfloor}/2^{\lfloor n/2 \rfloor}$.

(d) $\mathrm{E}\,N = g'(1) = \infty$. (It's also $\sum_{n=1}^{\infty} \Pr(N \geq n)$, where $\Pr(N \geq n) \sim 1/\sqrt{\pi n}$.)

(e) Let $p_m = \Pr(Z_n \geq -m)$ for all $n \geq 0$. Clearly $p_0 = 1/2$ and $p_m = (1 + p_{m-1} p_m)/2$ for $m > 0$; this recurrence has the solution $p_m = (m + 1)/(m + 2)$. So the answer is $1/((m + 1)(m + 2))$; it's another probability distribution with infinite mean.

(f) The generating function $g_m(z)$ for the number of times $-m$ is hit satisfies $g_0(z) = z/(2-z)$, $g_m(z) = (1+g_{m-1}(z)g_m(z))/2$ for $m > 0$. So $g_m(z) = h_m(z)/h_{m+1}(z)$ for $m \geq 0$, where $h_m(z) = 2m - (2m-1)z$, and $g'_m(1) = 2$. [A distribution with *finite* mean! See W. Feller, *An Intro. to Probability Theory* **2**, second edition (1971), XII.2.]

69. Each permutation of n elements corresponds to a configuration of $n+1$ balls in the urn. For Method 1, the number of corresponding "red balls" is the *position* of element 1; for Method 2, it is the *value* in position 1. For example, we'd put $3\,1\,2\,4$ into node $(2,3)$ with respect to Method 1 but into $(3,2)$ with respect to Method 2. (In fact, Methods 1 and 2 construct permutations that are inverses of each other.)

70. Start with the permutation $1\,2\,\ldots\,(c-1)$ at the root, and use Method 1 of the previous exercise to generate all $n!/(c-1)!$ permutations in which these elements retain that order. A permutation with j in position P_j for $1 \leq j < c$ stands for $P_j - P_{j-1}$ balls of color j, where $P_0 = 0$ and $P_c = n+1$; for example, if $c = 3$, the permutation $3\,1\,4\,2$ would correspond to node $(2,2,1)$. The resulting tuples $(A_1, \ldots, A_c)/(n+1)$ then form a martingale for $n = c,\ c+1,\ \ldots$, uniformly distributed (for each n) among all $\binom{n}{c-1}$ compositions of $n+1$ into c positive parts.

[We can also use this setup to deal with Pólya's two-color model when there are r red balls and b black balls at the beginning: Imagine $r+b$ colors, then identify the first r of them with red. This model was first studied by D. Blackwell and D. Kendall, *J. Applied Probability* **1** (1964), 284–296.]

71. If $m = r' - r$ and $n = b' - b$ we must move m times to the right and n times to the left; there are $\binom{m+n}{n}$ such paths. Every path occurs with the same probability, because the numerators of the fractions are $r \cdot (r+1) \cdot \ldots \cdot (r'-1) \cdot b \cdot (b+1) \cdot \ldots \cdot (b'-1) = r^{\overline{m}} b^{\overline{n}}$ in some order, and the denominators are $(r+b) \cdot (r+b+1) \cdot \ldots \cdot (r'+b'-1) = (r+b)^{\overline{m+n}}$.

The answer, $\binom{m+n}{n} r^{\overline{m}} b^{\overline{n}}/(r+b)^{\overline{m+n}}$, reduces to $1/(r'+b'-1)$ when $r = b = 1$.

72. Since all paths to (r,b) have the same probability, this expected value is the same as $E(X_1 X_2 \ldots X_m)$, which is obviously $1/(m+1)$. (Thus the X's are *very* highly correlated: This expected value would be $1/2^m$ if they were independent. Notice that the probability of an event such as $(X_2 = 1, X_5 = 0, X_6 = 1)$ is $E(X_2(1 - X_5)X_6) = 1/3 - 1/4$.)

[The far-reaching ramifications of such exchangeable random variables are surveyed in O. Kallenberg's book *Probabilistic Symmetries and Invariance Principles* (2005).]

73. $f(r,n) = r\binom{n+1}{r}\sum_k \binom{r-1}{k}(-1)^k q_{n+1-r+k}$, where $q_k = a_k/(k+1)$, by induction on r.

74. Node $(r, n+2-r)$ on level n is reached with probability $\langle{n \atop r-1}\rangle/n!$, proportional to an Eulerian number (see Section 5.1.3). (Indeed, we can associate the permutations of $\{1, \ldots, n+1\}$ that have exactly r *runs* with this node, using Method 1 as in exercise 69.)

Reference: Communications on Pure and Applied Mathematics **2** (1949), 59–70.

75. As before, let $R_n = X_0 + \cdots + X_n$ be the number of red balls at level n. Now we have $E(X_{n+1} \mid X_0, \ldots, X_n) = 1 - R_n/(n+2)$. Hence $E(R_{n+1} \mid R_n) = (n+1)R_n/(n+2) + 1$, and the definition $Z_n = (n+1)R_n - (n+2)(n+1)/2$ is a natural choice.

76. No. For example, let $Z_0 = X$, $Z'_0 = Y$, and $Z_1 = Z'_1 = X + Y$, where X and Y are independent with $EX = EY = 0$. Then $E(Z_1 \mid Z_0) = Z_0$ and $E(Z'_1 \mid Z'_0) = Z'_0$, but $E(Z_1 + Z'_1 \mid Z_0 + Z'_0) = 2(Z_0 + Z'_0)$. (On the other hand, if $\langle Z_n \rangle$ and $\langle Z'_n \rangle$ are both martingales with respect to some common sequence $\langle X_n \rangle$, then $\langle Z_n + Z'_n \rangle$ is also.)

77. $E(Z_{n+1} \mid Z_0, \ldots, Z_n) = E\big(E(Z_{n+1} \mid Z_0, \ldots, Z_n, X_0, \ldots, X_n) \mid Z_0, \ldots, Z_n\big)$, which equals $E\big(E(Z_{n+1} \mid X_0, \ldots, X_n) \mid Z_0, \ldots, Z_n\big)$ because Z_n is a function of $X_0, \ldots, X_n$;

and that equals $E(Z_n \mid Z_0, \ldots, Z_n) = Z_n$. (Furthermore $\langle Z_n \rangle$ is a martingale with respect to, say, a constant sequence. But not with respect to *every* sequence.)

A similar proof shows that any sequence $\langle Y_n \rangle$ that is fair with respect to $\langle X_n \rangle$ is also fair with respect to itself.

78. $E(Z_{n+1} \mid V_0, \ldots, V_n) = E(Z_n V_{n+1} \mid V_0, \ldots, V_n) = Z_n$.

The converse holds with $V_0 = Z_0$ and $V_n = Z_n/Z_{n-1}$ for $n > 0$, *provided* that $Z_{n-1} = 0$ implies $Z_n = 0$, and that we define $V_n = 1$ when that happens.

79. $Z_n = V_0 V_1 \ldots V_n$, where $V_0 = 1$ and each V_n for $n > 0$ is independently equal to q/p (with probability p) or to p/q (with probability q). Since $E V_n = q + p = 1$, $\langle V_n \rangle$ is multiplicatively fair. [See A. de Moivre, *The Doctrine of Chances* (1718), 102–154.]

80. (a) True; in fact $E(f_n(Y_0 \ldots Y_{n-1})Y_n) = 0$ for any function f_n.

(b) False: For example, let $Y_5 = \pm 1$ if $Y_3 > 0$, otherwise $Y_5 = 0$. (Hence permutations of a fair sequence needn't be fair. The statement is, however, true if the Y's are *independent* with mean zero.)

(c) False if $n_1 = 0$ and $m = 1$ (or if $m = 0$); otherwise true. (Sequences that satisfy $E((Y_{n_1} - E Y_{n_1}) \ldots (Y_{n_m} - E Y_{n_m})) = E(Y_{n_1} - E Y_{n_1}) \ldots E(Y_{n_m} - E Y_{n_m})$ are called *totally uncorrelated.* Such sequences, with $E Y_n = 0$ for all n, are not always fair; but fair sequences are always totally uncorrelated.)

81. Assuming that $X_0, \ldots, X_n$ can be deduced from $Z_0, \ldots, Z_n$, we have $a_n X_n + b_n X_{n-1} = Z_n = E(Z_{n+1} \mid Z_0, \ldots, Z_n) = E(a_{n+1} X_{n+1} + b_{n+1} X_n \mid X_0, \ldots, X_n) = a_{n+1}(X_n + X_{n-1}) + b_{n+1} X_n$ for $n \geq 1$. Hence $a_{n+1} = b_n$, $b_{n+1} = a_n - a_{n+1} = b_{n-1} - b_n$; and we have $a_n = F_{-n-1}$, $b_n = F_{-n-2}$ by induction, verifying the assumption.

[See J. B. MacQueen, *Annals of Probability* **1** (1973), 263–271.]

82. (a) $Z_n = A_n/C_n$, where $A_n = 4 - X_1 - \cdots - X_n$ is the number of aces and C_n is the number of cards remaining after you've seen n cards. Hence $E Z_{n+1} = (A_n/C_n)(A_n - 1)/(C_n - 1) + (1 - A_n/C_n)A_n/(C_n - 1) = A_n/C_n$. (In every generalization of Pólya's urn for which the nth step adds k_n balls of the chosen color, the ratio red/(red + black) is always a martingale, even when k_n is negative, as long as enough balls of the chosen color remain. This exercise represents the case $k_n = -1$.)

(b) This is the optional stopping principle in a bounded-time martingale.

(c) $Z_N = A_N/C_N$ is the probability that an ace will be next. ["Ace Now" is a variant of R. Connelly's game "Say Red"; see *Pallbearers Review* **9** (1974), 702.]

83. $Z_n = \sum_{k=1}^{n}(X_n - E X_n)$ is a martingale, for which we can study the bounded stopping rules $N'_n(x_0, \ldots, x_{n-1}) = [n < m] \cdot N_n(x_0, \ldots, x_{n-1})$ for any m. But Svante Janson suggests a direct computation, beginning with the formula $S_N = \sum_{n=1}^{\infty} X_n[N \geq n]$ where N might be ∞: We have $E(X_n[N \geq n]) = (E X_n)(E[N \geq n])$, because $[N \geq n]$ is a function of $\{X_0, \ldots, X_{n-1}\}$, hence independent of X_n. And since $X_n \geq 0$, we have $E S_N = \sum_{n=1}^{\infty} E(X_n[N \geq n]) = \sum_{n=1}^{\infty}(E X_n) E[N \geq n] = \sum_{n=1}^{\infty} E((E X_n)[N \geq n]) = E \sum_{n=1}^{\infty}(E X_n)[N \geq n]$, which is $E \sum_{n=1}^{N} E X_n$. (The equation might be '$\infty = \infty$'.)

[Wald's original papers, in *Annals of Mathematical Statistics* **15** (1944), 283–296, **16** (1945), 287–293, solved a somewhat different problem and proved more.]

84. (a) We have $f(Z_n) = f(E(Z_{n+1} \mid Z_0, \ldots, Z_n)) \leq E(f(Z_{n+1}) \mid Z_0, \ldots, Z_n)$ by Jensen's inequality. And the latter is $E(f(Z_{n+1}) \mid f(Z_0), \ldots, f(Z_n))$ as in answer 77. [Incidentally, D. Gilat has shown that every nonnegative submartingale is $\langle |Z_n| \rangle$ for some martingale $\langle Z_n \rangle$; see *Annals of Probability* **5** (1977), 475–481.]

(b) Again we get a submartingale, *provided* that we also have $f(x) \leq f(y)$ for $a \leq x \leq y \leq b$. [J. L. Doob, *Stochastic Processes* (1953), 295–296.]

85. Since $\langle B_n/(R_n + B_n)\rangle = \langle 1 - R_n/(R_n + B_n)\rangle$ is a martingale by (27), and since $f(x) = 1/x$ is convex for positive x, $\langle (R_n + B_n)/B_n\rangle = \langle R_n/B_n + 1\rangle$ is a submartingale by exercise 84. (A direct proof could also be given.)

86. The rule $N_{n+1}(Z_0, \ldots, Z_n) = [\max(Z_0, \ldots, Z_n) < x \text{ and } n + 1 < m]$ is bounded. If $\max(Z_0, \ldots, Z_{m-1}) < x$ then we have $Z_N < x$, where N is defined by (31); similarly, if $\max(Z_0, \ldots, Z_{m-1}) \geq x$ then $Z_N \geq x$. Hence $\Pr(\max(Z_0, \ldots, Z_n) \geq x) \leq (\mathrm{E}\, Z_N)/x$ by Markov's inequality; and $\mathrm{E}\, Z_N \leq \mathrm{E}\, Z_n$ in a submartingale.

87. This is the probability that Z_n becomes $3/4$, which also is $\Pr(\max(Z_0, \ldots, Z_n) \geq 3/4)$. But $\mathrm{E}\, Z_n = 1/2$ for all n, hence (33) tells us that it is at most $(1/2)/(3/4) = 2/3$.

(The exact value can be calculated as in the following exercise. It turns out to be $\sum_{k=0}^{\infty} \frac{2}{(4k+2)(4k+3)} = \frac{1}{2}H_{3/4} - \frac{1}{2}H_{1/2} + \frac{1}{3} = \frac{1}{4}\pi - \frac{1}{2}\ln 2 \approx .439$.)

88. (a) We have $S > 1/2$ if and only if there comes a time when there are more red balls than black balls. Since that happens if and only if the process passes through one of the nodes $(2, 1)$, $(3, 2)$, $(4, 3)$, $\ldots$, the desired probability is $p_1 + p_2 + \cdots$, where p_k is the probability that node $(k + 1, k)$ is hit before any of $(j + 1, j)$ for $j < k$.

All paths from the root to $(k+1, k)$ are equally likely, and the paths that meet our restrictions are equivalent to the paths in 7.2.1.6–(28). Thus we can use Eq. 7.2.1.6–(23) to show that $p_k = 1/(2k - 1) - 1/(2k)$; and $1 - 1/2 + 1/3 - 1/4 + \cdots = \ln 2$.

(b,c) If p_k is the probability of hitting node $((t - 1)k + 1, k)$ before any previous $((t - 1)j + 1, j)$, a similar calculation using the t-ary ballot numbers $C_{pq}^{(t)}$ yields $p_k = (t - 1)(1/(tk - 1) - 1/(tk))$. Then $\sum_{k=1}^{\infty} p_k = 1 - (1 - 1/t)H_{1-1/t}$ (see Appendix A).

Notes: We have $\Pr(S = 1/2) = 1 - \ln 2$, since S is always $\geq 1/2$. But we *cannot* claim that $\Pr(S \geq 2/3)$ is the sum of cases that pass through $(2, 1)$, $(4, 2)$, $(6, 3)$, etc., because the supremum might be $2/3$ even though the value $2/3$ is never reached. Those cases occur with probability $\pi/\sqrt{27}$; hence $\Pr(S = 2/3) \geq 2\pi/\sqrt{27} - \ln 3 \approx .111$. A determination of the exact value of $\Pr(S = 2/3)$ is beyond the scope of this book, because we've avoided the complications of measure theory by defining probability only in discrete spaces; we can't consider a limiting quantity such as S to be a random variable, by our definitions! But we *can* assign a probability to the event that $\max(Z_0, Z_1, \ldots, Z_n) > x$, for any given n and x, and we can reason about the limits of such probabilities.

With the help of deeper methods, E. Schulte-Geers and W. Stadje have proved that the supremum is reached within n steps, a.s. Hence $\Pr(S = 2/3) = 2\pi/\sqrt{27} - \ln 3$; indeed, $\Pr(S \text{ is rational}) = 1$, since only rationals are reached; and $\Pr(S = (t-1)/t) = (2-3/t)H_{1-1/t} - (1-2/t)H_{1-2/t} - (t-2)/(t-1)$. [*J. Applied Prob.* **52** (2015), 180–190.]

89. Set $Y_n = c_n(X_n - p_n)$, $a_n = -c_n p_n$, $b_n = c_n(1 - p_n)$. (Incidentally, when $c_1 = \cdots = c_n = 1$, exercise 1.2.10–22 gives an upper bound that has quite a different form.)

90. (a) Apply Markov's inequality to $\Pr(e^{(Y_1 + \cdots + Y_n)t} \geq e^{tx})$.

(b) $e^{yt} \leq e^{-pt}(q - y) + e^{qt}(y + p) = e^{f(t)} + ye^{g(t)}$ because the function e^{yt} is convex.

(c) We have $f'(t) = -p + pe^t/(q + pe^t)$ and $f''(t) = pqe^t/(q + pe^t)^2$; hence $f(0) = f'(0) = 0$. And $f''(t) \leq 1/4$, because the geometric mean of q and pe^t, $(pqe^t)^{1/2}$, is less than or equal to the arithmetic mean, $(q + pe^t)/2$.

(d) Set $c = b - a$, $p = -a/c$, $q = b/c$, $Y = Y/c$, $t = ct$, $h(t) = e^{g(ct)}/c$.

(e) In $\mathrm{E}((e^{c_1^2 t^2/4} + Y_1 h_1(t)) \ldots (e^{c_n^2 t^2/4} + Y_n h_n(t)))$ the terms involving $h_k(t)$ all drop out, because $\langle Y_n\rangle$ is fair. So we're left with the constant term, $e^{ct^2/4}$.

(f) Let $t = 2x/c$, to make $ct^2/4 - xt = -x^2/c$.

91. $\mathrm{E}(Z_{n+1} \mid X_0, \ldots, X_n) = \mathrm{E}(\mathrm{E}(Q \mid X_0, \ldots, X_n, X_{n+1}) \mid X_0, \ldots, X_n)$, and this is equal to $\mathrm{E}(Q \mid X_0, \ldots, X_n)$ by formula $(*)$ in answer 35. Apply exercise 77.

92. $Q_0 = \mathrm{E}\,X_m = 1/2$. If $n < m$ we have $Q_n = \mathrm{E}(X_m \mid X_0, \ldots, X_n)$, which is the same as $\mathrm{E}(X_{n+1} \mid X_0, \ldots, X_n)$ (see exercise 72); and this is $(1 + X_1 + \cdots + X_n)/(n+2)$, which is the same as Z_n in (27). If $n \geq m$, however, we have $Q_n = X_m$.

93. Everything goes through exactly as before, except that we must replace the quantity $(m-1)^t/m^{t-1}$ by the generalized expected value, which is $\sum_{k=1}^m \prod_{n=1}^t (1 - p_{nk})$.

94. If the X's are dependent, the Doob martingale still is well defined; but when we write its fair sequence as an average of $\Delta(x_1, \ldots, x_t)$ there is no longer a nice formula such as (40). In any formula for Δ that has the form $\sum_x p_x (Q(\ldots x_n \ldots) - Q(\ldots x \ldots))$, $\Pr(X_n = x_n, X_{n+1} = x_{n+1}, \ldots)/(\Pr(X_n = x_n)\Pr(X_{n+1} = x_{n+1}, \ldots))$ must equal $\sum_x p_x$, so it must be independent of x_n. Thus (41) can't be used.

95. False; the probability of only one red ball at level n is $1/(n+1) = \Omega(n^{-1})$. But there are *a.s.* more than 100 red balls, because that happens with probability $(n-99)/(n+1)$.

96. Exercise 1.2.10–21, with ϵn equal to the bound on $|X - n/2|$, tells us that (i) is q.s. and that (i), (ii), (iii) are a.s. To prove that (iv) isn't a.s., we can use Stirling's approximation to show that $\binom{n}{n/2\pm k}/2^n$ is $\Theta(n^{-1/2})$ when $k = \sqrt{n}$; consequently $\Pr(|X| < \sqrt{n}\,) = \Theta(1)$. A similar calculation shows that (ii) isn't q.s.

97. We need to show only that a *single* bin q.s. receives that many. The probability generating function for the number of items H that appear in any particular bin is $G(z) = ((n - 1 + z)/n)^N$, where $N = \lfloor n^{1+\delta} \rfloor$. If $r = \frac{1}{2}n^\delta$, we have

$$\Pr(H \leq r) \leq \left(\frac{1}{2}\right)^{-r} G\left(\frac{1}{2}\right) = 2^r\left(1 - \frac{1}{2n}\right)^{\lfloor 2nr \rfloor} \leq 2^r\left(1 - \frac{1}{2n}\right)^{2nr-1} \leq 2^{r+1}e^{-r},$$

by 1.2.10–(24). And if $r = 2n^\delta$ we have

$$\Pr(H \geq r) \leq 2^{-r} G(2) = 2^{-r}\left(1 + \frac{1}{n}\right)^{\lfloor nr/2 \rfloor} \leq 2^{-r}\left(1 + \frac{1}{n}\right)^{nr/2} \leq 2^{-r}e^{r/2},$$

by 1.2.10–(25). Both are exponentially small. [See Knuth, Motwani, and Pittel, *Random Structures & Algorithms* **1** (1990), 1–14, Lemma 1.]

98. Let $E_n = \mathrm{E}\,R$, where R is the number of reduction steps; and suppose $F(n) = k$ with probability p_k, where $\sum_{k=1}^n p_k = 1$ and $\sum_{k=1}^n k p_k = g \geq g_n$. (The values of $p_1, \ldots, p_n$, and g might be different, in general, every time we compute $F(n)$.) Let $\Sigma_a^b = \sum_{j=a}^b 1/g_j$. Clearly $E_0 = 0$. And if $n > 0$, we have by induction

$$E_n = 1 + \sum_{k=1}^n p_k E_{n-k} \leq 1 + \sum_{k=1}^n p_k \Sigma_1^{n-k} = 1 + \sum_{k=1}^n p_k(\Sigma_1^n - \Sigma_{n-k+1}^n)$$

$$= \Sigma_1^n + 1 - \sum_{k=1}^n p_k \Sigma_{n-k+1}^n \leq \Sigma_1^n + 1 - \sum_{k=1}^n p_k \frac{k}{g_n} \leq \Sigma_1^n.$$

[See R. M. Karp, E. Upfal, and A. Wigderson, *J. Comp. and Syst. Sci.* **36** (1988), 252.]

99. The same proof would work, provided that induction could be justified, if we were to do the sums from $k = -\infty$ to n and define $\Sigma_a^b = -\sum_{j=b+1}^{a-1} 1/g_j$ when $a > b$. (For example, that definition gives $-\Sigma_{n+3}^n = 1/g_{n+1} + 1/g_{n+2} \leq 2/g_n$.)

And in fact it does become a proof, by induction on m, that we have $E_{m,n} \leq \Sigma_1^n$ for all $m, n \geq 0$, where $E_{m,n} = \mathrm{E}\min(m, R)$. Indeed, we have $E_{0,n} = E_{m+1,0} = 0$; and $E_{m+1,n} = 1 + \sum_{k=-\infty}^n p_k E_{m,n-k}$ when $n > 0$. [This problem is exercise 1.6 in *Randomized Algorithms* by Motwani and Raghavan (1995). Svante Janson observes that the random variable $Z_m = \Sigma_1^{X_m} + \min(m, R)$ is a supermartingale, where X_m is the value of X after m iterations, as a consequence of this proof.]

100. (a) $\sum_{k=1}^m kp_k \leq \mathrm{E}\min(m,T) = p_1+2p_2+\cdots+mp_m+mp_{m+1}+\cdots+mp_\infty \leq \mathrm{E}T$.

(b) $\mathrm{E}\min(m,T) \geq mp_\infty$ for all m. (We assume that $\infty \cdot p = (p > 0?\ \infty: 0)$.)

101. (Solution by Svante Janson.) If $0 < t < \min(p_1,\ldots,p_m) = p$, we have $\mathrm{E}\,e^{tX} = \prod_{k=1}^m \mathrm{E}\,e^{tX_k} = \prod_{k=1}^m p_k/(e^{-t}-1+p_k) < \prod_{k=1}^m p_k/(p_k-t)$, because $e^{-t}-1 > -t$. Set $t = \theta/\mu$, and note that $p_k \ln(1-t/p_k) \geq p\ln(1-t/p) \geq \frac{1}{\mu}\ln(1-t\mu) = \frac{t}{\theta}\ln(1-\theta)$. By 1.2.10–(25), therefore, $\Pr(X \geq r\mu) \leq e^{-rt\mu}\prod_{k=1}^m p_k/(p_k-t) = \exp(-r\theta - \sum_{k=1}^m \ln(1-t/p_k)) \leq \exp(-r\theta - \sum_{k=1}^m (t/p_k)(\ln(1-\theta))/\theta) = \exp(-r\theta - \ln(1-\theta))$. Choose $\theta = (r-1)/r$ to get the desired bound re^{1-r}. (The bound is nearly sharp when $m=1$ and p is small, since $\Pr(X \geq r/p) = (1-p)^{\lceil r/p \rceil - 1} \approx e^{-r}$.)

102. Applying exercise 101 with $\mu \leq s_1 + \cdots + s_m$ and $r = \ln n$ gives probability $O(n^{-1}\log n)$ that $(s_1 + \cdots + s_m)r$ trials aren't enough. And if $r = f(n)\ln n$, where $f(n)$ is any increasing function that is unbounded as $n \to \infty$, the probability that $s_k r$ trials don't obtain coupon k is superpolynomially small. So is the probability that any one of a polynomial number of such failures will occur.

103. (a) The recurrence $p_{0ij} = [i=j]$, $p_{(n+1)ij} = \sum_{k=0}^2 p_{nik}([f_0(k)=j]+[f_1(k)=j])/2$ leads to generating functions $g_{ij} = \sum_{n=0}^\infty p_{nij}z^n$ that satisfy $g_{i0} - [i=0]+(g_{i0}+g_{i1})z/2$, $g_{i1} = [i=1] + (g_{i0} + g_{i2})z/2$, $g_{i2} = [i=2] + (g_{i1} + g_{i2})z/2$. From the solution $g_{i0} = A+B+C$, $g_{i1} = A-2B$, $g_{i2} = A+B-C$, $A = \frac{1}{3}/(1-z)$, $B = \frac{1}{6}(1-3[i=1])/(1+z/2)$, and $C = \frac{1}{2}([i=0] - [i=2])/(1-z/2)$, we conclude that the probability is $\frac{1}{3}+O(2^{-n})$; in fact it is always either $\lfloor 2^n/3 \rfloor/2^n$ or $\lceil 2^n/3 \rceil/2^n$. The former occurs if and only if $i \neq j$ and n is even, or $i+j = 2$ and n is odd.

(b) Letting $g_{012} = \frac{z}{2}(g_{001} + g_{112})$, $g_{001} = \frac{z}{2}([j=0] + g_{011})$, etc., yields the generating function $g_{012} = ([j\neq1] + [j=1]z)z^2/(4 - z^2)$. Hence each j occurs with probability $1/3$, and the generating function for N is $z^2/(2-z)$; mean $= 3$, variance $= 2$.

(c) Now $g_{001} = \frac{z}{2}([j=0] + g_{112})$, etc.; the output is never 1; 0 and 2 are equally likely; and N has the same distribution as before.

(d) Functional composition isn't commutative, so the stopping criterion is different: In the second case, 111 cannot occur unless the previous step had 000 or 222. The crucial difference is that, without stopping, process (b) becomes *fixed* at coalescence; process (c) continues to *change* $a_0a_1a_2$ as n increases (although all three remain equal).

(e) If T is even, $\mathrm{sub}(T)$ returns $(-1,0,1,2)$ with probability $(2,(2^T - 1)/3, (2^T - 4)/3, (2^T - 1)/3)/2^T$. Thus the supposed alternative to (b) will output 0 with probability $\frac{1}{4} + \frac{5}{32} + \frac{85}{4096} + \cdots = \frac{1}{3}\sum_{k=1}^\infty 2^{k+1}(2^{2^k} - 1)/2^{2^{k+1}} \approx 0.427$, *not* $1/3$.

(f) Change $\mathrm{sub}(T)$ to use consistent bits $X_T, X_{T-1}, \ldots, X_1$ instead of generating new random bits X each time; then the method of (b) is faithfully simulated. (The necessary consistency can be achieved by carefully resetting the seed of a suitable random number generator at appropriate times.)

[The technique of (f) is called "coupling from the past" in a monotone Monte Carlo simulation. It can be used to generate uniformly random objects of many important kinds, and it runs substantially faster than method (b) when there are thousands or millions of possible states instead of just three. See J. G. Propp and D. B. Wilson, *Random Structures & Algorithms* **9** (1996), 223–252.]

104. Let $q = 1-p$. The probability of output $(0,1,2)$ in (b) is $(q^2, 2pq, p^2)$; in (c) it is $(p^2+pq^2, 0, q^2+qp^2)$. In both cases N has generating function $(1-pq(2-z))z^2/(1-pqz^2)$, mean $3/(1 - pq) - 1$, variance $(5 - 2pq)pq/(1 - pq)^2$.

105. We have $g_0 = 1$ and $g_a = z(g_{a-1} + g_{a+1})/2$ for $0 < a < n/2$.

If $n = 2m$ is even, let $g_a = z^a t_{m-a}/t_m$ for $0 \le a \le m$. The polynomials t_k defined by $t_0 = t_1 = 1$, $t_{k+1} = 2t_k - z^2 t_{k-1}$ fill the bill, because they make $g_m = z g_{m-1}$. The generating function $T(w) = \sum_{m=0}^{\infty} t_m w^m = (1-w)/(1 - 2w + w^2 z^2)$ now shows, after differentiation by z, that we have $t'_m(1) = -m(m-1)$ and $t''_m(1) = (m^2 - 5m + 3)m(m-1)/3$; hence $t''_m(1) + t'_m(1) - t'_m(1)^2 = \frac{2}{3}(m^2 - m^4)$. The mean and variance, given a, are therefore $a - (m-a)(m-a-1) + m(m-1) = a(n-a)$ and $\frac{2}{3}((m-a)^2 - (m-a)^4 - m^2 + m^4) = \frac{1}{3}((n-a)^2 + a^2 - 2)a(n-a)$, respectively.

When $n = 2m - 1$ we can write $g_a = z^a u_{m-a}/u_m$ for $0 \le a \le m$, with $u_{m+1} = 2u_m - z^2 u_{m-1}$. In this case we want $u_0 = 1$ and $u_1 = z$, so that $g_m = g_{m-1}$. From $U(w) = \sum_{m=0}^{\infty} u_m w^m = (1 + (z-2)w)/(1 - 2w + w^2 z^2)$ we deduce $u'_m(1) = -m(m-2)$ and $u''_m(1) = m(m-1)(m^2 - 7m + 7)/3$. It follows that, also in this case, the mean number of steps in the walk is $a(n-a)$ and the variance is $\frac{1}{3}((n-a)^2 + a^2 - 2)a(n-a)$.

[The polynomials t_m and u_m in this analysis are disguised relatives of the classical Chebyshev polynomials defined by $T_m(\cos\theta) = \cos m\theta$, $U_m(\cos\theta) = \sin(m+1)\theta/\sin\theta$. Let us also write $V_m(\cos\theta) = \cos(m - \frac{1}{2})\theta/\cos\frac{1}{2}\theta$. Then $V_m(x) = (2 - 1/x)T_m(x) + (1/x - 1)U_m(x)$; and we have $t_m = z^m T_m(1/z)$, $u_m = z^m V_m(1/z)$.]

106. Before coalescing, the array $a_0 a_1 \ldots a_{d-1}$ always has the form $a^r(a+1)\ldots(b-1)b^s$ for some $0 \le a < b < d$, $r > 0$, and $s > 0$, where $r + s + b - a = d + 1$. Initially $a = 0$, $b = d-1$, $r = s = 1$. The behavior of the algorithm while $r + s = t$ is like a random walk on the t-cycle, as in the previous exercise, starting at $a = 1$. Let G_t be the generating function for that problem, which has mean $t - 1$ and variance $2\binom{t}{3}$. Then this problem has the generating function $G_2 G_3 \ldots G_d$; so its mean is $\sum_{k=2}^{d}(k-1) = \binom{d}{2}$, and the variance is $\sum_{k=2}^{d} 2\binom{k}{3} = 2\binom{d+1}{4}$.

107. (a) If the probabilities can be renumbered so that $p_1 \le q_1$ and $p_2 \le q_2$, the five events of Ω can have probabilities p_1, p_2, $q_1 - p_1$, $q_2 - p_2$, and q_3, because $p_3 = (q_1 - p_1) + (q_2 - p_2) + q_3$. But if that doesn't work, we can suppose that $p_1 < q_1 \le q_2 \le q_3 < p_2 \le p_3$. Then p_1, $q_1 - p_1$, $p_1 + p_2 - q_1$, $p_3 - q_3$, and q_3 are nonnegative.

(b) Give Ω's events the probabilities $\frac{1}{12}, \frac{2}{12}, \frac{3}{12}, \frac{6}{12}$.

(c) For example, let $p_1 = \frac{1}{9}$, $p_2 = p_3 = \frac{4}{9}$, $q_1 = q_2 = q_3 = \frac{1}{3}$.

108. Let $p_k = \Pr'(X = k)$ and $q_k = \Pr''(Y = k)$. The set $\bigcup_n \{\sum_{k \le n} p_k, \sum_{k \le n} q_k\}$ divides the unit interval $[0 \mathrel{..} 1]$ into countably many subintervals, which we take as the set Ω of atomic events ω. Let $X(\omega) = n$ if and only if $\omega \subseteq [\sum_{k<n} p_k \mathrel{..} \sum_{k \le n} p_k)$; a similar definition works for $Y(\omega)$. And $X(\omega) \le Y(\omega)$ for all ω.

109. (a) We're given that $p_1 + p_3 \le q_1 + q_3$, $p_2 + p_3 \le q_2 + q_3$, and $p_3 \le q_3$. (Also that $0 \le 0$ and $p_1 + p_2 + p_3 \le q_1 + q_2 + q_3$; but those inequalities always hold.) We must find a coupling with $p_{12} = p_{21} = p_{31} = p_{32} = 0$, because $1 \not\preceq 2$, $2 \not\preceq 1$, $3 \not\preceq 1$, and $3 \not\preceq 2$. In the previous problem we were given that $p_2 + p_3 \le q_2 + q_3$ and $p_3 \le q_3$, and we had to find a coupling with $p_{21} = p_{31} = p_{32} = 0$.

(b) Let $A^{\uparrow} = \{x \mid x \succeq a \text{ for some } a \in A\}$ and $B^{\downarrow} = \{x \mid x \preceq b \text{ for some } b \in B\}$. We're given that $\Pr'(X \in A^{\uparrow}) \le \Pr''(Y \in A^{\uparrow})$ for all A. Let $A = \{1, \ldots, n\} \setminus B^{\downarrow}$, so that $\Pr'(X \in B^{\downarrow}) = 1 - \Pr'(X \in A)$. The result follows because $A = A^{\uparrow}$.

(c) Remove all arcs $x_i \longrightarrow x_j$ from the network when $i \not\preceq j$. Then a blocking pair (I, J) has the property that $i \preceq j$ implies $i \in I$ or $j \in J$. Let $A = \{x \mid x \preceq a \text{ for some } a \notin J\}$ and $B = \{1, \ldots, n\} \setminus A$. Then $A \subseteq I$, $B \subseteq J$, and $B = B^{\downarrow}$. Hence $\sum_{i \in I} p_i + \sum_{j \in J} q_j \ge \sum_{i \in A} p_i + \sum_{j \in B} q_j \ge \sum_{i \in A} q_i + \sum_{j \in B} q_j = 1$.

[See K. Nawrotzki, *Mathematische Nachrichten* **24** (1962), 193–200; V. Strassen, *Annals of Mathematical Statistics* **36** (1965), 423–439.]

110. (a) The result is trivial if $r = 1$. Otherwise consider the probability distributions $p'_k = (p_k - r_k)/(1 - r)$ and $q'_k = (q_k - r_k)/(1 - r)$; use the coupling $p_{ij} = (1-r)p'_i q'_j + r_j[i{=}j]$. [See W. Doeblin, *Revue mathématique de l'Union Interbalkanique* **2** (1938), 77–105; R. L. Dobrushin, *Teoriya Veroyatnosteĭ i ee Primeneniĭâ* **15** (1970), 469–497.]

(b) Yes, because the (p', q') distribution satisfies the hypotheses of that exercise.

111. (a) Here are the 60 triples $1\pi\,3\pi\,4\pi$, with the minima in **bold** type:

134 163 123 126 142 142 153 145 163 154 245 **234** 534 563 623 526 632 652 534 643
356 645 246 **234** 435 463 524 423 642 532 461 351 361 641 251 231 341 531 321 421
512 412 415 315 316 615 216 216 415 316 623 526 652 452 564 354 465 364 256 265

(b) Both S_A and S_B lie in $A \cup B$. Each element of $A \cup B$ is equally likely to have the minimum value $a\pi$; exactly $|A \cap B|$ of those elements have that value as their sketch.

(c) $|A \cap B \cap C| / |A \cup B \cup C|$.

Notes: The ratio $|A \cap B|/|A \cup B|$ is a useful measure of similarity, called the "Jaccard index" because Paul Jaccard used it to compare different Swiss ecological sites according to the sets of plant species seen at each place [*Bulletin de la Société Vaudoise des Sciences Naturelles* **37** (1901), 249]. It is commonly used today to rank the similarity between web pages, based on a certain set of words in each page.

Minwise independence was introduced by Andrei Broder for that application in 1997, using $n = 2^{64}$ and a method of identifying roughly 1000 words A on a typical web page. By calculating, say, independent sketches $S_1(A)$, ..., $S_{100}(A)$ for each page, the number of j such that $S_j(A) = S_j(B)$ gives a highly reliable and quickly computable estimate of the Jaccard index. A perfectly minwise independent family is impossible in practice when n is huge, but the associated theory has led to approximate "minhash" algorithms that work well. See A. Z. Broder, M. Charikar, A. M. Frieze, and M. Mitzenmacher, *J. Computer and System Sciences* **60** (2000), 630–659. See also the related, independent work by K. Mulmuley, *Algorithmica* **16** (1996), 450–463.

112. (a) Such a rule breaks ties properly, provided that the number of π with ∞'s in B is a multiple of $n - m$. Each B can have its own rule.

(b) In fact we can produce families whose permutations are all obtained from $N/n = d$ "seeds" by cyclic shifts, as in exercise 111. Begin with $m = 1$ and a table of $N = \mathrm{lcm}(1, 2, \ldots, n)$ partial permutations whose entries π_{ij} for $1 \le i \le N$ and $1 \le j \le n$ are entirely blank, except that $\pi_{ij} = 1$ for each pair ij with $(j-1)d < i \le jd$ and $1 \le j \le n$. When $n = 4$, for instance, the initial tableau

$$1_{\sqcup\sqcup\sqcup} \quad 1_{\sqcup\sqcup\sqcup} \quad 1_{\sqcup\sqcup\sqcup} \quad {}_{\sqcup}1_{\sqcup\sqcup} \quad {}_{\sqcup}1_{\sqcup\sqcup} \quad {}_{\sqcup}1_{\sqcup\sqcup} \quad {}_{\sqcup\sqcup}1_{\sqcup} \quad {}_{\sqcup\sqcup}1_{\sqcup} \quad {}_{\sqcup\sqcup}1_{\sqcup} \quad {}_{\sqcup\sqcup\sqcup}1 \quad {}_{\sqcup\sqcup\sqcup}1 \quad {}_{\sqcup\sqcup\sqcup}1$$

represents $N = 12$ truncated permutations with $m = 1$. We'll insert some 2s next.

Let A be a subset of size $n - m$ that is all blank, in some π. Each A occurs equally often (as in uniform probing, Section 6.4); so the number of such π is $N/\binom{n}{n-m}$. Fortunately this is a multiple of $n - m$, because exercise 1.2.6–48 tells us that $N/((n - m)\binom{n}{n-m}) = N \sum_{k=0}^{m}(-1)^k \binom{m}{k}/(n - m + k)$.

Take $n-m$ such π and insert $m+1$ into different positions within them. Then find another such A, if possible, and repeat the process until no blank subsets of size $n - m$ remain. Then set $m \leftarrow m + 1$, and continue in the same way until $m = n$.

It's not hard to see that the insertions can be done so that $\pi_j, \pi_{d+j}, \ldots, \pi_{(n-1)d+j}$ are maintained as cyclic shifts of each other. When $n = 4$ the 2s are essentially forced:

$$12_{\sqcup\sqcup} \quad 1_{\sqcup}2_{\sqcup} \quad 1_{\sqcup\sqcup}2 \quad {}_{\sqcup}12_{\sqcup} \quad {}_{\sqcup}1_{\sqcup}2 \quad 21_{\sqcup\sqcup} \quad {}_{\sqcup\sqcup}12 \quad 2_{\sqcup}1_{\sqcup} \quad {}_{\sqcup}21_{\sqcup} \quad 2_{\sqcup\sqcup}1 \quad {}_{\sqcup}2_{\sqcup}1 \quad {}_{\sqcup\sqcup}21$$

But then there are two ways to fill the two cases with $A = \{3, 4\}$:

$$123_\sqcup \quad 1_\sqcup 2_\sqcup \quad 13_\sqcup 2 \quad _\sqcup 123 \quad _\sqcup 1_\sqcup 2 \quad 21_\sqcup 3 \quad 3_\sqcup 12 \quad 2_\sqcup 1_\sqcup \quad _\sqcup 213 \quad 23_\sqcup 1 \quad _\sqcup 2_\sqcup 1 \quad 3_\sqcup 21$$
$$12_\sqcup 3 \quad 1_\sqcup 2_\sqcup \quad 13_\sqcup 2 \quad 312_\sqcup \quad _\sqcup 1_\sqcup 2 \quad 213_\sqcup \quad _\sqcup 312 \quad 2_\sqcup 1_\sqcup \quad _\sqcup 213 \quad 2_\sqcup 31 \quad _\sqcup 2_\sqcup 1 \quad 3_\sqcup 21$$

Adopting the first of these leads to two ways to fill $A = \{2, 4\}$:

$$123_\sqcup \quad 132_\sqcup \quad 13_\sqcup 2 \quad _\sqcup 123 \quad _\sqcup 132 \quad 21_\sqcup 3 \quad 3_\sqcup 12 \quad 2_\sqcup 13 \quad _\sqcup 213 \quad 23_\sqcup 1 \quad 32_\sqcup 1 \quad 3_\sqcup 21$$
$$123_\sqcup \quad 1_\sqcup 23 \quad 13_\sqcup 2 \quad _\sqcup 123 \quad 31_\sqcup 2 \quad 21_\sqcup 3 \quad 3_\sqcup 12 \quad 231_\sqcup \quad _\sqcup 213 \quad 23_\sqcup 1 \quad _\sqcup 231 \quad 3_\sqcup 21$$

Here A is a cyclic shift of itself, but consistent placement is always possible.

[See Yoshinori Takei, Toshiya Itoh, and Takahiro Shinozaki, *IEICE Transactions on Fundamentals* **E83-A** (2000), 646–655, 747–755.]

113. (a) The probability is zero if $l \geq k$ or $r > n - k$. Otherwise the result follows if we can prove it in the "complete" case when $l = k - 1$ and $r = n - k$, because we can sum the probabilities of complete cases over all ways to specify which of the unconstrained elements are $< k$ and which are $> k$.

To prove the complete case, we may assume that $a_i = i$, $b = k$, and $c_j = k + j$ for $1 \leq i \leq l = k - 1$ and $1 \leq j \leq r = n - k$. The probability can be computed via the principle of inclusion and exclusion, because we know $\Pr(\min_{a \in A} a\pi = k\pi) = 1/(n - k + t) = P_B$ whenever $A = \{k, \ldots, n\} \cup B$ and B consists of t elements less than k. For example, if $k = 4$ the probability that $4\pi = 4$ and $\{1\pi, 2\pi, 3\pi\} = \{1, 2, 3\}$ is $P_\emptyset - P_{\{1\}} - P_{\{2\}} - P_{\{3\}} + P_{\{1,2\}} + P_{\{1,3\}} + P_{\{2,3\}} - P_{\{1,2,3\}}$; each of those probabilities is correct for truly random π.

(b) This event is the disjoint union of complete events of type (a). [See A. Z. Broder and M. Mitzenmacher, *Random Structures & Algorithms* **18** (2001), 18–30.]

Notes: The function $\psi(n) = \ln(\mathrm{lcm}(1, 2, \ldots, n)) = \sum_{p^k \leq n}[p\text{ prime}]\ln p$ was introduced by P. L. Chebyshev [see *J. de mathématiques pures et appliquées* **17** (1852), 366–390], who proved that it is $\Theta(n)$. Refinements by Ch.-J. de la Vallée Poussin [*Annales de la Société Scientifique de Bruxelles* **20** (1896), 183–256] showed that in fact $\psi(n) = n + O(ne^{-C\log n})$ for some positive constant C. Thus $\mathrm{lcm}(1, 2, \ldots, n)$ grows roughly as e^n, and we cannot hope to generate a list of minwise independent permutations when n is large; the length of such a list is 232,792,560 already for $19 \leq n \leq 22$.

114. First assume that $|S_j| = d_j + 1$ for all j, and let $g_j(x) = \prod_{s \in S_j}(x - s)$. We can replace $x_j^{d_j + 1}$ by $x_j^{d_j + 1} - g_j(x_j)$, without changing the value of $f(x_1, \ldots, x_n)$ when $x_j \in S_j$. Doing this repeatedly until every term of f has degree $\leq d_j$ in each variable x_j will produce a polynomial that has at least one nonroot in $S_1 \times \cdots \times S_n$, according to exercise 4.6.1–16. [See N. Alon, *Combinatorics, Probab. and Comput.* **8** (1999), 7–29.]

Now in general, if there were at most $|S_1| + \cdots + |S_n| - (d_1 + \cdots + d_n + n)$ nonroots, we could eliminate them one (or more) at a time, by removing an element from any S_j for which $|S_j| > d_j + 1$. Contradiction.

(This inequality also implies stronger lower bounds when the sets S_j are large. If, for example, $d_1 = \cdots = d_n = d$ and if each $|S_j| \geq s$, where $s = d + 1 + \lceil d/(n - 1) \rceil$, we can decrease each $|S_j|$ to s and increase the right-hand side. For further asymptotic improvements see Béla Bollobás, *Extremal Graph Theory* (1978), §6.2 and §6.3.)

115. Representing the vertex in row x and column y by (x, y), if all points could be covered we'd have $f(x, y) = \prod_{j=1}^{p}(x - a_j)\prod_{j=1}^{q}(y - b_j)\prod_{j=1}^{r}(x + y + c_j)(x - y + d_j) = 0$, for all $1 \leq x \leq m$ and $1 \leq y \leq n$ and for some choices of a_j, b_j, c_j, d_j. But f has degree $p + q + 2r = m + n - 2$, and the coefficient of $x^{m-1}y^{n-1}$ is $\pm\binom{r}{\lfloor r/2 \rfloor} \neq 0$.

116. Let $g_v = \sum\{x_e \mid v \in e\}$ for each vertex v, including x_e twice if e is a loop from v to itself. Apply the nullstellensatz with $f = \prod_v(1 - g_v^{p-1}) - \prod_e(1 - x_e)$ and with each $S_j = \{0, 1\}$, using mod p arithmetic. This polynomial has degree m, the number of edges and variables, because the first product has degree $(p - 1)n < m$; and the coefficient of $\prod_e x_e$ is $(-1)^m \neq 0$. Hence there is a solution x that makes $f(x)$ nonzero. The subgraph consisting of all edges with $x_e = 1$ in this solution is nonempty and satisfies the desired condition, because $g_v(x) \bmod p = 0$ for all v.

(This proof works also if we consider that a loop contributes just 1 to the degree. See N. Alon, S. Friedland, and G. Kalai, *J. Combinatorial Theory* **B37** (1984), 79–91.)

117. If $\omega = e^{2\pi i/m}$, we have $\mathrm{E}\,\omega^{jX} = \sum_{k=0}^n \binom{n}{k} p^k(1 - p)^{n-k}\omega^{jk} = (\omega^j p + 1 - p)^n$. Also $|\omega^j p + 1 - p|^2 = p^2 + (1 - p)^2 + p(1 - p)(\omega^j + \omega^{-j}) = 1 - 4p(1 - p)\sin^2(\pi j/m)$. Now $\sin \pi t \geq 2t$ for $0 \leq t \leq 1/2$. Hence, if $0 \leq j \leq m/2$ we have $|\omega^j p + 1 - p|^2 \leq 1 - 16p(1 - p)j^2/m^2 \leq \exp(-16p(1 - p)j^2/m^2)$; if $m/2 \leq j \leq m$ we have $\sin(\pi j/m) = \sin(\pi(m - j)/m)$. Thus $\sum_{j=1}^{m-1}|\mathrm{E}\,\omega^{jX}| \leq 2\sum_{j=1}^{m-1}\exp(-8p(1 - p)j^2n/m^2)$.

The result follows, since $\Pr(X \bmod m = r) = \frac{1}{m}\sum_{j=0}^{m-1}\omega^{-jr}\,\mathrm{E}\,\omega^{jX}$. [S. Janson and D. E. Knuth, *Random Structures & Algorithms* **10** (1997), 130–131.]

118. Indeed, (22) with $Y = X - x$ yields *more* (when we also apply exercise 47):

$$\Pr(X \geq x) \geq \Pr(X > x) \geq \frac{(\mathrm{E}\,X - x)^2}{\mathrm{E}(X - x)^2} = \frac{(\mathrm{E}\,X - x)^2}{\mathrm{E}\,X^2 - x(2\,\mathrm{E}\,X - x)}$$

$$\geq \frac{(\mathrm{E}\,X - x)^2}{\mathrm{E}\,X^2 - x\,\mathrm{E}\,X} \geq \frac{(\mathrm{E}\,X - x)^2}{\mathrm{E}\,X^2 - x^2}.$$

(The attribution of this result to Paley and Zygmund is somewhat dubious. They did, however, write an important series of papers [*Proc. Cambridge Philosophical Society* **26** (1930), 337–357, 458–474; **28** (1932), 190–205] in which a related inequality appeared in the proof of Lemma 19.)

119. Let $f(x, t) = \Pr(U \leq V \leq W$ and $V \leq (1 - t)U + tW)$, $g(x, t) = \Pr(U \leq W \leq V$ and $W < (1 - t)U + tV)$, $h(x, t) = \Pr(W < U \leq V$ and $U \leq (1 - t)W + tV)$. We want to prove that $f(x, t) + g(x, t) + h(x, t) = t$. Notice that, if $\overline{U} = 1 - U$, $\overline{V} = 1 - V$, $\overline{W} = 1 - W$, we have $\Pr(W \leq U \leq V$ and $U \geq (1 - t)W + tV) = \Pr(\overline{V} \leq \overline{U} \leq \overline{W}$ and $\overline{U} \leq t\overline{V} + (1 - t)\overline{W})$. Hence $\frac{x}{2} - h(x, t) = f(1 - x, 1 - t)$, and we may assume that $t \leq x$.

Clearly $g(x, t) = \int_0^x \frac{du}{x}\int_x^1 \frac{dv}{1-x}\,t(v - u) = \frac{t}{2}$. And $t \leq x$ implies that

$$f(x, t) = \int_{(x-t)/(1-t)}^x \frac{du}{x}\int_x^{(1-t)u+t} \frac{dv}{1-x}\,(1 - (v - (1 - t)u)/t) = t^2(1 - x)^2/(6(1 - t)x);$$

$$h(x, t) = \int_x^1 \frac{dv}{1-x}\left(\int_0^{vt} \frac{du}{x}\,u + \int_{vt}^x \frac{du}{x}\,\frac{t}{1-t}(v - u)\right) = \frac{t}{2} - f(x, t).$$

Instead of this elaborate calculation, Tamás Terpai has found a much simpler proof: Let $A = \min(U, V, W)$, $M = \langle UVW \rangle$, and $Z = \max(U, V, W)$. Then the conditional distribution of M, given A and Z, is a mixture of three distributions: Either $A = U$, $Z = V$, and M is uniform in $[A\,.\,.\,Z]$; or $A = U$, $Z = W$, and M is uniform in $[x\,.\,.\,Z]$; or $A = W$, $Z = V$, and M is uniform in $[A\,.\,.\,x]$. (These three cases occur with respective probabilities $(Z - A, Z - x, x - A)/(2Z - 2A)$, but we don't need to know that detail.) The overall distribution of M, being an average of conditional uniform distributions over all $A \leq x$ and $Z \geq x$, is therefore uniform. [See S. Volkov, *Random Struct. & Algorithms* **43** (2013), 115–130, Theorem 5.]

120. See J. Jabbour-Hattab, *Random Structures & Algorithms* **19** (2001), 112–127.

121. (a) $D(y\|x) = \frac{1}{5}\lg\frac{6}{5} + \frac{2}{15}\lg\frac{4}{5} \approx .0097$; $D(x\|y) = \frac{1}{6}\lg\frac{5}{6} + \frac{1}{6}\lg\frac{5}{4} \approx .0098$.

(b) We have $\mathrm{E}(\rho(X)\lg\rho(X)) \ge (\mathrm{E}\,\rho(X))\lg\mathrm{E}\,\rho(X)$ by Jensen's inequality (20); and $\mathrm{E}\,\rho(X) = \sum_t y(t) = 1$, so the logarithm evaluates to 0.

The question about zero is the hard part of this exercise. We need to observe that the function $f(x) = x\lg x$ is *strictly* convex, in the sense that equality holds in (19) only when $x = y$. Thus we have $(\mathrm{E}\,Z)\lg\mathrm{E}\,Z = \mathrm{E}(Z\lg Z)$ for a positive random variable Z only when Z is constant. Consequently $D(y\|x) = 0$ if and only if $x(t) = y(t)$ for all t.

(c) Let $\hat{x}(t) = x(t)/p$ and $\hat{y}(t) = y(t)/q$ be the distributions of X and Y within T. Then $0 \le D(\hat{y}\|\hat{x}) = \sum_{t\in T}\hat{y}(t)\lg(\hat{y}(t)/\hat{x}(t)) = \mathrm{E}(\lg\rho(Y)\,|\,Y \in T) + \lg(p/q)$.

(d) $D(y\|x) = (\mathrm{E}\lg m) - H_Y = \lg m - H_Y$. (Hence, by (b), the maximum entropy of any such random variable Y is $\lg m$, attainable only with the uniform distribution. Intuitively, H_Y is the number of bits that we learn when Y is revealed.)

(e) $I_{X,Y} = -H_Z - \sum_{u,v} z(u,v)(\lg x(u) + \lg y(v)) = -H_Z + \sum_u x(u)\lg(1/x(u)) + \sum_v y(v)\lg(1/y(v))$, because $\sum_v z(u,v) = x(u)$ and $\sum_u z(u,v) = y(v)$.

(f) Conditioning $I_{X,Z} = H_X + H_Z - H_{X,Z}$ on Y gives $0 \le I_{(X,Z)|Y} = H_{X|Y} + H_{Z|Y} - H_{(X,Z)|Y} = H_{X|Y} + (H_{Y,Z} - H_Y) - (H_{X,Y,Z} - H_Y)$.

122. (a) $D(y\|x) = \sum_{t=0}^{\infty}(3^t/4^{t+1})\lg(3^t/2^{t+1}) = \lg\frac{27}{16} \approx 0.755$; $D(x\|y) = \lg\frac{4}{3} \approx 0.415$.

(b) Let $q = 1 - p$ and $t = pn + u\sqrt{n}$. Then we have

$$y(t) = \frac{e^{-u^2/(2pq)}}{\sqrt{2\pi pqn}}\exp\left(\left(\frac{u}{2q} - \frac{u}{2p} + \frac{u^3}{6p^2} - \frac{u^3}{6q^2}\right)\frac{1}{\sqrt{n}} + O\left(\frac{1}{n}\right)\right);$$

$$\ln\rho(t) = -\frac{u^2}{2q} - \frac{1}{2}\ln q + \left(\frac{u}{2q} - \frac{u^3}{6q^2}\right)\frac{1}{\sqrt{n}} + O\left(\frac{1}{n}\right).$$

By restricting $|u| \le n^\epsilon$ and trading tails (see 7.2.1.5–(20)), we obtain

$$D(y\|x) = \frac{1}{\sqrt{2\pi pqn}}\int_{-\infty}^{\infty} e^{-u^2/(2pq)}\left(-\frac{u^2}{2q\ln 2} - \frac{1}{2}\lg q\right)du\sqrt{n} + O\left(\frac{1}{n}\right)$$

$$= \frac{1}{2\ln 2}\left(\ln\frac{1}{1-p} - p\right) + O\left(\frac{1}{n}\right).$$

In this case $D(x\|y)$ is trivially ∞, because $x(n+1) > 0$ but $y(n+1) = 0$.

123. Since $p_{k+1} = p_k y(t)/z_k(t)$ we have $\rho(t) = (1 - p_k)p_{k+1}/(p_k(1 - p_{k+1}))$. [This relation was the original motivation that led S. Kullback and R. A. Leibler to define $D(y\|x)$, in *Annals of Mathematical Statistics* **22** (1951), 79–86.]

124. Let $m = c^2 2^{D(y\|x)}$ and $g(t) = f(t)[\rho(t) \le m]$; thus $g(t) = f(t)$ except with probability Δ_c. We have $|\mathrm{E}(f) - \mathrm{E}_n(f)| = (\mathrm{E}(f) - \mathrm{E}(g)) + |\mathrm{E}(g) - \mathrm{E}_n(g)| + (\mathrm{E}_n(f) - \mathrm{E}_n(g))$. The Cauchy–Schwarz inequality (exercise 1.2.3–30) implies that the first and last are bounded by $\|f\|\sqrt{\Delta_c}$, because $f(t) - g(t) = f(t)[\rho(t) > m]$.

Now $\mathrm{var}(\rho(X)g(X)) \le \mathrm{E}(\rho(X)^2 g(X)^2) \le m\,\mathrm{E}(\rho(X)f(X)^2) = m\,\mathrm{E}(f(Y)^2) = m\|f\|^2$. Hence $(\mathrm{E}(g) - \mathrm{E}_n(g))^2 = \mathrm{var}\,\mathrm{E}_n(g) = \mathrm{var}(\rho(X)g(X))/n \le \|f\|^2/c^2$.

Consider now the case $c < 1$. From Markov's inequality we have $\Pr(\rho(X) > m) \le (\mathrm{E}\,\rho(X))/m = 1/m$. Also $\mathrm{E}(\rho(X)[\rho(X) \le m]) = \mathrm{E}[\rho(Y) \le m] = 1 - \Delta_c$. Consequently $\Pr(E_n(1) \ge a) \le \Pr(\max_{1 \le k \le n}\rho(X_k) > m) + \Pr(\sum_{k=1}^{n}\rho(X_k)[\rho(X_k) \le m] \ge na) \le n/m + \mathrm{E}(\sum_{k=1}^{n}\rho(X_k)[\rho(X_k) \le m])/(na) = c^2 + (1 - \Delta_c)/a$.

[S. Chatterjee and P. Diaconis, *Annals of Applied Prob.* **28** (2018), 1099–1135.]

125. (a) From $a_n^2 = a_{n-1}a_{n+1}$ we deduce that $a_n = cx^n$ for some $c \geq 0$ and $x \geq 0$.

(b) It remains log-convex $\Longleftrightarrow ca_1 \geq a_0^2$; it remains log-concave $\Longleftrightarrow ca_1 \leq a_0^2$. (The latter condition always holds in the important case $c = 0$.)

(c) If $a_{m-1}a_{m+1} > 0$ we have $a_m/a_{m-1} \geq a_{m+1}/a_m \geq \cdots \geq a_{n+1}/a_n$, because there are no internal zeros. (And the analogous result holds for log-convexity.)

(d) If $xz \geq y^2$ and $XZ \geq Y^2$ and $x, y, z, X, Y, Z > 0$, we have $(x + X)(z + Z) - (y+Y)^2 \geq (x+X)(y^2/x+Y^2/X) - (y+Y)^2 = (x/X)(Y - Xy/x)^2 \geq 0$. [L. L. Liu and Y. Wang, *Advances in Applied Mathematics* **39** (2007), 455.]

(e) Let $c_n = \sum_k \binom{n}{k} a_k b_{n-k}$. Clearly $c_1^2 \leq c_0 c_2$. And $c_n = \sum_k \binom{n-1}{k} a_{n-1-k} b_{k+1} + \sum_k \binom{n-1}{k} a_{k+1} b_{n-1-k}$, so we can apply (c) and induction on n to the shifted sequences. [H. Davenport and G. Pólya, *Canadian Journal of Mathematics* **1** (1949), 2–3.]

(f) Yes: Let $a_k = b_k = 0$ when $k < 0$, and $c_n = \sum_k a_k b_{n-k}$. Then we have

$$c_n^2 - c_{n-1}c_{n+1} = \sum_{0 \leq j \leq k} (a_j a_k - a_{j-1}a_{k+1})(b_{n-j}b_{n-k} - b_{n+1-j}b_{n-1-k}),$$

which is a special case of the Binet–Cauchy identity (exercise 1.2.3–46) with $m = 2$.

(g) Yes, but a more intricate proof seems to be needed. We have $c_n = t_{00}$, $c_{n+1} = t_{01} + t_{10}$, and $c_{n+2} = t_{02} + 2t_{11} + t_{20}$, where $t_{ij} = \sum_k \binom{n}{k} a_{k+i} b_{n-k+j}$; hence $c_{n+1}^2 - c_n c_{n+2} = (t_{01}^2 - t_{00}t_{02}) + (t_{10}^2 - t_{00}t_{20}) + 2(t_{01}t_{10} - t_{00}t_{11})$. We will show that each of these parenthesized terms is nonnegative.

Let $b_j' = \binom{n}{j} b_j$. Then the sequence $\langle b_j' \rangle$ is log-concave; and t_{i0} is the $(n+i)$th term of the sequence $\sum_k a_k b_{n-k}'$, which is log-concave by (f). Therefore $t_{10}^2 \geq t_{00}t_{20}$. A similar argument shows that $t_{01}^2 \geq t_{00}t_{02}$. Finally, Binet–Cauchy gives the identity

$$t_{01}t_{10} - t_{00}t_{11} = \sum_{p<q} \binom{n}{p}\binom{n}{q}(a_{p+1}a_q - a_p a_{q+1})(b_{n-p}b_{n-q+1} - b_{n-p+1}b_{n-q})$$

from the matrix product $T = AXB$, where $A_{ij} = a_{i+j}$, $X_{ij} = \binom{n}{j}[i+j=n]$, $B_{ij} = b_{i+j}$. [D. W. Walkup, *Journal of Applied Probability* **13** (1976), 79–80.]

126. The stated probability is $p_m = \binom{n}{m} m^m (n-m)^{n-m}/n^n$. We have $p_m/p_{m+1} = f_m/f_{n-m-1}$, where $f_m = (m/(m+1))^m$. Since $f_0 > f_1 > \cdots$, the minimum occurs when $m = \lfloor n/2 \rfloor$. And $p_{\lfloor n/2 \rfloor} = (1 + O(1/n))/\sqrt{\pi n/2}$, by exercise 1.2.11.2–9.

127. (a) Random binary vectors have $\Pr(X_1 + \cdots + X_n \leq \theta n) \leq x^{-\theta n}((1+x)/2)^n$ for $0 < x \leq 1$, by the tail inequality 1.2.10–(24). Set $x = \theta/(1-\theta)$ and multiply by 2^n.

(b) We have $\lg \binom{n}{\lfloor \theta n \rfloor} = H(\theta)n - \lg \sqrt{2\pi\theta(1-\theta)n} + O(1/n)$ by 1.2.11.2–(18).

(c) Let $p_{m'm''} = \Pr(x \oplus X' \oplus X''$ is sparse and $\nu X' = m', \nu X'' = m'')$. We will prove that each $p_{m'm''}$ is exponentially small, using several instructive methods.

First, let $\epsilon = \theta(1 - 2\theta)/3$. We can assume that $(\theta - \epsilon)n < m', m'' \leq \theta n$, because $\Pr(\nu X' \leq (\theta - \epsilon)n) = O(\sqrt{n} \, 2^{(H(\theta-\epsilon)-H(\theta))n})$ is exponentially small.

Second, let Y' and Y'' be random binary vectors whose bits are independently 1 with probabilities m'/n and m''/n. Each bit of $x \oplus Y' \oplus Y''$ is 1 with probability $m'/n(1 - m''/n) + (1 - m'/n)m''/n \geq 2(\theta - \epsilon)(1 - \theta) \geq \theta + \epsilon$ when x has a 0 bit, or $(m'/n)(m''/n) + (1 - m'/n)(1 - m''/n) \geq (\theta - \epsilon)^2 + (1 - \theta)^2 \geq \theta + \epsilon$ when x has a 1 bit. Therefore, by the tail inequality, we have $\Pr(x \oplus Y' \oplus Y''$ is sparse$) \leq \alpha^n$, where $\alpha = (1 + \epsilon/\theta)^\theta (1 - \epsilon/(1 - \theta))^{1-\theta}$. This is exponentially small, since $\alpha < 1$.

Finally, let Z' and Z'' be independent random bit vectors with $\nu Z' = m'$ and $\nu Z'' = m''$. Then $p_{m'm''} = \left(\binom{n}{m'}\binom{n}{m''}/S(n,\theta)^2\right) P_{m'm''}$, where $P_{m'm''}$ is the probability that $x \oplus Z' \oplus Z''$ is sparse. Then $\Pr(x \oplus Y' \oplus Y''$ is sparse$) \geq \Pr(x \oplus Y' \oplus Y''$ is sparse and $\nu Y' = m'$ and $\nu Y'' = m'') = \Omega(P_{m'm''}/n)$ by exercise 126. (Study this!)

[V. Guruswami, J. Håstad, and S. Kopparty, *IEEE Trans.* **IT-57** (2011), 718–725, used this result to prove the existence of efficient linear list-decodable codes.]

128. (a) $\Pr(k \text{ pings}) = \binom{n}{k}(\frac{1}{n})^k(1 - \frac{1}{n})^{n-k}$ is binomial, hence $\Pr(1 \text{ ping}) = (1 - \frac{1}{n})^{n-1}$.

(b) It waits T rounds, where $\Pr(T = k) = (1 - p)^{k-1}p$ has the geometric distribution with $p = \frac{1}{n}(1 - \frac{1}{n})^{n-1}$. Hence, for example by exercise 3.4.1–17, we have $\mathrm{E}\,T = 1/p = n^n/(n-1)^{n-1} = (n-1)\exp(n\ln(1/(1-1/n))) = en - \frac{1}{2}e + O(1/n)$. (The standard deviation, $en - \frac{1}{2}e - \frac{1}{2} + O(1/n)$, is approximately the same as the mean.)

(c) The hint suggests that we study the "coupon collector's distribution": If each box of cereal randomly contains one of n different coupons, how many boxes must we buy before we've got every coupon? The generating function for this distribution is

$$C(z) = \frac{nz}{n}\frac{(n-1)z}{n-z} \cdots \frac{z}{n-(n-1)z} = \frac{n}{n/z-0}\frac{n-1}{n/z-1} \cdots \frac{1}{n/z-(n-1)} = \binom{n/z}{n}^{-1},$$

because the time to acquire the next coupon, after we've already got k of them, is a geometric distribution with generating function $(n-k)z/(n-kz)$.

Let B be the number of boxes purchased. The upper tail inequality 1.2.10–(25) tells us that $\Pr(B \geq (1+\epsilon)n\ln n) \leq (n/(n-1/2))^{-(1+\epsilon)n\ln n}C(n/(n-1/2))$, which is

$$\frac{e^{(1+\epsilon)n\ln n\ln(1-1/(2n))}}{\binom{n-1/2}{n}} = \frac{e^{-\frac{1+\epsilon}{2}\ln n+O\left(\frac{\log n}{n}\right)}4^n}{\binom{2n}{n}} = \sqrt{\pi}\,n^{-\epsilon/2}\left(1 + O\left(\frac{\log n}{n}\right)\right)$$

by exercise 1.2.6–47. Thus B is a.s. less than $(1+\epsilon)n\ln n$.

Now let S be the number of successful accesses in $r = \lfloor(1+\epsilon)en\ln n\rfloor$ rounds. Then S is equivalent to r tosses of a biased coin for which the probability of success is $p = (1 - \frac{1}{n})^{n-1} = 1/e + O(1/n)$, by (a). So S has the binomial distribution, and $\Pr(S \leq (1 - \epsilon/2)rp) \leq e^{-\epsilon^2 rp/8}$ by exercise 1.2.10–22(b). This argument proves that S is q.s. greater than $(1 - \epsilon/2)rp = (1 + \epsilon/2 - \epsilon^2/2)n\ln n + O(\log n)$.

Consequently S attempts at coupon collecting will a.s. succeed.

(d) An argument similar to (c) applies, with $\epsilon \mapsto -\epsilon$ and $n - 1/2 \mapsto n + 1/2$.

[This exercise is based on a protocol analyzed in Jon Kleinberg and Éva Tardos's book *Algorithm Design* (Addison–Wesley, 2006), §13.1. See Uriel Feige and Jan Vondrák, *Theory of Computing* **6** (2010), 247–290, §3.1, for optimum contention resolution with a related (but different) model.]

129. The hint follows because $|\cot \pi z| \leq (e^\pi + 1)/(e^\pi - 1)$ and $|r(z)| = O(1/M^2)$ on the path of integration. The function $\pi \cot \pi z$ has no finite singularities except for simple poles at k for all integers k. Furthermore its residue is 1 at each of its poles. Therefore $\sum_{k=-\infty}^{\infty} r(k) + \sum_{j=1}^{t}(\text{Residue of } r(z)\pi \cot \pi z \text{ at } z_j) = \lim_{M \to \infty} O(1/M) = 0$.

Let the sums be S_1, S_2, S_3, S_4. We have $S_1 = \pi^2/4$, because the residue of $(\cot \pi z)/(2z - 1)^2$ at $1/2$ is $-\pi/4$. And $S_2 = \pi \coth \pi$, because the residue of $(\cot \pi z)/(z^2 + 1)$ at $\pm i$ is $-(\coth \pi)/2$. Similarly, the residue of $(\cot \pi z)/(z^2 + z + 1)$ at $(-1 \pm i\sqrt{3})/2$ is $-\alpha$, where $\alpha = \tanh(\sqrt{3}\pi/2)/\sqrt{3}$; hence $S_3 = 2\pi\alpha$. Finally, the residues of $(\cot \pi z)/((z^2 + z + 1)(2z - 1))$ at its poles are $\frac{2}{7}\alpha(1 \pm i\sqrt{3}/2)$ and 0; hence $S_4 = -\frac{2}{7}S_3$. (With hindsight, we can explain this "coincidence" by noting that $7/((k^2 + k + 1)(2k - 1)) = \frac{4}{2k-1} - \frac{2k+3}{k^2+k+1}$ and that $\sum_{k=-n}^{n+1} \frac{1}{2k-1} = \sum_{k=-n}^{n-1} \frac{2k+1}{k^2+k+1} = 0$.)

130. (a) Clearly $\mathrm{E}\,X^2 = \frac{1}{\pi}\int_{-\infty}^{\infty} t^2\,dt/(1+t^2) > \frac{2}{\pi}\int_1^{\infty} dt$, so $\mathrm{E}\,X^2 = \infty$. But $\mathrm{E}\,X = \frac{1}{\pi}\int_{-\infty}^{\infty} t\,dt/(1+t^2) = \frac{1}{2\pi}(\ln(1+\infty^2) - \ln(1+(-\infty)^2)) = \infty - \infty$ is undefined. Thus X has no mean (although it does have the median value 0).

(b) $1/2, 2/3$, and $5/6$, because $\Pr(|X| \le x) = \frac{1}{\pi}\int_{-x}^{x} \frac{dt}{1+t^2} = \frac{2}{\pi}\arctan x$ when $x \ge 0$.

(c) This follows directly from the fact that $\Pr(X \le x) = (\arctan x)/\pi + 1/2$.

(d) In step P4 of Algorithm 3.4.1P, V_1/V_2 is a random tangent, so it is a Cauchy deviate. Furthermore, by the theory underlying that algorithm, V_1/V_2 is the ratio of independent normal deviates; thus, $Z \leftarrow X/Y$ is Cauchy whenever X and Y are independently normal. The Cauchy distribution is also Student's t distribution with 1 degree of freedom; Section 3.4.1's recipe for generating it is to compute $Z \leftarrow X/|Y|$.

(e) We have $z \le Z \le z + dz \iff (z - qY)/p \le X \le (z + dz - qY)/p$. Hence

$$\Pr(z \le Z \le z + dz \text{ and } y \le Y \le y + dy) = \frac{1}{\pi}\frac{dz}{p}\frac{1}{(1+(z-qy/p)^2)}\frac{1}{\pi}\frac{dy}{1+y^2},$$

and we want to integrate this for $-\infty < y < \infty$. The integrand has poles at $y = \pm i$ and $y = (z \pm ip)/q$, and it is $O(1/M^4)$ when $|y| = M$. So we can integrate on a semicircular path, $y = t$ for $-M \le t \le M$ followed by $y = Me^{it}$ for $0 \le t \le \pi$, obtaining

$$\int_{-\infty}^{\infty} \frac{dy}{(p^2 + (z-qy)^2)(1+y^2)} = 2\pi i((\text{Residue at } i) + (\text{Residue at } \tfrac{z+pi}{q})) = \frac{1}{p(1+z^2)}.$$

Thus $\Pr(z \le Z \le z + dz) = \frac{1}{\pi}dz/(1 + z^2)$ as desired.

It follows by induction (see answer 42) that *any convex combination of independent Cauchy deviates is a Cauchy deviate*. In particular, the average of n independent Cauchy deviates is no more concentrated than a single deviate is; the "law of large numbers" doesn't always hold. [S. D. Poisson proved this special case in *Connaissance des Tems pour l'an 1827* (1824), 273–302. The distribution is named after A. L. Cauchy, not Poisson, because Cauchy clarified matters by publishing seven notes about it — one note per week! — in *Comptes Rendus Acad. Sci.* **37** (Paris, 1853), 64–68, ..., 381–385.]

(f) By (e), $c \cdot X$ is $|c_1| + \cdots + |c_n| = \|c\|_1$ times a Cauchy deviate. [This fact has important applications to dimension reduction and data streams; see P. Indyk, *JACM* **53** (2006), 307–323.]

(g) If $t \ge 0$ we get e^{-t}, using the residue of $e^{itz}/(1 + z^2)$ at $z = i$ and the semicircular path of part (e), because the integrand is $O(1/M^2)$ when $|z| = M$. If $t \le 0$ we can integrate in the opposite direction, getting e^{+t}. Hence the answer is $e^{-|t|}$.

131. (a) By exercise 129, $c = 1/(\pi \coth \pi)$. [Notice that $\coth \pi \approx 1.0037$ is nearly 1.]

(b) When $n \ne 0$, the method of exercise 129 tells us, somewhat surprisingly, that $\sum_{k=-\infty}^{\infty} 1/((1 + k^2)(1 + (n - k)^2)) = (2\pi \coth \pi)/(n^2 + 4)$. Thus $\Pr(X + Y = n) = 2c/(n^2 + 4)$. When n is even, this is exactly $\frac{1}{2}\Pr(2Z = n)$.

When $n = 0$, there's a double pole and the calculations are trickier. We can more easily compute $\Pr(X + Y \ne 0) = \sum_{n=1}^{\infty} \frac{4c}{n^2+4} = c(\pi \coth 2\pi - \frac{1}{2}) \approx .837717$. Thus $\Pr(X + Y = 0) \approx .162283$.

132. (a) $\binom{K}{k}\binom{N-K}{n-k}/\binom{N}{n}$. [Hence the probability generating function $g(z) = \sum_k p_k z^k$ is a hypergeometric function, $\binom{N-K}{n}F\binom{-K,-N}{N-K-n+1}|z)/\binom{N}{n}$; see Eq. 1.2.6–(39).]

(b) $g'(1) = nK/N$; $\{\lfloor((n+1)(K+1)-1)/(N+2)\rfloor, \lfloor(n+1)(K+1))/(N+2)\rfloor\}$; $n(N-n)(N-K)/(N^3 - N^2)$. (Note that $g''(1) = n(n-1)K(K-1)/(N(N-1))$.)

(c) Let $Q = X_1 + \cdots + X_n$ and $Z_m = \mathrm{E}(Q \mid X_1, \ldots, X_m)$. Then we have $Z_m = (K - X_1 - \cdots - X_m)(n - m)/(N - m) + X_1 + \cdots + X_m$. The associated fair sequence is $Y_m = Z_m - Z_{m-1} = \Delta_m(X_1 + \cdots + X_{m-1} - K) + c_m X_m$ for $1 \le m \le n$, where

$c_m = (N - n)/(N - m)$ and $\Delta_m = c_m - c_{m-1}$. Since Y_m changes by at most c_m when $\{X_1, \ldots, X_{m-1}\}$ are given and X_m varies, (37) tells us that $\Pr(Q \geq nK/N + x) = \Pr(Z_n - Z_0 \geq x) = \Pr(Y_1 + \cdots + Y_n \geq x) \leq e^{-2x^2/(c_1^2 + \cdots + c_n^2)} \leq e^{-2x^2/n}$.

133. (a) By induction on m: Suppose $m > 1$ and no t rows are shattered. Discard duplicate columns, and let $2b$ of the remaining ones have a "mate" whose bit in the bottom row is complemented. Let a of them have no mate. Then the first $m - 1$ rows contain $a + b \leq f(m - 1, t)$ distinct columns, by induction; and $b \leq f(m - 1, t - 1)$. Hence there are $a + 2b \leq f(m - 1, t) + f(m - 1, t - 1) = f(m, t)$ distinct columns.

(b) For example, let the columns be all length-m vectors that have at most $t-1$ 1s. [N. Sauer, *Journal of Combinatorial Theory* **A13** (1972), 143–145.]

134. (a) Use Chebyshev's inequality (18), because the variance is $p_j(1 - p_j) \leq 1/4$.

(b) Consider the $\binom{2m}{m}$ equally likely ways we could have gotten two samples $(\mathcal{X}, \mathcal{X}')$ from the same $2m$ atomic events. If A_j occurs $K = M_j(\mathcal{X}) + M_j(\mathcal{X}')$ times,

$$\Pr(\widehat{E}_j(\mathcal{X}, \mathcal{X}') > \epsilon) = \Pr\left(\sum\{\binom{K}{k}\binom{2m-K}{m-k}/\binom{2m}{m} \mid |k - K/2| > \epsilon m\}\right) \leq 2e^{-2(\epsilon m)^2/m}.$$

(c) $\Delta_{2m}(\mathcal{A}) \Pr(\widehat{E}_j(\mathcal{X}, \mathcal{X}') > \epsilon/2) \geq \Pr(\max_j \widehat{E}_j(\mathcal{X}, \mathcal{X}') \geq \epsilon/2 \text{ and } E(\mathcal{X}) > \epsilon) \geq \Pr(E_j(\mathcal{X}') \leq \epsilon/2 \text{ and } E_j(\mathcal{X}) > \epsilon \text{ and } E(\mathcal{X}) > \epsilon) \geq \frac{1}{2} \Pr(E_j(\mathcal{X}) > \epsilon \text{ and } E(\mathcal{X}) > \epsilon)$. [*Teoriya Veroyatnosteĭ i ee Primeneniĭa* **16** (1971), 264–279.]

135. (Notice that the smallest *non*-Baxter permutations are 3142 and its inverse, 2413.)

If P is a Baxter permutation, so are $P^R = p_n \ldots p_1$ and $P^C = \bar{p}_1 \ldots \bar{p}_n$, where $\bar{x} = n + 1 - x$. So is the permutation $P \setminus n$ obtained by deleting n; and so are the permutations $P \setminus x$ obtained by deleting x and subtracting 1 from each element that exceeds x, if $x = p_n$ or $x = 1$ or $x = p_1$. (Consider, for example, deleting n from P^-.)

Let's look at the $n+1$ permutations obtained by *inserting* $n+1$ into an n-element Baxter permutation. For example, when $n = 8$ and $P = 21836745$ the nine extensions are 921836745, 291836745, 219836745, 218936745, 218396745, 218369745, 218367945, 218367495, 218367459. Only four of these fail Baxter's property, namely 291836745, 218396745, 218369745, and 218367495; and we soon discover the general rule: $n + 1$ can be Baxterly inserted if and only if it's placed just before a left-to-right maximum, or just after a right-to-left maximum. (In our example, the left-to-right maxima are 2 and 8; the right-to-left maxima are 5, 7, and 8.)

Let $B_n(i, j, k)$ be the number of $(n+1)$-element Baxter permutations with exactly $i + 1$ left-to-right maxima, $j + 1$ left-to-right minima, k ascents, and $n - k$ descents. Such permutations correspond to floorplans with $n+1$ rooms, $i+1$ rooms touching the bottom of the frame, $j + 1$ rooms touching the left of the frame, $k + 2$ vertical bounds, and $n - k + 2$ horizontal bounds (see exercise 7.2.2.1–372). The reasoning above yields the interesting recurrence

$$B_1(i, j, k) = [i = j = k = 0], \quad B_{n+1}(i+1, j+1, k) = \sum_{i' > i} B_n(i', j, k) + \sum_{j' > j} B_n(i, j', k-1);$$

and the solution can be expressed as a determinant of binomial coefficients:

$$B_n(i, j, k) = \det \begin{pmatrix} \binom{n-j-1}{k-1} & \binom{n}{k-1} & \binom{n-i-1}{n-k+1} \\ \binom{n-j-1}{k} & \binom{n}{k} & \binom{n-i-1}{n-k} \\ \binom{n-j-1}{k+1} & \binom{n}{k+1} & \binom{n-i-1}{n-k-1} \end{pmatrix}, \quad \text{unless} \quad \begin{cases} i = 0 \text{ and } j = n \\ \text{or} \\ i = n \text{ and } j = 0. \end{cases}$$

Summing on i and j now gives the simpler formula

$$b_n(k) = t_{n+1}(k + 1)/t_{n+1}(1), \quad \text{where } t_n(k) = \binom{n}{k-1}\binom{n}{k}\binom{n}{k+1},$$

for the number of n-element Baxter permutations with exactly k ascents.

Since the terms with $k \approx n/2$ dominate the sum $b_n = \sum_k b_n(k)$, we obtain the asymptotic value

$$b_n = \frac{8^{n+2}}{\sqrt{12\pi n^4}}\left(1 - \frac{22}{3n} + O(n^{-2})\right),$$

due to A. M. Odlyzko. [See G. Baxter, *Proc. American Math. Soc.* **15** (1964), 851–855; F. R. K. Chung, R. L. Graham, V. E. Hoggatt, Jr., and M. Kleiman, *Journal of Combinatorial Theory* **A24** (1978), 382–394; W. M. Boyce, *Houston J. Math.* **7** (1981), 175–189; S. Dulucq and O. Guibert, *Discrete Math.* **180** (1998), 143–156.] R. L. Ollerton has found the recurrence $(n+2)(n+3)b_n = (7n^2 + 7n - 2)b_{n-1} + 8(n-1)(n-2)b_{n-2}$, with $b_1 = 1$, as well as the closed form $b_n = F\binom{1-n,-n,-1-n}{2,3} \mid -1)$. The initial terms are $(b_0, b_1, \dots) = (1, 1, 2, 6, 22, 92, 422, 2074, 10754, 58202, \dots)$.

136. It's true if $y \le x + \frac{1}{2}$, because $f(x+t) - f(x)$ increases from $f(t)$ to $-f(1-t)$ as x increases from 0 to $1-t$. But it fails when $x < \frac{1}{2}$ and $y = 1$.

137. (a) The sets $U = \{x \mid \Pr(X \le x) \ge \frac{1}{2}\}$ and $L = \{x \mid \Pr(X < x) \le \frac{1}{2}\}$ are intervals. Let $\underline{m} = \inf U$ and $\overline{m} = \sup L$; then $U \cap L = [\underline{m} .. \overline{m}]$. Since the distribution function $\Pr(X \le x)$ is right-continuous, $\underline{m} \in U$; similarly, $\overline{m} \in L$, because $\Pr(X < x)$ is left-continuous. Also $\underline{m} \le \overline{m}$; for if $\overline{m} < x < \underline{m}$ then $\Pr(X \le x) < \frac{1}{2} < \Pr(X < x)$.

(b) If $\underline{m} < \overline{m}$ then $\Pr(X < \underline{m}) \le \Pr(X < \overline{m}) = 1 - \Pr(X \ge \overline{m}) \le \frac{1}{2} \le \Pr(X \le \underline{m})$.

(c) $\Pr(X \le y) \ge \frac{1}{2}$ implies $y \ge \underline{m}$; $\Pr(X < x) \le \frac{1}{2}$ implies $x \le \overline{m}$; so it's true if $\underline{m} = \overline{m}$. But we might have $x > \underline{m}$ or $y < \overline{m}$.

(d) Suppose $m \in \text{med } X$ and $c < m$. (A similar argument applies when $c > m$.) Let $\Delta x = |x - c| - |x - m|$. If $x \ge m$ we have $\Delta x = m - c$. If $x < m$ we have $\Delta x = c - m + 2(x \dot{-} c)$; hence $E(\Delta X \mid X < m) \ge c - m$. Therefore $E(\Delta X) \ge (c-m)\Pr(X < m) + (m - c)\Pr(X \ge m) = (m - c)(2\Pr(X \ge m) - 1) \ge 0$. Equality holds if and only if $\Pr(X \ge m) = \frac{1}{2}$ and $\Pr(c < X < m) = 0$; the latter is the same as $\Pr(X \le c) = \Pr(X < m)$. [See M. Mitzenmacher and E. Upfal, *Probability and Computing* (2017), Theorem 3.9.]

(e) True by Cantelli's inequality, answer 48: If $m \ge \mu$ then $\frac{1}{2} \le \Pr(X \ge m) \le \sigma^2/(\sigma^2 + (m - \mu)^2)$. If $m \le \mu$ then $\frac{1}{2} \le \Pr(-X \ge -m) \le \sigma^2/(\sigma^2 + (\mu - m)^2)$.

(f) Call f a "C-function" if $I_t = \{x \mid f(x) \le t\}$ is connected and closed for all t. Every convex f is a C-function; for if $a \in I_t$ and $b \in I_t$, we have $pa + (1 - p)b \in I_t$ for $0 \le p \le 1$; also I_t is closed because f is continuous. (There also are rather wild C-functions, such as $f(x) = (x < 0? \ 3: x < 1? \ 2 - x: x \le 2? \ x - 1: x \le 3? \ \sqrt{x}: x).$).

Given a C-function f and a random variable X, let $\text{med } X = [\underline{m} .. \overline{m}]$ and $\text{med } f(X) = [\underline{M} .. \overline{M}]$. If $\underline{M} \le M \le \overline{M}$, then I_M is a closed interval and $\Pr(X \in I_M) = \Pr(f(X) \le M) \ge \frac{1}{2}$. Thus by (c), either $f(\underline{m}) \le M$ or $f(\overline{m}) \le M$. (For example, if $f(x) = -x$ we have $\underline{m} = -\overline{M}$ and $\overline{m} = -\underline{M}$.) [See M. Merkle, *Statistics & Probability Letters* **71** (2005), 277–281.]

138. Working in the slices of probability space where Y is constant, we have (by definition) $\text{var}(X \mid Y) = E(X^2 \mid Y) - (E(X \mid Y))^2$ and $\text{var}(E(X \mid Y)) = E(E(X \mid Y))^2 - (E(E(X \mid Y)))^2$. Hence $E(\text{var}(X \mid Y)) = E(E(X^2 \mid Y)) - E(E(X \mid Y))^2$. The complicated term $E(E(X \mid Y))^2$ fortuitously cancels out, giving $\text{var}(E(X \mid Y)) + E(\text{var}(X \mid Y)) = E(E(X^2 \mid Y)) - (E(E(X \mid Y)))^2 = E X^2 - (E X)^2$. [See *CMath*, pages 423–425.]

139. Let $x(z) = \sum_k \Pr(X_n = k)z^k$, $g_n(w, z) = \sum_{j,k} \Pr(R_n = j, S_n = k)w^j z^k$, $h_n(w, z) = \sum_{j,k} \Pr(S_n^+ = j, S_n = k)w^j z^k$; these generating functions involve negative values of k, so we treat them as "formal series." We shall prove that $g = h$, where

$$g = \sum_{n=0}^{\infty} g_n(w, z)t^n \quad \text{and} \quad h = \exp\left(\sum_{n=1}^{\infty} h_n(w, z)\frac{t^n}{n}\right);$$

that will suffice because $g_n(w,z) = r_n(wz, z^{-1})$ and $h_n(w,z) = s_n^+(wz) + s_n^-(z^{-1}) - 1$.

Let X be the operation that multiplies a formal series by $x(z)$, and let P be the operation that replaces $w^j z^k$ by $w^{\max(j,k)} z^k$. Notice that $h_n(w,z) = P(x(z)^n)$; furthermore we have $g_0(w,z) = 1$, $g_n(w,z) = PXg_{n-1}$ for $n > 0$. It follows that g is the unique formal series that satisfies $g = 1 + tPXg$. To finish the proof, we have $(1 - tX)h = \exp((1-P)\ln(1 - tx(z))) = 1 + \sum_{n=1}^{\infty}((1-P)\ln(1 - tx(z)))^n/n!$; hence $h - tPXh = P((1 - tX)h) = 1$. [J. G. Wendel, *Proc. Amer. Math. Soc.* **9** (1958), 905–908.]

140. (a) Let $q = 1 - p$. The expected number of marked elements that remain a max is $\sum_k \binom{n}{k} p^k q^{n-k} H_k = H_n + \ln p + O(q^n/n)$, by Theorem 1.2.7A. To this we add $\sum_{m=1}^{n} t_m$, where $t_m = \Pr(x_m \text{ unmarked and still a max}) = \sum_{j,k} \binom{m-1}{j}\binom{n-m}{k} p^{j+k} q^{n-j-k} / \binom{j+k}{j}$. (For example, $t_1 = q$; $t_2 = q^2 + (q - q^n)/(n-1)$; $t_m = t_{n+1-m}$.) The identity $\sum_k \binom{n}{k} p^k q^{n-k}/\binom{k+j}{j} = \left(1 - \sum_{k=0}^{j-1}\binom{n+j}{k} p^k q^{n+j-k}\right)/\left(p^j\binom{n+j}{j}\right)$ shows that, for fixed m, $t_m = \sum_{j=0}^{m-1} q^{m-j}(m-1)^{\underline{j}}/(n-m+j)^{\underline{j}} + O(q^n/n)$. Summing on m, and trading tails, yields $t_1 + \cdots + t_n = 2q/p + O(q^n/n)$. [For this result, as well as those of parts (b) and (c), see C. Banderier, R. Beier, and K. Mehlhorn, *LNCS* **2747** (2003), 198–207.]

(b) Say $m = \lfloor \sqrt{n} \rfloor$. If a of the first m elements are marked, and b of the last $n-m$, the probability that all a leave the first m positions is $q = b^{\underline{a}}/(a+b)^{\underline{a}} > ((b-a)/b)^a$; and in this case $\lambda(X) \geq m - a$. We q.s. have $a \leq \frac{3}{4}m$ and $b \geq \frac{1}{4}n + m$; consequently $q \geq \exp(a\ln(1 - a/b)) \geq \exp(-a^2/(b-a)) \geq \exp(-9/4)$ and $\lambda(X) = \Omega(\sqrt{n})$.

(c) Let $m = \lfloor \sqrt{8(n/p)\ln n} \rfloor$ and ignore all x_k with $k \leq m$ or $x_k \geq n-m$; at most $2m$ maxs are ignored. At most about $\ln pn$ of the marked elements are maxs. And if x_k is neither ignored nor marked, it's a max with probability $O(1/n)$; the reason is that q.s. at most $2pn$ are marked, of which $\geq pm/2$ precede x_k and $\geq pm/2$ exceed x_k.

(d) If $\bar{x}_k > \bar{x}_{k+1}$, swapping $\bar{x}_k \leftrightarrow \bar{x}_{k+1}$ and $\delta_k \leftrightarrow \delta_{k+1}$ doesn't decrease $\mathrm{E}\,\lambda(X)$.

(e) Let $m = \lfloor \sqrt{\epsilon n} \rfloor$ and $\Delta_k = \bar{x}_k - \bar{x}_{k-m}$, where $\bar{x}_k = 0$ for $k < 0$. If x_k is a max then either (*) $\epsilon < \Delta_k + \delta_k$ or (**) $\epsilon \geq \Delta_k + \delta_k > \max\{\delta_{k-1}, \ldots, \delta_{k-m}\}$. One can show that $\Pr(*) \leq \Pr(**)$; hence $\Pr(x_k \text{ is a max}) \leq \Delta_k/(2\epsilon) + 1/(m+1) + 1/k$. Sum on k.

See V. Damerow, B. Manthey, F. Meyer auf der Heide, H. Räcke, C. Scheideler, C. Sohler, and T. Tantau, *ACM Transactions on Algorithms* **8** (2012), 30:1–30:28, where a matching lower bound is also proved. Similarly, if each δ_k is a normal deviate with standard deviation σ, they showed that $\mathrm{E}\,\lambda(X) = O(\log n(1 + \sigma^{-1}\sqrt{\log n}))$.

141. We can assume that $p_1 + \cdots + p_n = 1$. Then $e^{\ln(\mathrm{E}\,X)} \geq e^{\mathrm{E}\ln X}$ (ln is concave).

142. (a) Let $p_j = \Pr(|X| = x_j)$. Since every term in the difference $M_q M_t - M_r M_s = \sum_{j<k} p_j p_k x_j^q x_k^q (x_k^{s-q} - x_j^{s-q})(x_k^{r-q} - x_j^{r-q})$ is nonnegative, we have $M_q M_t \geq M_r M_s$.

(b) The hint gives $(M_s/M_r)^{M_r/(s-r)} \geq x_1^{p_1 x_1^r} \ldots x_n^{p_n x_n^r}$. Similarly, but reversing the inequality because $q < r$, $(M_q/M_r)^{M_r/(q-r)} \leq x_1^{p_1 x_1^r} \ldots x_n^{p_n x_n^r}$. Take the M_rth root.

(c) The "fact" follows when $(q, r, s) = (0, 1/p, 1)$ in (b). Let $c = 1/\sum b_k^q$, and set $p_k = cb_k^q$, $x_k = a_k^p/b_k^q$; then $M_{1/p} = c\sum a_k b_k$, $M_1 = c\sum a_k^p$. (When $0 < p < 1$ and $q < 0$, the same relation holds but with $\leq$ changed to $\geq$ and $b_k = 0$ forbidden.)

(d) $|\mathrm{E}\,XY| \leq \mathrm{E}(|X||Y|) = \sum_{i,j} p_{ij}^{1/p+1/q} x_i y_j \leq (\mathrm{E}\,|X|^p)^{1/p}(\mathrm{E}\,|Y|^q)^{1/q}$, where $p_{ij} = \Pr(|X| = x_i \text{ and } |Y| = y_j)$ is the joint distribution of $|X|$ and $|Y|$.

Historical notes: This inequality and Jensen's inequality evolved in concert. The fact that $\mathrm{E}\,|X|^r \leq (\mathrm{E}\,|X|)^r$ for $0 < r < 1$, while $\mathrm{E}\,|X|^r \geq (\mathrm{E}\,|X|)^r$ for other values of r, was already implicit on page 155 of Reynaud and Duhamel's *Problèmes et développemens* (Paris: 1823). Rogers published his contributions in *Messenger of Math.* **17** (1887), 145–150 (with a few typographic errors). That inspired O. Hölder [*Göttinger Nachrichten* (1889), 38–47] to prove (20) for all f with $f''(x) \geq 0$, obtaining Rogers's identities as corollaries. Many related results are detailed in Hardy, Littlewood, and Pólya's book *Inequalities* (1934), Chapter 2. For example, if $p_j, a_{ij} \geq 0$ for $1 \leq i \leq m$ and $1 \leq j \leq n$, with $\sum p_j = 1$, their Theorem 10 states that

$$\sum_{i=1}^{m}\left(\prod_{j=1}^{n} a_{ij}^{p_j}\right) \leq \prod_{j=1}^{n}\left(\sum_{i=1}^{m} a_{ij}\right)^{p_j}. \qquad \text{[The case } n = 2,\ p_1 = \tfrac{1}{p},\ p_2 = \tfrac{1}{q},\ \text{is (c).]}$$

143. Let $M = \left(\mathrm{E}(|X| + |Y|)^p\right)^{1/p} = \left(\sum_{i,j}(p_{ij}(x_i + y_j)^p)\right)^{1/p}$, with the p_{ij} of answer 142(d). Then we have $M = \Sigma(x) + \Sigma(y)$, where $\Sigma(x) = \sum_{i,j} p_{ij}x_i(x_i + y_j)^{p-1}/M^{p-1} = \sum_{i,j}(p_{ij}^{1/p}x_i)(p_{ij}^{1/p}(x_i+y_j))^{p-1}/M^{p-1} \leq \left(\sum_{i,j} p_{ij}x_i^p\right)^{1/p}\left(\sum_{i,j}(p_{ij}(x_i+y_j)^p)\right)^{1/q}/M^{p-1} = (\mathrm{E}|X|^p)^{1/p}$. Add $\Sigma(y)$. [H. Minkowski, *Geometrie der Zahlen* (Leipzig, 1896), §40(I).]

144. (a) By convexity, $|x|^p = |\mathrm{E}(x+Y)|^p \leq \mathrm{E}|x+Y|^p$ for any x. Take E of both sides.

(b) By (a), $\mathrm{E}|X|^p = \mathrm{E}|X^+|^p \leq \mathrm{E}|X^+ - X^-|^p$.

(c) The hint follows because $(1 + x)^p + (1 - x)^p - 2x^p \geq 2$ for $0 \leq x \leq 1$. Consequently $\mathrm{E}|X|^p + \mathrm{E}|Y|^p \leq \mathrm{E}|X + Y|^p$ when $\mathrm{E}|X + Y|^p = \mathrm{E}|X - Y|^p$. Now use induction on n. [See J. A. Clarkson, *Trans. Amer. Math. Soc.* **40** (1936), 396–414.]

(d) $\mathrm{E}|X_1|^p + \cdots + \mathrm{E}|X_n|^p \leq \mathrm{E}|X_1^{\mathrm{sym}}|^p + \cdots + \mathrm{E}|X_n^{\mathrm{sym}}|^p \leq \mathrm{E}|X_1^{\mathrm{sym}} + \cdots + X_n^{\mathrm{sym}}|^p = \mathrm{E}|(X_1^+ + \cdots + X_n^+) - (X_1^- + \cdots + X_n^-)|^p \leq \mathrm{E}(2^{p-1}|X_1^+ + \cdots + X_n^+|^p) + \mathrm{E}(2^{p-1}|-(X_1^- + \cdots + X_n^-)|^p) = 2^p\,\mathrm{E}|X_1 + \cdots + X_n|^p$. [See A. Gut, *Probability: A Graduate Course* (Springer, 2013), Theorem 3.6.1. We've used the fact that $|x + y|^p < 2^{p-1}(|x|^p + |y|^p)$, which actually holds for $p \geq 1$ because the mapping $x \mapsto |x|^p$ is convex.]

145. We have $(a_1^2 + \cdots + a_n^2)^m = \sum_{k_1,\ldots,k_n} c(k_1,\ldots,k_n)a_1^{2k_1}\ldots a_n^{2k_n}$ by the multinomial theorem, Eq. 1.2.6–(42), where $c(k_1,\ldots,k_n) = \binom{m}{k_1,\ldots,k_n}$; $\mathrm{E}((a_1X_1 + \cdots + a_nX_n)^{2m}) = \sum_{k_1,\ldots,k_n} c'(k_1,\ldots,k_n)a_1^{k_1}\ldots a_n^{k_n}$, where $c'(k_1,\ldots,k_n) = \binom{2m}{k_1,\ldots,k_n}$ when each k_j is even, otherwise $c'(k_1,\ldots,k_n) = 0$. And $c'(2k_1,\ldots,2k_n)/c(k_1,\ldots,k_n) = (2m-1)!!/\prod_{j=1}^{m}(2k_j - 1)!!$. [A. Khintchine, *Math. Zeitschrift* **18** (1923), 109–116. More generally,

$$(a_1^2 + \cdots + a_n^2)^{p/2} \leq \mathrm{E}|a_1X_1 + \cdots + a_nX_n|^p \leq 2^{p/2}\pi^{-1/2}\Gamma\left(\tfrac{p+1}{2}\right)(a_1^2 + \cdots + a_n^2)^{p/2},$$

for all $p \geq 2$; see U. Haagerup, *Studia Mathematica* **70** (1981–1982), 231–283.]

146. For every binary vector $t = t_1 \ldots t_n$, let $T_n(t) = \sum_{k=1}^{n}(-1)^{t_k}X_k$. Also let $S_n = \sum_{k=1}^{n} X_k$, $S_n^{\mathrm{sym}} = \sum_{k=1}^{n} X_k^{\mathrm{sym}}$, $T_n^{\mathrm{sym}}(t) = \sum_{k=1}^{n}(-1)^{t_k}X_k^{\mathrm{sym}}$. By exercise 144 we have

$$2^{-2m}\,\mathrm{E}\,T_n(t)^{2m} \leq 2^{-2m}\,\mathrm{E}\,T_n^{\mathrm{sym}}(t)^{2m} = 2^{-2m}\,\mathrm{E}(S_n^{\mathrm{sym}})^{2m} \leq \mathrm{E}\,S_n^{2m}$$
$$\leq \mathrm{E}(S_n^{\mathrm{sym}})^{2m} = \mathrm{E}\,T_n^{\mathrm{sym}}(t)^{2m} \leq 2^{2m}\,\mathrm{E}\,T_n(t)^{2m}$$

for all t, because S_n^{sym} and $T_n^{\mathrm{sym}}(t)$ have the same distribution. Exercise 145 tells us that

$$\left(\sum_{k=1}^{n} x_k^2\right)^m \leq \frac{1}{2^n}\sum_{t}\left(\sum_{k=1}^{n}(-1)^{t_k}x_k\right)^{2m} \leq (2m-1)!!\left(\sum_{k=1}^{n} x_k^2\right)^m$$

for all sequences $x_1 \ldots x_n$ of atomic values. So the result follows by applying E. [*Fundamenta Mathematicæ* **29** (1937), 60–90; *Studia Mathematica* **7** (1938), 104–120.]

147. This is an application of the previous several exercises; see A. Gut, *Probability* (2013), Theorem 3.9.1. [H. P. Rosenthal, *Israel J. Mathematics* **8** (1970), 273–303.]

As to volume 4, well, I'm making progress
but it is the toughest of the lot.

— DONALD E. KNUTH, letter to Michael F. Yoder (19 November 1973)

SECTION 7.2.2

1. Although many formulations are possible, the following may be the nicest: (i) D_k is arbitrary (but hopefully finite), and P_l is always true. (ii) $D_k = \{1, 2, \ldots, n\}$ and $P_l = {}$'$x_j \neq x_k$ for $1 \leq j < k \leq l$'. (iii) For combinations of n things from N, $D_k = \{1, \ldots, N + 1 - k\}$ and $P_l = {}$'$x_1 > \cdots > x_l$'. (iv) $D_k = \{0, 1, \ldots, \lfloor n/k \rfloor\}$; $P_l = {}$'$x_1 \geq \cdots \geq x_l$ and $n - (n - l)x_l \leq x_1 + \cdots + x_l \leq n$'. (v) For restricted growth strings, $D_k = \{0, \ldots, k - 1\}$ and $P_l = {}$'$x_{j+1} \leq 1 + \max(x_1, \ldots, x_j)$ for $1 \leq j < l$'. (vi) For indices of left parentheses (see 7.2.1.6–(8)), $D_k = \{1, \ldots, 2k - 1\}$ and $P_l = {}$'$x_1 < \cdots < x_l$'.

2. True. (If not, set $D_1 \leftarrow D_1 \cap \{x \mid P_1(x)\}$.)

3. Let $D_k = \{1, \ldots, \text{max degree on level } k - 1\}$, and let $P_l(x_1, \ldots, x_l) = {}$'$x_1. \cdots .x_l$ is a label in T's Dewey decimal notation' (see Section 2.3).

4. We can restrict D_1 to $\{1, 2, 3, 4\}$, because the reflection $(9 - x_1) \ldots (9 - x_8)$ of every solution $x_1 \ldots x_8$ is also a solution. (H. C. Schumacher made this observation in a letter to C. F. Gauss, 24 September 1850.) Notice that Fig. 68 is left-right symmetric.

5. $try(l) = {}$ "If $l > n$, visit $x_1 \ldots x_n$. Otherwise, for $x_l \leftarrow \min D_l$, $\min D_l + 1$, $\ldots$, $\max D_l$, if $P_l(x_1, \ldots, x_l)$ call $try(l + 1)$."

This formulation is elegant, and fine for simple problems. But it doesn't give any clue about why the method is called "backtrack"! Nor does it yield efficient code for important problems whose inner loop is performed billions of times. We will see that the key to efficient backtracking is to provide good ways to update and downdate the data structures that speed up the testing of property P_l. The overhead of recursion can get in the way, and the actual iterative structure of Algorithm B isn't difficult to grasp.

6. Excluding cases with $j = r$ or $k = r$ from (3) yields respectively (312, 396, 430, 458, 458, 430, 396, 312) solutions. (With column r also omitted there are just (40, 46, 42, 80, 80, 42, 46, 40).)

7. Yes, almost surely for all $n > 16$. One such is $x_1 x_2 \ldots x_{17} = 2\ 17\ 12\ 10\ 7\ 14\ 3$ $5\ 9\ 13\ 15\ 4\ 11\ 8\ 6\ 1\ 16$. [See *Proc. Edinburgh Math. Soc.* **8** (1890), 43 and Fig. 52.] Preußer and Engelhardt found 34,651,355,392 solutions when $n = 27$.

8. Yes: $(42736815, 42736851)$; also therefore $(57263148, 57263184)$.

9. Yes, at least when $m = 4$; e.g., $x_1 \ldots x_{16} = 5\ 8\ 13\ 16\ 3\ 7\ 15\ 11\ 6\ 2\ 10\ 14\ 1\ 4$ $9\ 12$. There are no solutions when $m = 5$, but $7\ 10\ 13\ 20\ 17\ 24\ 3\ 6\ 23\ 11\ 16\ 21\ 4\ 9$ $14\ 2\ 19\ 22\ 1\ 8\ 5\ 12\ 15\ 18$ works for $m = 6$. (Are there solutions for all even $m \geq 4$? C. F. de Jaenisch, *Traité des applications de l'analyse mathématique au jeu des échecs* **2** (1862), 132–133, noted that all 8-queen solutions have four of each color. He proved that the number of white queens must be even, because $\sum_{k=1}^{4m}(x_k + k)$ is even.)

10. Let bit vectors a_l, b_l, c_l represent the "useful" elements of the sets in (6), with $a_l = \sum\{2^{x-1} \mid x \in A_l\}$, $b_l = \sum\{2^{x-1} \mid x \in B_l \cap [1 .. n]\}$, $c_l = \sum\{2^{x-1} \mid x \in C_l \cap [1 .. n]\}$. Then step W2 sets bit vector $s_l \leftarrow \mu\ \&\ \bar{a}_l\ \&\ \bar{b}_l\ \&\ \bar{c}_l$, where μ is the mask $2^n - 1$.

In step W3 we can set $t \leftarrow s_l\ \&\ (-s_l)$, $a_{l+1} \leftarrow a_l + t$, $b_{l+1} \leftarrow (b_l + t) \gg 1$, $c_{l+1} \leftarrow ((c_l + t) \ll 1)\ \&\ \mu$; and it's also convenient to set $s_l \leftarrow s_l - t$ at this time, instead of deferring this change to step W4.

(There's no need to store x_l in memory, or even to compute x_l in step W3 as an integer in $[1 .. n]$, because x_l can be deduced from $a_l - a_{l-1}$ when a solution is found.)

11. (a) Only when $n = 1$, because reflected queens can capture each other.

(b) Queens not in the center must appear in groups of four.

(c) The four queens occupy the same rows, columns, and diagonals in both cases.

(d) In each solution counted by c_n we can independently tilt (or not) each of the $\lfloor n/4 \rfloor$ groups of four. [*Mathematische Unterhaltungen und Spiele* **1**, second edition (Leipzig: Teubner, 1910), 249–258.]

12. With distinct x_k, $\sum_{k=1}^n (x_k + k) = 2\binom{n+1}{2} \equiv 0$ (modulo n). If the $(x_k + k) \bmod n$ are also distinct, the same sum is also $\equiv \binom{n+1}{2}$. But that's impossible when n is even.

Now suppose further that the numbers $(x_k - k) \bmod n$ are distinct. Then we have $\sum_{k=1}^n (x_k + k)^2 \equiv \sum_{k=1}^n (x_k - k)^2 \equiv \sum_{k=1}^n k^2 = n(n+1)(2n+1)/6$. And we also have $\sum_{k=1}^n (x_k + k)^2 + \sum_{k=1}^n (x_k - k)^2 = 4n(n+1)(2n+1)/6 \equiv 2n/3$, which is impossible when n is a multiple of 3. [See W. Ahrens, *Mathematische Unterhaltungen und Spiele* **2**, second edition (1918), 364–366, where G. Pólya cites a more general result of A. Hurwitz that applies to wraparound diagonals of other slopes.]

Conversely, if n isn't divisible by 2 or 3, we can let $x_n = n$ and $x_k = (2k) \bmod n$ for $1 \le k < n$. [The rule $x_k = (3k) \bmod n$ also works. See Édouard Lucas, *Récréations Mathématiques* **1** (1882), 84–86.]

13. The $(n+1)$ queens problem clearly has a solution with a queen in a corner if and only if the n queens problem has a solution with a queen-free main diagonal. Hence by the previous answer there's always a solution when $n \bmod 6 \in \{0, 1, 4, 5\}$.

Another nice solution was found by J. Franel [*L'Intermédiaire des Mathématiciens* **1** (1894), 140–141] when $n \bmod 6 \in \{2, 4\}$: Let $x_k = (n/2 + 2k - 3[2k \le n]) \bmod n + 1$, for $1 \le k \le n$. With this setup we find that $x_k - x_j = \pm(k - j)$ and $1 \le j < k \le n$ implies $(1 \text{ or } 3)(k - j) + (0 \text{ or } 3) \equiv 0$ (modulo n); hence $k - j = n - (1 \text{ or } 3)$. But the values of x_1, x_2, x_3, x_{n-2}, x_{n-1}, x_n give no attacking queens except when $n = 2$.

Franel's solution has empty diagonals, so it provides solutions also for $n \bmod 6 \in \{3, 5\}$. We conclude that only $n = 2$ and $n = 3$ are impossible.

[A more complicated construction for all $n > 3$ had been given earlier by E. Pauls, in *Deutsche Schachzeitung* **29** (1874), 129–134, 257–267. Pauls also explained how to find all solutions, in principle, by building the tree level by level (*not* backtracking).]

14. For $1 \le j \le n$, let $x_1^{(j)} \ldots x_m^{(j)}$ be a solution for m queens, and let $y_1 \ldots y_n$ be a solution for n toroidal queens. Then $X_{(i-1)n+j} = (x_i^{(j)} - 1)n + y_j$ (for $1 \le i \le m$ and $1 \le j \le n$) is a solution for mn queens. [I. Rivin, I. Vardi, and P. Zimmermann, *AMM* **101** (1994), 629–639, Theorem 2.]

15. More precisely, there's a constant $\sigma = e^{1-\alpha}$ such that, for any fixed ϵ with $0 < \epsilon < \sigma$, $Q(n)/n!$ is q.s. between $((1-\epsilon)\sigma)^n$ and $((1+\epsilon)\sigma)^n$. In fact, a subtle analysis [arXiv:2107.13460 [math.CO] (2021), 51 pages] shows that the average of all solutions approaches a fascinating probability distribution. P. Nobel, A. Agrawal, and S. Boyd have computed α accurately [arXiv:2112.03336 [math.CO] (2021), 14 pages].

16. Let the queen in row k be in cell k. Then we have a "relaxation" of the n queens problem, with $|x_k - x_j|$ becoming just $x_k - x_j$ in (3); so we can ignore the b vector in Algorithm B* or in exercise 10. We get

n =	0	1	2	3	4	5	6	7	8	9	10	11	12	13	14
$H(n)$ =	1	1	1	3	7	23	83	405	2113	12657	82297	596483	4698655	40071743	367854835

[N. J. Cavenagh and I. M. Wanless, *Discr. Appl. Math.* **158** (2010), 136–146, Table 2.]

17. It fails spectacularly in step L5. The minus signs, which mark decisions that were previously forced, are crucial tags for backtracking.

18. $x_4 \ldots x_8 = \overline{2}10\overline{4}0$, $p_0 \ldots p_4 = 33300$, and $y_1 y_2 y_3 = 130$. (If $x_i \le 0$ the algorithm will never look at y_i; hence the current state of $y_4 \ldots y_8$ is irrelevant. But $y_4 y_5$ happens to be 20, because of past history; y_6, y_7, and y_8 haven't yet been touched.)

19. We could say D_l is $\{-n, \ldots, -2, -1, 1, 2, \ldots, n\}$, or $\{k \mid k \neq 0 \text{ and } 2 - l \leq k \leq 2n - l - 1\}$, or anything in between. (But this observation isn't very useful.)

20. First we add a Boolean array $a_1 \ldots a_n$, where a_k means "k has appeared," as in Algorithm B*. It's $0 \ldots 0$ in step L1; we set $a_k \leftarrow 1$ in step L3, $a_k \leftarrow 0$ in step L5.

The loop in step L2 becomes "while $x_l < 0$, go to L5 if $l \geq n-1$ and $a_{2n-l-1} = 0$, otherwise set $l \leftarrow l+1$." After finding $l+k+1 \leq 2n$ in L3, and before testing x_{l+k+1} for 0, insert this: "If $l \geq n-1$ and $a_{2n-l-1} = 0$, while $l+k+1 \neq 2n$ set $j \leftarrow k$, $k \leftarrow p_k$."

21. (a) In any solution $x_k = n \iff x_{k+n+1} = -n \iff x^D_{n-k} = n$.

(b) $x_k = n - 1$ for some $k \leq n/2$ if and only if $x^D_k = n - 1$ for some $k > n/2$.

(c) Let $n' = n - [n \text{ is even}]$. Change '$l \geq n - 1$ and $a_{2n-l-1} = 0$' in the modified step L2 to '$(l = \lfloor n/2 \rfloor$ and $a_{n'} = 0)$ or $(l \geq n-1$ and $a_{2n-l-1} = 0)$'. Insert the following before the other insertion into step L3: "If $l = \lfloor n/2 \rfloor$ and $a_{n'} = 0$, while $k \neq n'$ set $j \leftarrow k$, $k \leftarrow p_k$." And in step L5 — this subtle detail is needed when n is even — go to L5 instead of L4 if $l = \lfloor n/2 \rfloor$ and $k = n'$.

22. The solutions $1\bar{1}$ and $21\bar{1}\bar{2}$ for $n = 1$ and $n = 2$ are self-dual; the solutions for $n = 4$ and $n = 5$ are $431\bar{1}2\bar{3}4\bar{2}$, $245\bar{2}31\bar{1}4\bar{3}5$, $451\bar{1}23\bar{4}2\bar{5}3$, and their duals. The total number of solutions for $n = 1, 2, \ldots$ is 1, 1, 0, 2, 4, 20, 0, 156, 516, 2008, 0, 52536, 297800, 1767792, 0, 75678864, $\ldots$; there are none when $n \bmod 4 = 3$, by a parity argument.

Algorithm L needs only obvious changes. To compute solutions by a streamlined method like exercise 21, use $n' = n - (0, 1, 2, 0)$ and substitute '$l = \lfloor n/4 \rfloor + (0, 1, 2, 1)$' for '$l = \lfloor n/2 \rfloor$', when $n \bmod 4 = (0, 1, 2, 3)$; also replace '$l \geq n - 1$ and $a_{2n-l-1} = 0$' by '$l \geq \lceil n/2 \rceil$ and $a_{\lfloor (4n+2-2l)/3 \rfloor} = 0$'. The case $n = 15$ is proved impossible with 397 million nodes and 9.93 gigamems.

23. `slums` → `sluff`, `slump`, `slurs`, `slurp`, or `sluts`; (`slums`, `total`) → (`slams`, `tonal`).

24. Build the list of 5-letter words and the trie of 6-letter words in step B1; also set $a_{01}a_{02}a_{03}a_{04}a_{05} \leftarrow 00000$. Use min $D_l = 1$ in step B2 and max $D_l = 5757$ in step B4. To test P_l in step B3, if word x_l is $c_1 c_2 c_3 c_4 c_5$, form $a_{l1} \ldots a_{l5}$, where $a_{lk} = trie[a_{(l-1)k}, c_k]$ for $1 \leq k \leq 5$; but jump to B4 if any a_{lk} is zero.

25. There are 5×26 singly linked lists, accessed from pointers h_{kc}, all initially zero. The xth word $c_{x1}c_{x2}c_{x3}c_{x4}c_{x5}$, for $1 \leq x \leq 5757$, belongs to 5 lists and has five pointers $l_{x1}l_{x2}l_{x3}l_{x4}l_{x5}$. To insert it, set $l_{xk} \leftarrow h_{kc_{xk}}$, $h_{kc_{xk}} \leftarrow x$, and $s_{kc_{xk}} \leftarrow s_{kc_{xk}} + 1$, for $1 \leq k \leq 5$. (Thus s_{kc} will be the length of the list accessed from h_{kc}.)

We can store a "signature" $\sum_{c=1}^{26} 2^{c-1}[trie[a, c] \neq 0]$ with each node a of the trie. For example, the signature for node 260 is $2^0 + 2^4 + 2^8 + 2^{14} + 2^{17} + 2^{20} + 2^{24} = {}^\#1124111$, according to (11); here $A \leftrightarrow 1, \ldots, Z \leftrightarrow 26$.

The process of running through all x that match a given signature y with respect to position z, as needed in steps B2 and B4, now takes the following form: (i) Set $i \leftarrow 0$. (ii) While $2^i \& y = 0$, set $i \leftarrow i + 1$. (iii) Set $x \leftarrow h_{z(i+1)}$; go to (vi) if $x = 0$. (iv) Visit x. (v) Set $x \leftarrow l_{xz}$; go to (iv) if $x \neq 0$. (vi) Set $i \leftarrow i + 1$; go to (ii) if $2^i \leq y$.

Let $trie[a, 0]$ be the signature of node a. We choose z and $y = trie[a_{(l-1)z}, 0]$ in step B2 so that the number of nodes to visit, $\sum_{c=1}^{26} s_{zc}[2^{c-1} \& y \neq 0]$, is minimum for $1 \leq z \leq 5$. For example, when $l = 3$, $x_1 = 1446$, and $x_2 = 185$ as in (10), that sum for $z = 1$ is $s_{11} + s_{15} + s_{19} + s_{1(15)} + s_{1(18)} + s_{1(21)} + s_{1(25)} = 296 + 129 + 74 + 108 + 268 + 75 + 47 = 997$; and the sums for $z = 2, 3, 4, 5$ are 4722, 1370, 5057, and 1646. Hence we choose $z = 1$ and $y = {}^\#1124111$; only 997 words, not 5757, need be tested for x_3.

The values y_l and z_l are maintained for use in backtracking. (In practice we keep x, y, and z in registers during most of the computation. Then we set $x_l \leftarrow x$, $y_l \leftarrow y$,

$z_l \leftarrow z$ before increasing $l \leftarrow l+1$ in step B3; and we set $x \leftarrow x_l$, $y \leftarrow y_l$, $z \leftarrow z_l$ in step B5. We also keep i in a register, while traversing the sublists as above; this value is restored in step B5 by setting it to the zth letter of word x, decreased by `'A'`.)

26. Here are the author's favorite 5×7 and 5×8, and the *only* 5×9's:

```
S M A S H E S     G R A N D E S T     P A S T E L I S T     V A R I S T O R S
P A R T I A L     R E N O U N C E     A C C I D E N C E     A G E N T I V A L
I M M E N S E     E P I S O D E S     M O R T G A G O R     C O E L O M A T E
E M E R G E D     B A S E M E N T     P R O R E F O R M     U N D E L E T E D
S A D N E S S     E Y E S O R E S     A N D E S Y T E S     O Y S T E R E R S
```

No 5×10 word rectangles exist, according to our ground rules.

27. $(1, 15727, 8072679, 630967290, 90962081, 625415)$ and $(15727.0, 4321.6, 1749.7, 450.4, 286.0)$. Total time ≈ 18.3 teramems.

28. Build a separate trie for the m-letter words; but instead of having trie nodes of size 26 as in (11), it's better to convert this trie into a *compressed* representation that omits the zeros. For example, the compressed representation of the node for prefix `'CORNE'` in (12) consists of five consecutively stored pairs of entries (`'T'`, 5013), (`'R'`, 171), (`'L'`, 9602), (`'D'`, 3878), (`'A'`, 3879), followed by $(0,0)$. Similarly, each shorter prefix with c descendants is represented by c consecutive pairs (character, link), followed by $(0,0)$ to mark the end of the node. Steps B3 and B4 are now very convenient.

Level l corresponds to row $i_l = 1 + (l-1) \bmod m$ and column $j_l = 1 + \lfloor (l-1)/m \rfloor$. For backtracking we store the n-trie pointer a_{i_l,j_l} as before, together with an index x_l into the compressed m-trie.

This method was used by M. D. McIlroy in 1975 (see answer 32). It finds all 5×6 word rectangles in just 400 gigamems; and its running time for "transposed" 6×5 rectangles turns out to be slightly less (380 gigamems). Notice that only one mem is needed to access each (character, link) pair in the compressed trie.

29. Yes, exactly 1618 of the 625415 solutions have repeated words. For example:

```
A C C E S S     A S S E R T     B E G G E D     M A G M A S     T R A D E S
M O O L A H     J A I L E R     R E A L E R     O N L I N E     R E V I S E
I M M U N E     U G L I F Y     A R T E R Y     D I O X I N     O T I O S E
N E E D E D     G E O D E S     W I E N I E     A S S E S S     T R A D E S
O T T E R S     A S S E R T     L E S S E R     L E S S E E     H O N E S T
```

30. The use of a single compressed trie both horizontally and vertically leads to a very pretty algorithm, which needs only 120 $M\mu$ to find all 541,968 solutions. De Morgan's example isn't among them, because the proper name `'ELLEN'` doesn't qualify as a word by our conventions. But some of the squares might be "meaningful," at least poetically:

```
B L A S T     W E E K S     T R A D E     S A F E R     A D M I T     Y A R D S
L U N C H     E V E N T     R U L E D     A G I L E     D R O N E     A P A R T
A N G E R     E E R I E     A L O N G     F I X E S     M O V E S     R A D I I
S C E N E     K N I F E     D E N S E     E L E C T     I N E P T     D R I L L
T H R E E     S T E E L     E D G E S     R E S T S     T E S T S     S T I L L
```

Just six of the solutions belong to the restricted vocabulary WORDS(500); three of them actually belong to WORDS(372), namely `**ASS | *IGHT | AGREE | SHEEP | STEPS`, where `***` is either `CLL` or `GLL` or `GRR`. (And `*** = GRL` gives an *unsymmetric* 5×5 in WORDS(372). There are $(1787056 - 541968)/2 = 622544$ unsymmetric squares in WORDS(5757).)

31. Yes, 27 of them. The search is greatly facilitated by noting that the NE-to-SW diagonal word must be one of the 18 palindromes in WORDS(5757). `'SCABS | CANAL | ANGLE | BALED | SLEDS'`, which belongs to WORDS(3025), has the most common words. [See the end of Chapter 18 in Babbage's *Passages from The Life of a Philosopher* (London: 1864).]

32. There are $(717, 120386, 2784632, 6571160, 1117161, 13077, 6)$ of sizes 2×2, $\ldots$, 8×8, and none larger than this. Each of these runs needed fewer than 6 gigamems of computation. Example solutions with words as common as possible are

```
                                            E S T A T E   C U R T A I L   N E R E I D E S
            I T S   A W A Y   H E A R T     S L A V E S   U T E R I N E   E T E R N I S E
T O         T H E   W E R E   E R R O R     T A L E N T   R E V E R T S   R E L O C A T E
O F         S E E   A R E A   A R G U E     A V E N U E   T R E B L E S   E R O T I Z E D
                    Y E A R   R O U T E     T E N U R E   A I R L I N E   I N C I T E R S
                            T R E E S     T E N U R E   I N T E N S E   D I A Z E P A M
                                            E S T E E M   L E S S E E S   E S T E R A S E
                                                                          S E E D S M E N
```

with the following numeric ranks of "minimax rarity" within their lists: TO = 2, SEE = 25, AREA = 86, ERROR = 438, ESTEEM = 1607, TREBLES = 5696, ETERNISE = 23623.

[Word squares go back thousands of years; 'SATOR|AREPO|TENET|OPERA|ROTAS', a famous 5×5 example that is found in many places including the ruins of Pompeii, actually has fourfold symmetry. But 6×6 squares appear to have been unknown until William Winthrop, the U.S. consul in Malta(!), published 'CIRCLE|ICARUS| RAREST|CREATE|LUSTRE|ESTEEM' in *Notes & Queries* (2) **8** (2 July 1859), page 8, claiming to have thereby "squared the circle." (If he had been told not to use a proper name like Icarus, he could have said 'CIRCLE|INURES|RUDEST|CREASE|LESSER|ESTERS'.)]

> *The conclusion to be drawn about exercises of this kind*
> *is that four letters are nothing at all; that five letters are so easy*
> *that nothing is worth notice unless the combination have meaning;*
> *that six letters, done in any way, are respectable;*
> *and that seven letters would be a triumph.*
> — AUGUSTUS DE MORGAN, in *Notes & Queries* (3 September 1859)

Henry Dudeney constructed several 7×7 examples and used them in clever puzzles, beginning with 'PALATED|ANEMONE|LEVANTS|AMASSES|TONSIRE|ENTERER|DESSERT' [*The Weekly Dispatch* (25 October and 8 November 1896)] and 'BOASTER|OBSCENE|ASSERTS| SCEPTRE|TERTIAN|ENTRANT|RESENTS' [*The Weekly Dispatch* (21 November and 5 December 1897)]. Years later he was particularly pleased to have found 'NESTLES|ENTRANT| STRANGE|TRAITOR|LANTERN|ENGORGE|STERNER' [*Strand* **55** (1918), 488; **56** (1919), 74; *The World's Best Word Puzzles* (1925), Puzzles 142 and 145]. M. Douglas McIlroy was the first to apply computers to this task [*Word Ways* **8** (1975), 195–197], discovering 52 examples such as 'WRESTLE|RENEWAL|ENPLANE|SELFDOM|TWADDLE|LANOLIN|ELEMENT'. Then he turned to the more difficult problem of *double word squares*, which are unsymmetric and contain $2n$ *distinct* words: He presented 117 double squares, such as 'REPAST|AVESTA|CIRCUS|INSECT|SCONCE|MENTOR', in *Word Ways* **9** (1976), 80–84. (His experiments allowed proper names, but avoided plurals and other derived word forms.)

For an excellent history of word squares and word cubes, chronicling the subsequent computer developments as well as extensive searches for 10×10 examples using vast dictionaries, see Ross Eckler, *Making the Alphabet Dance* (New York: St. Martin's Griffin, 1997), 188–203; *Tribute to a Mathemagician* (A K Peters, 2005), 85–91.

33. Working from bottom to top and right to left is equivalent to working from top to bottom and left to right on the word *reversals*. This idea does make the tries smaller; but unfortunately it makes the programs slower. For example, the 6×5 computation of answer 28 involves a 6347-node trie for the 6-letter words and a 63060-node compressed trie for the 5-letter words. Those sizes go down to 5188 and 56064, respectively, when we reverse the words; but the running time goes up from 380 $G\mu$ to 825 $G\mu$.

34. Leave out `face` and (of course) `dada`; the remaining eleven are fine.

35. Keep tables p_i, p'_{ij}, p''_{ijk}, s_i, s'_{ij}, s''_{ijk}, for $0 \le i, j, k < m$, each capable of storing a ternary digit, and initially zero. Also keep a table x_0, x_1, ... of tentatively accepted words. Begin with $g \leftarrow 0$. Then for each input $w_j = abcd$, where $0 \le a, b, c, d < m$, set $x_g \leftarrow abcd$ and also do the following: Set $p_a \leftarrow p_a \dotplus 1$, $p'_{ab} \leftarrow p'_{ab} \dotplus 1$, $p''_{abc} \leftarrow p''_{abc} \dotplus 1$, $s_d \leftarrow s_d \dotplus 1$, $s'_{cd} \leftarrow s'_{cd} \dotplus 1$, $s''_{bcd} \leftarrow s''_{bcd} \dotplus 1$, where $x \dotplus y = \min(2, x+y)$ denotes saturating ternary addition. Then if $s_{a'} p''_{b'c'd'} + s'_{a'b'} p'_{c'd'} + s''_{a'b'c'} p_{d'} = 0$ for all $x_k = a'b'c'd'$, where $0 \le k \le g$, set $g \leftarrow g+1$. Otherwise reject w_j and set $p_a \leftarrow p_a - 1$, $p'_{ab} \leftarrow p'_{ab} - 1$, $p''_{abc} \leftarrow p''_{abc} - 1$, $s_d \leftarrow s_d - 1$, $s'_{cd} \leftarrow s'_{cd} - 1$, $s''_{bcd} \leftarrow s''_{bcd} - 1$.

36. (a) The word bc appears in message $abcd$ if and only if $a \to b$, $b \to c$, and $c \to d$.

(b) For $0 \le k < r$, put vertex v into class k if the longest path from v has length k. Given any such partition, we can include all arcs from class k to class $j < k$ without increasing the path lengths. So it's a question of finding the maximum of $\sum_{0 \le j < k < r} p_j p_k$ subject to $p_0 + p_1 + \cdots + p_{r-1} = m$. The values $p_j = \lfloor (m+j)/r \rfloor$ achieve this (see exercise 7.2.1.4–68(a)). When $r = 3$ the maximum simplifies to $\lfloor m^2/3 \rfloor$.

37. (a) The factors of the period, 15 926 535 89 79 323 8314, begin at the respective boundary points 3, 5, 8, 11, 13, 15, 18 (and then $3 + 19 = 22$, etc.). Thus round 1 retains boundaries 5, 8, and 15. The second-round substrings $y_0 = 926$, $y_1 = 5358979$, $y_2 = 323831415$ have different lengths, so lexicographic comparison is unnecessary; the answer is $y_2 y_0 y_1 = x_{15} \ldots x_{33}$.

(b) Each substring consists of at least three substrings of the previous round.

(c) Let $a_0 = 0$, $b_0 = 1$, $a_{e+1} = a_e a_e b_e$, $b_{e+1} = b_e a_e b_e$; use a_e or b_e when $n = 3^e$.

(d) We use an auxiliary subroutine 'less(i)', which returns $[y_{i-1} < y_i]$, given $i > 0$: If $b_i - b_{i-1} \ne b_{i+1} - b_i$, return $[b_i - b_{i-1} < b_{i+1} - b_i]$. Otherwise, for $j = 0, 1, \ldots$, while $b_i + j < b_{i+1}$, if $x_{b_{i-1}+j} \ne x_{b_i+j}$ return $[x_{b_{i-1}+j} < x_{b_i+j}]$. Otherwise return 0.

The tricky part of the algorithm is to discard initial factors that aren't periodic. The secret is to let i_0 be the smallest index such that $y_{i-3} \ge y_{i-2} < y_{i-1}$; then we can be sure that a factor begins with y_i.

  O1. [Initialize.] Set $x_j \leftarrow x_{j-n}$ for $n \le j < 2n$, $b_j \leftarrow j$ for $0 \le j < 2n$, and $t \leftarrow n$.

  O2. [Begin a round.] Set $t' \leftarrow 0$. Find the smallest $i > 0$ such that less$(i) = 0$. Then find the smallest $j \ge i + 2$ such that less$(j - 1) = 1$ and $j \le t + 2$. (If no such j exists, report an error: The input x was equal to one of its cyclic shifts.) Set $i \leftarrow i_0 \leftarrow j \bmod t$. (Now a dip of the period begins at i_0.)

  O3. [Find the next factor.] Find the smallest $j \ge i + 2$ such that less$(j - 1) = 1$. If $j - i$ is even, go to O5.

  O4. [Retain a boundary.] If $i < t$, set $b'_{t'} \leftarrow b_i$; otherwise set $b'_k \leftarrow b'_{k-1}$ for $t' \ge k > 0$ and $b'_0 \leftarrow b_{i-t}$. Finally set $t' \leftarrow t' + 1$.

  O5. [Done with round?] If $j < i_0 + t$, set $i \leftarrow j$ and return to O3. Otherwise, if $t' = 1$, terminate; σx begins at item $x_{b'_0}$. Otherwise set $t \leftarrow t'$, $b_k \leftarrow b'_k$ for $0 \le k < t$, and $b_k \leftarrow b_{k-t} + n$ for $k \ge t$ while $b_{k-t} < 2n$. Return to O2. ∎

(e) Say that a "superdip" is a dip of odd length followed by zero or more dips of even length. Any infinite sequence y that begins with an odd-length dip has a unique factorization into superdips. Those superdips can, in turn, be regarded as atomic elements of a higher-level string that can be factored into dips. The result σx of Algorithm O is an infinite periodic sequence that allows repeated factorization into infinite periodic sequences of superdips at higher and higher levels, until becoming constant.

Notice that the first dip of σx ends at position i_0 in the algorithm, because its length isn't 2. Therefore we can prove the commafree property by observing that, if codeword $\sigma x''$ appears within the concatenation $\sigma x \sigma x'$ of two codewords, its superdip factors are also superdip factors of those codewords. This yields a contradiction if any of σx, $\sigma x'$, or $\sigma x''$ is a superdip. Otherwise the same observation applies to the superdip factors at the next level. [Eastman's original algorithm was essentially the same, but presented in a more complicated way; see *IEEE Trans.* **IT-11** (1965), 263–267. R. A. Scholtz subsequently discovered an interesting and totally different way to define the set of codewords produced by Algorithm O, in *IEEE Trans.* **IT-15** (1969), 300–306.]

38. Let $f_k(m)$ be the number of dips of length k for which $m > z_1$ and $z_k < m$. The number of such sequences with $z_{k-1} = j$ is $(m-j-1)\binom{m-j+k-3}{k-2} = (k-1)\binom{m-j+k-3}{k-1}$; summing for $0 \le j < m$ gives $f_k(m) = (k-1)\binom{m+k-2}{k}$. Thus $F_m(z) = \sum_{k=0}^{\infty} f_k(m)z^k = (mz-1)/(1-z)^m$. (The fact that $f_0(m) = -1$ in these formulas turns out to be useful!)

Algorithm O finishes in one round if and only if some cyclic shift of x is a superdip. The number of aperiodic x that finish in one round is therefore $n[z^n]G_m(z)$, where

$$G_m(z) = \frac{F_m(-z) - F_m(z)}{F_m(-z) + F_m(z)} = \frac{(1+mz)(1-z)^m - (1-mz)(1+z)^m}{(1+mz)(1-z)^m + (1-mz)(1+z)^m}.$$

To get the stated probability, divide by $\sum_{d\backslash n}\mu(d)m^{n/d}$, the number of aperiodic x. (See Eq. 7.2.1.1–(60). For $n = 3, 5, 7, 9$ these probabilities are 1, 1, 1, and $1-3/\binom{m^3-1}{3}$.)

39. If so, it couldn't have 0011, 0110, 1100, or 1001.

40. That section considered such representations of stacks and queues, but not of unordered sets, because large blocks of sequential memory were either nonexistent or ultra-expensive in olden days. Linked lists were the only decent option for families of variable-size sets, because they could more readily fit in a limited high-speed memory.

41. (a) The blue word x with $\alpha = $ d (namely 1101) appears in its P2 list at location 5e.
   (b) The P3 list for words of the form 010* is empty. (Both 0100 and 0101 are red.)

42. (a) The S2 list of 0010 has become closed (hence 0110 and 1110 are hidden).
   (b) Word 1101 moved to the former position of 1001 in its S1 list, when 1001 became red. (Previously 1011 had moved to the former position of 0001.)

43. In this case, which of course happens rarely, it's safe to set all elements of STAMP to zero and set $\sigma \leftarrow 1$. (Do *not* be tempted to save one line of code by setting all STAMP elements to -1 and leaving $\sigma = 0$. That might fail when σ reaches the value -1!)

44. (a) Set $r \leftarrow 5$. Then for $k \leftarrow 0, 1, \ldots, f-1$, set $t \leftarrow$ FREE$[k]$, $j \leftarrow$ MEM[CLOFF + $4t + m^4] - (\text{CLOFF} + 4t)$, and if $j < r$ set $r \leftarrow j$, $c \leftarrow t$; break out of the loop if $r = 0$.
   (b) If $r > 0$ set $x \leftarrow$ MEM[CLOFF + $4cl(\text{ALF}[x])$].
   (c) If $r > 1$ set $q \leftarrow 0$, $p' \leftarrow$ MEM[PP], and $p \leftarrow$ POISON. While $p < p'$ do the following steps: Set $y \leftarrow$ MEM$[p]$, $z \leftarrow$ MEM$[p+1]$, $y' \leftarrow$ MEM$[y+m^4]$, and $z' \leftarrow$ MEM$[z+m^4]$. (Here y and z point to the heads of prefix or suffix lists; y' and z' point to the tails.) If $y = y'$ or $z = z'$, delete entry p from the poison list; this means, as in (18), to set $p' \leftarrow p'-2$, and if $p \ne p'$ to store$(p, \text{MEM}[p'])$ and store$(p+1, \text{MEM}[p'+1])$. Otherwise set $p \leftarrow p+2$; if $y'-y \ge z'-z$ and $y'-y > q$, set $q \leftarrow y'-y$ and $x \leftarrow$ MEM$[z]$; if $y'-y < z'-z$ and $z'-z > q$, set $q \leftarrow z'-z$ and $x \leftarrow$ MEM$[y]$. Finally, after p has become equal to p', store(PP, p') and set $c \leftarrow cl(\text{ALF}[x])$. (Experiments show that this "max kill" strategy for $r > 1$ slightly outperforms a selection strategy based on r alone.)

45. (a) First there's a routine rem(α, δ, o) that removes an item from a list, following the protocol (21): Set $p \leftarrow \delta + o$ and $q \leftarrow$ MEM$[p+m^4] - 1$. If $q \ge p$ (meaning that list p isn't closed or being killed), store$(p + m^4, q)$, set $t \leftarrow$ MEM$[\alpha + o - m^4]$; and if $t \neq q$ also set $y \leftarrow$ MEM$[q]$, store(t, y), and store(ALF$[y] + o - m^4, t)$.

Now, to redden x we set $\alpha \leftarrow$ ALF$[x]$, store(α, RED); then rem$(\alpha, p_1(\alpha), \text{P1OFF})$, rem$(\alpha, p_2(\alpha), \text{P2OFF})$, ..., rem$(\alpha, s_3(\alpha), \text{S3OFF})$, and rem$(\alpha, 4cl(\alpha), \text{CLOFF})$.

(b) A simple routine close(δ, o) closes list $\delta + o$: Set $p \leftarrow \delta + o$ and $q \leftarrow$ MEM$[p + m^4]$; if $q \neq p - 1$, store$(p + m^4, p - 1)$.

Now, to green x we set $\alpha \leftarrow$ ALF$[x]$, store(α, GREEN); then close$(p_1(\alpha), \text{P1OFF})$, close$(p_2(\alpha), \text{P2OFF})$, ..., close$(s_3(\alpha), \text{S3OFF})$, and close$(4cl(\alpha), \text{CLOFF})$. Finally, for $p \le r < q$ (using the p and q that were just set within 'close'), if MEM$[r] \neq x$ redden MEM$[r]$.

(c) First set $p' \leftarrow$ MEM$[\text{PP}] + 6$, and store$(p' - 6, p_1(\alpha) + \text{S1OFF})$, store$(p' - 5, s_3(\alpha) + \text{P3OFF})$, store$(p' - 4, p_2(\alpha) + \text{S2OFF})$, store$(p' - 3, s_2(\alpha) + \text{P2OFF})$, store$(p' - 2, p_3(\alpha) + \text{S3OFF})$, store$(p' - 1, s_1(\alpha) + \text{P1OFF})$; this adds the three poison items (27).

Then set $p \leftarrow$ POISON and do the following while $p < p'$: Set y, z, y', z' as in answer 44(c), and delete poison entry p if $y = y'$ or $z = z'$. Otherwise if $y' < y$ and $z' < z$, go to C5 (a poisoned suffix-prefix pair is present). Otherwise if $y' > y$ and $z' > z$, set $p \leftarrow p + 2$. Otherwise if $y' < y$ and $z' > z$, store$(z + m^4, z)$, redden MEM$[r]$ for $z \le r < z'$, and delete poison entry p. Otherwise (namely if $y' > y$ and $z' < z$), store$(y + m^4, y)$, redden MEM$[r]$ for $y \le r < y'$, and delete poison entry p.

Finally, after p has become equal to p', store(PP, p').

46. Exercise 37 exhibits such codes explicitly for all odd n. The earliest papers on the subject gave solutions for $n = 2, 4, 6, 8$. Yoji Niho subsequently found a code for $n = 10$ but was unable to resolve the case $n = 12$ [*IEEE Trans.* **IT-19** (1973), 580–581].

This problem can readily be encoded in CNF and given to a SAT solver. The case $n = 10$ involves 990 variables and 8.6 million clauses, and is solved by Algorithm 7.2.2.2C in 10.5 gigamems. The case $n = 12$ involves 4020 variables and 175 million clauses. After being split into seven independent subproblems (by appending mutually exclusive unit clauses), it was proved *unsatisfiable* by that algorithm after about 86 teramems of computation.

So the answer is "No." But we can come close: Aaron Windsor used a SAT solver in 2021 to discover a binary commafree code for $n = 12$ that contains a representative of every cycle class except [000011001011].

47. (a) There are 28 commafree binary codes of size 3 and length 4; Algorithm C produces half of them, because it assumes that cycle class [0001] is represented by 0001 or 0010. They form eight equivalence classes, two of which are symmetric under the operation of complementation-and-reflection; representatives are $\{0001, 0011, 0111\}$ and $\{0010, 0011, 1011\}$. The other six are represented by $\{0001, 0110, 0111$ or $1110\}$, $\{0001, 1001, 1011$ or $1101\}$, $\{0001, 1100, 1101\}$, $\{0010, 0011, 1101\}$.

(b) Algorithm C produces half of the 144 solutions, which form twelve equivalence classes. Eight are represented by $\{0001, 0002, 1001, 1002, 1102, 2001, 2002, 2011, 2012, 2102, 2112, 2122$ or $2212\}$ and ($\{0102, 1011, 1012\}$ or $\{2010, 1101, 2101\}$) and ($\{1202, 2202, 2111\}$ or $\{2021, 2022, 1112\}$); four are represented by $\{0001, 0020, 0021, 0022, 1001, 1020, 1021, 1022, 1121$ or $1211, 1201, 1202, 1221, 2001, 2201, 2202\}$ and ($\{1011, 1012, 2221\}$ or $\{1101, 2101, 1222\}$).

(c) Algorithm C yields half of the 2304 solutions, which form 48 equivalence classes. Twelve classes have unique representatives that omit cycle classes [0123], [0103], [1213], one such being the code $\{0010, 0020, 0030, 0110, 0112, 0113, 0120, 0121, 0122, 0130, 0131, 0132, 0133, 0210, 0212, 0213, 0220, 0222, 0230, 0310, 0312, 0313, 0320, 0322, 0330, 0332, 0333, 1110, 1112, 1113, 2010, 2030, 2110, 2112, 2113, 2210, 2212, 2213,$

2230, 2310, 2312, 2313, 2320, 2322, 2330, 2332, 2333, 3110, 3112, 3113, 3210, 3212, 3213, 3230, 3310, 3312, 3313}. The others each have two representatives that omit classes [0123], [0103], [0121], one such pair being the code {0001, 0002, 0003, 0201, 0203, 1001, 1002, 1003, 1011, 1013, 1021, 1022, 1023, 1031, 1032, 1033, 1201, 1203, 1211, 1213, 1221, 1223, 1231, 1232, 1233, 1311, 1321, 1323, 1331, 2001, 2002, 2003, 2021, 2022, 2023, 2201, 2203, 2221, 2223, 3001, 3002, 3003, 3011, 3013, 3021, 3022, 3023, 3031, 3032, 3033, 3201, 3203, 3221, 3223, 3321, 3323, 3331} and its isomorphic image under reflection and (01)(23).

48. Algorithm C isn't fast enough to solve this problem. But Aaron Windsor used a SAT solver in 2021 to find such a code of size $139 = (5^4 - 5^2)/4 - 11$, and to prove that no such code of size 140 exists. (He also found, rather quickly, that an optimum ternary commafree code for $n = 6$ contains $(3^6 - 3^3 - 3^2 + 3^1)/6 - 3 = 113$ codewords.)

49. The 3-bit sequences 101, 111, 110 were rejected before seeing 000. In general, to make a uniformly random choice from q possibilities, the text suggests looking at the next $t = \lceil \lg q \rceil$ bits $b_1 \ldots b_t$. If $(b_1 \ldots b_t)_2 < q$, we use choice $(b_1 \ldots b_t)_2 + 1$; otherwise we reject $b_1 \ldots b_t$ and try again. [This simple method is optimum when $q \le 4$, and the best possible running time for other values of q uses more than half as many bits. But a better scheme is available for $q = 5$, using only $3\frac{1}{3}$ bits per choice instead of $4\frac{4}{5}$; and for $q = 6$, one random bit reduces to the case $q = 3$. See D. E. Knuth and A. C. Yao, *Algorithms and Complexity*, edited by J. F. Traub (Academic Press, 1976), 357–428, §2.]

50. It's the number of nodes on level $l+1$ (depth l) of the search tree. (Hence we can estimate the profile. Notice that $D = D_1 \ldots D_{l-1}$ in step E2 of Algorithm E.)

51. $Z_0 = C()$, $Z_{l+1} = c() + D_1 c(X_1) + D_1 D_2 c(X_1 X_2) + \cdots + D_1 \ldots D_l c(X_1 \ldots X_l) + D_1 \ldots D_{l+1} C(X_1 \ldots X_{l+1})$.

52. (a) True: The generating function is $z(z+1) \ldots (z+n-1)/n!$; see Eq. 1.2.10–(9).

(b) For instance, suppose $Y_1 Y_2 \ldots Y_l = 1457$ and $n = 9$. Alice's probability is $\frac{1}{1}\frac{1}{2}\frac{2}{3}\frac{1}{4}\frac{1}{5}\frac{5}{6}\frac{1}{7}\frac{7}{8}\frac{8}{9} = \frac{1}{3}\frac{1}{4}\frac{1}{6}\frac{1}{9}$. Elmo obtains $X_1 X_2 \ldots X_l = 7541$ with probability $\frac{1}{9}\frac{1}{6}\frac{1}{4}\frac{1}{3}$.

(c) The upper tail inequality (see exercise 1.2.10–22 with $\mu = H_n$) tells us that $\Pr(l \ge (\ln n)(\ln \ln n)) \le \exp(-(\ln n)(\ln \ln n)(\ln \ln \ln n) + O(\ln n)(\ln \ln n))$.

(d) If $k \le n/3$ we have $\sum_{j=0}^{k} \binom{n}{j} \le 2\binom{n}{k}$. By exercise 1.2.6–67, the number of nodes on the first $(\ln n)(\ln \ln n)$ levels is therefore at most $2\big(ne/((\ln n)(\ln \ln n))\big)^{(\ln n)(\ln \ln n)}$.

53. The key idea is to introduce recursive formulas analogous to (29):

$$m(x_1 \ldots x_l) = c(x_1 \ldots x_l) + \min\big(m(x_1 \ldots x_l x_{l+1}^{(1)})d, \ldots, m(x_1 \ldots x_l x_{l+1}^{(d)})d\big);$$

$$M(x_1 \ldots x_l) = c(x_1 \ldots x_l) + \max\big(M(x_1 \ldots x_l x_{l+1}^{(1)})d, \ldots, M(x_1 \ldots x_l x_{l+1}^{(d)})d\big);$$

$$\widehat{C}(x_1 \ldots x_l) = c(x_1 \ldots x_l)^2 + \sum_{i=1}^{d}\big(\widehat{C}(x_1 \ldots x_l x_{l+1}^{(i)})d + 2c(x_1 \ldots x_l)C(x_1 \ldots x_l x_{l+1}^{(i)})\big).$$

They can be computed via auxiliary arrays MIN, MAX, KIDS, COST, and CHAT as follows:

At the beginning of step B2, set $\texttt{MIN}[l] \leftarrow \infty$, $\texttt{MAX}[l] \leftarrow \texttt{KIDS}[l] \leftarrow \texttt{COST}[l] \leftarrow \texttt{CHAT}[l] \leftarrow 0$. Set $\texttt{KIDS}[l] \leftarrow \texttt{KIDS}[l] + 1$ just before $l \leftarrow l+1$ in step B3.

At the beginning of step B5, set $m \leftarrow c(x_1 \ldots x_{l-1}) + \texttt{KIDS}[l] \times \texttt{MIN}[l]$, $M \leftarrow c(x_1 \ldots x_{l-1}) + \texttt{KIDS}[l] \times \texttt{MAX}[l]$, $C \leftarrow c(x_1 \ldots x_{l-1}) + \texttt{COST}[l]$, $\widehat{C} \leftarrow c(x_1 \ldots x_{l-1})^2 + \texttt{KIDS}[l] \times \texttt{CHAT}[l] + 2 \times \texttt{COST}[l]$. Then, after $l \leftarrow l - 1$ is positive, set $\texttt{MIN}[l] \leftarrow \min(m, \texttt{MIN}[l])$, $\texttt{MAX}[l] \leftarrow \max(M, \texttt{MAX}[l])$, $\texttt{COST}[l] \leftarrow \texttt{COST}[l] + C$, $\texttt{CHAT}[l] \leftarrow \texttt{CHAT}[l] + \widehat{C}$. But when l reaches zero in step B5, return the values $m, M, C, \widehat{C} - C^2$.

54. Let $p(i) = p_{X_1 \ldots X_{l-1}}(y_i)$, and simply set $D \leftarrow D/p(I)$ instead of $D \leftarrow Dd$. Then node $x_1 \ldots x_l$ is reached with probability $\Pi(x_1 \ldots x_l) = p(x_1)p_{x_1}(x_2) \ldots p_{x_1 \ldots x_l}(x_l)$, and $c(x_1 \ldots x_l)$ has weight $1/\Pi(x_1 \ldots x_l)$ in S; the proof of Theorem E goes through as before. Notice that $p(I)$ is the *a posteriori* probability of having taken branch I.

    (The formulas of answer 53 should now use '$/p(i)$' instead of 'd'; and that algorithm should be modified appropriately, no longer needing the KIDS array.)

55. Let $p_{X_1 \ldots X_{l-1}}(y_i) = C(x_1 \ldots x_{l-1}y_i)/(C(x_1 \ldots x_{l-1}) - c(x_1 \ldots x_{l-1}))$. (Of course we generally need to know the cost of the tree before we know the exact values of these ideal probabilities, so we cannot achieve zero variance in practice. But the form of this solution shows what kinds of bias are likely to reduce the variance.)

56. The effects of lookahead, dynamic ordering, and reversible memory are all captured easily by a well-designed cost function at each node. But there's a fundamental difference in step C2, because different codeword classes can be selected for branching at the same node (that is, with the same ancestors $x_1 \ldots x_{l-1}$) after C5 has undone the effects of a prior choice. The level l never surpasses $L + 1$, but in fact the search tree involves hidden levels of branching that are implicitly combined into single nodes.

    Thus it's best to view Algorithm C's search tree as a sequence of *binary* branches: Should x be one of the codewords or not? (At least this is true when the "max kill" strategy of answer 44 has selected the branching variable x. But if $r > 1$ and the poison list is empty, an r-way branch is reasonable (or an $(r + 1)$-way branch when the slack is positive), because r will be reduced by 1 and the same class c will be chosen after x has been explored.)

    If x has been selected because it kills many other potential codewords, we probably should bias the branch probability as in exercise 54, giving smaller weight to the "yes" branch because the branch that includes x is less likely to lead to a large subtree.

57. Let $p_k = 1/D^{(k)}$ be the probability that Algorithm E terminates at the kth leaf. Then $\sum_{k=1}^{M}(1/M)\lg(1/(Mp_k))$ is the Kullback–Leibler divergence $D(q\|p)$, where q is the uniform distribution (see exercise MPR–121). Hence $\frac{1}{M}\sum_{k=1}^{M}\lg D^{(k)} \geq \lg M$. (The result of this exercise is essentially true in *any* probability distribution.)

58. Let ∞ be any convenient value $\geq n$. When vertex v becomes part of the path we will perform a two-phase algorithm. The first phase identifies all "tarnished" vertices, whose DIST must change; these are the vertices u from which every path to t passes through v. It also forms a queue of "resource" vertices, which are untarnished but adjacent to tarnished ones. The second phase updates the DISTs of all tarnished vertices that are still connected to t. Each vertex has LINK and STAMP fields in addition to DIST.

    For the first phase, set $d \leftarrow$ DIST(v), DIST(v) $\leftarrow \infty + 1$, R $\leftarrow \Lambda$, T $\leftarrow v$, LINK(v) $\leftarrow$ Λ, then do the following while T $\neq \Lambda$: (*) Set $u \leftarrow$ T, T $\leftarrow$ S $\leftarrow \Lambda$. For each $w \longrightarrow u$, if DIST(w) $< d$ do nothing (this happens only when $u = v$); if DIST(w) $\geq \infty$ do nothing (w is gone or already known to be tarnished); if DIST(w) $= d$, make w a resource (see below); otherwise DIST(w) $= d + 1$. If w has no neighbor at distance d, w is tarnished: Set LINK(w) $\leftarrow$ T, DIST(w) $\leftarrow \infty$, T $\leftarrow w$. Otherwise make w a resource (see below). Then set $u \leftarrow$ LINK(u), and return to (*) if $u \neq \Lambda$.

    The queue of resources will start at R. We will stamp each resource with v so that nothing is added twice to that queue. To make w a resource when DIST(w) $= d$, do the following (unless $u = v$ or STAMP(w) $= v$): Set STAMP(w) $\leftarrow v$; if R $= \Lambda$, set R $\leftarrow$ RT $\leftarrow w$; otherwise set LINK(RT) $\leftarrow w$ and RT $\leftarrow w$. To make w a resource when DIST(w) $= d + 1$ and $u \neq v$ and STAMP(w) $\neq v$, put it first on stack S as follows: Set STAMP(w) $\leftarrow v$; if S $= \Lambda$, set S $\leftarrow$ SB $\leftarrow w$; otherwise set LINK(w) $\leftarrow$ S, S $\leftarrow w$.

Finally, when $u = \Lambda$, we append S to R: Nothing needs to be done if $S = \Lambda$. Otherwise, if $R = \Lambda$, set $R \leftarrow S$ and $RT \leftarrow SB$; but if $R \neq \Lambda$, set $LINK(RT) \leftarrow S$ and $RT \leftarrow SB$. (These shenanigans keep the resource queue in order by DIST.)

Phase 2 operates as follows: Nothing needs to be done if $R = \Lambda$. Otherwise we set $LINK(RT) \leftarrow \Lambda$, $S \leftarrow \Lambda$, and do the following while $R \neq \Lambda$ or $S \neq \Lambda$: (i) If $S = \Lambda$, set $d \leftarrow DIST(R)$. Otherwise set $u \leftarrow S$, $d \leftarrow DIST(u)$, $S \leftarrow \Lambda$; while $u \neq \Lambda$, update the neighbors of u and set $u \leftarrow LINK(u)$. (ii) While $R \neq \Lambda$ and $DIST(R) = d$, set $u \leftarrow R$, $R \leftarrow LINK(u)$, and update the neighbors of u. In both cases "update the neighbors of u" means to look at all $w \,—\, u$, and if $DIST(w) = \infty$ to set $DIST(w) \leftarrow d+1$, $STAMP(w) \leftarrow v$, $LINK(w) \leftarrow S$, and $S \leftarrow w$. (It works!)

59. (a) Compute the generating function $g(z)$ (see exercise 7.1.4–209) and then $g'(1)$.

(b) Let (A, B, C) denote paths that touch (center, NE corner, SW corner). Recursively compute eight counts $(c_0, \ldots, c_7)$ at each node, where c_j counts paths π with $j = 4[\pi \in A] + 2[\pi \in B] + [\pi \in C]$. At the sink node $\boxed{\text{T}}$ we have $c_0 = 1$, $c_1 = \cdots = c_7 = 0$. Other nodes have the form $x = (\bar{e}?\ x_l{:}\ x_h)$ where e is an edge. Two edges go across the center and affect A; three edges affect each of B and C. Say that those edges have types 4, 2, 1, respectively; other edges have type 0. Suppose the counts for x_l and x_h are $(c'_0, \ldots, c'_7)$ and $(c''_0, \ldots, c''_7)$, and e has type t. Then count c_j for node x is $c'_j + [t=0]c''_j + [t\ \&\ j \neq 0](c''_0 + c''_{j-t})$.

(This procedure yields the following exact "Venn diagram" set counts at the root: $c_0 = |\overline{A} \cap \overline{B} \cap \overline{C}| = 765368538488901964\,8091604$; $c_1 = c_2 = |\overline{A} \cap \overline{B} \cap C| = |\overline{A} \cap B \cap \overline{C}| = 7755019053779199171839134$; $c_3 = |\overline{A} \cap B \cap C| = 7857706970503366819944024$; $c_4 = |A \cap \overline{B} \cap \overline{C}| = 4888524166534573765995071$; $c_5 = c_6 = |A \cap \overline{B} \cap C| = |A \cap B \cap \overline{C}| = 4949318991771252110605148$; $c_7 = |A \cap B \cap C| = 5010950157283718807987280$.)

60. Yes, the paths are less chaotic and the estimates are better:

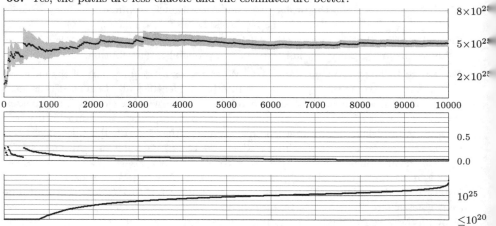

61. (a) Let x_k be the number of nodes at distance $k-1$ from the root.

(b) Let $Q_n^{(m)} = P_n^{(1)} + \cdots + P_n^{(m)}$. Then we have the joint recurrence $P_1^{(m)} = 1$, $P_{n+1}^{(m)} = Q_n^{(2m)}$; in particular, $Q_1^{(m)} = m$. And for $n \geq 2$, we have $Q_n^{(m)} = \sum_{k=1}^{n} a_{nk}\binom{m}{k}$ for certain constants a_{nk} that can be computed as follows: Set $t_k \leftarrow P_n^{(k)}$ for $1 \leq k \leq n$. Then for $k = 2, \ldots, n$ set $t_n \leftarrow t_n - t_{n-1}, \ldots, t_k \leftarrow t_k - t_{k-1}$. Finally $a_{nk} \leftarrow t_k$ for $1 \leq k \leq n$. For example, $a_{21} = a_{22} = 2$; $a_{31} = 6$, $a_{32} = 14$, $a_{33} = 8$. The numbers $P_n^{(m)}$ have $O(n^2 + n\log m)$ bits, so this method needs $O(n^5)$ bit operations to compute P_n.

(c) $P_n^{(m)}$ corresponds to random paths with $X_1 = m$, $D_k = 2X_k$, $X_{k+1} = \lceil 2U_k X_k \rceil$, where each U_k is an independent uniform deviate. Therefore $P_n^{(m)} = \mathrm{E}(D_1 \ldots D_{n-1})$ is the number of nodes on level n of an infinite tree. We have $X_{k+1} \geq 2^k U_1 \ldots U_k m$, by induction; hence $P_n^{(m)} \geq \mathrm{E}(2^{\binom{n}{2}} U_1^{n-2} U_2^{n-3} \ldots U_{n-2}^1 m^{n-1}) = 2^{\binom{n}{2}} m^{n-1}/(n-1)!$.

[M. Cook and M. Kleber have discussed similar sequences in *Electronic Journal of Combinatorics* **7** (2000), #R44, 1–16. See also K. Mahler's asymptotic formula for binary partitions, in *J. London Math. Society* **15** (1940), 115–123, which shows that $\lg P_n = \binom{n}{2} - \lg(n-1)! + \binom{\lg n}{2} + O(1)$.]

62. Random trials indicate that the expected number of 2-regular graphs is ≈ 3.115, and that the number of disjoint pairs is $(0, 1, \ldots, 9,$ and $\geq 10)$ approximately $(74.4, 4.3, 8.7, 1.3, 6.2, 0.2, 1.5, 0.1, 2.0, 0.0,$ and $12.2)$ percent of the time. If the cubes are restricted to cases where each color occurs at least five times, these numbers change to ≈ 4.89 and $(37.3, 6.6, 17.5, 4.1, 16.3, 0.9, 5.3, 0.3, 6.7, 0.2, 5.0)$.

However, the concept of "unique solution" is tricky, because a 2-regular graph with k cycles yields 2^k ways to position the cubes. Let's say that a set of cubes has a *strongly unique* solution if (i) it has a unique disjoint pair of 2-regular graphs, and furthermore (ii) both elements of that pair are n-cycles. Such sets occur with probability only about 0.3% in the first case, and 0.4% in the second.

[N. T. Gridgeman, in *Mathematics Magazine* **44** (1971), 243–252, showed that puzzles with four cubes and four colors have exactly 434 "types" of solutions.]

63. It's easy to find such examples at random, as in the second part of the previous answer, since strongly unique sets occur about 0.5% of the time (and weakly unique sets occur with probability $\approx 8.4\%$). For example, the pairs of opposite faces might be $(12, 13, 34)$, $(02, 03, 14)$, $(01, 14, 24)$, $(04, 13, 23)$, $(01, 12, 34)$.

(Incidentally, if we require each color to occur exactly *six* times, every set of cubes that has at least one solution will have at least *three* solutions, because the "hidden" pairs can be chosen in three ways.)

64. Each of these cubes can be placed in 16 different ways that contribute legitimate letters to all four of the visible words. (A cube whose faces contain only letters in $\{C, H, I, N, O, U, X, Z\}$ can be placed in 24 ways. A cube with a pattern like $\boxed{B \vartriangleright D}$ cannot be placed at all.) We can restrict the first cube to just two placements; thus there are $2 \cdot 16 \cdot 16 \cdot 16 \cdot 16 = 131072$ ways to place those cubes without changing their order. Of these, only 6144 are "compatible," in the sense that no right-side-up-only letter appears together with an upside-down-only letter in the same word.

The 6144 compatible placements can then each be reordered in $5! = 120$ ways. One of them, whose words before reordering are GRHTI, NCICY, OƎꓤMN, INNᴗO, leads to the unique solution. (There's a partial solution with three words out of four. There also are 39 ways to get two valid words, including one that has UNTIL adjacent to HOURS, and several with SYRUP opposite ECHOS.)

65. E. Robertson and I. Munro, in *Utilitas Mathematica* **13** (1978), 99–116, have reduced the exact cover problem to this problem.

66. Call the rays N, NE, E, SE, S, SW, W, NW; call the disks 1, 2, 3, 4 from inside to outside. We can keep disk 1 fixed. The sum of rays N, S, E, W must be 48. It is 16 (on disk 1) plus 13 or 10 (on disk 2) plus 8 or 13 (on disk 3) plus 11 or 14. So it is attained either as shown, or after rotating disks 2 and 4 clockwise by 45°. (Or we could rotate any disk by a multiple of 90°, since that keeps the desired sum invariant.)

Next, with optional $90°$ rotations, we must make the sum of rays $N + S$ equal to 24. In the first solution above it is 9 plus (6 or 7) plus (4 or 4) plus (7 or 4), hence never 24. But in the other solution it's 9 plus (4 or 6) plus (4 or 4) plus (5 or 9); hence we must rotate disk 2 clockwise by $90°$, and possibly also disk 3. However, $90°$ rotation of disk 3 would make the $NE + SW$ sum equal to 25, so we musn't move it.

Finally, to get NE's sum to be 12, via optional rotations by $180°$, we have 1 plus (2 or 5) plus (1 or 5) plus (3 or 4); we must shift disks 3 and 4. Hurrah: That makes all eight rays correct. Factoring twice has reduced 8^3 trials to $2^3 + 2^3 + 2^3$.

[See George W. Ernst and Michael M. Goldstein, *JACM* **29** (1982), 1–23. Such puzzles go back to the 1800s; three early examples are illustrated on pages 28 of Slocum and Botermans's *New Book of Puzzles* (1992). One of them, with six rings and six rays, factors from 6^5 trials to $2^5 + 3^5$. A five-ray puzzle would have defeated factorization.]

67. Call the cards $\mathbf{1525}$, $\mathbf{5113}$, $\ldots$, $\mathbf{3755}$. The key observation is that all 12 sums must be odd, so we can first solve the problem mod 2. For this purpose we may call the cards $\mathbf{1101}$, $\mathbf{1111}$, $\ldots$, $\mathbf{1111}$; only three cards now change under rotation, namely $\mathbf{1101}$, $\mathbf{0100}$, and $\mathbf{1100}$ (which are the mod 2 images of $\mathbf{1525}$, $\mathbf{4542}$, and $\mathbf{7384}$).

A second observation is that each solution gives $6 \times 6 \times 2$ others, by permuting rows and/or columns and/or by rotating all nine cards. Hence we can assume that the upper left card is $\mathbf{0011}$ ($\mathbf{8473}$). Then $\mathbf{0100}$ ($\mathbf{4542}$) must be in the first column, possibly rotated to $\mathbf{0001}$ ($\mathbf{4245}$), to preserve parity in the left two black sums. We can assume that it's in row 2. In fact, after retreating from 13 mod 2 to 13, we see that it *must* be rotated. Hence the bottom left card must be either $\mathbf{4725}$, $\mathbf{7755}$, or $\mathbf{3755}$.

Similarly we see that $\mathbf{1101}$ ($\mathbf{1525}$) must be in the first row, possibly rotated to $\mathbf{0111}$ ($\mathbf{2515}$); we can put it in column 2. It must be rotated, and the top right card must be $\mathbf{3454}$ or $\mathbf{3755}$. This leaves just six scenarios to consider, and we soon obtain the solution: $\mathbf{8473}$, $\mathbf{2515}$, $\mathbf{3454}$; $\mathbf{4245}$, $\mathbf{2547}$, $\mathbf{7452}$; $\mathbf{7755}$, $\mathbf{1351}$, $\mathbf{5537}$.

68. In general, let's say that a vertex labeling of a digraph is *stable* if v's label is the number of distinct labels among $\{w \mid v \longrightarrow w\}$, for all v. We wish to find all stable labelings that extend a given partial labeling. We may assume that no vertex is a sink.

Let $\Lambda(v)$ be a set of digits that includes every label that v could possibly have, in a solution to this extension problem. Initially, $\Lambda(v) = \{d\}$ if v's label is supposed to be d; otherwise $\Lambda(v) = \{1, \ldots, d^+(v)\}$. These sets are conveniently represented as the binary numbers $L(v) = \sum\{2^{k-1} \mid k \in \Lambda(v)\}$. Our goal is to reduce each $L(v)$ to a 1-bit number. A nice backtrack routine called "refine(v)" proves to be helpful in this regard.

Let $v_0 = v$ and let v_1, $\ldots$, v_n be v's successors. Let $a_j = L(v_j)$. Following the outline of Algorithm B, we let $x_l \subseteq a_l$ be a 1-bit number, accepted in step B3 only if $2^{\nu s_l - 1} \subseteq g_l$, where $s_l = x_1 \mid \cdots \mid x_l$ and where the goal sets g_l are defined by $g_n = a_0$, $g_l = (g_{l+1} \mid g_{l+1} \gg 1) \,\&\, (2^l - 1)$. We start with all $b_j \leftarrow 0$; then when visiting a solution $x_1 \ldots x_n$, we set $b_j \leftarrow b_j \mid x_j$ for $1 \le j \le n$, and $b_0 \leftarrow b_0 \mid 2^{\nu s_n - 1}$. After finding all solutions we'll have $b_j \subseteq a_j$ for all j; and whenever $b_j \ne a_j$ we can reduce $L(v_j) \leftarrow b_j$.

Operate in rounds, where all vertices are refined in round 1; subsequent rounds refine only the vertices whose parameters a_j have changed. In each round we first refine the vertices with smallest product $(\nu a_1) \ldots (\nu a_n)$, because they have the fewest potential solutions $x_1 \ldots x_n$. This method isn't guaranteed to succeed; but fortunately it does solve the stated problem, after 301 refinements in 6 rounds. [Such "Japanese arrow puzzles" were introduced by Masanori Natsuhara on page 75 of *Puzuraa* **128** (July 1992).]

69. (The 33rd boxed clue will, of course, have to point *outside* the 10×10 array. Maybe there's even a puzzle whose empty boxes are symmetrical, as in exercise 68.)

70. An extremely instructive analysis [*Combinatorics, Probability and Computing* **23** (2014), 725–748] leads to the recurrences $P_m = (5 + 9z)P_{m-2} - 4P_{m-4}$, $Q_m = (5 + 9z)Q_{m-2} - 4Q_{m-4}$, for $m \geq 6$, where the initial values are $(P_2, P_3, P_4, P_5) = (1, 1+z, 1+3z, 1+10z+9z^2)$; $(Q_2, Q_3, Q_4, Q_5) = (1-4z, 1-9z-6z^2, 1-19z-18z^2, 1-36z-99z^2-54z^3)$. The denominator $Q_m(z)$ has all real roots, exactly one of which is positive, namely $1/\rho_m$.

71. Suppose there are n questions, whose answers each lie in a given set S. A *student* supplies an answer list $\alpha = a_1 \ldots a_n$, with each $a_j \in S$; a *grader* supplies a Boolean vector $\beta = x_1 \ldots x_n$. There is a Boolean function $f_{js}(\alpha, \beta)$ for each $j \in \{1, \ldots, n\}$ and each $s \in S$. A graded answer list (α, β) is *valid* if and only if $F(\alpha, \beta)$ is true, where

$$F(\alpha, \beta) = F(a_1 \ldots a_n, x_1 \ldots x_n) = \bigwedge_{j=1}^{n} \bigwedge_{s \in S} ([a_j = s] \Rightarrow x_j \equiv f_{js}(\alpha, \beta)).$$

The *maximum score* is the largest value of $x_1 + \cdots + x_n$ over all graded answer lists (α, β) that are valid. A *perfect score* is achieved if and only if $F(\alpha, 1 \ldots 1)$ holds.

Thus, in the warmup problem we have $n = 2$, $S = \{A, B\}$; $f_{1A} = [a_2 = B]$; $f_{1B} = [a_1 = A]$; $f_{2A} = x_1$; $f_{2B} = \bar{x}_2 \oplus [u_1 = A]$. The four possible answer lists are:

$$
\begin{aligned}
\text{AA:} \quad & F = (x_1 \equiv [A = B]) \wedge (x_2 \equiv x_1) \\
\text{AB:} \quad & F = (x_1 \equiv [B = B]) \wedge (x_2 \equiv \bar{x}_2 \oplus [A = A]) \\
\text{BA:} \quad & F = (x_1 \equiv [B = A]) \wedge (x_2 \equiv x_1) \\
\text{BB:} \quad & F = (x_1 \equiv [B = A]) \wedge (x_2 \equiv \bar{x}_2 \oplus [B = A])
\end{aligned}
$$

Thus AA and BA must be graded 00; AB can be graded either 10 or 11; and BB has no valid grading. Only AB can achieve the maximum score, 2; but 2 isn't guaranteed.

In Table 666 we have, for example, $f_{1C} = [a_2 \neq A] \wedge [a_3 = A]$; $f_{4D} = [a_1 = D] \wedge [a_{15} = D]$; $f_{12A} = [\Sigma_A - 1 = \Sigma_B]$, where $\Sigma_s = \sum_{1 \leq j \leq 20} [a_j = s]$. It's amusing to note that $f_{14E} = [\{\Sigma_A, \ldots, \Sigma_E\} = \{2, 3, 4, 5, 6\}]$.

The other cases are similar (although often more complicated) Boolean functions — except for 20D and 20E, which are discussed further in exercise 72.

Notice that an answer list that contains both 10E and 17E must be discarded: It can't be graded, because 10E says '$x_{10} \equiv \bar{x}_{17}$' while 17E says '$x_{17} \equiv x_{10}$'.

By suitable backtrack programming, we can prove first that no perfect score is possible. Indeed, if we consider the answers in the order (3, 15, 20, 19, 2, 1, 17, 10, 5, 4, 16, 11, 13, 14, 7, 18, 6, 8, 12, 9), many cases can quickly be ruled out. For example, suppose $a_3 = C$. Then we must have $a_1 \neq a_2 \neq \cdots \neq a_{16} \neq a_{17} = a_{18} \neq a_{19} \neq a_{20}$, and early cutoffs are often possible. (We might reach a node where the remaining choices for answers 5, 6, 7, 8, 9 are respectively $\{C, D\}$, $\{A, C\}$, $\{B, D\}$, $\{A, B, E\}$, $\{B, C, D\}$, say. Then if answer 8 is forced to be B, answer 7 can only be D; hence answer 6 is also forced to be A. Also answer 9 can no longer be B.) An instructive little propagation algorithm will make such deductions nicely at every node of the search tree. On the other hand, difficult questions like 7, 8, 9, are best *not* handled with complicated mechanisms; it's better just to wait until all twenty answers have been tentatively selected, and to check such hard cases only when the checking is easy and fast. In this way the author's program showed the impossibility of a perfect score by exploring just 52859 nodes, after only 3.4 megamems of computation.

The next task was to try for score 19 by asserting that only x_j is false. This turned out to be impossible for $1 \leq j \leq 18$, based on very little computation whatsoever (especially, of course, when $j = 6$). The hardest case, $j = 15$, needed just 56 nodes and fewer than 5 kilomems. But then, ta da, three solutions were found: One for $j = 19$ (185 kilonodes, 11 megamems) and two for $j = 20$ (131 kilonodes, 8 megamems), namely

1	2	3	4	5	6	7	8	9	10	11	12	13	14	15	16	17	18	19	20	
D	C	E	A	B	E	B	C	E	A	B	E	A	E	D	B	D	A	b	B	(i)
A	E	D	C	A	B	C	D	C	A	C	E	D	B	C	A	D	A	A	c	(ii)
D	C	E	A	B	A	D	C	D	A	E	D	A	E	D	B	D	B	E	e	(iii)

(The incorrect answers are shown here as lowercase letters. The first two solutions establish the truth of 20B and the falsity of 20E.)

72. Now there's only *one* list of answers with score ≥ 19, namely (iii). But that is paradoxical — because it claims 20E is false; hence the maximum score *cannot* be 19!

Paradoxical situations are indeed possible when the global function F of answer 71 is used recursively within one or more of the local functions f_{js}. Let's explore a bit of recursive territory by considering the following two-question, two-letter example:

1. (A) Answer 1 is incorrect.   (B) Answer 2 is incorrect.
2. (A) Some answers can't be graded consistently.   (B) No answers achieve a perfect score.

Here we have $f_{1A} = \bar{x}_1$; $f_{1B} = \bar{x}_2$; $f_{2A} = \exists a_1 \exists a_2 \forall x_1 \forall x_2 \neg F(a_1 a_2, x_1 x_2)$; $f_{2B} = \forall a_1 \forall a_2 \neg F(a_1 a_2, 11)$. (Formulas quantified by $\exists a$ or $\forall a$ expand into $|S|$ terms, while $\exists x$ or $\forall x$ expand into two; for example, $\exists a \forall x g(a, x) = (g(A, 0) \wedge g(A, 1)) \vee (g(B, 0) \wedge g(B, 1))$ when $S = \{A, B\}$.) Sometimes the expansion is undefined, because it has more than one "fixed point"; but in this case there's no problem because f_{2A} is true: Answer AA can't be graded, since 1A implies $x_1 \equiv \bar{x}_1$. Also f_{2B} is true, because both BA and BB imply $x_1 \equiv \bar{x}_2$. Thus we get the maximum score 1 with either BA or BB and grades 01.

On the other hand the simple one-question, one-letter questionnaire '**1.** (A) The maximum score is 1' has an *indeterminate* maximum score. For in this case $f_{1A} = F(A, 1)$. We find that if $F(A, 1) = 0$, only $(A, 0)$ is a valid grading, so the only possible score is 0; similarly, if $F(A, 1) = 1$, the only possible score is 1.

OK, suppose that the maximum score for the modified Table 666 is m. We know that $m < 19$; hence (iii) isn't a valid grading. It follows that 20E is true, which means that *every valid graded list of score m has x_{20} false.* And we can conclude that $m = 18$, because of the following two solutions (which are the only possibilities with 20C false):

1	2	3	4	5	6	7	8	9	10	11	12	13	14	15	16	17	18	19	20
B	A	d	A	B	E	D	C	D	A	E	D	A	E	D	E	D	B	E	c
A	E	D	C	A	B	C	D	C	A	C	E	D	B	a	C	D	A	A	c

But wait: If $m = 18$, we can score 18 with 20A true and two errors, using (say)

1	2	3	4	5	6	7	8	9	10	11	12	13	14	15	16	17	18	19	20
D	e	D	A	B	E	D	e	C	A	E	D	A	E	D	B	D	C	C	A

or 47 other answer lists. This *contradicts* $m = 18$, because x_{20} is true.

End of story? No. This argument has implicitly been predicated on the assumption that 20D is false. What if m is indeterminate? Then a new solution arises

1	2	3	4	5	6	7	8	9	10	11	12	13	14	15	16	17	18	19	20
D	C	E	A	B	E	D	C	E	A	E	B	A	E	D	B	D	A	d	D

of score 19. With (iii) it yields $m = 19$! If m is determinate, we've shown that m cannot actually be defined consistently; but if m is indeterminate, it's definitely 19.

> *Question 20 was designed to create difficulties. [:-)]*
>
> — DONALD R. WOODS (2001)

73. The 29 words `spark`, `often`, `lucky`, `other`, `month`, `ought`, `names`, `water`, `games`, `offer`, `lying`, `opens`, `magic`, `brick`, `lamps`, `empty`, `organ`, `noise`, `after`, `raise`, `drink`, `draft`, `backs`, `among`, `under`, `match`, `earth`, `roofs`, `topic` yield this: "The success or failure of backtrack often depends on the skill and ingenuity of the programmer. ... Backtrack programming (as many other types of programming) is somewhat of an art." — Solomon W. Golomb, Leonard D. Baumert.

That solution can be found interactively, using inspired guesses based on a knowledge of English and its common two-letter and three-letter words. But could a computer that knows common English words discover it without understanding their meanings?

We can formulate that question as follows: Let $w_1, \ldots, w_{29}$ be the unknown words from `WORDS`(1000), and let $q_1, \ldots, q_{29}$ be the unknown words of the quotation. (By coincidence there happen to be just 29 of each.) We can restrict the q's to words that appear, say, 32 times or more in the British National Corpus. That gives respectively (85, 562, 1863, 3199, 4650, 5631, 5417, 4724, 3657, 2448) choices for words of (2, 3, ..., 11) letters; in particular, we allow 3199 possibilities for the five-letter words $q_7, q_{11}, q_{21}, q_{22}$, because they aren't required to lie in `WORDS`(1000). Is there a unique combination of words w_i and q_j that meets the given anacrostic constraints?

This is a challenging problem, whose answer turns out (surprisingly?) to be *no*. In fact, here is the first solution found by the author's machine(!): "The success or failure of backtrack often depends on roe skill and ingenuity at the programmer. ... Backtrack programming (as lacy offal types of programming) as somewhat al an art." (The OSPD4 includes 'al' as the name of the Indian mulberry tree; the BNC has 'al' 3515 times, mostly in unsuitable contexts, but that corpus is a blunt instrument.) Altogether 720 solutions satisfy the stated constraints; they differ from the "truth" only in words of at most five letters.

Anacrostic puzzles, which are also known by other names such as double-crostics, were invented in 1933 by E. S. Kingsley. See E. S. Spiegelthal, *Proceedings of the Eastern Joint Computer Conference* **18** (1960), 39–56, for an interesting early attempt to solve them — *without* backtracking — on an IBM 704 computer.

74. Instead of considering 1000 possibilities for $\underline{}_{131\,132\,133\,134\,135}$, it suffices to consider the 43 pairs xy such that $cxyab$ is in `WORDS`(1000) and abc is a common three-letter word. (Of these pairs `ab`, `ag`, ..., `ve`, only `ar` leads to a solution. And indeed, the 720 solutions factor into three sets of 240, corresponding to choosing `earth`, `harsh`, or `large` as the keyword for $\underline{}_{131\,132\,133\,134\,135}$.) Similar reductions, but not so dramatic, occur with respect to $\underline{}_{137\,139}, \underline{}_{118\,119}, \underline{}_{46\,48}$, and $\underline{}_{32\,35}$.

75. The following algorithm uses an integer utility field `TAG`(u) in the representation of each vertex u, representing the number of times u has been "tagged." The operations "tag u" and "untag u" stand respectively for `TAG`$(u) \leftarrow$ `TAG`$(u) + 1$ and `TAG`$(u) \leftarrow$ `TAG`$(u) - 1$. Vertices shown as '⊙' in the 21 examples have a nonzero `TAG` field, indicating that the algorithm has decided *not* to include them in this particular H.

State variables v_l (a vertex), i_l (an index), and a_l (an arc) are used at level l for $0 \le l < n$. We assume that $n > 1$.

R1. [Initialize.] Set $\mathtt{TAG}(u) \leftarrow 0$ for all vertices u. Then set $v_0 \leftarrow v$, $i \leftarrow i_0 \leftarrow 0$, $a \leftarrow a_0 \leftarrow \mathtt{ARCS}(v)$, $\mathtt{TAG}(v) \leftarrow 1$, $l \leftarrow 1$, and go to R4.

R2. [Enter level l.] (At this point $i = i_{l-1}$, $v = v_i$, and $a = a_{l-1}$ is an arc from v to v_{l-1}.) If $l = n$, visit the solution $v_0 v_1 \ldots v_{n-1}$ and set $l \leftarrow n - 1$.

R3. [Advance a.] Set $a \leftarrow \mathtt{NEXT}(a)$, the next neighbor of v.

R4. [Done with level?] If $a \neq \Lambda$, go to R5. Otherwise if $i = l - 1$, go to R6. Otherwise set $i \leftarrow i + 1$, $v \leftarrow v_i$, $a \leftarrow \mathtt{ARCS}(v)$.

R5. [Try a.] Set $u \leftarrow \mathtt{TIP}(a)$ and tag u. If $\mathtt{TAG}(u) > 1$, return to R3. Otherwise set $i_l \leftarrow i$, $a_l \leftarrow a$, $v_l \leftarrow u$, $l \leftarrow l + 1$, and go to R2.

R6. [Backtrack.] Set $l \leftarrow l - 1$, and stop if $l = 0$. Otherwise set $i \leftarrow i_l$, $v \leftarrow v_i$. Untag all neighbors of v_k, for $l \geq k > i$. Then set $a \leftarrow \mathtt{NEXT}(a_l)$; while $a \neq \Lambda$, untag $\mathtt{TIP}(a)$ and set $a \leftarrow \mathtt{NEXT}(a)$. Finally set $a \leftarrow a_l$ and return to R3. ∎

This instructive algorithm differs subtly from the conventional structure of Algorithm B. Notice in particular that $\mathtt{TIP}(a_l)$ is not untagged in step R6; that vertex won't be untagged and chosen again until some previous decision has been reconsidered.

76. Let G have N vertices. For $1 \leq k \leq N$, perform Algorithm R on the kth vertex v of G, except that step R1 should tag the first $k - 1$ vertices so that they are excluded. (You'll need to make it work when $n = 1$. A tricky shortcut can be used: If we untag all neighbors of $v = v_0$ after Algorithm R stops, the net effect will be to tag only v.)

The n-omino placement counts 1, 4, 22, 113, 571, 2816, 13616, 64678, 302574 are computed almost instantly, for small n. (Larger n are discussed in Section 7.2.3.)

77. (a) All but the 13th and 18th, which require an upward or leftward step.

(b) True. If $u \in H$ and $u \neq v$, let p_u be any node of H that's one step closer to v.

(c) Again true: The oriented spanning trees are also ordinary spanning trees.

(d) The same algorithm works, except that step R4 must return to itself after setting $a \leftarrow \mathtt{ARCS}(v)$. (We can no longer be sure that $\mathtt{ARCS}(v) \neq \Lambda$.)

78. Extend Algorithm R to terminate immediately if $\mathtt{WT}(v) \geq U$, otherwise to visit the singleton solution v. Also set $w \leftarrow \mathtt{WT}(v)$ in step R1. Replace steps R2 and R5 by

R2′. [Enter level l.] If $w \geq L$, visit the solution $v_0 v_1 \ldots v_{l-1}$.

R5′. [Try a.] Set $u \leftarrow \mathtt{TIP}(a)$ and tag u. If $\mathtt{TAG}(u) > 1$ or $w + \mathtt{WT}(u) \geq U$, return to R3. Otherwise set $i_l \leftarrow i$, $a_l \leftarrow a$, $v_l \leftarrow u$, $w \leftarrow w + \mathtt{WT}(u)$, $l \leftarrow l + 1$, and go to R2.

In step R6, set $w \leftarrow w - \mathtt{WT}(v_l)$ just before setting $i \leftarrow i_l$.

79. (a) $(0, j)$ and $(1, j)$ for $j \geq 44$; $(2, j)$ for $j \geq 32$; $(4, j)$, $(8, j)$, $(10, j)$ for $j < 12$.

(b) True, each of the Boolean functions $r_{i,j}$ is clearly monotone.

(c) The "couplers" can be simulated by playing s_j^* and g_j^* instead of s_j and g_j (as if the organist had assistants). Therefore the problem can be *factored* into independent subproblems for the Pedal, Swell, and Great separately: Let there be P_n, S_n, G_n playable sounds on the Pedal, Swell, and Great, and define $P(z) = \sum_n P_n z^n$, $S(z) = \sum_n S_n z^n$, $G(z) = \sum_n G_n z^n$; then $Q(z) = \sum_n Q_n z^n$ is the convolution $P(z) S(z) G(z)$.

(d) $p_0 = p_{12} = c_0 = c_1 = c_{15} = 1$ gives $(0,0)$, $(0,12)$, $(0,24)$, $(1,0)$, $(1,12)$; $s_0 = s_{19} = s_{28} = c_3 = c_4 = 1$ gives (the beautiful) $(3,0)$, $(3,19)$, $(3,28)$, $(4,19)$, $(4,28)$; etc.

(e) It's unplayable if and only if $i \in \{2, 14, 15\}$ or $i' \in \{0, 1, 2, 14, 15\}$ or ($i \neq i'$ and either $3 \leq i, i' \leq 8$ or $9 \leq i, i' \leq 15$).

(f) $Q_1 = 812 - 112 = 700$, because we can't have $(14, j)$ or $(15, j)$ without $(13, j)$.

(g) $Q_{811} = 12$ sounds lack only one pipe: With all inputs 1 except p_j, for $12 \le j <$ 24, only $r_{2,j}$ is 0. (Thankfully there isn't enough wind pressure to actually play this.)

(h) Brute-force backtrack programs can be written, using the monotonicity property (b) for cutoffs, in order to check small values and to list the actual sounds. But the best way to compute P_n, S_n, G_n, and Q_n is to use generating functions.

For example, let $G(z) = G_0(z) + G_1(z) + \cdots + G_{63}(z)$, where $G_k(z)$ for $k = (c_{14}c_{13}c_{12}c_{11}c_{10}c_9)_2$ enumerates the sounds for a given setting of console switches, excluding sounds already enumerated by $G_j(z)$ for $j < k$. Then $G_0(z) = 1$; $G_k(z) = 0$ if $c_{13}c_{14} = 1$; otherwise $G_k(z) = f(c_9 + c_{11} + c_{12} + c_{13} + 3c_{14})$ when $c_{10} = 0$, and $G_k(z) = g(c_9 + 1 + c_{11} + c_{12} + c_{13} + 3c_{14}, 1 + c_{11} + c_{12} + c_{13} + 3c_{14})$ when $c_{10} = 1$, where

$$f(n) = (1 + z^n)^{56} - 1, \qquad g(m, n) = (1 + z^n)^{12}((1 + z^m)^{44} - 1).$$

Thus $G(z) = 1 + 268z + 8146z^2 + 139452z^3 + \cdots + 178087336020z^{10} + \cdots + 12z^{374} + z^{380}$.

Similarly, with $S(z) = \sum_{k=0}^{63} S_k(z)$ and $k = (c_8 c_7 c_6 c_5 c_4 c_3)_2$, we have $S_0(z) = 1$; $S_{32}(z) = (1 + z)^{44} - 1$; otherwise $S_k(z) = f(c_3 + c_5 + c_6 + c_7)$ when $c_4 = c_8 = 0$, $S_k(z) = g(c_3 + c_4 + c_5 + c_6 + c_7 + c_8, \max(c_3, c_4) + c_5 + c_6 + c_7)$ when $c_4 + c_8 > 0$. Thus $S(z) = 1 + 312z + 9312z^2 + 155720z^3 + \cdots + 180657383126z^{10} + \cdots + 12z^{308} + z^{312}$. [Curiously we have $S_n > G_n$ for $1 \le n \le 107$.]

The generating functions for $P(z) = \sum_{k=0}^{31} P_k(z)$, with $k = (c_{16}c_{15}c_2c_1c_0)_2$, are trickier. Let $h(w, z) = (1 + 3wz^2 + 2w^2z^3 + w^2z^4 + w^3z^4)^8((1 + 2wz^2 + w^2z^3)^4 - 1)$. Then $P_{31}(z) = h(z, z^2)$, and there are three main cases when $0 < k < 31$: If $c_0 c_{15} = c_1 c_{16} = 0$, then $P_k(z) = (1 + z^{c_{15} + c_{16}})^{32} - (1 + z^{c_{15} + c_{16}})^{20}$ if $c_0 + c_1 + c_2 = 0$, otherwise $P_k(z) = (1 + z^{c_0 + c_1 + c_2 + c_{15} + c_{16}})^{32} - 1$. If $c_0 = c_{15}$, $c_1 = c_{16}$, $c_2 = 0$, then $P_k(z) = q(z^{c_0 + c_1})$,

$$q(z) = (1 + 3z^2 + 2z^3 + z^4)^8(1 + 2z^2 + z^3)^4 - 2(1 + 2z^2 + z^3)^8(1 + z^2)^4 + (1 + z^2)^8.$$

Otherwise we have $P_k(z) = h(z^{c_0 + c_1 + c_2 + c_{15} + c_{16} - 2}, z)$. Thus $P(z) = 1 + 120z + 2336z^2 + 22848z^3 + \cdots + 324113168z^{10} + \cdots + 8z^{119} + z^{120}$. And $Q(z) = 1 + 700z + 173010z^2 + 18838948z^3 + 1054376915z^4 + 38386611728z^5 + 1039287557076z^6 + 22560539157160z^7 + 410723052356833z^8 + 6457608682396156z^9 + 89490036797524716z^{10} + \cdots + 12z^{811} + z^{812}$. So $(Q_2/\binom{812}{2}, \ldots, Q_{10}/\binom{812}{10}) \approx (.5, .2, .06, .01, .003, .0005, .00009, .00002, .000003)$.

> *Dr Pell was wont to say, that in the Resolution of Questiones,*
> *the main matter is the well stating them:*
> *which requires a good mother-witt & Logick: as well as Algebra:*
> *for let the Question be but well-stated, and it will worke of it selfe:*
> *... By this way, an man cannot intangle his notions, & make a false Steppe.*
> — JOHN AUBREY, *An Idea of Education of Young Gentlemen* (c. 1684)

SECTION 7.2.2.1

1. (a) Note first that Algorithm 6.2.2T has its own LLINK and RLINK fields, for left and right children; they shouldn't be confused with the links of the doubly linked list. After all deletions are done, LLINK(k) will be the largest search-tree ancestor of k that's less than k; RLINK(k) will be the smallest ancestor of k that's greater than k; but if there's no such ancestor, the link will be 0. (For example, in Fig. 10 of Section 6.2.2, RLINK(LEO) would be PISCES and LLINK(AQUARIUS) would be the list head.)

(b) There are $C_n = \binom{2n}{n} \frac{1}{n+1}$ classes (the Catalan number), one for each binary tree.

(c) The size of each class is the number of topological sortings of the partial order generated by the relations $k \prec$ LLINK(k), $k \prec$ RLINK(k). And this number equals 1 only in the 2^{n-1} "degenerate" trees of height n (see exercise 6.2.2–5).

2. (a) (Solution by X. Lou.) We can prove that LLINK(a_k) $= a_k - 1$ and RLINK(a_k) $= (a_k+1) \bmod (n+1)$ when a_k is undeleted; hence that undeletion sets RLINK($a_k - 1$) and LLINK($(a_k + 1) \bmod (n + 1)$) to the correct value a_k. (If $a_k - 1$ wasn't deleted *before* a_k, LLINK(a_k) never changed. Otherwise LLINK(a_k) became $a_k - 1$ when $a_k - 1$ was undeleted, by induction on k. A similar argument works for RLINK.) Notice that each LLINK and RLINK is reset exactly once, except that LLINK(1) and RLINK(n) remain 0.

(Programmers are advised to use this amazing fact only with *great* care, because the lists are malformed during the process and fully reconstructed only at the end.)

(b) No. For example, delete 1, 2, 3; then undelete 1, 3, 2.

(c) Yes. The argument of (a) applies to each maximal interval of affected elements.

3. (a) $(x_1, \ldots, x_6) = (1, 0, 0, 1, 1, 0)$. (In general the solutions to linear equations won't always be 0 or 1. For example, the equations $x_1 + x_2 = x_2 + x_3 = x_1 + x_3 = 1$ imply that $x_1 = x_2 = x_3 = \frac{1}{2}$; hence the corresponding exact cover problem is unsolvable.)

(b) In practice, m is much larger than n. Example (5) is just a "toy problem"! The best we can hope to achieve from n simultaneous equations is to express n of the variables in terms of the other $m - n$; that leaves 2^{m-n} cases to try.

4. If G is bipartite, the exact covers are the ways to choose the vertices of one part. (Hence there are 2^k solutions, if G has k components.) Otherwise there are no solutions. (Algorithm X will discover that fact quickly, although Algorithm 7B is faster.)

5. Given a hypergraph, find a set of vertices that hits each hyperedge exactly once. (In an ordinary graph this is the scenario of exercise 4.)

Similarly, the so-called hitting set problem is dual to the vertex cover problem.

6. The header nodes, numbered 1 through N, are followed by L ordinary nodes and $M + 1$ spacers; hence the final node Z is number $L + M + N + 1$. (There also are $N + 1$ records for the horizontal list of items; those "records" aren't true "nodes.")

7. Node 23 is a spacer; '-4' indicates that it follows the 4th option. (Any nonpositive number would work, but this convention aids debugging.) Option 5 ends at node 25.

8. (*Secondary* items, which are introduced in the text after (24), are also handled by the steps below. Such items should occur *after* all of the primary items have been listed on the first line, and separated from them by some distinguishing mark.)

I1. [Read the first line.] Set $N_1 \leftarrow -1$, $i \leftarrow 0$. Then, for each item name α on the first line, set $i \leftarrow i+1$, $\texttt{NAME}(i) \leftarrow \alpha$, $\texttt{LLINK}(i) \leftarrow i - 1$, $\texttt{RLINK}(i-1) \leftarrow i$. If α names the first secondary item, also set $N_1 \leftarrow i - 1$. (In practice α is limited to at most 8 characters, say. One should report an error if $\alpha = \texttt{NAME}(j)$ for some $j < i$.)

I2. [Finish the horizontal list.] Set $N \leftarrow i$. If $N_1 < 0$ (there were no secondary items), set $N_1 \leftarrow N$. Then set $\texttt{LLINK}(N+1) \leftarrow N$, $\texttt{RLINK}(N) \leftarrow N+1$, $\texttt{LLINK}(N_1+1) \leftarrow N+1$, $\texttt{RLINK}(N+1) \leftarrow N_1+1$, $\texttt{LLINK}(0) \leftarrow N_1$, $\texttt{RLINK}(N_1) \leftarrow 0$. (The active secondary items, if any, are accessible from record $N + 1$.)

I3. [Prepare for options.] Set $\texttt{LEN}(i) \leftarrow 0$ and $\texttt{ULINK}(i) \leftarrow \texttt{DLINK}(i) \leftarrow i$ for $1 \leq i \leq N$. (These are the header nodes for the N item lists, which are initially empty.) Then set $M \leftarrow 0$, $p \leftarrow N + 1$, $\texttt{TOP}(p) \leftarrow 0$. (Node p is the first spacer.)

I4. [Read an option.] Terminate with $Z \leftarrow p$ if no input remains. Otherwise let the next line of input contain the item names $\alpha_1 \ldots \alpha_k$, and do the following for $1 \leq j \leq k$: Use an algorithm from Chapter 6 to find the index i_j for which $\texttt{NAME}(i_j) = \alpha_j$. (Report an error if unsuccessful. Complain also if an item name appears more than once in the same option, because a duplicate might make Algorithm X fail spectacularly.) Set $\texttt{LEN}(i_j) \leftarrow \texttt{LEN}(i_j) + 1$, $q \leftarrow \texttt{ULINK}(i_j)$, $\texttt{ULINK}(p+j) \leftarrow q$, $\texttt{DLINK}(q) \leftarrow p+j$, $\texttt{DLINK}(p+j) \leftarrow i_j$, $\texttt{ULINK}(i_j) \leftarrow p+j$, $\texttt{TOP}(p+j) \leftarrow i_j$.

I5. [Finish an option.] Set $M \leftarrow M+1$, $\texttt{DLINK}(p) \leftarrow p+k$, $p \leftarrow p+k+1$, $\texttt{TOP}(p) \leftarrow -M$, $\texttt{ULINK}(p) \leftarrow p - k$, and return to step I4. (Node p is the next spacer.) ∎

9. Set $\theta \leftarrow \infty$, $p \leftarrow \texttt{RLINK}(0)$. While $p \neq 0$, do the following: Set $\lambda \leftarrow \texttt{LEN}(p)$; if $\lambda < \theta$ set $\theta \leftarrow \lambda$, $i \leftarrow p$; and set $p \leftarrow \texttt{RLINK}(p)$. (We could exit the loop immediately if $\theta = 0$.)

10. If $\texttt{LEN}(p) > 1$ and $\texttt{NAME}(p)$ doesn't begin with '#', set $\lambda \leftarrow M + \texttt{LEN}(p)$ instead of $\texttt{LEN}(p)$. (Similarly, the "nonsharp preference" heuristic favors nonsharp items.)

11. Item a is selected at level 0, trying option $x_0 = 12$, '$a\ d\ g$', and leading to (7). Then item b is selected at level 1, trying $x_1 = 16$, '$b\ c\ f$'. Hence, when the remaining item e is selected at level 2, it has no options in its list, and backtracking becomes necessary. Here are the current memory contents — substantially changed from Table 1:

i:	0	1	2	3	4	5	6	7
$\texttt{NAME}(i)$:	—	a	b	c	d	e	f	g
$\texttt{LLINK}(i)$:	0	0	0	0	3	0	5	6
$\texttt{RLINK}(i)$:	0	2	3	5	5	0	0	0

x:	0	1	2	3	4	5	6	7
$\texttt{LEN}(x)$:	—	2	1	1	1	0	0	1
$\texttt{ULINK}(x)$:	—	20	16	9	27	5	6	25
$\texttt{DLINK}(x)$:	—	12	16	9	27	5	6	25

x:	8	9	10	11	12	13	14	15
$\texttt{TOP}(x)$:	0	3	5	-1	1	4	7	-2
$\texttt{ULINK}(x)$:	—	3	5	9	1	4	7	12
$\texttt{DLINK}(x)$:	10	3	5	14	20	21	25	18

x:	16	17	18	19	20	21	22	23
$\texttt{TOP}(x)$:	2	3	6	-3	1	4	6	-4
$\texttt{ULINK}(x)$:	2	9	6	16	12	4	18	20
$\texttt{DLINK}(x)$:	2	3	6	22	1	27	6	25

x:	24	25	26	27	28	29	30
$\texttt{TOP}(x)$:	2	7	-5	4	5	7	-6
$\texttt{ULINK}(x)$:	16	7	24	4	10	25	27
$\texttt{DLINK}(x)$:	2	7	29	4	5	7	—

12. Report that x is out of range if $x \leq N$ or $x > Z$ or $\mathtt{TOP}(x) \leq 0$. Otherwise set $q \leftarrow x$ and do "print '$\mathtt{NAME}(\mathtt{TOP}(q))$'" and set $q \leftarrow q+1$; if $\mathtt{TOP}(q) \leq 0$ set $q \leftarrow \mathtt{ULINK}(q)$" until $q = x$. Then set $i \leftarrow \mathtt{TOP}(x)$, $q \leftarrow \mathtt{DLINK}(i)$, and $k \leftarrow 1$. While $q \neq x$ and $q \neq i$, set $q \leftarrow \mathtt{DLINK}(q)$ and $k \leftarrow k+1$. If $q \neq i$, report that the option containing x is 'k of $\mathtt{LEN}(i)$' in item i's list; otherwise report that it's not in that list.

[Algorithm C extends Algorithm X to colors. If $\mathtt{COLOR}(q) \neq 0$, also print '$:c$' where $c = \mathtt{COLOR}(q)$ if $\mathtt{COLOR}(q) > 0$, otherwise $c = \mathtt{COLOR}(\mathtt{TOP}(q))$.]

13. For $0 \leq j < l$, node x_j is part of an option in the solution. By setting $r \leftarrow x_j$ and then $r \leftarrow r+1$ until $\mathtt{TOP}(r) < 0$, we'll know exactly what that option is: It's option number $-\mathtt{TOP}(r)$, which begins at node $\mathtt{ULINK}(r)$. (Many applications of Algorithm X have a custom-made output routine, to convert $x_0 \ldots x_{l-1}$ into an appropriate format — presenting it directly as a sudoku solution or a box packing, etc.)

Exercise 12 explains how to provide further information, not only identifying the option of x_j but also showing its position in the search tree.

14. (a) The options are '$S_j M_k$', for all $0 \leq j, k < n$ except $j = k$ or $j = (k+1) \bmod n$.

(b) There are $(u_3, \ldots, u_{10}) = (1, 2, 13, 80, 579, 4738, 43387, 439792)$ solutions. The running time for $n = 10$ is about 180 (or 275) mems per solution with (or without) MRV.

[This problem has a rich history: E. Lucas presented and named it in his *Théorie des Nombres* (1891), 215, 491–495. An equivalent problem had, however, already been posed by P. G. Tait, and solved by A. Cayley and T. Muir; see *Trans. Royal Soc. Edinburgh* **28** (1877), 159, and *Proc. Royal Soc. Edinburgh* **9** (1878), 338–342, 382–391, **11** (1880), 187–190. In particular, Muir found the recurrence relation

$$(n-1)u_{n+1} = (n^2 - 1)u_n + (n+1)u_{n-1} + (-1)^n \cdot 4, \quad \text{for } n > 1.$$

Clearly $u_2 = 0$; a careful consideration of initial values shows that the choices $u_0 = 1$ and $u_1 = -1$ give mathematically clean expressions, such as the explicit formula

$$u_n = \sum_{k=0}^{n} (-1)^k \frac{2n}{2n-k} \binom{2n-k}{k} (n-k)!.$$

(See J. Touchard, *Comptes Rendus Acad. Sci.* **198** (Paris, 1934), 631–633; I. Kaplansky, *Bull. Amer. Math. Soc.* **49** (1943), 784–785.) The kth term of this formula can also be written $n! \sum_j (-1)^{j+k} 2^{k-2j} / ((k-2j)!\, j!\, (n-1)^{\underline{j}})$; hence we have the curious identity

$$\frac{u_n}{n!} = \sum_{j=0}^{n/2} \frac{(-1)^j}{j!} \frac{T_{n-2j}}{(n-1)^{\underline{j}}} = T_n - \frac{T_{n-1}}{n-1} + \frac{T_{n-2}/2!}{(n-1)(n-2)} - \frac{T_{n-3}/3!}{(n-1)(n-2)(n-3)} + \cdots,$$

where $T_n = \sum_{k=0}^{n} (-2)^k / k!$ is the sum of the first $n+1$ terms of the power series for e^{-2}. The ménage numbers therefore satisfy the interesting asymptotic formula

$$u_n = \frac{n!}{e^2} \left(1 - \frac{1}{n-1} + \frac{1/2!}{(n-1)(n-2)} + \cdots + \frac{(-1)^k/k!}{(n-1)\ldots(n-k)} + O(n^{-k-1}) \right)$$

for all fixed $k \geq 0$, discovered by I. Kaplansky and J. Riordan (*Scripta Mathematica* **12** (1946), 113–124). In fact, M. Wyman and L. Moser proved that the sum of this series for $0 \leq k < n$ differs from u_n by less than $1/2$ (*Canadian J. Math.* **10** (1958), 468–480). Among many other things, they also found a (complicated) expression for the exponential generating function $\sum_n u_n z^n / n!$. The *ordinary* generating function $\sum_n u_n z^n$ has the surprisingly nice form $((1-z)/(1+z)) F(z/(1+z)^2)$, where $F(z) = \sum_{n\geq 0} n! z^n$; see P. Flajolet and R. Sedgewick, *Analytic Combinatorics* (2009), 368–372.]

15. Omit the options with $i = n - [n \text{ even}]$ and $j > n/2$.

(Other solutions are possible. For example, we could omit the options with $i = 1$ and $j \geq n$; that would omit $n-1$ options instead of only $\lfloor n/2 \rfloor$. However, the suggested rule turns out to make Algorithm X run about 10% faster.)

16. The two solutions are 'r_1 c_2 a_3 b_{-1}' 'r_2 c_4 a_6 b_{-2}' 'r_3 c_1 a_4 b_2' 'r_4 c_3 a_7 b_1' 'a_2' 'a_5' 'a_8' 'b_{-3}' 'b_0' 'b_3'; 'r_1 c_3 a_4 b_{-2}' 'r_2 c_1 a_3 b_1' 'r_3 c_4 a_7 b_{-1}' 'r_4 c_2 a_6 b_2' 'a_2' 'a_5' 'a_8' 'b_{-3}' 'b_0' 'b_3'. At the top levels, the MRV heuristic causes Algorithm X to branch first on the slack variables a_2, a_8, b_{-3}, and b_3, which each have at most two possibilities. (And that's actually a pretty strange way to tackle the four queens problem!)

17. Branch first on r_3, which has four options. If 'r_3 c_1 a_4 b_2', there's just one option for c_2, then c_3, then r_2, so we get the first solution: 'r_3 c_1 a_4 b_2' 'r_1 c_2 a_3 b_{-1}' 'r_4 c_3 a_7 b_1' 'r_2 c_4 a_6 b_{-2}'. If 'r_3 c_2 a_5 b_1', c_3 is forced, then r_2 can't be covered. If 'r_3 c_3 a_6 b_0', r_2 is forced, then c_2 can't be covered. If 'r_3 c_4 a_7 b_{-1}', we cruise to the second solution: 'r_3 c_4 a_7 b_{-1}' 'r_1 c_3 a_4 b_{-2}' 'r_2 c_1 a_3 b_1' 'r_4 c_2 a_6 b_2'. (And that's a good way.)

18. 'c e' 'a d f' 'b g' (as before) and 'b c f' 'a d g' (new).

19. When all primary items have been covered in step X2, accept a solution only if $\text{LEN}(i) = 0$ for all of the active secondary items, namely the items accessible from $\text{RLINK}(N+1)$. [This algorithm is called the "second death" method, because it checks that all of the purely secondary options have been killed off by primary covering.]

20. For $1 \leq k < m$, set $t \leftarrow k \,\&\, (-k)$; include secondary item y_k in option α_j for $k \leq j < \min(m, k+t)$ and in option β_j for $k - t \leq j < k$.

Equivalently, to set up option α_j, include a and set $t \leftarrow j$; while $t > 0$, include y_t and set $t \leftarrow t \,\&\, (t-1)$. To set up option β_j, include b and set $t \leftarrow -1-j$; while $t > -m$, include y_{-t} and set $t \leftarrow t \,\&\, (t-1)$.

If $j > k$, options α_j and β_k both contain $y_{j \,\&\, -2^{\lfloor \lg(j-k) \rfloor}}$.

21. The options α_j^i will contain the primary item a_i. Simply do $k-1$ pairwise orderings, with secondary items y_k^i to ensure that $j_k \leq j_{k+1}$. If m is a power of 2, it turns out that the options for $1 < i < k$ each have exactly $\lg m$ secondary items. For example, if $m = 4$ and $k > 2$, the options α_j^2 are 'a_2 y_1^1 y_2^1', 'a_2 y_2^1 y_1^2', 'a_2 y_3^1 y_2^2', 'a_2 y_3^2 y_2^2'.

(The author attempted to knock out options for $\alpha^{i'}$ with $i' < i - 1$ or $i' > i+1$, by adding additional secondary items, but that turned out to be a bad idea.)

Of course, this method doesn't compete with the lightning-quick methods for combination generation in Section 7.2.1.3. For instance, when $m = 20$ and $k = 8$ it needs 1.1 Gμ to crank out the $\binom{27}{8} = 2220075$ coverings, about 500 mems per solution.

22. (a) Let $n' = \lfloor n/2 \rfloor + 1$. By rotation/reflection we can assume that the queen in column n' (the middle column) is in row i and the queen in row n' is in column j, where $1 \leq i < j < n'$. We obtain a suitable exact cover problem by leaving out the options $o(i,j) =$ 'r_i c_j a_{i+j} b_{i-j}' for $i = j$ or $i + j = n + 1$; also omit $o(i,j)$ for $i > j$ when $j = n'$; $j > i$ when $i = n'$; and $(i,j) = (n'-1, n')$ or $(n', 1)$. Then include secondary items to force the pairwise ordering of $\alpha_k = o(k+1, n')$ and $\beta_k = o(n', k+2)$, for $0 \leq k < m = n' - 2$.

(b) Now we assume a queen in (j, j), where $1 \leq j < n'$, and that the queen in row n is closer to the bottom right corner than the queen in column n. So we omit options $o(i,j)$ for $i+j = n+1$ or $i = j \geq n'$ or $(i,j) = (n,2)$ or $(i,j) = (n-1,n)$; we make item b_0 primary; and we let $\alpha_k = o(n, n-k-1)$, $\beta_k = o(n-k-2, n)$ for $0 \leq k < m = n - 3$.

(c) This time we want queens in (i,i) and $(j, n+1-j)$ where $1 \leq i < j < n'$. We promote a_{n+1} and b_0 to primary; omit $o(i,j)$ when $i = j \geq n'-1$ or $i = n+1-j \geq n'$ or $(i,j) = (1,n)$; and let $\alpha_k = o(k+1, k+1)$, $\beta_k = o(k+2, n-k-1)$ for $0 \leq k < m = n' - 2$.

In case (a) there are $(0, 0, 1, 8, 260, 9709, 371590)$ solutions for $n = (5, 7, \ldots, 17)$; Algorithm X handles $n = 17$ in 3.4 Gμ. [In case (b) there are $(0, 0, 1, 4, 14, 21, 109, 500, 2453, 14498, 89639, 568849)$ for $n = (5, 6, \ldots, 16)$; and $n = 16$ costs 6.0 Gμ. In case (c), similarly, there are $(1, 0, 3, 6, 24, 68, 191, 1180, 5944, 29761, 171778, 1220908)$ solutions; $n = 16$ costs 5.5 Gμ.]

23. (a) Consider the queens in column a of row 1, row b of column n, column $\bar{c}$ of row n, and row $\bar{d}$ of column 1, where $\bar{x} = n + 1 - x$. (These four queens are distinct, because no queen is in a corner. Notice also that neither $\bar{a}$ nor $\bar{b}$ nor $\bar{c}$ nor $\bar{d}$ can equal a.) Repeated rotations and/or reflections will change these numbers from (a, b, c, d) to

$$(b, c, d, a), \ (c, d, a, b), \ (d, a, b, c), \ (\bar{d}, \bar{c}, \bar{b}, \bar{a}), \ (\bar{c}, \bar{b}, \bar{a}, \bar{d}), \ (\bar{b}, \bar{a}, \bar{d}, \bar{c}), \ (\bar{a}, \bar{d}, \bar{c}, \bar{b}).$$

Those eight 4-tuples are usually distinct, and in such cases we can save a factor of 8 by eliminating all but one of them. There always is a solution with $a \leq b, c, d < \bar{a}$; and those inequalities can be enforced by doing three simultaneous pairwise comparisons, between the options for row 1 and the respective options for column n, row n, and column 1. For example, the options that correspond to $a = 1$ when $n = 16$ are 'r_1 c_2 a_3 b_{-1}'; 'r_2 c_{16} a_{18} b_{-14} x_1 x_2 x_4'; 'r_{15} c_{16} a_{31} b_{-1} x_1 x_2 x_4'; 'r_{16} c_2 a_{18} b_{14} y_1 y_2 y_4'; 'r_{16} c_{14} a_{30} b_2 y_1 y_2 y_4'; 'r_2 c_1 a_3 b_1 z_1 z_2 z_4'; 'r_{15} c_1 a_{16} b_{14} z_1 z_2 z_4'. (Here $m = n/2 - 1 = 7$.)

With this change, the number of solutions for $n = 16$ drops from 454376 to 64374 (ratio ≈ 7.06), and the running time drops from 4.3 Gμ to 1.2 Gμ (ratio ≈ 3.68).

[The author experimented with further restrictions, so that solutions were allowed only if (i) $a < b, c, d$; (ii) $a = b < c, d$; (iii) $a = b = c < d$; (iv) $a = b = c = d$; (v) $a = c < b, d$. Five options were given for each value of $a < n/2 - 1$, and m was 6 instead of 7. The number of solutions decreased to 59648; but the running time increased to 1.9 Gμ. Thus a point of diminishing returns had been reached. (A completely canonical reduction would have produced 57188 solutions, with considerable difficulty.)]

(b) This case is almost identical to (a), because the queen in the center vacates all other diagonal cells. Requiring $a \leq b, c, d < \bar{a}$ reduces the number of solutions for $n = 17$ from 4067152 to 577732 (ratio ≈ 7.04), and run time to 3.2 Gμ (ratio ≈ 4.50).

24. We simply combine compatible options into (a) pairs, (b) quadruplets, and force a queen in the center when n is odd. For example, when $n = 4$ we replace (23) by (a) 'r_1 c_2 a_3 b_{-1} r_4 c_3 a_7 b_1'; 'r_1 c_3 a_4 b_{-2} r_4 c_2 a_6 b_2'; 'r_2 c_1 a_3 b_1 r_3 c_4 a_7 b_{-1}'; 'r_2 c_4 a_6 b_{-2} r_3 c_1 a_4 b_2'; (b) 'r_1 c_2 a_3 b_{-1} r_2 c_4 a_6 b_{-2} r_4 c_3 a_7 b_1 r_3 c_1 a_4 b_2'; 'r_2 c_1 a_3 b_1 r_3 c_4 a_7 b_{-1} r_1 c_3 a_4 b_{-2} r_4 c_2 a_6 b_2'. The options when $n = 5$ are (a) 'r_1 c_2 a_3 b_{-1} r_5 c_4 a_9 b_1'; 'r_1 c_4 a_5 b_{-3} r_5 c_2 a_7 b_3'; 'r_2 c_1 a_3 b_1 r_4 c_5 a_9 b_{-1}'; 'r_2 c_5 a_7 b_{-3} r_4 c_1 a_5 b_3'; 'r_3 c_3 a_6 b_0'; (b) 'r_1 c_2 a_3 b_{-1} r_2 c_5 a_7 b_{-3} r_5 c_4 a_9 b_1 r_4 c_1 a_5 b_3'; 'r_2 c_1 a_3 b_1 r_1 c_4 a_5 b_{-3} r_4 c_5 a_9 b_{-1} r_5 c_2 a_7 b_3'; 'r_3 c_3 a_6 b_0'.

An n-queen solution is either *asymmetric* (changed by 180° rotation) or *singly symmetric* (changed by 90° rotation but not 180°) or *doubly symmetric* (unchanged by 90° rotation). Let $Q_a(n)$, $Q_s(n)$, $Q_d(n)$ be the number of such solutions that are essentially different; then $Q(n) = 8Q_a(n) + 4Q_s(n) + 2Q_d(n)$ when $n > 1$. Furthermore there are $4Q_s(n) + 2Q_d(n)$ solutions to (a) and $2Q_d(n)$ solutions to (b). Hence we can determine the individual values just by counting solutions, and we obtain these results for small n:

$n =$	4	5	6	7	8	9	10	11	12	13	14	15	16	17
$Q_a(n) =$	0	1	0	4	11	42	89	329	1765	9197	45647	284743	1846189	11975869
$Q_s(n) =$	0	0	1	2	1	4	3	12	18	32	105	310	734	2006
$Q_d(n) =$	1	1	0	0	0	0	0	0	4	4	0	0	32	64

We can reduce the solutions to (a) by a factor of 2, by simply eliminating the options that contain $\{r_1, c_k\}$ for $k \geq \lceil n/2 \rceil$. We can reduce the solutions to (b) by a factor of $2^{\lfloor n/4 \rfloor}$, by simply eliminating the options that contain $\{r_j, c_k\}$ for $j < \lceil n/2 \rceil$ and $k \geq \lceil n/2 \rceil$. With these simplifications, the computation of $Q_{\mathrm{d}}(16)$ needs only 70 Kμ; and then the computation of $Q_{\mathrm{s}}(16)$ needs only 5 Mμ. Only 20 Mμ are needed to determine that $Q_{\mathrm{d}}(32) = 2^7 \cdot 1589$.

25. With 64 items, one for each cell of the chessboard, let there be 92 options, one for each of the 92 solutions to the eight queens problem (see Fig. 68). Every option names eight of the 64 items; so an 8-coloring is equivalent to solving this exact cover problem. Algorithm X needs only 25 kilomems and a 7-node search tree to show that such a mission is impossible. [In fact no *seven* solutions can be disjoint, because each solution touches at least three of the twenty cells 13, 14, 15, 16, 22, 27, 31, 38, 41, 48, 51, 58, 61, 68, 72, 77, 83, 84, 85, 86. See Thorold Gosset, *Messenger of Mathematics* **44** (1914), 48. However, Henry E. Dudeney found the illustrated way to occupy all but two cells, in *Tit-Bits* **32** (11 September 1897), 439; **33** (2 October 1897), 3.]

```
12345678
78563412
46718235
23854167
84236751
51672384
67481523
512784
```

```
07348652
18650437
75421860
26835071
34072186
52183704
80564213
61207345
```

26. This is an exact cover problem with $92 + 312 + 396 + \cdots + 312 = 3284$ options (see exercise 7.2.2–6). Algorithm X needs about 32 megamems to find the solution shown, and about 1.3 Tμ to find all 11,092 of them.

27. Let u_{jh} and d_{jh} be secondary items for $1 \leq j \leq 2n$ and $1 \leq h \leq \lceil n/2 \rceil$. Insert the gadget

$$u_{j1}\ u_{j2}\ \cdots\ u_{j\lceil i/2\rceil}\ u_{(j+1)\lceil i/2\rceil}\ \cdots\ u_{k\lceil i/2\rceil}\ \cdots\ u_{k2}\ u_{k1}$$

into each option (16); also append similar options, but with 'u' changed to 'd', except when $i = n$. [Solutions whose planar graph "splits" will be obtained more than once. One such example is 12 10 8 6 4 11 9 7 5 4 6 8 10 12 5 7 9 11 3 1 2 1 3 2.]

28. (a) Denoting that formula by $\rho(c_0, t_0; \ldots; c_l, t_l)$, notice that if $c'_j = t_j + 1 - c_j$ we have $\rho(c_0, t_0; \ldots; c_l, t_l) + \rho(c'_0, t_0; \ldots; c'_l, t_l) = 1$. Consequently the completion ratio is $1/2$ if and only if $c'_j = c_j$ for all j, namely when $t_j = 2c_j - 1$.

(b) The ratio $\rho(c_0, t_0; \ldots; c_l, t_l)$ never has an odd denominator, because $p/q + p'/q'$ has an even denominator whenever q and p' are odd and q' is even. But we can get arbitrarily close to $1/3$, since $\rho(2, 4; \ldots; 2, 4) = 1/3 + 1/(24 \cdot 4^l)$.

29. If T has only a root node, let there be one column, no rows. Otherwise let T have $d \geq 1$ subtrees $T_1, \ldots, T_d$, and assume that we've constructed matrices with rows R_j and columns C_j for each T_j. Let $C = C_1 \cup \cdots \cup C_d$. The matrix for T is obtained by appending three new columns $\{0, 1, 2\}$ and the following new rows: (i) '0 1 2 and all columns of $C \backslash C_j$', for $1 \leq j \leq d$; (ii) 'j and all columns of C', for $j \in \{0, 1\}$. The matrix for the example tree has 15 columns and 14 rows.

```
011111000000000
101111000000000
110111000000000
111100000000000
111010000000000
000000011111000
000000101111000
000000110111000
000000111100000
000000111010000
000000111111111
111111000000111
111111111111100
111111111111010
```

30. Yes, assuming that duplicate options are permitted. Use the previous construction, but change '$C \backslash C_j$' to 'C' if T_j is a solution node. (Without duplicate options, no two solution nodes can be siblings.)

31. (a) In step I4 of answer 8, insert $p+j$ into the rth position of the list for i_j, instead of at the bottom, where r is uniform between 1 and $\mathtt{LEN}(i_j)$.

(b) In answer 9, when $\lambda < \theta$ also set $r \leftarrow 1$; when $\lambda = \theta$, set $r \leftarrow r+1$, and change $i \leftarrow p$ with probability $1/r$.

32. (a) No. Otherwise there would be an option with no primary items.

(b) Yes, but only if there are two options with the same primary items.

(c) Yes, but only if there are two options whose union is also an option, when restricted to primary items.

(d) The number of places, j, where $x = 1$ and $x' = 0$ must be the same as the number where $x = 0$ and $x' = 1$. For if A has exactly k primary items in every option, exactly jk primary items are being covered in different ways.

(e) Again distances must be even, because every solution also solves the restricted problem, which is uniform. (Consequently it makes sense to speak of the *semidistance* $d(x, x')/2$ between solutions of a quasi-uniform exact covering problem. The semidistance in a polyform packing problem is the number of pieces that are packed differently.)

33. (Solution by T. Matsui.) Add one new column at the left of A, all 0s. Then add two rows of length $n + 1$ at the bottom: $10 \ldots 0$ and $11 \ldots 1$. This $(m + 2) \times (n + 1)$ matrix A' has one solution that chooses only the last row. All other solutions choose the second-to-last row, together with rows that solve A.

34. (Solution by T. Matsui.) Assume that all 1s in column 1 appear in the first t rows, where $t > 3$. Add two new columns at the left, and two new rows $1100 \ldots 0$, $1010 \ldots 0$ of length $n + 2$ at the bottom. For $1 \le k \le t$, if row k was $1\alpha_k$, replace it by $010\alpha_k$ if $k \le t/2$, $011\alpha_k$ if $k > t/2$. Insert 00 at the left of the remaining rows $t + 1$ through m.

This construction can be repeated (with suitable row and column permutations) until no column sum exceeds 3. If the original column sums were $(c_1, \ldots, c_n)$, the new A' has $2T$ more rows and $2T$ more columns than A did, where $T = \sum_{j=1}^{n}(c_j \doteq 3)$.

One consequence is that the exact cover problem is NP-complete even when restricted to cases where all row and column sums are at most 3.

Notice, however, that this construction is *not* useful in practice, because it disguises the structure of A: It essentially *destroys* the minimum remaining values heuristic, because all columns whose sum is 2 look equally good to the solver!

35. Take a matrix with column sums $(c_1, \ldots, c_n)$, all ≤ 3, and extend it with three columns of 0s at the right. Then add the following four rows: $(x_1, \ldots, x_n, 0, 1, 1)$, $(y_1, \ldots, y_n, 1, 0, 1)$, $(z_1, \ldots, z_n, 1, 1, 0)$, and $(0, \ldots, 0, 1, 1, 1)$, where $x_j = [c_j < 3]$, $y_j = [c_j < 2]$, $z_j = [c_j < 1]$. The bottom row must be chosen in any solution.

36. The following modifications (which work also with Algorithm C) will find *all* solutions in lexicographic order; we can terminate early if we want only the first one.

Set $\text{LL} \leftarrow 0$ in step X1. (We will use the MRV heuristic, but only on levels $> \text{LL}$.)

If $\text{RLINK}(0) = 0$ and $l = \text{LL} + 1$ in step X2, visit the current solution as usual. Otherwise, however, set $\text{LL} \leftarrow \text{LL} + 1$ and do the following while $l > \text{LL}$ (because the current solution was not found lexicographically): Set $l \leftarrow l - 1$, $i \leftarrow \text{TOP}(x_l)$; uncover the items $\ne i$ in the option that contains x_l (as in X6); uncover i (as in X7).

In step X3, if $l = \text{LL}$ simply set $i \leftarrow \text{RLINK}(0)$. Otherwise use exercise 9, say.

If $l < \text{LL}$ after setting $l \leftarrow l - 1$ in step X8, set $\text{LL} \leftarrow l$.

To get the lexicographically smallest solution to the n queens problem, make sure that the first n items are $r_1, r_2, \ldots, r_n$. (The other primary items, c_j, can follow in *any* order.) The first solution for $n = 32$, found after 4.2 Gμ, has queens in columns 1, 3, 5, 2, 4, 9, 11, 13, 15, 6, 18, 24, 26, 30, 25, 31, 28, 32, 27, 29, 16, 19, 10, 8, 17, 12, 21, 7, 14, 23, 20, 22. (Without MRV the computation would have taken 35.6 Gμ.)

[The analogous problem for $n = 48$ is already quite difficult; that case was first solved by Wolfram Schubert. The best results currently known for large n have been obtained via sophisticated methods of integer programming: In November 2017, Matteo Fischetti and Domenico Salvagnin were the first to solve the case $n = 56$ and many larger cases, although $n = 62$ was still unsolved; see arXiv:1907.08246 [cs.DS] (2019), 14 pages. See also OEIS A141843 for the latest developments.]

37. (a) Let $a_{i,j} = 0$ if $i \leq 0$ or $j \leq 0$; otherwise

$$a_{i,j} = \text{mex}(\{a_{i,j-k} \mid k > 0\} \cup \{a_{i-k,j} \mid k > 0\} \cup \{a_{i-k,j-k} \mid k > 0\} \cup \{a_{i+k,j-k} \mid k > 0\})$$

where 'mex' is defined in exercise 7.1.3–8. It is not difficult to verify that $a_{i,q_i} = 1$ and that each of the sequences $\langle a_{i,n} \rangle$, $\langle a_{n,j} \rangle$ for $n \geq 1$ is a permutation of the positive integers. (See OEIS A065188 and Alec Jones's A269526.)

(b) The following exercise gives strong empirical evidence for this conjecture. And in the *full* plane, the analogous spiral sequence *can* be analyzed: See F. M. Dekking, J. Shallit, and N. J. A. Sloane, *Electronic J. Combinatorics* **27** (2020), #P1.52, 1–27.

38. The following method, inspired by Eq. 7.2.2–(6) and the previous exercise, uses binary vectors a, b, c, where c has both positive and negative subscripts.

G1. [Initialize.] Set $r \leftarrow 0$, $s \leftarrow 1$, $t \leftarrow 0$, $n \leftarrow 0$. (We've computed q_k for $1 \leq k \leq n$.)

G2. [Try for $q_n \leq n$.] (At this point $a_k = 1$ for $1 \leq k < s$ and $a_s = 0$; also $c_k = 1$ for $-r < k \leq t$ and $c_{-r} = c_{t+1} = 0$; each vector contains n 1s.) Set $n \leftarrow n+1$, $k \leftarrow s$.

G3. [Found?] If $k > n - r$ go to G4. Otherwise if $a_k = b_{k+n} = c_{k-n} = 0$, go to G5. Otherwise set $k \leftarrow k+1$ and repeat this step.

G4. [Make $q_n > n$.] Set $t \leftarrow t+1$, $q_n \leftarrow n+t$, $a_{n+t} \leftarrow b_{2n+t} \leftarrow c_t \leftarrow 1$, and return to G2.

G5. [Make $q_n \leq n$.] Set $q_n \leftarrow k$, $a_k \leftarrow b_{k+n} \leftarrow c_{k-n} \leftarrow 1$. If $k = s$, set $s \leftarrow s+1$ repeatedly until $a_s = 0$. If $k = n - r$, set $r \leftarrow r+1$ repeatedly until $c_{-r} = 0$. Return to G2. ∎

In step G2 we have $s \approx n - r \approx t \approx n/\phi$; hence the running time is extremely short. Empirically, in fact, the calculation of q_n requires at most 19 accesses to the bit vectors (averaging about 5.726 accesses), for each n. Agreement with exercise 37 is very close:

$$(q_{999999997}, \ldots, q_{1000000004}) = (618033989, 1618033985, 618033988,$$
$$1618033988, 1618033990, 1618033992, 1618033994, 618033991).$$

Moreover, it's likely that $q_n \in [n/\phi - 3 \mathinner{.\,.} n/\phi + 5] \cup [n\phi - 2 \mathinner{.\,.} n\phi + 1]$ for all n.

39. (a) With probability $(1 - p)^n$, no items will be selected; in such cases we must restart the clause generator, because options can't be empty. Ten random trials with $m = 500$, $n = 100$, and $p = .05$ gave respectively (444, 51, 138, 29, 0, 227, 26, 108, 2, 84) solutions, costing about 100 megamems per solution.

Although the exercise did not call for a mathematical analysis, we can derive a formula for the expected number of solutions by computing the probability that a given subset of the options is an exact cover, then summing over all subsets. If the subset has k items, and if each item in each option were present with probability p, this probability would be $(kp(1 - p)^{k-1})^n$. However, we've excluded empty options; the true probability $f(n, p, k)$ turns out to be $k!\{{n \atop k}\}(p(1-p)^{k-1})^n/(1 - (1-p)^n)^k$. The sum $\sum_k \binom{m}{k} f(n, p, k)$, when $(m, n, p) = (500, 100, .05)$, is approximately 3736.96 with the incorrect formula and 297.041 with the correct one.

[In unpublished notes, Robin Pemantle and Boris Pittel have independently derived asymptotic results for $m = an$ and $p = r/n$, for fixed a and r as $n \to \infty$. The behavior of Algorithm X with this random model is not easy to analyze, but an analysis may be within reach because of the recursive structure.]

(b) This case has completely different behavior. In the first place, n must obviously be a multiple of r. In the second place, we'll need more options to get even one solution when $n = 100$ and $r = 5$, because conveniently small options don't exist.

Proof: The total number of set partitions into twenty subsets of size 5 is $P = 100!/(20! \cdot 5!^{20}) \approx 10^{98}$; the total number of possible options is $N = \binom{100}{5} = 75287520$. The probability that any particular set partition occurs as a solution is the probability that twenty given options occur in a random sample of m, with replacement, namely $g(N, m, 20) = \sum_k \binom{20}{k}(-1)^k(N - k)^m/N^m = \sum_t \{{m \atop t}\}t!\binom{N-20}{t-20}/N^m$. If m isn't extremely large, this is almost the same as the probability without replacement, namely $\binom{N-20}{m-20}/\binom{N}{m} \approx (m/N)^{20}$. The expected number of solutions when $m = (500, 1000, 1500)$, respectively, is $P\,g(N, m, 20) \approx (.000002, 2.41, 8500)$.

40. Set $f_m \leftarrow 0$ and $f_{k-1} \leftarrow f_k \mid r_k$ for $m \geq k > 1$. The bits of u_k represent items that are being changed for the last time.

Let $u_k = u' + u''$, where $u' = u_k \,\&\, p$. If $u_k \neq 0$ at the beginning of step N4, we compress the database as follows: For $N \geq j \geq 1$, if $s_j \,\&\, u' \neq u'$, delete (s_j, c_j); otherwise if $s_j \,\&\, u'' \neq 0$, delete (s_j, c_j) and insert $((s_j \,\&\, \bar{u}_k) \mid u', c_j)$.

To delete (s_j, c_j), set $(s_j, c_j) \leftarrow (s_N, c_N)$ and $N \leftarrow N - 1$.

When this improved algorithm terminates in step N2, we always have $N \leq 1$. Furthermore, if we let $p_k = r_1 \mid \cdots \mid r_{k-1}$, the size of N never exceeds 2^{ν_k}, where $\nu_k = \nu\langle p_k r_k f_k\rangle$ is the size of the "frontier" (see exercise 7.1.4–55).

[In the special case of n queens, represented as an exact cover problem as in (23), this algorithm is due to I. Rivin, R. Zabih, and J. Lamping, *Inf. Proc. Letters* **41** (1992), 253–256. They proved that the frontier for n queens never has more than $3n$ items.]

41. The author has had reasonably good results using a triply linked binary search tree for the database, with randomized search keys. (Beware: The swapping algorithm used for deletion was difficult to get right.) This implementation was, however, limited to exact cover problems whose matrix has at most 64 columns; hence it could do n queens via (23) only when $n < 12$. When $n = 11$ its database reached a maximum size of 75,009, and its running time was about 25 megamems. But Algorithm X was noticeably better: It needed only about 12.5 Mμ to find all $Q(11) = 2680$ solutions.

In theory, this method will need only about 2^{3n} steps as $n \to \infty$, times a small polynomial function of n. A backtracking algorithm such as Algorithm X, which enumerates each solution explicitly, will probably run asymptotically slower (see exercise 7.2.2–15). But in practice, a breadth-first approach needs too much space.

On the other hand, this method did beat Algorithm X on the n queen bees problem of exercise 7.2.2–16: When $n = 11$ its database grew to 364,864 entries; it computed $H(11) = 596,483$ in just 30 Mμ, while Algorithm X needed 440 Mμ.

42. The set of solutions for s_j can be represented as a regular expression α_j instead of by its size, c_j. Instead of inserting $(s_j + t, c_j)$ in step N3, insert $\alpha_j k$. If inserting (s, α), when (s_i, α_i) is already present with $s_i = s$, change $\alpha_i \leftarrow \alpha_i \cup \alpha$. [Alternatively, if only one solution is desired, we could attach a single solution to each s_j in the database.]

43. Let $i = (i_1 i_0)_3$ and $j = (j_1 j_0)_3$; then cell (i, j) belongs to box $(i_1 j_1)_3$. Mathematically, it's cleaner to consider the matrices $a'_{ij} = a_{ij} - 1$, $b'_{ij} = b_{ij} - 1$, $c'_{ij} = c_{ij} - 1$, which are the "multiplication tables" of interesting binary operators on $\{0, \ldots, 8\}$. We have $a'_{ij} = ((i_0 i_1)_3 + j) \bmod 9$; $b'_{ij} = ((i_0 + j_1) \bmod 3, (i_1 + j_0) \bmod 3)_3$; and $c'_{ij} = ((i_0 + i_1 + j_1) \bmod 3, (i_0 - i_1 + j_0) \bmod 3)_3$. (Furthermore the latter two operators are "isotopic": $c'_{ij} = b'_{(i\pi)(j\pi-)}\pi$, when $(i_1, i_0)_3\pi = (i_1, (i_0 + i_1) \bmod 3)_3$.)

[A pattern like (28c) appeared in a Paris newspaper of 1895, in connection with magic squares. But no properties of its 3×3 subsquares were mentioned; it was a sudoku solution purely by coincidence. See C. Boyer, *Math. Intelligencer* **29**, 2 (2007), 63.]

44. No. The 33rd digit is 0. [A sudoku whose clues are π's first 32 digits was first constructed by Johan de Ruiter in 2007; see www.puzzlepicnic.com/puzzle?346. Furthermore, π's first 22 digits can actually be arranged *in a circle* to give a uniquely solvable sudoku, if we also require the elements of both main diagonals to be distinct! See Aad Thoen and Aad van de Wetering, *Exotische Sudoku's* (2016), 144.]

45. Step X3 chooses p_{44}, p_{84}, p_{74}, p_{24}, p_{54}, p_{14}, p_{82}, p_{42}, p_{31}, p_{32}, p_{40}, p_{45}, p_{46}, p_{50}, p_{72}, p_{60}, p_{00}, p_{62}, p_{61}, p_{65}, p_{35}, p_{67}, p_{70}, p_{71}, p_{75}, p_{83}, p_{13}, p_{03}, p_{18}, p_{16}, p_{07}, p_{01}, p_{05}, p_{15}, p_{21}, p_{25}, p_{76}, p_{36}, p_{33}, p_{37}, p_{27}, p_{28}, p_{53}, p_{56}, p_{06}, p_{08}, p_{58}, p_{77}, p_{88}, in that order.

46. The lists for items p_{44}, p_{84}, r_{33}, r_{44}, r_{48}, r_{52}, r_{59}, r_{86}, r_{88}, c_{22}, c_{43}, b_{07}, b_{32}, b_{39}, b_{43}, b_{54}, and b_{58} have length 1 when Algorithm X begins to tackle puzzle (29a). Step X3 will branch on whichever item was placed first in step X1. (The author's sudoku setup program puts p before r before c before b in that step.)

47. r_{13}, c_{03}, b_{03}, b_{24}, b_{49}, b_{69}. The latter three were hidden already in (32).

48. In case (a) we list the available columns; in case (b) we list the available rows:

(Notice that "hidden" singles and pairs, etc., become "naked" in this representation. Similar plots, which relate boxes to values, are also possible; but they're trickier, because boxes aren't orthogonal to rows or columns.)

49. (a) For columns, remove all items r_{ik} and b_{xk}, as well as c_{jk} with $j \neq j_0$; let $u_j \relbar v_k$ when an option contains '$p_{ij_0} c_{j_0 k}$'. For boxes, remove all r_{ik}, c_{jk}, and b_{xk} with $x \neq x_0$; let $u_j \relbar v_k$ when an option contains '$p_{(3\lfloor x_0/3 \rfloor + \lfloor j/3 \rfloor)(3(x \bmod 3) + (j \bmod 3))} b_{x_0 k}$'.

(b) The $n - q$ *non*-neighbors of a hidden q-tuple (e.g., $\{u_3, u_8, u_1\}$) are "naked."

(c) By (b) it suffices to list the naked ones (and only those for which $q < r$). Let's denote the option in (30) by ijk. In row 4 we find the naked pair $\{u_3, u_8\}$, hence we can delete options 411, 417, 421, 427, 471; also the naked triple $\{u_1, u_3, u_8\}$, so we can also delete option 424. There's no nakedness in the columns. The naked triple $\{u_0, u_3, u_6\}$ in box 4 allows deletion of options 341, 346, 347, 351, 356, 357.

(d) Let $u_i \relbar v_j$ if there's an option that contains '$r_{ik_0} c_{jk_0}$'. When $k_0 = 9$ there's a naked pair $\{u_1, u_5\}$, so we can delete options 079 and 279.

[Many other reductions have been proposed. For example, (33) has a "pointing pair" in box 4: Since '4' and '8' must occupy that box in row 3, we can remove options 314, 324, 328, 364, 368, 378. Classic references are the early tutorials by W. Gould, *The Times Su Doku Book 1* (2005); M. Mepham, *Solving Sudoku* (2005). A comprehensive theory, applicable also to many other problems, has been developed by D. Berthier, *Pattern-Based Constraint Satisfaction and Logic Puzzles* (2012).]

50. Such a puzzle must add a 7 or 8 in one of 18 places, because (29c) has just 2 solutions. So there are 36 of them (18 isomorphic pairs).

```
9 3 4 5 1 7     6
7 6 2 4 9 3 1 7 5
7 5 1 7     4 9 3
2 7 5 9 7 1 6 3 4
6 4 9     3 5   1
1 7 3       5   9
4 1 7 6 5 9 3
3 2 7 1     9 5 6
5 9 6 3     7 4 1
```

51. We can solve this problem with Algorithm M, using options (30) with $k \neq 8$ and giving multiplicity 2 to each of the items r_{i7}, c_{j7}, b_{x7}. There are six solutions, all of which extend the partial solution shown. Only one yields a sudoku square when we change half of the 7s to 8s.

52. (Solution by F. Stappers.) Puzzles claiming to be "the world's hardest sudoku" keep appearing in online forums. Rated by search tree size with Algorithm X, the toughest among nearly 27,000 such extreme puzzles is shown here in a canonical form. (It's number 6539 in a list available from sites.google.com/site/sudoeleven/ (2011).) Its randomized search tree sizes are 24400 ± 1900 — astonishingly high for sudoku; and its mean running time is about 12 Mμ.)

```
1 2   3     4
5     4     1
      2       6
7
      7       3 1
        5 4 7
4     5     3
8
  9   4
```

53. (a) Every shidoku solution is equivalent to one of the two special solutions A or B below (which incidentally have respectively 32 and 16 automorphisms, in the sense of exercise 114). We can't uniquely specify either solution unless we have at least one clue in each of the regions $\{A, B, C, D\}$ of C.

$$A = \begin{array}{|c|c|c|c|}\hline 1&2&3&4\\\hline 3&4&1&2\\\hline 2&1&4&3\\\hline 4&3&2&1\\\hline\end{array}, \qquad B = \begin{array}{|c|c|c|c|}\hline 1&2&3&4\\\hline 3&4&2&1\\\hline 2&1&4&3\\\hline 4&3&1&2\\\hline\end{array}, \qquad C = \begin{array}{|c|c|c|c|}\hline A&A&B&B\\\hline C&C&D&D\\\hline A&A&B&B\\\hline C&C&D&D\\\hline\end{array}.$$

(b) Only $4^4 = 256$ sets of four clues meet the conditions of (a), for each of A and B; we can test them all. Reducing by the automorphisms leaves two for A and eleven for B:

(There also are 22 essentially different shidoku puzzles with five irredundant clues, and a unique puzzle with six. The latter, which is solved by A, is shown above at the bottom left; it cannot omit a clue without having an empty region in either C or C^T. These results were discovered by Ed Russell in 2006.)

54. For example, removing clues one at a time shows that only 10 of the 32 givens are actually essential. The best strategy for finding all minimal X is probably to examine candidate sets in order of decreasing cardinality: Suppose $W \subseteq X$, and suppose that previous tests have shown that the solution is unique, given X, but not given $X \setminus w$ for any $w \in W$. Thus X is minimal if $W = X$. Otherwise let $X \setminus W = \{x_1, \ldots, x_t\}$, and test $X \setminus x_i$ for each i. Suppose the solution turns out to be unique if and only if $i > p$. Then we schedule the $t - p$ candidate pairs $(W \cup \{x_1, \ldots, x_p\}, X \setminus x_i)$, $p < i \leq t$, for processing in the next round. With suitable caching of previous results, we can avoid testing the same subset of clues more than once. Furthermore we can readily modify Algorithm X so that it backtracks immediately after discovering a single unwanted solution.

All 777 minimal subsets were found in this manner, involving 15441 invocations of Algorithm X, but needing a total of only about 1.5 gigamems of computation. Altogether (1, 22, 200, 978, 2780, 4609, 4249, 1950, 373, 22) candidate pairs were examined in rounds (32, 31, ..., 23); and exactly (8, 154, 387, 206, 22) solutions were found of sizes $(27, 26, 25, 24, 23)$. The lexicographically last 23-clue subset, which is illustrated below, turns out to be a fairly tough puzzle, with 220 nodes in its search tree.

(Let $f(x_1, \ldots, x_{32})$ be the monotone Boolean function '[the solution is unique, given the clues with $x_j = 1$]'. This problem essentially asks for f's prime implicants.)

(29a)
```
. . . 1 . . . . .
4 1 . . . 9 . . .
. 6 5 . . . . . .
5 . . 8 . . 9 . .
. 7 . . . . 3 2 .
. 3 8 . 4 . . . .
. . 2 6 . 4 . . .
. . . 3 . . . . .
3 . . . . 7 . 5 .
```
; (28a)
```
1 2 3 . . . . . .
. . . 7 8 9 . . .
. . . . . . . . .
2 3 4 . . . . . .
. . . . . . 5 6 7
. . . . 5 6 7 . .
. . . . . . . . .
. . . . . . . . .
9 1 . . . . . . 8
```
; (28b)
```
1 . . . . . 6 . 8
. 5 . . . . . 1 .
. . . 9 . . . 4 .
3 . 5 . . . . . 7
. . . . . . 9 . .
8 . . . . . 1 . .
. . . . . . . 7 .
6 4 . . . . 8 . 2
. . 3 . . . . . 5
```
.

55. If only one of those nine appearances has been specified, the other eight can always be permuted into another solution. And the entire diagram can be partitioned into nine disjoint sets of nine, all with the same property, thus requiring at least $2 \cdot 9$ clues.

This argument proves that all 18-clue characterizations must have a very special form. The interesting solution above makes a particularly satisfying puzzle. (The author found it with the help of a SAT solver; see Section 7.2.2.2.)

The same argument shows that (28b) needs at least 18 clues. But this time the corresponding SAT instance is unsatisfiable. Moreover, any 19-clue solution must have three clues in just one critical group of nine; the associated SAT instance, which insists on having at least one clue in each of the 2043 subsets of at most 18 cells that can be rearranged into new solutions, also is unsatisfiable. (Proved in 177 Mμ.) But hurrah, the special structure does lead to 20-clue examples, like the one above.

(The constructions for (28b) apply also to (28c), via the isotopism in answer 43.)

56. (We assume that a decent sudoku problem has only one solution.) An example with 40 irredundant clues, shown here, was first discovered by Mladen Dobrichev in 2014, after examining a huge number of cases. (Incidentally, the solution to this problem has no automorphisms.) An example with 41 irredundant clues would be a big surprise.
```
1 2 . 3 4 5 6 7 .
3 4 5 . . 6 1 8 2
. 1 . 5 8 2 . . 6
. 8 6 . . . . . 1
. 2 . . . 7 . . 5
. 3 7 . . 5 . 2 8
. 8 . . . 6 . 7 .
. . . . . . . . .
2 . 7 . 8 3 6 1 5
```

57. There are only $2 \cdot 3! \cdot 3! \cdot 3! \cdot 3! = 2592$ possibilities for each box. So we can set up an exact cover problem with $9 \cdot 2592$ options, each of which names a box, nine row-column pairs, three horizontal trios, and three vertical trios. We can assume by symmetry that there's only one option for box 0, namely 'b_0 r_{01} c_{01} r_{04} c_{14} r_{07} c_{27} r_{18} c_{08} r_{12} c_{12} r_{15} c_{25} r_{26} c_{06} r_{29} c_{19} r_{23} c_{23} h_{147} h_{258} h_{369} v_{168} v_{249} v_{357}'. Furthermore row 0 can be restricted to $\mathtt{1472AB3CD}$, where $\{\mathtt{A}, \mathtt{C}\} = \{5, 6\}$ and $\{\mathtt{B}, \mathtt{D}\} = \{8, 9\}$. That reduces the number of options to 16417; and Algorithm X quickly $((58+54)\mathrm{M}\mu)$ finds 864 solutions.

Such solutions were first discovered by A. Thoen and A. van de Wetering; see Thoen's book *Sudoku Patterns* (2019), §2.7. All 864 are isomorphic under sudoku-solution-preserving permutations of rows and columns. One of the nicest is

```
1 4 7 2 5 9 3 6 8
8 2 5 7 3 6 9 1 4
6 9 3 4 8 1 5 7 2
2 6 9 3 4 8 1 5 7
7 3 4 9 1 5 8 2 6
5 8 1 6 7 2 4 9 3
3 5 8 1 6 7 2 4 9
9 1 6 8 2 4 7 3 5
4 7 2 5 9 3 6 8 1
```
,

which has a remarkable inner symmetry between diagonally adjacent boxes:

58. Use the standard 729 sudoku options (30); but also include queen items '$a'_{(i+j)k}$ $b'_{(i-j)k}$' in option (i, j, k) when $k \leq 7$. Furthermore, in order to avoid getting each solution $7! \, 2! = 10080$ times, force row 0 by adding a new primary item '$*$' and new secondary items '$*_j$' for $0 \leq j < 9$, together with 20 options '$* \; *_0{:}f(0, p, q) \cdots *_8{:}f(8, p, q)$' for $0 \leq p < q < 9$, $p + q < 9$, where $f(j, p, q) = (j = p?\; 8{:}\; j = q?\; 9{:}\; 1 + j - [j > p] - [j > q])$. Include '$*_j{:}k$' in option $(0, j, k)$. There are only four solutions, found in 3 Gμ, centrally symmetric and reducing under transposition to only two. (See Appendix E, and Thoen's book *Sudoku Patterns* (2019), §3.4.)

59. When ps precede rs precede cs precede bs in X1, the tree sizes are 1105, 910, 122.

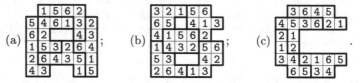

(34a); (34b); (34c).

60. Using the options (30), items r_{ik} and c_{jk} should be *secondary* when row i or column j contains fewer than 6 cells. The puzzles are fun to solve by hand; but in a pinch, Algorithm X will traverse search trees of sizes 23, 26, and 16 to find the answers:

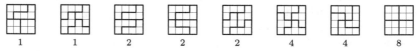

(a); (b); (c).

[These are the first of 26 elegant puzzles announced by Serhiy and Peter Grabarchuk on Martin Gardner's 100th birthday (21 October 2014) and posted at puzzlium.com.]

61. Exactly 1315 of the $\binom{25}{5} = 53130$ ways to retain five clues result in a unique solution, and 175 of them involve all five digits. The lexicographically first is Fig. A–2(a).

62. Follow the hint; the undesired *straight* n-ominoes can be rejected easily in step R2 by examining v_{n-1} and v_0. This quickly produces (16, 105, 561, 2804, 13602) box options, for $n = (3, 4, 5, 6, 7)$, which can be fed to Algorithm X to get jigsaw patterns.

There are no patterns for $n = 3$. But $n = 4$ has 33 patterns, which divide into eight equivalence classes under rotation and/or reflection:

1	1	2	2	2	4	4	8

(The number of symmetries is shown below each arrangement; notice that $8/1 + 8/1 + 8/2 + 8/2 + 8/2 + 8/4 + 8/4 + 8/8 = 33$.) Similarly, $n = 5$ has 266 equivalence classes, representing $256 \cdot (8/1) + 7 \cdot (8/2) + 3 \cdot (8/4) = 2082$ total patterns; $n = 6$ has 40237 classes, representing $39791 \cdot (8/1) + 439 \cdot (8/2) + 7 \cdot (8/4) = 320098$ patterns in all.

The computation gets more serious in the case $n = 7$, when Algorithm X needs about 1.9 Tμ to generate the 132,418,528 jigsaw patterns. These patterns include 16,550,986 classes with no symmetry, and 2660 with one nontrivial symmetry. The latter break down into 2265 that are symmetric under 180° rotation, 354 that are symmetric under horizontal reflection, and 41 that are symmetric under diagonal reflection. Here are some typical symmetric examples:

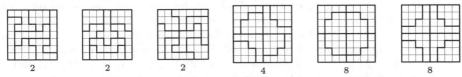

(It's not difficult to generate all of the *symmetric* solutions for slightly higher values of n; three of the classes for $n = 8$, shown above, have more than 2 symmetries. And the case $n = 9$ contains two patterns with 8-fold symmetry *besides* the standard sudoku boxes: See Fig. A–2(b) and (c), where the latter might be called windmill sudoku! For complete counts for $n = 8$ and $n = 9$, with straight n-ominoes allowed, see Bob Harris's preprint "Counting nonomino tilings," presented at G4G9 in 2010.)

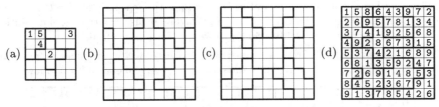

Fig. A–2. Jigsaw sudoku patterns.

63. A simple modification of exercise 7.2.2–76 will generate the 3173 boxes that have the desired rainbow property. An exact cover problem, given those 3173 options, shows (after 1.2 Gμ of computation) that the boxes can be packed in 98556 ways. If we restrict the options to the 3164 that aren't sudoku boxes, the number of packings goes down to 42669, of which 24533 are faultfree. Figure A–2(d) is a faultfree example.

64. (a) When $n = 4$, one of the eight classes in answer 62 (the 2nd) has *no* solutions; another (the 5th) is clueless. When $n = 5$, eight of the 266 classes have no solution; six are clueless. When $n = 6$, 1966 of 40237 are vacuous and 28 are clueless.

(Maxime's original puzzle appeared in the newsletter of Chicago Area Mensa [*ChiMe* **MM**, 3 (March 2000), 15]. Algorithm X solves it with a 40-node search tree. But the tree size would have been 215 if he'd put `ABCDEF` in the next row down!)

(b) (Solution by Bob Harris, `www.bumblebeagle.org/dusumoh/proof/`, 2006.) The clueless jigsaw for $n = 4$ generalizes to all larger n, as illustrated here for $n = 7$: First $a = 3$; hence $b = 3$; ...; hence $f = 3$. Then $g = 4$; hence $h = 4$; ...; hence $l = 4$. And so on. Finally we know where to place the 2's and the 1's. (This proof shows that, for odd $n > 3$, there's always an $n \times n$ jigsaw sudoku whose clues lie entirely on the main diagonal. Is there also a general construction that works for *even* values of n? An 8×8 example appears in exercise 65.)

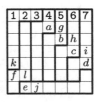

65. (The author designed these puzzles with the aid of exercises 62 and 64. Similar puzzles have been contrived by J. Henle, *Math. Intelligencer* **38**, 1 (2016), 76–77.)

66. (Puzzles like this might be too difficult for humans, but not for Algorithm C.) Extend the 729 options (30) by adding '$ij{:}k$', where ij is a new secondary item for $0 \le i,j < 9$. Also add eighteen new primary items k for $1 \le k \le 9$ and s_j for $0 \le j < 9$, where k represents card k and s_j represents a slot in the $3{\times}3$ array. Each item k has nine options, for the nine slots in which it might be placed; for example, the options for item 2 are '2 s_0 00:2 11:3 22:4 20:1', '2 s_1 03:2 14:3 25:4 23:1', ..., '2 s_8 66:2 77:3 88:4 86:1'.

There are 9! ways to place the cards in slots; but only $9!/(3!\,3!) = 10080$ are actually different, because the rows and columns can be permuted independently without changing the number of sudoku solutions. Suppose card c_j goes into slot s_j; then we can assume without loss of generality that $c_0 = 1$ and that $c_4 = \min(c_4, c_5, c_7, c_8)$. (To incorporate these constraints, give only one option for card 1 and only eight options for cards 2–9; use ordering tricks like (26) to ensure that $c_4 < c_5$, $c_4 < c_7$, $c_4 < c_8$.)

With this understanding, puzzle (i) has only one solution, and only when $c_0 \ldots c_8 = 192435768$. (That solution has six automorphisms, in the sense of exercise 114.) Puzzle (ii) has a unique solution when $c_0 \ldots c_8 = 149523786$. It also has ten sudoku solutions when the slot permutation is 149325687; so we can't use *that* placement.

67. (a) (Solution by A. E. Brouwer, `homepages.cwi.nl/~aeb/games/sudoku/nrc.html`, 2006.) The four new boxes force also aaaaaaaaa, ..., eeeeeeeee to be rainbows.

e	a	a	a	e	b	b	b	e
c				c				c
c				c				c
c				c				c
e	a	a	a	e	b	b	b	e
d				d				d
d				d				d
d				d				d
e	a	a	a	e	b	b	b	e

(i)

3	2	7	1	5	4	8	6	9
6	1	5	8	2	9	4	7	3
8	9	4	3	7	6	2	1	5
9	6	2	7	1	5	3	8	4
7	4	3	9	8	2	1	5	6
5	8	1	4	6	3	7	9	2
1	3	6	2	9	8	5	4	7
4	7	9	5	3	1	6	2	8
2	5	8	6	4	7	9	3	1

(ii)

3	1	6	8	9	4	7	2	5
5	7	8	3	2	6	4	1	9
4	2	9	5	1	7	3	8	6
7	4	1	6	3	9	2	5	8
2	9	5	7	8	1	6	3	4
8	6	3	4	5	2	9	7	1
9	8	7	1	4	3	5	6	2
6	5	2	9	7	8	1	4	3
1	3	4	2	6	5	8	9	7

(b) Introduce new primary items b'_{yk} for $0 \le y < 9$ and $1 \le k \le 9$. Add b'_{yk} to option (30) with $y = 3\lfloor i\tau/3 \rfloor + \lfloor j\tau/3 \rfloor$, where τ is the permutation (03)(12)(58)(67).

(c) With items b'_{yk} only considered for $y \in \{0,2,6,8\}$, Algorithm X's search tree grows from 77 nodes to 231 for (i), and from 151 nodes to 708 for (ii).

[Puzzle (ii) is a variant of an 11-clue example constructed by Brouwer. The minimum number of clues necessary for hypersudoku is unknown.]

(d) True. (That's the permutation τ in (b), applied to both rows and columns.)

68. (a) A simple backtrack program generates all convex n-ominoes whose top cell(s) are in row 0 and whose leftmost cell(s) are in column 0. [This problem has respectively (1, 2, 6, 19, 59, 176, 502) solutions for $1 \le n \le 7$; see M. Bousquet-Mélou and J.-M. Fédou, *Discrete Math.* **137** (1995), 53–75, for the generating function.] The resulting (1, 4, 22, 113, 523, 2196, 8438) placements into an $n \times n$ box yield exact cover problems as in answer 62. Considering symmetries, we find $1 \cdot (8/4) = 2$ patterns when $n = 2$; $1{\cdot}(8/1)+1{\cdot}(8/4) = 10$ patterns when $n = 3$; $10{\cdot}(8/1)+7{\cdot}(8/2)+4{\cdot}(8/4)+1{\cdot}(8/8) = 117$ when $n = 4$; $355{\cdot}(8/1)+15{\cdot}(8/2)+4{\cdot}(8/4) = 2908$ when $n = 5$; $20154{\cdot}(8/1)+342{\cdot}(8/2)+8 \cdot (8/4) = 162616$ when $n = 6$; $2272821 \cdot (8/1)+1181 \cdot (8/2)+5 \cdot (8/4) = 18187302$ when $n = 7$. (Exercise 62 had different results because it disallowed straight n-ominoes.)

(b) There are 325 such nonominoes touching row 0 and column 0, leading to 12097 placements and $1014148 \cdot (8/1) + 119 \cdot (8/2) + 24 \cdot (8/4) + 1 \cdot (8/8) = 8113709$ patterns. If we exclude the 3×3 nonomino, and its 49 placements, the number of patterns goes down to $675797 \cdot (8/1) = 5406376$.

[Convex polyominoes were introduced by Klarner and Rivest; see answer 303.]

69. Say that an "N_k" is a suitable nonomino placement that has k Bs and $9 - k$ Ls. Only two cases give seven wins for B: 1 N_6, 6 N_5, 2 N_0; 7 N_5, 1 N_1, 1 N_0. With the given voting pattern there are respectively (1467, 2362, 163, 2) options for N_6, N_5, N_1, N_0. Algorithm M provides the desired multiplicities. After 12 Mμ of computation we find that there are no solutions in case 1 but 60 solutions in case 2, one of which is shown.

(Of course the author does not recommend secret deals such as this! The point is that unfair gerrymandering is easy to do and hard to detect. Indeed, a trial of 1000 random voter patterns, each with 5/4 split in the nine standard 3×3 districts, included 696 cases that could be gerrymandered to seven Big-Endian districts using only convex nonominoes that fit in a 5×5. Eight of those cases could also achieve a 4×4 fit.)

[Similar studies, using realistic data, go back to R. S. Garfinkel's Ph.D. thesis *Optimal Political Districting* (Baltimore: Johns Hopkins University, 1968).]

70. In (a), four pieces change; in (b) the solution is unique:

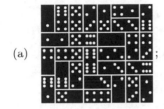 ;  .

(a) (b)

Notice that the spot patterns ⠃, ⠆, and ⣿ are rotated when a domino is placed vertically; these visual clues, which would disambiguate (a), don't show up in the matrix.

(Dominosa was invented by O. S. Adler [Reichs Patent #71539 (1893); see his booklet *Sperr-Domino und Dominosa* (1912), 23–64, written with F. Jahn]. Similar "quadrille" problems had been studied earlier by E. Lucas and H. Delannoy. See Lucas's *Récréations Mathématiques* **2** (1883), 52–63; W. E. Philpott, *JRM* **4** (1971), 229–243.)

71. Define 28 vertices Dxy for $0 \le x \le y \le 6$; 28 vertices ij for $0 \le i < 7$, $0 \le j < 8$, and $i + j$ even; and 28 similar vertices ij with $i + j$ odd. The matching problem has 49 triples of the form $\{Dxy, ij, i(j+1)\}$ for $0 \le i, j < 7$, as well as 48 of the form $\{Dxy, ij, (i+1)j\}$ for $0 \le i < 6$ and $0 \le j < 8$, corresponding to potential horizontal or vertical placements. For example, the triples for exercise 70(a) are $\{D06, 00, 01\}$, $\{D56, 01, 02\}$, ..., $\{D23, 66, 67\}$; $\{D01, 00, 10\}$, $\{D46, 01, 11\}$, ..., $\{D12, 57, 67\}$.

72. Model (i) has $M = 56!/8!^7 \approx 4.10 \times 10^{42}$ equally likely possibilities; model (ii) has $N = 1292697 \cdot 28! \cdot 2^{21} \approx 8.27 \times 10^{41}$, because there are 1292697 ways to pack 28 dominoes in a 7×8 frame. (Algorithm X will quickly list them all.) The expected number of solutions per trial in model (i) is therefore $N/M \approx 0.201$.

Ten thousand random trials with model (i) gave 216 cases with at least one solution, including 26 where the solution was unique. The total number $\sum x$ of solutions was 2256; and $\sum x^2 = 95918$ indicated a heavy-tailed distribution whose empirical standard deviation is ≈ 3.1. The total running time was about 250 Mμ.

Ten thousand random trials with model (ii), using random choices from a precomputed list of 1292697 packings, gave 106 cases with a unique solution; one case had 2652 of them! Here $\sum x = 508506$ and $\sum x^2 = 144119964$ indicated an empirical mean of ≈ 51 solutions per trial, with standard deviation ≈ 109. Total time was about 650 Mμ.

73. From 66110144/26611514/52132140/55322200/53242006/36430565/33643054 we get 730,924 solutions, which is the current record. This array, found by Michael Keller in 2004, has the surprising property that *every* candidate placement, except for the '21' in '521', occurs in at least one solution. (In fact, in at least 31,370 solutions!)

74. One way to obtain candidate arrays is to formulate an MCC problem: Given one of the 1292697 matchings of answer 72, let there be options 'P_{uv} xy $t_u{:}x$ $t_v{:}y$', 'P_{uv} xy $t_u{:}y$ $t_v{:}x$' for uv in the matching, and 'Q_{uv} D_{xy} $t_u{:}x$ $t_v{:}y$', 'Q_{uv} D_{xy} $t_u{:}y$ $t_v{:}x$' for uv not in the matching; here $0 \le x \le y \le 6$, and duplicate options are omitted when $x = y$. Give each D_{xy} multiplicity 3. Also add 28 further options '# D_{xy}', where # has multiplicity 15 (because 15 pairs xy should have only two spurious appearances).

For fun, the author chose a *tatami tiling* for the matching (see exercise 7.1.4–215), and obtained one candidate every 70 Mμ or so when the nonsharp variant of Algorithm M was applied with randomization as in exercise 31. Surprisingly, the first 10000 candidates yielded 2731 solutions, of which the hardest (with a 572-node search tree) was 15133034/21446115/22056105/65460423/22465553/61102332/63600044.

[See www.solitairelaboratory.com/puzzlelaboratory/DominoGG.html.]

75. (a) $(x \circ y) \circ x = (x \circ y) \circ (y \circ (x \circ y)) = y$.

(b) All five are legitimate. (The last two are gropes because $f(t + f(t)) = t$ for $0 \le t < 4$ in each case; they are isomorphic if we interchange any two elements. The third is isomorphic to the second if we interchange $1 \leftrightarrow 2$. There are 18 grope tables of order 4, of which (4, 12, 2) are isomorphic to the first, third, and last tables shown here.)

(c) For example, let $x \circ y = (-x - y) \bmod n$. (More generally, if G is any group and if $\alpha \in G$ satisfies $\alpha^2 = 1$, we can let $x \circ y = \alpha x^- \alpha y^- \alpha$. If G is commutative and $\alpha \in G$ is arbitrary, we can let $x \circ y = x^- y^- \alpha$.)

(d) For each option of type (i) in an exact covering, define $x \circ x = x$; for each of type (ii), define $x \circ x = y$, $x \circ y = y \circ x = x$; for each of type (iii), define $x \circ y = z$, $y \circ z = x$, $z \circ x = y$. Conversely, every grope table yields an exact covering in this way.

(e) Such a grope covers n^2 items with k options of size 1, all other options of size 3. [F. E. Bennett proved, in *Discrete Mathematics* **24** (1978), 139–146, that such gropes exist for *all* k with $0 \le k \le n$ and $k \equiv n^2$ (modulo 3), except when $k = n = 6$.]

Notes: The identity $x \circ (y \circ x) = y$ seems to have first been considered by E. Schröder in *Math. Annalen* **10** (1876), 289–317 [see '(C_0)' on page 306], but he didn't do much with it. In a class for sophomore mathematics majors at Caltech in 1968, the author defined gropes and asked the students to discover and prove as many theorems about them as they could, by analogy with the theory of groups. The idea was to "grope for results." The official modern term for a grope is a real jawbreaker: *semisymmetric quasigroup*.

76. (a) Eliminate the n items for xx; use only the $2\binom{n}{3}$ options of type (iii) for which $y \ne z$. (Idempotent gropes are equivalent to "Mendelsohn triples," which are families of $n(n - 1)/3$ three-cycles (xyz) that include every ordered pair of distinct elements. N. S. Mendelsohn proved [*Computers in Number Theory* (New York: Academic Press, 1971), 323–338] that such systems exist for all $n \not\equiv 2$ (modulo 3), except when $n = 6$.

(b) Use only the $\binom{n+1}{2}$ items xy for $0 \le x \le y < n$; replace options of type (ii) by 'xx xy' and 'xy yy' for $0 \le x < y < n$; replace those of type (iii) by 'xy xz yz' for $0 \le x < y < z < n$. (Such systems, Schröder's '(C_1) and (C_2)', are called totally symmetric quasigroups; see S. K. Stein, *Trans. Amer. Math. Soc.* **85** (1957), 228–256, §8. If idempotent, they're equivalent to Steiner triple systems.)

(c) Omit items for which $x = 0$ or $y = 0$. Use only the $2\binom{n-1}{3}$ options of type (iii) for $1 \le x < y, z < n$ and $y \ne z$. (Indeed, such systems are equivalent to idempotent gropes on the elements $\{1, \ldots, n - 1\}$.)

77. Use primary items v and v' for each vertex of G and H; also secondary items ee' for each pair of edges e and e' in G and the *complement* of H. There are n^2 options, namely '$v\ v'\ \bigcup_{e(v),e'(v')} e(v)e'(v')$', where $e(v)$ ranges over all edges $v \!-\! u$ in G and $e'(v')$ ranges over all nonedges $v' \!\not\!-\! u'$ in H. (The solutions to this problem are the one-to-one matchings $v \longleftrightarrow v'$ of the vertices such that $u \!-\! v$ implies $u' \!-\! v'$.)

78. For example, CATALANDAUBOREL, GRAMARKOFFKNOPP, ABELWEIERSTRASS, BERTRAND-HERMITE, CANTORFROBENIUS, GLAISHERHURWITZ, HADAMARDHILBERT, HENSELKIRCHHOFF, JENSENSYLVESTER, MELLINSTIELTJES, NETTORUNGESTERN, MINKOWSKIPERRON.

79. In an $n \times n$ array for word search, every k-letter word generates $(n+1-k) \cdot n \cdot 4$ horizontal/vertical options and $(n+1-k)^2 \cdot 4$ diagonal options. So the desired answer is $(2, 5, 6, 5, 3, 5, 0, 1) \cdot (1296, 1144, 1000, 864, 736, 616, 504, 400) = 24320$.

80. Item q is selected at level 0, trying option $x_0 = 8$, 'q x y:A p'. We cover q, then cover x, then purify y to color A, and cover p; but at level 1 we find that item r's list is empty. So we backtrack: Uncover p, unpurify y, uncover x — and try option $x_0 = 20$, 'q x:A', hence purifying x to color A. This time at level 1 we try $x_1 = 12$, 'p r x:A y'. That causes us to cover p, then cover r, and then (since x is already purified) to cover y. At level 2 we discover that we've found a solution! Here's what's in memory:

i:	0	1	2	3	4	5	6
NAME(i):	—	p	q	r	x	y	—
LLINK(i):	0	0	1	0	6	4	4
RLINK(i):	0	3	3	0	6	6	4

x:	0	1	2	3	4	5	6
LEN(x), TOP(x):	—	1	2	1	2	0	0
ULINK(x):	—	12	20	23	18	5	—
DLINK(x):	—	12	8	23	14	5	10
COLOR(x):	—	—	—	—	—	—	0

x:	7	8	9	10	11	12	13
TOP(x):	1	2	4	5	−1	1	3
ULINK(x):	1	2	4	5	7	1	3
DLINK(x):	12	20	14	15	15	1	23
COLOR(x):	0	0	0	A	0	0	0

x:	14	15	16	17	18	19	20
TOP(x):	4	5	−2	1	4	−3	2
ULINK(x):	4	5	12	12	14	17	8
DLINK(x):	18	24	18	1	4	21	2
COLOR(x):	−1	0	0	0	0	B	0

x:	21	22	23	24	25		
TOP(x):	4	−4	3	5	−5		
ULINK(x):	18	20	3	5	23		
DLINK(x):	4	24	3	5	—		
COLOR(x):	A	0	0	B	0		

81. Almost true, if TOP and COLOR are stored in the same octabyte (so that only one is charged to read both). The only difference is when processing the input, because Algorithm X has no COLOR fields to initialize but Algorithm C zeroes them out.

82. True; the LEN field of secondary items doesn't affect the computation.

83. Before setting $i \leftarrow$ TOP(x_0) in step C6 when $l = 0$, let node x be the spacer at the right of x_0's option, and set $j \leftarrow$ TOP($x - 1$). If $j > N_1$ (that is, if x_0's option ends with the secondary item j), and if COLOR($x - 1$) = 0, cover(j).

84. Let CUTOFF (initially ∞) point to the spacer at the end of the best solution found so far. We'll essentially remove all nodes $>$ CUTOFF from further consideration.

Whenever a solution is found, let node PP be the spacer at the end of the option for which $x_k = \max(x_0, \ldots, x_{l-1})$. If PP $\neq$ CUTOFF, set CUTOFF $\leftarrow$ PP, and for $0 \leq k < l$ remove all nodes $>$ CUTOFF from the list for TOP(x_k). (It's easy to do this because the list is sorted.) Minimax solutions follow the last change to CUTOFF.

Begin the subroutine 'uncover'(i)' by removing all nodes $>$ CUTOFF from item i's list. After setting $d \leftarrow$ DLINK(q) in unhide'(p), set DLINK(q) $\leftarrow d \leftarrow x$ if $d >$ CUTOFF. Make the same modifications also to the subroutine 'unpurify(p)'.

Subtle point: Suppose we're uncovering item i and encounter an option 'i j $\ldots$' that should be restored to the list of item j; and suppose that the original successor 'j a $\ldots$' of that option for item j lies below the cutoff. We know that 'j a $\ldots$' contains at least one primary item, and that every primary item was covered before we changed the cutoff. Hence 'j a $\ldots$' was *not* restored, and we needn't worry about removing it. We merely need to correct the DLINK, as stated above.

85. Now let CUTOFF be the spacer just *before* the best solution known. When resetting CUTOFF, backtrack to level $k - 1$, where x_k maximizes $\{x_0, \ldots, x_{l-1}\}$.

86. The steps below also estimate the profile of the search tree. Running time is estimated in terms of "updates" and "cleansings." The user specifies a random seed and a desired number of trials; the final estimates are the averages of the (unbiased) estimates from each trial. Here we specify only how to make a single trial.

In step C1, also set $D \leftarrow 1$.

In step C2, estimate that the search tree has D nodes at level l. If RLINK(0) $= 0$, also estimate that there are D solutions.

In step C3, let θ be the number of options in the list of the chosen item i. If $\theta = 0$, estimate that there are 0 solutions, and go to C7.

At the end of step C4, let k be uniformly random in $[0 .. \theta - 1]$; then set $x_l \leftarrow$ DLINK(x_l), k times.

Just before setting $l \leftarrow l + 1$ at the end of step C5, suppose you've just done U updates and C cleansings. (An "update" occurs when 'cover' sets LLINK(r) or 'hide' sets ULINK(d). A "cleansing" occurs when 'commit' calls 'purify' or 'purify' sets COLOR(q) $\leftarrow -1$.) Estimate that level l does $D(U' + \theta \cdot U)$ updates and DC cleansings, where U' is the number of updates just done in step C4. Then set $D \leftarrow \theta \cdot D$.

Step C6 now should do absolutely nothing. Steps C7 and C8 don't change.

Upon termination, all data structures will have been returned to their original state, ready for another random trial. These steps will have estimated the number of nodes, updates, and cleansings at each level. Sum those estimates to get the *total* estimated number of nodes, updates, and cleansings.

87. Use $2n$ primary items a_i, d_j for the "across" and "down" words, together with n^2 secondary items ij for the individual cells. Also use W secondary items w, one for each legal word. The XCC problem has $2Wn$ options, namely 'a_i $i1{:}c_1 \ldots in{:}c_n$ $c_1 \ldots c_n$' and 'd_j $1j{:}c_1 \ldots nj{:}c_n$ $c_1 \ldots c_n$' for $1 \leq i, j \leq n$ and each legal word $c_1 \ldots c_n$. (See (110).)

We can avoid having both a solution and its transpose by introducing W further secondary items $w@$ and appending $c_1 \ldots c_n@$ at the right of each option for a_1 and d_1. Then exercise 83's variant of Algorithm C will never choose a word for d_1 that it has already tried for a_1. (Think about it.)

But this construction is *not* a win for "dancing links," because it causes massive amounts of data to go in and out of the active structure. For example, with the five-letter words of WORDS(5757), it correctly finds all 323,264 of the double word squares, but its running time is 15 *tera*mems! Much faster is to use the algorithm of exercise

7.2.2–28, which needs only 46 gigamems to discover all of the 1,787,056 unrestricted word squares; the double word squares are easily identified among those solutions.

88. One could do a binary search, trying varying values of W. But the best way is to use the construction of exercise 87 together with the minimax variant of Algorithm C in exercise 84. This works perfectly, when the options for most common words come first.

Indeed, this method finds the double square 'BLAST|EARTH|ANGER|SCOPE|TENSE' and proves it best in just 64 Gμ, almost as fast as the specialized method of exercise 7.2.2–28. (That square contains ARGON, the 1720th most common five-letter word, in its third column; the next-best squares use PEERS, which has rank 1800.)

89. The "minimax" method of exercise 88 finds the first five squares of

```
                                  CHESTS   HERTZES
                 SHOW    START     LUSTRE   OPERATE
      MAY  SHOW  NONE    THREE     OBTAIN   MIMICAL
  IS  AGE  NONE  ROOFS   ASSET     ARENAS   ACERATE
  TO  AGE  OPEN  ASSET   PEERS     CIRCLE   GENETIC
      NOT  WEST  PEERS             ASSESS   ENDMOST
                                            RESENTS
```

in respectively 200 Kμ, 15 Mμ, 450 Mμ, 25 Gμ, 25.6 Tμ. It struggles to find the best 6×6, because too few words are cut off from the search; and it thrashes miserably with the 24 thousand 7-letter words, because those words yield only seven extremely esoteric solutions. For those lengths it's best to cull the 2038753 and 14513 *unrestricted* word squares, which the method of exercise 7.2.2–28 finds in respectively 4.6 Tμ and 8.7 Tμ.

90. An XCC problem works nicely, as in answer 88: There are $2p$ primary items a_i and d_i for the final words, and $pn + W$ secondary items ij and w for the cells and potential words, where $0 \le i < p$ and $1 \le j \le n$. The Wp options going across are 'a_i $i1{:}c_1$ $i2{:}c_2$ $\ldots$ $in{:}c_n$ $c_1 \ldots c_n$'. The Wp options going down are 'd_i $i1{:}c_1$ $((i+1)$ mod $p)2{:}c_2$ $\ldots$ $((i+n-1)$ mod $p)n{:}c_n$ $c_1 \ldots c_n$' for left-leaning stairs; 'd_i $i1{:}c_n$ $((i+1)$ mod $p)2{:}c_{n-1}$ $\ldots$ $((i+n-1)$ mod $p)n{:}c_1$ $c_1 \ldots c_n$' for right-leaning stairs. The modification to Algorithm C in exercise 83 saves a factor of $2p$; and the minimax modification in exercise 84 hones in quickly on optimum solutions.

There are no left word stairs for $p = 1$, since we need two distinct words. The left winners for $2 \le p \le 10$ are: 'WRITE|WHOLE'; 'MAKES|LIVED|WAXES'; 'THERE|SHARE| WHOLE|WHOSE'; 'STOOD|THANK|SHARE|SHIPS|STORE'; 'WHERE|SHEEP|SMALL|STILL|WHOLE| SHARE'; 'MAKES|BASED|TIRED|WORKS|LANDS|LIVES|GIVES'; 'WATER|MAKES|LOVED|GIVEN| LAKES|BASED|NOTES|TONES'; 'WHERE|SHEET|STILL|SHALL|WHITE|SHAPE|STARS|WHOLE| SHORE'; 'THERE|SHOES|SHIRT|STONE|SHOOK|START|WHILE|SHELL|STEEL|SHARP'. They all belong to WORDS(500), except that $p = 8$ needs WORDS(504) for NOTED.

The right winners have a bit more variety: 'SPOTS'; 'STALL|SPIES'; 'STOOD|HOLES| LEAPS'; 'MIXED|TEARS|SLEPT|SALAD'; 'YEARS|STEAM|SALES|MARKS|DRIED'; 'STEPS| SEALS|DRAWS|KNOTS|TRAPS|DROPS'; 'TRIED|FEARS|SLIPS|SEAMS|DRAWS|ERECT|TEARS'; 'YEARS|STOPS|HOOKS|FRIED|TEARS|SLANT|SWORD|SWEEP'; 'START|SPEAR|SALES|TESTS| STEER|SPEAK|SKIES|SLEPT|SPORT'; 'YEARS|STOCK|HORNS|FUELS|BEETS|SPEED|TEARS| PLANT|SWORD|SWEEP'. They belong to WORDS(1300) except when p is 2 or 3.

[Arrangements equivalent to left word stairs were introduced in America under the name "Flower Power" by Will Shortz in *Classic Crossword Puzzles* (Penny Press, February 1976), based on Italian puzzles called "Incroci Concentrici" in *La Settimana Enigmistica*. Shortly thereafter, in *GAMES* magazine and with $p = 16$, he called them "Petal Pushers," usually based on six-letter words but occasionally going to seven. Left word stairs are much more common than the right-leaning variety, because the latter mix end-of-word with beginning-of-word letter statistics.]

91. Consider all "kernels" $c_1 \ldots c_{14}$ that can appear as illustrated, within a right word stair of 5-letter words. Such kernels arise for a given set of words only if there are letters $x_1 \ldots x_{12}$ such that $x_3 x_4 x_5 c_2 c_3$, $c_4 c_5 c_6 c_7 c_8$, $c_9 c_{10} c_{11} c_{12} x_6$, $c_{13} c_{14} x_7 x_8 x_9$, $x_1 x_2 x_5 c_5 c_9$, $c_1 c_2 c_6 c_{10} c_{13}$, $c_3 c_7 c_{11} c_{14} x_{10}$, and $c_8 c_{12} x_7 x_{11} x_{12}$ are all in the set. Thus it's an easy matter to set up an XCC problem that will find the multiset of kernels, after which we can extract the set of *distinct* kernels.

$$
\begin{array}{llllll}
x_1 & & & & & \\
x_2 & c_1 & & & & \\
x_3 & x_4 & x_5 & c_2 & c_3 & \\
c_4 & c_5 & c_6 & c_7 & c_8 & \\
c_9 & c_{10} & c_{11} & c_{12} & x_6 & \\
 & c_{13} & c_{14} & x_7 & x_8 & x_9 \\
 & & x_{10} & x_{11} & & \\
 & & & x_{12} & & \\
\end{array}
$$

Construct the digraph whose arcs are the kernels, and whose vertices are the 9-tuples that arise when kernel $c_1 \ldots c_{14}$ is regarded as the transition

$$c_1 c_2 c_3 c_4 c_5 c_6 c_7 c_9 c_{10} \;\rightarrow\; c_3 c_7 c_8 c_9 c_{10} c_{11} c_{12} c_{13} c_{14}.$$

This transition contributes two words, $c_4 c_5 c_6 c_7 c_8$ and $c_1 c_2 c_6 c_{10} c_{13}$, to the word stair. Indeed, *right word stairs of period p are precisely the p-cycles in this digraph for which the $2p$ contributed words are distinct.*

Now we can solve the problem, if the graph isn't too big. For example, WORDS(1000) leads to a digraph with 180524 arcs and 96677 vertices. We're interested only in the oriented cycles of this (very sparse) digraph; so we can reduce it drastically by looking only at the largest induced subgraph for which each vertex has positive in-degree and positive out-degree. (See exercise 7.1.4–234, where a similar reduction was made.) And wow: That subgraph has only 30 vertices and 34 arcs! So it is totally understandable, and we deduce quickly that the longest right word stair belonging to WORDS(1000) has $p = 5$. That word stair, which we found directly in answer 90, corresponds to the cycle

SEDYEARST $\rightarrow$ DRSSTEASA $\rightarrow$ SAMSALEMA $\rightarrow$ MESMARKDR $\rightarrow$ SKSDRIEYE $\rightarrow$ SEDYEARST.

A similar approach applies to left word stairs, but the kernel configurations are reflected left-to-right; transitions then contribute the words $c_8 c_7 c_6 c_5 c_4$ and $c_1 c_2 c_6 c_{10} c_{13}$. The digraph from WORDS(500) turns out to have 136771 arcs and 74568 vertices; but this time 6280 vertices and 13677 arcs remain after reduction. Decomposition into strong components makes the task simpler, because every cycle belongs to a strong component. Still, we're stuck with a giant component that has 6150 vertices and 12050 arcs.

The solution is to reduce the current subgraph repeatedly as follows: Find a vertex v of out-degree 1. Backtrack to discover a simple path, from v, that contributes only distinct words. If there is no such path (and there usually isn't, and the search usually terminates quickly), remove v from the graph and reduce it again.

With this method one can rapidly show that an optimum left word stair from WORDS(500) has period length 36: 'SHARE|SPENT|SPEED|WHEAT|THANK|CHILD|SHELL| SHORE|STORE|STOOD|CHART|GLORY|FLOWS|CLASS|NOISE|GAMES|TIMES|MOVES|BONES| WAVES|GASES|FIXED|TIRED|FEELS|WALLS|WORLD|ROOMS|WORDS|DOORS|PARTY|WANTS| WHICH|WHERE|SHOES|STILL|STATE', with 36 other words that go down. Incidentally, GLORY and FLOWS have ranks 496 and 498, so they just barely made it into WORDS(500).

Larger values of W are likely to lead to quite long cycles from WORDS(W). Their discovery won't be easy, but the search will no doubt be instructive.

92. Use $3p$ primary items a_i, b_i, d_i for the final words; $pn + 2W$ secondary items ij, w, $w@$ for the cells and potential words, with $0 \le i < p$ and $1 \le j \le n$ (somewhat as in answer 90). The Wp options going across are 'a_i $i1{:}c_1$ $i2{:}c_2$ $\ldots$ $in{:}c_n$ $c_1 \ldots c_n$

$c_1 \ldots c_n$@'. The $2Wp$ options going down in each way are 'b_i $i1:c_1$ $((i+1) \bmod p)2:c_2$ $\ldots$ $((i+n-1) \bmod p)n:c_n$ $c_1 \ldots c_n$' and 'd_i $i1:c_n$ $((i+1) \bmod p)2:c_{n-1}$ $\ldots$ $((i+n-1) \bmod p)n:c_1$ $c_1 \ldots c_n$'. The items w@ at the right of the a_i options save us a factor of p.

Use Algorithm C (modified). We can't have $p = 1$. Then comes 'SPEND | SPIES'; 'WAVES | LINED | LEPER'; 'LOOPS | POUTS | TROTS | TOONS'; 'SPOOL | STROP | STAID | SNORT | SNOOT'; 'DIMES | MULES | RIPER | SIRED | AIDED | FINED'; 'MILES | LINTS | CARES | LAMED | PIPED | SANER | LIVER'; 'SUPER | ROVED | TILED | LICIT | CODED | ROPED | TIMED | DOMED'; 'FORTH | LURES | MIRES | POLLS | SLATS | SPOTS | SOAPS | PLOTS | LOOTS'; 'TIMES | FUROR | RUNES | MIMED | CAPED | PACED | LAVER | FINES | LIMED | MIRES'. (Lengthy computations were needed for $p \geq 8$.)

93. Now $p \leq 2$ is impossible. A construction like the previous one allows us again to save a factor of p. (There's also top/bottom symmetry, but it is somewhat harder to exploit.) Examples are relatively easy to find, and the winners are 'MILES | GALLS | BULLS'; 'FIRES | PONDS | WALKS | LOCKS'; 'LIVES | FIRED | DIKES | WAVED | TIRES'; 'BIRDS | MARKS | POLES | WAVES | WINES | FONTS'; 'LIKED | WARES | MINES | WINDS | MALES | LOVES | FIVES'; 'WAXES | SITES | MINED | BOXES | CAVES | TALES | WIRED | MALES'; 'CENTS | HOLDS | BOILS | BALLS | MALES | WINES | FINDS | LORDS | CARES'; 'LOOKS | ROADS | BEATS | BEADS | HOLDS | COOLS | FOLKS | WINES | GASES | BOLTS'. [Such patterns were introduced by Harry Mathews in 1975, who gave the four-letter example 'TINE | SALE | MALE | VINE'. See H. Mathews and A. Brotchie, *Oulipo Compendium* (London: Atlas, 1998), 180–181.]

94. Set up an XCC problem with primary items k, p_k, and secondary items x_k, for $0 \leq k < 16$, and with options 'j p_k $x_k{:}a$ $x_{(k+1) \bmod 16}{:}b$ $x_{(k+3) \bmod 16}{:}c$ $x_{(k+4) \bmod 16}{:}d$' for $0 \leq j, k < 16$, where $j = (abcd)_2$. The solution (0000011010111011) is essentially unique (except for cyclic permutation, reflection, and complementation). [See C. Flye Sainte-Marie, *L'Intermédiaire des Mathématiciens* **3** (1896), 155–161.]

95. Use $2m$ primary items a_k, b_k, and m secondary items x_k, for $0 \leq k < m$. Define m^2 options of size $2 + n$, namely 'a_j b_k $x_j{:}t_1$ $x_{(j+1) \bmod m}{:}t_2$ $\cdots$ $x_{(j+n-1) \bmod m}{:}t_n$', where $t_1 t_2 \ldots t_n$ is the kth binary vector of interest. However, save a factor of m by omitting the options with $j = 0$ and $k > 0$, and the options with $j > 0$ and $k = 0$.

The case $(7, 0, 3)$ has 137216 solutions, found in 8.5 gigamems; the case $(7, 3, 4)$ has 41280 solutions, found in 3.2 gigamems. (We can make the items b_k secondary instead of primary. This makes the search tree a bit larger. But it actually *saves* a little time, because the MRV heuristic causes branching on a_j and maintains a good focus; less time is spent computing that heuristic when b_k isn't primary. Alternatively we could make the items a_k secondary (or even omit them entirely, which would have the same effect). But that would be a disaster! For example, the running time for case $(7, 0, 3)$ would then increase to nearly 50 *tera*mems, because focus is lost.)

Section 7.2.1 discusses other "universal cycles," which can be handled similarly.

96. In fact, there are 80 solutions for which the bottom four rows are the complements of the top four. (This problem extends the idea of "ourotoruses" in exercise 7.2.1.1–109. One can also consider windows that aren't rectangles. For example, the thirty-two ways to fill a cross of five cells can be identified with 32 positions of the generalized torus whose offsets are $(4, \pm4)$; see exercise 7–137.)

```
00000110
00010111
11001010
10001110
11111001
11101000
00110101
01110001
```

97. Use primary items jk, p_{jk}, and secondary items $d_{j,k}$, for $0 \leq j < 3$ and $0 \leq k < 9$, with the following three options for each $0 \leq i, j < 3$ and $0 \leq k, k' < 9$: 'jk $p_{j'k'}$ $d_{j',k'}{:}i$ $d_{j',k'+1}{:}(i+a)$ $d_{j'+1,k'}{:}(i+b)$ $d_{j'+1,k'+1}{:}(i+c)$', for $0 \leq j' \leq 1$, and 'jk $p_{2k'}$ $d_{2,k'}{:}i$ $d_{2,k'+1}{:}(i+a)$ $d_{0,k'-3}{:}(i+b-1)$ $d_{0,k'-2}{:}(i+c-1)$', where $9j+k = (abc)_3$; sums involving i are mod 3, while sums involving k' are mod 9. We can assume that 00 is paired with p_{00}. Then there are $2 \cdot 2898 = 5796$ solutions D; all have $D \neq D^T$.

98. Given a 3SAT problem with clauses $(l_{i1} \vee l_{i2} \vee l_{i3})$ for $1 \le i \le m$, with each $l_{ij} \in \{x_1, \bar{x}_1, \ldots, x_n, \bar{x}_n\}$, construct an XCC problem with $3m$ primary items ij ($1 \le i \le m$, $1 \le j \le 3$) and n secondary items x_k ($1 \le k \le n$), having the following options: (i) '$l_{i1}\ l_{i2}$', '$l_{i2}\ l_{i3}$', '$l_{i3}\ l_{i1}$'; (ii) '$l_{ij}\ x_k{:}1$' if $l_{ij} = x_k$, '$l_{ij}\ x_k{:}0$' if $l_{ij} = \bar{x}_k$. That problem has a solution if and only if the given clauses are satisfiable.

99. True — but perhaps with many more secondary items and much longer options: Let x be a secondary item to which a color has been assigned, in some XCC problem A; and let O be the options in which x appears. Replace A by a new problem A', by deleting item x and adding new secondary items $x_{\{o,p\}}$ for each $o, p \in O$ for which x gets different colors in A. And for each $o \in O$, replace item x in o by the set of all $x_{\{o,p\}}$ that apply. If A' still involves colors, replace it by A'' in a similar way, until all colors disappear.

100. (a) There are five solutions: 00112, 00122, 01112, 01122, 11111.

(b) Let there be five primary items, $\{\#1, \#2, \#3, \#4, \#5\}$, and five secondary items, $\{x_1, x_2, x_3, x_4, x_5\}$. Item $\#1$ enforces the binary constraint $x_1 \le x_2$, and has the options '$\#1\ x_1{:}0\ x_2{:}0$'; '$\#1\ x_1{:}0\ x_2{:}1$'; '$\#1\ x_1{:}0\ x_2{:}2$'; '$\#1\ x_1{:}1\ x_2{:}1$'; '$\#1\ x_1{:}1\ x_2{:}2$'; '$\#1\ x_1{:}2\ x_2{:}2$'. Similar options for $\#2$, $\#3$, and $\#4$ will enforce the constraints $x_2 \le x_3$, $x_3 \le x_4$, and $x_4 \le x_5$. Finally, the options '$\#5\ x_1{:}0\ x_3{:}1\ x_5{:}2$'; '$\#5\ x_1{:}0\ x_3{:}2\ x_5{:}1$'; '$\#5\ x_1{:}1\ x_3{:}0\ x_5{:}2$'; '$\#5\ x_1{:}1\ x_3{:}1\ x_5{:}1$'; '$\#5\ x_1{:}1\ x_3{:}2\ x_5{:}0$'; '$\#5\ x_1{:}2\ x_3{:}0\ x_5{:}1$'; '$\#5\ x_1{:}2\ x_3{:}1\ x_5{:}0$' will enforce the ternary constraint $x_1 + x_3 + x_5 = 3$.

(c) Use primary items $\#j$ for $1 \le j \le m$, one for each constraint, and secondary items x_k for $1 \le k \le n$, one for each variable. If constraint C_j involves the d variables $x_{i_1}, \ldots, x_{i_d}$, include options '$\#j\ x_{i_1}{:}a_1\ \ldots\ x_{i_d}{:}a_d$' for each legal d-tuple $(a_1, \ldots, a_d)$.

(Of course this construction isn't efficient for all instances of CSP; furthermore, we can often find substantially better ways to encode a particular CSP as an XCC instance, because this method uses only one primary item in each option. But the idea that underlies this construction is a useful mental tool when formulating particular problems.)

101. Notice that the final sentence implies two further clues:

- Somebody trains a zebra.   • Somebody prefers to drink just plain water.

Let there be primary items $\#k$ for $1 \le k \le 16$, one for each clue. And let the $5 \cdot 5$ secondary items N_j, J_j, P_j, D_j, C_j represent the nationality, job, pet, drink, and color associated with house j, for $0 \le j < 5$. There are respectively (5, 5, 5, 5, 1, 5, 1, 5, 4, 5, 8, 5, 8, 8, 5, 5) options for clues (1, $\ldots$, 16), typified by '$\#1\ N_j$:England C_j:red', for $0 \le j < 5$; '$\#5\ N_0$:Norway'; '$\#9\ C_i$:white C_{i+1}:green', for $0 \le i < 4$; '$\#14\ J_i$:nurse P_{i+1}:fox', '$\#14\ P_i$:fox J_{i+1}:nurse', for $0 \le i < 4$; '$\#15\ P_j$:zebra', for $0 \le j < 5$.

A more complex formulation enforces the redundant "all-different" constraint by introducing $5 \cdot 5$ additional secondary items to represent the *inverses* of N_j, J_j, P_j, D_j, C_j. For example, the options for $\#1$ then become '$\#1\ N_j$:England $N_{\text{England}}^-{:}j\ C_j$:red $C_{\text{red}}^-{:}j$'. (With those additional items, Algorithm C will infer C_1:blue immediately from $\#5$ and $\#11$; but without them, $\#5$ doesn't immediately make N_1:Norway illegal. They reduce the search tree size from 112 to 32 nodes. However, the time they save during the search just barely compensates for the extra time that they consume in step C1.)

The inverses alone are *not* sufficient; they don't forbid, say, $N_{\text{England}}^- = N_{\text{Japan}}^-$.

[The author of this now-famous puzzle is unknown. Its first known publication, in *Life International* **35** (17 December 1962), 95, used cigarettes instead of occupations.]

102. As in answer 7.2.2–68, let's find all stable extensions of a given partially labeled digraph. And let's allow sinks too; we can assume that every vertex with out-degree $d \le 1$ is labeled d. The following XCC formulation is based on ideas of R. Bittencourt.

Let Δ be the maximum out-degree. Introduce primary items H_v, I_v, E_{vd}, and secondary items v, h_{vd}, i_{vd}, for $0 \le d \le \Delta$ and all vertices v. The color of v will be $\lambda(v)$, the label of v; the color of h_{vd} will denote the Boolean quantity '[v sees d]', meaning that $\lambda(w) = d$ for some w with $v \longrightarrow w$; and the color of i_{vd} will denote '[$\lambda(v) = d$]'. The options for H_v are 'H_v v:d $\bigcup_{k=0}^{\Delta}\{h_{vk}{:}e_k\}$' where $e_0 + \cdots + e_\Delta = d$. The options for I_v are 'I_v v:d $\bigcup_{k=0}^{\Delta}\{i_{vk}{:}[k=d]\}$ $\bigcup_{u \longrightarrow v}\{h_{ud}{:}1\}$'. And the options for E_{vd} are 'E_{vd} h_{vd}:1 $i_{w_k d}$:1 $\bigcup_{j=1}^{k-1}\{i_{w_j d}{:}0\}$' for $1 \le k \le d^+(v)$ and 'E_{vd} h_{vd}:0 $\bigcup_{j=1}^{d^+(v)}\{i_{w_j d}{:}0\}$', when $v \longrightarrow w_1$, $\ldots$, $v \longrightarrow w_{d^+(v)}$. For example, if the vertices of the puzzle in exercise 7.2.2–68 are named 00, $\ldots$, 99, some of the options of its unique solution are 'H_{00} 00:3 h_{000}:0 h_{001}:0 h_{002}:0 h_{003}:0 h_{004}:1 h_{005}:0 h_{006}:0 h_{007}:1 h_{008}:0 h_{009}:1'; 'I_{00} 00:3 i_{000}:0 $\ldots i_{002}$:0 i_{003}:1 i_{004}:0 $\ldots i_{009}$:0 h_{013}:1 h_{033}:1 h_{053}:1 h_{703}:1 h_{803}:1'; 'E_{004} h_{004}:1 i_{104}:0 $\ldots i_{404}$:0 i_{504}:1'.

Of course many of those options can be greatly simplified, because many of the quantities are known from the given labels. We know the color of i_{vd} when $\lambda(v)$ is given; we know the color of h_{vd} when v sees d in the given puzzle. We don't need I_v when v is labeled; we don't even need E_{vd}, when v is known to see d. If v has out-degree d and already sees some label twice, we know that i_{vd} is 0. And so on. In the pi day puzzle such simplifications reduce 60 thousand options on $1200 + 1831$ items to 11351 options on $880 + 1216$ items. That's still a lot, and Algorithm C needs 135 Mμ to input them; but then it finds the solution and proves it unique after 25 more Mμ. (The highly tuned method of answer 7.2.2–68 needed only 7 Mμ to prove uniqueness. But that method solves only a small class of problems that happen to reduce nicely.)

Bittencourt notes that further speedup is possible when two arrows point in the same direction. (This happens 123 times in the pi day puzzle.) In general if $v \longrightarrow w$ implies $u \longrightarrow w$, we must have $\lambda(u) \ge \lambda(v)$; and this condition can be enforced by introducing a new primary variable whose options allow u and v to have only appropriate combinations of colors.

103. (a) An all-interval row always has $x_{n-1} = (x_0 + 1 + \cdots + (n-1)) \bmod n = (x_0 + n(n-1)/2) \bmod n = (x_0 + [n\,\text{even}]\,n/2) \bmod n$.

(b) Let j, p_j, d_k, q_k be primary items and let x_j be a secondary item, for $0 \le j < n$ and $1 \le k < n$. There's an option 'j p_t x_j:t' for $0 \le j, t < n$, omitted when ($j = 0$ and $t \ne 0$) or ($j = n-1$ and $t \ne n/2$). And there's an option 'd_k q_t x_{t-1}:i x_t:$(i+k) \bmod n$' for $1 \le k, t < n$ and $0 \le i < n$. Then the tone row and its intervals are permutations.

There are (1, 2, 4, 24, 288, 3856) solutions for $n = (2, 4, 6, 8, 10, 12)$. [These values were first computed by D. H. Lehmer, *Proc. Canadian Math. Congress* **4** (1959), 171–173, for $n = 12$ and E. N. Gilbert *SIAM Review* **7** (1965), 189–198, for $n < 12$.]

For larger n, Algorithm C is *not* at all competitive with a straightforward backtrack algorithm, which uses Algorithm 7.2.1.2X to find all suitable permutations of the $n-1$ intervals: That method needs only 100 Mμ to find all 89328 solutions when $n = 14$, compared to 107 Gμ by Algorithm C! With backtracking we can generate all 2755968 solutions for $n = 16$ in 4.7 Gμ, and all 103653120 solutions for $n = 18$ in 281 Gμ.

(c) The intervals between adjacent classes in x^Q are the same as those of x, except that $x_k - x_{k-1}$ is replaced by $x_0 - x_{n-1}$. And we know that $x_0 - x_{n-1} = \pm n/2$.

(d) True; both are $x_{k-1} \ldots x_0 x_{n-1} \ldots x_k$. (Also $(cx)^R = c(x^R)$; $(cx)^Q = c(x^Q)$.)

(e) The solution for $n = 2$ has every possible symmetry; and both solutions x for $n = 4$ are equivalent to x^R, $-x^Q$, and $-x^{QR}$. But for $n > 4$ one can show that x is equivalent to at most one of the $4\varphi(n)$ rows cx, cx^R, cx^Q, cx^{QR} besides itself. We obviously can't have $x \equiv cx$ when $c \ne 1$. An elementary but nontrivial proof shows also that $x \equiv cx^R$ implies $c \bmod n = 1$; $x \equiv cx^Q$ implies $c \bmod n = n-1$; $x \equiv cx^{QR}$ implies $c \bmod n =$

$n/2 + 1$ and $n \bmod 8 = 4$. (See Richard Stong in *AMM*, to appear.) Gilbert stated incorrectly [page 196] that no solutions of the latter kind exist; he had overlooked 12-tone rows such as $0\,3\,9\,12\,4\,11\,8\,7\,5\,10\,6$, $0\,1\,4\,9\,3\,11\,10\,8\,5\,7\,2\,6$, $0\,1\,8\,11\,10\,3\,9\,5\,7\,4\,2\,6$, for which $x \equiv 7x^{QR}$. Similarly, the 20-tone row $0\,1\,3\,11\,2\,19\,13\,9\,12\,7\,14\,18\,4\,17\,16\,8\,6\,15\,5\,10$ satisfies $x \equiv 11x^{QR}$.)

At any rate, the transformations of (c) partition the solutions into clusters of size $2\varphi(n)$ when there's symmetry, $4\varphi(n)$ when there's not. Gilbert enumerated the cases of symmetry when $n < 12$; R. Morris and D. Starr did it when $n = 12$ [*J. Music Theory* **18** (1974), 364–389]. For $n = (6, 8, 10, 12, 14, 16, 18)$ the number of clusters with $x \equiv x^R$ turns out to be respectively $(1, 1, 6, 22, 48, 232, 1872)$; the number of clusters with $x \equiv -x^Q$ turns out to be $(0, 0, 2, 15, 0, 0, 1346)$; also $n = 12$ has 15 cases with $x \equiv 7x^{QR}$.

104. (a) We may assume that $x_0 = 0$. There's a constant c_r such that $y_{kr} \equiv x_{k-1} + c_r$ (modulo n) for $1 \le k \le n$. Thus $y_r = x_{r-1} \equiv c_r$; $y_{r^2} = x_{(r^2-1) \bmod p} \equiv x_{r-1} + c_r \equiv 2c_r$; $y_{r^3} = x_{(r^3-1) \bmod p} \equiv x_{(r^2-1) \bmod p} + c_r \equiv 3c_r$; etc. Let r be primitive modulo p, so that $\{r \bmod p, \ldots, r^n \bmod p\} = \{1, \ldots, p-1\}$, and let $R = r^d$ where $c_r d \bmod n = 1$. Then we've proved $R^{x \cdot (r^k-1) \bmod p} \equiv (r^k \bmod p)$ (modulo p) for $1 \le k \le n$; that is, $R^{x_{k-1}} \equiv k$.

Now suppose $x_k - x_{k-1} \equiv x_l - x_{l-1}$ (modulo n). Then $R^{x_k} R^{x_{l-1}} \equiv R^{x_{k-1}} R^{x_l}$ (modulo p); consequently $(k+1)l \equiv k(l+1)$ (modulo p), hence $k = l$.

(b) $x^{(n)} = x^R$. [See the papers by Lehmer and Gilbert in answer 103.]

105. There are just five solutions; the latter two are flawed by being disconnected:

Historical notes: The earliest known word search puzzle was "Viajando" by Henrique Ramos of Brazil, published in *Almanaque de Seleções Recreativas* (1966), page 43. Such puzzles were independently invented in America by Norman E. Gibat (1968). Jo Ouellet of Canada developed "Wonderword," which puts the unused letters to use, in 1970.

106. When Algorithm C is generalized to allow non-unit item sums as in Algorithm M, it needs just 24 megamems to prove that there are exactly eight solutions — which all are rotations of the two shown here.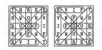

107. To pack w given words, use primary items $\{Pij, Ric, Cic, Bic, \#k \mid 1 \le i, j \le 9, 1 \le k \le w, c \in \{\texttt{A}, \texttt{C}, \texttt{E}, \texttt{M}, \texttt{O}, \texttt{P}, \texttt{R}, \texttt{T}, \texttt{U}\}\}$ and secondary items $\{ij \mid 1 \le i, j \le 9\}$. There are 729 options '$Pij\ Ric\ Cjc\ Bbc\ ij{:}c$', where $b = 3\lfloor (i-1)/3 \rfloor + \lceil j/3 \rceil$, together with an option '$\#k\ i_1 j_1{:}c_1 \ \ldots \ i_l j_l{:}c_l$' for each placement of an l-letter word $c_1 \ldots c_l$ into cells $(i_1, j_1), \ldots, (i_l, j_l)$. Furthermore, it's important to use the sharp preference heuristic (exercise 10) in step C3 of the algorithm.

A brief run then establishes that `COMPUTER` and `CORPORATE` cannot both be packed. But all of the words *except* `CORPORATE` do fit together; the (unique) solution shown is found after only 7.3 megamems, most of which are needed simply to input the problem. [This exercise was inspired by a puzzle in *Sudoku Masterpieces* (2010) by Huang and Snyder.]

108. (a, b) The author's best solutions, thought to be minimal (but there is no proof), are below. In both cases, and in Fig. 71, an interactive method was used: After the longest words were placed strategically by hand, Algorithm C packed the others nicely.

[Solution (b) applies an idea by which Leonard Gordon was able to pack the names of presidents 1–42 with one less column. See A. Ross Eckler, *Word Ways* **27** (1994), 147; see also page 252, where **OBAMA** miraculously fits into Gordon's 15×15 solution!]

109. To pack w given words, use $w + m(n-1) + (m-1)n$ primary items $\{\#k \mid 1 \le k \le w\}$ and $\{Hij, Vij \mid 1 \le i \le m, \ 1 \le j \le n\}$, but with Hin and Vmj omitted; Hij represents the edge between cells (i,j) and $(i,j+1)$, and Vij is similar. There also are $2mn$ secondary items $\{ij, ij' \mid 1 \le i \le m, \ 1 \le j \le n\}$. Each horizontal placement of the kth word $c_1 \ldots c_l$ into cells $(i, j+1), \ldots, (i, j+l)$ generates the option

'$\#k \ ij:. \ ij':0 \ i(j+1):c_1 \ i(j+1)':1 \ Hi(j+1) \ i(j+2):c_2 \ i(j+2)':1 \ Hi(j+2) \ \ldots$
$$Hi(j+l-1) \ i(j+l):c_l \ i(j+l)':1 \ i(j+l+1):. \ i(j+l+1)':0'$$

with $3l + 4$ items, except that '$ij:. \ ij':0$' is omitted when $j = 0$ and '$i(j+l+1):. \ i(j+l+1)':0$' is omitted when $j+l = n$. Each vertical placement is similar. For example,

'$\#1 \ 11:Z \ 11':1 \ V11 \ 21:E \ 21':1 \ V21 \ 31:R \ 31':1 \ V31 \ 41:O \ 41':1 \ 51:. \ 51':0$'   (∗)

is the first vertical placement option for **ZERO**, if **ZERO** is word #1. When $m = n$, however, we save a factor of 2 by omitting all of the vertical placements of word #1.

To enforce the tricky condition (ii), we also include $3m(n-1) + 3(m-1)n$ options:

'$Hij \ ij':0 \ i(j+1)':1 \ ij:.$'   '$Vij \ ij':0 \ (i+1)j':1 \ ij:.$'

'$Hij \ ij':1 \ i(j+1)':0 \ i(j+1):.$'   '$Vij \ ij':1 \ (i+1)j':0 \ (i+1)j:.$'

'$Hij \ ij':0 \ i(j+1)':0 \ ij:. \ i(j+1):.$'   '$Vij \ ij':0 \ (i+1)j':0 \ ij:. \ (i+1)j:.$'

This construction works nicely because each edge must encounter either a word that crosses it or a space that touches it. (Beware of a slight glitch: A valid solution to the puzzle might have several compatible choices for Hij and Vij in "blank" regions.)

Important: As in answer 107, the sharp preference heuristic should be used here, because it gives an enormous speedup.

The XCC problem for our 11-word example has 1192 options, $123 + 128$ items, and 9127 solutions, found in 29 Gμ. But only 20 of those solutions are connected; and they yield only the three distinct word placements below. A slightly smaller rectangle, 7×9, also has three valid placements. The smallest rectangle that admits a solution to (i) and (ii) is 5×11; that placement is *unique*, but it has two components:

```
      F    F          F TWO             FIVE
ZERO     SIX        ONE      S     TWO        I
  I   U    V          U  NINE        U        G
  G   R  TEN       ZERO              ZERO     H
  H      H  I         I   F   E             N TEN
TWO      R  N         G  SIX  N      SEVEN    I
  N   E    E          H   V            I      N
  SEVEN               THREE           X    THREE
```

```
  E T                 F SIX  F T
FIVE      SIX         ONE     EIGHT
  G NINE              U  V  T V R T
  H     V F           R E E   E E W
TWO     ZERO          NINE  ZERO
  N     N U
THREE        R
```

Suppose there are w words of total length s. Aaron Windsor suggests adding options 'E ij:. ij':0' for $1 \le i \le m$ and $1 \le j \le n$, where E is a new primary item representing an empty cell. All solutions to the MCC problem with the number of E's in the interval $[mn - s + w - 1 \mathinner{.\,.} mn]$ are then either connected or contain a cycle.

Instead of generating all solutions to (i) and (ii) and discarding the disconnected ones, there's a much faster way to guarantee connectedness throughout the search; but it requires major modifications to Algorithm C. Whenever no H or V is forced, we can list all active options that are connected to word #1 and not smaller than choices that could have been made earlier. Then we branch on them, instead of branching on an item. For example, if $(*)$ above is used to place ZERO, it will force H00 and H20 and V30. The next decision will be to place either EIGHT or ONE, in the places where they overlap ZERO. (However, we'll be better off if we order the words by decreasing length, so that for instance #1 is EIGHT and #11 is ONE.) Interested readers are encouraged to work out the instructive details. This method needs only 630 Mμ to solve the example problem, as it homes right in on the three connected solutions.

110. Gary McDonald found this remarkable 20×20 solution in 2017:

```
WILSON  TAFT               P
    I   A   O   C   JOHNSON
    X   Y   R   L   E       L
  T H COOLIDGE  F   A       K
REAGAN  O      V   F   R
  U  R  R  ROOSEVELT
  M  R  T  B    B   L   R HAYES
  A  I  E  U   ADAMS  U     I
  N  S  R  C    M   N  O  R S
     N     O    H HARDING   E
        N  A  O            GRANT
  F     MONROE  J           H
  I     A   V  WASHINGTON
  L MCKINLEY  C         A  W
  L  L      R   K  PIERCE
MADISON      BUSH       F  R
  O  N          O       I
  R  TYLER  VAN BUREN
  E  O                  L
  LINCOLN        KENNEDY
```

A 19×19 is surely impossible, although no proof is known. L. Gordon had previously fit the names of presidents 1–42 into an 18×22 rectangle [*Word Ways* **27** (1994), 63].

111. (a) Set up an XCC problem as in answer 109, but with just three words AAA, AAAA, AAAAA; then adjust the multiplicities and apply Algorithm M. The two essentially distinct answers are shown below; one of them is disconnected, hence disqualified.

(b) Similarly, we find four essentially different answers, only two of which are OK:

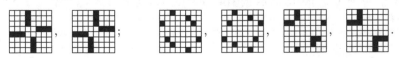

Algorithm M handles case (b) with ease (5 Gμ). But it does not explore the space of possibilities for case (a) intelligently, and costs 591 Gμ.

112. (a) Yes: IMMATURE, MATURING, COMMUTER, GROUPING, TROUPING, AUTHORING, and THRUMMING. A straightforward backtracking program will quickly determine the presence or absence of any given string of letters.

(b) Let's put DANCING and LINKS in there too. Then we obtain an array with 24 words from WORDS(5757) (like LOVER, ROSIN, SALVO, TOADS, TROVE); also ASKING, DOSING, LOSING, ORDAIN, SAILOR, SIGNAL, SILVER; also LANCING, LOANING, SOAKING, and even ORTOLAN. (Notice that TORTO occurs in two ways.)

```
C G N
N I K
L A S
V O D
E R T
T O W
```

To find such arrays, as suggested by R. Bittencourt, we can let word k be $c_0 \ldots c_{t-1}$, and introduce primary items W_{kl} for $1 \le l < t$ to represent the placement of $c_{l-1}c_l$. Let X_u be a secondary item, for each cell u of the array, to be colored with some letter. Represent the king path for word k by giving color u to P_{kl} and color l to Q_{ku} when c_l is in cell u, where P_{kl} and Q_{ku} are additional secondary items. There also are secondary items D_{kv}, for each internal vertex v. For example, if the cells and vertices are numbered rowwise, two of the options chosen for DANCING and LINKS in the example above are 'W_{03} X_3:N X_0:C P_{02}:3 P_{03}:0 Q_{03}:2 Q_{00}:3' and 'W_{12} X_4:I X_2:N P_{11}:4 P_{12}:2 Q_{14}:1 Q_{12}:2 D_{11}'. The 'D_{11}' in the latter will prevent another step of word 1 between cells 2 and 4.

We can save a factor of nearly 4 by restricting the placement of, say, $c_{l-1}c_l$ in word 0 when $l = \lfloor t_0/2 \rfloor$, so that c_{l-1} lies in the upper left quadrant and c_l isn't in the rightmost column. Then W_{0l} has only 26 options instead of the usual 94.

It turns out that exactly 10 essentially different Torto arrays contain DANCING, LINKS, TORTO, WORDS, and SOLVER; exactly 1444 contain THE, ART, OF, COMPUTER, and PROGRAMMING. They're found by Algorithm C in 713 Gμ and 126 Gμ, respectively.

(c) Yes, in 140 ways (but we can't add ELEVEN). Similarly, we can pack ZERO, ONE, ..., up to EIGHT, in 553 ways. And FIRST, ..., SIXTH can be packed in 72853 ways, sometimes without using more than 16 of the 18 cells. (These computations took (16, 5, 1.5) Tμ. Interesting words lurk in these arrays—can you spot them? See Appendix E.)

```
F X N | F S X | E T V
S I N | Z I E | F H X
G E V | G E V | F I T
H R E | H R N | O R S
U T N | T O U | U D E
F O W | W N F | N O C
```

[The name 'Torto' was trademarked by Coquetel/Ediouro of Rio de Janeiro in 1977, and an example appeared in issue #1 of *Coquetel Total* magazine that year. Monthly puzzles still appear regularly in Coquetel's magazine *Desafio Cérebro*. Bittencourt posed the problem of constructing Torto arrays from a given list of required words in 2011; see blog.ricbit.com/2011/05/torto-reverso.html.]

113. First, we can find all sets of six or fewer letters that could be on such a block, by solving an MCC problem with 25 primary items TREES, ..., DEQUE of multiplicity [1..26] and one primary item # of multiplicity [0..6]. There are 22 options, '# ABOVE AVAIL GRAPH STACK TABLE VALUE' through '# EMPTY', one for each potential letter (listing all words that include that letter). This covering problem has 3223 solutions, found in 4 Mμ and ranging alphabetically from {A, B, C, D, E, I} to {E, L, R, T} to {L, N, R, T, U, V}.

Then we set up an XCC problem with 25 primary items TREES, ..., DEQUE and five primary items 1, ..., 5, together with $5 \cdot 22$ secondary items A_j, ..., Y_j for $1 \le j \le 5$. Each word has an option for each permutation of its letters (see Algorithm 7.2.1.2L), showing which letters it needs for that permutation of the blocks. (For example, QUEUE will have 30 options, beginning with 'QUEUE E_1:1 E_2:1 Q_3:1 U_4:1 U_5:1', which means that block 1 should have an E, ..., block 5 should have a U.) Break symmetry by giving only one of the 120 options for one of the words (FIRST, for example). Each of the 3223 potential sets of letters has five options of size 23, showing exactly which letters are present if block j uses that set; for example, the five options for $\{\mathtt{A},\mathtt{B},\mathtt{C},\mathtt{D},\mathtt{E},\mathtt{I}\}$ are 'j $\mathtt{A}_j{:}1 \ldots \mathtt{E}_j{:}1\ \mathtt{F}_j{:}0 \ldots \mathtt{I}_j{:}1 \ldots \mathtt{Y}_j{:}0$' for $1 \leq j \leq 5$. There are 18486 options altogether, of total length 403357; Algorithm C solves them in 225 Gμ.

For these words the five blocks must be $\{\mathtt{E},\mathtt{F},\mathtt{G},\mathtt{L},\mathtt{O},\mathtt{S}\}$, $\{\mathtt{C},\mathtt{E},\mathtt{T},\mathtt{R},\mathtt{U},\mathtt{Y}\}$, $\{\mathtt{A},\mathtt{L},\mathtt{M},$ $\mathtt{N},\mathtt{Q},\mathtt{R}\}$, $\{\mathtt{A},\mathtt{B},\mathtt{E},\mathtt{P},\mathtt{S},\mathtt{T}\}$, $\{\mathtt{D},\mathtt{H},\mathtt{K},\mathtt{T},\mathtt{U},\mathtt{V}\}$. (The XCC problem actually has 8 solutions, because TIMES, TREES, and VALUE can each be formed in two ways from those blocks.)

[This exercise is based on an idea by E. Riekstiņš, who realized that a classic puzzle called Castawords could be extended to words of length 5.]

114. Besides the primary items p_{ij}, r_{ik}, c_{jk}, b_{xk} of (30), introduce R_{ik}, C_{jk}, and B_{xk} for the permuted array, as well as u_k and v_l to define a permutation. Also introduce secondary items π_k to record the permutation and ij to record the value at cell (i,j). The permutation is defined by 81 options '$u_k\ v_l\ \pi_k{:}l$' for $1 \leq k,l \leq 9$. And there are $9^4 = 6561$ other options, one for each cell (i,j) of the board and each pair (k,l) of values before and after α is applied. If $(ij)\alpha = i'j'$, let $x' = 3\lfloor i'/3\rfloor + \lfloor j'/3\rfloor$. Then option (i,j,k,l) is normally '$p_{ij}\ r_{ik}\ c_{jk}\ b_{xk}\ R_{i'l}\ C_{j'l}\ B_{x'l}\ ij{:}k\ i'j'{:}l\ \pi_k{:}l$'. However, if $i' = i$ and $j' = j$, that option is shortened to '$p_{ij}\ r_{ik}\ c_{jk}\ b_{xk}\ R_{il}\ C_{jl}\ B_{xl}\ ij{:}k\ \pi_k{:}l$'; and it is omitted when $i = i'$, $j = j'$, $k \neq l$. The options $(0,j,k,l)$ are also omitted when $k \neq j + 1$, in order to force '123456789' on the top row.

With that top row and with $\alpha =$ transposition, Algorithm C produces 30,258,432 solutions in 2.2 teramems. (These solutions were first enumerated in 2005 by E. Russell; see www.afjarvis.staff.shef.ac.uk/sudoku/sudgroup.html.)

115. A similar method applies, but with additional items b'_{yk} and $B'_{y'l}$ as in answer 67(b). The number of solutions is (a) 7784; (b) 16384; (c) 372; (d) 32. Here are examples of (a) and (d); the latter is shown with labels $\{0, \ldots, 7, *\}$, to clarify its structure. [Enumerations (a), (b), (c) were first carried out by Bastian Michel in 2007.]

(a)

1	2	3	4	5	6	7	8	9
9	7	4	3	1	8	5	6	2
8	5	6	9	7	2	1	3	4
5	8	2	1	3	9	4	7	6
4	1	7	8	6	5	2	9	3
6	3	9	2	4	7	8	5	1
7	4	1	5	9	3	6	2	8
3	6	8	7	2	4	9	1	5
2	9	5	6	8	1	3	4	7

(d)

7	0	2	5	1	3	*	4	6
5	3	6	*	7	4	2	0	1
*	1	4	2	0	6	7	5	3
2	5	7	0	6	1	3	*	4
0	4	3	7	*	5	1	6	2
6	*	1	3	4	2	5	7	0
1	7	5	4	2	0	6	3	*
3	2	0	6	5	*	4	1	7
4	6	*	1	3	7	0	2	5

116. (a) Any triangle in $\mu(G)$ must be in G, because $u' \not\!\!\!- v'$.

(b) Suppose $\mu(G)$ can be c-colored with some coloring function α, where $\alpha(w) = c$. If $\alpha(v) = c$ for any $v \in V$, change it to $\alpha(v')$. This gives a $(c - 1)$-coloring of G. [Hence a triangle-free graph on n vertices can have chromatic number $\Omega(\log n)$. One can show nonconstructively that the triangle-free chromatic number can actually be $\Omega(n/\log n)^{1/2}$; but currently known methods of explicit construction for large n achieve only $\Omega(n^{1/3})$. See N. Alon, *Electronic J. Combinatorics* **1** (1994), #R12, 1–8.]

(c) If G is χ-critical, so is $\mu(G)$: Let $e \in E$ and suppose α is a $(c - 1)$-coloring of $G \setminus e$. Then we get c-colorings of all but one edge of $\mu(G)$ in several ways: (i) Set $\alpha(v') \leftarrow c$ for all $v \in V$, and $\alpha(w) \leftarrow 1$. (ii) Let $u \in e$, and set $\alpha(u) \leftarrow \alpha(w) \leftarrow c$; also set $\alpha(v') = \alpha(v)$ for all $v \in V$, either before or after changing $\alpha(u)$. If you want to remove an edge of $\mu(G)$ that's in G, use (i); otherwise use (ii).

[See J. Mycielski, *Colloquium Mathematicum* **3** (1955), 161–162; H. Sachs, *Einführung in die Theorie der endlichen Graphen* (1970), §V.5.]

117. (a) Use the answer to (b), with each clique consisting of a single edge.

(b) Each vertex v has d options '$v\ c_{1j} \ \ldots\ c_{kj}$' for $1 \le j \le d$, where the cliques containing v are $\{c_1, \ldots, c_k\}$.

(c) We save a factor of $9! = 362880$ by fixing the colors of the queens in the top row. Then there are 262164 solutions, found by Algorithm X in 8.3 Tμ with method (a) but in only 0.6 Tμ with method (b).

(d) Insert '$v'{:}j$' into the jth option for v, where v' is secondary. (This reduces the running time for method (a) in part (c) to 5.0 Tμ, *without* fixing any colors.)

(e) Using (d) to save a factor of $c!$, we get $(2!\cdot 1,\ 3!\cdot 5,\ 4!\cdot 520,\ 5!\cdot 23713820)$ solutions, in approximately $(600, 4000, 130000, 4100000000)$ mems. [Monte Carlo estimates can be made for larger cases by combining exercises 86 and 122; the true branching factor at each level can be determined by rejecting options that involve illegal purification. It appears that M_6 can be 6-colored in approximately $6! \cdot 2.0 \times 10^{17}$ ways.]

(f) Now (d) saves a factor of $(c-1)!$, despite having no solutions; the running times are roughly $(100, 600, 5000, 300000)$ mems. (But then for 5-coloring M_6 it's 45 Tμ!)

(g) There are $\big(1! \cdot 1,\ 2! \cdot 1,\ 3! \cdot (5\text{ or }7),\ 4! \cdot (1432,\ 1544,\ 1600,\ 2200,\ 2492,\ 2680,\ 3744,\ 4602,\text{ or }6640)\big)$ such colorings, depending on which edge is deleted.

118. In general, colorings of a hypergraph can be found with the construction of the previous exercise, but using Algorithm M and giving multiplicity $[0 \mathrel{{.}\,{.}} (r{-}1)]$ to each hyperedge of size r. In this case, however, there are 380 independent sets of size 16 (see exercise 7.1.4– 242); we can simply use them as options to an exact cover problem with 64 items. There are four solutions, having a curious symmetry so that only two are "essentially different": One is shown, and the other is obtained by keeping A and C fixed but *transposing* the B's and D's.

```
A B C D C D A B
B D B D C A C A
C B A C D B A D
D D A B A B C C
A A D C D C B B
B C D B A C D A
C A C A B D B D
D C B A B A D C
```

119. Exactly three interior edges are white in every solution. Any other placement of the all-white piece defines those three edges. That leaves no way to place all three of the two-white pieces.

120. (a) Call the types 0, 1, $\ldots$, 9, and use Algorithm C to find all ways to place a given type at the center of a 5×5 array. There are respectively $(16, 8, 19, 8, 8, 8, 10, 8, 16, 24)$ ways to do this; and the *intersection* of all solutions for a given type shows that

```
?????   0490?   ?????   68568   21721   32032   2032?   49049   0320?   17217
?????   2032?   ??0??   0490?   ?6856   17217   ?217?   0320?   21721   68568
??0??,  ?217?,  ??2??,  2032?,  9049?,  68568,  8568?,  21721,  ?6856,  049??
??2??   8568?   ?????   ?217?   320??   049??   490??   ?6856   9049?   20???
?????   490??   ?????   8568?   172??   20???   032??   9049?   320??   ?2???
```

are the respective neighborhoods that are forced near a given type in any infinite tiling. Consequently every such tiling contains at least one 5; and if we place 5 at the origin everything in the entire plane is forced. The result is a torus in the sense of exercise 7–137, with a periodic supertile of size 12:

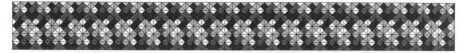

(b) Similarly, there's again a unique tiling, this time with a 13-cell supertile:

121. (a) Marek Tyburec noticed in 2017 that there are no 2×2 solutions with βUS at lower right; similarly, there are no 3×4 solutions with βUS at lower left. Hence βUS can appear only in the top row, or at the left of the next-to-top row.

(b) Let (A_k, B_k, C_k, D_k) be the $(2^k - 1) \times (2^k - 1)$ tilings defined by $(\alpha a, \alpha b, \alpha c, \alpha d)$ when $k = 1$, otherwise by placing $(\delta Na, \delta Nb, \delta Nc, \delta Nd)$ in the middle and placing A_{k-1}, B_{k-1}, C_{k-1}, D_{k-1} at the corners as in answer 2.3.4.3–5. The unique tiling requested here has δRD in the middle and $D_{k-1}, C_{k-1}, B_{k-1}, A_{k-1}$ at the corners.

(c) With δRU or δLD in the middle, another solution has $C_{k-1}, D_{k-1}, A_{k-1}$, B_{k-1} at the corners. With δLU or δSU, there's a third solution with B_{k-1}, A_{k-1}, D_{k-1}, C_{k-1} at the corners. And δSU also has 54 additional solutions with C_{k-2} in the upper left corner; they use $\{DL, DP, DS, DT, UL, UP, UR, US, UT\}$ in the upper half when choices need to be made, and independently $\{R, YR, L, P, S, T\}$ in the lower half.

(d) Only one of each survives. As in (b), its four quadrants are $D_\infty, C_\infty, B_\infty, A_\infty$.

[Each of the other 86 types occurs in A_6, hence in every sufficiently large tiling. Incidentally, the "dragon sequence" (see answer 4.5.3–41) arises in the colors at the edges of $A_\infty, B_\infty, C_\infty, D_\infty$.]

122. A new global variable Θ, initially v, is the current "color threshold." Every item has a new field CTH in addition to NAME, LLINK, and RLINK. That field is normally zero in primary items, although it has a special use in step C3 as described below. In secondary items, CTH will be used to undo changes to Θ.

Insert 'CTH$(i) \leftarrow \Theta$; if $c = \Theta$, set $\Theta \leftarrow \Theta + 1$' just after '$i \leftarrow$ TOP(p)' in the purify routine (55). Insert '$\Theta \leftarrow$ CTH(i)' just after '$i \leftarrow$ TOP(p)' in the unpurify routine (57). Modify the commit routine (54) so that it jumps to the end of the uncommit routine (56), if COLOR$(p) > \Theta$, without changing j or p. (The effect is to avoid committing to any option that would have set a color value greater than Θ, by jumping from step C5 into the appropriate place within step C6.*)

Finally, change step C3 so that it never chooses an item i for which CTH$(i) > \Theta$. That step should then go to C8 if no item is choosable. (This mechanism prohibits branching on primary items for which the assumption of total symmetry between all colors $\geq \Theta$ isn't yet valid. Exercise 126 has an example.)

123. When, say, $m = 4$ and $n = 10$, Algorithm C takes 49 megamems to produce 1048576 solutions. The modified algorithm (where we set $v = 1$) takes 2 megamems to produce 43947 solutions. (Notice that the value vectors $q_1 \ldots q_n$ are equivalent to the *restricted growth strings* $a_1 \ldots a_n$ of 7.2.1.5–4, with $q_k = a_k + 1$.)

124. Let (x, y) denote a $\triangle$ triangle, and let $(x, y)'$ denote the $\triangledown$ triangle that lies immediately to its right. (Think of a square cell (x, y) that has been subdivided into right triangles by its main diagonal, then slanted and yscaled by $\sqrt{3}/2$.) For example, an $m \times n$ parallelogram has $2mn$ triangles (x, y) and $(x, y)'$ for $0 \leq x < m$ and $0 \leq y < n$, Cartesianwise; the 3×2 case is illustrated.

The boundary edges of triangle (x, y) are conveniently denoted by $/xy$, $\backslash xy$, and $-xy$. Then the boundary edges of $(x, y)'$ are $/(x+1)y$, $\backslash xy$, and $-x(y+1)$.

[A "barycentric" alternative with three coordinates is also of interest, because it's more symmetrical: Each triangle corresponds to an ordered triple of integers (x, y, z) such that $x + y + z = 1$ or 2, under the correspondence $(x, y) \leftrightarrow (x, y, 2 - x - y)$ and

---

* Backtrack programs often run into such cases where it is permissible, even desirable, to *jump into the middle of a loop.* See Examples 6c and 7a in the author's paper "Structured programming with **go to** statements," *Computing Surveys* **6** (1974), 261–301.

$(x, y)' \leftrightarrow (x, y, 1 - x - y)$. The twelve symmetries are then the six permutations of $\{x, y, z\}$ with an optional flip between (x, y, z) and $(\bar{x}, \bar{y}, \bar{z}) = (1 - x, 1 - y, 1 - z)$.]

[One can also use "barycentric even/odd coordinates," inspired by exercise 145, which are ordered triples (x, y, z) with $|x + y + z| \le 1$. Cases with x, y, z odd represent triangles, with $(x, y) \leftrightarrow (2x - 1, 2y - 1, 3 - 2x - 2y)$, $(x, y)' \leftrightarrow (2x - 1, 2y - 1, 1 - 2x - 2y)$. Cases with x, y, z even represent vertices. Cases with just one even coordinate represent edges (the average of two adjacent triangles). Cases with two even coordinates could represent directed edges.]

125. Every original triangle (x, y) or $(x, y)'$ expands to k^2 triangles of the forms $(kx + p, kx + q)$ or $(kx + p', kx + q')'$ for $0 \le p, q, p', q' < k$. Those obtained from (x, y) have $p + q < k$ and $p' + q' < k - 1$ (of which there are $\binom{k+1}{2}$ and $\binom{k}{2}$, respectively). The others are obtained from $(x, y)'$.

126. Let there be 24 primary items 01', 02, 02', ..., 32 for the triangles, and 24 primary items aaa, aab, ..., ddd for the tiles, together with 42 secondary items \01, -02, /02, ..., /41 for the edges. There are $24 \cdot 64$ options '01' aaa -02:a /11:a \01:a', '01' aab -02:a /11:a \01:b', '01' aab -02:a /11:b \01:a', ..., '32 ddd -32:d /32:d \32:d' — one for each way to place a tile. Finally, to force the boundary conditions, add another primary item '*', and another option '* -20:a -30:a /40:a ... \10:a'.

Algorithm C finds 11,853,792 solutions, after 340 Gμ of computation; this total includes 72 different versions of every distinct solution, hence there really are just 164,636 of them (a number that was unknown until Toby Gottfried computed it in 2001).

Using exercise 119 we can remove all options for aaa except '20 aaa -20:a /20:a \20:a'. Algorithm C then finds $11853792/12 = 987,816$ solutions, in 25 Gμ.

Furthermore, using exercise 122 (with $v = $ b), and not allowing step C3 to branch on a tile name until $\Theta = $ e (because there's total symmetry with respect to triangle locations but not tile names), finds every distinct solution just once, in 6.9 Gμ.

Finally, we can allow branching on aab whenever $\Theta \ge$ c, and in general on a piece name whenever Θ exceeds all colors in its name. This reduces the runtime to 4.5 Gμ.

[MacMahon specifically designed pattern (59b) to include all three of the nonwhite solid-color triangles in the center. If we fix them in those positions, an unmodified Algorithm C quickly finds 2138 solutions. There also are 2670 solutions with those three fixed in positions $\{11', 21', 12'\}$ instead of $\{12, 21, 22\}$.]

127. Every color appears in $(3 \cdot 24)/4 = 18$ places among the triangles, hence $18 - 2k$ times on the border when it occurs k times in the interior of a solution. Consequently no color occurs an odd number of times on the border. That leaves 2099200 possibilities.

All of those 2099200 are actually completable. (MacMahon would have been very happy to have known this!) The number of cases can be reduced to only 4054, using the methods of Section 7.2.3, because there are 576 symmetries: cyclic shifting and/or reflection and/or permutation of colors. The Monte Carlo procedure of Algorithm 7.2.2E not only finds solutions in each of those cases, it finds oodles of them. In fact, we can be confident that *every all-even-but-not-constant border specification has more than four times as many solutions as the pure-white border does.*

(More precisely, the pure-white border 000000000000 has 11853792 solutions, without reducing by symmetry; the next-smallest border, 000000000011, has 48620416; the next-smallest, 000000000101, has 49941040; and so on. There are more than 100 million solutions in the vast majority of cases, but probably never more than 500 million. Incidentally, 001022021121 is the only valid color pattern that has exactly three automorphisms.)

128. We can pack them into the 11-triangle region obtained by deleting triangle $(2,1)'$ from the 2×3 parallelogram in answer 124, in such a way that the edge colors satisfy $-00 = -20$, $/01 = /30$, $-02 = -12$. There are 1032 ways to do this, one of which is shown. This yields a "supertile" that nicely tiles the plane, in combination with its 180° rotation: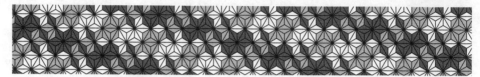

129. First consider rotation symmetry. Only 180° rotation applies, because of the four single-color tiles. To generate all of the strong solutions, assume that rotation changes a ↔ d, b ↔ c, and combine the options of answer 126 into pairs such as '02 abc -02:a /02:b \02:c 31' bdc -32:d /41:c \31:b'. The resulting 768 options have 68,024,064 solutions (found in about 0.5 Tμ); but many of those solutions are essentially the same (that is, obtainable from each other by rotation, reflection and/or color permutation).

It's somewhat tricky to count the essentially distinct patterns; canonical representations can be obtained by distinguishing six types of solutions: (1) 02 aaa (hence 31' ddd) and 03 bbb (hence 30' ccc), and /12:a or /12:c. [The cases /12:b or /12:d are equivalent to these, if we reflect and swap a ↔ b, c ↔ d.] (2) 02 aaa, 23 bbb [or equivalently 03' bbb]. (3) 02 aaa, 13' bbb, and \03:a or \03:c. (4) 02 aaa, and bbb in 12, 12', 22, 22', or 13. (5) 13 aaa, 02' bbb, and \12:a or \12:c. (6) 13 aaa, 12 bbb. Each type is easy, yielding $80768 + 164964 + 77660 + 819832 + 88772 + 185172 = 1417168$ solutions.

[Notice that the illustrated example of strong symmetry actually tiles the plane without rotation; that is, it has $-04 = -20$, $-14 = -30$, $/03 = /41$, ..., $\backslash 10 = \backslash 32$. Exactly 40208 of the essentially distinct solutions satisfy this additional proviso.]

To generate the weak solutions, introduce new secondary items b_{xy}, b'_{xy} for each triangle (x,y) or $(x,y)'$ with $y > 1$, representing color changes within the triangle. Typical options are now '02 aad -02:a /02:a \02:d b02:5', '02 aad -02:a /02:d \02:a b02:3', '02 aad -02:d /02:a \02:a b02:6', '02 abc -02:a /02:b \02:c b02:7', '31' bdc -32:c /41:b \31:d b02:7', '31' ccd -32:c /41:c \31:d b02:5'. We may assume that ddd is opposite aaa, ccc is opposite bbb. Algorithm C generates each weak-not-strong solution twice, each strong solution once; the six types yield a total of $24516 + 45818 + 22202 + 341301 + 44690 + 130676 = 609203$ weak-not-strong solutions.

Turning now to reflections of the hexagon, there are two essentially different possibilities: Top-bottom reflection preserves the values of four edges, but all triangles change; left-right reflection preserves the values of four triangles and two edges. Therefore *strong reflection symmetry is impossible*. (In the first case, all triangles change, hence all colors change. In the second case, two colors must be fixed. With colors a and d fixed but b ↔ c, eight triangles aaa, aad, abc, acb, bcd, bdc, dda, ddd must be fixed.)

Weak symmetry under top-bottom reflection can be assumed as before to take aaa to ddd, bbb to ccc. Again there are six types: [1] 02' aaa, 22' bbb, -13:a or -13:c. [2] 02' aaa, bbb in 12', 03', 13, 13', or 23. [3] 12' aaa, bbb in 03 or 03'. [4] 03 aaa, 23 bbb, -13:a or -13:c. [5] 03 aaa, bbb in 13 or 13'. [6] 03' aaa, 13' bbb, -13:a or -13:c. Surprisingly, some placements are "special": They have strong rotational symmetry, as well as weak top-down symmetry! Algorithm C, which generates the special ones once and the others twice, produces respectively (88, 0, 0, 98, 0, 75) + 2(1108, 12827, 8086, 3253, 12145, 4189) solutions. Here are examples of the $88 + 98 + 75 = 261$ special placements, which belong simultaneously to types [1] and (5), [4] and (3), [6] and (1):

Weak left-right symmetry is similar, but there now are some fixed triangles. If aaa is fixed, assume that ddd is also fixed; three such types arise, with $46975 + 35375 + 25261 = 107611$ solutions. Otherwise assume that ddd is opposite aaa; six types of this kind yield (75, 0, 98, 0, 0, 88) strong and (3711, 56706, 5889, 60297, 38311, 9093) non-strong solutions. So there's a grand total of 281618 essentially distinct weak-not-strong placements with left-right symmetry — of which 194 are top-down symmetric too.

[Arrangements that have strong and weak symmetry were first discovered by Kate Jones, who presented them in the 1991 user manual for Multimatch® III, an attractively produced set of triangular tiles.]

130. The nicest coordinate system for an octahedron is probably to number the faces 000, 001, ..., 111 in binary, and to let the vertices be $\{$0**, 1**, *0*, *1*, **0, **1$\}$; the edges are $\{xy*, x*y, *xy\}$ for $x, y \in \{0, 1\}$. Construct 512 options '000 aaa *00:a 0*0:a 00*:a', '000 aab *00:a 0*0:b 00*:a', '000 aab *00:b 0*0:a 00*:a', ..., with face-name items 000, ..., 111 primary and tile-name items aaa, ..., ddd secondary. Algorithm C quickly finds 2723472 solutions, which include 45356 distinct sets of eight. Those 45356 sets become, in turn, new options for Algorithm X (or C), with 24 primary tile-name items; now we get 1615452 solutions, which are the desired partitions.

Many symmetries are present, of course; we'll study how to distinguish nonisomorphic representatives in Section 7.2.3. One of the most interesting solutions,

   ,

has four color-swap symmetries, with all the solid-color triangles on one octahedron.

131. (a) Each triangle edge is either a (straight) or b (a wave) or c (a hump) or d (a dip). We can set this up with options and items as in answer 126, except that the edge-match condition is now a ↦ a, b ↦ b, c ↦ d, d ↦ c; to get proper matching, the options of ▽ triangles should state the *mate* color, as in '01' abc -02:a /11:b \01:d'.

Every solution corresponds to 24 equivalent solutions, because we get a factor of 6 by rotating the hexagon, a factor of two by interchanging humps with dips, and another factor of two by reflection. (Reflection is a bit tricky, because a wave becomes an anti-wave when a piece is flipped over. However, every reflected piece has its own anti-piece, which yields the desired anti-solution.) Thus we can force aaa to be in position 02. Treating c and d symmetrically as in answer 126 (with $v = $ c) produces exactly 2,231,724 canonical solutions and needs only 30 gigamems of running time.

[This puzzle is manufactured by Kadon Enterprises under the name Trifolia®.]

(b) A similar setup, letting c and d represent 0 spots and 3 spots so that it's easy to treat them symmetrically, now has mates a ↦ b, b ↦ a, c ↦ d, d ↦ c; hence one option is '01' abc -02:b /11:a \01:d'. The boundary colors in directions / and \ are a; in direction – they are b. The solutions to this problem typically form groups of eight (not 24): We can swap c ↔ d, reflect left-right, reflect top-down, or rotate by 180°;

the latter two are combined with swapping $\mathtt{a} \leftrightarrow \mathtt{b}$. Without attempting to remove any symmetries, we get 3,419,736,176 solutions, after 20.6 teramems of computation.

Left-right reflection always gives a distinct solution, whether we swap $\mathtt{c} \leftrightarrow \mathtt{d}$ or not (because there are at least eight pieces that stay fixed, and only four places to put them). But the illustrated example shows that some solutions are fixed under 180° rotation; we can find them by adding 15 new primary items, such as $\mathtt{\#/23}$, and $15 \cdot 4$ new options, such as '$\mathtt{\#/23}$ $\mathtt{/23{:}x}$ $\mathtt{/20{:}x}$' for $x \in \{\mathtt{a}, \mathtt{b}, \mathtt{c}, \mathtt{d}\}$. Altogether 18656 solutions have that symmetry; such cases form groups of four, not eight. Similarly, 169368 cases turn out to have top-down symmetry. It follows from "Burnside's lemma" that the total number of essentially different solutions is $(3419736176 + 18656 + 169368)/8 = 427490525$.

To double the speed of all these computations, take $v = \mathtt{c}$ in exercise 122.

132. This challenging problem was first resolved by Peter Esser in April 2002, and presented online at $\mathtt{www.polyforms.eu/coloredpolygons/triindex.html\#trios24}$. [See *JRM* **9** (1977), 209. One can show that the only solutions to the Diophantine equation $d + d(d-1) + d(d-1)(d-2)/3 = m^2$ are $d = 1$, 2, and 24, using advanced methods found in N. P. Smart, *The Algorithmic Resolution of Diophantine Equations* (1998).]

133. This problem is like exercise 126, but considerably simpler because squares are easier than triangles. There are $24 \cdot 81$ options '$\mathtt{00}$ $\mathtt{aaaa}$ $\mathtt{h00{:}a}$ $\mathtt{v10{:}a}$ $\mathtt{h01{:}a}$ $\mathtt{v00{:}a}$', ..., '$\mathtt{53}$ $\mathtt{ccba}$ $\mathtt{h53{:}a}$ $\mathtt{v63{:}c}$ $\mathtt{h54{:}c}$ $\mathtt{v53{:}b}$', where $\mathtt{h}xy$ and $\mathtt{v}xy$ denote the horizontal and vertical edges between squares. We save a factor of 4 by limiting $\mathtt{aaaa}$ to four positions on the border, and another factor of 2 by making $\mathtt{b}$ and $\mathtt{c}$ equivalent (exercise 122 with $v = \mathtt{b}$). The resulting 13328 solutions are found in 15 $\mathrm{G}\mu$.

[Today it's easy to count them; but this problem has a tortured history! T. H. O'Beirne missed two of the 20 possible ways to place the internal white edges, when he analyzed the situation by hand in *New Scientist* **9** (2 February 1961), 288–289. A few years later, the problem of solution counts for MacMahon squares was probably the very first large computation ever undertaken at Stanford Artificial Intelligence Laboratory; Gary Feldman found 12261 placements, during a 40-hour computer run (see *Stanford AI Project*, Memo 12 (16 January 1964), 8 pages). That number was believed to be correct until May 1977, when the true value was obtained by H. Fernández Long in Argentina.]

Instead of denoting squares by xy and edges by $\{\mathtt{h}xy, \mathtt{v}xy\}$, it's convenient to use "even/odd coordinates" instead (see exercise 145). In that system, a pair of odd numbers $(2x+1)(2y+1)$ denotes a square, and the edge between two adjacent squares is represented by the midpoint between them. For example, the $24 \cdot 81$ options sketched above would then take the form

'$\mathtt{11}$ $\mathtt{aaaa}$ $\mathtt{01{:}a}$ $\mathtt{12{:}a}$ $\mathtt{21{:}a}$ $\mathtt{10{:}a}$', ..., '$\mathtt{b7}$ $\mathtt{ccba}$ $\mathtt{a7{:}a}$ $\mathtt{b8{:}c}$ $\mathtt{c7{:}c}$ $\mathtt{b6{:}b}$'.

Such coordinates are easier to work with under reflection and rotation.

134. (O, P, Q, ..., Z) occur respectively (0, 1672, 22, 729, 402, 61, 36, 48, 174, 259, 242, 0) times, sometimes twice in the same solution; one solution features *four* pentominoes.

[Kate Jones introduced such questions in the Multimatch® I user manual (1991).]

135. Indeed, the total number of solutions is enormous; Monte Carlo estimates predict $\approx 9 \times 10^8$ of them for any fixed placements of $\mathtt{aaaa}$, $\mathtt{bbbb}$, $\mathtt{cccc}$ that aren't obviously impossible. Therefore it's natural to impose extra conditions. The elegant wrapping below permutes colors cyclically and has solid colors on every edge of the cube! Investigations by H. L. Nelson, F. Fink, and M. Risueño showed that 61 such solutions are possible; see W. E. Philpott, *JRM* **7** (1974), 266–275. See answer 145 for an even/odd coordinate system that is useful for representing this problem internally.

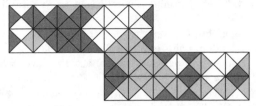

(Wrapping the surface of a symmetrical polyhedron is a nice way to avoid awkward boundary conditions when arranging MacMahon-like tiles. Dario Uri devised 39 such problems in 1993, together with ingenious mechanical frames for building the results. Here, for example, are a rhombic triacontahedron (30 rhombuses) and a stellated dodecahedron (60 isosceles triangles), based on all possible ways to put distinct colors from {red, green, blue, yellow, black} on the edges. His report "Tessere di Mac Mahon su superfici tridimensionali" is online at www.uriland.it.)

136. The main challenge is to find a good way to represent the faces and edges of a dodecahedron. Perhaps the nicest is to represent the faces by vertices of an icosahedron, with the three-dimensional coordinates $(0, (-1)^b\phi, (-1)^c)\sigma^a$, where $(x, y, z)\sigma = (z, x, y)$; let abc stand for this face, for $0 \le a < 3$ and $0 \le b, c < 2$. A face is adjacent to its five nearest neighbors; we can represent the edge between abc and $a'b'c'$ as the midpoint $(abc + a'b'c')/2$. These 30 midpoints have two forms, either $ab = (0, (-1)^b\phi, 0)\sigma^a$ or $abcd = \frac{1}{2}((-1)^b, (-1)^c\phi, (-1)^d\phi^2)\sigma^a$. The corresponding XCC problem can now be formulated as usual, with 120 options for each face. For example, a typical option for face 201 is '201 01243 20:3 1100:0 2001:1 2101:2 1110:4'.

We can force the first tile to be in a particular place by default. Algorithm C needs only 9 megamems to solve the resulting problem, and produces 60 solutions.

Of course many of those solutions are equivalent. There are 120 transformations that preserve the dodecahedron and icosahedron as represented above, generated by three reflection matrices and two orthogonal matrices,

$$D_0 = \begin{pmatrix} -1 & 0 & 0 \\ 0 & +1 & 0 \\ 0 & 0 & +1 \end{pmatrix}, \quad D_1 = \begin{pmatrix} +1 & 0 & 0 \\ 0 & -1 & 0 \\ 0 & 0 & +1 \end{pmatrix}, \quad D_2 = \begin{pmatrix} +1 & 0 & 0 \\ 0 & +1 & 0 \\ 0 & 0 & -1 \end{pmatrix},$$

$$P = \begin{pmatrix} 0 & 0 & 1 \\ 1 & 0 & 0 \\ 0 & 1 & 0 \end{pmatrix}, \quad Q = \frac{1}{2} \begin{pmatrix} 1 & -\phi & 1/\phi \\ \phi & 1/\phi & -1 \\ 1/\phi & 1 & \phi \end{pmatrix}.$$

Applying any combination of these, and remapping the colors to agree with the default placement, gives an equivalent solution. It turns out, as Conway discovered by hand(!), that there are just three inequivalent solutions, having respectively 4, 6, and 12 automorphisms (hence occurring 30, 20, and 10 times in the output of Algorithm C):

[See M. R. Boothroyd and J. H. Conway, Eureka: *The Archimedeans' Journal* **22** (1959), 15–17, 22–23. Conway has named them the "quintominal dodecahedra."]

137. (a) This is an easy application of Algorithm C, with $14 + 12$ items and $7 \cdot (1 + 6 \times 6) = 259$ options. (Clever reasoning also allows it to be established by hand, with a search tree of size 15.)

(b) No. Again Algorithm C gives the answer quickly.

(c) Thousands of random trials indicate that about 93% of the $\binom{120}{7}$ choices have no solution; about 5% have just one solution; about 1% have two solutions; and the remaining 1% have three or more.

(d) About 0.4% of all cases work, as in the example shown. *Historical notes:* Milton Bradley Company introduced Drive Ya Nuts in 1970; the name of its inventor has unfortunately been forgotten. It was preceded by a much more difficult puzzle with 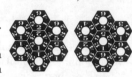 19 hexagons in three concentric rings, called Super Dom [H. Hydes, *British Patent 149473* (19 August 1920)], and by several similar puzzles [H. Hydes and F. R. B. Whitehouse, *British Patent 173588* (29 December 1921); G. H. Haswell, *U.S. Patent 1558165* (20 October 1925)], featuring both kinds of edge-matching rules.

138. (a) We can name the tiles ABcd, ABdc, ACbd, ..., DCba. Assuming that ABcd is in the top left corner, a straightforward application of Algorithm C (with 2118 options involving $48 + 48$ items) will output 42680 solutions, in 13 gigamems. As in other such problems, however, these outputs include many that are essentially the same. Up to 96 equivalent solutions are related by the operations of shifting any cell to the top-left position and/or flipping horizontally and/or flipping vertically, then remapping the colors. For instance, the given example has six automorphisms: We can shift it two columns right, then map $A \mapsto C \mapsto D \mapsto A$, $a \mapsto c \mapsto d \mapsto a$; we can also shift two rows down, reflect left-right, then $A \leftrightarrow D$ and $a \leftrightarrow d$. Hence it contributes $96/6 = 16$ cases to the total of 42680. Altogether there are (79, 531, 5, 351, 6, 68, 12, 4) cases with respectively (1, 2, 3, 4, 6, 8, 12, 24) automorphisms, hence $79+531+5+351+6+68+12+4 = 1056$ essentially different solutions. One with 24 symmetries is shown below (it leads to itself if we move right 1 and down 2, and/or reflect horizontally or vertically).

(b) Now Algorithm C, given 1089 options involving $49+60$ items, quickly finds just six solutions — three different pairs related by transposition, each of which is symmetric under 90° rotation, all with heads and tails in the same places.

(c) Take any of the three solutions to (b), reflect it top-down, interchange heads with tails, and swap $B \leftrightarrow D$, $b \leftrightarrow d$. For example, the dual of the given solution is shown below. Alternating all-heads with all-tails, in checkerboard fashion, yields uncountably many tilings of the plane.

[These tiles are believed to have originated in 1990 with a puzzle called "Super Heads & Tails," designed by Howard Swift and produced in a limited edition.]

139. (a) Say that two sets of nine are essentially the same if one can be obtained from the other by remapping the colors, and/or reflecting all of the pieces, and/or interchanging heads with tails. For example, $4! \times 2 \times 2 = 96$ different choices of nine are equivalent to the set

   (∗)

By considering canonical forms, as in exercise 138(a), we find 14124 equivalence classes, of which (13157, 882, 7, 78) have the respective sizes (96/1, 96/2, 96/3, 96/4).

     (b) There are exactly (9666, 1883, 1051, 537, 380, 213, 147, 68, 60, 27, 29, 9, 24, 4, 8, 2, 5, 4, 1, 1, 1, 1, 1, 1, 1, 0, 0, 0, 1) classes with (0, 1, 2, ..., 27) solutions; the amazing one with 27 is represented by (∗) above. Two of the 1883 puzzles with unique solutions are particularly interesting because they have four automorphisms:

In each case we can flip the pieces and/or swap heads ↔ tails, then remap the colors to get the original tiles.

     [This problem was first solved by Jacques Haubrich in 1996, who considered color remapping only (hence he had 54498 equivalence classes). Haubrich has collected 435 inequivalent puzzles, from around the world, that consist of nine tiles with two heads opposite two tails. But only 17 of them have all tiles different and all four objects different on each tile; for example, at least one tile such as `ABcb` is usually present. The first "pure" `HHtt` puzzle in his collection was made by the Hoek Loos company in 1974.]

140. (a) We save a factor of 4! by applying exercise 122 with $v = \mathbf{a}$. Then Algorithm C gives respectively (10, 5, 6) solutions. The true numbers, however, are (5, 3, 3), because the shapes are symmetrical — and because the middle solution has an additional symmetry: It goes into itself if we rotate by 180° and permute the colors.

     (b) The scaled-up versions of ⬡, ⌐, ⌐ are impossible. But we have

  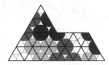

with respectively (4, 4, 3) solutions; and there are *unique* solutions to the other five:

(c) These shapes, with respectively (7, 9, 48, 2, 23, 28, 18) solutions, are a bit easier to handle. The "wave" has six solutions with central symmetry; the "bar" has four.

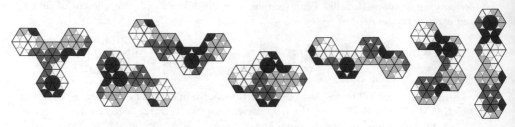

[Vertex-colored triangles have been named 'Trioker' by Marc Odier; see French Patent 1582023 (1968), *U.S. Patent 3608906* (1971), and the book *Surprenant Triangles*, which he published with Yves Roussel in 1976. They also are sold as Multimatch® IV.]

141. (a) Using exercise 122 with $v = $ a yields respectively (138248, 49336, 147708) solutions in (1390, 330, 720) gigamems. Then we divide by (8, 4, 4) to remove symmetries of the board, getting (17281, 12334, 36927) solutions that are essentially distinct. [These numbers were first computed by Toby Gottfried in (1998, 1999, 2002). He had been interested in the puzzle ever since seeing the 5×5 version that was sold by Skor-Mor in 1970 under the name "Nitty Gritty." The puzzle is extremely difficult to solve by hand, in spite of the many solutions; Langford himself was unable to solve the 3×8 case.]

The 12334 solutions for 4×6 include 180 that have matching colors at the left and right. Each of these patterns therefore tiles a "cylinder"; and the 180 form 30 families of 6 that are equivalent to each other by rotating the cylinder. Similarly, 1536 of the 36927 solutions for 3×8 are cylindrical, making 192 families of 8. The example illustrated is one of 42 that have the same solid color at both left and right.

(b) Any solution can be used to tile the plane in combination with its mirror reflections and its 180° rotation (which is a reflection of a reflection).

The 17281 solutions include 209 for which the hole is surrounded by a single color. Six of these have matching colors at two opposite sides; the one illustrated will tile the plane in conjunction with its mate, which is obtained by swapping b ↔ c.

The 4×6 example illustrated is the unique solution for which both pairs of opposite sides induce exactly the same color partition (the restricted growth strings 0121120 and 01220). Thus it too will tile the plane together with its b ↔ c mate.

[Vertex-matched squares, with *incomplete* sets of tiles, first appeared in puzzles devised by E. L. Thurston, *U.S. Patents 487797* (1892), *490689* (1893).]

142. Each boundary between the square cells containing octagons now has *two* secondary items that receive color. For example, a typical option for Algorithm C is now '10 aabc a_{10}:a r_{10}:a l_{11}:b a_{11}:b b_{21}:c l_{21}:c r_{20}:a b_{20}:a', where a_{xy}, b_{xy}, l_{xy}, and r_{xy} denote the half edges above, below, left, and right of (x, y). The number of solutions, again using exercise 122 with $v = $ a, is $2 \cdot (132046861, 1658603, 119599)$ in cases (i), (ii), (iii), found in (2607, 10223, 77) gigamems. Case (i) includes $2 \cdot (193920, 10512, 96)$ "cylindrical" arrangements in which the colors match at top/bottom, left/right, both; one of the 96 "toroidal" examples is shown. Case (ii) includes $2 \cdot 5980$ cylindrical arrangements that match at left/right. Case (iii) has no cylindrical examples.

[Many other possibilities arise, because neighboring octagons can match without lying in a square grid. Kadon Enterprises offers attractive sets called 'Doris®'.]

143. (a) *simplex*(8, 6, 8, 2, 0, 0, 0); *simplex*(7, 4, 7, 3, 0, 0, 0); *simplex*(5, 5, 5, 4, 0, 0, 0).

(b, c) Nonnegative integers $x_0x_1x_2x_3x_4x_5$ define such a polygon if and only if the boundary path returns to its starting point, which means that $x_0 + x_1 = x_3 + x_4$ and $x_1 + x_2 = x_4 + x_5$. Rotating by $60°$ replaces $x_0x_1x_2x_3x_4x_5$ by $x_5x_0x_1x_2x_3x_4$; reflecting left $\leftrightarrow$ right replaces $x_0x_1x_2x_3x_4x_5$ by $x_0x_5x_4x_3x_2x_1$. Hence we get a canonical form by insisting that $x_0 \geq x_3 \geq x_5 \geq x_1$: *Every sequence of nonnegative integers* (a, b, c, d) *with* $a \geq b \geq c \geq d$ *defines the boundary* $x_0x_1x_2x_3x_4x_5$ *of a unique convex triangular polygon*, where $x_0 = a$, $x_1 = d$, $x_2 = a - b + c$, $x_3 = b$, $x_4 = a - b + d$, $x_5 = c$. Furthermore, that polygon contains exactly $N = (a + c + d)^2 - b^2 - c^2 - d^2$ triangles.

Given N, the following algorithm visits all relevant (a, b, c, d). For $c = 0, 1, \ldots,$ while $2c^2 \leq N$ do the following: For $d = 0, 1, \ldots,$ while $d \leq c$ and $2c(c + 2d) \leq N$, let $x = N + c^2 + d^2$. If x mod $4 \neq 2$, for every divisor q of x such that $q \equiv x$ (modulo 2) and $q^2 \leq x$, set $a \leftarrow (x/q+q)/2 - c - d$ and $b \leftarrow (x/q-q)/2$. Visit (a, b, c, d) if $a \geq b$ and $b \geq c$.

When $N = 24$ this algorithm visits six (a, b, c, d), namely $(7, 5, 0, 0)$, $(5, 1, 0, 0)$, $(12, 12, 1, 0)$, $(6, 6, 2, 0)$, $(2, 2, 2, 2)$, $(4, 4, 3, 0)$. The fourth, sixth, and second are the shapes of exercise 140. The other three cannot be tiled properly with Langford's 24 tiles.

[See OEIS sequence A096004, contributed by P. Boddington in 2004.]

(d) Yes. One way is $simplex(a + c + d, a + c, a + d, a - b + c + d, 0, 0, 0)$.

144. The constraints are severe, because a solid color is needed at transitions between regimes. Algorithm C (with $v = $ a as in answer 142) quickly finds $2 \cdot 102$ solutions to (ii). But surprisingly many arrangements arise in case (i); Algorithm C finds $2 \cdot 37586004$ of them, *not* so quickly (643 teramems)!

(These tiles suggest many intriguing questions. For example, suppose we restrict consideration to making a big hexagon from 24 small ones. There are 2^{24} ways to specify whether each position should be matched at vertices or edges; but very few of those specifications are actually realizable. Can the realizable ones be nicely characterized?)

145. Suppose $0 \leq i \leq l$, $0 \leq j \leq m$, and $0 \leq k \leq n$. Let $(2i, 2j, 2k)$ represent vertex (i, j, k); let $(u+v)/2$ represent the edge between adjacent vertices u and v; let $(a+b)/2$ represent the face containing parallel edges a and b; let $(e + f)/2$ represent the cell containing parallel faces e and f. Thus, the triple (x, y, z) represents a vertex, edge, face, or cell when it has respectively 0, 1, 2, or 3 odd coordinates.

For example, $(2i, 2j+1, 2k)$ represents the edge between vertices (i, j, k) and $(i, j+1, k)$; $(2i+1, 2j, 2k+1)$ represents the face whose vertices are (i, j, k), $(i+1, j, k)$, $(i, j, k+1)$, $(i+1, j, k+1)$; and $(2i+1, 2j+1, 2k+1)$ represents the cell whose eight vertices are $(i + (0 \text{ or } 1), j + (0 \text{ or } 1), k + (0 \text{ or } 1))$.

Notice that $(a + b)/2$ represents the vertex between adjacent parallel edges a and b; $(e + f)/2$ represents the edge between adjacent parallel faces e and f; $(p+q)/2$ represents the face between adjacent cells p and q.

(We can use a similar convention in two dimensions, as an alternative to the 'H' and 'V' items in situations like answer 109.)

146. (a) Each color occurs four times on the "visible" faces and at most twice on the "hidden" faces. So the five adjacencies account for all six occurrences of five colors.

(b) For every partition of $\{a, b, c, d, e, f\}$ into three pairs $\{u, u'\}$, $\{v, v'\}$, $\{w, w'\}$, there are two chiral cubes having u opposite u', v opposite v', w opposite w'. Order the colors so that $u < u'$, $u < v$, $v < v'$, $v < w$, $v < w'$; there are 30 ways to do this. The cube named $uu'vv'ww'$ is the one that can be placed with u on top, u' on the bottom, v in front, v' in the back, w at left, w' at the right. For example, the cubes in $(*)$ are named aebfcd, acbfde, acbdef, afbdec, abcedf, aebcfd.

(c) We can set this up for Algorithm C by specifying $6 \cdot 30 \cdot 24$ options, one for each cube position, cube name, and cube placement. There are 6 primary items for the positions; 30 secondary items for the names; $4 \cdot 6$ primary items u_c, d_c, f_c, b_c for colors on the top, bottom, front, and back, where $c \in \{a, b, c, d, e, f\}$; and 6 secondary items h_k for the colors hidden between positions k and $k+1$. For example, the leftmost cube in (∗) corresponds to the option '1 aebfcd u_a d_e f_b b_f h_0:c h_1:d'.

If we eliminate all but one option for position 1 (thus saving a factor of 720), there are 2176 solutions. Each solution is, however, potentially equivalent to 95 others, because there are 16 possible rotations/reflections together with 6 cyclic permutations (followed by remapping the colors of the leftmost cube). For example, the solution illustrated has 12 such automorphisms. Further study shows that only 33 solutions are "essentially different" — of which $(17, 9, 3, 1, 3)$ have $(1, 2, 4, 6, 12)$ automorphisms.

(d) Yes, in lots and lots of ways. The $720 \cdot 2176$ solutions obtained *without* fixing the leftmost cube involve 15500 different 6-tuples of cubes; and the exact cover problem for which those 6-tuples are the options has 163,088,368 solutions.

[This problem was posed by Martin Gardner in *Scientific American* **204**, 3 (March 1961), 168–174 (long before the "Instant Insanity" craze), and he extended it to question (c) in *Scientific American* **235**, 3 (September 1978), 26. A solution to (d) that involves five symmetrical arrangements was found by Zoltan Perjés in 1981; see Gardner's book *Fractal Music, Hypercards, and More* (1992), 97.]

147. (a) The "even/odd coordinates" of exercise 145 are ideal for representing the cube positions and the faces between them. For example, the colors in the $1 \times 2 \times 2$ brick that was illustrated with the exercise are nicely represented by the $3 \times 5 \times 5$ array

$$
\begin{bmatrix} ..... \\ .a.a. \\ ..... \\ .a.a. \\ ..... \end{bmatrix}
\begin{bmatrix} .d.d. \\ c.e.c \\ .f.f. \\ c.d.c \\ .e.e. \end{bmatrix}
\begin{bmatrix} ..... \\ .b.b. \\ ..... \\ .b.b. \\ ..... \end{bmatrix},
$$

where entry $(0, 1, 1) =$ a, entry $(1, 0, 1) =$ d, entry $(1, 1, 0) =$ c, ..., entry $(2, 3, 3) =$ b. The cubes in positions $(1, 1, 1)$, $(1, 1, 3)$, $(1, 3, 1)$, $(1, 3, 3)$ of this example have the respective names abcedf, abcefd, abcdfe, abcdef. In a similar way an $l \times m \times n$ brick has colors represented by a $(2l + 1) \times (2m + 1) \times (2n + 1)$ tensor; and the tensor

$$
\begin{bmatrix} .... \\ .a.a.a.a. \\ .... \\ .a.a.a.a. \\ .... \\ .a.a.a.a. \\ .... \end{bmatrix}
\begin{bmatrix} .c.c.c.c.c. \\ b.f.d.f.d.b \\ .e.e.b.b.f. \\ b.c.d.f.e.b \\ .f.f.e.d.d. \\ b.e.d.b.e.b \\ .c.c.c.c.c. \end{bmatrix}
\begin{bmatrix} .... \\ .d.b.e.e.e. \\ .... \\ .d.b.c.c.c. \\ .... \\ .d.b.f.f.f. \\ .... \end{bmatrix}
\begin{bmatrix} .c.c.c.c.c. \\ b.f.d.b.f.b \\ .e.e.f.d.d. \\ b.c.d.e.f.b \\ .f.f.b.b.e. \\ b.e.d.e.d.b \\ .c.c.c.c.c. \end{bmatrix}
\begin{bmatrix} .... \\ .a.a.a.a. \\ .... \\ .a.a.a.a. \\ .... \\ .a.a.a.a. \\ .... \end{bmatrix}
$$

represents a "magnificent brick" whose faces are colored a, b, c (each twice).

(b) Let there be lmn primary items $(2i+1)(2j+1)(2k+1)$ for the cube positions, 30 secondary items for the cube names, and $lm(n+1) + l(m+1)n + (l+1)mn$ secondary items xyz for the cube faces, where $0 \le x \le 2l$, $0 \le y \le 2m$, $0 \le z \le 2n$, $(x \bmod 2) + (y \bmod 2) + (z \bmod 2) = 2$. For example, the option for position 135 in solution (a) is '135 acbefd 035:a 125:b 134:d 136:f 145:e 235:c'. We also introduce six primary items to enforce the rule about solid colors on the brick's faces. Each of them has six options, one for each color c; for example, the options for the top face are 'top 101:c 103:c 105:c

107:c 109:c 301:c 303:c 305:c 307:c 309:c'. The number of solutions is reduced by a factor of 720 if we remove all but one of the 720 options for position 111.

It turns out that the brick's face colors have an interesting property in every solution: A repeated face color occurs only on opposite, parallel faces. The example $1 \times 2 \times 2$ brick has face colors $\mathsf{ab} \times \mathsf{cc} \times \mathsf{de}$; the $2 \times 3 \times 5$ brick in (a) has colors $\mathsf{aa} \times \mathsf{bb} \times \mathsf{cc}$.

A brick is considered to be essentially the same as any other that's obtained from it by rotation, reflection, and/or permutation of colors. The example $1 \times 2 \times 2$ brick above has 8 automorphisms; for example, we can reflect top $\leftrightarrow$ bottom and swap $\mathsf{d} \leftrightarrow \mathsf{e}$. The $2 \times 3 \times 5$ brick above has 2 automorphisms: The nontrivial one reflects front $\leftrightarrow$ back, top $\leftrightarrow$ bottom, $\mathsf{e} \leftrightarrow \mathsf{f}$.

There's *another* $1 \times 2 \times 2$ brick, whose face colors are $\mathsf{ab} \times \mathsf{cd} \times \mathsf{ef}$. It has 16 automorphisms. Thus it occurs only once among the three solutions found by Algorithm C when $(l, m, n) = (1, 2, 2)$; the other two solutions are equivalent to each other.

There's a *unique* $1 \times 2 \times 3$ brick, easily found by hand. It has colors $\mathsf{ab} \times \mathsf{cc} \times \mathsf{dd}$, and 8 automorphisms. (Clearly $1 \times m \times n$ is possible only if $mn \le 6$.)

The $2 \times 2 \times 2$ bricks are especially interesting because MacMahon himself and his friend J. R. J. Jocelyn considered this case (with six different face colors), when they introduced the 30 6-color cubes in U.K. Patent 8275 of 1892. They observed that one can choose any "prototype" cube and replicate it at twice the size, by assembling eight of the other cubes. This can be done in two ways — using, in fact, the same eight cubes. But those two solutions are isomorphic, in 24 different ways. [See *Proc. London Math. Soc.* **24** (1893), 145–155. Their 8-cube puzzle was sold under the name "Mayblox."]

Gerhard Kowalewski, in *Alte und neue mathematische Spiele* (1930), 14–19, found a $2 \times 2 \times 2$ brick with face colors $\mathsf{aa} \times \mathsf{bb} \times \mathsf{cd}$. Ferdinand Winter, in *Mac Mahons Problem: Das Spiel der 30 bunten Würfel* (1933), 67–87, found another, with face colors $\mathsf{aa} \times \mathsf{bc} \times \mathsf{de}$. And there's also a fourth solution, having Winter's face colors:

MacMahon
```
[.....][.c.c.][.....][.c.c.][.....]
[.a.a.][e.b.f][.d.d.][e.a.f][.b.b.] ;
[.....][.f.e.][.....][.f.e.][.....]
[.a.a.][e.b.f][.c.c.][e.a.f][.b.b.]
[.....][.d.d.][.....][.d.d.][.....]
```

Kowalewski
```
[.....][.b.b.][.....][.b.b.][.....]
[.a.a.][c.e.d][.d.c.][c.f.d][.a.a.] ;
[.....][.f.f.][.....][.e.e.][.....]
[.a.a.][c.e.d][.d.c.][c.f.d][.a.a.]
[.....][.b.b.][.....][.b.b.][.....]
```

Winter
```
[.....][.b.b.][.....][.b.b.][.....]
[.a.a.][d.c.e][.f.f.][d.c.e][.a.a.] ;
[.....][.e.d.][.....][.e.d.][.....]
[.a.a.][d.f.e][.b.b.][d.f.e][.a.a.]
[.....][.c.c.][.....][.c.c.][.....]
```

Fourth
```
[.....][.b.b.][.....][.b.b.][.....]
[.a.a.][d.f.e][.c.c.][d.f.e][.a.a.] .
[.....][.e.d.][.....][.e.d.][.....]
[.a.a.][d.f.e][.b.b.][d.f.e][.a.a.]
[.....][.c.c.][.....][.c.c.][.....]
```

These solutions have respectively $(24, 8, 4, 8)$ automorphisms; hence Algorithm C finds $48/24 + 48/8 + 48/4 + 48/8 = 26$ solutions to the case $l = m = n = 2$.

Larger cases have solutions that are, perhaps, even more remarkable; but there's room here for only a brief summary. For each feasible case of $l \times m \times n$ bricks with particular face colors, we list the number of different solutions with $(1, 2, 4, 8)$ automorphisms. *Case* $2 \times 2 \times 3$: $\mathsf{aa} \times \mathsf{bb} \times \mathsf{cc}$, $(0, 0, 1, 0)$; $\mathsf{aa} \times \mathsf{bc} \times \mathsf{dd}$, $(0, 2, 6, 1)$; $\mathsf{aa} \times \mathsf{bc} \times \mathsf{de}$, $(0, 1, 6, 0)$; $\mathsf{ab} \times \mathsf{cd} \times \mathsf{ee}$, $(0, 1, 2, 0)$; $\mathsf{ab} \times \mathsf{cd} \times \mathsf{ef}$, $(0, 0, 2, 0)$. *Case* $2 \times 2 \times 4$: $\mathsf{aa} \times \mathsf{bb} \times \mathsf{cc}$, $(0, 0, 1, 0)$; $\mathsf{aa} \times \mathsf{bb} \times \mathsf{cd}$, $(0, 0, 1, 0)$; $\mathsf{aa} \times \mathsf{bc} \times \mathsf{dd}$, $(0, 3, 4, 2)$; $\mathsf{aa} \times \mathsf{bc} \times \mathsf{de}$, $(0, 11, 14, 2)$; $\mathsf{ab} \times \mathsf{cd} \times \mathsf{ee}$, $(0, 2, 2, 3)$; $\mathsf{ab} \times \mathsf{cd} \times \mathsf{ef}$, $(0, 1, 1, 1)$. *Case* $2 \times 2 \times 5$: $\mathsf{aa} \times \mathsf{bc} \times \mathsf{dd}$, $(0, 5, 4, 0)$; $\mathsf{aa} \times \mathsf{bc} \times \mathsf{de}$, $(0, 18, 9, 0)$; $\mathsf{ab} \times \mathsf{cd} \times \mathsf{ee}$, $(0, 0, 1, 0)$; $\mathsf{ab} \times \mathsf{cd} \times \mathsf{ef}$, $(0, 2, 5, 1)$. *Case* $2 \times 3 \times 3$: $\mathsf{aa} \times \mathsf{bb} \times \mathsf{cc}$, $(2, 15, 4, 0)$; $\mathsf{aa} \times \mathsf{bb} \times \mathsf{cd}$, $(4, 8, 1, 0)$; $\mathsf{aa} \times \mathsf{bc} \times \mathsf{de}$, $(1, 4, 1, 2)$. *Case* $2 \times 3 \times 4$: $\mathsf{aa} \times \mathsf{bb} \times \mathsf{cd}$,

$(6, 8, 1, 0)$; aa × bc × de, $(0, 6, 0, 0)$; ab × cc × dd, $(0, 4, 2, 0)$; ab × cc × de, $(0, 2, 0, 0)$; ab × cd × ee, $(0, 2, 0, 0)$; ab × cd × ef, $(0, 7, 0, 0)$. *Case* $2 \times 3 \times 5$: aa × bb × cc, $(0, 2, 0, 0)$.

(Conspicuous by its absence is the case $l = m = n = 3$. There's no $3 \times 3 \times 3$ brick, although we can come close: A $3 \times 3 \times 3$ without a corner can be made from 26 of the 30; or without the middle cube and the one above it, from 25.)

148. There are eleven such cubes, and they can be matched in many pleasant ways:

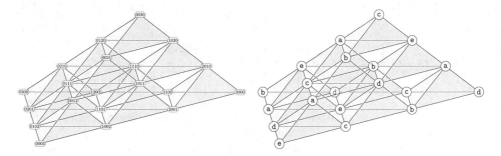

$$
\begin{bmatrix} \cdots \\ \cdots \\ \cdots \\ \cdots\text{c}\cdots \\ \cdots \\ \cdots \end{bmatrix}
\begin{bmatrix} \cdots \\ \cdots \\ \cdots\text{a}\cdots \\ \cdots\text{a.c}\cdots \\ \cdots\text{c}\cdots \\ \cdots \end{bmatrix}
\begin{bmatrix} \cdots \\ \text{.a.b.a.} \\ \cdots \\ \text{.b.a.b.} \\ \cdots \\ \text{.a.b.a.} \end{bmatrix}
\begin{bmatrix} \text{.a.a.a.} \\ \text{a.b.a.c} \\ \text{.c.b.c.} \\ \text{a.b.a.c} \\ \text{.b.a.a.} \\ \text{a.c.b.c} \\ \text{.c.c.c.} \end{bmatrix}
\begin{bmatrix} \cdots \\ \text{.b.c.b.} \\ \cdots \\ \text{.c.b.c.} \\ \cdots \\ \text{.b.c.b.} \end{bmatrix}
\begin{bmatrix} \cdots \\ \cdots \\ \cdots\text{b}\cdots \\ \cdots\text{b.c}\cdots \\ \cdots\text{c}\cdots \\ \cdots \end{bmatrix}
\begin{bmatrix} \cdots \\ \cdots \\ \cdots \\ \cdots\text{c}\cdots \\ \cdots \\ \cdots \end{bmatrix}
$$

149. Label the vertices with nonnegative barycentric coordinates $wxyz$, where $w + x + y + z = 3$. Also label the ten unit tetrahedra with barycentric coordinates $stuv$, where $s + t + u + v = 2$; the vertices $wxyz$ of tetrahedron $stuv$ are then $stuv + \{1000, 0100, 0010, 0001\}$. Introduce ten primary items $stuv$ for the tetrahedra, and ten more abcd, abdc, abce, adec, ..., bcde, bced for the different colorings. And introduce 20 secondary items $wxyz$ for the vertices.

Then the admissible vertex colors are the solutions to the XCC problem with 1200 options '$stuv\ \alpha\ v_1{:}p_1\ \ldots\ v_4{:}p_4$', where α is a coloring, $v_1 v_2 v_3 v_4$ are the vertices of $stuv$, and $p_1 p_2 p_3 p_4$ is an even permutation of α's colors. Curiously, this problem has 2880 solutions (found in 500 Mμ) — and they're all equivalent to the one below, under the $5!\, 4! = 2880$ automorphisms present.

(This problem was posed in 2015 by J. McComb, and solved by J. Scherphuis.)

150. Notice that there are fourteen distinct pieces, with four pairs of two. So we use Algorithm M, with 14 primary items for pieces and 64 for cells. We also introduce secondary items for edges between cells, with colors to indicate the presence or absence of links. The final two pieces must obviously be adjacent, hence we can combine them into a "super-piece" of size 11; then all interfaces between adjacent cells are identical. We can remove symmetry by forcing the super-piece to be in one of 18 positions.

Then 43 solutions are found, in 7 Gμ. Here are some typical examples:

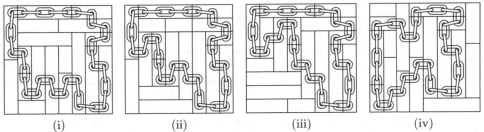

(i)   (ii)   (iii)   (iv)

Solution (i) appears in Hoffmann's *Puzzles Old and New*, puzzle 3–18. Solution (iii) avoids most of the lower left quadrant, and solution (iv) avoids the entire right column. If we ignore blank spaces, the links form eight different paths, all of length 34. Paths (i), (ii), (iii), (iv) occur in respectively 1, 15, 9, 3 of the 43 solutions. [The Endless Chain Puzzle was distributed circa 1887 by Reason Manufacturing Company.]

151. (a) The key idea is to start by *factoring* this problem, by considering only the task of edge-matching between adjacent dominoes, while ignoring the loop details.

Algorithm M applies, with primary items 1–9 and a–i for the distinct on-off patterns of attachment points, as well as primary items ij for each cell to be covered ($0 \le i < 8, 0 \le j < 9$), and two special primary items H, V. There are 63+64 secondary items h_{ij} and v_{ij}, to indicate path/nopath at internal attachment points. Typical options:

$$\text{`a 10 11 } v_{12}\text{:1 } h_{21}\text{:1 } h_{20}\text{:1, } h_{10}\text{:0 } h_{11}\text{:1 H',}$$

$$\text{`a 11 21 } h_{11}\text{:0 } v_{12}\text{:0 } v_{22}\text{:1, } h_{31}\text{:1 } v_{21}\text{:1 } v_{11}\text{:1 V';}$$

the goal is to find an exact cover with multiplicities 1 for patterns 1–9, multiplicities 3 for patterns a–i, and multiplicities 18 for H and V. (There are millions of solutions.)

Once that task is solved, we need to assign the actual dominoes whose subpaths jointly define a single loop. A (nontrivial) program, whose structure has a lot in common with Algorithm X, will find such assignments in microseconds (although a full day might be needed to actually *write* that program).

(b) Now H and V should have multiplicities 32 and 4. (Also, we can save about half of Algorithm M's running time by omitting vertical placements at odd height.) The algorithm finds 6420 solutions; suitable domino assignments are then found in a flash.

[These 36 path dominoes were first studied by Ed Pegg Jr. in 1999, and first placed into a single-loop 8 × 9 array by Roger Phillips later that year.]

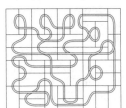
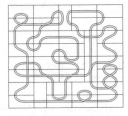
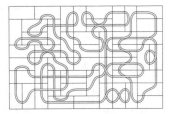

152. This (factored) problem is like the previous one, but with an additional pattern j of multiplicity 11, and a blank pattern of multiplicity 1, but without H or V. One needs to be lucky to find a solution; the author struck it rich with Algorithm M after 35.1 Tμ.

[Notice that exactly 32 of the 48 path dominoes have no crossings. Thus it is irresistible to try to place them on a chessboard, so as to form a single noncrossing loop. Unfortunately, Algorithm M tells us that such a mission is impossible, even with multiple loops, because the corresponding factored problem has no solution. *Something interesting, however, can surely be done with those 32.*]

153. (a) Algorithm M quickly verifies the uniqueness of the solution below, if we add a blank *monomino* of multiplicity 4. ["Line puzzles" like this were invented by Bill Darrah; several of his ingenious designs were made by Binary Arts in 1994 and 1999.]

(b) There are 30 patterns, three for each distinct choice of three connection points.

(c) Trials with random choices of respectively (2, 2, 4)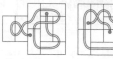
sets of (2, 3, 4) distinct connection points usually give no solutions at all. But one of the author's first 1000 trials was suitable, and it led to a nice puzzle whose solution is shown.

154. The integer solutions to $P(n) = n(n+1)^2(n+2)/12 = m^2$ involve perfect squares u^2 and v^2 with $v^2 \approx 3u^2$. If $|v^2 - 3u^2|$ is sufficiently small, v/u must be a convergent to the continued fraction $\sqrt{3} = 1 + //1, 2, 1, 2, 1, 2, 1, 2, \ldots //$ (see exercise 4.5.3–42).

Pursuing this idea, let $\theta = 2 + \sqrt{3}$, $\hat{\theta} = 2 - \sqrt{3}$, $\langle a_n \rangle = \langle (\theta^n + \hat{\theta}^n)/2 \rangle = \langle 1, 2, 7, 26, 97, \ldots \rangle$ and $\langle b_n \rangle = \langle (\theta^n - \hat{\theta}^n)/(2\sqrt{3}) \rangle = \langle 0, 1, 4, 15, 56, \ldots \rangle$. Notice that $a_n^2 = 3b_n^2 + 1$; $(a_n + 3b_n)^2 = 3(a_n + b_n)^2 - 2$. We find that $P(n)$ is a perfect square if and only if $n = 6b_m^2$ for some m (thus $n = 0, 6, 96, 1350, 18816, \ldots$) or $n = (a_m + 3b_m)^2$ for some m (thus $n = 1, 25, 361, 5041, 70225, \ldots$).

[See R. Wainwright, in *Puzzlers' Tribute* (A K Peters, 2002), 277–281; also Erich Friedman's survey in `erich-friedman.github.io/mathmagic/0607.html`.]

155. (a) Algorithm M finds $8 \cdot 7571$ solutions, in 60 Gμ.

(b) The maximum is 35 (not easy to find!), and the minimum is 5. [This exercise was suggested by Robert Reid, who found a minimum solution by hand in 2000.]

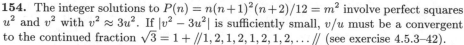

156. At level l of backtracking, branch on all ways to fill the leftmost unfilled cell of the topmost unfilled row. Even though no MRV heuristic is used, this method needs just 2.0 teramems (and negligible memory) to find 18656 solutions. The search tree has 61636037366 nodes.

We can save a factor of 8 by removing symmetry: The 1×1 square can be confined to cells (i, j) with $i < 18$ and $j \geq 35 - i$. Furthermore, if (i, j) is on the diagonal $(j = 35 - i)$, the context of the 1×1 square must be either ⊤ or ⊣, and we can insist on the former. Now we find 2332 solutions (and 6975499717 nodes), in just 235 gigamems.

By contrast, the MCC problem (61) for $n = 8$ has 1304 items and 7367 options of total length 205753, when we restrict the options of #1 to $i < 18$ and $j \geq 35 - i$. It needs 490.6 teramems to find 2566 solutions; postprocessing reduces that number to 2332, because 468 of those 2566 have #1 in position (i, j) with $j = 35 - i$.

We conclude that a dancing-links approach is decidedly *not* the method of choice for this partridge problem; straightforward backtracking with bitwise operations is more than 2000 times faster! Indeed, we might consider ourselves fortunate to pay "only" a 2000-fold cost penalty, since each of the 841 options for #8 in (61) contributes 65 nodes to doubly linked lists. Such updating and downdating keeps the dancers extremely busy.

[*Historical notes:* The 2332 solutions for $n = 8$ were first found by Bill Cutler in 1996, using a refinement of the backtrack approach described above. At that time no solutions for $n < 11$ had been known, although Wainwright knew how to solve $12 \leq n \leq 15$ in 1981, and C. H. Jepsen and S. Ahearn had presented constructions for $11 \leq n \leq 33$ in *Crux Mathematicorum* **19** (1993), 189–191. The puzzle can surely be solved for all $n > 7$, but no proof is yet known.]

157. Algorithm M readily shows the nonexistence of perfect packings, but the back-track method of exercise 156 is much better to show that we can't pack all but one 2×2. That method also shows that we *can* pack all but two of them:

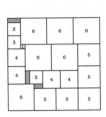

158. The following solutions can be proved optimum with bitwise backtracking as in exercise 156:

159. Replace # by four primary items $\#_0, \#_1, \#_2, \#_3$ representing "quadrants," and use $\#_{2\lfloor i/4\rfloor + \lfloor j/4\rfloor}$ in place of # in (64). Then partition into ten separate cases, in which the multiplicities $m_0 m_1 m_2 m_3$ of $\#_0 \#_1 \#_2 \#_3$ are respectively (2012, 2111, 2120, 3002, 3011, 3020, 3110, 4010, 4001, 5000). (Omit options containing $\#_k$ of multiplicity 0.) These cases produce (134, 884, 33, 23, 34, 1, 16, 0, 22, 0) solutions, in (95, 348, 60, 23, 75, 8, 19, 2, 10, 0) megamems. (Notice that $4 \cdot 134 + 4 \cdot 884 + 8 \cdot 33 + 4 \cdot 23 + 8 \cdot 34 + 8 \cdot 1 + 4 \cdot 16 + 8 \cdot 0 + 4 \cdot 22 + 4 \cdot 0 = 4860$.) The running time has decreased by a factor of 20.

[For larger values of n we could divide the cells into nine regions: eight octants, plus a special region containing the diagonals (and the middle row, column if n is odd).]

160. There are 589 components, among which are 388 isolated vertices and one giant of size 3804. The other 200 components have sizes ranging from 2 to 12. (For example, the first three solutions in (65) belong to the giant component; the other belongs to a component of size 8.)

161. In general, consider the problem of finding all the m-vertex dominating sets of a graph G; the $n \times n$ m-queen problem is the special case where G is the queen graph of order n. Then the options (64) have the form '# v v_1 ... v_t', where $\{v_1, \ldots, v_t\}$ are the vertices adjacent to v, and # is a special primary item of multiplicity m.

Variant (i) is equivalent to asking for all *kernels* of size m (all of the maximal independent sets). Let there be a secondary item e for every edge in G; the options are then '# v v_1 ... v_t e_1 ... e_t', where e_j is the edge between v and v_j. An 8×8 chessboard has $8 \cdot 91 = 728$ kernels of size 5. (It also has 6912, 2456, and 92 kernels of sizes 6, 7, and 8; see exercise 7.1.4–241(a).)

For variant (ii) we simply shorten v's option to '# v_1 ... v_t'; some other option must then cover v. Exactly 352 of the 5-queen solutions satisfy (ii).

Variant (iii) seems a bit harder to formulate. Let there be a secondary item $\hat{v}$ for each vertex v. The option for choosing v can then be '# v $\hat{v}{:}1$ v_1 ... v_t $\hat{u}_1{:}0$ ... $\hat{u}_s{:}0$', where $\{u_1, \ldots, u_s\} = V \setminus \{v, v_1, \ldots, v_t\}$ is the set of vertices *not* adjacent to v. The 8×8 chessboard has 20 clique-dominators of size 5.

[Chapter 10 of the classic work *Mathematische Unterhaltungen und Spiele* by W. Ahrens (1910) is an excellent survey of early work on queen-domination problems.]

162. Formulate these as MCC problems, by starting with the ordinary options for the n queens problem (see (23)), then adding additional options such as '# r_j c_{k+1} a_{j+k+1} b_{j-k-1} r_{j+1} c_{k+3} a_{j+k+3} b_{j-k-3} r_{j+2} c_k a_{j+k+2} b_{j-k+2} r_{j+3} c_{k+2} a_{j+k+5} b_{j-k+1}' to represent a contained $\mathcal{Q}_4$, for $1 \le j, k \le n-3$. Here # is a new primary item, which is given the desired multiplicity.

(a) 15; one can, in fact, get disjoint $\mathcal{Q}_4$ and $\mathcal{Q}_5$ in a $\mathcal{Q}_{15}$.

(b, c) 17. Put a queen in the center, make a pinwheel! [See Ahrens (1910), 258.]

(d) 22; see below. Algorithm M proves $n = 21$ impossible after 1.2 teramems.

(e) 16; there are four essentially different solutions.

(f) 19; see below. Only 35 Gμ to show that $n = 18$ is too small.

(g) 20(!). Once you know this, Algorithm X will find all 18 solutions in 2 Mμ.

(h) 22; there are 28 essentially different solutions.

(i) 25; see below. (After 6 teramems, we learn that $n = 24$ doesn't work.)

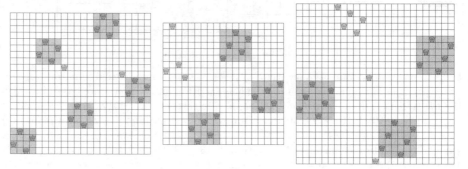

163. Sometimes Algorithm M is called on to choose zero or more items from an empty list. Then it sets $\texttt{FT}[l] \leftarrow i$ and $x_l \leftarrow i$, where i is the item whose list is empty; but step M5 doesn't actually tweak anything. The peculiar rule in (71) ensures that step M8 doesn't actually untweak anything as we backtrack.

164. If $x_j \le N$, node x_j is the header for item x_j; there's no further option for such j.

[A good implementation will also extend answer 12, so that the relative positions of each x_j in the search tree are identified. For this purpose one can add a new array $\texttt{SCORE}$, setting $\texttt{SCORE}[l] \leftarrow \theta_i$ and $\texttt{FT}[l] \leftarrow 0$ at the end of step M3. When printing the jth step x_j of a solution, the old answer 12 is used if $\texttt{FT}[j] = 0$; otherwise that answer is modified as follows: If $x \le N$ and $(x = \texttt{FT}[j]$ or $x = \texttt{TOP}(\texttt{FT}[j]))$, print 'null $\texttt{NAME}(x)$'; otherwise print option x as before. Conclude by looping with $i \leftarrow 0$, $q \leftarrow \texttt{FT}[j]$ rather than $i \leftarrow \texttt{TOP}(x)$, $q \leftarrow \texttt{DLINK}(i)$; report '$k$ of $\texttt{SCORE}[j]$' rather than 'k of $\texttt{LEN}(i)$'.]

165. (a) To cover 2 of 4, we have 3 choices at the root, then 3 or 2 or 1 at the next level, hence $(1, 3, 6)$ cases at levels $(0, 1, 2)$. To cover 5 of 7, there are $(1, 3, 6, 10, 15, 21)$ cases at levels $(0, 1, \ldots, 5)$. Thus the search profile with item 1 first is $(1, 3, 6, 6 \cdot 3, 6 \cdot 6, 6 \cdot 10, 6 \cdot 15, 6 \cdot 21)$. The other way is better: $(1, 3, 6, 10, 15, 21, 21 \cdot 3, 21 \cdot 6)$.

(b) With item 1 first the profile is $(a_0, a_1, \ldots, a_p, a_p a_1, \ldots, a_p a_q)$, where $a_j = \binom{j+d}{d}$. We should branch on item 2 first because $a_{p+1} < a_p a_1$, $a_{p+2} < a_p a_2$, $\ldots$, $a_q < a_p a_{q-p}$, $a_q a_1 < a_p a_{q-p+1}$, $\ldots$, $a_q a_{p-1} < a_p a_{q-1}$. (These inequalities follow because the sequence $\langle a_j \rangle$ is strongly log-concave: It satisfies the condition $a_j^2 > a_{j-1} a_{j+1}$ for all $j \ge 1$. See exercise MPR–125.)

166. (a) The "monus" operation $x \mathbin{\dot-} y = \max(x - y, 0)$ is good for situations like this:

$$\theta_p = (\text{LEN}(p) + 1) \mathbin{\dot-} (\text{BOUND}(p) \mathbin{\dot-} \text{SLACK}(p)).$$

(b) It's better to branch on p' (although this may be counterintuitive).

[The author's implementation of step M3 breaks ties by first preferring an item with smaller SLACK, then preferring longer LEN when the SLACKs are equal. Thus, his MRV replaces answer 9 by this: Set $\theta \leftarrow \infty$, $p \leftarrow \text{RLINK}(0)$. While $p \neq 0$, do the following: Set $\lambda \leftarrow \theta_p$; if $\lambda < \theta$ or ($\lambda = \theta$ and $\text{SLACK}(p) < \text{SLACK}(i)$) or ($\lambda = \theta$ and $\text{SLACK}(p) = \text{SLACK}(i)$ and $\text{LEN}(p) > \text{LEN}(i)$) set $\theta \leftarrow \lambda$, $i \leftarrow p$; then set $p \leftarrow \text{RLINK}(p)$.

167. Step M3 isn't precisely defined; therefore *any* change to v_p could possibly affect the behavior. But let's assume that step M3 is implemented as in exercise 166.

Even so, there can be differences. A minor difference arises, for instance, if there are *no* options: A primary item with multiplicity $[0..1]$ will be inactivated by covering in step M4; with multiplicity $[0..2]$, it will become inactive at the end of step M5.

There can also be more significant differences. Suppose there's just one option, 'a', and one primary item. If a has multiplicity 1, we simply cover a as in Algorithm X. But if a has multiplicity $[1..2]$, we'll do some tweaking and untweaking — even entering a new level, and taking a null branch there.

On the other hand, the differences can't get much worse. Let $\text{BOUND}_0(p)$ and $\text{BOUND}_1(p)$ denote the values of $\text{BOUND}(p)$ when the upper bound v_p has respectively been specified as M_p and $M_p+\delta$. If the same options are chosen, we'll have $\text{BOUND}_1(p) = \text{BOUND}_0(p) + \delta$ throughout the algorithm, because $\text{BOUND}(p)$ is adjusted appropriately whenever the algorithm recursively reduces the problem by removing an option. Also $\text{SLACK}_1(p) = \text{SLACK}_0(p) + \delta$. One can then prove, by induction on the computation, that the same options are indeed chosen (possibly with different amounts of tweaking).

Any two values of v_p that are $M_p + 2$ or more will be totally equivalent.

168. Introduce a new primary item '!' and a new secondary item '+'. Replace the two copies of α by '! +:0', '! α', 'α +:1'. [Similarly, three copies of α can be replaced by '! +:0', '! α', '!! ++:0', '!! α +:1', 'α ++:1', after introducing '!!' and '++'.]

169. Let there be one primary item, #, together with one secondary item for each vertex. And let there be one option, '# v v_1:0 ... v_d:0' for each vertex v, where v_1 through v_d are the neighbors of v. Finally, let # have multiplicity t. [Notice that the secondary items in this construction are colored either with 0 or not at all!]

170. Introduce the primary item $!v$ for each vertex, and give it $d + 1$ options: '# $!v$ v:1 v_1:0 ... v_d:0', '$!v$ v:0 v_1:1', '$!v$ v:0 v_1:0 v_2:1', ..., '$!v$ v:0 v_1:0 ... v_{d-1}:0 v_d:1'.

171. Let there be ten primary items v, for $0 \leq v < 10$; also fifteen primary items $\#uv$, with multiplicity $[1..5]$, for each edge $u - v$, where the edges are $0 - 1 - 2 - 3 - 4 - 0$, $0 - 5$, $1 - 6$, $2 - 7$, $3 - 8$, $4 - 9$, and $5 - 7 - 9 - 6 - 8 - 5$. Let there be $26 \cdot 10$ secondary items a_v through z_v, for $0 \leq v < 10$; also $26 \cdot 30$ secondary items a_{uv} through z_{uv}, for $u \mathbin{\not\!-} v$; also a secondary item w for each word in, say, WORDS(1000). There are 26 options, '$\#uv$ a_u a_v' through '$\#uv$ z_u z_v', for each edge. And there are 10 options for each word; for example, the options for added are 'v a_v:1 b_v:0 c_v:0 d_v:1 e_v:1 f_v:0 ... z_v:0 a_{02} a_{03} a_{06} a_{07} a_{08} a_{09} d_{02} ... e_{09} added', where $0 \leq v < 10$.

Every solution to this MCC problem will be obtained 120 times, because the Petersen graph has 120 automorphisms. But symmetry can be broken by choosing the labels of 0, 1, and 3 at levels 0, 1, and 2, and by ordering the label ranks so that $r_0 > r_1$, $r_0 > r_2$, $r_0 > r_3$, $r_0 > r_6$, $r_1 > r_4$, $r_1 > r_5$, $r_3 > r_7$, $r_3 > r_8$, $r_3 > r_9$.

There are two solutions in WORDS(834), namely muddy, thumb, books, knock, ended, apply, fifth, grass, civil, (refer or fewer), found in 3.5 Tμ.

172. A construction analogous to answer 170 generates all solutions to the *weaker* problem where connectivity isn't tested; it's easy to remove the unconnected solutions from Algorithm M's output. Consider cycles first: There are $1 + \binom{d}{2}$ options for each primary item !v, namely '!v v:0' and '# !v v:1 v_1:a_1 ... v_d:a_d', where $a_1 \ldots a_d$ is a binary vector with $a_1 + \cdots + a_d = 2$. For the path problem, the options for the starting vertex should have $a_1 + \cdots + a_d = 1$, not 2. The options for all other vertices that aren't adjacent to the starting vertex should have d additional options '# E !v v:1 v_1:a_1 ... v_d:a_d', with $a_1 + \cdots + a_d = 1$, where E is a new primary item signifying the end vertex.

(a) Paths of length l are obtained when the multiplicity of # is set to $l + 1$.

First let's restrict consideration to paths that start in the corner cell $(0,0)$. Then every essentially distinct path occurs twice—reflected about the diagonal. (i) There are 16 distinct snake-in-the-box king paths of length 31 from a given corner, found in 6 Tμ. One of them, illustrated below, also *ends* at a corner; hence it occurs four times, not two—twice in each direction. These paths are optimum, because we can divide the board into sixteen 2×2 subsquares, each of which can contain at most two kings. (ii) A single run, with the multiplicity of # set to $[32 .. 33]$, suffices to find the 13 distinct knight solutions of length 31 in 58 Gμ, simultaneously showing that length 32 is impossible. One of the most remarkable solutions is shown below. (iii) With bishops we should first eliminate all squares of the wrong parity, because they cannot be connected to the start. Then the 32 solutions of length 12 are found in just 13 Mμ. (It's not difficult to prove by hand that an $n \times n$ board has exactly 2^{n-3} bishop solutions of length $2n - 4$, when n is even.) (iv) Rook solutions are even easier to enumerate by hand: There are $(n - 1)!^2$ of them, because we always have $n - k$ choices at steps $2k - 1$ and $2k$. (Algorithm M finds the $7!^2 = 25401600$ solutions in 625 Gμ, while generating also 21488110 disconnected impostors.) However, $(n - 2)!^2 - (n - 2)!$ of those solutions are counted twice, because they go from corner to corner and have no symmetry. Hence there are $25401600 - 517680/2 = 25142760$ distinct rook solutions of length 14. (v) Finally, there are 134 distinct queen solutions of length 11—found and proved optimum in 17 Gμ, despite having 16788 options of total length 454380(!). The unique solution that occupies opposite corners is shown here. (You may enjoy finding another unique 11-step path, which begins slowly by moving just one diagonal step.)

 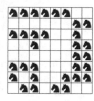   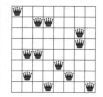

Now let's consider paths that start in cell $(0,1)$ and do not end in a corner. (i) Five solutions with 32 kings are found (in 3.7 Tμ); but they all have 3-cycles and are disconnected. (ii) Knights, however, yield a big surprise: There's a unique path of length 33, doubly counted! (Found in 43 Gμ.) (iii) Bishop paths can't have length 12 unless they start or end in a corner. (iv) There are $N = (n - 1)!^2 - 2(n - 2)!^2$ solutions where the rook first moves down, and N where it first moves sideways. Of these, $2N_c$ end at $(n - 1, n - 2)$ and are double-counted by central symmetry, where $N_c = (2^{\lfloor n/2 \rfloor - 1}(\lfloor n/2 \rfloor - 1)!)^2$; $N_t = 2(n-2)!$ end at $(1,0)$ and are *not* double-counted by transposition; N_t end at $(n - 2, n - 1)$ and aren't double-counted by dual transposition.

So there are $2N - N_c - (2(n-2)!^2 - N_t) = 47691936$ equivalence classes when $n = 8$.
(v) Another nice surprise greets us, namely a unique queen path of length 12!

The next step is to consider paths that start in $(0, 2)$ and don't end in the 12 types of cells already considered. And so on, for seven more cases. Of course rook counting gets hairier and hairier; we shall omit it. Unexpectedly, there's also another maximum queen path(!). All of these computations are fast, except that the kings need 6.3 Tμ.

(b) Cycles are similar, but symmetry now becomes even trickier. (i) The six distinct 31-cycles of a king are asymmetric, so they each appear eight times when reflected and/or rotated. (ii) But the four distinct 32-cycles of a knight include two that are equivalent to their transpose, and one (shown below) with central symmetry. (iii,v) A bishop has 36 distinct 12-cycles, and a queen has five 13-cycles, all asymmetric.

(iv) A rook, on the other hand, has oodles of 16-cycles, some of which (like the one illustrated) even have 4-fold symmetry under both horizontal and vertical reflection. Every rook snake-in-the-box 16-cycle can be represented uniquely as $(p_0q_0\ p_0q_1\ p_1q_1\ p_1q_2\ \ldots\ p_7q_7\ p_7q_0)$, where $p_0p_1\ldots p_7$ and $q_0q_1\ldots q_7$ are permutations of $\{0, 1, \ldots, 7\}$ with $p_0 = 0$ and $q_0 < q_1$. Consequently there are $8!^2/16 = 101606400$ of them, if symmetry isn't taken into account. That cycle is equivalent to its transpose if and only if $p_j = q_{(k-j)\bmod 8}$ for some k and all j; there are $8!/2 = 20160$ such cases. It is equivalent to its 180° rotation if and only if $p_j + p_{4+j} = q_j + q_{4+j} = 7$ for $0 \le j < 4$; there are $6 \cdot 4 \cdot 2 \cdot 8 \cdot 6 \cdot 4 \cdot 2/2 = 9216$ such cases. And it is equivalent to both, in $6 \cdot 4 \cdot 2 \cdot 8/2 = 192$ cases. Hence by "Burnside's lemma" there are $(101606400 + 0 + 9216 + 0 + 20160 + 0 + 20160 + 0)/8 = 12706992$ equivalence classes of rook cycles.

 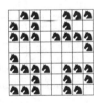  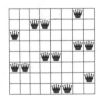

[T. R. Dawson introduced this problem for knights, and presented an example path of length 31 and an example cycle of length 32, in *L'Echiquier* (2) **2** (1930), 1085; **3** (1931), 1150. C. C. Verbeek posed the problem of maximizing the number of queens such that each is "attacked by exactly two others" in *Elsevier's Weekly* (June 1971); if we allow several queens in the same row, arguing that the first doesn't attack the third, 14 queens are actually possible (see P. Torbijn, *Cubism For Fun* **17** (1991), 19). The name 'snake-in-the-box' was coined by W. H. Kautz, *IRE Trans.* **EC-7** (1958), 177–180, for the case where G is an n-cube. The term 'coil-in-the-box' is often used nowadays for a snake-in-the-box cycle.]

Nikolai Beluhov proved in 2018 that, if $n \ge 6$ is even, all snake-in-the-box king paths of the maximal length $n^2/2 - 1$ on $n \times n$ boards have an interesting structure, which can be characterized completely. In fact, he showed that exactly $2n+(n \bmod 4)/2$

such paths are distinct under symmetry. Furthermore, there are exactly six distinct snake-in-the-box king *cycles* of length $n^2/2 - 1$, when $n \geq 8$ is a multiple of 4.

With arguments of a different kind, Beluhov has also proved that the longest snake-in-the-box paths and cycles of a *knight*, on an $m \times n$ board, have length $mn/2 - O(m+n)$. [To appear.]

173. (a) Write '$k \!-\! ij$' if clue k is a (knight or bishop) move away from cell (i, j). For each row, column, and box, compute "quotas" r_i, c_j, and b_x, equal to 3 minus the number of pieces already present among the given clues. Also compute the quota p_k for each clue k, equal to the label minus the number of neighboring cells already occupied. There is no solution if any quota is negative.

Say that cell (i, j) of box x is *known* if it is occupied, or if $r_i = 0$ or $c_j = 0$ or $b_x = 0$, or if $p_k = 0$ for some $k \!-\! ij$. Introduce primary items R_i, C_j, B_x, P_k for each row, column, box, or clue with a positive quota, having multiplicities r_i, c_j, b_x, p_k. There is one option for each unknown cell, namely '$R_i\, C_j\, B_x \bigcup \{P_k \mid k \!-\! ij\}$'.

(b, c, d) See Fig. A–3. The knight puzzles with labels ≥ 6, and the bishop puzzles with labels 0, 10, and 12, are due to N. Beluhov; the others represent the author's best early attempts, not necessarily minimum. Solutions can be found in Appendix E.

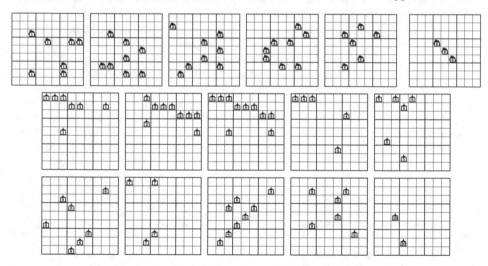

Fig. A–3. A gallery of knight and bishop sudoku puzzles.

[These variants of sudoku were devised by David Nacin and first published in *MAA Focus* **38**, 6 (Dec. 2018/Jan. 2019), 36; see also `quadratablog.blogspot.com`.]

174. Beluhov's remarkable solution, which he obtained with the help of a SAT solver, is also a pair of "rainbow puzzles" — every possible knight label occurs exactly once(!):

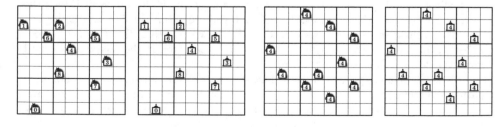

[Also shown are his 10-clue puzzles in which all the labels are equal.]

175. We can allow an option α to be repeated twice by simply replacing it by three options 'α x', '$\#$ x', '$\#$ α', where $\#$ is a new primary item and x is a new secondary item. (If α contains uncolored secondary items $y_1, \ldots, y_s$, we should first replace them by $y_1{:}c, \ldots, y_s{:}c$, where c is a new color.)

In general if α is the ith option and if $a_i = a + 1 > 1$, replace α by the $2a + 1$ options 'α x_{1i}', '$\#_{1i}$ x_{1i}', '$\#_{1i}$ α x_{2i}', '$\#_{2i}$ x_{2i}', '$\#_{2i}$ α x_{3i}', $\ldots$, '$\#_{ai}$ x_{ai}', '$\#_{ai}$ α', where $\#_{ti}$ and x_{ti} are new primary and secondary items.

176. (a) Introduce $3N$ items $\{A_j, B_j, \#_j \mid 1 \le j \le N\}$, to be used in M options $\{A_j \mid a_{ij} \ge 1\} \cup \{B_j \mid a_{ij} = 2\}$ for $1 \le i \le M$. (For example, the option for row (2, 1, 0, 2, 0, $\ldots$) would be 'A_1 B_1 A_2 A_4 B_4'.) Add $2N$ further options '$\#_j$ A_j', '$\#_j$ B_j' for $1 \le j \le N$. Use Algorithm M with multiplicities $(2, 1, 1)$ for $(A_j, B_j, \#_j)$.

(b) The same construction works, but with multiplicities $(3, 1, 1)$.

(c) Now use $4N$ primary items $\{A_j, B_j, \#_j, \#'_j\}$ and N secondary items x_j. Change the $2N$ special options to '$\#_j$ A_j', '$\#_j$ B_j x_j', '$\#'_j$ A_j x_j', '$\#'_j$ B_j', for $1 \le j \le N$. Use multiplicities $(4, 2, 1, 1)$.

(d) With $7N$ primary items $\{A_j, B_j, \#_{1j}, \ldots, \#_{5j}\}$ and $4N$ secondary items $\{x_{1j}, x_{2j}, x_{3j}, x_{4j}\}$, the special options are '$\#_{1j}$ A_j', '$\#_{1j}$ B_j x_{1j}', '$\#_{2j}$ A_j x_{1j}', '$\#_{2j}$ B_j x_{2j}', $\ldots$, '$\#_{5j}$ A_j x_{4j}', '$\#_{5j}$ B_j', and the multiplicities are $(11, 5, 1, 1, 1, 1, 1)$.

177. (a) The $2^s 3^t - 1$ nonzero vectors $a_1 \ldots a_s b_1 \ldots b_t$ with $0 \le a_i \le 1$ and $0 \le b_i \le 2$ form the rows of a matrix A. Allow the $2^t - 1$ rows with $a_i = 0$ and $b_i \ne 2$ to be repeated, via answer 175; also encode the 2's via answer 176. That leads to $s + 3t + 2^t - 1$ primary items, $2^t - 1$ secondary items, and a total of $2^s 3^t - 1 + 2t + 2(2^t - 1)$ options. (There are 91914202 multipartitions when $s = t = 5$. Algorithm M generates them at a rate of about 1300 mems per solution; that's only about seven times slower than the special-purpose Algorithm 7.2.1.5M.)

(b) This problem is easier, because we simply disallow using an option twice. That leaves us with $s + 3t$ primary items and $2^s 3^t - 1 + 2t$ options.

(Exercise 7.2.1.5–73 enumerates the number of solutions $P(s, t)$ for part (a). The same argument gives a similar recurrence for the number $Q(s, t)$ of solutions to part (b):

$$Q(s, 0) = \varpi_s; \qquad 2Q(s, t+1) = Q(s+2, t) + Q(s+1, t) - \sum_k \binom{n}{k} Q(s, k).$$

With this formula one finds quickly, for example, that $Q(5, 5) = 75114998$.)

178. (a) Since $360 = 2^3 \cdot 3^2 \cdot 5$, we need first to extend exercise 176 to matrices of 0s, 1s, 2s, and 3s. Encoding $a_{ij} = 3$ in option i can be done by using items A_j, B_j, C_j. To ensure a total of 3 in that column, let $\#_j$ and $\#'_j$ be new primary items, and give multiplicity $(3, 1, 1, 1, 1)$ to $(A_j, B_j, C_j, \#_j, \#'_j)$; also let x_j be secondary. Then the special options '$\#_j$ A_j', '$\#_j$ B_j x_j', '$\#'_j$ A_j x_j', '$\#'_j$ C_j' will fix everything up.

This makes an MCC problem with 29 options, $9 + 1$ items, and 34 solutions.

(b) Now use exercise 175 to allow the options for factors 3 and 2×3 to be repeated at most twice, and to allow the option for factor 2 to be repeated at most thrice. The MCC problem now has 37 options, $13 + 5$ items, and 52 solutions. [These solutions were first studied by John Wallis; see exercise 7.2.1.7–28.]

179. From $1000 + 0110 + 0001$ we get four solutions $100000 + \{011100, 011100\} + \{000011, 000011\}$; from $1110 + 0001$ we get two solutions $111100 + \{000011, 000011\}$; and from $1010 + 0101$ we get $101000 + 010111$.

180. The text showed that $o_1 = 'i_1'$ and that i_2 and o_5 exist, when $t = 4$ and $t' \geq 1$. Continuing that example, if $s_2 = 5$ so that $t' \geq 2$, then option o_2 intersects only $\{o_1, \ldots, o_5\}$; hence $o_2 = 'i_1\ i_2'$, and i_2 cannot occur in *more* than 4 options. Its appearances must therefore be in $\{o_2, o_3, o_4, o_5\}$.

Furthermore, o_3 must be '$i_1\ i_2\ i_3\ \ldots$' for some third item, i_3, since we can't have $o_3 = o_2$. Consequently there's an option $o_6 = 'i_2\ i_3\ \ldots'$. And so on.

181. $(c_0, c_1, c_2, c_3, c_4) = (188, 248, 320, 425, 566)/96$, by the initial values in the text.

182.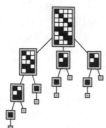

(To establish the lower bound in Theorem E, make n copies of this problem, on disjoint four-tuples of items. This yields 7^n solutions, in a search tree with $(5 \cdot 7^n - 3)/2$ nodes. Notice that the branching factor never exceeds 3 in this construction.)

183. (Can one, for example, often make the branching factor $t = 4$?)

184. Yes. If we can write $t = a_{n-1}\varpi_{n-1} + a_{n-2}\varpi_{n-2} + \cdots + a_0\varpi_0$, with $0 \leq a_j \leq \binom{n-1}{j}$ for $0 \leq j < n$, we get such a problem by letting the options consist of (i) all $2^{n-1} - 1$ subsets of $\{1, \ldots, n-1\}$; (ii) exactly a_j subsets of $\{1, \ldots, n\}$ of size $n-j$ that contain n.

To write t in that form, suppose $t = \binom{n-1}{n-1}\varpi_{n-1} + \cdots + \binom{n-1}{n-k+1}\varpi_{n-k+1} + a_{n-k}\varpi_{n-k} + t'$, where $0 \leq a_{n-k} < \binom{n-1}{n-k}$ and $0 \leq t' < \varpi_{n-k}$. Then, by induction, we can write $t' = a_{n-k-1}\varpi_{n-1-k} + \cdots + a_0\varpi_0$, with $0 \leq a_j \leq \binom{n-1}{j} \leq \binom{n-1}{j}$.

For example, $10000 = 1\cdot4140 + 6\cdot877 + (1\cdot203 + 7\cdot52 + 2\cdot15 + (0\cdot5 + (0\cdot2 + (1\cdot1))))$.

185. We get the most solutions when we have the most options, namely the $2^{N_1+N_2} - 2^{N_2}$ subsets that aren't entirely secondary. Then the solutions are the set partitions that include at most one entirely secondary block; and the number of such set partitions is seen to be $\sum_m \{{N_1 \atop m}\}(m+1)^{N_2}$, when we consider their restricted growth strings.

186. (a) The list for i consists of all 2^{n-1} subsets that contain i. So there are $\binom{n-1}{k-1}$ operations hide(p) on options p of size k; and $u_n = 1 + \sum_k \binom{n-1}{k-1}(k-1) = (n-1)2^{n-2}+1$.

(b) The lists get shorter, so the algorithm does $u_{n-1} + \cdots + u_{n-(k-1)}$ updates.

(c) Sum $u_n + \sum_k \binom{n-1}{k-1}(s_{n-1} - s_{n-k})$, where $s_n = \sum_{k=1}^{n} u_k = (n-2)2^{n-1}+n+1$. For example, $(v_0, v_1, \ldots, v_5) = (0, 1, 3, 12, 57, 294)$; $(x_0, x_1, \ldots, x_5) = (0, 1, 4, 18, 90, 484)$.

187. (a) We have $X'(z) = \sum_n x_{n+1}z^n/n! = V'(z) + e^z X(z)$, where $V(z) = \sum_n v_n z^n/n!$. The given function solves this differential equation and has $X(0) = 0$.

(b) Similarly, we have $T'_{r,s}(z) = e^z T_{r,s}(z) + z^r$ and $T_{r,s}(0) = 0$.

(c) Integrate by parts.

(d) For example, $T_{1,3}(z) = 4e^{e^z-1} + 2T_{0,0}(z) - ze^{2z} - (2z+1)e^z - 2z - 3$, by (c).

188. By induction, $\widehat{\varpi}_{nk}$ is the number of n-element, single-tail set partitions (equivalence relations) for which $n > 1$ and $1 \not\equiv 2, \ldots, 1 \not\equiv k$. (For example, if we know that 22 single-tail partitions of $\{1, 2, 3, 4, 5\}$ have $1 \not\equiv 2$, and that 6 such partitions of $\{1, 2, 3, 4\}$ have $1 \not\equiv 2$, then 6 single-tail partitions of $\{1, 2, 3, 4, 5\}$ must have $1 \not\equiv 2$ and $1 \equiv 3$; hence 16 of them have $1 \not\equiv 2$ and $1 \not\equiv 3$.) Therefore $\widehat{\varpi}_{nn} = \widehat{\varpi}_{n-1}$, for all $n \geq 1$.

[Leo Moser played with this triangular array in 1968 and found the generating function $\sum_n \widehat{\varpi}_n z^n/n! = e^{e^z} \int_0^z e^{-e^t}\,dt$; he showed his results to R. K. Guy, who told

N. J. A. Sloane; see OEIS sequences A046936 and A298804. If we start with '0, 0, 1' on the diagonal instead of '0, 1', we get Gould's $\langle a_{n2} \rangle = \langle 0, 0, 1, 1, 4, 14, 54, 233, \dots \rangle$; etc.]

189. (a) $|e^{e^z}| = |e^{e^x \cos y + ie^x \sin y}| = \exp(e^x \cos y)$; $|e^{-e^z}| = \exp(e^{-x} \cos y)$.

(b) $|\int_0^\theta \exp(-\xi e^{i\phi}) d(\xi e^{i\phi}) + \int_\xi^\infty e^{-e^t} dt| = O(\xi \exp(-e^x \cos y)) + O(\exp(-e^\xi))$; $|e^{e^z}| = O(\exp(e^\xi))$; and we have $x = \xi \cos\theta \geq \xi - 2.25/\xi$, $\cos y \geq \cos \frac{3}{2}$.

(c) We have $\int_z^\infty e^{-e^t} dt = \int_0^\infty e^{-e^t} dt - \int_0^1 e^{-e^{uz}} d(uz) = \hat{g}/3 - I$. Let $\max |e^{e^{uz}}|$ for $0 \leq u \leq 1$ be $\exp(-e^{u_0 x} \cos u_0 y)$. If $\cos u_0 y \geq 0$ we have $|I| = O(\xi)$. Otherwise if $\cos y - \cos u_0 y \leq 1$ we have $|e^{e^z} I| \leq \xi \exp(e^x \cos y - e^{u_0 x} \cos u_0 y) \leq \xi \exp(e^x \cos y - e^x \cos u_0 y) \leq \xi \exp(e^x)$. Otherwise we use a more delicate argument: Since $\cos(a-b) - \cos(a+b) = 2(\sin a)(\sin b)$, we have $|\sin \frac{u_0-1}{2} y| = \frac{1}{2} |(\cos y - \cos u_0 y)/\sin \frac{u_0+1}{2} y| \geq \frac{1}{2}$, hence $u_0 \leq 1 - \pi/(3y)$. And in this range, $u_0 x \leq x - \frac{\pi}{3} x/y = \xi \cos\theta - \frac{\pi}{3} \cot\theta \leq \xi - c\xi^{1/3} + O(1)$, where $c^3 = \frac{3}{8} \pi^2$.

The desired bound now holds in each case because $x = \xi\sqrt{1 - \sin^2\theta} \leq \xi - 9/(8\xi)$.

(d) If $\frac{\pi}{2} \leq \theta \leq \pi$, $|e^{e^z}| \exp(-e^{u_0 x} \cos u_0 y) = O(1)$. Since $\rho_{n-1}/(n-1)! = \frac{1}{2\pi i} \oint R(z) \, dz/z^n$, and since $\varpi_{n-1}/(n-1)! = \Theta(e^{e^\xi}/(\xi^{n-1}\sqrt{\xi n}))$ by 7.2.1.5–(26), we have $|\rho_{n-1}/\varpi_{n-1}| = O(\sqrt{\xi n} \exp(-c_2 e^\xi/\xi))$ for all $c_2 < \frac{9}{8}$. And $-e^\xi/\xi = -n/\xi^2 < -n/\ln^2 n$.

[These results, and considerably more, were proved by W. Asakly, A. Blecher, C. Brennan, A. Knopfmacher, T. Mansour, and S. Wagner, *J. Math. Analysis and Applic.* **416** (2014), 672–682. In particular, they proved that a_{nk}/ϖ_n rapidly approaches the constant $\hat{g}_k = \int_0^\infty t^{k-1} e^{1-e^t} dt/k! = \int_0^\infty e^{-x} \ln^k(1+x) \, dx/k!$, for all $k > 0$.]

Historical notes: Leonhard Euler computed the constant $\hat{g}$ when he argued that this value can be assigned to the divergent series $\sum_{n=0}^\infty (-1)^n n!$ [*Novi Comment. Acad. Sci. Pet.* **5** (1754), 205–237]. Benjamin Gompertz, who did not know the constant $\hat{g}$ explicitly, studied the probability distributions $F(x) = 1 - a^{1-b^x}$ for $a, b > 0$ and $x \geq 0$ [*Philos. Trans.* **115** (1825), 513–585]. His name came to be associated with $\hat{g}$ because, for example, a random variable with $a = e$ in his distribution has $E\,X = \hat{g}/\ln b$.

190. Empirically, these signs are essentially periodic, but with a slowly increasing period length as n grows. For example, the signs for $4000 \leq n \leq 4100$ are $+^2-^4+^4-^5+^4-^4+^5-^4+^4-^5+^4-^4+^4-^5+^4-^4+^5-^4+^4-^5+^4$ $-^4+^4-^5$. The quantities $\hat{\varpi}_{nk} - \hat{g}\varpi_{nk}$ for $1 \leq k \leq n \leq 100$ have the interesting sign pattern shown at the right. (See exercise 188.) Complex variables are evidently interacting here somehow!

191. The mean is $G'(1) = 1 + \hat{g}$; the variance is $G''(1) + G'(1) - G'(1)^2 = 2\hat{g}_2 + \hat{g} - \hat{g}^2 \approx 0.773$. [Incidentally, $G(z)$ can also be written $e\Gamma(1+z) - \sum_{k=1}^\infty (-1)^k ez/((k+z)k!)$.]

192. Let $\xi e^\xi = n$ as in 7.2.1.5–(24). Then, when $x = e^\xi - 1 + t$ and t is small, we have $e^{-x}(\ln(1+x))^n \approx A \exp(-(1+\xi)t^2/(2n))$, where $A = \exp(n \ln \xi + 1 - e^\xi)$. Trading tails and integrating over $-\infty < t < \infty$ gives $\hat{g}_n \sim A\sqrt{2\pi n/(1+\xi)}/n!$.

193. At level 0, when given the complete graph K_{t+1}, the algorithm does $t+1$ updates when covering i in step X4, and t updates when covering each of t values of j in step X5. Thus $U(t+1) = 1 + t + t^2 + tU(t-1)$.

194. (a) In general we have $X(2q+1) = (2q)(2q-2)\dots(2)(a_0 + a_2/2 + a_4/(2\cdot4) + \dots + a_{2q}/(2\cdot4\cdot\dots\cdot(2q))) = 2^q q! S - R$, where $S = \sum_{n\geq 0} a_{2n}/(2^n n!)$ and $R = a_{2q+2}/(2q+2) + a_{2q+4}/((2q+2)\cdot(2q+4)) + \cdots$. Hence when $a_t = 1$ we have $S = e^{1/2}$ and $0 < R < 1$. [This result was noticed in 1999 by Michael Somos; see OEIS A010844.]

(b) In general, $X(2q) = ((2q)!/(2^q q!))S - R$, where $S = X(0) + a_1 + a_3/3 + a_5/(3\cdot5) + a_7/(3\cdot5\cdot7) + \cdots$ and $R = a_{2q+1}/(2q+1) + a_{2q+3}/((2q+1)\cdot(2q+3)) + \cdots$.

When $a_t = X(0) = 1$, $S - 1 = 1 + 1/3 + 1/(3 \cdot 5) + \cdots = e^{1/2} \operatorname{erf}(\sqrt{1/2})/((\frac{1}{2})^{1/2}/(\frac{1}{2})!)$, and $0 < R < 1$. So the answer is $\lfloor (1 + \sqrt{e\pi/2}\operatorname{erf}(\sqrt{1/2}))(2q)!/(2^q q!) \rfloor$.

(c) $2^q q! C - 2q + O(1)$, where $C = \sum_{n \geq 0}(1 + 2n + 4n^2)/(2^n n!) = 5e^{1/2} \approx 8.24361$.

(d) $((2q)!/(2^q q!))C' - 2q + O(1)$, where $C' = 3 + 5\sqrt{e\pi/2}\operatorname{erf}(\sqrt{1/2}) \approx 10.05343$.

195. Assume that $q, r > 1$, and let v be the unique vertex of degree 2. The algorithm will try to match v with the vertex at its left; that leaves a problem of matching the independent graphs K_{2q} and K_{2r}. If $q \leq r$, each matching of K_{2q} will initiate a computation of the matchings of K_{2r}; otherwise each matching of K_{2r} will initiate the matchings of K_{2q}. So the running time of this phase will be C' updates per solution, where C' is the constant of answer 194(d) and there are $(2q)!(2r)!/(2^q q! \, 2^r r!)$ solutions.

The algorithm will also try to match v with the vertex at its right. That leaves a problem of independently matching K_{2q+1} and K_{2r-1}, and there are no solutions. The running time of this phase will be C times $\min(2^q q!, 2^{r-1}(r-1)!)$, where C is the constant of answer 194(c). (Curiously, it's actually negligible compared to the other phase.)

196. (a) $b_1 \ldots b_9 = 135778899$. (Draw the bipartite graph, and rotate it $180°$.)

(b) Let $\bar{k} = n + 1 - k$ for $1 \leq k \leq n$. Then '$X_j \, Y_k$' is a dual option if and only if '$Y_{\bar{j}} \, X_{\bar{k}}$' is an original option; $q_1 \ldots q_n$ is the inverse of an original solution if and only if $\bar{q}_n \ldots \bar{q}_1$ is a dual solution.

(c) $1 + a_1(n + 1)$, because each Y_k for $1 \leq k \leq a_1$ appears in n options.

(d) $a_1(a_2 - 1)(a_3 - 2)\ldots(a_n - n + 1)$. [This number must therefore be equal to $b_1(b_2 - 1)(b_3 - 2)\ldots(b_n - n + 1)$ — and that's *not* an obvious fact!]

(e) Let $\Pi_j = \prod_{i=1}^{j}(a_i - i + 1)$. From (c), the answer is $1 + (\sum_{j=1}^{n}(n + 3 - j)\Pi_j) - \Pi_n$.

(f) $1 + (\sum_{j=1}^{n}(n + 3 - j)n^j) - n! \approx (4e - 1)n!$. [Perfect matchings of $K_{n,n}$.]

(g) $6 \cdot 2^n - 2n - 7$, because $\Pi_j = 2^j$ for $1 \leq j < n$, and $\Pi_n = 2^{n-1}$.

(h) Now $\Pi_n = \lfloor \frac{n+1}{2} \rfloor \lfloor \frac{n+2}{2} \rfloor$; and the total number of updates, divided by Π_n, is therefore $6 + 4/1! + 5/2! + \cdots + O(n^2/(n/2)!) \approx 4e - 1$.

(i) If $b_1 < a_1$, the first branch is on Y_n, not X_1; and $1 + b_1(n + 1)$ updates are made at root level. (The example problem in (a) branches on Y_9, then X_2, then Y_8, etc.)

197. (a, b). Induction; σ_{st} can in fact be any permutation that takes $s \mapsto t$ and doesn't increase any other element.

(c) $C(a_1, \ldots, a_n) = \prod_{j=1}^{n}(z + a_j - j)$, by (a), since we gain a cycle in that product representation if and only if $t_j = j$. $I(a_1, \ldots, a_n) = \prod_{j=1}^{n}(1 + z + \cdots + z^{a_j - j})$, by (b). [See exercise 7.2.1.5–29; also M. Dworkin, *J. Combinatorial Theory* **B71** (1997), 17–53.]

198. (a) If $s > a_r$ we have $\pi_{rs} = 0$. Otherwise let q be the smallest j with $a_j \geq s$; then $q \leq r$. Each permutation of $P(a_1, \ldots, a_n)$ with $p_r = s$ corresponds to one of $P(a'_1, \ldots, a'_{r-1}, a'_{r+1}, \ldots, a'_n)$, where $a'_j = a_j - [j \geq q]$. Thus $(a_r + 1 - r)\pi_{rs} = \prod_{j=q}^{r-1}(a_j - j)/(a_j + 1 - j)$.

(b) We have $q' \geq q$ when $s' > s$. Consequently $\pi_{rs}/\pi_{rs'} = \prod_{j=q}^{q'-1}(a_j - j)/(a_j + 1 - j)$ for all $r \geq q'$, if $\pi_{rs'} > 0$. [In such cases the parameters r and s are said to be "quasi-independent."]

$$
\begin{array}{ccccccccc}
\frac{1}{2} & \frac{1}{2} & 0 & 0 & 0 & 0 & 0 & 0 & 0 \\
\frac{1}{8} & \frac{1}{8} & \frac{1}{4} & \frac{1}{4} & \frac{1}{4} & 0 & 0 & 0 & 0 \\
\frac{1}{8} & \frac{1}{8} & \frac{1}{4} & \frac{1}{4} & \frac{1}{4} & 0 & 0 & 0 & 0 \\
\frac{1}{12} & \frac{1}{12} & \frac{1}{6} & \frac{1}{6} & \frac{1}{6} & \frac{1}{3} & 0 & 0 & 0 \\
\frac{1}{12} & \frac{1}{12} & \frac{1}{6} & \frac{1}{6} & \frac{1}{6} & \frac{1}{3} & 0 & 0 & 0 \\
\frac{1}{24} & \frac{1}{24} & \frac{1}{12} & \frac{1}{12} & \frac{1}{12} & \frac{1}{6} & \frac{1}{2} & 0 & 0 \\
\frac{1}{72} & \frac{1}{72} & \frac{1}{36} & \frac{1}{36} & \frac{1}{36} & \frac{1}{18} & \frac{1}{6} & \frac{1}{3} & \frac{1}{3} \\
\frac{1}{72} & \frac{1}{72} & \frac{1}{36} & \frac{1}{36} & \frac{1}{36} & \frac{1}{18} & \frac{1}{6} & \frac{1}{3} & \frac{1}{3} \\
\frac{1}{72} & \frac{1}{72} & \frac{1}{36} & \frac{1}{36} & \frac{1}{36} & \frac{1}{18} & \frac{1}{6} & \frac{1}{3} & \frac{1}{3}
\end{array}
$$

199. Assume by symmetry that $m \leq \lceil n/2 \rceil$. With the MRV heuristic it's not difficult to see that every branch at level l for $l < m$ is on some a_i for $i \leq m$, with exactly $(n - l)(m - 1 - l)$ descendants. Hence there are $n^{\underline{l}}(m - 1)^{\underline{l}}$ nodes on level l. The total number of nodes when $m \approx n/2$ is huge, $\Theta((n - 2)!)$; and there are no solutions.

200. (a) When all n^3 options are present, $\det Q(X) = \sum \text{sign}(p)v_{1p_1q_1}\ldots v_{np_nq_n}$, summed over all permutations $p = p_1\ldots p_n$ and all n-tuples $q = q_1\ldots q_n$ with $q_j \notin X$. Summing $(-1)^{|X|}\det Q(X)$ yields $\sum \text{sign}(p)v_{1p_1q_1}\ldots v_{np_nq_n}$ where both p and q are permutations. (This is essentially an application of the inclusion-exclusion principle.) Set $v_{ijk} \leftarrow 0$ if option '$a_i\,b_j\,c_k$' isn't present.

(b) Assign a random integer in $[0\mathinner{\ldotp\ldotp}p)$ to each of the M given options, where p is a prime greater than $2M$, and evaluate $s = S \bmod p$. If $s \ne 0$, S is nonzero. If $s = 0$, S is nonzero with probability less than $1 - (1-1/p)^M < M/p < 1/2$, by exercise 4.6.1–16, because S is linear in each variable. Repeating r times will fail with probability $< 2^{-r}$.

[In practice, 2^n is often an overestimate because many of the determinants are obviously zero. For example, if $Q(X)$ has an all-zero row or column, so does $Q(X')$ for all $X' \supseteq X$. This method shines on unsolvable examples such as those of exercise 199. Björklund's paper, *STACS* **27** (2010), 95–106, has more general results.]

201. (a) "Given n people seated at a circular table, how many seating arrangements do not require anybody to move more than one place left or right?"

(b) Two solutions in which everybody moves, plus L_n solutions (a Lucas number) in which at least one person remains in the same seat.

(c) An interesting recursive structure leads to the answer $5L_{n+2} + 10n - 33$. [This analysis depends on using the given ordering to break ties in step X3 when several lists have the minimum length.]

202.

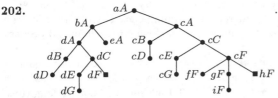

203. (a) Yes; $T \oplus T' \oplus T''$ is the search tree corresponding to $A \oplus A' \oplus A''$.

(b) No; $\vphantom{}$ = $\vphantom{}$ $\oplus$ $\vphantom{}$ $\ne$ $\vphantom{}$ $\oplus$ $\vphantom{}$ = $\vphantom{}$.

204. By definition of $T \oplus T'$, we have $\text{subtree}(\alpha\alpha') = \text{subtree}(\alpha) \oplus \text{subtree}(\alpha')$. Hence $\deg(\alpha\alpha') = \min(\deg(\alpha), \deg(\alpha'))$.

Let $\text{ancestors}(\alpha) = \{\alpha_0,\ldots,\alpha_l\}$ and $\text{ancestors}(\alpha') = \{\alpha'_0,\ldots,\alpha'_{l'}\}$. Suppose $\alpha\alpha'$ is dominant in $T \oplus T'$ and $\deg(\alpha\alpha') = d$. If $0 \le k < l$, some ancestor $\alpha_k\alpha'_{k'}$ of $\alpha\alpha'$ has $\deg(\alpha_k) = \deg(\alpha_k\alpha'_{k'}) < d$; hence α is dominant. Similarly, α' is dominant.

We've proved the "only if" part, but the converse is false: $\vphantom{}$ $\oplus$ $\vphantom{}$ = $\vphantom{}$.

205. The first statement follows easily from the definition (see exercise 202). Suppose $\alpha\alpha' = \alpha_l\alpha'_{l'} \in T \oplus T'$, as in answer 204, where neither α nor α' is dominant, and where $l + l'$ is minimum. Then $l > 0$ and $l' > 0$, because α_0 and α'_0 are dominant.

Assume that the parent of $\alpha\alpha'$ is $\alpha\alpha'_{l'-1}$. Then $\alpha'_{l'-1}$ is dominant, and α_l isn't. So there's a $k < l$ such that $\deg(\alpha_k) = \max(\deg(\alpha_0),\ldots,\deg(\alpha_l))$. Hence there's a maximum $k' < l'$ such that $\alpha_k\alpha'_{k'}$ is an ancestor of $\alpha\alpha'$. Then $\deg(\alpha'_{k'}) \le \deg(\alpha'_{l'-1}) < \deg(\alpha)$, and $\alpha_k\alpha'_{k'+1}$ is also an ancestor. But $\alpha_k\alpha'_{l'}$ isn't. Contradiction.

A similar contradiction arises when the parent of $\alpha\alpha'$ is $\alpha_{l-1}\alpha'$.

206. Replace each solution node of T by a copy of T'.

207. (a) If $\lambda_j = 4$ we now prefer the 5-way branch on i, because $\lambda'_i = 7/2 < 11/3 = \lambda'_j$. If $\lambda_j = 3$ we prefer $\min(i,j)$, because $\lambda'_i = 3 = \lambda'_j$. If $\lambda_j = 2$ we still prefer the binary branch on j to the ternary branch on i. And if $\lambda_j = 1$ or 0 we certainly prefer j.

(b) Include two new fields, ACT and STAMP, initially zero, in each item node. (They can share an octabyte, if ACT is a short float and STAMP is a tetrabyte.) A global variable TIME serves as the "convenient clock." Another global, BUMP (which is a short float, initially 10^{-32}), is the amount by which we advance activity scores. Whenever i is covered or uncovered, or whenever LEN(i) is changed, we check to see if STAMP(i) = TIME; if not, we set ACT(i) ← ACT(i) + BUMP and STAMP(i) ← TIME.

The "clock" advances at the beginning of steps X4, X5, X6, and X7. This means that TIME ← (TIME + 1) mod 2^{32} and BUMP ← BUMP/ρ. (Furthermore, if BUMP $\geq 10^{29}$, we divide BUMP and *all* ACT fields by 10^{64}, to avoid overflow. We limit ρ to be at most .999, so that each α_i is at most 1000.)

These changes allow us to replace the definition of λ in step X3 (answer 9) by
$$\lambda \leftarrow (\text{LEN}(p) \leq 1?\ \text{LEN}(p):\ 1 + \text{LEN}(p)/(1 + \mu\,\text{ACT}(p)/\text{BUMP})).$$

(c) Consider (90) first. After branching on 00 and trying option '00 01', we have $\alpha_{00} = \alpha_{02} = \rho$, $\alpha_{01} = 1 + \rho$, $\alpha_{04} = \alpha_{05} = \alpha_{06} = 1$, and the other α's are zero. We want $\lambda'_{05} = 1 + 3/(1 + \mu\alpha_{05})$ to be less than $\lambda'_{10} = 1 + 2$; that is, $\mu > 1/2$. Later, after trying option '00 02', we'll have $\alpha_{05} > 1$ and $\alpha_{06} > 1$; again, item 01 isn't chosen.

Problem (92) is trickier. After trying '00 01', the nonzero α's are $\alpha_{00} = \alpha_{02} = \rho$, $\alpha_{01} = 1 + \rho$, and $\alpha_{03} = \alpha_{04} = \alpha_{05} = 1$. We'll prefer the 3-way branch on 02 to the 2-way branch on 20 if $\mu > 1/(2\rho)$; and we'll even prefer the 4-way branch on 04 (or 05) to that 2-way branch, if $\mu > 1$. In either case we'll reach a solution to problem 0 before starting on problem 1. The same calculations then take us to problem 2 only when problem 1 has been solved; etc. (Furthermore, when coming back down there will be no incentive to go back up. In fact, 4-way branches will be done on the items $k3$ because of their high activity scores.)

(d) The normal Algorithm X finds all 212 solutions in 92 Gμ, with a 54-meganode search tree. This modification finds them in 51 Gμ, if we set $\mu = 1/8$ and $\rho = .99$, with a 26-meganode search tree. (With $\mu = 1/2$ and $\rho = .9$, the time is 62 Gμ. In long runs, the α scores tend to approach $1/(1-\rho)$; so increases in ρ usually imply decreases in μ.)

208. The original problem has primary items ij for $0 \leq i, j \leq$ e, and eight kinds of options '$\{ij + \delta \mid \delta \in S_k\}$' for all cells $ij + \delta$ that are in range, where $S_0 = \{01, 11, 21, 31, 10\}$, $S_1 = \{00, 01, 02, 03, 11\}$, $S_2 = \{00, 10, 20, 30, 21\}$, $S_3 = \{10, 11, 12, 13, 02\}$, $S_4 = \{01, 11, 21, 31, 20\}$, $S_5 = \{00, 01, 02, 03, 12\}$, $S_6 = \{00, 10, 20, 30, 11\}$, $S_7 = \{10, 11, 12, 13, 01\}$. Options that involve the center cell 77 come only from S_0.

The modified problem adds secondary items V_{ij} and H_{ji}, for $0 \leq i \leq$ b, $1 \leq j \leq$ d. It inserts V_{ij}, $H_{(i+1)j}$, $V_{i(j+1)}$, H_{ij} respectively into the options with S_4, S_5, S_6, S_7.

(The 16 solutions to this problem represent $2^2 + 2^4 + 2^5 + 2^2 + 2^3 + 2^2 + 2^5 + 2^3 + 2^5 + 2^3 + 2^2 + 2^4 + 2^3 + 2^4 + 2^2 + 2^4 = 212$ solutions to the original. We're lucky that none of those solutions has an 'H' that includes 77.)

209. With the modified options '0 1 A', '0 2 B', '1 4 5 B', '2 3 4 A', obtained from the bipairs ('0 1', '2 3 4'; '0 2', '1 3 4') and ('0 1', '2 4 5'; '0 2', '1 4 5'), we get the balanced search tree shown here.

210. Add a new primary item #A and give it multiplicity [0..2]. Insert it into options α', β', γ'. Then use the nonsharp preference variant of Algorithm M.

211. No bipairs. (But Langford has bitriples, and all three have "biquadruples.")

212. (a) Order the options first by their smallest item, and secondly by lexicographic order among those with the same smallest item.

(b) Yes. For example, we can let $1 < 2$, and $1 < 4 < 0 < 5$.

213. Yes, *provided* that we regard a proper prefix of a string as lexicographically *larger* than that string (contrary to the conventions of a dictionary). Otherwise the condition fails when α is a prefix of α' (although exercise 212 remains valid).

Suppose the items of α and β are respectively represented by the digits j and k in rgs(π), the restricted growth string of π. Then j will also represent α' in rgs(π'), and both strings will be equal up to the point where j first appears.

Let β' be represented by k' in rgs(π'); then $k' > j$. Consider the leftmost place where rgs(π) differs from rgs(π'). If that digit is j in rgs(π), it is k' in rgs(π'). Otherwise it is k in rgs(π); but then it is j in rgs(π'), and α is a prefix of α'.

214. We can find all solutions Σ that reduce to a given strong solution Σ_0, by repeatedly reversing the construction in the proof of Theorem S — replacing joint occurrences of α and β by joint occurrences of α' and β', for all canonical bipairs, in all possible ways. (It's a reachability problem: to find all nodes of an acyclic digraph, given the sinks.)

Notice that different strong solutions can lead to the same nonstrong solution. For example, in the 2DM problem with options $\{xX, xY, yX, yY, yZ, zY, zZ\}$, where uv stands for 'u v', we might have the canonical bipairs $(yX, xY; yY, xX)$, $(yZ, zY; yY, zZ)$. The strong solutions $\{xY, yX, zZ\}$ and $\{xX, yZ, zY\}$ both lead to the nonstrong $\{xX, yY, zZ\}$. (However, in that same problem, we could have made the bipairs $(yY, xY; yY, xX)$, $(yY, zZ; yZ, zY)$ canonical. Then there would have been only one strong solution.)

215. (a) This is the number of 4-cycles, of which there are $3\binom{2q+1}{4}$: Four vertices $i < j < k < l$ can form three 4-cycles, with either j or k or l opposite i.

(b) For convenience, denote options by ij instead of 'i j'. If $i < j < k < l$, we exclude (i, j, k, l) unless $\min(ij, ik, il, jk, jl, kl) = ij$ or kl. We exclude (i, k, j, l) unless $\min(ij, ik, il, jk, jl, kl) = ik$ or jl. We exclude (i, l, j, k) unless $\min(ij, ik, il, jk, jl, kl) = il$ or jk. Hence exactly two of the three possibilities are excluded.

(c) When $i < j < k < l$ they are (i, k, j, l) and (i, l, j, k).

(d) The root has $2q$ children, branching on 0. All of them are leaves except for the branch '0 1'. That one has $2q - 2$ children, all of which are leaves except for the branch '2 3'. And so on, with $2(q - l)$ nodes on level $l > 0$.

(e) Use only (i, j, k, l) for $k = i + 1 < \min(j, l)$ and i even.

(f) Put '1 $2q$' first, then '2 $2q-1$', ..., then 'q $q+1$', then the others. When we branch on '0 k' at the root, for $1 \le k \le 2q$, no options remain for item $2q + 1 - k$.

(g) '0 k' and '$2q+1-k$ l' are excluded, for all $l \notin \{0, k, 2q+1 - k\}$. (Altogether $(2q)(2q - 2)$ cases.) [Is it perhaps feasible to order the options *dynamically*?]

216. The search tree is almost always smaller than that of answer 215(c), which in fact has the worst case on every level. But it rarely seems to go below half of the worst-case size. (The author discovered the trick of answer 215(f) by studying randomly generated examples that had unusually small trees.)

Algorithm X needs 540 Gμ to prove that K_{21} has no perfect matching. It has potentially $2\binom{21}{4} = 11970$ excludable quadruples. We can use Algorithm 3.4.2S to sample just m of them; then the running time for $m = (2000, 4000, 6000, 8000,$ and $10000)$ decreases to about $(40$ Gμ, 1.6 Gμ, 145 Mμ, 31 Mμ, 12 M$\mu)$, respectively.

217. Each delta $\alpha - \alpha'$ has k positive terms and k negative terms; we can assume that $1 \le k \le 4$. Furthermore it suffices to work with "normalized" deltas, which are lexicographically smallest under rotation, reflection, and negation. The pentominoes (O, P, ..., Z) have $(10, 64, 81, 73, 78, 25, 23, 24, 22, 3, 78, 24)$ normalized deltas, of which $(1, 7, 3, 3, 2, 0, 1, 0, 1, 0, 4, 0)$ have $k = 1$. Two of the deltas are shared by four different pentominoes: $00+01-23-33$ (Q, S, W, Z); $00-02$ (P, Q, R, Y). Eleven are shared by three.

A common delta is necessary but not sufficient; if $\alpha - \alpha' = \beta' - \beta$, we still need to fill in cancelled terms that don't clash. For example, $00 - 23$ is common to Q and W, but it doesn't yield a bipair. Furthermore (although the exercise didn't state this!), we don't want the 10-cell region to have a hole; the delta $00 + 01 - 12 - 22$ is common to P, U, and Y, but only PY makes a useful bipair. A delta can arise in more than one way: From $00 + 01 + 02 + 03 - 20 - 21 - 22 - 23$ we can make a Q with either 10 or 13, and a Y with either 11 or 12; symmetry (and hole removal) yields only one bipair, not four.

The complete catalog has 34 essentially distinct entries. Eighteen of them

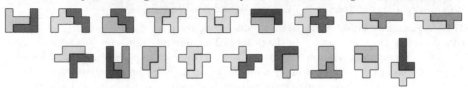

have 10-cell shapes with left-right symmetry. Fourteen have transposition symmetry:

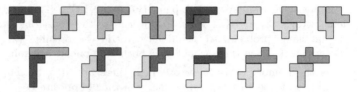

The other two are especially interesting because they are asymmetric:

$$ \textsf{P} \equiv \textsf{P} \; ; \qquad \textsf{Y} \equiv \textsf{Y} . $$

(These two each lead to eight varieties when rotated and reflected, not just four. See J. C. P. Miller in Eureka: *The Archimedeans' Journal* **23** (1960), 14–15.)

218. If the only options involving p are 'p i:0' and 'p i:1', we can't eliminate item i. [But if they all involve, say, i:0, we *could* eliminate it; Algorithm P doesn't go that far.]

219. If option o contains i, but neither p nor q, it can be in a solution only with two other options $\{o', o''\}$ that contain $\{p, q\}$. But o' and o'' must then both contain j. [This argument is like the "naked pairs" of sudoku lore. It's tempting to go further, by also eliminating items i and j; but that could increase the number of solutions.]

220. Let the option be 'i_1 $i_2[:c_2]$ ... $i_t[:c_t]$'. We've already covered item $i = i_1$, which is represented by node x. Nodes $x+1$, $x+2$, ... represent the other items, possibly with spacers that were inserted when this option was shortened (see exercise 222). We want to commit $i_2, \ldots, i_t$, and to determine whether this causes LEN(p) to become 0 for some primary $p \notin \{i_2, \ldots, i_t\}$. The tricky part is to be sure that $p \notin \{i_2, \ldots, i_t\}$; to accomplish this, we set COLOR$(i_j) \leftarrow x$ for $1 < j \le t$. [In detail: Set $p \leftarrow x + 1$; while $p > x$, set $j \leftarrow$ TOP(p), and if $j \le 0$ set $p \leftarrow$ ULINK(p), otherwise set COLOR$(j) \leftarrow x$, $p \leftarrow p+1$.]

Then we make a second pass over the option: Set $p \leftarrow x+1$. While $p > x$, set $j \leftarrow$ TOP(p), and if $j \le 0$ set $p \leftarrow$ ULINK(p), otherwise commit$'(p, j)$ and set $p \leftarrow p+1$. Here commit$'(p, j)$ emulates (54): Set $c \leftarrow$ COLOR(p), $q \leftarrow$ DLINK(j); while $q \ne j$, hide$'''(q)$ unless COLOR$(q) = c > 0$, and set $q \leftarrow$ DLINK(q). And hide$'''(p)$ is just like hide(p), but it detects blocking if LEN(y) becomes 0 for some $y \le N_1$ with COLOR$(y) \ne x$.

Finally, a third pass undoes our changes: Set $p \leftarrow x - 1$. While $p \ne x$, set $j \leftarrow$ TOP(p), and if $j \le 0$ set $p \leftarrow$ DLINK(p), otherwise uncommit$'(p, j)$ and set $p \leftarrow p - 1$. Here uncommit$'(p, j)$ undoes commit$'(p, j)$ in the obvious way.

It is possible to switch immediately from committing to uncommitting as soon as blocking is detected, by jumping into the middle of a loop (see answer 122).

221. While $S > 0$, set $x \leftarrow S$, $S \leftarrow \text{TOP}(x)$, $\text{TOP}(x) \leftarrow i$, and do the following: Set $q \leftarrow x$; while $q \geq x$, set $j \leftarrow \text{TOP}(q)$, and if $j \leq 0$ set $q \leftarrow \text{ULINK}(q)$; otherwise if $j \leq N_1$ and $\text{LEN}(j) = 1$, go to P9; otherwise set $u \leftarrow \text{ULINK}(q)$, $d \leftarrow \text{DLINK}(q)$, $\text{ULINK}(d) \leftarrow u$, $\text{DLINK}(u) \leftarrow d$, $\text{LEN}(j) \leftarrow \text{LEN}(j) - 1$, $q \leftarrow q + 1$.

222. Set $p \leftarrow \text{DLINK}(i)$, and do the following steps while $p \neq i$: Set $p' \leftarrow \text{DLINK}(p)$, $q \leftarrow p+1$. While $q \neq p$, set $j \leftarrow \text{TOP}(q)$, and if $j \leq 0$ set $q \leftarrow \text{ULINK}(q)$; otherwise if $j = S$, exit this loop; otherwise set $q \leftarrow q + 1$. Then if $q \neq p$, set $\text{ULINK}(p) \leftarrow p+1$, $\text{DLINK}(p) \leftarrow p-1$, $\text{TOP}(p) \leftarrow 0$ (thereby making a spacer); otherwise set $q \leftarrow p+1$ and perform the loop in answer 221 while $q \neq p$ (instead of while $q \geq x$). Finally set $p \leftarrow p'$.

223. In accordance with the conventions of exercise 8, we first declare the items of the reduced problem: For $1 \leq i \leq N$, output the distinguishing mark for secondary items, if $i = N_1 + 1$; and output the name of item i, if $\text{LEN}(i) > 0$ or $i = N = 1$. Then we output the remaining options: For $1 \leq i \leq N$, if $\text{LEN}(i) > 0$, set $p \leftarrow \text{DLINK}(i)$ and do the following while $p \neq i$: Set $q \leftarrow p - 1$ and while $\text{DLINK}(q) = q - 1$ set $q \leftarrow q - 1$. If $\text{TOP}(q) \leq 0$ (hence i was the leftmost item to survive, in the option following the spacer node q), output the option as explained below. Then set $p \leftarrow \text{DLINK}(p)$ and repeat.

To output the (possibly shortened) option that follows node q, set $q \leftarrow q + 1$; then, while $\text{TOP}(q) \geq 0$, output the name of item $\text{TOP}(q)$ if $\text{TUP}(q) > 0$, followed by $:c$ if $\text{COLOR}(q) = c > 0$, and set $q \leftarrow q + 1$. (Afterwards, $-\text{TOP}(q)$ is the number of the corresponding option in the original input.)

224. Use $3n - 3$ items $p_1, x_1, i_1, \ldots, p_{n-1}, x_{n-1}, i_{n-1}$ (in that order), with the options '$i_{n-k}\ p_k\ x_k$', '$i_{n-k}\ p_k\ x_{k+1}$', '$i_{n-k}\ x_k$', '$i_{n-k}\ p_{k+1}$', for $1 \leq k < n - 1$, and also '$i_1\ p_{n-1}$', 'x_{n-1}', '$i_1\ x_{n-1}$'. During round k, for $1 \leq k < n$, item i_{n-k} is forced by p_k.

225. Some options, like 'Z 01 02 11 20 21' and 'U 30 31 41 50 51', are obviously useless because they cut off a region of fewer than five cells. More of these options are discarded in the larger problem — but only because of piece U. Eight options, like 'O 10 11 12 13 14', are useless because they block a corner cell.

The smaller problem also has numerous options like 'P 02 12 13 22 23', which turn out to be useless because they block piece X. (That piece has been confined to just eight placements, in order to break symmetry. It has more freedom in the larger problem, and can't be blocked there.) Round 2 also discovers that options like 'O 22 23 24 25 26' would block X, since round 1 has disabled one of X's eight choices.

226. Since $\Sigma_1' = \sum_{k=1}^{2n}(2n + 1 - k)a_k$, it's clear that $\Sigma_1 + \Sigma_1' = (2n + 1)\sum_{k=1}^{2n} a_k = (2n+1)(n+1)n$. Similarly $S + S' = (2n + 1)\sum_{k=1}^{2n} a_k^2 = (2n+1)^2(n+1)n/3$.

The relation $\Sigma_2' - (2n+1)\Sigma_1' = \Sigma_2 - (2n+1)\Sigma_1$ holds for *any* sequence $a_1 \ldots a_{2n}$.

227. (a) $\$(ij^2 + ik^2)$. (b) $\$(i^2j + i^2k)$. [$\$(C - ij^2 - ik^2)$, for large C, will *maximize* Σ_2.]

228. Well, it certainly surprised the author. Intuitively, we expect small $\Sigma_1 = \sum ka_k$ to be correlated with small $\Sigma_2 = \sum k^2 a_k$, but not nearly so well. For some mysterious reason, Langford pairings with the same Σ_1 tend to have the same Σ_2, and vice versa!

That's not always true. For example, $2\,8\,6\,2\,3\,5\,7\,4\,3\,6\,8\,5\,4\,1\,7\,1$ and $3\,5\,7\,4\,3\,8\,6\,5\,4\,1\,7\,1\,2\,6\,8\,2$ have the same Σ_1 but different Σ_2; $1\,5\,1\,7\,4\,8\,9\,5\,1\,1\,4\,1\,0\,7\,6\,3\,8\,2\,9\,3\,2\,6\,1\,1\,1\,0$ and $1\,4\,1\,6\,7\,1\,0\,4\,5\,9\,1\,1\,6\,8\,7\,5\,2\,3\,1\,0\,2\,9\,3\,8\,1\,1$ have the same Σ_2 but different Σ_1. Yet such exceptions are rare. When $n = 7$, the four pairings that have $\Sigma_1 = 444$ are the same as the four that have $\Sigma_2 = 4440$; the six pairings that have the larger value $\Sigma_1 = 448$ are the same as the six that have $\Sigma_2 = 4424$, which is *smaller* than 4440. What is going on?

The special nature of Langford pairings does allow us to prove certain curious facts. For example, let j_k be the index of the first occurrence of k. The other occurrence is at $j_k + k + 1$; hence $\sum_{k=1}^{n} j_k = (3n-1)n/4$. Also $\sum_{k=1}^{n} j_k^2 = (4n^2-1)n/3 - \frac{1}{2}\Sigma_1$.

229. These pairings can be found by Algorithm 7.2.2L (or its reverse-order variant). But we can also find them via dancing links, using the sharp minimax modification of Algorithm X (or C) in exercise 85: Order options (16) so that 'i s_j s_k' precedes 'i' $s_{j'}$ $s_{k'}$' when $j' < j$, or when $j' = j$ and $i' < i$ (for lex max) or $i < i'$ (for lex min). Then repeatedly (i) use the minimax algorithm to fill the smallest undetermined slot s_j; (ii) move the option that minimally covered s_j to the front of the list, and remove all other options that involve s_j.

Thus we find 1 2 1 3 2 4 8 3 12 13 4 10 14 15 16 8 9 6 11 5 7 12 10 13 6 5 9 14 7 15 11 16 in sixteen such steps, all of which are easy (and need less than 110 Kμ) except for the placements of 8 in s_7 (4.5 Mμ) and 12 in s_9 (500 Kμ). The total time (6 Mμ) includes 465 Kμ just for inputting the data in step X1. After placing 8 items, only 12 solutions remain, so it's slightly faster to switch gears when finishing. (This pairing has $\Sigma_1 = $ \$5240, $\Sigma_2 = $ \$119192, $S = $ \$60324; somewhat high but not extreme.)

The lexicographic maximum turns out to be (108) — partially explaining why it is so "remarkable." It can be obtained in the same fashion, in fewer than 2 Mμ.

230. Assume that all solutions to the exact cover problem contain the same number of options, d. (For example, $d = 16$ in Fig. 74.) Then we can replace each cost \$$c$ by the complementary cost, \$$(C - c)$, where C is sufficiently large to make this nonnegative. Solve the problem with the complementary costs; then subtract its total cost from Cd. [It's convenient to implement a special version of Algorithm X\$ that does this automatically, with appropriate changes to the presentation of intermediate and final results.]

231. (a) MAPLE
ARRAY   ($139);
SMOKE
TYPES

(b) HAPPY
EXILE   ($176);
ALLOW
PELTS

(c) JAMBS   MAGMA
EQUIP or EQUIP   ($197).
TUMOR   OUNCE
SASSY   WAKED

Algorithm X\$ needs 6 Gμ, 80 Gμ, and 483 Gμ to find these; Algorithm X needs 5 Gμ, 95 Gμ, and 781 Gμ to visit all solutions, of which there are 27, 8017, and 310077. (Section 7.2.2's trie-based methods are *much* faster: They need just 12 Mμ, 628 Mμ, 13 Gμ.)

232. No. Algorithm X\$ finds 96 solutions of minimum cost \$84; but the true solution in Fig. 74(a) actually costs \$86 by this measure. The effects of 16 rounding errors, each potentially changing the result by nearly \$1, have invalidated everything. [Therefore the author used \$$\lfloor 2^{32} d(i,j) \rfloor$ when preparing Fig. 74. This was safe, because the distance between the first 8 solutions and the 9th was greater than 16 — in fact, *much* greater, although a difference of only 17 would have been convincing.]

233. With costs \$$\lfloor 2^{32} \ln d(i,j) \rfloor$, we get the same answers (but faster: $1.2 + 0.2$ Gμ).

234. By that measure, *every* placement of n nonattacking queens (or rooks!) costs

$$\sum_{k=1}^{n}((k-c)^2 + (p_k - c)^2) = 2\sum_{k=1}^{n}(k-c)^2 = \frac{n(n^2-1)}{6}, \qquad \text{where } c = (n+1)/2.$$

235. Now the roles are reversed: We're more interested in the periphery than in the center, and the minimum is easier to compute than the maximum. The minimum cost, \$127760, is achievable in four ways, each symmetric; hence we must take $K = 17$, not $K = 9$. This computation took only 1.3 Gμ. (The two examples below have different

sets of distances, which coincidentally yield the same total cost.) But there's a unique
way to get the maximum cost, \$187760, discovered (with $K = 9$) in 9.7 Gμ:

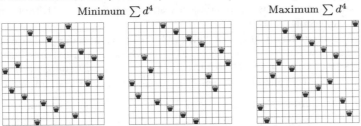

Minimum $\sum d^4$ Maximum $\sum d^4$

236. The idea is first to minimize the longest distance; then, placing a queen at that
distance in all possible ways, to minimize the next-longest distance; and so on. In other
words, if the options are in nondecreasing order by cost, it's almost like the search for
lexicographically minimax solutions, iteratively as in answer 229.

However, there's a catch: Many options have the same cost. Different orderings of
equal-cost options can lead to wildly different lex-min solutions. For example, suppose
there are four options, '1' for \$1, '2' for \$2, '1 3' for \$3, and '2 3' for \$3. In that order,
the minimax solution omits the final option and costs $3^N + 2^N$, which is not optimum.

The solution is to add to each option a primary item describing its cost, and
to use Algorithm M iteratively by specifying the number of queens of highest costs,
keeping this as low as possible until the problem has no solutions. Here are the best
such ways to place n queens, for $n = 17, 18,$ and 19:

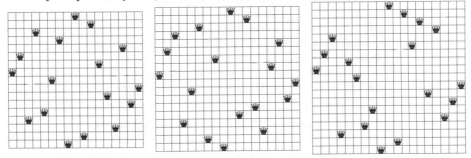

The author was able to reach $n = 47$ with dancing-links-based methods, in an
afternoon. But he knew that integer programming is significantly faster for "linear"
applications such as the n queens problem (see answer 36). So he enlisted the help of
Matteo Fischetti; and sure enough, Matteo was able to extend the results dramatically.
Here, for example, are optimum placements for $n = 32, 64,$ and 128:

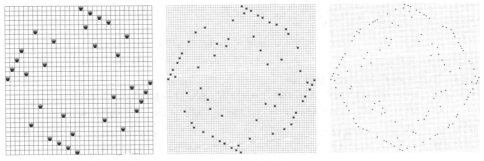

It appears likely that these optimum queen placements have rotational symmetry only when $n = 1, 4, 5, 16$, and 32. But the solutions for $n = 64$ and 128 do have 2^6 and 2^{12} equivalent mates, because they contain respectively 6 and 12 "tiltable squares" in the sense of exercise 7.2.2–11(c).

(The limiting behavior may not "kick in" until N is quite large. For example, the optimum solution when $n = 16$ and $N = 20$ is *not* the symmetrical one illustrated; the placements 8 11 4 7 5 12 1 16 14 2 15 10 3 13 6 9 have total cost $\approx 2.08 \times 10^{21}$, which beats $\approx 2.09 \times 10^{21}$. The limiting shape turns out to be optimum if and only if $N \geq 21$.)

237. False. For example, the square shown here is the smallest of ≈ 3 billion solutions for which $02 \equiv 20$, $03 \equiv 30$, $12 \equiv 21$, $13 \equiv 31$, $42 \equiv 24$, $43 \equiv 34$.
$$\begin{bmatrix} 1 & 2 & 1 & 1 & 3 \\ 1 & 1 & 0 & 0 & 3 \\ 1 & 0 & 1 & 0 & 3 \\ 1 & 0 & 3 & 6 & 9 \\ 3 & 1 & 3 & 9 & 1 \end{bmatrix}$$

238.
$$\begin{bmatrix} 1 & 1 & 3 \\ 3 & 0 & 7 \\ 1 & 3 & 9 \end{bmatrix} \begin{bmatrix} 2 & 1 & 1 & 1 \\ 1 & 0 & 3 & 1 \\ 1 & 1 & 9 & 3 \end{bmatrix} \begin{bmatrix} 2 & 1 & 2 & 1 & 1 \\ 1 & 0 & 3 & 0 & 1 \\ 1 & 1 & 3 & 9 & 3 \end{bmatrix} \begin{bmatrix} 1 & 1 & 1 & 2 & 1 & 1 \\ 1 & 0 & 0 & 1 & 0 & 3 \\ 3 & 3 & 1 & 1 & 7 & 1 \end{bmatrix} \begin{bmatrix} 1 & 1 & 1 & 1 & 2 & 1 & 1 \\ 1 & 0 & 0 & 0 & 4 & 0 & 3 \\ 3 & 1 & 9 & 3 & 1 & 7 & 1 \end{bmatrix};$$

$$\begin{bmatrix} 9 & 9 & 7 \\ 7 & 8 & 7 \\ 7 & 3 & 3 \end{bmatrix} \begin{bmatrix} 8 & 9 & 9 & 9 \\ 8 & 6 & 9 & 9 \\ 7 & 7 & 1 & 7 \end{bmatrix} \begin{bmatrix} 9 & 8 & 9 & 9 & 9 \\ 9 & 8 & 8 & 9 & 7 \\ 7 & 7 & 3 & 1 & 7 \end{bmatrix} \begin{bmatrix} 9 & 8 & 9 & 9 & 9 & 9 \\ 9 & 8 & 8 & 5 & 7 & 9 \\ 7 & 7 & 3 & 3 & 7 & 1 \end{bmatrix} \begin{bmatrix} 9 & 8 & 9 & 9 & 9 & 9 & 9 \\ 9 & 8 & 6 & 8 & 5 & 9 & 7 \\ 7 & 7 & 3 & 3 & 1 & 7 \end{bmatrix}.$$

The problems for $n = 7$ have 1759244 options; yet they were solved in 20 Gμ without preprocessing. Special methods would, however, be required for $n \geq 8$.

239. Introduce primary items k and jk, for $1 \leq k \leq n$ and for all j with $k \in S_j$. When $S_j = \{k_1, \ldots, k_t\}$, there's an option '$jk_1 \ldots jk_t$' of cost w_j, together with t options '$k_i\ jk_i$' of "infinitesimal" cost ϵ^j for $1 \leq i \leq t$; also t "slack" options 'jk_i' of cost 0.

For example, suppose the only sets that cover 1 are S_1, S_2, S_3, S_4; and suppose that an optimum set cover uses S_2 and S_4 but neither S_1 nor S_3. Then a maximum-cost solution to this exact cover problem will use option '11 ...' of cost w_1, '31 ...' of cost w_3, '1 21' of cost ϵ^2, and '41' of cost 0 (because the alternative with '21' and '1 41' has smaller additional cost $0 + \epsilon^4$).

[See M. Gondran and M. Minoux, *Graphs and Algorithms* (1984), exercise 10.35. When finding the k best solutions instead of a single optimum, all solutions that become identical when ϵ is set to zero should be counted just once.]

240. Add $\{\text{WY}, \text{CO}, \text{NM}\}$ and either ID or UT or AZ. Or add $\{\text{ID}, \text{UT}, \text{CO}, \text{OK}\}$. Or add $\{\text{SD}, \text{MO}\}$ and either $\{\text{IA}, \text{OK}\}$ or $\{\text{NE}, \text{AR}\}$ (a surprise to the author when he posed this problem).

241. No, although it does find the cases where regions of fewer than 6 vertices are cut off. Round 1 discovers that New England can be shrunk to a single item; then Round 2 is able to remove options such as 'LA AR TN VA MD PA'. Altogether 3983 options and 5 items are removed, at a cost of 8 Gμ.

242. Before visiting a solution in step R2′, use depth-first search to find the connected components of the residual graph. Reject the solution if any such component has a size d for which $d < L \cdot \lceil d/(U-1) \rceil$.

243. Let $W = w_1 + \cdots + w_n$ be the sum of all weights. Then we have $\sum_{k=1}^{d} (x_k - r)^2 = \sum_{k=1}^{d} x_k^2 - 2rW + r^2 d$, because $\sum_{k=1}^{d} x_k = W$ in an exact cover problem.

244. True: Let G have m edges and n vertices. A solution with k edges between vertices of the same option has total interior cost $n(t-1) - 2k$, total exterior cost $2(m-k)$.

[But answer 246 shows that this can fail with options of different sizes.]

245. For (a), exercise 242 gives $42498 - 25230 = 17268$ options of size 7. Minimum cost \$58 is discovered in 101 Mμ. For (b), there are $1176310 - 1116759 = 59551$ options with population in $[43 . . 45]$ million. In the optimum solution shown below, which was found in 7.7 Gμ, all populations lie in the range $[43.51 . . 44.24]$ million.

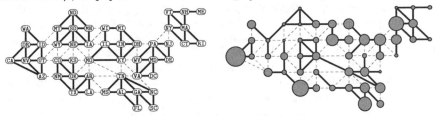

246. Minimum exterior cost ($90 and $74, found in 612 and 11 Mμ):

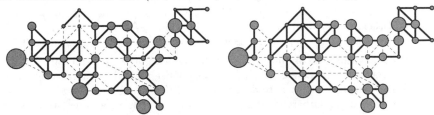

Minimum interior cost ($176 and $230, found in 1700 and 100 Mμ):

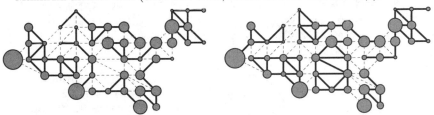

247. Use the procedure of answer 8 for raw data entry, but also set COST(j) ← ⟨the cost of the current option⟩ for $p < j \leq p + k$ at the beginning of step I5.

Then assign taxes "greedily" by doing the following for $k = 1, 2, \ldots, n$: If item k has no options, terminate with an unsolvable problem. Otherwise let c be the minimum cost of k's options, and set COST(k) ← c; this is the "tax" on k. If $c > 0$, subtract c from the cost of every option on k's list; this will affect all nodes of those options.

(The modified costs will be used internally. But all results reported to the user should be expressed in terms of the original costs, by adding the taxes back in.)

After all taxes have been assigned, sort the options by their (new) costs. (The "natural list merge sort," exercise 5.2.4–12, works well for this purpose, with the COST fields in spacer nodes serving as links.)

Finally, achieve (118) by re-inserting all nodes, in order of cost.

[Taxes could be assessed in many other ways. In general we seek real numbers u_1, $\ldots$, u_n such that $c_j \geq \sum\{u_i \mid \text{item } i \text{ in option } j\}$ for $1 \leq j \leq m$, where $u_1 + \cdots + u_n$ is maximum. This is a linear programming problem, which happens to be dual to the (fractional) exact cover problem of minimizing $c_1 x_1 + \cdots + c_m x_m$ such that $x_1, \ldots, x_m \geq 0$ and $\sum\{x_j \mid \text{item } i \text{ in option } j\} = 1$ for $1 \leq i \leq n$. An "optimum" taxation scheme, found by a linear programming solver, might make Algorithm C\$ significantly faster than it is with the greedy scheme above, even on highly nonlinear XCC problems; careful tests have not yet been made. See M. Gondran and J. L. Laurière, *Revue Française d'Automatique, Informatique et Recherche Opérationnelle* **8**, V-1 (1974), 27–40.]

248. Set $t \leftarrow \infty$, $c \leftarrow 0$, $j \leftarrow \mathtt{RLINK(0)}$, and do the following while $j > 0$: Set $p \leftarrow \mathtt{DLINK}(j)$ and $c' \leftarrow \mathtt{COST}(p)$. If $p = j$ or $c' \geq \vartheta$, go to C8$. Otherwise set $s \leftarrow 1$, $p \leftarrow \mathtt{DLINK}(p)$, and loop as follows: If $p = j$ or $\mathtt{COST}(p) \geq \vartheta$, exit the loop; otherwise if $s = t$, set $s \leftarrow s+1$ and exit; otherwise if $s \geq L$, set $s \leftarrow \mathtt{LEN}(j)$ and exit; otherwise set $s \leftarrow s+1$, $p \leftarrow \mathtt{DLINK}(p)$, and continue. After exiting the loop, if $s < t$ or ($s = t$ and $c < c'$), set $t \leftarrow s$, $i \leftarrow j$, and $c \leftarrow c'$. Finally set $j \leftarrow \mathtt{RLINK}(j)$.

[The author uses $L = 10$. He considered doing a complete search, thereby avoiding the frequent updates to LEN in (13), (15), etc.; but that turned out to be a bad idea.]

249. After we've seen t costs, we know only that the remaining $dk - t$ are nonnegative. The following algorithm sorts incoming costs into the rightmost positions of a buffer $b_0 b_1 \ldots b_{dk-1}$, maintaining the best possible lower bound l: Set $l \leftarrow t \leftarrow 0$. When seeing a new cost c, set $p \leftarrow t$, $y \leftarrow 0$, $r \leftarrow 1$, and do this while $rp > 0$: Set $x \leftarrow b_{dk-p}$. If $c \leq x$, set $r \leftarrow 0$. Otherwise if $p \bmod k = 0$, set $l \leftarrow l+x-y$; set $y \leftarrow b_{dk-p-1} \leftarrow x$, $p \leftarrow p-1$. After $rp = 0$, set $b_{dk-p-1} \leftarrow c$, $t \leftarrow t+1$; if $p \bmod k = 0$, set $l \leftarrow l+c-y$. Stop if $l \geq \theta$.

250. Keep a separate "accumulator" for each character in Z, and another for z if it is present. Look at each active item i: If $\mathtt{NAME}(i)$ begins with a character of Z, add $\mathtt{COST(DLINK}(i))$ to the appropriate accumulator. Otherwise if $z = 1$, add that cost to the accumulator for z. Otherwise if $z > 1$, use exercise 249 to accumulate costs that are separated by z. If any of the accumulators becomes $\geq T - C_l$, go to C8$.

(When Z or z hints are given, step C1$ should verify that they are legitimate.)

251. When all items have been covered, step Z2 will see the signature $\mathtt{S[0]} = 0$, which was initialized in step Z1; $\mathtt{Z[0]} = 1$ is the "success" node 'T'.

252.

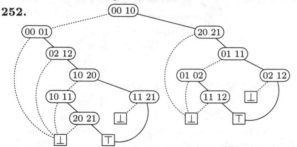

Notice that this free ZDD is *not* ordered, because '02 12' appears above '20 21' in the left branch but below '20 21' in the right branch. See exercise 264.

253. Introduce a global variable COUNT; also auxiliary variables $c_0 c_1 \ldots$ indexed by the current level l; also integer variables $\mathtt{C[}t\mathtt{]}$ indexed by cache location t. Set COUNT $\leftarrow 0$ and $\mathtt{C[0]} \leftarrow 1$ in step Z1. If a cache hit occurs in Z2, set COUNT $\leftarrow$ COUNT $+ \mathtt{C[}t\mathtt{]}$; otherwise set $c_l \leftarrow$ COUNT. Set $\mathtt{C[}m_l\mathtt{]} \leftarrow$ COUNT $- c_l$ in step Z7.

254. (a) If the options include d different colors for item i, a subproblem has $d + 2$ distinct cases: Either item i does not appear in any remaining options, or its list has not been purified, or its list has been purified to a particular color. So we reserve $\lceil \lg(d + 2) \rceil$ bits for i in the signature. If, for example, $d = 4$, those three bits will contain one of the codes 000, 001, 010, 011, 100, 101.

[In order to recognize the relevant case, Algorithm Z's version of the 'purify' operation in (55) should set $\mathtt{COLOR}(i) \leftarrow c$ in the header node for i; the 'unpurify' in (57) should set $\mathtt{COLOR}(i) \leftarrow 0$; and step Z1 should set $\mathtt{COLOR}(i) \leftarrow 0$. That initialization step should also remap i's colors so that they appear internally as $1, 2, \ldots, d$.]

(b) In large problems σ will occupy several octabytes. Give each item i a new field $\mathtt{SIG}(i)$, which is an index to a code table, and a new field $\mathtt{WD}(i)$. If $\mathtt{LEN}(i) \neq 0$, item i will contribute $\mathtt{CODE[SIG}(i) + \mathtt{COLOR}(i)\mathtt{]}$ to octabyte $\mathtt{WD}(i)$ of σ.

[If hashing is used for the cache lookup in step Z2, the CODE table can also contain random bits, for convenience in computing a good hash function.]

(c) Operation hide$'(p)$ doesn't remove node q from list TOP(q), if that list has been purified. But if TOP(q) is included in the signature, we'll *never* get a cache hit for solutions with different colors, even when subproblems don't actually depend on those colors. Therefore we need to know when a secondary item has no active options in its list.

(d) The trick is to decrease LEN(i), while still retaining the nodes on list i. If LEN(i) becomes zero, when i is a secondary item, we can then remove it from the list of active secondary items (whose head is $N + 1$, by answer 8).

[We can also use this trick in the 'hide' routine: Let hide$''''(p)$ be like hide(p) except that DLINK(u) and ULINK(d) remain unmodified when COLOR$(q) < 0$; LEN(x) is decreased as usual.] Of course unpurify and unhide$''''$ should undo purify and hide$''''$.

Some delicate maneuvers are needed to avoid deactivating a secondary item twice, and to reactivate it at precisely the right time when unpurifying. (The author's implementation temporarily sets the LEN to -1.)

255. Let $V_n = \sum_{k=0}^{n}(n-1-2k)\binom{n-k}{k}$, $W_n = \sum_{k=0}^{n}(1+(n-1-2k)+(n-1-2k)^2)\binom{n-k}{k}$. Using the fact that $\sum_{k=0}^{n}\binom{k}{r}\binom{n-k}{k} = [z^n]\,z^{2r}/(1-z-z^2)^{r+1}$, we obtain the closed forms $V_n = ((n-5)F_{n+1}+2(n+1)F_n)/5$ and $W_n = ((5n^2+7n+25)F_{n+1}-6(n+1)F_n)/25$. (See the derivation of 1.2.8–(17).) When N is even, Algorithm Z performs $W_N - 1$ updates and outputs a ZDD with $V_N + 2$ nodes. When N is odd, it performs W_N updates and outputs the trivial ZDD '$\perp$'.

256. Let $T(N)$, $Z(N)$, and $C(N)$ be the time, ZDD size, and cache size needed for K_N. With (89) the algorithm first spends $T(2q) + T(2r)$ time to create a ZDD of size $Z(2q) + Z(2r)$. Then it spends $\min(T(2q + 1), T(2r - 1))$ time to learn that no more ZDD nodes are desirable. The cache size is $C(2q) + C(2r) + \min(C(2q + 1), C(2r - 1))$.

257. (a) There are $2^{n-1}+1$ signatures: $11\ldots1$ and all n-bit strings beginning with 0.

(b)

Each nonzero signature σ has $2^{\nu\sigma-1}$ branches.

258. See (84). Now it's $V_n = v_n + \sum_{k=1}^{n-1}\binom{n-1}{k}v_k = ((72n - 342)5^n + (375n - 875)4^n + 600\cdot3^n+1800n2^n+1550)/3600$. [For example, $V_{16} = 40454337297$; $\varpi_{16} = 10480142147$.]

259. (a) The signatures at level l are $\{X_{l+1},\ldots,X_n\}$ together with all $\binom{n}{l}$ l-element subsets of $\{Y_1,\ldots,Y_n\}$. So there are 2^n of them; also $2 + \sum_{l=0}^{n}(n-l)\binom{n}{l} = n2^{n-1} + 2$ ZDD nodes; and $((n^2 + 3n + 4)2^n - 4)/4$ updates.

(b) Now the signatures are $\{X_{l+1},\ldots,X_n\}$ plus l-element subsets of $\{Y_1,\ldots,Y_{l+1}\}$. So we get $\binom{n}{2} + 1$ cache memos; $n^2 + 2$ ZDD nodes; $(2n^3 + 15n^2 + n)/6$ updates.

260. The ménage problem, with $\approx n!/e^2$ solutions, leads to unexpected running times: We seem to get roughly order $n^{3/2}\rho^n$ updates, where $\rho \approx 3.1$; but better results are obtained for $n \geq 13$ when the MRV heuristic is *not* used in step Z3! Then the running time may well be $\Theta(ne^n)$, although the ZDD size apparently grows as $n\rho^n$ with $\rho \approx 2.56$.

The other problem, with $L_n + 2$ solutions, needs just $6n + 9$ memos, $8n - 9$ ZDD nodes, and $34n - 58$ updates.

261. (a) Introduce primary items v^- and v^+ for each vertex v, representing the possibility of passing through v; but omit v^- for $v \in S$, and v^+ for $v \in T$. Also introduce secondary items v, whose color (if nonzero) represents the path number. The main options are '$u^+ \ v^- \ u{:}k \ v{:}k$', for each arc $u \longrightarrow v$ and for $1 \le k \le m$. There also are options '$v^- \ v{:}0$' for all $v \notin S$, and '$v^+ \ v{:}0$' for all $v \notin T$.

Moreover, we need a way to number each path canonically, so that we don't get $m!$ equivalent solutions. (The method of exercise 122 does not work with Algorithm Z.) If $S = \{s_1, \ldots, s_p\}$, introduce primary items x_k and secondary items y_k for $1 \le k \le p$, with the following options: '$x_k \ s_k{:}0 \ y_{k-1}{:}j \ y_k{:}j$' and '$x_k \ s_k{:}(j{+}1) \ y_{k-1}{:}j \ y_k{:}(j{+}1)$', for $1 \le k \le p$ and $0 \le j < k$. [Omit the item $y_{k-1}{:}j$ when $k = 1$; omit options with $y_p \ne m$.]

Many of these options can never be used. Algorithm P readily removes them.

(b) Remove unreachable vertices and unreachable arcs from G, if necessary, so that the only sources and sinks are $S = \{s_1, \ldots, s_m\}$ and $T = \{t_1, \ldots, t_m\}$. Then use items v^-, v^+, v and the main options of the construction in part (a); but omit any option that specifies $s_j{:}k$ or $t_j{:}k$ for $j \ne k$.

(c) This is a trick question, because each path contains exactly one vertex on the diagonal. The problem therefore factors neatly into two independent subproblems. It suffices to find $n-1$ vertex-disjoint paths from $S = \{(0, 1), \ldots, (0, n-1), (1, n), \ldots, (n-1, n)\}$ to $T = \{(1, 1), \ldots, (n-1, n-1)\}$ in the digraph with vertices (i, j) for $0 \le i \le j \le n$, $(i, j) \notin \{(0, 0), (0, n), (n, n)\}$, and arcs $(i, j) \longrightarrow (i+1, j)$, $(i, j) \longrightarrow (i, j-1)$.

If this problem has P_n solutions, given by a ZDD Z with M_n nodes, the original problem has P_n^2 solutions, given by a ZDD Z'' with $2M_n$ nodes. We obtain Z'' by replacing $\top$ in Z with the root of Z', where Z' specifies the reflections of the paths of Z.

Algorithm Z needs just 7 gigamems to find $P_{16} = 992340657705109416$ and $M_{16} = 3803972$. (In fact, P_n is known to be $\prod_{1 \le i \le j \le k \le n}(i+j+k-1)/(i+j+k-2)$, the number of plane partitions that are totally symmetric: N. Beluhov [to appear] has found a nice way to glue six triangular diagrams together, in kaleidoscope fashion, which establishes a one-to-one correspondence linking these paths to symmetrical diamond tilings like those of exercise 262(b).)

(d) There are exactly 47356 solutions. Algorithm C finds them in 278 Gμ, without preprocessing; but it needs only 760 Mμ, after Algorithm P has removed redundant options. Algorithm Z, by contrast, handles the problem in 92 Gμ, using 7 gigabytes of memo-cache memory (without preprocessing); 940 Mμ and 90 megabytes (with). Hence Algorithm Z is undesirable for problem (d), but essential for problem (c).

262. (a) The ordering of the primary items — the cells of S_n — is critical: Rowwise ordering (left-to-right, top-to-bottom) causes exponential growth; but columnwise ordering (top-to-bottom, left-to-right) yields *linear* ZDD size, and $\Theta(n^2)$ running time.

Furthermore, it turns out to be better *not* to use the MRV heuristic, when $n \ge 18$. Then the number of ZDD nodes is $154440n - 2655855$ for all $n \ge 30$. Only 2.2 Gμ are needed for $n = 32$. There are $68719476736 = (\sqrt{2})^{72}$ solutions for S_{16}, via exercise 7.1.4–208; for S_{32} there are $15232655601559677139083020722034115329 \approx 1.552^{200}$.

(An Aztec diamond of order m has exactly $2^{m(m+1)/2}$ domino tilings; moreover, as $m \to \infty$, the dominoes at the corners are q.s. aligned, except within an "arctic circle" of radius $m/\sqrt{2}$. See W. Jockusch, J. Propp, and P. Shor, arXiv:math/9801068 [math.CO] (1995), 44 pages; H. Cohn, N. Elkies, and J. Propp, *Duke Math. J.* **85** (1996), 117–166. See also D. Grensing, I. Carlsen, and H.-Chr. Zapp, *Philos. Mag.* **A41** (1980), 777–781.)

[Tilings of the more general shapes S_{mn} considered here, where we replace 16 by $2m$ and 7 by $m-1$, are more mysterious. M. Ciucu observes that $R_{(2m)(n-2m)} \subseteq S_{mn} \subseteq$

$R_{(2m)(n+2m)}$, where R_{kn} is a $k \times n$ rectangle; furthermore both $R_{(2m)(n+2m)} \setminus S_{mn}$ and $S_{mn} \setminus R_{(2m)(n-2m)}$ are tilable. Richard Stanley has shown, in *Discrete Applied Math.* **12** (1985), 81–87, that $R_{(2m)n}$ has $\sim a_{2m}\mu_{2m}^{n+1}$ tilings, for fixed m as $n \to \infty$, where

$$a_k = \frac{(1+\sqrt{2})^{k+1} - (1-\sqrt{2})^{k+1}}{2\sqrt{2}}, \quad \mu_{2m} = \prod_{j=1}^{m}\left(\cos\theta_j + \sqrt{1+\cos^2\theta_j}\right), \quad \theta_j = \frac{j\pi}{2m+1}.$$

Hence S_{mn} has $\Theta(\mu_{2m}^n)$ tilings in that limit. But if $m = \alpha n$ as $n \to \infty$, the limiting "arctic curve" outside which dominoes tend to be frozen remains to be discovered.]

    There is, incidentally, a beautiful connection between domino tilings and vertex-disjoint paths, discovered by D. Randall (unpublished):

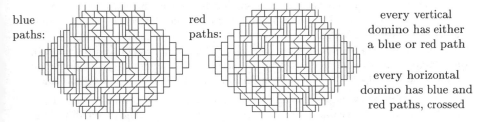

blue paths: red paths: every vertical domino has either a blue or red path

every horizontal domino has blue and red paths, crossed

    (b) In this case the triangle coordinates of answer 124 yield linear growth if we use items (x, y) for $0 \le x < n+8$, $0 \le y < 16$, $x+y \ge 8$; $(x, y)'$ for $0 \le x < n+8$, $0 \le y < 16$, $7 \le x+y < n+15$. The options are '(x, y) (x', y')', where $(x', y') = (x, y) - \{(0,0), (0,1), (1,0)\}$ and both items exist. Then the ZDD size (without MRV) turns out to be $257400n - 1210061$, for all $n \ge 7$.

    The convex triangular regions that can be tiled with diamonds are precisely those that have equally many $\triangle$ and $\triangledown$ triangles, namely the generalized hexagons T_{lmn} with sides (l, m, n, l, m, n) for some $l, m, n \ge 0$. These tilings are equivalent to plane partitions that fit in an $l \times m \times n$ box. In fact you can "see" this equivalence, because the diagrams resemble cubies packed into a corner of the box! (David Klarner made this discovery in the 1970s, but didn't publish it.) Therefore every tiling of T_n has respectively $(1, 2, \ldots, 8, 7, \ldots, 1)$ vertical diamonds in rows $(1, 2, \ldots, 15)$, hence 64 in all; and these occurrences are nested. For example, the middle diagram corresponds to the reverse plane partition shown here. (See exercise 5.1.4–36, from which it follows that the generalized hexagon T_{lmn} has exactly $\Pi_{lmn} = \prod_{i=1}^{l}\prod_{j=1}^{m}\prod_{k=1}^{n}(i+j+k-1)/(i+j+k-2)$ tilings. In particular, we have $\Pi_{888} = 5055160684040254910720$; $\Pi_{88(16)} = 206571578891401218269399172539062$5.)

```
00012457
1134569c
12368abc
25789bbc
4578accc
459aaccc
569aaccc
bbbbcccc
```

    [In *New York J. of Math.* **4** (1998), 137–165, H. Cohn, M. Larsen, and J. Propp studied random tilings of T_{lmn} when l, m, and n approach infinity with constant scaling, and conjectured that they are q.s. "frozen" outside of the largest enclosed ellipse. See also the more general results of C. Boutillier, *Annals of Probability* **37** (2009), 107–142.]

263.

	parameters	solutions	items	options	Alg C time, space		Alg Z time, space		ZDD
a)	organ-pipe order	14772512	$32 + 58$	256	40 Gμ	23 KB	55 Gμ	4.1 GB	56M
b)	6×10	2339	$72 + 0$	2032	4.1 Gμ	230 KB	3.1 Gμ	23 MB	11K
b)	8×8, square	16146	$77 + 1$	2327	20 Gμ	264 KB	14 Gμ	101 MB	59K
b)	8×8, straight	24600	$77 + 1$	2358	36 Gμ	267 KB	26 Gμ	177 MB	93K
b)	8×8, skew	23619	$77 + 1$	2446	28 Gμ	275 KB	20 Gμ	137 MB	84K
b)	8×8, ell	60608	$77 + 1$	2614	68 Gμ	291 KB	44 Gμ	276 MB	183K
b)	8×8, tee	25943	$77 + 1$	2446	35 Gμ	275 KB	25 Gμ	166 MB	92K
c)	aaa placed	987816	$49 + 42$	1514	25 Gμ	149 KB	18 Gμ	646 MB	2.2M

(d)	$(7,0,3)$	137216	$64+128$	3970	8.5 Gμ	642 KB	1.7 Gμ	20 MB	210K
(d)	$(7,3,4)$	41280	$70+140$	4762	3.2 Gμ	769 KB	1.0 Gμ	13 MB	122K
(e)	$p=6$, WORDS(1200)	1	$12+1230$	14400	17 Gμ	2 MB	25 Gμ	91 MB	14
(f)	kill symmetry	44*	$12+36$	1188	1.3 Gμ	110 KB	0.9 Gμ	10 MB	186
(g)	unmodified	18	$1165+66$	4889	202 Gμ	509 MB	234 Gμ	8.9 GB	2049
(g)	modified	1	$1187+66$	5143	380 Gμ	537 MB	424 Gμ	15 GB	336
(g)	preprocessed	18	$446+66$	666	223 Mμ	66 KB	1.8 Mμ	136 KB	574

* includes solutions that touch all cells

264. Let the primary items be linearly ordered, and let $r(o)$ be the smallest primary item in option o. If $(\bar{o}?\ l\colon h)$ is a ZDD node, every option o' in the subZDD rooted at h has $r(o') > r(o)$, because o covers $r(o)$ and smaller items have already been covered. Moreover, if $l \neq 0$, the option o' in node l has $r(o') = r(o)$; and o' precedes o in the input.

Thus, if we use a stable sorting algorithm to sort the options by decreasing $r(o)$, the ZDD will respect the reverse of this ordering. [This result was proved by Nishino, Yasuda, Minato, and Nagata in their original paper. Unfortunately, the algorithm is usually too slow without MRV, except in special situations like those of exercise 262.]

265. Every solution below any given ZDD node covers the same primary items. If all items are primary, no two visible nodes have the same signature. And the nodes of the chain below every visible node are distinct, because they branch on different options.

Now suppose we have three primary items $\{p, q, r\}$, and one secondary item s, with options 'p', '$p\ r$', '$p\ s$', '$q\ r$', '$q\ s$'. If we don't use MRV, we'll branch on p. Choice 1, 'p', leads to a subproblem with signature 0111 that outputs $I_2 = (\overline{q}\overline{r}?\ 0\colon 1)$, $I_3 = (\bar{p}?\ 0\colon 2)$. Choice 2, '$p\ r$', leads to a subproblem with signature 0101 that outputs $I_4 = (\overline{q}\overline{s}?\ 0\colon 1)$, $I_5 = (\overline{p}\overline{r}?\ 3\colon 4)$. Choice 3, '$p\ s$', leads to a subproblem with signature 0110 that outputs $I_6 = (\overline{q}\overline{r}?\ 0\colon 1)$, $I_7 = (\overline{p}\overline{s}?\ 5\colon 6)$. And $I_6 = I_2$.

A similar example, with items $\{q_1, q_2, q_3, r_1, r_2, r_3\}$ in place of $\{q, r\}$, and with 23 options 'p', '$p\ r_i$', '$p\ s$', '$q_i\ q_j$', '$r_i\ r_j$', '$q_i\ r_i$', '$q_i\ r_j$', '$q_j\ r_i$', '$q_i\ s$', for $1 \leq i < j \leq 3$, fails when MRV dictates the choices.

266. Let the given shape be specified as a set of integer pairs (x, y). These pairs might simply be listed one by one in the input; but it's much more convenient to accept a more compact specification. For example, the utility program with which the author prepared the examples of this book was designed to accept UNIX-like specifications such as '[14-7]2 5[0-3]' for the eight pairs $\{(1,2), (4,2), (5,2), (6,2), (7,2), (5,0), (5,1), (5,3)\}$. (Notice that a pair is included only once, if it's specified more than once.) The range $0 \leq x, y < 62$ has proved to be sufficient in almost all instances, with such integers encoded as single "extended hexadecimal digits" 0, 1, $\ldots$, 9, a, b, $\ldots$, z, A, B, $\ldots$, Z. The specification '[1-3][1-k]' is one way to define a 3×20 rectangle.

Similarly, each of the given polyominoes is specified by stating its piece name and a set T of typical positions that it might occupy. Such positions (x, y) are specified using the same conventions that were used for the shape; they needn't lie within that shape.

The program computes *base placements* by rotating and/or reflecting the elements of that set T. The first base placement is the shifted set $T_0 = T - (x_{\min}, y_{\min})$, whose coordinates are nonnegative and as small as possible. Then it repeatedly applies an elementary transformation, either $(x, y) \mapsto (y, x_{\max} - x)$ or $(x, y) \mapsto (y, x)$, to every existing base placement, until no further placements arise. (That process becomes easy when each base placement is represented as a sorted list of packed integers $(x \ll 16) + y$.) For example, the typical positions of the straight tromino might be specified as '1[1-3]'; it will have two base placements, $\{(0,0), (0,1), (0,2)\}$ and $\{(0,0), (1,0), (2,0)\}$.

After digesting the input specifications, the program defines the items of the exact cover problem, which are (i) the piece names; (ii) the cells xy of the given shape.

Finally, it defines the options: For each piece p and for each base placement T' of p, and for each offset (δ_x, δ_y) such that $T' + (\delta_x, \delta_y)$ lies fully within the given shape, there's an option that names the items $\{p\} \cup \{(x + \delta_x, y + \delta_y) \mid (x, y) \in T'\}$.

(The output of this program is often edited by hand, to take account of special circumstances. For example, some items may change from primary to secondary; some options may be eliminated in order to break symmetry. The author's implementation also allows the specification of secondary items with color controls, along with base placements that include such controls.)

Historical notes: Early algorithms for polyomino packing failed to realize the essentially unity between cells to be covered and pieces to be covered; their treatment of cells was quite different from their treatment of pieces. The fact that both cells and pieces are primary items of a "pure" exact cover problem was first noticed in connection with the Soma cube, by C. Peter-Orth [*Discrete Mathematics* **57** (1985), 105–121]. The base placements of tiles that are to be translated (but not rotated or reflected) are called "aspects" in *Tilings and Patterns* by Grünbaum and Shephard (1987).

267. RUSTY. [Leigh Mercer posed a similar question to Martin Gardner in 1960.]

268. As in the 3×20 example considered in the text, we can set up an exact cover problem with $12 + 60$ items, and with options for every potential placement of each piece. This gives respectively (52, 292, 232, 240, 232, 120, 146, 120, 120, 30, 232, 120) options for pieces (O, P, ..., Z) in Conway's nomenclature, thus 1936 options in all.

To reduce symmetry, we can insist that the X occurs in the upper left corner; then it contributes just 10 options instead of 30. But some solutions are still counted twice, when X is centered in the middle row. To prevent this we can add a *secondary item* 's': Append 's' to the five options that correspond to those centered appearances; also append 's' to the 60 options that correspond to placements where the Z is flipped over.

Without those changes, Algorithm X would use 10.04 Gμ to find 4040 solutions; with them, it needs just 2.93 Gμ to find 1010.

This approach to symmetry breaking in pentomino problems is due to Dana Scott [Technical Report No. 1 (Princeton University Dept. of Electrical Engineering, 10 June 1958)]. Another way to break symmetry would be to allow X anywhere, but to restrict the W to its 30 *unrotated* placements. That works almost as well: 2.96 Gμ.

269. There's a unique way to pack P, Q, R, U, X into a 5×5 square, and to pack the other seven into a 5×7. (See below.) With independent reflections, together with rotation of the square, we obtain 16 of the 1010. There's also a unique way to pack P, R, U into a 5×3 and the others into a 5×9 (noticed by R. A. Fairbairn in 1967), yielding 8 more. And there's a unique way to pack O, Q, T, W, Y, Z into a 5×6, plus two ways to pack the others via a bipair, yielding another 16. (These paired 5×6 patterns were apparently first noticed by J. Pestieau; see answer 286.) Finally, the packings in the next exercise give us 264 decomposable 5×12s altogether.

[Similarly, C. J. Bouwkamp discovered that S, V, T, Y pack uniquely into a 4×5, while the other eight can be put into a 4×10 in five ways, thus accounting for 40 of the 368 distinct 4×15s. See *JRM* **3** (1970), 125.]

270. Without symmetry reduction, 448 solutions are found in 1.24 Gμ. But we can restrict X to the upper left corner, as in answer 268, flagging its placements with 's' when centered in the middle row or middle column (but not both). Again the 's' is appended to flipped Z's. Finally, when X is placed in dead center, we append *another* secondary item 'c', and append 'c' to the 90°-rotated placements of W. This yields 112 solutions, after 0.35 Gμ.

Or we could leave X unhindered but curtail W to 1/4 of its placements. That's easier to do (although not *quite* as clever) and it finds those 112 in 0.44 Gμ.

Incidentally, there *aren't* actually any solutions with X in dead center.

271. The exact cover problem analogous to that in exercise 268 has $12 + 60$ items and $(56, 304, 248, 256, 248, 128, 152, 128, 128, 32, 248, 128)$ options. It finds 9356 solutions after 16.42 Gμ of computation, without symmetry reduction. But if we insist that X be centered in the upper left quarter, by removing all but 8 of its placements, we get 2339 solutions after just 4.11 Gμ. (The alternative of restricting W's rotations is *not* as effective in this case: 5.56 Gμ.) These solutions were first enumerated by C. B. and Jenifer Haselgrove [Eureka: *The Archimedeans' Journal* **23** (1960), 16–18].

272. (a) Obviously only $k = 5$ is feasible. All such packings can be obtained by omitting all options of the cover problem that straddle the "cut." That leaves 1507 of the original 2032 options, and yields 16 solutions after 104 Mμ. (Those 16 boil down to just the two 5×6 decompositions that we already saw in answer 269.)

(b) Now we remove the 763 options for placements that don't touch the boundary, and obtain just the two solutions below, after 100 Mμ. (This result was first noticed by Tony Potts, who posted it to Martin Gardner on 9 February 1960.)

(c) With 1237 placements/options, the *unique* solution is now found after 83 Mμ.

(d) There are respectively $(0, 9, 3, 47, 16, 8, 3, 1, 30, 22, 5, 11)$ solutions for pentominoes (O, P, Q, ..., Z). (The I/O pentomino can be "framed" by the others in 11 ways; but all of those packings also have at least one other interior pentomino.)

(e) Despite many ways to cover all boundary cells with just seven pentominoes, none of them lead to an overall solution. Thus the minimum is eight; 207 of the 2339 solutions attain it. To find them we might as well generate and examine all 2339.

(f) The question is ambiguous: If we're willing to allow the X to touch unnamed pieces at a corner, but not at an edge, there are 25 solutions (8 of which happen to be answers to part (a)). In each of these solutions, X also touches the outer boundary. (The cover and frontispiece of Clarke's book show a packing in which X doesn't touch the boundary, but it *doesn't* solve this problem: Using Golomb's piece names, there's an edge where X meets I, and there's a point where X meets P.) There also are two packings in which the edges of X touch only F, N, U, and the boundary, but not V.

On the other hand, there are just 6 solutions if we allow only F, N, U, V to touch X's corner points. One of them, shown below, has X touching the short side and seems to match the quotation best. These 6 solutions can be found in just 47 Mμ, by introducing 60 secondary items as sort of an "upper level" to the board: All placements of X occupy the normal five lower-level cells, plus up to 16 upper-level cells that touch them; all placements of F, N, U, V are unchanged; all placements of the other seven pieces occupy both the lower and the upper level. This nicely forbids them from touching X.

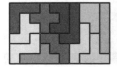  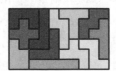 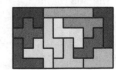

273. (a) We could set this up as twelve separate exact cover problems, one for each pentomino omitted. But it's more interesting to consider all cases simultaneously, by giving a "free pass" to one pentomino as follows: Add a new primary item '#', and twelve new options '# O', '# P', ..., '# Z'. The sixty items ij are demoted to secondary status.

To remove symmetry, delete 3/4 of the options for piece V; also make its new option '# V s', and add 's' to 3/4 of the options for piece W, where 's' is a new secondary item. That makes a total of 1194 options, involving $13 + 61$ items.

If Algorithm X branches first on #, the effect is equivalent to 12 separate runs; the search tree has 7.9 billion nodes, and the run time is 16.8 teramems. But if we use the nonsharp preference heuristic (see answer 10), the algorithm is able to save some time by making decisions that are common to several subcases. Its search tree then has 7.3 billion nodes, and the run time is 15.1 teramems. Of course both methods give the same answer, which is huge: 118,034,464.

(b) Now keep items ij primary, but introduce 60 new secondary items ij'. There are 60 new options '$ij\ ij'\ (i{+}1)j'\ i(j{+}1)'\ (i{+}1)(j{+}1)''$', where we omit items containing $(i{+}1)$ when $i = 2$ or $(j{+}1)$ when $j = 19$. This problem has 1254 options involving $73{+}61$ items. Its search tree (with deprecated # branching) has about 950 million nodes; it finds 4,527,002 solutions, after about 1.5 teramems of computation.

A related, but much simpler, problem asks for packings in which exactly one hole appears in each of the column pairs $\{1,2\}$, $\{5,6\}$, $\{9,\mathsf{a}\}$, $\{\mathsf{d},\mathsf{e}\}$, $\{\mathsf{h},\mathsf{i}\}$. That one has 1224 options, $78{+}1$ items, 20 meganodes, 73 gigamems, and 23642 solutions. Here's one:

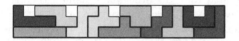

(c) A setup like the one in (a) yields 1127 options, $13{+}58$ items, 1130 meganodes, 2683 gigamems, 22237 solutions. (One of the noteworthy solutions is illustrated above.)

274. Restrict X to five essentially different positions; if X is on the diagonal, also keep Z unflipped by using the secondary item 's' as in answer 268. There are respectively (16146, 24600, 23619, 60608, 25943) solutions, found in (20.3, 36.3, 28.0, 68.3, 35.2) $G\mu$.

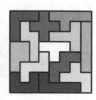

In each case the tetromino can be placed anywhere that doesn't immediately cut off a region of one or two squares. [The twelve pentominoes first appeared in print when H. E. Dudeney published *The Canterbury Puzzles* in 1907. His puzzle #74, "The Broken Chessboard," presented the first solution shown above, with pieces checkered in black and white. That parity restriction, with the further condition that no piece is turned over, would reduce the number of solutions to only 4, findable in 120 $M\mu$.]

The 60-element subsets of the chessboard that *can't* be packed with the pentominoes have been characterized by M. Reid in *JRM* **26** (1994), 153–154.

The earliest known polyomino puzzle appeared in P. F. Catel's *Verzeichniß von sämmtlichen Waaren* (Berlin, 1785), #11: 4 Z pentominoes + 4 ells make a 6×6 square.

275. Yes, in seven essentially different ways. To remove symmetry, we can make
the O vertical and put the X in the right half. (The pentominoes will have a total
of $6 \times 2 + 5 \times 3 + 4 = 31$ black squares; therefore the tetromino *must* be .)

276. These shapes can't be packed in a rectangle. But we can use the "supertile"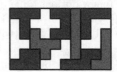
to make an infinite strip $\cdots$  $\cdots$. [See B. Grünbaum and G. C. Shephard,
Tilings and Patterns (1987), 508.] We can also tile the plane with a supertile like ,
or even use a generalized torus such as 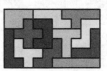 (see exercise 7–137). That supertile was
used in 2009 by George Sicherman to make tetromino wallpaper.

277. The 2339 solutions contain 563 that satisfy the "tatami" condition: No four pieces
meet at any one point. Each of those 563 leads to a simple 12-vertex graph coloring
problem; for example, the SAT methods of Section 7.2.2.2 typically need at most two
or three kilomems to decide each case.

It turns out that exactly 94 are three-colorable, including the second solution to
exercise 272(b). Here are the three for which W, X, Y, Z all have the same color:

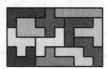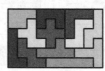

278. The 2339 solutions in answer 271 restrict X to the upper left quarter; we must
be careful not to include bipairs that might swap X out of that region. One way (see
exercise 212) is to order the items: Put X first, then the other piece names, then the
place names from 00 to 59. All swaps involving X will then move it up or left.

The 34 bipairs of the catalog now result in an exact cover problem with the same
primary items and options as before, but with 2804 new secondary items. They limit
the number of solutions to 1523; but the running time increases to 4.26 Gμ.

[The proof idea of Theorem S yields an interesting directed acyclic graph with
2339 vertices and 937 arcs. It has 1528 source vertices, 1523 sink vertices, and 939
isolated vertices (both sources and sinks). If we ignore the arc directions, there are
1499 components, of which the largest has size 10. That component contains the
leftmost solution below, which belongs to four different bipairs. There also are two components of size 8, with three nonoverlapping bipairs. The rightmost solution belongs to
a component of size 6, which would grow to size 8 if X were allowed to move downward.]

279. It's also possible to wrap *two* cubes of size $\sqrt{5} \times \sqrt{5} \times \sqrt{5}$,
as shown by F. Hansson; see *Fairy Chess Review* **6** (1947–
1948), problems 7124 and 7591. A full discussion appears in
FGbook, pages 685–689.

280. (Notice that width 3 would be impossible, because every faultfree placement of
the V needs width 4 or more.) We can set up an exact cover problem for a 4×19
rectangle in the usual way; but then we make cell $(x, y+15)$ identical to $(3-x, y)$ for
$0 \le x < 4$ and $0 \le y < 5$, essentially making a half-twist when the pattern begins to
wrap around. There are 60 symmetries, and care is needed to remove them properly.
The easiest way is to put X into a fixed position, and allow W to rotate at most $90°$.

This exact cover problem has 850 solutions, 502 of which are faultfree. Here's one of the 29 strongly three-colorable ones, shown before and after its ends are joined:

   top: bottom:

281. Both shapes have 8-fold symmetry, so we can save a factor of nearly 8 by placing the X in (say) the north-northwest octant. If X thereby falls on the diagonal, or in the middle column, we can insist that the Z is not flipped, by introducing a secondary item 's' as in answer 270. Furthermore, if X occurs in dead center — this is possible only for shape (i) — we use 'c' as in that answer to prohibit also any rotation of the W.

Thus we find (a) 10 packings, in 3.5 Gμ; (b) 7302 packings, in 353 Gμ; for instance

   ,      ;      .

It turns out that the monomino must appear in or next to a corner, as shown. [The first solution to shape (i) with monomino in the corner was sent to Martin Gardner by H. Hawkins in 1958. The first solution of the other type was published by J. A. Lindon in *Recreational Mathematics Magazine* #6 (December 1961), 22. Shape (ii) was introduced and solved much earlier, by G. Fuhlendorf in *The Problemist: Fairy Chess Supplement* **2**, 17 and 18 (April and June, 1936), problem 2410.]

282. It's easy to set up an exact cover problem in which the cells touching the polyomino are primary items, while other cells are secondary, and with options restricted to placements that contain at least one primary item. Postprocessing can then remove spurious solutions that contain holes. Typical answers for (a) are

representing respectively (9, 2153, 37, 2, 17, 28, 18, 10, 9, 2, 4, 1) cases. For (b) they're

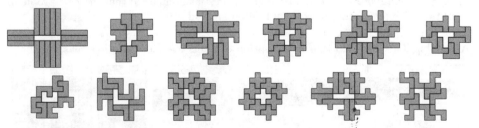

representing (16, 642, 1, 469, 551, 18, 24, 6, 4, 2, 162, 1). The total number of fences is respectively (3120, 1015033, 8660380, 284697, 1623023, 486, 150, 2914, 15707, 2, 456676, 2074), after weeding out respectively (0, 0, 16387236, 398495, 2503512, 665, 600, 11456, 0, 0, 449139, 5379) cases with holes. (See *MAA Focus* **36**, 3 (June/July

2016), 26; **36**, 4 (August/September 2016), 33.) Of course we can also make fences for one shape by using *other* shapes; for example, there's a beautiful way to fence a Z with 12 Ps, also a unique way to fence one pentomino with only *three* copies of another.

283. The small fences of answer 282(a) already meet this condition — except for the X, which has *no* tatami fence. The large fences for T and U in 282(b) are also good. But the other nine fences can no longer be as large:

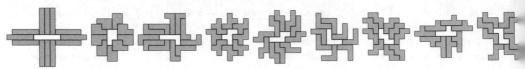

[The tatami condition can be incorporated into the exact cover problem by introducing a secondary item $/ij$ for each interior point ij. Add this item to every placement option that has a convex corner at ij and occupies either the cell to the northeast or the cell to the southwest. However, for this exercise it's best simply to apply the tatami condition directly to each ordinary solution, before postprocessing for hole-removal.]

284. This problem is readily solved with the "second death" algorithm of exercise 19, by letting the four designated piece names be the *only* primary items. The answers to both (a) and (b) are unique. [See M. Gardner, *Scientific American* **213**, 4 (October 1965), 96–102, for Golomb's conjectures about minimum blocking configurations on larger boards.]

285. This exercise, with 3×30, 5×18, 6×15, and 9×10 rectangles, yields four increasingly difficult benchmarks for the exact cover problem, having respectively (46, 686628, 2567183, 10440433) solutions. Symmetry can be broken as in answer 270. The 3×30 case was first resolved by J. Haselgrove; the 9×10 packings were first enumerated by A. Wassermann and P. Östergård, independently. [See *New Scientist* **12** (1962), 260–261; J. Meeus, *JRM* **6** (1973), 215–220; and *FGbook* pages 455, 468–469.] Algorithm X needs (.006, 5.234, 15.576, 63.386) teramems to find them.

286. Two solutions are now equivalent only when related by 180° rotation. Thus there are $2 \cdot 2339/64 = 73.09375$ solutions per problem, on average. The minimum (42) and maximum (136) solution counts occur for the cases

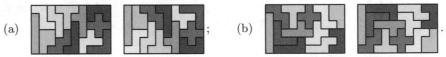

(a)   ;   (b)   .

[In *U.S. Patent 2900190* (1959, filed 1956), J. Pestieau remarked that these 64 problems would give his pentomino puzzle "unlimited life and utility."]

287. Let $c = (12, 11, \ldots, 1)$ for pieces $(O, P, \ldots, Z)$ when assigning costs to each option. Algorithm X$, when told that every option contains one piece and five cells, finds

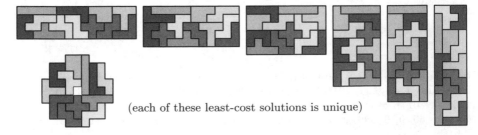

(each of these least-cost solutions is unique)

in respectively (1.5, 3.4, 3.3, 2.9, 3.2, 1.4, 1.1) $G\mu$. The corresponding times for Algorithm X are (3.7, 10.0, 16.4, 16.4, 10.0, 3.7, 2.0) $G\mu$. (However, we could reduce symmetry when applying Algorithm X, then calculate the values of four or eight different reflections or rotations whenever a solution is found; that would often be faster.)

288. When symmetry is removed efficiently, Algorithm X needs 63 $T\mu$ to visit all of the essentially different solutions. But Algorithm X\$ wins this competition, by discovering

(which both are uniquely optimum) in 28.9 $T\mu$ and 25.1 $T\mu$, respectively.

289. (a) One of the $8 \cdot 2422 \cdot 85 \cdot 263 \cdot 95 \cdot 224 \cdot 262 \cdot 226 \cdot 228 \cdot 96 \cdot 105 \cdot 174$ solutions is shown in Fig. A–4. (It isn't hard to keep pentominoes of the same shape from touching.)

(b) Now there are $1472 \cdot 5915 \cdot 596 \cdot 251 \cdot 542 \cdot 204 \cdot 170 \cdot 226 \cdot 228 \cdot 96 \cdot 651 \cdot 316$.

(c) The first seven columns left of the middle line can yield six 12-cell regions only by using all 72 cells. Thus the problem *factors* neatly into ten independent problems of the form (i). That problem has 7712 solutions with six connected regions; Algorithm X\$ needs a search tree of only 622 nodes to determine that there are just 11 minimum-perimeter solutions. Three of them are symmetrical; and the nicest is shown in (ii). (And two of the solutions, such as (iii), *maximize* the total perimeter.)

(i) = ; (ii) = ; (iii) = .

Unfortunately (36) can't be expanded into the desired 720-cell shape based on (ii), because the scaled-up Q can't be packed. But the *alternative* form of (36) does lead to $16 \cdot 2139 \cdot 6 \cdot 97 \cdot 259 \cdot 111 \cdot 44 \cdot 64 \cdot 79 \cdot 12 \cdot 17 \cdot 111$ solutions, such as the one in Fig. A–4.

290. There are no ways to fill 2×20; $4 \cdot 66$ ways to fill 4×10; $4 \cdot 84$ ways to fill 5×8. None of the solutions are symmetrical. [See R. K. Guy, *Nabla* **7** (1960), 99–101.]

291. The puzzles for January, April, September, and December (say) are equivalent; thus only $4 \cdot 31 = 124$ puzzles need to be solvable, not 366. Only 53 of the 220 pentomino triples are unsuitable: First reject all 55 that include X, and all 10 that are subsets of $\{O, R, S, W, Z\}$; then restore $P\{O, Q, S, T, U, V, Y\}X$ and ORS, OSW, RSW; then reject RTZ and TWZ. Of the remaining 167 triples, PQV is by far the easiest: Every PQV puzzle has at least 1778 solutions! The hardest is QTX, which allows only about 33 solutions per day, on average. [This puzzle was designed by Marcel Gillen, © 2018, who made it with pentominoes R, U, W for the 2018 International Puzzle Party.]

292. Most of the hexominoes will have three black cells and three white cells, in any "checkering" of the board. However, eleven of them (shown as darker gray in the illustration) will have a two-to-four split. Thus the total number of black cells will always be an even number between 94 and 116, inclusive. But a 210-cell rectangle

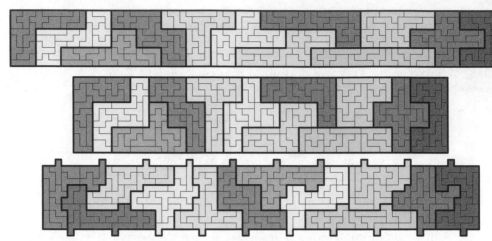

Fig. A–4. Pentominoes of pentominoes.

always contains exactly 105 black cells. [See *The Problemist: Fairy Chess Supplement* **2**, 9–10 (1934–1935), 92, 104–105; *Fairy Chess Review* **3**, 4–5 (1937), problem 2622.]

Benjamin's triangular shape, on the other hand, has $1+3+5+\cdots+19 = 10^2 = 100$ cells of one parity and $\binom{21}{2} - 10^2 = 110$ of the other. It can be packed with the 35 hexominoes in a huge number of ways, probably not feasible to count exactly.

293. The parity considerations in answer 292 tell us that this is possible only for the "unbalanced" hexominoes, such as the one shown. And in fact, Algorithm X readily finds solutions for all eleven of those, too numerous to count. Here's an example:

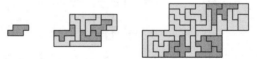

[See *Fairy Chess Review* **6** (April 1947) through **7** (June 1949), problems 7252, 7326, 7388, 7460, 7592, 7728, 7794, 7865, 7940, 7995, 8080. See also the similar problem 7092.]

294. Each castle must contain an odd number of the eleven unbalanced hexominoes (see answer 292). Thus we can begin by finding all sets of seven hexominoes that can be packed into a castle: This amounts to solving $\binom{11}{1} + \binom{11}{3} + \binom{11}{5} + \binom{11}{7} = 968$ exact cover problems, one for each potential choice of unbalanced elements. Each of those problems is fairly easy; the 24 balanced hexominoes provide secondary items, while the castle cells and the chosen unbalanced elements are primary. In this way we obtain 39411 suitable sets of seven hexominoes, with only a moderate amount of computation.

That gives us *another* exact cover problem, having 35 items and 39411 options. This secondary problem turns out to have exactly 1201 solutions (found in just 115 Gμ), each of which leads to at least one of the desired overall packings. Here's one:

In this example, two of the hexominoes in the rightmost castle can be flipped vertically; and of course the entire contents of each castle can independently be flipped horizontally. Thus we get 64 packings from this particular partition of the hexominoes (or maybe $64 \cdot 5!$, by permuting the castles), but only two of them are "really" distinct. Taking multiplicities into account, there are 1803 "really" distinct packings altogether.

[Frans Hansson found the first way to pack the hexominoes into five equal shapes, using ▨ as the container; see *Fairy Chess Review* **8** (1952–1953), problem 9442. His container admits 123189 suitable sets of seven, and 9298602 partitions into five suitable sets instead of only 1201. Even more packings are possible with the container ▨, which has 202289 suitable sets and 3767481163 partitions!]

In 1965, M. J. Povah packed all of the hexominoes into containers of shape ▨, using *seven* sets of *five*; see *The Games and Puzzles Journal* **2** (1996), 206.

295. By exercise 292, m must be odd, and less than 35. F. Hansson posed this question in *Fairy Chess Review* **7** (1950), problem 8556. He gave a solution for $m = 19$,

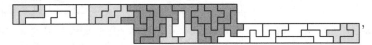

and claimed without proof that 19 is maximum. The 13 dark gray hexominoes in this diagram cannot be placed in either "arm"; so they must go in the center. (Medium gray indicates pieces that have parity restrictions in the arms.) Thus we cannot have $m \geq 25$.

When $m = 23$, there are 39 ways to place all of the hard hexominoes, such as

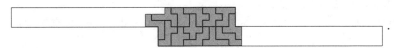

However, none of these is completable with the other 22; hence $m \leq 21$.

When $m = 21$, the hard hexominoes can be placed in 791792 ways, without creating a region whose size isn't a multiple of 6 and without creating more than one region that matches a particular hexomino. Those 791792 ways have 69507 essentially distinct "footprints" of occupied cells, and the vast majority of those footprints appear to be impossible to fill. But in 2016, George Sicherman found the remarkable packing

which not only solves $m = 21$, it yields solutions for $m = 19, 17, 15, 11, 9, 7, 5,$ and 3 by simple modifications. Sicherman also found separate solutions for $m = 13$ and $m = 1$.

296. Stead's original solution makes a very pleasant three-colored design:

[See *Fairy Chess Review* **9** (1954), 2–4; also *FGbook*, pages 659–662.]

This problem is best solved via the techniques of dynamic programming (Section 7.7), *not* with Algorithm X, because numerous subproblems are equivalent.

297. Yes — in fact, there are so many ways, further conditions ought to be imposed. Torbijn's original quest, to leave a hexomino-shaped "hole" in one square, turns out to have been impossible. But there's a nice alternative: We can add the two *trominoes*.

A. van de Wetering showed in 1991 that exactly 13710 sets of six hexominoes can fit into a single square. [See *JRM* **23** (1991), 304–305.] Similarly, exactly 34527 sets of five hexominoes will fit, when supplemented by two trominoes that both occupy two black cells. So we're left with a secondary covering problem, with 35 primary items and 48237 options, as in answer 294. That problem has 163 solutions (found in 3 Tμ).

Another alternative, also suggested by van de Wetering, is to place six empty cells symmetrically. He also was able to add a monomino and one of the pentominoes: The secondary covering problems associated with pentominoes (O, P, ..., Z) turn out to have (94, 475, 1099, 0, 0, 2, 181, 522, 0, 0, 183, 0) solutions.

298. Make options for the pentominoes in cells xy for $0 \le x < 8$, $0 \le y < 10$ as in exercise 266, and also for the tetrominoes in cells xy for $1 \le x < 7$, $1 \le y < 9$. In the latter options include also items xy':0 for all cells xy *in* the tetromino, as well as xy':1 for all other cells xy *touching* the tetromino, where the items xy' for $0 \le x < 8$ and $0 \le y < 10$ are secondary. We can also assume that the center of the X pentomino lies in the upper left corner. There are 168 solutions, found after 1.5 Tμ of computation. (Another way to keep the tetrominoes from touching would be to introduce secondary items for the *vertices* of the grid. Such items are more difficult to implement, however, because they behave differently under the rotations of answer 266.)

[Many problems that involve placing the tetrominoes and pentominoes together in a rectangle were explored by H. D. Benjamin and others in the *Fairy Chess Review*, beginning already with its predecessor *The Problemist: Fairy Chess Supplement* **2**, 16 (February 1936), problem 2171. But this question seems to be new; it was inspired by Michael Keller's 15×18 pentomino + hexomino construction in *World Game Review* **9** (1989), 3. See also P. Torbijn's elegant 13×23 packing of all the n-ominoes for $1 \le n \le 6$, in *Cubism For Fun* **25**, part 1 (1990), 11.]

299. P. J. Torbijn and J. Meeus [*JRM* **32** (2003), 78–79] have exhibited solutions for rectangles of sizes 6×45, 9×30, 10×27, and 15×18; thus intuition suggests that enormously many solutions ought to be possible for this case too. But Peter Esser has surprisingly proved that *no* packing of the 35 hexominoes into a 5×54 rectangle will occupy all 114 of the border cells. Indeed, the pieces can individually occupy at most (6, 5, 5, 4, 4, 4, 3, 3, 3, 3, 3, 3, 3, 2, 2, 2, 2, 2, 2, 2, 2, 1, 1, $5 + x_{24}$, $4 + x_{25}$, $4 + x_{26}$, $4 + x_{27}$, $3 + x_{28}$, $3 + x_{29}$, $3 + x_{30}$, $2 + x_{31}$, $2 + x_{32}$, $4 + 2x_{33}$, $3 + 2x_{34}$, $3 + 2x_{35}$) border cells, respectively, under an appropriate numbering of the pieces, where $x_k = 1$ only if piece k is in a corner. Since there are only four corners, we can occupy at most $6 + 5 + \cdots + 4 + 3 + 3 + (1 + 2 + 2 + 2) = 114$ border cells — but only if $x_{33} = x_{34} = x_{35} = 1$. Unfortunately, those last three pieces (namely ⌐, ⌐, ⌐) can't simultaneously occupy corners.

300. Make options as usual (exercise 266), but also include 100 new options 'xy Rx Cy' for $0 \le x, y < 10$. Then use Algorithm M, assigning multiplicity 4 to each Rx and Cy. Remove symmetry by confining X to the upper left corner, and by insisting that O be horizontal. (a) One of the 31 solutions (found in 12 Gμ) is shown below. (b) This case has 5347 solutions (found in 4.6 Tμ); and if we insist on filling also all cells just *above* the diagonals, the solution turns out to be *unique* (see below). (c) Instead of focusing on diagonals, Aad van de Wetering noticed that we can require the empty spaces to be *symmetrical*. For example, there are 1094 solutions (found in 19.2 Tμ)

whose empty spaces are diagonally symmetric. Three of them, like the one shown here, are also rather close (92%) to being *centrally symmetric* (that is, under 180° rotation).

Three others, like the fourth example above, leave a 4×4 hole in the corner. Moreover, there are 98 solutions (found in 3.2 Tμ) whose empty spaces have 100% central symmetry. One of them has a large "moat" between two blocks of pentominoes; another has connected pentominoes, with holes of size at least 6.

Furthermore, van de Wetering reported that he had found "by accident" a solution where each of the four 5×5 quadrants of the 10×10 contained exactly three pentominoes. This additional stipulation is, indeed, easy to add to our MCC formulation: We omit options that cross quadrant boundaries, append a new item Q_t to each option in the tth quadrant, and give multiplicity 3 to each Q_t. It turns out that there actually are 1,124,352 inequivalent solutions(!), found by Algorithm M in 23 Tμ.

But van de Wetering also discovered a class of solutions that's even more interesting: He packed the empty spaces entirely with "ghost" pentominoes, all different!

To obtain such remarkable solutions, use primary items #xy, !xy, #Rx, and #Cy for $0 \le x, y < 10$, as well as O, P, ..., Z; use secondary items xy as well as O′, P′, ..., Z′. Items #Rx and #Cy have multiplicity 4. Specify two options for each pentomino placement, such as 'V !00 00:1 !01 01:1 !02 02:1 !10 10:1 !20 20:1' for V in the corner and 'V′ !00 00:0 !01 01:0 !02 02:0 !10 10:0 !20 20:0' for its ghost in that place. Also specify 200 further options, '#xy #Rx #Cy xy:0' and '#xy xy:1', for $0 \le x, y < 10$. Algorithm M with the nonsharp heuristic will then make intelligent choices. There are (amazingly) 357 solutions, found in 322 teramems with a search tree of 32 giganodes. The first solution above is one of six that cover exactly six cells of each main diagonal, answering a question that had been posed by Aad Thoen. The second solution is one of two for which all seven of the "unambiguously named pentominoes" T, U, V, W, X, Y, Z are among the ghosts. The third solution is one of two that respects 5×5 quadrants. [*Note:* A similar question, but with *identical* polyominoes, was Erich Friedman's "problem of the month" in May 2007; see erich-friedman.github.io/mathmagic/0507.html.]

301. (a) Algorithm M produces $4 \cdot 13330$ solutions when we specify the desired multiplicities for cell items. Symmetry under reflection can be removed by restricting, say, W to only 1/4 of its options.

(b) Consider the conflict graph on vertices O, P, ..., Z, defined by declaring pieces to be adjacent when they appear in the same cell. We can achieve $\le d$ levels if and only if we can color that graph with $\le d$ colors. The conflict graph for the given arrangement has the 4-clique {Q, X, Y, Z}; so it can't be 3-colored.

(c, d) A SAT solver such as Algorithm 7.2.2.2D quickly determines that exactly (587, 12550, 193) of the conflict graphs for the 13330 distinct solutions to (a) have

chromatic numbers (3, 4, 5). The first example below can be (uniquely) 3-colored
$\texttt{O V Y Z} \mid \texttt{P R W X} \mid \texttt{Q S T U}$; the second example has the clique $\{\texttt{Q, R, S, W, Y}\}$.

OU	XY	UW	WZ	SZ
OUX	UXY	UXY	SWZ	SVW
OT	XY	RZ	SZ	VW
ORT	RTY	RTV	PSV	PQV
OT	QR	PQ	PQ	PQ

QY	QR	TU	TX	TU
RSY	QRY	RUX	UTX	UVX
SY	QW	RW	TX	VZ
SWY	QSW	PVZ	PVZ	PVZ
OW	OS	OZ	OP	OP

302. (a) There are 94. (But 16 of them have interior "holes" and can't be used in (b).)

(b) The two solutions are related by rotating four of the pieces:

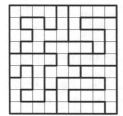 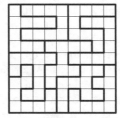 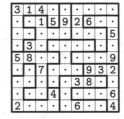

(c) Sixteen different jigsaw sudoku diagrams can be used. The first of them collaborates with π as shown above; the others probably do too. [Appendix E has the answer. This exercise was suggested by E. Timmermans, *Cubism For Fun 85* (2011), 4–9.]

303. (a) Represent the tree as a sequence $a_0 a_1 \ldots a_{2n-1}$ of nested parentheses; then a_0 will match a_{2n-1}. The left boundary of the corresponding parallomino is obtained by mapping each '(' into N or E, according as it is immediately followed by '(' or ')'. The right boundary, similarly, maps each ')' into N or E according as it is immediately *preceded* by ')' or '('. For example, if we take 7.2.1.6–(1) and enclose it in an additional pair of parentheses, the corresponding parallomino is shown below with part (d).

(b) This series $wxy + w^2(xy^2 + x^2y) + w^3(xy^3 + 2x^2y^2 + x^3y) + \cdots$ can be written $wxyH(w, wx, wy)$, where $H(w, x, y) = 1/(1 - x - y - G(w, x, y))$ generates a sequence of "atoms" corresponding to places x, y, G where the juxtaposed boundary paths have the respective forms $\frac{\text{E}}{\text{E}}$, $\frac{\text{N}}{\text{N}}$, or $\frac{\text{N}}{\text{E}}\langle\text{inner}\rangle\frac{\text{E}}{\text{N}}$. The area is thereby computed by diagonals between corresponding boundary points. (In the example from (a), the area is $1+1+1+1+2+2+2+2+2+2+2+2+2+1+1$; there's an "outer" G, whose H is $yxyGy$, and an "inner" G, whose H is $xyyxyxxy$.) Thus we can write G as a continued fraction,

$$G(w, x, y) = wxy/(1 - wx - wy - w^3xy/(1 - w^2x - w^2y - w^5xy/(\cdots))).$$

[A completely different form is also possible, namely $G(w, x, y) = x\frac{J_1(w,x,y)}{J_0(w,x,y)}$, where

$$J_0(w, x, y) = \sum_{n=0}^{\infty} \frac{(-1)^n y^n w^{n(n+1)/2}}{(1-w)(1-w^2)\ldots(1-w^n)(1-xw)(1-xw^2)\ldots(1-xw^n)};$$

$$J_1(w, x, y) = \sum_{n=1}^{\infty} \frac{(-1)^{n-1} y^n w^{n(n+1)/2}}{(1-w)(1-w^2)\ldots(1-w^{n-1})(1-xw)(1-xw^2)\ldots(1-xw^n)}.$$

This form, derived via *horizontal* slices, disguises the symmetry between x and y.]

(c) Let $G(w, z) = G(w, z, z)$. We want $[z^n]G'(1, z)$, where differentiation is with respect to the first parameter. From the formulas in (b) we know that $G(1, z) =$

$z(C(z) - 1)$, where $C(z) = (1 - \sqrt{1-4z})/(2z)$ generates the Catalan numbers. Partial derivatives $\partial/\partial w$ and $\partial/\partial z$ then give $G'(1, z) = z^2/(1-4z)$ and $G_{\prime}(1, z) = 1/\sqrt{1-4z}-1$.

(d) This problem has four symmetries, because we can reflect about either diagonal. When $n = 5$, Algorithm X finds 801×4 solutions, of which 129×4 satisfy the tatami condition, and 16×4 are strongly three-colorable. (The tatami condition is easily enforced via secondary items in this case, because we need only stipulate that the upper right corner of one parallomino doesn't match the lower left corner of another.) When $n = 6$ there are oodles and oodles of solutions. All of the trees/parallominoes thereby appear together in an attractive compact pattern.

 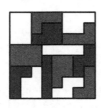 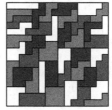

[*References:* J. Levine, *Scripta Mathematica* **24** (1959), 335–338; D. A. Klarner and R. L. Rivest, *Discrete Math.* **8** (1974), 31–40; E. A. Bender, *Discrete Math.* **8** (1974), 219–226; I. P. Goulden and D. M. Jackson, *Combinatorial Enumeration* (New York: Wiley, 1983), exercise 5.2.2; M.-P. Delest and G. Viennot, *Theoretical Comp. Sci.* **34** (1984), 169–206; W.-J. Woan, L. Shapiro, and D. G. Rogers, *AMM* **104** (1997), 926–931; P. Flajolet and R. Sedgewick, *Analytic Combinatorics* (2009), 660–662.]

304. E. D. Demaine and M. L. Demaine [*Graphs and Combinatorics* **23** (2007), Supplement, 195–208] show the NP-completeness also of several other related problems, such as to exactly pack given boxes of sizes $\{1 \times x_1, \ldots, 1 \times x_n\}$ into a given rectangle.

305. A scheme of "even/odd coordinates" (see exercise 145 and answer 133) works beautifully to represent the space occupied by a windmill domino: Encode the large square in row i and column j by the ordered pair $(2i+1)(2j+1)$; encode the small "tilted" square that overlaps two adjacent large squares by the midpoint between them. Then, for example, '15' is the large square in row 0 and column 2; '25' is the small tilted square whose top and bottom halves are the bottom and top quarters of 15 and 35. Large squares have area 4; small tilted squares have area 2; the encoding of each square specifies the coordinates of its center point. The relevant coordinates xy in an $m \times n$ box satisfy $0 < x < 2n$ and $0 < y < 2m$, where x and y are integers that aren't both even.

Therefore the possible placements of the leftmost windmill domino are either $\{13, 15, 12, 23\} + (2k, 2l)$, $\{33, 53, 23, 32\} + (2k, 2l)$, $\{33, 31, 34, 23\} + (2k, 2l)$, or $\{31, 11, 41, 32\} + (2k, 2l)$, where k and l are nonnegative integers.

(a) Here it suffices to use a 5×5 box, and to require that the small squares of each option are either $\{34, 45\}$, $\{47, 56\}$, $\{76, 65\}$, or $\{63, 54\}$. Each piece has exactly four such options; for example, if we call the leftmost piece '0', its options are 'O 35 37 34 45', 'O 57 77 47 56', 'O 53 33 63 54', 'O 75 73 76 65'. The problem has $4 \cdot 183$ solutions, in groups of four that are related by $90°$ rotation. Here are six of the eight classes of equivalent solutions whose large squares form a symmetric shape:

(b) Algorithm X quickly finds $501484 = 2 \cdot 4 + 4 \cdot 125369$ solutions, including four classes that are symmetric under reflection and 125369 unsymmetric classes. One of the symmetric examples is shown below; also one of the 164 asymmetric classes whose small squares do at least form a symmetric shape.

(c) The $288 = 2 \cdot 4 + 4 \cdot 70$ solutions include four symmetric classes (like the one shown) and 70 that have no symmetry.

(d) We can set this up as a 7×7 problem in which the small squares form a rectangle whose corners are $\{47, 74, 8b, b8\}$. It has $2 \cdot 2696$ solutions, all asymmetric; $2 \cdot 95$ of them fit in a 5×5 box, and $2 \cdot 3$ of them have large squares that form the symmetric shape shown.

(e) Now there are two possibilities: We might have an 8×8 box, with small squares in the rectangle whose corners are $\{34, 43, cd, dc\}$; or we might have a 9×9 box, with small squares confined to the rectangle $\{45, 54, de, ed\}$. The first case has $69120 = 2 \cdot 4 + 4 \cdot 17278$ solutions, four with reflective symmetry; the second case has a whopping $157398 = 2 \cdot 75 + 4 \cdot 39312$ solutions, with 75 classes unchanged under reflection. Symmetric solutions of both types are shown.

 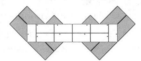 

306. Introduce items 0 to 9 and xy as in the previous answer, as well as pxy and #xy; again x and y aren't both even, and $0 < x < 2n$, $0 < y < 2m$. Here pxy and #xy are primary, but the xy items are secondary. Options of the first kind, like '0 p35 35:1 p37 37:1 p34 34:1 p45 45:1', specify placement of a piece. Options of the second kind, 'pxy xy:0', allow square xy to be empty. Options of the third kind, either '#xy xy:0' or '#xy xy:1 $(x-2)y$:a $(x+2)y$:b $x(y-2)$:c $x(y+2)$:d' for binary variables a, b, c, d with $a + b + c + d = 2$, and where both x and y are odd, enforce the snake condition for large squares. Options of the fourth kind, either '#xy xy:0' or '#xy xy:1 $(x-1)(y-1)$:a $(x-1)(y+1)$:b $(x+1)(y-1)$:c $(x+1)(y+1)$:d' and where $x + y$ is odd, enforce the snake condition for small squares. Nonsharp branching (exercise 10) should be used.

Those options unfortunately produce a huge number of spurious solutions containing 4-cycles. One can rule out the 4-cycle whose large squares have a given $x'y'$ as midpoint by using Algorithm M and introducing a new primary item #$x'y'$ whose multiplicity is $[0..3]$. (Notice that x' and y' are both even.) This primary item is appended to every option of type 3 that begins with '#xy xy:1', where xy is one of the four squares touching point $x'y'$. The 4-cycles of small squares can be ruled out similarly, with new primary items #xy!, where $x + y$ is even.

Every snake-in-the-box cycle of 20 large squares will fit into a box of size 3×9, 4×8, 5×7, or 6×6; and Algorithm M finds respectively $(0, 0, 4 \cdot 9, 8 \cdot 8)$ solutions in those four cases. Six of the eight 6×6 equivalence classes are, however, spurious solutions, because their small squares form an 8-cycle and a 12-cycle instead of a single 20-cycle. Thus there are eleven essentially different solutions. Two of each size are shown below. [The middle two examples show two of the large squares touching at a corner.

The definition of snake-in-the-box cycles allows this to happen; but five of the eleven solutions don't have this "defect." See *Cubism For Fun* **41** (October 1996), 30–32.]

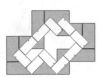

307. "Factoring" with the residues $(i - j) \bmod 3$ and $(i + j) \bmod 3$, we see that the domino must go into adjacent cells with $(i - j) \bmod 3 \neq 1$ and $(i+j) \bmod 3 \neq 2$. That means either $\{(3i, 3j), (3i, 3j + 1)\}$ or $\{(3i + 1, 3j + 2), (3i + 2, 3j + 2)\}$. Conversely, it's easy to insert straight trominoes after placing a domino into any of those cell pairs.

308. (a) Each shape now has integer pairs of the forms (x, y) and $(x, y)'$. One elementary transformation, which rotates by $60°$, takes $(x, y) \mapsto (x + y, -x)'$ and $(x, y)' \mapsto (x+y+1, -x)$; the shape's triangles should be shifted afterwards so that all coordinates are nonnegative and as small as possible. The other elementary transformation, which is a reflection, simply takes $(x, y) \mapsto (y, x)$ and $(x, y)' \mapsto (y, x)'$.

For convenience, let's write just xy for (x, y). One tetriamond is the triangle of size 2, $\{00, 01, 10, 00'\}$. It has two base placements; the other one is $\{01', 10', 11', 11\}$. Another tetriamond is "straight," $\{00, 00', 10, 10'\}$, and it has six base placements. (Three of them, such as $\{00, 00', 01, 01'\}$, involve reflection; hence that tetriamond has two one-sided versions.) The remaining tetriamond is "bent," $\{00', 01, 10, 10'\}$, a hexagon minus a diamond. Its six base placements are all obtained by rotation.

(b) Four of the 20-iamonds are convex, namely those parameterized by $(6, 4, 0, 0)$, $(10, 10, 1, 0)$, $(4, 2, 1, 0)$, and $(5, 5, 2, 0)$ in the notation of exercise 143. But only $(4, 2, 1, 0)$ can be packed with the four pentiamonds — in fact in two ways, differing by a bipair.

(c) The convex 30-iamonds $(15, 15, 1, 0)$ and $(7, 7, 1, 1)$ cannot be packed. But $(4, 2, 1, 1)$, $(5, 5, 3, 0)$, $(3, 3, 3, 1)$ have respectively 3, 1, and 4 distinct solutions.

309. (a) (A, ..., L) have respectively (6, 3, 6, 1, 6, 6, 12, 12, 6, 12, 12, 12) placements.

(The hexiamonds have also been given *descriptive* names: A = lobster (or heart); B = butterfly (or spool); C = chevron (or bat); D = hexagon; E = crown (or boat); F = snake (or wave); G = hook (or shoe); H = signpost (or pistol or airplane); I = bar (or rhomboid); J = crook (or club or ladle); K = yacht (or steps); L = sphinx (or funnel).)

(b) Hexiamonds K and L are special, because they contain four triangles of one kind (Δ or ∇) and two of the other (∇ or Δ). The other hexiamonds are balanced, with three of each kind.

Eleven convex polygons are 72-iamonds, by exercise 143. Those with height less than 4, namely $(36, 36, 1, 0)$, $(19, 17, 0, 0)$, $(18, 18, 2, 0)$, and $(12, 12, 3, 0)$, are unsolvable. So is $(9, 3, 0, 0)$, which is out of balance by 6. The other six are solvable; for example,

$(11, 7, 0, 0)$	$(8, 8, 2, 2)$	$(9, 9, 4, 0)$
$2 \cdot 76$ solutions	$4 \cdot 856$ solutions	$2 \cdot 74$ solutions

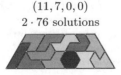  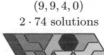

$(6,2,2,1)$ $(6,6,3,2)$ $(6,6,6,0)$

$2 \cdot 5885$ solutions $2 \cdot 5916$ solutions $4 \cdot 156$ solutions

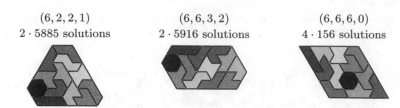

The shape $(6,2,2,1)$ is out of balance by 4. Consequently we can restrict K and L to about half of the positions where they would otherwise fit. The running time to find all solutions (without removing symmetry) thereby decreases, from 168 $G\mu$ to 135 $G\mu$; thus the parity theory helps here, but not as much as might be expected.

What about the one-sided hexiamonds (with "flipped" versions of F through L, making 19 in all)? There are six convex polygons made up of $6 \cdot 19 = 114$ triangles, and again the small-height ones $(57,57,1,0)$, $(28,28,1,1)$, $(19,19,3,0)$ are unsolvable. The case $(13,9,1,0)$ has 1,687,429 solutions (found by Algorithm X in 11 $T\mu$). Shape $(8,8,3,3)$ has 4,790,046 distinct solutions (103 $T\mu$); $(9,5,2,1)$ has 17,244,919 (98 $T\mu$).

$(13,9,1,0)$ $(9,5,2,1)$ $(8,8,3,3)$

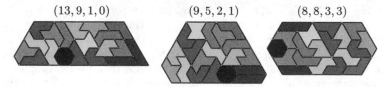

Historical notes: T. Scrutchin [*U.S. Patent 895114* (1908)] described an early puzzle based on assembling checkered polyiamonds of sizes 3–7 into a large equilateral triangle. The complete set of hexiamonds was perhaps first invented by Charles H. Lewis, who submitted a paper about them to the *American Mathematical Monthly* in April 1958. His paper wasn't judged worthy of publication; but a copy survives in the files of Martin Gardner, to whom he had sent a preprint. (He'd been inspired by Martin's exposition of polyominoes in December 1957.) Lewis named his pieces *hexotinoes*, and said that they belonged to the family of "polotinoes," which began with the monotino, the dotino, the trotino, three tetrotinoes, and four pentotinoes. He knew the parity rule, and he exhibited one of the ways to pack all 12 hexotinoes into a 6×6 rhombus.

Other people came up with similar ideas independently a few years later. It was T. H. O'Beirne who coined the names "polyiamond" and "hexiamond"—to the eternal dismay of language purists—first in letters to Richard Guy in 1960, then in his popular weekly columns in *New Scientist* [**12** (1961), 261, 316–317, 379, 706–707]. He introduced an intriguing problem about packing the one-sided hexiamonds into the rosette shape formed by 19 hexagons (12 surrounding 6 surrounding 1); see pages 452–455 of *FGbook* for details. Martin Gardner wrote about the subject in *Scientific American* **211**, 6 (December 1964), 123–130, and hexiamonds were soon sold as pleasing puzzles in Japan, Germany, the USA, and elsewhere. The 24 heptiamonds also have many aficionados, but they are beyond the scope of this book.

The earliest papers about hexiamonds considered mostly standard shapes like parallelograms, or shapes that are decidedly non-convex. Polygon $(6,2,2,1)$ above, the "diaper," may have first appeared as problem 130 in the Russian magazine *Nauka i Zhizn'* #6 (1969), 146; #7 (1969), 101; Michael Beeler enumerated its solutions in HAKMEM (M.I.T. A.I. Laboratory, 1972), Hack 112. Polygon $(6,6,3,2)$ has apparently not occurred previously in print, although it has more solutions than the others.

310. The container holds $4m+2$ triangles; $m = 18$ doesn't work, so we need at least six empty cells. The author's favorite way constrains them to be well-separated "teeth":

311. H. Postl found a nice proof that N must be at least 190: Replace hexiamonds A, G, K by the heptiamond that includes a hexagon. The twelve resulting pieces contain 75 triangles; enlarge them by appending quarter-size triangles around all the edges. This adds 91 trapezoids and 163 quarter-triangles. The latter must occupy at least $91 + (163 - 91)/3 = 115$ triangles, because we can't fill a triangle without using a trapezoid.

Exercise 7–137 explains how to obtain many generalized toruses that are composed of 95 rhombuses; so we might as well make the repeating pattern as square as possible by choosing $(a, b, c, d) = (11, -4, -1, 9)$, as in the solution below. There are (astonishingly) 321530 such packings, each of which represents 24 different solutions when the heptiamonds revert to $\{A, G, K\}$. The example shown is one of only 1768 solutions for which the three resulting "females" attract three neighboring "males."

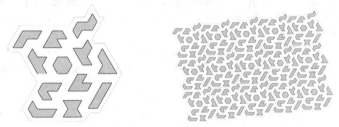

[The smallest region for *pentomino* wallpaper has 143 cells. See A. Thoen and A. van de Wetering, *Facets of Pentominoes* (2018), 95.]

312. Adrian Struyk wrapped the octahedron with hexiamonds, and showed it to Martin Gardner in 1964. An attractive solution by Walter Stead (1970, unpublished),

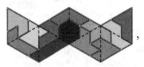

doesn't bend any piece in more than two places. (Incidentally, Thijs Notenboom showed in 1967 how to wrap the *icosahedron* with the four *pentiamonds*.)

313. The whirled versions of pieces (A, ..., L) can be packed in respectively (13, 2·2, 10, 6·55, 19, 2·10, 9, 10, 2·10, 18, 6, 20) ways. But with flipped whirls, the one-sided pieces lead to different shapes, and the counts for (F, G, ..., L) change to (2·6, 7, 8, 2·0, 25, 7, 8). Here's how the pattern of answer 310 looks when scaled up by $\sqrt{12}$:

[The "whirl" in this exercise is the case $n = 3$ of an n-whirl, which has $n^2 + 3$ triangles for $n \geq 2$. In 1936, Maurits Escher visited the Alhambra and saw a pattern related to the whirl tessellation. He was subsequently inspired to develop it much further; see *The World of M. C. Escher* (1971), plates 84 and 199.]

314. To make the same shape from two pairs $\{a,b\}$ and $\{c,d\}$ of polyiamonds (or polyominoes, etc.), choose an n-celled region A into which any solution will fit. Use four primary items $\{a,b,c,d\}$ and $6n$ secondary items 0α, 1α, $a\alpha$, $b\alpha$, $c\alpha$, $d\alpha$ for each cell α. For each placement '$a\ \alpha_1\ \ldots\ \alpha_s$' in A, and each of the 2^s sequences $q_1 \ldots q_s$ with $q_k \in \{c,d\}$, create the option '$a\ 0\alpha_1\ q_1\alpha_1\ \ldots\ 0\alpha_s\ q_s\alpha_s\ a\beta_1\ \ldots\ a\beta_{n-s}$', where $\{\beta_1,\ldots,\beta_{n-s}\} = A \setminus \{\alpha_1,\ldots,\alpha_s\}$. Also create similar options for each placement of b, c, d, with the roles of $(0,a,c,d)$ replaced respectively by $(0,b,c,d)$, $(1,c,a,b)$, $(1,d,a,b)$.

Choose one of $\{a,b,c,d\}$ (one-sided if possible) and restrict it to a single placement. For the pentiamond problem, the author chose the piece a that includes a tetrahedron, and placed it in the center of a 70-iamond A. There are three separate cases, depending on which piece is called b; they yielded three huge exact cover problems, each of which had 15300 options of length 76 (thus total length 1.2 million). Yet Algorithm X solved each problem in at most 1.5 Gμ, including 0.3 Gμ just to load the data.

The answer, as Sicherman observed, is unique. [See Ed Pegg Jr.'s blog, `www.mathpuzzle.com/30November2008.html`. Solomon Golomb, in *Recreational Math. Mag.* #5 (October 1961), 3–12, had shown that the twelve pentominoes can be partitioned into three sets of four, each of which make congruent pairs.]

315. Proceed as in answer 308, but simply let $(x,y) \mapsto (x+y, x_{\max} - x)$; ignore $(x,y)'$.

[There's also an even/odd coordinate system for hexagons, with hexagon xy represented by $(2x+1, 2y+1)$, and the edge between adjacent hexagons represented by their average. Then $60°$ rotation takes $(x,y) \mapsto (x+y-1, x_{\max} - x + 1)$.]

316. There are $12 \cdot 12290$ solutions, and it's not hard to find one by hand. (The first solutions were discovered independently by T. Marlow and E. Schwartz in 1966; the total number was found by K. Noshita in 1974.) The example shown here has the trihexes "maximally separated." [The seven tetrahexes pack the rhomboid $\{xy \mid 0 \le x < 4,\ 0 \le y < 7\}$ in $2 \cdot 9$ ways, and the skew triangle $\{xy \mid 0 \le x < 7,\ x \le y < 7\}$ in $2 \cdot 5$ ways; but they can't pack the triangle $\{xy \mid 0 \le x < 7,\ 0 \le y < 7 - x\}$.]

317. The scaled-up "bar," "wave," and "propeller" cannot be packed. But the "bee," "arch," "boot," and "worm" are doable in respectively $2 \cdot 2$, 1, 10, and 4 ways, such as

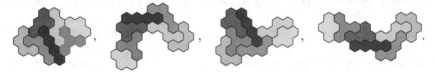

[This problem was introduced by E. Schwartz in 1966 and independently by G. Edgar in 1967, who showed their solutions to Martin Gardner. Edgar pointed out that the rosettes can actually be placed in *two* ways — either rising or falling slightly from left to right when put together. The three one-sided tetrahexes therefore lead to *distinct* scaled-up shapes. Only one of those two is packable, for the boot and the worm; *both* are impossible for the wave. The slight tilting accounts for some of the remarkable properties of R. W. Gosper's "flowsnake" fractal; see M. Gardner, *Scientific Amer.* **235**,6 (December 1976), 124–128, 133; A. Vince, *SIAM J. Discrete Math.* **6** (1993), 501–521.]

318. The "holes" in the T-grid correspond to vertices of the infinite triangular grid; and every hexagon of the T-grid is inside exactly one of the triangles made by those

vertices. More formally, we can let

$$\Delta\,(x,y) \leftrightarrow \text{hexagon}\,(x-y, x+2y+1); \quad \nabla\,(x,y)' \leftrightarrow \text{hexagon}\,(x-y, x+2y+2).$$

Adjacent triangles correspond to adjacent hexagons. The hexiamond hexahexes are

319. One way is to replace each square by a 3×3 array, representing $\triangle, \triangledown, \triangleright, \triangleleft$ by
$\begin{smallmatrix}\texttt{ooo}\\\texttt{oxo}\\\texttt{oxo}\end{smallmatrix}$, $\begin{smallmatrix}\texttt{oxo}\\\texttt{xoo}\\\texttt{ooo}\end{smallmatrix}$, $\begin{smallmatrix}\texttt{oxo}\\\texttt{oox}\\\texttt{ooo}\end{smallmatrix}$, $\begin{smallmatrix}\texttt{ooo}\\\texttt{oxo}\\\texttt{oxo}\end{smallmatrix}$. But it uses only 4 pixels out of 9. A more compact scheme is able to
use 4 pixels out of every 8: We rotate the pieces by $45°$ and represent $\triangleleft, \triangle, \triangleright, \triangledown$ by
$\begin{smallmatrix}\texttt{xo}\\\texttt{xo}\end{smallmatrix}$, $\begin{smallmatrix}\texttt{xx}\\\texttt{oo}\end{smallmatrix}$, $\begin{smallmatrix}\texttt{ox}\\\texttt{ox}\end{smallmatrix}$, $\begin{smallmatrix}\texttt{oo}\\\texttt{xx}\end{smallmatrix}$, separated by $\begin{smallmatrix}\texttt{oo}\\\texttt{oo}\end{smallmatrix}$. For example, the 14 tetraboloes take the following forms:

```
· A A ·      B B · ·      · C · · ·      · D D ·      E · · · ·      F · · · · ·       · G G
· A A ·      B B · ·      · C · · ·      D · · D      E · · · ·      F · · F F ·       G · ·
A · · A      · · B B      C · · · ·      D · · D      · E E · ·      · F F · · F       G · ·
A · · A      · · B B      C · · C C      · D D ·      · E E · ·      · · · · · F       · G G
             · C C ·                     · · · E E                    · G G

· · H H · ·      I I · · I I · ·      J J · · J J ·      · K · ·      · · · L       · M M · ·      N N · · · ·
H H · · H H      · · I I · · I I      · J J · · J      · K · ·      L L · L       · · M M · ·      · · N N · ·
· · · · H H                           · · · · · J      K · · K      · L L ·       M M · · M M      · N N · ·
                                                       K · · K      · L L                          · · N N
                                                       · K K                                       · · · · N N
```

This scheme sets up a one-to-one correspondence between n-aboloes and $2n$-ominoes
on the "H-grid," which is the set of all pixels (x, y) with $\lfloor x/2 \rfloor + \lfloor y/2 \rfloor$ even. (Each
$2n$-omino is kingwise connected; it actually consists of n dominoes.)

Formally speaking, let's divide every square cell into four quarters, by cutting at
the diagonals. Then every n-abolo occupies $2n$ quarters; and the (north, east, south,
west) quarters of cell (x, y), in polyabolo coordinates, correspond respectively to cells
$(2x - 2y, 2x + 2y) + ((0, 1), (1, 1), (1, 0), (0, 0))$ of the H-grid.

[After first seeing the H-grid versions of the tetraboloes, the author felt a foolish
but irresistible urge to pack them into a 10×12 box, putting seven of them in the
H-grid and the other seven in the complementary H-grid, leaving eight vacant pixels
at the sides. This corresponds to putting the tetraboloes into two layers of a certain
frame that's capable of holding 29 halfsquares. It turned out that there are $8 \cdot 305$ ways
to do this (found by Algorithm X in 10 Gμ). For example:

```
· D D · · M M L L M M ·
D G G D C B B M M L L N
D G G D C B B M M L L N
G D D B B C H K L N N J
G C C B B C H K L N N J
· G G C C F K H N K J E
· F F A A F K H N K J E
F A A F F H H K K E E J
F A A I I H H I I E E J
· I I A A I I E E J J ·
```

Nowadays, polyaboloes are often called "polytans," based on their connection to classical tangram puzzles from 18th-century China. T. H. O'Beirne introduced polyaboloes
in *New Scientist* **13** (18 January 1962), 158–159.]

320. Every convex polyabolo can be characterized by six more-or-less independent
parameters: We start with an $m \times n$ rectangle, then cut off triangles of sizes a, b, c, d at
the lower left, lower right, upper right, and upper left corners, where $a+b \le n, b+c \le m,$
$c + d \le n$, and $d + a \le m$. The number of halfsquares is $N = 2mn - a^2 - b^2 - c^2 - d^2$.
To avoid duplicates, we require $m \le n$, and insist that (a, b, c, d) be lexicographically
greater than or equal to (b, a, d, c), (c, d, a, b), (d, c, b, a). Furthermore, if $m = n$, this
4-tuple (a, b, c, d) should also be lexicographically greater than or equal to (a, d, c, b),
(b, c, d, a), (c, b, a, d), (d, a, b, c).

The smallest positive area achievable with $m < n$ is $2m(n - m)$ halfsquares; and when $m = n$ the smallest is $2n - 1$. Thus we must have $n \le (N + 2)/2$, and it's feasible to backtrack through a finite number of cases.

There are 63 solutions when $N = 56$. But most of them are unpackable, because of an important property noted by T. H. O'Beirne in 1962: Exactly five of the tetraboloes, namely $\{E, G, J, K, L\}$, have an odd number of unmatched $\sqrt{2}$ sides in each direction. It follows that $a + c$ (and $b + d$) must be odd.

Just 10 of the 63 solutions pass this extra test. Two of those ten — $(1 \times 29; 1, 1, 0, 0)$ and $(3 \times 11; 3, 1, 0, 0)$ — don't work. But the other eight are achievable:

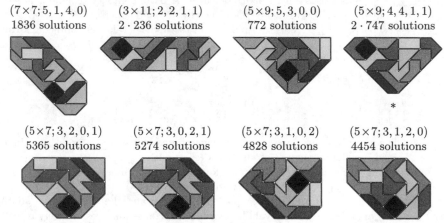

$(7 \times 7; 5, 1, 4, 0)$	$(3 \times 11; 2, 2, 1, 1)$	$(5 \times 9; 5, 3, 0, 0)$	$(5 \times 9; 4, 4, 1, 1)$
1836 solutions	$2 \cdot 236$ solutions	772 solutions	$2 \cdot 747$ solutions

$(5 \times 7; 3, 2, 0, 1)$	$(5 \times 7; 3, 0, 2, 1)$	$(5 \times 7; 3, 1, 0, 2)$	$(5 \times 7; 3, 1, 2, 0)$
5365 solutions	5274 solutions	4828 solutions	4454 solutions

Most of them were cracked by E. S. Ainley in 1965; but H. Picciotto found '∗' in 1989.

[This enumeration problem was first studied by F. T. Wang and C.-C. Hsiung, *AMM* **49** (1942), 596–599, who proved that there are 20 convex 16-aboloes. The totals for general N are OEIS sequence A245676, contributed by E. Fox-Epstein in 2014.]

321. [In a letter to Martin Gardner dated 12 March 1967, O'Beirne said that he now knew of 13 solutions, with help from several readers. "Are these the lot?" The answer is yes: The total is indeed 13. The solution shown here leads to three of the others, via tricky rearrangements.]

322. (i) We can reduce polysticks to (disconnected) polyominoes, by 3-fold enlargement: Let vertex ij of a square grid correspond to pixel $(3i)(3j)$; and let the line segment between adjacent vertices $ij - i'j'$ correspond to the two pixels between $(3i)(3j)$ and $(3i')(3j')$. Placements can intersect each other only at internal pixels where two parallel segments touch; we can prevent crossing by making such pixels secondary.

For example, to pack the 6×6 array in the example, we use the pixels xy for $0 \le x, y \le 18$, where x or y is a multiple of 3; item xy is secondary if 3 divides *both* x and y. One of the options for the T-shaped tetrastick is '04 05 07 08 16 26 36 46 56'; one of the options for the V-shaped tetrastick is '34 35 36 37 38 49 59 69 79 89'. The secondary item 36 ensures that these options won't both be chosen simultaneously.

(ii) Instead of scaling up by 3, we can scale up by 2, as in the even/odd coordinate system, by letting vertex ij correspond to pixel $(2i)(2j)$. Then segment $ij - i'j'$ corresponds to pixel $(i + i')(j + j')$; and the 6×6 example involves primary items xy for $0 \le x, y \le 12$ with $x + y$ odd, together with secondary items xy with x and y both even. The example T and V options in this scheme become '03 05 14 24 34' and '23 24 25 36 46 56'; now it's the secondary item 24 that keeps them from interacting.

Scheme (i) can be used without change to answer 266. Scheme (ii) is almost twice as fast; but answer 266 must then be modified so that it never shifts by odd amounts. (Notice, for example, that the O and X tetrasticks each have only one base placement in scheme (ii), namely '01 10 12 21' and '12 21 23 32'. Shifting by 11 would change O to X and vice versa!) Thus, 90° rotation must be redefined as $(x, y) \mapsto (y, x_{\max} + (x_{\max} \ \& \ 1) - x)$, in the modified answer 266; also, δ_x and δ_y must be even.

[Polysticks were named and explored by B. R. Barwell in *JRM* **22** (1990), 165–175. They had actually been studied in the 1940s by H. D. Benjamin and T. R. Dawson, who already knew how to pack the pieces for $n \le 4$ into a 6×6 grid; see G. P. Jelliss, *JRM* **29** (1998), 140–142. See also *FGbook*, pages 457–472.]

323. (a) For example, the vertices (m, n) of an ordinary square grid can be skewed to

$$(m, n)' = (m - (n \bmod 2)\epsilon, n - (m \bmod 2)\epsilon), \quad \text{where } \epsilon \text{ is the degree of skew.}$$

Notice that each square of the skewed grid has a clockwise or counterclockwise "spin."

(b) There's a nice way to represent each square as a 5-pixel cross, and each rhombus as a 3-pixel diagonal. For example, here are pixel equivalents of the tetraskews:

```
                      k · · · · · ·     · · 1 · · · ·    q · · Q ·       · S s · · · ·
· I · · i I · · i     · k · · · ·       · 1 · · · · ·    · q Q Q Q       S S S s · · ·
I I I i I I I i ·     · K k · k K ·    1 L 1 · · L ·     · q Q Q q       · S · S o · o
· I i · · I i · ·     K K K k K K K    L L L 1 L L L    Q Q Q q ·        · · S S S s ·
                      · K k · · K ·     · L · · 1 L ·    · Q q · ·       · · · S s · ·

· · t T · · t         · · u U · · u    v · · V v · ·     · · · Y · · ·    · · · Z · · z
· t T T T t ·         · u U U U u ·    · v V V V v ·     · · Y Y Y · ·    · · Z Z Z z ·
t · t T t · ·         u · · U u U ·    · · v V · V v     · Y y Y · Y ·   · Z z Z z · ·
· · · t · · ·         · · · · U U U    · · · · V V V    Y Y Y y Y Y Y   Z Z Z z · · ·
· · · t · ·           · · · · · U ·    · · · · · V ·     · Y · · y Y ·    · Z · · z · ·
```

(Lowercase letters indicate the rhombuses here only for clarity; all pixels are either "in" or "out." The shapes fit together only when squares and rhombuses alternate properly.)

(c) The 4×10 frame in the example has 486 solutions; the analogous 5×8 frame has 572; these were first enumerated by Brendan Owen in 2000. There are 3648 ways to fit the pieces into a 2×21 frame, but 2×20 is too tight.

However, those counts can be divided by 2, because solutions to this problem come in pairs. Consider an arrangement of ten *unskewed* tetrominoes that involves one square, one straight, two skews, two tees, and four ells. It can be skewed in four ways, because we have two choices for which cells should be rhombuses and two choices for the spins; and it will be a valid skewed solution if and only if the resulting ten tetraskews are distinct. Changing the spins of a valid solution always gives another valid solution in which $K \leftrightarrow L$, $S \leftrightarrow Z$, $U \leftrightarrow V$ are swapped. Every solution therefore has a *dual*, which looks rather different but is well defined.

For example, the 486 solutions to the 4×10 rectangle problem correspond to exactly 226 unskewed arrangements that are distinct under reflections, 17 of which actually yield *two* dual pairs of skewed solutions, in which the roles of squares and rhombuses are reversed! Here's one such case:

[Michael Keller named the polyskews in 1993, and found a way to pack the tetraskews into two 4×5 frames, thus solving the 4×10 and 5×8 rectangles simultaneously. (See *World Game Review* **12** (1994), 12. That problem has just 24 solutions.) Generalizations to 3D await investigation.]

References: Polyforms live on many excellent and well-illustrated websites — notably `puzzler.sourceforge.net` by David Goodger; `www.polyforms.eu` by Peter Esser; `www.iread.it/lz/polymultiforms2.html` by Livio Zucca; `userpages.monmouth.com/~colonel/polycur.html` by George Sicherman; `www.recmath.org/PolyPages/` by Andrew Clarke; `abarothsworld.com/Puzzles.htm` by Abaroth. In particular, Abaroth's page "Squaring the Hexagon" discusses many ways to reduce one polyform to another. See also Ed Pegg Jr.'s chapter in *Tribute to a Mathemagician* (2005), 119–125.

324. The same ideas apply, but with three coordinates instead of two, and with the elementary transformations $(x, y, z) \mapsto (y, x_{\max} - x, z)$, $(x, y, z) \mapsto (y, z, x)$.

Pieces $(1, 2, \ldots, 7)$ have respectively $(12, 24, 12, 12, 12, 12, 8)$ base placements, leading to $144 + 144 + 72 + 72 + 96 + 96 + 64$ options for the $3 \times 3 \times 3$ problem.

325. It's tempting, but wrong, to try to compute the Somap by considering only the 240 solutions that restrict the tee and the claw as suggested in the text; the pairwise semidistances between these special solutions will miss many of the actual adjacencies. To decide if $u - v$, one must compare u to the 48 solutions equivalent to v.

(a) The strong Somap has vertex degrees $7^1 6^7 5^{19} 4^{31} 3^{59} 2^{63} 1^{45} 0^{15}$; so an "average" solution has $(1 \cdot 7 + 7 \cdot 6 + \cdots + 15 \cdot 0)/240 \approx 2.57$ strong neighbors. (The unique vertex of degree 7 has the level-by-level structure $\begin{smallmatrix}333\\534\\552\end{smallmatrix}\,\begin{smallmatrix}114\\652\\662\end{smallmatrix}\,\begin{smallmatrix}174\\652\\662\end{smallmatrix}$ from bottom to top.) This graph has two edges between $\begin{smallmatrix}333\\534\\552\end{smallmatrix}\,\begin{smallmatrix}614\\752\\772\end{smallmatrix}$ and $\begin{smallmatrix}333\\534\\752\end{smallmatrix}\,\begin{smallmatrix}614\\752\\772\end{smallmatrix}$, so it's actually a multigraph.

The full Somap has vertex degrees $21^2 18^1 16^9 15^{13} 14^{10} 13^{16} 12^{17} 11^{12} 10^{16} 9^{28} 8^{26} 7^{25} 6^{26} 5^{16} 4^{17} 3^3 2^1 1^1 0^1$, giving an average degree ≈ 9.14. (Its unique isolated vertex is $\begin{smallmatrix}333\\432\\462\end{smallmatrix}\,\begin{smallmatrix}455\\466\\762\end{smallmatrix}\,\begin{smallmatrix}115\\715\\772\end{smallmatrix}$, and its only pendant vertex is $\begin{smallmatrix}333\\435\\222\end{smallmatrix}\,\begin{smallmatrix}755\\465\\462\end{smallmatrix}\,\begin{smallmatrix}771\\711\\466\end{smallmatrix}$. Two other noteworthy solutions, $\begin{smallmatrix}333\\466\\466\end{smallmatrix}\,\begin{smallmatrix}412\\435\\762\end{smallmatrix}\,\begin{smallmatrix}115\\795\\772\end{smallmatrix}$ and $\begin{smallmatrix}333\\466\\466\end{smallmatrix}\,\begin{smallmatrix}412\\435\\765\end{smallmatrix}\,\begin{smallmatrix}112\\792\\772\end{smallmatrix}$, are the only ones that contain the two-piece substructure . There are 14 instances of repeated edges.)

(b) The Somap has just two components, namely the isolated vertex and the 239 others. The latter has just three bicomponents, namely the pendant vertex, its neighbor, and the 237 others. Its diameter is 8 (or 21, if we use the edge lengths 2 and 3).

The strong Somap has a much sparser and more intricate structure. Besides the 15 isolated vertices, there are 25 components of sizes $\{8 \times 2, 6 \times 3, 4, 3 \times 5, 2 \times 6, 7, 8, 11, 16, 118\}$. Using the algorithm of Section 7.4.1.2, the large component breaks down into nine bicomponents (one of size 2, seven of size 1, the other of size 109); the 16-vertex component breaks into seven; and so on, totalling 58 bicomponents altogether.

(One can also consider "physical" Somaps with 480 vertices, by saying that solutions are equivalent under rotation but not reflection. There are no repeated edges. The degree sequences are $7^2 6^{14} \ldots 0^{30}$ and $21^4 18^2 \ldots 0^2$, double what we had before.)

[The Somap was first constructed by R. K. Guy, J. H. Conway, and M. J. T. Guy, without computer help. It appears on pages 910–913 of Berlekamp, Conway, and Guy's *Winning Ways*, where all of the strong links are shown, and where enough other links are given to establish near-connectedness. Each vertex in that illustration has been given a code name; for example, the seven special solutions mentioned in part (a) have code names B5f, W4e, W2f, R7d, LR7g, YR3a, and R3c, respectively.]

326. Let the cubie coordinates be $51z$, $41z$, $31z$, $32z$, $33z$, $23z$, $13z$, $14z$, $15z$, for $z \in \{1, 2, 3\}$. Replace matrix A of the exact cover problem by a simplified matrix A' having only items $(1, 2, 3, 4, 5, 6, 7, S)$, where S is the sum of all items xyz of A where $x \cdot y \cdot z$ is odd. Any solution to A yields a solution to A' with item sums $(1, 1, 1, 1, 1, 1, 1, 10)$. But that's impossible, because the S counts of pieces $(1, \ldots, 7)$ are at most $(1, 2, 2, 1, 1, 1, 1)$. [See the Martin Gardner reference in answer 333.]

327. (a) The solution counts, ignoring symmetry reduction, are: 4×5 corral (2), gorilla (2), smile (2), 3×6 corral (4), face (4), lobster (4), castle (6), bench (16), bed (24), doorway (28), piggybank (80), five-seat bench (104), piano (128), shift 2 (132), 4×4 coop (266), shift 1 (284), bathtub (316), shift 0 (408), grand piano (526), tower 4 (552), tower 3 (924), canal (1176), tower 2 (1266), couch (1438), tower 1 (1520), stepping stones (2718). So the 4×5 corral, gorilla, and smile are tied for hardest, while stepping stones are the easiest. (The bathtub, canal, bed, and doorway each have four symmetries; the couch, stepping stones, tower 4, shift 0, bench, 4×4 coop, castle, five-seat bench, piggybank, lobster, piano, gorilla, face, and smile each have two. To get the number of *essentially distinct* solutions, divide by the number of symmetries.)

(b) Notice that the stepping stones, canal, bed, and doorway appear also in (a). The solution counts are: W-wall (0), almost W-wall (12), bed (24), apartments 2 (28), doorway (28), clip (40), tunnel (52), zigzag wall 2 (52), zigzag wall 1 (92), underpass (132), chair (260), stile (328), fish (332), apartments 1 (488), goldfish (608), canal (1176), steps (2346), stepping stones (2718); hence "almost W-wall" is the hardest of the possible shapes. Notice that the stepping stones, chair, steps, and zigzag wall 2 each have two symmetries, while the others in Fig. 75(b) all have four. The $3\times3\times3$ cube, with its 48 symmetries, probably is the easiest possible shape to make from the Soma pieces.

[Piet Hein himself published the tower 1, shift 2, stile, and zigzag wall 1 in his original patent; he also included the bathtub, bed, canal, castle, chair, steps, stile, stepping stones, shift 1, five-seat bench, tunnel, W-wall, and both apartments in his booklet for Parker Brothers. Parker Brothers distributed four issues of *The SOMA®* *Addict* in 1970 and 1971, giving credit for new constructions to Noble Carlson (fish, lobster), Mrs. C. L. Hall (piano, clip, underpass), Gerald Hill (towers 2–4), Craig Kenworthy (goldfish), John W. M. Morgan (piano, face, gorilla, smile), Rick Murray (grand piano), and Dan Smiley (doorway, zigzag wall 2). Sivy Farhi published a booklet called *Somacubes* in 1977, containing the solutions to more than one hundred Soma cube problems including the bench, the couch, and the piggybank.]

328. By eliminating symmetries, there are (a) 421 distinct cases with cubies omitted on both layers, and (b) 129 with cubies omitted on only one layer. All are possible, except in the one case where the omitted cubies disconnect a corner cell. The easiest of type (a) omits $\{000, 001, 200\}$ and has 3599 solutions; the hardest omits $\{100, 111, 120\}$ and has $2 \cdot 45$ solutions. The easiest of type (b) omits $\{000, 040, 200\}$ and has 3050 solutions; the hardest omits $\{100, 110, 140\}$ and has $2 \cdot 45$ solutions. (The two examples illustrated have $2 \cdot 821$ and $4 \cdot 68$ solutions. Early Soma solvers seem to have overlooked them!)

329. (a) The 60 distinct cases are all quite easy. The easiest has 3497 solutions and uses $\{002, 012, 102\}$ on the top level; the hardest has 268 solutions and uses $\{002, 112, 202\}$.

(b) Sixteen of the 60 possibilities are disconnected. Three of the others are also impossible — namely those that omit $\{01z, 13z, 21z\}$ or $\{10z, 11z, 12z\}$ or $\{10z, 11z, 13z\}$. The easiest has 3554 solutions and omits $\{00z, 01z, 23z\}$; the hardest of the possibles has only 8 solutions and omits $\{00z, 12z, 13z\}$.

(The two examples illustrated have $2 \cdot 132$ and $2 \cdot 270$ solutions.)

330. T. Bundgård and C. McFarren found in 1999 that all but 216 are realizable [www.fam-bundgaard.dk/SOMA/NEWS/N990308.HTM]. Five cases have unique $(2 \cdot 1)$ solutions:

331. Every polycube has a minimum enclosing box for which it touches all six faces. If those box dimensions $a \times b \times c$ aren't too large, we can generate such polycubes uniformly at random in a simple way: First choose 27 of the abc possible cubies; try again if that choice doesn't touch all faces; otherwise try again if that choice isn't connected.

For example, when $a = b = c = 4$, about 99.98% of all choices will touch all faces, and about 0.1% of those will be connected. This means that about $.001 \binom{64}{27} \approx 8 \times 10^{14}$ of the 27-cubie polycubes have a $4 \times 4 \times 4$ bounding box. Of these, about 5.8% can be built with the seven Soma pieces.

But most of the relevant polycubes have a larger bounding box; and in such cases the chance of solvability goes down. For example, $\approx 6.2 \times 10^{18}$ cases have bounding box $4 \times 5 \times 5$; $\approx 3.3 \times 10^{18}$ cases have bounding box $3 \times 5 \times 7$; $\approx 1.5 \times 10^{17}$ cases have bounding box $2 \times 7 \times 7$; and only 1% or so of those cases are solvable.

Section 7.2.3 will discuss the enumeration of polycubes by their size.

332. Each interior position of the penthouse and pyramid that might or might not be occupied can be treated as a secondary item in the corresponding exact cover problem. We obtain $2 \cdot 10$ solutions for the staircase; $(223, 8 \cdot 286)$ solutions for the penthouse with hole at the (bottom, middle); and $2 \cdot 32$ solutions for the pyramid, of which $2 \cdot 2$ have all three holes on the diagonal and $2 \cdot 3$ have no adjacent holes.

333. A full simulation of gravity would be quite complex, because pieces can be prevented from tipping with the help of their neighbors above and/or at their side. If we assume a reasonable coefficient of friction and an auxiliary weight at the top, it suffices to define stability by saying that a piece is stable if and only if at least one of its cubies is immediately above either the floor or a stable piece.

The given shapes can be packed in respectively $2 \cdot 202$, $2 \cdot 21$, $2 \cdot 270$, $8 \cdot 223$, and $2 \cdot 122$ ways, of which $2 \cdot 202$, $2 \cdot 8$, $2 \cdot 53$, $8 \cdot 1$, and $2 \cdot 6$ are stable. Going from the bottom level to the top, the layers $\begin{smallmatrix}4\cdots7\\3\cdots6\end{smallmatrix}$ $\begin{smallmatrix}4477\\3366\end{smallmatrix}$ $\begin{smallmatrix}54\cdots\\31\cdots\end{smallmatrix}$ $\begin{smallmatrix}22\cdots\\21\cdots\end{smallmatrix}$ give a decently stable cot; a fragile vulture comes from $\begin{smallmatrix}2\cdots7\\3\cdots7\end{smallmatrix}$ $\begin{smallmatrix}2447\\3177\end{smallmatrix}$ $\begin{smallmatrix}2244\\1156\end{smallmatrix}$; a delicate mushroom comes from $\begin{smallmatrix}\cdots7\end{smallmatrix}$ $\begin{smallmatrix}572\\577\end{smallmatrix}$ $\begin{smallmatrix}552\\3\cdot6\end{smallmatrix}$ $\begin{smallmatrix}322\\311\end{smallmatrix}$; and a delicate cantilever from $\begin{smallmatrix}222\end{smallmatrix}$ $\begin{smallmatrix}255\end{smallmatrix}$ $\begin{smallmatrix}5\\7\end{smallmatrix}$ $\begin{smallmatrix}634\\674\end{smallmatrix}$ $\begin{smallmatrix}333\\664\end{smallmatrix}$. The author's cherished set of Skjøde Skjern Soma pieces, made of rosewood and purchased in 1967, includes a small square base that nicely stabilizes both mushroom and cantilever. The vulture needs a book on top.

[The casserole and cot are due respectively to W. A. Kustes and J. W. M. Morgan. The mushroom, which is hollow, is the same as B. L. Schwartz's "penthouse," but turned upside down; John Conway noticed that it then has a unique stable solution. See Martin Gardner, *Knotted Doughnuts* (1986), Chapter 3.]

334. Infinitely many cubies lie behind a wall; but it suffices to consider only the hidden ones whose distance is at most $27 - v$ from the v visible ones. For example, the W-wall has $v = 25$, and the two invisible cubies are $\{332, 331\}$ if we use the coordinates of answer 326. We're allowed to use any of $\{241, 242, 251, 252, 331, 332, 421, 422, 521, 522\}$ at distance 1, and $\{341, 342, 351, 352, 431, 432, 531, 532, 621, 622\}$ at distance 2. (The stated projection doesn't have left-right symmetry.) The X-wall is similar, but it has $v = 19$ and potentially $(9, 7, 6, 3, 3, 2, 1)$ hidden cubies at distances 1 to 7 (omitting cases like 450, which is invisible at distance 2 but "below ground").

Using secondary items for the optional cubies, we must examine each solution to the exact cover problem and reject those that are disconnected or violate the gravity constraint of exercise 333. Those ground rules yield 282 solutions for the W-wall, 612 for the X-wall, and a whopping 1,130,634 for the cube itself. (These solutions fill respectively 33, 275, and 13842 different sets of cubies.) Here are examples of some of the more exotic shapes that are possible, as seen from behind and below:

There also are ten surprising ways to make the cube façade if we allow hidden "underground" cubies: The remarkable construction   raises the entire cube one level *above* the floor, and is gravitationally stable, by exercise 333's criteria! Unfortunately, though, it falls apart — even with a heavy book on top.

[The false-front idea was pioneered by Jean Paul Francillon, whose construction of a fake W-wall was announced in *The SOMA® Addict* **2**, 1 (spring 1971).]

335. (a) Each of 13 solutions occurs in 48 equivalent arrangements. To remove the symmetry, place piece 7 horizontally, either (i) at the bottom or (ii) in the middle. In case (ii), add a secondary 's' item as in answer 268, and append 's' also to all placements of piece 6 that touch the bottom more than the top. Run time: 400 Kμ.

[This puzzle was number 3–39 in Hoffmann's *Puzzles Old and New* (1893). Another $3 \times 3 \times 3$ polycube dissection of historical importance, "Mikusiński's Cube," was described by Hugo Steinhaus in the 2nd edition of his *Mathematical Snapshots* (1950). That one consists of the ell and the two twist pieces of the Soma cube, plus the pentacubes B, C, and f of exercise 340; it has 24 symmetries and just two solutions.]

(b) Yes: Michael Reid, circa 1995, found the remarkable set

which also makes $9 \times 3 \times 1$ uniquely(!). George Sicherman carried out an exhaustive analysis of all relevant flat polyominoes in 2016, finding exactly 320 sets that are unique for $3 \times 3 \times 3$, of which 19 are unique also for $9 \times 3 \times 1$. In fact, one of those 19,

  ⊆ ⊆ ⊆ ⊆ ⊆   ,

is the long-sought "Holy Grail" of $3 \times 3 \times 3$ cube decompositions: Its pieces not only have flatness and double uniqueness, they are nested (!!). There's also Yoshiya Shindo's

      ,

known as the "Neo Diabolical Cube" (1995); notice that it has 24 symmetries, not 48.

336. This piece can be modeled by a polycube with $20 + 20 + 27 + 3$ cubies, where we want to pack nine of them into a $9 \times 9 \times 9$ box. Divide that box into 540 primary cells (which must be filled) and 189 secondary cells (which will contain the 27 cubies of the simulated dowels). Answer 324 now yields an exact cover problem with 1536 options; and Algorithm X needs only 33 Mμ to discover 24 solutions, all equivalent by symmetry. (Or we could modify answer 324 so that all offsets have multiples of 3 in each coordinate; then there would be only 192 options, and the running time would go down to 8 Mμ.) One packing is $\begin{smallmatrix}122 & 567 & 557\\123 & 163 & 867\\443 & 849 & 899\end{smallmatrix}$, with dowels at $\begin{smallmatrix}010 & 070 & 000\\400 & 529 & 800\\030 & 080 & 000\end{smallmatrix}$.

One might be tempted to factor this problem, by first looking at all ways to pack nine solid bent trominoes into a $3 \times 3 \times 3$ box. That problem has 5328 solutions, found in about 5 Mμ; and after removing the 48 symmetries we're left with just 111 solutions, into which we can try to model the holes and dowels. But such a procedure is rather complicated, and it doesn't really save much time, if any.

Ronald Kint-Bruynseels, who designed this remarkable puzzle, also found that it's possible to drill holes in the solid cubies, parallel to the other two, without destroying the uniqueness of the solution(!). [*Cubism For Fun* **75** (2008), 16–19; **77** (2008), 13–18.]

337. Let's use even/odd coordinates as in exercise 145, so that each final face has one coordinate in $\{0,6\}$ and two coordinates in $\{1,3,5\}$. The first goal has red spots on faces 330, 105, 501, 015, 033, 051, 611, 615, 651, 655, 161, 165, 363, 561, 565, 116, 136, 156, 516, 536, 556. The other goal has green spots on 19 of those 21 faces;   red   green
but 303 replaces 033 and 633 replaces 363. (For simplicity, we'll ignore
alternative setups; there are 16 ways to put spots on dice, not just two.)

Nine bent tricubes will pack a $3 \times 3 \times 3$ cube in 5328 ways. (They fall into 111 equivalence classes of size 48, under rotation and reflection; but that fact is irrelevant here.) Take any such solution and color its 54 external faces with the red solution. Then see if its pieces can be rearranged to give the green solution.

Notice that each bent tricube has fourteen square faces; but the two "inner" faces are never visible in the final assembly. That assembly will specify from 2 to 7 of the 12 potential faces, leaving 5 to 10 faces unconstrained. Altogether we'll have 21 faces specified red, 33 specified blank, and 54 still free.

It turns out that 371 of the 5328 red solutions can be rearranged into green solutions; in fact one case leads to 6048 different green solutions! And there are 52 combinations of red+green solutions that leave 18 faces unspecified, such as this:

We're free to put anything we like on those 18 faces — giving red or green spots that are false clues, and/or concealing a *third* pattern that the puzzler is challenged to achieve.

(The classic "Spots Puzzle" in Hoffmann's *Puzzles Old and New* (1893), No. 3–17, distributed by E. Wolff & Son's pencil company, assembled a single die from *straight* tricubes. Lavery's elegant "Twice Dice" was produced by Pentangle Puzzles in 1990.)

338. The straight tetracube ▭▭▭▭ and the square tetracube ▭▭, together with the size-4 Soma pieces in (39), make a complete set.

We can fix the tee's position in the twin towers, saving a factor of 32; and each of the resulting 40 solutions has just one twist with the tee. Hence there are five inequivalent solutions, and $256 \cdot 5$ altogether.

The double claw has $6 \cdot 63$ solutions. But the cannon, with $4 \cdot 1$ solutions, can be formed in essentially only one way. (*Hint:* Both twists are in the barrel.)

There are no solutions to 'up 3'. But 'up 4' and 'up 5' each have $8 \cdot 218$ solutions (related by turning them upside down). Gravitationally, four of those 218 are stable for 'up 5'; the stable solution for 'up 4' is unique, and unrelated to those four.

References: Jean Meeus, *JRM* **6** (1973), 257–265; Nob Yoshigahara, *Puzzle World No. 1* (San Jose: Ishi Press International, 1992), 36–38.

339. All but 48 are realizable. The unique "hardest" realizable case, ▦, has $2 \cdot 2$ solutions. The "easiest" case is the $2 \times 4 \times 4$ cuboid, with $11120 = 16 \cdot 695$ solutions.

340. (a) A, B, C, D, E, F, a, b, c, d, e, f, j, k, l, ..., z. (It's a little hard to see why reflection doesn't change piece 'l'. In fact, S. S. Besley once patented the pentacubes under the impression that there were 30 different kinds! See *U.S. Patent 3065970* (1962), where Figs. 22 and 23 illustrate the same piece in slight disguise.)

Historical notes: R. J. French, in *Fairy Chess Review* **4** (1940), problem 3930, was first to show that there are 23 different pentacube shapes, if mirror images are considered to be identical. The full count of 29 was established somewhat later by F. Hansson and others [*Fairy Chess Review* **6** (1948), 141–142]; Hansson also counted the $35 + 77 = 112$ mirror-inequivalent hexacubes. Complete counts of hexacubes (166) and heptacubes (1023) were first established soon afterwards by J. Niemann, A. W. Baillie, and R. J. French [*Fairy Chess Review* **7** (1948), 8, 16, 48].

(b) The cuboids $1 \times 3 \times 20$, $1 \times 4 \times 15$, $1 \times 5 \times 12$, and $1 \times 6 \times 10$ have of course already been considered. The $2 \times 3 \times 10$ and $2 \times 5 \times 6$ cuboids can be handled by restricting X to the bottom upper left, and sometimes also restricting Z, as in answers 268 and 270; we obtain 12 solutions (in 350 Mμ) and 264 solutions (in 2.5 Gμ), respectively.

The $3 \times 4 \times 5$ cuboid is more difficult. Without symmetry-breaking, we obtain 3940×8 solutions in about 200 Gμ. To do better, notice that O can appear in four essentially different positions. With four separate runs we can find $5430/2 + 1348/4 + 716/2 + 2120/4 = 3940$ solutions, in $35.7 + 10.0 + 4.5 + 7.1 \approx 57$ Gμ.

[The fact that solid pentominoes will fill these cuboids was first demonstrated by D. Nixon and F. Hansson, *Fairy Chess Review* **6** (1948), problem 7560 and page 142. Exact enumeration was first performed by C. J. Bouwkamp in 1967; see *J. Combinatorial Theory* **7** (1969), 278–280, and *Indagationes Math.* **81** (1978), 177–186.]

(c) Almost *any* subset of 25 pentacubes can probably do the job. But a particularly nice one is obtained if we simply omit o, q, s, and y, namely those that don't fit in a $3 \times 3 \times 3$ box. R. K. Guy proposed this subset in *Nabla* **7** (1960), 150, although he wasn't able to pack a $5 \times 5 \times 5$ at that time.

The same idea occurred independently to J. E. Dorie, who trademarked the name "Dorian cube" [*U.S. Trademark 1,041,392* (1976)].

An amusing way to form such a cube is to make 5-level prisms in the shapes of the P, Q, R, U, and X pentominoes, using pieces $\{a, e, j, m, w\}$, $\{f, k, l, p, r\}$, $\{A, d, D, E, n\}$, $\{c, C, F, u, v\}$, $\{b, B, t, x, z\}$; then use the packing in answer 269(!). This solution can be found with six very short runs of Algorithm X, taking only 300 megamems overall.

Another nice way, due to Torsten Sillke, is more symmetrical: There are 70,486 ways to partition the pieces into five sets of five that allow us to build an X-prism in the center (with piece x on top), surrounded by four P-prisms.

One can also assemble a Dorian cube from five cuboids, using one $1 \times 3 \times 5$, one $2 \times 2 \times 5$, and three $2 \times 3 \times 5$s. Indeed, there are zillions more ways, too many to count.

341. (a) Make an exact cover problem in which a and A, b and B, ..., f and F are required to be in symmetrical position; there are respectively $(86, 112, 172, 112, 52, 26)$ placements for such 10-cubie "super-pieces." Furthermore, the author decided to force piece m to be in the middle of the top wall. Solutions were found immediately! So piece x was placed in the exact center, as an additional desirable constraint. Then there were exactly 20 solutions; the one below has also n, o, and u in mirror-symmetrical locations.

(b) The super-pieces now have $(59, 84, 120, 82, 42, 20)$ placements; the author also optimistically forced j, k, and m to be symmetrical about the diagonal, with m in the northwest corner. A long and apparently fruitless computation (34.3 teramems) ensued; but — hurrah — two closely related solutions were discovered at the last minute.

(c) This computation, due to Torsten Sillke [see *Cubism For Fun* **27** (1991), 15], goes much faster: The quarter-of-a-box shown here can be packed with seven non-x pentacubes in 55356 ways, found in 1.3 Gμ. As in answer 294, this yields a new exact cover problem, with 33412 different options.

Another 11.8 Gμ then yields seven suitable partitions into four sets of seven, one of which is illustrated below. [See also *Cubism For Fun* **49** (1999), 26.]

```
          1 1 1 q q q q
          1 o o o o o q
          f f u u u F F
          D f u m u F d
  1 1 f D D D m m m d d d F q q
  1 f f C C D D m d d c c F F r
  v v v B C C C x c c c b r r r
  v w B B B x x x b b b b r z
  v w w A A A x a a a z z z
  k k w w E E A n a e e y z j j
  k k s s s E E n e e y y y y j
          s E n n n e y
          s s p t t t y
          k s p p t j y
          k k p p t j j
                (a)

          m o o o o o s
          m m x q q q q
          m x x x b b b
          r n x e e b a
  m m m r n e e a a a a b q s
  t m r r n n n e a D D D b q s
  t t t r E p p p v C C D D s s
  t w w E E E p p v F C C C s z
  w w B E A A v v v F F F z z z
  w 1 B B A d c f f k k F z j j
  1 1 B A A d c c f k k k u u j
          A d d c f f k
          B B d c u u u
          1 1 1 y u j u
          1 y y y y j j
                (b)

          v E z z t A A
          E E z s t t t
          E z z s t F F
          f f s s a F k
  v E E f B f s w a k k F t A
  v E f f B B w w a k k D F F A
  v v v B B w w x a a D D y A A
  u u u j j j x x x D D y y y
  u p u j m j C x c d o o o o
  p p e m m m C b c d d n n n 1
  p p e e m C C b c c d d n 1 1
          e C q b b b c d
          e e q b r n n
          p e q r r r 1
          p q q r 1 1 1
                (c)
```

342. As in previous exercises, the key is to reduce the search space drastically, by asking for solutions of a special form. (Such solutions aren't unlikely, because pentacubes are so versatile.) Here we can break the given shape into four pieces: Three modules of size $3^3 + 2^3$ to be packed with seven pentacubes, and one of size $4^3 - 3 \cdot 2^3$ to be packed with eight pentacubes. The first problem has 13,587,963 solutions, found with 2.5 Tμ of computation; they involve 737,695 distinct sets of seven pentacubes. The larger problem has 15,840 solutions, found with 400 Mμ and involving 2075 sets of eight. Exactly covering those sets yields 1,132,127,589 suitable partitions; the first one found, $\{a, A, b, c, j, q, t, y\}$, $\{B, C, d, D, e, k, o\}$, $\{E, f, l, n, r, v, x\}$, $\{F, m, p, s, u, w, z\}$, works fine. (We need only one partition, so we needn't have computed more than a thousand or so solutions to the smaller problem.)

Pentacubes galore: Since the early 1970s, Ekkehard Künzell and Sivy Farhi have independently published booklets that contain hundreds of solved pentacube problems.

343. We can use an instructive variety of methods to deduce that the tallest towers have heights $(h_O, h_P, \ldots, h_Z) = (12, 29, 28, 28, 29, 25, 26, 23, 24, 17, 28, 27)$: Case O is trivial. A perfect tower for P was published by S. Farhi in *Pentacubes*, 5th edition (1981), Fig. 78. And it's easy to show that $h_W \le 24$, because r, t, v, x, z can't be placed.

Factorization yields most of the upper bounds. For example, let the cells of a tower for R be $\{00k, 01k, 11k, 12k, 21k \mid 1 \le k \le h\}$, and add a new "weight" column to the exact-cover matrix, representing the sum of all items/columns $00k$ and $12k$. (Thus the option 'y 212 311 312 412 512' has weight 4.) An exact cover by disjoint options/rows will then make the new column sum $2h$. But the maximum weights of the pentacubes (a, A, $\ldots$, f, F, j, k, $\ldots$, z) are respectively (1, 1, 1, 1, 3, 3, 3, 3, 2, 2, 2, 2, 2, 2, 1, 1, 3, 5, 3, 4, 2, 3, 0, 3, 0, 0, 0, 4, 0). Their sum is 57; hence $h_R \le 57/2 < 29$.

Similar arguments prove that $h_U < 27$, $h_V < 24$, $h_X < 18$, $h_Z < 28$. But case T is more complicated. Let's introduce a column for the weights $(100 \cdot 00k) + (100 \cdot 02k) + (10 \cdot 11k) + (101 \cdot 21k)$, and compute the 29 maximum weights (312, 312, 310, 310, 311, 311, 221, 221, 210, 210, 220, 220, 220, 210, 211, 210, 310, 505, 323, 414, 300, 323, 400, 400, 400, 300, 200, 414, 400). The heaviest 27 sum to 8296, which is less than $311 \cdot 27$; hence $h_T < 27$. And if $h_T = 26$, further study shows that we must omit x and two of $\{e, E, k, m\}$. Moreover, each piece must use an option of maximum weight, except that c and C should use weight 310. These restrictions narrow down the search considerably; Algorithm X is able to prove that $h_T < 26$ in 11 Tμ (and Algorithm M in 7.6 Tμ).

It's difficult to prove that $h_Q < 29$, and even harder to prove that $h_Y < 29$. But in both cases a suitable weighted factorization makes the calculations feasible. (See www.math.uni-bielefeld.de/~sillke/POLYCUBE/TOWER/pentacube.)

Such weights also greatly accelerate the *successful* searches, for towers of maximum height. Here are some that were hardest-to-find (add piece 's' atop the first one):

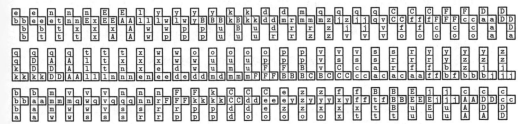

344. Reduce the placements that occupy the center cell from 72 to 3. That problem has 2528 solutions, found by Algorithm X in 25 $G\mu$; and those solutions form 1264 mirror-symmetric pairs. [See C. J. Bouwkamp and D. A. Klarner, *JRM* **3** (1970), 10–26.]

345. A variation of even/odd coordinates works nicely: Let the pieces fill 13 cells like $(x, y, z) + \{(\pm 1, \pm 1, \pm 3), (1, \pm 1, \pm 1)\}$, xyz odd, where the items (x, y, z) for $0 \le x, y \le 10$ and $0 \le z \le 6$ are primary for x, y, z even and secondary for x, y, z odd. The solution is unique. [This puzzle, marketed as "Vier Farben Block," was designed by T. Geerinck in 2004.]

```
001122 001122 001122 001122
001122 888899 888899 001122
334444 834894 83b89b 33bbbb
334444 a34a94 a3ba9b 33nnnn
556677 aaaa99 aaaa99 556677
556677 556677 556677 556677
```

346. (a) Shifting by multiples of $(0, 1, 1)$ gives N disjoint tripods whose corners are on layer 0 of the torus, filling all cells of that layer except for a (possibly broken) diagonal, and also filling all cells of such a diagonal on layer 1. We can plug the holes on layer 0 by appropriately placing N tripods whose corners are on layer $N - 1$. And so on.

(b) Here's a way to pack twelve of them into a $3 \times 6 \times 6$ torus. (Is 7/9 optimum?)

```
012600      066678      0..6..
112371      917778      .1..7.
222348      9a2888      ..2..8
933345      9ab399      9..3..
0a4445      aab64a      .a..4.
01b555      bbb675      ..b..5
```

(c) Place 13 tripods in a $6 \times 6 \times 6$ torus, with corners at $(0, 0, 0)$, $(0, 1, 1)$, $(0, 2, 2)$, $(1, 1, 3)$, $(1, 2, 4)$, $(2, 3, 2)$, $(2, 4, 4)$, $(3, 3, 3)$, $(3, 4, 5)$, $(4, 4, 0)$, $(4, 5, 1)$, $(5, 0, 5)$, $(5, 5, 3)$.

(d) One can place $2r(l, m, n)$ nonoverlapping tripods in a $2l \times 2m \times 2n$ torus, by putting the tripod corners at the positions of the pod corners, plus $(0, 0, 0)$ and (l, m, n).

(e) With one primary item # and lmn secondary items xyz, and with options such as '# 123 023 103 113 120 121 122' (one for each pod with $0 \le x < l, 0 \le y < m, 0 \le z < n$), we can find solutions with t pods by giving multiplicity t to #. Furthermore we can save time by letting the items 000 and $(l-1)(m-1)(n-1)$ be primary, because those two pods can be assumed to be present. In this way we find $444 \mapsto 8$, $445 \mapsto 9$, $446 \mapsto 9$, $455 \mapsto 10$, $456 \mapsto 10$, $466 \mapsto 12$, $555 \mapsto 11$, $556 \mapsto 12$, $566 \mapsto 13$, $666 \mapsto 14$. (Algorithm M can determine that $r(6, 6, 6) < 15$ in reasonable time, 253 $G\mu$, despite its rather weak heuristics for pruning the search. But the SAT solver Algorithm 7.2.2.2C solves this problem in only 2 $G\mu$; it can also establish that $r(7, 7, 7) = 19$ in 169 $G\mu$, while Algorithm M as it stands would be hopeless for that task.)

[*Notes:* Sherman Stein initiated the study of tripods (actually an n-dimensional generalization called "semicrosses") in *IEEE Trans.* **IT-30** (1984), 356–363; see also his paper with W. Hamaker on pages 364–368. They proved that the function $r(n) = r(n, n, n)$ is $\Omega(n^{1.516})$, and that $r(l, n, n)/n$ approaches a limit as $n \to \infty$. The initial values $(r(1), \ldots, r(9)) = (1, 2, 5, 8, 11, 14, 19, 23, 28)$ were found by C. Morgan, in an undergraduate project at the University of Warwick in 2000; see also S. Szabó, *Ann. Univ. Sci. Budapestinensis, Sect. Computatorica* **41** (2013), 307–322. With extensive computations, P. R. J. Östergård and A. Pöllänen have proved that $r(10) = 32$ and (surprisingly) that $r(11) = 38$ [*Discrete and Computational Geometry* **61** (2019), 271–284]. See also A. Tiskin, *Discrete Math.* **307** (2007), 1973–1981, who showed among other things that $r(12) \geq 43$, $r(n) = \Omega(n^{1.534})$, $r(n) = O(n^2/(\log n)^{1/15})$.]

347. Fourteen proofs have been given by S. Wagon, *AMM* **94**, (1987), 601–617. [For generalizations, see R. J. Bower and T. S. Michael, *Math. Magazine* **79** (2006), 14–30.]

348. See F. W. Barnes's complete solution, *Discrete Mathematics* **133** (1994), 55–78.

349. Let $t = s/4$. Each brick of an m-brick packing contains at least one of the 27 "special points" $\{(it, jt, kt) \mid 0 < i, j, k < 4\}$, because a, b, and c exceed t. Hence $m \leq 27$.

In a packing with $m = 27$, each of the "special lines" l_{*jk}, l_{i*k}, l_{ij*} with two coordinates fixed will be totally full, because the bricks collectively occupy $27(a+b+c)$ units of space on those lines. The special lines also intersect the bricks in 27 segments of each length a, b, c; hence each special line has a segment of each length.

Thus we're led to solve an XCC problem with primary items p_{ijk}, l_{*jk}, l_{i*k}, l_{ij*} and secondary items x_{ijk}, y_{ijk}, z_{ijk}, and with options like '$p_{ijk}\, x_{ijk}{:}\pi_1\, y_{ijk}{:}\pi_2\, z_{ijk}{:}\pi_3$' and '$l_{i*k}\, y_{i1k}{:}\pi_1\, y_{i2k}{:}\pi_2\, y_{i3k}{:}\pi_3$', where $\pi_1\pi_2\pi_3$ is a permutation of $\{a, b, c\}$. That problem has 7712 solutions, when we fix one of the six options for p_{111}.

Only 168 of those solutions, in 21 equivalence classes under the 48 symmetries of the cube, actually pack properly when $(a, b, c) = (2, 3, 4)$. And it can be shown that those 21 solutions will solve Hoffman's problem for arbitrary (a, b, c). Here, for example, is the unique solution that is "self-dual" — isomorphic to itself when $a \leftrightarrow c$:

```
ABC  ABC  ABC  ABC  ABL  AKL  JKL  JKL  JKL  JTU  STU  STU  STU  STU
DEF  DEF  DEF  DEF  DNO  MNO  MNO  MNO  MNO  MEW  VWX  VWX  VWX  VWX
GHI  GHI  GHI  GHI  GHR  GHR  PQR  PQR  PQR  PZR  YZ&  YZ&  YZ&  YZ&
```

[See Hoffman's exposition in *The Mathematical Gardner* (1981), 212–225.]

350. Set this up for Algorithm M with 28 instances of a $3 \times 4 \times 5$ brick and 48 instances of a single cubie. We can omit all options where a brick lies 1 or 2 units from a face but not on the face, because the brick could move outward in such solutions. We can also force the placement of a brick at corner $(0, 0, 0)$. Furthermore, an empty corner would imply at least 27 cubies there; hence we can omit placing a cubie in any corner except $(11, 11, 11)$. This problem, with 715 options of size 61 and 1721 options of size 2, has 112 solutions(!), found in 440 Gμ. (The author's first attempt, in 2004, took much longer.)

There are three species of solutions: (i) Pack seven bricks into $5 \times 7 \times 12$; arrange four of those in a pinwheel (see exercise 365), leaving a $2 \times 2 \times 12$ hole. (ii) Pack 12 into $5 \times 12 \times 12$; add a pinwheel of four $5 \times 7 \times 7$s, each of which is a pinwheel of four $3 \times 4 \times 5$s. (iii) Assemble the bricks in a bizarre way that includes two such $5 \times 7 \times 7$s:

```
ABCD  ABCD  ABCD  ABCD  ABCD  OPQ   OPQ   OPQ   OWQ   ZW&   ZW&   ZW&
EFG   EFG   EFG   EFG   EF L  R  L  R  L  R TU  X TU  X TU  X TU  X TU
HIJK  HIJK  HIJK  HIJK  HM N  SM N  SM N  SV N  SV Y  @V Y  @V Y  @V Y
```

Types (i), (ii), (iii) contribute 6+10+4 nonisomorphic solutions. [George Miller's puzzle with bricks of tricolored faces is called Perfect Packing, because 28 is a perfect number.]

351. (Generalizing exercise 349, Hoffman observed that such a construction would yield a nice geometrical way to prove the inequality $(abcde)^{1/5} \le (a+b+c+d+e)/5$.)

352. None. But any eleven of the "hypersolid pentominoes" can easily be squeezed in;

for example,

```
Q X W W .    T S S S U    S S Z R U    Q Q Q Q .
X X X W W    T T T . U    Z Z Z R R    0 0 0 0 0
. X P P W    T P P P U    Z Y R R U    Y Y Y Y .
```

is one way to pack all but **V**.

353. There are exactly 9 (including a mirror pair). They pack a $3 \times 3 \times 3$ cube in $48 \cdot 8789$ ways, such as $\begin{smallmatrix}000\\112\\123\end{smallmatrix} \mid \begin{smallmatrix}434\\525\\567\end{smallmatrix} \mid \begin{smallmatrix}548\\786\\876\end{smallmatrix}$. [See J. Lou, Danish patent 126840 (1973).]

354. (a) Let cell (x, y) of a polyomino correspond to $(-x, x, y, -y)$. Let cell (x, y) of a polyhex, as represented in exercise 315, correspond to $(0, x, y, -x - y)$.

(b) A polysphere is planar if and only if the differences between its adjacent cells lie in a plane. Each of those differences has the form $e_{ij} = e_i - e_j$, where $e_1 = (1, 0, 0, 0)$, $\ldots$, $e_4 = (0, 0, 0, 1)$. Three such differences can't be linearly independent yet lie in a plane; the linearly dependent cases are polyominoes and/or polyhexes.

(c) Every connected graph has at least one vertex whose removal doesn't disconnect the graph. So the result follows by induction on n.

(d) An orthogonal matrix fixes $w + x + y + z$ if and only if its row and column sums are 1. The matrices (i) T and (ii) R below respectively rotate by $120°$ about $x = y = z$ and by $90°$ about $(x = y) \wedge (w = z)$.

$$T = \begin{pmatrix} 1 & 0 & 0 & 0 \\ 0 & 0 & 1 & 0 \\ 0 & 0 & 0 & 1 \\ 0 & 1 & 0 & 0 \end{pmatrix}; \quad R = \frac{1}{2}\begin{pmatrix} 1 & -1 & 1 & 1 \\ 1 & 1 & 1 & -1 \\ -1 & 1 & 1 & 1 \\ 1 & 1 & -1 & 1 \end{pmatrix}; \quad R^2 = \begin{pmatrix} 0 & 0 & 0 & 1 \\ 0 & 0 & 1 & 0 \\ 0 & 1 & 0 & 0 \\ 1 & 0 & 0 & 0 \end{pmatrix}; \quad H = \frac{1}{6}\begin{pmatrix} 5 & -1 & -1 & 3 \\ -1 & -1 & 5 & 3 \\ -1 & 5 & -1 & 3 \\ 3 & 3 & 3 & -3 \end{pmatrix}.$$

(e) The matrices (i) R^2 and (ii) H above respectively rotate by $180°$ about $(x = y) \wedge (w = z)$ and about $(x = y) \wedge (w = 3z - 2x)$. Thus H can be used when $z = 0$.

(f) Suppose $V' = \{v'_1, \ldots, v'_n\}$ is a rotation of $V = \{v_1, \ldots, v_n\} \subset S$, where $v_k = (w_k, x_k, y_k, z_k)$, $v'^T_k = (w'_k, x'_k, y'_k, z'_k)^T = Q v^T_k$, $v_1 = v'_1 = (0, 0, 0, 0)$, and $v_2 = e_{12} = (1, -1, 0, 0)$. The matrix $Q = (q_{ij})$ is orthogonal, with row and column sums and determinant 1. By applying an even permutation to the coordinates of v' and the rows of Q, we can assume without loss of generality that $v'_2 = e_{12} = v_2$. Hence $q_{k1} = q_{k2} + \delta_{k1} - \delta_{k2}$, $q_{11} = q_{22}$. If $Q \ne I$ we have $v_p - v_q = e_{ij} \ne e_{i'j'} = v'_p - v'_q$ for some p, q, i, j, i', and j', with $i < j$. By orthogonality, $e_{12} \cdot e_{ij} = e_{12} \cdot e_{i'j'} \in \{-1, 0, +1\}$.

If $e_{12} \cdot e_{ij} = 1$, there are six cases, depending on (i, j, i', j'): $(1, 3, 1, 4)$ implies $Q = TH$; $(1, 4, 1, 3)$ implies $Q = HT^2$; $(1, 3, 4, 2)$ implies $Q = T^2RT$ or THR^3T^2; $(1, 4, 3, 2)$ implies $Q = T^2RT$ or HR; $(1, 3, 3, 2)$ and $(1, 4, 4, 2)$ are impossible.

If $e_{12} \cdot e_{ij} = 0$, we have $(i, j, i', j') = (3, 4, 4, 3)$ and Q is forced to be TR. Finally, the case (i, j, i', j') for $e_{12} \cdot e_{ij} = -1$ is the same as the case (i, j, j', i') for $e_{12} \cdot e_{ij} = +1$.

Note: Some authors represent S as the set of integer triples (X, Y, Z) with $X + Y + Z$ even. The Hadamard transform provides an isomorphism between these representations: If $-2M$ is the upper left 4×4 submatrix of 7.2.1.1–(21), we have $M^2 = I$, $\det M = 1$, and M takes $(-x - y - z, x, y, z) \mapsto (0, x + z, y + z, x + y) = (0, X, Y, Z)$.

355. (a) Normalize the given polysphere by subtracting $(x_{\min}, y_{\min}, z_{\min})$, to get *its* base placement. Then, for each base placement P, form up to three others until no more can be formed: (i) Replace each xyz by yzx. (ii) Replace each xyz by $(x + y + z)(t - z)(t - x)$, for some large t; then normalize. (iii) If $z = 0$ in each cell of P, replace each $xy0$ by $yx0$.

[The (X, Y, Z) representation mentioned in answer 354 suggests "polyjubes" — George Sicherman's name for the sets of *edge-connected cubes* that don't touch face-to-face. Transformation (iii) does not apply to polyjubes; hence there are 5 trijubes and

28 tetrajubes. Polyjubes are also equivalent to "polyrhons" — the connected sets of rhombic dodecahedra, which are the Voronoi regions of the face-centered cubic lattice. See S. Coffin, *The Puzzling World of Polyhedral Dissection* (1990), Figure 167.]

(b) Phenalene has eight base placements; in lexicographic order they are $\{000, 001, 010\}$, $\{000, 001, 100\}$, $\{000, 010, 100\}$, $\{001, 010, 011\}$, $\{001, 010, 100\}$, $\{001, 100, 101\}$, $\{010, 100, 110\}$, $\{011, 101, 110\}$. The straight trisphere has six base placements, namely $\{000, 001, 002\}$, $\{000, 010, 020\}$, $\{000, 100, 200\}$, $\{002, 011, 020\}$, $\{002, 101, 200\}$, $\{020, 110, 200\}$. The bent trisphere has twelve, from $\{001, 010, 101\}$ to $\{011, 100, 110\}$. And phenanthrene has twenty-four, from $\{000, 001, 011\}$ to $\{020, 101, 110\}$.

(c) There are 853 connected subsets, with 475 different base placements. (Each placement with $\max(x + y + z) = (1, 2, 3)$ occurs respectively $(10, 4, 1)$ times.) They form 25 distinct tetraspheres — five from tetrominoes and six additional planar pieces from tetrahexes, plus four nonplanar nonchiral pieces and five chiral pairs:

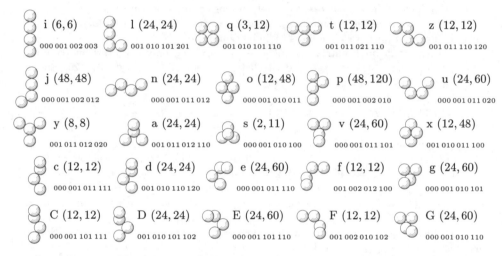

i (6,6)	l (24,24)	q (3,12)	t (12,12)	z (12,12)
000 001 002 003	001 010 101 201	001 010 101 110	001 011 021 110	001 011 110 120

j (48,48)	n (24,24)	o (12,48)	p (48,120)	u (24,60)
000 001 002 012	000 001 011 012	000 001 010 011	000 001 002 010	000 001 011 020

y (8,8)	a (24,24)	s (2,11)	v (24,60)	x (12,48)
001 011 012 020	001 011 012 110	000 001 010 100	000 001 011 101	001 010 011 100

c (12,12)	d (24,24)	e (24,60)	f (12,12)	g (24,60)
000 001 011 111	001 010 110 120	000 001 011 110	001 002 012 100	000 001 010 101

C (12,12)	D (24,24)	E (24,60)	F (12,12)	G (24,60)
000 001 101 111	001 010 101 102	000 001 101 110	001 002 010 102	000 001 010 110

Each piece has been given an identifying letter. This chart shows the number of base placements and the number of occurrences in $simplex(3, 3, 3, 3, 3, 0, 0)$, as well as the lexicographically smallest base placement. Notice that j and p have 48 base placements, while a polycube can have at most 48. Piece s is $simplex(1, 1, 1, 1, 1, 0, 0)$, a tetrahedron with four equidistant spheres. Piece x is perhaps the most fascinating to play with.

[The tetraspheres were first enumerated by K. Takizawa; then T. Sillke enumerated the nonplanar polyspheres of larger sizes. See B. Wiezorke, *Cubism For Fun* **25**, part 3 (1990), 10–17; G. Bell, *Cubism For Fun* **81** (2010), 18–23; OEIS A038174.]

356. (a) The n-tetrahedron, which is the same as $simplex(n - 1, n - 1, n - 1, n - 1, n-1, 0, 0)$, has base placement $\{xyz \mid x, y, z \geq 0, x+y+z < n\}$; $\binom{n+2}{3}$ cells. (It has one other base placement, namely $\{(n-1-x)(n-1-y)(n-1-z) \mid x, y, z \geq 0, x+y+z < n\}$.)

One of the 12 base placements of the $m \times n$ roof is $\{x(y+k)(m-1-y) \mid k \geq 0, 0 \leq x < n - k, 0 \leq y < m - k\}$. If $m \leq n$, it has $m(m + 1)(3n - m + 1)/6$ cells.

The stretched $m \times n$ roof is based on slicing the face-centered cubic lattice into layers with constant $y - z$. (Each cell has two neighbors on its own layer, four neighbors on each adjacent layer, and two neighbors that are two layers away.) One of its 12 base placements is $\{(x+m-1-y)(y+k)y \mid k \geq 0, 0 \leq x < n - k, 0 \leq y < m - k\}$.

(b) Let's call the four shapes T_4, $R_{3\times4}$, $S_{3\times4}$, and $S_{4\times3}$. Here are the stats:

Shape	Total multisets(sets)	All planar (balanced)	Mixed (balanced)	Mixed (chiral)	All nonplanar (balanced)	All nonplanar (chiral)
T_4	2952(1211)	174(34)	308(115)	2442(1062)	2(0)	26(0)
$R_{3\times4}$	11531(6274)	372(69)	1250(583)	9818(5608)	3(0)	88(14)
$S_{3\times4}$	1184(480)	51(6)	108(48)	1014(426)	1(0)	10(0)
$S_{4\times3}$	266(52)	2(0)	27(8)	234(44)	1(0)	2(0)

For example, $\{j, j, p, p, t\}$ is one of 174 multisets of five planar pieces that can make T_4. [In fact, the solution is unique — and $\{j, j, p, p, t\}$ also uniquely solves $R_{3\times4}$ and $S_{3\times4}$! G. Bell used this fact as the basis for his elegant Triple Pyradox puzzle; see *Cubism For Fun* **94** (2014), 10–13.] Of those 174 cases, 34 have five *different* pieces; for instance, $\{n, o, p, u, y\}$ is one of only seven that contains y, the "propeller."

Many other suitable sets of five mix planar pieces with nonplanar ones. Of these, 115 (like $\{g, G, i, s, x\}$) are closed under reflection; that one has 24 solutions, all essentially the same. The other 1062 form 531 mirror-image pairs (like $\{d, e, f, G, i\}$ and $\{D, E, F, g, i\}$); every solution for a chiral set has 12 equivalents, not 24.

Algorithm M discovers all such solutions quickly, if we assign multiplicity $[0 . . 5]$ to each piece. There are respectively (88927, 77783, 3440, 996) solutions to (T_4, $R_{3\times4}$, $S_{3\times4}$, $S_{4\times3}$), without symmetry removal; they're found in (840, 607, 48, 13) $M\mu$.

Six of the multisets — three mirror pairs — are actually able to make *all four* shapes. These versatile combinations of pieces are $\{e, g, g, p, p\}$ and $\{E, G, G, p, p\}$, $\{g, j, p, p, p\}$ and $\{G, j, p, p, p\}$, $\{g, p, p, p, p\}$ and $\{G, p, p, p, p\}$.

There's an obvious, yet interesting, way to make T_4 with the "pure" multiset $\{s, s, s, s, s\}$. The only other pure multiset that works is $\{p, p, p, p, p\}$, which is able to form both T_4 and $R_{3\times4}$, as well as many other shapes noted by W. Schneider in 1995.

[A 2×7 roof also has 20 cells. So we might want to consider additional stats:

$R_{2\times7}$	3940(1628)	608(116)	1296(512)	1970(1000)	14(0)	52(0)
$S_{2\times7}$	426(84)	58(4)	48(20)	306(60)	2(0)	12(0)
$S_{7\times2}$	4(0)	0(0)	0(0)	0(0)	2(0)	2(0)

The long and skinny $S_{7\times2}$ can be made in only two ways, both with x in the middle, surrounded by g's or G's. The set $\{i, j, n, o, p\}$ packs both $S_{2\times7}$ and $S_{7\times2}$, as well as T_4.]

(c) Let's name the trispheres 1, 2, 3, 4, according to the squared distance between the two farthest-apart cells; thus the pieces in exercise 355 are 2, 4, 1, 3. The pyramid P_4 is buildable from 296 such multisets, many of which allow huge numbers of solutions. (For example, each of the ten multisets that contain $\{1, 1, 2, 2, 3, 3, 4, 4\}$ leads to more than 30,000 solutions; $\{1, 1, 2, 2, 2, 3, 3, 4, 4, 4\}$ has more than 120,000!) Most interesting are the cases with unique solution ($\{2, 2, 4, 4, 4, 4, 4, 4, 4, 4\}\ddagger$, $\{1, 1, 1, 4, 4, 4, 4, 4, 4, 4\}$, $\{1, 2, 2, 2, 2, 2, 2, 2, 2, 2\}$), or with just two solutions ($\{2, 2, 2, 2, 2, 2, 2, 2, 2, 2\}\dagger$, $\{1, 1, 3, 3, 3, 3, 3, 3, 3, 3\}$, $\{2, 4, 4, 4, 4, 4, 4, 4, 4, 4\}\ddagger$); $\dagger$ = noted by L. Gordon (1986); $\ddagger$ = noted by J. Becker (2009). The stretched pyramid S_4 has 213 such multisets, all of which can also make P_4. Unique solutions occur for $\{1, 1, 1, 3, 4, 4, 4, 4, 4, 4\}$ and $\{1, 3, 3, 3, 3, 3, 3, 3, 4, 4\}$; almost for $\{3, 3, 3, 3, 3, 3, 3, 3, 4, 4\}$.

Historical notes: The first polysphere puzzle may have been "Pyramystery," copyright by Piet Hein in 1967 when his Soma cube was becoming popular. Pyramystery had the six pieces $\{1, 1, 3, 4, o, p\}$; Hein knew that it could form T_4, as well as two copies of T_3, and several planar designs. A similar puzzle of unknown origin, called

Kugelpyramide, may have been created earlier, because it was seen by B. Wiezorke in 1968. Kugelpyramide's pieces, $\{1, 3, 4, 4, o, p\}$ were slightly different. With either Pyramystery or Kugelpyramide one can make T_4, $T_3 + T_3$, $R_{3\times4}$, $R_{2\times7}$, and $S_{2\times7}$; and with the not-thought-of pieces $\{1, 2, 3, 4, o, p\}$, one could have made also $S_{3\times4}$ but not $T_3 + T_3$. The first puzzle to mix polyomino-type polyspheres with polyhex-type polyspheres — a nonobvious possibility — was Tetra, by A. Kuwagaki and S. Takenaka; see *Sugaku Seminar* **11**, 7 (July 1972), cover, 34–38; also *U.S. Patent 3837652* (1974). That patent describes making P_3 from the dispheres and trispheres, and making the 44-ball octahedron $P_4 P_3^R$ from the planar tetraspheres $\{i, j, l, n, o, p, q, t, u, y, z\}$. In those early days, the stretched roofs and pyramids weren't known to be possible; they were first introduced by Leonard Gordon, in his WARP-30 puzzle (Kadon Enterprises, 1986).

(d) The unique base placement is $\{xyz \mid x, y, z \in \{0, 1, 2, 3\}, x \neq y \neq z \neq x\}$. Stats are $95(0)$ $5(0)$ $13(0)$ $70(0)$ $3(0)$ $4(0)$. Only pieces a, c, d, q, u will fit in this shape. Here's how to make it with $\{a, a, c, d, u, u\}$, $\{c, c, c, C, C, C\}$, or $\{u, u, u, u, u, u\}$:

$a_2 a_2$		a_1	a_2		$a_1 a_1$			$C_2 c_3$	C_2	c_3	$C_2 c_3$		$u_5 u_3$	u_1	u_3	$u_3 u_3$
c	a_2	c		u_2			$a_1 u_1$	c_1	C_3	c_1	C_3		$C_2 c_3$	u_5	u_6 u_1	u_6
d d						c		u_2	c	u_1	$C_1 c_2$		c_1	C_3 c_1	C_3	$u_5 u_5$
	d u_2		d	u_2	$u_1 u_1$			$C_1 c_2$	C_1	c_2	$C_1 c_2$		$u_4 u_4$	u_4	u_6

(Note that $\{q, q, q, q, q, q\}$ is trivial.) This is a hollow object that can't stand on its own.

357. Truncated octahedra are the Voronoi regions of the "body-centered cubic lattice," which is less tight than the face-centered cubic lattice: It can be represented as the set of all integer triples (x, y, z) with x mod $2 = y$ mod $2 = z$ mod 2. Two truncated octahedra whose centers are two such points are adjacent if and only if the distance between those points is either $\sqrt{3}$ (eight neighbors, joined at hexagonal faces) or 2 (six neighbors, joined at square faces). There are 2 displatts, 6 trisplatts, and 44 tetrasplatts — including 9 chiral pairs. [See M. Owen and M. Richards, *Eureka* **47** (1987), 53–58.]

Base placements can be found almost as in exercise 324, except that we must set $(x, y, z) \mapsto (y, 2\lceil x_{\max}\rceil - x, z)$. Furthermore, each base placement should be normalized, by adding $(\pm1, \pm1, \pm1)$ if needed, so that $x_{\min} + y_{\min} + z_{\min} \leq 1$.

[One might also consider truncating further, leaving only the union of four small hexagonal prisms between diametrically opposite hexagonal faces. This yields a sub-family of polysplatts called "polycrunches" — named and enumerated by G. Sicherman: Adjacent crunches, with centers $\sqrt{3}$ apart, are pasted together where the prisms meet. The polycrunch family has 1 monocrunch, 1 dicrunch, 3 tricrunches, and 14 tetra-crunches (including 2 chiral pairs). The tricrunches have respectively (4, 12, 12) base placements; the tetracrunches have respectively (4, 6, 6, 8, 12, 12, 12, 12, 24, ..., 24).]

358. This fascinating packing is considerably more difficult than the other. For example, there are *six* distinct trihexaspheres, having respective angles of $(60°$, $90°$, $\arccos(-1/3) \approx 109.5°$, $120°$, $\arccos(-5/6) \approx 146.4°$, $180°)$ and respective maximum squared distances $(1, 2, 8/3, 3, 11/3, 4)$. G. Bell has discovered a convenient way to represent *magnified* polyhexaspheres *within* the face-centered cubic lattice: Consider the subset $\widehat{S}$ of S whose elements have the special form $\alpha j + \beta k + \gamma_l$ for integers j, k, l, where $\alpha = (0, 3, -3, 0)$, $\beta = (0, 0, 3, -3)$, $\gamma_{2l} = (6l, -2l, -2l, -2l)$, and $\gamma_{2l+1} = (6l+3, -3-2l, -2l, -2l)$. Two cells of $\widehat{S}$ are called adjacent if the distance between them is $\sqrt{18}$. Thus each cell v of layer l has six neighbors $v \pm \{(0, 3, -3, 0), (0, 0, 3, -3), (0, -3, 0, 3)\}$ on the same level; three neighbors $v + A[l$ even$] + B[l$ odd$]$ on level $l + 1$, where $A = \{(3, -3, 0, 0), (3, 0, -3, 0), (3, 0, 0, -3)\}$ and $B = \{(3, 1, -2, -2), (3, -2, 1, -2), (3, -2, -2, 1)\}$; and three neighbors $v - A[l$ odd$] - B[l$ even$]$ on level $l - 1$.

All of the tetraspheres are tetrahexaspheres, because they fit on at most two levels. But many of the pentaspheres, for example the planar one for pentomino T, are not pentahexaspheres. A polyomino polyhexasphere exists if and only if the polyomino fits in a $2 \times k$ box: Connected subsets of $\{(0,0,3k,-3k),(-3,-1,2+3k,2-3k)\}$ are OK.

The matrices T and $R^2 H R^2$ of answer 354 are rotations of $\widehat{S}$. Therefore we can obtain equivalent base placements in the manner of answer 355, replacing each xyz by either yzx or $(y+\frac{2}{3}w)(x+\frac{2}{3}w)(z+\frac{2}{3}w)$, where $w = -x-y-z$. Normalize a placement by adding or subtracting 666 or $3\overline{3}0$ or $03\overline{3}$ or $\overline{3}03$. But the analysis is still incomplete: Are further transformations of base placements needed? How many n-hexaspheres are possible, for $n = 4, 5, \ldots$? [See *Cubism For Fun* **106** (2018), 24–29.]

359. First we realize that every edge of the square must touch at least three pieces; hence the pieces must in fact form a 3×3 arrangement. Consequently any correct placement would also lead to a placement for nine pieces of sizes $(17 - k) \times (20 - k)$, $\ldots, (24 - k) \times (25 - k)$, into a $(65 - 3k) \times (65 - 3k)$ box. Unfortunately, however, if we try, say, $k = 16$, Algorithm X quickly gives a contradiction.

But aha — a closer look shows that the pieces have *rounded corners*. Indeed, there's just enough room for pieces to get close enough together so that, if they truly were rectangles, they'd make a 1×1 overlap at a corner.

So we can take $k = 13$ and make nine pieces of sizes $4 \times 7, \ldots, 11 \times 12$, consisting of rectangles *minus* their corners. Those pieces can be packed into a 26×26 square, as if they were polyominoes (see exercise 266), but with the individual cells of the enclosing rectangle treated as secondary items because they needn't be covered. (Well, the eight cells adjacent to corners can be primary.) We can save a factor of 8 by insisting that the 9×11 piece appear in the upper left quarter, with its long side horizontal.

Algorithm X solves that problem in 620 gigamems — but it finds 43 solutions, most of which are unusable, because the missing corners give too much flexibility. The unique correct solution is easily identified, because a 1×1 overlap between rectangles in one place must be compensated by a 1×1 empty cell between rectangles in another. The resulting cross pattern (like the X pentomino) occurs in just one of the 43.

360. Let there be mn primary items p_{ij} for $0 \le i < m$ and $0 \le j < n$, one for each cell that should be covered exactly once. Also introduce m primary items x_i for $0 \le i < m$, as well as n primary items y_j for $0 \le j < n$. The exact cover problem has $\binom{m+1}{2} \cdot \binom{n+1}{2}$ options, one for each subrectangle $[a\mathinner{.\,.}b] \times [c\mathinner{.\,.}d]$ with $0 \le a < b \le m$ and $0 \le c < d \le n$. The option for that subrectangle contains $2 + (b-a)(d-c)$ items, namely x_a, y_c, and p_{ij} for $a \le i < b$, $c \le j < d$. The solutions correspond to reduced decompositions when we insist that each x_i be covered $[1\mathinner{.\,.}n]$ times and that each y_j be covered $[1\mathinner{.\,.}m]$ times. (We can save a little time by omitting x_0 and y_0.)

The 3×5 problem has 20165 solutions, found in 18 Mμ. They include respectively (1071, 3816, 5940, 5266, 2874, 976, 199, 22, 1) cases with $(7, 8, \ldots, 15)$ subrectangles.

[See C. J. Bloch, *Environment and Planning* **B6** (1979), 155–190, for a complete catalog of all reduced decompositions into at most seven subrectangles.]

361. The minimum is $m + n - 1$. Proof (by induction): The result is obvious when $m = 1$ or $n = 1$. Otherwise, given a decomposition into t subrectangles, $k \ge 1$ of them must be confined to the nth column. If two of those k are contiguous, we can combine them; the resulting dissection of order $t - 1$ reduces to either $(m - 1) \times n$ or $m \times n$, hence $t - 1 \ge (m - 1) + n - 1$. On the other hand if none of them are contiguous, the reduction of the first $n - 1$ columns is $m \times (n - 1)$; hence $t \ge m + (n - 1) - 1 + k$.

Close examination of this proof shows that a reduced decomposition has minimum order t if and only if its boundary edges form $m - 1$ horizontal lines and $n - 1$ vertical lines that don't cross each other. (In particular, the "tatami condition" is satisfied; see exercise 7.1.4–215.) See C. F. Earl, *Environment and Planning* **B5** (1978), 179–187.

362. Simply remove the offending subrectangles, so that the cover problem has only $\left(\binom{m+1}{2}-1\right)\left(\binom{n+1}{2}-1\right)$ options. Now there are 13731 3×5 solutions, found in 11 Mμ, and (410, 1974, 3830, 3968, 2432, 900, 194, 22, 1) cases with (7, 8, ..., 15) subrectangles.

363. Introduce additional primary items X_i for $0 < i < m$, to be covered $[1..n-1]$ times, as well as Y_j for $0 < j < n$, to be covered $[1..m-1]$ times. Then add items X_i for $a < i < b$ and Y_j for $c < j < d$ to the constraint for subrectangle $[a..b] \times [c..d]$.

Now the 3×5 problem has just 216 solutions, found in 1.9 megamems. They include (66, 106, 44) instances with (7, 8, 9) subrectangles. Just two of the solutions are symmetric under left-right reflection, namely ⊞ and its top-bottom reflection.

364. We can delete non-tromino options from the exact cover problem, thereby getting all faultfree tromino tilings that are reduced. If we also delete the constraints on x_i and y_j — and if we require X_i and Y_j to be covered $[1..n]$ and $[1..m]$ times instead of $[1..n-1]$ and $[1..m-1]$ — we obtain *all* of the $m \times n$ faultfree tromino tilings.

It is known that such nontrivial tilings exist if and only if $m, n \geq 7$ and mn is a multiple of 3. [See K. Scherer, *JRM* **13** (1980), 4–6; R. L. Graham, *The Mathematical Gardner* (1981), 120–126.] So we look at the smallest cases in order of mn: When $(m,n) = (7,9), (8,9), (9,9), (7,12), (9,10)$, we get respectively (32, 32), (48, 48), (16, 16), (706, 1026), (1080, 1336) solutions. Hence the assertion is false; a smallest counterexample is shown.

365. Augment the exact cover problem of answer 362 by introducing $\binom{m+1}{2} + \binom{n+1}{2} - 2$ secondary items x_{ab} and y_{cd}, for $0 \leq a < b \leq m$ and $0 \leq c < d \leq n$, $(a,b) \neq (0,m)$, $(c,d) \neq (0,n)$. Include item x_{ab} and y_{cd} in the option for subrectangle $[a..b] \times [c..d]$. Furthermore, cover x_i $[1..m-i]$ times, not $[1..n]$; cover y_j $[1..n-j]$ times.

366. The hint follows because $[a..b] \times [0..d]$ cannot coexist motleywise with its left-right reflection $[a..b] \times [n-d..n]$. Thus we can forbid half of the solutions.

Consider, for example, the case $(m,n) = (7,7)$. Every solution will include x_{67} with some y_{cd}. If it's y_{46}, say, left-right reflection would produce an equivalent solution with y_{13}; therefore we disallow the option $(a,b,c,d) = (6,7,4,6)$. Similarly, we disallow $(a,b,c,d) = (6,7,c,d)$ whenever $7 - d < c$.

Reflection doesn't change the bottom-row rectangle when $c+d = 7$, so we haven't broken all the symmetry. But we can complete the job by looking also at the top-row rectangle, namely the option where x_{01} occurs with some $y_{c'd'}$. Let's introduce new secondary items t_1, t_2, t_3, and include t_c in the option that has x_{67} with $y_{c(7-c)}$. Then we include t_1, t_2, and t_3 in the option that has x_{01} with $y_{c'd'}$ for $c' + d' > 7$. We also add t_1 to the option with x_{01} and y_{25}; and we add both t_1 and t_2 to the option with x_{01} and y_{34}. This works beautifully, because no solution can have $c = c'$ and $d = d'$.

In general, we introduce new secondary items t_c for $1 \leq c < n/2$, and we disallow all options $x_{(m-1)m}\, y_{cd}$ for which $c + d > n$. We put t_c into the option that contains $x_{(m-1)m}\, y_{c(n-c)}$; t_1 thru $t_{\lfloor (n-1)/2 \rfloor}$ into the option that contains $x_{01}\, y_{c'd'}$ when $c'+d' > n$; and t_1 thru $t_{c'-1}$ into the option that contains $x_{01}\, y_{c'(n-c')}$. (Think about it.)

For example, when $m = n = 7$ there now are 717 options instead of 729, 57 secondary items instead of 54. We now find 352546 solutions after only 13.2 gigamems of computation, instead of 705092 solutions after 26.4. The search tree now has just 7.8 meganodes instead of 15.7.

(It's tempting to believe that the same idea will break top-bottom symmetry too. But that would be fallacious: Once we've fixed attention on the bottommost row while breaking left-right symmetry, we've lost all symmetry between top and bottom.)

367. From any $m \times n$ dissection of order t we get two $(m+2) \times (n+2)$ dissections of order $t + 4$, by enclosing it within two $1 \times (m+1)$ tiles and two $1 \times (n+1)$ tiles. So the claim follows by induction and the examples in exercise 365, together with a 5×6 example of order 10 — of which there are 8 symmetrical instances such as the one shown here. (This construction is faultfree, and it's also "tight": The order of every $m \times n$ dissection is at least $m + n - 1$, by exercise 361.)

In general, Helmut Postl observes that we can create nested motley dissections by motley-dissecting *any* subrectangle of a motley dissection (taking care not to repeat any internal boundary coordinates) and reducing the result. For example, one of the $2 \cdot (6+3+3+3+1+9+3) = 56$ ways to nest a pinwheel within the second motley 4×4 is shown here.

368. The number of subrectangles $[a..b) \times [c..d)$ that have either $c = k$ or $d = k$, given k, is ≥ 2 when $k \in \{0, n\}$ and ≥ 3 when $0 < k < n$. Hence $2t \geq 2 + 3(n-1) + 2$.

369. All 214 of the 5×7 motley dissections have order 11, which is far short of $\binom{6}{2} - 1 = 14$; and there are no 5×8s, 5×9s, or 5×10s. Surprisingly, however, 424 of the 696 dissections of size 6×12 do have the optimum order 20, and 7×17 dissections with the optimum order 27 also exist. Examples of these remarkable patterns are shown. (The case $m = 7$ is still not fully explored except for small n. For example, the total number of motley 7×17 dissections is unknown. No 7×18s exist, by exercise 368. If we restrict attention to *symmetrical* dissections, the maximum orders for $5 \leq m \leq 8$ are 11 (5×7); 19 (6×11); 25 (7×15); 33 (8×21).)

370. The basic idea is to combine complementary options into a single option whenever possible. More precisely: (i) If $a + b = m$ and $c + d = n$, we retain the option as usual; it is self-complementary. (ii) Otherwise, if $a + b = m$ or $c + d = n$, reject the option; merging would be non-motley. (iii) Otherwise, if $a + b > m$, reject the option; we've already considered its complement. (iv) Otherwise, if $b = 1$ and $c + d < n$, reject the option; its complement is illegal. (v) Otherwise, if $b > m/2$ and $c < n/2$ and $d > n/2$, reject the option; it intersects its complement. (vi) Otherwise merge the option with its complement. For example, when $(m, n) = (4, 5)$, case (i) arises when $(a, b, c, d) = (1, 3, 2, 3)$; the option is '$x_1\ y_2\ p_{12}\ p_{22}\ x_{13}\ y_{23}$' as in answer 366. Case (ii) arises when $(a, b, c, d) = (1, 3, 0, 1)$. Case (iii) arises when $(a, b) = (2, 3)$. Case (iv) arises when $(a, b, c, d) = (0, 1, 0, 1)$; the complement $(3, 4, 4, 5)$ isn't a valid subrectangle in answer 366. Case (v) arises when $(a, b, c, d) = (1, 3, 1, 3)$; cells p_{22} and p_{23} occur also in the complement $(1, 3, 2, 4)$. And case (vi) arises when $(a, b, c, d) = (0, 1, 4, 5)$; the merged option is the union of '$x_0\ y_4\ p_{04}\ x_{01}\ y_{45}\ t_1\ t_2$' and '$x_3\ y_0\ p_{30}\ x_{34}\ y_{01}$'. (Well, x_0 and y_0 are actually omitted, as suggested in answer 360.)

Size 8×16 has (6703, 1984, 10132, 1621, 47) solutions, of orders (26, ..., 30).

371. (a) Again we merge compatible options, as in answer 370. But now $(a, b, c, d) \to (c, d, n-b, n-a) \to (n-b, n-c, n-b, n-a) \to (n-b, n-a, c, d)$, so we typically must merge *four* options instead of two. The rules are: Reject if $a = n - 1$ and $c + d > n$, or $c = n - 1$ and $a + b < n$, or $b = 1$ and $c + d < n$, or $d = 1$ and $a + b > n$. Also reject if (a, b, c, d) is lexicographically greater than any of its three successors. But accept, without merging, if $(a, b, c, d) = (c, d, n-b, n-a)$. Otherwise reject if $b > c$ and $b+d > n$, or if $b > n/2$ and $c < n/2$ and $d > n/2$, because of intersection. Also reject if $a + b = n$ or $c + d = n$, because of the motley condition. Otherwise merge four options into one.

For example, the merged option when $n = 4$ and $(a, b, c, d) = (0, 1, 2, 4)$ is 'x_0 y_2 p_{02} p_{03} x_{01} y_{24} t_1 x_2 y_3 p_{23} p_{33} x_{24} y_{34} x_3 y_0 p_{30} p_{31} x_{34} y_{24} p_{00} p_{10} x_{02} y_{01}', except that x_0 and y_0 are omitted. Notice that it's important not to include an item x_i or y_j twice, when merging in cases that have $a = c$ or $b = d$ or $a = n - d$ or $b = n - c$.

(b) With bidiagonal symmetry it's possible to have $(a, b, c, d) = (c, d, a, b)$ but $(a, b, c, d) \neq (n - d, n - c, n - b, n - a)$, or vice versa. Thus we'll sometimes merge two options, we'll sometimes merge four, and we'll sometimes accept without merging. In detail: Reject if $a = n - 1$ and $c + d > n$, or $c = n - 1$ and $a + b > n$, or $b = 1$ and $c + d < n$, or $d = 1$ and $a + b < n$. Also reject if (a, b, c, d) is lexicographically greater than any of its three successors. But accept, without merging, if $a = c = n - d = n - b$. Otherwise reject if $b > c$ or $b > n - d$ or $a + b = n$ or $c + d = n$. Otherwise merge two or four distinct options into one.

Examples when $n = 4$ are: 'x_1 y_1 p_{11} p_{12} p_{21} p_{22} x_{13} y_{13}'; 'x_0 y_3 p_{03} x_{01} y_{34} t_1 x_3 y_0 p_{30} x_{34} y_{01}'; 'x_0 y_2 p_{02} x_{34} y_{23} t_1 x_1 y_3 p_{13} x_{12} y_{34} x_3 y_1 p_{31} x_{34} y_{12} x_2 y_0 p_{20} x_{23} y_{01}'; again with x_0 and y_0 suppressed.

(c) The unique solution for $n = 10$ is shown. [The total number of such patterns for $n = (10, 11, \ldots, 16)$ turns out to be $(1, 0, 3, 6, 28, 20, 354)$. All 354 of the 16×16 solutions are found in only 560 megamems; they have orders 34, 36, and 38–44. Furthermore the number of $n \times n$ motley dissections with symmetry (a), for $n = (3, 4, 5, \ldots, 16)$, turns out to be $(1, 0, 2, 2, 8, 18, 66, 220, 1024, 4178, 21890, 102351, 598756, 3275503)$, respectively. Algorithm M needs 3.3 teramems when $n = 16$; those patterns have orders $4k$ and $4k + 1$ for $k = 8, 9, \ldots, 13$.]

372. (a) This fact, and the others noted below, can be proved by induction on the number of rooms: If the lower right corner of the upper left room is a $\perp$ junction, we can "flatten" and remove that room by bringing its right bound left; otherwise we can bring its bottom bound up. All floorplans can be built up by reversing this flattening process.

Let the rooms be $r_1 \ldots r_n$ in diagonal order and $r_{p_1} \ldots r_{p_n}$ in antidiagonal order (left to right). Then $r_i \Downarrow r_j \iff i < j$ and i follows j in the permutation $p = p_1 \ldots p_n$; $r_i \Rightarrow r_j \iff i < j$ and i precedes j in p. The number of horizontal bounds is the number of *descents* in p, plus 2. The number of vertical bounds is the number of *ascents*, plus 2.

(b) Here's the twin tree structure for the example. Notice that its leftward and rightward chains are the ordered sequences of rooms adjacent to the bounds.

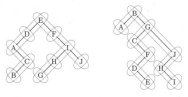

Every twin tree structure arises in a remarkably simple way: Let $p = p_1 p_2 \ldots p_n$ be any permutation of $\{1, 2, \ldots, n\}$. Obtain T_0 by inserting p_1, p_2, $\ldots$, p_n into an initially empty binary tree; obtain T_1 similarly by inserting p_n, $\ldots$, p_2, p_1. Those trees can be constructed in linear time (exercise 6.2.2–50); and it's easy to see that they are twins, both with inorder $12 \ldots n$. Although different permutations can yield the same twin tree, exactly one *Baxter permutation* (exercise MPR–135) does so; and it can be computed from the twin tree in linear time(!). Thus there are nice one-to-one correspondences between floorplans, twin trees, and Baxter permutations.

[Floorplans are important in VLSI layout, where rooms correspond to modules and bounds correspond to channels. Twin trees were introduced by S. Dulucq and O. Guibert in *Discrete Math.* **157** (1996), 91–106, purely for their combinatorial interest, then applied to floorplans by B. Yao, H. Chen, C.-K. Cheng, and R. Graham in *ACM Trans. Design Aut. Electronic Syst.* **8** (2003), 55–80. See also J. M. Hart, *Int. J. Comp. Inf. Sciences* **9** (1980), 307–321; H. Murata, K. Fujiyoshi, T. Watanabe, and Y. Kajitani, *Proc. Asia South Pacific Design Aut. Conf.* **2** (1997), 625–633; E. Ackerman, G. Barequet, and R. Y. Pinter, *Discrete Applied Mathematics* **154** (2006), 1674–1684; and the author's programs FLOORPLAN-TO-TWINTREE, TWINTREE-TO-BAXTER, BAXTER-TO-FLOORPLAN, available online (2021).]

373. The reduction of a perfectly decomposed rectangle is a motley dissection. Thus we can find all perfectly decomposed rectangles by "unreducing" all motley dissections.

For example, the only motley dissection of order 5 is the 3×3 pinwheel. Thus the perfectly decomposed $m \times n$ rectangles of order 5 with integer dimensions are the positive integer solutions to $x_1 + x_2 + x_3 = m$, $y_1 + y_2 + y_3 = n$ such that the ten values x_1, x_2, x_3, $x_1 + x_2$, $x_2 + x_3$, y_1, y_2, y_3, $y_1 + y_2$, $y_2 + y_3$ are distinct. Those equations are readily factored into two easy backtrack problems, one for m and one for n, each producing a list of five-element sets $\{x_1, x_2, x_3, x_1 + x_2, x_2 + x_3\}$; then we search for all pairs of disjoint solutions to the two subproblems. In this way we quickly see that the equations have just two essentially different solutions when $m = n = 11$, namely $(x_1, x_2, x_3) = (1, 7, 3)$ and $(y_1, y_2, y_3) = (2, 4, 5)$ or $(5, 4, 2)$. The smallest perfectly decomposed squares of order 5 therefore have size 11×11, and there are two of them (shown below); they were discovered by M. van Hertog, who reported them to Martin Gardner in May 1979. (Incidentally, a 12×12 square can also be perfectly decomposed.)

There are no solutions of order 6. Those of orders 7, 8, 9, 10 must come respectively from motley dissections of sizes 4×4, 4×5, 5×5, and 5×6. By looking at them all, we find that the smallest $n \times n$ squares respectively have $n = 18$, 21, 24, and 28. Each of the order-t solutions shown here uses rectangles of dimensions $\{1, 2, \ldots, 2t\}$, except in the case $t = 9$: There's a *unique* perfectly decomposed 24×24 square of order 9, and it uses the dimensions $\{1, 2, \ldots, 17, 19\}$.

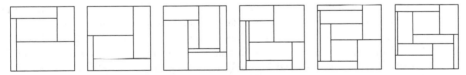

[W. H. Cutler introduced perfectly decomposed rectangles in *JRM* **12** (1979), 104–111.]

374. (a) False (but close). Let the individual dimensions be z_1, $\ldots$, z_{2t}, where $z_1 \leq \cdots \leq z_{2t}$. Then we have $\{w_1, h_1\} = \{z_1, z_{2t}\}$, $\{w_2, h_2\} = \{z_2, z_{2t-1}\}$, $\ldots$, $\{w_t, h_t\} = \{z_t, z_{t+1}\}$; consequently $z_1 < \cdots < z_t \leq z_{t+1} < \cdots < z_{2t}$. But $z_t = z_{t+1}$ is possible.

(b) False (but close). If the reduced rectangle is $m \times n$, one of its subrectangles might be $1 \times n$ or $m \times 1$; a motley dissection must be *strict*.

(c) True. Label the rectangles $\{a, b, c, d, e\}$ as shown. Then there's a contradiction: $w_b > w_d \iff w_e > w_c \iff h_e < h_c \iff h_d < h_b \iff w_b < w_d$.

(d) The order can't be 6, because the reduction would then have to be a pinwheel together with a 1×3 subrectangle, and the argument in (c) would still apply. Thus the order must be 7, and we must show that the second dissection of exercise 365 doesn't work. Labeling its regions $\{a, \ldots, g\}$ as shown, we have $h_d > h_a$; hence $w_a > w_d$. Also $h_e > h_b$; so $w_b > w_e$. Oops: $w_f > w_g$ and $h_f > h_g$.

In the other motley 4×4 dissection of exercise 365 we obviously have

$$w_4 < w_5, \quad w_4 < w_6, \quad w_6 < w_7, \quad h_4 < h_3, \quad h_3 < h_1, \quad h_4 < h_2;$$

therefore $h_4 > h_5$, $h_4 > h_6$, $h_6 > h_7$, $w_4 > w_3$, $w_3 > w_1$, $w_4 > w_2$. Now $h_5 < h_6 \iff w_5 > w_6 \iff w_2 > w_3 \iff h_2 < h_3 \iff h_6 + h_7 < h_5$. Hence $h_5 < h_6$ implies $h_5 > h_6$; we must have $h_5 > h_6$, thus also $h_2 > h_3$. Finally $h_2 < h_1$, because $h_7 < h_5$.

(e) The condition is clearly necessary. Conversely, given any such pair of solutions, the rectangles $w_1 \times \alpha h_1, \dots, w_t \times \alpha h_t$ are incomparable for all large enough α.

[Many questions remain unanswered: Is it NP-hard to determine whether or not a given motley dissection supports an incomparable dissection? Is there a motley dissection that supports incomparable dissections having two different permutation labels? Can a *symmetric* motley dissection ever support an incomparable dissection?]

375. (a) By exercise 374(d), the widths and heights must satisfy

$$w_5 = w_2 + w_4, \quad w_6 = w_3 + w_4, \quad w_7 = w_1 + w_3 + w_4;$$
$$h_3 = h_4 + h_5, \quad h_2 = h_4 + h_6 + h_7, \quad h_1 = h_4 + h_5 + h_6.$$

To prove the hint, consider answer 374(a). Each z_j for $1 \le j \le t$ can be either h or w; then z_{2t+1-j} is the opposite. So there are 2^t ways to shuffle the h's and w's together.

For example, suppose all the h's come first, namely $h_7 < \cdots < h_1 \le w_1 < \cdots < w_7$:

$$1 \le h_7, \quad h_7 + 1 \le h_6, \quad h_6 + 1 \le h_5, \quad h_5 + 1 \le h_4, \quad h_4 + 1 \le h_4 + h_5,$$
$$h_4 + h_5 + 1 \le h_4 + h_6 + h_7, \quad h_4 + h_6 + h_7 + 1 \le h_4 + h_5 + h_6,$$
$$h_4 + h_5 + h_6 \le w_1, \quad w_1 + 1 \le w_2, \quad w_2 + 1 \le w_3, \quad w_3 + 1 \le w_4,$$
$$w_4 + 1 \le w_2 + w_4, \quad w_2 + w_4 + 1 \le w_3 + w_4, \quad w_3 + w_4 + 1 \le w_1 + w_3 + w_4.$$

The least semiperimeter in this case is the smallest value of $w_1 + w_2 + w_3 + w_4 + h_7 + h_6 + h_5 + h_4$, subject to those inequalities; and one easily sees that the minimum is 68, achieved when $h_7 = 2$, $h_6 = 3$, $h_5 = 4$, $h_4 = 5$, $w_1 = 12$, $w_2 = 13$, $w_3 = 14$, $w_4 = 15$.

Consider also the alternating case, $w_1 < h_7 < w_2 < h_6 < w_3 < h_5 < w_4 \le h_4 < w_2 + w_4 < h_4 + h_5 < w_3 + w_4 < h_4 + h_6 + h_7 < w_1 + w_3 + w_4 < h_4 + h_5 + h_6$. This case turns out to be infeasible. (Indeed, any case with $h_6 < w_3 < h_5$ requires $h_4 + h_5 < w_3 + w_4$, hence it needs $h_4 < w_4$.) Only 52 of the 128 cases are actually feasible.

Each of the 128 subproblems is a classic example of linear programming, and a decent LP solver will resolve it almost instantly. The minimum semiperimeter with seven subrectangles is 35, obtained uniquely in the case $w_1 < w_2 < w_3 < h_7 < h_6 < h_5 < h_4 \le w_4 < w_5 < w_6 < w_7 < h_3 < h_2 < h_1$ (or the same case with $w_4 \leftrightarrow h_4$) by setting $w_1 = 1$, $w_2 = 2$, $w_3 = 3$, $h_7 = 4$, $h_6 = 5$, $h_5 = 6$, $h_4 = w_4 = 7$. The next-best case has semiperimeter 43. In one case the best-achievable semiperimeter is 103!

To find the smallest square, we simply add the constraint $w_1 + w_2 + w_3 + w_4 = h_7 + h_6 + h_5 + h_4$ to each subproblem. Now only four of the 128 are feasible. The minimum side, 34, occurs uniquely when $(w_1, w_2, w_3, w_4, h_7, h_6, h_5, h_4) = (3, 7, 10, 14, 6, 8, 9, 11)$.

(b) With eight subrectangles the reduced pattern is 4×5. We can place a 4×1 column at the right of either the 4×4 pattern or its transpose; or we can use one of the first two 4×5 patterns in exercise 365. (The other six patterns can be ruled out, using arguments similar to those of answer 374.) The labeled diagrams are

For each of these four choices there are 256 easy subproblems to consider. The best semiperimeters are respectively $(44, 44, 44, 56)$; the best square sizes are respectively — and surprisingly — $(27, 36, 35, 35)$. [With eight subrectangles we can dissect a significantly smaller square than we can with seven! Furthermore, no smaller square can be incomparably dissected, integerwise, because nine subrectangles would be too many.] One way to achieve 44 is with $(w_1, w_2, w_3, w_4, w_5, h_8, h_7, h_6, h_5) = (4, 5, 6, 7, 8, 1, 2, 3, 8)$ in the third diagram. The only way to achieve a square of side 27 is with $(w_1, w_2, w_3, w_4, w_5, h_8, h_7, h_6, h_5) = (1, 3, 5, 7, 11, 4, 6, 8, 9)$ in the first diagram.

These linear programs usually have integer solutions; but sometimes they don't. For example, the optimum for the second diagram in the case $h_8 < h_7 < w_1 < h_6 < w_2 < w_3 < w_4 < h_5$ turns out to be $97/2$, achievable when $(w_1, w_2, w_3, w_4, w_5, h_8, h_7, h_6, h_5) = (7, 11, 13, 15, 17, 3, 5, 9, 17)/2$. The minimum rises to 52, if we restrict to integer solutions, achieved by $(w_1, w_2, w_3, w_4, w_5, h_8, h_7, h_6, h_5) = (4, 6, 7, 8, 9, 1, 3, 5, 9)$.

[The theory of incomparable dissections was developed by A. C. C. Yao, E. M. Reingold, and B. Sands in *JRM* **8** (1976), 112–119. For generalizations to three dimensions, see C. H. Jepsen, *Mathematics Magazine* **59** (1986), 283–292.]

376. This is an incomparable dissection in which exercise 374(d) applies. Let's try first to solve the equations $a(x+y+z) = bx = c(w+x) = d(w+x+y) = (a+b)w = (b+c)y = (b+c+d)z = 1$, by setting $b = x = 1$. We find successively $c = 1/(w+1)$, $a = (1-w)/w$, $y = (w+1)/(w+2)$, $d = (w+2)/((w+1)(w+3))$, $z = (w+1)(w+3)/((w+2)(w+4))$. Therefore $x + y + z - 1/a = (2w+3)(2w^2+6w-5)/((w-1)(w+2)(w+4))$, and we must have $2w^2+6w = 5$. The positive root of this quadratic is $w = (\sqrt{} - 3)/2$, where $\sqrt{} = \sqrt{19}$.

Having decomposed the rectangle $(a+b+c+d) \times (w+x+y+z)$ into seven different rectangles of area 1, we normalize it, dividing (a, b, c, d) by $a + b + c + d = \frac{7}{15}(\sqrt{}+1)$ and dividing (w, x, y, z) by $w+x+y+z = \frac{5}{6}(\sqrt{}-1)$. This gives the desired tiling (shown), with rectangles of dimensions $\frac{1}{14}(7-\sqrt{}) \times \frac{1}{15}(7+\sqrt{})$, $\frac{5}{42}(-1+\sqrt{}) \times \frac{1}{15}(1+\sqrt{})$, $\frac{5}{21} \times \frac{3}{5}$, $\frac{1}{21}(8-\sqrt{}) \times \frac{1}{15}(8+\sqrt{})$, $\frac{1}{21}(8+\sqrt{}) \times \frac{1}{15}(8-\sqrt{})$, $\frac{5}{42}(1 + \sqrt{}) \times \frac{1}{15}(-1 + \sqrt{})$, $\frac{1}{14}(7 + \sqrt{}) \times \frac{1}{15}(7 - \sqrt{})$.

[See W. A. A. Nuij, *AMM* **81** (1974), 665–666. To get eight different rectangles of area 1/8, we can shrink one dimension by 7/8 and attach a rectangle $(1/8) \times 1$. Then to get nine of area 1/9, we can shrink the *other* dimension by 8/9 and attach a $(1/9) \times 1$ sliver. And so on. The eight-rectangle problem also has two other solutions, supported by the third and fourth 4×5 patterns in exercise 375(b).]

377. (a) We can obtain $h \times w$ except when w is odd and h is not a multiple of 3. For if w is even, we can concatenate $w/2$ instances of size $h \times 2$; if h is a multiple of 3, we can concatenate $h/3$ instances of size $3 \times w$; otherwise we can't use concatenation to obtain w as the sum of two even numbers, or h as the sum of two multiples of 3.

(b) The shapes $2{\times}3$, $2{\times}4$, $2{\times}5$, $3{\times}4$, $3{\times}5$, $3{\times}6$, $3{\times}7$ are necessary and sufficient. (And then $\Lambda(S) = \{h{\times}w \mid h > 1, w > 3\} \cup \{2h{\times}3 \mid h \geq 1\}$.)

(c) $S = \{2{\times}4, 3{\times}8, 4{\times}2, 8{\times}3\}$.

(d) $h{\times}w \in S$ if and only if $h = an'$ for some a with $\lfloor m/n' \rfloor < a < 2\lfloor m/n' \rfloor + 2$ and $w = bn''$ for some b with $\lfloor m/n'' \rfloor < b < 2\lfloor m/n'' \rfloor + 2$, where $n' = n/\gcd(n, w)$ and $n'' = n/\gcd(n, h)$.

378. Consider first a one-dimensional analog: If A is a set of positive integers, let $\Lambda(A)$ be the integers obtainable by adding together one or more elements of A. We can prove that any set B of positive integers has a finite subset A such that $B \subseteq \Lambda(A)$. For if B is empty, there's nothing to prove; otherwise let $b = \min(B)$. Let q_r be the smallest element of B such that $q_r \bmod b = r$, for $0 \le r < b$, or let q_r be undefined if no such element exists. Then every element of B is some q_r plus a multiple of $q_0 = b$.

Therefore in two dimensions, there's a finite set $X = \{h_1 \times w_1, \ldots, h_t \times w_t\} \subseteq T$ such that the width of every element of T is in $\Lambda(X^*)$, where $X^* = \{w_1, \ldots, w_t\}$ is the set of widths in X. Let $p = h_1 \ldots h_t$ be the product of all heights in X. It follows that $p \times w \in \Lambda(X)$ whenever $h \times w \in T$.

For $0 \le r < p$, let T_r be the elements $h \times w$ of T with $h \bmod p = r$, and let Q_r be a finite subset of T_r such that every element of T_r has a width in $\Lambda(Q_r^*)$. Let q be the largest height of any element of any Q_r. Notice that if $h \times w \in T$ with $h > q$, and if $h' \times w' \in Q_{h \bmod p}$, we have $h \times w' \in \Lambda(X \cup Q_r)$, because $p \times w' \in \Lambda(X)$ and $h - h'$ is a positive multiple of p. Hence $h \times w \in \Lambda(\{h \times w' \mid h' \times w' \in Q_r\}) \subseteq \Lambda(X \cup Q_r)$.

Finally, for $1 \le i \le q$, let T_i' be the elements $h \times w$ of T with $h = i$, and let P_i be a finite subset of T_i' such that every element of T_i' has a width in $\Lambda(P_i^*)$. Then every element of T belongs to $\Lambda(X \cup Q_0 \cup \cdots \cup Q_{p-1} \cup P_1 \cup \cdots \cup P_q)$.

[This argument extends to any number of dimensions. See N. G. de Bruijn and D. A. Klarner, *Philips Research Reports* **30** (1975), 337*–343*; Michael Reid, *J. Combinatorial Theory* **A111** (2005), 89–105.]

379. A 2×5 packing is obvious; thus the basis contains 2×5 (and 5×2). The case $5 \times w$ and $w > 2$ has a packing only if $5 \times (w - 2)$ does. The case $h = 3$ is clearly impossible.

The case $h = 7$ is more interesting: 7×10 follows by concatenation, while 7×15 has 80 distinct and easily found solutions. Hence the basis contains 7×15 and 15×7.

This basis is complete: We've shown that if h is not a multiple of 5, $h \times w$ is possible whenever w is a multiple of 5, except when $h = 1$ or $h = 3$ or (h is odd and $w = 5$). If h and w are both multiples of 5, $h \times w$ is possible except when h or w equals 5 and the other is odd. [See W. R. Marshall, *J. Combinatorial Theory* **A77** (1997), 181–192; M. Reid, *J. Combinatorial Theory* **A80** (1997), 106–123.]

380. The minimum basis consists of 15×15 (see Fig. 73) plus 39 pairs $\{h \times w, w \times h\}$, where $(h, w) \in \{(5, 10), (9, 20), (9, 30), (9, 45), (9, 55), (10, 14), (10, 16), (10, 23), (10, 27), (11, 20), (11, 30), (11, 35), (11, 45), (12, 50), (12, 55), (12, 60), (12, 65), (12, 70), (12, 75), (12, 80), (12, 85), (12, 90), (12, 95), (13, 20), (13, 30), (13, 35), (13, 45), (14, 15), (15, 16), (15, 17), (15, 19), (15, 21), (15, 22), (15, 23), (17, 20), (17, 25), (18, 25), (18, 35), (22, 25)\}$. (This problem has a long history, going back to the discovery by David Klarner that ten *one-sided* Y pentominoes can be packed uniquely in a 5×10 box [*Fibonacci Quarterly* **3** (1965), 20]. Klarner eventually found 14 of the 39 basic pairs by hand, including the difficult case $(12, 80)$. The other nine cases $(12, w)$ were found by J. Bitner [*JRM* **7** (1974), 276–278], using a frontier-transition method that works much faster than Algorithm X in cases where h is much less than w. The complete set was nailed down by T. Sillke in 1992 [unpublished], then independently by J. Fogel, M. Goldenberg, and A. Liu [*Mathematics and Informatics Quarterly* **11** (2001), 133–137].)

381. Algorithm X quickly finds examples for $n = 7, 11, 12, 13, 15, 16, 17$; hence it's possible for all $n \ge 11$. [J. B. Kelly discovered the case $n = 7$ in *AMM* **73** (1966), 468. Are *all* packable rectangles consequences of this basis?]

382. Let the back corner in the illustration be the point 777, and write just '*abcdef*' instead of $[a .. b] \times [c .. d] \times [e .. f)$. The subcuboids are 670517 (270601) 176705 (012706) 051767 (060127), 561547 (260312) 475615 (122603) 154756 (031226), 351446 (361324) 463514 (243613) 144635 (132436), 575757 (020202), 454545 (232323) — with the 11 mirror images in parentheses — plus the central cubie 343434. Notice that each of the 28 possible intervals is used in each dimension, except $[0 .. 4)$, $[1 .. 6)$, $[2 .. 5)$, $[3 .. 7)$, $[0 .. 7)$.

> *I started from a central cube and built outwards, all the while*
> *staring at the 24-cell in Hilbert's Geometry and the Imagination.*
> — SCOTT KIM, letter to Martin Gardner (December 1975)

383. (Solution by Helmut Postl.) We can use the 7-tuples $(2, 10, 27, 17, 11, 20, 5)$, $(1, 14, 18, 8, 21, 24, 6)$, $(3, 19, 16, 7, 34, 9, 4)$ to "unreduce" the 1st, 2nd, 3rd coordinates. For example, subcuboid 670517 becomes $5 \times (1+14+18+8+21) \times (19+16+7+34+9+4)$. The resulting dissection, of a $92 \times 92 \times 92$ cube into blocks of sizes $1 \times 70 \times 87$, $2 \times 77 \times 88$, $3 \times 80 \times 86$, $4 \times 67 \times 91$, $5 \times 62 \times 89$, $6 \times 79 \times 90$, $7 \times 8 \times 17$, $9 \times 51 \times 65$, $10 \times 38 \times 71$, $11 \times 21 \times 34$, $12 \times 15 \times 22$, $13 \times 25 \times 30$, $14 \times 39 \times 66$, $16 \times 18 \times 27$, $19 \times 33 \times 75$, $20 \times 47 \times 61$, $23 \times 32 \times 48$, $24 \times 36 \times 76$, $26 \times 37 \times 50$, $28 \times 40 \times 43$, $29 \times 31 \times 42$, $35 \times 44 \times 53$, $41 \times 45 \times 54$, makes a fiendishly difficult puzzle.

How were those magic 7-tuples discovered? An exhaustive search such as that of exercise 374 was out of the question. Postl first looked for 7-tuples that led to very few dimensions in the "popular" ranges $[13 \mathinner{.\,.} 23]$ and $[29 \mathinner{.\,.} 39]$. With luck, a large set of other 7-tuples would lead to no conflict in the 23 relevant subtotals; and with further luck, some of those wouldn't conflict with each other.

(Postl also proved that no $91 \times 91 \times 91$ decomposition is possible.)

384. The exact cover problem of answer 365 is readily extended to 3D: The option for every admissible subcuboid $[a \mathinner{.\,.} b) \times [c \mathinner{.\,.} d) \times [e \mathinner{.\,.} f)$ has $6 + (b-a)(d-c)(f-e)$ items, namely x_a y_c z_e x_{ab} y_{cd} z_{ef} and the cells p_{ijk} that are covered.

We can do somewhat better, as in exercise 366: Most of the improvement in that answer can be achieved also 3Dwise, if we simply omit cases where $a = l - 1$ and either $c + d > m$ or $e + f > n$. Furthermore, if $m = n$ we can omit cases with $(e, f) < (c, d)$.

Without those omissions, Algorithm M handles the case $l = m = n = 7$ in 98 teramems, producing 2432 solutions. With them, the running time is reduced to 43 teramems, and 397 solutions are found.

(The $7 \times 7 \times 7$ problem can be factored into subproblems, based on the patterns that appear on the cube's six visible faces. These patterns reduce to 5×5 pinwheels, and it takes only about 40 Mμ to discover all 152 possibilities. Furthermore, those possibilities reduce to only 5 cases, under the 48 symmetries of a cube. Each of those cases can then be solved by embedding the 5×5 reduced patterns into 7×7 unreduced patterns, considering $15^3 = 3375$ possibilities for the three faces adjacent to vertex 000. Most of those possibilities are immediately ruled out. Hence each of the five cases can be solved by Algorithm C in about 70 Gμ — making the total running time about 350 Gμ. However, this 120-fold increase in speed cost the author two man-days of work.)

All three methods showed that, up to isomorphism, exactly 56 distinct motley cubes of size $7 \times 7 \times 7$ are possible. Each of those 56 dissections has exactly 23 cuboids. Nine of them are symmetric under the mapping $xyz \mapsto (7-x)(7-y)(7-z)$; and one of those nine, namely the one in exercise 382, has six automorphisms.

[These runs confirm and slightly extend the work of W. H. Cutler in *JRM* **12** (1979), 104–111. His computer program found exactly 56 distinct possibilities, when restricting the search to solutions that have exactly 23 cuboids.]

385. No; there are infinitely many. For example, Postl has constructed a primitive $11 \times 11 \times 13$ by pasting Kim's $7 \times 7 \times 7$ to its mirror image, perturbing a few planes normal to the splice, and reducing.

386. The twelve possible symmetries can be represented as the permutations of $\{0, 1, 2, 3, 4, 5\}$ defined by $x \mapsto (ax + b) \bmod 6$, where $a = \pm 1$ and $0 \le b < 6$; let's denote that permutation by b or $\bar{b}$, according to the sign of a. There are ten symmetry classes, depending on the automorphisms that are present: (i) all twelve; (ii) $\{0,\bar0,2,\bar2,4,\bar4\}$; (iii) $\{0,\bar1,2,\bar3,4,\bar5\}$; (iv) $\{0,1,2,3,4,5\}$; (v) $\{0,3,\bar0,\bar3\}$ or $\{0,3,\bar2,\bar5\}$ or $\{0,3,\bar4,\bar1\}$; (vi) $\{0,2,4\}$; (vii) $\{0,3\}$; (viii) $\{0,\bar0\}$ or $\{0,\bar2\}$ or $\{0,\bar4\}$; (ix) $\{0,\bar1\}$ or $\{0,\bar3\}$ or $\{0,\bar5\}$; (x) $\{0\}$.

(i)	(ii)	(iii)	(iv)	(v)	(vi)	(vii)	(viii)	(ix)	(x)
full	triaxial-a	triaxial-b	60°	biaxial	120°	180°	axial-a	axial-b	none

(i)	(ii)	(iii)	(iv)	(v)	(vi)	(vii)	(viii)	(ix)	(x)
full	triaxial-a	triaxial-b	60°	biaxial	120°	180°	axial-a	axial-b	none

(Types (ii), (iii) and (viii), (ix) depend on whether a reflection is left-right or top-down. Notice that there are $12/k$ base placements when there are k automorphisms.)

387. The 24 potential symmetries S can be represented as signed permutations of $\{\pm1,\pm2,\pm3\}$, meaning that coordinates are permuted and/or complemented. Using the notation of answer 7.2.1.2–20, they are 123, $1\bar2\bar3$, $\bar12\bar3$, ..., $\bar3\bar2\bar1$, where the number of inversions of the permutation plus the number of complementations is even.

Each of those symmetries is a rotation in 3-space about some line through the origin. (After a polycube has been rotated by one of its symmetries, we should shift the result, if necessary, to bring it into the original position.) For example, $\bar132$ takes $(x,y,z)\mapsto(c-x,z,y)$; it's a rotation of 180° about the diagonal line $x=c/2$, $y=z$. It's a symmetry of the bent tricube $\{000,001,010\}$ when $c=0$; it's a symmetry of the L-twist $\{000,001,100,110\}$ when $c=1$.

All subgroups of this group are easily found by constructing the BDD for the Boolean function whose 24 variables are the potential symmetries. Indeed, all subsets of any set S that are closed under any given binary operator $\star$ on that set are the solutions to $\bigwedge_{x,y\in S}(\neg x\vee\neg y\vee(x\star y))$. In this case the resulting BDD (found in 2.5 Mμ) has 197 nodes, and it characterizes exactly 30 subgroups.

Two subgroups T and T' are said to be *conjugate* if $T'=t^-Tt$ for some $t\in S$. Such subgroups are considered to be equivalent, because they amount to viewing the objects from a different direction. The distinct conjugacy classes of subgroups according to this equivalence relation are called the "symmetry types," and there are 11 of them:

(i)	(ii)	(iii)	(iv)	(v)	(vi)	(vii)	(viii)	(ix)	(x)	(xi)

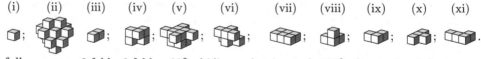

full	even	8-fold	6-fold	90°	bidiagonal	tricentral	120°	diagonal	axial	none

Class (ii) consists of the 12 symmetries whose permutations are even. The smallest polycube which admits these symmetries and no more — and hence it has just two base placements — contains 20 cubies, with 12 surrounding a central core of 8. Class (iv) has one symmetry for each permutation of the three coordinates. Classes (iii), (v), (vi), (vii), (ix), (x), (xi) correspond to the eight symmetry types of a square, with reflections implemented by "turning the square over" to the opposite side. In this interpretation biaxial symmetry becomes "tricentral," because it corresponds to central symmetry about each coordinate axis. The former class called "180°" is now the same as "axial," when viewed from either of the two other axes. [Many of these twelve examples have reflective symmetries too; but those don't count. Under the full set of 48 hyperoctahedral symmetries, when reflections are allowed, there are 33 symmetry types(!), nicely presented by W. F. Lunnon in *Graph Theory and Computing* (Academic Press, 1972), 101–108. Lunnon also exhibited the ten symmetry types for polyhexes on pages 87–100.]

388. The directed path of four weak clues in (a) is equivalent to the five strong clues $(1, 2, 3, 4, 5)$. Then there are "hidden singles" in columns 1 and 2, leading to a "naked single" in cell $(4, 2)$, etc.; we cruise to victory without branching. Puzzle (b) has a naked single in $(4, 2)$ — and we notice, by the way, that the middle cell needn't be 5 even though it is greater than each of its four neighbors. Then $(4, 4)$ is naked, and so on; again everything is forced. Puzzle (c) begins with hidden singles, which place the three missing 1s and then the 5 in row 0. After we fix cell $(4, 2)$, the rest falls into place.

a)
```
4  5  1  3  2
            ∧
5> 4  2> 1  3
3  1  5  2  4
      ∨
2  3< 4  5  1
   ∨
1< 2  3  4  5
```

b)
```
3> 1  4  5  2
2  3  1  4  5
            ∧
5  2< 3> 1  4
            ∨
4  5  2  3  1
            ∧
1  4< 5  2  3
```

c)
```
3  5  1  2< 4
4  1  5  3  2
2  3  4  5  1 .
5  4  2  1  3
1  2< 3  4  5
```

[*Historical note:* Futoshiki was invented by Yoshihiko Asao, who called it Dainarism ("Greater Than"); see *Puzzle Communication Nikoli* **92** (September 2000).]

389. In general, given a digraph in which each vertex v is supposed to be given an integer label $l(v)$ with $l(v) \geq a(v)$, where the lower bounds $a(v)$ have been specified, we can refine them as follows: For each vertex with $d^+(v) > 0$, push $v \Rightarrow S$, where S is an initially empty stack. Then while S is nonempty, repeatedly do this: Pop $S \Rightarrow v$; for each w with $v \longrightarrow w$ and $a(w) \leq a(v)$, set $a(w) \leftarrow a(v)+1$, and push $w \Rightarrow S$ if $d^+(w) > 0$.

A similar algorithm will refine a given set of upper bounds $b(v)$. For futoshiki, we apply these algorithms with $a(v) = 1$ and $b(v) = n$ initially, except that $a(v) = b(v) = l$ when a strong clue has specified v's label. (*Note:* This method isn't clever enough to prove that the middle element of puzzle (b) must be 3 or more. But it's still very useful.)

390. In both cases we use primary items p_{ij}, r_{ik}, and c_{jk} for $0 \leq i, j < n$ and $1 \leq k \leq n$, as we did for sudoku. There will be one option analogous to (30) for every (i, j) and for every $k \in [a_{ij} \mathinner{\ldotp\ldotp} b_{ij}]$, where the bounds a_{ij} and b_{ij} are calculated as in exercise 389.

(a) Suppose there are w weak clues, where the tth weak clue is $l(i_t j_t) < l(i'_t j'_t)$. Introduce $(n - 3)w$ secondary items g_{td} for $1 < d < n - 1$ and $1 \leq t \leq w$. Such an item informally means that $l(i_t j_t) > d$ and $d \geq l(i'_t j'_t)$; so we don't want it to appear twice. We include g_{td} in each option for ij with $d < k$, and in each option for $i'j'$ with $d \geq k$.

For example, the options for cells $(0, 0)$ and $(0, 1)$ in puzzle 388(b) are 'p_{00} r_{02} c_{02} g_{12} g_{13}', 'p_{00} r_{03} c_{03} g_{13}', 'p_{00} r_{04} c_{04}', 'p_{00} r_{05} c_{05}'; 'p_{01} r_{01} c_{11}', 'p_{01} r_{02} c_{12}', 'p_{01} r_{03} c_{13} g_{12}', 'p_{01} r_{04} c_{14} g_{12} g_{13}'. Another option is 'p_{22} r_{23} c_{23} g_{23} g_{33} g_{43} g_{53}'.

(b) Introduce w primary items g_t, and $3n^2$ secondary items P_{ij}, R_{ik}, C_{jk}. The options for p_{ij}, r_{ik}, and c_{jk} are 'p_{ij} r_{ik} c_{jk} $P_{ij}{:}k$ $R_{ik}{:}j$ $C_{jk}{:}i$' for $0 \leq i, j < n$ and $a_{ij} \leq k \leq b_{ij}$. The options for g_t are 'g_t $P_{i_t j_t}{:}k$ $P_{i'_t j'_t}{:}k'$ $R_{i_t k}{:}j_t$ $R_{i'_t k'}{:}j'_t$ $C_{j_t k}{:}i_t$ $C_{j'_t k'}{:}i'_t$' for $k < k'$, where k and k' are within the bounds for $l(i_t j_t)$ and $l(i'_t j'_t)$.

Experience shows that formulation (a) is a clear winner over formulation (b).

391. Given $5 \cdot 5 \cdot 5$ options 'p_{ij} r_{ik} c_{jk}' as in answer 390, Algorithm X needs just 230 megamems to generate $161280 = 5! \cdot 4! \cdot 56$ solutions. [Euler enumerated them in his major paper on latin squares [*Verhandelingen Genootschap Wetenschappen Vlissingen*

9 (1782), 85–239, §148], though he was nearly blind at the time.] Every 5×5 latin square has 40 pairs of adjacent elements, leading to a string of 40 inequality signs; and we can sort those 161280 strings. Only 115262 distinct strings actually occur; and only 82148 of them occur just once. The other 79132 cannot be identified by weak clues only.

392. Here are the first examples found of each type, and the total number of cases:

	(a) Unique solution		(b) No solutions		(c) Multiple solutions	
	(long path)	(no long path)	(long path)	(no long path)	(long path)	(no long path)
	2976	4000	369404	405636	1888424	242985880

(More detailed counting shows exactly (369404, 2976, 4216, 3584, ..., 80) cases with at least one long path and (0, 1, 2, 3, ..., 1344) solutions; (405636, 4000, 4400, 1888, ..., 72) cases with no long path and (0, 1, 2, 3, ..., 24128) solutions.) Example (i) below is one way to get the maximum number of solutions, using six particularly unhelpful clues.

The most interesting cases, of course, are those that make valid puzzles. They fall into equivalence classes under rotation and/or reflection and/or complementation; thus sixteen examples are typically equivalent to any given one. However, there are 46 equivalence classes with only eight members, self-dual under transposition, of which 26 have long paths (as in (ii), (iii), (iv) below) and 18 do not (as in (v), (vi), (vii)). Thus $(173+26)+(241+18) = 458$ essentially different futoshiki puzzles with six weak clues are valid; however, many of these are really the same, under row-and-column permutations that preserve all clues. The most difficult symmetric instance is probably (vii), because exercise 390 needs a 374-node search tree to solve it. (A clever solver will, however, deduce immediately that all diagonal elements of a symmetric puzzle must be 3!)

(i)   (ii)   (iii)   (iv)   (v)   (vi)   (vii)

393. The $5^6 = 15625$ ways to label six cells can be reduced to $\varpi_6 = 203$, by limiting consideration to restricted growth strings (Section 7.2.1.5), multiplying the results for every such string by $5^{\underline{k}}$ when it has k different labels. (In fact, only 202 such strings are relevant, because the last one (123456) will be multiplied by $5^{\underline{6}} = 0$ and never used.) Running through each subset of five cells, we find respectively (1877807500, 864000, 0, 0, 1296000, 10368000, ..., 144000) cases that have (0, 1, 2, 3, 4, 5, ..., 336) solutions.

0 solutions	1 solution	4 solutions	5 solutions	336 solutions	336 solutions

Every case with a unique solution is obtained from the example shown by independently permuting the rows, columns, and labels. (Indeed, $864000 = 5!^3/2$.)

394. Let there be h strong clues and $k = 5 - h$ weak clues. Four solutions are obtained only in (144, 2016, 2880) cases for $h = (1, 2, 3)$. In every such case, two rows and two columns are completely free from clues; thus the four solutions arise from swapping those two rows and/or those two columns. As in answer 392, most of the cases belong to classes of 16 puzzles that are equivalent under rotation, transposition, and/or complementation. But when $h = 3$ there are 30 classes of size 8, having transposition symmetry (see (iii) and (iv) below); also 6 self-dual classes of size 8 (see (v)). Hence there are $9 + 126 + (36 + 162) = 333$ inequivalent 4-solution 5-clue futoshikis altogether.

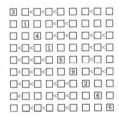

| (i) | (ii) | (iii) | (iv) | (v) | (vi) |

[This exercise was inspired by a talk that Dan Katz gave at the Joint Mathematics Meetings in January 2012. He observed, among other things, that valid puzzles exist with $h + k = 6$ for all values $0 \le h \le 6$. Indeed, we can start with example (iv) in answer 392, and repeatedly insert a clue (5, 1, 5, 1, 4, 2) while removing an inequality.]

[The minimum number of strong clues needed to specify an $n \times n$ latin square is known to be $\lfloor n^2/4 \rfloor$ for $n \le 8$. See R. Bean, arXiv:math/0403005 [math.CO] (2004).]

395. Let L solve (vi) in answer 394. [See Appendix E if you're stuck.] The only way to distinguish L from fifteen other latin squares that have the same string of 40 inequality signs is to give at least one clue 2 or 3 in a boundary row or column, at least one clue 4 or 5 in a boundary row or column, and at least one 4 or 5 in cells $\{(1,1), (1,3), (3,1), (3,3)\}$.

396. For example, here's one that Algorithm P+X solves in 90 Mμ. (See Appendix E.)

397. (a) Assuming an $m \times n$ grid, let there be $(m+1)(n+1) - 4$ primary "endpoint" items ij for $0 \le i \le m$, $0 \le j \le n$, and $[i=0] + [i=m] + [j=0] + [j=n] \le 1$; also "sheep" items s_{ij} when a sheep is in cell ij; also "start-stop" items $+$ and $-$. Let there be mn secondary items x_{ij} for $0 \le i < m$ and $0 \le j < n$, one for each cell. Three kinds of options are used: (i) There are $14(m-1)(n-1)$ "junction" options 'ij $x_{(i-1)(j-1)}{:}a$ $x_{(i-1)j}{:}b$ $x_{ij}{:}c$ $x_{i(j-1)}{:}d$', for $0 < i < m$ and $0 < j < n$ and $0 \le a, b, c, d \le 1$ and $(a = b$ or $b = c$ or $c = d)$. (ii) There are $2m + 2n - 4$ sets of four "boundary" options typified by '02 $x_{01}{:}0$ $x_{02}{:}0$', '02 $x_{01}{:}0$ $x_{02}{:}1$ $-$', '02 $x_{01}{:}1$ $x_{02}{:}0$ $+$', '02 $x_{01}{:}1$ $x_{02}{:}1$', for $0 \le i \le m$, $0 \le j \le n$, and $[i=0] + [i=m] + [j=0] + [j=n] = 1$; adjacent boundary cells, like x_{01} and x_{02} in this example, are listed in clockwise order. (For example, one of the options at the right boundary when $n = 5$ is '35 $x_{24}{:}0$ $x_{34}{:}1$ $-$'; one of the options at the left is '20 $x_{20}{:}1$ $x_{10}{:}0$ $+$'.) (iii) Each sheep has up to six "sheep" options, 's_{ij} $x_{ij}{:}1$ $x_{(i-1)j}{:}a$ $x_{i(j+1)}{:}b$ $x_{(i+1)j}{:}c$ $x_{i(j-1)}{:}d$', where $a + b + c + d = 2$; the x items are omitted if the corresponding cells lie outside of the grid, in which case their values are assumed to be 1. For example, the topmost sheep has only three options in the example puzzles, namely 's_{03} x_{03}:1 x_{04}:b x_{13}:c x_{02}:d', where $b + c + d = 1$.

This XCC problem for the rightmost example puzzle has five solutions:

To eliminate the spurious ones, we traverse the fence from '$+$' to '$-$', accepting a solution only if that path contains all of the color transitions between adjacent cells.

(b) There's a unique solution if we put k sheep into a diagonal of length k; but that puzzle is trivial, not "interesting." Random trials show that about one configuration in every 10,000 makes a suitable puzzle; the author found the first three examples below in that way. The fourth example was contrived by hand. All are solvable by hand:

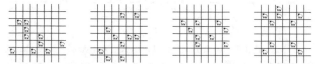

[E. Olson invented this game; see J. Henle, *Math. Intelligencer* **40**, 1 (2018), 69–70.]

398. The blanks in rows 0 and 4 of (c) can be filled with 3 and 5 in two ways.

[Tetsuya Miyamoto invented KenKen® in 2004, as an aid to education. The special case where all operations are multiplication, and all cages are rectangular, had been published by Ryuoh Yano in *Puzzle Communication Nikoli* **92** (September 2000).]

399. Set up an XCC problem with $3n^2$ primary items p_{ij}, r_{ik}, c_{jk} and $3n^2$ secondary items P_{ij}, R_{ik}, C_{jk}, and with n^2 options 'p_{ij} r_{ik} c_{jk} P_{ij}:k R_{ik}:j C_{jk}:i' for $0 \le i, j < n$ and $1 \le k \le n$, as in answer 390(b). Also, if there are w cages, introduce primary items g_t for $1 \le t \le w$. Let C_t be the cells of the tth cage, and let there be an option

$$\text{'}g_t \bigcup \{\{P_{i_t j_t}:l(i_t, j_t), R_{i_t l(i_t, j_t)}:j_t, C_{j_t l(i_t, j_t)}:i_t\} \mid (i_t, j_t) \in C_t\}\text{'}$$

for every feasible way to assign labels $l(i_t, j_t)$ to the cells of C_t. For example, there are two labelings that satisfy the clue '15×' in the third cage in puzzle 398(a), namely either $l(0, 3) = 3$ and $l(0, 4) = 5$ or $l(0, 3) = 5$ and $l(0, 4) = 3$; the two options for g_3 are therefore 'g_3 P_{03}:3 R_{03}:3 C_{33}:0 P_{04}:5 R_{05}:4 C_{45}:0' and 'g_3 P_{03}:5 R_{05}:3 C_{35}:0 P_{04}:3 R_{03}:4 C_{43}:0'. The cage of that puzzle whose clue is '9×' has just one option: 'g_4 P_{10}:3 R_{13}:0 C_{03}:1 P_{11}:1 R_{11}:1 C_{11}:1 P_{21}:3 R_{23}:1 C_{13}:2'.

The option for a one-cell cage is trivial, and the options for two-cell cages are also easy. The options for larger cages are readily listed by a straightforward backtrack algorithm: We can represent unchosen labels in each row and column by bit vectors, just as unchosen values in the queens problem were represented in Algorithm 7.2.2B*. Simple upper and lower bounds on the final sum or product, given a partial labeling, yield satisfactory cutoffs in the analog to step B3* of that algorithm, based on the λ and ρ functions of Section 7.1.3. The ten-cell '34560×' cage of puzzle 398(b) turns out to have 288 options, with 31 items each; the links will dance merrily around them all.

(Incidentally, this formulation doesn't require the cells of a cage to be connected.)

400. The formulation in answer 399 makes it easy to omit the options for any cage. Thus Algorithm C almost instantaneously breezes through those 2048 problems, and finds that exactly 499 of them are uniquely solvable. The number of such puzzles with $(5, 6, \ldots, 11)$ given clues is $(14, 103, 184, 134, 52, 11, 1)$; for example, one can solve it when given only the clues '15×', '6+', '3−', '5+', '5', in five cages! Exactly $(14, 41, 6)$ of those 499 puzzles have $(5, 6, 7)$ *minimal* clues; minimal-clue puzzles correspond to the prime implicants of the associated monotone Boolean function.

Similar remarks apply to puzzle 398(b), which can be solved uniquely *without* knowing either of the clues '34560×' or '2' — although the reader probably made heavy use of those clues when solving it. (On the other hand, its clue '9+' cannot be omitted.)

401. There are 36 ways to cover a 4×4 board with dominoes, but nearly all of them are unsuitable. For example, ▦ can't define the cages of a valid kenken problem, because the middle rows of any solution could be swapped to give another solution. And no two dominoes can cover a 2×2 region whose solution has the form $\begin{smallmatrix}ab\\ba\end{smallmatrix}$. Therefore we're left with only two cage patterns, ▦ and its transpose.

A given cage pattern can be filled with two clues of each type in $8!/2!^4 = 2520$ ways. Most of those ways are obviously impossible, because ÷ cannot be applied to the pairs $\{2,3\}$ or $\{3,4\}$. It turns out that $(1620, 847, 52, 1)$ of the cases give a kenken puzzle with respectively $(0, 1, 2, 4)$ solutions. Notable examples are

and ,

where the first is the "most difficult," in the sense that its search tree via the construction of exercise 399 has the most nodes (134). The second is the one with four solutions.

402. The solution follows answer 403. The author constructed this puzzle by first designing the cages, then generating a dozen or so random latin squares via exercise 86 until finding one that had a unique solution. Then the domino clues were permuted at random, ten times; the most difficult of those ten puzzles (77 meganodes) was selected.

The construction of answer 399 gives an XCC problem with 10914 options, $486 + 432$ items, and 163288 total entries. There are respectively $(720, 684, 744, 1310, 990, 360, 792, 708, 568, 1200, 606, 30)$ options for the pentominoes (O, P, ..., Z); preprocessing with Algorithm P reduces those counts to $(600, 565, 96, 1122, 852, 248, 744, 656, 568, 1144, 606, 26)$. Overall, the reduced problem has 8927 options, $484 + 432$ items, and 134530 total entries. The total time to find the solution and prove its uniqueness was 9 Gμ for Algorithm P and 293 Gμ for Algorithm C. (Without preprocessing, Algorithm C would have taken 6.4 Tμ, and its search tree would have had 2 giganodes. Could a human being solve this puzzle by hand?)

403. The author's best attempt, shown below, manages to match 35 digits before deviating in the final cage. The construction of answer 399 fails spectacularly on this particular instance, because the monster cage for '79+' has 3,978,616,320 options! We can, however, work around that problem by simply making row 7 unconstrained and subtracting $1+2+\cdots+9 = 45$ from the cage total. (A latin square is determined by any $n-1$ of its rows.) Then Algorithm C solves the problem handily, with a cost of 2 Gμ (from 184422 options), and with a search tree of only 252 nodes. (See Appendix E.

Surprisingly, the non-π clue '3780×' in the bottom row affects row 1 of the solution.)

404. Such puzzles can be defined on any N-vertex graph G, some of whose vertices are labeled with elements of $\{1, 2, \ldots, N\}$; the problem is to extend such a labeling to a full Hamiltonian path, in all possible ways. We imagine an additional vertex ∞, which is adjacent to all the others. A Hamiltonian path in G is then equivalent to a Hamiltonian *cycle* in $G \cup \infty$, with ∞ interposed between the first and last vertices of the path.

For $1 \le k \le N$, let v_k be the vertex labeled k, or $v_k = \Lambda$ if there's no such vertex. Also let $v_0 = v_{N+1} = \infty$. We define an XCC problem with two kinds of primary items: (i) $-v$ and $+v$ for all unlabeled vertices v; (ii) s_k for $0 \le k \le N$, except when both $v_k \ne \Lambda$ and $v_{k+1} \ne \Lambda$. We also introduce secondary items p_v for all unlabeled v, and q_k for all unused labels k. (Thus the example has 35 primary items $\{-00, +00, -10, +10, -11, \ldots, +33, s_1, \ldots, s_7, s_9, \ldots, s_{16}\}$, and 20 secondary items $\{p_{00}, \ldots, p_{33}, q_2, q_4, \ldots, q_{15}, q_{16}\}$.) The options for s_k are 's_k $-u$ $p_u{:}k$ $q_k{:}u$ $+v$ $p_v{:}k{+}1$ $q_{k+1}{:}v$' for all pairs of unlabeled vertices u — v such that u might be labeled k and v might be labeled $k+1$. However, we omit $-u$ $p_u{:}k$ $q_k{:}u$ if $v_k \ne \Lambda$, and we omit $+v$ $p_v{:}k{+}1$ $q_{k+1}{:}v$ if $v_{k+1} \ne \Lambda$. For example, four of the options in the 4×4 toy problem are

$$\text{'}s_3 +10\ p_{10}{:}4\ q_4{:}10\text{'},\qquad \text{'}s_6 -31\ p_{31}{:}6\ q_6{:}31 +30\ p_{30}{:}7\ q_7{:}30\text{'},$$
$$\text{'}s_4 -11\ p_{11}{:}4\ q_4{:}11\text{'},\qquad \text{'}s_6 -30\ p_{30}{:}6\ q_6{:}30 +31\ p_{31}{:}7\ q_7{:}31\text{'};$$

the bottom two appear in the solution, but the top two do not. The secondary items are colored so that interdependent options will always link up properly.

Suppose $l < k < r$ and $v_l \ne \Lambda$, $v_{l+1} = \cdots = v_k = \cdots = v_{r-1} = \Lambda$, $v_r \ne \Lambda$. The statement "u might be labeled k" in the specification above means more precisely that there is a simple path of length $k - l$ from v_l to u and a simple path of length $r - k$ from u to v_r. (This condition is necessary for u to be labeled k, but not sufficient. It is, however, sufficient for our purposes.) A simple path of length 1 is equivalent to adjacency. A simple path of length > 1 can be decided using the algorithm in the following exercise; but if that algorithm is taking too long, we can proceed safely by assuming that a simple path does exist. The value of $\min(k - l, r - k)$ is usually small.

[Gyora Benedek invented Hidato® in 2005 and began to publish examples in 2008. Similar brainteasers sprang up later, based on other kinds of paths; but king moves $P_m \boxtimes P_n$ have a special appeal because they can cross each other.]

405. For $l = 0, 1, \ldots, L$, find the set $\mathcal{S}_l$ of all pairs (S, w) such that at least one simple path from v to w runs through the vertices of $S \cup v$, where S is an l-element set. Clearly $\mathcal{S}_0 = \{(\emptyset, v)\}$; and $\mathcal{S}_{l+1} = \{(S \cup w, w) \mid w - u \text{ and } w \notin S \text{ for some } (S, u) \in \mathcal{S}_l\}$.

If at most 58 vertices w are reachable from v in $\leq l$ steps, we can represent each pair (S, w) in a single octabyte, with 6 bits for w and 58 bits for S. These octabytes can be stored in two stacks, alternately at the low and high ends of a sequential list.

406. The moves from 12 to 19 are forced, as are those on several other diagonals. So everything is quickly filled in, except for blanks between 42 and 51. Aha.

407. Using exercise 404, Algorithm C finds the 52 solutions quickly (1500 kilomems). Only one of them has '18' in row 3, column 3; and that clue makes a puzzle with a nicely symmetric solution (see Appendix E). [We could also put '27' in cell $(2,4)$; or '18' in $(4,3)$; or '17' in $(4,4)$. But that would destroy the smile.]

408.

(a)

					6
28					
11		24	33		

(b)

2		6		10
1		5		9
22		18		13
21		17		14
25		30		36
26		29		35

(See Appendix E for solutions. Are the numbers 5 and 18 best possible for 6×6?)

409. Yes! (This puzzle is fiendishly difficult to solve by hand, although that *has* actually been done. Algorithm C finds the unique solution in 330 $M\mu$, with a search tree of 161612 nodes. (If you give up, the solution can be found in Appendix E.) A "pidato puzzle" like this is presumably possible only because 10×10 hidato solutions are quite abundant. Indeed, the actual number of 10×10 king paths is 7218332206501318903432956545877450 95696; it can be determined with ZDD technology, as explained in Section 7.1.4.)

		31				41			
59			26		53				
	58			97	93				
23	84					50			
	21		100		49				
19		67	81		89		47		
18	68			79	3				
							9		
		77							

410. Puzzles (a), (b), (d) have unique solutions; remarkably, all 12 of the clues in (b) are essential. But (c) has 40 solutions, including two whose loop doesn't touch a corner.

(a) (b) (c) 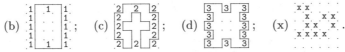 (d) (x) .

Pattern (x), incidentally, has unique solutions for $x = 0, 1, 2$, but none for $x = 3$.

[*Historical note:* Slitherlink was invented by Nikoli editor Nobuhiko Kanamoto, who combined the puzzle ideas of Ayato Yada and Kazuyuki Yuzawa. See *Puzzle Communication Nikoli* **26** (June 1989).]

411. False; for instance, $\begin{smallmatrix}3&2\\2&3\end{smallmatrix}$ has two. [But such cases are somewhat mysterious. There are 93 of size 5×5, including three that give two loops despite 8-fold symmetry. A 6×6 example yields *four* loops; can you find them? (See Appendix E.) Are *three* loops possible? If $m+1$ and $n+1$ are relatively prime, N. Beluhov has proved that an $m \times n$ slitherlink diagram with all clues given cannot have more than one solution.]

```
1 2 2 2 1     3 2 2 2 3     3 2 2 2 3     3 2 2 2 2 2
2 1 0 1 2     2 1 1 1 2     2 3 2 3 2     2 2 2 2 3 2
2 0 0 0 2     2 1 0 1 2     2 2 0 2 2     2 2 2 2 2 2
2 1 0 1 2     2 1 1 1 2     2 3 2 3 2     2 2 2 2 2 2
1 2 2 2 1     3 2 2 2 3     3 2 2 2 3     2 3 2 2 2 2
                                          2 2 2 2 2 3
```

412. With an $m \times n$ grid it's convenient to use the $(2m + 1)(2n + 1)$ pairs xy for $0 \leq x \leq 2m$ and $0 \leq y \leq 2n$, with xy representing either (i) a vertex, if x and y are both even; (ii) a cell, if x and y are both odd; or (iii) an edge, if $x+y$ is odd. The edge between two adjacent vertices is their midpoint. The four edges surrounding a cell are obtained by adding $(\pm 1, 0)$ and $(0, \pm 1)$ to the coordinates of the cell.

To obtain the weak solutions for any slitherlink diagram on a planar graph, introduce one primary item for each vertex, one primary item for each face in which the number of edges is specified, and one secondary item for each edge. There are $1 + \binom{d}{2}$ options for each vertex v of degree d, namely '$v \; e_1{:}x_1 \; \ldots \; e_d{:}x_d$' where $x_j \in \{0, 1\}$ and $x_1 + \cdots + x_d = 0$ or 2. There are $\binom{d}{k}$ options for each face f of degree d that should have k edges in the path, namely '$f \; e_1{:}x_1 \; \ldots \; e_d{:}x_d$' with $x_j \in \{0, 1\}$ and $x_1 + \cdots + x_d = k$.

For example, the options for vertex 00 in the diagram of exercise 410(i) are '00 01:1 10:1' and '00 01:0 10:0'. The options for cell 11 are '11 01:1 10:1 12:1 21:0', '11 01:1 10:1 12:0 21:1', '11 01:1 10:0 12:1 21:1', '11 01:0 10:1 12:1 21:1'.

This construction yields $(2, 2, 104, 2)$ weak solutions for puzzles 410(a) to 410(d). (In cases (a), (b), (d) we can delete or insert the 4-cycle that surrounds the middle cell.)

413. (Solution simplified by R. Molinari.) Let each record for an item include two new fields U and V. The U and V fields of a secondary item that represents edge $u \!-\! v$ will point to the primary items u and v. The U and V fields of a primary item that represents vertex v are renamed MATE and INNER. MATE(v) is zero until v first becomes the endpoint of an edge, after which it points to the other endpoint of the path fragment containing that edge. INNER(v) is nonzero when v lies within a path fragment.

Introduce two new global variables: Global variable F is the current number of fragments. Global variable E is the edge that closed a loop, or zero if there's no loop.

For example, suppose two edges currently have color 1, say $v_1 \!-\! v_2$ and $v_3 \!-\! v_4$. Then we've set MATE(v_1) $\leftarrow v_2$, MATE(v_2) $\leftarrow v_1$, MATE(v_3) $\leftarrow v_4$, MATE(v_4) $\leftarrow v_3$, and F $\leftarrow$ 2. If now $v_2 \!-\! v_5$ joins the fray, we set MATE(v_5) $\leftarrow v_1$, MATE(v_1) $\leftarrow v_5$, and INNER(v_2) $\leftarrow 1$; but we leave MATE(v_2) unchanged. Subsequent edges to v_2 are rejected.

When the 'purify' routine (55) is called to give color 1 to a new edge i, it will refuse to do so when E is nonzero, because a loop has already been closed. Furthermore, when E $= 0$, it will know that edge i shouldn't be chosen if U(i) and V(i) are mates and F $\neq 1$, because that would close a loop disjoint from other fragments. On the other hand, it *will* close the loop if F $= 1$, also setting E $\leftarrow i$.

All of these operations are nicely and easily undone when we need to 'unpurify'. For example, suppose edge i loses color 1 when $u = $ U(i) and $v = $ V(i). If $v = $ MATE(u), we unclose the loop (and set E $\leftarrow$ 0) if $i = $ E; otherwise we zero the mates and set F $\leftarrow$ F $- 1$. If MATE(u) $\neq$ MATE(v), we set MATE(MATE(u)) $\leftarrow u$, MATE(MATE(v)) $\leftarrow v$, and INNER(u) $\leftarrow$ INNER(v) $\leftarrow 0$, F $\leftarrow$ F $+ 1$. The case MATE(u) $= $ MATE(v) is easy too.

Caution: Algorithm P must be modified so that it never discards redundant items, when it is used to preprocess a problem for this extension of Algorithm C.

414. After the forced moves have been made as shown, only two edges are undecided between the vertices of rows 1 and 2. A strongest possible algorithm will know that those two edges must either both be present or both absent. (In fact, a truly strongest possible algorithm will force both to be present as soon as *any* edge in or between rows 0 and 1 has been chosen.)

In general, consider the graph G consisting of the original vertices V and all the currently undecided edges. If X is any proper subset of V, connected or not, any loop will contain an even number of edges between X and $V \setminus X$. Thus any cutset of size two will force a relation between two undecided edges. An algorithm that dynamically maintains minimum cutsets of G (see Section 7.5.3) will therefore be helpful.

415. Instead of solving millions of puzzles, we can use the ZDD technology of Section 7.1.4 to list all the loops in $P_6 \square P_6$, of which there are 1222363. Say that the "signature" of a loop is the full sequence of 25 clues — the number of edges around each cell. It turns out that 93 pairs of loops have the same signature (see exercise 411); those 186 loops cannot be the solution to any 5×5 slitherlink puzzle. Let S be the set of 1222270 distinct signatures, and let S' be the subset of 1222177 that give a valid 25-clue puzzle.

Suppose $s' \in S'$ has $t > 0$ entries equal to digit d; and for $s \in S$ let $p(s, s')$ be the binary "projection vector" $x_1 \ldots x_t$, where $x_k = 1$ if and only if s has d in the kth cell where s' has d. For example, if $d = 1$, the signatures s and s' shown above have $t = 10$ and $p(s, s') = 1011101111$. Form the set $P(s') = \{p(s, s') \mid s \neq s'\}$. Then s', with all clues restricted to digit d, is a valid puzzle if and only if $11 \ldots 1 \notin P(s')$. Moreover, the valid puzzles contained in that one are precisely those whose projections aren't contained in any element of $P(s')$. (If we regard $P(s')$ as a family of sets, such projections are the elements of $\wp \nearrow P(s')$, in the notation of exercise 7.1.4–236.) We can find those vectors, and the minimal ones, with a reachability algorithm such as Algorithm 7.1.3R.

$$s = \begin{matrix} 2\,1\,2\,3\,1 \\ 2\,1\,3\,1\,1 \\ 2\,1\,2\,3\,3 \\ 1\,1\,0\,1\,1 \\ 1\,2\,1\,1\,2 \end{matrix}, \quad s' = \begin{matrix} 2\,2\,2\,3\,1 \\ 2\,2\,1\,1\,1 \\ 2\,1\,1\,2\,3 \\ 2\,3\,2\,1\,1 \\ 2\,2\,1\,1\,2 \end{matrix}.$$

In this way we discover exactly (9310695, 833269, 242772, 35940, 25) valid puzzles for $d = (0, 1, 2, 3, 4)$, of which exactly (27335, 227152, 11740, 17427, 25) have no redundant clues. The minimum number of clues, in such irredundant homogeneous puzzles, is respectively (7, 8, 11, 4, 1); and the maximum number is respectively (12, 14, 18, 10, 1). Many of the extreme cases make pleasant little puzzles:

```
. . . . .    . . . . .   . . . . .   . . . . .   . . . . .   . . . . .   . . . . .
 0       0    0   0  0         1       1 1  1        2            2 2          3  3
.   .   .    .   .   .   . . . . .   . . . . .   . . . . .   . . . . .   . . . . .
 0       0    0   0         1 1     1 1   1      2 2 2 2     2 2   2 2       3
.   .   .    .   .   .   . . . . .   . . . . .   . . . . .   . . . . .   . . . . .
 0       0    0   0  0      1 1      1    1      2 2 2 2     2 2   2 2     3 3 3     3
.   .   .    .   .   .   . . . . .   . . . . .   . . . . .   . . . . .   . . . . .
   0        0   0         1 1      1 1 1   1        2        2 2 2 2        3    3  3
. . . . .    . . . . .   . . . . .   . . . . .   . . . . .   . . . . .   . . . . .
 0     0      0   0  0        1       1 1  1        2           2   2 2      3  3  3
```

(See Appendix E. This minimum-1s puzzle is one of two based on signature s' above.)

416. Of course $d = 4$ is trivial. So is $d = 0$; but that case has an amusing sparse construction. The following puzzles generalize to all n with $(n + d) \bmod 4 = 1$:

```
. . . . . . .   . . . . . . . . . . . .   . . . . . . . . . . . .   . . . . . . . . . . . . .
 0   0  0  0  0  0   1 1 1 1 1 1 1 1 1 1 1   2 2 2 2 2 2 2 2 2 2 2     3 3 3 3 3 3 3 3 3 3 3 3 3
.   .   .   .   . 1   1 1 1 1 1 1 1 1 1 1     2 2 2 2 2 2 2 2 2 2 2   3
 0   0  0  0  0    1 1   1 1 1 1 1 1 1 1   1 2 2 2 2 2 2 2 2 2 2 2 2  3
.   .   .   .   . 1 1 1   1 1 1 1 1 1 1     2 2 2 2 2 2 2 2 2 2 2 2   3 3 3 3 3 3 3 3 3 3 3 3 3
 0   0  0  0  0  1 1 1   1 1 1 1 1 1 1      2 2 2 2   2 2 2 2 2       3
.   .   .   .   . 1 1 1   1 1 1 1 1 1 1     2 2 2 2   2 2 2 2 2      3 3 3 3 3 3 3 3 3 3 3 3 3
 0   0  0  0  0  1 1   1 1 1 1 1 1 1 1   1 2 2 2 2 2 2 2 2 2 2 2 2   3
.   .   .   .   . 1 1   1 1 1 1 1 1 1 1   1 2 2 2 2 2 2 2 2 2 2 2 2  3 3 3 3 3 3 3 3 3 3 3 3 3
 0   0  0  0  0  1 1 1   1 1 1 1 1 1 1      2 2 2 2 2 2 2 2 2 2 2 2  3
.   .   .   .   . 1 1 1   1 1 1 1 1 1 1     2 2 2 2 2 2 2 2 2 2 2 2  3 3 3 3 3 3 3 3 3 3 3 3 3
 0   0  0  0  0  1 1 1   1 1 1 1 1 1 1    1 2 2 2 2 2 2 2 2 2 2 2 2  3
.   .   .   .   . 1 1   1 1 1 1 1 1 1 1   1 2 2 2 2 2 2 2 2 2 2 2 2  3 3 3 3 3 3 3 3 3 3 3 3 3
 0   0  0  0  0    1 1 1 1 1 1 1 1 1 1 1                             3
. . . . . . .    1 1 1 1 1 1 1 1 1 1 1     . . . . . . . . . . . .  3
 0   0  0  0  0                                                     3 3 3 3 3 3 3 3 3 3 3 3 3
```

(See the solutions in Appendix E.) N. Beluhov, who found these patterns for $d = 2$ and 3, has raised interesting problems of optimum density: Let $\underline{\beta}(d) = \liminf_{n \to \infty} \|S\|/n^2$ and $\overline{\beta}(d) = \limsup_{n \to \infty} \|S\|/n^2$, where S ranges over all valid $n \times n$ slitherlink puzzles that are d-homogeneous, and where $\|S\|$ denotes the number of clues. Clearly $\|S\| \le n^2/2$ when $d = 3$, because no 2×2 subsquare can contain more than two 3s. Furthermore $\|S\| \ge n^2/4 - O(n)$ when $d = 0$. For we must eliminate at least $n^2 + 2n$ of the $2n(n+1)$ edges if all but one cycle is to be cut; each 0 eliminates at most four. If $n > 5$ we obtain a valid puzzle with only fourteen 1s, by placing a suitable 4×6 pattern in the upper left corner. Similarly, there's a valid puzzle with only four 3s, if $n > 3$. Therefore these constructions prove that $\overline{\beta}(0) = \overline{\beta}(1) = \overline{\beta}(2) = 1$; $\overline{\beta}(3) = 1/2$; $\underline{\beta}(1) = \underline{\beta}(3) = \underline{\beta}(4) = \overline{\beta}(4) = 0$; $\underline{\beta}(0) = 1/4$.

```
. . . . .
 1 1  1
1       1
 1 1  1
. . . . .
```

The intriguing case of $\beta(2)$ remains unknown. Beluhov proved that it is at most $\frac{11}{16}$, using a construction for $n = 4k$ that's illustrated here for $n = 12$. Palmer Mebane has constructed this 2-homogeneous puzzle on an 8×8 board that has only 24 clues [see puzsq.jp/main/puzzle_play.php?pid=14178].

```
 2       2 2 2 2 2 2
 2 2 2 2 2 2 2 2 2 2 2
 2       2 2 2 2 2 2 2   2
 2 2 2 2 2 2 2 2   2
             2   2   2
 2 2 2 2 2   2   2
 2 2 2 2   2 2   2
 2 2 2 2 2 2 2 2   2 2
 2 2                 2 2
 2 2 2 2 2 2 2 2 2 2 2
 2                         2
```

```
 2                   2
 2                       2
     2 2 2 2
       2 2 2       2
       2 2   2
     2 2 2     2
   2 2                 2
```

417. The pattern for $d = 3$ in answer 416 works also for $d = 0$, if we remove one clue from the top row. Fascinating diagrams arise when such patterns are attempted for $d = 1$; Beluhov's largest example so far is the 30×30 puzzle obtained when removing the 1 in column 26 of row 0. (Such puzzles are extremely difficult for the algorithm of answer 413 to handle; but SAT solvers have no trouble with them.)

418. (a) $6 \cdot 26^{12} \approx 5.7 \times 10^{17}$, from the central cell and 12 complementary pairs.

(b, c, d, e) As in answer 415, we define the projection $p(s, s') = x_1 \ldots x_{13}$, where $x_k = 1$ if and only if s and s' agree in the kth pair (or in the center, when $k = 13$). We obtain altogether 2,692,250,947 puzzles, of which 199,470,026 are minimal. The minimal ones include $(1, 24, 0, 7, 42, 1648, 13428, 257105, \ldots, 184, 8)$ that have respectively $(1, 2, 3, 4, 5, 6, 7, 8, \ldots, 19, 20)$ clues; here are some choice specimens:

```
 .  .  .  .  .  .    .  .  0 .  .  .      .  .  .  .  0 .    .  .  0 0 .  .       .  .  .  .  .  .       .  .  .  .  .  .       .  3 2 1 .  3
          0             .  .  0 .        .  .  .  .  .      .  0 .  1 0 .    .  .  .  .  .  1      .  3 .  2 0 1 .       .  2 1 .  2 2
     .  4 .  .  .                            .  .  0 .          .  .  .  .  . 1 1 3 2 3          .  .  .  .  .  .       .  2 2 .  2 2
                           .  3 .            .  2 3 .  .  1    .  3 .  .  .      .  2 3 0 .  1       .  2 1 .  2 2
          .  4 .           .  3 .            .  3 3 .                                                   .  3 .  2 2 3
```

419. To design this puzzle, the author began with the signature of the desired loop (see answer 415), then removed pairs of centrally opposite clues, more-or-less at random, until no redundant pairs remained. The construction of exercise 412 produced 2267 options on 404+573 items from the final clue set; and Algorithm P needed just 17 Mμ to remove 1246 of those options. Then the algorithm of exercise 413 discovered the solution, and proved it unique, with 5.5 Gμ of computation and a search tree of 15 meganodes. (It's another big win for preprocessing: Otherwise that algorithm would have taken 37 Tμ, with a 78-giganode search tree!) *Reference:* D. E. Knuth, *Computer Modern Typefaces* (Addison–Wesley, 1986), 158–159.

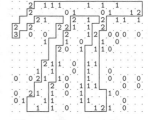

420. (Solution by Palmer Mebane.) In any solution, each cell is either inside or outside the loop. *Lemma: Every 2 has exactly two neighbors inside.* (For if the 2 is outside, the neighbors opposite its two edges are inside; otherwise the neighbors opposite its two *non*edges are inside.) Let S be the set of cells next to a 2. Color each 2 alternately red or blue; then each cell of S is a neighbor of exactly one red 2 and exactly one blue 2. In particular, that's true for each *inside* cell of S. Thus, by the lemma, there are equally many red and blue cells. But that contradicts $m \bmod 4 = n \bmod 4 = 1$!

[This exercise is due to N. Beluhov, who observes that solutions aplenty exist when m is odd and $n \bmod 4 = 3$.]

421.

(1 of 44)   (1 of 7)   (1 of 1)   (1 of 7)   (1 of 5)

[*Historical note:* Masyu was invented by Ryuoh Yano, who developed a white-circles-only version, together with Mitsuhiro Ase, who contributed the black circles. See *Puzzle Communication Nikoli* **84** (April 1999); **90** (March 2000).]

422. Now we use the $(2m-1)(2n-1)$ pairs xy for $0 \le x \le 2m-2$ and $0 \le y \le 2n-2$. Cell (i,j) corresponds to $x = 2i$ and $y = 2j$ (a "vertex"); clue (i,j) corresponds to $x = 2i+1$ and $y = 2j+1$. Edges are as before, and we use the same options to ensure that either 0 or 2 edges touch every vertex in a solution. The only essential change from answer 412 is the treatment of clues, since masyu clues are different from slitherlink clues.

A black masyu clue in (i,j) has four options, corresponding to north-west, north-east, south-west, and south-east legs; for example, the north-west option is

$$\text{`}C(i,j) \; N(i,j)\text{:}1 \; NN(i,j)\text{:}1 \; W(i,j)\text{:}1 \; WW(i,j)\text{:}1\text{'},$$

where $C(i,j) = (2i+1)(2j+1)$, $N(i,j) = C(i,j) - 10$, $NN(i,j) = C(i,j) - 30$, $W(i,j) = C(i,j) - 01$, $WW(i,j) = C(i,j) - 03$. Edges off the grid have "color" 0, so this option is omitted when $i \le 1$ or $j \le 1$.

A white masyu clue in (i,j) has six options, three for north-south orientation and three for east-west. The three for east-west are

$$\text{`}C(i,j) \; E(i,j)\text{:}1 \; EE(i,j)\text{:}0 \; W(i,j)\text{:}1 \; WW(i,j)\text{:}0\text{'},$$
$$\text{`}C(i,j) \; E(i,j)\text{:}1 \; EE(i,j)\text{:}0 \; W(i,j)\text{:}1 \; WW(i,j)\text{:}1\text{'},$$
$$\text{`}C(i,j) \; E(i,j)\text{:}1 \; EE(i,j)\text{:}1 \; W(i,j)\text{:}1 \; WW(i,j)\text{:}0\text{'}.$$

Again we omit an option that would set an off-board edge to 1. An off-board edge item that sets color 0 is silently dropped.

For example, the options for the black clue in exercise 421's puzzle are '15 14:1 34:1 03:1 01:1', '15 14:1 34:1 05:1 07:1'. The options for the white clue in the bottom row are '97 87:1 85:1 83:0', '97 87:1 85:1 83:1'. That puzzle has 15 clue options altogether, and 119 vertex options '00 01:1 10:1', '00 01:0 10:0', '02 01:1 03:1 12:0', ..., '88 78:0 87:0'.

423. Obtain a representative of each class of equivalent variables, for example by adapting Algorithm 2.3.3E. This calculation may show that certain variables are constant. A contradiction might also arise — for example, if there's a white clue in a corner; in such cases the masyu puzzle has no solution.

The vertex options of answer 422 can now be eliminated, at all vertices for which a clue was given. The clue options can also be consolidated, so that equivalent variables don't appear together, and so that constants are suppressed. Every option that tries to set a variable both true and false is, of course, eliminated.

For example, variables 14, 50, 70, 85, and 87 in the puzzle of exercise 421 are forced to be true; variables 61 and 76 are forced to be false. We can eliminate variables 05, 16, 27, 36, 54, 65, and 74 because $05 = {\sim}03$, $16 = 36 = {\sim}25$, $27 = 25$, $54 = 74 = {\sim}63$, $65 = 63$. The options for the black clue become '15 01:1 03:1 34:1', '15 03:0 07:1 34:1'. The options for the white clue in the bottom row become '97 83:0', '97 83:1'.

Caveat: These simplifications are very nice, but they mess up the single-loop-detection mechanism of answer 413 — because that answer uses several fields of item nodes as key elements of its data structure! To keep that algorithm happy, we must append a special option that covers all of the supposedly eliminated vertex items and constant-edge items; this option is '04 26 60 64 86 87:1 85:1 76:0 50:1 70:1 61:0 14:1' in the example. We also need pairs of options such as '#25 16:1 36:1 27:0 25:0' and '#25 16:0 36:0 27:1 25:1', to keep all variables of an equivalence class in sync.

A tenfold speedup is achieved even on small puzzles like the 8×10 in exercise 426.

424. As in answer 415, we can begin with the 1222363 loops that are potential solutions. But this time the "signature" of a loop is the maximum set of clues that it supports. Such a signature turns out to have at most 24 clues; indeed, only puzzle (i) in

Fig. A–5, along with its rotations or reflections, attains this maximum. (At the other extreme, 64 loops have an entirely *empty* signature, despite having lengths up to 28.)

Let S be the set of 905472 distinct signatures; and let S' be the subset of 93859 that aren't contained in (or equal to) the signature of any other loop. These are the signatures of loops that can solve a valid 6×6 puzzle. If $s' \in S'$ has t clues, we define the projection vector $p(s, s') = x_1 \ldots x_t$ for $s \in S$ by setting $x_j = 1$ when s agrees with s' in the jth cell where s' has a clue. For example, when s' is puzzle (i) and s is its transpose, the projection $p(s, s')$ is 00001100001110111101100011.

Form the set $P(s') = \{p(s, s') \mid s \neq s'\}$. We know that $11 \ldots 1 \notin P(s')$, because s' isn't dominated by any other signature. Moreover, the valid puzzles having the loop of s' as their solution are precisely those whose clues are not contained in any element of $P(s')$. We can find such puzzles, and the minimal ones, with a reachability computation like Algorithm 7.1.3R, whose running time is $O(2^t)$. For example, the loop of (i) turns out to be the solution to 8924555 puzzles(!). Four of them, such as (ii) and (iii), are minimal with only four clues; three of them, such as (iv), are minimal with eleven.

Most elements of S' have far fewer than 24 clues. Hence it isn't difficult to determine that there are exactly 1,166,086,477 valid 6×6 masyu puzzles altogether, of which 4,366,185 are minimal. (There are (80, 1212, 26188, 207570, $\ldots$, 106) minimal puzzles with (3, 4, 5, 6, $\ldots$, 12) clues. One of the 3s is puzzle (v); it also has the shortest loop. One of the 12s is puzzle (vi); it also has the *longest* loop — a Hamiltonian cycle. (A Hamiltonian cycle can actually be forced by only four clues; see puzzle (xvii).)

The valid puzzles include 5571407 that are pure white, 4820 that are pure black. The white clues can take on 22032015 different patterns; the black clues can assume only 39140. A surprisingly large number of 6×6 puzzles, 37472, can be "inverted," remaining valid when white and black are swapped. If we restrict consideration to minimal puzzles, these figures become: 574815 pure white, 1914 pure black, 2522171 white patterns, 22494 black patterns, 712 invertible. The latter include many amusing and amazing pairs, such as (vii)–(viii), (ix)–(x), (xi)–(xii), as well as self-dual examples such as (xiii), (xiv), (xv), (xvi); there are 49 essentially distinct invertible puzzles of size 6×6. [Considerably larger invertible puzzles have been published in the anonymous blog uramasyu.blog80.fc2.com/, every few days since 2006.]

The author thinks puzzle (vi) may well be the hardest 6×6, although its search tree via exercise 423 has only 212 nodes. (That tree has 1001 nodes with exercise 422.)

425. A "balanced" $n \times n$ masyu solution of order k clearly requires $2 \leq k \leq \lfloor n^2/4 \rfloor$. All such k turn out to be achievable, for $n \leq 6$, except that the upper limit $\lfloor n^2/4 \rfloor$ is not. Solutions for $k = 2$ exist for all $n \geq 3$; solutions for $k = 3$ exist for all $n \geq 4$; solutions for $k = 4$, due to B. S. Ho, exist for all $n \geq 5$; solutions for $k = 5$ and $k = 6$, due to G. J. H. Goh, exist for all $n \geq 6$. (See (xviii)–(xxiv) in Fig. A–5.) Goh has also discovered analogous constructions for $k = 7, 8, 9, 10$.

426. The clue in the corner must obviously be '●'. That leaves us with 2^{28} other possibilities to consider, many of which can be rejected immediately because certain local patterns are impossible. (For example, there cannot be three consecutive '●'s.) Consider the Boolean function of $x_0 x_1 \ldots x_{27}$ that's true if and only if the diagram has at least one solution, with '●' when $x_j = 1$ and '○' when $x_j = 0$.

One can easily verify that there's no solution when $x_0 x_1$ or $x_1 x_3$ or $x_0 \bar{x}_1 x_4$ or $\ldots$ or $\bar{x}_3 \bar{x}_4 \bar{x}_5$ or $x_6 x_7$ or $\bar{x}_7 \bar{x}_8 x_{10} \bar{x}_{11}$, etc.; also when we replace x_j by x_{j+12}. We can also rule out extreme cases such as $\bar{x}_1 x_{26}$.

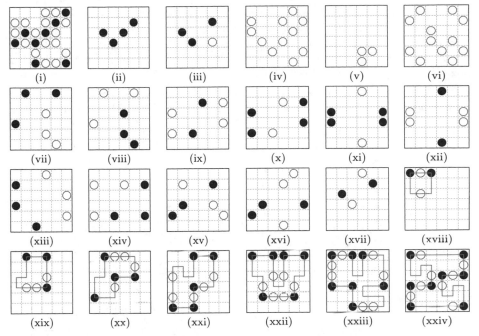

Fig. A-5. A gallery of interesting 6×6 masyu puzzles.

After compiling several dozen such "bad" configurations, the author applied BDD technology: Less than a megamem sufficed to generate a BDD of size 715, which showed that exactly 10239 vectors $x_0 x_1 \ldots x_{27}$ were not yet ruled out. The masyu solver of exercise 423 tossed off those cases with search trees of 3 nodes per problem, on average; and it turned out that exactly (10232, 1, 1, 1, 4) vectors had (0, 1, 2, 3, 4) solutions. The unique winning puzzle is shown here (and solved in Appendix E).

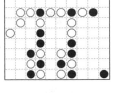

427. Here's an example with $8 \cdot 15$ white clues (solved in Appendix E):

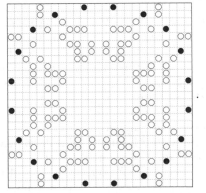

It turns out to be problematic for the method of exercise 423, which severely loses focus and takes forever to prove that there's only one solution. One can, however, exploit symmetry by modifying Algorithm C as follows: Whenever a color setting is made on the rightmost branch of the search tree, all settings that are equivalent to it by symmetry can be forced. Then uniqueness is proved in about 36 Mμ, provided that the primary items are suitably ordered. [This exercise was inspired by Nikoli's *Giant Logic Puzzles for Geniuses* (Puzzlewright Press, 2016), #53.]

428. (Solution by N. Beluhov.) $3n - 12$ black clues suffice when $n \bmod 4 = 0$; $5n - 21$ white clues suffice when $n \bmod 4 = 1$. (Are these constants 3 and 5 the best possible?)

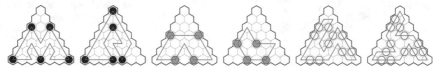

(a) ; (b) .

429. (a) Incidentally, each of these puzzles is minimal (all clues important):

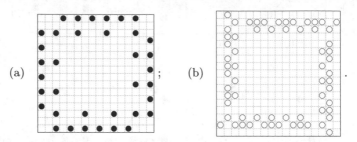

(b) In fact, *two* permutations of the colors are possible in each case:

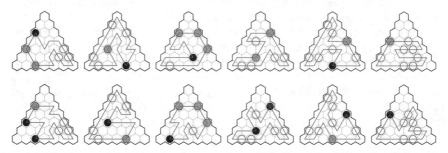

430. (a) The lower right corner must contain 5. See Appendix E for the other cells.

(b) Set $c_{nk} \leftarrow 0$ for all n and k. Now do this for $3 \leq x < 512$: Set $k \leftarrow n \leftarrow 0$; for $0 \leq t < 9$ set $k \leftarrow k+1$, $n \leftarrow n+t+1$ if $x \mathbin{\&} (1 \ll t) \neq 0$; finally if $k > 1$, set $C_{nkc_{nk}} \leftarrow x$ and $c_{nk} \leftarrow c_{nk} + 1$. The n-in-k combinations are now C_{nkj} for $0 \leq j < c_{nk}$.

The maximum c_{nk}, 12, is obtained for $(n, k) = (20, 4)$ or $(25, 5)$. Notice that $c_{nk} = c_{(45-n)(9-k)}$ when $1 < k < 8$. Cases with $c_{nk} = 1$ are called "restricted" or "magic blocks"; they're extremely helpful when present (but our example doesn't have any).

(c) The middle must be 7 9 8 (an odd digit < 9, 9, then an even digit).

(d) The tables from (b) convert kakuro to generalized kakuro. Introduce a primary item ij for each cell to be filled. Let there be H horizontal blocks, and assume that horizontal block h has c_h combinations X_{hp} of length k_h, for $1 \leq h \leq H$ and $1 \leq p \leq c_h$. Introduce $c_h k_h$ primary items H_{hpx}, for $x \in X_{hp}$, to represent the elements of block h's pth combination. (For example, the primary items for the first horizontal block of our example are H_{111}, H_{114}, H_{122}, H_{123} because the two combinations are $\{1, 4\}$ and

$\{2,3\}$.) Similarly, introduce primary items V_{vqy} for the elements of the qth combination Y_{vq} of vertical block v, for $1 \le v \le V$ and $1 \le q \le d_v$.

Also introduce secondary items H_h and V_v for $1 \le h \le H$ and $1 \le v \le V$, one for each block. The "color" of such an item represents the choice of combination to be used.

The options for cell ij are '$ij\ H_{hpx}\ H_h{:}p\ V_{vqx}\ V_v{:}q$', where h and v indicate the horizontal and vertical blocks through ij, for $1 \le p \le c_h$ and $1 \le q \le d_v$ and $x \in X_{hp} \cap Y_{vq}$. (Thus, the options for the upper left blank cell in our example are '$11\ H_{111}\ H_1{:}1\ V_{111}\ V_1{:}1$', '$11\ H_{114}\ H_1{:}1\ V_{124}\ V_1{:}2$', '$11\ H_{122}\ H_1{:}2\ V_{122}\ V_1{:}2$'. Set intersections are easily computed from the bitmaps X_{hp} and V_{vq}.)

Additional options are also necessary to "absorb" the combinations not used. These are '$\bigcup\{H_{hpx} \mid x \in X_{hp}\}\ H_h{:}p'$' for $1 \le p, p' \le c_h$ and $p \ne p'$; '$\bigcup\{V_{vqy} \mid y \in Y_{vq}\}$ $V_v{:}q'$' for $1 \le q, q' \le d_v$ and $q \ne q'$. (Thus the options for $h = 1$ in our example are 'H_{111} $H_{114}\ H_1{:}2$', '$H_{122}\ H_{123}\ H_1{:}1$'.) This instructive construction deserves careful study.

431. There are 18 solutions, because of two ways to complete the middle left portion and (independently) nine ways to complete the lower left corner. (The digits that *are* uniquely determined by his conditions are shown below.) We can freeze most of those digits, and extract two much smaller problems, then insert a few wildcards as in exercise 433 until obtaining uniqueness. One suitable patch, shown below, changes seven clues and has the solution found in Appendix E. (In this problem, preprocessing greatly improves the focus, reducing the search tree size from 115 million to just 343!)

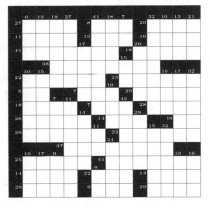

[Funk had copyrighted a Cross Sums Puzzle already in September 1935; see *Canadian Patent Office Record and Register of Copyrights and Trade Marks* **63** (1935), 2253.]

432. (a) We save a lot of time by considering only "restricted growth strings" as solutions (see Section 7.2.1.5). That is, we can assume that the top row is '12'; then the second row is either '213' or '234' or '312' or '314' or '34x' for $1 \le x \le 5$; etc. Altogether there are $(5, 28, 33, 11, 1)$ such strings with maximum element $(3, 4, 5, 6, 7)$. Thus we know that the blanks can be filled in $5 \cdot 9^3 + 28 \cdot 9^4 + 33 \cdot 9^5 + 11 \cdot 9^6 + 9^7 = 1432872$ ways. And we can quickly compute the 1432872 sequences of block sums from those restricted growth strings, using a table of 9! permutations built by Algorithm 7.2.1.2L. Exactly 78690 of those sequences, about 5.5%, occur uniquely and define a kakuro puzzle.

Every kakuro puzzle has a *dual*, obtained by replacing all clue-sums s for blocks of length k by $10k - s$; the dual is solved by changing each digit d to $10 - d$. Thus, if a puzzle of type (a) is defined by horizontal and vertical sums $s_1 s_2 s_3 / t_1 t_2 t_3$, its dual is defined by $(20-s_1)(30-s_2)(30-s_3)/(20-t_1)(30-t_2)(20-t_3)$. Diagonal symmetry also makes $s_1 s_2 s_3 / t_1 t_2 t_3$ equivalent to $s_3 s_2 s_1 / t_3 t_2 t_1$ and $t_1 t_2 t_3 / s_1 s_2 s_3$; so we get up to eight equivalent puzzles from each sequence. There are 9932 essentially distinct puzzles, only one of which has four symmetries, namely $6\,15\,14/14\,15\,6$; 190 have one symmetry, and the remaining 9741 are asymmetric. (The asymmetric ones are, of course, more difficult to solve, because a symmetric puzzle will have a symmetric solution.) The example $5\,19\,6/6\,10\,14$ in exercise 430 is asymmetrical; but it's relatively easy because it has a forced move in the lower right corner. The easiest puzzles, with *four* forced moves, are $4\,15\,12/12\,15\,4$ and $4\,15\,16/12\,15\,8$, both symmetric. Altogether 4011 of the asymmetric puzzles have no forced moves. And of those, 570 have no "magic blocks." And of those, puzzle $6\,19\,6/8\,11\,10$ is the hardest, in the sense that it maximizes the number of nodes (79) in Algorithm C's search tree, using the construction of answer 430(d).

(b) Similarly, this shape has $2 \cdot 9^3 + 42 \cdot 9^4 + 186 \cdot 9^5 + 234 \cdot 9^6 + 105 \cdot 9^7 + 18 \cdot 9^8 + 9^9 = 43038576$ sequences of block sums, of which $6840 \approx 0.016\%$ are unique. Those 6840 yield 49 equivalence classes under the symmetries $s_1 s_2 s_3 / t_1 t_2 t_3 \mapsto s_2 s_1 s_3 / t_1 t_2 t_3$, $s_3 s_2 s_1 / t_1 t_2 t_3$, $s_1 s_2 s_3 / t_2 t_1 t_3$, $s_1 s_2 s_3 / t_3 t_2 t_1$, $t_1 t_2 t_3 / s_1 s_2 s_3$, $(30 - s_1)(30 - s_2)(30 - s_3) / (30 - t_1)(30 - t_2)(30 - t_3)$. All but 3 of those 49 puzzles are asymmetric; $7\,11\,20/7\,11\,20$ and $7\,19\,20/7\,19\,20$ are self-transpose, and $7\,15\,23/10\,15\,20$ is self-dual. They aren't great, because they all have at least one forced move from 7 opposite 20 or from its dual.

[It's extremely difficult to find a kakuro puzzle whose spaces make a 4×4 grid. But Johan de Ruiter discovered in 2010 that there are five essentially different ways. For example, $11\,15\,23\,29/12\,15\,23\,28$ has a 488-node search tree, so it's a nice little challenge.]

433. A slight extension to the construction of answer 430(d) allows "wildcard" blocks, with unspecified length and with the universal combination $\{1, \ldots, 9\}$ as their X or Y. The items H_{h1x} or V_{v1y} for such wildcards are secondary, not primary. Algorithm C now pumps out 89638 solutions (in 150 Mμ); and 12071 of the corresponding sum sequences $s_1 \ldots s_7 / t_1 \ldots t_7$ occur once only and yield valid puzzles. (The easiest ones, $16\,4\,18\,(d+14)\,16\,16\,16/9\,34\,24\,6\,d\,12\,15$ for $7 \le d \le 9$, have a search tree of only 47 nodes. A median puzzle such as $16\,4\,20\,18\,16\,16\,15/9\,22\,24\,6\,17\,12\,15$ needs 247 nodes. And the hardest, $16\,4\,23\,19\,16\,16\,13/9\,25\,24\,6\,17\,11\,15$, needs 1994.)

[The author tried 10000 experiments in which all 21 cells of this diagram were simply filled at random, and their block sums recorded. Those 10000 problems had ≈ 75 solutions, on average, with standard deviation ≈ 1200. Only five of them led to valid puzzles; the most difficult one, $15\,3\,21\,16\,27\,8\,10/9\,22\,28\,11\,21\,5\,4$, needed 1168 nodes.]

434. In 700 Mμ, a BDD with 64 variables and 124487 nodes characterizes 93,158,227,648 solutions. N. Beluhov proved in 2018 that there are at most 38 blocks, achieved for example as shown, by listing all cases with 38 or more. He also observed that the maximum for $n \times n$ kakuro is $n^2/3 - O(n)$, using a similar construction with (i, j) black $\iff (i + j) \bmod 3 = 0$ except near the boundary.

435. The search tree for this one has 566 nodes. (See Appendix E.)

436. (a) Any solution with a black seed works also with that cell white.

(b) A solution with a non-articulation point would work also with that cell black.

437. Introduce a primary item $*$ to make the seeds white; also primary items Ric and
Cjc for each character c that occurs more than once in row i or column j. Introduce
secondary items ij for $0 \le i < m$ and $0 \le j < n$, representing cell (i, j). For example,
the first option for puzzle 436(α) is '$*$ 01:0 02:0 10:0 13:0 14:0 21:0 31:0 32:0'.

Suppose row i contains character c in columns $j_1, \ldots, j_t$, where $t > 1$. Then Ric
normally has $t + 1$ options 'Ric ij_1:e_1 $\ldots$ ij_t:e_t u_1:0 $\ldots$ u_s:0' for $e_1 + \cdots + e_t \ge t - 1$,
where $\{u_1, \ldots, u_s\}$ are the non-seed neighbors of the cells being colored 1. However,
this option is suppressed if it would assign two colors to the same item. For example,
if $i = 1$, $t = 3$, and $j_1 j_2 j_3 = 123$, there is only one option 'R1c 11:1 12:0 13:1 01:0 03:0
10:0 14:0 21:0 23:0' (but with entries deleted that color a seed with 0), because the
other three options are contradictory.

Of course the options for Cjc are similar. For example, the options for C3L in
puzzle 436(α) are 'C3L 23:0 33:1 34:0' and 'C3L 33:0 23:1 22:0 24:0'.

[Notice, incidentally, that this XCC problem is a special case of 2SAT. Therefore
it can be solved in linear time. Furthermore, by Theorem 7.1.1S, the median of any
three solutions is also a solution — a curious fact!]

438. The basic idea is to abandon partial solutions that cut off any white cells from
the first seed. Connectedness can be assured by maintaining a triply linked spanning
tree, rooted at that seed, with the help of new fields in each item record. Changes to
the spanning tree need not be undone when unblackening a cell while backtracking;
any spanning tree on the currently nonblack cells is satisfactory.

[This method can be patched to handle the rare instances that have *no* seeds.
To ensure uniqueness, as in exercise 436(b), each solution should also be tested for
articulation points. Hopcroft and Tarjan's algorithm for bicomponents does that
efficiently. See Section 7.4.1.2; also *The Stanford GraphBase*, pages 90–99.]

439. (a) Property (ii) states that U is a vertex cover (or equivalently that $V \setminus U$ is
independent). Thus (i) and (ii) together state that U is a connected vertex cover.
Adding property (iii) gives us a *minimal* connected vertex cover. [Minimal connected
vertex covers were introduced by M. R. Garey and D. S. Johnson in *SIAM J. Applied
Math.* **32** (1977), 826–834, who proved that it is NP-complete to decide if a planar
graph with maximum degree 4 has a connected vertex cover of a given size.]

(b) This is the thrust of exercise 436(b). [N. Beluhov has proved constructively
that every $m \times n$ hitori cover for $m, n > 1$ solves at least one valid puzzle, using an
alphabet of at most $\max(m, n)$ letters.]

440. False (if neither A is alone in its column). Consider $\begin{smallmatrix} A & B & A \\ B & C & A \\ A & C & C \end{smallmatrix}$ or $\begin{smallmatrix} 0 & A & B & C & D & A & 1 \\ B & 2 & 3 & 4 & 5 & 6 & D \\ B & A & B & C & D & A & D \end{smallmatrix}$.

441. When $n = 1$ any single letter a is trivially a valid puzzle. When $n > 1$ the possibilities are (i) aαa for every string α of $n - 2$ distinct letters containing an a (thus
$(n - 2)d^{n-2}$ puzzles); (ii) aαb for a $\ne$ b and every string α of $n - 2$ distinct letters
containing a and b (thus $(n - 2)^2 d^{n-2}$ puzzles); altogether $(n - 2)^2 d^{n-2}$ valid puzzles.

442. A "frontier-based" algorithm analogous to those of answers 7.1.4–55 and 7.1.4–225
will produce an unreduced ZDD for the family f of all *complements* $V \setminus U$ of connected
vertex covers, from which a variant of Algorithm 7.1.4R will give a ZDD. Then the
NONSUB subroutine of answer 7.1.4–237 will produce a ZDD for $f^\uparrow$, the complements of
hitori covers (the black cells of potential solutions). In the most complicated case, $m =$

$n = 9$, an unreduced ZDD of size 203402 is reduced quickly to 55038 nodes; then 550 Gμ of computation produces a ZDD of size 1145647 for the family of maximal black cells. Those ZDDs make it easy to count and generate hitori covers; we obtain the totals

$$\begin{pmatrix} 1 & 2 & 1 & 1 & 1 & 1 & 1 & 1 & 1 \\ 2 & 4 & 6 & 12 & 20 & 36 & 64 & 112 & 200 \\ 1 & 6 & 11 & 30 & 75 & 173 & 434 & 1054 & 2558 \\ 1 & 12 & 30 & 110 & 382 & 1270 & 4298 & 14560 & 49204 \\ 1 & 20 & 75 & 382 & 1804 & 7888 & 36627 & 166217 & 755680 \\ 1 & 36 & 173 & 1270 & 7888 & 46416 & 287685 & 1751154 & 10656814 \\ 1 & 64 & 434 & 4298 & 36627 & 287685 & 2393422 & 19366411 & 157557218 \\ 1 & 112 & 1054 & 14560 & 166217 & 1751154 & 19366411 & 208975042 & 2255742067 \\ 1 & 200 & 2558 & 49204 & 755680 & 10656814 & 157557218 & 2255742067 & 32411910059 \end{pmatrix}.$$

Further statistics about these fascinating patterns are also of interest:

$$\begin{pmatrix} [1..1] & [1..1] & [2..2] & [2..2] & [2..2] & [2..2] & [2..2] & [2..2] & [2..2] \\ [1..1] & [1..1] & [1..2] & [2..2] & [2..3] & [2..3] & [3..4] & [3..4] & [3..5] \\ [2..2] & [1..2] & [2..4] & [2..4] & [3..6] & [4..6] & [4..8] & [5..8] & [5..10] \\ [2..2] & [2..2] & [2..4] & [4..5] & [4..7] & [5..8] & [6..9] & [7..10] & [8..12] \\ [2..2] & [2..3] & [3..6] & [4..7] & [5..9] & [6..10] & [8..12] & [9..14] & [10..15] \\ [2..2] & [2..3] & [4..6] & [5..8] & [6..10] & [8..12] & [9..14] & [11..16] & [12..18] \\ [2..2] & [3..4] & [4..8] & [6..9] & [8..12] & [9..14] & [11..17] & [12..19] & [14..21] \\ [2..2] & [3..4] & [5..8] & [7..10] & [9..14] & [11..16] & [12..19] & [14..21] & [16..24] \\ [2..2] & [3..5] & [5..10] & [8..12] & [10..15] & [12..18] & [14..21] & [16..24] & [18..27] \end{pmatrix} \begin{pmatrix} 10 & 1 & 1 & 1 & 1 & 1 & 1 & 1 & 1 \\ 0 & 0 & 0 & 0 & 0 & 0 & 0 & 0 & 0 \\ 10 & 3 & 2 & 5 & 1 & 6 & 2 & 10 \\ 10 & 2 & 0 & 2 & 0 & 2 & 0 & 2 \\ 10 & 5 & 2 & 10 & 2 & 21 & 1 & 46 \\ 10 & 1 & 0 & 2 & 0 & 1 & 0 & 2 \\ 10 & 6 & 2 & 21 & 1 & 48 & 1 & 150 \\ 10 & 2 & 0 & 1 & 0 & 1 & 0 & 3 \\ 10 & 10 & 2 & 46 & 2 & 150 & 3 & 649 \end{pmatrix}$$

The left-hand matrix shows how many black cells can occur in hitori covers. The right-hand matrix shows how many hitori covers have both horizontal and vertical symmetry; when $m \neq n$, such covers are counted just once in the previous totals, while the unsymmetrical covers are counted twice or four times. When $m = n$, such covers are counted either once (if there's 8-fold symmetry) or twice (otherwise); there are respectively (1, 0, 1, 0, 2, 0, 2, 0, 11) $n \times n$ hitori covers with 8-fold symmetry. Further types of 4-fold symmetry are possible when $m = n$: There's 90° rotational symmetry (but not 8-fold) in (0, 0, 0, 1, 1, 3, 11, 30, 106) pairs of cases; there's symmetry about both diagonals (but not 8-fold) in (0, 0, 0, 0, 0, 1, 4, 9, 49) pairs of cases. Figure A–6 shows some of the winners in this beauty contest for symmetrical hitori covers.

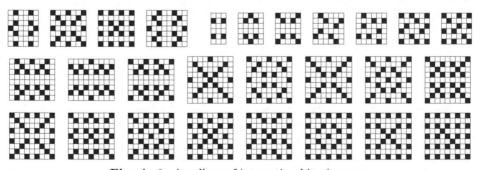

Fig. A–6. A gallery of interesting hitori covers.

Fourfold horizontal and vertical symmetry is impossible when m and n are both even, because it forces at least 12 white cells near the center. The number of $2 \times n$

hitori covers can readily be shown to satisfy the recurrence $X_n = 2X_{n-2} + 2X_{n-3}$, growing as $\Theta(r^n)$ where $r \approx 1.76929$.

443. (Solution by N. Beluhov.) Let there be s black cells, of which a lie in the interior, b on the boundary but not in a corner, and c in a corner. One can show that $b + 2c \le m+n+2-[m\,\text{even}]-[n\,\text{even}]-[mn\,\text{odd}]$. Therefore the number of edges in $P_m \square P_n \,|\, U$ is $m(n-1) + (m-1)n - 4a - 3b - 2c = 2mn - m - n - 4s + b + 2c \le 2mn - 4s + 1$. But $P_m \square P_n \,|\, U$ is connected, so it has at least $mn - s - 1$ edges.

[Beluhov has also proved that the number of black cells is always at least $mn/5 - O(m+n)$. One can obtain a small hitori cover by blackening (i,j) when $i + 2j$ is a multiple of 5, and possibly a few more cells; this cover has at most $mn/5 + 2$ black cells.]

444. No. By exercise 443, the solution has at most $\lfloor (n^2/3+2)/n \rfloor$ black cells in some row. This is at most $n/3$, when $n > 5$; hence $2n/3$ elements of that row are white. Conversely, the puzzle illustrated here for $n = 9$ can be generalized to $3k \times 3k$ for all $k > 1$. (It's a simplification of a construction by N. Beluhov. Notice that every nonzero element is a seed!)

445. Array (α) below is a seedless puzzle that corresponds to (ii), if you change its lowercase letters to uppercase. (The lowercase letters are convenient for our purposes in understanding seedlessness, because they indicate the cells that we'll want to darken.) When every black cell has a different letter to be hidden, a seedless puzzle must fill each white cell (i,j) with a hidden letter from either row i or column j.

Given a hitori cover, its "RC problem" is to put either R or C into each white cell so that the number of Rs in each row is at most the number of black cells in that row, and the number of Cs is similar but for columns. Array (β) shows the RC solution that corresponds to (α); this is one of four ways to solve the RC problem for (ii).

Suppose a hitori cover has s black cells. Every solution to its RC problem has at most s white cells marked R and at most s marked C; so we must have $s \ge n^2/3$ in an $n \times n$ cover. Consequently s must be 12 when $n = 6$, by exercise 443. In particular, pattern (i) can't lead to a seedless puzzle. Also, equality must hold when we said "at most."

It's easy to formulate the RC problem as an MCC problem, by introducing a primary item ij for each white cell (i,j), also primary items R_i and C_j for each nonwhite row i and column j. In the problem for pattern (ii) we have, for example, two options '23 R_2' and '23 C_3' for item 23. The multiplicity of C_3 is 2. (This is actually a bipartite matching problem; we use Algorithm M only because of the multiplicities.)

Array (γ) shows a seedless puzzle different from (α) that comes from the same RC solution (β). Indeed, (β) yields $3!1!2!2!1!3! \cdot 3!1!2!2!1!3! = 20736$ different seedless puzzles, because the letters chosen in each row and column can be permuted arbitrarily.

All such permutations yield valid puzzles. *Proof:* Each of the 12 letters occurs thrice. To solve the puzzle we must blacken each letter at least once, preserving white connectedness. One successful solution is to kill two birds with each stone; any other way would blacken 13 or more. But no 6×6 hitori cover has more than 12 black cells.

Pattern (iii) has eight RC solutions, and 20736 seedless puzzles for each of them.

Pattern (iv) has no RC solutions. But pattern (v) has the unique solution (δ), and one of its $3!0!3!2!1!3! \cdot 2!2!1!3!1!3! = 62208$ seedless puzzles is (ϵ).

(α) (β) (γ) (δ) (ϵ)

[N. Beluhov has proved that valid $n \times n$ seedless puzzles exist $\iff n \bmod 6 = 0$.]

446. There are only 1804 hitori covers, according to answer 442; but the exact probability appears to be difficult to compute. Experiments with millions of random numbers show convincingly, however, that the probability is $\approx .0133$. It drops to $\approx .0105$ with radix 8, and even further to $\approx .0060$ with radix 16; the "sweet spot" appears to be radix 10(!). [Also, the probability for decimal 4×4 is $\approx .0344$; for 6×6 only $\approx .0020$.]

447. Yes, when $2 \le m \le 4$ and $n = 6$! (Johan discovered the 4×6, and the 5×5 for e, in 2017. The cases 2×6, 3×2, and 4×5 also work for e. By exercise 443, we can assume that $m, n \le 15$.)

448. There are just two answers. (Also a nice 6×6 with only one not-so-common word.)

T	A	S	T	E
U	P	P	E	R
F	R	I	A	R
T	O	R	S	O
S	N	E	E	R

I	D	L	E	D
S	W	E	A	R
L	E	A	S	E
E	L	V	E	S
S	L	E	D	S

S	C	H	E	M	A
H	A	U	L	E	D
I	S	S	U	E	D
R	E	T	A	K	E
T	I	L	T	E	R
S	N	E	E	R	S

449. A few more nuggets: Johan noticed (i) in the (appropriately named) 1990 movie *Home Alone*; and he found (ii) in the King James Bible, Luke 9:56. George Sicherman hit on Falstaff's famous repartee (iii) in *1 Henry IV*, Act V, Scene 4, Line 119. The author found (iv) within the graffiti on page 278 of *CMath*; also (v), an inspiring remark by Francis Sullivan, on page 2 of *Computing in Science and Engineering* **2**, 1 (January/February 2000). Example (vi) appears in the front matter to Volume 1. And example (vii), also 11×3, shows that a nice hitori can involve lowercase letters, spaces, and punctuation; it's a quote from Samuel Rogers's poem *Human Life* (1819).

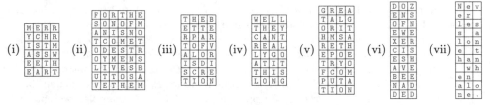

The current record for largest literary hitori nugget, $12 \times 5 = 60$, was found by Gary McDonald in September 2019: "Ruth intimated that, as far as she could judge, he was a very eligible swain." [Charles Dickens, *Martin Chuzzlewit*.]

450. The solutions are characterized by 25 items {tot, tibi, ..., caelo, 1a, 1b, 1c, ..., 5a, 5b, 5c, 6a, 6b} and 80 options 'tot 1a', 'tot 1b 1c', ..., 'tot 4b 4c', 'tot 5a', 'tot 6a', 'tot 6b'; 'tibi 1b 1c', 'tibi 1c 2a', ..., 'tibi 5c 6a'; ..., 'sidera 1a 1b 1c', ..., 'sidera 5a 5b 5c'; 'caelo 1a 1b 1c', 'caelo 1b 1c 2a', ..., 'caelo 4b 4c 5a', 'caelo 6a 6b'.

SECTION 7.2.2.2

1. (a) $\emptyset$ (no clauses). (b) $\{\epsilon\}$ (one clause, which is empty).

2. Letting $1 \leftrightarrow$ lazy, $2 \leftrightarrow$ happy, $3 \leftrightarrow$ unhealthy, $4 \leftrightarrow$ dancer, we're given the respective clauses $\{31\bar{4}, \bar{1}42, 3\bar{4}2, \bar{2}4\bar{3}, \bar{1}3\bar{2}, 2\bar{3}1, \bar{1}4\bar{3}\}$, matching R' in (7). So all known Pincusians dance happily, and none are lazy. But we know nothing about their health. [And we might wonder why travelers have bothered to describe so many empty sets.]

3. $f(j-1, n) + f(k-1, n)$, where $f(p, n) = \sum_{d=1}^{q}(n-pd) = p\binom{q}{2} + q(n \bmod p) \approx n^2/(2p)$, if we set $q = \lfloor n/p \rfloor$.

4. Those constraints are unsatisfiable if and only if we remove a subset of either $\{357, 456, \bar{3}5\bar{7}, \bar{4}5\bar{6}\}$, $\{246, 468, \bar{2}4\bar{6}, \bar{4}6\bar{8}\}$, $\{246, 357, 468, \bar{4}5\bar{6}\}$, or $\{456, \bar{2}4\bar{6}, \bar{3}5\bar{7}, \bar{4}6\bar{8}\}$.

5. No polynomial upper bound for $W(3, k)$ is currently known. Clearly $W(3, k)$ is less than $\overline{W}(3, k)$, the minimum n that guarantees either three equally spaced 0s or k *consecutive* 1s. An analysis by R. L. Graham in *Integers* **6** (2006), A29:1–A29:5, beefed up by a subsequent theorem of T. F. Bloom in *J. London Math. Society* (2) **93** (2016), 643–663, shows that $\overline{W}(3, k) = \exp O(k(\log k)^4)$.

6. Let each x_i be 0 with probability $p = (2 \ln k)/k$, and let n be at most $k^2/(\ln k)^3$. There are two kinds of "bad events": A_i, a set of three equally spaced 0s, occurs with probability $P = p^3$; and A'_j, a set of k equally spaced 1s, occurs with probability $P' = (1-p)^k \le \exp(-kp) = 1/k^2$. In the lopsidependency graph, which is bipartite, each A_i is adjacent to at most $D = 3k^3/((k-1)(\ln k)^3)$ nodes A'_j; each A'_j is adjacent to at most $d = \frac{3}{2}k^3/(\ln k)^3$ nodes A_i. By Theorem L, we want to show that, for all sufficiently large values of k, $P \le y(1-x)^D$ and $P' \le x(1-y)^d$, for some x and y.

Choose x and y so that $(1-x)^D = 1/2$ and $y = 2P$. Then $x = \Theta((\log k)^3/k^2)$ and $y = \Theta((\log k)^3/k^3)$; hence $(1-y)^d = \exp(-yd + O(y^2 d)) = O(1)$. [See T. Brown, B. M. Landman, and A. Robertson, *J. Combinatorial Theory* **A115** (2008), 1304–1309.]

7. Yes, for all n, when $x_1 x_2 x_3 \ldots = 001001001 \ldots$.

8. For example, let $x_{i,a}$ signify that $x_i = a$, for $1 \le i \le n$ and $0 \le a < b$. The relevant clauses are then $x_{i,0} \vee \cdots \vee x_{i,b-1}$ for $1 \le i \le n$; and $\bar{x}_{i,a} \vee \bar{x}_{i+d,a} \vee \cdots \vee \bar{x}_{i+(k_a-1)d,a}$, for $1 \le i \le n - (k_a - 1)d$ and $d \ge 1$. Optionally include the clauses $\bar{x}_{i,a} \vee \bar{x}_{i,a'}$ for $0 \le a < a' < b$. (Whenever the relevant clauses are satisfiable, we can also satisfy the optional ones by falsifying some variables if necessary.)

[V. Chvátal found $W(3, 3, 3) = 27$. Kouril's paper shows that $W(2, 4, 8) = 157$, $W(2, 3, 14) = 202$, $W(2, 5, 6) = 246$, $W(4, 4, 4) = 293$, and lists many smaller values.]

9. $W(2, 2, k) = 3k - (2, 0, 2, 2, 1, 0)$ when $k \bmod 6 = (0, 1, 2, 3, 4, 5)$. The sequence $2^{k-1}02^{k-1}12^{k-1}$ is maximal when $k \perp 6$; also $2^{k-1}02^{k-1}12^{k-3}$ when $k \bmod 6 = 3$; also $2^{k-1}02^{k-2}12^{k-1}$ when $k \bmod 6 = 4$; otherwise $2^{k-1}02^{k-2}12^{k-2}$. [See B. Landman, A. Robertson, and C. Culver, *Integers* **5** (2005), A10:1–A10:11, where many other values of $W(2, \ldots, 2, k)$ are also established.]

10. If the original variables are $\{1, \ldots, n\}$, let the new ones be $\{1, \ldots, n\} \cup \{1', \ldots, n'\}$. The new problem has positive clauses $\{11', \ldots, nn'\}$. Its negative clauses are, for example, $\bar{2}'\bar{6}\bar{7}9'$ if $2\bar{6}\bar{7}9$ was an original clause. The original problem is equivalent because it can be obtained from the new one by resolving away the primed variables.

[One can in fact construct an equivalent monotonic problem of size $O(m+n)$ in which $(x_1 \vee \cdots \vee x_k)$ is a positive clause if and only if $(\bar{x}_1 \vee \cdots \vee \bar{x}_k)$ is a negative clause. Such a problem, "not-all-equal SAT," is equivalent to 2-colorability of hypergraphs. See L. Lovász, *Congressus Numerantium* **8** (1973), 3–12; H. Kleine Büning and T. Lettmann, *Propositional Logic* (Cambridge Univ. Press, 1999), §3.2, Problems 4–8.]

11. For each variable i, the only way to match vertices of the forms ij' and ij'' is to choose all of its true triples or all of its false triples.

Furthermore, the only way to match $j'1$ is to choose one of the satisfiability triples for clause j. Suppose $\bar{l}_k j$ belongs to the chosen triple; then we must also have chosen the true triples for literal l_k. Thus a perfect matching implies satisfiable clauses.

Conversely, if all clauses are satisfied, with l_k true in clause j, there always are exactly two ways to match $\bar{l}_k j$ with $j'1$ while matching wj, xj, yj, zj, and the other two $\bar{l}j$ vertices with $j'2$, ..., $j'7$. (It's a beautiful construction! Notice that no vertex appears in more than three triples.)

12. Equation (13) says $S_1(y_1, \ldots, y_p) = S_{\geq 1}(y_1, \ldots, y_p) \wedge S_{\leq 1}(y_1, \ldots, y_p)$. If $p \leq 4$, use $\bigwedge_{1 \leq j < k \leq p}(\bar{y}_j \vee \bar{y}_k)$ for $S_{\leq 1}(y_1, \ldots, y_p)$; otherwise $S_{\leq 1}(y_1, \ldots, y_p)$ can be encoded recursively via the clauses $S_{\leq 1}(y_1, y_2, y_3, t) \wedge S_{\leq 1}(\bar{t}, y_4, \ldots, y_p)$, where t is a new variable. [This method saves half of the auxiliary variables in the answer to exercise 7.1.1–55(b).]

Note: Langford's problem involves primary items only; in an exact cover problem with *nonprimary* items, such items only need the constraint $S_{\leq 1}(y_1, \ldots, y_p)$.

13. (a) $S_1(x_1, x_2, x_3, x_4, x_5, x_6) \wedge S_1(x_7, x_8, x_9, x_{10}, x_{11}) \wedge S_1(x_{12}, x_{13}) \wedge S_1(x_{14}, x_{15}, x_{16}) \wedge S_1(x_1, x_7, x_{12}, x_{14}) \wedge S_1(x_2, x_8, x_{13}, x_{15}) \wedge S_1(x_1, x_3, x_9, x_{16}) \wedge S_1(x_2, x_4, x_7, x_{10}) \wedge S_1(x_3, x_5, x_8, x_{11}, x_{12}) \wedge S_1(x_4, x_6, x_9, x_{13}, x_{14}) \wedge S_1(x_5, x_{10}, x_{15}) \wedge S_1(x_6, x_{11}, x_{16})$.

(b) Duplicate clauses occur when options intersect more than once. We avoid them if we simply generate clauses $\bar{x}_i \vee \bar{x}_j$ for every pair (i, j) of intersecting options.

(c) When *langford*(4) is generated in this way, it has 85 distinct clauses in 16 variables, namely $(x_1 \vee x_2 \vee x_3 \vee x_4 \vee x_5 \vee x_6) \wedge (x_7 \vee x_8 \vee x_9 \vee x_{10} \vee x_{11}) \wedge \cdots \wedge (x_6 \vee x_{11} \vee x_{16}) \wedge (\bar{x}_1 \vee \bar{x}_2) \wedge (\bar{x}_1 \vee \bar{x}_3) \wedge \cdots \wedge (\bar{x}_{15} \vee \bar{x}_{16})$.

But *langford'*(4) cannot use the trick of (b). It has 85 (nondistinct) clauses in 20 variables, beginning with 123456, $\overline{1}\overline{2}$, $\overline{1}\overline{3}$, $\overline{1}\overline{1}'$, $\overline{2}\overline{3}$, $\overline{2}\overline{1}'$, $\overline{3}\overline{1}'$, $1'\overline{4}$, $1'\overline{5}$, $1'\overline{6}$, $\overline{4}\overline{5}$, $\overline{4}\overline{6}$, $\overline{5}\overline{6}$, ..., if we denote the auxiliary variables by $1'$, $2'$, ... Two of those clauses ($\overline{1}\overline{3}$ and $\overline{4}\overline{6}$) are repeated. (Incidentally, *langford'*(12) has 1548 clauses, 417 variables, 3600 literals.)

14. (Answer by M. Heule.) Those clauses sometimes help to focus the search. For example, if we're trying to color the complete graph K_n with n colors (or pigeons), we don't want to waste time trying $v_2 = 1$ when v_1 is already 1.

On the other hand, other instances of SAT often run slower when redundant clauses are present, because more updates to the data structures are needed.

We might also take an opposite approach, and replace (17) by nd clauses that force every color class to be a *kernel*. (See exercise 21.) Such clauses sometimes speed up a proof of uncolorability.

15. There are $N = n(n+1)$ vertices (j, k) for $0 \leq j \leq n$ and $0 \leq k < n$. If $(j, k) = (1, 0)$ we define $(j, k) \!\!-\!\! (n, i)$ for $x \leq i < n$, where $x = \lfloor n/2 \rfloor$. Otherwise we define the following edges: $(j, k) \!\!-\!\! (j+1, k+1)$ if $j < n$ and $k < n-1$; $(j, k) \!\!-\!\! (j+1, k)$ if $j < n$ and $j \neq k$; $(j, k) \!\!-\!\! (j, k+1)$ if $k < n-1$ and $j \neq k+1$; $(j, k) \!\!-\!\! (n, n-1)$ if $j = 0$; $(j, k) \!\!-\!\! (n-j, 0)$ if $k < n-1$ and $j = k$; $(j, k) \!\!-\!\! (n+1-j, 0)$ if $j > 0$ and $j = k$; $(j, k) \!\!-\!\! (n-j, n-j-1)$ if $k = n-1$ and $0 < j < k$; $(j, k) \!\!-\!\! (n+1-j, n-j)$ if $k = n-1$ and $0 < j < n$. Finally, $(0, 0) \!\!-\!\! (1, 0)$, and $(0, 0) \!\!-\!\! (n, i)$ for $1 \leq i \leq x$. That makes a grand total of $3N - 6$ edges. (It's a maximal planar graph; see exercise 7–46.)

16. There's a unique 4-clique for all $n \geq 3$, namely $\{(0, n-2), (0, n-1), (1, n-1), (n, n-1)\}$. All other vertices, except $(0, 0)$ and $(1, 0)$, are surrounded by neighbors that form an induced cycle of length 4 or more (usually 6). [See J.-L. Lauriere, *Artificial Intelligence* **10** (1978), 117.]

17. Let $mcgregor(n)$ be the clauses (15) and (16) for the graph. Add clauses (18) and (19), for symmetric threshold functions to bound the number of variables v_1 for color 1; the kth vertex x_k can be specified by the ordering in answer 20. Then if, for instance, we can satisfy those clauses together with the unit clause s_r^N, where $N = n(n+1)$, we have proved that $f(n) < r$. Similarly, if we can satisfy them together with $\bar{s}_r^N$, we have proved that $g(n) \geq r$. Additional unit clauses that specify the colors of the four clique vertices will speed up the computation: Four cases should be run, one with each clique vertex receiving color 1. If all four cases are unsatisfiable, we've proved that $f(n) \geq r$ or $g(n) < r$, respectively. Binary search with different values of r will identify the optimum.

For speedier $g(n)$, first find a maximum independent set instead of a complete 4-coloring; then notice that the colorings for $f(n)$ already achieve this maximum.

The results turn out to be $f(n) = (2, 2, 3, 4, 5, 7, 7, 7, 8, 9, 10, 12, 12, 12)$ for $n = (3, 4, \ldots, 16)$, and $g(n) = (4, 6, 10, 13, 17, 23, 28, 35, 42, 50, 58, 68, 77, 88)$.

18. Assuming that $n \geq 4$, first assign to vertex (j, k) the following "default color": $1 + (j+k) \bmod 3$ if $j \leq k$; $1 + (j + k + 1 - n) \bmod 3$ if $k < j/2$; otherwise $1 + (j + k + 2 - n) \bmod 3$. Then make the following changes to exceptional vertices: Vertex $(1, 0)$ is colored 2 if $n \bmod 6 = 0$ or 5, otherwise 3. Vertex $(n, n-1)$ is colored 4. For $k \leftarrow 0$ up to $n-2$, change the color of vertex (n, k) to 4, if its default color matches vertex $(0, 0)$ when $k \leq n/2$ or vertex $(1, 0)$ when $k > n/2$. And make final touchups for $1 \leq j < n/2$, depending again on $n \bmod 6$:

Case 0: Give color 4 to vertex $(2j, j-1)$ and color 1 to vertex $(2j+1, j)$.

Case 1: Give color 4 to vertex $(2j, j)$ and color 2 to vertex $(2j+1, j)$.

Case 2: Give color 4 to vertex $(2j, j)$ and color 1 to vertex $(2j+1, j)$. Also give $(n, n-2)$ the color 1 and $(n-1, n-3)$ the color 4.

Cases 3, 4, 5: Give color 4 to vertex $(2j+1, j)$.

For example, the coloring for the case $n = 10$ (found by Bryant) is shown in Fig. A–7(a).

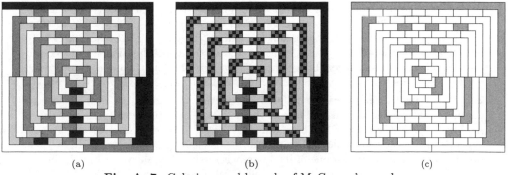

(a)　　　　　　　(b)　　　　　　　(c)

Fig. A–7. Colorings and kernels of McGregor's graph.

The color distribution is $(\lfloor n^2/3 \rfloor, \lfloor n^2/3 \rfloor, \lfloor n^2/3 \rfloor, 5k) + ((0, 1, k, -1), (1, k, 1, 0), (-1, k+1, 1, 2), (0, k, 1, 2), (1, k+1, 1, 2), (0, 2, k+1, 3))$, for $n \bmod 6 = (0, 1, 2, 3, 4, 5)$, $k = \lfloor n/6 \rfloor$. Since this construction achieves all of the optimum values for $f(n)$ and $g(n)$, when $n \leq 16$, it probably is optimum for all n. Moreover, the value of $g(n)$ agrees with the size of the maximum independent set in all known cases. A further conjecture is that the maximum independent set is *unique*, whenever $n \bmod 6 = 0$ and $n > 6$.

19. Use the clauses of $mcgregor(n)$, together with $(v_1 \lor v_2 \lor v_3 \lor \bar{v}_x) \land (v_1 \lor v_2 \lor v_4 \lor \bar{v}_x) \land$ $(v_1 \lor v_3 \lor v_4 \lor \bar{v}_x) \land (v_2 \lor v_3 \lor v_4 \lor \bar{v}_x)$ for each vertex, together with clauses from (20) and (21) that require at least r of the vertices v_x to be true. Also assign unique colors to the four clique vertices. (One assignment, not four, is sufficient to break symmetry here, because $h(n)$ is a more symmetrical property than $f(n)$ or $g(n)$.) These clauses are satisfiable if and only if $h(n) \geq r$. The SAT computation goes faster if we also provide clauses that require each color class to be a *kernel* (see exercise 21).

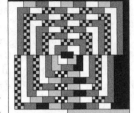

The values $h(n) = (1, 3, 4, 8, 9, 13)$ for $n = (3, 4, \ldots, 8)$ are readily obtained in this way. Furthermore, if we extend color class 4 in the construction of answer 18 to a suitable kernel, we find $h(9) \geq 17$ and $h(10) \geq 23$. The resulting diagram for $n = 10$, illustrated in Fig. A–7(b), nicely exhibits 2^{23} solutions to McGregor's original coloring problem, all at once.

A good SAT solver also shows that $h(9) \leq 18$ and $h(10) \leq 23$, thus proving that $h(10) = 23$. And Armin Biere's solver proved in 2013 that $h(9) = 18$, by discovering the surprising solution shown here. (This exercise was inspired by Frank Bernhart, who sent a diagram like Fig. A–7(b) to Martin Gardner in 1975; his diagram achieved 2^{21} solutions.)

20. Arrange the vertices (j, k) of answer 15 in the following order $v_0, v_1, \ldots$: $(n, n-1)$; $(0, n-1)$, $(0, n-2)$, $\ldots$, $(0, 0)$; $(1, n-1)$, $(1, n-2)$, $\ldots$, $(1, 1)$; $\ldots$; $(n-2, n-1)$, $(n-2, n-2)$; $(n-1, n-2)$, $(n-2, n-3)$, $\ldots$, $(2, 1)$; $(n-1, n-1)$; $(2, 0), (3, 1), \ldots$, $(n, n-2)$; $(3, 0), (4, 1), \ldots$, $(n, n-3)$; $(1, 0); (4, 0), \ldots$, $(n, n-4)$; $\ldots$; $(n-1, 0), (n, 1)$; $(n, 0)$. Then if $V_t = \{v_0, \ldots, v_{t-1}\}$, let the "frontier" F_t consist of all vertices $\in V_t$ that have at least one neighbor $\notin V_t$. We can assume that (v_0, v_1, v_2) are colored $(0, 1, 2)$, because they are part of the 4-clique.

All 4-colorings of V_t that have a given sequence of colors on F_t can be enumerated if we know the corresponding counts for F_{t-1}. The stated ordering ensures that F_t never will contain more than $2n-1$ elements; in fact, at most 3^{2n-2} sequences of colors are feasible, for any given t. Since 3^{18} is less than 400 million, it's quite feasible to do these incremental calculations. The total (obtained with about 6 gigabytes of memory and after about 500 gigamems of computation) turns out to be 898,431,907,970,211.

This problem is too large to be handled efficiently by BDD methods when $n = 10$, but BDD calculations for $n \leq 8$ can be used to check the algorithm. The frontiers essentially represent level-by-level slices of a QDD for this problem. The 4-coloring counts for $3 \leq n \leq 9$ are respectively 6, 99, 1814, 107907, 9351764, 2035931737, 847019915170.

21. With one Boolean variable v for every vertex of a graph G, the kernels are characterized by the clauses (i) $\bar{u} \lor \bar{v}$ whenever $u - v$; (ii) $v \lor \bigvee_{u-v} u$ for all v. Adding to these the clauses for the symmetric threshold function $S_{\leq r}(x_1, \ldots, x_N)$, we can find the least r for which all clauses are satisfiable. The graph of Fig. 76 yields satisfiability for $r = 17$; and one of its 46 kernels of size 17 is shown in Fig. A–7(c).

[BDD methods are slower for this problem; but they enumerate *all* 520,428,275,749 of the kernels, as well as the generating function $46z^{17} + 47180z^{18} + \cdots + 317z^{34} + 2z^{35}$.]

22. Eight colors are needed. The coloring $\begin{smallmatrix}12771\\22788\\33668\\34655\\14451\end{smallmatrix}$ is "balanced," with each color used at least thrice.

23. Writing k for x_k and $\frac{k}{j}$ for s_j^k, the clauses from (18)–(19) are $\bar{1}\,\bar{1}\,_{1\,2}$, $\bar{1}\,\bar{1}\,_{2\,3}$, $\bar{2}\,\bar{2}\,_{1\,2}$, $\bar{2}\,\bar{2}\,_{2\,3}$, $\bar{3}\,\bar{3}\,_{1\,2}$, $\bar{3}\,\bar{3}\,_{2\,3}$, $\bar{4}\,\bar{4}\,_{1\,2}$, $\bar{4}\,\bar{4}\,_{2\,3}$; $\bar{1}^1_1$, $\bar{2}^1_2$, $\bar{3}^1_3$, $\bar{2}^{\bar{1}\,2}_{1\,1}$, $\bar{3}^{\bar{1}\,2}_{2\,2}$, $\bar{4}^{\bar{1}\,2}_{3\,3}$, $3^{\bar{1}\,1}_{1\,1}$, $\bar{4}^{\bar{2}\,3}_{2\,2}$, $5^{\bar{2}\,3}_{3\,3}$, $\bar{4}^{\bar{3}\,4}_{1\,1}$, $5^{\bar{3}\,4}_{2\,2}$, $6^{\bar{3}\,4}_{3\,3}$, $5^{\bar{4}}_1$, $6^{\bar{4}}_2$, $7^{\bar{4}}_3$.

Similarly, (20) and (21) define the clauses $\bar{7}^6_1$, $\bar{6}^6_1$, $\bar{6}7^6_2$; $\bar{5}^5_1$, $\bar{4}^5_1$, $\bar{4}5^5_2$; $\bar{3}^4_1$, $\bar{2}^4_1$, $\bar{2}3^4_2$; $\bar{1}^3_1$, $\bar{6}^3_{11}$, $\bar{6}\bar{1}^3_{12}$, $\bar{6}^3_{22}$, $\bar{6}\bar{1}^3_{23}$; $\bar{5}^2_{11}$, $\bar{4}^2_{11}$, $\bar{5}^2_{22}$, $\bar{4}^2_{22}$, $\bar{4}5^2_{112}$, $\bar{4}5^2_{123}$, $\bar{4}5^2_{213}$, $\bar{2}^2_{224}$; $\bar{2}^3_{41}$, $\bar{2}^3_{32}$, $\bar{2}^3_{23}$. So this tree-based method apparently needs one more variable and two more clauses when $(n, r) = (7, 4)$. But the next exercise shows that (18) and (19) don't really win!

24. (a) The clause $(\bar{b}_1^2 \vee \bar{b}_r^3)$ appears only if $t_3 = r$; and $t_3 \leq n/2$.

(b) For example, $t_3 = \min(r, 4) < r$ when $n = 11$ and $r = 5$.

(c) In this case t_k is the number of leaves below node k, and the only auxiliary variables that survive pure literal elimination are $b_{t_k}^k$. We're left with just $n-1$ surviving clauses, namely $(\bar{b}_{t_{2k}}^{2k} \vee \bar{b}_{t_{2k+1}}^{2k+1} \vee b_{t_k}^k)$ for $1 < k < n$, plus $(\bar{b}_{t_2}^2 \vee \bar{b}_{t_3}^3)$.

(d) If $2^k \leq n \leq 2^k + 2^{k-1}$ we have $(n', n'') = (n - 2^{k-1}, 2^{k-1})$; on the other hand if $2^k + 2^{k-1} \leq n \leq 2^{k+1}$ we have $(n', n'') = (2^k, n - 2^k)$. (Notice that $n'' \leq n' \leq 2n''$.)

(e) No pure literals are removed in this completely balanced case (which is the easiest to analyze). We find $a(2^k, 2^{k-1}) = (k-1)2^k$ and $c(2^k, 2^{k-1}) = (2^{k-2} + k - 1)2^k$.

(f) One can show that $a(n, r) = (r \leq n''? \; b(n', r) + b(n'', r): r \leq n'? \; b(n', n'') + b(n'', n''): b(n', n-r) + b(n'', n-r))$, where $b(1, 1) = 0$ and $b(n, r) = r + b(n', \min(r, n')) + b(n'', \min(r, n''))$ for $n \geq 2$. Similarly, $c(n, r) = (r \leq n''? \; r + f(n', 0, r) + f(n'', 0, r): r \leq n'? \; n'' + f(n', r - n'', r) + f(n'', 0, n''): n - r + f(n', r - n'', n') + f(n'', r - n', n''))$, where $f(n, l, r) = \sum_{k=l+1}^r \min(k+1, n''+1, n+1- k) + (r \leq n''? \; r + f(n', 0, r) + f(n'', 0, r): r \leq n'? \; n'' + f(n', 0, r) + f(n'', 0, n''): r < n? \; n - r + f(n', 0, n') + f(n'', 0, n''): f(n', (n' + l) \dot{-} r, n') + f(n'', (n'' + l) \dot{-} r, n''))$ for $n \geq 2$ and $f(1, 0, 1) = 0$. The desired results follow by induction from these recurrence relations.

Incidentally, ternary branching can give further savings. We can, for example, handle the case $n = 6$, $r = 3$ with 17 clauses in the 6 variables $b_1^2, b_2^2, b_3^2, b_1^3, b_2^3, b_3^3$.

25. From (18) and (19) we obtain $5n - 12$ clauses in $2n - 4$ variables, with a simple lattice-like structure. But (20) and (21) produce a more complex tree-like pattern, with $2n - 4$ variables and with $\lfloor n/2 \rfloor$ nodes covering just two leaves. So we get $\lfloor n/2 \rfloor$ nodes with 3 clauses, $n \bmod 2$ nodes with 5 clauses, $\lceil n/2 \rceil$ nodes with 7 clauses, and 2 clauses from (21), totalling $5n - 12$ as before (assuming that $n > 3$). In fact, all but $n - 2$ of the clauses are binary in both cases.

26. Imagine the boundary conditions $s_j^0 = 1$, $s_j^{r+1} = 0$, $s_0^k = 0$, for $1 \leq j \leq n - r$ and $1 \leq k \leq r$. The clauses say that $s_1^k \leq \cdots \leq s_{n-r}^k$ and that $x_{j+k}s_j^k \leq s_j^{k+1}$; so the hint follows by induction on j and k.

Setting $j = n - r$ and $k = r + 1$ shows that we cannot satisfy the new clauses when $x_1 + \cdots + x_n \geq r + 1$. Conversely, if we can satisfy F with $x_1 + \cdots + x_n \leq r$ then we can satisfy (18) and (19) by setting $s_j^k \leftarrow [x_1 + \cdots + x_{j+k-1} \geq k]$.

27. Argue as in the previous answer, but imagine that $b_0^k = 1$, $b_{r+1}^1 = 0$; prove the hint by induction on j and $n - k$ (beginning with $k = n - 1$, then $k = n - 2$, and so on).

28. For example, the clauses for $\bar{x}_1 + \cdots + \bar{x}_n \leq n - 1$ when $n = 5$ are $(x_1 \vee s_1^1)$, $(x_2 \vee \bar{s}_1^1 \vee s_1^2)$, $(x_3 \vee \bar{s}_1^2 \vee s_1^3)$, $(x_4 \vee \bar{s}_1^3 \vee s_1^4)$, $(x_5 \vee \bar{s}_1^4)$. We may assume that $n \geq 4$; then the first two clauses can be replaced by $(x_1 \vee x_2 \vee s_1^2)$, and the last two by $(x_{n-1} \vee x_n \vee \bar{s}_1^{n-2})$, yielding $n - 2$ clauses of length 3 in $n - 3$ auxiliary variables.

29. We can assume that $1 \leq r_1 \leq \cdots \leq r_n = r < n$. Sinz's clauses (18) and (19) actually do the job nicely if we also assert that s_j^k is false whenever $k = r_i + 1$ and $j = i - r_i$.

30. The clauses now are $(\bar{s}_j^k \vee s_{j+1}^k)$, $(\bar{x}_{j+k} \vee \bar{s}_j^k \vee s_j^{k+1})$, $(s_j^k \vee \bar{s}_j^{k+1})$, $(x_{j+k} \vee s_j^k \vee \bar{s}_{j+1}^k)$, hence they define the quantities $s_j^k = [x_1 + \cdots + x_{j+k-1} \geq k]$; implicitly $s_0^k = s_j^{r+1} = 0$ and $s_j^0 = s_{n-r+1}^k = 1$. The new clauses in answer 23 are $1\frac{2}{1}, 2\frac{3}{1}, 3\frac{4}{1}, 1\frac{2}{2}, 2\frac{3}{2}, 3\frac{4}{2}, 1\frac{2}{3}, 2\frac{3}{3}, 3\frac{4}{3}; 1\frac{\bar{1}}{1}, 2\frac{\bar{2}}{1}, 3\frac{\bar{3}}{1}, 4\frac{\bar{4}}{1}, 2\frac{\bar{1}}{1}{2}, 3\frac{\bar{2}}{1}{2}, 4\frac{\bar{3}}{1}{2}, 5\frac{\bar{4}}{1}{2}, 3\frac{\bar{1}}{2}{3}, 4\frac{\bar{2}}{2}{3}, 5\frac{\bar{3}}{2}{3}, 6\frac{\bar{4}}{2}{3}, 4\frac{1}{3}, 5\frac{2}{3}, 6\frac{3}{3}, 7\frac{4}{3}$.

With (20) and (21) we can identify b'^k_j with $\bar b^k_{l_k+1-j}$, when $l_k > 1$ leaves are below node k. Then b^k_j is true if *and only if* the leaves below k have j or more 1s. For example, answer 23 gets the new clauses $7^{\bar6}_2,\, 6^{\bar6}_2,\, 67^{\bar6}_1;\ 5^{\bar5}_2,\, 4^{\bar5}_2,\, 45^{\bar5}_1;\ 3^{\bar4}_2,\, 2^{\bar4}_2,\, 23^{\bar4}_1;\ 1^{\bar3}_3,$ $\frac{6\,\bar3}{2\,3},\, \frac{16\,\bar3}{1\,2\,2},\, \frac{6\,\bar3}{1\,2},\, \frac{16\,\bar3}{1\,1\,1};\ \frac{4\,\bar2}{2\,4},\, \frac{5\,\bar2}{2\,4},\, \frac{4\,\bar2}{1\,3},\, \frac{45\,\bar2}{2\,2\,3},\, \frac{5\,\bar2}{1\,3},\, \frac{45\,\bar2}{1\,2\,2},\, \frac{45\,\bar2}{2\,1\,2},\, \frac{4\,5}{1\,1};\ \frac{2\,3}{4\,1},\, \frac{2\,3}{3\,2},\, \frac{2\,3}{2\,3}.$

Furthermore, (20) and (21) can be unified in the same way with the weaker constraints $r' \leq x_1 + \cdots + x_n \leq r$. If we want, say, $2 \leq x_1 + \cdots + x_7 \leq 4$, we can simply replace the final four clauses of the previous paragraph by $\frac{4\,5\,\bar2}{1\,1\,1},\, \frac{2\,3}{2\,1},\, \frac{2\,3}{1\,2}$. Under the conventions of (18) and (19), by contrast, these weaker constraints would generate a comparable number of new clauses, namely $\frac{1\,\bar2}{1\,1},\, \frac{1\,\bar2}{2\,2},\, \frac{1\,\bar2}{3\,3},\, \frac{1\,\bar2}{4\,4},\, \frac{1\,\bar2}{5\,5}$ and $1^{\bar1}_1,\, 2^{\bar2}_1,\, 3^{1\,\bar2}_{1\,2},\, 3^{1\,\bar2}_{2\,3},\, 4^{2\,\bar2}_{2\,3},$ $4^{1\,\bar1}_{3\,4},\, 5^{2\,\bar2}_{3\,4},\, 5^{1\,\bar1}_{4\,5},\, 6^{2\,\bar2}_{4\,5},\, 6^1_5,\, 7^2_5$; but those clauses involve the new variables $\tfrac14,\, \tfrac15,\, \tfrac24,\, \tfrac25$.

31. We can use the constraints on the second line of (10), together with the constraints of exercise 30 that force $x_1 + \cdots + x_n = r$. Then we seek n for which this problem is satisfiable, while the same problem with $x_n = 0$ is not. The following small values can be used to check the calculations:

r	1	2	3	4	5	6	7	8	9	10	11	12	13	14	15	16	17	18	19	20	21	22	23	24	25	26	27
$F_3(r) =$	1	2	4	5	9	11	13	14	20	24	26	30	32	36	40	41	51	54	58	63	71	74	82	84	92	95	100
$F_4(r) =$	1	2	3	5	6	8	9	10	13	15	17	19	21	23	25	27	28	30	33	34	37	40	43	45	48	50	53
$F_5(r) =$	1	2	3	4	6	7	8	9	11	12	13	14	16	17	18	19	24	25	27	28	29	31	33	34	36	37	38
$F_6(r) =$	1	2	3	4	5	7	8	9	10	12	13	14	15	17	18	19	20	22	23	24	25	26	29	32	33	35	36

Furthermore, significant speedup is possible if we also make use of previously computed values $F_t(1), \ldots, F_t(r-1)$. For example, when $t = 3$ and $r \geq 5$ we must have $x_{a+1} + \cdots + x_{a+8} \leq 4$ for $0 \leq a \leq n-8$, because $F_3(5) = 9$. These additional subinterval constraints blend beautifully with those of exercise 30, because $x_{a+1} + \cdots + x_{a+p} \leq q$ for $0 \leq a \leq n - p$ implies $\bar s^k_{b+p-q} \vee s^{k-q}_b$ for $0 \leq b \leq n+1-p+q-r$ and $q < k \leq r$.

We can also take advantage of left-right symmetry by appending the unit clause $\bar s^{\lceil r/2 \rceil}_{\lceil (n-r)/2 \rceil}$ when r is odd; $s^{r/2}_{n/2-r/2+1}$ when n and r are both even.

Suitable benchmark examples arise when computing, say, $F_3(27)$ or $F_4(36)$. But for large cases, general SAT-based methods do not seem to compete with the best special-purpose backtrack routines. For example, Gavin Theobald and Rodolfo Niborski have obtained the value $F_3(41) = 194$, which seems well beyond the reach of these ideas.

[See P. Erdős and P. Turán, *J. London Math. Soc.* (2) **11** (1936), 261–264; errata, **34** (1959), 480; S. S. Wagstaff, Jr., *Math. Comp.* **26** (1972), 767–771.]

32. Use (15) and (16), and optionally (17), but omit variable v_j unless $j \in L(v)$.

33. To double-color a graph with k colors, change (15) to the set of k clauses $v_1 \vee \cdots \vee v_{j-1} \vee v_{j+1} \vee \cdots \vee v_k$, for $1 \leq j \leq k$; similarly, $\binom{k}{2}$ clauses of length $k - 2$ will yield a triple coloring. Small examples reveal that C_{2l+1} for $l \geq 2$ can be double-colored with five colors: $\{1,2\}(\{3,4\}\{5,1\})^{l-1}\{2,3\}\{4,5\}$; furthermore, seven colors suffice for triple coloring when $l \geq 3$: $\{1,2,3\}(\{4,5,6\}\{7,1,2\})^{l-2}\{3,4,5\}\{6,7,1\}\{2,3,4\}\{5,6,7\}$. The following exercise proves that those colorings are in fact optimum.

34. (a) We can obviously find a q-tuple coloring with $q\chi(G)$ colors. And McGregor's graph has a four-clique, hence $\chi^*(G) \geq 4$.

(b) Any q-tuple coloring with p colors yields a solution to the fractional exact cover problem, if we let $\lambda_j = \sum_{i=1}^p [S_j$ is the set of vertices colored $i]/q$. Conversely, the theory of linear equalities tells us that there is always an optimum solution with rational $\{\lambda_1, \ldots, \lambda_N\}$; such a solution yields a q-tuple coloring when each $q\lambda_j$ is an integer.

(c) $\chi^*(C_n) = \chi(C_n) = 2$ when n is even; and $\chi^*(C_{2l+1}) \le 2 + 1/l = n/\alpha(C_{2l+1})$, because there's an l-tuple coloring with n colors as in the previous exercise. Also $\chi^*(G) \ge n/\alpha(G)$ in general: $n = \sum_v \sum_j \lambda_j [v \in S_j] = \sum_j \lambda_j |S_j| \le \alpha(G) \sum_j \lambda_j$.

(d) For the hint, let $S = \{v_1, \ldots, v_l\}$ where vertices are sorted by their colors. Since vertex v_j belongs to C_i with $|C_i| \ge |\{v_j, \ldots, v_l\}|$, we have $t_{v_j} \le 1/(l+1-j)$.

So $\chi(G) \le k = \sum_v t_v = \sum_v t_v \sum_j \lambda_j [v \in S_j] = \sum_j \lambda_j \sum_v t_v [v \in S_j] \le \sum_j \lambda_j H_{\alpha(G)}$.

[See David S. Johnson, *J. Computer and System Sci.* **9** (1974), 264–269; L. Lovász, *Discrete Math.* **13** (1975), 383–390. The concept of fractional covering is due to A. J. W. Hilton, R. Rado, and S. H. Scott, *Bull. London Math. Soc.* **5** (1973), 302–306.]

35. (a) The double coloring below proves that $\chi^*(G) \ge 7/2$; and it is optimum because NV and its neighbors induce the wheel W_5. (Notice that $\chi^*(W_n) = 1 + \chi^*(C_n)$.)

(b) By part (c) of the previous exercise, $\chi^*(G) \ge 25/4$. Furthermore there is a quadruple coloring with 25 colors:

AEUY ABUV BCVW CDWX DEXY
AEFJ ABFG BCGH CDHI DEIJ
FJKO FGKL GHLM HIMN IJNO
KOPT KLPQ LMQR MNRS NOST
PTUY PQUV QRVW RSWX STXY

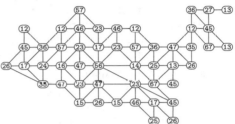

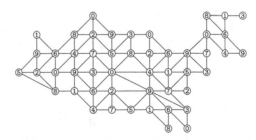

[Is $\overline{C_5 \boxtimes C_5}$ the smallest graph for which $\chi^*(G) < \chi(G) - 1$?]

36. A few more binary color constraints analogous to (16) yield the corresponding SAT problem. We can also assume that the upper right corner is colored 0, because that region touches $n + 4 = 14$ others; at least $n + 6$ colors are needed. The constraints elsewhere aren't very tight (see exercise 38(b)); thus we readily obtain an optimum radio coloring with $n + 6$ colors for the McGregor graphs of all orders $n > 4$, such as the one below. An $(n+7)$th color is necessary and sufficient when $n = 3$ or 4.

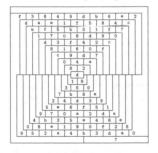

37. The 10-coloring shown here is optimum, because Missouri (MO) has degree 8.

38. By looking at solutions for $n = 10$, say, which can be obtained quickly via Algorithm W (WalkSAT), it's easy to discover patterns that work in general: (a) Let (x, y) have color $(2x + 4y) \bmod 7$. (Seven colors are clearly necessary when $n \ge 3$.) (b) Let (x, y, z) have color $(2x + 6y) \bmod 9$. (Nine colors are clearly necessary when $n \ge 4$.)

39. Let $f(n)$ denote the fewest consecutive colors. SAT solvers readily verify that $f(n) = (1, 3, 5, 7, 8, 9)$ for $n = (0, 1, 2, 3, 4, 5)$. Furthermore we can exploit symmetry to show that $f(6) > 10$: One can assume that 000000 is colored 0, and that the colors of 000001, ..., 100000 are increasing; that leaves only three possibilities for each of the latter. Finally, we can verify that $f(6) = 11$ by finding a solution that uses only the colors $\{0, 1, 3, 4, 6, 7, 9, 10\}$.

But $f(7)$ is known only to be ≥ 11 and ≤ 15.

[$L(2, 1)$ labelings were named by J. R. Griggs and R. K. Yeh, who initiated the theory in *SIAM J. Discrete Math.* **5** (1992), 586–595. The best known upper bounds, including the fact that $f(2^k - k - 1) \leq 2^k$, were obtained by M. A. Whittlesey, J. P. Georges, and D. W. Mauro, who also solved exercise 38(a); see *SIAM J. Discrete Math.* **8** (1995), 499–506.]

40. No; the satisfiable cases are $z = 0$, 1, 2, 3, 4, 5, 6, 7, 8, 9, 10, 12, 14, 15, 21. [The statement would have been true if we'd also required $(x_m \vee \cdots \vee x_2) \wedge (y_n \vee \cdots \vee y_2)$.]

41. First there are mn ANDs to form $x_i y_j$. A bin that contains t bits initially will generate $\lfloor t/2 \rfloor$ carries for the next bin, using $(t - 1)/2$ adders. (For example, $t = 6$ will invoke 2 full adders and one half adder.) The respective values of t for $bin[2]$, $bin[3]$, $\ldots$, $bin[m + n + 1]$ are (1, 2, 4, 6, $\ldots$, $2m - 2$, $2m - 1$, $\ldots$, $2m - 1$, $2m - 2$, $2m - 3$, $\ldots$, 5, 3, 1), with $n - m$ occurrences of $2m - 1$. That makes a total of $mn - m - n$ full adders and m half adders; altogether we get $mn + 2(mn - m - n) + m$ instances of AND, $mn - m - n$ instances of OR, and $2(mn - m - n) + m$ instances of XOR.

42. Ternary XOR requires quaternary clauses, but ternary clauses suffice for median:

$(t \vee u \vee v \vee \bar{x})$	$(t \vee u \vee \bar{v} \vee x)$	$(t \vee u \vee \bar{y})$	$(\bar{t} \vee \bar{u} \vee y)$
$(t \vee \bar{u} \vee \bar{v} \vee \bar{x})$	$(t \vee \bar{u} \vee v \vee x)$	$(t \vee v \vee \bar{y})$	$(\bar{t} \vee \bar{v} \vee y)$
$(\bar{t} \vee u \vee \bar{v} \vee \bar{x})$	$(\bar{t} \vee u \vee v \vee x)$	$(u \vee v \vee \bar{y})$	$(\bar{u} \vee \bar{v} \vee y)$
$(\bar{t} \vee \bar{u} \vee v \vee \bar{x})$	$(\bar{t} \vee \bar{u} \vee \bar{v} \vee x)$		

These clauses specify respectively that $x \leq t \oplus u \oplus v$, $x \geq t \oplus u \oplus v$, $y \leq \langle tuv \rangle$, $y \geq \langle tuv \rangle$.

43. $x = y = 3$ works when $n = 2$, but the cases $3 \leq n \leq 7$ are unsatisfiable. We can use $x = 3(2^{n-2} + 1)$, $y = 7(2^{n-3} + 1)$ for all $n \geq 8$. (Such solutions aren't at all rare. For example, $(x, y) = (^\#\text{C4466223}, {}^\#\text{E26E7647})$ is one of 293 instances when $n = 32$.)

44. First scout the territory quickly by looking at all $\binom{N+1}{2} \approx 660$ billion cases with at most six zeros in x or y; here $N = \binom{32}{26} + \binom{32}{27} + \cdots + \binom{32}{32}$. This uncovers the remarkable pair $x = 2^{32} - 2^{26} - 2^{22} - 2^{11} - 2^8 - 2^4 - 1$, $y = 2^{32} - 2^{11} + 2^8 - 2^4 + 1$, whose product is $2^{64} - 2^{58} - 2^{54} - 2^{44} - 2^{33} - 2^8 - 1$. Now a SAT solver finishes the job by showing that the clauses for 32×32 bit multiplication are unsatisfiable in the presence of the further constraint $\bar{x}_1 + \cdots + \bar{x}_{32} + \bar{y}_1 + \cdots + \bar{y}_{32} + \bar{z}_1 + \cdots + \bar{z}_{64} \leq 15$. (The LIFO version of the clauses worked much faster than FIFO in the author's experiments with Algorithm L. Symmetry was broken by separate runs with $x_k \ldots x_1 = 01^{k-1}$, $y_k \ldots y_1 = 1^k$.)

45. Use the clauses for $xy = z$ in the factorization problem, with $m = \lfloor t/2 \rfloor$, $n = \lceil t/2 \rceil$, and $x_j = y_j$ for $1 \leq j \leq m$; append the unit clause $(\bar{y}_n)$ if $m < n$.

46. The two largest, 285000288617375^2 and 301429589329949^2, have 97 bits; the next square binary palindrome, 1178448744881657^2, has 101. [This problem is *not* easy for SAT solvers; number theory does much better. Indeed, M. Coriand has discovered a nice way to find all n-bit examples by considering only $O(2^{n/4})$ cases, because the left and right halves of a binary number are nearly forced by the left and right *quarters* of its square. The first eight square binary palindromes were found by G. J. Simmons, *JRM* **5** (1972), 11–19; see OEIS sequence A003166 for many further results.]

47. Each wire has a "top" and a "bottom." There are $n + g + 2h$ tops of wires, and $m + 2g + h$ bottoms of wires. Hence the total number of wires is $n + g + 2h = m + 2g + h$, and we must have $n + h = m + g$.

48. The wires compute $q^1 \leftarrow q$, $q^2 \leftarrow q$, $x \leftarrow p \oplus q^1$, $y \leftarrow q^2 \oplus r$, $z \leftarrow x \oplus y$. Let p denote "p stuck at 1" while $\bar{p}$ denotes "p stuck at 0." The pattern $pqr = 000$ detects p, q^1, q^2, r, x, y, z; 001 detects p, q^1, q^2, $\bar{r}$, x, $\bar{y}$, $\bar{z}$; 010 detects p, $\bar{q}^1$, $\bar{q}^2$, r, $\bar{x}$, $\bar{y}$, z; 011 detects p, $\bar{q}^1$, $\bar{q}^2$, $\bar{r}$, $\bar{x}$, y, $\bar{z}$; 100 detects $\bar{p}$, q^1, q^2, r, $\bar{x}$, y, $\bar{z}$; 101 detects $\bar{p}$, q^1, q^2, $\bar{r}$, $\bar{x}$, $\bar{y}$, z; 110 detects $\bar{p}$, $\bar{q}^1$, $\bar{q}^2$, r, x, $\bar{y}$, $\bar{z}$; 111 detects $\bar{p}$, $\bar{q}^1$, $\bar{q}^2$, $\bar{r}$, x, y, z. Notice that the stuck-at faults for q aren't detectable (because $z = (p \oplus q) \oplus (q \oplus r) = p \oplus r$); but we can detect faults on its clones q^1, q^2. (In Fig. 77 the opposite happens.)

Three patterns such as $\{100, 010, 001\}$ suffice for all of the detectable faults.

49. One finds, for example, that the faults b_3^2, $\bar{c}_1^2$, $\bar{s}^2$, and $\bar{q}$ are detected *only* by the pattern $y_3 y_2 y_1 x_2 x_1 = 01111$; $\bar{a}_2^2$, $\bar{a}_3^2$, b_3^2, $\bar{p}$, $\bar{c}_2^2$, $\bar{z}_5$ are detected only by 11011 or 11111.

All covering sets can be found by setting up a CNF with 99 positive clauses, one for each detectable fault; for example, the clause for $\bar{z}_5$ is $x_{27} \vee x_{31}$, while the clause for x_2^2 is $x_4 \vee x_5 \vee x_{12} \vee x_{13} \vee x_{20} \vee x_{21} \vee x_{28} \vee x_{29}$. We can find minimum covers from a BDD for these clauses, or by using a SAT solver with additional clauses such as (20) and (21) to limit the number of positive literals. Exactly fourteen sets of five patterns suffice, the most memorable being $\{01111, 10111, 11011, 11101, 11110\}$. (Indeed, every minimum set includes at least three of these five patterns.)

50. Primed variables for tarnished wires are x_2', b_2', b_3', s', p', q', z_3', c_2', z_4', z_5'. Those wires also have sharped variables $x_2^\sharp$, $b_2^\sharp$, $\ldots$, $z_5^\sharp$; and we need sharped variables $x_2^{1\sharp}$, $x_2^{3\sharp}$, $x_2^{4\sharp}$, $b_2^{1\sharp}$, $b_2^{2\sharp}$, $b_3^{1\sharp}$, $b_3^{2\sharp}$, $s^{1\sharp}$, $s^{2\sharp}$, $c_2^{1\sharp}$, $c_2^{2\sharp}$ for fanout wires. The primed variables are defined by clauses such as $(\bar{p}' \vee a_3) \wedge (\bar{p}' \vee b_2') \wedge (p' \vee \bar{a}_3 \vee \bar{b}_2')$, which corresponds to $p' \leftarrow a_3 \wedge b_2'$. Those clauses are appended to the 49 clauses listed after (23) in the text. Then there are two clauses (25) for nine of the ten primed-and-sharped variables; however, in the case of x_2 we use the unit clauses $(x_2') \wedge (\bar{x}_2)$ instead, because the variable $x_2^\sharp$ doesn't exist. There are five fanout clauses (26), namely $(\bar{x}_2^{1\sharp} \vee x_2^{3\sharp} \vee x_2^{4\sharp}) \wedge (\bar{b}_2^\sharp \vee b_2^{1\sharp} \vee b_2^{2\sharp}) \wedge \cdots \wedge (\bar{c}_2^\sharp \vee c_2^{1\sharp} \vee c_2^{2\sharp})$. There are eleven clauses $(\bar{x}_2^{3\sharp} \vee b_2^\sharp) \wedge (\bar{x}_2^{4\sharp} \vee b_3^\sharp) \wedge (\bar{b}_2^{1\sharp} \vee s^\sharp) \wedge \cdots \wedge (\bar{b}_3^{2\sharp} \vee z_5^\sharp) \wedge (\bar{c}_2^{2\sharp} \vee z_5^\sharp)$ for tarnished inputs to gates. And finally there's $(x_2^{1\sharp}) \wedge (z_3^\sharp \vee z_4^\sharp \vee z_5)$.

51. (The complete set of 196 patterns found by the author in 2013 included the inputs $(x, y) = (2^{32} - 1, 2^{31} + 1)$ and $(\lceil 2^{63/2} \rceil, \lceil 2^{63/2} \rceil)$ as well as the two number-theoretic patterns mentioned in the text. Long runs of carries are needed in the products.)

52. $(z_{1,2} \vee z_{2,2} \vee \cdots \vee z_{M,2}) \wedge (\bar{z}_{i,2} \vee \bar{q}_{i,1}) \wedge (\bar{z}_{i,2} \vee \bar{p}_{i,2}) \wedge (\bar{z}_{i,2} \vee \bar{q}_{i,3}) \wedge (\bar{z}_{i,2} \vee \bar{p}_{i,4}) \wedge \cdots \wedge (\bar{z}_{i,2} \vee \bar{q}_{i,20})$, for $1 \leq i \leq M$. The second subscript of z is k in the kth case, $1 \leq k \leq P$.

53. On the left is the binary expansion of π, and on the right is the binary expansion of e, 20 bits at a time (see Appendix A).

One way to define $f(x)$ for all 20-bit x is to write $\pi/4 = \sum_{k=1}^\infty u_k/2^{20k}$ and $e/4 = \sum_{l=1}^\infty v_l/2^{20l}$, where each u_k and v_l is a 20-bit number. Let k and l be smallest such that $x = u_k$ and $x = v_l$. Then $f(x) = [k \leq l]$.

Equation (27) has actually been contrived to *sustain* an illusion of magic: Many simple Boolean functions are consistent with the data in Table 2, even if we require four-term DNFs of three literals each. But only two of them, like (27), have the additional property that they actually agree with the definition of $f(x)$ in the previous paragraph for ten more cases, using u_k up to $k = 22$ and v_l up to $l = 20$! One might almost begin to suspect that a SAT solver has discovered a deep new connection between π and e.

54. (a) The function $\bar{x}_1 x_9 x_{11} \bar{x}_{18} \vee \bar{x}_6 \bar{x}_{10} \bar{x}_{12} \vee \bar{x}_4 x_{10} \bar{x}_{12}$ matches all 16 rows of Table 2; but adding the 17th row makes a 3-term DNF impossible.

(b) 21 rows are impossible, but (27) satisfies 20 rows.

(c) $\bar{x}_1\bar{x}_5\bar{x}_{12}x_{17} \vee \bar{x}_4x_8\bar{x}_{13}\bar{x}_{15} \vee \bar{x}_6\bar{x}_9\bar{x}_{12}x_{16} \vee \bar{x}_6\bar{x}_{13}\bar{x}_{16}x_{20} \vee x_{13}x_{14}\bar{x}_{16}$ does 28, which is max. (Incidentally, this problem makes no sense for sufficiently large M, because the equation $f(x) = 1$ probably does not have exactly 2^{19} solutions.)

55. Using (28)–(31) with $p_{i,j} = 0$ for all i and j, and also introducing clauses like (20) and (21) to ensure that $q_{i,1} + \cdots + q_{i,20} \le 3$, leads to solutions such as

$$f(x_1,\ldots,x_{20}) = \bar{x}_1\bar{x}_7\bar{x}_8 \vee \bar{x}_2\bar{x}_3\bar{x}_4 \vee \bar{x}_4\bar{x}_{13}\bar{x}_{14} \vee \bar{x}_6\bar{x}_{10}\bar{x}_{12}.$$

(There are no monotone *increasing* solutions with ≤ 4 terms of *any* length.)

56. We can define f consistently from only a subset of the variables if and only if no entry on the left agrees with any entry on the right, when restricted to those coordinate positions. For example, the first 10 coordinates do not suffice, because the top entry on the left begins with the same 10 bits as the 14th entry on the right. The first 11 coordinates do suffice (although two entries on the right actually agree in their first 12 bits).

Let the vectors on the left be u_k and those on the right be v_l, as in answer 53, and form the 256×20 matrix whose rows are $u_k \oplus v_l$ for $1 \le k,l \le 16$. We can solve the stated problem if and only if we can find five columns for which that matrix isn't 00000 in any row. This is the classical *covering problem* (but with rows and columns interchanged): We want to find five columns that cover every row.

In general, such an $m \times n$ covering problem corresponds to an instance of SAT with m clauses and n variables x_j, where x_j means "select column j." The clause for a particular row is the OR of the x_j for each column j in which that row contains 1. For example, in Table 2 we have $u_1 \oplus v_1 = 01100100111101111000$, so the first clause is $x_2 \vee x_3 \vee x_6 \vee \cdots \vee x_{17}$. To cover with at most five columns, we add suitable clauses according to (20) and (21); this gives 396 clauses of total length 2894, in 75 variables.

(Of course $\binom{20}{5}$ is only 15504; we don't need a SAT solver for this simple task! Yet Algorithm D needs only 578 kilomems, and Algorithm C finds an answer in 353 Kμ.)

There are 12 solutions: We can restrict to coordinates x_j for j in $\{1,4,15,17,20\}$, $\{1,10,15,17,20\}$, $\{1,15,17,18,20\}$, $\{4,6,7,10,12\}$, $\{4,6,9,10,12\}$, $\{4,6,10,12,19\}$, $\{4,10,12,15,19\}$, $\{5,7,11,12,15\}$, $\{6,7,8,10,12\}$, $\{6,8,9,10,12\}$, $\{7,10,12,15,20\}$, or $\{8,15,17,18,20\}$. (Incidentally, BDD methods show that the number of solutions to the covering problem has the generating function $12z^5 + 994z^6 + 13503z^7 + \cdots + 20z^{19} + z^{20}$, counting by the size of the covering set.)

57. Table 2 specifies a partially defined function of 20 Boolean variables, having $2^{20} - 32$ "don't-cares." Exercise 56 shows how to embed it in a partially defined function of only 5 Boolean variables, in twelve different ways. So we have twelve different truth tables:

```
11110110 0*1*010* 10000111 10*0*1*0      00100101 11110*0* 1011**** **0**00*
011*011* 1*110100 10*001*1 1000**10      100*1**0 11*00010 1100**0* *0**0101
011*1*11 010*100* 10*0*000 *101*011      **1*1000 1*101100 1*100*10 0*****1*
10101110 0*100*1* 1*001*00 1**00***      1*1*1*10 10001100 0*101*1* **1*0*10
10101110 0*1*0*10 1*0*1*00 0**01***      1*01*00* 1101*0*0 0011*11* 1*100*0*
1*01110* 00**110* 11**0*00 10*****0      001*1001 *1**1*1* 11*0*010 01011001
```

And the tenth of these yields $f(x) = ((x_8 \oplus (x_9 \vee x_{10})) \vee ((x_6 \vee x_{12}) \oplus \bar{x}_{10})) \oplus x_{12}$.

58. These clauses are satisfiable whenever the other clauses are satisfiable (except in the trivial case when $f(x) = 0$ for all x), because we don't need to include both x_j and $\bar{x}_j$ in the same term. Furthermore they reduce the space of possibilities by a factor of $(3/4)^N$. So they seem worthwhile. (On the other hand, their effect on the running time appears to be negligible, at least with respect to Algorithm C in small-scale trials.)

59. $f(x) \oplus \hat{f}(x) = x_2 \bar{x}_3 \bar{x}_6 \bar{x}_{10} \bar{x}_{12} (\bar{x}_8 \vee x_8 (x_{13} \vee x_{15}))$ is a function of eight variables that has 7 solutions. Thus the probability is $7/256 = .02734375$.

60. A typical example with 32 given values of $f(x)$, chosen randomly, yielded

$$\hat{f}(x_1, \ldots, x_{20}) = x_4 \bar{x}_7 \bar{x}_{12} \vee \bar{x}_6 x_8 \bar{x}_{11} x_{14} x_{20} \vee \bar{x}_9 \bar{x}_{12} x_{18} \bar{x}_{19} \vee \bar{x}_{13} \bar{x}_{16} \bar{x}_{17} x_{19},$$

which of course is way off; it differs from $f(x)$ with probability $102752/2^{18} \approx .39$. With 64 training values, however,

$$\hat{f}(x_1, \ldots, x_{20}) = x_2 \bar{x}_{13} \bar{x}_{15} x_{19} \vee \bar{x}_3 \bar{x}_9 \bar{x}_{19} \bar{x}_{20} \vee \bar{x}_6 \bar{x}_{10} \bar{x}_{12} \vee \bar{x}_8 x_{10} \bar{x}_{12}$$

comes closer, disagreeing only with probability $404/2^{11} \approx .197$.

61. We can add 24 clauses $(p_{a,1} \vee q_{a,1} \vee p_{a,2} \vee \bar{q}_{a,2} \vee p_{a,3} \vee \bar{q}_{a,3} \vee \cdots \vee p_{b,1} \vee q_{b,1} \vee \cdots \vee p_{c,1} \vee q_{c,1} \vee \cdots \vee p_{d,1} \vee q_{d,1} \vee \cdots \vee \bar{p}_{d,10} \vee q_{d,10} \vee \cdots \vee p_{d,20} \vee q_{d,20})$, one for each permutation $abcd$ of $\{1, 2, 3, 4\}$; the resulting clauses are satisfiable only by other functions $f(x)$.

But the situation is more complicated in larger examples, because a function can have many equivalent representations as a short DNF. A general scheme, to decide whether the function described by a particular setting $p'_{i,j}$ and $q'_{i,j}$ of the ps and qs is unique, would be to add more complicated clauses, which state that $p_{i,j}$ and $q_{i,j}$ give a different solution. Those clauses can be generated by the Tseytin encoding of

$$\bigvee_{i=1}^{M} \bigwedge_{j=1}^{N} ((\bar{p}_{i,j} \wedge \bar{x}_j) \vee (\bar{q}_{i,j} \wedge x_j)) \oplus \bigvee_{i=1}^{M} \bigwedge_{j=1}^{N} ((\bar{p}'_{i,j} \wedge \bar{x}_j) \vee (\bar{q}'_{i,j} \wedge x_j)).$$

62. Preliminary experiments by the author, with $N = 20$ and $p = 1/8$, seem to indicate that more data points are needed to get convergence by this method, but the SAT solver tends to run about 10 times faster. Thus, locally biased data points appear to be preferable unless the cost of observing the hidden function is relatively large.

Incidentally, the chance that $x^{(k)} = x^{(k-1)}$ was relatively high in these experiments $((7/8)^{20} \approx .069)$; so cases with $y^{(k)} = 0$ were bypassed.

63. With Tseytin encoding (24), it's easy to construct $6r + 2n - 1$ clauses in $2r + 2n - 1$ variables that are satisfiable if and only if α fails to sort the binary sequence $x_1 \ldots x_n$. For example, the clauses when $\alpha = [1{:}2][3{:}4][1{:}3][2{:}4][2{:}3]$ are $(x_1 \vee \bar{l}_1) \wedge (x_2 \vee \bar{l}_1) \wedge (\bar{x}_1 \vee \bar{x}_2 \vee l_1) \wedge (\bar{x}_1 \vee h_1) \wedge (\bar{x}_2 \vee h_1) \wedge (x_1 \vee x_2 \vee \bar{h}_1) \wedge \cdots \wedge (l_4 \vee \bar{l}_5) \wedge (h_3 \vee \bar{l}_5) \wedge (\bar{l}_4 \vee \bar{h}_3 \vee l_5) \wedge (\bar{l}_4 \vee h_5) \wedge (\bar{h}_3 \vee h_5) \wedge (l_4 \vee h_3 \vee \bar{h}_5) \wedge (g_1 \vee g_2 \vee g_3) \wedge (\bar{g}_1 \vee l_3) \wedge (\bar{g}_1 \vee \bar{l}_5) \wedge (\bar{g}_2 \vee l_5) \wedge (\bar{g}_2 \vee \bar{h}_5) \wedge (\bar{g}_3 \vee h_5) \wedge (\bar{g}_3 \vee h_4)$. They're unsatisfiable, so α always sorts properly.

64. Here we reverse the policy of the previous answer, and construct clauses that are *satisfiable* when they describe a sorting network: Let the variable $C_{i,j}^t$ stand for the existence of comparator $[i{:}j]$ at time t, for $1 \le i < j \le n$ and $1 \le t \le T$. Also, adapting (20) and (21), let variables $B_{j,k}^t$ be defined for $1 \le j \le n - 2$ and $1 \le k \le n$, with clauses

$$(\overline{B}_{2j,k}^t \vee \overline{B}_{2j+1,k}^t) \wedge (\overline{B}_{2j,k}^t \vee B_{j,k}^t) \wedge (\overline{B}_{2j+1,k}^t \vee B_{j,k}^t) \wedge (B_{2j,k}^t \vee B_{2j+1,k}^t \vee \overline{B}_{j,k}^t); \qquad (*)$$

in this formula we substitute $\{C_{1,k}^t, \ldots, C_{k-1,k}^t, C_{k,k+1}^t, \ldots, C_{k,n}^t\}$ for the $n - 1$ "leaf nodes" $\{B_{n-1,k}^t, \ldots, B_{2n-3,k}^t\}$. These clauses prohibit comparators from clashing at time t, and they make $B_{1,k}^t$ false if and only if line k remains unused.

If $x = x_1 \ldots x_n$ is any binary vector, let $y_1 \ldots y_n$ be the result of sorting x (so that $(y_1 \ldots y_n)_2 = 2^{\nu x} - 1$). The following clauses $F(x)$ encode the fact that comparators $C_{i,j}^t$ transform $x \mapsto y$: $(\overline{C}_{i,j}^t \vee \overline{V}_{x,i}^t \vee V_{x,i}^{t-1}) \wedge (\overline{C}_{i,j}^t \vee \overline{V}_{x,i}^t \vee V_{x,j}^{t-1}) \wedge (\overline{C}_{i,j}^t \vee V_{x,i}^t \vee \overline{V}_{x,i}^{t-1} \vee \overline{V}_{x,j}^{t-1}) \wedge (\overline{C}_{i,j}^t \vee \overline{V}_{x,j}^t \vee V_{x,i}^{t-1} \vee V_{x,j}^{t-1}) \wedge (\overline{C}_{i,j}^t \vee V_{x,j}^t \vee \overline{V}_{x,i}^{t-1}) \wedge (\overline{C}_{i,j}^t \vee V_{x,j}^t \vee \overline{V}_{x,j}^{t-1}) \wedge (B_{1,i}^t \vee \overline{V}_{x,i}^t \vee V_{x,i}^{t-1}) \wedge$

$(B_{1,i}^t \lor V_{x,i}^t \lor \overline{V}_{x,i}^{t-1})$, for $1 \le i < j \le n$ and $1 \le t \le T$; here we substitute x_j for $V_{x,j}^0$ and also substitute y_j for $V_{x,j}^T$, thereby simplifying the boundary conditions.

Furthermore, we can remove all variables $V_{x,i}^t$ when x has i leading 0s and $V_{x,j}^t$ when x has j trailing 1s, replacing them by 0 and 1 respectively and simplifying further.

Finally, given any sequence $\alpha = [i_1\!:\!j_1]\ldots[i_r\!:\!j_r]$ of initial comparators, T further parallel stages will yield a sorting network if and only if the clauses (∗), together with $\bigwedge_x F(x)$ over all x producible by α, are simultaneously satisfiable.

Setting $n = 9$, $\alpha = [1\!:\!6][2\!:\!7][3\!:\!8][4\!:\!9]$, and $T = 5$, we obtain 85768 clauses in 5175 variables, if we leave out the ten vectors x that are already sorted. Algorithm C finds them unsatisfiable after spending roughly 200 megamems; therefore $\hat{T}(9) > 6$. (Algorithm L fails spectacularly on these clauses, however.) Setting $T \leftarrow 6$ quickly yields $\hat{T}(9) \le 7$. D. Bundala and J. Závodný [*LNCS* **8370** (2014), 236–247] used this approach to prove in fact that $\hat{T}(11) = 8$ and $\hat{T}(13) = 9$. Then T. Ehlers and M. Müller extended it [*LNCS* **9136** (2015), 167–176], to prove that $\hat{T}(17) = 10$, with the surprising optimum network shown here.

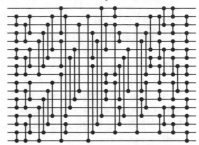

65. (a) The goal is to express the transition equation in CNF. There are $\binom{8}{4}$ clauses like $(\bar{x}' \lor \bar{x}_a \lor \bar{x}_b \lor \bar{x}_c \lor \bar{x}_d)$, one for each choice of four neighbors $\{a, b, c, d\} \subseteq \{\text{NW}, \text{N}, \ldots, \text{SE}\}$. Also $\binom{8}{7}$ clauses like $(\bar{x}' \lor x_a \lor \cdots \lor x_g)$, one for each choice of seven. Also $\binom{8}{6}$ like $(\bar{x}' \lor x \lor x_a \lor \cdots \lor x_f)$, for each choice of six. Also $\binom{8}{3}$ like $(x' \lor \bar{x}_a \lor \bar{x}_b \lor \bar{x}_c \lor x_d \lor \cdots \lor x_h)$, complementing just three. And finally $\binom{8}{2}$ like $(x' \lor \bar{x} \lor \bar{x}_a \lor \bar{x}_b \lor x_c \lor \cdots \lor x_g)$, complementing just two and omitting any one of the others. Altogether $70 + 8 + 28 + 56 + 28 = 190$ clauses of average length $(70\cdot5+8\cdot8+28\cdot8+56\cdot9+28\cdot9)/190 \approx 7.34$.

(b) Here we let $x = x_{ij}$, $x_{\text{NW}} = x_{(i-1)(j-1)}$, $\ldots$, $x_{\text{SE}} = x_{(i+1)(j+1)}$, $x' = x'_{ij}$. There are seven classes of auxiliary variables a_k^{ij}, $\ldots$, g_k^{ij}, each of which has two children; the meaning is that the sum of the descendants is $\ge k$. We have $k \in \{2, 3, 4\}$ for the a variables, $k \in \{1, 2, 3, 4\}$ for the b and c variables, and $k \in \{1, 2\}$ for d, e, f, g.

The children of a^{ij} are $b^{(i|1)j}$ and c^{ij}. The children of b^{ij} are $d^{i(j-(j\&2))}$ and $e^{i(j+(j\&2))}$. The children of c^{ij} are $f^{i'j'}$ and g^{ij}, where $i' = i+2$ and $j' = (j-1)\,|\,1$ if i is odd, otherwise $i' = i$ and $j' = j-(j\&1)$. The children of d^{ij} are $x_{(i-1)(j+1)}$ and $x_{i(j+1)}$. The children of e^{ij} are $x_{(i-1)(j-1)}$ and $x_{i(j-1)}$. The children of f^{ij} are $x_{(i-1)j}$ and $x_{(i-1)(j+1)}$. Finally, the children of g^{ij} are $x_{i'j}$ and $x_{i''j''}$, where $i' = i+1-((i\&1)\ll 1)$; and $(i'', j'') = (i+1, j\oplus 1)$ if i is odd, otherwise $(i'', j'') = (i-1, j-1+((j\&1)\ll 1))$. (OK — this isn't elegant. But hey, it works!)

If the children of p are q and r, the clauses that define p_k are $(p_k \lor \bar{q}_{k'} \lor \bar{r}_{k''})$ for $k' + k'' = k$ and $(\bar{p}_k \lor q_{k'} \lor r_{k''})$ for $k' + k'' = k+1$. In these clauses we omit $\bar{q}_0$ or $\bar{r}_0$; we also omit q_m or r_m when q or r has fewer than m descendants.

For example, these rules define d_1^{35} and d_2^{35} by the following six clauses:

$$(d_1^{35} \lor \bar{x}_{26}),\ (d_1^{35} \lor \bar{x}_{36}),\ (d_2^{35} \lor \bar{x}_{26} \lor \bar{x}_{36}),\ (\bar{d}_1^{35} \lor x_{26} \lor x_{36}),\ (\bar{d}_2^{35} \lor x_{26}),\ (\bar{d}_2^{35} \lor x_{36}).$$

The variables b_k^{ij} are defined only when i is odd; d_k^{ij} and e_k^{ij} only when i is odd and $j \bmod 4 < 2$; f_k^{ij} only when $i + j$ is even. Thus the total number of auxiliary variables per cell (i, j), ignoring small corrections at boundary points, is $3+4/2+4+2/4+2/4+2/2+2 = 13$ of types a through g, not 19, because of the sharing; and the total number of clauses per cell to define them is $21 + 16/2 + 16 + 6/4 + 6/4 + 6/2 + 6 = 57$, not 77.

Finally we define x'_{ij} from a_2^{ij}, a_3^{ij}, a_4^{ij}, by means of six clauses

$$(\bar{x}'_{ij} \vee \bar{a}_4^{ij}), \ (\bar{x}'_{ij} \vee a_2^{ij}), \ (\bar{x}'_{ij} \vee x_{ij} \vee a_3^{ij}), \ (x'_{ij} \vee a_4^{ij} \vee \bar{a}_3^{ij}), \ (x'_{ij} \vee \bar{x}_{ij} \vee \bar{y}_{ij}), \ (y_{ij} \vee a_4^{ij} \vee \bar{a}_2^{ij}),$$

where y_{ij} is another auxiliary variable (introduced only to avoid clauses of size 4).

66. All solutions to (a) can be characterized by a BDD of 8852 nodes, from which we can obtain the generating function $38z^{28} + 550z^{29} + \cdots + 150z^{41}$ that enumerates them (with a total computation time of only 150 megamems or so). Part (b), however, is best suited to SAT, and X_0 must have at least 38 live cells. Typical answers are

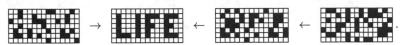

67. Either ▨ or ▨ at lower left will produce the X_0 of (37) at time 1. But length 22 is impossible: With $r = 4$ we can verify that all the live cells in X_4 lie in some 3×3 subarray. Then with $r = 22$ we need to rule out only $(\binom{9}{3} + \binom{9}{4} + \binom{9}{5}) \times 6 = 2016$ possibilities, one for each viable X_4 within each essentially different 3×3 subarray.

68. The author believes that $r = 12$ is impossible, but his SAT solvers have not yet been able to verify this conjecture. Certainly $r = 11$ is achievable, because we can continue with the text's fifth example after prepending

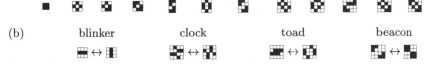

69. Since only 8548 essentially different 4×4 bitmaps are possible (see Section 7.2.3), an exhaustive enumeration is no sweat. The small stable patterns arise frequently, so they've all been named:

(a) block tub boat ship snake bee-hive carrier barge loaf eater long boat long ship pond

(b) blinker clock toad beacon

(A glider is also considered to be stable, although it's not an oscillator.)

70. (a) A cell with three live neighbors in the stator will stay alive.

(b) A $4 \times n$ board doesn't work; Fig. A–8 shows the 5×8 examples.

(c) Again, the smallest-weight solutions with smallest rectangles are shown in Fig. A–8. Oscillators with these rotors are plentiful on larger boards; the first examples of each kind were found respectively by Richard Schroeppel (1970), David Buckingham (1972), Robert Wainwright (1985).

71. Let the variables $X_t = x_{ijt}$ characterize the configuration at time t, and suppose we require $X_r = X_0$. There are $q = 8r$ automorphisms σ that take $X_t \mapsto X_{(t+p) \bmod r}\tau$, where $0 \le p < r$ and τ is one of the eight symmetries of a square grid.

Any global permutation of the $N = n^2 r$ variables leads via Theorem E to a canonical form, where we require the solution to be lexicographically less than or equal to the $q - 1$ solutions that are equivalent to it under automorphisms.

Such lexicographic tests can be enforced by introducing $(q-1)(3N-2)$ new clauses of length ≤ 3, as in (169) — and often greatly simplified using Corollary E.

These additional clauses can significantly speed up a proof of unsatisfiability. On the other hand they can also slow down the search, if a problem has abundant solutions.

In practice it's usually better to insist only on solutions that are *partially* canonical, by using only some of the automorphisms and by requiring lexicographic order only on some of the variables.

72. (a) The two 7×7s, shown in Fig. A–8, were found by R. Wainwright (trice tongs, 1972) and A. Flammenkamp (jam, 1988).

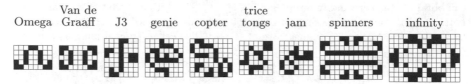

Van de   trice
Omega Graaff   J3   genie   copter   tongs   jam   spinners   infinity

Fig. A–8. Noteworthy minimal oscillators of periods 2 and 3.

(b) Here the smallest examples are 9×13 and 10×15; the former has four L-rotors surrounding long stable lines. Readers will also enjoy discovering 10×10 and 13×13 instances that have full eightfold symmetry. (When encoding such symmetrical problems by using exercise 65(b), we need only compute the transitions between variables x_{tij} for $1 \le i \le \lceil m/2 \rceil$ and $1 \le j \le \lceil n/2 \rceil$; every other variable is identical to one of these. However, the auxiliary variables $a^{ij}, \ldots, g^{ij}$ shouldn't be coalesced in this way.)

(c,d) Champion heavyweights have small rotors. What a cool four-way snake dance!

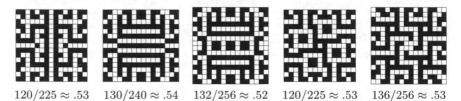

$120/225 \approx .53$ $130/240 \approx .54$ $132/256 \approx .52$ $120/225 \approx .53$ $136/256 \approx .53$

73. (a) They don't have three A neighbors; and they don't have three B neighbors.

(b) Two examples appear in Fig. A–9, where they are packed as snugly as possible into a 12×15 box. This pattern, found by R. W. Gosper about 1971, is called the *phoenix*, since its living cells repeatedly die and rise again. It is the smallest mobile flipflop; the same idea yields the next smallest (also seen in Fig. A–9), which is 10×12.

(c) The nonblank one comes from a 1×4 torus; the checkerboard from an 8×8. Here are some amazing $m \times n$ ways to satisfy the constraints for small m and n:

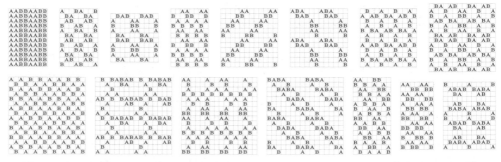

Notice that infinite one-dimensional examples are implied by several of these motifs; the checkerboard, in fact, can be fabricated by placing ⬚ diagonals together.

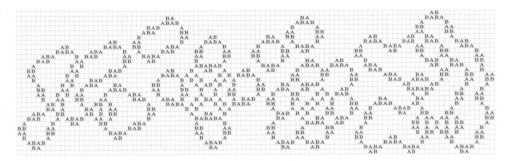

Fig. A-9. Mobile flipflops: An ideal way to tile the floor of a workspace for hackers.

74. Call a cell *tainted* if it is A with more than one A neighbor or B with more than one B neighbor. Consider the topmost row with a tainted cell, and the leftmost tainted cell in that row. We can assume that this cell is an A, and that its neighbors are S, T, U, V, W, X, Y, Z in the pattern $\begin{smallmatrix} S\,T\,U \\ V\,A\,W \\ X\,Y\,Z \end{smallmatrix}$. Three of those eight neighbors are type B, and at least four are type A; several cases need to be considered.

Case 1: W = X = Y = Z = A. Then we must have S = U = V = B and T = 0 (blank), because S, T, U, V aren't tainted. The three left neighbors of V can't be type A, since V already has three A neighbors; nor can they be type B, since V isn't tainted. Hence the tainted X, which must have two B neighbors in the three cells below it, cannot also have two or more A neighbors there.

Case 2: T = A or V = A. If, say, T = A then X = Y = Z = A, and neither V nor W can be type B.

Case 3: S ≠ A, U = A. Then W can't be type B, and S must be tainted.

Case 4: S = A, U ≠ A. At least one of W, X, Y, Z is B; at least three are A; so exactly three are A. The B can't be Y, which has four A neighbors. Nor can it be W or Z: That would force V to be blank, hence T = U = B; consequently W = A, Z = B. Since W is tainted, at least two of its right neighbors must be A, contradicting Z = B.

Thus X = B in Case 4. Either T or V is also B, while the other is blank; say T is blank. The three left neighbors of V cannot be A. So they must either all be B (tainting the cell left of S) or all blank. In the latter case the upper neighbors of T must be BBA in that order, since T is blank. But that taints the B above T. A symmetric argument applies if V is blank.

Case 5: S = U = A. Then W ≠ A, and at least two of {X, Y, Z} are A. Now Y = Z = A forces T = V = X = B and W blank, tainting V.

Similarly, X = Y = A forces T = W = Z = B and V blank; this case is more difficult. The three lower neighbors of Y must be AAB, in that order, lest a B be surrounded by four A's. But then the left neighbors of X are BBB; hence so are the left neighbors of V, tainting the middle one.

Finally, therefore, Case 5 implies that X = Z = A. Either T, V, W, or Y is blank; the other three are B. The blank can't be T, since T's upper three neighbors can't be A. It can't be W or Y, since V and T aren't tainted. So T = W = Y = B and V is blank. The left neighbors of S cannot be A, because S isn't tainted. So the cell left of X must be A. Therefore X must have at least four A neighbors; but that's impossible, because Y already has three.

Diagonally adjacent A's are rare. (In fact, they cannot occur in rectangular grids of size 15×18 or 16×17.) But diligent readers will be able to spot them in Fig. A–9, which exhibits an astonishing variety of different motifs that are possible in large grids.

75. Let the cells alive at times $p - 2$, $p - 1$, p be of types X, Y, Z, and consider the topmost row in which a live cell ever appears. Without loss of generality, the leftmost cell in that row is type Z. The cell below that Z can't be of type Y, because that Y would have three X neighbors and four Y neighbors besides Z and the blank to its left.

Thus the picture must look like $\frac{\text{ZYX}}{\text{YXYX}}$, where the three predecessors of Z and the topmost Y are filled in. But there's no room for the three predecessors of the topmost X.

76. The smallest known example, a 28×33 pattern found by Jason Summers in 2012, is illustrated here using the letters $\{F, A, B\}$, $\{B, C, D\}$, $\{D, E, F\}$ for cells that are alive when $t \bmod 3 = 0$, 1, 2. His ingenious construction leads in particular to an infinite solution based on a 7×24 torus. An amazing infinite 7×7 toroidal pattern also exists, but little else is yet known.

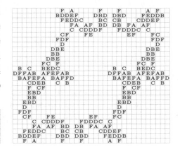

77. If the first four cells in row 4 of X_0 (and of X_5) contain a, b, c, d, we need $a + b \neq 1$, $a + b + c \neq 1$, $b + c + d \neq 2$. In clause form this becomes $\bar{a} \vee b$, $a \vee \bar{b}$, $b \vee \bar{c}$, $\bar{c} \vee d$, $\bar{b} \vee c \vee \bar{d}$.

Similarly, let the last four elements of column 5 be (f, g, h, i); then we want $f + g + h \neq 2$, $g + h + i \neq 2$, $h + i \neq 2$. These conditions simplify to $\bar{f} \vee \bar{g}$, $\bar{f} \vee \bar{h}$, $\bar{g} \vee \bar{i}$, $\bar{h} \vee \bar{i}$.

78. The "9^2 phage" in Fig. A–10 is a minimal example.

79. (Solution by T. G. Rokicki.) A tremendous battle flares up, raging wildly on all fronts. When the dust finally settles at time 1900, 11 gliders are escaping the scene (1 going in the original NE direction, 3 going NW, 5 going SW, and 2 going SE), leaving behind 16 blocks, 1 tub, 2 loaves, 3 boats, 4 ships, 8 beehives, 1 pond, 15 blinkers, and 1 toad. (One should really watch this with a suitable applet.)

80. Paydirt is hit on 10×10 and 11×11 boards, with $X_8 = X_9$; see Fig. A–10. The minimal example, "symeater19," has a close relative, "symeater20," which consists simply of two blocks and two carriers, strategically placed. (The first of these, also called "eater 2," was discovered by D. Buckingham in the early 1970s; the other by S. Silver in 1998.) They both have the additional ability to eat the glider if it is moved one or two cells to the right of the position shown, or one cell to the left.

It is important to realize that the diagonal track of a glider does *not* pass through the corners of pixels, bisecting them; the axis of a glider's symmetry actually passes through the *midpoints* of pixel edges, thereby cutting off small triangles whose area is $1/8$ of a full pixel. Consequently, any eater that is symmetric about a diagonal will eat gliders in two adjacent tracks. The two in Fig. A–10 are exceptional because they're quadruply effective. Furthermore symeater20 will eat from the opposite direction; and either of its carriers can be swapped to another position next to the blocks.

81. Two eaters make "ssymeater14" (Fig. A–10); and "ssymeater22" is narrower.

82. (a) If $X \rightarrow X'$, then $x'_{ij} = 1$ only if we have $\sum_{i'=i-1}^{i+1} \sum_{j'=j-1}^{j+1} x_{i'j'} \geq 3$.

(b) Use the same inequality, and induction on j.

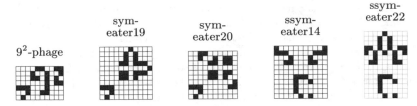

Fig. A–10. Various examples of minimal still lifes that eat gliders and spaceships.

(c) (Proof of the hint by John Conway, 1970.) In the transitions

$$X = \;\;\to\;\;\to\;\; = X'',$$

we must have ▦ in the center of X'; hence we must have ▦ at the lower left of X. But then the center of X' is ▦.

83. Work with $(2r + 1 - 2t) \times (2r + 1 - 2t)$ grids x_{tij} centered at cell (i_0, j_0), for $0 \le t \le r = f(i_0, j_0)$; and assume that $x_{tij} = 0$ whenever $f(i, j) > t$. For example, if $(i_0, j_0) = (1, 2)$, only 14 of the x_{3ij} can be alive, namely when $(i, j) = (-2 .. -1, 2)$, $(-2 .. 0, 1)$, $(-2 .. 1, 0)$, $(-2 .. 2, -1)$. The case $(i_0, j_0) = (1, 2)$ leads to 5031 readily satisfiable clauses on 1316 variables, including the unit clause x_{612}, when the state transitions are encoded as in answer 65; all but 106 of those variables are auxiliary.

84. (a) Use a glider, positioned properly with its tip at $(0, 0)$.

(b) Similarly, a spaceship reaches these cells in the minimum possible time.

(c) Consider patterns $A_n = $ ▦ and $B_n = $ ▦ of width $2n + 1$, illustrated here for $n = 3$. Then B_j works when $j \bmod 4 \in \{1, 2\}$; A_j and B_{j-1} work when $j \bmod 4 \in \{2, 3\}$; A_{j-1} works when $j \bmod 4 \in \{0, 3\}$.

(d) The pattern ▦ assembles a suitable glider at time 3.

(e) A SAT solver found the pattern shown here, which launches an appropriate spaceship (plus some construction debris that vanishes at $t = 5$).

[It appears likely that $f^*(i, j) = f(i, j)$ for all i and j. But the best general result at present, based on space-filling constructions such as Tim Coe's "Max," is that $f^*(i, j) = f(i, j) + O(1)$. There's no known way to prove even the special cases that, say, $f^*(j, 2j) = 6j$ or that $f^*(-j, 2j) = 3j$ for all $j \ge 0$.]

85. (a) Let X be a 12×12 bitmap. We must show that the clauses $T(X, X')$ of exercise 65, together with 92 unary clauses $x'_{23}, \bar{x}'_{24}, x'_{25}, \ldots$ from the given pattern, are unsatisfiable. (The pattern is symmetrical; but Life's rules often produce symmetrical states from unsymmetrical ones.) Thus 2^{144-8} different conceivable predecessor states need to be ruled out. Fortunately Algorithm C needs fewer than 100 Mμ to do that.

(b) Most states have thousands of predecessors (see the following exercise); so Algorithm C can almost always find one in, say, 500 Kμ. Therefore one can prove, for example, that no 6×6 Gardens of Eden exist, by rapidly finding a predecessor for each of the 2^{36} patterns. (Only about $2^{36}/8$ patterns actually need to be tried, by symmetry.) Furthermore, if we run through those patterns in Gray code order, changing the polarity of just one assumed unary clause $\pm x'_{ij}$ at each step, the mechanism of Algorithm C goes even faster, because it tends to find nearby solutions to nearby problems. Thus thousands of patterns can be satisfied per second, and the task is feasible.

Such an approach is out of the question for 10×10 bitmaps, because $2^{100} \gg 2^{36}$. But we *can* find all 10×10 Gardens of Eden for which there is $90°$-rotational symmetry, by trying only about $2^{25}/2$ patterns, again using Gray code. Aha: Eight such patterns have no predecessor, and four of them correspond to the given orphan.

[See C. Hartman, M. J. H. Heule, K. Kwekkeboom, and A. Noels, *Electronic J. Combinatorics* **20**, 3 (2013), #P16, 1–19. The existence of Gardens of Eden with respect to many kinds of cellular automata was first proved nonconstructively by E. F. Moore, *Proc. Symp. Applied Math.* **14** (1962), 17–33.]

86. The 80 cells outside the inner 8×8 can be chosen in $N = 11{,}984{,}516{,}506{,}952{,}898$ ways. (A BDD of size 53464 proves this.) So the answer is $N/2^{100-64} \approx 174{,}398$.

87. Instead of using subscripts t and $t + 1$, we can write the transition clauses for $X \to X'$ in the form $(@ \vee \overline{A0} \vee A0')$, etc. Let Alice's states be $\{\alpha_1, \ldots, \alpha_p\}$ and let Bob's be $\{\beta_1, \ldots, \beta_q\}$. The clauses $(@ \vee \bar{\alpha}_i \vee \alpha_i')$ and $(\overline{@} \vee \bar{\beta}_i \vee \beta_i')$ say that your state doesn't change unless you are bumped. If state α corresponds to the command 'Maybe go to s', the clause $(\overline{@} \vee \bar{\alpha} \vee \alpha' \vee s')$ defines the next possible states after bumping. The analogous clause for 'Critical, go to s' or 'Set $v \leftarrow b$, go to s' is simply $(\overline{@} \vee \bar{\alpha} \vee s')$; and the latter also generates the clause $(\overline{@} \vee \bar{\alpha} \vee v')$ if $b = 1$, $(\overline{@} \vee \bar{\alpha} \vee \bar{v}')$ if $b = 0$. The command 'If v go to s_1, else to s_0' generates $(\overline{@} \vee \bar{\alpha} \vee \bar{v} \vee s_1') \wedge (\overline{@} \vee \bar{\alpha} \vee v \vee s_0')$. And for each variable v, if the states whose commands set v are $\alpha_{i_1}, \ldots, \alpha_{i_h}$, the clauses

$$(\overline{@} \vee v \vee \alpha_{i_1} \vee \cdots \vee \alpha_{i_h} \vee \bar{v}') \wedge (\overline{@} \vee \bar{v} \vee \alpha_{i_1} \vee \cdots \vee \alpha_{i_h} \vee v')$$

encode the fact that v isn't changed by other commands.

Bob's program generates similar clauses — but they use $@$, not $\overline{@}$, and β, not α.

Incidentally, when other protocols are considered in place of (40), the initial state X_0 analogous to (41) is constructed by putting Alice and Bob into their smallest possible states, and by setting all shared variables to 0.

88. For example, let all variables be false except A0$_0$, B0$_0$, @$_0$, A1$_1$, B0$_1$, A1$_2$, B1$_2$, A1$_3$, B2$_3$, @$_3$, A2$_4$, B2$_4$, @$_4$, A3$_5$, B2$_5$, l_5, A3$_6$, B3$_6$, l_6.

89. No; we can find a counterexample to the corresponding clauses as in the previous exercise: A0$_0$, B0$_0$, A0$_1$, B1$_1$, A0$_2$, B2$_2$, b_2, @$_2$, A1$_3$, B2$_3$, b_3, A1$_4$, B3$_4$, b_4, A1$_5$, B4$_5$, b_5, @$_5$, A2$_6$, B4$_6$, a_6, b_6, @$_6$, A5$_7$, B4$_7$, a_7, b_7, A5$_8$, B2$_8$, a_8, b_8, l_8, A5$_9$, B5$_9$, a_9, b_9, l_9.

(This protocol was the author's original introduction to the fascinating problem of mutual exclusion [see *CACM* **9** (1966), 321–322, 878], about which Dijkstra had said "Quite a collection of trial solutions have been shown to be incorrect.")

90. Alice starves in (43) with $p = 1$ and $r = 3$ in (47), if she moves to A1 and then Bob remains in B0 whenever he is bumped. The A2 $\wedge$ B2 deadlock mentioned in the text for (45) corresponds to (47) with $p = 4$ and $r = 6$. And in (46), successive moves to B1, (B2, A1, A2, B3, B1, A4, A5, A0)$^\infty$ will starve poor Bob.

91. A cycle (47) with no maybe/critical states for Alice can certainly starve her. Conversely, given (i), (ii), (iii), suppose Alice is in no maybe/critical state when $t \geq t_0$; and let $t_0 < t_1 < t_2 < \cdots$ be times with @$_{t_i} = 1$ but with @$_t = 0$ for at least one t between t_i and t_{i+1}. Then we must have $X_{t_i} = X_{t_j}$ for some $i < j$, because the number of states is finite. Hence there's a starvation cycle with $p = t_i$ and $r = t_j$.

92. For $0 \leq i < j \leq r$ we want clauses that encode the condition $X_i \neq X_j$. Introduce new variables σ_{ij} for each state σ of Alice or Bob, and v_{ij} for each shared variable v. Assert that at least one of these new variables is true. (For the protocol (40) this clause would be $(A0_{ij} \vee \cdots \vee A4_{ij} \vee B0_{ij} \vee \cdots \vee B4_{ij} \vee l_{ij})$.) Also assert the binary clauses $(\bar{\sigma}_{ij} \vee \sigma_i) \wedge (\bar{\sigma}_{ij} \vee \bar{\sigma}_j)$ for each σ, and the ternary clauses $(\bar{v}_{ij} \vee v_i \vee v_j) \wedge (\bar{v}_{ij} \vee \bar{v}_i \vee \bar{v}_j)$ for each v.

The transition clauses can also be streamlined, because we needn't allow cases where $X_{t+1} = X_t$. Thus, for example, we can omit $B0_{t+1}$ from the clause $(@_t \vee \overline{B0_t} \vee B0_{t+1} \vee B1_{t+1})$ of (42); and we can omit the clause $(@_t \vee \overline{B1_t} \vee \bar{l}_t \vee B1_{t+1})$ entirely.

[If r is large, encodings with $O(r(\log r)^2)$ clauses are possible via sorting networks, as suggested by D. Kroening and O. Strichman, *LNCS* **2575** (2003), 298–309. The most practical scheme, however, seems to be to add the ij constraints one by one as needed; see N. Eén and N. Sörensson, *Electronic Notes in Theoretical Computer Science* **89** (2003), 543–560.]

93. For the Φ in (50), for example, we can use $(x_1 \vee x_2 \vee \cdots \vee x_{16}) \wedge (\bar{x}_1 \vee \overline{A0'}) \wedge \cdots \wedge (\bar{x}_1 \vee \overline{A6'}) \wedge (\bar{x}_2 \vee \overline{B0'}) \wedge \cdots \wedge (\bar{x}_2 \vee \overline{B6'}) \wedge (\bar{x}_3 \vee A0') \wedge (\bar{x}_3 \vee a') \wedge \cdots \wedge (\bar{x}_{16} \vee B6') \wedge (\bar{x}_{16} \vee \bar{b}')$.

94. $(X \to X' \to \cdots \to X^{(r)}) \wedge \Phi(X) \wedge \Phi(X') \wedge \cdots \wedge \Phi(X^{(r-1)}) \wedge \neg\Phi(X^{(r)})$. [This important technique is called "k-induction"; see Mary Sheeran, Satnam Singh, and Gunnar Stålmarck, *LNCS* **1954** (2000), 108–125. One can, for example, add the clause $(\overline{A5} \vee \overline{B5})$ to (50) and prove the resulting formula Φ by 3-induction.]

95. The critical steps have $a = b = 1$, by the invariants, so they have no predecessor.

96. The only predecessor of $A5_2 \wedge B5_2 \wedge a_2 \wedge b_2 \wedge \bar{l}_2$ is $A5_1 \wedge B4_1 \wedge a_1 \wedge b_1 \wedge \bar{l}_1$; and the only predecessor of *that* is $A5_0 \wedge B3_0 \wedge a_0 \wedge b_0 \wedge \bar{l}_0$. The case l_2 is similar.

But *without* the invariants, we could find arbitrarily long paths to $A5_r \wedge B5_r$. In fact the longest such *simple* path has $r = 33$: Starting with $A2_0 \wedge B2_0 \wedge \bar{a}_0 \wedge \bar{b}_0 \wedge l_0$, we could successively bump Alice and Bob into states A3, A5, A6, A0, A1, A2, A3, B3, B4, A5, B3, A6, B4, A0, B3, A1, A2, A3, A5, A6, A0, A1, A2, B4, A3, A5, A6, A0, B5, A1, A2, A3, A5, never repeating a previous state. (Of course all of these states are unreachable from the real X_0, because none of them satisfy Φ.)

97. No. Removing each person's final step in a path to $A6 \wedge B6$ gives a path to $A5 \wedge B5$.

98. (a) Suppose $X_0 \to \cdots \to X_r = X_0$ is impure and $X_i = X_j$ for some $0 \le i < j < r$. We may assume that $i = 0$. If either of the two cycles $X_0 \to \cdots \to X_j = X_0$ or $X_j \to \cdots \to X_r = X_j$ is impure, it is shorter.

(b) In those states she would have had to be previously in A0 or A5.

(c) Generate clauses $(\bar{g}_0)$, $(\bar{g}_t \vee g_{t-1} \vee @_{t-1})$, $(\bar{h}_0)$, $(\bar{h}_t \vee h_{t-1} \vee \overline{@_{t-1}})$, $(\bar{f}_t \vee g_t)$, $(\bar{f}_t \vee h_t)$, $(\bar{f}_t \vee \alpha_0 \vee \bar{\alpha}_t)$, $(\bar{f}_t \vee \bar{\alpha}_0 \vee \alpha_t)$, $(\bar{f}_t \vee v_0 \vee \bar{v}_t)$, $(\bar{f}_t \vee \bar{v}_0 \vee v_t)$, for $1 \le t \le r$; and $(f_1 \vee f_2 \vee \cdots \vee f_r)$. Here v runs through all shared variables, and α runs through all states that can occur in a starvation cycle. (For example, Alice's states with respect to protocol (49) would be restricted to A3 and A4, but Bob's are unrestricted.)

(d) With exercise 92 we can determine that the longest simple path, using only states that can occur in a starvation cycle for (49), is 15. And the clauses of (c) are unsatisfiable when $r = 15$ and invariant (50) is used. Thus the only possible starvation cycle is made from two simple pure cycles; and those are easy to rule out.

99. Invariant assertions define the values of a and b at each state. Hence mutual exclusion follows as in exercise 95. For starvation-freedom, we can exclude states A0, A6, A7, A8 from any cycle that starves Alice. But we need also to show that the state $A5_t \wedge B0_t \wedge l_t$ is impossible; otherwise she could starve while Bob is maybe-ing. For that purpose we can add $\neg((A6 \vee A7 \vee A8) \wedge (B6 \vee B7 \vee B8)) \wedge \neg(A8 \wedge \bar{l}) \wedge \neg(B8 \wedge l) \wedge \neg((A3 \vee A4 \vee A5) \wedge B0 \wedge l) \wedge \neg(A0 \wedge (B3 \vee B4 \vee B5) \wedge \bar{l})$ to the invariant $\Phi(X)$. The longest simple path through allowable states has length 42; and the clauses of exercise

98(c) are unsatisfiable when $r = 42$. Notice that Alice and Bob never compete when setting the common variable l, because states A7 and B7 cannot occur together.

(See Dijkstra's *Cooperating Sequential Processes*, cited in the text.)

100. Bob is starved by the moves B1, (A1, A2, A3, B2, A4, B3, A0, B4, B1)$^\infty$. But an argument similar to the previous answer shows that Alice cannot be.

[The protocol obviously provides mutual exclusion as in exercise 95. It was devised independently in the late 1970s by J. E. Burns and L. Lamport, as a special case of an N-player protocol using only N shared bits; see *JACM* **33** (1986), 337–339.]

101. The following solution is based on G. L. Peterson's elegant protocol for N processes in *ACM Transactions on Programming Languages and Systems* **5** (1983), 56–65:

A0. Maybe go to A1.
A1. Set $a_1 \leftarrow 1$, go to A2.
A2. If b_2 go to A2, else to A3.
A3. Set $a_2 \leftarrow 1$, go to A4.
A4. Set $a_1 \leftarrow 0$, go to A5.
A5. If b_1 go to A5, else to A6.
A6. Set $a_1 \leftarrow 1$, go to A7.
A7. If b_1 go to A8, else to A9.
A8. If b_2 go to A7, else to A9.
A9. Critical, go to A10.
A10. Set $a_1 \leftarrow 0$, go to A11.
A11. Set $a_2 \leftarrow 0$, go to A0.

(Alice and Bob might need an app to help them deal with this.)

B0. Maybe go to B1.
B1. Set $b_1 \leftarrow 1$, go to B2.
B2. If a_1 go to B2, else to B3.
B3. Set $b_2 \leftarrow 1$, go to B4.
B4. Set $b_1 \leftarrow 0$, go to B5.
B5. If a_2 go to B5, else to B6.
B6. Set $b_1 \leftarrow 1$, go to B7.
B7. If a_1 go to B8, else to B12.
B8. If a_2 go to B9, else to B12.
B9. Set $b_1 \leftarrow 0$, go to B10.
B10. If a_1 go to B11, else to B6.
B11. If a_2 go to B10, else to B6.
B12. Critical, go to B13.
B13. Set $b_1 \leftarrow 0$, go to B14.
B14. Set $b_2 \leftarrow 0$, go to B0.

102. The clauses for, say, 'B5. If a go to B6, else to B7.' should be $(@ \vee \overline{B5} \vee \bar{a} \vee \alpha_1 \vee \cdots \vee \alpha_p \vee B6') \wedge (@ \vee \overline{B5} \vee a \vee \alpha_1 \vee \cdots \vee \alpha_p \vee B7') \wedge (@ \vee \overline{B5} \vee B6' \vee B7')$, where α_1, $\ldots$, α_p are the states in which Alice sets a.

103. See, for example, any front cover of *SICOMP*, or of *SIAM Review* since 1970.

104. Assume that $m \le n$. The case $m = n$ is clearly impossible, because all four corners must be occupied. When m is odd and $n = m + k + 1$, put m bishops in the first and last columns, then k in the middle columns of the middle row. When m is even and $n = m + 2k + 1$, put m in the first and last columns, and two in the middle rows of columns $m/2 + 2j$ for $1 \le j \le k$. There's no solution when m and n are both even, because the maximum number of independent bishops of each color is $(m + n - 2)/2$. [R. Berghammer, *LNCS* **6663** (2011), 103–106.]

105. (a) We must have $(x_{ij}, x'_{ij}) = (1, 0)$ for t pairs ij, and $(0, 1)$ for t other pairs; otherwise $x_{ij} = x'_{ij}$. Hence there are 2^{mn-2t} solutions.

(b) Use $2mn$ variables y_{ij}, y'_{ij} for $1 \le i \le m$ and $1 \le j \le n$, with binary clauses $(\bar{y}_{ij} \vee \bar{y}'_{ij})$, together with $m + n + 2(m + n - 1)$ sets of cardinality constraints such as (20) and (21) to enforce the balance condition $\sum \{y_{ij} + \bar{y}'_{ij} \mid ij \in L\} = |L|$ for each row, column, and diagonal line L.

(c) $T(m, n) = 1$ when $\min(m, n) < 4$, because only the zero matrix qualifies in such cases. Other values can be enumerated by backtracking, if they are small enough. (The asymptotic behavior is unknown.)

n	$=$	4	5	6	7	8
$T(4, n) =$		3	7	17	35	77
$T(5, n) =$		7	31	109	365	1367
$T(6, n) =$		17	109	877	6315	47607
$T(7, n) =$		35	365	6315	107637	1703883
$T(8, n) =$		77	1367	47607	1703883	66291089

(d) Suppose $m \le n$. Any solution with nonzero first row and column has all entries zero except that $y_{1t} = -y_{t1} = y_{(k+1-t)1} =$

$-y_{kt} = y_{k(k+1-t)} = -y_{(k+1-t)k} = y_{tk} = -y_{1(k+1-t)}$, for some t and k with $1 < t \le k/2 \le m/2$. So the answer is $2 \sum_{k=4}^{m} \lfloor k/2 - 1 \rfloor (m+1-k)(n+1-k)$, which simplifies to $q(q-1)(4q(n-q) - 5n + 2q + 3 + (m \bmod 2)(6n - 8q - 5))/3$ when $q = \lfloor m/2 \rfloor$.

[The answer in the case $(m, n) = (25, 30)$ is 36080; hence a random 25×30 image will have an average of $36080/256 \approx 140.9$ tomographically equivalent "neighbors" that differ from it in exactly eight pixel positions. Figure 79 has five such neighbors, one of which is shown in answer 111 below.]

(e) We can make all entries nonzero except on the main diagonals (see below). This is optimum, because the diagonal lines for $a_1, a_3, \ldots, a_{4n-1}, b_1, b_3, \ldots, b_{4n-1}$ must each contain a different 0. So the answer is $2n(n-1)$. (But the maximum for odd sized boards is unknown; for $m = n = (5, 7, 9)$ it turns out to be $(6, 18, 33)$.)

```
0+++---0      0+++0---0
-0++--0+      ----+++0+     0++--00      0++--00
--0+-0++      0-+-+--++     --++000      --++000
---00+++      ++-++0---     0+--00+      0+-0-0+
+++00---      -+-+--0++     -00+0-+      -0-+00+
++0-+0--      +0-0+0+--     +0-0+0-      +000+--
+0--++0-      --+--+++0     +0+0-0-      +0+-00-
0---+++0      ++++-0---     0--0++0      0--0++0
              0-0--+++0
```

(f) The smallest counterexamples are 7×7 (see above).

106. In an $m \times n$ problem we must have $0 \le r_i \le n$, $0 \le c_j \le m$, and $0 \le a_d, b_d \le \min\{d, m, n, m+n-d\}$. So the total number B of possibilities, assuming that $m \le n$, is $(n+1)^m (m+1)^n ((m+1)! \, (m+1)^{n-m} m!)^2$, which is $\approx 3 \cdot 10^{197}$ when $(m, n) = (25, 30)$. Since $2^{750}/B \approx 2 \cdot 10^{28}$, we conclude that a "random" 25×30 digital tomography problem usually has more than 10^{28} solutions. (Of course there are other constraints too; for example, the fact that $\sum r_i = \sum c_j = \sum a_d = \sum b_d$ reduces B by at least a factor of $(n+1)(m+1)^2$.)

107. (a) $(r_1, \ldots, r_6) = (11, 11, 11, 9, 9, 10)$; $(c_1, \ldots, c_{13}) = (6, 5, 6, 2, 4, 4, 6, 5, 4, 2, 6, 5, 6)$; $(a_1, \ldots, a_6) = (11, 10, 9, 9, 11, 11)$; $(b_1, \ldots, b_{12}) = (6, 1, 6, 5, 7, 5, 6, 2, 6, 5, 7, 5)$.

(b) There are two others, namely the following one and its left-right reversal:

[*Reference:* P. Gerdes, *Sipatsi* (Maputo: U. Pedagógica, 2009), page 62, pattern #122.]

108. Here are four of the many possibilities:

109. **F1.** [Initialize.] Find one solution $y_1 \ldots y_n$, or terminate if the problem is unsatisfiable. Then set $y_{n+1} \leftarrow 1$ and $d \leftarrow 0$.

F2. [Advance d.] Set d to the smallest $j > d$ such that $y_j = 1$.

F3. [Done?] If $d > n$, terminate with $y_1 \ldots y_n$ as the answer.

F4. [Try for smaller.] Try to find a solution with additional unit clauses to force $x_j = y_j$ for $1 \le j < d$ and $x_d = 0$. If successful, set $y_1 \ldots y_n \leftarrow x_1 \ldots x_n$. Return to F2. ∎

Even better is to incorporate a similar procedure into the solver itself; see exercise 275.

110. Algorithm B actually gives these directly:

```
001111111011101111100101111101111011111101110110110111111111100101111011110111111100110111111110111
1111111110111111110011001111110011110111111111010111111110111101111111001100111110110111101111111
```

111. This family of problems appears to provide an excellent (though sometimes formidable) series of benchmark tests for SAT solvers. The suggested example has solutions

(a) colexicographically first;   (b) minimally different;   (c) colexicographically last;

and several of the entries in (a) were by no means easy. An even more difficult case arises if we base lexicographic order on a rook path that spirals out from the center (thus favoring solutions that are mostly 0 or mostly 1 in the middle):

(a) spiral rook path;   (b) "spirographically" first;   (c) "spirographically" last.

Here many of the entries have never yet been solved by a SAT solver, as of 2013, although again IP solvers have no great difficulty. In fact, the "lexicographic pure cutting plane" procedure of E. Balas, M. Fischetti, and A. Zanette [*Math. Programming* **A130** (2011), 153–176; **A135** (2012), 509–514] turns out to be particularly effective on such problems.

112. Reasonably tight upper and lower bounds would also be interesting.

113. Given an $N \times N \times N$ contingency problem with binary constraints $C_{JK} = X_{*JK}$, $R_{IK} = X_{I*K}$, $P_{IJ} = X_{IJ*}$, we can construct an equivalent $n \times n$ digital tomography problem with $n = N^2 + N^3 + N^4$ as follows: First construct a four-dimensional tensor $Y_{IJKL} = X_{(I \oplus L)JK}$, where $I \oplus L = 1 + (I + L - 1) \bmod N$, and notice that $Y_{*JKL} = Y_{IJK*} = X_{*JK}$, $Y_{I*KL} = X_{(I \oplus L)*K}$, $Y_{IJ*L} = X_{(I \oplus L)J*}$. Then define x_{ij} for $1 \leq i, j \leq n$ by the rule $x_{ij} = Y_{IJKL}$ when $i = I - N^2 K + N^3 L$, $j = NJ + N^2 K + N^3 L$, otherwise $x_{ij} = 0$. This rule makes sense; for if $1 \leq I, I', J, J', K, K', L, L' \leq N$ and $I - N^2 K + N^3 L = I' - N^2 K' + N^3 L'$ and $NJ + N^2 K + N^3 L = NJ' + N^2 K' + N^3 L'$, we have $I \equiv I'$ (modulo N); hence $I = I'$ and $K \equiv K'$; hence $K = K'$, $L = L'$, $J = J'$.

Under this correspondence the marginal sums are $r_i = Y_{I*KL}$ when $i = I - N^2 K + N^3 L$, $c_j = Y_{*JKL}$ when $j = NJ + N^2 K + N^3 L$, $a_d = Y_{IJ*L}$ when $d + 1 = I + NJ + 2N^3 L$, $b_d = Y_{IJK*}$ when $d - n = I - NJ - 2N^2 K$, otherwise zero. [See S. Brunetti, A. Del Lungo, P. Gritzmann, and S. de Vries, *Theoretical Comp. Sci.* **406** (2008), 63–71.]

114. (a) From $x_{7,23} + x_{7,24} = x_{7,23} + x_{7,24} + x_{7,25} = x_{7,24} + x_{7,25} = 1$ we deduce $x_{7,23} = x_{7,25} = 0$ and $x_{7,24} = 1$, revealing $n_{7,23} = n_{7,25} = 5$. Now $x_{6,23} + x_{6,24} = x_{6,24} + x_{6,25} = x_{4,24} + x_{5,24} + x_{6,24} + x_{6,25} = 1$; hence $x_{4,24} = x_{5,24} = 0$, revealing $n_{4,24} = n_{5,24} = 2$. So $x_{6,23} = x_{6,25} = 0$, and the rest is easy.

(b) Let $y_{i,j}$ mean "cell (i,j) has been probed safely, revealing $n_{i,j}$." Consider the clauses C obtained by appending $\bar{y}_{i,j}$ to each clause of the symmetric function $[\sum_{i'=i-1}^{i+1}\sum_{j'=j-1}^{j+1} x_{i',j'} = n_{i,j}]$, for all i,j with $x_{i,j} = 0$. Also include $(\bar{x}_{i,j} \vee \bar{y}_{i,j})$, as well as clauses for the symmetric function $S_N(x)$ if we're told the total number N of mines.

Given any subset F of mine-free cells, the clauses $C_F = C \wedge \bigwedge\{y_{i,j} \mid (i,j) \in F\}$ are satisfiable precisely by the configurations of mines that are consistent with the data $\{n_{i,j} \mid (i,j) \in F\}$. Therefore cell (i,j) is safe if and only if $C_F \wedge x_{i,j}$ is unsatisfiable.

A simple modification of Algorithm C can be used to "grow" F until no further safe cells can be added: Given a solution to C_F for which neither $x_{i,j}$ nor $\bar{x}_{i,j}$ was obtained at root level (level 0), we can try to find a "flipped" solution by using the complemented value as the decision at level 1. Such a solution will be found if and only if the flipped value is consistent; otherwise the unflipped value will have been forced at level 0. By changing default polarities we can favor solutions that flip many variables at once. Whenever a literal $\bar{x}_{i,j}$ is newly deduced at root level, we can force $y_{i,j}$ to be true, thus adding (i,j) to F. We reach an impasse when a set of solutions has been obtained for C_F that covers both settings of every unforced $x_{i,j}$.

For problem (i) we start with $F = \{(1,1)\}$, etc. Case (iv) by itself uncovers only 56 cells in the lower right corner. The other results, each obtained in $< 6\,\mathrm{G}\mu$, are:

(i), (ii) (iii) (v)

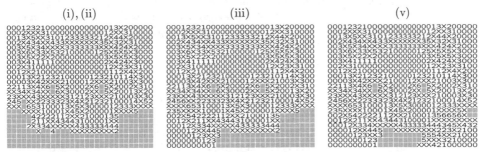

Notice that the Cheshire cat's famous smile defies logic and requires much guesswork!

[For aspects of Minesweeper that are NP-complete and coNP-complete, see Kaye, Scott, Stege, and van Rooij, *Math. Intelligencer* **22**, 2 (2000), 9–15; **33**, 4 (2011), 5–17.]

115. Several thousand runs of the algorithm in the previous exercise, given that the total number of mines is 10, indicate success probabilities $.490 \pm .007$, $.414 \pm .004$, $.279 \pm .003$, when the first guess is respectively in a corner, in the center of an edge, or in the center.

116. The smallest is the "clock" in answer 69(b). Other noteworthy possibilities are

as well as the "phoenix" in Fig. A–9.

117. (a) Set $x_0 = x_{n+1} = 0$, and let (a, b, c) be respectively the number of occurrences of $(01, 10, 11)$ as a substring of $x_0 x_1 \ldots x_{n+1}$. Then $a + c = b + c = \nu x$ and $c = \nu^{(2)} x$; hence $a = b = \nu x - \nu^{(2)} x$ is the number of runs.

(b) In this case the complete binary tree will have only $n-1$ leaves, corresponding to $\{x_1 x_2, \ldots, x_{n-1} x_n\}$; therefore we want to replace n by $n - 1$ in (20) and (21).

The clauses of (20) remain unchanged unless $t_k \leq 3$. When $t_k = 2$ they become $(\bar{x}_{2k-n+1} \vee \bar{x}_{2k-n+2} \vee b_1^k) \wedge (\bar{x}_{2k-n+2} \vee \bar{x}_{2k-n+3} \vee b_1^k) \wedge (\bar{x}_{2k-n+1} \vee \bar{x}_{2k-n+2} \vee \bar{x}_{2k-n+3} \vee b_2^k)$. When $t_k = 3$ we have $2k = n-1$, and they become $(\bar{b}_1^{2k} \vee b_1^k) \wedge (\bar{x}_1 \vee \bar{x}_2 \vee b_1^k) \wedge (\bar{b}_1^{2k} \vee b_2^k) \wedge (\bar{b}_1^{2k} \vee \bar{x}_1 \vee \bar{x}_2 \vee b_2^k) \wedge (\bar{b}_2^{2k} \vee \bar{x}_1 \vee \bar{x}_2 \vee b_3^k)$.

The clauses of (21) remain unchanged except in simple cases when $n \leq 3$.

(c) Now the leaves represent $\overline{x_i x_{i+1}} = \bar{x}_i \vee \bar{x}_{i+1}$. So we change (20), when $t_k = 2$, to $(x_{2k-n+1} \vee b_1^k) \wedge (x_{2k-n+2} \vee b_1^k) \wedge (x_{2k-n+3} \vee b_1^k) \wedge (x_{2k-n+2} \vee b_2^k) \wedge (x_{2k-n+1} \vee x_{2k-n+3} \vee b_2^k)$. And there are eight clauses when $t_k = 3$: $(\bar{b}_1^{2k} \vee b_1^k) \wedge (x_1 \vee b_1^k) \wedge (x_2 \vee b_1^k) \wedge (\bar{b}_2^{2k} \vee b_2^k) \wedge (\bar{b}_1^{2k} \vee x_1 \vee b_2^k) \wedge (\bar{b}_1^{2k} \vee x_2 \vee b_2^k) \wedge (\bar{b}_2^{2k} \vee x_1 \vee b_3^k) \wedge (\bar{b}_2^{2k} \vee x_2 \vee b_3^k)$.

118. Let $p_{i,j} = $ [the pixel in row i and column j should be covered], and introduce variables $h_{i,j}$ when $p_{i,j} = p_{i,j+1} = 1$, $v_{i,j}$ when $p_{i,j} = p_{i+1,j} = 1$. The clauses are (i) $(h_{i,j} \vee h_{i,j-1} \vee v_{i,j} \vee v_{i-1,j})$, whenever $p_{i,j} = 1$, omitting variables that don't exist; (ii) $(\bar{h}_{i,j} \vee \bar{h}_{i,j-1})$, $(\bar{h}_{i,j} \vee \bar{v}_{i,j})$, $(\bar{h}_{i,j} \vee \bar{v}_{i-1,j})$, $(\bar{h}_{i,j-1} \vee \bar{v}_{i,j})$, $(\bar{h}_{i,j-1} \vee \bar{v}_{i-1,j})$, $(\bar{v}_{i,j} \vee \bar{v}_{i-1,j})$, whenever $p_{i,j} = 1$, omitting clauses whose variables don't both exist; and (iii) $(h_{i,j} \vee h_{i+1,j} \vee v_{i,j} \vee v_{i,j+1})$, whenever $p_{i,j} + p_{i,j+1} + p_{i+1,j} + p_{i+1,j+1} \geq 3$, omitting variables that don't exist. (The example has 10527 clauses in 2874 variables, but it's quickly solved.)

119. There's symmetry between l and $\bar{l}$, also between l and $10 - l$; so we need consider only $l = (1, 2, 3, 4, 5)$, with respectively $(4, 4, 6, 6, 8)$ occurrences. The smallest result is $F \mid 5 = \{123, 234, 678, 789, 246, 468, 147, 369, \overline{123}, \overline{234}, \overline{34}, \overline{46}, \overline{67}, \overline{678}, \overline{789}, \overline{13}, \overline{246}, \overline{37}, \overline{468}, \overline{79}, \overline{147}, \overline{28}, \overline{369}, \overline{19}\}$.

120. True.

121. The main point of interest is that an empty clause is typically discovered in the *midst* of step A3; partial backtracking must be done when taking back the changes that were made before this interruption.

> **A3.** [Remove $\bar{l}$.] Set $p \leftarrow F(\bar{l})$ (which is $F(l \oplus 1)$, see (57)). While $p \geq 2n + 2$, set $j \leftarrow C(p)$, $i \leftarrow SIZE(j)$, and if $i > 1$ set $SIZE(j) \leftarrow i - 1$, $p \leftarrow F(p)$. But if $i = 1$, interrupt that loop and set $p \leftarrow B(p)$; then while $p \geq 2n + 2$, set $j \leftarrow C(p)$, $i \leftarrow SIZE(j)$, $SIZE(j) \leftarrow i + 1$, $p \leftarrow B(p)$; and finally go to A5.

> **A4.** [Deactivate l's clauses.] Set $p \leftarrow F(l)$. While $p \geq 2n + 2$, set $j \leftarrow C(p)$, $i \leftarrow START(j)$, $p \leftarrow F(p)$, and for $i \leq s < i + SIZE(j) - 1$ set $q \leftarrow F(s)$, $r \leftarrow B(s)$, $B(q) \leftarrow r$, $F(r) \leftarrow q$, and $C(L(s)) \leftarrow C(L(s)) - 1$. Then set $a \leftarrow a - C(l)$, $d \leftarrow d + 1$, and return to A2.

> **A7.** [Reactivate l's clauses.] Set $a \leftarrow a + C(l)$ and $p \leftarrow B(l)$. While $p \geq 2n + 2$, set $j \leftarrow C(p)$, $i \leftarrow START(j)$, $p \leftarrow B(p)$, and for $i \leq s < i + SIZE(j) - 1$ set $q \leftarrow F(s)$, $r \leftarrow B(s)$, $B(q) \leftarrow F(r) \leftarrow s$, and $C(L(s)) \leftarrow C(L(s)) + 1$. (The links dance a little here.)

> **A8.** [Unremove $\bar{l}$.] Set $p \leftarrow F(\bar{l})$. While $p \geq 2n + 2$, set $j \leftarrow C(p)$, $i \leftarrow SIZE(j)$, $SIZE(j) \leftarrow i + 1$, $p \leftarrow F(p)$. Then go to A5. ∎

122. Pure literals are problematic when we want all solutions, so we don't take advantage of them here. Indeed, things get simpler; only the move codes 1 and 2 are needed.

> **A1*.** [Initialize.] Set $d \leftarrow 1$.

A2*. [Visit or choose.] If $d > n$, visit the solution defined by $m_1 \ldots m_n$ and go to A6*. Otherwise set $l \leftarrow 2d + 1$ and $m_d \leftarrow 1$.

A3*. [Remove $\bar{l}$.] Delete $\bar{l}$ from all active clauses; but go to A5* if that would make a clause empty.

A4*. [Deactivate l's clauses.] Suppress all clauses that contain l. Then set $d \leftarrow d + 1$ and return to A2*.

A5*. [Try again.] If $m_d = 1$, set $m_d \leftarrow 2$, $l \leftarrow 2d$, and go to A3*.

A6*. [Backtrack.] Terminate if $d = 1$. Otherwise set $d \leftarrow d - 1$ and $l \leftarrow 2d + (m_d \;\&\; 1)$.

A7*. [Reactivate l's clauses.] Unsuppress all clauses that contain l.

A8*. [Unremove $\bar{l}$.] Reinstate $\bar{l}$ in all the active clauses that contain it. Then go back to A5*. ∎

It's no longer necessary to update the values $\mathtt{C}(k)$ for $k < 2n+2$ in steps A4* and A7*.

123. For example, we might have

$$p = 0 \;\; 1 \;\; 2 \;\; 3 \;\; 4 \;\; 5 \;\; 6 \;\; 7 \;\; 8 \;\; 9 \;\; 10 \;\; 11 \;\; 12 \;\; 13 \;\; 14 \;\; 15 \;\; 16 \;\; 17 \;\; 18 \;\; 19 \;\; 20$$
$$\mathtt{L}(p) = 3 \;\; 9 \;\; 7 \;\; 8 \;\; 7 \;\; 5 \;\; 6 \;\; 5 \;\; 3 \;\; 4 \;\; 3 \;\; 8 \;\; 2 \;\; 8 \;\; 6 \;\; 9 \;\; 6 \;\; 4 \;\; 7 \;\; 4 \;\; 2$$

and $\mathtt{START}(j) = 21 - 3j$ for $0 \le j \le 7$; $W_2 = 3$, $W_3 = 7$, $W_4 = 4$, $W_5 = 0$, $W_6 = 5$, $W_7 = 1$, $W_8 = 6$, $W_9 = 2$. Also $\mathtt{LINK}(j) = 0$ for $1 \le j \le 7$ in this case.

124. Set $j \leftarrow W_{\bar{l}}$. While $j \ne 0$, a literal other than $\bar{l}$ should be watched in clause j, so we do the following: Set $i \leftarrow \mathtt{START}(j)$, $i' \leftarrow \mathtt{START}(j-1)$, $j' \leftarrow \mathtt{LINK}(j)$, $k \leftarrow i + 1$. While $k < i'$, set $l' \leftarrow \mathtt{L}(k)$; if l' isn't false (that is, if $|l'| > d$ or $l' + m_{|l'|}$ is even, see (57)), set $\mathtt{L}(i) \leftarrow l'$, $\mathtt{L}(k) \leftarrow \bar{l}$, $\mathtt{LINK}(j) \leftarrow W_{l'}$, $W_{l'} \leftarrow j$, $j \leftarrow j'$, and exit the loop on k; otherwise set $k \leftarrow k + 1$ and continue that loop. If k reaches i', however, we cannot stop watching $\bar{l}$; so we set $W_{\bar{l}} \leftarrow j$, exit the loop on j, and go on to step B5.

125. Change steps B2 and B4 to be like A2* and A4* in answer 122.

126. Starting with active ring $(6\,9\,7\,8)$, the unit clause 9 will be found (because 9 appears before 8); the clause $9\bar{3}\bar{6}$ will become $\bar{6}\bar{3}9$; the active ring will become $(7\,8\,6)$.

127. Before: 11414545; after: 1142. (And then 11425, etc.)

128.

Active ring	$x_1x_2x_3x_4$	Units	Choice	Changed clauses
$(1\,2\,3\,4)$	– – – –		$\bar{1}$	$21\bar{3}$
$(2\,3\,4)$	0 – – –		$\bar{2}$	$\bar{3}12, 32\bar{4}$
$(3\,4)$	0 0 – –	$\bar{3}$	$\bar{3}$	$\bar{4}23, 431$
(4)	0 0 0 –	$4, \bar{4}$	Backtrack	
$(3\,4)$	0 – – –		2	$3\bar{2}4$
$(3\,4)$	0 1 – –	$\bar{4}$	$\bar{4}$	$341, \bar{1}42$
(3)	0 1 – 0	$3, \bar{3}$	Backtrack	
$(4\,3)$	– – – –		1	$4\bar{1}2, \bar{2}\bar{1}3$
$(2\,4\,3)$	1 – – –		$\bar{2}$	
$(4\,3)$	1 0 – –	4	4	$32\bar{4}, 1\bar{4}\bar{2}$
(3)	1 0 – 1	$3, \bar{3}$	Backtrack	
$(4\,3)$	1 – – –		2	$3\bar{1}2$
$(4\,3)$	1 1 – –	3	3	$4\bar{2}3, \bar{1}32, \bar{4}3\bar{1}$
(4)	1 1 1 –	$4, \bar{4}$	Backtrack	

129. Set $j \leftarrow W_l$, then do the following steps while $j \neq 0$: (i) Set $p \leftarrow$ START$(j) + 1$; (ii) if $p =$ START$(j - 1)$, return 1; (iii) if L(p) is false (that is, if $x_{|L(p)|} = $ L(p) & 1), set $p \leftarrow p + 1$ and repeat (ii); (iv) set $j \leftarrow$ LINK(j). If j becomes zero, return 0.

130. Set $l \leftarrow 2k + b$, $j \leftarrow W_l$, $W_l \leftarrow 0$, and do the following steps while $j \neq 0$: (i) Set $j' \leftarrow$ LINK(j), $i \leftarrow$ START(j), $p \leftarrow i + 1$; (ii) while L(p) is false, set $p \leftarrow p + 1$ (see answer 129; this loop will end before $p =$ START$(j - 1)$); (iii) set $l' \leftarrow$ L(p), L$(p) \leftarrow l$, L$(i) \leftarrow l'$; (iv) set $p \leftarrow W_{l'}$ and $q \leftarrow W_{\bar{l}'}$, and go to (vi) if $p \neq 0$ or $q \neq 0$ or $x_{|l'|} \geq 0$; (v) if $t = 0$, set $t \leftarrow h \leftarrow |l'|$ and NEXT$(t) \leftarrow h$, otherwise set NEXT$(|l'|) \leftarrow h$, $h \leftarrow |l'|$, NEXT$(t) \leftarrow h$ (thus inserting $|l'| = l' \gg 1$ into the ring as its new head); (vi) set LINK$(j) \leftarrow p$, $W_{l'} \leftarrow j$ (thus inserting j into the watch list of l'); (vii) set $j \leftarrow j'$.

[The tricky part here is to remember that t can be zero in step (v).]

131. For example, the author tried selecting a variable x_k for which $s_{2k} \cdot s_{2k+1}$ is maximum, where s_l is the length of l's watch list plus ε, and the parameter ε was 0.1. This reduced the runtime for $waerden(3, 10; 97)$ to 139.8 gigamems, with 8.6 meganodes. Less dramatic effects occurred with $langford(13)$: 56.2 gigamems, with 10.8 meganodes, versus 99.0 gigamems if the $minimum$ $s_{2k} \cdot s_{2k+1}$ was chosen instead.

132. The unsatisfiable clauses $(\bar{x}_1 \vee x_2)$, $(x_1 \vee \bar{x}_2)$, $(\bar{x}_3 \vee x_4)$, $(x_3 \vee \bar{x}_4)$, ..., $(\bar{x}_{2n-1} \vee x_{2n})$, $(x_{2n-1} \vee \bar{x}_{2n})$, $(\bar{x}_{2n-1} \vee \bar{x}_{2n})$, $(x_{2n-1} \vee x_{2n})$ cause it to investigate all 2^n settings of x_1, x_3, ..., x_{2n-1} before encountering a contradiction and repeatedly backtracking.

(Incidentally, the successive move codes make a pretty pattern. If the stated clauses are ordered randomly, the algorithm runs significantly faster, but it still apparently needs nonpolynomial time. What is the growth rate?)

133. (a) Optimum backtrack trees for n-variable SAT problems can be calculated with $\Theta(n3^n)$ time and $\Theta(3^n)$ space by considering all 3^n partial assignments, "bottom up." In this 9-variable problem we obtain a tree with 67 nodes (the minimum) if we branch first on x_3 and x_5, then on x_6 if $x_3 \neq x_5$; unit clauses arise at all other nodes.

(b) Similarly, the worst tree turns out to have 471 nodes. But if we require the algorithm to branch on a unit clause whenever possible, the worst size is 187. (Branch first on x_1, then on x_4, then x_7; avoid opportunities for unit clauses.)

134. Let each BIMP list be accessed by ADDR, BSIZE, CAP, and K fields, where ADDR is the starting address in MEM of a block that's able to store CAP items, and CAP $= 2^K$; ADDR is a multiple of CAP, and BSIZE is the number of items currently in use. Initially CAP $= 4$, K $= 2$, BSIZE $= 0$, and ADDR is a convenient multiple of 4. The $2n$ BIMP tables therefore occupy $8n$ slots initially. If MEM has room for 2^M items, those tables can be allocated so that the doubly linked lists AVAIL$[k]$ initially contain $a_k = (0$ or $1)$ available blocks of size 2^k for each k, where $2^M - 8n = (a_{M-1} \ldots a_1 a_0)_2$.

Resizing is necessary when BSIZE $=$ CAP and we need to increase BSIZE. Set $a \leftarrow$ ADDR, $k \leftarrow$ K, CAP $\leftarrow 2^{k+1}$, and let $b \leftarrow a \oplus 2^k$ be the address of a's buddy. If b is a free block of size 2^k, we're in luck: We remove b from AVAIL$[k]$; then if a & $2^k = 0$, nothing needs to be done, otherwise we copy BSIZE items from a to b and set ADDR $\leftarrow b$.

In the unlucky case when b is either reserved or free of size $< 2^k$, we set p to the address of the first block in AVAIL$[k']$, where AVAIL$[t]$ is empty for $k < t < k'$ (or we panic if MEM's capacity is exceeded). After removing p from AVAIL$[k']$, we split off new free blocks of sizes 2^{k+1}, ..., $2^{k'-1}$ if $k' > k + 1$. Finally we copy BSIZE items from block a to block p, set ADDR $\leftarrow p$, and put a into AVAIL$[k]$. (We needn't try to "collapse" a with its buddy, since the buddy isn't free.)

135. They're the complements of the literals in BIMP$(\bar{l})$.

136. Before, $\{(1,2),(4,2),(4,5),(5,1),(5,7),(6,9)\}$; after, $\{(1,2),(4,2),(6,9)\}$.

137. If p in a TIMP list points to the pair (u,v), let's write $u = \mathtt{U}(p)$ and $v = \mathtt{V}(p)$.

(a) Set $N \leftarrow n - G$, $x \leftarrow \mathtt{VAR}[N]$, $j \leftarrow \mathtt{INX}[X]$, $\mathtt{VAR}[j] \leftarrow x$, $\mathtt{INX}[x] \leftarrow j$, $\mathtt{VAR}[N] \leftarrow X$, $\mathtt{INX}[X] \leftarrow N$. Then do the following for $l = 2X$ and $l = 2X{+}1$, and for all p in $\mathtt{TIMP}(l)$: $u \leftarrow \mathtt{U}(p)$, $v \leftarrow \mathtt{V}(p)$, $p' \leftarrow \mathtt{LINK}(p)$, $p'' \leftarrow \mathtt{LINK}(p')$; $s \leftarrow \mathtt{TSIZE}(\bar{u}) - 1$, $\mathtt{TSIZE}(\bar{u}) \leftarrow s$, $t \leftarrow$ pair s of $\mathtt{TIMP}(\bar{u})$; if $p' \neq t$, swap pairs by setting $u' \leftarrow \mathtt{U}(t)$, $v' \leftarrow \mathtt{V}(t)$, $q \leftarrow \mathtt{LINK}(t)$, $q' \leftarrow \mathtt{LINK}(q)$, $\mathtt{LINK}(q') \leftarrow p'$, $\mathtt{LINK}(p) \leftarrow t$, $\mathtt{U}(p') \leftarrow u'$, $\mathtt{V}(p') \leftarrow v'$, $\mathtt{LINK}(p') \leftarrow q$, $\mathtt{U}(t) \leftarrow v$, $\mathtt{V}(t) \leftarrow \bar{l}$, $\mathtt{LINK}(t) \leftarrow p''$, $p' \leftarrow t$. Then set $s \leftarrow \mathtt{TSIZE}(\bar{v}) - 1$, $\mathtt{TSIZE}(\bar{v}) \leftarrow s$, $t \leftarrow$ pair s of $\mathtt{TIMP}(\bar{v})$; if $p'' \neq t$, swap pairs by setting $u' \leftarrow \mathtt{U}(t)$, $v' \leftarrow \mathtt{V}(t)$, $q \leftarrow \mathtt{LINK}(t)$, $q' \leftarrow \mathtt{LINK}(q)$, $\mathtt{LINK}(q') \leftarrow p''$, $\mathtt{LINK}(p') \leftarrow t$, $\mathtt{U}(p'') \leftarrow u'$, $\mathtt{V}(p'') \leftarrow v'$, $\mathtt{LINK}(p'') \leftarrow q$, $\mathtt{U}(t) \leftarrow \bar{l}$, $\mathtt{V}(t) \leftarrow u$, $\mathtt{LINK}(t) \leftarrow p$.

Notice that we do *not* make the current pairs of $\mathtt{TIMP}(l)$ inactive. They won't be accessed by the algorithm until it needs to undo the swaps just made.

(b) In VAR and in each TIMP list, the active entries appear first. The inactive entries follow, in the same order as they were swapped out, because inactive entries never participate in swaps. Therefore we can reactivate the most-recently-swapped-out entry by simply increasing the count of active entries. We must, however, be careful to do this "virtual unswapping" in precisely the reverse order from which we did the swapping.

Thus, for $l = 2X + 1$ and $l = 2X$, and for all p in $\mathtt{TIMP}(l)$, proceeding in the reverse order from (a), we set $u \leftarrow \mathtt{U}(p)$, $v \leftarrow \mathtt{V}(p)$, $\mathtt{TSIZE}(\bar{v}) \leftarrow \mathtt{TSIZE}(\bar{v}) + 1$, and $\mathtt{TSIZE}(\bar{u}) \leftarrow \mathtt{TSIZE}(\bar{u}) + 1$.

(The number N of free variables increases implicitly, because $N + E = n$ in step L12. Thus nothing needs to be done to VAR or INX. These efficient techniques based on swapping are examples of "sparse-set representations"; see 7.2.2–(16) thru (23).)

138. Because $\bar{v} \in \mathtt{BIMP}(\bar{u})$, (62) will be used to make u nearly true. That loop will *also* make v nearly true, because $v \in \mathtt{BIMP}(u)$ is equivalent to $\bar{u} \in \mathtt{BIMP}(\bar{v})$.

139. Introduce a new variable BSTAMP analogous to ISTAMP, and a new field $\mathtt{BST}(l)$ analogous to $\mathtt{IST}(l)$ in the data for each literal l. At the beginning of step L9, set $\mathtt{BSTAMP} \leftarrow \mathtt{BSTAMP} + 1$, then set $\mathtt{BST}(l) \leftarrow \mathtt{BSTAMP}$ for $l = \bar{u}$ and all $l \in \mathtt{BIMP}(\bar{u})$. Now, if $\mathtt{BST}(\bar{v}) \neq \mathtt{BSTAMP}$ and $\mathtt{BST}(v) \neq \mathtt{BSTAMP}$, do the following for all $w \in \mathtt{BIMP}(v)$: If w is fixed in context NT (it must be fixed true, since $\bar{w}$ implies $\bar{v}$), do nothing. Otherwise if $\mathtt{BST}(\bar{w}) = \mathtt{BSTAMP}$, perform (62) with $l \leftarrow u$ and exit the loop on w (because $\bar{u}$ implies both w and $\bar{w}$). Otherwise, if $\mathtt{BST}(w) \neq \mathtt{BSTAMP}$, append w to $\mathtt{BIMP}(\bar{u})$ and u to $\mathtt{BIMP}(\bar{w})$. (Of course (63) must be invoked when needed.)

Then increase BSTAMP again, and do the same thing with u and v reversed.

140. Unfortunately, no: We might have $\Omega(n)$ changes to BSIZE on each of $\Omega(n)$ levels of the search tree. However, the ISTACK will never have more entries than the total number of cells in all BIMP tables (namely 2^M in answer 134).

141. Suppose $\mathtt{ISTAMP} \leftarrow (\mathtt{ISTAMP} + 1) \bmod 2^e$ in step L5. If $\mathtt{ISTAMP} = 0$ after that operation, we can safely set $\mathtt{ISTAMP} \leftarrow 1$ and $\mathtt{IST}(l) \leftarrow 0$ for $2 \le l \le 2n{+}1$. (A similar remark applies to BSTAMP and $\mathtt{BST}(l)$ in answer 139.)

142. (The following operations, performed after $\mathtt{BRANCH}[d]$ is set in step L2, will also output '|' to mark levels of the search where no decision was made.) Set $\mathtt{BACKL}[d] \leftarrow F$, $r \leftarrow k \leftarrow 0$, and do the following while $k < d$: While $r < \mathtt{BACKF}[k]$, output '6+(R_r & 1)' and set $r \leftarrow r{+}1$. If $\mathtt{BRANCH}[k] < 0$, output '|'; otherwise output '2BRANCH$[k]$+(R_r & 1)' and set $r \leftarrow r + 1$. While $r < \mathtt{BACKL}[k + 1]$, output '4 + ($R_r$ & 1)' and set $r \leftarrow r + 1$. Then set $k \leftarrow k + 1$.

143. The following solution treats `KINX` and `KSIZE` as the unmodified algorithm treats `TIMP` and `TSIZE`. It deals in a somewhat more subtle way with `CINX` and `CSIZE`: If clause c originally had size k, and if j of its literals have become false while none have yet become true, `CSIZE`(c) will be $k - j$, but the nonfalse literals will not necessarily appear at the beginning of list `CINX`(c). As soon as j reaches $k - 2$, or one of the literals becomes true, clause c becomes inactive and it disappears from the `KINX` tables of all free literals. The algorithm won't look at `CINX`(c) or `CSIZE`(c) again until it unfixes the literal that deactivated c. Thus a big clause is inactive if and only if it has been satisfied (contains a true literal) or has become binary (has at most two nonfalse literals).

We need to modify only the three steps that involve `TIMP`. The modified step L1, call it L1′, inputs the big clauses in a straightforward way.

Step L7′ removes the formerly free variable X from the data structures by first deactivating all of the active big clauses that contain L: For each of the `KSIZE`(L) numbers c in `KINX`(L), and for each of the `CSIZE`(c) free literals u in `CINX`(c), we swap c out of u's clause list as follows: Set $s \leftarrow$ `KSIZE`$(u) - 1$, `KSIZE`$(u) \leftarrow s$; find $t \leq s$ with `KINX`$(u)[t] = c$; if $t \neq s$ set `KINX`$(u)[t] \leftarrow$ `KINX`$(u)[s]$ and `KINX`$(u)[s] \leftarrow c$. [*Heuristic:* If the number of free literals remaining in c is small compared to c's original size, for example if say 15 or 20 original literals have become false, the remaining nonfalse literals can usefully be swapped into the first `CSIZE`(c) positions of `CINX`(c) when c is being deactivated. The author's experimental implementation does this when `CSIZE`(c) is at most θ times the original size, where the parameter θ is normally $25/64$.]

Then step L7′ updates clauses for which L has become false: For each of the `KSIZE`$(\bar{L})$ numbers c in `KINX`$(\bar{L})$, set $s \leftarrow$ `CSIZE`$(c) - 1$ and `CSIZE`$(c) \leftarrow s$; if $s = 2$, find the two free literals (u, v) in `CINX`(c), swap them into the first positions of that list, put them on a temporary stack, and swap c out of the clause lists of u and v as above.

Finally, step L7′ does step L8′ = L8 for all (u, v) on the temporary stack. [The maximum size of that stack will be the maximum of `KSIZE`(l) over all l, after step L1′; so we allocate memory for that stack as part of step L1′.]

In step L12′ we set $L \leftarrow R_E$, $X \leftarrow |L|$, and reactivate the clauses that involve X as follows: For each of the `KSIZE`$(\bar{L})$ numbers c in `KINX`$(\bar{L})$, proceeding in reverse order from the order used in L7′, set $s \leftarrow$ `CSIZE`(c), `CSIZE`$(c) \leftarrow s + 1$; if $s = 2$, swap c back into the clause lists of v and u, where $u =$ `CINX`$(c)[0]$ and $v =$ `CINX`$(c)[1]$. For each of the `KSIZE`(L) numbers c in `KINX`(L), and for each of the `CSIZE`(c) free literals u in `CINX`(c), again proceeding in reverse order from the order used in L7′, swap c back into the clause list of u. The latter operation simply increases `KSIZE`(u) by 1.

ParamILS advises changing α from 3.5 to 0.001(!) in (195).

144. False; $h'(l) = 0.1$ if and only if the *complement*, $\bar{l}$, doesn't appear in any clause.

145. By symmetry we know that $h(l) = h(\bar{l}) = h(10 - l)$ for $1 \leq l \leq 9$ at depth 0, and the `BIMP` tables are empty. The first five rounds of refinement respectively give $(h(1), \ldots, h(5)) \approx (4.10, 4.10, 6.10, 6.10, 8.10)$, $(5.01, 4.59, 6.84, 6.84, 7.98)$, $(4.80, 4.58, 6.57, 6.57, 8.32)$, $(4.88, 4.54, 6.72, 6.67, 8.06)$, and $(4.85, 4.56, 6.63, 6.62, 8.23)$, slowly converging to the limiting values

$$(4.85810213, 4.55160111, 6.66761920, 6.63699698, 8.16778057).$$

But when $d = 1$, the successively refined values of $(h(1), h(\bar{1}), \ldots, h(4), h(\bar{4}))$ are erratic and divergent: $(2.10, 9.10, 3.10, 6.60, 3.10, 13.60, 4.10, 11.10)$, $(5.63, 3.37, 9.24, 2.57, 5.48, 5.67, 8.37, 4.87)$, $(1.42, 10.00, 2.31, 10.42, 1.28, 17.69, 1.94, 16.07)$, $(8.12, 1.43, 12.42, 1.30, 7.51, 2.41, 12.02, 1.81)$, $(0.32, 14.72, 0.42, 16.06, 0.30, 26.64, 0.43, 24.84)$.

They eventually oscillate between limits that favor either positive or negative literals:

$$(0.1017, 20.6819, 0.1027, 21.6597, 0.1021, 32.0422, 0.1030, 33.0200) \quad \text{and}$$
$$(8.0187, 0.1712, 11.9781, 0.1361, 11.9781, 0.2071, 15.9374, 0.1718).$$

[Equations (64) and (65), which were inspired by survey propagation, first appeared in unpublished work of S. Mijnders, B. de Wilde, and M. J. H. Heule in 2010. The calculations above indicate that we needn't take $h(l)$ too seriously, although it does seem to yield good results in practice. The author's implementation also sets $h'(l) \leftarrow \Theta$ if the right-hand side of (65) exceeds a threshold parameter Θ, which is 20.0 by default.]

146. Good results have been obtained with the simple formula $h(l) = \varepsilon + \text{KSIZE}(\bar{l}) + \sum_{u \in \text{BIMP}(l), \, u \text{ free}} \text{KSIZE}(\bar{u})$, which estimates the potential number of big-clause reductions that occur when l becomes true. The parameter ε is typically set to 0.001.

147. ∞, 600, 60, 30, 30.

148. If a problem is easy, we don't care if we solve it in 2 seconds or in .000002 seconds. On the other hand if a problem is so difficult that it can be solved only by looking ahead more than we can accomplish in a reasonable time, we might as well face the fact that we won't solve it anyway. There's no point in looking ahead at 60 variables when $d = 60$, because we won't be able to deal with more than 2^{50} or so nodes in any reasonable search tree.

149. The idea is to maintain a binary string $\text{SIG}(x)$ for each variable x, representing the highest node of the search tree in which x has participated. Let $b_j = [\text{BRANCH}[j] = 1]$, and set $\sigma \leftarrow b_0 \ldots b_{d-1}$ at the beginning of step L2, $\sigma \leftarrow b_0 \ldots b_d$ at the beginning of step L4. Then x will be a participant in step X3 if and only if $\text{SIG}(x)$ is a prefix of σ.

We update $\text{SIG}(x)$ when $x = |u|$ or $x = |v|$ in step L9, by setting $\text{SIG}(x) \leftarrow \sigma$ unless $\text{SIG}(x)$ is a prefix of σ. The initial value of $\text{SIG}(x)$ is chosen so that it is never a prefix of any possible σ.

(Notice that $\text{SIG}(x)$ needn't change when backtracking. In practice we can safely maintain only the first 32 bits of σ and of each string $\text{SIG}(x)$, together with their exact lengths, because lookahead computations need not be precise. In answer 143, updates occur not in step L9 but in step L7'; they are done for all literals $u \neq \overline{L}$ that appear in any big clause containing $\overline{L}$ that is being shortened for the first time.)

150. Asserting 7 at level 22 will also 22fix $\bar{1}$, because of the clause $\overline{1}4\overline{7}$. Then $\overline{1}$ will 22fix 3 and 9, which will 22fix $\bar{2}$ and $\bar{6}$, then $\bar{8}$; and clause 258 becomes false. Therefore $\overline{7}$ becomes proto true; and (62) makes 3, 6, 9 all proto true, contradicting $\overline{3}\overline{6}9$.

151. For example, one such arrangement is

$$
\begin{array}{c|cccccccccccccccc}
l: & 2 & \bar{8} & 9 & 3 & \bar{1} & 6 & \bar{7} & \bar{4} & 4 & 7 & \bar{6} & 1 & \bar{3} & \bar{9} & 8 & \bar{2} \\
o(l): & 4 & 2 & 10 & 14 & 6 & 16 & 8 & 12 & 22 & 26 & 18 & 28 & 20 & 24 & 32 & 30
\end{array}.
$$

[Digraphs that are obtainable in this way are called "partial orderings of dimension ≤ 2," or *permutation posets*. We've actually seen them in exercise 5.1.1–11, where the set of arcs was represented as a set of *inversions*. Permutation posets have many nice properties, which we shall study in Section 7.4.2. For example, if we reverse the order of the list and complement the offsets, we reverse the directions on the arrows. All but two of the 238 connected partially ordered sets on six elements are permutation posets. Unfortunately, however, permutation posets don't work well with lookahead when they aren't also forests. For example, after 10fixing '9' and its consequences, we would want to remove those literals from the R stack when 14fixing '3'; see (71). But then we'd want them back when 6fixing '$\bar{1}$'.]

152. A single clause such as '12' or '123' would be an example, except that the autarky test in step X9 would solve the problem before we ever get to step X3. The clauses $\{12\bar{3}, 1\bar{2}3, \bar{1}23, \bar{1}\bar{2}\bar{3}, 245, 3\bar{4}\bar{5}\}$ do, however, work: Level 0 branches on x_1, and level 1 discovers an autarky with x_2 and x_3 both true but returns $l = 0$. Then level 2 finds all clauses satisfied, although both of the free variables x_4 and x_5 are newbies.

[Indeed, the absence of free participants means that the fixed-true literals form an autarky. If $\text{TSIZE}(l)$ is nonzero for any free literal l, some clause is unsatisfied. Otherwise all clauses are satisfied unless some free l has an unfixed literal $l' \in \text{BIMP}(l)$.]

153. Make the CAND array into a heap, with an element x of *least* rating $r(x)$ at the top. (See Section 5.2.3; but start indices at 0, with $r(\text{CAND}[k]) \leq \min(r(\text{CAND}[2k+1]), r(\text{CAND}[2k+2]))$.) Then, while $C > C_{\max}$, delete the top of the heap (namely CAND[0]).

154. The child $\longrightarrow$ parent relations in the subforest will be $d \longrightarrow c \longrightarrow a$, $b \longrightarrow a$, $\bar{c} \longrightarrow \bar{d}$, and either $\bar{a} \longrightarrow \bar{b}$ or $\bar{a} \longrightarrow \bar{c}$. Here's one suitable sequence, using the latter:

$$\begin{array}{lcccccccc} \text{preorder} & \bar{b} & a & b & c & d & \bar{d} & \bar{c} & \bar{a} \\ 2\cdot\text{postorder} & 2 & 10 & 4 & 8 & 6 & 16 & 14 & 12 \end{array}$$

155. First construct the dependency graph on the $2C$ candidate literals, by extracting a subset of arcs from the BIMP tables. (This computation needn't be exact, because we're only calculating heuristics; an upper bound can be placed on the number of arcs considered, so that we don't spend too much time here. However, it is important to have the arc $u \longrightarrow v$ if and only if $\bar{v} \longrightarrow \bar{u}$ is also present.)

Then apply Tarjan's algorithm [see Section 7.4.1.2, or SGB pages 512–519]. If a strong component contains both l and $\bar{l}$ for some l, terminate with a contradiction. Otherwise, if a strong component contains more than one literal, choose a representative l with maximum $h(l)$; the other literals of that component regard l as their parent. Be careful to ensure that l is a representative if and only if $\bar{l}$ is also a representative.

The result will be a sequence of candidate literals $l_1 l_2 \ldots l_S$ in topological order, with $l_i \longrightarrow l_j$ only if $i > j$. Compute the "height" of each l_j, namely the length of the longest path from l_j to a sink. Then every literal of height $h > 0$ has a predecessor of height $h - 1$, and we let one such predecessor be its parent in the subforest. Every literal of height 0 (a sink) has a null parent. Traversal of this subforest in double order (exercise 2.3.1–18) now makes it easy to build the LL table in preorder while filling the LO table in postorder.

156. If $\bar{l}$ doesn't appear in any clause of F, then $A = \{l\}$ is clearly an autarky.

157. Well, *any* satisfying assignment is an autarky. But more to the point is the autarky $\{1, 2\}$ for $F = \{1\bar{2}3, \bar{1}24, \bar{3}\bar{4}\}$.

158. BIMP(l) and TIMP(l) will be empty, so w will be zero when Algorithm X looks ahead on l. Thus l will be forced true, at depth $d = 0$. (But pure literals that arise in subproblems for $d > 0$ won't be detected unless they're among the preselected candidates.)

159. (a) False (consider $A = \{1\}$, $F = \{1, 2, \bar{1}\bar{2}\}$); but true if we assume that $F \mid A$ is computed as a multiset (so that $F \mid A$ would be $\{2, 2\} \not\subseteq F$ in that example).

(b) True: Suppose $A = A' \cup A''$, $A' \cap A'' = \emptyset$, and A'' or $\overline{A}''$ touches $C \in F \mid A'$. Then $C \cap A' = \emptyset$ and $C \cup C' \in F$, where $C' \subseteq \overline{A}'$. Since A or $\overline{A}$ touches $C \cup C'$, some $a \in C \cup C'$ is in A; hence $a \in A''$.

160. (a) If the gray clauses are satisfiable, let all black literals be true. [Notice, incidentally, that the suggested example coloring works like a charm in (7).]

(b) Given any set A of strictly distinct literals, color l black if $l \in A$, white if $\bar{l} \in A$, otherwise gray. Then A is an autarky if and only if condition (a) holds. [E. A. Hirsch, *Journal of Automated Reasoning* **24** (2000), 397–420.]

161. (a) If F' is satisfiable, so is F. If F is satisfiable with at least one blue literal false, so is F'. If F is satisfiable with all the blue literals true, make all the black literals true (but keep gray literals unchanged). Then F' is satisfied, because every clause of F' that contains a black or blue literal is true, hence every clause that contains a white literal is true; the remaining clauses, whose literals are only orange and gray, each contain at least one true gray literal. [The black-and-blue condition is equivalent to saying that A is a *conditional autarky*, namely an autarky of $F \mid L$. Tseytin's notion of "extended resolution" is a special case, because the literals of A and L need not appear in F. See S. Jeannicot, L. Oxusoff, and A. Rauzy, *Revue d'intelligence artificielle* **2** (1988), 41–60, Section 6; O. Kullmann, *Theoretical Comp. Sci.* **223** (1999), 1–72, Sections 3, 4, and 14.]

(b) Without affecting satisfiability, we are allowed to add or delete any clause $C = (a \vee \bar{l}_1 \vee \cdots \vee \bar{l}_q)$ for which all clauses containing $\bar{a}$ also contain l_1 or $\cdots$ or l_q. (Such a clause is said to be "blocked" with respect to a, because C produces nothing but tautologies when it is resolved with clauses that contain $\bar{a}$.)

(c) Without affecting satisfiability, we are allowed to add or delete any or all of the clauses $(\bar{l} \vee a_1), \ldots, (\bar{l} \vee a_p)$, if A is an autarky of $F' \mid l$; that is, we can do this if A is *almost* an autarky, in the sense that every clause that touches $\overline{A}$ but not A contains l.

(d) Without affecting satisfiability, we are allowed to add or delete the clause $(\bar{l} \vee a)$ whenever every clause that contains $\bar{a}$ also contains l.

162. Construct a "blocking digraph" with $l' \hookrightarrow l$ when every clause that contains literal $\bar{l}$ also contains l'. (If l is a pure literal, we'll have $l' \hookrightarrow l$ for *all* l'; this case can be handled separately. Otherwise all in-degrees will be less than k in a kSAT problem, and the blocking digraph can be constructed in $O(k^2 m)$ steps if there are m clauses.)

(a) Then $(l \vee l')$ is a blocked binary clause if and only if $\bar{l} \hookrightarrow l'$ or $\bar{l}' \hookrightarrow l$. (Hence we're allowed in such cases to add both $\bar{l} \longrightarrow l'$ and $\bar{l}' \longrightarrow l$ to the *dependency* digraph.)

(b) Also $A = \{a, a'\}$ is an autarky if and only if $a \hookrightarrow a' \hookrightarrow a$. (Moreover, any strong component $\{a_1, \ldots, a_t\}$ with $t > 1$ is an autarky of size t.)

163. Consider the recurrence relations $T_n = 1 + \max(T_{n-1}, T_{n-2}, 2U_{n-1})$, $U_n = 1 + \max(T_{n-1}, T_{n-2}, U_{n-1} + V_{n-1})$, $V_n = 1 + U_{n-1}$ for $n > 0$, with $T_{-1} = T_0 = U_0 = V_0 = 0$. We can prove that T_n, U_n, V_n are upper bounds on the step counts, where U_n refers to cases where F is known to have a nonternary clause, and V_n refers to cases when $s = 1$ and R2 was entered from R3: The terms T_{n-1} and T_{n-2} represent autarky reductions in step R2; otherwise the recursive call in R3 costs U_{n-1}, not T_{n-1}, because at least one clause contains $\bar{l}_s$. We also have $V_n = 1 + U_{n-1}$, not $1 + T_{n-1}$, because the preceding step R3 either had a clause containing l_2 not l_1 or a clause containing $\bar{l}_1$ not $\bar{l}_2$.

Fibonacci numbers provide the solution: $T_n = 2F_{n+2} - 3 + [n = 0]$, $U_n = F_{n+3} - 2$, $V_n = F_{n+2} - 1$. [Algorithm R is a simplification of a procedure devised by B. Monien and E. Speckenmeyer, *Discrete Applied Mathematics* **10** (1985), 287–295, who introduced the term "autarky" in that paper. A Stanford student, Juan Bulnes, had discovered a Fibonacci-bounded algorithm for 3SAT already in 1976; his method was, however, unattractive, because it also required $\Omega(\phi^n)$ *space*.]

164. If $k < 3$, $T_n = n$ is an upper bound; so we may assume that $k \geq 3$. Let $U_n = 1 + \max(T_{n-1}, T_{n-2}, U_{n-1} + V_{n-1,1}, \ldots, U_{n-1} + V_{n-1,k-2})$, $V_{n,1} = 1 + U_{n-1}$, and $V_{n,s} = 1 + \max(U_{n-1}, T_{n-2}, U_{n-1} + V_{n-1,s-1})$ for $s > 1$, where $V_{n,s}$ refers to an entry at R2 from R3. The use of U_{n-1} in the formula for $V_{n,s}$ is justified, because the previous R3 either had a clause containing l_{s+1} not l_s or one containing $\bar{l}_s$ not $\bar{l}_{s+1}$. One can show by induction that $V_{n,s} = s + U_{n-1} + \cdots + U_{n-s}$, $U_n = V_{n,k-1}$; and $T_n = U_n + U_{n-k}+1 = 2U_{n-1}+1$ if $n \geq k$. For example, the running time when $k = 4$ is bounded by Tribonacci numbers, whose growth rate 1.83929^n comes from the root of $x^3 = x^2 + x + 1$.

165. Clause $\overline{134}$ in the example tells us that $1, 3, 4 \notin A$. Then $13\bar{6}$ implies $6 \notin A$. But $A = \{2, 5\}$ works, so it is maximum. There always is a maximum (not just maximal) positive autarky, because the union of positive autarkies is a positive autarky.

Each clause $(v_1 \vee \cdots \vee v_s \vee \bar{v}_{s+1} \vee \cdots \vee \bar{v}_{s+t})$ of F, where the v's are positive, tells us that $v_1 \notin A$ and $\cdots$ and $v_s \notin A$ implies $v_{s+j} \notin A$, for $1 \leq j \leq t$. Thus it essentially generates t Horn clauses, whose core is the set of all positive literals not in any positive autarky. A simple variant of Algorithm 7.1.1C will find this core in linear time; namely, we can modify steps C1 and C5 in order to get t Horn clauses from a single clause of F.

[By complementing a subset of variables, and prohibiting another subset, we can find the largest autarky A contained in any given set of strictly distinct literals. This exercise is due to unpublished work of O. Kullmann, V. W. Marek, and M. Truszczyński.]

166. Assume first that $\texttt{PARENT}(l_0) = \Lambda$, so that $H(l_0) = 0$ at the beginning of X9 (see X6). Since $l_0 = \texttt{LL}[j]$ is not fixed in context T, we have $R_F = l_0$ by (62). And $A = \{R_F, R_{F+1}, \ldots, R_{E-1}\}$ is an autarky, because no clause touched by A or $\bar{A}$ is entirely false or contains two unfixed literals. Thus we're allowed to force l_0 true (which is what "do step X12 with $l \leftarrow l_0$" means).

On the other hand if $w = 0$ and $\texttt{PARENT}(l_0) = p$, so that $H(l_0) = H(p) > 0$ in X6, the set $A = \{R_F, \ldots, R_{E-1}\}$ is an autarky with respect to the clauses of $F \mid p$. Hence the additional clause $(l_0 \vee \bar{p})$ doesn't make the clauses any less satisfiable, by the black and blue principle. (Notice that $(\bar{l}_0 \vee p)$ is already a known clause; so in this case l_0 is essentially being made equal to its parent.)

[The author's implementation therefore goes further and includes the step

$$\texttt{VAL}[|l_0|] \leftarrow \texttt{VAL}[|p|] \oplus ((l_0 \oplus p) \,\&\, 1), \tag{$*$}$$

which promotes the truth degree of l_0 to that of p. This step violates the invariant relation (71), but Algorithm X doesn't rely on (71).]

167. If a literal l is fixed in context T during the lookahead, it is implied by l_0. In step X11 we have a case where l is also implied by $\bar{l}_0$; hence we're allowed to force its truth, if l isn't already proto true. In step X6, $\bar{l}_0$ is implied by l_0, so l_0 must be false.

168. The following method works well in $\texttt{march}$: Terminate happily if $F = n$. (At this point in Algorithm L, F is the number of fixed variables, all of which are really true or really false.) Otherwise find $l \in \{\texttt{LL}[0], \ldots, \texttt{LL}[S-1]\}$ with $l \bmod 2 = 0$ and maximum $(H(l) + .1)(H(l+1) + .1)$. If l is fixed, set $l \leftarrow 0$. (In that case, Algorithm X found at least one forced literal, although U is now zero; we want to do another lookahead before branching again.) Otherwise, if $H(l) > H(l+1)$, set $l \leftarrow l+1$. (A subproblem that is less reduced will tend to be more satisfiable.)

169. When a and b are positive, the function $f(x) = e^{-ax} + e^{-bx} - 1$ is convex and decreasing, and it has the unique root $\ln \tau(a, b)$. Newton's method for solving this equation refines an approximation x by computing $x' = x + f(x)/(ae^{-ax} + be^{-bx})$. Notice that x is less than the root if and only if $f(x) > 0$; furthermore $f(x) > 0$ implies $f(x') > 0$, because $f(x') > f(x) + (x' - x)f'(x)$ when f is convex. In particular we have $f(1/(a+b)) > 0$, because $f(0) = 1$ and $0' = 1/(a+b)$, and we can proceed as follows:

K1. [Initialize.] Set $j \leftarrow k \leftarrow 1$, $x \leftarrow 1/(a_1 + b_1)$.

K2. [Done?] (At this point (a_j, b_j) is the best of $(a_1, b_1), \ldots, (a_k, b_k)$, and $e^{-a_j x} + e^{-b_j x} \geq 1$.) Terminate if $k = s$. Otherwise set $k \leftarrow k+1$, $x' \leftarrow 1/(a_k + b_k)$.

K3. [Find α, β.] If $x' < x$, swap $j \leftrightarrow k$ and $x \leftrightarrow x'$. Then set $\alpha \leftarrow e^{-a_j x'}$ and $\beta \leftarrow e^{-b_j x'}$. Go to K2 if $\alpha + \beta \leq 1$.

K4. [Newtonize.] Set $x \leftarrow x' + (\alpha + \beta - 1)/(a_j \alpha + b_j \beta)$, $\alpha' \leftarrow e^{-a_k x'}$, $\beta' \leftarrow e^{-b_k x'}$, $x' \leftarrow x' + (\alpha' + \beta' - 1)/(a_k \alpha' + b_k \beta')$, and return to K3. ∎

(The floating point calculations should satisfy $e^u \leq e^v$ and $u + w \leq v + w$ when $u < v$.)

170. If the problem is unsatisfiable, Tarjan's algorithm discovers l and $\bar{l}$ in the same strong component. If it's satisfiable, Algorithm X finds autarkies (because w is always zero), thus forcing the value of all literals at depth 0.

171. It prevents double-looking on the same literal twice at the same search tree node.

172. When Algorithm Y concludes normally, we'll have $T = \text{BASE} + \text{LO}[j]$, even though BASE has changed. This relation is assumed to be invariant in Algorithm X.

173. The run reported in the text, using nonoptimized parameters (see exercise 513), did 29,194,670 double-looks (that is, executions of step Y2), and exited 23,245,231 times to X13 in step Y8 (thus successfully forcing l_0 false in about 80% of those cases). Disabling Algorithm Y (i) increased the running time from 0.68 teramems to 1.13 teramems, with 24.3 million nodes. Disabling wraparound (ii) increased the time to 0.85 teramems, with 13.3 million nodes. Setting $Y = 1$, which disabled wraparound only in Algorithm Y, yielded 0.72 teramems, 11.3 meganodes. (Incidentally, the loops of Algorithm X wrapped around 40% of the time in the regular run, with a mean of 0.62 and maximum of 12; those of Algorithm Y had 20% wraparound, with a mean of 0.25; the maximum $Y = 8$ was reached only 28 times.) Disabling the lookahead forest (iii) gave surprisingly good results: 0.70 teramems, 8.5 meganodes; there were fewer nodes [hence a more discriminating lookahead], but more time spent per node because of duplicated effort, although strong components were not computed. (Structured problems that have numerous binary clauses tend to generate more helpful forests than random 3SAT problems do.) Disabling compensation resolvents (iv) made very little difference: 0.70 teramems, 9.9 meganodes. But disabling windfalls (v) raised the cost to 0.89 teramems and 13.5 meganodes. And branching on a random $l \in \text{LL}$ (vi) made the running time soar to 40.20 teramems, with 594.7 meganodes. Finally, disabling Algorithm X altogether (vii) was a disaster, leading to an estimated run time of well over 10^{20} mems.

The weaker heuristics of exercise 175 yield 3.09 teramems and 35.9 meganodes.

174. Setting Y to a huge value such as PT will never get to step Y2. (But for (ii), (iii), ..., (vii) one must change the programs, not the parameters as they stand.)

175. Precompute the weights, by setting $K_2 = 1$ and $K_s \leftarrow \gamma K_{s-1} + .01$, for s between 3 and the maximum clause size. (The extra .01 keeps this from being zero.) The third line of (72) must change to "take account of c for all c in $\text{KINX}(\bar{L})$," where that means "set $s \leftarrow \text{CSIZE}(c) - 1$; if $s \geq 2$, set $\text{CSIZE}(c) \leftarrow s$ and $w \leftarrow w + K_s$; otherwise if all literals of c are fixed false, set a flag; otherwise if some literal u of c isn't fixed (there will be just one), put it on a temporary stack." Before performing the last line of (72), go to CONFLICT if the flag is set; otherwise, for each unfixed u on the temporary stack, set $W_i \leftarrow u$ and $i \leftarrow i + 1$ and perform (62) with $l \leftarrow u$; go to CONFLICT if some u on the temporary stack is fixed false. (A "windfall" in this more general setting is a clause for which all but one literal has been fixed false as a consequence of l_0 being fixed true.)

Of course those changes to CSIZE need to be undone; a simulated false literal that has been "virtually" removed from a clause must be virtually put back. Fortunately, the invariant relation (71) makes this task fairly easy: We set $G \leftarrow F$ in step X5, and insert the following restoration loop at the very beginning of (72): "While $G > F$, set $u \leftarrow R_{G-1}$; stop if u is fixed in context T; otherwise set $G \leftarrow G - 1$, and increase CSIZE(c) by 1 for all $c \in$ KINX($\bar{u}$)." The restoration loop should also be performed, with $T \leftarrow$ NT, just before terminating Algorithm X in steps X7 or X13.

[The additional step (*) in answer 166 can't be used, because (71) is now crucial.]

Algorithm Y should change in essentially the same way as Algorithm X.

[See O. Kullmann, Report CSR 23-2002 (Swansea: Univ. of Wales, 2002), §4.2.]

176. (a) $a_j - a_{j+1}$, $a_j - b_j$, $a_j - b_{j+1}$, $b_j - c_j$, $b_j - d_j$, $c_j - d_j$, $c_j - e_j$, $d_j - f_j$, $e_j - d_{j+1}$, $e_j - f_{j+1}$, $f_j - c_{j+1}$, $f_j - e_{j+1}$.

(b) Let $(t_j, u_j, v_j, w_j, a_j, b_j, c_j, d_j, e_j, f_j)$ have colors $(1, 2, 1, 1, 1, 2, 1, 3, 3, 2)$ when j is even, $(2, 1, 2, 2, 3, 2, 3, 1, 1, 2)$ when j is odd. The lower bounds are obvious.

(c) Vertices a_j, e_j, f_j can't all have the same color, because b_j, c_j, d_j have distinct colors. Let α_j denote the colors of $a_j e_j f_j$. Then $\alpha_j = 112$ implies $\alpha_{j+1} = 332$ or 233; $\alpha_j = 121$ implies $\alpha_{j+1} = 233$ or 323; $\alpha_j = 211$ implies $\alpha_{j+1} = 323$ or 332; $\alpha_j = 123$ implies $\alpha_{j+1} = 213$ or 321. Since $\alpha_1 = \alpha_{q+1}$, the colors of α_1 must be distinct, and we can assume that $\alpha_1 = 123$. But then α_j will be an odd permutation whenever j is even.

[See Rufus Isaacs, *AMM* **82** (1975), 233–234. Unpublished notes of E. Grinberg show that he had independently investigated the graph J_5 in 1972.]

177. There are 20 independent subsets of $V_j = \{a_j, b_j, c_j, d_j, e_j, f_j\}$ when $q > 1$; eight of them contain none of $\{b_j, c_j, d_j\}$ while four contain b_j. Let A be a 20×20 transition matrix, which indicates when $R \cup C$ is independent for each independent subset $R \subseteq V_j$ and $C \subseteq V_{j+1}$. Then I_q is trace(A^q); and the first eight values are 8, 126, 1052, 11170, 112828, 1159416, 11869768, 121668290. The characteristic polynomial of A, $x^{12}(x^2 - 2x - 1)(x^2 + 2x - 1)(x^4 - 8x^3 - 25x^2 + 20x + 1)$, has nonzero roots $\pm 1 \pm \sqrt{2}$ and $\approx -2.91, -0.05, +0.71, +10.25$; hence $I_q = \Theta(r^q)$, where $r \approx 10.24811166$ is the dominant root. *Note:* The number of *kernels* of $L(J_q)$ is respectively 2, 32, 140, 536, 2957, 14336, 70093, 348872, for $1 \leq q \leq 8$, and its growth rate is $\approx 4.93^q$.

178. With the first ordering, the top $18k$ levels of the search tree essentially represent all of the ways to 3-color the subgraph $\{a_j, b_j, c_j, d_j, e_j, f_j \mid 1 \leq j \leq k\}$; and there are $\Theta(2^k)$ ways to do that, by answer 176. But with the second ordering, the top $6kq$ levels essentially represent all of the independent sets of the graph; and there are $\Omega(10 \cdot 2^k)$ of those, by answer 177.

Empirically, Algorithm B needs respectively 1.54 megamems, 1.57 gigamems, and 1.61 teramems to prove unsatisfiability when $q = 9, 19$, and 29, using the first ordering; but it needs 158 gigamems already for $q = 5$ with the second! Additional clauses, which require color classes to be kernels (see answer 14), reduce that time to 492 megamems.

Algorithm D does badly on this sequence of problems: When $q = 19$, it consumes 37.6 gigamems, even with the "good" ordering. And when $q = 29$, its cyclic method of working somehow transforms the good ordering into a bad ordering on many of the variables at depths 200 or more. It shows no sign of being anywhere near completion even after spending a *petamem* on that problem!

Algorithm L, which is insensitive to the ordering, needs 2.42 megamems, 2.01 gigamems, and 1.73 teramems when $q = 9, 19$, and 29. Thus it appears to take $\Theta(2^q)$ steps, and to be slightly slower than Algorithm B as q grows, although exercise 232 shows that a clairvoyant lookahead procedure could theoretically do much better.

Algorithm C triumphs here, as shown in Fig. 92.

179. This is a straightforward exact cover problem. If we classify the solutions according to how many asterisks occur in each coordinate, it turns out that exactly (10, 240, 180, 360, 720, 480, 1440, 270, 200, 480) of them are respectively of type (00088, 00268, 00448, 00466, 02248, 02266, 02446, 04444, 22228, 22246).

By complementation, we see that 4380 choices of 8 clauses are unsatisfiable; hence $q_8 = 1 - 4380/\binom{80}{8} = 1 - 4380/28987537150 \approx 0.9999998$.

180. With N variables y_j, one for each possible clause C_j, the function $f(y_1, \ldots, y_N) = [\bigwedge \{C_j \mid y_j = 1\}$ is satisfiable$]$ is $\bigvee_x f_x(y)$, where $f_x(y) = [x$ satisfies $\bigwedge \{C_j \mid y_j = 1\}]$ is simply $\bigwedge \{\bar{y}_j \mid x$ makes C_j false$\}$. For instance if $k = 2$ and $n = 3$, and if C_1, C_7, C_{11} are the clauses $(x_1 \vee x_2)$, $(x_1 \vee \bar{x}_3)$, $(x_2 \vee \bar{x}_3)$, then $f_{001}(y_1, \ldots, y_{12}) = \bar{y}_1 \wedge \bar{y}_7 \wedge \bar{y}_{11}$.

Each function f_x has a very simple BDD, but of course the OR of 2^n of them will not be simple. This problem is an excellent example where no natural ordering of the clause variables is evident, but the method of sifting is able to reduce the BDD size substantially. In fact, the clauses for $k = 3$ and $n = 4$ can be ordered cleverly so that the corresponding 32-variable BDD for satisfiability has only 1362 nodes! The author's best result for $k = 3$ and $n = 5$, however, was a BDD of size 2,155,458. The coefficients of its generating function (exercise 7.1.4–25) are the desired numbers Q_m.

The largest such count, $Q_{35} = 3,449,494,339,791,376,514,416$, is so enormous that we could not hope to enumerate the relevant sets of 35 clauses by backtracking.

181. The previous exercise essentially computed the generating function $\sum_m Q_m z^m$; now we want the *double* generating function $\sum_{l,m} T_{l,m} w^l z^m$, where $T_{l,m}$ is the number of ways to choose m different k-clauses in such a way that these clauses are satisfied by exactly l vectors $x_1 \ldots x_n$. To do this, instead of taking the OR of the simple functions f_x, we compute the BDD base that contains all of the symmetric Boolean functions $S_l(f_{0\ldots0}, \ldots, f_{1\ldots1})$ for $0 \leq l \leq 2^n$, as follows (see exercise 7.1.4–49): Consider the subscript x to be a binary integer, so that the functions are f_x for $0 \leq x < 2^n$. Start with $S_l = 0$ for $-1 \leq l \leq 2^n$, except that $S_0 = 1$. Then do the following for $x = 0, \ldots, 2^n - 1$ (in that order): Set $S_l = f_x? S_{l-1}: S_l$ for $l = x + 1, \ldots, 0$ (in that order).

After this computation, the generating function for S_l will be $\sum_m T_{l,m} z^m$. In the author's experiments, the sifting algorithm found an ordering of the 80 clauses for $k = 3$ and $n = 5$ so that only about 6 million nodes were needed when x had reached 24; afterwards, however, sifting took too long, so it was turned off. The final BDD base had approximately 87 million nodes, with many nodes shared between the individual functions S_l. The total running time was about 22 gigamems.

182. $T_0 = 32$ and $T_1 = 28$ and $T_m = 0$ for $71 \leq m \leq 80$. Otherwise $\min T_m < \max T_m$.

183. Let $t_m = \Pr(T_m = 1)$, and suppose that we obtain clauses one by one until reaching an unsatisfiable set. The fact that t_m gets reasonably large suggests that we probably have accumulated a *uniquely* satisfiable set just before stopping. (That probability is $2^{-k} N \sum_m t_m/(N-m)$, which turns out to be ≈ 0.8853 when $k = 3$ and $n = 5$.)

However, except for the fact that both Figs. 85 and 86 are bell-shaped curves with roughly the same tendency to be relatively large or small at particular values of m, there is apparently no strong mathematical connection. The probabilities in Fig. 86 sum to 1; but the sum of probabilities in Fig. 85 has no obvious significance.

When n is large, uniquely satisfiable sets are encountered only rarely. The final set before stopping a.s. has at most $f(n)$ solutions, for certain functions f; but how fast does the smallest such f grow? [See D. J. Aldous, *J. Theoretical Probability* **4** (1991), 197–211, for related ideas.]

184. The probability $\hat{q}_m$ is $\widehat{Q}_m/N^m$, where $\widehat{Q}_m$ counts the choices $(C_1,\ldots,C_m)$ for which $C_1 \wedge \cdots \wedge C_m$ is satisfiable. The number of such choices that involve t distinct clauses is $t!\,{m \brace t}$ times Q_t, because ${m \brace t}$ enumerates set partitions; see Eq. 3.3.2–(5).

185. $\hat{q}_m = \sum_{t=0}^{N} {m \brace t} t!\, q_t {N \choose t}/N^m \geq q_m \sum_{t=0}^{N} {m \brace t} t! {N \choose t}/N^m = q_m$.

186. $\sum_m \sum_t {m \brace t} t!\, q_t {N \choose t} N^{-m}$ can be summed on m, since $\sum_m {m \brace t} N^{-m} = 1/(N-1)^{\underline{t}}$ by Eq. 1.2.9–(28). Similarly, the derivative of 1.2.9–(28) shows that $\sum_m m{m \brace t} N^{-m} = (N/(N-1) + \cdots + N/(N-t))/(N-1)^{\underline{t}}$.

187. In this special case, $q_m = [0 \leq m < N]$ and $p_m = [m = N]$; hence $S_{n,n} = N = 2^n$ (and the variance is zero). By (78), we also have $\widehat{S}_{n,n} = NH_N$; indeed, the coupon collector's test (exercise 3.3.2–8) is an equivalent way to view this situation.

188. Now $q_m = 2^m n^{\underline{m}}/(2n)^m$. It follows by (78) that $\widehat{S}_{1,n} = \sum_{m=0}^{n} 2^m n^{\underline{m}}/(2n-1)^m$, because $N = 2n$. The identity $2^m n^{\underline{m}}/(2n-1)^{\underline{m}} = 2q_m - q_{m+1}$ yields the surprising fact that $\widehat{S}_{1,n} = (2q_0 - q_1) + (2q_1 - q_2) + \cdots = 1 + S_{1,n}$; and we also have $\widehat{S}_{1,n} - 1 = \frac{2n}{2n-1} S_{1,n-1}$. Hence, by induction, we obtain the (even more surprising) closed forms

$$S_{1,n} = 4^n \Big/ {2n \choose n}, \qquad \widehat{S}_{1,n} = 4^n \Big/ {2n \choose n} + 1.$$

So random 1SAT problems become unsatisfiable after $\sqrt{\pi n} + O(1)$ clauses, on average.

189. With the autosifting method in the author's experimental BDD implementation, the number of BDD nodes, given a sequence of m distinct clauses when $k = 3$ and $n = 50$, increased past 1000 when m increased from 1 to about 30, and it tended to peak at about 500,000 when m was slightly more than 100. Then the typical BDD size fell to about 50,000 when $m = 150$, and to only about 500 when $m = 200$.

BDD methods break down when n is too large, but when they apply we can count the total number of solutions remaining after m steps. In the author's tests with $k = 3$, $n = 50$, and $m = 200$, this number varied from about 25 to about 2000.

190. For example, $S_1(x_1,\ldots,x_n)$ can't be expressed in $(n-1)$CNF: All clauses of length $n-1$ that are implied by $S_1(x_1,\ldots,x_n)$ are also implied by $S_{\leq 1}(x_1,\ldots,x_n)$.

191. Let $f(x_0,\ldots,x_{2^n-1}) = 1$ if and only if $x_0 \ldots x_{2^n-1}$ is the truth table of a Boolean function of n variables that is expressible in kCNF. This function f is the conjunction of 2^n constraints $c(t)$, for $0 \leq t = (t_0 \ldots t_{2^n-1})_2 < 2^n$, where $c(t)$ is the following condition: If $x_t = 0$, then $\bigvee\{x_y \mid 0 \leq y < 2^n, (y \oplus t) \& m = 0\}$ is 0 for some n-bit pattern m that has $\nu m = k$. By combining these constraints we can compute the BDD for f when $n = 4$ and $k = 3$; it has 880 nodes, and 43,146 solutions.

Similarly we have the following results, analogous to those in Section 7.1.1:

	$n=0$	$n=1$	$n=2$	$n=3$	$n=4$	$n=5$	$n=6$
1CNF	2	4	10	28	82	244	730
2CNF	2	4	16	166	4,170	224,716	24,445,368
3CNF	2	4	16	256	43,146	120,510,132	4,977,694,100,656

And if we consider equivalence under complementation and permutation, the counts are:

1CNF	2	3	4	5	6	7	8
2CNF	2	3	6	14	45	196	1,360
3CNF	2	3	6	22	253	37,098	109,873,815

192. (a) $S(p) = \sum_{m=0}^{N} p^m (1-p)^{N-m} Q_m$. (b) We have $\int_0^N (t/N)^m (1 - t/N)^{N-m} \, dt = NB(m+1, N-m+1) = \frac{N}{N+1}\Big/{N \choose m}$, by exercises 1.2.6–40 and 41; hence $\overline{S}_{k,n} = \frac{N}{N+1} \sum_{m=0}^{N} q_m = \frac{N}{N+1} S_{k,n}$. [See B. Bollobás, *Random Graphs* (1985), Theorem II.4.]

194. A similar question, about proofs of *unsatisfiability* when $\alpha > \limsup_{n\to\infty} S_{3,n}/n$, is also wide open.

195. $EX = 2^n \Pr(0\ldots0 \text{ satisfies all}) = 2^n(1 - 2^{-k})^m = \exp(n \ln 2 + m \ln(1 - 2^{-k})) < 2\exp(-2^{-k-1}n \ln 2)$. Thus $S_k(\lfloor (2^k \ln 2)n \rfloor, n) = \Pr(X > 0) \leq \exp(-\Omega(n))$. [*Discrete Applied Math.* **5** (1983), 77–87. Conversely, in *J. Amer. Math. Soc.* **17** (2004), 947–973, D. Achlioptas and Y. Peres use the second moment principle to show that $(2^k \ln 2 - O(k))n$ random kSAT clauses are almost always satisfiable by vectors x with $\nu x \approx n/2$. Careful study of "covering assignments" (see exercise 364) leads to the sharp bounds

$$2^k \ln 2 - \frac{1 + \ln 2}{2} - O(2^{-\frac{k}{3}}) \leq \liminf_{n\to\infty} \alpha_k(n) \leq \limsup_{n\to\infty} \alpha_k(n) \leq 2^k \ln 2 - \frac{1 + \ln 2}{2} + O(2^{-\frac{k}{3}});$$

see A. Coja-Oghlan and K. Panagiotou, *Advances in Math.* **288** (2016), 985–1068.]

196. The probability is $((n - t)^{\underline{k}}/n^{\underline{k}})^{\alpha n + O(1)} = e^{-kt\alpha}(1 + O(1/n))$ that $\alpha n + O(1)$ random kSAT clauses omit t given letters. Let $p = 1 - (1 - e^{-ka})^k$. By inclusion and exclusion, the first clause will be easy with probability $p(1 + O(1/n))$, and the first two will both be easy with probability $p^2(1 + O(1/n))$. Thus if $X = \sum_{j=1}^{m}[\text{clause } j \text{ is easy}]$, we have $EX = pm + O(1)$ and $EX^2 = p^2m^2 + O(m)$. Hence, by Chebyshev's inequality, $\Pr(|X - pm| \geq r\sqrt{m}) = O(1/r^2)$.

197. By Stirling's approximation, $\ln q(a, b, A, B, n) = nf(a, b, A, B) + g(a, b, A, B) - \frac{1}{2}\ln 2\pi n - (\delta_{an} - \delta_{(a+b)n}) - (\delta_{bn} - \delta_{(b+B)n}) - (\delta_{An} - \delta_{(a+A)n}) - (\delta_{Bn} - \delta_{(A+B)n}) - \delta_{(a+b+A+B)n}$, where δ_n is positive and decreasing. And we must have $f(a, b, A, B) \leq 0$, since $q(a, b, A, B, n) \leq 1$. The O estimate is uniform when $0 < \delta \leq a, b, A, B \leq M$.

198. Consider one of the N^M possible sequences of M 3SAT clauses, where $N = 8\binom{n}{3}$ and $M = 5n$. By exercise 196 it contains $g = 5(1 - (1 - e^{-15})^3)n + O(n^{3/4})$ easy clauses, except with probability $O(n^{-1/2})$. Those clauses, though rare, don't affect the satisfiability; and all $\binom{M}{g}$ of the ways to insert them among the $r = M - g$ others are equally likely, so they tend to dampen the transition.

Let $l \leq r$ be maximum so that the first l noneasy clauses are satisfiable, and let $p(l, r, g, m)$ be the probability that, when drawing m balls from an urn that contains g green balls and r red balls, at most l balls are red. Then $S_3(m, n) = \sum p(l, r, g, m)/N^M$ and $S_3(m', n) = \sum p(l, r, g, m')/N^M$, summed over all N^M sequences.

To complete the proof we shall show that

$$p(l, r, g, m + 1) = p(l, r, g, m) - O(n^{-1/2}) \qquad \text{when } 3.5n < m < 4.5n;$$

hence $S_3(m + 1, n) = S_3(m, n) - O(n^{-1/2})$, $S_3(m, n) - S_3(m', n) = O((m' - m)n^{-1/2})$. Notice that $p(l, r, g, m) = p(l, r, g, m+1)$ when $m < l$ or $m > l + g$; thus we may assume that l lies between $3.4n$ and $4.6n$. Furthermore the difference

$$d_m = p(l, r, g, m) - p(l, r, g, m + 1) = \frac{\binom{m}{l}\binom{r+g-m-1}{r-l-1}}{\binom{r+g}{r}} = \frac{\binom{m}{l}\binom{r+g-m}{r-l}}{\binom{r+g}{r}}\frac{r - l}{r + g - m}$$

has a decreasing ratio $d_m/d_{m-1} = (m/(m-l))((l+g+1-m)/(r+g-m))$ when m increases from l to $l + g$. So $\max d_m$ occurs at $m \approx l(r + g)/r$, where this ratio is ≈ 1. Now exercise 197 applies with $a = l/n$, $b = \rho g/n$, $A = (r-l)/n$, $B = (1-\rho)g/n$, $\rho = l/r$.

[D. B. Wilson, in *Random Structures & Algorithms* **21** (2002), 182–195, showed that similar methods apply to many other threshold phenomena.]

199. (a) Given the required letters $\{a_1, \ldots, a_t\}$, there are m ways to place the leftmost a_1, then $m-1$ ways to place the leftmost a_2, and so on; then there are at most N ways to fill in each of the remaining $m-t$ slots.

(b) By inclusion and exclusion: There are $(N-k)^m$ words that omit k of the letters.

(c) $N^{-m} \sum_k \binom{t}{k} (-1)^k \sum_j \binom{m}{j} N^{m-j} (-k)^j = \sum_j \binom{m}{j} (-1)^{j+t} N^{-j} A_j$, where $A_j = \sum_k \binom{t}{k} (-1)^{t-k} k^j = \{{j \atop t}\} t!$ by Eq. 1.2.6–(53).

200. (a) The unsatisfiable digraph must contain a strong component with a path
$$\bar{l}_t \longrightarrow l_1 \longrightarrow \cdots \longrightarrow l_t \longrightarrow l_{t+1} \longrightarrow \cdots \longrightarrow l_l = \bar{l}_t,$$
where $l_1, \ldots, l_t$ are strictly distinct. This path yields an s-snare $(C; t, u)$ if we set s to the smallest index such that $|l_{s+1}| = |l_u|$ for some u with $1 \le u < s$.

(b) No: $(x \vee y) \wedge (\bar{y} \vee x) \wedge (\bar{x} \vee y)$ and $(x \vee y) \wedge (\bar{y} \vee x) \wedge (\bar{x} \vee \bar{y})$ are both satisfiable.

(c) Apply exercise 199(a) with $t = s+1$, $N = 2n(n-1)$; note that $m^{\underline{s+1}} \le m^{s+1}$.

201. (a) Set $(l_i, l_{i+1}) \leftarrow (x_1, x_2)$ or $(\bar{x}_2, \bar{x}_1)$, where $0 \le i < 2t$ (thus $4t$ ways).

(b) Set $(l_i, l_{i+1}, l_{i+2}) \leftarrow (x_1, x_2, x_3)$ or $(\bar{x}_3, \bar{x}_2, \bar{x}_1)$, where $0 \le i < 2t$; also $(\bar{l}_1, l_t, l_{t+1})$ or $(l_{t-1}, l_t, \bar{l}_{2t-1}) \leftarrow (x_1, x_2, x_3)$ or $(\bar{x}_3, \bar{x}_2, \bar{x}_1)$ (total $4t + 4$ ways, if $t>2$).

(c) (l_1, l_{t-1}, l_t) or $(\bar{l}_{2t-1}, \bar{l}_{t+1}, \bar{l}_t) \leftarrow (x_1, x_{t-1}, x_t)$ or $(\bar{x}_{t-1}, \bar{x}_1, x_t)$ (4 ways).

(d) l_i or $\bar{l}_{2t-i} \leftarrow x_i$ or $\bar{x}_{t-i}$, for $1 \le i \le t$ (4 ways, if you understand this notation).

(e) By part (a), it is $2t \times 4t = 8t^2$.

(f) Parts (b) and (c) combine to give $N(3, 2) = (2t + 2) \times (4t + 4) + 2 \times 4 = 8(t^2 + 2t + 2)$ when $t > 2$. From part (d), $N(t, t) = 8$. Also $N(2t - 1, 2t) = 8$; this is the number of snakes that specify the same $2t$ clauses. (Incidentally, when $t = 5$ the generating function $\sum_{q,r} N(q, r) w^q z^r$ is $1 + 200w^2 z^1 + (296w^3 + 7688w^4) z^2 + (440w^4 + 12800w^5 + 55488w^6) z^3 + (640w^5 + 12592w^6 + 66560w^7 + 31104w^8) z^4 + (8w^5 + 736w^6 + 8960w^7 + 32064w^8 + 6528w^9) z^5 + (32w^6 + 704w^7 + 4904w^8 + 4512w^9) z^6 + (48w^7 + 704w^8 + 1232w^9) z^7 + (64w^8 + 376w^9) z^8 + 80w^9 z^9 + 8w^9 z^{10}$.)

(g) The other l's can be set in at most $2^{2t-1-q}(n-q)^{\underline{2t-1-q}} = R/(2^q n^{\underline{q}})$ ways.

(h) We may assume that $r < 2t$. The r chosen clauses divide into connected components, which are either paths or a "central" component that contains either $(\bar{x}_0 \vee x_1)$ and $(\bar{x}_{t-1} \vee x_t)$ or $(\bar{x}_t \vee x_{t+1})$ and $(\bar{x}_{2t-1} \vee x_0)$. Thus q equals r plus the number of components, minus 1 if the central component includes a cycle. If the central component is present, we must set $l_t \leftarrow x_t$ or $\bar{x}_t$, and there are at most 8 ways to complete the mapping of that component. And $N(r, r) = 16(r+1-t)$ for $t < r < 2t$.

Cases with $k > 0$ paths can be chosen in at most $\binom{2t+2}{2k}$ ways, because we choose the starting and ending points, and they can be mapped in at most $2^k k! \binom{2t+2}{2k}$ ways; so they contribute $\sum_{k>0} O(t^{4k} k/(k!^3 n^k)) = O(t^4/n)$ to $(2n)^r p_r$. The noncyclic central components, which can be chosen in $\Theta(t^4)$ ways, also contribute $O(t^4/n)$.

202. (a) $m(m-1) \ldots (m-r+1)/m^r \ge 1 - \binom{r}{2}/m$; $(2n(n-1)-r)^{m-r}/(2n(n-1))^{m-r} \ge 1 - (m-r)r/(2n(n-1))$ when $r \le m < 2n(n-1)$; and both factors are ≤ 1.

(b) The term of (95) for $r = 0$ is 1 plus a negligible error. The contribution of $O(t^4/n)$ for $r > 0$ is $O(n^{4/5+1/6-1})$, because $\sum_{r \ge 0} (1 + n^{-1/6})^{-r} = n^{1/6} + 1$. And the contributions of (96) to (95) for $r \ge t$ are exponentially small, because in that range we have $(1 + n^{-1/6})^{-t} = \exp(-t \ln(1 + n^{-1/6})) = \exp(-\Omega(n^{1/30}))$. Finally, then, by the second moment principle MPR–(22), $S_2(\lfloor n + n^{5/6} \rfloor, n) \le 1 - \Pr(X > 0) \le 1 - (\mathrm{E}\,X)^2/(\mathrm{E}\,X^2) = 1 - 1/((\mathrm{E}\,X^2)/(\mathrm{E}\,X)^2) = 1 - 1/(1 + O(n^{-1/30})) = O(n^{-1/30})$.

203. (a) $\mathrm{E}\,X = d^n\,\mathrm{E}\,X(1, \ldots, 1)$, by symmetry; and $\mathrm{E}\,X(1, \ldots, 1) = (1-p)^m$, because each set of q clauses is falsified with probability p. So $\mathrm{E}\,X = \exp((r \ln(1-p) + 1)n \ln d)$ is exponentially small when $r \ln(1-p) + 1 < 0$; and we know that $\Pr(X > 0) \le \mathrm{E}\,X$.

(b) Let $\theta_s = \binom{s}{2}/\binom{n}{2} = \frac{s(s-1)}{n(n-1)}$, and consider a random constraint set, given that $X(1,\ldots,1) = 1$. With probability θ_s, both u and v have color 1 and the constraint is known to be satisfied. But with probability $1-\theta_s$, it holds with probability $\binom{d^2-2}{q}/\binom{d^2-1}{q}$. Thus $p_s = (\theta_s + (1-\theta_s)(d^2 - pd^2 - 1)/(d^2-1))^m$.

(c) We have $\Pr(X > 0) \ge d^n(1-p)^m / \mathrm{E}(X \mid X(1,\ldots,1) = 1)$, from the inequality and symmetry; and the denominator is $\sum_{s=0}^n \binom{n}{s}(d-1)^{n-s}p_s$. We can replace p_s by the simpler value $p'_s = (1 - p + ps^2/n^2)^m$, because $p_s < (\theta_s + (1-\theta_s)(1-p))^m = (1-p+\theta_s p)^m < p'_s$. And we can divide the simplified sum by $d^n(1-p)^m$.

(d) We have $\sum_{s=0}^{3n/d} t_s = e^{O(m/d^2)} \sum_{s=0}^{3n/d} \binom{n}{s}(\frac{1}{d})^s(1 - \frac{1}{d})^{n-s}$, because $s^2/n^2 = O(1/d^2)$ when $s \le 3n/d$. This sum is $\ge 1 - (e^2/27)^{n/d}$ by exercise 1.2.10–22; and the crucial assumption that $\alpha > \frac{1}{2}$ makes $m/d^2 \to 0$.

(e) Transition between increase and decrease occurs when $x_s \approx 1$; and we have

$$x_s = \frac{n-s}{s+1}\frac{1}{d-1}\left(1 + \frac{(2s+1)p}{(1-p)n^2 + ps^2}\right)^m \approx \exp\left(\ln\frac{1-\sigma}{\sigma} + \left(\frac{2pr\sigma}{1-p+p\sigma^2} - 1\right)\ln d\right)$$

when $s = \sigma n$. Let $f(\sigma) = 2pr\sigma/(1 - p + p\sigma^2) - 1$, and notice that $f'(\sigma) > 0$ for $0 \le \sigma < 1$ because $p \le \frac{1}{2}$. Furthermore our choice of r makes $f(\frac{1}{2}) < 0 < f(1)$. Setting $g(\sigma) = f(\sigma)/\ln\frac{\sigma}{1-\sigma}$, we seek values of σ with $g(\sigma) = 1/\ln d$. There are three such roots, because $g(1/N) \approx -f(0)/\ln N \ge 1/\ln N$; $g(\frac{1}{2} \pm 1/N) \approx \mp f(\frac{1}{2})N/4$; and $g(1 - 1/N) \approx f(1)/\ln N$.

(f) At the second peak, where $s = n - n/d^{f(1)}$, we have (see exercise 1.2.6–67)

$$t_s < \left(\frac{ned}{n-s}\right)^{n-s}\left(\frac{1}{d}\right)^n\left(1 + \frac{p}{1-p}\right)^m = \exp((-\epsilon + O(1/d^{f(1)}))n\ln d),$$

which is exponentially small. And when $s = 3n/d$, $t_s < \left(\frac{ne}{sd}\right)^s e^{O(m/d^2)} = O((e/3)^{3n/d})$ is also exponentially small. Consequently $\sum_{s=3n/d}^n t_s$ is exponentially small.

[This derivation holds also when the random constraints are k-ary instead of binary, with $q = pd^k$ and $\alpha > 1/k$. See *J. Artificial Intelligence Res.* **12** (2000), 93–103.]

204. (a) If the original literals $\pm x_j$ that involve variable x_j correspond to $\sigma_1 X_{i(1)}, \ldots, \sigma_p X_{i(p)}$, with signs σ_h, add the clauses $(-\sigma_h X_{i(h)} \vee \sigma_{h^+} X_{i(h^+)})$ for $1 \le h \le p$ to enforce consistency, where $h^+ = 1+(h \bmod p)$. (This transformation, due to C. A. Tovey, works even in degenerate cases. For example, if $m = 1$ and if the given clause is $(x_1 \vee x_1 \vee \bar{x}_2)$, the transformed clauses are $(X_1 \vee X_2 \vee X_3)$, $(\bar{X}_1 \vee X_2)$, $(\bar{X}_2 \vee X_1)$, $(X_3 \vee \bar{X}_3)$.)

(b) (Solution by E. Wynn.) The following 44 clauses in 35 variables are satisfiable if and only if each variable is false: $a_i \vee \bar{b}_i \vee c_i$, $\bar{a}_i \vee \bar{b}_i \vee c_i$, $\bar{b}_i \vee \bar{c}_i \vee d_i$, $\bar{c}_i \vee d_i \vee e_i$, $d_i \vee \bar{e}_i \vee f_i$, $\bar{e}_i \vee \bar{f}_i \vee g_i$, $\bar{f}_i \vee g_i \vee h_i$, $\bar{f}_i \vee g_i \vee \bar{h}_i$, for $i \in \{1, 2\}$; $b_1 \vee b_2 \vee \bar{A}$, $A \vee B \vee \bar{C}$, $A \vee \bar{B} \vee D$, $A \vee \bar{D} \vee E$, $\bar{B} \vee \bar{D} \vee \bar{E}$, $B \vee C \vee \bar{F}_1$, $C \vee \bar{E} \vee G_1$, $C \vee F_1 \vee \bar{G}_1$; $F_j \vee G_j \vee \bar{F}_{j+1}$, $F_j \vee G_j \vee \bar{G}_{j+1}$, for $1 \le j \le 6$; $D \vee E \vee \bar{a}_1$, $F_2 \vee G_2 \vee \bar{a}_2$, $F_3 \vee G_3 \vee h_1$, $F_4 \vee G_4 \vee h_2$, $a_1 \vee h_1 \vee \bar{d}_1$, $a_2 \vee h_2 \vee \bar{d}_2$, $F_5 \vee G_5 \vee \bar{g}_1$, $F_6 \vee G_6 \vee \bar{g}_2$.

(c) Add the clauses of (b), and the clauses $F_j \vee G_j \vee \bar{F}_{j+1}$, $F_j \vee G_j \vee \bar{G}_{j+1}$ for $7 \le j \le \lceil 3m/2 \rceil + 3$, to the $4m$ clauses of (a). We can stick the literals $\{F_7, G_7, \ldots\}$, which are always false, into the 2-clauses without using any variable five times, obtaining at most $(7m+39)$ 3-clauses in $N \approx 7m + 30$ variables.

205. (a) After $F_0 = \{\epsilon\}$, $F_1 = F_0 \sqcup F_0$, $F_2 = F_0 \sqcup F_1$, $F_3 = F_0 \sqcup F_2$, $F_4 = F_3 \sqcup F_3'$, $F_5 = F_4 \sqcup F_4''$, always putting the new variable into the four shortest possible clauses, we get $F_5 = \{345, 2\bar{3}4, 1\bar{2}\bar{3}, \bar{1}\bar{2}\bar{3}, 3'\bar{4}5, 2'\bar{3}'\bar{4}, 1'\bar{2}'\bar{3}', \bar{1}'\bar{2}'\bar{3}', 3''4''\bar{5}, 2''\bar{3}''4'', 1''\bar{2}''\bar{3}'', \bar{1}''\bar{2}''\bar{3}'', 3'''\bar{4}''\bar{5}, 2'''\bar{3}'''\bar{4}''', 1'''\bar{2}'''\bar{3}''', \bar{1}'''\bar{2}'''\bar{3}'''\}$.

(b) Let $F_0 = \{\epsilon\}$, $F_1 = F_0 \sqcup F_0$, $F_2 = F_0 \sqcup F_1$, $F_3 = F_0 \sqcup F_2$, $F_4 = F_0 \sqcup F_3$, $F_5 = F_1 \sqcup F_4$, $F_6 = F_0 \sqcup F_5$, $F_7 = F_0 \sqcup F_6$, $F_8 = F_4 \sqcup F_7'$, $F_9 = F_0 \sqcup F_8$, $F_{10} = F_7 \sqcup F_9'$, $F_{11} = F_7 \sqcup F_{10}'$, $F_{12} = F_0 \sqcup F_{11}$, $F_{13} = F_9 \sqcup F_{12}''$, $F_{14} = F_{10} \sqcup F_{12}^{(3)}$, $F_{15} = F_{12} \sqcup F_{14}^{(4)}$, $F_{16} = F_{13} \sqcup F_{14}^{(6)}$, $F_{17} = F_{14} \sqcup F_{15}^{(7)}$, $F_{18} = F_{16} \sqcup F_{17}^{(13)}$. (Here '$x^{(3)}$' stands for '$x'''$', etc.) Then F_{18} consists of 257 unsatisfiable 4-clauses in 234 variables.

(Is there a shorter solution? This problem was first solved by J. Stříbrná in her M.S. thesis (Prague: Charles University, 1994), with 449 clauses. The $\sqcup$ method was introduced by S. Hoory and S. Szeider, *Theoretical Computer Science* **337** (2005), 347–359, who presented an unsatisfiable 5SAT problem that uses each variable at most 7 times. It's not known whether 7 can be decreased to 6 when every clause has size 5.)

206. Suppose F and F' are minimally unsatisfiable, and delete a clause of $F \sqcup F'$ that arose from F'; then we can satisfy $F \sqcup F'$ with x true.

Conversely, if $F \sqcup F'$ is minimally unsatisfiable, F and F' can't both be satisfiable. Suppose F is unsatisfiable but F' is satisfied by L'. Removing a clause of $F \sqcup F'$ that arose from F' is satisfiable only with x true; but then we can use L' to satisfy $F \sqcup F'$. Hence F and F' are both unsatisfiable. Finally, if $F \setminus C$ is unsatisfiable, so is $(F \sqcup F') \setminus (C \mid \bar{x})$, because any solution would satisfy either $F \setminus C$ or F'.

207. The five clauses of $C(x, y, z; a, b, c) = \{x\bar{a}b, y\bar{b}c, z\bar{c}a, abc, \bar{a}\bar{b}\bar{c}\}$ resolve to the single clause xyz. Thus $C(x, y, y; 1, 2, 3) \cup C(x, \bar{y}, \bar{y}; 4, 5, 6) \cup C(\bar{x}, z, z; 7, 8, 9) \cup C(\bar{x}, \bar{z}, \bar{z}; a, b, c)$ is a solution. [K. Iwama and K. Takaki, *DIMACS* **35** (1997), 315–333, noted that the 16 clauses $\{\bar{x}\bar{y}\bar{z}\} \cup C(x, x, x; 1, 2, 3) \cup C(y, y, y; 4, 5, 6) \cup C(z, z, z; 7, 8, 9)$ involve each variable exactly four times, and proved that no set of twelve clauses does so.]

208. Make m clones of all but one of the 20 clauses in answer 207, and put the other $3m$ cloned literals into the $3m$ binary clauses of answer 204(a). This gives $23m$ 3-clauses in which every literal occurs twice, except that the $3m$ literals $\bar{X}_i$ occur only once.

To complete the solution, we "pad" them with additional clauses that are always satisfiable. For example, we could introduce $3m$ more variables u_i, with new clauses $\bar{X}_i u_i \bar{u}_{i+1}$ for $1 \le i \le 3m$ and $\{u'_{3j} u'_{3j+1} u'_{3j+2}, \bar{u}'_{3j} \bar{u}'_{3j+1} \bar{u}'_{3j+2}\}$ for $1 \le j \le m$ (treating subscripts mod $3m$), where u'_i denotes (i even? u_i: $\bar{u}_i$).

209. Since the multiset of kt literals in any t clauses contains at least t different variables, the "marriage theorem" (Theorem 7.5.1H) implies that we can choose a different variable in each clause, easily satisfying it. [*Discr. Applied Math.* **8** (1984), 85–89.]

210. [P. Berman, M. Karpinski, A. D. Scott, *Electronic Colloquium on Computational Complexity* (2003), TR22.] This answer uses the magic number $\varepsilon = \delta^7 \approx 1/58$, where δ is the smallest root of $\delta((1 - \delta^7)^6 + (1 - \delta^7)^7) = 1$. We will assign random values to each variable so that $\Pr[\text{all clauses are satisfied}] > 0$.

Let $\eta_j = (1 - \varepsilon)^j / ((1 - \varepsilon)^j + (1 - \varepsilon)^{13-j})$, and observe that $\eta_j \le \delta(1 - \varepsilon)^j$ for $0 \le j \le 13$. If variable x occurs d^+ times and $\bar{x}$ occurs d^- times, let x be true with probability η_{d^-}, false with probability $1 - \eta_{d^-} = \eta_{13-d^-} \le \delta(1 - \varepsilon)^{13-d^-} \le \delta(1 - \varepsilon)^{d^+}$.

Let $\text{bad}(C) = [\text{clause } C \text{ is falsified by the random assignment}]$, and construct the lopsidependency graph for these events as in exercise 351. Then, if the literals of $C = (l_1 \vee \cdots \vee l_7)$ have contrary appearances in $d_1, \ldots, d_7$ other clauses, we have

$$\Pr(\text{bad}(C)) \le (\delta(1-\varepsilon)^{d_1}) \ldots (\delta(1-\varepsilon)^{d_7}) = \varepsilon(1-\varepsilon)^{d_1+\cdots+d_7} \le \varepsilon(1-\varepsilon)^{\text{degree}(C)},$$

because C has at most $d_1 + \cdots + d_7$ neighbors. Theorem L, with parameter $\theta_i = \varepsilon$ for each event $\text{bad}(C)$, now tells us that $\Pr[\text{all } m \text{ clauses are satisfied}] \ge (1 - \varepsilon)^m$.

[See H. Gebauer, T. Szabó, and G. Tardos, *JACM* **63** (2016), 43:1–43:32, for asymptotic results that apply to kSAT as $k \to \infty$.]

211. If m clauses in n variables are given, so that $3m = 4n$, let $N = 8n$. Consider N "colors" named jk or $\overline{jk}$, where $1 \le j \le n$ and k is one of the four clauses that contains $\pm x_j$. Let σ be a permutation on the colors, consisting of 4-cycles that involve the same variable, with the properties that (i) $(jk)\sigma = jk'$ for some k' and (ii) $(\overline{jk})\sigma = \overline{(jk)\sigma}$.

There are $4n$ vertices of K_N named jk, having the respective color lists

$$L(jk,1) = \{jk, \overline{jk}\}, \quad L(jk,2) = \{jk, (jk)\sigma\}, \quad L(jk,3) = \{\overline{jk}, (jk)\sigma\}.$$

The other $3m$ vertices of K_N are named a_k, b_k, c_k for each clause k. If that clause is, say, $x_2 \vee \bar{x}_5 \vee x_6$, the color lists are

$$L(a_k,1) = \{2k, \overline{5k}, 6k\}, \quad L(b_k,1) = L(c_k,1) = \{2k, \overline{2k}, 5k, \overline{5k}, 6k, \overline{6k}\};$$
$$L(a_k,2) = \{\overline{(2k)\sigma}\}, \quad L(b_k,2) = \{\overline{(5k)\sigma}\}, \quad L(c_k,2) = \{\overline{(6k)\sigma}\};$$
$$L(a_k,3) = \{\overline{(2k)\sigma^2}, (2k)\sigma\}, \quad L(b_k,3) = \{\overline{(5k)\sigma^2}, (5k)\sigma\}, \quad L(c_k,3) = \{\overline{(6k)\sigma^2}, (6k)\sigma\}.$$

Then $K_N \mathbin{\square} K_3$ is list-colorable if and only if the clauses are satisfiable. (For example, $(jk,1)$ is colored $jk \iff ((jk)\sigma, 1)$ is colored $(jk)\sigma \iff (a_k,1)$ is not colored jk.)

212. (a) Let $x_{ijk} = 1$ if and only if $X_{ij} = k$. [*Note:* Another equivalent problem is to find an exact cover with options $\{ \{Pij, Rik, Cjk\} \mid p_{ij} = r_{ik} = c_{jk} = 1\}$. This is a special case of 3D matching. Incidentally, the 3D matching problem can be formulated as the problem of finding a binary tensor (x_{ijk}) such that $x_{ijk} \le y_{ijk}$ and $x_{i**} = x_{*j*} = x_{**k} = 1$, given (y_{ijk}).]

(b) $c_{31} = c_{32} = r_{13} = r_{14} = 0$ forces $x_{13*} = 0 \ne p_{13}$ when $r = c = \begin{pmatrix} 1100 \\ 0110 \\ 0011 \\ 1001 \end{pmatrix}$, $p = \begin{pmatrix} 1010 \\ 1100 \\ 0101 \\ 0011 \end{pmatrix}$.

(c) Make $L(I,J) = \{1, \ldots, N\}$ for $M < I \le N$, $1 \le J \le N$. It is well known (Theorem 7.5.1L) that a latin rectangle can always be extended to a latin square.

(d) Index everything by the set $\{1, \ldots, N\} \cup \bigcup_{I,J} \{(I,J,K) \mid K \in L(I,J)\}$. The elements (I,J,K) where $K = \min L(I,J)$ are called *headers*. Set $p_{ij} = 1$ if and only if (i) $i = j = (I,J,K)$ is not a header; or (ii) $i = (I,J,K)$ is a header, and $j = J$ or $j = (I,J,K')$ is not a header; or (iii) $j = (I,J,K)$ is a header, and $i = I$ or $i = (I,J,K')$ is not a header. Set $r_{ik} = c_{ik} = 1$ if and only if (i) $1 \le i, k \le N$; or (ii) $i = (I,J,K)$ and $k = (I,J,K')$, and if i is not a header then ($K' = K$ or K' is the largest element $< K$ in $L(I,J)$). [*Reference:* SICOMP **23** (1994), 170–184.]

213. The hinted probability is $(1 - (1-p)^{n'}(1-q)^{n-n'})^m$, where $n' = b_1 + \cdots + b_n$. Thus if $p \le q$, every x has probability at least $(1 - (1-p)^n)^m$ of satisfying every clause. This is huge, unless n is small or m is large: If m is less than α^n, where α is any constant less than $1/(1-p)$, then when $n > -1/\lg(1-p)$ the probability $(1 - (1-p)^n)^m > \exp(\alpha^n \ln(1 - (1-p)^n)) > \exp(-2(\alpha(1-p))^n) > 1 - 2(\alpha(1-p))^n$ is exponentially close to 1. Nobody needs a SAT solver for such an easy problem.

Even if, say, $p = q = k/(2n)$, so that the average clause size is k, a clause is empty — hence unsatisfiable — with probability $e^{-k} + O(n^{-1})$; and indeed a clause has exactly r elements with the Poisson probability $e^{-k}k^r/r! + O(n^{-1})$ for fixed r. So the model isn't very relevant. [See J. Franco, *Information Proc. Letters* **23** (1986), 103–106.]

214. (a) $T(z) = ze^z + 2T(pz)(e^{(1-p)z} - 1)$.

(b) If $f(z) = \prod_{m=1}^{\infty}(1 - e^{(p-1)z/p^m})$ and $\tau(z) = f(z)T(z)e^{-z}$, we have $\tau(z) = zf(z) + 2\tau(pz) = zf(z) + 2pzf(pz) + 4p^2zf(p^2z) + \cdots$.

(c) See P. Jacquet, C. Knessl, and W. Szpankowski, *Combinatorics, Probability, and Computing* **23** (2014), 829–841. [The sequence $\langle T_n \rangle$ was first studied by A. T. Goldberg, *Courant Computer Science Report* **16** (1979), 48–49.]

215. Since any given $x_1 \ldots x_l$ is a partial solution in $(8\binom{n}{3} - \binom{l}{3})^m$ of the $(8\binom{n}{3})^m$ possible cases, level l contains $P_l = 2^l(1 - \frac{1}{8}l^3/n^3)^m$ nodes on the average. When $m = 4n$ and $n = 50$, the largest levels are $(P_{31}, P_{32}, \ldots, P_{36}) \approx (6.4, 6.9, 7.2, 7.2, 6.8, 6.2) \times 10^6$, and the mean total tree size $P_0 + \cdots + P_{50}$ is about 85.6 million.

If $l = 2tn$ and $m = \alpha n$ we have $P_l = 2^{f(t)n}$, where $f(t) = 2t + \alpha \lg(1 - t^3) + O(1/n)$ for $0 \leq t \leq 1/2$. The maximum $f(t)$ occurs when $\ln 4 = 3\alpha t^2/(1 - t^3)$, at which point $t = t_\alpha = \beta - \frac{1}{2}\beta^4 + \frac{5}{8}\beta^7 + O(\beta^{10})$, where $\beta = \sqrt{\ln 4/(3\alpha)}$; for example, $t_4 \approx 0.334$. Now

$$\frac{P_{L+k}}{P_L} = \exp\left(-\frac{\gamma k^2}{n} + O\left(\frac{k}{n}\right) + O\left(\frac{k^3}{n^2}\right)\right), \quad \gamma = \frac{(\ln 2)^2}{6\alpha}\left(1 + \frac{2}{t_\alpha^3}\right), \quad \text{when } L = 2t_\alpha n;$$

by trading tails, the expected total tree size is $\sqrt{\pi n/\gamma}\, P_L(1 + O(1/\sqrt{n}))$.

[This question was first studied by C. A. Brown and P. W. Purdom, Jr., *SICOMP* **10** (1981), 583–593; K. M. Bugrara and C. A. Brown, *Inf. Sciences* **40** (1986), 21–37.]

216. If the search tree has q two-way branches, it has fewer than $2nq$ nodes; we shall find an upper bound on $\mathrm{E}\,q$. Consider such branches after values have been assigned to the first l variables $x_1, \ldots, x_l$, and also to s additional variables $y_1, \ldots, y_s$ because of unit-clause forcing; the branch therefore occurs on level $t = l + s$. The values can be assigned in 2^t ways, and the y's can be chosen in $\binom{n-1-l}{s}$ ways. For $1 \leq i \leq s$ the m given clauses must contain $j_i \geq 1$ clauses chosen (with replacement) from the $F = \binom{t-1}{2}$ that force the value of y_i from other known values. The other $m - j_1 - \cdots - j_s$ must be chosen from the $R = 8\binom{n}{3} - sF - \binom{t}{3} - 2\binom{t}{2}(n - t)$ remaining clauses that aren't entirely false and don't force anything further. Thus the expected number of two-way branches is at most

$$P_{lt} = 2^t\binom{n-l-1}{s} \sum_{j_1, \ldots, j_s \geq 1}\binom{m}{j_1, \ldots, j_s, m-j}\frac{F^j R^{m-j}}{N^m}, \quad j = j_1 + \cdots + j_s, \quad N = 8\binom{n}{3},$$

summed over $0 \leq l \leq t < n$. Let $b = F/N$ and $c = R/N$; the sum on $j_1, \ldots, j_s$ is

$$m!\,[z^m]\,(e^{bz} - 1)^s e^{cz} = \sum_r\binom{s}{r}(-1)^{s-r}(c + rb)^m = s!\,c^m\sum_q\binom{m}{q}\begin{Bmatrix} q \\ s \end{Bmatrix}\left(\frac{b}{c}\right)^q.$$

These values P_{lt} are almost all quite small when $m = 200$ and $n = 50$, rising above 100 only when $l \geq 45$ and $t = 49$; $\sum P_{lt} \approx 4404.7$.

If $l = xn$ and $t = yn$, we have $b \approx \frac{3}{8}y^2/n$ and $c \approx 1 - \frac{1}{8}(3(y-x)y^2 + y^3 + 6y^2(1-y))$. The asymptotic value of $[z^{\alpha n}]\,(e^{\beta z/n} - 1)^{\delta n}e^{\gamma z}$ can be found by the saddle point method: Let ζ satisfy $\beta \delta e^\zeta/(e^\zeta - 1) + \gamma = \alpha\beta/\zeta$, and let $\rho^2 = \alpha/\zeta^2 - \delta e^\zeta/(e^\zeta - 1)^2$. Then the answer is approximately $(e^\zeta - 1)^{\delta n}e^{\gamma\zeta n/\beta}\sqrt{n}/(\sqrt{2\pi}\rho\beta(\zeta n/\beta)^{\alpha n+1})$.

[For exact formulas and lower bounds, see *SICOMP* **12** (1983), 717–733. The total time to find all solutions grows approximately as $(2(\frac{7}{8})^\alpha)^n$ when $\alpha < 4.5$, according to H.-M. Méjean, H. Morel, and G. Reynaud, *SICOMP* **24** (1995), 621–649.]

217. True, unless both l and $\bar{l}$ belong to A or to B (making A or B tautological). For if L is a set of strictly distinct literals that covers both A and B, we know that neither A nor B nor L contains both l and $\bar{l}$; hence $L \setminus \{l, \bar{l}\}$ covers $(A \setminus \{l, \bar{l}\}) \cup (B \setminus \{l, \bar{l}\}) = C$.

(This generalization of resolution is, however, useless if $C \supseteq A$ or $C \supseteq B$, because a large clause is easier to cover than any of its subsets. Thus we generally assume that $l \in A$ and $\bar{l} \in B$, and that C isn't tautological, as in the text.)

218. x? B: A. [Hence $(x \vee A) \wedge (\bar{x} \vee B)$ always implies $A \vee B$.]

219. If C' or C'' is tautological ($\wp$), we define $\wp \diamond C = C \diamond \wp = C$. Otherwise, if there's a unique literal l such that C' has the form $l \vee A'$ and C'' has the form $\bar{l} \vee A''$, we define $C' \diamond C'' = A' \vee A''$ as in the text. If there are two or more such literals, strictly distinct, we define $C' \diamond C'' = \wp$. And if there are no such literals, we define $C' \diamond C'' = C' \vee C''$.

[This operation is obviously commutative but not associative. For example, we have $(\bar{x} \diamond \bar{y}) \diamond (x \vee y) = \wp$ while $\bar{x} \diamond (\bar{y} \diamond (x \vee y)) = \epsilon$.]

220. (a) True: If $C \subseteq C'$ and $C' \subseteq C''$ and $C'' \neq \wp$ then $C' \neq \wp$; hence every literal of C appears in C' and in C''. [The notion of subsumption goes back to a paper by Hugh McColl, *Proc. London Math. Soc.* **10** (1878), 16–28.]

(b) True: Otherwise we'd necessarily have $(C \diamond C') \vee \alpha \vee \alpha' \neq \wp$ and $C \neq \wp$ and $C' \neq \wp$ and $C \diamond C' \neq C \vee C'$; hence there's a literal l with $C = l \vee A$, $C' = \bar{l} \vee A'$, and the literals of $A \vee A' \vee \alpha \vee \alpha'$ are strictly distinct. So the result is easily checked, whether or not α or α' contains l or $\bar{l}$. (Notice that we always have $C \diamond C' \subseteq C \vee C'$.)

(c) False: $\bar{x}y \subseteq \wp$ but $x \diamond \bar{x}y = y \not\subseteq x = x \diamond \wp$. Also $\epsilon \subseteq \bar{x}$ but $x \diamond \epsilon = x \not\subseteq \epsilon = x \diamond \bar{x}$.

(d) Such examples are possible if $C \neq \epsilon$: We have $x, \bar{x} \vdash y$ (and also $x, \bar{x} \vdash \wp$), although the only clauses obtainable from x and $\bar{x}$ by resolution are x, $\bar{x}$, and ϵ. (On the other hand we do have $F \vdash \epsilon$ *if and only if* there's a refutation chain (104) for F.)

(e) Given a resolution chain $C'_1, \ldots, C'_{m+r}$, we can construct another chain $C_1, \ldots, C_{m+r}$ in which $C_i \subseteq C'_i$ for $1 \leq i \leq m+r$. Indeed, if $i > m$ and $C'_i = C'_j \diamond C'_k$, it's easy to see that either $C_j \diamond C_j$ or $C_k \diamond C_k$ or $C_j \diamond C_k$ will subsume C'_i.

(f) It suffices by (e) to prove this when $\alpha_1 = \cdots = \alpha_m = \alpha$; and by induction we may assume that $\alpha = l$ is a single literal. Given a resolution chain $C_1, \ldots, C_{m+r}$ we can construct another one $C'_1, \ldots, C'_{m+r}$ such that $C'_i = C_i \vee l$ for $1 \leq i \leq m$ and $C'_i \subseteq C_i \vee l$ for $m+1 \leq i \leq m+r$, with $C'_i = C'_j$ or C'_k or $C'_j \diamond C'_k$ whenever $C_i = C_j \diamond C_k$.

221. Algorithm A recognizes '1' as a pure literal, but then finds a contradiction because the *other* two clauses are unsatisfiable. The resolution refutation uses only the other two clauses. (This is an example of an unnecessary branch. Indeed, a pure literal never appears in a refutation tree, because it can't be canceled; see the next exercise.)

222. If A is an autarky that satisfies C, it also satisfies every clause on the path to ϵ from a source vertex labeled C, because all of the satisfied literals cannot simultaneously vanish. For the converse, see *Discrete Appl. Math.* **107** (2000), 99–137, Theorem 3.16.

223. (The author has convinced himself of this statement, but he has not been able to construct a formal proof.)

224. At every leaf labeled by an axiom A of $F \mid \bar{x}$ that is not an axiom of F, change the label to $A \cup x$; also include x in the labels of all this leaf's ancestors. We obtain a resolution tree in which the leaves are labeled by axioms of F. The root is labeled x, if any labels have changed; otherwise it is still labeled ϵ.

[See J. A. Robinson, *Machine Intelligence* **3** (1968), 77–94.]

225. Let's say that a regular resolution tree for clause A is *awkward* if at least one of its nodes resolves on one of the variables in A. An awkward tree T for A can always be transformed into a regular non-awkward tree T' for some clause $A' \subseteq A$, where T' is smaller than T. *Proof:* Suppose T is awkward, but none of its subtrees are. Without loss of generality we can find a sequence of subtrees $T_0, \ldots, T_p, T'_1, \ldots, T'_p$, where $T_0 = T$ and T_{j-1} for $1 \leq j \leq p$ is obtained from T_j and T'_j by resolving on the variable x_j; furthermore $x_p \in A$. We can assume that the labels of T_j and T'_j are A_j and A'_j, where $A_j = x_j \cup R_j$ and $A'_j = \bar{x}_j \cup R'_j$; hence $A_{j-1} = R_j \cup R'_j$. Let $B_p = A_p$; and for

$j = p-1, p-2, \ldots, 1$, let $B_j = B_{j+1}$ if $x_j \notin B_{j+1}$, otherwise obtain B_j by resolving B_{j+1} with A'_j. It follows by induction that $B_j \subseteq x_p \cup A_{j-1}$. Thus $B_1 \subseteq x_p \cup A_0 = A$, and we've derived B_1 with a non-awkward tree smaller than T.

Now we can prove more than was asked: If T is any resolution tree that derives clause A, and if $A \cup B$ is any clause that contains A, there's a non-awkward regular resolution tree T_r no larger than T that derives some clause $C \subseteq A \cup B$. The proof is by induction on the size of T: Suppose $A = A' \cup A''$ is obtained at the root of T by resolving the clauses $x \cup A'$ with $\bar{x} \cup A''$ that label the subtrees T' and T''. Find non-awkward regular trees T'_r and T''_r that derive C' and C'', where $C' \subseteq x \cup A' \cup B$ and $C'' \subseteq \bar{x} \cup A'' \cup B$. If $x \in C'$ and $\bar{x} \in C''$, we obtain the desired T_r by resolving T'_r and T''_r on x. Otherwise we can either let $C = C'$ and $T_r = T'_r$, or $C = C''$ and $T_r = T''_r$. [It's interesting to apply this construction to the highly irregular resolutions in (105).]

226. Initially α is the root, $C(\alpha) = \epsilon$, $\|\alpha\| = N$, and $s = 0$. If α isn't a leaf, we have $C(\alpha) = C(\alpha') \diamond C(\alpha'')$ where $x \in C(\alpha')$ and $\bar{x} \in C(\alpha'')$ for some variable x. The Prover names x, and changes $\alpha \leftarrow \alpha'$ or $\alpha \leftarrow \alpha''$ if the Delayer sets $x \leftarrow 0$ or $x \leftarrow 1$, respectively. Otherwise $\min(\|\alpha'\|, \|\alpha''\|) \leq \|\alpha\|/2$, and the Prover can keep going.

227. The proof is by induction on the number of variables, n: If F contains the empty clause, the game is over, the Delayer has scored 0, and the root is labeled 0. Otherwise the Prover names x, and the Delayer considers the smallest possible labels (m, m') on the roots of refutations for $F \mid x$ and $F \mid \bar{x}$. If $m > m'$, the reply $x \leftarrow 0$ guarantees m points; and the reply $x \leftarrow *$ is no better, because $m' + 1 \leq m$. If $m < m'$, the reply $x \leftarrow 1$ guarantees m'; and if $m = m'$, the reply $x \leftarrow *$ guarantees $m + 1$. Thus an optimum Delayer can always score at least as many points as the root label of any branch of a refutation tree constructed by the Prover. Conversely, if the Prover always names an optimal x, the Delayer can't do better.

(This exercise was suggested by O. Kullmann. One can compute the optimum score "bottom up" by considering all 3^n possible partial assignments as in answer 133.)

228. We need only assume the transitivity clauses T_{ijk} of (100) when $i < j$ and $k < j$. [Notice further that T_{ijk} is tautological when $i = j$ or $k = j$, thus useless for resolution.]

229. Using the binary-relation interpretation, these clauses say that $j \nprec j$, that the transitive law "$i \prec j$ and $j \prec k$ implies $i \prec k$" holds whenever $i \leq k$ and $j < k$, and that every j has a successor such that $j \prec k$. The latter axiom combines with the finiteness of m to imply that there must be a cycle $j_0 \prec j_1 \prec \cdots \prec j_{p-1} \prec j_p = j_0$.

Consider the *shortest* such cycle, and renumber the subscripts so that $j_p = \max\{j_0, \ldots, j_p\}$. We cannot have $p \geq 2$, because (100') implies $j_{p-2} \prec j_p$, yielding a shorter cycle. Hence $p = 1$; but that contradicts (99).

230. Call the axioms I_j, T_{ijk}, and M_{jm} as in the text. If I_{j_0} is omitted, let $x_{ij} = [j = j_0]$ for all i and j. If $T_{i_0 j_0 k_0}$ is omitted, let $x_{ij} = [j \in A]$ for all $i \notin A = \{i_0, j_0, k_0\}$; also let $x_{i_0 j} = [j = j_0]$, $x_{j_0 j} = [j = k_0]$, and (if $i_0 \neq k_0$) $x_{k_0 j} = [j = i_0]$. Finally, if $M_{j_0 m}$ is omitted, let $x_{ij} = [p_i < p_j]$, where $p_1 \ldots p_m = 1 \ldots (j_0 - 1)(j_0 + 1) \ldots m j_0$. (The same construction shows that the clauses of answer 228 are minimally unsatisfiable.)

231. Since $G_{11} = M_{1m}$, we can assume that $j > 1$. Then $G_{(j-1)j} = G_{(j-1)(j-1)} \diamond I_{j-1}$. And if $1 \leq i < j-1$ we have $G_{ij} = (\cdots((G_{(j-1)j} \diamond A_{ijj}) \diamond A_{ij(j+1)}) \diamond \cdots) \diamond A_{ijm}$, where $A_{ijk} = G_{i(j-1)} \diamond T_{i(j-1)k} = G_{ij} \vee \bar{x}_{(j-1)k}$. These clauses make it possible to derive $B_{ij} = (\cdots((G_{ij} \diamond T_{jij}) \diamond T_{ji(j+1)}) \diamond \cdots) \diamond T_{jim} = G_{jj} \vee \bar{x}_{ji}$ for $1 \leq i < j$, from which we obtain $G_{jj} = (\cdots((M_{jm} \diamond B_{1j}) \diamond B_{2j}) \diamond \cdots) \diamond B_{(j-1)j}$. Finally $G_{mm} \diamond I_m = \epsilon$.

232. It suffices to exhibit a backtrack tree of depth $6 \lg q + O(1)$. By branching on at most 6 variables we can find the color-triplet α_1 in answer 176(c).

　　Suppose we know that $\alpha_j = \alpha$ and $\alpha_{j+p} = \alpha'$, where α' cannot be obtained from α in p steps; this is initially true with $j = 1$, $\alpha = \alpha' = \alpha_1$, and $p = q$. If $p = 1$, a few more branches will find a contradiction. Otherwise at most 6 branches will determine α_l, where $l = j + \lfloor p/2 \rfloor$; and either α_l will be unreachable from α in $\lfloor p/2 \rfloor$ steps, or α' will be unreachable from α_l in $\lceil p/2 \rceil$ steps, or both. Recurse.

233. $C_9 = C_6 \diamond C_8$, $C_{10} = C_1 \diamond C_9$, $C_{11} = C_3 \diamond C_{10}$, $C_{12} = C_7 \diamond C_{10}$, $C_{13} = C_4 \diamond C_{11}$, $C_{14} = C_2 \diamond C_{12}$, $C_{15} = C_{13} \diamond C_{14}$, $C_{16} = C_5 \diamond C_{15}$, $C_{17} = C_6 \diamond C_{15}$, $C_{18} = C_8 \diamond C_{15}$, $C_{19} = C_{12} \diamond C_{17}$, $C_{20} = C_{11} \diamond C_{18}$, $C_{21} = C_{16} \diamond C_{19}$, $C_{22} = C_{20} \diamond C_{21}$.

234. Reply $x_{jk} \leftarrow *$ to any query that doesn't allow the Prover to violate (107). Then the Prover can violate (106) only after every hole has been queried.

235. Let $C(k, A) = (\bigvee_{j=0}^{k} \bigvee_{a \in A} x_{ja})$, so that $C(0, \{1, \ldots, m\}) = (x_{01} \vee \cdots \vee x_{0m})$ and $C(m, \emptyset) = \epsilon$. The chain consists of m stages for $k = 1, \ldots, m$, where stage k begins by deriving the clauses $\bar{x}_{ka} \vee C(k - 1, A)$ from the clauses of stage $k - 1$, for all $(m - k)$-element subsets A of $\{1, \ldots, m\} \setminus a$; every such clause requires k resolutions with (107). Stage k concludes by deriving $C(k, A)$ for all $(m - k)$-element subsets A of $\{1, \ldots, m\}$, each using one resolution from (106) and $k - 1$ resolutions from the beginning of the stage. (See (103).) Thus stage k involves a total of $\binom{m}{m-k}(k^2 + k)$ resolutions.

　　For example, the resolutions when $m = 3$ successively yield $\overline{11}\,02\,03$, $\overline{12}\,01\,03$, $\overline{13}\,01\,02$; $01\,02\,11\,12$, $01\,03\,11\,13$, $02\,03\,12\,13$ (stage 1); $\overline{21}\,02\,11\,12$, $\overline{21}\,02\,12$, $\overline{21}\,03\,11\,13$, $\overline{21}\,03\,13$, $\overline{22}\,01\,12\,11$, $\overline{22}\,01\,11$, $\overline{22}\,03\,12\,13$, $\overline{22}\,03\,13$, $\overline{23}\,01\,13\,11$, $\overline{23}\,01\,11$, $\overline{23}\,02\,13\,12$, $\overline{23}\,02\,12$; $01\,11\,21\,22$, $01\,11\,21$, $02\,12\,22\,23$, $02\,12\,22$, $03\,13\,23\,22$, $03\,13\,23$ (stage 2); and $\overline{31}\,11\,21$, $\overline{31}\,21$, $\overline{31}$, $\overline{32}\,12\,22$, $\overline{32}\,22$, $\overline{32}$, $\overline{33}\,13\,23$, $\overline{33}\,23$, $\overline{33}$; $32\,33$, 33, ϵ (stage 3).

　　[Stephen A. Cook constructed such chains in 1972 (unpublished).]

236. The symmetry of the axioms should allow exhaustive verification by computer for $m = 2$, possibly also for $m = 3$. The construction certainly seems hard to beat. Cook conjectured in 1972 that any minimum-length resolution proof would include, for every subset S of $\{1, \ldots, m\}$, at least one clause C such that $\bigcup_{\pm x_{jk} \in C} \{k\} = S$.

237. The idea is to define $y_{jk} = x_{jk} \vee (x_{jm} \wedge x_{mk})$ for $0 \le j < m$ and $1 \le k < m$, thus reducing from $m + 1$ pigeons to m. First we append $6m(m - 1)$ new clauses

$$(x_{jm} \vee z_{jk}) \wedge (x_{mk} \vee z_{jk}) \wedge (\bar{x}_{jm} \vee \bar{x}_{mk} \vee \bar{z}_{jk}) \wedge (\bar{x}_{jk} \vee y_{jk}) \wedge (y_{jk} \vee z_{jk}) \wedge (x_{jk} \vee \bar{y}_{jk} \vee \bar{z}_{jk}),$$

involving $2m(m - 1)$ new variables y_{jk} and z_{jk}. Call these clauses $A_{jk}, \ldots, F_{jk}$.

　　Now if P_j stands for (106) and H_{ijk} for (107), we want to use resolution to derive $P'_j = (y_{j1} \vee \cdots \vee y_{j(m-1)})$ and $H'_{ijk} = (\bar{y}_{ik} \vee \bar{y}_{jk})$. First, P_j can be resolved with D_{j1}, $\ldots$, $D_{j(m-1)}$ to get $P'_j \vee x_{jm}$. Next, $P_m \diamond H_{jmm} = x_{m1} \vee \cdots \vee x_{m(m-1)} \vee \bar{x}_{jm}$ can be resolved with $G_{jk} = C_{jk} \diamond E_{jk} = \bar{x}_{jm} \vee \bar{x}_{mk} \vee y_{jk}$ for $1 \le k < m$ to get $P'_j \vee \bar{x}_{jm}$. One more step yields P'_j. (The intuitive "meaning" guides these maneuvers.)

　　From $B_{jk} \diamond F_{jk} = x_{jk} \vee x_{mk} \vee \bar{y}_{jk}$, we obtain $Q_{ijk} = \bar{x}_{ik} \vee \bar{y}_{jk}$ after resolving with H_{ijk} and H_{imk}. Then $(Q_{ijk} \diamond F_{ik}) \diamond A_{ik} = x_{im} \vee \bar{y}_{ik} \vee \bar{y}_{jk} = R_{ijk}$, say. Finally, $(R_{jik} \diamond H_{ijm}) \diamond R_{ijk} = H'_{ijk}$ as desired. (When forming R_{jik} we need Q_{jik} with $j > i$.)

　　We've done $5m^3 - 6m^2 + 3m$ resolutions to reduce $m + 1$ to m. Repeating until $m = 0$, with fresh y and z variables each time, yields ϵ after about $\frac{5}{4}m^4$ steps.

　　[See Stephen A. Cook, *SIGACT News* **8**, 4 (October 1976), 28–32.]

238. The function $(1 - cx)^{-x} = \exp(cx^2 + c^2 x^3/2 + \cdots)$ is increasing and $> e^{cx^2}$. Setting $c = \frac{1}{2n}$, $W = \sqrt{2n \ln r}$, and $b = \lceil W \rceil$ makes $f \le r < \rho^{-b}$. Also $W \ge w(\alpha_0)$

when $n \geq w(\alpha_0)^2$ and $r \geq 2$; hence $w(\alpha_0 \vdash \epsilon) \leq W + b \leq \sqrt{8n \ln r} + 1$ as desired. The '-2' in the lemma handles the trivial cases that arise when $r < 2$.

(It is important to realize that we don't change n or W in the induction proof. Incidentally, the exact minimum of $W + b$, subject to $r = (1 - W/(2n))^{-b}$, occurs when

$$W = 2n(1 - e^{-2T(z)}) = 4nz + \frac{2nz^3}{3} + \cdots, \qquad b = \frac{\ln r}{2T(z)} = (\ln r)\left(\frac{1}{2z} - \frac{1}{2} - \frac{z}{4} - \cdots\right),$$

where $z^2 = (\ln r)/(8n)$ and $T(z)$ is the tree function. Thus it appears likely that the proof of Lemma B supports the stronger result $w(\alpha_0 \vdash \epsilon) < \sqrt{8n \ln r} - \frac{1}{2} \ln r + 1$.)

239. Let α_0 consist of all 2^n nontautological clauses of length n. The shortest refutation is the complete binary tree with these leaves, because every nontautological clause must appear. Algorithm A shows that $2^n - 1$ resolutions suffice to refute any clauses in n variables; hence $\|\alpha_0 \vdash \epsilon\| = 2^n - 1$, and this is the worst case.

240. If A' has t elements and $\partial A'$ has fewer than t, the sequence of $5t$ integers f_{ij} for its neighbors must include at least $2t$ repeats of values seen earlier. (In fact there are at least $2t + 1$ repeats, because $2t$ would leave at least t in the boundary; but the calculations are simpler with $2t$, and we need only a rather crude bound.)

The probability p_t that some such A' exists is therefore less than $\binom{m+1}{t}\binom{5t}{2t}\left(\frac{3t}{m}\right)^{2t}$, because there are $\binom{m+1}{t}$ ways to select A', $\binom{5t}{2t}$ to select the repeating slots, and at most $(3t)^{2t}$ out of m^{2t} ways to fill those slots. Also $\binom{m+1}{t} = \binom{m}{t} + \binom{m}{t-1} < 2\binom{m}{t}$ when $t \leq \frac{1}{2}m$.

By exercise 1.2.6–67 we have $p_t \leq 2\left(\frac{me}{t}\right)^t\left(\frac{5te}{2t}\right)^{2t}\left(\frac{3t}{m}\right)^{2t} = 2(ct/m)^t$, where $c = 225e^3/4 \approx 1130$. Also $p_0 = p_1 = 0$. Thus the sum of p_t for $t \leq m/3000$ is less than $2\sum_{t=2}^{\infty}(c/3000)^t \approx .455$; and the probability of strong expansion exceeds $.544$.

241. If $0 < |A'| \leq m/3000$, we can put one of its elements into a hole $b_k \in \partial A'$. Then we can place the other elements in the same way, since b_k isn't their neighbor.

242. The proof of Theorem B remains valid when these new axioms are added.

243. (a) The probability that F' has t elements and $V(F')$ has fewer than t is at most $\binom{\alpha n}{t}\binom{n}{t}\left(\frac{t}{n}\right)^{3t} \leq \left(\frac{\alpha e^2 t}{n}\right)^t$. The sum of this quantity for $1 \leq t \leq \lg n$ is $O(n^{-1})$, and so is the sum for $\lg n \leq t \leq n/(2\alpha e^2)$.

(b) If the condition in (a) holds, there's a matching from F' into $V(F')$, by Theorem 7.5.1H; hence we can satisfy F' by assigning to its variables, one by one. If F is unsatisfiable we'll therefore need to invoke more than $n/(2\alpha e^2)$ of its axioms.

(c) The probability p_t that F' has t elements and $2|V(F')| - 3|F'| < \frac{1}{2}|F'|$ is at most $\binom{\alpha n}{t}\binom{n}{\lambda t}\left(\frac{\lambda t}{n}\right)^{3t} \leq (\alpha e^{1+\lambda}\lambda^{3-\lambda}(t/n)^{1/4})^t$, where $\lambda = \frac{7}{4}$. We have $(e^{1+\lambda}\lambda^{3-\lambda})^4 < 10^6$; so $p_t < c^t$ when $t \leq n'$, where $c < 1$, and $\sum_{t=n'/2}^{n'} p_t$ is exponentially small.

(d) Since $n' < n/(2\alpha e^2)$, every refutation a.s. contains a clause C with $n'/2 \leq \mu(C) < n'$. The minimal axioms F' on which C depends have $|F'| = \mu(C)$. Let k be the number of "boundary" variables that occur in just one axiom of F'. If v is such a variable, we can falsify C and the axiom containing v, while the other axioms of F' are true; hence V must contain v or $\bar{v}$. We have $|V(F')| = k + |\text{nonboundary}| \leq k + \frac{1}{2}(3|F'| - k)$, because each nonboundary variable occurs at least twice. Therefore $k \geq 2|V(F')| - 3|F'| \geq n'/4$, q.s. (Notice the similarities to the proof of Theorem B.)

244. We have $[A \cup B]^0 = [A]^0[B]^0 \cup [A]^1[B]^1$ and $[A \cup B]^1 = [A]^0[B]^1 \cup [A]^1[B]^0$, where concatenation of sets has the obvious meaning. These relations hold also when $A = \emptyset$ or $B = \emptyset$, because $[\emptyset]^0 = \{\epsilon\}$ and $[\emptyset]^1 = \emptyset$.

245. (a) When conditioning on $\bar{e}_{uv}$, simply delete the edge $u \,\text{---}\, v$ from G. When conditioning on e_{uv}, also complement $l(u)$ and $l(v)$. The graph might become disconnected; in that case, there will be exactly two components, one even and one odd, with respect to the sums of their labels. The axioms for the even component are satisfiable and may be discarded.

For example, $\alpha(G) \,|\, \{b, \bar{e}\}$ corresponds to while $\alpha(G) \,|\, \{b, e\}$ corresponds to . We toss out the left component in the first case, the right one in the other.

(b) If $C \in \alpha(v)$ we may take $V' = \{v\}$. And we have $\mu(\epsilon) = |V|$, because the axioms $\bigcup_{v \in V \setminus u} \alpha(v)$ are satisfiable for all $u \in V$.

(c) If $u \in V'$ and $v \notin V'$, there's an assignment that falsifies C and some axiom of $\alpha(u)$ while satisfying all $\alpha(w)$ for $w \in V' \setminus u$, because $|V'|$ is minimum. Setting $e_{uv} \leftarrow \bar{e}_{uv}$ will satisfy $\alpha(u)$ without affecting the axioms $\alpha(w)$ (which don't contain e_{uv}).

(d) By (b), every refutation of $\alpha(G)$ must contain a clause C with $\frac{1}{3}m \le \mu(C) < \frac{2}{3}m$. The corresponding V' has $|V'|/(|V'| + |\partial V'|) < (\frac{2}{3} + 8)/9$, hence $|\partial V'| > \frac{1}{26}|V'|$.

[Property (i) is interesting but irrelevant for this proof. Notice that $\alpha(G)$ has exactly $\frac{8}{3}n \approx 2.67n$ 3SAT clauses in $n = 3m/2$ variables when G is cubic; every literal occurs four times. G. Tseytin proved lower bounds for refutations of $\alpha(G)$ by *regular* resolution in 1966, before graphs with property (iii) were known; A. Urquhart obtained them for general resolution in *JACM* **34** (1987), 209–219, and the simplified argument given here is due to Ben-Sasson and Wigderson. The fact that $\alpha(G)$ requires exponentially long refutation chains, although the same axioms can be refuted easily by working with linear equations mod 2, amounts to a proof that backtracking is a poor way to deal with linear equations! Suitable Ramanujan graphs $raman(2, q, 3, 0)$ can be found by the algorithms of the Stanford GraphBase for infinitely many prime numbers q. We can also obtain the same lower bounds with the multigraphs $raman(2, q, 1, 0)$ and $raman(2, q, 2, 0)$. Section 7.4.3 will explore expander graphs in detail.]

246. Let's write $[a_1 \ldots a_k]^\ell$ for what exercise 244 calls $[\{a_1, \ldots, a_k\}]^\ell$. With new variables x, y, z we can introduce $\{xa, x\bar{b}, \bar{x}\bar{a}b, y\bar{a}, yb, \bar{y}a\bar{b}, zx, zy, \bar{z}\bar{x}\bar{y}\}$ and resolve those clauses to $[zab]^1$, which means $z = a \oplus b$. So we can assume that '$z \leftarrow a \oplus b$' is a legal primitive operation of "extended resolution hardware," when z is a new variable. Furthermore we can compute $a_1 \oplus \cdots \oplus a_k$ in $O(k)$ steps, using $z_0 \leftarrow 0$ (which is the clause $[z_0]^1$, namely $\bar{z}_0$) and $z_k \leftarrow z_{k-1} \oplus a_k$ when $k \ge 1$.

Let the edge variables $E(v)$ be $a_1, \ldots, a_d$, where d is the degree of v. We compute $s_v \leftarrow a_1 \oplus \cdots \oplus a_d$ by setting $s_{v,0} \leftarrow 0$, $s_{v,k} \leftarrow s_{v,k-1} \oplus a_k$, and $s_v \leftarrow s_{v,d}$. We can resolve s_v with the axioms $\alpha(v)$ in $O(2^d)$ steps, to get the singleton clause $[s_v]^{l(v) \oplus 1}$, meaning $s_v = l(v)$. Summing over v, these operations therefore take $O(N)$ steps.

On the other hand, we can also compute $z_n \leftarrow \bigoplus_v s_v$ and get zero (namely '$\bar{z}_n$'). Doing this cleverly, by omnisciently knowing G, we can in fact compute it in $O(mn)$ steps: Start with any vertex v and set $z_1 \leftarrow s_v$ (more precisely, set $z_{1,k} \leftarrow s_{v,k}$ for $0 \le k \le d$). Given z_j for $1 \le j < n$, with all its subvariables $z_{j,k}$, we then compute $z_{j+1} \leftarrow z_j \oplus s_u$, where u is the unused vertex with $s_{u,1} = z_{j,1}$. We can arrange the edges into an order so that if z_j has p edge variables in common with s_u, then $z_{j,k} = s_{u,k}$ for $1 \le k \le p$. Suppose the other variables of z_j and s_u are respectively $a_1, \ldots, a_q$ and $b_1, \ldots, b_r$; we want to merge them into the sequence $c_1, \ldots, c_{q+r}$ that will be needed later when z_{j+1} is used. So we set $z_{j+1,0} \leftarrow 0$, $z_{j+1,k} \leftarrow z_{j+1,k-1} \oplus c_k$, $z_{j+1} \leftarrow z_{j+1,q+r}$.

From the clauses constructed in the previous paragraph, resolution can deduce $[z_{j,k}s_{u,k}]^1$ for $1 \le k \le p$, and hence $[z_{j+1,0}z_{j,p}s_{u,p}]^1$ (namely that $z_{j+1,0} = z_{j,p} \oplus s_{u,p}$). Furthermore, if $c_k = a_i$, and if we know that $z_{j+1,k-1} = z_{j,s} \oplus s_{u,t}$ where $s = p + i - 1$

and $t = p + k - i$, resolution can deduce that $z_{j+1,k} = z_{j,s+1} \oplus s_{u,t}$; a similar formula applies when $c_k = b_i$. Thus resolution yields $z_{j+1} \leftarrow z_j \oplus s_u$ as desired. Ultimately we deduce both z_n and $\bar{z}_n$ from the singleton clauses $s_v = l(v)$.

247. Eliminating x_2 from $\{12, \bar{1}2, \bar{1}\bar{2}\}$ gives $\{\bar{1}\}$; eliminating x_1 then gives $\emptyset$. So those five clauses are satisfiable.

248. We have $F(x_1, \ldots, x_n) = (x_n \vee A_1') \wedge \cdots \wedge (x_n \vee A_p') \wedge (\bar{x}_n \vee A_1'') \wedge \cdots \wedge (\bar{x}_n \vee A_q'') \wedge A_1''' \wedge \cdots \wedge A_r''' = (x_n \vee G') \wedge (\bar{x}_n \vee G'') \wedge G'''$, where $G' = A_1' \wedge \cdots \wedge A_p'$, $G'' = A_1'' \wedge \cdots \wedge A_q''$, and $G''' = A_1''' \wedge \cdots \wedge A_r'''$ depend only on $\{x_1, \ldots, x_{n-1}\}$. Hence $F' = (G' \vee G'') \wedge G'''$; and the clauses of $G' \vee G'' = \bigwedge_{i=1}^{p} \bigwedge_{j=1}^{q} (A_i' \vee A_j'')$ are the resolvents eliminating x_n.

249. After learning $C_7 = \bar{2}\bar{3}$ as in the text, we set $d \leftarrow 2$, $l_2 \leftarrow \bar{2}$, $C_j = 2\bar{3}$, learn $C_8 = \bar{3}$, and set $d \leftarrow 1$, $l_1 \leftarrow \bar{3}$. Then $l_2 \leftarrow \bar{4}$ (say); and $l_3 \leftarrow \bar{1}$, $l_4 \leftarrow \bar{2}$. Now $C_i = 1234$ has been falsified; after $l_4 \leftarrow 2$ and $C_j = 1\bar{2}$ we learn $C_9 = 134$, set $l_3 \leftarrow 1$, and learn $C_{10} = 134 \diamond \bar{1}3 = 34$. Finally $l_2 \leftarrow 4$, we learn $C_{11} = 3$; $l_1 \leftarrow 3$, and we learn $C_{12} = \epsilon$.

250. $l_1 \leftarrow 1$, $l_2 \leftarrow 3$, $l_3 \leftarrow \bar{2}$, $l_4 \leftarrow 4$; learn $\bar{1}2\bar{3}$; $l_3 \leftarrow 2$, $l_4 \leftarrow 4$; learn $\bar{1}\bar{2}\bar{3}$ and $\bar{1}\bar{3}$; $l_2 \leftarrow \bar{3}$, $l_3 \leftarrow \bar{2}$, $l_4 \leftarrow 4$; learn $\bar{1}23$; $l_3 \leftarrow 2$, $l_4 \leftarrow 4$; learn $\bar{1}\bar{2}3$, $\bar{1}3$, $\bar{1}$; $l_1 \leftarrow \bar{1}$, $l_2 \leftarrow 3$, $l_3 \leftarrow \bar{4}$, $l_4 \leftarrow 2$; learn $1\bar{3}4$; $l_3 \leftarrow 4$, $l_4 \leftarrow \bar{2}$, $l_4 \leftarrow 2$.

251. Algorithm I has the property that $\bar{l}_{i_1}, \ldots, \bar{l}_{i_{k-1}}, l_{i_k}$ are on the stack whenever the new clause $l_{i_1} \vee \cdots \vee l_{i_k}$ has been learned, if $i_1 < \cdots < i_k = d$ and step I4 returns to I2. These literals limit our ability to exploit the new clause; so it appears to be impossible to solve this problem without doing more resolutions than Stålmarck did.

However, we can proceed as follows. Let M_{imk}'' be the clause $x_{m1} \vee \cdots \vee x_{m(k-1)} \vee x_{ik} \vee \cdots \vee x_{i(m-1)} \vee \bar{x}_{im}$, for $1 \le i, k < m$. Using ij to stand for x_{ij}, the process for $m = 3$ begins by putting $\bar{1}\bar{1}$, $\bar{1}\bar{2}$, 13, $\bar{2}\bar{1}$, $\bar{2}\bar{2}$, 23, $\bar{3}\bar{1}$, $\bar{3}\bar{2}$, 33 on the stack. Then step I3 has $C_i = I_3$, step I4 has $C_j = M_{33}$; so step I5 learns $I_3 \diamond M_{33} = M_{32}$. Step I4 now changes $\bar{3}\bar{2}$ to 32 and chooses $C_j = T_{232}$; so I5 learns $M_{32} \diamond T_{232} = M_{232}''$. Step I4 changes $\bar{3}\bar{1}$ to 31 and chooses $C_j = T_{231}$; now we learn $M_{232}'' \diamond T_{231} = M_{231}''$. Next, we learn $M_{231}'' \diamond M_{23} = M_{22}$; and after changing $\bar{2}\bar{2}$ to 22 we also learn M_{21}.

The stack now contains $\bar{1}\bar{1}$, $\bar{1}\bar{2}$, 13, 21. We add $\bar{3}\bar{1}$, $\bar{3}\bar{2}$, and proceed to learn $M_{32} \diamond T_{132} = M_{132}''$, $M_{132}'' \diamond T_{131} = M_{131}''$, $M_{131}'' \diamond M_{13} = M_{12}$. The stack now contains $\bar{1}\bar{1}$, 12, and we've essentially reduced m from 3 to 2.

In a similar way, $O(m^2)$ resolutions will learn $M_{i(m-1)}$ for $i = m - 1, \ldots, 1$; and they'll leave $\bar{x}_{11}, \ldots, \bar{x}_{1(m-2)}, x_{1(m-1)}$ on the stack so that the process can continue.

252. No; large numbers of clauses such as $\bar{x}_{12} \vee \bar{x}_{23} \vee \cdots \vee \bar{x}_{89} \vee x_{19}$ are generated by the elimination process. Although these clauses are valid, they're not really helpful.

Exercise 373 proves, however, that the proof *is* completed in polynomial time if we restrict consideration to the transitivity clauses of exercise 228(!).

253. A conflict arises when we follow a chain of forced moves:

t	L_t	level	reason		t	L_t	level	reason
0	$\bar{6}$	1	Λ		5	$\bar{7}$	2	$\bar{5}7\bar{9}$
1	4	1	46		6	$\bar{1}$	2	$\bar{1}5\bar{9}$
2	5	2	Λ		7	8	2	678
3	$\bar{3}$	2	$\bar{3}4\bar{5}$		8	2	2	123
4	9	2	369		9	$\bar{2}$	2	$\bar{2}5\bar{8}$

Now $\bar{2}\bar{5}\bar{8} \rightarrow \bar{2}5\bar{8} \diamond 123 = 13\bar{5}\bar{8} \rightarrow 13\bar{5}67 \rightarrow 3\bar{5}679 \rightarrow 3\bar{5}69 \rightarrow 3\bar{5}6 \rightarrow \bar{4}5\bar{6}$; so we learn $\bar{4}56$ (which can be simplified to $\bar{5}6$, because $\bar{4}$ is "redundant" as explained in exercise 257).

Setting $L_2 \leftarrow \bar{5}$, with reason $\overline{456}$ or $\overline{56}$, now forces 7, $\bar{1}$, 3, 9, $\bar{2}$, $\bar{8}$, 8, all at level 1; this conflict soon allows us to learn the *unit* clause 6. (Next we'll inaugurate level 0, setting $L_0 \leftarrow 6$. No "reasons" need to be given at level 0.)

254. Deducing 3, 2, 4, $\bar{4}$ at level 1, it will find $\overline{24} \diamond \overline{43} = \overline{23}$ and $\overline{23} \diamond 2\bar{3} = \bar{3}$, learning $\bar{3}$. (Or it might learn $\bar{3}$ after deducing $\bar{2}$.) Then it will deduce $\bar{3}$, $\bar{1}$, 2, $\bar{4}$ at level 0.

255. For example, $\{\overline{124}, \overline{235}, 456, 45\bar{6}\}$. [Since the clause c' that is learned by the procedure described in the text contains just one literal l from the conflict level d, the trail position for $\bar{l}$ has been called a "unique implication point" (UIP). If l isn't the decision literal for its level, we could resolve c' with l's reason and find another UIP; but each new resolution potentially increases the b array and limits the amount of backjumping. Therefore we stop at the first UIP.]

256. If it is false, literals 50, 26, …, 30 are true; hence also $\overline{25}$, 23, and 29, a conflict. Consequently we can obtain '**' by starting with $\overline{23} \, \overline{26} \ldots \overline{50}$ and resolving with 23 25 27, 25 27 29, and $\overline{25} \, \overline{30} \ldots \overline{70}$. [Similarly, and more simply, one can learn (122) by resolving $\overline{11} \, \overline{16} \ldots \overline{56}$ with 31 61 91, 41 66 91, and 56 61 66.]

257. (a) Suppose $\bar{l}'$ on level $d' > 0$ is redundant. Then some l'' in the reason for l' is also on level d'; and l'' is either in c or redundant. Use induction on trail position.

(b) We can assume that the stamp value s used when resolving conflicts is a multiple of 3, and that all stamps are $\leq s$. Then we can stamp literal l with $S(|l|) \leftarrow s + 1$ if $\bar{l}$ is known to be redundant, or $s + 2$ if $\bar{l}$ is known to be nonredundant and not in c. (These stamps serve as a "memo cache" to avoid repeated work.) While building c we can also stamp *levels* as well as literals, setting $LS[d'] \leftarrow s$ if level d' has exactly one of the b_i, or $s + 1$ if it has more than one.

Then for $1 \leq j \leq r$, $\bar{b}_j$ is redundant if and only if $LS[lev(b_j)] = s + 1$ and $red(\bar{b}_j)$ is true, where $lev(l) = \text{VAL}(|l|) \gg 1$ and where $red(\bar{l})$ is the following recursive procedure: "If l is a decision literal, return false. Otherwise let $(l \vee \bar{a}_1 \vee \cdots \vee \bar{a}_k)$ be l's reason. For $1 \leq i \leq k$ with $lev(a_i) > 0$, if $S(|a_i|) = s + 2$ return false; if $S(|a_i|) < s$ and either $LS[lev(a_i)] < s$ or $red(\bar{a}_i)$ is false, set $S(|a_i|) \leftarrow s + 2$ and return false. But if none of these conditions hold, set $S(|l|) \leftarrow s + 1$ and return true."

[See Allen Van Gelder, *LNCS* **5584** (2009), 141–146.]

258. That statement is true in Table 3, but false in general. Indeed, consider the sequel to Table 3: The decision $L_{44} = \overline{57}$ causes the watch list of 57 to be examined, thus forcing 15, 78, and 87 (among other literals) in some order because of the clauses 15 57 36, 78 57 36, 87 57 27. Then $\overline{96}$ will be forced by the clause $\overline{96} \, \overline{87} \ldots \overline{15}$; and the second literal of that clause at the time of forcing will be $\overline{15}$, regardless of trail order, if the watched literals of that clause were $\overline{96}$ and $\overline{15}$ (making it invisible to $\overline{78}$ and $\overline{87}$).

259. $1 + \rho^6 + \rho^7 < \rho + \rho^2$ when $.7245 < \rho < .7548$. (There can in fact be any number of crossover points: Consider the polynomial $(1 - \rho - \rho^2)(1 - \rho^3 - \rho^6)(1 - \rho^9 - \rho^{18})$.)

260. First, to get a random permutation in the heap we can use a variant of Algorithm 3.4.2P: For $k \leftarrow 1, 2, \ldots, n$, let j be a random integer in $[0 \ldots k - 1]$ and set $\text{HEAP}[k - 1] \leftarrow \text{HEAP}[j]$, $\text{HEAP}[j] \leftarrow k$. Then set $\text{HLOC}(\text{HEAP}[j]) \leftarrow j$ for $0 \leq j < n$.

Next, set $F \leftarrow 0$ and $W_l \leftarrow 0$ for $2 \leq l \leq 2n + 1$ and $c \leftarrow 3$. Do the following for each input clause $l_0 l_1 \ldots l_{k-1}$: Terminate unsuccessfully if $k = 0$, or if $k = 1$ and $0 \leq \text{VAL}(|l_0|) \neq l_0 \& 1$. If $k = 1$ and $\text{VAL}(|l_0|) < 0$, set $\text{VAL}(|l_0|) \leftarrow l_0 \& 1$, $\text{TLOC}(|l_0|) \leftarrow F$, $F \leftarrow F + 1$. If $k > 1$, set $\text{MEM}[c + j] \leftarrow l_j$ for $0 \leq j < k$; also $\text{MEM}[c - 1] \leftarrow k$, $\text{MEM}[c - 2] \leftarrow W_{l_0}$, $W_{l_0} \leftarrow c$, $\text{MEM}[c - 3] \leftarrow W_{l_1}$, $W_{l_1} \leftarrow c$, $c \leftarrow c + k + 3$.

Finally, set $\texttt{MINL} \leftarrow \texttt{MAXL} \leftarrow c+2$ (allowing two cells for extra data in the preamble of the first learned clause). Of course we must also ensure that $\texttt{MEM}$ is large enough.

261. (Throughout this answer, l_j is an abbreviation for $\texttt{MEM}[c+j]$.) Set $q \leftarrow 0$ and $c \leftarrow W_{\bar{l}}$. While $c \neq 0$, do the following: Set $l' \leftarrow l_0$. If $l' \neq \bar{l}$ (hence $l_1 = \bar{l}$), set $c' \leftarrow l_{-3}$; otherwise set $l' \leftarrow l_1$, $l_0 \leftarrow l'$, $l_1 \leftarrow \bar{l}$, $c' \leftarrow l_{-2}$, $l_{-2} \leftarrow l_{-3}$, and $l_{-3} \leftarrow c'$. If $\texttt{VAL}(|l_0|) \geq 0$ and $\texttt{VAL}(|l_0|) + l_0$ is even (that is, if l_0 is true), perform the steps

$$\text{if } q \neq 0, \text{ set } \texttt{MEM}[q-3] \leftarrow c, \text{ else set } W_{\bar{l}} \leftarrow c; \text{ then set } q \leftarrow c. \qquad (*)$$

Otherwise set $j \leftarrow 2$; while $j < l_{-1}$ and $\texttt{VAL}(|l_j|) \geq 0$ and $\texttt{VAL}(|l_j|) + l_j$ is odd, set $j \leftarrow j+1$. If now $j < l_{-1}$, set $l_1 \leftarrow l_j$, $l_j \leftarrow \bar{l}$, $l_{-3} \leftarrow W_{l_1}$, $W_{l_1} \leftarrow c$. But if $j = l_{-1}$, do $(*)$ above; jump to C7 if $\texttt{VAL}(|l_0|) \geq 0$; otherwise set $L_F \leftarrow l_0$, etc. (see step C4) and $c \leftarrow c'$.

Finally, when $c = 0$, do $(*)$ above to terminate $\bar{l}$'s new watch list.

262. To delete $k = \texttt{HEAP}[0]$ in C6: Set $h \leftarrow h - 1$ and $\texttt{HLOC}(k) \leftarrow -1$. Stop if $h = 0$. Otherwise set $i \leftarrow \texttt{HEAP}[h]$, $\alpha \leftarrow \texttt{ACT}(i)$, $j \leftarrow 0$, $j' \leftarrow 1$, and do the following while $j' < h$: Set $\alpha' \leftarrow \texttt{ACT}(\texttt{HEAP}[j'])$; if $j' + 1 < h$ and $\texttt{ACT}(\texttt{HEAP}[j'+1]) > \alpha'$, set $j' \leftarrow j'+1$ and $\alpha' \leftarrow \texttt{ACT}(\texttt{HEAP}[j'])$; if $\alpha \geq \alpha'$, set $j' \leftarrow h$, otherwise set $\texttt{HEAP}[j] \leftarrow \texttt{HEAP}[j']$, $\texttt{HLOC}(\texttt{HEAP}[j']) \leftarrow j$, $j \leftarrow j'$, and $j' \leftarrow 2j+1$. Then set $\texttt{HEAP}[j] \leftarrow i$ and $\texttt{HLOC}(i) \leftarrow j$.

In C7, set $k \leftarrow |l|$, $\alpha \leftarrow \texttt{ACT}(k)$, $\texttt{ACT}(k) \leftarrow \alpha + \texttt{DEL}$, $j \leftarrow \texttt{HLOC}(k)$, and if $j > 0$ perform the "siftup" operation: "Looping repeatedly, set $j' \leftarrow (j-1) \gg 1$ and $i \leftarrow \texttt{HEAP}[j']$, exit if $\texttt{ACT}(i) \geq \alpha$, else set $\texttt{HEAP}[j] \leftarrow i$, $\texttt{HLOC}(i) \leftarrow j$, $j \leftarrow j'$, and exit if $j = 0$. Then set $\texttt{HEAP}[j] \leftarrow k$ and $\texttt{HLOC}(k) \leftarrow j$."

To insert k in C8, set $\alpha \leftarrow \texttt{ACT}(k)$, $j \leftarrow h$, $h \leftarrow h + 1$; if $j = 0$ set $\texttt{HEAP}[0] \leftarrow k$ and $\texttt{HLOC}(k) \leftarrow 0$; otherwise perform the siftup operation.

263. (This answer also sets the level stamps $\texttt{LS}[d]$ needed in answer 257, assuming that the $\texttt{LS}$ array is initially zero.) Let "bump l" mean "increase $\texttt{ACT}(|l|)$ by $\texttt{DEL}$" as in answer 262. Also let $blit(l)$ be the following subroutine: "If $\texttt{S}(|l|) = s$, do nothing. Otherwise set $\texttt{S}(|l|) \leftarrow s$, $p \leftarrow lev(l)$. If $p > 0$, bump l; then if $p = d$, set $q \leftarrow q+1$; else set $r \leftarrow r+1$, $b_r \leftarrow \bar{l}$, $d' \leftarrow \max(d', p)$, and if $\texttt{LS}[p] \leq s$ set $\texttt{LS}[p] \leftarrow s + [\texttt{LS}[p] = s]$."

When step C7 is entered from C4, assuming that $d > 0$, set $d' \leftarrow q \leftarrow r \leftarrow 0$, $s \leftarrow s + 3$, $\texttt{S}(|l_0|) \leftarrow s$, bump l_0, and do $blit(l_j)$ for $1 \leq j < k$. Also set $t \leftarrow \max(\texttt{TLOC}(|l_0|), \dots, \texttt{TLOC}(|l_{k-1}|))$. Then, while $q > 0$, set $l \leftarrow L_t$, $t \leftarrow t - 1$; if $\texttt{S}(|l|) = s$ then set $q \leftarrow q - 1$, and if $R_l \neq \Lambda$ let clause R_l be $l_0 l_1 \dots l_{k-1}$ and do $blit(l_j)$ for $1 \leq j < k$. Finally set $l' \leftarrow L_t$, and while $\texttt{S}(|l'|) \neq s$ set $t \leftarrow t - 1$ and $l' \leftarrow L_t$.

The new clause can now be checked for redundancies as in answer 257. To install it during step C9, there's a subtle point: *We must watch a literal that was defined on level d'.* Thus we set $c \leftarrow \texttt{MAXL}$, $\texttt{MEM}[c] \leftarrow \bar{l'}$, $k \leftarrow 0$, $j' \leftarrow 1$; and for $1 \leq j \leq r$ if $\texttt{S}(|b_j|) = s$ set $k \leftarrow k+1$ and do this: If $j' = 0$ or $lev(b_j) < d'$, set $\texttt{MEM}[c + k + j'] \leftarrow \bar{b}_j$; otherwise set $\texttt{MEM}[c+1] \leftarrow \bar{b}_j$, $j' \leftarrow 0$, $\texttt{MEM}[c-2] \leftarrow W_{\bar{l'}}$, $W_{\bar{l'}} \leftarrow c$, $\texttt{MEM}[c-3] \leftarrow W_{\bar{b}_j}$, $W_{\bar{b}_j} \leftarrow c$. Finally set $\texttt{MEM}[c-1] \leftarrow k+1$, $\texttt{MAXL} \leftarrow c + k + 6$.

264. We can maintain a "history code" array, setting H_F to 0, 2, 4, or 6 when L_F is set, and then using $H_t + (L_t \mathbin{\&} 1)$ as the move code that represents trail location t for $0 \leq t < F$. History codes 6, 4, and 0 are appropriate in steps C1, C4, and C6, respectively; in C9, use code 2 if l' was a decision literal, otherwise use code 6.

[These move codes do *not* increase lexicographically when the trail is flushed and restarted; hence they don't reveal progress as nicely as they do in the other algorithms.]

265. (1) A literal L_t on the trail with $G \leq t < F$ has become true, but the watch list of $\bar{L}_t$ has not yet been examined. (2) If l_0 is true, so that c is satisfied, step C4 doesn't remove c from the watch list of l_1 when l_1 becomes false. (This behavior is justified, because c won't be examined again until l_1 has become free during the backtracking step C8.) (3) A clause that becomes a reason for l_0 remains on the watch list of its false l_1. (4) During a full run, a clause that triggers a conflict is allowed to keep both of its watched literals false.

In general, a false watched literal must be defined at the highest trail level of all literals in its clause.

266. If $U < p$, where U is a uniform deviate between 0 and 1, do this: Set j to a random integer with $0 \le j < h$, and $k \leftarrow$ HEAP$[j]$. If $j = 0$, or if VAL$(k) \ge 0$, use the normal C6. Otherwise branch on k (and don't bother to remove k from the heap).

267. As in Algorithm L, let there be a sequential table BIMP(l) for each literal l, containing all literals l' such that $\bar{l} \vee l'$ is a binary clause. Furthermore, when the propagation algorithm sets $L_F \leftarrow l'$ because $l' \in$ BIMP(l), we may set $R_{l'} \leftarrow -l$, instead of using a positive clause number as the "reason." (Notice that a binary clause therefore need not be represented explicitly in MEM, if it is represented implicitly in the BIMP tables. The author's implementation of Algorithm C uses BIMP tables only to expedite binary clauses that appear in the original input. This has the advantage of simplicity, since the exact amount of necessary space can be allocated permanently for each table. Learned binary clauses are comparatively rare in practice; thus they can usually be handled satisfactorily with watched literals, instead of by providing the elaborate buddy-system scheme that was important in Algorithm L.)

Here, more precisely, is how the inner loop goes faster with BIMPs. We want to carry out binary propagations as soon as possible, because of their speed; hence we introduce a breadth-first exploration process analogous to (62):

$$\text{Set } H \leftarrow F; \text{ take account of } l' \text{ for all } l' \in \text{BIMP}(l_0);$$
$$\text{while } H < F, \text{ set } l_0 \leftarrow L_H, \, H \leftarrow H+1, \text{ and} \qquad (**)$$
$$\text{take account of } l' \text{ for all } l' \in \text{BIMP}(l_0).$$

Now "take account of l'" means "if l' is true, do nothing; if l' is false, go to C7 with conflict clause $\bar{l} \vee l'$; otherwise set $L_F \leftarrow l'$, TLOC$(|l'|) \leftarrow F$, VAL$(|l'|) \leftarrow 2d + (l' \& 1)$, $R_{l'} \leftarrow -l$, $F \leftarrow F+1$." We do $(**)$ just before setting $c \leftarrow c'$ in answer 261. Furthermore, we set $E \leftarrow F$ just after $G \leftarrow 0$ in step C1 and just after $F \leftarrow F+1$ in steps C6 and C9; and if $G \le E$ after $G \leftarrow G+1$ in step C4, we do $(**)$ with $l_0 \leftarrow \bar{l}$.

Answer 263 is modified in straightforward ways so that "clause R_l" is treated as if it were the binary clause $(l \vee \bar{l}')$ when R_l has the negative value $-l'$.

268. If MEM$[c-1] = k \ge 3$ is the size of clause c, and if $1 < j < k$, we can delete the literal l in MEM$[c+j]$ by setting $k \leftarrow k-1$, MEM$[c-1] \leftarrow k$, $l' \leftarrow$ MEM$[c+k]$, MEM$[c+j] \leftarrow l'$, and MEM$[c+k] \leftarrow l+f$, where f is a flag (typically 2^{31}) that distinguishes a deleted literal from a normal one. (This operation does not need to be done when the current level d is zero; hence we can assume that $k \ge 3$ and $j > 1$ before deletion. The flag is necessary so that global operations on the entire set of clauses, such as the purging algorithm, can pass safely over deleted literals. The final clause in MEM should be followed by 0, an element that's known to be unflagged.)

269. (a) If the current clause contains a literal $l = \bar{L}_t$ that is not in the trivial clause, where t is maximum, resolve the current clause with $R_{\bar{l}}$ and repeat.

(b) $(\bar{u}_1 \vee b_j) \wedge (l_j \vee \bar{l}_{j-1} \vee \bar{b}_j)$ for $1 \le j \le 9$, $(l_0 \vee \bar{u}_2 \vee \bar{u}_3) \wedge (\bar{l}_9 \vee \bar{l}_8 \vee \bar{b}_{10})$; $l' = l_0$.

(c) If $r \ge d' + \tau$, where τ is a positive parameter, learn the trivial clause instead of $(\bar{l}' \vee \bar{b}_1 \vee \cdots \vee \bar{b}_r)$. (The watched literals should be $\bar{l}'$ and $\bar{u}_{d'}$.)

Notice that this procedure will learn more than simple backtrack à la Algorithm D does, even when the trivial clause is *always* substituted (that is, even when $\tau = -\infty$), because it provides for backjumping when $d' < d + 1$.

270. (a) Consider the clauses $3\bar{2}$, $43\bar{2}$, $5\bar{4}3\bar{1}$, $6\bar{5}4\bar{1}$, $\bar{6}5\bar{4}$, with initial decisions $L_1 \leftarrow 1$, $L_2 \leftarrow 2$. Then $L_3 \leftarrow 3$ with reason $R_3 \leftarrow 3\bar{2}$; similarly $L_4 \leftarrow 4$, $L_5 \leftarrow 5$. If $L_6 \leftarrow 6$, the conflict clause $\bar{6}5\bar{4}$ allows us to strengthen R_6 to $5\bar{4}\bar{1}$; but if $L_6 \leftarrow \bar{6}$, with $R_{\bar{6}} \leftarrow \bar{6}5\bar{4}$, we don't notice that $6\bar{5}4\bar{1}$ can be strengthened. In either case we can, however, strengthen R_5 to $4\bar{3}\bar{1}$, before learning the clause $\bar{2}1$.

(b) After doing $blit(l_j)$ to the literals of R_l, we know that $R_l \setminus l$ is contained in $\{\bar{b}_1, \ldots, \bar{b}_r\}$ together with $q + 1$ unresolved false literals that have been stamped at level d. (Exercise 268 ensures that $p \neq 0$ within each $blit$.) Thus we can subsume clause R_l on the fly if $q + r + 1 < k$ and $q > 0$.

In such cases the procedure of answer 268 can be used to delete l from $c = R_l$. But there's a complication, because $l = l_0$ is a watched literal ($j = 0$ in that answer), and all other literals are false. After l is deleted, it will be essential to watch a false literal l' that is defined at trail level d. So we find the largest $j' \leq k$ such that $\mathtt{VAL}(\mathtt{MEM}[c + j']) \geq 2d$, and we set $l' \leftarrow \mathtt{MEM}[c + j']$. If $j' \neq k$, we also set $\mathtt{MEM}[c + j'] \leftarrow \mathtt{MEM}[c + k]$; we can assume that $j' > 1$. Finally, after setting $\mathtt{MEM}[c] \leftarrow l'$ and $\mathtt{MEM}[c + k] \leftarrow l + f$ as in answer 268, we also delete c from the watch list W_l, and insert it into $W_{l'}$.

[This enhancement typically saves 1%–10% of the running time, but sometimes it saves a lot more. It was discovered in 2009, independently by two different groups of researchers: See H. Han and F. Somenzi, *LNCS* **5584** (2009), 209–222; Y. Hamadi, S. Jabbour, and L. Saïs, *Int. Conf. Tools with Artif. Int.* (ICTAI) **21** (2009), 328–335.]

271. We shall check for discards only if the current clause C_i is not trivial (see exercise 269), and if the first literal of C_{i-1} does not appear in the trail. (Indeed, experience shows that almost every permissible discard falls into this category.) Thus, let C_{i-1} be $l_0 l_1 \ldots l_{k-1}$ where $\mathtt{VAL}(|l_0|) < 0$; we want to decide if $\{\bar{l}', \bar{b}_1, \ldots, \bar{b}_r\} \subseteq \{l_1, \ldots, l_{k-1}\}$.

The secret is to use the stamp fields that have already been set up. Set $j \leftarrow k-1$, $q \leftarrow r + 1$, and do the following while $q > 0$ and $j \geq q$: If $l_j = \bar{l}'$, or if $0 \leq \mathtt{VAL}(|l_j|) \leq 2d' + 1$ and $\mathtt{S}(|l_j|) = s$, set $q \leftarrow q - 1$; in any case set $j \leftarrow j - 1$. Then discard if $q = 0$.

272. Reflection isn't as easy to implement as it may seem, unless C is a unit clause, because C^R must be placed carefully in $\mathtt{MEM}$ and it must be consistent with the trail. Furthermore, experience shows that it's best not to learn the reflection of *every* learned clause, because excess clauses make unit propagation slower. The author has obtained encouraging results, however, by doing the following operations just before returning to C3 in step C9, whenever the length of C doesn't exceed a given parameter R:

Assign ranks to the literals of C^R by letting $\mathrm{rank}(l) = \infty$ if l is on the trail, $\mathrm{rank}(l) = d''$ if $\bar{l}$ is on the trail at level $d'' < d'$, $\mathrm{rank}(l) = d$ otherwise. Let u and v be two of the highest ranking literals, with $\mathrm{rank}(u) \geq \mathrm{rank}(v)$. Put them into the first two positions of C^R, so that they will be watched. Do nothing further if $\mathrm{rank}(v) > d'$. Otherwise, if $\mathrm{rank}(v) < d'$, backjump to level $\mathrm{rank}(v)$ and set $d' \leftarrow \mathrm{rank}(v)$. Then if $\mathrm{rank}(u) = \mathrm{rank}(v) = d'$, treat C^R as a conflict clause by going to step C7 with $c \leftarrow C^R$. (That is a rare event, but it can happen.) Otherwise, if u doesn't appear in the current trail, set $L_F \leftarrow u$, $\mathtt{TLOC}(|u|) \leftarrow F$, $R_u \leftarrow C^R$, $F \leftarrow F + 1$. (Possibly $F = E + 2$ now.)

(For example, this method with $R \leftarrow 6$ roughly halved the running time of $waerden(3, 10; 97)$ and $waerden(3, 13; 160)$ with parameters (193) except for $\rho \leftarrow .995$.)

A similar idea works with the clauses $langford(n)$, and in general whenever the input clauses have an automorphism of order 2.

273. (a) We can convert Algorithm C into a "clause learning machine" by keeping the process going after F reaches n in step C5: Instead of terminating, start over again by essentially going back to step C1, except that the current collection of clauses should be retained, and the OVAL polarities should be reset to random bits. Learned clauses of size K or less, where K is a parameter, should be written to a file. Stop when you've found a given number of short clauses, or when you've exceeded a given time limit.

For example, here's what happened when the author first tried to find $W(3, 13)$: Applying this algorithm to $waerden(3, 13; 158)$ with $K = 3$, and with a timeout limit of $30\,G\mu$ (gigamems), yielded the five clauses $65\,68\,70$, $68\,78\,81$, $78\,81\,90$, $78\,79\,81$, $79\,81\,82$. So fifteen clauses $65\,68\,70$, $66\,69\,71$, ..., $81\,83\,84$ could be added to $waerden(3, 13; 160)$, as well as their fifteen reflections $96\,93\,91$, $95\,92\,90$, ..., $80\,78\,77$. Then the algorithm "C^R" of exercise 272 proved this augmented set unsatisfiable after an additional $107\,G\mu$. In a second experiment, using $K = 2$ with $waerden(3, 13; 159)$ led to three binary clauses $76\,84$, $81\,86$, and $84\,88$. Shifting and reflecting gave twelve binary clauses, which in company with $waerden(3, 13; 160)$ were refuted by C^R in another $80\,G\mu$. (For comparison, Algorithm C^R refuted $waerden(3, 13; 160)$ unaided in about $120\,G\mu$, compared to about $270\,G\mu$ for both Algorithm C and Algorithm L.) Optimum strategies for learning useful clauses from satisfiable subproblems are far from clear, especially because running times are highly variable. But this method does show promise, especially on more difficult problems — when more time can be devoted to the preliminary learning.

(b) Short clauses that can be learned from satisfiable instances of, say, $X_0 \to X_1 \to \cdots \to X_{r-1}$, when X_0 is *not* required to be an initial state, can be shifted and used to help refute $X_0 \to X_1 \to \cdots \to X_r$.

274. With care, circular reasoning can (and must) be avoided. But the author's elaborate experiments with such ideas (and with the related notion of "better conflicts") were disappointing; they didn't beat the running time of the simpler algorithm. However, an intriguing idea by Allen Van Gelder [*Journal on Satisfiability, Boolean Modeling and Computation* **8** (2012), 117–122] shows promise.

275. When a solution has been found, let k be minimum such that $x_k = 1$ and the value of x_k has not been assigned at level 0. If no such k exists, we stop. Otherwise we are entitled to force variables x_1 through x_{k-1} all to have their current values, at level 0, because we know that this doesn't produce an unsatisfiable problem. So we fix those values, and we restart the solution process at level 1 with the tentative decision '$x_k = 0$'. If a conflict occurs, we'll know that $x_k = 1$ at level 0; if not, we'll have a solution with $x_k = 0$. In either case we can increase k. (This method is considerably better than that of answer 109, because *every learned clause remains valid*.)

276. True. Unit propagation essentially transforms $F \wedge L$ into $F \mid L$.

277. Otherwise $F \wedge C_1 \wedge \cdots \wedge C_{t-1} \vdash_1 \epsilon$ fails (unit propagation wouldn't start).

278. For example, $(46, \bar{5}6, \bar{5}4, 6, 4, \epsilon)$. (Six steps are necessary.)

279. True, because the dependency digraph contains a literal l with $l \longrightarrow^* \bar{l} \longrightarrow^* l$.

280. (a) They're satisfied if and only if $x_1 \ldots x_n$ has at least j 0s and at least k 1s. [The problem $cook(k, k)$ was introduced by Stephen A. Cook (unpublished) in 1971.]

(b) Take all positive $(j - t)$-clauses on $\{1, \ldots, n - 1 - t\}$ for $t = 1, 2, \ldots, j$.

(c) Suppose the very first decision is $L_0 \leftarrow x_n$. The algorithm will proceed to act as if the input were $cook(j, k) \mid x_n = cook(j, k - 1)$. Furthermore, with these clauses, every clause that it learns initially will include $\bar{x}_n$. Therefore, by induction, the unit clause $(\bar{x}_n)$ will be learned clause number $\binom{n-2}{j-1}$. All previously learned clauses are subsumed by this one, hence they're no longer relevant. The remaining problem is $cook(j,k) \mid \bar{x}_n = cook(j-1,k)$; so the algorithm will finish after learning $\binom{n-2}{j-2}$ more.

Similarly, if the first decision is $L_0 \leftarrow \bar{x}_n$, the $\binom{n-2}{j-2}$th learned clause will be (x_n).

281. Stålmarck's refutation corresponds to the sequence $(M'_{jk1}, M'_{jk2}, \ldots, M'_{jk(k-1)}, M_{j(k-1)})$ for $j = 1, \ldots, k-1$, for $k = m, m-1, \ldots, 1$. ($M'_{jk(k-1)}$ can be omitted.)

282. First learn the exclusion clauses (17). In the next clauses we shall write a_j, b_j, $\ldots$, as shorthand for $a_{j,p}$, $b_{j,p}$, $\ldots$, where p is a particular color, $1 \leq p \leq 3$. Notice that the $12q$ edges appear in $4q$ triangles, namely $\{b_j, c_j, d_j\}$, $\{a_j, a_{j'}, b_{j'}\}$, $\{f_j, e_{j'}, c_{j'}\}$, $\{e_j, f_{j'}, d_{j'}\}$, for $1 \leq j \leq q$, where j' is $j+1$ (modulo q). For every such triangle $\{u, v, w\}$, learn $(\bar{u}_{p'} \vee v_p \vee w_p)$ and then $(u_p \vee v_p \vee w_p)$, where p' is $p+1$ (modulo 3).

Now for $j = 1, 2, \ldots, q$, learn $(a_j \vee f_j \vee a_{j'} \vee e_{j'})$, $(a_j \vee e_j \vee a_{j'} \vee f_{j'})$, $(e_j \vee f_j \vee e_{j'} \vee f_{j'})$, $(\bar{a}_j \vee \bar{e}_j \vee \bar{e}_{j'})$, $(\bar{a}_j \vee \bar{f}_j \vee \bar{f}_{j'})$, $(\bar{e}_j \vee \bar{f}_j \vee \bar{a}_{j'})$, as well as eighteen more:

$$(\bar{u}_1 \vee \bar{v}_1 \vee u'_j \vee v'_j), (\bar{u}_2 \vee \bar{v}_2 \vee u'_{j'} \vee v'_{j'}), \quad \text{if } j \geq 3 \text{ is odd};$$
$$(\bar{u}_1 \vee \bar{v}_1 \vee \bar{u}'_j), (\bar{u}_2 \vee \bar{v}_2 \vee \bar{u}'_{j'}), \quad \text{if } j \geq 3 \text{ is even};$$

here $u, v \in \{a, e, f\}$ and $u', v' \in \{a, e, f\}$ yield 3×3 choices of (u, v, u', v'). Then we're ready to learn $(\bar{a}_j \vee \bar{e}_j)$, $(\bar{a}_j \vee \bar{f}_j)$, $(\bar{e}_j \vee \bar{f}_j)$ for $j \in \{1, 2\}$ and $(a_j \vee e_j \vee f_j \vee a_{j'})$, $(a_j \vee e_j \vee f_j)$ for $j \in \{1, q\}$. All of these clauses are to be learned for $1 \leq p \leq 3$.

Next, for $j = q, q-1, \ldots, 2$, learn $(\bar{a}_j \vee \bar{e}_j)$, $(\bar{a}_j \vee \bar{f}_j)$, $(\bar{e}_j \vee \bar{f}_j)$ for $1 \leq p \leq 3$ and then $(a_{j-1} \vee e_{j-1} \vee f_{j-1} \vee a_j)$, $(a_{j-1} \vee e_{j-1} \vee f_{j-1})$ for $1 \leq p \leq 3$. We have now established all clauses in the hint.

The endgame consists of the following for $1 \leq p \leq 3$: For all choices of p' and p'' with $\{p, p', p''\} = \{1, 2, 3\}$ (thus two choices), and for $j = 2, 3, \ldots, q$, learn three clauses

$$(\bar{a}_{1,p} \vee \bar{e}_{1,p'} \vee \bar{a}_{j,p} \vee e_{j,p''}), (\bar{a}_{1,p} \vee \bar{e}_{1,p'} \vee \bar{a}_{j,p'} \vee e_{j,p}), (\bar{a}_{1,p} \vee \bar{e}_{1,p'} \vee \bar{a}_{j,p''} \vee e_{j,p'}), \quad j \text{ even};$$
$$(\bar{a}_{1,p} \vee \bar{e}_{1,p'} \vee \bar{a}_{j,p} \vee e_{j,p'}), (\bar{a}_{1,p} \vee \bar{e}_{1,p'} \vee \bar{a}_{j,p'} \vee e_{j,p''}), (\bar{a}_{1,p} \vee \bar{e}_{1,p'} \vee \bar{a}_{j,p''} \vee e_{j,p}), \quad j \text{ odd};$$

then learn $(\bar{a}_{1,p} \vee \bar{e}_{1,p'})$. Finally learn $\bar{a}_{1,p}$.

[Not all of these clauses are actually necessary. For example, the exclusion clauses for b's, c's, and d's aren't used. This certificate doesn't assume that the symmetry-breaking unit clauses $b_{1,1} \wedge c_{1,2} \wedge d_{1,3}$ of $fsnark(q)$ are present; indeed, those clauses don't help it much. The actual clauses learned by Algorithm C are considerably longer and somewhat chaotic (indeed mysterious); it's hard to see just where an "aha" occurs!]

283. A related question is to ask whether the expected length of learned clauses is $O(1)$ as $q \to \infty$.

284. It's convenient to represent each unit clause (l) in $F \cup C_1 \cup \cdots \cup C_t$ as if it were the binary clause $(l \vee \bar{x}_0)$, where x_0 is a new variable that is always true. We borrow some of the data structures of Algorithm C, namely the trail array L, the reason array R, and the fields TLOC, S, VAL associated with each variable. We set $\text{VAL}(k) = 0$, 1, or -1 when x_k has been forced true, forced false, or not forced, respectively.

To verify the clause $C_i = (a_1 \vee \cdots \vee a_k)$, we begin with $\text{VAL}(j) \leftarrow 0$ for $0 \leq j \leq n$, $L_0 \leftarrow 0$, $L_1 \leftarrow \bar{a}_1, \ldots, L_k \leftarrow \bar{a}_k$, $E \leftarrow F \leftarrow k+1$, $G \leftarrow 0$, and $\text{VAL}(|L_p|) \leftarrow L_p \,\&\, 1$ for $0 \leq p < F$; then we carry out unit propagation as in Algorithm C, expecting to reach a conflict before $G = F$. (Otherwise verification fails.)

A conflict arises when a clause $c = l_0 \ldots l_{k-1}$ forces l_0 at a time when $\bar{l}_0$ has already been forced. Now we mimic step C7 (see exercise 263), but the operations are much simpler: Mark c, stamp $\text{S}(|l_j|) \leftarrow i$ for $0 \leq j < k$, and set $p \leftarrow \max(\text{TLOC}(|l_1|), \ldots,$

$\text{TLOC}(|l_{k-1}|)$). Now, while $p \geq E$, we set $l \leftarrow L_p$, $p \leftarrow p - 1$, and if $\text{S}(|l|) = i$ we also "resolve with the reason of l" as follows: Let clause R_l be $l_0 l_1 \ldots l_{k-1}$, mark R_l, and set $\text{S}(|l_j|) \leftarrow i$ for $1 \leq j < k$.

[Wetzler, Heule, and Hunt have suggested an interesting improvement, which will often mark significantly fewer clauses at the expense of a more complicated algorithm: Give preference to already-marked clauses when doing the unit propagations, just as Algorithm L prefers binary implications to the implications of longer clauses (see (62)).]

285. (a) $j = 77$, $s_{77} = 12 + 2827$, $m_{77} = 59$, $b_{77} = 710$.

(b) $j = 72$, $s_{72} = 12 + 2048$, $m_{72} = 99 + 243 + 404 + 536 = 1282$, $b_{72} = 3 + 40 + 57 + 86 = 186$. (The RANGE statistic is rather coarse when $\alpha = \frac{1}{2}$, because many different signatures yield the same value.)

(c) $j = 71$, $s_{71} = 12 + 3087$, $m_{71} = 243$, $b_{71} = 40$.

286. The maximum, 738, is achieved uniquely by the RANGE-oriented solution with $\alpha = \frac{15}{16}$, except that we can optionally include also the signatures $(6, 0)$ and $(7, 0)$ for which $a_{pq} = 0$. [This solution optimizes the worst case of clause selection, because the stated problem implicitly assumes that the secondary heuristic is bad. If we assume, however, that the choice of tie-breakers based on clause activity is at least as good as a random choice, then the expected number $738 + 45 \cdot \frac{10}{59} \approx 745.6$ from $\alpha = \frac{15}{16}$ is *not* as good as the expected number $710 + 287 \cdot \frac{57}{404} \approx 750.5$ from $\alpha = \frac{9}{16}$.]

287. When a conflict is detected in step C7 (with $d > 0$), keep going as in step C3; but remember the first clause C_d that detected a conflict at each level d.

Eventually step C5 will find $F = n$. That's when clauses get their RANGE scores, if we're doing a full run because we want to purge some of them. (Sometimes, however, it's also useful to do a few full runs at the very beginning, or just after a restart, because some valuable clauses might be learned.)

New clauses can be learned in the usual way from the remembered clauses C_d, in decreasing order of d, except that "trivial" clauses (exercise 269) are considered only at the lowest such level. We must keep track of the minimum backjump level d', among all of these conflicts. And if several new clauses have the same d', we must remember all of the literals that will be placed at the end of the trail after we eventually jump back.

288. Step C5 initiates a full run, then eventually finds $F = n$. At this point we're done, in the unlikely event that no conflicts have arisen. Otherwise we set $\text{LS}[d] \leftarrow 0$ for $0 \leq d < n$ and $m_j \leftarrow 0$ for $1 \leq j < 256$. The activity $\text{ACT}(c)$ of each learned clause c has been maintained in $\text{MEM}[c - 5]$, as a 32-bit floating point number. The following steps compute $\text{RANGE}(c)$, which will be stored in $\text{MEM}[c - 4]$ as an integer, for all learned c in increasing order, assuming that c's literals are $l_0 l_1 \ldots l_{s-1}$:

If $R_{l_0} = c$, set $\text{RANGE}(c) \leftarrow 0$. Otherwise set $p \leftarrow r \leftarrow 0$, and do the following for $0 \leq k < s$: Set $v \leftarrow \text{VAL}(|l_k|)$. If $v < 2$ and $v + l_k$ is even, set $\text{RANGE}(c) \leftarrow 256$ and exit the loop on k (because c is permanently satisfied, hence useless). If $v \geq 2$ and $\text{LS}[lev(l_k)] < c$, set $\text{LS}[lev(l_k)] \leftarrow c$ and $r \leftarrow r + 1$. Then if $v \geq 2$ and $\text{LS}[lev(l_k)] = c$ and $l_k + v$ is even, set $\text{LS}[lev(l_k)] \leftarrow c + 1$ and $p \leftarrow p + 1$. After k reaches s, set $r \leftarrow \min(\lfloor 16(p + \alpha(r - p)) \rfloor, 255)$, $\text{RANGE}(c) \leftarrow r$, and $m_r \leftarrow m_r + 1$.

Now resolve conflicts (see answer 287), giving $\text{ACT}(c) \leftarrow 0$ and $\text{RANGE}(c) \leftarrow 0$ to all newly learned clauses c, and jump back to trail level 0. (A round of purging is a major event, something like spring cleaning. It is possible that $d' = 0$, in which case one or more literals have been appended to trail level 0 and their consequences have not yet been explored.) Find the median range j as defined in (124), where T is half the total current number of learned clauses. If $j < 256$ and $T > s_j$, find $h = T - s_j$ clauses with RANGE$(c) = j$ and ACT(c) as small as possible, and bump their range up to $j + 1$. (This can be done by putting the first $m_j - h$ of them into a heap, then repeatedly bumping the least active as the remaining h are encountered; see exercise 6.1–22.)

Finally, go again through all the learned clauses c, in order of increasing c, ignoring c if RANGE$(c) > j$, otherwise copying it into a new location $c' \le c$. (Permanently false literals, which are currently defined at level 0, can also be removed at this time; thus the clause's size in MEM$[c' - 1]$ might be less than MEM$[c - 1]$. It is possible, but unlikely, that a learned clause becomes reduced to a unit in this way, or even that it becomes empty.) The activity score in MEM$[c - 5]$ should be copied into MEM$[c' - 5]$; but RANGE(c) and the watch links in MEM$[c - 2]$ and MEM$[c - 3]$ needn't be copied.

When copying is complete, all the watch lists should be recomputed from scratch, as in answer 260, including original clauses as well as the learned clauses that remain.

289. By induction, $y_k = (2 - 2^{1-k})\Delta + (2(k - 2) + 2^{2-k})\delta$ for all $k \ge 0$.

290. Set $k \leftarrow$ HEAP$[0]$; then if VAL$(k) \ge 0$, delete k from the heap as in answer 262, and repeat this loop.

291. OVAL(49) will be the even number 36, because of the propagations on level 18 that led to (115).

292. If AGILITY $\ge 2^{32} - 2^{13}$, then (127) either subtracts $2^{19} - 1$ or adds 1. Hence there's a minuscule chance that AGILITY will overflow by passing from $2^{32} - 1$ to 2^{32} (zero). (But overflow won't be a calamity even if — unbelievably — it happens. So this is one "bug" in the author's program that he will *not* try to fix.)

293. Maintain integers u_f, v_f, and θ_f, where θ_f has 64 bits. Initially $u_f = v_f = M_f = 1$. When $M \ge M_f$ in step C5, do this: Set $M_f \leftarrow M_f + v_f$. If $u_f \& -u_f = v_f$, set $u_f \leftarrow u_f + 1$, $v_f \leftarrow 1$, $\theta_f \leftarrow 2^{32}\psi$; otherwise set $v_f \leftarrow 2v_f$ and $\theta_f \leftarrow \theta_f + (\theta_f \gg 4)$. Flush if AGILITY $\le \theta_f$.

294. We have, for example, $g_{1100} = \frac{z}{3}(g_{0100} + g_{1000} + g_{1110})$, and $g_{01*1} = 1$. The solution is $g_{00*1} = g_{01*0} = g_{11*1} = A/D$, $g_{00*0} = g_{10*1} = g_{11*0} = B/D$, $g_{10*0} = C/D$, where $A = 3z - z^2 - z^3$, $B = z^2$, $C = z^3$, $D = 9 - 6z - 3z^2 + z^3$. Hence the overall generating function is $g = (6A + 6B + 2C + 2D)/(16D)$; and we find $g'(1) = 33/4$, $g''(1) = 147$. Thus mean$(g) = 8.25$, var$(g) = 87.1875$, and the standard deviation is ≈ 9.3.

295. Consider all $3\binom{n}{3}$ clauses $\bar{x}_i \lor x_j \lor x_k$ for distinct $\{i, j, k\}$, plus two additional clauses $(\bar{x}_1 \lor \bar{x}_2 \lor \bar{x}_3) \land (\bar{x}_4 \lor \bar{x}_5 \lor \bar{x}_6)$ to make the solution $0 \ldots 0$ unique. Only the two latter clauses cause the variables X_t and Y_t in the proof of Theorem U to deviate from each other. [C. Papadimitriou, *Computational Complexity* (1994), Problem 11.5.6. These clauses spell trouble for a lot of other SAT algorithms too.]

296. The hinted ratio $2(2p+q+1)(2p+q)/(9(p+1)(p+q+1))$ is ≈ 1 when $p \approx q$ (more precisely when $p = q - 7 + O(1/q)$). And $f(q + 1, q + 1)/f(q, q) = 2(n - q)(3q + 3)^3/(27(q+1)^2(2q+2)^2)$ is ≈ 1 when $q \approx n/3$. Finally, $f(n/3, n/3) = \frac{3}{4\pi n}(3/4)^n(1+O(1/n))$ by Stirling's approximation, when $n = 3q$.

297. (a) $G_q(z) = (z/3)^q C(2z^2/9)^q = G(z)^q$ where $G(z) = (3 - \sqrt{9 - 8z^2})/(4z)$, by Eqs. 7.2.1.6–(18) and (24). [See *Algorithmica* **32** (2002), 620–622.]

(b) $G_q(1) = 2^{-q}$ is the probability that Y_t actually reaches 0, for some finite t.

(c) If the Y process does stop, $G_q(z)/G_q(1) = (2G(z))^q$ describes the distribution of stopping times. Hence $G_q'(1)/G_q(1) = 2qG'(1) = 3q$ is the mean length of the random walk, *given* that it terminates. (The variance, incidentally, is $24q$. A random Y-walker who doesn't finish quickly is probably doomed to wander forever.)

(d) The generating function for T, the stopping time of the Y process, is $T(z) = \sum_q \binom{n}{q} 2^{-n} G_q(z)$; and T is finite with probability $T(1) = (\frac{3}{4})^n$ by (b). If we restrict consideration to such scenarios, the mean $T'(1)/T(1)$ is n; and Markov's inequality tells us that $\Pr(T \geq N \mid \text{the algorithm terminates}) \leq n/N$.

(e) The algorithm succeeds with probability $p > \Pr(T < N) \geq (1 - n/N)(3/4)^n$, when it is given satisfiable clauses. So it fails after $K(4/3)^n$ trials with probability less than $\exp(K(4/3)^n \ln(1 - p)) < \exp(-K(4/3)^n p) < \exp(-K/2)$ when $N = 2n$.

298. Change $1/3$ and $2/3$ in (129) to $1/k$ and $(k-1)/k$. The effect is to change $G(z)$ to $(z/k)C((k-1)z^2/k^2)$, with $G(1) = 1/(k-1)$ and $G'(1) = k/((k-1)(k-2))$. As before, $T(1) = 2^{-n}(1 + G(1))^n$ and $T'(1)/T(1) = nG'(1)/(1 + G(1))$. So the generalized Corollary W gives success probability $> 1 - e^{-K/2}$ when we apply Algorithm P $K(2 - 2/k)^n$ times with $N = \lfloor 2n/(k-2) \rfloor$.

299. In this case $G(z) = (1 - \sqrt{1 - z^2})/z$; thus $G(1) = T(1) = 1$. But $G'(1) = \infty$, so we must use a different method. The probability of failure if $N = n^2$ is

$$\frac{1}{2^n} \sum_{p,q} \binom{n}{q} \frac{q}{2p+q} \binom{2p+q}{p} \frac{[2p+q>n^2]}{2^{2p+q}} = \sum_{t>n^2} \frac{2^{-n-t}}{t} \sum_{p} \binom{n}{t-2p} \binom{t}{p}(t-2p)$$

$$\leq \sum_{t>n^2} \frac{2^{-n-t}}{t} \binom{t}{\lfloor t/2 \rfloor} \sum_{p} \binom{n}{t-2p}(t-2p) = \frac{n}{4} \sum_{t>n^2} \frac{2^{-t}}{t} \binom{t}{\lfloor t/2 \rfloor}$$

$$< \frac{n}{4} \sum_{t>n^2} \sqrt{\frac{2}{\pi t^3}} = \frac{n}{\sqrt{8\pi}} \int_{n^2}^{\infty} \frac{dx}{\lceil x \rceil^{3/2}} < \frac{n}{\sqrt{8\pi}} \int_{n^2}^{\infty} \frac{dx}{x^{3/2}} = \frac{1}{\sqrt{2\pi}}.$$

[See C. Papadimitriou, *Computational Complexity* (1994), Theorem 11.1.]

300. In this algorithm, variables named with uppercase letters (except C and N) denote bit vectors of some fixed size (say 64); each bit position represents a separate trial. The notation U_r stands for a vector of *random* bits, each of which is 1 with probability $1/r$, independently of all other bits and all previous U's. The maximum number of flips per bit position in this variant of Algorithm P is only *approximately* equal to N.

P1'. [Initialize.] Set $X_i \leftarrow U_2$ for $1 \leq i \leq n$. Also set $t \leftarrow 0$.

P2'. [Begin pass.] Set $Z \leftarrow 0$ and $j \leftarrow 0$. (Flipped positions are remembered in Z.)

P3'. [Move to next clause.] If $j = m$, go to P5'. Otherwise set $j \leftarrow j + 1$.

P4'. [Flip.] Let C_j be the clause $(l_1 \vee \cdots \vee l_k)$. Set $Y \leftarrow \bar{L}_1 \& \cdots \& \bar{L}_k$, where L_i denotes X_h if $l_i = x_h$ and L_i denotes $\bar{X}_h$ if $l_i = \bar{x}_h$. (Thus Y has 1s in positions that violate clause C_j.) Set $Z \leftarrow Z \mid Y$ and $t \leftarrow t + (Y \& 1)$. Then for $r = k, k-1, \ldots, 2$ set $Y' \leftarrow Y \& U_r$, $L_r \leftarrow L_r \oplus Y'$, $Y \leftarrow Y - Y'$. Finally set $L_1 \leftarrow L_1 \oplus Y$ and return to P3'.

P5'. [Done?] If $Z \neq -1$, terminate successfully: One solution is given by the bits $(X_1 \& B) \ldots (X_n \& B)$, where $B = \bar{Z} \& (Z + 1)$. Otherwise, if $t > N$, terminate unsuccessfully. Otherwise return to P2'. ∎

The shenanigans in step P4' have the effect of flipping the offending bits of each literal with probability $1/k$, thus distributing the 1s of Y in an unbiased fashion.

301. In practice we can assume that all clauses have limited size, so that (say) $k \leq 4$ in step P4'. The clauses can also be sorted by size.

A traditional random number generator produces bits U_2; and one can use $U_2 \& U_2$ to get U_4. The method of exercise 3.4.1–25 can be used for other cases; for example,

$$U_2 \& (U_2 \mid (U_2 \& (U_2 \mid (U_2 \& (U_2 \mid (U_2 \& (U_2 \mid (U_2 \& U_2)))))))) $$

is a sufficiently close approximation to U_3. The random numbers needed in step P1′ must be of top quality; but those used in step P4′ don't have to be especially accurate, because most of their bits are irrelevant. We can precompute the latter, making tables of 2^d values for each of U_2, U_3, U_4, and running through them cyclically by means of table indices U2P, U3P, U4P as in the code below, where $\text{UMASK} = 2^{d+3} - 1$. The values of U2P, U3P, and U4P should be initialized to (truly) random bits whenever step P2′ starts a new pass over the clauses.

Here is sample code for the inner loop, step P4′, for clauses with $k = 3$. The octabyte in memory location $L + 8(i-1)$ is the address in memory where X_h is stored, plus 1 if it should be complemented; for example, if l_2 is $\bar{x}_3$, the address $X + 3 \times 8 + 1$ will be in location $L + 8$, where L is a global register. Register mone holds the constant -1.

LDOU	$1,L,0	addr(L_1)	XOR	$9,$6,$0	$\bar{L}_3$	STOU	$6,$3,0	$\lvert L_3\rvert \oplus Y'$
LDOU	$4,$1,0	$\lvert L_1\rvert$	AND	$7,$7,$8		SUBU	$7,$7,$0	
LDOU	$2,L,8	addr(L_2)	AND	$7,$7,$9	Y	LDOU	$0,U2,U2P	
LDOU	$5,$2,0	$\lvert L_2\rvert$	OR	Z,Z,$7	$Z\,\vert\,Y$	ADD	U2P,U2P,8	
LDOU	$3,L,16	addr(L_3)	AND	$0,$7,1	$Y\,\&\,1$	AND	U2P,U2P,UMASK	
LDOU	$6,$3,0	$\lvert L_3\rvert$	ADD	T,T,$0	new t	AND	$0,$0,$7	$U_2\,\&\,Y$
ZSEV	$0,$1,mone		LDOU	$0,U3,U3P		XOR	$5,$5,$0	
XOR	$7,$4,$0	$\bar{L}_1$	ADD	U3P,U3P,8		STOU	$5,$2,0	$\lvert L_2\rvert \oplus Y'$
ZSEV	$0,$2,mone		AND	U3P,U3P,UMASK		SUBU	$7,$7,$0	
XOR	$8,$5,$0	$\bar{L}_2$	AND	$0,$0,$7	$U_3\,\&\,Y$	XOR	$4,$4,$7	
ZSEV	$0,$3,mone		XOR	$6,$6,$0		STOU	$4,$1,0	$\lvert L_1\rvert \oplus Y$ ∎

302. Assume that literals are represented internally as in Algorithm A, and that all clauses have strictly distinct literals. An efficient implementation actually requires more arrays than are stated in the text: We need to know exactly which clauses contain any given literal, just as we need to know the literals of any given clause.

> **W4.** [Choose l.] Set $g \leftarrow [U \geq p]$, $c \leftarrow \infty$, $j \leftarrow z \leftarrow 0$, and do the following while $j < k$: Set $j \leftarrow j + 1$. Then if $c_{\lvert l_j\rvert} < c$ and either $c_{\lvert l_j\rvert} = 0$ or $g = 1$, set $c \leftarrow c_{\lvert l_j\rvert}$ and $z \leftarrow 0$. Then if $c_{\lvert l_j\rvert} \leq c$, set $z \leftarrow z + 1$, and if $zU < 1$ also set $l \leftarrow l_j$. (Here each random fraction U should be independent of the others.)

> **W5.** [Flip l.] Set $s \leftarrow 0$. For each j such that C_j contains l, make clause C_j happier as follows: Set $q \leftarrow k_j$, $k_j \leftarrow q+1$; and if $q = 0$, set $s \leftarrow s+1$ and delete C_j from the f array (see below); or if $q = 1$, decrease the cost of C_j's critical variable (see below). Then set $c_{\lvert l\rvert} \leftarrow s$ and $x_{\lvert l\rvert} \leftarrow \bar{x}_{\lvert l\rvert}$. For each j such that C_j contains $\bar{l}$, make clause C_j sadder as follows: Set $q \leftarrow k_j - 1$, $k_j \leftarrow q$; and if $q = 0$, insert C_j into the f array (see below); or if $q = 1$, increase the cost of C_j's critical variable (see below). Set $t \leftarrow t + 1$ and return to W2. ∎

To insert C_j into f, we set $f_r \leftarrow j$, $w_j \leftarrow r$, and $r \leftarrow r + 1$ (as in step W1). To delete it, we set $h \leftarrow w_j$, $r \leftarrow r - 1$, $f_h \leftarrow f_r$, $w_{f_r} \leftarrow h$.

Whenever we want to update the cost of C_j's critical variable in step W5, we know that C_j has exactly one true literal. Thus, if the literals of C_j appear sequentially in a master array M, it's easy to locate the critical variable $x_{\lvert M_i\rvert}$: We simply set $i \leftarrow \text{START}(j)$; then while M_i is false (namely while $x_{\lvert M_i\rvert} = M_i\ \&\ 1$), set $i \leftarrow i + 1$.

A slight refinement is advantageous when we will be increasing $c_{\lvert M_i\rvert}$: If $i \neq \text{START}(j)$, swap $M_{\text{START}(j)} \leftrightarrow M_i$. This change significantly shortens the search when $c_{\lvert M_i\rvert}$ is subsequently decreased. (In fact, it reduced the total running time by more than 5% in the author's experiments with random 3SAT problems.)

303. In this case $D = 3 - z - z^2 = A/z$, and we have $g'(1) = 3$, $g''(1) = 73/4$. Thus mean$(g) = 3$ and var$(g) = 12.25 = 3.5^2$.

304. If $\nu x = x_1 + \cdots + x_n = a$, there are $a(n - a)$ unsatisfied clauses; hence there are two solutions, $0\ldots0$ and $1\ldots1$. If $x_1\ldots x_n$ isn't a solution, Algorithm P will change a to $a \pm 1$, each with probability $\frac{1}{2}$. Thus the probability generating function g_a for future flips is 1 when $a = 0$ or $a = n$, otherwise it is $z(g_{a-1} + g_{a+1})/2$. And the overall generating function is $g = \sum_a \binom{n}{a} g_a/2^n$. Clearly $g_a = g_{n-a}$.

Exercise MPR–105 determines g_a and proves that the mean number of flips, $g'_a(1)$, is $a(n - a)$ for $0 \le a \le n$. Thus $g'(1) = 2^{-n} \sum_{a=0}^{n} \binom{n}{a} g'_a(1) = \frac{1}{2}\binom{n}{2}$.

Turning now to Algorithm W, again with $x_1 + \cdots + x_n = a$, the cost of x_i is $a - 1$ when $x_i = 1$, $n - a - 1$ when $x_i = 0$. Therefore $g_1 = g_{n-1} = z$ in this case. And for $2 \le a \le n - 2$, $a \ne n/2$, we will move closer to a solution with probability q and farther from a solution with probability p, where $p + q = 1$ and $p = p'/2 \le 1/2$; here p' is the greed-avoidance parameter of Algorithm W. Thus for $2 \le a \le n/2$ we have $g_a = g_{n-a} = z(qg_{a-1} + pg_{a+1})$.

If $p' = 0$, so that the walk is 100% greedy, Algorithm W zooms in on the solution, with $g_a = z^a$. Exercise 1.2.6–68 with $p = 1/2$ tells us that $g'(1) = n/2 - m\binom{n}{m}/2^n = n/2 - \sqrt{n/2\pi} + O(1)$ in that case. On the other hand if $p' = 1$, so that the walk is greedy only when $a = 1$ or $a = n - 1$, we're almost in the situation of Algorithm P but with n decreased by 2. Then $g'(1) = 2^{-n} \sum_{a=1}^{n-1} \binom{n}{a}(1 + (a - 1)(n - 2) - (a - 1)^2) = n(n - 5)/4 + 2 + (2n - 4)/2^n$; greed triumphs.

What happens as p' rises from 0 to 1? Let's decrease n by 2 and use the rule $g_a = z(qg_{a-1} + pg_{a+1})$ for $1 \le a \le n/2$, so that the calculations resemble those we did for Algorithm P but with p now $\le 1/2$ instead of $p = 1/2$. Functions t_k and u_k can be defined as in MPR–105; but the new recurrences are $t_{k+1} = (t_k - pz^2 t_{k-1})/q$ and $u_{k+1} = (u_k - pz^2 u_{k-1})/q$. Hence

$$T(w) = \frac{q - pw}{q - w + pz^2w^2}; \qquad U(w) = \frac{q - (1 - qz)w}{q - w + pz^2w^2}.$$

Differentiating with respect to z, then setting $z = 1$, now yields

$$t'_k(1) = \frac{2pq(1 - (p/q)^k)}{(q - p)^2} - \frac{2pk}{q - p}, \qquad u'_k(1) = \frac{(2p - (p/q)^k)q}{(q - p)^2} - \frac{2p(k - 1/2)}{q - p}.$$

It follows that $g'_a(1) = a/(q - p) - 2pq((p/q)^{m-a} - (p/q)^m)/(q - p)^2$ for $0 \le a \le n/2$ when n is even, $a/(q - p) - q((p/q)^{m-a} - (p/q)^m)/(q - p)^2$ when n is odd. The overall totals when $n = 1000$ and $p' = (.001, .01, .1, .5, .9, .99, .999)$ are respectively $\approx (487.9, 492.3, 541.4, 973.7, 4853.4, 44688.2, 183063.4)$.

305. That little additional clause reverses the picture! Now there's only one solution, and greediness fails badly when $\nu x > n/2$ because it keeps trying to move x away from the solution. To analyze the new situation in detail, we need $3(n - 1)$ generating functions g_{ab}, where $a = x_1 + x_2$ and $b = x_3 + \cdots + x_n$. The expected number of flips will be $g'(1)$, where $g = 2^{-n} \sum_{a=0}^{2} \sum_{b=0}^{n-2} \binom{2}{a}\binom{n-2}{b} g_{ab}$.

The behavior of Algorithm P is ambiguous, because the unsatisfied clause found in step P2 depends on the clause ordering. The most favorable case arises when $a = 2$, because we can decrease a to 1 by working on the special clause $\bar{x}_1 \vee \bar{x}_2$. Any other clause is equally likely to increase or decrease $a + b$. So the best-case generating functions maximize the chance of reaching $a = 2$: $g_{00} = 1$, $g_{01} = \frac{z}{2}(g_{00} + g_{11})$, $g_{02} = \frac{z}{2}(g_{01} + g_{12})$, $g_{10} = \frac{z}{2}(g_{00} + g_{20})$, $g_{11} = \frac{z}{2}(g_{10} + g_{21})$, $g_{12} = \frac{z}{2}(g_{11} + g_{22})$, and $g_{2b} = zg_{1b}$. The solution has $g_{1b} = (z/(2 - z^2))^{b+1}$; and we find mean$(g) = 183/32 = 5.71875$.

The worst case arises whenever $g_{20} \neq zg_{10}$ and $g_{21} \neq zg_{11}$; for example we can take $g_{20} = \frac{z}{2}(g_{10}+g_{21})$, $g_{21} = \frac{z}{2}(g_{20}+g_{22})$, together with the other seven equations from the best case. Then $g_{01} = g_{10} = z(4-3z^2)/d$, $g_{02} = g_{11} = g_{20} = z^2(2-z^2)/d$, and $g_{12} = g_{21} = z^3/d$, where $d = 8-8z^2+z^4$. Overall, $g = (1+z)^2(2-z^2)/(4d)$ and mean$(g) = 11$.

(This analysis can be extended to larger n: The worst case turns out to have $g_{ab} = (z/2)^{a+b}t_{n-a-b}/t_n$, in the notation of the previous exercise, giving $n(3n-1)/4$ flips on average. The best case has g_{1b} as before; hence $g'_{0b} = 3b+2-2^{1-b}$, $g'_{1b} = 3b+3$, and $g'_{2b} = 3b+4$ when $z = 1$. The best average number of flips therefore turns out to be *linear*, with mean$(g) = \frac{3}{2}n - \frac{8}{9}(3/4)^n$.)

The analysis becomes more exciting, but trickier, when we use Algorithm W. Let $p = p'/2$ and $q = 1 - p$ as in the previous answer. Clearly $g_{00} = 1$, $g_{01} = g_{10} = zg_{00}$, $g_{02} = \frac{z}{2}(g_{01}+g_{12})$, and $g_{22} = zg_{12}$; but the other four cases need some thought. We have

$$g_{11} = \frac{z}{4}\left(\left(\tfrac{1}{2} + q\right)(g_{01} + g_{10}) + g_{12} + 2pg_{21}\right),$$

since the costs for $x_1x_2x_3x_4 = 1010$ are 1211 and the unsatisfied clauses are $(\bar{x}_1 \vee x_4)$, $(\bar{x}_3 \vee x_4)$, $(\bar{x}_1 \vee x_2)$, $(\bar{x}_3 \vee x_2)$; in the former two clauses we flip each literal equally often, but in the latter two we flip x_2 with probability p and the other with probability q. A similar but simpler analysis shows that $g_{21} = \frac{z}{4}(g_{11}+3g_{22})$ and $g_{20} = \frac{z}{5}(3g_{10}+2g_{21})$.

The most interesting case is $g_{12} = \frac{z}{3}(pg_{02} + 2pg_{11} + 3qg_{22})$, where the costs are 2122 and the problematic clauses are $(\bar{x}_1 \vee x_2)$, $(\bar{x}_3 \vee x_2)$, $(\bar{x}_4 \vee x_2)$. If $p = 0$, Algorithm W will always decide to flip x_2; but then we'll be back in state 12 after the next flip.

Indeed, setting $p = 0$ yields $g_{00} = 1$, $g_{01} = g_{10} = z$, $g_{02} = \frac{1}{2}z^2$, $g_{11} = \frac{3}{4}z^2$, $g_{20} = \frac{3}{5}z^2+\frac{3}{40}z^4$, $g_{21} = \frac{3}{16}z^3$, and $g_{12} = g_{22} = 0$. The weighted total therefore turns out to be $g = (40 + 160z + 164z^2 + 15z^3 + 3z^4)/640$. Notice that the greedy random walk never succeeds after making more than 4 flips, in this case; so we should set $N = 4$ and restart after each failure. The probability of success is $g(1) = 191/320$. (This strategy is actually quite good: It succeeds after making an average of $1577/382 \approx 4.13$ flips and choosing random starting values $x_1x_2x_3x_4$ about $320/191$ times.)

If p is positive, no matter how tiny, the success probability for $N = \infty$ is $g(1) = 1$. But the denominator of g is $48 - 48z^2 + 26pz^2 + 6pz^4 - 17p^2z^4$, and we find that mean$(g) = (1548+2399p-255p^2)/(1280p-680p^2) = (6192+4798p'-255p'^2)/(2560p' - 680p'^2)$. Taking $p' = (.001, .01, .1, .5, .9, .99, .999)$ in this formula gives, respectively, the approximate values $(2421.3, 244.4, 26.8, 7.7, 5.9, 5.7, 5.7)$.

(Calculations for $n = 12$ show that g is a polynomial of degree 8 when $p = 0$, with $g(1) \approx .51$ and $g'(1) \approx 2.40$. Thus, setting $N = 8$ yields success after about 16.1 flips and 1.95 initializations. When $p > 0$ we have $g'(1) \approx 1.635p^{-5} + O(p^{-4})$ as $p \to 0$, and the seven values of p' considered above yield respectively $(5 \times 10^{16}, 5 \times 10^{11}, 5 \times 10^6, 1034.3, 91.1, 83.89, 83.95)$ flips — surprisingly *not* monotone decreasing in p'. These WalkSAT statistics can be compared with 17.97 to 105 flips for Algorithm P.)

306. (a) Since $l(N) = E_N + (1 - q_N)(N + l(N))$, we have $q_N l(N) = E_N + N - Nq_N = p_1 + 2p_2 + \cdots + Np_N + Np_{N+1} + \cdots + Np_\infty = N - (q_1 + \cdots + q_{N-1})$.

(b) If $N = m + k$ and $k \geq 0$ we have $E_N = m^2/n$, $q_1 + \cdots + q_{N-1} = km/n$, and $q_N = m/n$; hence $l(N) = n + k(n - m)/m$.

(c) If $N \leq n$, $l(N) = (N - \binom{N}{2}/n)/(N/n) = n - \frac{N-1}{2}$; otherwise $l(N) = l(n) = \frac{n+1}{2}$.

(d) From $q_N = p_1(N - q_1 - \cdots - q_{N-1})$ and $q_{N+1} = p_1(N + 1 - q_1 - \cdots - q_N)$ we deduce $p_{N+1} = p_1(1 - q_N)$, hence $1 - q_{N+1} = (1 - p_1)(1 - q_N)$. So it's a geometric distribution, with $p_t = p(1 - p)^{t-1}$ for $t \geq 1$. (The fact that $l(1) = l(2) = \cdots$ is called the "memoryless property" of the geometric distribution.)

(e) Choose $p_1, \ldots, p_n$ arbitrarily, with $q_n = p_1 + \cdots + p_n \leq 1$. Then, arguing as in (d), $p_{n+1}, p_{n+2}, \ldots$ are defined by $1 - q_N = (1 - 1/l(n))^{N-n}(1 - q_n)$ for $N \geq n$.

(f) Since $l(n+1) - l(n) = (n - (q_1 + \cdots + q_n))(1 - 1/q_n) \leq 0$, we must have $q_n = 1$ and $l(n) = l(n+1)$. (The case $l(n) < l(n+1)$ is impossible.)

(g) Let $x = p_1$ and $y = p_2$. By part (f), the conditions are equivalent to $0 < x \leq x + y < 1$ and $x(3 - 2x - y) > 1$. Hence $0 < (2x-1)(1-x) - xy \leq (2x-1)(1-x)$; we get the general solution by first choosing $\frac{1}{2} < x < 1$, then $0 \leq y < (2x-1)(1-x)/x$.

(h) If $N^* = \infty$ and $l(n) < \infty$, we can find n' with $q_{n'}l(n') = p_1 + 2p_2 + \cdots + n'p_{n'} + n'p_{n'+1} + \cdots + n'p_\infty > l(n)$. Hence $l(N) \geq q_N l(N) \geq q_{n'}l(n') > l(n)$ for all $N \geq n'$.

(i) We have $q_{n+k} = k/(k+1)$ for $k \geq 0$; hence $l(n+k) = (k+1)(n+H_k)/k$. The minimum occurs when $l(n+k) \approx l(n+k-1)$, namely when $n \approx k - H_k$; thus $k = n + \ln n + O(1)$. For example, the optimum cutoff value when $n = 10$ is $N^* = 23$. (Notice that $E_\infty = \infty$, yet $l = l(N^*) \approx 14.194$ in this case.)

(j) Let $p_t = [t > 1]/2^{t-1}$. Then $l(N) = (3 - 2^{2-N})/(1 - 2^{1-N})$ decreases to 3.

(k) Clearly $l \leq L$. For $N \leq L$ we have $l(N) = (N - (q_1 + \cdots + q_{N-1}))/q_N \geq (N - (1 + \cdots + (N-1))/L)/(N/L) = L - (N-1)/2 \geq (L+1)/2$. And for $N = \lfloor L \rfloor + k + 1$, similarly, $l(N) \geq N - (1 + \cdots + \lfloor L \rfloor + kL)/L = \lfloor L + 1 \rfloor (1 - \lfloor L \rfloor/(2L)) \geq (L+1)/2$.

307. (a) $E\,X = E N_1 + (1 - q_{N_1})(N_1 + E\,X')$, where X' is the number of steps for the sequence $(N_2, N_3, \ldots)$. For numerical results, start with $j \leftarrow 0$, $s \leftarrow 0$, $\alpha \leftarrow 1$; then, while $\alpha > \epsilon$, set $j \leftarrow j + 1$, $\alpha \leftarrow (1 - q_{N_j})\alpha$, and $s \leftarrow s + E N_j + \alpha N_j$. (Here ϵ is tiny.)

(b) Let $P_j = (1 - q_{N_1}) \ldots (1 - q_{N_{j-1}}) = \Pr(X > T_j)$, and note that $P_j \leq (1 - p_n)^{j-1}$ where $n = \min\{t \mid p_t > 0\}$. Since $q_N l(N) = E_N + (1 - q_N)N$, we have

$$E\,X = q_{N_1} l(N_1) + (1 - q_{N_1})(q_{N_2} l(N_2) + (1 - q_{N_2})(q_{N_3} l(N_3) + \cdots))$$
$$= \sum_{j=1}^{\infty} P_j q_{N_j} l(N_j) = \sum_{j=1}^{\infty} (P_j - P_{j+1}) l(N_j).$$

(c) $E\,X \geq \sum_{j=1}^{\infty}(P_j - P_{j+1})l(N^*) = l$.

(d) We can assume that $N_j \leq n$ for all j; otherwise the strategy would do even worse. For the hint, let $\{N_1, \ldots, N_r\}$ contain r_m occurrences of m, for $1 \leq m \leq n$, and suppose $t_m = r_m + \cdots + r_n$. If $t_m < n/(2m)$, the probability of failure would be $(1 - m/n)^{t_m} \geq 1 - t_m m/n > 1/2$. Hence we have $t_m \geq n/(2m)$ for all m, and $N_1 + \cdots + N_r = t_1 + \cdots + t_n \geq nH_n/2$.

Now there's some m such that the first $r - 1$ trials fail on $p^{(m)}$ with probability $> \frac{1}{2}$. For this m we have $E\,X > \frac{1}{2}(N_1 + \cdots + N_{r-1}) \geq \frac{1}{2}(N_1 + \cdots + N_r - n)$.

308. (a) $2^{a+1} - 1$; and we also have $S_{2^a + b} = S_{b+1}$ for $0 \leq b < 2^a - 1$ (by induction).

(b) The sequence (u_n, v_n) in (131) has $1 + \rho k$ entries with $u_n = k$; and $\rho 1 + \cdots + \rho n = n - vn$ by Eq. 7.1.3–(61). From the double generating function $g(w, z) = \sum_{n \geq 0} w^{vn} z^n = (1 + wz)(1 + wz^2)(1 + wz^4)(1 + wz^8) \ldots$ we deduce that $\sum_{k \geq 0} z^{2k+1-vk} = zg(z^{-1}, z^2)$.

(c) $\{n \mid S_n = 2^a\} = \{2^{a+1}k + 2^{a+1} - 1 - vk \mid k \geq 0\}$; hence $\sum_{n \geq 0} z^n[S_n = 2^a] = z^{2^{a+1}-1}g(z^{-1}, z^{2^{a+1}}) = z^{2^{a+1}-1}(1 + z^{2^{a+1}-1})(1 + z^{2^{a+2}-1})(1 + z^{2^{a+3}-1}) \ldots$

(d) When 2^a occurs for the 2^bth time, we've had $2^{a+b-c} - [c > a]$ occurrences of 2^c, for $0 \leq c \leq a + b$. Consequently $\Sigma(a, b, 1) = (a + b - 1)2^{a+b} + 2^{a+1}$.

(e) The exact value is $\sum_{c=0}^{a+b} 2^{a+b-c} 2^c + \sum_{c=1}^{\rho k} 2^{a+b+c}$; and $\rho k \leq \lambda k = \lfloor \lg k \rfloor$.

(f) The stated formula is $E \min_k \{\Sigma(a, b, k) \mid \Sigma(a, b, k) \geq X\}$, if we penalize the algorithm so that it *never* succeeds unless it is run with the particular cutoff $N = 2^a$.

(g) We have $Q \le (1 - q_t)^{2^b} \le (1 - q_t)^{1/q_t} < e^{-1}$; hence $\mathrm{E}\,X < (a + b - 1)2^{a+b} + 2^{a+1} + \sum_{k=1}^{\infty}(a + b + 2k - 1)2^{a+b}e^{-k} = 2^{a+b}((a+b)e/(e-1) + e(3-e)/(e-1)^2 + 2^{1-b})$. Furthermore we have $2^{a+b} < 8l - 4l[b=0]$, by exercise 306(k).

309. No—far from it. If Algorithm C were to satisfy the hypotheses of exercise 306, it would have to do *complete* restarts: It would not only have to flush *every* literal from the trail, it would also have to forget all the clauses that it has learned, and reinitialize the random heap. [But reluctant doubling appears to work well also outside of Vegas.]

310. A method analogous to (131) can be used: Let $(u'_1, v'_1) = (1, 0)$; then define $(u'_{n+1}, v'_{n+1}) = (u'_n \ \& \ -u'_n = 1 \ll v'_n? \ (\mathrm{succ}(u'_n), 0)\colon (u'_n, v'_n + 1))$. Here 'succ' is the Fibonacci-code successor function that is defined by six bitwise operations in answer 7.1.3–158. Finally, let $S'_n = F_{v'_n + 2}$ for $n \ge 1$. (This sequence $\langle S'_n \rangle$, like $\langle S_n \rangle$, is "nicely balanced"; hence it is universal as in exercise 308. For example, when F_a appears for the first time, there have been exactly F_{a+2-c} occurrences of F_c, for $2 \le c \le a$.)

311. Because $\langle R_n \rangle$ does surprisingly well in these tests, it seems desirable to consider also its Fibonacci analog: If $f_n = \mathrm{succ}(f_{n-1})$ is the binary Fibonacci code for n, we can call $\langle \rho' n \rangle = \langle \rho f_n \rangle = (0, 1, 2, 0, 3, 0, 1, 4, 0, \dots)$ the "Fibonacci ruler function," and let $\langle R'_n \rangle = (1, 2, 3, 1, 5, 1, 2, 8, 1, \dots)$ be the "ruler of Fibonaccis," where $R'_n = F_{2+\rho' n}$.

The results $(E_S, E_{S'}, E_R, E_{R'})$ for $m = 1$ and $m = 2$ are respectively $(315.1, 357.8, 405.8, 502.5)$ and $(322.8, 284.1, 404.9, 390.0)$; thus S beats S' beats R beats R' when $m = 1$, while S' beats S beats R' beats R when $m = 2$. The situation is, however, reversed for larger values of m: R beats R' beats S beats S' when $m = 90$, while R' beats R beats S' beats S when $m = 89$.

In general, the reluctant methods shine for small m, while the more "aggressive" ruler methods forge ahead as m grows: When $n = 100$, S beats R if and only if $m \le 13$, and S' beats R' if and only if $m \le 12$. The doubling methods are best when m is a power of 2 or slightly less; the Fibonacci methods are best when m is a Fibonacci number or slightly less. The worst cases occur at $m = 65 = 2^6 + 1$ for S and R (namely 1402.2 and 845.0); they occur at $m = 90 = F_{11} + 1$ for S' and R' (namely 1884.8 and 805.9).

312. $T(m, n) = m + b2^b h_0(\theta)/\theta + 2^b g(\theta)$, where $b = \lceil \lg m \rceil$, $\theta = 1 - m/n$, $h_a(z) = \sum_n z^n [S_n = 2^a]$, and $g(z) = \sum_{n \ge 1} S_n z^n = \sum_{a \ge 0} 2^a h_a(z)$.

313. If l is flipped, the number of unsatisfied clauses increases by the cost of $|l|$ and decreases by the number of unsatisfied clauses that contain l; and the latter is at least 1.

Consider the following interesting clauses, which have the unique solution 0000:

$$x_1 \lor \bar{x}_2, \quad \bar{x}_1 \lor x_2, \quad x_2 \lor \bar{x}_3, \quad \bar{x}_2 \lor x_3, \quad x_3 \lor \bar{x}_4, \quad \bar{x}_3 \lor x_4, \quad \bar{x}_1 \lor \bar{x}_4.$$

"Uphill" moves $1011 \mapsto 1111$ and $1101 \mapsto 1111$ are forced; also $0110 \mapsto 1110$ or 0111.

314. (Solution by Bram Cohen, 2012.) Consider the 10 clauses $\bar{1}23\bar{4}567$, $\bar{1}2\bar{3}4\bar{5}67$, $12\bar{3}4\bar{5}$, $123\bar{4}6$, $123\bar{4}7$, $\bar{1}2\bar{3}4$, $\bar{1}2\bar{3}5$, $\bar{1}2\bar{3}6$, $\bar{1}2\bar{4}5$, $\bar{1}2\bar{4}6$, and 60 more obtained by the cyclic permutation (1234567). All binary $x = x_1 \dots x_7$ with weight $\nu x = 2$ have cost-free flips leading to weight 3, but no such flips to weight 1. Since the only solution has weight 0, Algorithm W loops forever whenever $\nu x > 1$. (Is there a smaller example?)

315. Any value with $0 \le p < 1/2$ works, since each graph component is either K_1 or K_2.

316. No; $\max \theta(1 - \theta)^d$ for $0 \le \theta < 1$ is $d^d/(d + 1)^{d+1}$, when $\theta = 1/(d + 1)$. [But Theorem J for $d > 2$ *is* a consequence of the improved Theorem L in exercise 356(c).]

317. Number the vertices so that the neighbors of vertex 1 are $2, \dots, d'$, and let $G_j = G \setminus \{1, \dots, j\}$. Then $\alpha(G) = \alpha(G_1) - \Pr(A_1 \cap \bar{A}_2 \cap \dots \cap \bar{A}_m)$, and the latter probability is $\le \Pr(A_1 \cap \bar{A}_{d'+1} \cap \dots \cap \bar{A}_m) = \Pr(A_1 \mid \bar{A}_{d'+1} \cap \dots \cap \bar{A}_m)\alpha(G_{d'}) \le p\alpha(G_{d'})$.

Let $\rho = (d-1)/d$. By induction we have $\alpha(G_j) > \rho\alpha(G_{j+1})$ for $1 \le j < d'$, because vertex $j+1$ has degree $< d$ in G_j. If $d' = 1$ then $\alpha(G) \ge \alpha(G_1) - p\alpha(G_1) > \rho\alpha(G_1) > 0$. Otherwise if $d' \le d$, $\alpha(G) \ge \alpha(G_1) - p\alpha(G_{d'}) > \alpha(G_1) - p\rho^{1-d'}\alpha(G_1) \ge \alpha(G_1) - p\rho^{1-d}\alpha(G_1) = \rho\alpha(G_1) > 0$. Otherwise we must have $d' = d+1$, with vertex 1 of degree d, and $\alpha(G) > \alpha(G_1) - p\rho^{-d}\alpha(G_1) = \frac{d-2}{d-1}\alpha(G_1) \ge 0$.

318. Let $f_n = M_G(p)$ where G is the graph of a complete t-ary tree with t^n leaves; thus G has t^k vertices at distance k from the root, for $0 \le k \le n$. Then

$$f_0 = 1 - p, \quad f_1 = (1-p)^t - p, \quad \text{and} \quad f_{n+1} = f_n^t - pf_{n-1}^{t^2} \text{ for } n > 1.$$

By Theorem S, it suffices to show that $f_n \le 0$ for some n.

The key idea is to let $g_0 = 1 - p$ and $g_{n+1} = f_{n+1}/f_n^t = 1 - p/g_n^t$. Assuming that $g_n > 0$ for all n, we have $g_1 < g_0$ and $g_n - g_{n+1} = p/g_n^t - p/g_{n+1}^t > 0$ when $g_{n+1} < g_n$. Hence $\lim_{n\to\infty} g_n = \lambda$ exists, with $0 < \lambda < 1$. Furthermore $\lambda = 1 - p/\lambda^t$, so that $p = \lambda^t(1-\lambda)$. But then $p \le t^t/(t+1)^{t+1}$ (see answer 316 with $\theta = 1 - \lambda$).

[One must admit, however, that the limit is not often reached until n is extremely large. For example, even if $t = 2$ and $p = .149$, we don't have $f_n < 0$ until $n = 45$. Thus G must have at least 2^{45} vertices before this value of p is too large for Lemma L.]

319. Let $x = 1/(d-1)$. Since $e^x > 1 + x = d/(d-1)$, we have $e > (d/(d-1))^{d-1}$.

320. (a) Let $f_m(p)$ be the Möbius polynomial when $p_1 = \cdots = p_m = p$. Then we have $f_m(p) = f_{m-1}(p) - pf_{m-2}(p)$, and one can show by induction that $f_m(1/(4\cos^2\theta)) = \sin((m+2)\theta)/((2\cos\theta)^{m+1}\sin\theta)$. The threshold decreases to $1/4$ as $m \to \infty$.

(b) $1/(4\cos^2\frac{\pi}{2m})$; the Möbius polynomial $g_m(p) = f_{m-1}(p) - pf_{m-3}(p)$ satisfies the same recurrence as $f_m(p)$, and equals $2\cos m\theta/(2\cos\theta)^m$ when $p = 1/(4\cos^2\theta)$.

[In terms of the classical Chebyshev polynomials, $g_m(p) = 2p^{m/2}T_m(1/(2\sqrt{p}))$ and $f_m(p) = p^{(m+1)/2}U_{m+1}(1/(2\sqrt{p}))$.]

321. Let $\theta = (2 - \sqrt{2})/2$, $\theta' = \theta(1-\theta) = (\sqrt{2}-1)/2$, and $c = (p-\theta)/(1-\theta)$. The method of answer 345 gives $(\Pr(\overline{A}\overline{B}\overline{C}\overline{D}), \Pr(A\overline{B}\overline{C}\overline{D}), \Pr(AB\overline{C}\overline{D}), \Pr(A\overline{B}C\overline{D}),$ $\Pr(ABC\overline{D}), \Pr(ABCD)) = (0, \theta'(1-c)^3, 2\theta'(1-c)^2c, \theta^2(1-c)^2+2\theta'(1-c)^3, \theta^2(1-c)c+ 3\theta'(1-c)c^2, \theta^2c^2 + 4\theta'c^3)$. Other cases are symmetric to these six. When $p = 3/10$ the six probabilities are $\approx (0, .20092, .00408, .08815, .00092, .00002)$.

322. (a) Let $a_j = \sum_i w_i[ij \in A]$, $b_j = \sum_k y_k[jk \in B]$, $c_l = \sum_k y_k[kl \in C]$, and $d_l = \sum_i w_i[li \in D]$. Then when $X = j$ and $Z = l$, the best way to allocate the events is

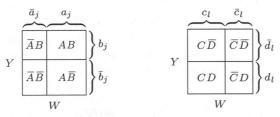

within W and Y. Hence $\Pr(\overline{A}\cap\overline{B}\cap\overline{C}\cap\overline{D}) = \sum_{j,l} x_j z_l((\bar{a}_j+\bar{d}_l)\dot{-}1)((\bar{b}_j+\bar{c}_l)\dot{-}1)$, which is zero if and only if we have $a_j + d_l \ge 1$ or $b_j + c_l \ge 1$ for all j and l with $x_j z_l > 0$.

(b) Since $\sum_j x_j(a_j, b_j) = (p, p)$, the point (p, p) lies in the convex hull of the points (a_j, b_j). So there must be points $(a, b) = (a_j, b_j)$ and $(a', b') = (a_{j'}, b_{j'})$ such that the line from (a, b) to (a', b') intersects the region $\{(x, y) \mid 0 \le x, y \le p\}$; in other words $\mu a + (1-\mu)a' \le p$ and $\mu b + (1-\mu)b' \le p$. Similarly we can find c, d, c', d', ν.

(c) Fact: If $a \geq \frac{2}{3}$ and $b' \geq \frac{2}{3}$, then $\mu = \frac{1}{2}$; hence $a = b' = \frac{2}{3}$ and $a' = b = 0$. Notice also that there are 16 symmetries, generated by (i) $a \leftrightarrow b$, $c \leftrightarrow d$; (ii) $a \leftrightarrow a'$, $b \leftrightarrow b'$, $\mu \leftrightarrow 1 - \mu$; (iii) $c \leftrightarrow c'$, $d \leftrightarrow d'$, $\nu \leftrightarrow 1 - \nu$; (iv) $a \leftrightarrow d$, $b \leftrightarrow c$, $\mu \leftrightarrow \nu$.

If $c \leq c'$ and $d \leq d'$, or if $c \leq \frac{1}{3}$ and $d \leq \frac{1}{3}$, we can assume (by symmetry) that the Fact applies; this gives a solution to all the constraints, with $c = d = c' = d' = \frac{1}{3}$.

For the remaining solutions we may assume that $a, b' > \frac{1}{3} > a', b$. Suppose the line from (a, b) to (a', b') intersects the line from $(0, 0)$ to $(1, 1)$ at the point (α, α); dividing a, b, a', b' by 3α gives a solution in which $\mu a + (1 - \mu)a' = \mu b + (1 - \mu)b' = \frac{1}{3}$. Similarly, we can assume that $d, c' > \frac{1}{3} > d', c$ and that $\nu c + (1 - \nu)c' = \nu d + (1 - \nu)d' = \frac{1}{3}$. Consequently $a + d \geq 1$ and $b' + c' \geq 1$. Symmetry also allows us to assume that $a + d' \geq 1$. In particular, $a > \frac{2}{3}$; and, by the Fact, $b' < \frac{2}{3}$. So $a' + d \geq 1$, $d > \frac{2}{3}$, $c' < \frac{2}{3}$.

Now extend the lines that connect (a, b) to (a', b') and (c, d) to (c', d'), by increasing a, b', c', d while decreasing a', b, c, d', until $a' = 1 - d$ and $a = 1 - d'$, and until either $a = 1$ or $b = 0$, and either $d = 1$ or $c = 0$. The only solution of this kind with $b' + c' \geq 1$ occurs when $a = d = 1$, $a' = b = c = d' = 0$, $b' = c' = 1/2$, $\mu = \frac{1}{3}$, $\nu = \frac{2}{3}$.

(d) For the first solution, we can let W, X, Y, Z be uniform on $\{0, 1, 2\}$, $\{0, 1\}$, $\{0, 1, 2\}$, and $\{0\}$, respectively; and let $A = \{10, 20\}$, $B = \{11, 12\}$, $C = \{00\}$, $D = \{00\}$. (For example, $WXYZ = 1110$ gives event B.) The second solution turns out to be the same, but with (X, Y, Z, W) in place of (W, X, Y, Z). Notice that the solution applies also to P_4, where the threshold is $\frac{1}{3}$. [See STOC **43** (2011), 242.]

323. *cbc*. In this simple case, we just eliminate all strings in which c is followed by a.

324. For $1 \leq j \leq n$, and for each v such that $v = x_j$ or $v - x_j$, let $i \prec j$ for each $i < j$ such that $v = x_i$. (If several values of i qualify, it suffices to consider only the largest one. Several authors have used the term "dependence graph" for this partial ordering.) The traces equivalent to α correspond to the topological sortings with respect to $\prec$, because those arrangements of the letters are precisely the permutations that preserve the empilement.

In (136), for example, with $x_1 \ldots x_n = bcebafdc$, we have $1 \prec 2$, $1 \prec 4$, $2 \prec 4$, $4 \prec 5$, $3 \prec 6$, $2 \prec 7$, $3 \prec 7$, $2 \prec 8$, $4 \prec 8$, and $7 \prec 8$. Algorithm 7.2.1.2V produces 105 solutions, 12345678 (*bcebafdc*) through 36127485 (*efbcdbca*).

325. Every such trace α yields an acyclic orientation, if we let $u \longrightarrow v$ when u appears at a lower level in α's empilement. Conversely, the topological sortings of any acyclic orientation are all equivalent traces; so this correspondence is one-to-one. [See Ira M. Gessel, *Discrete Mathematics* **232** (2001), 119–130.]

326. True: x commutes with y if and only if y commutes with x.

327. Each trace α is represented by its height $h = h(\alpha) \geq 0$, and by h linked lists $L_j = L_j(\alpha)$ for $0 \leq j < h$. The elements of L_j are the letters on level j of α's empilement; these letters have disjoint territories, and we keep each list in alphabetic order so that the representation is unique. The canonical string representing α is then $L_0 L_1 \ldots L_{h-1}$. (For example, in (136) we have $L_0 = be$, $L_1 = cf$, $L_2 = bd$, $L_3 = ac$, and the canonical representation is *becfbdac*.) We also maintain the sets $U_j = \bigcup \{T(a) \mid a \in L_j\}$ as bit vectors; in (136), for example, they are $U_0 = {}^\#36$, $U_1 = {}^\#1b$, $U_2 = {}^\#3c$, $U_3 = {}^\#78$.

To multiply α by β, do the following for $k = 0, 1, \ldots, h(\beta) - 1$ (in that order), and for each letter $b \in L_k(\beta)$ (in any order): Set $j \leftarrow h(\alpha)$; then while $j > 0$ and $T(b) \mathbin{\&} U_{j-1}(\alpha) = 0$, set $j \leftarrow j - 1$. If $j = h(\alpha)$, set $L_j(\alpha)$ empty, $U_j(\alpha) \leftarrow 0$, and $h(\alpha) \leftarrow h(\alpha) + 1$. Insert b into $L_j(\alpha)$, and set $U_j(\alpha) \leftarrow U_j(\alpha) + T(b)$.

328. Do the following for $k = h(\beta) - 1, \ldots, 1, 0$ (in that order), and for each letter $b \in L_k(\beta)$ (in any order): Set $j \leftarrow h(\alpha) - 1$; while $j > 0$ and $T(b)$ & $U_j(\alpha) = 0$, set $j \leftarrow j - 1$. Report failure if b isn't in $L_j(\alpha)$. Otherwise remove b from that list and set $U_j(\alpha) \leftarrow U_j(\alpha) - T(b)$; if $U_j(\alpha)$ is now zero, set $h(\alpha) \leftarrow h(\alpha) - 1$.

If there was no failure, the resulting α is the answer.

329. Do the following for $k = 0, 1, \ldots, h(\alpha) - 1$ (in that order), and for each letter $a \in L_k(\alpha)$ (in any order): Report failure if a isn't in $L_0(\beta)$. Otherwise remove a from that list, set $U_0(\beta) \leftarrow U_0(\beta) - T(a)$, and renormalize the representation of β.

Renormalization involves the following steps: Set $j \leftarrow c \leftarrow 1$. While $U_{j-1}(\beta) \neq 0$ and $c \neq 0$, terminate if $j = h(\beta)$; otherwise set $c \leftarrow 0$, $j \leftarrow j+1$, and then, for each letter b in $L_{j-1}(\beta)$ such that $T(b)$ & $U_{j-2}(\beta) = 0$, move b from $L_{j-1}(\beta)$ to $L_{j-2}(\beta)$ and set $U_{j-2}(\beta) \leftarrow U_{j-2}(\beta) + T(b)$, $U_{j-1}(\beta) \leftarrow U_{j-1}(\beta) - T(b)$, $c \leftarrow 1$. Finally, if $U_{j-1}(\beta) = 0$, set $U_{i-1}(\beta) \leftarrow U_i(\beta)$ and $L_{i-1}(\beta) \leftarrow L_i(\beta)$ for $j \leq i < h(\beta)$, then set $h(\beta) \leftarrow h(\beta) - 1$.

If there was no failure, the resulting β is the answer.

330. Let the territorial universe be $V \cup E$, the vertices plus edges of G, and let $T(a) = \{a\} \cup \{\{a, b\} \mid a - b\}$. [G. X. Viennot, in 1985, called this subgraph a *starfish*.] Alternatively, we can get by with just two elements in each set $T(a)$ if and only if $G = L(H)$ is the line graph of some other multigraph H. Then each vertex a of G corresponds to an edge $u - v$ in H, and we can let $T(a) = \{u, v\}$.

[*Notes:* The smallest graph G that *isn't* a line graph is the "claw" $K_{1,3}$. Since sets of independent vertices in the line graph G are sets of disjoint edges in H, also called *matchings* of H, the Möbius polynomial of G is also known as the "matching polynomial" of H. Such polynomials are important in theoretical chemistry and physics. When all territories have $|T(a)| \leq 2$, all roots of the polynomial $M_G^*(z)$ in (149) are real and positive, by exercise 341. But $M_{\text{claw}}(z, z, z, z) = 1 - 4z + 3z^2 - z^3$ has complex roots ≈ 0.317672 and $1.34116 \pm 1.16154i$.]

331. If α is a string with $k > 0$ occurrences of the substring ac, there are 2^k ways to decompose α into factors $\{a, b, c, ac\}$, and the expansion includes $+\alpha$ and $-\alpha$ each exactly 2^{k-1} times. Thus we're left with the sum of all strings that don't contain 'ac'.

332. No: If b commutes with a and c, but $ac \neq ca$, we're dealing with strings that contain no adjacent pairs ba or cb; hence cab qualifies, but it's equivalent to the smaller string bca. [Certain graphs do define traces with the stated property, as we've seen in (135) and (136). Using the next exercise we can conclude that the property holds if and only if no three letters $a < b < c$ have $a \not\!\!- b$, $b \not\!\!- c$, and $a - c$ in the graph G of clashes. Thus the letters can be arranged into a suitable linear order if and only if G is a cocomparability graph; see Section 7.4.2.]

333. To show that $\sum_{\alpha \in A, \beta \in B}(-1)^{|\beta|}\alpha\beta = 1$, let $\gamma = a_1 \ldots a_n$ be any nonempty string. If γ cannot be factored so that $a_1 \ldots a_k \in A$ and $a_{k+1} \ldots a_n \in B$, then γ doesn't appear. Otherwise γ has exactly two such factorizations, one in which k has its smallest possible value and the other in which k is one greater; these factorizations cancel each other in the sum. [*Discrete Mathematics* **14** (1976), 215–239; *Manuscripta Mathematica* **19** (1976), 211–243. See also R. Fröberg, *Mathematica Scandinavica* **37** (1975), 29–39.]

334. Equivalently we want to generate all strings of length n on the alphabet $\{1, \ldots, m\}$ that satisfy the following criterion, which strengthens the adjacent-letter test of exercise 332: If $1 \leq i < j \leq n$, $x_i \not\!\!- x_j$, $x_{i+1} \not\!\!- x_j$, $\ldots$, $x_{j-1} \not\!\!- x_j$, then $x_i \leq x_j$. [See A. V. Anisimov and D. E. Knuth, *Int. J. Comput. Inf. Sci.* **8** (1979), 255–260.]

T1. [Initialize.] Set $x_0 \leftarrow 0$ and $x_k \leftarrow 1$ for $1 \leq k \leq n$.

T2. [Visit.] Visit the trace $x_1 \ldots x_n$.

T3. [Find k.] Set $k \leftarrow n$. While $x_k = m$ set $k \leftarrow k - 1$. Terminate if $k = 0$.

T4. [Advance x_k.] Set $x_k \leftarrow x_k + 1$ and $j \leftarrow k - 1$.

T5. [Is x_k valid?] If $x_j > x_k$ and $x_j \not\!\!- x_k$, return to T4. If $j > 0$ and $x_j < x_k$ and $x_j \not\!\!- x_k$, set $j \leftarrow j - 1$ and repeat this step.

T6. [Reset $x_{k+1} \ldots x_n$.] While $k < n$ do the following: Set $k \leftarrow k + 1$, $x_k \leftarrow 1$; while $x_{k-1} > x_k$ and $x_{k-1} \not\!\!- x_k$, set $x_k \leftarrow x_k + 1$. Then go back to T2. ∎

335. Given such an ordering, we have $M_G = \det(I - A)$, where the entry in row u and column v of A is $v[u \geq v$ or $u\!\!-\!\!v]$. The determinant in the given example is

$$
\det \begin{pmatrix}
1 & -b & -c & 0 & 0 & 0 \\
0 & 1-b & 0 & -d & 0 & 0 \\
0 & -b & 1-c & -d & -e & 0 \\
0 & -b & -c & 1-d & 0 & -f \\
0 & -b & -c & -d & 1-e & -f \\
0 & -b & -c & -d & -e & 1-f
\end{pmatrix}
+ \det \begin{pmatrix}
-a & -b & -c & 0 & 0 & 0 \\
0 & 1 & c & -d & 0 & 0 \\
0 & 0 & 1 & -d & -e & 0 \\
0 & 0 & 0 & 1-d & 0 & -f \\
0 & 0 & 0 & -d & 1-e & -f \\
0 & 0 & 0 & -d & -e & 1-f
\end{pmatrix},
$$

after expanding the first column, then subtracting the first row from all other rows in the right-hand determinant. Therefore this rule satisfies recurrence (142).

[The result also follows from MacMahon's Master Theorem, exercise 5.1.2–20, using the characterization of lexicographically smallest traces in answer 334. According to Theorem 5.1.2B, such traces are in one-to-one correspondence with multiset permutations whose two-line representation does not contain $\genfrac{}{}{0pt}{}{v}{u}$ when $v > u$ and $v \not\!\!- u$. Is there a similar determinantal expression when G is *not* a cocomparability graph?]

336. (a) If α is a trace for G and β is a trace for H, we have $\mu_{G \oplus H}(\alpha\beta) = \mu_G(\alpha)\mu_H(\beta)$. Hence $M_{G \oplus H} = M_G M_H$. (b) In this case $\mu_{G\!-\!H}(\alpha\beta) = \mu_G(\alpha)$ if $\beta = \epsilon$, $\mu_H(\beta)$ if $\alpha = \epsilon$; otherwise it's zero. Therefore $M_{G\!-\!H} = M_G + M_H - 1$.

[These rules determine M_G recursively whenever G is a cograph (see exercise 7–90). In particular, complete bipartite and k-partite graphs have simple Möbius series, exemplified by $M_G = (1-a)(1-b)(1-c) + (1-d)(1-e) + (1-f) - 2$ when $G = K_{3,2,1}$.]

337. Substituting $a_1 + \cdots + a_k$ for a in M_G gives $M_{G'}$. (Each trace for G' is obtained by putting subscripts on the a's of the traces for G.)

338. The proof of Theorem F needs only minor changes: We limit α to traces that contain no elements of A, and we define α' and β' by letting a be the smallest letter $\notin A$ in the bottom level of γ's empilement. If γ has no such letter, there's only one factorization, with $\alpha = \epsilon$. Otherwise we pair up cancelling factorizations. [Incidentally, the sum of all traces whose *sinks* are in A must be written in the other order: $M_G^{-1} M_{G \setminus A}$.]

339. (a) "Push down" on piece x_j and factor out what comes through the floor.

(b) Factor out the pyramid for the smallest label, and repeat on what's left.

(c) This is a general convolution principle for labeled objects [see E. A. Bender and J. R. Goldman, *Indiana Univ. Math. J.* **20** (1971), 753–765]. For example, when $l = 3$ the number of ways to get a labeled trace of length n from three labeled pyramids is $\sum_{i,j,k} \binom{n}{i,j,k} P_i P_j P_k / 3! = n! \sum_{i,j,k} (P_i/i!)(P_j/j!)(P_k/k!)/3!$, with $i+j+k = n$ in both of these sums. We divide by $3!$ so that the topmost pyramid labels will be increasing.

(d) Sum the identity in (c) for $l = 0, 1, 2, \ldots$.

(e) $T(z) = \sum_{n \geq 0} t_n z^n = 1/M_G(z)$ by Theorem F, and $P(z) = \sum_{n \geq 1} p_n z^n / n$.

Note: If we retain the letter names, writing for example $M_G(z) = 1 - (a+b+c)z + acz^2$ instead of $M_G(z) = 1 - 3z + z^2$, the formal power series $-\ln M_G(z)$ exhibits the pyramids of length n in the coefficient of z^n, but only in the sense of *commutative* algebra (not trace algebra). For example, the coefficient of z^3 obtained from $\sum_{k \geq 1} (1 - M_G(z))^k/k$ with trace algebra includes the nonpyramidal term $bac/6$.

340. Let $w((i_1 \ldots i_k)) = (-1)^{k-1} a_{i_1 i_2} a_{i_2 i_3} \ldots a_{i_k i_1}$; thus $w(\pi) = (-a_{13} a_{34} a_{42} a_{21})$ $(-a_{57} a_{75})(a_{66})$ in the given example. The permutation polynomial is then $\det A$, by definition of the determinant. (And we get the *permanent*, if we omit the $(-1)^{k-1}$.)

341. The hint is true when $n = 2$, since the first involution polynomials are $w_{11} x$ and $w_{11} w_{22} x^2 - w_{12}$. And there's a recurrence: $W(S) = w_{ii} x W(S \setminus i) - \sum_{j \neq i} W(S \setminus \{i, j\})$.

So we can prove the existence of $n + 1$ roots $s_1 < r_1 < \cdots < r_n < s_{n+1}$ by induction: Let $W_n(x)$ be the polynomial for $\{1, \ldots, n\}$. Then $W_{n+1}(x)$ is $w_{(n+1)(n+1)} x W_n(x)$ minus n polynomials $w_{(n+1)j} W(\{1, \ldots, n\} \setminus j)$, each with roots $q_k^{(j)}$ that are nicely sandwiched between the roots of W_n. Furthermore $q_{n-k}^{(j)} = -q_k^{(j)}$ and $r_{n+1-k} = -r_k$, for $1 \leq k \leq n/2$. It follows that $W_{n+1}(r_n) < 0$, $W_{n+1}(r_{n-1}) > 0$, and so on, with $(-1)^k W_{n+1}(r_{n+1-k}) > 0$ for $1 \leq k \leq n/2$. Moreover, $W_{n+1}(0) = 0$ when n is even; $(-1)^k W_{n+1}(0) > 0$ when $n = 2k - 1$; and $W_{n+1}(x) > 0$ for all large x. Hence the desired s_k exist. [See Heilmann and Lieb, *Physical Review Letters* **24** (1970), 1412.]

342. If we replace $(i_1 \ldots i_k)$ by $a_{i_1 i_2} a_{i_2 i_3} \ldots a_{i_k i_1}$ (as in answer 340, but without the $(-1)^{k-1}$), then M_{G_n} becomes $\det(I - A)$. Replacing a_{ij} by $a_{ij} x_j$ gives the determinant in MacMahon's Master Theorem. And if $x_1 = \cdots = x_n = x$, we get the polynomial $\det(I - xA)$, whose roots are the reciprocals of the roots of A's characteristic polynomial.

343. The formulas in answer 336 show that $M_G(p_1, \ldots, p_m)$ increases whenever any p_j decreases, with respect to a cograph G. The only graph on ≤ 4 vertices that isn't a cograph is P_4 (see exercise 7–90); then $M_G(p_1, p_2, p_3, p_4) = 1 - p_1 - p_2 - p_3 - p_4 + p_1 p_3 + p_1 p_4 + p_2 p_4 = (1 - p_1)(1 - p_3 - p_4) - p_2(1 - p_4)$. In this case also we can conclude that $M_G(p_1, \ldots, p_4) > 0$ implies $(p_1, \ldots, p_4) \in \mathcal{R}(G)$. But when $G = P_5$, we find $M_G(1 - \epsilon, 1 - \epsilon, \epsilon, 1 - \epsilon, 1 - \epsilon) > 0$ for $0 \leq \epsilon < \phi^{-2}$; yet $(1 - \epsilon, 1 - \epsilon, \epsilon, 1 - \epsilon, 1 - \epsilon)$ is never in $\mathcal{R}(G)$ because $M_G(0, 0, \epsilon, 1 - \epsilon, 1 - \epsilon) = -(1 - \epsilon)^2$.

344. (a) If some minterm, say $B_1 \overline{B}_2 \overline{B}_3 B_4$, has negative "probability," then $p_1 p_4 \times (1 - \pi_2 - \pi_3 + \pi_{23}) < 0$; hence $M_G(0, p_2, p_3, 0) < 0$ violates the definition of $\mathcal{R}(G)$.

(b) In fact, more is true: $\pi_{I \cup J} = \pi_I \pi_J$ when $i \not\!\!\frown j$ for $i \in I$, $j \in J$, and $I \cap J = \emptyset$.

(c) It's $M_G(p_1[1 \in J], \ldots, p_m[m \in J])$, by (140) and (141). This important fact, already implicit in the solution to part (a), implies that $\beta(G \mid J) > 0$ for all J.

(d) Writing just 'J' for '$G|J$', we shall prove that $\alpha(i \cup J)/\beta(i \cup J) \geq \alpha(J)/\beta(J)$ for $i \notin J$, by induction on $|J|$. Let $J' = \{j \in J \mid i \not\!\!\frown j\}$. Then we have

$$\alpha(i \cup J) = \alpha(J) - \Pr\left(A_i \cap \bigcap_{j \in J} \overline{A}_j\right) \geq \alpha(J) - \Pr\left(A_i \cap \bigcap_{j \in J'} \overline{A}_j\right) \geq \alpha(J) - p_i \alpha(J'),$$

because of (133). Also $\beta(i \cup J) = \beta(J) - p_i \beta(J')$. Hence $\alpha(i \cup J)\beta(J) - \alpha(J)\beta(i \cup J) \geq (\alpha(J) - p_i \alpha(J'))\beta(J) - \alpha(J)(\beta(J) - p_i \beta(J')) = p_i(\alpha(J)\beta(J') - \alpha(J')\beta(J))$, which is ≥ 0 by induction since $J' \subseteq J$.

[This argument proves that Lemma L holds whenever $(p_1, \ldots, p_m)$ leads to a legitimate probability distribution with $\beta(G) > 0$; hence such probabilities are in $\mathcal{R}(G)$.]

(e) By induction, we have $\beta(i \cup J) = \beta(J) - \theta_i \beta(J') \prod_{i \not\frown j}(1 - \theta_j) \geq \beta(J) - \theta_i \beta(J') \prod_{j \in J \setminus J'}(1 - \theta_j) \geq (1 - \theta_i)\beta(J)$, because $\beta(J)/\beta(J') \geq \prod_{j \in J \setminus J'}(1 - \theta_j)$.

345. (Solution by A. D. Scott and A. D. Sokal.) Set $p'_j = (1 + \delta)p_j$ where $\delta \leq 0$ is the slack of $(p_1, \ldots, p_m)$. Then $M_G(p'_1, \ldots, p'_m) = 0$, but it becomes positive if any p'_j is decreased. Define events $B'_1, \ldots, B'_m$ by the construction in exercise 344. Let $C_1, \ldots, C_m$ be independent binary random variables such that $\Pr(C_j = 1) = q_j$, where $(1 - p'_j)(1 - q_j) = 1 - p_j$. Then the events $B_j = B'_j \vee C_j$ satisfy the desired conditions: $\Pr(B_i \mid \overline{B}_{j_1} \cap \cdots \cap \overline{B}_{j_k}) = \Pr(B_i \mid \overline{B}'_{j_1} \cap \cdots \cap \overline{B}'_{j_k}) = \Pr(B_i) = p_i$; and $\Pr(B_1 \vee \cdots \vee B_m) \geq \Pr(B'_1 \vee \cdots \vee B'_m) = 1$.

346. (a) By (144), $K_{a,G}$ is the sum of all traces on the probabilities of $G \setminus a$ whose sources are neighbors of a. Decreasing p_j doesn't decrease any trace.

(b) Suppose vertex $a = 1$ has neighbors $2, \ldots, j$. If we've recursively computed $M_{G \setminus a^*}$ and $M_{G \setminus a}$, finding that $(p_{j+1}, \ldots, p_m) \in \mathcal{R}(G \setminus a^*)$ and $(p_2, \ldots, p_m) \in \mathcal{R}(G \setminus a)$, then we know $K_{a,G}$; and the monotonicity property in (a) implies that $(p_1, \ldots, p_m) \in \mathcal{R}(G)$ if and only if $a K_{a,G} < 1$.

The graph $G = $ (a—b, c—d, e—f grid) in exercise 335 can, for example, be processed as follows:

$$M_{abcdef} = M_{bcdef}\left(1 - a\frac{M_{def}}{M_{bcdef}}\right) = (1-a')(1-b')\ldots(1-f'), \quad a' = \frac{a}{(1-b')(1-c')},$$

$$M_{bcdef} = M_{cdef}\left(1 - b\frac{M_{cef}}{M_{cdef}}\right) = (1-b')(1-c')\ldots(1-f'), \quad b' = \frac{b(1-c'')}{(1-c')(1-d')},$$

$$M_{cdef} = M_{def}\left(1 - c\frac{M_f}{M_{def}}\right) = (1-c')(1-d')(1-e')(1-f'), \quad c' = \frac{c}{(1-d')(1-e')},$$

$$M_{cef} = M_{ef}\left(1 - c\frac{M_f}{M_{ef}}\right) = (1-c'')(1-e')(1-f'), \quad c'' = \frac{c}{(1-e')},$$

$$M_{def} = M_{ef}\left(1 - d\frac{M_e}{M_{ef}}\right) = (1-d')(1-e')(1-f'), \quad d' = \frac{d(1-e'')}{(1-e')(1-f')},$$

$$M_{ef} = M_f\left(1 - e\frac{M_e}{M_f}\right) = (1-e')(1-f'), \quad e' = \frac{e}{(1-f')},$$

$$M_e = M_\epsilon\left(1 - e\frac{M_\epsilon}{M_\epsilon}\right) = (1-e''), \quad e'' = e,$$

$$M_f = M_\epsilon\left(1 - f\frac{M_\epsilon}{M_\epsilon}\right) = (1-f'), \quad f' = f,$$

with $M_\epsilon = 1$. (The equations on the left are derived top-down, then the equations on the right are evaluated bottom-up. We have $(a, b, \ldots, f) \in \mathcal{R}(G)$ if and only if $f' < 1$, $e'' < 1$, $e' < 1$, $\ldots$, $a' < 1$.) Even better is to traverse this graph in another order, using the rule $M_{G \oplus H} = M_G M_H$ (exercise 336) when subgraphs aren't connected:

$$M_{cdabef} = M_{dabef}\left(1 - c\frac{M_b M_f}{M_{dabef}}\right) = (1-c')(1-d')\ldots(1-f'), \quad c' = \frac{c}{(1-a')(1-d')(1-e')},$$

$$M_{dabef} = M_{ab}M_{ef}\left(1 - d\frac{M_a M_e}{M_{ab} M_{ef}}\right) = (1-d')(1-a')(1-b')(1-e')(1-f'), \quad \text{(see below)}$$

$$M_{ab} = M_b\left(1 - a\frac{M_\epsilon}{M_b}\right) = (1-a')(1-b'), \quad a' = \frac{a}{(1-b')},$$

$$M_a = M_\epsilon\left(1 - a\frac{M_\epsilon}{M_\epsilon}\right) = (1-a''), \quad a'' = a,$$

$$M_b = M_\epsilon\left(1 - b\frac{M_\epsilon}{M_\epsilon}\right) = (1-b'), \quad b' = b,$$

where $d' = d M_a M_\epsilon/(M_{ab} M_{ef}) = d(1-a'')(1-e'')/((1-a')(1-b')(1-e')(1-f'))$, and $M_{ef}, M_e, M_f, M_\epsilon$ are as before. In this way we can often solve the problem in linear time. [See A. D. Scott and A. D. Sokal, *J. Stat. Phys.* **118** (2005), 1151–1261, §3.4.]

347. (a) Suppose $v_1 — v_2 — \cdots — v_k — v_1$ is an induced cycle. We can assume that $v_1 \succ v_2$. Then, by induction on j, we must have $v_1 \succ \cdots \succ v_j$ for $1 < j \leq k$; for if $v_{j+1} \succ v_j$ we would have $v_{j+1} — v_{j-1}$ by (∗). But now $v_k — v_1$ implies that $k = 3$.

(b) Let the vertices be $\{1, \ldots, m\}$, with territory sets $T(a) \subseteq U$ for $1 \leq a \leq m$; and let U be a tree such that each $U \mid T(a)$ is connected. Let U_a be the least common ancestor of $T(a)$ in U. (Thus the nodes of $T(a)$ appear at the top of the subtree rooted at U_a.) Since $U_a \in T(a)$, we have $a — b$ when $U_a = U_b$.

Writing $s \succ_U t$ for the ancestor relation in U, we now define $a \succ b$ if $U_a \succ_U U_b$ or if $U_a = U_b$ and $a < b$. Then (∗) is satisfied: If $t \in T(a) \cap T(b)$, we have $U_a \succ_U t$ and $U_b \succ_U t$, hence $U_a \succeq_U U_b$ or $U_b \succeq_U U_a$, hence $a \succ b$ or $b \succ a$. And if $a \succ b \succ c$ and $t \in T(a) \cap T(c)$, we have $U_a \succeq_U U_b \succeq_U U_c$; consequently $U_b \in T(a) \cap T(b)$, because U_b lies on the unique path between t and U_a in U and $T(a)$ is connected.

(c) Processing the nodes in any order such that a is eliminated before b whenever U_a is a proper ancestor of U_b will then lead only to subproblems in which the algorithm needs no "double-primed" variables.

For example, using $(a, b, \ldots, g)$ instead of $(1, 2, \ldots, 7)$ in order to match the notation in exercise 346, suppose U is the tree rooted at p having the edges $p — q$, $p — r$, $r — s$, $r — t$, and let $T(a) = \{p, q, r, t\}$, $T(b) = \{p, r, s\}$, $T(c) = \{p, q\}$, $T(d) = \{q\}$, $T(e) = \{r, s\}$, $T(f) = \{s\}$, $T(g) = \{t\}$. Then $a \succ b \succ c \succ d$, $c \succ e \succ f$, $e \succ g$. The algorithm computes $M_{abcdefg} = (1 - a') M_{bcdefg}$, $M_{bcdefg} = (1 - b') M_{cdefg}$, etc., where $a' = aM_f/M_{bcdefg}$, $b' = bM_{dfg}/M_{cdefg} = b(M_d M_f M_g)/(M_{cd} M_{ef} M_g)$, etc.

In general, the tree ordering guarantees that no "double-primed" variables are needed. Thus the formulas reduce to $v' = v/\prod_{u—v,\, v \succ u}(1 - u')$ for each vertex v.

(d) For example, we have $p_1 = a$, $\ldots$, $p_7 = g$, $\theta_1 = a'$, $\ldots$, $\theta_7 = g'$ in (c). The values of the θ's, which depend on the ordering $\succ$, are uniquely defined by the given equations; and we have $M_G(p_1, \ldots, p_m) = (1 - \theta_1) \ldots (1 - \theta_m)$ in any case. [W. Pegden, *Random Structures & Algorithms* **41** (2012), 546–556.]

348. There is at least one singularity at $z = \rho e^{i\theta}$ for some θ. If $0 < r < \rho$, the power series $f(z) = \sum_{n=0}^{\infty} f^{(n)}(re^{i\theta})(z - re^{i\theta})^n/n!$ has radius of convergence $\rho - r$. If $z = \rho$ isn't a singularity, the radius of convergence for $\theta = 0$ would exceed $\rho - r$. But $|f^{(n)}(re^{i\theta})| = |\sum_{m=0}^{\infty} m^{\underline{n}} a_n (re^{i\theta})^{m-n}| \leq f^{(n)}(r)$. [*Mathematische Annalen* **44** (1894), 41–42.]

349. Typical generating functions are $g_{00000001} = 1$; $g_{01100110} = z(g_{00100110} + g_{01010110} + g_{01100110} + g_{01111110})/4$ (in Case 1) or $g_{01100110} = z(g_{00000110} + g_{00010110} + g_{01000110} + g_{01100110})/4$ (in Case 2). These systems of 128 linear equations have solutions whose denominators involve one or more of the polynomials $4 - z$, $2 - z$, $16 - 12z + z^2$, $4 - 3z$, $64 - 80z + 24z^2 - z^3$, $8 - 8z + z^2$ in Case 1 (see exercise 320); the denominators in Case 2 are powers of $4 - z$.

Setting $g(z) = \sum_x g_x(z)/128$ leads to $g(z) = 1/((2 - z)(8 - 8z + z^2))$ in Case 1, with mean 7 and variance 42; $g(z) = (1088 - 400z + 42z^2 - z^3)/(4 - z)^6$ in Case 2, with mean $1139/729 \approx 1.56$ and variance $1139726/729^2 \approx 2.14$.

[The upper bound $E_1 + \cdots + E_6$ is achieved by the distribution of Case 1, because it matches the extreme distribution (148) of the path graph P_6. Incidentally, if Case 1 is generalized from $n = 7$ to arbitrary n, the mean is $n(n - 1)/6$ and the variance is $(n + 3)(n + 2)n(n - 1)/90$.]

350. (a) The generating function for N is $\prod_{k=1}^{n}(1 - \xi_k)/(1 - \xi_k z)$; so the mean and variance, in general, are $\sum_{k=1}^{n} \xi_k/(1 - \xi_k)$ and $\sum_{k=1}^{n} \xi_k/(1 - \xi_k)^2$. In particular, the means are (i) n; (ii) $n/(2n - 1)$; (iii) $n/(2^n - 1)$; (iv) $H_{2n} - H_n + \frac{1}{2n} = \ln 2 + O(1/n)$; (v) $\frac{1}{2}\left(\frac{1}{n+1} + \frac{1}{2n} - \frac{1}{2n+1}\right) = \frac{1}{2n} + O(1/n^2)$. The variance in case (i) is $2n$; otherwise it's asymptotically the same as the mean, times $1 + O(1/n)$.

(b) In this case the mean and variance are $\xi/(1-\xi)$ and $\xi/(1-\xi)^2$, where $\xi = \Pr(A_m) = 1 - (1-\xi_1)\dots(1-\xi_n)$. This value ξ is (i) $1 - 2^{-n}$; (ii) $1 - (1 - \frac{1}{2n})^n = 1 - e^{-1/2} + O(1/n)$; (iii) $1 - (1 - 2^{-n})^n = n/2^n + O(n^2/4^n)$; (iv) $1/2$; (v) $1/(2n+2)$. Hence the respective means are (i) $2^n - 1$; (ii) $e^{1/2} - 1 + O(1/n)$; (iii) $n/2^n + O(n^2/4^n)$; (iv) 1; (v) $1/(2n+1)$. And the variances are (i) $4^n - 2^n$; (ii) $e - e^{1/2} + O(1/n)$; (iii) $n/2^n + O(n^2/4^n)$; (iv) 2; (v) $1/(2n+1) + 1/(2n+1)^2$.

(c) Since G is $K_{n,1}$, exercises 336 and 343 imply that $(\xi_1,\dots,\xi_n,\xi) \in \mathcal{R}(G)$ if and only if $\xi < \frac{1}{2}$. This condition holds in cases (ii), (iii), and (v).

351. (Solution by Moser and Tardos.) We require $i \mathrel{-\!\!\!-} j$ if there's a setting of the variables such that A_i is false and A_j is true, provided that some change to the variables of Ξ_j might make A_i true. And vice versa with $i \leftrightarrow j$.

(The Local Lemma can be proved also for *directed* lopsidependency graphs; see Noga Alon and Joel H. Spencer, *The Probabilistic Method* (2008), §5.1. But the theory of traces, which we use to analyze Algorithm M, is based on undirected graphs, and no algorithmic extension to the directed case is presently known.)

352. Answer 344(e), with $M_G = \beta(i \cup J)$, $M_{G\setminus i} = \beta(J)$, proves that $M_{G\setminus i}/M_G \geq 1 - \theta_i$.

353. (a) There are $n+1$ sorted strings in Case 1, namely $0^k 1^{n-k}$ for $0 \leq k \leq n$. There are F_{n+2} solutions in Case 2 (see, for example, exercise 7.2.1.1–91).

(b) At least $2^n M_G(1/4)$, where G is the path P_{n-1}. By exercise 320 we have $M_G(1/4) = f_{n-1}(1/4) = (n+1)/2^n$; so Case 1 matches the lower bound.

(c) There are *no* lopsidependencies. Hence the relevant G is the empty graph on $m = n-1$ vertices; $M_G(1/4) = (3/4)^{n-1}$ by exercise 336; and indeed, $F_{n+2} \geq 3^{n-1}2^{2-n}$.

354. Differentiate (151) and set $z \leftarrow 1$.

355. If $A = A_j$ is an isolated vertex of G, then $1 - p_j z$ is a factor of the polynomial $M_G^*(z)$ in (149), hence $1 + \delta \leq 1/p_j$; and $E_j = p_j/(1-p_j) \leq 1/\delta$. Otherwise $M_G(p_1,\dots,p_{j-1},p_j(1+\delta),p_{j+1},\dots,p_m) = M_G^*(1) - \delta p_j M_{G\setminus A^*}^*(1) > M_G^*(1+\delta) = 0$; so $E_j = p_j M_{G\setminus A^*}^*(1)/M_G^*(1) > 1/\delta$.

356. (a) We prove the hint by induction on $|S|$. It's obvious when $S = \emptyset$; otherwise let $X = S \cap \bigcup_{i \in U_j} U_j$ and $Y = S \setminus X$. We have

$$\Pr(A_i \mid \overline{A}_S) = \frac{\Pr(A_i \cap \overline{A}_X \cap \overline{A}_Y)}{\Pr(\overline{A}_X \cap \overline{A}_Y)} \leq \frac{\Pr(A_i \cap \overline{A}_Y)}{\Pr(\overline{A}_X \cap \overline{A}_Y)} \leq \frac{\Pr(A_i)\Pr(\overline{A}_Y)}{\Pr(\overline{A}_X \cap \overline{A}_Y)} = \frac{\Pr(A_i)}{\Pr(\overline{A}_X \mid \overline{A}_Y)}$$

by (133). Suppose i belongs to the cliques $U_{j_0}, \dots, U_{j_r}$ where $j = j_0$. Let $X_0 = \emptyset$ and $X_k = (S \cap U_{j_k}) \setminus X_{k-1}$, $Y_k = Y \cup X_1 \cup \dots \cup X_{k-1}$ for $1 \leq k \leq r$. We have $\Pr(A_l \mid \overline{A}_{Y_k}) \leq \theta_{l j_k}$ for all $l \in X_k$, since $|Y_k| < |S|$ when $X_k \neq \emptyset$; hence $\Pr(\overline{A}_{X_k} \mid \overline{A}_{Y_k}) \geq (1 + \theta_{i j_k} - \Sigma_{j_k})$. Thus $\Pr(\overline{A}_X \mid \overline{A}_Y) = \Pr(\overline{A}_{X_1} \mid \overline{A}_{Y_1})\Pr(\overline{A}_{X_2} \mid \overline{A}_{Y_2})\dots\Pr(\overline{A}_{X_r} \mid \overline{A}_{Y_r}) \geq \prod_{k \neq j, i \in U_k} (1 + \theta_{ik} - \Sigma_k)$, by the chain rule (exercise MPR-14); the hint follows.

Finally let $W_k = U_1 \cup \dots \cup U_k$ for $1 \leq k \leq t$. The hint implies that

$$\Pr(\overline{A}_1 \cap \dots \cap \overline{A}_m) = \Pr(\overline{A}_{W_1})\Pr(\overline{A}_{W_2} \mid \overline{A}_{W_1})\dots\Pr(\overline{A}_{W_t} \mid \overline{A}_{W_{t-1}})$$
$$\geq (1 - \Sigma_1)(1 - \Sigma_2)\dots(1 - \Sigma_t) > 0.$$

(b) The extreme events $B_1, \dots, B_m$ of Theorem S satisfy the hint of (a). Thus $\Pr(B_i \mid \bigcap_{k \notin U_j} \overline{B}_k) \leq \theta_{ij}$ for all $i \in U_j$; hence $q_i = \Pr(B_i \mid \bigcap_{k \neq i} \overline{B}_k) \leq \theta_{ij}/(1 + \theta_{ij} - \Sigma_j)$. Furthermore $E_i = q_i/(1 - q_i)$ in (152), because $q_i = p_i M_{G\setminus i^*}/M_{G\setminus i}$.

(c) Let $U_1, \ldots, U_t$ be the *edges* of G, with $\theta_{ik} = \theta_i$ when $U_k = \{i, j\}$. Then $\Sigma_k = \theta_i + \theta_j < 1$, and the sufficient condition in (a) is that $\Pr(A_i) \le \theta_i \prod_{j \ne k, i \!-\! j}(1 - \theta_j)$ whenever $i \!-\! k$. (But notice that Theorem M does not hold for such larger p_i.)

[K. Kolipaka, M. Szegedy, and Y. Xu, *LNCS* **7408** (2012), 603–614.]

357. If $r > 0$, we have $x = r/(1-p)$, $y = r/(1-q)$. But $r = 0$ is possible only on the axes of Fig. 94: Either $(p, q) = (0, 1)$, $x = 0$, $0 < y \le 1$, or $(p, q) = (1, 0)$, $0 < x \le 1$, $y = 1$.

358. Suppose $x \ge y$ (hence $p \ge q$ and $x > 0$). Then $p \le r$ if and only if $1 - y \le y$.

359. Instead of computing π_l by formula (154), represent it as two numbers (π_l^+, π_l'), where π_l^+ is the product of the nonzero factors and π_l' is the number of zero factors. Then the quantity $\pi_{\bar{l}}$ needed in (156) is $\pi_{\bar{l}}^+ [\pi_{\bar{l}}' = 0]$; and the quantity $\pi_l/(1 - \eta_{C \to l})$ is $\pi_l^+ [\pi_l' = 1]$ if $\eta_{C \to l} = 1$, otherwise it's $\pi_l^+ [\pi_l' = 0]/(1 - \eta_{C \to l})$. A similar method can be used to separate out the zero factors of $\prod_{l \in C} \gamma_{l \to C}$ in (157).

360. We may assume that $\eta_3 = 0$. Since $\pi_l = 1$ implies that $\eta_{C \to l} = \gamma_{\bar{l} \to C} = 0$, we have $\eta_{C \to 1} = \eta_{C \to \bar{2}} = \eta_{C \to 3} = \eta_{C \to \bar{4}} = \gamma_{\bar{1} \to C} = \gamma_{2 \to C} = \gamma_{3 \to C} = \gamma_{4 \to C} = 0$ for all C. Consequently, as in (159), all but three of the values $\eta_{C \to l}$ are zero; let x, y, z denote the others. Also let $\eta_{\bar{1}} = a$, $\eta_2 = b$, $\eta_4 = c$, $\eta_{\bar{3}} = d$. Then $\pi_{\bar{1}} = (1-a)(1-x)$, $\pi_2 = (1-b)(1-y)$, $\pi_4 = (1-c)(1-z)$, and $\pi_{\bar{3}} = 1 - d$. A fixed point is obtained if $x = d(b + cd(1-b) + ad^2(1-b)(1-c))/(1 - d^3(1-a)(1-b)(1-c))$, etc. If d is 0 or 1 then $x = y = z = d$. [Are there any other fixed points, say with $\pi_1 \ne 1$?]

361. The π's and γ's will also be either 0 or 1, and we exclude the case $\pi_l = \pi_{\bar{l}} = 0$; thus each variable v is either 1, 0, or $*$, depending on whether $(\pi_v, \pi_{\bar{v}})$ is $(0, 1)$, $(1, 0)$, or $(1, 1)$.

Any assignment of 1, 0, or $*$ to the variables is permissible, provided that every clause has at least one literal that's true or two that are $*$. (Such partial assignments are called "covering," and they're usually possible even with unsatisfiable clauses; see exercise 364.) All survey messages $\eta_{C \to l}' = \eta_{C \to l}$ are zero except when clause C has l as its only non-false literal. The reinforcement message η_l can be either 0 or 1, except that it must be 1 if l is true ($\pi_l = 0$) and all messages $\eta_{C \to l}$ are 0.

If we also want $\eta_l' = \eta_l$, we take $\kappa = 1$ in (158), and $\eta_l = 1 - \pi_l$.

362. Create a linked list L, containing all literals that are to be forced true, including all literals that are in 1-clauses of the original problem. Do the following steps while L is nonempty: Remove a literal l from L; remove all clauses that contain l; and remove $\bar{l}$ from all the clauses that remain. If any of those clauses has thereby been reduced to a single literal, (l'), check to see if l' or $\bar{l}'$ is already present in L. If $\bar{l}'$ is present, a contradiction has arisen; we must either terminate unsuccessfully or restart step S8 with increased ψ. But if $\bar{l}'$ and l' are both absent, put l' into L.

363. (a) True; indeed, this is an important invariant property of Algorithm C.

(b) $W(001) = 1$, $W(\ast\ast\ast) = p_1 p_2 p_3$, otherwise $W(x) = 0$.

(c) Statements (i) and (iii) are true, but not (ii); consider $x = 10\ast$, $x' = 00\ast$, and the clause 123.

(d) All eight subsets of $\{1, \bar{2}, \bar{3}\}$ are stable except $\{\bar{2}, \bar{3}\}$, because x_1 is constrained in 100. The other seven are partially ordered as shown. (This diagram illustrates L_7, the smallest lattice that is lower semimodular but not modular.)

(e)

$x_2 x_3 = 00$	01	0*	10	11	1*	*0	*1	**
$x_1 = 0$ 0	$q_1 q_2$	0	$q_1 q_3$	$q_1 q_2 q_3$	$q_1 q_2 p_3$	0	$q_1 p_2 q_3$	$q_1 p_2 p_3$
$x_1 = 1$ $q_2 q_3$	$q_1 q_2 q_3$	$q_1 q_2 p_3$	$q_1 q_2 q_3$	$q_1 q_2 q_3$	$q_1 q_2 p_3$	$q_1 p_2 q_3$	$q_1 p_2 q_3$	$q_1 p_2 p_3$
$x_1 = *$ 0	$p_1 q_2 q_3$	$p_1 q_2 p_3$	$p_1 q_2 q_3$	$p_1 q_2 q_3$	$p_1 q_2 p_3$	$p_1 p_2 q_3$	$p_1 p_2 q_3$	$p_1 p_2 p_3$

(f) One solution is $\{\bar{1}23\bar{4}5, \bar{1}4, \bar{2}5, \bar{3}45, \bar{3}45\}$. (For these clauses the partial assignment $\{3\}$ is stable, but it is "unreachable" below $\{1, 2, 3, 4, 5\}$.)

(g) If $L = L' \setminus l$ and $L' \in \mathcal{L}$ but $L \notin \mathcal{L}$, introduce the clause $(x_l \vee \bigvee_{k \in L'} \bar{x}_k)$.

(h) True, because $L' = L \setminus l'$ and $L'' = L \setminus l''$, where $|l'|$ and $|l''|$ are unconstrained with respect to L. A variable that's unconstrained with respect to L is also unconstrained with respect to any subset of L.

(i) Suppose $L' = L'^{(0)} \prec \cdots \prec L'^{(s)} = \{1, \ldots, n\}$ and $L'' = L''^{(0)} \prec \cdots \prec L''^{(t)} = \{1, \ldots, n\}$. Then $L'^{(s-i)} \cap L''^{(t-j)}$ is stable for $0 \le i \le s$ and $0 \le j \le t$, by induction on $i + j$ using (h).

(j) It suffices to consider the case $L = \{1, \ldots, n\}$. Suppose the unconstrained variables are x_1, x_2, x_3. Then, by induction, the sum is $q_1 q_2 q_3 + p_1 + p_2 + p_3 - (p_1 p_2 + p_1 p_3 + p_2 p_3) + p_1 p_2 p_3 = 1$, using "inclusion and exclusion" to compensate for terms that are counted more than once. A similar argument works with any number of unconstrained variables.

Notes: See F. Ardila and E. Maneva, *Discrete Mathematics* **309** (2009), 3083–3091. The sum in (j) is ≤ 1 when each $p_k + q_k \le 1$ for $1 \le k \le n$, because it is monotone. Because of (i), the stable sets below L form a lower semimodular lattice, with

$$L' \wedge L'' = L' \cap L'' \quad \text{and} \quad L' \vee L'' = \bigcap\{L''' \mid L''' \supseteq L' \cup L'' \text{ and } L''' \sqsubseteq L\}.$$

E. Maneva and A. Sinclair noted in *Theoretical Comp. Sci.* **407** (2008), 359–369 that a random satisfiability problem is satisfiable with probability $\le \mathrm{E}\sum W(X)$, the expected total weight of partial assignments having the given distribution, because of identity (j); this led them to sharper bounds than had previously been known.

364. (a) True if and only if all clauses have length 2 or more.

(b) 001 and $***$ are covering; these are the partial assignments of nonzero weight, when $q_1 = \cdots = q_n = 0$ in the previous exercise. Only 001 is a core.

(c) $***$ is the only covering and the only core; $W(0101) = W(0111) = q_3$.

(d) In fact, every stable partial assignment L' has a unique covering assignment L with $L \sqsubseteq L'$, namely $L = \bigcap\{L'' \mid L'' \sqsubseteq L'\}$, obtained by successively removing unconstrained literals (in any order)}.

(e) If L' and L'' are adjacent we have $L' \cap L'' \sqsubseteq L'$ and $L' \cap L'' \sqsubseteq L''$.

(f) Not necessarily. For example, the clauses $\{\bar{1}234, \bar{1}2\bar{3}4, \bar{1}2\bar{3}\bar{4}, 1\bar{2}\bar{3}4, 12\bar{3}\bar{4}, 123\bar{4}\}$ define $\bar{S}_2(x_1, x_2, x_3, x_4)$; there are two clusters but only an empty core.

[A. Braunstein and R. Zecchina introduced the notion of covering assignments in *J. Statistical Mechanics* (June 2004), P06007:1–18.]

365. If L is any of the six solutions in (8), and if q is odd, then $qL - d$ is a covering assignment for $0 \le d < q$ and $8q - d \le n < 9q - d$. (For example, if $L = \{\bar{1}, \bar{2}, 3, 4, \bar{5}, \bar{6}, 7, 8\}$ the partial assignment $3L - 1 = \{\bar{2}, \bar{5}, 8, 11, \bar{14}, \bar{17}, 20, 23\}$ works for $n \in [23 \ldots 25]$.) Thus all $n > 63$ are "covered." [Do all nonempty coverings of *waerden*$(3, 3; n)$ have this form?]

366. Eliminating variable 1 (x_1) by resolution yields the erp rule $\bar{x}_1 \leftarrow (x_2 \vee \bar{x}_3) \wedge (x_3 \vee x_4)$, and new clauses $\{2\bar{3}4, 2\bar{3}\bar{4}, 234, \bar{2}34\}$. Then eliminating 2 (x_2) yields $x_2 \leftarrow (x_3 \vee x_4) \wedge (\bar{x}_3 \vee x_4)$ and new clauses $\{34, \bar{3}4\}$. Now 4 (x_4) is pure; so $x_4 \leftarrow 1$, and $F' = \emptyset$ is satisfiable. (Going backwards in the erp rules will then make $x_4 \leftarrow 1$, $x_2 \leftarrow 1$, $x_1 \leftarrow 0$, regardless of x_3.)

367. (We can choose whichever of the two assignments is most convenient, for example by picking the shortest, since either one is a valid erp rule.) Any solution will either satisfy all the clauses on the right side of $\bar{x}$ or all the clauses on the right side of x, or both. For if a solution falsifies both $C_i \setminus x$ and $C'_j \setminus \bar{x}$, it falsifies $C_i \diamond C'_j$.

In either case the value of x will satisfy all of the clauses $C_1, \ldots, C_a, C'_1, \ldots, C'_b$.

368. If (l) is a clause, subsumption removes all other clauses that contain l. Then resolution (with $p = 1$) will remove $\bar{l}$ from all q of its clauses, and (l) itself.

369. Let $C_i = (l \vee \alpha_i)$ and $C'_j = (\bar{l} \vee \beta_j)$. Each omitted clause $C_i \diamond C'_j = (\alpha_i \vee \beta_j)$, where $1 < i \le p$ and $r < j \le q$, is redundant, because it is a consequence of the non-omitted clauses $(\alpha_i \vee \bar{l}_1), \ldots, (\alpha_i \vee \bar{l}_r), (l_1 \vee \cdots \vee l_r \vee \beta_j)$ via hyperresolution. [This technique is called "substitution," because we essentially replace $|l|$ by its definition.]

370. $(a \vee b) \wedge (a \vee \bar{b} \vee \bar{c}) \wedge (\bar{a} \vee b \vee c) = (a \vee \bar{c}) \wedge (b \vee c)$. (See the discussion following 7.1.1–(27). In general, advanced preprocessors use the theory of DNF minimization, in its dual form, to find irredundant minimum forms for CNF. Such techniques are not implemented, however, in the examples of preprocessing considered in this section.)

371. One scenario starts by eliminating variable 1, replacing eight clauses by eight new ones: 2347, $\bar{2}347$, 2359, $\bar{2}359$, 3457, $\bar{3}457$, 4579, $\bar{4}579$. Then 8 is eliminated, replacing another eight by eight: 2456, $\bar{2}456$, 2567, $\bar{2}567$, 2579, $\bar{2}579$, 4679, $\bar{4}679$. Then come self-subsumptions: $2347 \mapsto 237$ (via 234), $3457 \mapsto 357$ (345), $357 \mapsto 35$ ($35\bar{7}$); and 35 subsumes 345, 357. Further self-subsumptions yield $2359 \mapsto 239$, $\bar{2}359 \mapsto \bar{2}39$, $\bar{2}579 \mapsto \bar{2}79$, $\bar{2}456 \mapsto \bar{2}46$, $246 \mapsto 46$; and 46 subsumes 456, $46\bar{7}9$, $\bar{2}46$. Similarly, $\bar{2}567 \mapsto \bar{2}67$, $\bar{4}579 \mapsto \bar{4}59$, $\bar{2}347 \mapsto \bar{2}37$, $\bar{3}457 \mapsto \bar{3}57$, $\bar{3}57 \mapsto \bar{3}5$; and $\bar{3}5$ subsumes $\bar{3}45$, $\bar{3}57$. Then $2\bar{4}56 \mapsto 2\bar{4}6$, $2\bar{4}6 \mapsto \bar{4}6$; and $\bar{4}6$ subsumes $\bar{4}56$, $2\bar{4}6$, $\bar{4}679$. Also $2567 \mapsto 267$, $4579 \mapsto 459$, $2579 \mapsto 279$.

Round 2 of variable elimination first gets rid of 4, replacing six clauses by just four using exercise 369: 236, $\bar{2}36$, 569, $\bar{5}69$. Then variable 3 goes away; ten clauses become eight, again via exercise 369: 256, $\bar{2}56$, 257, $\bar{2}57$, 259, $\bar{2}59$, 569, $\bar{5}69$. And the ten clauses that now contain 2 or $\bar{2}$ resolve into just four: 5679, $5\bar{6}79$, $\bar{5}679$, $\bar{5}\bar{6}79$.

After eliminating 7 and 9, only four clauses remain, namely 56, $5\bar{6}$, $\bar{5}6$, $\bar{5}\bar{6}$; and they quickly produce a contradiction.

372. (This problem is surprisingly difficult.) Are the clauses $\{\bar{1}5, \bar{1}6, \bar{2}5, \bar{2}6, \bar{3}7, \bar{3}8, \bar{4}7, \bar{4}8, 123, 124, 134, 234, 567, 568, 578, 678\}$ as "small" as possible?

373. Using the notation of (102), elimination of $x_{1m}, x_{2m}, \ldots, x_{mm}$ produces new clauses M'_{imk} for $1 \le i, k < m$ as well as $M_{m(m-1)}$. Then elimination of $x_{m(m-1)}$ gives $(M_{i(m-1)} \vee M_{m(m-2)})$ for $1 \le i < m$. This clause self-subsumes to $M_{i(m-1)}$, using $M'_{im1}, \ldots, M'_{im(m-2)}$. And $M_{i(m-1)}$ subsumes each M'_{imk}, so we've reduced m to $m-1$.

374. As in (57), variables are numbered 1 to n, and literals from 2 to $2n + 1$. But we will now number the clauses from $2n + 2$ to $m + 2n + 1$. The literals of clauses will be stored in cells, somewhat as in Algorithm A, but with additional links: Each cell p contains not only a literal $\mathrm{L}(p)$, a clause number $\mathrm{C}(p)$, and forward/backward pointers $\mathrm{F}(p)$ and $\mathrm{B}(p)$ to other cells with the same literal, but also left/right pointers $\mathrm{S}(p)$ and $\mathrm{D}(p)$ to other cells in the same *clause*. (Think "sinister" and "dexter.") Cells 0 and 1 are reserved for special use; cell l, for $2 \le l < 2n + 2$, serves as the head of the doubly linked list of cells that contain the literal l; cell c, for $2n + 2 \le c < m + 2n + 2$, serves as the head of the doubly linked list of cells that contain the elements of clause c; and cell p, for $m + 2n + 2 \le p < M$, either is available for future use or holds literal and clause data for a currently active clause.

Free cells are accessed via a global pointer AVAIL. To get a new $p \Leftarrow$ AVAIL when AVAIL $\ne 0$, we set $p \leftarrow$ AVAIL, AVAIL $\leftarrow$ S(AVAIL); but if AVAIL $= 0$, we set $p \leftarrow M$ and $M \leftarrow M + 1$ (assuming that M never gets too large). To free one or more cells from p' to p'' that are linked together via left links, we set $\mathrm{S}(p') \leftarrow$ AVAIL and AVAIL $\leftarrow p''$.

The number of active clauses containing literal l, TALLY(l), can therefore be computed as follows: Set $t \leftarrow 0$, $p \leftarrow$ F(l); while not $lit(p)$, set $t \leftarrow t+1$ and $p \leftarrow$ F(p); set TALLY(l) $\leftarrow t$; here '$lit(p)$' stands for '$p < 2n+2$'. The number of literals in clause c, SIZE(c), can be computed by a similar loop, using '$cls(p)$' to stand for '$p < m+2n+2$': Set $t \leftarrow 0$, $p \leftarrow$ S(c); while not $cls(p)$, set $t \leftarrow t+1$ and $p \leftarrow$ S(p); set SIZE(c) $\leftarrow t$. After initialization, the TALLY and SIZE statistics can be updated dynamically as local changes are made. (TALLY(l) and SIZE(c) can be maintained in L(l) and C(c).)

To facilitate resolution, the literals of each clause are required to increase from left to right; in other words, we must have L(p) $<$ L(q) whenever $p =$ S(q) and $q =$ D(p), unless $cls(p)$ or $cls(q)$. But the clauses within literal lists need not appear in any particular order. We might even have C(F(p)) $>$ C(q) but C(F(p')) $<$ C(q'), when C(p) $=$ C(p') and C(q) $=$ C(q').

To facilitate subsumption, each literal l is assigned a 64-bit *signature* SIG(l) $= (1 \ll U_1) \mid (1 \ll U_2)$, where U_1 and U_2 are independently random 6-bit numbers. Then each clause c is assigned a signature that is the bitwise OR of the signatures of its literals: Set $t \leftarrow 0$, $p \leftarrow$ S(c); while not $cls(p)$, set $t \leftarrow t \mid$ SIG(L(p)) and $p \leftarrow$ S(p); set SIG(c) $\leftarrow t$. (See the discussion of Bloom's superimposed coding in Section 6.5.)

(a) To resolve c with c', where c contains l and c' contains $\bar{l}$, we essentially want to do a list merge. Set $p \leftarrow 1$, $q \leftarrow$ S(c), $u \leftarrow$ L(q), $q' \leftarrow$ S(c'), $u' \leftarrow$ L(q'), and do the following while $u + u' > 0$: If $u = u'$, copy(u) and bump(q,q'); if $u = \bar{u}' = l$, bump(q,q'); if $u = \bar{u}' \neq l$, terminate unsuccessfully; otherwise if $u > u'$, copy(u) and bump(q); otherwise copy(u') and bump(q'). Here 'copy(u)' means 'set $p' \leftarrow p$, $p \Leftarrow$ AVAIL, S(p') $\leftarrow p$, L(p) $\leftarrow u$'; 'bump(q)' means 'set $q \leftarrow$ S(q); if $cls(q)$ set $u \leftarrow 0$, otherwise set $u \leftarrow$ L(q)'; 'bump(q')' is similar, but it uses q' and u'; and 'bump(q,q')' means 'bump(q) and bump(q')'. Unsuccessful termination occurs when clauses c and c' resolve to a tautology; we set $p \leftarrow 0$, after first returning cells p through S(1) to free storage if $p \neq 1$. Successful termination with $u = u' = 0$ means that the resolved clause consists of the literals in cells from p through S(1), linked only via S pointers.

(b) Find a literal l in C with minimum TALLY(l). Set $p \leftarrow$ F(l), and do the following while not $lit(p)$: Set $c' \leftarrow$ C(p); if $c' \neq c$ and $\sim$SIG(c') & SIG(c) $= 0$ and SIZE(c') $\geq$ SIZE(c), do a detailed subsumption test; then set $p \leftarrow$ F(p). The detailed test begins with $q \leftarrow$ S(c), $u \leftarrow$ L(q), $q' \leftarrow$ S(c'), $u' \leftarrow$ L(q'), and does the following steps while $u' \geq u > 0$: bump(q') while $u' > u$; then bump(q,q') if $u' = u$. When the loop terminates, c subsumes c' if and only if $u \leq u'$.

(c) Use (b), but set $p \leftarrow$ F($l = \bar{x}$? x: l), and use $((\text{SIG}(c)\ \&\ \sim\text{SIG}(\bar{x})) \mid \text{SIG}(x))$ in place of SIG(c). Also modify the detailed test, by inserting 'if $u = \bar{x}$ then $u \leftarrow x$' just after each occurrence of '$u \leftarrow$ L(q)'.

[The algorithm in (b) was introduced by A. Biere, *LNCS* **3542** (2005), 59–70, §4.2. "False hits," in which the detailed test is performed but no actual (self-)subsumption is detected, tend to occur less than 1% of the time in practice.]

375. Let each literal l have another field STAMP(l), initially zero; and let s be a global "time stamp" that is initially zero. To make the test, set $s \leftarrow s+1$ and $\sigma \leftarrow 0$; then set STAMP(u) $\leftarrow s$ and $\sigma \leftarrow \sigma \mid$ SIG(u) for all u such that ($\bar{l}u$) is a clause. If $\sigma \neq 0$, set $\sigma \leftarrow \sigma \mid$ SIG(l) and run through all clauses c that contain l, doing the following: If SIG(c) & $\sim\sigma = 0$, and if each of c's literals $u \neq l$ has STAMP(u) $= s$, exit with $C_1 = c$ and $r =$ SIZE(c) $- 1$. If C_1 has thereby been found, set $s \leftarrow s+1$ and STAMP($\bar{u}$) $\leftarrow s$ for all $u \neq l$ in c. Then a clause ($\bar{l} \lor \beta_j$) implicitly has $j \leq r$ in the notation of exercise 369 if and only if β_j is a single literal u with STAMP(u) $= s$.

Given a variable x, test the condition first for $l = x$; if that fails, try $l = \bar{x}$.

376. Highest priority is given to the common operations of unit conditioning and pure literal elimination, which are "low-hanging fruit." Give each variable x two new fields, STATE(x) and LINK(x). A "to-do stack," containing all such easy pickings, begins at TODO and follows LINKs until reaching Λ. The nonzero states are called FF (forced false), FT (forced true), EQ (eliminated quietly), and ER (eliminated by resolution). Variable x is on the to-do stack only if STATE(x) is FF, FT, or EQ.

Whenever a unit clause (l) is detected, with STATE($|l|$) $= 0$, we set STATE($|l|$) $\leftarrow$ $(l \,\&\, 1?\,\text{FF}:\text{FT})$, LINK($|l|$) $\leftarrow$ TODO, and TODO $\leftarrow |l|$. But if STATE($|l|$) $= (l \,\&\, 1?\,\text{FT}:\text{FF})$, we terminate, because the clauses are unsatisfiable.

Whenever a literal with TALLY($\bar{l}$) $= 0$ is detected, we do the same thing if STATE($|l|$) $= 0$. But if STATE($|l|$) $= (l \,\&\, 1?\,\text{FT}:\text{FF})$, we simply set STATE($|l|$) $\leftarrow$ EQ instead of terminating. (In that case TALLY(l) is also 0.)

To clear the to-do stack, we do the following while TODO $\neq \Lambda$: Set $x \leftarrow$ TODO and TODO $\leftarrow$ LINK(x); if STATE(x) $=$ EQ, do nothing (no erp rule is needed to eliminate x); otherwise set $l \leftarrow$ (STATE(x) $=$ FT? x: $\bar{x}$), output the erp rule $l \leftarrow 1$, and use the doubly linked lists to delete all clauses containing l and to delete $\bar{l}$ from all clauses. (Those deletions update TALLY and SIZE fields, so they often contribute new entries to the to-do stack. Notice that if clause c loses a literal, we must recompute SIG(c). If clause c disappears, we set SIZE(c) $\leftarrow 0$, and never use c again.)

Subsumption and strengthening are next in line. We give each clause c a new field LINK(c), which is nonzero if and only if c appears on the "exploitation stack." That stack begins at EXP and follows LINKs until reaching the nonzero sentinel value Λ'. All clauses are initially placed on the exploitation stack. Afterwards, whenever a literal $\bar{l}$ is deleted from a clause c, either during unit conditioning or self-subsumption, we test if LINK(c) $= 0$; if so, we put c back on the stack by setting LINK(c) $\leftarrow$ EXP and EXP $\leftarrow c$.

To clear the exploitation stack, we first clear the to-do stack. Then, while EXP $\neq$ Λ', we set $c \leftarrow$ EXP, EXP $\leftarrow$ LINK(c), and do the following if SIZE(c) $\neq 0$: Remove clauses subsumed by c; clear the to-do stack; and if SIZE(c) is still nonzero, strengthen clauses that c can improve, clear the to-do stack, and set TIME(c) $\leftarrow T$ (see below).

All of this takes place before we even think about the elimination of variables. But rounds of variable elimination form the "outer level" of computation. Each variable x has yet another field, STABLE(x), which is nonzero if and only if we need not attempt to eliminate x. This field is initially zero, but set nonzero when x is eliminated or its elimination has been abandoned. It is reset to zero whenever a variable is later "touched," namely when x or $\bar{x}$ appears in a deleted or self-subsumed clause. (In particular, every variable that appears in a new clause produced by resolution will be touched, because it will appear in at least one of the clauses that were replaced by new ones.)

If a round has failed to eliminate any variables, or if it has eliminated them all, we're done. But otherwise there's still work to do, because the new clauses can often be subsumed or strengthened. (Indeed, some of them might actually be duplicates.) Hence two *more* fields are introduced: TIME(l) for each literal and TIME(c) for each clause, initially zero. Let T be the number of the current elimination round. We set TIME(l) $\leftarrow T$ for all literals l in all clauses that are replaced by resolution, and TIME(c) $\leftarrow T$ is also set appropriately as mentioned above.

Introduce yet another field, EXTRA(c), initially zero. It is reset to zero whenever TIME(c) $\leftarrow T$, and set to 1 whenever c is replaced by a new clause. For every literal l such that STATE($|l|$) $= 0$ and TIME(l) $= T$ at the end of round T, set EXTRA(c) $\leftarrow$ EXTRA(c) $+ 4$ for all clauses c that contain l, and EXTRA(c) $\leftarrow$ EXTRA(c) $\,|\, 2$ for all clauses c that contain $\bar{l}$. Then run through all clauses c for which SIZE(c) > 0 and

TIME$(c) < T$. If SIZE$(c) =$ EXTRA$(c) \gg 2$, remove clauses subsumed by c and clear the exploitation stack. Also, if EXTRA$(c) \mathbin{\&} 3 \neq 0$, we may be able to use c to strengthen other clauses — unless EXTRA$(c) \mathbin{\&} 1 = 0$ and EXTRA$(c) \gg 2 <$ SIZE$(c) - 1$. Self-subsumption using l need not be attempted when EXTRA$(c) \mathbin{\&} 1 = 0$ unless TIME$(\bar{l}) = T$ and EXTRA$(c) \gg 2 =$ SIZE$(c) - [$TIME$(l) = T]$. Finally, reset EXTRA(c) to zero (even if TIME$(c) = T$). [See Niklas Eén and Armin Biere, *LNCS* **3569** (2005), 61–75.]

377. Each vertex v of G corresponds to variables v_1, v_2, v_3 in F; each edge $u - v$ corresponds to clauses $(\bar{u}_1 \vee v_2)$, $(\bar{u}_2 \vee v_3)$, $(\bar{u}_3 \vee \bar{v}_1)$, $(u_2 \vee v_1)$, $(u_3 \vee \bar{v}_2)$, $(\bar{u}_1 \vee \bar{v}_3)$. The longest paths in the dependency digraph for F have the form $t_1 \to u_2 \to v_3 \to \bar{w}_1$ or $t_1 \to \bar{u}_3 \to \bar{v}_2 \to \bar{w}_1$, where $t - u - v - w$ is a walk in G.

[A similar method reduces the question of finding an oriented cycle of length r in a given digraph to the question of finding a failed literal in some dependency digraph. The cycle detection problem has a long history; see N. Alon, R. Yuster, and U. Zwick, *Algorithmica* **17** (1997), 209–223. So any surprisingly fast algorithm to decide whether or not failed literals exist — that is, faster than $n^{2\omega/(\omega+1)}$ when $m = O(n)$ and matrix multiplication takes $O(n^\omega)$ — would lead to surprisingly fast algorithms for other problems.]

378. The erp rule $l \leftarrow l \vee (\bar{l}_1 \wedge \cdots \wedge \bar{l}_q)$ will change any solution of $F \setminus C$ into a solution of F. [See M. Järvisalo, A. Biere, and M. Heule, *LNCS* **6015** (2010), 129–144.]

(In practice it's sometimes possible to remove tens of thousands of blocked clauses. For example, all of the exclusion clauses (17) in the coloring problem are blocked, as are many of the clauses that arise in fault testing. Yet the author has yet to see a *single* example where blocked clause elimination is actually helpful in combination with transformations 1–4, which are already quite powerful by themselves.)

379. (Solution by O. Kullmann.) In general, *any* set F of clauses can be replaced by another set F', whenever there's a variable x such that the elimination of x from F yields exactly the same clauses as the elimination of x from F'. In this case the elimination of a has this property. The erp rule $a \leftarrow a \vee (\bar{b} \wedge \bar{c} \wedge d)$ is necessary and sufficient.

380. (a) Reverse self-subsumption weakens it to $(a \vee b \vee c \vee d)$, then to $(a \vee b \vee c \vee d \vee e)$, which is subsumed by $(a \vee d \vee e)$. [In general one can show that reverse self-subsumption from C leads to a subsumed clause if and only if C is certifiable from the other clauses.]

(b) Again we weaken to $(a \vee b \vee c \vee d \vee e)$; but now we find this blocked by c.

(c) No erp rule is needed in (a), but we need $c \leftarrow c \vee (\bar{a} \wedge \bar{b})$ in (b). [Heule, Järvisalo, and Biere, *LNCS* **6397** (2010), 357–371, call this "asymmetric elimination."]

381. By symmetry, we'll remove the final clause. (Without it, the given clauses state that $x_1 \leq x_2 \leq \cdots \leq x_n$; with it, they state that all variables are equal.) Assume more generally that, for $1 \leq j < n$, every clause other than $(\bar{x}_j \vee x_{j+1})$ that contains $\bar{x}_j$ also contains either x_n or $\bar{x}_i$ for some $i < j$. For $1 \leq j \leq n - 1$ we can then weaken $(x_1 \vee \cdots \vee x_j \vee \bar{x}_n)$ to $(x_1 \vee \cdots \vee x_{j+1} \vee \bar{x}_n)$. Finally, $(x_1 \vee \cdots \vee x_{n-1} \vee \bar{x}_n)$ can be eliminated because it is blocked by x_{n-1}.

Although we've eliminated only one clause, $n - 1$ erp rules are actually needed to undo the process: $x_1 \leftarrow x_1 \vee x_n$; $x_2 \leftarrow x_2 \vee (\bar{x}_1 \wedge x_n)$; $x_3 \leftarrow x_3 \vee (\bar{x}_1 \wedge \bar{x}_2 \wedge x_n)$; $\ldots$; $x_{n-1} \leftarrow x_{n-1} \vee (\bar{x}_1 \wedge \cdots \wedge \bar{x}_{n-2} \wedge x_n)$. (Those rules, applied in reverse order, can however be simplified to $x_j \leftarrow x_j \vee x_n$ for $1 \leq j < n$, because $x_1 \leq \cdots \leq x_n$ in any solution.) [See Heule, Järvisalo, Biere, *EasyChair Proc. in Computing* **13** (2013), 41–46.]

382. See M. J. H. Heule, M. Järvisalo, and A. Biere, *LNCS* **6695** (2011), 201–215.

383. (a) In a learning step, let $\Phi' = \Phi$ and $\Psi' = \Psi \cup C$. In a forgetting step, let $\Phi' = \Phi$ and $\Psi = \Psi' \cup C$. In a hardening step, let $\Phi' = \Phi \cup C$ and $\Psi = \Psi' \cup C$. In a softening step, let $\Phi = \Phi' \cup C$ and $\Psi' = \Psi \cup C$. In all four cases it is easy to verify that $(\mathrm{sat}(\Phi) \iff \mathrm{sat}(\Phi \cup \Psi))$ implies $(\mathrm{sat}(\Phi) \iff \mathrm{sat}(\Phi') \iff \mathrm{sat}(\Phi' \cup \Psi'))$, where $\mathrm{sat}(G)$ means "G is satisfiable," because $\mathrm{sat}(G \cup G') \implies \mathrm{sat}(G)$. Thus the assertions are invariant.

(b) Each erp rule allows us to go one step backward, until reaching F.

(c) The first (softening) step is fine, because both $\Phi = (x)$ and $\Phi \setminus (x) = 1$ are satisfiable, and because the erp rule unconditionally makes x true. But the second (learning) step is flawed, because $\mathrm{sat}(\Phi \cup \Psi)$ does not imply $\mathrm{sat}(\Phi \cup \Psi \cup C)$ when $\Phi \cup \Psi = (x)$ and $C = (\bar{x})$. (This example explains why the criterion for learning is not simply '$\mathrm{sat}(\Phi) \implies \mathrm{sat}(\Phi \cup C)$' as it essentially is for softening.)

(d) Yes, because C is also certifiable for $\Phi \cup \Psi$.

(e) Yes, after softening it. No erp rule is needed, because $\Phi \setminus C \vdash C$.

(f) A soft clause can be discarded whether or not it is subsumed. To discard a hard clause that is subsumed by a soft clause, first harden the soft one. To discard a hard C that is subsumed by a hard C', weaken C and then discard it. (The weakening step is clearly permissible, and no erp rule is needed.)

(g) If C contains $\bar{x}$ and C' contains x and $C \setminus \bar{x} \subseteq C' \setminus x$, we can learn the soft clause $C \diamond C' = C' \setminus x$, then use it to subsume C' as in (f).

(h) Forget all soft clauses that contain x or $\bar{x}$. Then let $C_1, \ldots, C_p$ be the hard clauses containing x, and $C'_1, \ldots, C'_q$ those containing $\bar{x}$. Learn all the (soft) clauses $C_i \diamond C'_j$, and harden them, noting that they don't involve x. Weaken each C_i, with erp rule $x \leftarrow x \vee \overline{C}_i$, and forget it; also weaken and forget each C'_j, with erp rule $x \leftarrow x \wedge C'_j$. (One can show that either of the erp rules in (161) would also suffice.)

(i) Whenever $\Phi \cup \Psi$ is satisfiable, so is $\Phi \cup \Psi \cup \{(x \vee z), (y \vee z), (\bar{x} \vee \bar{y} \vee \bar{z})\}$, because we can always set $z \leftarrow \bar{x} \vee \bar{y}$.

[*Reference:* M. Järvisalo, M. Heule, and A. Biere, *LNCS* **7364** (2012), 355–370. Notice that, by exercise 368, parts (f) and (h) justify the use of unit conditioning.]

384. Whenever we have a solution to $\Phi \setminus C$ that falsifies C, we will show that Φ is satisfied by making l true; hence softening C is permissible, with erp rule $l \leftarrow l \vee \overline{C}$.

To prove that claim, notice that a problem could arise only in a hard clause C' that contains $\bar{l}$. But if all other literals of C' are false in the given solution, then all literals of $C \diamond C'$ are false, contradicting the assumption that $(\Phi \setminus C) \wedge \overline{C \diamond C'} \vdash_1 \epsilon$.

(Such clauses C are "resolution certifiable" with respect to $\Phi \setminus C$. Blocked clauses are a very special case. Similarly, we can safely learn any clause that is resolution certifiable with respect to $\Phi \cup \Psi$.)

385. (a) True, because $\overline{C} \wedge l \vdash_1 \epsilon$ when $l \in C$.

(b) $\bar{1}$ is implied, not certifiable; $\bar{1}2$ is certifiable, not absorbed; $\bar{1}23$ is absorbed.

(c,d) If C is any clause and l is any literal, then $F \wedge \overline{C} \vdash_1 l$ implies $F' \wedge \overline{C} \vdash_1 l$, because unit propagation in F carries over to unit propagation in F'.

386. (a) The trail contained exactly $\mathrm{score}(F, C, l)$ literals when decision $\bar{l}$ was made at level d during the helpful round. The clause learned from the ensuing conflict causes at least one new literal to be implied at level $d' < d$.

(b) The score can't decrease when F grows.

(c) Each $l \in C$ needs at most n helpful rounds to make $\mathrm{score}(F, C, l) = \infty$.

(d) Suppose, for example, $F = (a \vee \bar{d}) \wedge (a \vee b \vee e \vee l) \wedge (\bar{a} \vee c) \wedge (\bar{b}) \wedge (c \vee d \vee \bar{e} \vee l)$ and $C = (a \vee b \vee c \vee d \vee l)$. The helpful sequences of decisions are $(\bar{a}, \bar{c}, \bar{l})$, $(\bar{c}, \bar{l})$, $(\bar{d}, \bar{a}, \bar{c}, \bar{l})$, $(\bar{d}, \bar{c}, \bar{l})$, and they occur with probabilities $\frac{1}{10}\frac{1}{6}\frac{1}{4}$, $\frac{1}{10}\frac{1}{4}$, $\frac{1}{10}\frac{1}{8}\frac{1}{6}\frac{1}{4}$, $\frac{1}{10}\frac{1}{8}\frac{1}{4}$.

In general if a decision is to be made and j elements of $\overline{C}$ are not yet in the trail, the probability that suitable decisions will be made at random is at least

$$f(n,j) = \min\left(\frac{j-1}{2n}f(n-1,j-1),\ \frac{j-2}{2(n-1)}f(n-2,j-2),\ \ldots,\right.$$

$$\left.\frac{1}{2(n-j+2)}f(n-j+1,1),\ \frac{1}{2(n-j+1)}\right) = \frac{(j-1)!}{2^j n^{\underline{j}}}.$$

(e) The waiting time to absorb each clause C_i is upper-bounded by a geometric distribution whose mean is $\le 4n^{|C_i|}$, repeated at most $|C_i|n$ times.

References: K. Pipatsrisawat and A. Darwiche, *Artif. Intell.* **175** (2011), 512–525; A. Atserias, J. K. Fichte, and M. Thurley, *J. Artif. Intell. Research* **40** (2011), 353–373.

387. We may assume that G and G' have no isolated vertices. Letting variable vv' mean that v corresponds to v', we need the clauses $(\overline{uv'} \vee \overline{vv'})$ for $u < v$ and $(\overline{vu'} \vee \overline{vv'})$ for $u' < v'$. Also, for each $u < v$ with $u \,—\, v$ in G, we introduce auxiliary variables $uu'vv'$ for each edge $u' \,—\, v'$ in G', with clauses $(\overline{uu'vv'} \vee uu') \wedge (\overline{uu'vv'} \vee vv') \wedge (\bigvee\{uu'vv' \mid u' \,—\, v' \text{ in } G'\})$. The variables vv' and $uu'vv'$ can be restricted to cases where $\deg(u) \le \deg(u')$ and $\deg(v) \le \deg(v')$.

388. (a) Can the complete graph K_k be embedded in G? (b) Can G be embedded in the complete k-partite graph $K_{n,\ldots,n}$, where G has n vertices? (c) Can the cycle C_n be embedded in G?

389. This is similar to a graph embedding problem, with G' the 4×4 (king $\cup$ knight) graph and with G defined by edges T — H, H — E, E — ⊔, ..., N — G; however, we allow $v' = w'$ when $v \ne w$, and labels must match. The adjacent Ms can be avoided by changing 'PROGRAMMING' to either 'PROGRAMXING' or 'PROGRAXMING'.

Algorithm C needs fewer than 10 megamems to find the first solution below. Furthermore, if the blank space can also be moved, the algorithm will rather quickly also find solutions with just five knight moves (the minimum), or 17 of them (the max):

U	P	C	F
M	M	O	⊔
I	T	R	A
N	G	E	H

M	M	I	N
A	P	O	G
H	R	⊔	F
U	T	E	C

H	N	U	F
E	M	O	I
G	T	⊔	P
A	R	M	C

390. Let $d(u,v)$ be the distance between vertices u and v. Then $d(v,v) = 0$ and

$$d(u,v) \le j+1 \iff d(u,w) \le j \text{ for some } w \in N(v) = \{w \mid w \,—\, v\}$$

if $u \ne v$. In parts (a), (d), we introduce variables v_j for each vertex v and $0 \le j \le k$. In part (c) we do this for $0 \le j < n$. But parts (b), (e), (f) use just n variables, $\{v \mid v \in V\}$.

(a) Clauses $(s_0) \wedge \bigwedge_{v \in V \setminus s}((\overline{v}_0) \wedge \bigwedge_{j=0}^{k-1}(\overline{v}_{j+1} \vee \bigvee_{w \in N(v)} w_j))$ are satisfied only if $v_j \le [d(s,v) \le j]$; hence the additional clause (t_k) is also satisfied only if $d(s,t) \le k$. Conversely, if $d(s,t) \le k$, all clauses are satisfied by setting $v_j \leftarrow [d(s,v) \le j]$.

(b) There's a path from s to t if and only if there's a subset $H \subseteq V$ such that $s \in H$, $t \in H$, and every vertex v of the induced graph $G \mid H$ has degree $2 - [v=s] - [v=t]$. [The vertices on a shortest path from s to t yield one such H. Conversely, given H, we can find vertices $v_j \in H$ such that $s = v_0 \,—\, v_1 \,—\, \cdots \,—\, v_k = t$.]

We can represent that criterion via clauses on the binary variables $v = [v \in H]$ by asserting $(s) \wedge (t)$, together with clauses to ensure that $\Sigma(v) = 2 - [v=s] - [v=t]$ for all $v \in H$, where $\Sigma(v) = \sum_{w \in N(v)} w$ is the degree of v in $G \mid H$. The number of such clauses for each v is at most $6|N(v)|$, because we can append $\overline{v}$ to each clause of (18) and (19) with $r = 2$, and $|N(v)|$ additional clauses will rule out $\Sigma(v) < 2$. Altogether there are $O(m)$ clauses, because $\sum_{v \in V} |N(v)| = 2m$.

[Similar but simpler alternatives, such as (i) to require $\Sigma(v) \in \{0, 2\}$ for all $v \in V \setminus \{s, t\}$, or (ii) to require $\Sigma(v) \geq 2$ for all $v \in H \setminus \{s, t\}$, do *not* work: Counterexamples are (i) s⬡t and (ii) s⬠t. Another solution, more cumbersome, associates a Boolean variable with each *edge* of G.]

(c) Let s be any vertex; use (a) with $k = n - 1$, plus (v_{n-1}) for all $v \in V \setminus s$.

(d) Clauses $(s_0) \wedge \bigwedge_{j=0}^{k-1} \bigwedge_{v \in V} \bigwedge_{w \in N(v)} (\bar{v}_j \vee w_{j+1})$ are satisfied only if we have $v_j \geq [d(s, v) \leq j]$; hence the additional unit clause $(\bar{t}_k)$ cannot also be satisfied when $d(s, t) \leq k$. Conversely, if $d(s, t) > k$ we can set $v_j \leftarrow [d(s, v) \leq j]$.

(e) $(s) \wedge (\bigwedge_{v \in V} \bigwedge_{w \in N(v)} (\bar{v} \vee w)) \wedge (\bar{t})$.

(f) Letting s be any vertex, use $(s) \wedge (\bigwedge_{v \in V} \bigwedge_{w \in N(v)} (\bar{v} \vee w)) \wedge (\bigvee_{v \in V \setminus s} \bar{v})$.

[Similar constructions work with digraphs and strong connectivity. Parts (d)–(f) of this exercise were suggested by Marijn Heule. Notice that parts (a) and (c)–(f) construct renamed Horn clauses, which work very efficiently (see exercise 444).]

391. (a) Let $d - 1 = (q_{l-1} \ldots q_0)_2$. To ensure that $(x_{l-1} \ldots x_0)_2 < d$ we need the clauses $(\bar{x}_i \vee \bigvee \{\bar{x}_j \mid j > i, q_j = 1\})$ whenever $q_i = 0$. The same holds for y.

To enforce $x \neq y$, introduce the clause $(a_{l-1} \vee \cdots \vee a_0)$ in auxiliary variables $a_{l-1} \ldots a_0$, together with $(\bar{a}_j \vee x_j \vee y_j) \wedge (\bar{a}_j \vee \bar{x}_j \vee \bar{y}_j)$ for $0 \leq j < l$ (see (172)).

(b) Now $x \neq y$ is enforced via clauses of length $2l$, which state that we don't have $x = y = k$ for $0 \leq k < d$. For example, the appropriate clause when $l = 3$ and $k = 5$ is $(\bar{x}_2 \vee \bar{y}_2 \vee x_1 \vee y_1 \vee \bar{x}_0 \vee \bar{y}_0)$.

(c) Use the clauses of (b) for $0 \leq k < 2d - 2^l$, plus clauses of length $2l - 2$ for $d \leq k < 2^l$ stating that we don't have $(x_{l-1} \ldots x_1)_2 = (y_{l-1} \ldots y_1)_2 = k - 2^{l-1}$. (The encodings in (b) and (c) are identical when $d = 2^l$.)

[See A. Van Gelder, *Discrete Applied Mathematics* **156** (2008), 230–243.]

392. (a) [Puzzle (*ii*) was introduced by Sam Loyd in the *Boston Herald*, 13 November 1904; page 27 of his *Cyclopedia* (1914) states that he'd created a puzzle like (*i*) at age 9! Puzzle (*iv*) is by H. E. Dudeney, *Strand* **42** (1911), 108, slightly modified. Puzzle (*iii*) is from the Grabarchuks' *Big, Big, Big Book of Brainteasers* (2011), #196; puzzle (*v*) was designed by Serhiy A. Grabarchuk in 2015.]

(i)   (ii)   (iii)   (iv)   (v)

(b) [Puzzle (*vi*) is an instance of the odd-even transposition sort, exercise 5.3.4–37. Eight order-reversing connections would be impossible with only eight columns, instead of the nine in (*vii*), because the permutation has too many inversions.]

(vi)   (vii)   (viii)

(c) Let $d_j = \sum_{i=1}^{j}(|T_i| - 1)$ and $d = d_t$. We introduce variables v_i for $1 \le i \le d$, and the following clauses for $1 \le j \le t$ and $d_{j-1} < i \le d_j$: $(\bar{v}_{i'} \vee \bar{v}_i)$ for $1 \le i' \le d_{j-1}$; the clauses of answer 390(b) on variables v_i, where s is the $(i - d_{j-1})$th element of T_j and t is the last element. These clauses ensure that the sets $V_j = \{v \mid v_{d_{j-1}+1} \vee \cdots \vee v_{d_j}\}$ are disjoint, and that V_j contains a connected component $S_j \supseteq T_j$.

We also assert $(\bar{v}_i)$ for $1 \le i \le d$, whenever T_j is a singleton set $\{v\}$.

[For the more general "Steiner tree packing" problem, see M. Grötschel, A. Martin, and R. Weismantel, *Math. Programming* **78** (1997), 265–281.]

393. A construction somewhat like that of answer 392(c) can be used with five different 8×8 graphs, one for the moves of each white-black pair S_j. But we need to keep track of the edges used, not vertices, in order to prohibit edges that cross each other. Additional clauses will rule that out.

394. Call these clauses *langford'''(n)*. [Steven Prestwich described a similar method in *Trends in Constraint Programming* (Wiley, 2007), 269–274.] Typical results are:

variables	clauses	Algorithm D	Algorithm L	Algorithm C	
langford'''(9)	206	1157	131 Mμ	18 Mμ	22 Mμ	(UNSAT)
langford'''(13)	403	2935	1425 Gμ	44 Gμ	483 Gμ	(UNSAT)
langford'''(16)	584	4859	713 Kμ	42 Mμ	343 Kμ	(SAT)
langford'''(64)	7352	120035	(huge)	(big)	71 Mμ	(SAT)

395. The color of each vertex v gets binary axiom clauses $(\bar{v}^{j+1} \vee v^j)$ for $1 \le j < d-1$, as in (164). And for each edge $u \!-\! v$ in the graph, we want d clauses $(\bar{u}^{j-1} \vee u^j \vee \bar{v}^{j-1} \vee v^j)$ for $1 \le j \le d$, omitting $\bar{u}^0$ and $\bar{v}^0$ when $j = 1$, u^d and v^d when $j = d$.

[The surprising usefulness of order encoding in graph coloring was first noticed by N. Tamura, A. Taga, S. Kitagawa, and M. Banbara in *Constraints* **14** (2009), 254–272.]

396. First we have $(\bar{x}^{j+1} \vee x^j)$ and $(\widehat{\bar{x}^{j+1}} \vee \hat{x}^j)$ for $1 \le j < d$. Then we have "channeling" clauses to ensure that $j \le x < j+1 \iff j\pi \le x\pi < j\pi + 1$ for $0 \le j < d$:

$$(\bar{x}^j \vee x^{j+1} \vee \hat{x}^{j\pi}) \wedge (\bar{x}^j \vee x^{j+1} \vee \widehat{\bar{x}^{j\pi+1}}) \wedge (\widehat{\bar{x}^{j\pi}} \vee \hat{x}^{j\pi+1} \vee x^j) \wedge (\widehat{\bar{x}^{j\pi}} \vee \hat{x}^{j\pi+1} \vee \bar{x}^{j+1}).$$

(These clauses should be either shortened or omitted in boundary cases, because x^0 and $\hat{x}^0$ are always true, while x^d and $\hat{x}^d$ are always false. We obtain $6d-8$ clauses for each x.)

With such clauses for every vertex of a graph, together with clauses based on adjacent vertices and cliques, we obtain encodings for n-coloring the $n \times n$ queen graph that involve $2(n^3 - n^2)$ variables and $\frac{5}{3}n^4 + 4n^3 + O(n^2)$ clauses, compared to $n^3 - n^2$ variables and $\frac{5}{3}n^4 - n^3 + O(n^2)$ clauses with single cliques and (162) alone. Typical running times with Algorithm C and single cliques are 323 Kμ, 13.1 Mμ, 706 Gμ for $n = 7, 8, 9$; with double clique-ing they become 252 Kμ, 1.97 Mμ, 39.8 Gμ, respectively.

The double clique hints turn out to be mysteriously ineffective when π is the standard organ-pipe permutation $(0\pi, 1\pi, \ldots, (d-1)\pi) = (0, 2, 4, \ldots, 5, 3, 1)$ instead of its inverse. Random choices of π when $n = 8$ yielded significant improvement almost half the time, in the author's experiments; but they had negligible effect in 1/3 of the cases.

Notice that the example π for $d = 4$ yields $x^1 = \bar{x}_0$, $x^3 = x_3$, $\hat{x}^1 = \bar{x}_2$, $\hat{x}_3 = x_1$. Hence the direct encoding is essentially present as part of this redundant representation, and the hints $(\bar{u}^3 \vee \bar{v}^3) \wedge (u^1 \vee v^1) \wedge (\widehat{\bar{u}^3} \vee \widehat{\bar{v}^3}) \wedge (\hat{u}^1 \vee \hat{v}^1)$ for 2-cliques $\{u, v\}$ are equivalent to (16). But the hints $(u^2 \vee v^2 \vee w^2) \wedge (\bar{u}^2 \vee \bar{v}^2 \vee \bar{w}^2) \wedge (\hat{u}^2 \vee \hat{v}^2 \vee \hat{w}^2) \wedge (\widehat{\bar{u}^2} \vee \widehat{\bar{v}^2} \vee \widehat{\bar{w}^2})$ that apply when $\{u, v, w\}$ is a triangle give additional logical power.

397. There are $(p-2)d$ binary clauses $(\bar{y}_j^{i+1} \vee y_j^i)$ for $1 \le i < p-1$, together with the $(2p-2)d$ clauses $(\bar{x}_i^j \vee x_i^{j+1} \vee y_j^i) \wedge (\bar{x}_{i-1}^j \vee x_{i-1}^{j+1} \vee \bar{y}_j^i)$ for $1 \le i < p$, all for $0 \le j < d$. The hint clauses $(x_0^{p-1} \vee \cdots \vee x_{p-1}^{p-1}) \wedge (\bar{x}_0^{d-p+1} \vee \cdots \vee \bar{x}_{p-1}^{d-p+1})$ are also valid.

(This setup corresponds to putting p pigeons into d holes, so we can usually assume that $p \le d$. If $p \le 4$ it is better to use $\binom{p}{2}d$ clauses as in exercise 395. Notice that we obtain an interesting representation of *permutations* when $p = d$. In that case y is the inverse permutation; hence $(2d-2)p$ additional clauses corresponding to $y_j = i$ $\implies x_i = j$ are also valid, as well as two hint clauses for y.)

A related idea, but combined with direct encoding of the x's, was presented by I. Gent and P. Nightingale in *Proceedings of the International Workshop on Modelling and Reformulating Constraint Satisfaction Problems* **3** (2004), 95–110.

398. We could construct $(3p-4)d$ binary clauses that involve y_j^i, as in exercise 397. But it's better just to have $(3p-6)d$ clauses for the at-most-one constraints $x_{0k} + x_{1k} + \cdots + x_{(p-1)k} \le 1$, $0 \le k < d$.

399. (a) $d^2 - t$ preclusion clauses (binary); or $2d$ support clauses (total length $2(d+t)$).

(b) If unit propagation derives $\bar{v}_j$ from $(\bar{u}_i \vee \bar{v}_j)$, we knew u_i; hence (17) gives $\bar{u}_{i'}$ for all $i' \ne i$, and $\bar{v}_j$ follows from the support clause that contains it.

(c) If unit propagation derives $\bar{v}_j$ from its support clause, we knew $\bar{u}_i$ for all $i \ne j$; hence (15) gives u_j, and $\bar{v}_j$ follows from (16). Or if unit propagation derives u_i from that support clause, we knew v_j and $\bar{u}_{i'}$ for all $i' \notin \{i, j\}$; hence $\bar{u}_j$ from (16), u_i from (15).

(d) A trivial example has no legal pairs; then unit propagation never gets started from binary preclusions, but the (unit) support clauses deduce all. A more realistic example has $d = 3$ and all pairs legal except $(1,1)$ and $(1,2)$, say; then we have $(15) \wedge (17) \wedge (\bar{u}_1 \vee \bar{v}_1) \wedge (\bar{u}_1 \vee \bar{v}_2) \wedge (\bar{v}_3) \not\vdash_1 \bar{u}_1$ but $(15) \wedge (17) \wedge (\bar{u}_1 \vee v_3) \wedge (\bar{v}_3) \vdash_1 \bar{u}_1$.

[Preclusion was introduced by S. W. Golomb and L. D. Baumert, *JACM* **12** (1965), 521–522. The support encoding was introduced by I. P. Gent, *European Conf. on Artificial Intelligence* **15** (2002), 121–125, based on work of S. Kasif, *Artificial Intelligence* **45** (1990), 275–286.]

400. This problem has n variables $q_1, \ldots, q_n$ with n values each; thus there are n^2 Boolean values, with $q_{ij} = [q_i = j] = $ [there's a queen in row i and column j]. The constraint between q_i and q_j is that $q_i \notin \{q_j, q_j + i - j, q_j - i + j\}$; so it turns out that there are n at-least-one clauses, plus $(n^3 - n^2)/2$ at-most-one clauses, plus either $n^3 - n^2$ support clauses or $n^3 - n^2 + \binom{n}{3}$ preclusion clauses. In this problem each support clause has at least $n - 2$ literals, so the support encoding is much larger.

Since the problem is easily satisfiable, it makes sense to try WalkSAT. When $n = 20$, Algorithm W typically finds a solution from the preclusion clauses after making fewer than 500 flips; its running time is about $500\,K\mu$, including about $200\,K\mu$ just to read the input. With the support clauses, however, it needs about 10 times as many flips and consumes about 20 times as many mems, before succeeding.

Algorithm L is significantly worse: It consumes $50\,M\mu$ with preclusion clauses, $11\,G\mu$ with support clauses. Algorithm C is the winner, with about $400\,K\mu$ (preclusion) versus $600\,K\mu$ (support).

Of course $n = 20$ is pretty tame; let's consider $n = 100$ queens, when there are 10,000 variables and more than a million clauses. Algorithm L is out of the picture; in the author's experiments, it showed no indication of being even close to a solution after $20\,T\mu$! But Algorithm W solves that problem in $50\,M\mu$, via preclusion, after making only about 5000 flips. Algorithm C wins again, polishing it off in $29\,M\mu$. With the support clauses, nearly 100 million literals need to be input, and Algorithm W is hopelessly inefficient; but Algorithm C is able to finish after about $200\,\mathrm{M}\mu$.

The preclusion clauses actually allow us to omit the at-most-one clauses in this problem, because two queens in the same row will be ruled out anyway. This trick improves the run time when $n = 100$ to $35\,\mathrm{M}\mu$ for Algorithm W.

We can also append support clauses for the columns as well as the rows. This idea roughly halves the search space, but it gives no improvement because twice as many clauses must be handled. *Bottom line:* Support clauses don't support n queens well.

(However, if we seek *all* solutions to the n queens problem instead of stopping with the first one, using a straightforward extension of Algorithm D (see exercise 122), the support clauses proved to be definitely better in the author's experiments.)

401. (a) $y^j = x^{2j-1}$. (b) $z^j = x^{3j-1}$. In general $w = \lfloor (x+a)/b \rfloor \iff w^j = x^{bj-a}$.

402. (a) $\bigwedge_{j=1}^{\lfloor d/2 \rfloor} (\bar{x}^{2j-1} \vee x^{2j})$; (b) $\bigwedge_{j=1}^{\lceil d/2 \rceil} (\bar{x}^{2j-2} \vee x^{2j-1})$; omit $\bar{x}^0$ and x^d.

403. (a) $\bigwedge_{j=1}^{d-1} (\bar{x}^j \vee \bar{y}^j \vee z^j)$; (b) $\bigwedge_{j=1}^{d-1} ((\bar{x}^j \vee z^j) \wedge (\bar{y}^j \vee z^j))$; (c) $\bigwedge_{j=1}^{d-1} ((x^j \vee \bar{z}^j) \wedge (y^j \vee \bar{z}^j))$; (d) $\bigwedge_{j=1}^{d-1} (x^j \vee y^j \vee \bar{z}^j)$.

404. $\bigwedge_{j=0}^{d-a} (\bar{x}^j \vee x^{j+a} \vee \bar{y}^j \vee y^{j+a})$. (As usual, omit literals with superscript 0 or d.)

405. (a) If $a < 0$ we can replace ax by $(-a)\bar{x}$ and c by $c + a - ad$, where $\bar{x}$ is given by (165). A similar reduction applies if $b < 0$. Cases with a, b, or $c = 0$ are trivial.

(b) We have $13x + 8\bar{y} \leq 63 \iff \text{not } 13x + 8\bar{y} \geq 64 \iff \text{not } (P_0 \text{ or } \ldots \text{ or } P_{d-1}) \iff \text{not } P_0 \text{ and } \ldots \text{ and not } P_{d-1}$, where $P_j = `x \geq j$ and $\bar{y} \geq \lceil (64 - 13j)/8 \rceil$'. This approach yields $\bigwedge_{j=0}^{7} (\bar{x}^j \vee y^{8-\lceil (64-13j)/8 \rceil})$, which simplifies to $(\bar{x}^1 \vee y^1) \wedge (\bar{x}^2 \vee y^3) \wedge (\bar{x}^3 \vee y^4) \wedge (\bar{x}^4 \vee y^6) \wedge (\bar{x}^5)$. (Notice that we could have defined $P_j = `\bar{y} \geq j$ and $x \geq \lceil (64 - 8j)/13 \rceil$' instead, thereby obtaining the less efficient encoding $(\bar{x}^5) \wedge (y^7 \vee \bar{x}^5) \wedge (y^6 \vee \bar{x}^4) \wedge (y^5 \vee \bar{x}^4) \wedge (y^4 \vee \bar{x}^3) \wedge (y^3 \vee \bar{x}^2) \wedge (y^2 \vee \bar{x}^2) \wedge (y^1 \vee \bar{x}^1)$; it's better to discriminate on the variable with the larger coefficient.)

(c) Similarly, $13\bar{x} + 8y \leq 90$ gives $(x^5 \vee \bar{y}^7) \wedge (x^4 \vee \bar{y}^5) \wedge (x^3 \vee \bar{y}^4) \wedge (x^2 \vee \bar{y}^2) \wedge (x^1)$. (The (x, y) pairs legal for both (b) and (c) are $(1, 1)$, $(2, 3)$, $(3, 4)$, $(4, 6)$.)

(d) $\bigwedge_{j=\max(0, \lceil (c+1-b(d-1))/a \rceil)}^{\min(d-1, \lceil (c+1)/a \rceil)} (\bar{x}^j \vee \bar{y}^{\lceil (c+1-aj)/b \rceil})$, when $a \geq b > 0$ and $c \geq 0$.

406. (a) $(\bigwedge_{j=\lceil (a+1)/(d-1) \rceil}^{\lfloor \sqrt{a+1} \rfloor} (\bar{x}^j \vee \bar{y}^{\lceil (a+1)/j \rceil})) \wedge (\bigwedge_{j=\lceil (a+1)/(d-1) \rceil}^{\lceil \sqrt{a+1} \rceil - 1} (\bar{x}^{\lceil (a+1)/j \rceil} \vee \bar{y}^j))$.

(b) $(\bigwedge_{j=l+1}^{\lfloor \sqrt{a-1} \rfloor + 1} (x^j \vee y^{\lfloor (a-1)/(j-1) \rfloor + 1})) \wedge (\bigwedge_{j=l+1}^{\lceil \sqrt{a-1} \rceil} (x^{\lfloor (a-1)/(j-1) \rfloor + 1} \vee y^j)) \wedge (x^l) \wedge (y^l)$, where $l = \lfloor (a - 1)/(d - 1) \rfloor + 1$. [Both formulas belong to 2SAT.]

407. (a) We always have $\lfloor x/2 \rfloor + \lceil x/2 \rceil = x$, $\lfloor x/2 \rfloor + \lfloor y/2 \rfloor \leq \frac{x+y}{2} \leq \lfloor x/2 \rfloor + \lfloor y/2 \rfloor + 1$, and $\lceil x/2 \rceil + \lceil y/2 \rceil - 1 \leq \frac{x+y}{2} \leq \lceil x/2 \rceil + \lceil y/2 \rceil$. (Similar reasoning proves the correctness of Batcher's odd-even merge network; see Eq. 5.3.4–(3).)

(b) Axiom clauses like (164) needn't be introduced for u and v, or even for z; so they aren't counted here, although they could be added if desired. Let $a_d = d^2 - 1$ be the number of clauses in the original method; then the new method has fewer clauses when $a_{\lceil d/2 \rceil} + a_{\lfloor d/2 \rfloor + 1} + 3(d - 2) < a_d$, namely when $d \geq 7$. (The new method for $d = 7$ involves 45 clauses, not 48; but it introduces 10 new auxiliary variables.) Asymptotically, we can handle $d = 2^t + 1$ with $3t2^t + O(2^t) = 3d \lg d + O(d)$ clauses and $d \lg d + O(d)$ auxiliary variables.

(c) $x + y \geq z \iff (d - 1 - x) + (d - 1 - y) \leq (2d - 2 - z)$; so we can use the same method, but complemented (namely with $x^j \mapsto \bar{x}^{d-j}$, $y^j \mapsto \bar{y}^{d-j}$, $z^j \mapsto \bar{z}^{2d-1-j}$).

[See N. Tamura, A. Taga, S. Kitagawa, and M. Banbara, *Constraints* **14** (2009), 254–272; R. Asín, R. Nieuwenhuis, A. Oliveras, and E. Rodríguez-Carbonell, *Constraints* **16** (2011), 195–221.]

408. (a) No; makespan 11 is best, achievable as follows (or via left-right reflection):

M1: | J1 | J3 | M1: | J3 | J1 |

M2: | J3 | J2 | J1 | M2: | J2 | J3 | J1 |

M3: | J2 | J3 | J1 | M3: | J1 | J3 | J2 |

(b) If j is the last job processed by machine i, that machine must finish at time $\le \sum_{k=1}^{n} w_{ik} + \sum_{k=1}^{m} w_{kj} - w_{ij}$, because j uses some other machine whenever i is idle. [See D. B. Shmoys, C. Stein, and J. Wein, *SICOMP* **23** (1994), 631.]

(c) Clearly $0 \le s_{ij} \le t - w_{ij}$. And if $ij \ne i'j'$ but $i = i'$ or $j = j'$, we must have either $s_{ij} + w_{ij} \le s_{i'j'}$ or $s_{i'j'} + w_{i'j'} \le s_{ij}$ whenever $w_{ij} w_{i'j'} \ne 0$.

(d) When $w_{ij} > 0$, introduce Boolean variables s_{ij}^k for $1 \le k \le t - w_{ij}$, with the axiom clauses $(\bar{s}_{ij}^{k+1} \vee s_{ij}^k)$ for $1 \le k < t - w_{ij}$. Then include the following clauses for all relevant i, j, i', and j' as in (c): For $0 \le k \le t + 1 - w_{ij} - w_{i'j'}$, assert $(\bar{p}_{iji'j'} \vee \bar{s}_{ij}^k \vee s_{i'j'}^{k+w_{ij}})$ if $ij < i'j'$ or $(p_{i'j'ij} \vee \bar{s}_{ij}^k \vee s_{i'j'}^{k+w_{ij}})$ if $ij > i'j'$, omitting $\bar{s}_{ij}^0$ in the first of these ternary clauses and omitting $s_{i'j'}^{t+1-w_{i'j'}}$ in the last.

[This method, introduced by N. Tamura, A. Taga, S. Kitagawa, and M. Banbara in *Constraints* **14** (2009), 254–272, was able to solve several open shop scheduling problems in 2008 that had resisted attacks by all other approaches.]

Since the left-right reflection of any valid schedule is also valid, we can also save a factor of two by arbitrarily choosing one of the p variables and asserting $(p_{iji'j'})$.

(e) Any schedule for W and T yields a schedule for $\lfloor W/k \rfloor$ and $\lceil T/k \rceil$, if we examine time slots 0, k, $2k$, ... [With this observation we can narrow down the search for an optimum makespan by first working with simpler problems; the number of variables and clauses for $\lfloor W/k \rfloor$ and T/k is about $1/k$ times the number for W and T, and the running time also tends to obey this ratio. For example, the author solved a nontrivial 8×8 problem by first working with $\lfloor W/8 \rfloor$ and getting the respective results (U, S, U) for $t = (128, 130, 129)$, where 'U' means "unsatisfiable" and 'S' means "satisfiable"; running times were about $(75, 10, 1250)$ megamems. Then with $\lfloor W/4 \rfloor$ it was (S, U, U) with $t = (262, 260, 261)$ and runtimes $(425, 275, 325)$; with $\lfloor W/2 \rfloor$ it was (U, S, U) with $t = (526, 528, 527)$ and runtimes $(975, 200, 900)$. Finally with the full W it was (U, S, S) with $t = (1058, 1060, 1059)$ and runtimes $(2050, 775, 300)$, establishing 1059 as the optimum makespan while doing most of the work on small subproblems.]

Notes: Further savings are possible by noting that any clauses learned while proving that t is satisfiable are valid also when t is decreased. Difficult random problems can be generated by using the following method suggested by C. Guéret and C. Prins in *Annals of Operations Research* **92** (1999), 165–183: Start with work times w_{ij} that are as near equal as possible, having constant row and column sums s. Then choose random rows $i \ne i'$ and random columns $j \ne j'$, and transfer δ units of weight by setting $w_{ij} \leftarrow w_{ij} - \delta$, $w_{i'j} \leftarrow w_{i'j} + \delta$, $w_{ij'} \leftarrow w_{ij'} + \delta$, $w_{i'j'} \leftarrow w_{i'j'} - \delta$, where $\delta \le w_{ij}$ and $\delta \le w_{i'j'}$; this operation clearly preserves the row and column sums. Choose δ at random between $p \cdot \min\{w_{ij}, w_{i'j'}\}$ and $\min\{w_{ij}, w_{i'j'}\}$, where p is a parameter. The final weights are obtained after making r such transfers. Guéret and Prins suggested choosing $r = n^3$, and $p = .95$ for $n \ge 6$; but other choices give useful benchmarks too.

409. (a) If $S \subseteq \{1, \ldots, r\}$, let $\Sigma_S = \sum_{j \in S} a_j$. We can assume that job n runs on machines 1, 2, 3 in that order. So the minimum makespan is $2w_{2n} + x$, where x is the smallest Σ_S that is $\geq \lceil(a_1 + \cdots + a_r)/2\rceil$. (The problem of finding such an S is well known to be NP-hard [R. M. Karp, *Complexity of Computer Computations* (New York: Plenum, 1972), 97–100]; hence the open shop scheduling problem is NP-complete.)

(b) Makespan $w_{2n} + w_{4n}$ is achievable if and only if $\Sigma_S = (a_1 + \cdots + a_r)/2$ for some S. Otherwise we can achieve makespan $w_{2n} + w_{4n} + 1$ by running jobs $1, \ldots, n$ in order on machine 1 and letting $s_{3(n-1)} = 0$, $s_{4n} = w_{2n}$; also $s_{2j} = w_{2n} + w_{4n}$, if machine 1 is running job j at time w_{2n}. The other jobs are easily scheduled.

(c) $\lfloor 3n/2 \rfloor - 2$ time slots are clearly necessary and sufficient. (If all row and column sums of W are equal to s, can the minimum makespan be $\geq \frac{3}{2}s$?)

(d) The "tight" makespan s is always achievable: By renumbering the jobs we can assume that $a_j \leq b_j$ for $1 \leq j \leq k$, $a_j \geq b_j$ for $k < j \leq n$, $b_1 = \max\{b_1, \ldots, b_k\}$, $a_n = \max\{a_{k+1}, \ldots, a_n\}$. Then if $b_n \geq a_1$, machine 1 can run jobs $(1, \ldots, n)$ in order while machine 2 runs $(n, 1, \ldots, n-1)$; otherwise $(2, \ldots, n, 1)$ and $(1, \ldots n)$ suffice.

If $a_1 + \cdots + a_n \neq b_1 + \cdots + b_n$, we can increase a_n or b_n to make them equal. Then we can add a "dummy" job with $a_{n+1} = b_{n+1} = \max\{a_1 + b_1, \ldots, a_n + b_n\} \doteq s$, and obtain an optimum schedule in $O(n)$ steps as explained above.

Results (a), (b), (d) are due to T. Gonzalez and S. Sahni, who introduced and named the open shop scheduling problem in *JACM* **23** (1976), 665–679. Part (c) is a subsequent observation and open problem due to Gonzalez (unpublished).

410. Using half adders and full adders as we did in (23) allows us to introduce intermediate variables w_j such that $(x_2x_1x_0)_2 + (x_2x_1x_000)_2 + (x_2x_1x_0000)_2 + (\bar{y}_2\bar{y}_1\bar{y}_0000)_2 \leq (w_7w_6 \ldots w_0)_2$, and then to require $(\bar{w}_7)\wedge(\bar{w}_6)$. In slow motion, we successively compute $(c_0z_0)_2 \geq x_0 + x_1$, $(c_1z_1)_2 \geq x_0 + x_1 + \bar{y}_0$, $(c_2z_2)_2 \geq c_0 + z_1$, $(c_3z_3)_2 \geq x_1 + x_2 + \bar{y}_1$, $(c_4z_4)_2 \geq c_1 + c_2 + z_3$, $(c_5z_5)_2 \geq x_2 + \bar{y}_2 + c_3$, $(c_6z_6)_2 \geq c_4 + z_5$, $(c_7z_7)_2 \geq c_5 + c_6$; then $w_7w_6 \ldots w_0 = c_7z_7z_6z_4z_2z_0x_1x_0$. In slower motion, each step $(c_iz_i)_2 \geq u + v$ expands to $z_i \geq u \oplus v$, $c_i \geq u \wedge v$; each step $(c_iz_i)_2 \geq t + u + v$ expands to $s_i \geq t \oplus u$, $p_i \geq t \wedge u$, $z_i \geq v \oplus s$, $q_i \geq v \wedge s$, $c_i \geq p_i \vee q_i$. And at the clause level, $t \geq u \wedge v \iff (t \vee \bar{u} \vee \bar{v})$; $t \geq u \vee v \iff (t \vee \bar{u}) \wedge (t \vee \bar{v})$; $t \geq u \oplus v \iff (t \vee \bar{u} \vee v) \wedge (t \vee u \vee \bar{v})$. [Only about half of (24) is needed when inequalities replace equalities. Exercise 42 offers improvements.]

We end up with 44 binary and ternary clauses; 10 of them can be omitted, because z_0, z_2, z_4, z_6, and z_7 are pure literals, and the clause for c_7 can be omitted if we simply require $c_5 = c_6 = 0$. But the order encoding of exercise 405 is clearly much better. The log encoding becomes attractive only with larger integers, as in the following exercise. [See J. P. Warners, *Information Processing Letters* **68** (1998), 63–69.]

411. Use $m + n$ new variables to represent an auxiliary number $w = (w_{m+n} \ldots w_1)_2$. Form clauses as in exercise 41 for the product $xy = w$; but retain only about half of the clauses, as in answer 410. The resulting $9mn - 5m - 10n$ clauses are satisfiable if $w = xy$; and we have $w \geq xy$ whenever they are satisfiable. Now add $3m + 3n - 2$ further clauses as in (169) to ensure that $z \geq w$. The case $z \leq xy$ is similar.

412. Mixed-radix representations are also of interest in this connection. See, for example, N. Eén and N. Sörensson, *J. Satisfiability, Bool. Modeling and Comp.* **2** (2006), 1–26; T. Tanjo, N. Tamura, and M. Banbara, *LNCS* **7317** (2012), 456–462.

413. There's only one, namely $\bigwedge_{\sigma_1,\ldots,\sigma_n \in \{-1,1\}}(\sigma_1x_1 \vee \sigma_1y_1 \vee \cdots \vee \sigma_nx_n \vee \sigma_ny_n)$. *Proof:* Some clause must contain only positive literals, because $f(0, \ldots, 0) = 0$. This clause must be $(x_1 \vee y_1 \vee \cdots \vee x_n \vee y_n)$; otherwise it would be false in cases where f is true. A similar argument shows that *every* clause $(\sigma_1x_1 \vee \sigma_1y_1 \vee \cdots \vee \sigma_nx_n \vee \sigma_ny_n)$ must be present. And no clause for f can contain both x_j and $\bar{y}_j$, or both $\bar{x}_j$ and y_j.

414. Eliminating first a_{n-1}, then a_{n-2}, etc., yields $2^n - 1$ clauses. (The analogous result for $x_1 \ldots x_n < y_1 \ldots y_n$ is $2^n + 2^{n-1} + 1$. A preprocessor will probably eliminate a_{n-1}.)

415. Construct clauses for $1 \le k \le n$ that represent 'a_{k-1} implies $x_k < y_k + a_k$':

$$\left(\bar{a}_{k-1} \vee \bigvee_{j=1}^{d-1} (\bar{x}_k^j \vee y_k^j)\right) \wedge \left(\bar{a}_{k-1} \vee a_k \vee \bigvee_{j=0}^{d-1} (\bar{x}_k^j \vee y_k^{j+1})\right), \quad \text{omitting } \bar{x}_k^0 \text{ and } y_k^d;$$

also omit $\bar{a}_0$. For the relation $x_1 \ldots x_n \le y_1 \ldots y_n$ we can omit the d clauses that contain the (pure) literal a_n. But for $x_1 \ldots x_n < y_1 \ldots y_n$, we want $a_n = 0$; so we omit a_n and the $d - 1$ clauses $(\bar{a}_{n-1} \vee \bar{x}_n^j \vee y_n^j)$. [The clauses (169) are due to K. Sakallah, *Handbook of Satisfiability* (2009), Chapter 10, (10.32).]

416. The other clauses are $\bigwedge_{i=1}^m ((u_i \vee \bar{v}_i \vee \bar{a}_0) \wedge (\bar{u}_i \vee v_i \vee \bar{a}_0))$ and $(a_0 \vee a_1 \vee \cdots \vee a_n)$. [See A. Biere and R. Brummayer, *Proceedings, International Conference on Formal Methods in Computer Aided Design* **8** (IEEE, 2008), 4 pages [FMCAD 08].]

417. The four clauses $(\bar{s} \vee \bar{t} \vee u) \wedge (\bar{s} \vee t \vee v) \wedge (s \vee \bar{t} \vee \bar{u}) \wedge (s \vee t \vee \bar{v})$ ensure that s is true if and only if $t? u: v$ is true. But we need only the first two of these, as in (173), when translating a branching program, because the other two are blocked in the initial step. Removing them makes the other two blocked on the second step, etc.

418. A suitable branching program for h_n when $n = 3$, beginning at I_{11}, is $I_{11} = (\bar{1}? 21:22)$, $I_{21} = (\bar{2}? 31:32)$, $I_{22} = (\bar{2}? 32:33)$, $I_{31} = (\bar{3}? 0:42)$, $I_{32} = (\bar{3}? 42:43)$, $I_{33} = (\bar{3}? 43:1)$, $I_{42} = (\bar{1}? 0:1)$, $I_{43} = (\bar{2}? 0:1)$. It leads via (173) to the following clauses for row i, $1 \le i \le m$: $(r_{i,1,1})$; $(\bar{r}_{i,k,j} \vee x_{ik} \vee r_{i,k+1,j}) \wedge (\bar{r}_{i,k,j} \vee \bar{x}_{ik} \vee r_{i,k+1,j+1})$, for $1 \le j \le k \le n$; $(\bar{r}_{i,n+1,1}) \wedge (r_{i,n+1,n+1})$ and $(\bar{r}_{i,n+1,j+1} \vee x_{ij})$ for $1 \le j < n$. Also the following clauses for column j, $1 \le j \le n$: $(c_{i,1,1})$; $(\bar{c}_{j,k,i} \vee x_{kj} \vee c_{j,k+1,i}) \wedge (\bar{c}_{j,k,i} \vee \bar{x}_{kj} \vee c_{j,k+1,i+1})$, for $1 \le i \le k \le m$; $(\bar{c}_{j,m+1,1}) \wedge (c_{j,m+1,m+1})$ and $(\bar{c}_{j,m+1,i+1} \vee x_{ij})$ for $1 \le i < m$.

419. (a) There are exactly $n-2$ solutions: $x_{ij} = [j=1][i \ne m-1] + [j=2][i=m-1] + [j=k][i=m-1]$, for $2 < k \le n$.

(b) There are exactly $m-2$ solutions: $\bar{x}_{ij} = [j>1][i=m-1] + [j=1][i=m-2] + [j=1][i=k]$, for $1 \le k < m-2$ or $k = m$.

420. Start via (24) with $(\bar{x}_1 \vee x_2 \vee s) \wedge (x_1 \vee \bar{x}_2 \vee s) \wedge (x_1 \vee x_2 \vee \bar{s}) \wedge (\bar{x}_1 \vee \bar{x}_2 \vee \bar{s})$; $(x_1 \vee \bar{c}) \wedge (x_2 \vee \bar{c}) \wedge (\bar{x}_1 \vee \bar{x}_2 \vee c)$; $(\bar{s} \vee x_3 \vee t) \wedge (s \vee \bar{x}_3 \vee t) \wedge (s \vee x_3 \vee \bar{t}) \wedge (\bar{s} \vee \bar{x}_3 \vee \bar{t})$; $(s \vee \bar{c}') \wedge (x_3 \vee \bar{c}') \wedge (\bar{s} \vee \bar{x}_3 \vee c')$; $(\bar{c}) \wedge (\bar{c}')$. Propagate $(\bar{c})$ and $(\bar{c}')$, obtaining $(\bar{x}_1 \vee \bar{x}_2) \wedge (\bar{s} \vee \bar{x}_3)$; remove subsumed clauses $(\bar{x}_1 \vee \bar{x}_2 \vee \bar{s})$, $(\bar{s} \vee \bar{x}_3 \vee \bar{t})$; remove blocked clause $(s \vee x_3 \vee \bar{t})$; remove clauses containing the pure literal t; rename s to a_1.

421. Start via (173) with $(\bar{a}_5 \vee x_1 \vee a_4) \wedge (\bar{a}_5 \vee \bar{x}_1 \vee a_3) \wedge (\bar{a}_4 \vee \bar{x}_2 \vee a_2) \wedge (\bar{a}_3 \vee x_2 \vee a_2) \wedge (\bar{a}_3 \vee \bar{x}_2) \wedge (\bar{a}_2 \vee \bar{x}_3) \wedge (a_5)$. Propagate (a_5).

422. (a) x_1 implies $\bar{x}_2$, then a_1, then $\bar{x}_3$; x_2 implies $\bar{x}_1$, then a_1, then $\bar{x}_3$.

(b) x_1 implies a_3, then $\bar{x}_2$, then a_2, then $\bar{x}_3$; x_2 implies $\bar{a}_3$, then $\bar{x}_1$, a_4, a_2, $\bar{x}_3$.

423. No; consider $x_1? (x_2? x_3: x_4): (x_2? x_4: x_3)$ with $L = (\bar{x}_3) \wedge (\bar{x}_4)$. (But Abío, Gange, Mayer-Eichberger, and Stuckey have shown [*LNCS* **9676** (2016), 1–17] that weak forcing is always achieved if $(\bar{a}_j \vee a_l \vee a_h)$ is added to (173). Furthermore, a *forcing* encoding *can* always be constructed, via the extra clauses defined in exercise 436. Notice that, in the presence of failed literal tests, weak forcing corresponds to forcing.)

424. The clause $\bar{1}\bar{3}\bar{4}$ is redundant (in the presence of $\bar{1}\bar{2}\bar{3}$ and $\bar{2}\bar{3}\bar{4}$); it cannot be omitted, because $\{\bar{2}\bar{3}, \bar{2}\bar{3}, 12\} \not\vdash_1 \bar{3}$. The clause $\bar{2}\bar{3}\bar{4}$ is also redundant (in the presence of $\bar{1}\bar{3}\bar{4}$ and 12); it *can* be omitted, because $\{\bar{1}\bar{4}, 34, 1\} \vdash_1 \bar{4}$, $\{\bar{1}\bar{3}, 34, 1\} \vdash_1 \bar{3}$, and $\{\bar{1}\bar{2}, \bar{1}, 12\} \vdash_1 2$.

425. If x is in the core, $F \vdash_1 x$, because Algorithm 7.1.1C does unit propagation. Otherwise F is satisfied when all core variables are true and all noncore variables are false.

426. (a) True. Suppose the clauses involving a_m are $(a_m \vee \alpha_i)$ for $1 \le i \le p$ and $(\bar{a}_m \vee \beta_j)$ for $1 \le j \le q$; then G contains the pq clauses $(\alpha_i \vee \beta_j)$ instead. If $F \,|\, L \vdash_1 l$ we want to prove that $G \,|\, L \vdash_1 l$. This is clear if unit propagation from $F \,|\, L$ doesn't involve a_m. Otherwise, if $F \,|\, L \vdash_1 a_m$, unit propagation has falsified some α_i; every subsequent propagation step from $F \,|\, L$ that uses $(\bar{a}_m \vee \beta_j)$ can use $(\alpha_i \vee \beta_j)$ in a propagation step from $G \,|\, L$. A similar argument applies when $F \,|\, L \vdash_1 \bar{a}_m$.

(Incidentally, the elimination of an auxiliary variable also preserves "honesty.")

(b) False. Let $F = (x_1 \vee x_2 \vee a_1) \wedge (x_1 \vee x_2 \vee \bar{a}_1)$, $L = \bar{x}_1$ or $\bar{x}_2$.

427. Suppose $n = 3m$, and let f be the symmetric function $[\nu x < m$ or $\nu x > 2m]$. The prime clauses of f are the $N = \binom{n}{m,m,m} \sim 3^{n+3/2}/(2\pi n)$ ORs of m positive literals and m negative literals. There are $N' = \binom{n}{m-1,m,m+1} = \frac{m}{m+1} N$ ways to specify that $x_{i_1} = \cdots = x_{i_m} = 1$ and $x_{i_{m+1}} = \cdots = x_{i_{2m-1}} = 0$; and this partial assignment implies that $x_j = 1$ for $j \notin \{i_1, \ldots, i_{2m-1}\}$. Therefore at least one of the $m+1$ clauses $(\bar{x}_{i_1} \vee \cdots \vee \bar{x}_{i_m} \vee x_{i_{m+1}} \vee \cdots \vee x_{i_{2m-1}} \vee x_j)$ must be present in any set of prime clauses that forces f. By symmetry, any such set must include at least N'/m prime clauses.

On the other hand, f is characterized by $O(n^2)$ forcing clauses (see answer 436).

428. (a) $(y \vee z_{j1} \vee \cdots \vee z_{jd})$ for $1 \le j \le n$; $(\bar{x}_{ij} \vee \bar{z}_{ik} \vee \bar{z}_{jk})$ for $1 \le i < j \le n$, $1 \le k \le d$.

(b) Imagine a circuit with $2N(N+1)$ gates g_{lt}, one for each literal l of G_{nd} and for each $0 \le t \le N$, meaning that literal l is known to be true after t rounds of unit propagation, if we start with given values of the x_{ij} variables only. Thus we set $g_{l0} \leftarrow 1$ if $l = x_{ij}$ and x_{ij} is true, or if $l = \bar{x}_{ij}$ and x_{ij} is false; otherwise $g_{l0} \leftarrow 0$. And

$$g_{l(t+1)} \leftarrow g_{lt} \vee \bigvee \{ g_{\bar{l}_1 t} \wedge \cdots \wedge g_{\bar{l}_k t} \mid (l \vee l_1 \vee \cdots \vee l_k) \in G_{nd} \}, \quad \text{for } 0 \le t < N.$$

Given values of the x_{ij}, the literal y is implied if and only if the graph has no d-coloring; and at most N rounds make progress. Thus there's a monotone chain for $g_{yN} = \bar{f}_{nd}$.

[This exercise was suggested by S. Buss and R. Williams in 2014, based on a similar construction by M. Gwynne and O. Kullmann.]

429. Let Σ_k be the sum of the assigned x's in leaves descended from node k. Unit propagation will force $b_j^k \leftarrow 1$ for $1 \le j \le \Sigma_k$, moving from leaves toward the root. Then it will force $b_j^k \leftarrow 0$ for $j = \Sigma_k + 1$, moving downwards from the root, because $r = \Sigma_2 + \Sigma_3$ and because (21) starts this process when $k = 2$ or 3.

430. Imagine boundary conditions as in answer 26, and assume that $x_{j_1}, \ldots, x_{j_r}$ have been assigned 1, where $j_1 < \cdots < j_r$. Unit propagation forces $s_{j_k+1-k}^k \leftarrow 1$ for $1 \le k \le r$; then it forces $s_{j_k-k}^k \leftarrow 0$ for $r \ge k \ge 1$. So unassigned x's are forced to zero.

431. Equivalently $x_1 + \cdots + x_m + \bar{y}_1 + \cdots + \bar{y}_n \le n$; so we can use (18)–(19) or (20)–(21).

432. The clauses of answer 404(b) can be shown to be forcing. But not those of 404(a) when $a > 1$; for example, if $a = 2$ and we assume $\bar{x}^2$, unit propagation doesn't yield y^2.

433. Yes. Imagine, for example, the partial assignment $x = 1{*}{*}{*}10{*}{*}1$, $y = 10{*}00{*}1{*}{*}$. Then y_3 must be 1; otherwise we'd have $10010001 \le x \le y \le 100001111$. In this situation unit propagation from the clauses that correspond to $1 \le \langle a_1 01 \rangle$, $a_1 \le \langle a_2 \bar{x}_2 0 \rangle$, $a_2 \le \langle a_3 \bar{x}_3 y_3 \rangle$, $a_3 \le \langle a_4 \bar{x}_4 0 \rangle$, $a_4 \le \langle a_5 00 \rangle$ forces $a_1 = 1$, $a_2 = 1$, $a_4 = 0$, $a_3 = 0$, $y_3 = 1$.

In general if a given partial assignment is consistent with $x \le y$, we must have $x{\downarrow} \le y{\uparrow}$, where $x{\downarrow}$ and $y{\uparrow}$ are obtained from x and y by changing all unassigned variables to 0 and 1, respectively. If that partial assignment forces some y_j to a particular value, the value must be 1; and we must in fact have $x{\downarrow} > y'{\uparrow}$, where y' is like y but with $y_j = 0$ instead of $y_j = {*}$. If $x_j \ne 1$, unit propagation will force $a_1 = \cdots = a_{j-1} = 1$, $a_k = \cdots = a_j = 0$, $y_j = 1$, for some $k \ge j$.

Similar remarks apply when x_i is forced, because $x \leq y \iff \bar{y} \leq \bar{x}$.

434. (a) Clearly p_k is equivalent to $\bar{x}_1 \wedge \cdots \wedge \bar{x}_k$, q_k is equivalent to $\bar{x}_k \wedge \cdots \wedge \bar{x}_n$, and r_k implies that a run of exactly l 1s begins at x_k.

(b) When $l = 1$, if $x_k = 1$ unit propagation will imply $\bar{p}_j$ for $j \geq k$ and $\bar{q}_j$ for $j \leq k$, hence $\bar{r}_j$ for $j \neq k$; then r_k is forced, making $x_j = 0$ for all $j \neq k$. Conversely, $x_j = 0$ forces $\bar{r}_j$; if this holds for all $j \neq k$, then r_k is forced, making $x_k = 1$.

But when $l = 2$ and $n = 3$, the clauses fail to force $x_2 = 1$ by unit propagation. They also fail to force $x_1 = 0$ when we have $l = 2$, $n = 4$, and $x_3 = 1$.

435. The following construction with $O(nl)$ clauses is satisfactory when l is small: Begin with the clauses for p_k and q_k (but not r_k) in exercise 434(a); include also $(\bar{x}_k \vee p_{k-l})$ for $l < k \leq n$, and $(\bar{x}_k \vee q_{k+l})$ for $1 \leq k \leq n - l$. Append $(\bar{p}_{k-l} \vee \bar{q}_{k+l} \vee x_k)$ for $1 \leq k \leq n$, omitting $\bar{p}_j$ for $j < 1$ and omitting $\bar{q}_j$ for $j > n$. Finally, append

$$(x_k \vee \bar{x}_{k+1} \vee x_{k+d}) \qquad \text{for } 0 \leq k < n \text{ and } 1 < d < l, \qquad (*)$$

omitting x_j when $j < 1$ or $j > n$.

To reduce to $O(n \log l)$ clauses, suppose $2^{e+1} < l \leq 2^{e+2}$, where $e \geq 0$. The clauses $(*)$ can be replaced by $(\bar{x}_k \vee \bar{y}_k^{(e)} \vee \bar{z}_k^{(e)})$ for $1 \leq k \leq n$, if $\bar{x}_{k-d}$ implies $y_k^{(e)}$ for $1 \leq d \leq \lfloor l/2 \rfloor$ and $\bar{x}_{k+d}$ implies $z_k^{(e)}$ for $1 \leq d \leq \lceil l/2 \rceil$. And to achieve the latter, we introduce clauses $(\bar{y}_k^{(t)} \vee y_k^{(t+1)})$, $(\bar{y}_{k-2^t}^{(t)} \vee y_k^{(t+1)})$, $(\bar{z}_k^{(t)} \vee z_k^{(t+1)})$, $(\bar{z}_{k+2^t}^{(t)} \vee z_k^{(t+1)})$, $(x_{k-1} \vee y_k^{(0)})$, $(x_{k+2^e-1-\lfloor l/2 \rfloor} \vee y_k^{(0)})$, $(x_{k+1} \vee z_k^{(0)})$, $(x_{k-2^e+1+\lceil l/2 \rceil} \vee z_k^{(0)})$, for $1 \leq k \leq n$ and $0 \leq t < e$, always omitting x_j or $\bar{y}_j$ or $\bar{z}_j$ when $j < 1$ or $j > n$.

436. Let the variables q_k for $0 \leq k \leq n$ and $q \in Q$ represent the sequence of states, and let t_{kaq} represent a transition when $1 \leq k \leq n$ and when T contains a triple of the form (q', a, q). The clauses, F, are the following, for $1 \leq k \leq n$: (i) $(\bar{t}_{kaq} \vee x_k^a) \wedge (\bar{t}_{kaq} \vee q_k)$, where x_k^0 denotes $\bar{x}_k$ and x_k^1 denotes x_k; (ii) $(\bar{q}_{k-1} \vee \bigvee\{t_{kaq'} \mid (q, a, q') \in T\})$, for $q \in Q$; (iii) $(\bar{q}_k \vee \bigvee\{t_{kaq} \mid (q', a, q) \in T\})$; (iv) $(\bar{x}_k^a \vee \bigvee\{t_{kaq} \mid (q', a, q) \in T\})$; (v) $(\bar{t}_{kaq'} \vee \bigvee\{q_{k-1} \mid (q, a, q') \in T\})$, for $a \in A$, $q' \in Q$. And (vi) $(\bar{q}_0)$ for $q \in Q \backslash I$, $(\bar{q}_n)$ for $q \in Q \backslash O$.

It is clear that if $F \vdash_1 \bar{x}_k^a$, no string $x_1 \ldots x_n \in L$ can have $x_k = a$. Conversely, assume that $F \nvdash_1 \bar{x}_k^a$, and in particular that $F \nvdash_1 \epsilon$. To prove the forcing property, we want to show that some string of L has $x_k = a$. It will be convenient to say that a literal l is 'n.f.' (not falsified) if $F \nvdash_1 \bar{l}$; thus x_k^a is assumed to be n.f.

By (iv), there's a $(q', a, q) \in T$ such that t_{kaq} is n.f. Hence q_k is n.f., by (i). If $k = n$ we have $q \in O$ by (vi); otherwise some $t_{(k+1)bq'}$ is n.f., by (ii), hence x_{k+1}^b is n.f. Moreover, (v) tells us that there's $(q'', a, q) \in T$ with q_{k-1}'' n.f. If $k = 1$ we have $q'' \in I$; otherwise some $t_{(k-1)cq''}$ is n.f., by (iii), and x_{k-1}^c is n.f. Continuing this line of reasoning yields $x_1 \ldots x_n \in L$ with $x_k = a$ (and with $x_{k+1} = b$ if $k < n$, $x_{k-1} = c$ if $k > 1$).

The same proof holds even if we add unit clauses to F that assign values to one or more of the x's. Hence F is forcing. [See F. Bacchus, *LNCS* **4741** (2007), 133–147.]

For example, the language L_2 of exercise 434 yields $20n + 4$ clauses with $8n + 3$ auxiliary variables: $F = \bigwedge_{k=1}^{n} \big((\bar{t}_{k00} \vee \bar{x}_k) \wedge (\bar{t}_{k00} \vee 0_k) \wedge (\bar{t}_{k11} \vee x_k) \wedge (\bar{t}_{k11} \vee 1_k) \wedge (\bar{t}_{k12} \vee x_k) \wedge (\bar{t}_{k12} \vee 2_k) \wedge (\bar{t}_{k02} \vee \bar{x}_k) \wedge (\bar{t}_{k02} \vee 2_k) \wedge (\bar{0}_{k-1} \vee t_{k00} \vee t_{k11}) \wedge (\bar{1}_{k-1} \vee t_{k12}) \wedge (\bar{2}_{k-1} \vee t_{k02}) \wedge (\bar{0}_k \vee t_{k00}) \wedge (\bar{1}_k \vee t_{k11}) \wedge (\bar{2}_k \vee t_{k02} \vee t_{k12}) \wedge (x_k \vee t_{k00} \vee t_{k02}) \wedge (\bar{x}_k \vee t_{k11} \vee t_{k12}) \wedge (\bar{t}_{k00} \vee 0_{k-1}) \wedge (\bar{t}_{k11} \vee 0_{k-1}) \wedge (\bar{t}_{k12} \vee 1_{k-1}) \wedge (\bar{t}_{k02} \vee 2_{k-1}) \big) \wedge (\bar{1}_0) \wedge (\bar{2}_0) \wedge (\bar{0}_n) \wedge (\bar{1}_n)$.

The clauses produced by this general-purpose construction can often be significantly simplified by preprocessing to eliminate auxiliary variables. (See exercise 426.)

437. Each variable x_k now becomes a set of $|A|$ variables x_{ka} for $a \in A$, with clauses like (15) and (17) to ensure that exactly one value is assigned. The same construction is then valid, with the same proof, if we simply replace 'x_k^a' by 'x_{ka}' throughout. (Notice that unit propagation will often derive partial information such as $\bar{x}_{ka}$, meaning that $x_k \neq a$, although the precise value of x_k may not be known.)

438. Let $l_{\leq j} = l_1 + \cdots + l_j$. Exercise 436 does the job via the following automaton: $Q = \{0, 1, \ldots, l_{\leq t} + t - 1\}$, $I = \{0\}$, $O = \{l_{\leq t} + t - 1\}$; $T = \{(l_{\leq j} + j, 0, l_{\leq j} + j) \mid 0 \leq j < t\} \cup \{(l_{\leq j} + j + k, 1, l_{\leq j} + j + k + 1) \mid 0 \leq j < t, 0 \leq k < l_{j+1}\} \cup \{(l_{\leq j} + j - 1, 0, l_{\leq j} + j - [j=t]) \mid 1 \leq j \leq t\}$.

439. We obviously want the clauses $(\bar{x}_j \vee \bar{x}_{j+1})$ for $1 \leq j < n$; and we can use, say, (18) and (19) with $r = t$, to force 0s whenever the number of 1s reaches t. The difficult part is to force 1s from partial patterns of 0s; for example, if $n = 9$ and $t = 4$, we can conclude that $x_4 = x_6 = 1$ as soon as we know that $x_3 = x_7 = 0$.

An interesting modification of (18) and (19) turns out to work beautifully, namely with the clauses $(\bar{t}_j^k \vee t_{j+1}^k)$ for $1 \leq j < 2t - 1$ and $1 \leq k \leq n - 2t + 1$, together with $(x_{2j+k-1} \vee \bar{t}_{2j-1}^k \vee t_{2j-1}^{k+1})$ for $1 \leq j \leq t$ and $0 \leq k \leq n - 2t + 1$, omitting $\bar{t}_{2j-1}^0$ and t_{2j-1}^{n-2t+2}.

440. It's convenient to introduce $\binom{n+1}{2}|N|$ variables P_{ik} for all $P \in N$ and for $1 \leq i \leq k \leq n$, as well as $\binom{n+1}{3}|N|^2$ variables QR_{ijk} for $Q, R \in N$ and for $1 \leq i < j \leq k \leq n$, although almost all of them will be eliminated by unit propagation. The clauses are: (i) $(\overline{QR}_{ijk} \vee Q_{i(j-1)}) \wedge (\overline{QR}_{ijk} \vee R_{jk})$; (ii) $(\overline{P}_{kk} \vee \bigvee\{x_k^a \mid P \to a \in U\})$; (iii) $(\overline{P}_{ik} \vee \bigvee\{QR_{ijk} \mid i < j \leq k, P \to QR \in W\})$, if $i < k$; (iv) $(\bar{x}_k^a \vee \bigvee\{P_{kk} \mid P \to a \in U\})$; (v) $(\overline{P}_{ik} \vee \bigvee\{PR_{i(k+1)l} \mid k < l \leq n, R \in N\} \vee \bigvee\{QP_{hik} \mid 1 \leq h < i, Q \in N\})$, if $i > 1$ or $k < n$; (vi) $(\overline{QR}_{ijk} \vee \bigvee\{P_{ik} \mid P \to QR \in W\})$; (vii) $(\overline{P}_{1n})$ for $P \in N \setminus S$.

The forcing property is proved by extending the argument in answer 436: Assume that x_k^a is n.f.; then some P_{kk} with $P \to a$ is also n.f. Whenever P_{ik} is n.f. with $i > 1$ or $k < n$, some $PR_{i(k+1)l}$ or QP_{hik} is n.f.; hence some "larger" P'_{il} or P'_{hk} is also n.f. And if P_{1n} is n.f., we have $P \in S$.

Furthermore we can go "downward": Whenever P_{ik} is n.f. with $i < k$, there's QR_{ijk} such that $Q_{i(j-1)}$ and R_{jk} are n.f.; on the other hand if P_{kk} is n.f., there's $a \in A$ such that x_k^a is n.f. Our assumption that x_k^a is n.f. has therefore shown the existence of $x_1 \ldots x_n \in L$ with $x_k = a$.

[See C.-G. Quimper and T. Walsh, *LNCS* **4741** (2007), 590–604].

441. See O. Bailleux, Y. Boufkhad, and O. Roussel, *LNCS* **5584** (2009), 181–194.

442. (a) $F \mid L_q^- = F \mid l_1 \mid \ldots \mid l_{q-1} \mid \bar{l}_q$ contains ϵ if and only if $F \mid l_1 \mid \ldots \mid l_{q-1}$ contains ϵ or the unit clause (l_q).

(b) If $F \not\vdash_1 l$ and $F \mid \bar{l} \vdash_1 \epsilon$, the failed literal elimination technique will reduce F to $F \mid l$ and continue looking for further reductions. Thus we have $F \vdash_2 l$ if and only if unit propagation plus failed literal elimination will deduce either ϵ or l.

(c) Use induction on k; both statements are obvious when $k = 0$. Suppose we have $F \vdash_{k+1} \bar{l}$ via $l_1, \ldots, l_p = \bar{l}$, with $F \mid L_q^- \vdash_k \epsilon$ for $1 \leq q \leq p$. If $p > 1$ we have $F \mid l \mid L_q^- \vdash_k \epsilon$ for $1 \leq q < p$; it follows that $F \mid l \vdash_{k+1} l_{p-1}$ and $F \mid l \vdash_{k+1} \bar{l}_{p-1}$. If $p = 1$ we have $F \mid l \vdash_k \epsilon$. Hence $F \mid l \vdash_{k+1} \epsilon$ in both cases.

Now we want to prove that $F \mid l \vdash_{k+1} \epsilon$ and $F \vdash_{k+2} \epsilon$, given $F \vdash_{k+1} l'$ and $F \vdash_{k+1} \bar{l}'$. If $F \mid L_q^- \vdash_k \epsilon$ for $1 \leq q \leq p$, with $l_p = l'$, we know that $F \mid L_q^- \vdash_{k+1} \epsilon$. Furthermore we can assume that $F \not\vdash_{k+1} \bar{l}$; hence $l \neq \bar{l}_q$ for $1 \leq q \leq p$, and $l \neq l_p$. If $l = l_q$ for some $q < p$, then $F \mid l \mid L_r^- \vdash_k \epsilon$ for $1 \leq r < q$ and $F \mid L_r^- \vdash_k \epsilon$ for $q < r \leq p$; otherwise $F \mid l \mid L_q^- \vdash_k \epsilon$ for $1 \leq q \leq p$. In both cases $F \mid l \vdash_{k+1} l'$ and $F \vdash_{k+2} l'$. Essentially the same proof shows that $F \mid l \vdash_{k+1} \bar{l}'$ and $F \vdash_{k+2} \bar{l}'$.

(d) True, by the last relation in part (c).

(e) If all clauses of F have more than k literals, $L_k(F)$ is empty; hence $L_0(R') = L_1(R') = L_2(R') = \emptyset$. But $L_k(R') = \{\bar{1}, 2, 4\}$ for $k \geq 3$; for example, $R' \vdash_3 \bar{1}$ because $R' \,|\, 1 \vdash_2 \epsilon$, because $R' \,|\, 1 \vdash_2 3$ and $R' \,|\, 1 \vdash_2 \bar{3}$.

(f) Unit propagation can be done in $O(N)$ steps if N is the total length of all clauses; this handles the case $k = 1$.

For $k \geq 2$, procedure $P_k(F)$ calls $P_{k-1}(F \,|\, x_1)$, $P_{k-1}(F \,|\, \bar{x}_1)$, $P_{k-1}(F \,|\, x_2)$, etc., until either finding $P_{k-1}(F \,|\, \bar{l}) = \{\epsilon\}$ or trying both literals for each variable of F. In the latter case, P_k returns F. In the former case, if $P_{k-1}(F \,|\, l)$ is *also* $\{\epsilon\}$, P_k returns $\{\epsilon\}$; otherwise it returns $P_k(F \,|\, l)$. The set L_k contains all literals for which we've reduced F to $F|l$, unless $P_k(F) = \{\epsilon\}$. (In the latter case, *every* literal is in L_k.)

To justify this procedure we must verify that the order of testing literals doesn't matter. If $F \,|\, \bar{l} \vdash_k \epsilon$ and $F \,|\, \bar{l}' \vdash_k \epsilon$, we have $F \,|\, l \,|\, \bar{l}' \vdash_k \epsilon$ and $F \,|\, l' \,|\, \bar{l} \vdash_k \epsilon$ by (c); hence $P_k(F \,|\, l) = P_k(F \,|\, l \,|\, l') = P_k(F \,|\, l' \,|\, l) = P_k(F \,|\, l')$.

[See O. Kullmann, *Annals of Math. and Artificial Intell.* **40** (2004), 303–352.]

443. (a) If $F \,|\, L \vdash \epsilon$ then $F \,|\, L \vdash l$ for all literals l; so if $F \in \mathrm{PC}_k$ we have $F \,|\, L \vdash_k l$ and $F \,|\, L \vdash_k \bar{l}$ and $F \,|\, L \vdash_k \epsilon$, proving that $\mathrm{PC}_k \subseteq \mathrm{UC}_k$.

Suppose $F \in \mathrm{UC}_k$ and $F \,|\, L \vdash l$. Then $F \,|\, L \,|\, \bar{l} \vdash \epsilon$, and we have $F \,|\, L \,|\, \bar{l} \vdash_k \epsilon$. Consequently $F \,|\, L \vdash_{k+1} l$, proving that $\mathrm{UC}_k \subseteq \mathrm{PC}_{k+1}$.

The satisfiable clause sets $\emptyset$, $\{1\}$, $\{1, \bar{1}2\}$, $\{12, \bar{1}2\}$, $\{12, \bar{1}2, 1\bar{2}, \bar{1}\bar{2}3\}$, $\{123, \bar{1}23, 1\bar{2}3, \bar{1}\bar{2}3\}$, $\{123, \bar{1}23, 1\bar{2}3, \bar{1}\bar{2}3, 12\bar{3}, \bar{1}2\bar{3}, 1\bar{2}\bar{3}, \bar{1}\bar{2}\bar{3}4\}$, $\ldots$, show that $\mathrm{PC}_k \neq \mathrm{UC}_k \neq \mathrm{PC}_{k+1}$.

(b) $F \in \mathrm{PC}_0$ if and only if $F = \emptyset$ or $\epsilon \in F$. (This can be proved by induction on the number of variables in F, because $\epsilon \notin F$ implies that F has no unit clauses.)

(c) If F has only one clause, it is in UC_0. More interesting examples are $\{1\bar{2}, \bar{1}2\}$; $\{1234, \bar{1}2\bar{3}\bar{4}\}$; $\{12\bar{3}4, 12\bar{3}\bar{4}, 1\bar{2}34, \bar{1}234\}$; $\{12, \bar{1}\bar{2}, 34\bar{5}, \bar{3}\bar{4}5\}$; etc. In general, F is in UC_0 if and only if it contains all of its prime clauses.

(d) True, by induction on n: If $F \,|\, L \vdash l$ then $F \,|\, L \,|\, \bar{l} \vdash \epsilon$, and $F \,|\, L \,|\, \bar{l}$ has $\leq n - 1$ variables; so $F \,|\, L \,|\, \bar{l} \in \mathrm{PC}_{n-1} \subseteq \mathrm{UC}_{n-1}$. Hence we have $F \,|\, L \,|\, \bar{l} \vdash_{n-1} \epsilon$ and $F \,|\, L \vdash_n l$.

(e) False, by the examples in (c).

(f) $R' \in \mathrm{UC}_2 \setminus \mathrm{PC}_2$. For example, we have $R' \,|\, 1 \vdash_2 2$ and $R' \,|\, 1 \vdash_2 \bar{2}$.

[See M. Gwynne and O. Kullmann, arXiv:1406.7398 [cs.CC] (2014), 67 pages.]

444. (a) Complementing a variable doesn't affect the algorithm's behavior, so we can assume that F consists of unrenamed Horn clauses. Then all clauses of F will be Horn clauses of length ≥ 2 whenever step E2 is reached. Such clauses are always satisfiable, by setting all remaining variables false; so step E3 cannot find both $F \vdash_1 l$ and $F \vdash_1 \bar{l}$.

(b) For example, $\{12, \bar{2}3, 1\bar{2}\bar{3}, \bar{1}23\}$.

(c) Every unsatisfiable F recognized by SLUR must be in UC_1. Conversely, if $F \in \mathrm{UC}_1$, we can prove that F is satisfiable and in UC_1 whenever step E2 is reached.

[Essentially the same argument proves that a generalized algorithm, which uses $\vdash_k$ instead of $\vdash_1$ in steps E1 and E3, always classifies F if and only if $F \in \mathrm{UC}_k$. See M. Gwynne and O. Kullmann, *Journal of Automated Reasoning* **52** (2014), 31–65.]

(d) If step E3 interleaves unit propagation on $F \,|\, l$ with unit propagation on $F \,|\, \bar{l}$, stopping when either branch is complete and ϵ was not detected in the other, the running time is proportional to the number of cells used to store F, using data structures like those of Algorithm L. (This is an unpublished idea of Klaus Truemper.)

[SLUR is due to J. S. Schlipf, F. S. Annexstein, J. V. Franco, and R. P. Swaminathan, *Information Processing Letters* **54** (1995), 133–137.]

445. (a) Since the lexicographic constraints (169) are forcing, a succinct certificate is $(\bar{x}_{1m}, \bar{x}_{2m}, \ldots, \bar{x}_{(m-1)m}, \bar{x}_{2(m-1)}, \bar{x}_{3(m-1)}, \ldots, \bar{x}_{(m-1)(m-1)}, \bar{x}_{3(m-2)}, \bar{x}_{4(m-2)}, \ldots, \bar{x}_{(m-1)(m-2)}, \ldots, \bar{x}_{(m-1)2}, \emptyset)$. The first $m-1$ steps can be replaced by 'x_{0m}'.

(b) $(\bar{x}_{(m-1)1}, \bar{x}_{(m-2)2}, \ldots, \bar{x}_{1(m-1)}, \emptyset)$.

(c) $(x_{01}, x_{12}, \ldots, x_{(m-2)(m-1)}, \emptyset)$.

446. $Z(m,n) - 1$, because a 4-cycle corresponds to a quad.

447. For general m and n we can add the $m^3n^3/3!$ constraints $(\bar{x}_{ij} \vee \bar{x}_{i'j'} \vee \bar{x}_{i''j'} \vee \bar{x}_{i''j''} \vee \bar{x}_{ij''})$ to (184), for $1 \le i < i' < i'' \le m$ and distinct $\{j, j', j''\} \subseteq \{1, \ldots, n\}$. The 19-edge graph illustrated here works when $m = n = 8$; and Algorithm C finds girth ≥ 8 unsatisfiable with 20 edges, after only 400 megamems of calculation (using lexicographic row/column symmetry).

448. Each pair of points can occur together in at most one line. If the lines contain respectively $l_1, \ldots, l_n$ points, we therefore have $\binom{l_1}{2} + \cdots + \binom{l_n}{2} \le \binom{m}{2} = 3n$. A Steiner triple system achieves equality, with $l_1 = \cdots = l_n = 3$. Since $\binom{l-1}{2} + \binom{l'+1}{2} < \binom{l}{2} + \binom{l'}{2}$ when $l \ge l' + 2$, we can't have $l_1 + \cdots + l_n > 3n$. Thus $Z(m,n) = 3n + 1$.

[If m is even and $\binom{m}{2} = 3n$, we can't cover all the pairs with triples, because no point can be in more than $(m-2)/2$ triples. Daniel Horsley proved in 2015 that $Z(m,n) = 3n + \lfloor 1 - m/14 \rfloor$ in such cases.]

449. It's wise to try first for symmetric solutions with $x_{ij} = x_{ji}$, roughly halving the number of variables; then the matrices below are found quickly. Such solutions are impossible when $n = 9$, 12, 13 (and also when $n = 15$ and 16 if we insist on five 1s in the top row). The case $n = 13$ corresponds to the projective plane of order 3; indeed, a projective plane of order q is equivalent to a maximum quad-free matrix with $m = n = q^2 + q + 1$ and $Z(n,n) = (q+1)n + 1$.

```
                                                                                              1111000000000000
                                                                          111100000000000     1000111000000000
                                                        11110000000000    100011100000000     1000000111000000
                                        1111000000000   100001110000000   100000011100000     1000000000111000
                        11110000000     100011100000    100000001110000   100000000011100     1000100000001010
        1111000000      100011100       100000011100    100000000011100   010010010000000     0100100000100101
1111000 1000110000      100001110       100000000111    010010010000000   001010001000000     0010010000010001
111100000 100001100     010010010       010010010000    001010001000000   000010110000000     0001010010000100
100011100 100000011     010001001       001010001000    000101000100000   000100010010000     0100100001001000
100001110 010010010     001010001       001001001000    010001001000000   010001001000000     0010001000010100
100000011 010001001     001001010       000110001000    001001001001000   001001001010000     0010000100100100
010010010 001010001     000110001       000101000110    000110010001000   000110001001000     0010100010010010
001010001 001001010     000100101       000100101010    000010100100100   000010100100100     0001001000010010
000110001 000110001                     000010010100010 000100101000010   000100101100010     0001010100000100
000100101 000100101                                     000001001010100   000001001010001     0000001100100001
                                                                                              0000010010010001
```

450. To prove the hint, add the unary clause $(\bar{x}_{15})$ to the others; this problem is rapidly found to be unsatisfiable, hence no line has more than 4 points. On the other hand, a line with fewer than 3 points is impossible because $Z(9, 10) = 32$. The same arguments show that every point belongs to either 3 or 4 lines. Thus exactly four lines contain four points, and exactly four points lie on such lines.

If $p \in l$ and l is a 4-point line, every other line containing p must contain 2 of the remaining 6 points. And the four 4-point lines contain at least $4 \times 4 - \binom{4}{2} = 10$ points altogether. Hence, pigeonwise, we see that each of the four 4-point lines contains exactly one of the four 4-line points.

Now we may call the 4-line points $\{a, b, c, d\}$, and the 4-point lines $\{A, B, C, D\}$. The other points may be called $\{ab, ac, ad, bc, bd, cd\}$, with $A = \{a, ab, ac, ad\}$, $B = \{b, ab, bc, bd\}$, $C = \{c, ac, bc, cd\}$, $D = \{d, ad, bd, cd\}$. The other lines can be called $\{AB, AC, AD, BC, BD, CD\}$; and we have $AB = \{a, b, cd\}$, $AC = \{a, c, ad\}$, etc.

451. One of the colors can be placed uniquely, by the previous exercise. So we're left with the simple problem of two-coloring the remaining 66 squares and avoiding both 0-quads and 1-quads. That problem is unsatisfiable with $\sum x_{ij}$ odd. The author then constructed a $33 + 33 + 33$ solution by hand, using the fact that each color class must be unable to use the deleted square. [See M. Beresin, E. Levine, and J. Winn, *The College Mathematics Journal* **20** (1989), 106–114 and the cover; J. L. Lewis, *JRM* **28** (1997), 266–273.]

452. Any such solution must have exactly 81 cells of each color, because R. Nowakowski proved in 1978 that $Z(18, 18) = 82$. The solution exhibited here was found by B. Steinbach and C. Posthoff [*Multiple-Valued Logic and Soft Computing* **21** (2013), 609–625], exploiting 90° rotational symmetry.

453. (a) If $R \subseteq \{1, \ldots, m\}$ and $C \subseteq \{1, \ldots, n\}$, let $V(R, C) = \{u_i \mid i \in R\} \cup \{v_j \mid j \in C\}$. If X is decomposable, there's no path from a vertex in $V(R, C)$ to a vertex not in $V(R, C)$; hence the graph isn't connected. Conversely, if the graph isn't connected, let $V(R, C)$ be one of its connected components. Then $0 < |R| + |C| < m + n$, and we've decomposed X.

(b) False in general, unless every row and column of X' contains a positive element. Otherwise, clearly true by the definition of lexicographic order.

(c) True: A direct sum is certainly decomposable. Conversely, let X be decomposable via R and C. We may assume that $1 \in R$ or $1 \in C$; otherwise we could replace R by $\{1, \ldots, m\} \setminus R$ and C by $\{1, \ldots, n\} \setminus C$. Let $i \geq 1$ and $j \geq 1$ be minimal such that $i \notin R$ and $j \notin C$. Then $x_{i'j} = 0$ for $1 \leq i' < i$ and $x_{ij'} = 0$ for $1 \leq j' < j$. The lexicographic constraints now force $x_{i'j'} = 0$ for $1 \leq i' < i$, $j' \geq j$; also for $i' \geq i$, $1 \leq j' < j$. Consequently $X = X' \oplus X''$, where X' is $(i-1) \times (j-1)$ and X'' is $(m + 1 - i) \times (n + 1 - j)$. (Degenerate cases where $i = 1$ or $j = 1$ or $i = m + 1$ or $j = n + 1$ need to be considered, but they work fine. This result allows us to "read off" the block decomposition of a lexicographically ordered matrix.)

Reference: A. Mader and O. Mutzbauer, *Ars Combinatoria* **61** (2001), 81–95.

454. We have $f(x) \leq f(x\tau) \leq f(x\tau\tau) \leq \cdots \leq f(x\tau^k) \leq \cdots$; eventually $x\tau^k = x$.

455. (a) Yes, because C only causes 1001 and 1011 to be nonsolutions. (b) No, because F might have been satisfied only by 0011. (c) Yes as in (a), although (187) might no longer be an endomorphism of $F \wedge C$ as it was in that case. (d) Yes; if 0110 is a solution, so are 0101 and 1010. [Of course this exercise is highly artificial: We're unlikely to know that a weird mapping such as (187) is an endomorphism of F unless we know a lot more about the set of solutions.]

456. Only $(1 + 2 \cdot 7)(1 + 2)(1 + 8) = 405$, out of 65536 possibilities (about 0.06%).

457. We have $\min_{0 < k < 16}(k^k 16^{16-k}) = 6^6 16^{10} \approx 51.3 \times 10^{15}$. For general n, the minimum occurs when $k = 2^n/e + O(1)$; and it is $2^{2^n(n-x)}$ where $x = 1/(e \ln 2) + O(2^{-n}) < 1$.

458. The operation of assigning values to each variable of an autarky, so that all clauses containing those variables are satisfied, while leaving all other variables unchanged, is an endomorphism. (For example, consider the operation that makes a pure literal true.)

459. $\mathrm{sweep}(X_{ij}) = -\infty$ when $i = 0$ or $j = 0$. And for $1 \leq i \leq m$ and $1 \leq j \leq n$ we have $\mathrm{sweep}(X_{ij}) = \max(x_{ij} + \mathrm{sweep}(X_{(i-1)(j-1)}), \mathrm{sweep}(X_{(i-1)j}), \mathrm{sweep}(X_{i(j-1)}))$.

[Let the 1s in the matrix be $x_{i_1 j_1}, \ldots, x_{i_r j_r}$, with $1 \leq i_1 \leq \cdots \leq i_r \leq m$ and with $j_{q+1} < j_q$ when $i_{q+1} = i_q$. Richard Stanley has observed (unpublished) that $\mathrm{sweep}(X)$ is the number of rows that occur when the Robinson–Schensted–Knuth algorithm is used to insert the sequence $n - j_1, \ldots, n - j_r$ into an initially empty tableau.]

460. We introduce auxiliary variables s_{ij}^t that will become true if $\mathrm{sweep}(X_{ij}) > t$. They are implicitly true when $t < 0$, false when $t = k$. The clauses are as follows, for $1 \leq i \leq m$, $1 \leq j \leq n$, and $0 \leq t \leq \min(i - 1, j - 1, k)$: $(\bar{s}_{(i-1)j}^t \vee s_{ij}^t)$, if $i > 1$ and

$t < k$; $(\bar{s}^{t}_{i(j-1)} \vee s^{t}_{ij})$, if $j > 1$ and $t < k$; and $(\bar{x}_{ij} \vee \bar{s}^{t-1}_{(i-1)(j-1)} \vee s^{t}_{ij})$. Omit $\bar{s}^{t-1}_{0(j-1)}$ and $\bar{s}^{t-1}_{(i-1)0}$ and $\bar{s}^{-1}_{(i-1)(j-1)}$ and s^{k}_{ij} from that last clause, if present.

461. $\bigwedge_{i=1}^{m-1} \bigwedge_{j=1}^{n-1} (x_{ij} \vee \bar{c}_{(i-1)j} \vee c_{ij}) \wedge \bigwedge_{i=1}^{m} \bigwedge_{j=1}^{n-1} (\bar{c}_{(i-1)j} \vee \bar{x}_{ij} \vee x_{i(j+1)})$, omitting $\bar{c}_{0j}$. These clauses take care of τ_1; interchange $i \leftrightarrow j$, $m \leftrightarrow n$ for τ_2.

462. Let $\tilde{X}_{ij}$ denote the *last* $m+1-i$ rows and the last $n+1-j$ columns of X; and let $t_{ij} = \mathrm{sweep}(X_{(i-1)(j-1)}) + \mathrm{sweep}(\tilde{X}_{(i+1)(j+1)})$. For τ_1 we must prove $1 + t_{i(j+1)} \le k$, given that $1 + t_{ij} \le k$. It's true because $\mathrm{sweep}(X_{(i-1)j}) = \mathrm{sweep}(X_{(i-1)(j-1)})$ when column j begins with $i-1$ zeros, and we have $\mathrm{sweep}(\tilde{X}_{(i+1)(j+2)}) \le \mathrm{sweep}(\tilde{X}_{(i+1)(j+1)})$.

Let $X' = X\tau_3$ have the associated sweep sums t'_{ij}. We must prove that $t'_{ij} \le k$ and $1 + t'_{(i+1)(j+1)} \le k$, if $1 + t_{ij} \le k$, $1 + t_{i(j+1)} \le k$, $1 + t_{(i+1)j} \le k$, and $t_{(i+1)(j+1)} \le k$. The key point is that $\mathrm{sweep}(X'_{ij}) = \max(\mathrm{sweep}(X_{(i-1)j}), \mathrm{sweep}(X_{i(j-1)}))$, since $x'_{ij} = 0$. Also $\mathrm{sweep}(\tilde{X}'_{(i+1)(j+1)}) \le 1 + \mathrm{sweep}(\tilde{X}_{(i+2)(j+1)})$.

(Notice that τ_1 and τ_2 might actually *decrease* the sweep, but τ_3 preserves it.)

463. If row $i + 1$ is entirely zero but row i isn't, τ_2 will apply. Therefore the all-zero rows occur at the top. And by τ_1, the first nonzero row has all its 1s at the right.

Suppose rows 1 through i have $r_1, \ldots, r_i$ 1s, all at the right, with $r_i > 0$. Then $r_1 \le \cdots \le r_i$, by τ_2. If $i < n$ we can increase i to $i+1$, since we can't have $x_{(i+1)j} > x_{(i+1)(j+1)}$ when $j \le n - r_i$, by τ_1; and we can't have it when $j > n - r_i$, by τ_3.

Thus all the 1s are clustered at the right and the bottom, like the diagram of a partition but rotated $180°$; and the sweep is the size of its "Durfee square" (see Fig. 91 in Section 7.2.1.4). Hence the maximum number of 1s, given sweep k, is $k(m + n - k)$.

[Under the partial ordering $(i, j) \prec (i', j')$ when $i < i'$ and $j < j'$, binary matrices of sweep $\le k$ correspond to sets of cells with all chains of length $\le k$. Significant lattice and matroid properties of such "Sperner k-families" have been studied by C. Greene and D. J. Kleitman, *J. Combinatorial Theory* **A20** (1976), 41–68.]

464. By answer 462, τ_1 can be strengthened to τ'_1, which sets $x_{i(j+1)} \leftarrow 1$ but leaves $x_{ij} = 1$. Similarly, τ_2 can be strengthened to τ'_2. These endomorphisms preserve the sweep but increase the weight, so they can't apply to a matrix of maximum weight. [One can prove, in fact, that max-weight binary matrices of sweep k are precisely equivalent to k disjoint shortest paths from the leftmost cells in row m to the rightmost cells in row 1. Hence every integer matrix of sweep k is the sum of k matrices of sweep 1.]

465. If not, there's a cycle $x_0 \to x_1 \to \cdots \to x_p = x_0$ of length $p > 1$, where $x_i \tau_{uv_i} \mapsto x_{i+1}$. Let uv be the largest of $\{uv_1, \ldots, uv_{p-1}\}$. Then none of the other τ's in the cycle can change the status of edge uv. But that edge must change status at least twice. (See also the more general result in Theorem 7.2.2.1S.)

466. Notice first that v_{11} must be true, if $m \ge 2$. Otherwise h_{11}, v_{21}, h_{22}, v_{32}, $\ldots$ would successively be forced by unit propagation, until reaching a contradiction at the edge of the board. And v_{31} must also be true, if $m \ge 4$, by a similar argument. Thus the entire first column must be filled with verticals, except the bottom row when m is odd.

Then we can show that the remainder of row 1 is filled with horizontals, except for the rightmost column when n is even. And so on.

The unique solution when m and n are both even uses v_{ij} if and only if $i + j$ is even and $1 \le j \le \min(i, m - i, n/2)$, or $i + j$ is odd and $v_{i(n+1-j)}$ is used. When m is odd, add a row of horizontals below the $(m-1) \times n$ solution. When n is odd, remove the rightmost column of verticals in the $m \times (n+1)$ solution.

467. The 8×7 covering is the reflection of the 7×8 covering (shown here) about its southwest-to-northeast diagonal. Both solutions are unique.

468. (a) Typical running times with Algorithm C for sizes 6×6, 8×8, ..., 16×16 are somewhat improved: $39 \, K\mu$, $368 \, K\mu$, $4.3 \, M\mu$, $48 \, M\mu$, $626 \, M\mu$, $8 \, G\mu$.

(b) Now they're even better, but still growing exponentially: $30 \, K\mu$, $289 \, K\mu$, $2.3 \, M\mu$, $22 \, M\mu$, $276 \, M\mu$, $1.7 \, G\mu$.

469. For instance (v_{11}), (v_{31}), (v_{51}), (h_{12}), (h_{14}), (v_{22}), (v_{42}), (h_{23}), (v_{33}), ϵ.

470. There can't be a cycle $x_0 \to x_1 \to \cdots \to x_p = x_0$ of length $p > 1$, because the largest vertex whose mate is changed always gets smaller and smaller mates.

471. We must pair $2n$ with 1, then $2n - 1$ with 2, ..., then $n + 1$ with n.

472. We can number the vertices from 1 to mn in such a way that every 4-cycle switches as desired. For example, we can make $(i, j) < (i, j + 1) \iff (i, j) < (i + 1, j) \iff (i, j) \bmod 4 \in \{(0, 0), (0, 1), (1, 1), (1, 2), (2, 2), (2, 3), (3, 3), (3, 0)\}$. One such numbering in the 4×4 case is shown here.

16	15	1	2
4	14	13	3
5	6	12	11
9	7	8	10

473. For every even-length cycle $v_0 - v_1 - \cdots - v_{2r-1} - v_0$ with $v_0 = \max v_i$ and $v_1 > v_{2r-1}$, assert $(\overline{v_0 v_1} \vee v_1 v_2 \vee \overline{v_2 v_3} \vee \cdots \vee v_{2r-1} v_0)$.

474. (a) $(2n) \cdot (2n - 2) \cdot \ldots \cdot 2 = 2^n n!$. (b) $(17\overline{3})(\overline{1}7\overline{3})(25\overline{2}\overline{5})(4\overline{4})(6)(\overline{6})$.

(c) Using 0, 1, ..., f for the 4-tuples 0000, 0001, ..., 1111, we must have $f(0) = f(9) = f(5)$; $f(2) = f(b) = f(7)$; $f(4) = f(8) = f(d)$; and $f(6) = f(a) = f(f)$; in other words, the truth table of f must have the form $abcdeagceagcfehg$, where $a, b, c, d, e, f, g, h \in \{0, 1\}$. So there are 2^8 f's.

(d) Change '$=$' to '$\neq$' in (c). There are no such truth tables, because (191) contains odd cycles; all cycles of an antisymmetry must have even length.

(e) The 128 binary 7-tuples are partitioned into sixteen "orbits" $\{x, x\sigma, x\sigma^2, \ldots\}$, with eight of size 12 and eight of size 4. For example, one of the 4s is $\{0011010, 0010110, 0111110, 0110010\}$; one of the 12s is $\{0000000, 0011101, \ldots, 1111000\}$. Hence there are 2^{16} functions with this symmetry, and 2^{16} others with this antisymmetry.

475. (a) $2^{n+1} n!$. (There are $2^{n+1} n!/a$, if f has a automorphisms+antiautomorphisms.)

(b) $(x\bar{z})(\bar{x}z)$, because (surprisingly) $(x \vee y) \wedge (x \oplus z) = (\bar{z} \vee y) \wedge (\bar{z} \oplus \bar{x})$.

(c) In general if σ is any permutation having a cycle of length l, and if p is a prime divisor of l, some power of σ will have a cycle of length p. (Repeatedly raise σ to the qth power for all primes $q \neq p$, until all cycle lengths are powers of p. Then, if the longest remaining cycle has length p^e, compute the p^{e-1}st power.)

(d) Suppose $f(x_1, x_2, x_3)$ has the symmetry $(x_1 \bar{x}_2 x_3)(\bar{x}_1 x_2 \bar{x}_3)$. Then $f(0, 0, 0) = f(1, 1, 0) = f(0, 1, 1)$, $f(1, 1, 1) = f(0, 0, 1) = f(1, 0, 0)$, so $(x_1 \bar{x}_2)(\bar{x}_1 x_2)$ is a symmetry.

(e) A similar argument shows that $(ux)(vw)(\bar{u}\bar{x})(\bar{v}\bar{w})$ is a symmetry.

(f) If σ is an antisymmetry of f, then σ^2 is a symmetry. If f has a nontrivial symmetry, it has a symmetry of prime order p, by (c). And if $p \neq 2$, it has one of order 2, by (d) and (e), unless $n > 5$.

(g) Let $f(x_1, \ldots, x_6) = 1$ only when $x_1 \ldots x_6 \in \{001000, 001001, 001011, 010000, 010010, 010110, 100000, 100100, 100101\}$. (Another interesting example, for $n = 7$, has $f = 1 \iff x_1 \ldots x_7$ is a cyclic shift of 0000001, 0001101, or 0011101; 21 symmetries.)

476. We want clauses that specify r-step chains in n variables, having a single output x_{n+r}. For $0 < t < t' < 2^n$, introduce new variables $\Delta_{tt'} = x_{(n+r)t} \oplus x_{(n+r)t'}$. (See (24).) Then for each signed involution σ, not the identity, we want a clause that says "σ is not a symmetry of f," namely $(\bigvee \{\Delta_{tt'} \mid t < t' \text{ and } t' = t\sigma\})$. (Here t is considered to be the same as its binary representation $(t_1 \ldots t_n)_2$, as in exercise 477.)

Also, if σ has no fixed points — this is true if and only if σ takes $x_i \mapsto \bar{x}_i$ for at least one i — we have further things to do: In case (b), we want a clause that says "σ

is not an antisymmetry," namely $(\bigvee\{\overline{\Delta_{tt'}} \mid t < t' \text{ and } t' = t\sigma\})$. But in case (a), we need further variables a_j for $1 \le j \le T$, where T is the number of signed involutions that are fixedpoint-free. We append the clause $(a_1 \vee \cdots \vee a_T)$, and also $(\bar{a}_j \vee \Delta_{tt'})$ for all $t < t'$ such that $t' = t\sigma$ when σ corresponds to index j. Those clauses say, "there's at least one signed involution that is an antisymmetry."

There are no solutions when $n \le 3$. Answers for (a) are $(((x_1 \oplus x_2) \vee x_3) \wedge x_4) \oplus x_1$ and $((((\bar{x}_1 \oplus x_2) \wedge x_3) \oplus x_4) \wedge x_5) \oplus x_1$; in both cases the signed involution $(1\bar{1})(2\bar{2})$ is obviously an antisymmetry. Answers for (b) are $((x_1 \oplus x_2) \vee x_3) \wedge (x_4 \vee x_1)$ and $(((x_1 \wedge x_2) \oplus x_3) \wedge x_4) \oplus (x_5 \vee x_1)$. [Is there a simple formula that works for all n?]

477. Use the following variables for $1 \le h \le m$, $n < i \le n+r$, and $0 < t < 2^n$: $x_{it} = $ (tth bit of truth table for x_i); $g_{hi} = [g_h = x_i]$; $s_{ijk} = [x_i = x_j \circ_i x_k]$, for $1 \le j < k < i$; $f_{ipq} = \circ_i(p,q)$ for $0 \le p, q \le 1$, $p+q > 0$. (We don't need f_{i00}, because every operation in a normal chain takes $(0,0) \mapsto 0$.) The main clauses for truth table computations are

$$\left(\bar{s}_{ijk} \vee (x_{it} \oplus a) \vee (x_{jt} \oplus b) \vee (x_{kt} \oplus c) \vee (f_{ibc} \oplus \bar{a})\right), \text{ for } 0 \le a,b,c \le 1 \text{ and } 1 \le j < k < i.$$

Simplifications arise in special cases: For example, if $b = c = 0$, the clause is omitted if $a = 0$, and the term f_{i00} is omitted if $a = 1$. Furthermore if $t = (t_1 \ldots t_n)_2$, and if $j \le n$, the (nonexistent) variable x_{jt} actually has the known value t_j; again we omit either the whole clause or the term $(x_{jt} \oplus b)$, depending on b and t. For example, there usually are eight main clauses that involve s_{ijk}; but there's only one that involves s_{i12} when $t < 2^{n-2}$, namely $(\bar{s}_{i12} \vee \bar{x}_{i1})$, because the truth tables for x_1 and x_2 begin with 2^{n-2} 0s. (All such simplifications would be done by a preprocessor if we had defined additional variables f_{i00} and x_{jt}, and fixed their values with unit clauses.)

There also are more mundane clauses, namely $(\bar{g}_{hi} \vee \bar{x}_{it})$ or $(\bar{g}_{hi} \vee x_{it})$ according as $g_h(t_1, \ldots, t_n) = 0$ or 1, to fix the outputs; also $(\bigvee_{i=n+1}^{n+r} g_{hi})$ and $(\bigvee_{k=1}^{i-1} \bigvee_{j=1}^{k-1} s_{ijk})$, to ensure that each output appears in the chain and that each step has two operands.

Additional clauses are optional, but they greatly shrink the space of possibilities: $(\bigvee_{k=1}^{m} g_{ki} \vee \bigvee_{i'=i+1}^{n+r} \bigvee_{j=1}^{i-1} s_{i'ji} \vee \bigvee_{i'=i+1}^{n+r} \bigvee_{j=i+1}^{i'-1} s_{i'ij})$ ensures that step i is used at least once; $(\bar{s}_{ijk} \vee \bar{s}_{i'ji})$ and $(\bar{s}_{ijk} \vee \bar{s}_{i'ki})$ for $i < i' \le n+r$ avoid reapplying an operand.

Finally, we can rule out trivial binary operations with the clauses $(f_{i01} \vee f_{i10} \vee f_{i11})$, $(f_{i01} \vee \bar{f}_{i10} \vee \bar{f}_{i11})$, $(\bar{f}_{i01} \vee f_{i10} \vee \bar{f}_{i11})$. (But beware: These clauses, for $n < i \le n+r$, will make it impossible to compute the trivial function $g_1 = 0$ in fewer than three steps!)

Further clauses such as $(\bar{s}_{ijk} \vee f_{i01} \vee \bar{x}_{it} \vee x_{jt})$ are true, but unhelpful in practice.

478. We can insist that the (j,k) pairs in steps $n+1, \ldots, n+r$ appear in colexicographic order; for example, a chain step like $x_8 = x_4 \oplus x_5$ need never follow $x_7 = x_2 \wedge x_6$. The clauses, for $n < i < n+r$, are $(\bar{s}_{ijk} \vee \bar{s}_{(i+1)j'k'})$ if $1 \le j' < j < k = k' < i$ or if $1 \le j < k$ and $1 \le j' < k' < k < i$. (If $(j,k) = (j',k')$, we could insist further that $f_{i01}f_{i10}f_{i11}$ is lexicographically less than $f_{(i+1)01}f_{(i+1)10}f_{(i+1)11}$. But the author didn't go that far.)

Furthermore, if $p < q$ and if each output function is unchanged when x_p is swapped with x_q, we can insist that x_p is used before x_q as an operand. Those clauses are

$$\left(\bar{s}_{ijq} \vee \bigvee_{n < i' < i} \bigvee_{1 \le j' < k' < i'} [j' = p \text{ or } k' = p] s_{i'j'k'}\right) \text{ whenever } j \ne p.$$

For example, when answer 477 is applied to the full-adder problem, it yields M_r clauses in N_r variables, where $(M_4, M_5) = (942, 1662)$ and $(N_4, N_5) = (82, 115)$. The symmetry-breaking strategy above, with $(p,q) = (1,2)$ and $(2,3)$, raises the number of clauses to M'_r, where $(M'_4, M'_5) = (1025, 1860)$. Algorithm C reported 'unsat' after $(1015, 291)$ kilomems using (M_4, M'_4) clauses; 'sat' after $(250, 268)$ kilomems using (M_5, M'_5). With larger problems, such symmetry breakers give significant speedup when proving unsatisfiability, but they're often a handicap in satisfiable instances.

479. (a) Using the notation of the previous answer, we have $(M_8, M_8', N_8) = (14439, 17273, 384)$ and $(M_9, M_9', N_9) = (19719, 24233, 471)$. The running times for the 'sat' cases with M_9 and M_9' clauses were respectively $(16, 645, 1259)$ and $(66, 341, 1789)$ megamems — these stats are the $(\min, \text{median}, \max)$ of nine runs with different random seeds. The 'unsat' cases with M_8 and M_8' were dramatically different: $(655631, 861577, 952218)$ and $(8858, 10908, 13171)$. Thus $s(4) = 9$ in 7.1.2–(28) is optimum.

(b) But $s(5) = 12$ is *not* optimum, despite the beauty of 7.1.2–(29)! The $M_{11} = 76321$ clauses in $N_{11} = 957$ variables are 'sat' in 680 Gμ, yielding an amazing chain:

$$x_6 = x_1 \oplus x_2, \qquad x_{10} = x_6 \vee x_7, \qquad x_{14} = \bar{x}_8 \wedge x_{11},$$
$$x_7 = x_1 \oplus x_3, \qquad x_{11} = x_4 \oplus x_9, \qquad z_1 = x_{15} = x_{10} \oplus x_{14},$$
$$x_8 = x_4 \oplus x_5, \qquad x_{12} = x_9 \oplus x_{10}, \qquad z_2 = x_{16} = x_{12} \wedge \bar{x}_{15}.$$
$$x_9 = x_3 \oplus x_6, \qquad z_0 = x_{13} = x_5 \oplus x_{11},$$

And $(M_{10}', N_{10}) = (68859, 815)$ turns out to be 'unsat' in 1773 gigamems; this can be reduced to 309 gigamems by appending the unit clause $(g_{3(15)})$, since $C(S_{4,5}) = 10$.

Hence we can evaluate $x_1 + \cdots + x_7$ in only $5 + 11 + 2 + 1 = 19$ steps, by computing $(u_1 u_0)_2 = x_5 \mid x_6 + x_7$, $(v_2 v_1 z_0)_2 - x_1 + x_2 + x_3 + x_4 + u_0$, $(w_2 z_1)_2 = u_1 + v_1$, $z_2 = v_2 \oplus w_2$.

(c) The solver finds an elegant 8-step solution for $(M_8, N_8) = (6068, 276)$ in 6 Mμ:

$$x_4 = x_1 \vee x_2, \qquad x_6 = x_3 \oplus x_4, \qquad x_8 = x_3 \oplus x_5, \qquad S_1 = x_{10} = x_6 \wedge x_8,$$
$$x_5 = x_1 \oplus x_2, \quad \overline{S}_0 = x_7 = x_3 \vee x_4, \qquad S_3 = x_9 = \bar{x}_6 \wedge x_8, \qquad S_2 = x_{11} = x_7 \oplus x_8.$$

The corresponding $(M_7', N_7) = (5016, 217)$ problem is 'unsat' in 97 Mμ.

(d) The total cost of evaluating the S's independently is $3 + 7 + 6 + 7 + 3 = 26$, using the optimum computations of Fig. 9 in Section 7.1.2. Therefore the author was surprised to discover a 9-step chain for S_1, S_2, and S_3, using the footprint heuristic:

$$x_5 = x_1 \oplus x_2, \qquad x_8 = x_5 \oplus x_7, \qquad S_2 = x_{11} = \bar{x}_8 \wedge x_9,$$
$$x_6 = x_1 \oplus x_3, \qquad x_9 = x_6 \vee x_7, \qquad S_3 = x_{12} = x_8 \wedge \bar{x}_{10},$$
$$x_7 = x_3 \oplus x_4, \qquad x_{10} = x_2 \oplus x_9, \qquad S_1 = x_{13} = x_8 \wedge x_{10}.$$

This chain can solve problem (d) in 13 steps; but SAT technology does it in 12(!):

$$x_5 = x_1 \oplus x_2, \qquad x_9 = x_6 \vee x_7, \qquad S_1 = x_{13} = x_8 \wedge x_{10},$$
$$x_6 = x_1 \oplus x_3, \qquad x_{10} = x_2 \oplus x_9, \qquad S_4 = x_{14} = x_1 \wedge \bar{x}_{11},$$
$$x_7 = x_3 \oplus x_4, \qquad x_{11} = x_5 \vee x_9, \qquad \overline{S}_0 = x_{15} = x_4 \vee x_{11},$$
$$x_8 = x_5 \oplus x_7, \qquad S_3 = x_{12} = x_8 \wedge \bar{x}_{10}, \qquad S_2 = x_{16} = \bar{x}_8 \wedge x_{11}.$$

The nonexistence of an 11-step solution can be proved via Algorithm C by a long computation (11034 gigamems), during which 99,999,379 clauses are learned(!).

(e) This solution (found in 342 Gμ) matches the lower bound in exercise 7.1.2–80:

$$x_7 = x_1 \oplus x_2, \qquad x_{11} = x_4 \oplus x_{10}, \qquad x_{15} = \bar{x}_9 \wedge x_{12},$$
$$x_8 = x_3 \oplus x_4, \qquad x_{12} = x_5 \oplus x_{10}, \qquad x_{16} = x_{13} \oplus x_{15},$$
$$x_9 = x_1 \oplus x_5, \qquad x_{13} = x_8 \vee x_{11}, \qquad x_{17} = x_{14} \wedge x_{16}.$$
$$x_{10} = x_6 \oplus x_8, \qquad x_{14} = x_7 \oplus x_{12},$$

(f) This solution (found in 7471 Gμ) also matches that lower bound:

$$x_7 = x_1 \wedge x_2, \qquad x_{11} = x_5 \oplus x_6, \qquad x_{15} = x_8 \oplus x_{13},$$
$$x_8 = x_1 \oplus x_2, \qquad x_{12} = x_4 \oplus x_{11}, \qquad x_{16} = x_{10} \oplus x_{14},$$
$$x_9 = x_3 \oplus x_4, \qquad x_{13} = x_9 \oplus x_{11}, \qquad x_{17} = x_7 \oplus x_{16},$$
$$x_{10} = x_5 \wedge x_6, \qquad x_{14} = x_9 \vee x_{12}, \qquad x_{18} = x_{15} \vee x_{17}.$$

Here x_{18} is the normal function $\overline{S}_{0,4} = S_{1,2,3,5,6}$. We beat exercise 7.1.2–28 by one step.

(g) A solution in $t(3) = 12$ steps is found almost instantaneously (120 megamems); but 11 steps are too few ('unsat' in 301 gigamems).

480. (a) Let $x_1 x_2 x_3 x_4 = x_l x_r y_l y_r$. The truth tables for z_l and z_r are 0011010010001000 and 01**1*00*011*011, where the *s ("don't-cares") are handled by simply *omitting* the corresponding clauses $(\bar{g}_{hi} \vee \pm x_{it})$ in answer 477.

Less than 1 gigamem of computation proves that a six-step circuit is 'unsat'. Here's a seven-stepper, found in just 30 Mμ: $x_5 = x_2 \oplus x_3$, $x_6 = x_3 \vee x_4$, $x_8 = x_1 \oplus x_6$, $x_7 = x_1 \vee x_5$, $x_9 = x_6 \oplus x_7$, $z_l = x_{10} = x_7 \wedge x_8$, $z_r = x_{11} = x_3 \oplus x_9$. (See exercise 7.1.2–60 for a six-step solution that is based on a *different* encoding.)

(b) Now we have the truth tables $z_l = 0011010001001000010010010000011$, $z_r = 01**1*001*00*0111*00*011*01101**$, if $x_4 x_5 = y_l y_r$. One of many 9-step solutions is found in 6.9 gigamems: $x_6 = x_1 \oplus x_2$, $x_7 = x_2 \oplus x_5$, $x_8 = x_4 \oplus x_6$, $x_9 = \bar{x}_4 \wedge x_7$, $x_{10} = x_1 \oplus x_9$, $x_{11} = x_8 \vee x_9$, $x_{12} = x_3 \oplus x_{10}$, $z_r = x_{13} = x_3 \oplus x_{11}$, $z_l = x_{14} = x_{11} \wedge \bar{x}_{12}$.

The corresponding clauses for only 8 steps are proved 'unsat' after 190 Gμ of work. (Incidentally, the encoding of exercise 7.1.2–60 does *not* have a 9-step solution.)

(c) Let c_n be the minimum cost of computing the representation $z_l z_r$ of $(x_1 + \cdots + x_n) \bmod 3$. Then $(c_1, c_2, c_3, c_4) = (0, 2, 5, 7)$, and $c_{n-3} \le c_n + 9$. Hence $c_n \le 3n - 4$ for all $n \ge 2$. [This result is due to A. Kojevnikov, A. S. Kulikov, and G. Yaroslavtsev, whose paper in *LNCS* **5584** (2009), 32–44, also inspired exercises 477–479.]

Conjecture: For $n \ge 3$ and $0 \le a \le 2$, the minimum cost of evaluating the (single) function $[(x_1 + \cdots + x_n) \bmod 3 = a]$ is $3n - 5 - [(n + a) \bmod 3 = 0]$. (It's true for $n \le 5$. Here's a 12-step computation when $n = 6$ and $a = 0$, found in 2014 by Armin Biere: $x_7 = x_1 \oplus x_2$, $x_8 = x_3 \oplus x_4$, $x_9 = x_1 \oplus x_5$, $x_{10} = x_3 \oplus x_5$, $x_{11} = x_2 \oplus x_6$, $x_{12} = x_8 \oplus x_9$, $x_{13} = x_8 \vee x_{10}$, $x_{14} = x_7 \oplus x_{13}$, $x_{15} = \bar{x}_{12} \wedge x_{13}$, $x_{16} = \bar{x}_{11} \wedge x_{14}$, $x_{17} = x_{11} \oplus x_{15}$, $S_{0,3,6} = x_{18} = x_{16} \vee x_{17}$. The case $n = 6$ and $a \ne 0$, which lies tantalizingly close to the limits of today's solvers, is still unknown. What is $C(S_{1,4}(x_1, \ldots, x_6))$?)

481. (a) Since $z \oplus z' = \langle x_1 x_2 x_3 \rangle$ and $z' = x_1 \oplus x_2 \oplus x_3$, this circuit is called a "modified full adder." It costs one less than a normal full adder, since $z' = (x_1 \oplus x_2) \oplus x_3$ and $z = (x_1 \oplus x_2) \vee (x_1 \oplus x_3)$. (And it's the special case $u = 0$ of the more general situation in exercise 7.1.2–28.) Part (b) describes a "modified double full adder."

(b) The function z_2 has 20 don't-cares, so there are many eight-step solutions (although 7 are impossible); for example, $x_6 = x_1 \oplus x_5$, $x_7 = x_2 \oplus x_5$, $z_3 = x_8 = x_3 \oplus x_6$, $x_9 = x_4 \oplus x_6$, $x_{10} = x_1 \vee x_7$, $x_{11} = \bar{x}_3 \wedge x_9$, $z_2 = x_{12} = x_6 \oplus x_{11}$, $z_1 = x_{13} = x_{10} \oplus x_{11}$.

(c) Letting $y_{2k-1} y_{2k} = [\![x_{2k-1} x_{2k}]\!]$, it suffices to show that the binary representation of $\Sigma_n = \nu[\![y_1 y_2]\!] + \cdots + \nu[\![y_{2n-1} y_{2n}]\!] + y_{2n+1}$ can be computed in at most $8n$ steps. Four steps are enough when $n = 1$. Otherwise, letting $c_0 = y_{2n+1}$, we can compute z's bits with $\nu[\![y_{4k-3} y_{4k-2}]\!] + \nu[\![y_{4k-1} y_{4k}]\!] + c_{k-1} = 2\nu[\![z_{2k-1} z_{2k}]\!] + c_k$ for $1 \le k \le \lfloor n/2 \rfloor$. Then $\Sigma_n = 2(\nu[\![z_1 z_2]\!] + \cdots + \nu[\![z_{n-1} z_n]\!]) + c_{n/2}$ if n is even, $\Sigma_n = 2(\nu[\![z_1 z_2]\!] + \cdots + \nu[\![z_{n-2} z_{n-1}]\!] + z_n) + c'$ if n is odd, where $\nu[\![y_{2n-1} y_{2n}]\!] + c_{\lfloor n/2 \rfloor} = 2z_n + c'$, at a cost of $4n$ in both cases. The remaining sum costs at most $8\lfloor n/2 \rfloor$ by induction. [See E. Demenkov, A. Kojevnikov, A. S. Kulikov, and G. Yaroslavtsev, *Information Processing Letters* **110** (2010), 264–267.]

482. (a) $\sum_{j=1}^{k} (2y_j - 1)$ is odd when k is odd, and it's ± 1 when $k = 1$.

(b) Adapting Sinz's cardinality clauses as in exercises 29 and 30, we only need the auxiliary variables $a_j = s_j^{j-1}$, $b_j = s_j^j$, and $c_j = s_j^{j+1}$, because $s_j^{j+2} = 0$ and $s_{j+2}^j = 1$. The clauses are then $(\bar{b}_j \vee a_{j+1}) \wedge (\bar{c}_j \vee b_{j+1}) \wedge (b_j \vee \bar{c}_j) \wedge (a_{j+1} \vee \bar{b}_{j+1})$, for $1 \le j < t/2 - 1$; and $(\bar{y}_{2j-2} \vee a_j) \wedge (\bar{y}_{2j-1} \vee \bar{a}_j \vee b_j) \wedge (\bar{y}_{2j} \vee \bar{b}_j \vee c_j) \wedge (\bar{y}_{2j+1} \vee \bar{c}_j) \wedge (\bar{y}_{2j-2} \vee \bar{c}_{j-1}) \wedge (y_{2j-1} \vee c_{j-1} \vee \bar{b}_j) \wedge (y_{2j} \vee b_j \vee \bar{a}_{j+1}) \wedge (y_{2j+1} \vee a_{j+1})$ for $1 \le j < t/2$, omitting $\bar{a}_1$, c_0, and the two clauses that contain y_0.

(c) Use the construction in (b) with $y_j = x_{jd}$ for $1 \le d \le n/3$ and independent auxiliary variables $a_{j,d}$, $b_{j,d}$, $c_{j,d}$. Also, assuming that $n \ge 720$, break symmetry by asserting the unit clause (x_{720}). (That's much better than simply asserting (x_1).)

This problem was shown to be satisfiable if and only if $n < 1161$ by B. Konev and A. Lisitsa [*Artificial Intelligence* **224** (2015), 103–118], thereby establishing the case $C = 2$ of a well-known conjecture by Paul Erdős [*Michigan Math. J.* **4** (1957), 291–300, Problem 9]. Algorithm C can prove unsatisfiability for $n = 1161$ in less than 600 gigamems, using the parameters of exercise 512.

483. Using a direct encoding as in (15), with v_{jk} meaning that v_j has color k, we can generate the clauses $(\bar{v}_{jk})$ for $1 \le j < k \le d$ and $(\bar{v}_{j(k+1)} \vee \bigvee_{i=k}^{j-1} v_{ik})$ for $2 \le k < j \le n$. A similar but slightly simpler scheme works with the order encoding, when v_{jk} means that v_j has color $> k$. [See Ramani, Markov, Sakallah, and Aloul, *Journal of Artificial Intelligence Research* **26** (2006), 289–322. The vertices might be ordered in such a way that $\mathrm{degree}(v_1) \ge \cdots \ge \mathrm{degree}(v_n)$, for example.]

It's not difficult to color the Mycielski graph M_c with c colors (which is the minimum), *without* any symmetry breaking. For example, the 191-vertex graph M_{12} leads to 2,446,271 clauses in 36852 variables (total length 4.9 million); yet 12-color solutions are found by Algorithms C, W, and L respectively in 2.6, 523, and 12200 megamems. The symmetry breaking clauses actually would *retard* that calculation, because those clauses are much longer. On the other hand, when we try to succeed with only $c - 1$ colors, those clauses are extremely helpful: The runtime needed by Algorithm C to show that M_6 isn't 5-colorable goes down from 124 Gμ to 32 Mμ! Furthermore, Algorithm L does better here: Its runtime for that problem goes down from 7.5 Gμ to 28 Mμ.

484. (a) A type (iii) move will work if and only if $v_1 \!-\! v_4$, $v_2 \!-\! v_4$, $v_2 \!-\! v_3$.

(b) For $0 \le t < n - 1$ we have the clause $(\bigvee_{k=1}^{n-t-1} q_{t,k} \vee \bigvee_{l=1}^{n-t-3} s_{t,l})$, as well as the following for $1 \le i < j < n - t$, $1 \le k < n - t$, $1 \le l < n - t - 2$: $(\bar{q}_{t,k} \vee x_{t,k,k+1})$; $(\bar{q}_{t,k} \vee \bar{x}_{t+1,i,j} \vee x_{t,i',j'})$; $(\bar{s}_{t,l} \vee x_{t,l,l+3})$; $(\bar{s}_{t,l} \vee \bar{x}_{t+1,i,j} \vee x_{t,i'',j''})$; here $i' = i + [i \ge k]$, $j' = j + [j \ge k]$, and $\{i'', j''\}$ are the min and max of $\{i + [i \ge l + 3] + 3[i = l], j + [j \ge l + 3] + 3[j = l]\}$. Finally there's a unit clause $(\bar{x}_{0,i,j})$ for all $1 \le i < j \le n$ with $v_i \ne v_j$.

(These clauses essentially compute [G is quenchable], which is a monotone Boolean function of the $\binom{n}{2}$ elements above the diagonal in the adjacency matrix of G. The prime implicants of this function correspond to certain spanning trees, of which there are respectively 1, 1, 2, 6, 28, 164, 1137, ... when $n = 1, 2, 3, 4, 5, 6, 7, \ldots$.)

485. Let $t' = t + 1$. Instances of commutativity are: $(q_{t,k}, q_{t',k'}) \leftrightarrow (q_{t,k'+1}, q_{t',k})$ if $k < k'$; $(s_{t,l}, s_{t',l'}) \leftrightarrow (s_{t,l'+1}, s_{t',l})$ if $l + 2 < l'$; $(q_{t,k}, s_{t',l'}) \leftrightarrow (s_{t,l'+1}, q_{t',k})$ if $k < l'$; $(s_{t,l}, q_{t',k'}) \leftrightarrow (q_{t,k'+1}, s_{t',l})$ if $l + 2 < k'$; $(s_{t,l}, s_{t',l}) \leftrightarrow (q_{t,l+3}, s_{t',l})$. These can be broken by appending the clauses $(\bar{q}_{t,k'+1} \vee \bar{q}_{t',k})$, $(\bar{s}_{t,l'+1} \vee \bar{s}_{t',l})$, ..., $(\bar{q}_{t,l+3} \vee \bar{s}_{t',l})$.

Endomorphisms are also present in the two cases $(q_{t,k}, q_{t',k}) \leftrightarrow (q_{t,k+1}, q_{t',k})$ and $(s_{t,k+1}, q_{t',k}) \leftrightarrow (q_{t,k+1}, s_{t',k})$, *provided* that *both* pairs of transitions are legal. These are exploited by the clauses $(\bar{q}_{t,k+1} \vee \bar{q}_{t',k} \vee x_{t,k,k+1})$ and $(\bar{q}_{t,k+1} \vee \bar{s}_{t',k} \vee x_{t,k+1,k+4})$.

486. This game is a special case of graph quenching, so we can use the previous two exercises. Algorithm C finds a solution after about 1.2 gigamems, without the symmetry-breaking clauses; this time goes down to roughly 85 *mega*mems when those clauses are added. Similarly, the corresponding 17-card problem after A♣ × J♣ is found to be unsatisfiable, after 15 Gμ without and 400 Mμ with. (A♣ ×× 10♣ fails too.)

Those SAT problems have respectively (1242, 20392, 60905), (1242, 22614, 65590), (1057, 15994, 47740), (1057, 17804, 51571) combinations of (variables, clauses, cells), and they are *not* handled easily by Algorithms A, B, D, or L. In one solution *both*

$q_{0,11}$ and $s_{0,7}$ are true, thus providing two ways to win(!), when followed by $q_{1,15}$, $s_{2,13}$, $q_{3,12}$, $s_{4,10}$, $s_{5,7}$, $q_{6,7}$, $s_{7,5}$, $q_{8,5}$, $s_{9,4}$, $q_{10,5}$, $s_{11,3}$, $q_{12,3}$, $s_{13,1}$, $s_{14,1}$, $q_{15,1}$, $q_{16,1}$.

Notes: This mildly addictive game is an interesting way to waste time in case you ever get lost with a pack of cards on a desert island. If you succeed in reducing the original 18 piles to a single pile, you can continue by dealing 17 more cards and trying to reduce the new 18 piles. And if you succeed also at that, you have 17 more cards for a third try, since $52 = 18 + 17 + 17$. Three consecutive wins is a Grand Slam.

In a study of ten thousand random deals, just 4432 turned out to be winnable. Computer times (with symmetry breaking) varied wildly, from 1014 Kμ to 37 Gμ in the satisfiable cases (median 220 Mμ) and from 46 Kμ to 36 Gμ in the others (median 848 Mμ). The most difficult winnable and unwinnable deals in this set were respectively

9♠ 7♣ 3♣ K♦ 7♠ 3♡ 2♦ 8♣ 6♡ J♦ 8♠ 2♡ 6♠ 4♦ 5♠ 4♡ 10♦ Q♠   and
A♡ Q♡ 2♦ 9♦ 7♣ 7♦ 8♡ K♣ 3♦ 10♣ 3♣ 3♠ Q♠ 8♣ 2♣ K♠ 6♦ 5♣ .

Students in Stanford's graduate problem seminar investigated this game in 1989 [see K. A. Ross and D. E. Knuth, Report STAN-CS-89-1269 (Stanford Univ., 1989), Problem 1]. Ross posed an interesting question, still unsolved: Is there a sequence of (say) nine "poison cards," such that all games starting with those cards are lost?

The classic game Idle Year is also known by many other names, including Tower of Babel, Tower of London, Accordion, Methuselah, and Skip Two. Albert H. Morehead and Geoffrey Mott-Smith, in *The Complete Book of Solitaire and Patience Games* (1949), 61, suggested that moves shouldn't be too greedy.

487. Every queen in a set of eight must attack at least 14 vacant cells. Thus $|\partial S|$ gets its minimum value $8 \times 14 = 112$ when the queens occupy the top row. Solutions to the 8 queens problem, when queens are independent, all have $|\partial S| \leq 176$. The maximum $|\partial S|$ is 184, achieved symmetrically for example in Fig. A–11(a). (This problem is *not* at all suitable for SAT solvers, because the graph has 728 edges. The best way to proceed is to run through all $\binom{64}{8}$ possibilities with the revolving-door Gray code (Algorithm 7.2.1.3R), because incremental changes to $|\partial S|$ are easy to compute when a queen is deleted or inserted. The total time by that method is only 601 gigamems.)

The maximum of $|\partial_{\text{out}} S|$ is obviously $64 - 8 = 56$. The minimum, which corresponds to Turton's question, is 45; it can be achieved symmetrically as in Fig. A–11(b), leaving $64 - 8 - 45 = 11$ cells unattacked (shown as black queens). In this case SAT solvers win: The revolving-door method needs 953 gigamems, but SAT methods show the impossibility of 44 after only 2.2 Gμ of work. With symmetry reduction as in the following exercise, this goes down to 900 Mμ although there are 789 variables and 4234 clauses. [Bernd Schwarzkopf, in *Die Schwalbe* **76** (August 1982), 531, computed all solutions of minimum $|\partial_{\text{out}} S|$, given $|S|$, for $n \times n$ boards with $n \leq 8$. Extensions of Turton's problem to larger n have been surveyed by B. Lemaire and P. Vitushinskiy in two articles, written in 2011 and accessible from www.ffjm.org. Optimum solutions for $n > 16$ are conjectured but not yet known.]

All sets S of eight queens trivially have $|\partial_{\text{in}} S| = 8$.

488. Let variables w_{ij} and b_{ij} represent the presence of white or black queens on cell (i, j), with clauses $(\bar{w}_{ij} \vee \bar{b}_{i'j'})$ when $(i, j) = (i', j')$ or $(i, j) \!-\!\!\!-\! (i', j')$. Also, if each army is to have at least r queens, add clauses based on (20) and (21) to ensure that $\sum w_{ij} \geq r$ and $\sum b_{ij} \geq r$. Optionally, add clauses based on Theorem E to ensure that k of the w variables for the top row are lexicographically greater than or equal to the corresponding k variables in fifteen symmetrical variants. (For instance, if $k = 3$, we might require $w_{11} w_{12} w_{13} \geq b_{1n} b_{2n} b_{3n}$, thus partially breaking the symmetries.)

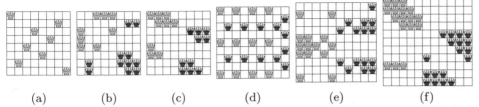

| (a) | (b) | (c) | (d) | (e) | (f) |

Fig. A–11. Optimum queen placements of various kinds.

The maximum army sizes for $3 \leq n \leq 13$ are known to be (1, 2, 4, 5, 7, 9, 12, 14, 17, 21, 24); see OEIS sequence A250000. An extra black queen can actually be included in the cases $n = 3, 4, 6, 8, 10, 11$, and 13. Solutions appear in Fig. A–11; the construction shown in Fig. A–11(d) generalizes to armies of $2q(q+1)$ queens whenever $n = 4q + 1$, while the one in part (c) belongs to another family of constructions that achieve the higher asymptotic density $\frac{7}{48}n^2$.

When $n = 8$ and $r = 9$, Algorithm C typically finds a solution in about 10 megamems ($k = 0$), or about 30 megamems ($k = 3$); but with $r = 10$ it typically proves unsatisfiability in about 1800 Mμ ($k = 0$) or 850 Mμ ($k = 3$) or 550 Mμ ($k = 4$) or 600 Mμ ($k = 5$). Thus the symmetry breaking constraints are helpful for unsatisfiability in this case, but not for the easier satisfiability problem. On the other hand, the extra constraints do turn out to be helpful for both the satisfiable and unsatisfiable variants when n is larger. The "sweet spot" turns out to be $k = 6$ when $n = 10$ and $n = 11$; unsatisfiability was proved in those cases, with $r = 15$ and $r = 18$, after about 185 Gμ and 3500 Gμ, respectively. [B. M. Smith, K. E. Petrie, and I. P. Gent obtained similar results using CSP methods in *LNCS* **3011** (2004), 271–286.]

(This problem was posed by S. Ainley in his *Mathematical Puzzles* (1977), problem C1. He mentioned solutions for $n \leq 30$ that have never yet been beaten, although he obtained them by hand. See also Martin Gardner, *Math Horizons* **7**, 2 (November 1999), 2–16, for generalizations to coexisting armies of sizes r and s. D. M. Kane has proved, among other things, that the maximum value of s, if $r = 3q^2 + 3q + 1$, is asymptotically $n^2 - (6q + 3)n + O(1)$ [arXiv:1703.04538 [math.CO] (2017), 19 pages].)

489. $T_0 = 1$, $T_1 = 2$, $T_n = 2T_{n-1} + (2n - 2)T_{n-2}$ (see Eq. 5.1.4–(40)). The generating function $\sum_n T_n z^n / n!$ and the asymptotic value are given in exercise 5.1.4–31.

490. Yes. For example, using the signed permutation $\bar{4}13\bar{2}$, we're allowed to assume that some solution satisfies $\bar{x}_4 x_1 x_3 \bar{x}_2 \leq \bar{x}'_4 x'_1 x'_3 \bar{x}'_2$ for every endomorphism — because the solution with lexicographically smallest $\bar{x}_4 x_1 x_3 \bar{x}_2$ has this property. Notice that the signed permutation $\bar{1}\bar{2}\ldots\bar{n}$ converts '$\leq$' to '$\geq$'.

491. Let σ be the permutation $(1\,2\,3\,4\,\bar{1}\,\bar{2}\,\bar{3}\,\bar{4})$. Then $\sigma^4 = (1\,\bar{1})(2\,\bar{2})(3\,\bar{3})(4\,\bar{4})$; and by Theorem E we need only search for solutions that satisfy $x_1 x_2 x_3 x_4 \leq \bar{x}_1 \bar{x}_2 \bar{x}_3 \bar{x}_4$. We're therefore allowed to append the clause $(\bar{x}_1)$ without affecting satisfiability.

(We actually are allowed to assert that $x_1 = x_2 = x_4 = 0$, because 0000 and 0010 are the lex-leaders of the two 8-cycles when σ is written as a permutation of states.)

In general if an automorphism σ is a permutation of literals having a cycle that contains both v and $\bar{v}$, for some variable v, we can simplify the problem by assigning a fixed value to v and then by restricting consideration to automorphisms that don't change v. (See the discussion of Sims tables in Section 7.2.1.2.)

492. Suppose $x_1 \ldots x_n$ satisfies all clauses of F; we want to prove that $(x_1 \ldots x_n)\tau = x'_1 \ldots x'_n$ also satisfies them all. And that's easy: If $(l_1 \vee \cdots \vee l_k)$ is a clause, we have

$l_1' = l_1\tau, \ldots, l_n' = l_n\tau$; and we know that $(l_1\tau \vee \cdots \vee l_k\tau)$ is true because it's subsumed by a clause of F. [See S. Szeider, *Discrete Applied Math.* **130** (2003), 351–365.]

493. Using the global ordering $p_1 \ldots p_9 = 543219876$ and Corollary E, we can add clauses to assert that $x_5 = 0$ and $x_4x_3x_2x_1 \leq x_6x_7x_8x_9$. A contradiction quickly follows, even if we stipulate only the weaker relation $x_4 \leq x_6$, because that forces $x_6 = 1$.

494. Exercise 475(d) shows that $(uv)(\bar{u}\bar{v})$ is a symmetry of the underlying Boolean function, although not necessarily of the clauses F. [This observation is due to Aloul, Ramani, Markov, and Sakallah in the cited paper.] The other symmetries allow us to assert (i) $(\bar{x}_i \vee x_j) \wedge (\bar{x}_j \vee \bar{x}_k)$, (ii) $(\bar{x}_i \vee \bar{x}_j) \wedge (\bar{x}_j \vee \bar{x}_k)$, (iii) $(\bar{x}_i \vee \bar{x}_j) \wedge (\bar{x}_j \vee x_k)$.

495. Suppose, for example, that $m = 3$ and $n = 4$. The variables can then be called 11, 12, 13, 14, 21, ..., 34; and we can give them the global ordering 11, 12, 21, 13, 22, 31, 14, 23, 32, 24, 33, 34. To assert that $21\,22\,23\,24 \leq 31\,32\,33\,34$, we use the involution that swaps rows 2 and 3; this involution is $(21\,31)(22\,32)(23\,33)(24\,34)$ when expressed in form (192) with signs suppressed. Similarly we can assert that $12\,22\,13 \leq 13\,23\,33$ because of the involution $(12\,13)(22\,23)(32\,33)$ that swaps columns 2 and 3. The same argument works for any adjacent rows or columns. And we can replace '$\leq$' by '$\geq$', by complementing all variables.

For general m and n, consider any global ordering for which x_{ij} precedes or equals $x_{i'j'}$ when $1 \leq i \leq i' \leq m$ and $1 \leq j \leq j' \leq n$. The operation of swapping adjacent rows makes the global lexicographic order increase if and only if it makes the upper row increase lexicographically; and the same holds for columns.

[See Ilya Shlyakhter, *Discrete Applied Mathematics* **155** (2007), 1539–1548.]

496. No; that reasoning would "prove" that m pigeons cannot fit into m holes. The fallacy is that his orderings on rows and columns aren't simultaneously consistent with a *single* global ordering, as in the previous exercise.

497. A BDD with 71,719 nodes makes it easy to calculate the total, 818,230,288,201, as well as the generating function $1 + z + 3z^2 + 8z^3 + 25z^4 + \cdots + 21472125415z^{24} + 31108610146z^{25} + \cdots + 10268721131z^{39} + 6152836518z^{40} + \cdots + 24z^{60} + 8z^{61} + 3z^{62} + z^{63} + z^{64}$. (The relatively small coefficients of z^{39} and z^{40} help account for the fact that $\geq$ was chosen in (185)–(186); problems with sparse solutions tend to favor $\geq$.)

[Pólya's theorem in Section 7.2.3 shows that exactly 14,685,630,688 inequivalent matrices exist; compare this to $2^{64} \approx 1.8447 \times 10^{19}$ without any symmetry reduction.]

498. Consider the global ordering $x_{01}, x_{11}, \ldots, x_{m1}; x_{12}, x_{22}, \ldots, x_{m2}; x_{02}, x_{23}, x_{33}, \ldots, x_{m3}, x_{03}, x_{13}; \ldots; x_{(m-1)m}, x_{mm}, x_{0m}, \ldots, x_{(m-2)m}$. There's a column symmetry that fixes all elements preceding $x_{(j-1)j}$ and takes $x_{(j-1)j} \mapsto x_{(j-1)k}$.

499. No. The unusual global ordering in answer 498 is not consistent with ordinary lexicographic row or column ordering. [Nor can the analogous clauses $(x_{ii} \vee \bar{x}_{ij})$ for $1 \leq i \leq m$ and $i < j \leq n$ be appended to (185) and (186). No quad-free matrix for $m = n = 4$ and $r = 9$ satisfies all those constraints simultaneously.]

500. If F_0 has a solution, then it has a solution for which l is true. But $(F_0 \cup F_1) \mid l$ might be unsolvable. (For example, let $F_0 = (\bar{x}_1 \vee x_2) \wedge (\bar{x}_2 \vee x_1)$, which has the symmetry $\bar{1}\bar{2}$; so we can take $S = (\bar{x}_1)$, $l = \bar{x}_1$. Combine that with $F_1 = (x_1)$.)

501. Let x_{ij} denote a queen in cell (i, j), for $1 \leq i \leq m$ and $1 \leq j \leq n$. Also let $r_{ij} = [x_{i1} + \cdots + x_{ij} \geq 1]$ and $r_{ij}' = [x_{i1} + \cdots + x_{i(j+1)} \geq 2]$, for $1 \leq i \leq m$ and $1 \leq j < n$. Using (18) and (19) we can easily construct about $8mn$ clauses that define the r's in terms of the x's and also ensure that $x_{i1} + \cdots + x_{in} \leq 2$. Thus $r_{i(n-1)}' = [x_{i1} + \cdots + x_{in} = 2]$; call this condition r_i.

Similar conditions c_j, a_d, and b_d are readily established for column j, and for the diagonals with $i+j = d+1$ or $i-j = d-n$, for $1 \le i \le m$, $1 \le j \le n$, and $1 \le d < m+n$. Then condition (ii) corresponds to the mn clauses $(x_{ij} \vee r_i \vee c_j \vee a_{i+j-1} \vee b_{i-j+n})$.

Finally we have clauses from (20) and (21) to ensure that $\sum x_{ij} \le r$.

When $m = n$, the lower bound $r \ge n - [n \bmod 4 = 3]$ has been established by A. S. Cooper, O. Pikhurko, J. R. Schmitt, and G. S. Warrington [*AMM* **121** (2014), 213–221], who also used backtracking to show that $r \ge 12$ on an 11×11 board. SAT methods, with symmetry breaking, yield that result much more quickly (after about 9 teramems of computation); but this problem, like the tomography problem of Fig. 79, is best solved by integer programming techniques when m and n are large.

If we call the upper left corner white, solutions with $m = n = r - 1$ and all queens on white squares appear to exist for all $n > 2$, and they are found almost instantly. However, no general pattern is apparent. In fact, when n is odd it appears possible to insist that the queens all appear in odd-numbered rows *and* in odd-numbered columns.

Here are examples of optimum placements on smallish boards. The solutions for 8×9, 8×10, 8×13, 10×10, and 12×12 also work for sizes 8×8, 9×10, 8×12, 9×9, and 11×11, respectively.

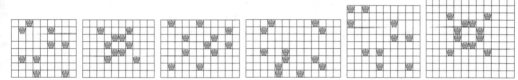

This placement of ten queens on a 10×10 board can be described by the "magic sequence" $(a_1, \ldots, a_5) = (1, 3, 7, 5, 9)$, because the queens appear in positions (a_i, a_{i+1}) and (a_{i+1}, a_i) for $1 \le i < n/2$ as well as in (a_1, a_1) and $(a_{n/2}, a_{n/2})$. The magic sequences $(1, 3, 9, 13, 15, 5, 11, 7, 17)$ and $(9, 3, 1, 19, 5, 11, 15, 25, 7, 21, 23, 13, 17)$ likewise describe optimum placements for $n = 18$ and 26. No other magic sequences are known; none exist when $n = 34$.

502. For each j, construct independent cardinality constraints for the relation $x_1^{(j)} + \cdots + x_n^{(j)} \le r_j$, using say (20) and (21), where $x_k^{(j)} = (s_{jk}?\ \bar{x}_k : x_k)$.

503. The Hamming distance $d(x, y) = \nu(x \oplus y)$ between binary vectors of length n satisfies $d(x, y) + d(\bar{x}, y) = n$. Thus there is no x with $d(x, s_j) \ge r_j + 1$ for all j if and only if there is no x with $d(\bar{x}, s_j) \le n - 1 - r_j$ for all j. [See M. Karpovsky, *IEEE Transactions* **IT-27** (1981), 462–472.]

504. (a) Assume that $n \ge 4$. For strings of length $2n$ we have $d(z, w) + d(z, \bar{w}) = 2n$; hence $d(z, w) \le n$ and $d(z, \bar{w}) \le n$ if and only if $d(z, w) = d(z, \bar{w}) = n$. Every string z with $z_{2k-1} \ne z_{2k}$ for $1 \le k \le n$ satisfies $d(z, w_j) = n$ for $1 \le j \le n$. Conversely, if $d(z, w_j) = d(z, w_k) = n$ and $1 \le j < k \le n$, then $z_{2j-1} + z_{2j} = z_{2k-1} + z_{2k}$. Thus if $z_{2j-1} = z_{2j}$ for some j we have $z = 00 \ldots 0$ or $11 \ldots 1$, contradicting $d(z, w_1) = n$.

(b) For each string $\hat{x} = \bar{x}_1 x_1 \bar{x}_2 x_2 \ldots \bar{x}_n x_n$ that satisfies part (a) we have $d(\hat{x}, y) = 2\bar{l}_1 + 2\bar{l}_2 + 2\bar{l}_3 + n - 3$, which is $\le n + 1$ if and only if $(l_1 \vee l_2 \vee l_3)$ is satisfied.

(c) Let $s_j = w_j$ and $r_j = n$ for $1 \le j \le 2n$; let $s_{2n+k} = y_k$ and $r_{2n+k} = n + 1$ for $1 \le k \le m$, where y_k is the string in (b) for the kth clause of F. This system has a closest string $\hat{x} = \bar{x}_1 x_1 \bar{x}_2 x_2 \ldots \bar{x}_n x_n$ if and only if $x_1 \ldots x_n$ satisfies every clause. [A similar construction in which all strings have length $2n + 1$ and all r_j are equal to $n + 1$ is obtained if we append the bit $[n < j \le 2n]$ to each s_j. See M. Frances and A. Litman, *Theory of Computing Systems* **30** (1997), 113–119.]

(d) Boilerplate 11000000, 00110000, 00001100, 00000011, 00111111, 11001111, 11110011, 00000011, at distance ≤ 4; for the clauses, 01011000, 00010110, 01000101, 10010001, 10100100, 00101001, 10001010, and possibly 01100010, at distance ≤ 5.

505. (For $k = 0, 1, \ldots, n - 1$ one can set j to a uniform integer in $[0 \ldots k]$ and INX$[k + 1] \leftarrow j$; also if $j = k$ set VAR$[k] \leftarrow k + 1$, otherwise $i \leftarrow$ VAR$[j]$, VAR$[k] \leftarrow i$, INX$[i] \leftarrow k$, VAR$[j] \leftarrow k + 1$.) With nine random seeds, typical runtimes for D3 are $(1241, 873, 206, 15, 748, 1641, 1079, 485, 3321)\,M\mu$. They're much less variable for the unsatisfiable K0, namely $(1327, 1349, 1334, 1330, 1349, 1322, 1336, 1330, 1317)\,M\mu$; and even for the satisfiable W2: $(172, 192, 171, 174, 194, 172, 172, 170, 171)\,M\mu$.

506. (a) *Almost* true: That sum is the total number of clauses of length ≥ 2, because every such clause of length k contributes $1/\binom{k}{2}$ to the weights of $\binom{k}{2}$ edges.

(b) Each of the $12^2 - 2 = 142$ cells of the mutilated 12×12 board contributes one positive clause $(v_1 \vee \cdots \vee v_k)$ and $\binom{k}{2}$ negative clauses $(\bar{v}_i \vee \bar{v}_j)$, when that cell can be covered by k potential dominoes $\{v_1, \ldots, v_k\}$. So the weight between u and v is 2, $4/3$, or $7/6$ when dominoes u and v overlap in a cell that can be covered in 2, 3, or 4 ways. Exactly 6 cells can be covered in just 2 ways (and exactly 10^2 in 4 ways).

(The largest edge weights in all of Fig. 95 are $37/6$, between 20 pairs of vertices in K6. At the other extreme, 95106 of the 213064 edges in X3 have the tiny weight $1/8646$, and 200904 of them have weight at most twice that much.)

507. Consider, for example, the clauses $(u \vee \bar{t})$, $(v \vee \bar{t})$, $(\bar{u} \vee \bar{v} \vee t)$, $(u \vee \bar{t}')$, $(v \vee \bar{t}')$, $(\bar{u} \vee \bar{v} \vee t')$ from (24). Looking ahead from $t = 1$ yields the windfall $(\bar{t} \vee t')$, and looking ahead from $t' = 1$ yields $(\bar{t}' \vee t)$. Henceforth Algorithm L knows that t equals t'.

508. According to (194), the purging parameters were $\Delta_{\rm p} = 1000$ and $\delta_{\rm p} = 500$; thus we have learned approximately $1000k + 500\binom{k}{2}$ clauses when doing the kth purging phase. After $1000L$ clauses this works out to be $\approx (\sqrt{16L + 9} - 3)/2$ phases, which is ≈ 34.5 when $L = 323$. (And the actual number was indeed 34.)

509. One remedy for overfitting is to select training examples at random. In this case such randomness is already inherent, because of the different seeds used while training.

510. (a) From Fig. 96 or Fig. 97 or Table 7 we know that T1 $<$ T2 $<$ L6 in the median rankings; thus T2 obscures L6 and T1.

(b) Similarly, L8 $<$ M3 $<$ Q2 $<$ X6 $<$ F2 $<$ X4 $<$ X5; X6 obscures L8 and X4.

(c) X7 obscures K0, K2, and (indirectly) A2, because K2 obscures K0 and A2.

511. (a) Nine random runs finished in only $(4.9, 5.0, 5.1, 5.1, 5.2, 5.2, 5.3, 5.4, 5.5)\,M\mu(!)$.

(b) Nine random runs now each were aborted after a teramem of trials. (No theoretical explanation for this discrepancy, or for the wildness of P4 in Fig. 97, is known.)

(c) $(0.2, \ldots, 0.5, \ldots, 3.2)\,M\mu$ without; $(0.3, \ldots, 0.5, \ldots, 0.7)\,M\mu$ with.

512. A training run with ParamILS in 2015 suggested the parameters

$$\alpha = 0.7, \quad \rho = 0.998, \quad \varrho = 0.99995, \quad \Delta_{\rm p} = 100000, \quad \delta_{\rm p} = 2000,$$
$$\tau = 10, \quad w = 1, \quad p = 0, \quad P = 0.05, \quad \psi = 0.166667, \qquad (*)$$

which produce the excellent results in Fig. A–12.

513. After training on $rand(3, 1062, 250, 314159)$, ParamILS chose the values $\alpha = 3.5$ and $\Theta = 20.0$ in (195), together with distinctly different values that favor double lookahead, namely $\beta = .9995$, $Y = 32$. [The untuned values $\alpha = 3.3$, $\beta = .9985$, $\Theta = 25.0$, and $Y = 8$ had been used by the author when preparing exercise 173.]

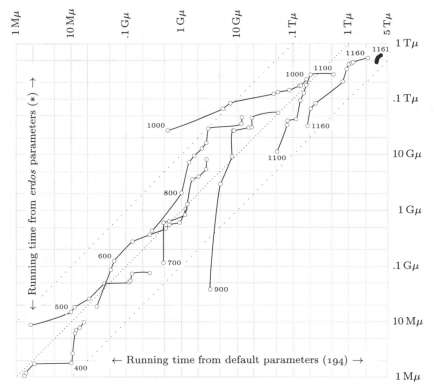

Fig. A–12. Running times for Algorithm C, with and without special parameter tuning.

514. ParamILS suggests $p = .85$ and $N = 5000n$; that gives a median time $\approx 690\,\mathrm{M}\mu$. (But those parameters give horrifically *bad* results on most other problems.)

515. Use variables S_{ijk} meaning that cell (i,j) in the solution holds k, and Z_{ij} meaning that cell (i,j) is blank in the puzzle. The 729 S variables are constrained by $4 \times 81 \times \left(1 + \binom{9}{2}\right) = 11{,}988$ clauses like (13). From condition (i), we need only 41 variables Z_{ij}. Condition (ii) calls for 15 clauses such as $(Z_{11} \vee \cdots \vee Z_{19})$, $(Z_{11} \vee \cdots \vee Z_{51} \vee Z_{49} \vee \cdots \vee Z_{19})$, $(Z_{15} \vee \cdots \vee Z_{55})$, $(Z_{44} \vee Z_{45} \vee Z_{46} \vee Z_{54} \vee Z_{55})$, when equal Z's are identified via (i). Condition (iii), similarly, calls for 28 clauses such as $(\bar{Z}_{11} \vee \bar{Z}_{12} \vee \bar{Z}_{13})$, $(\bar{Z}_{11} \vee \bar{Z}_{21} \vee \bar{Z}_{31})$, $(\bar{Z}_{45} \vee \bar{Z}_{55})$. Condition (vi) is enforced by 34,992 clauses epitomized by $(\bar{S}_{111} \vee \bar{Z}_{11} \vee \bar{S}_{122} \vee \bar{Z}_{12} \vee \bar{S}_{412} \vee \bar{Z}_{41} \vee \bar{S}_{421} \vee \bar{Z}_{42})$.

For conditions (iv) and (v), we introduce auxiliary variables $V_{ijk} = S_{ijk} \wedge \bar{Z}_{ij}$, meaning that k is visible in (i,j); $R_{ik} = V_{i1k} \vee \cdots \vee V_{i9k}$, meaning that k is visible in row i; $C_{jk} = V_{1jk} \vee \cdots \vee V_{9jk}$, meaning that k is visible in column j. Also $B_{bk} = \bigvee_{\langle i,j \rangle = b} V_{ijk}$, meaning that k is visible in box b; here $\langle i,j \rangle = 1 + 3\lfloor(i-1)/3\rfloor + \lfloor(j-1)/3\rfloor$. Then $P_{ijk} = Z_{ij} \wedge \bar{R}_{ik} \wedge \bar{C}_{jk} \wedge \bar{B}_{\langle i,j \rangle k}$ means that k is a possible way to fill cell (i,j) without conflict. These 1701 auxiliary variables are defined with 8262 clauses.

Condition (iv) is enforced by nine 9-ary clauses for each i and j, stating that we mustn't have exactly one of $\{P_{ij1}, \ldots, P_{ij9}\}$ true. Condition (v) is similar, enforced by three sets of 81×9 clauses of length 9; for example, one of those clauses is

$$(P_{417} \vee P_{427} \vee P_{437} \vee P_{517} \vee \bar{P}_{527} \vee P_{537} \vee P_{617} \vee P_{627} \vee P_{637}).$$

("We aren't obviously forced to put 7 into box 4 by using cell $(5, 2)$.")

Finally, some of the symmetry is usefully broken by asserting the unary clauses $(S_{1kk}) \wedge (\bar{Z}_{11}) \wedge (Z_{12})$. Altogether there are 2,471 variables, 58,212 clauses, 351,432 cells.

(This problem was suggested by Daniel Kroening. There are zillions of solutions, and about one in every five or six appears to be completable uniquely to the setting of the S variables. Thus we can obtain as many "hard sudoku" puzzles as we like, by adding additional unary clauses such as $(S_{553}) \wedge (\bar{Z}_{17})$ more-or-less at random, then weeding out ambiguous cases via dancing links. The clauses are readily handled by Algorithms L or C, but they're often too difficult for Algorithm D. That algorithm did, however, find the uniquely completable solution (a) below after only 9.3 Gμ of work.)

If we beef up condition (iii), insisting now that no box contains a row or column with more than *one* blank, condition (vi) becomes superfluous. We get solutions such as (b) below, remarkable for having no forced moves in spite of 58 visible clues, yet uniquely completable. That puzzle is, however, quite easy; only 2, 4, 7 are unplaced.

```
1....6.8.      1.3.56.89      1.3.5.7..      1.3.56.89
5.87214.6      59738.61.      .5.79...1      68.3.91.5
.6.38.2.1      68.1.93.5      7....125.      .9518.63.
84...3..5      956.318.7      ..1..5.76      3.896..51
..5.6.8..      .315.896.      ..5.7.1..      .195.836.
6..8...42      2.896.153      47.1...5..     56..319.8
3.6.48.2.      8.96.5.31      .185....7      .56.9381.
4.76321.8      .65.13298      5...87.1.      8.16.5.93
.8.5....4      31.89.5.6      ..7.1.8.5      93.81.5.6
   (a)            (b)            (c)            (d)
```

We might also try to strengthen conditions (iv) and (v) by requiring at least *three* ways to make each choice, not just two. Then we get solutions like (c) above. Unfortunately, however, that one is completable in 1237 ways! Even if we also strengthen condition (iii) as in (b), we get solutions like (d), which can be completed in 12 ways. No uniquely completable sudoku puzzles are known to have such ubiquitous threefold ambiguity.

516. This conjecture can be expressed in several equivalent forms. R. Impagliazzo and R. Paturi [*J. Comp. Syst. Sci.* **62** (2001), 367–375] defined $s_k = \inf\{\lg \tau \mid$ we can know an algorithm to solve kSAT in τ^n steps$\}$, and stated the *exponential time hypothesis*: $s_3 > 0$. They also defined $s_\infty = \lim_{k\to\infty} s_k$, and proved that $s_k \le (1-d/k)s_\infty$ for some positive constant d. They conjectured that $s_\infty = 1$; this is the *strong exponential time hypothesis*. An alternative formulation [C. Calabro, R. Impagliazzo, and R. Paturi, *IEEE Conf. on Comput. Complexity* **21** (2006), 252–260] was found later: "If $\tau < 2$, there is a constant α such that no knowable randomized algorithm can solve every SAT problem with $\le \alpha n$ clauses in fewer than τ^n steps, where n is the number of variables."

517. (a) (Solution by Günter Rote.) Replace the jth ternary clause $(l_j \vee l'_j \vee l''_j)$ by three ternary equations $l_j + a_j + c_j = 1$, $\bar{l}'_j + a_j + b_j = 1$, $\bar{l}''_j + c_j + d_j = 1$, where a_j, b_j, c_j, and d_j are new variables.

(b) Remove equations of length > 3 by using the fact that $l_1 + \cdots + l_k = 1$ if and only if $l_1 + \cdots + l_j + t = 1$ and $l_{j+1} + \cdots + l_k + \bar{t} = 1$, where t is a new variable. Also, if a, b, c, and d are new variables with $a + b + d = a + c + \bar{d} = 1$, beef up short equations using $l + l' = 1 \iff l + l' + a = 1$ and $l = 1 \iff \bar{l} + b + c = 1$.

[Thomas J. Schaefer proved the NP-completeness of 1-in-3 SAT as a special case of considerably more general results, in *STOC* **10** (1978), 216–226.]

518. (a) $A = \begin{pmatrix} x\,y\,y \\ y\,x\,y \\ y\,y\,x \end{pmatrix}$, where $x = \begin{smallmatrix} -1 & 0 \\ 1 & 0 \end{smallmatrix}$, $y = \begin{smallmatrix} 1 & 1 \\ -1 & 1 \end{smallmatrix}$.

(b) Twice in the n variable rows and n variable columns; once in the $3m$ output rows and $3m$ input columns; never in the $3m$ input rows and $3m$ output columns.

(c) By (a), each way to choose 2s in different rows and columns contributes zero to the permanent unless, in every clause, the subset of chosen inputs is nonempty and matches the chosen outputs. In the latter case it contributes $16^m 2^n$. [See A. Ben-Dor and S. Halevi, *Israel Symp. Theory of Computing Systems* **2** (IEEE, 1993), 108–117.]

519. The unsatisfiable problem corresponding to D1 and D2 has median running time $2099\,\mathrm{M}\mu$ (losing to both *factor_fifo* and *factor_lifo*). The satisfiable one corresponding to D3 and D4 is unstable (as in Fig. 97), with median $903\,\mathrm{M}\mu$ (winning over both).

520. (Solution by Sven Mallach, 2015, using solvers X and Y, where X was CPLEX 12.6 and Y was GUROBI 6, both used with emphasis on mixed-integer-program feasibility, constant objective function, and solution limit 1.) With a time cutoff of 30 minutes on a single-threaded Xeon computer, neither X nor Y could solve any of the 46 problems A1, A2, C1, C2, C3, C4, C5, C6, C8, D1, D2, E1, E2, F1, F2, G1, G2, G5, G6, G7, G8, K7, K8, M5, M7, M8, O1, O2, P0, P1, P2, Q7, S3, S4, T5, T6, T7, T8, W2, W4, X1, X3, X5, X6, X7, X8. (In particular, this list includes P0, S4, and X1, which are extremely easy for Algorithm C.) On the other hand both X and Y solved the *langford* problems L3 and L4 — which were the toughest for Algorithm C — in less than a second.

Algorithm C performs about $20\,\mathrm{G}\mu$ per minute on a comparable Xeon. In these experiments it significantly outperformed the geometric methods except on problems K0, K1, K2, L3, L4, and P4 (and some easy cases such as B2).

Of course we must keep in mind that the particular clauses in Table 6 aren't necessarily the best ways to solve the corresponding combinatorial problems with an IP solver, just as they aren't necessarily the best encodings for a SAT solver. We are comparing here only black-box clause-solving speeds.

521. A variety of simple schemes have been surveyed by S. Jabbour, J. Lonlac, L. Saïs, and Y. Salhi, arXiv:1402.1956 [cs.AI] (2014), 13 pages.

522. For cycles of length T we can introduce $27T$ variables xyz_t for $1 \le x, y, z \le 3$ and $0 \le t < T$, signifying that vertex (x, y, z) occupies slot t in the path. Binary exclusion clauses $\neg xyz_t \vee \neg x'y'z'_{t'}$, when $xyz = x'y'z'$ and $t \ne t'$ or when $xyz \ne x'y'z'$ and $t = t'$, ensure that no vertex appears twice in the path, and that no two vertices occupy the same slot. A valid path is specified via the adjacency clauses

$$\neg xyz_t \vee \bigvee \{x'y'z'_{(t+1)\,\mathrm{mod}\,T} \mid 1 \le x', y', z' \le 3 \text{ and } |x' - x| + |y' - y| + |z' - z| = 1\}.$$

We represent the shadows by introducing 36 variables $a!b*$, $ba!*$, $a!*b$, $b*a!$, $*a!b$, $*ba!$ for $1 \le a \le 2$ and $1 \le b \le 3$; here $a!*b$ (for example) means that the shadow of (x, z) coordinates has a transition between (a, b) and $(a+1, b)$. These variables appear in ternary clauses such as $(\neg xyz_t \vee \neg(x+1)yz_{t'} \vee x!*z) \wedge (\neg xyz_t \vee \neg(x+1)yz_{t'} \vee x!y*)$ whenever $x < 3$ and $t' \equiv t \pm 1$ (modulo T). To exclude loops we append clauses like

$$\neg 1!1* \vee \neg 2!1* \vee \neg 31!* \vee \neg 32!* \vee \neg 2!3* \vee \neg 22!* \vee \neg 1!2* \vee \neg 11!*;$$

this one excludes the loop in the example illustration. There are 39 such loop-defeating clauses, one for each of the 13 simple cycles in each shadow.

Finally we can break symmetry by asserting the unary clauses 121_{T-1}, 111_0, 112_1 without loss of generality, after verifying that no solution can avoid all eight corners.

Clearly T must be an even number, because the graph is bipartite; also $T < 27$. If the method of exercise 12 is used for the exclusions, we obtain a total of 6264 clauses, 822 variables, and 17439 cells when $T = 16$; there are 9456 clauses, 1242 variables, and 26199 cells when $T = 24$. These clauses are too difficult for Algorithm D. But Algorithm L resolves them almost instantaneously for any given T; they turn out to be satisfiable if and only if $T = 24$, and in that case there are two essentially different solutions. One of these cycles, due to John Rickard (who introduced this problem at Cambridge University, circa 1990), is beautifully symmetric, and it is illustrated on the cover of Peter Winkler's book *Mathematical Mind-Benders* (2007). It can be represented by the delta sequence $(322\bar{3}133\bar{1}\bar{2}112\bar{3}\bar{2}\bar{2}3\,\bar{1}\bar{3}\bar{3}12\bar{1}\bar{1}\bar{2})$, where '$k$' and '$\bar{k}$' change coordinate k by $+1$ or -1. The other is unsymmetric and represented by $(332\bar{1}\bar{2}1\bar{3}\bar{3}\bar{1}221\bar{2}323\bar{1}\bar{1}31\bar{2}\bar{1}3\bar{2})$.

523. (Solution by Peter Winkler.) With coordinates (x, y, z) for $1 \leq x \leq m$, $1 \leq y \leq n$, $1 \leq z \leq 2$, any cycle with loopless shadows must contain at least two steps $(x, y, 1)$ — $(x, y, 2)$ and $(x', y', 1)$ — $(x', y', 2)$. We can assume that $x < x'$ and that $x' - x$ is minimum. The $m \times 2$ shadow contains $(x, 1)$ — $(x, 2)$ and $(x', 1)$ — $(x', 2)$, together with (say) the path $(x, 1)$ — $\cdots$ — $(x', 1)$, but without the edge $(x'', 2)$ — $(x''+1, 2)$ for some x'' with $x \leq x'' < x'$. The unique shortest path from (x, y) to (x', y') in the $m \times n$ shadow contains some edge (x'', y'') — $(x''+1, y'')$; hence $(x'', y'', 1)$ — $(x''+1, y'', 1)$ must occur twice in the cycle.

524. This problem involves clauses very much like those for a cyclic path, but simpler; we have $T = 27$ and no "wrap-around" conditions. With typically 1413 variables, 10410 clauses, and 28701 cells, Algorithm L shines again, needing only a gigamem or two to handle each of several cases that break symmetry based on starting and ending points. There are four essentially different solutions, each of which can be assumed to start at 111; one ends at 333, another at 133, another at 113, and the other at 223. Using the delta sequence notation above, they are: $332\bar{3}\bar{3}2331\bar{3}\bar{3}2\bar{3}3\bar{2}\bar{3}\bar{3}133\bar{2}\bar{3}3233$ (which is reflected ternary code); $31\bar{3}133\bar{1}\bar{1}2113\bar{3}1\bar{3}13231\bar{3}133\bar{1}\bar{1}$; $32\bar{3}231\bar{3}\bar{2}3\bar{2}\bar{3}132\bar{3}233\bar{2}\bar{2}122\bar{1}\bar{2}\bar{2}$; $1122\bar{1}\bar{1}213\bar{1}211\bar{2}\bar{2}\bar{1}\bar{1}31122\bar{1}\bar{1}2\bar{1}$.

[Such paths, and more generally spanning trees that have loopless shadows, were invented in 1983 by Oskar van Deventer, who called them "hollow mazes"; see *The Mathemagician and Pied Puzzler* (1999), 213–218. His *Mysterians* puzzle is based on an amazing Hamiltonian path on $P_5 \,\square\, P_5 \,\square\, P_5$ that has loopless shadows.]

525. The author's best solution, as of July 2015, had 100 variables, 400 clauses, and 1200 literals (cells); it was derived from Tseytin's examples of exercise 245, applied to a more-or-less random 4-regular graph of girth 6 on 50 vertices. Tseytin's construction, with one odd vertex and 49 even ones, yields 400 clauses of 4SAT, which are quite challenging indeed. It can be simplified to a 3SAT problem by insisting further that every even vertex must have degree exactly 2 in the subgraph specified by true edges. (See K. Markström, *J. Satisfiability, Boolean Modeling and Comp.* **2** (2006), 221–227).

That simplified problem still turned out to be fairly challenging: It was proved unsatisfiable by Algorithm L in 3.3 Tμ and by Algorithm C in 1.9 Tμ. (But by applying the endomorphisms of exercise 473, which broke symmetry by adding 142 clauses of length 6, the running time went down to just 263 Mμ and 949 Mμ, respectively.)

Another class of small-yet-difficult problems is worth mentioning, although it doesn't fit the specifications of this exercise [see I. Spence, *ACM J. Experimental Algorithmics* **20** (2015), 1.4:1–1.4:14]: Every instance of 3D matching whose representation as an exact cover problem has $3n$ items and $5n$ options, with five options for each item and three items in each option, can be represented as a SAT problem in $3n$ variables, $10n$

binary clauses, and $2n$ quinary clauses, hence only $30n$ total literals. This 5SAT problem has the same number of literals as the 3SAT problem discussed above, when $n = 40$; yet it is considerably more difficult if the matching problem is unsatisfiable. (The problem of this kind that defeated all the SAT solvers in the 2014 competition corresponds to an instance of 3D matching that is solved almost instantaneously by the dancing links method: Algorithm 7.2.2.1X needs fewer than 60 Mμ to prove it unsatisfiable. On the other hand, if we encode that 3D matching problem with $3n$ quinary at-least-one and $3n \cdot 10$ binary at-most-one clauses, as in (13), instead of using only $2n$ for at-least-one and $n \cdot 10$ for at-most-one, Algorithm L will be almost as good as dancing links.)

526. We prove by induction on $|F|$ that it's possible to leave at most $w(F)$ clauses unsatisfied, where $w(F) = \sum_{C \in F} 2^{-|C|}$: If all clauses of the multiset F are empty we have $w(F) = |F|$, and the result holds. Otherwise suppose the variable x appears in F. Let $l = x$ if $w(\{C \mid x \in C \in F\}) \geq w(\{C \mid \bar{x} \in C \in F\})$; otherwise $l = \bar{x}$. A simple calculation shows that $w(F \mid l) \leq w(F)$. [*J. Computer and System Sciences* **9** (1974), 256–278, Theorem 3.]

TABLES OF NUMERICAL QUANTITIES

Table 1

QUANTITIES THAT ARE FREQUENTLY USED IN STANDARD SUBROUTINES
AND IN ANALYSIS OF COMPUTER PROGRAMS (40 DECIMAL PLACES)

$$\sqrt{2} = 1.41421\ 35623\ 73095\ 04880\ 16887\ 24209\ 69807\ 85697-$$
$$\sqrt{3} = 1.73205\ 08075\ 68877\ 29352\ 74463\ 41505\ 87236\ 69428+$$
$$\sqrt{5} = 2.23606\ 79774\ 99789\ 69640\ 91736\ 68731\ 27623\ 54406+$$
$$\sqrt{10} = 3.16227\ 76601\ 68379\ 33199\ 88935\ 44432\ 71853\ 37196-$$
$$\sqrt[3]{2} = 1.25992\ 10498\ 94873\ 16476\ 72106\ 07278\ 22835\ 05703-$$
$$\sqrt[3]{3} = 1.44224\ 95703\ 07408\ 38232\ 16383\ 10780\ 10958\ 83919-$$
$$\sqrt[4]{2} = 1.18920\ 71150\ 02721\ 06671\ 74999\ 70560\ 47591\ 52930-$$
$$\ln 2 = 0.69314\ 71805\ 59945\ 30941\ 72321\ 21458\ 17656\ 80755+$$
$$\ln 3 = 1.09861\ 22886\ 68109\ 69139\ 52452\ 36922\ 52570\ 46475-$$
$$\ln 10 = 2.30258\ 50929\ 94045\ 68401\ 79914\ 54684\ 36420\ 76011+$$
$$1/\ln 2 = 1.44269\ 50408\ 88963\ 40735\ 99246\ 81001\ 89213\ 74266+$$
$$1/\ln 10 = 0.43429\ 44819\ 03251\ 82765\ 11289\ 18916\ 60508\ 22944-$$
$$\pi = 3.14159\ 26535\ 89793\ 23846\ 26433\ 83279\ 50288\ 41972-$$
$$1° = \pi/180 = 0.01745\ 32925\ 19943\ 29576\ 92369\ 07684\ 88612\ 71344+$$
$$1/\pi = 0.31830\ 98861\ 83790\ 67153\ 77675\ 26745\ 02872\ 40689+$$
$$\pi^2 = 9.86960\ 44010\ 89358\ 61883\ 44909\ 99876\ 15113\ 53137-$$
$$\sqrt{\pi} = \Gamma(1/2) = 1.77245\ 38509\ 05516\ 02729\ 81674\ 83341\ 14518\ 27975+$$
$$\Gamma(1/3) = 2.67893\ 85347\ 07747\ 63365\ 56929\ 40974\ 67764\ 41287-$$
$$\Gamma(2/3) = 1.35411\ 79394\ 26400\ 41694\ 52880\ 28154\ 51378\ 55193+$$
$$e = 2.71828\ 18284\ 59045\ 23536\ 02874\ 71352\ 66249\ 77572+$$
$$1/e = 0.36787\ 94411\ 71442\ 32159\ 55237\ 70161\ 46086\ 74458+$$
$$e^2 = 7.38905\ 60989\ 30650\ 22723\ 04274\ 60575\ 00781\ 31803+$$
$$\gamma = 0.57721\ 56649\ 01532\ 86060\ 65120\ 90082\ 40243\ 10422-$$
$$\ln \pi = 1.14472\ 98858\ 49400\ 17414\ 34273\ 51353\ 05871\ 16473-$$
$$\phi = 1.61803\ 39887\ 49894\ 84820\ 45868\ 34365\ 63811\ 77203+$$
$$e^\gamma = 1.78107\ 24179\ 90197\ 98523\ 65041\ 03107\ 17954\ 91696+$$
$$e^{\pi/4} = 2.19328\ 00507\ 38015\ 45655\ 97696\ 59278\ 73822\ 34616+$$
$$\sin 1 = 0.84147\ 09848\ 07896\ 50665\ 25023\ 21630\ 29899\ 96226-$$
$$\cos 1 = 0.54030\ 23058\ 68139\ 71740\ 09366\ 07442\ 97660\ 37323+$$
$$-\zeta'(2) = 0.93754\ 82543\ 15843\ 75370\ 25740\ 94567\ 86497\ 78979-$$
$$\zeta(3) = 1.20205\ 69031\ 59594\ 28539\ 97381\ 61511\ 44999\ 07650-$$
$$\ln \phi = 0.48121\ 18250\ 59603\ 44749\ 77589\ 13424\ 36842\ 31352-$$
$$1/\ln \phi = 2.07808\ 69212\ 35027\ 53760\ 13226\ 06117\ 79576\ 77422-$$
$$-\ln \ln 2 = 0.36651\ 29205\ 81664\ 32701\ 24391\ 58232\ 66946\ 94543-$$

Table 2

QUANTITIES THAT ARE FREQUENTLY USED IN STANDARD SUBROUTINES
AND IN ANALYSIS OF COMPUTER PROGRAMS (40 HEXADECIMAL PLACES)

The names at the left of the "=" signs are given in decimal notation.

$$0.1 = 0.1999\ 9999\ 9999\ 9999\ 9999\ 9999\ 9999\ 9999\ 9999\ 999A-$$
$$0.01 = 0.028F\ 5C28\ F5C2\ 8F5C\ 28F5\ C28F\ 5C28\ F5C2\ 8F5C\ 28F6-$$
$$0.001 = 0.0041\ 8937\ 4BC6\ A7EF\ 9DB2\ 2D0E\ 5604\ 1893\ 74BC\ 6A7F-$$
$$0.0001 = 0.0006\ 8DB8\ BAC7\ 10CB\ 295E\ 9E1B\ 089A\ 0275\ 2546\ 0AA6+$$
$$0.00001 = 0.0000\ A7C5\ AC47\ 1B47\ 8423\ 0FCF\ 80DC\ 3372\ 1D53\ CDDD+$$
$$0.000001 = 0.0000\ 10C6\ F7A0\ B5ED\ 8D36\ B4C7\ F349\ 3858\ 3621\ FAFD-$$
$$0.0000001 = 0.0000\ 01AD\ 7F29\ ABCA\ F485\ 787A\ 6520\ EC08\ D236\ 9919+$$
$$0.00000001 = 0.0000\ 002A\ F31D\ C461\ 1873\ BF3F\ 7083\ 4ACD\ AE9F\ 0F4F+$$
$$0.000000001 = 0.0000\ 0004\ 4B82\ FA09\ B5A5\ 2CB9\ 8B40\ 5447\ C4A9\ 8188-$$
$$0.0000000001 = 0.0000\ 0000\ 6DF3\ 7F67\ 5EF6\ EADF\ 5AB9\ A207\ 2D44\ 268E-$$
$$\sqrt{2} = 1.6A09\ E667\ F3BC\ C908\ B2FB\ 1366\ EA95\ 7D3E\ 3ADE\ C175+$$
$$\sqrt{3} = 1.BB67\ AE85\ 84CA\ A73B\ 2574\ 2D70\ 78B8\ 3B89\ 25D8\ 34CC+$$
$$\sqrt{5} = 2.3C6E\ F372\ FE94\ F82B\ E739\ 80C0\ B9DB\ 9068\ 2104\ 4ED8-$$
$$\sqrt{10} = 3.298B\ 075B\ 4B6A\ 5240\ 9457\ 9061\ 9B37\ FD4A\ B4E0\ ABB0-$$
$$\sqrt[3]{2} = 1.428A\ 2F98\ D728\ AE22\ 3DDA\ B715\ BE25\ 0D0C\ 288F\ 1029+$$
$$\sqrt[3]{3} = 1.7137\ 4491\ 23EF\ 65CD\ DE7F\ 16C5\ 6E32\ 67C0\ A189\ 4C2B-$$
$$\sqrt[4]{2} = 1.306F\ E0A3\ 1B71\ 52DE\ 8D5A\ 4630\ 5C85\ EDEC\ BC27\ 3436+$$
$$\ln 2 = 0.B172\ 17F7\ D1CF\ 79AB\ C9E3\ B398\ 03F2\ F6AF\ 40F3\ 4326+$$
$$\ln 3 = 1.193E\ A7AA\ D030\ A976\ A419\ 8D55\ 053B\ 7CB5\ BE14\ 42DA-$$
$$\ln 10 = 2.4D76\ 3776\ AAA2\ B05B\ A95B\ 58AE\ 0B4C\ 28A3\ 8A3F\ B3E7+$$
$$1/\ln 2 = 1.7154\ 7652\ B82F\ E177\ 7D0F\ FDA0\ D23A\ 7D11\ D6AE\ F552-$$
$$1/\ln 10 = 0.6F2D\ EC54\ 9B94\ 38CA\ 9AAD\ D557\ D699\ EE19\ 1F71\ A301+$$
$$\pi = 3.243F\ 6A88\ 85A3\ 08D3\ 1319\ 8A2E\ 0370\ 7344\ A409\ 3822+$$
$$1° = \pi/180 = 0.0477\ D1A8\ 94A7\ 4E45\ 7076\ 2FB3\ 74A4\ 2E26\ C805\ BD78-$$
$$1/\pi = 0.517C\ C1B7\ 2722\ 0A94\ FE13\ ABE8\ FA9A\ 6EE0\ 6DB1\ 4ACD-$$
$$\pi^2 = 9.DE9E\ 64DF\ 22EF\ 2D25\ 6E26\ CD98\ 08C1\ AC70\ 8566\ A3FE+$$
$$\sqrt{\pi} = \Gamma(1/2) = 1.C5BF\ 891B\ 4EF6\ AA79\ C3B0\ 520D\ 5DB9\ 383F\ E392\ 1547-$$
$$\Gamma(1/3) = 2.ADCE\ EA72\ 905E\ 2CEE\ C8D3\ E92C\ D580\ 46D8\ 4B46\ A6B3-$$
$$\Gamma(2/3) = 1.5AA7\ 7928\ C367\ 8CAB\ 2F4F\ EB70\ 2B26\ 990A\ 54F7\ EDBC+$$
$$e = 2.B7E1\ 5162\ 8AED\ 2A6A\ BF71\ 5880\ 9CF4\ F3C7\ 62E7\ 160F+$$
$$1/e = 0.5E2D\ 58D8\ B3BC\ DF1A\ BADE\ C782\ 9054\ F90D\ DA98\ 05AB-$$
$$e^2 = 7.6399\ 2E35\ 376B\ 730C\ E8EE\ 881A\ DA2A\ EEA1\ 1EB9\ EBD9+$$
$$\gamma = 0.93C4\ 67E3\ 7DB0\ C7A4\ D1BE\ 3F81\ 0152\ CB56\ A1CE\ CC3B-$$
$$\ln \pi = 1.250D\ 048E\ 7A1B\ D0BD\ 5F95\ 6C6A\ 843F\ 4998\ 5E6D\ DBF4-$$
$$\phi = 1.9E37\ 79B9\ 7F4A\ 7C15\ F39C\ C060\ 5CED\ C834\ 1082\ 276C-$$
$$e^\gamma = 1.C7F4\ 5CAB\ 1356\ BF14\ A7EF\ 5AEB\ 6B9F\ 6C45\ 60A9\ 1932+$$
$$e^{\pi/4} = 2.317A\ CD28\ E395\ 4F87\ 6B04\ B8AB\ AAC8\ C708\ F1C0\ 3C4A+$$
$$\sin 1 = 0.D76A\ A478\ 4867\ 7020\ C6E9\ E909\ C50F\ 3C32\ 89E5\ 1113+$$
$$\cos 1 = 0.8A51\ 407D\ A834\ 5C91\ C246\ 6D97\ 6871\ BD29\ A237\ 3A89+$$
$$-\zeta'(2) = 0.F003\ 2992\ B55C\ 4F28\ 88E9\ BA28\ 1E4C\ 405F\ 8CBE\ 9FEE+$$
$$\zeta(3) = 1.33BA\ 004F\ 0062\ 1383\ 7171\ 5C59\ E690\ 7F1B\ 180B\ 7DB1+$$
$$\ln \phi = 0.7B30\ B2BB\ 1458\ 2652\ F810\ 812A\ 5A31\ C083\ 4C9E\ B233+$$
$$1/\ln \phi = 2.13FD\ 8124\ F324\ 34A2\ 63C7\ 5F40\ 76C7\ 9883\ 5224\ 4685-$$
$$-\ln \ln 2 = 0.5DD3\ CA6F\ 75AE\ 7A83\ E037\ 67D6\ 6E33\ 2DBC\ 09DF\ AA82-$$

Several interesting constants with less common names have arisen in connection with the analyses in the present book. Those constants have been evaluated to 40 decimal places in Eq. 7.2.2.1–(86) and in the answer to exercise MPR–19(d).

Table 3
VALUES OF HARMONIC NUMBERS, BERNOULLI NUMBERS,
AND FIBONACCI NUMBERS, FOR SMALL VALUES OF n

n	H_n	B_n	F_n	n
0	0	1	0	0
1	1	1/2	1	1
2	3/2	1/6	1	2
3	11/6	0	2	3
4	25/12	−1/30	3	4
5	137/60	0	5	5
6	49/20	1/42	8	6
7	363/140	0	13	7
8	761/280	−1/30	21	8
9	7129/2520	0	34	9
10	7381/2520	5/66	55	10
11	83711/27720	0	89	11
12	86021/27720	−691/2730	144	12
13	1145993/360360	0	233	13
14	1171733/360360	7/6	377	14
15	1195757/360360	0	610	15
16	2436559/720720	−3617/510	987	16
17	42142223/12252240	0	1597	17
18	14274301/4084080	43867/798	2584	18
19	275295799/77597520	0	4181	19
20	55835135/15519504	−174611/330	6765	20
21	18858053/5173168	0	10946	21
22	19093197/5173168	854513/138	17711	22
23	444316699/118982864	0	28657	23
24	1347822955/356948592	−236364091/2730	46368	24
25	34052522467/8923714800	0	75025	25
26	34395742267/8923714800	8553103/6	121393	26
27	312536252003/80313433200	0	196418	27
28	315404588903/80313433200	−23749461029/870	317811	28
29	9227046511387/2329089562800	0	514229	29
30	9304682830147/2329089562800	8615841276005/14322	832040	30

For any x, let $H_x = \sum_{n \geq 1} \left(\frac{1}{n} - \frac{1}{n+x} \right)$. Then

$$H_{1/2} = 2 - 2\ln 2,$$

$$H_{1/3} = 3 - \tfrac{1}{2}\pi/\sqrt{3} - \tfrac{3}{2}\ln 3,$$

$$H_{2/3} = \tfrac{3}{2} + \tfrac{1}{2}\pi/\sqrt{3} - \tfrac{3}{2}\ln 3,$$

$$H_{1/4} = 4 - \tfrac{1}{2}\pi - 3\ln 2,$$

$$H_{3/4} = \tfrac{4}{3} + \tfrac{1}{2}\pi - 3\ln 2,$$

$$H_{1/5} = 5 - \tfrac{1}{2}\pi\phi^{3/2}5^{-1/4} - \tfrac{5}{4}\ln 5 - \tfrac{1}{2}\sqrt{5}\ln\phi,$$

$$H_{2/5} = \tfrac{5}{2} - \tfrac{1}{2}\pi\phi^{-3/2}5^{-1/4} - \tfrac{5}{4}\ln 5 + \tfrac{1}{2}\sqrt{5}\ln\phi,$$

$$H_{3/5} = \tfrac{5}{3} + \tfrac{1}{2}\pi\phi^{-3/2}5^{-1/4} - \tfrac{5}{4}\ln 5 + \tfrac{1}{2}\sqrt{5}\ln\phi,$$

$$H_{4/5} = \tfrac{5}{4} + \tfrac{1}{2}\pi\phi^{3/2}5^{-1/4} - \tfrac{5}{4}\ln 5 - \tfrac{1}{2}\sqrt{5}\ln\phi,$$

$$H_{1/6} = 6 - \tfrac{1}{2}\pi\sqrt{3} - 2\ln 2 - \tfrac{3}{2}\ln 3,$$

$$H_{5/6} = \tfrac{6}{5} + \tfrac{1}{2}\pi\sqrt{3} - 2\ln 2 - \tfrac{3}{2}\ln 3,$$

and, in general, when $0 < p < q$ (see exercise 1.2.9–19),

$$H_{p/q} = \frac{q}{p} - \frac{\pi}{2}\cot\frac{p}{q}\pi - \ln 2q + 2\sum_{1 \leq n < q/2}\cos\frac{2pn}{q}\pi \cdot \ln\sin\frac{n}{q}\pi.$$

INDEX TO NOTATIONS

In the following formulas, letters that are not further qualified have the following significance:

j, k	integer-valued arithmetic expression
m, n	nonnegative integer-valued arithmetic expression
p, q	binary-valued arithmetic expression (0 or 1)
x, y	real-valued arithmetic expression
z	complex-valued arithmetic expression
f	integer-valued, real-valued, or complex-valued function
G, H	graph
S, T	set or multiset
$\mathcal{F}, \mathcal{G}$	family of sets
u, v	vertex of a graph
α, β	string of symbols

The place of definition is either a page number in the present volume or a section number in another volume. Many other notations, such as K_n for the complete graph on n vertices, appear in the main index at the close of this book. See also 'Notational conventions' in that index.

Formal symbolism	Meaning	Where defined
$V \leftarrow E$	give variable V the value of expression E	§1.1
$U \leftrightarrow V$	interchange the values of variables U and V	§1.1
A_n or $A[n]$	the nth element of linear array A	§1.1
A_{mn} or $A[m, n]$	the element in row m and column n of rectangular array A	§1.1
$(R?\ a{:}\ b)$	conditional expression: denotes a if relation R is true, b if R is false	336
$[R]$	characteristic function of relation R: $(R?\ 1{:}\ 0)$	§1.2.3
δ_{jk}	Kronecker delta: $[j = k]$	§1.2.3
$[z^n]\, f(z)$	coefficient of z^n in power series $f(z)$	§1.2.9
$z_1 + z_2 + \cdots + z_n$	sum of n numbers (even when n is 0 or 1)	§1.2.3
$a_1 a_2 \ldots a_n$	product or string or vector of n elements	
$(x_1, \ldots, x_n)$	vector of n elements	
$\langle x_1 x_2 \ldots x_{2k-1} \rangle$	median value (the middle value after sorting)	§7.1.1

Formal symbolism	Meaning	Where defined
$\sum_{R(k)} f(k)$	sum of all $f(k)$ such that relation $R(k)$ is true	§1.2.3
$\prod_{R(k)} f(k)$	product of all $f(k)$ such that relation $R(k)$ is true	§1.2.3
$\min_{R(k)} f(k)$	minimum of all $f(k)$ such that relation $R(k)$ is true	§1.2.3
$\max_{R(k)} f(k)$	maximum of all $f(k)$ such that relation $R(k)$ is true	§1.2.3
$\bigcup_{R(k)} S(k)$	union of all $S(k)$ such that relation $R(k)$ is true	
$\sum_{k=a}^{b} f(k)$	shorthand for $\sum_{a \le k \le b} f(k)$	§1.2.3
$\{a \mid R(a)\}$	set of all a such that relation $R(a)$ is true	
$\sum \{f(k) \mid R(k)\}$	another way to write $\sum_{R(k)} f(k)$	
$\{a_1, a_2, \ldots, a_n\}$	the set or multiset $\{a_k \mid 1 \le k \le n\}$	
$[x \mathinner{..} y]$	closed interval: $\{a \mid x \le a \le y\}$	§1.2.2
$(x \mathinner{..} y)$	open interval: $\{a \mid x < a < y\}$	§1.2.2
$[x \mathinner{..} y)$	half-open interval: $\{a \mid x \le a < y\}$	§1.2.2
$(x \mathinner{..} y]$	half-closed interval: $\{a \mid x < a \le y\}$	§1.2.2
$|S|$	cardinality: the number of elements in S	
$|x|$	absolute value of x: $(x \ge 0?\ x:\ -x)$	
$|z|$	absolute value of z: $\sqrt{z\bar{z}}$	§1.2.2
$|\alpha|$	length of α: m if $\alpha = a_1 a_2 \ldots a_m$	
$|l|$	base variable of literal l: $|v| = |\bar{v}| = v$	186
$\lfloor x \rfloor$	floor of x, greatest integer function: $\max_{k \le x} k$	§1.2.4
$\lceil x \rceil$	ceiling of x, least integer function: $\min_{k \ge x} k$	§1.2.4
$x \bmod y$	mod function: $(y = 0?\ x:\ x - y\lfloor x/y \rfloor)$	§1.2.4
$\{x\}$	fractional part (used in contexts where a real value, not a set, is implied): $x \bmod 1$	§1.2.11.2
$x \equiv x' \ (\text{modulo } y)$	relation of congruence: $x \bmod y = x' \bmod y$	§1.2.4
$j \backslash k$	j divides k: $k \bmod j = 0$ and $j > 0$	§1.2.4
$S \setminus T$	set difference: $\{s \mid s$ in S and s not in $T\}$	
$S \setminus t$	shorthand for $S \setminus \{t\}$	
$G \setminus U$	G with vertices of the set U removed	§7
$G \setminus v$	G with vertex v removed	§7
$G \setminus e$	G with edge e removed	§7
G / e	G with edge e shrunk to a point	§7.2.1.6
$S \cup t$	shorthand for $S \cup \{t\}$	
$S \uplus T$	multiset sum; e.g., $\{a, b\} \uplus \{a, c\} = \{a, a, b, c\}$	§4.6.3
$\gcd(j, k)$	greatest common divisor: $(j = k = 0?\ 0:\ \max_{d \backslash j, d \backslash k} d)$	§1.1
$j \perp k$	j is relatively prime to k: $\gcd(j, k) = 1$	§1.2.4

Formal symbolism	Meaning	Where defined
A^T	transpose of rectangular array A: $A^T[j,k] = A[k,j]$	
α^R	left-right reversal of string α	
α^T	conjugate of partition α	§7.2.1.4
x^y	x to the y power (when $x > 0$): $e^{y \ln x}$	§1.2.2
x^k	x to the k power: $(k \geq 0? \prod_{j=0}^{k-1} x: 1/x^{-k})$	§1.2.2
x^-	inverse (or reciprocal) of x: x^{-1}	§1.3.3
$x^{\bar{k}}$	x to the k rising: $\Gamma(x+k)/\Gamma(k) =$ $(k \geq 0? \prod_{j=0}^{k-1}(x+j): 1/(x+k)^{\overline{-k}})$	§1.2.5
$x^{\underline{k}}$	x to the k falling: $x!/(x-k)! =$ $(k \geq 0? \prod_{j=0}^{k-1}(x-j): 1/(x-k)^{\underline{-k}})$	§1.2.5
$n!$	n factorial: $\Gamma(n+1) = n^{\underline{n}}$	§1.2.5
$\binom{x}{k}$	binomial coefficient: $(k < 0? \ 0: x^{\underline{k}}/k!)$	§1.2.6
$\binom{n}{n_1,\ldots,n_m}$	multinomial coefficient (when $n = n_1 + \cdots + n_m$)	§1.2.6
$\left[\begin{smallmatrix} n \\ m \end{smallmatrix}\right]$	Stirling cycle number: $\sum_{0 < k_1 < \cdots < k_{n-m} < n} k_1 \ldots k_{n-m}$	§1.2.6
$\left\{\begin{smallmatrix} n \\ m \end{smallmatrix}\right\}$	Stirling subset number: $\sum_{1 \leq k_1 \leq \cdots \leq k_{n-m} \leq m} k_1 \ldots k_{n-m}$	§1.2.6
$\left\langle\begin{smallmatrix} n \\ m \end{smallmatrix}\right\rangle$	Eulerian number: $\sum_{k=0}^{m}(-1)^k \binom{n+1}{k}(m+1-k)^n$	§5.1.3
$\left|\begin{smallmatrix} n \\ m \end{smallmatrix}\right|$	m-part partitions of n: $\sum_{1 \leq k_1 \leq \cdots \leq k_m} [k_1 + \cdots + k_m = n]$	§7.2.1.4
$(\ldots a_1 a_0.a_{-1} \ldots)_b$	radix-b positional notation: $\sum_k a_k b^k$	§4.1
$\Re z$	real part of z	§1.2.2
$\Im z$	imaginary part of z	§1.2.2
$\bar{z}$	complex conjugate: $\Re z - i \Im z$	§1.2.2
$\neg p$ or $\sim p$ or $\bar{p}$	complement: $1 - p$	§7.1.1
$\sim x$ or $\bar{x}$	bitwise complement	§7.1.3
$p \wedge q$	Boolean conjunction (and): pq	§7.1.1
$x \wedge y$	minimum: $\min\{x, y\}$	§7.1.1
$x \mathbin{\&} y$	bitwise AND	§7.1.3
$p \vee q$	Boolean disjunction (or): $\overline{\bar{p}\bar{q}}$	§7.1.1
$x \vee y$	maximum: $\max\{x, y\}$	§7.1.1
$x \mid y$	bitwise OR	§7.1.3
$p \oplus q$	Boolean exclusive disjunction (xor): $(p + q) \bmod 2$	§7.1.1
$x \oplus y$	bitwise XOR	§7.1.3
$x \mathbin{\dot-} y$	saturated subtraction, x monus y: $\max\{0, x - y\}$	§1.3.1′
$x \ll k$	bitwise left shift: $\lfloor 2^k x \rfloor$	§7.1.3
$x \gg k$	bitwise right shift: $x \ll (-k)$	§7.1.3
$x \ddagger y$	"zipper function" for interleaving bits, x zip y	§7.1.3

Formal symbolism	Meaning	Where defined
$\log_b x$	logarithm, base b, of x (defined when $x > 0$, $b > 0$, and $b \neq 1$): the y such that $x = b^y$	§1.2.2
$\ln x$	natural logarithm: $\log_e x$	§1.2.2
$\lg x$	binary logarithm: $\log_2 x$	§1.2.2
λn	binary logsize (when $n > 0$): $\lfloor \lg n \rfloor$	§7.1.3
$\exp x$	exponential of x: $e^x = \sum_{k=0}^{\infty} x^k/k!$	§1.2.9
ρn	ruler function (when $n > 0$): $\max_{2^m \backslash n} m$	§7.1.3
νn	sideways sum (when $n \geq 0$): $\sum_{k \geq 0} \big((n \gg k) \,\&\, 1\big)$	§7.1.3
$\langle X_n \rangle$	the infinite sequence $X_0, X_1, X_2, \ldots$ (here the letter n is part of the symbolism)	§1.2.9
$f'(x)$	derivative of f at x	§1.2.9
$f''(x)$	second derivative of f at x	§1.2.10
$H_n^{(x)}$	harmonic number of order x: $\sum_{k=1}^{n} 1/k^x$	§1.2.7
H_n	harmonic number: $H_n^{(1)}$	§1.2.7
F_n	Fibonacci number: $(n \leq 1?\ n{:}\ F_{n-1} + F_{n-2})$	§1.2.8
B_n	Bernoulli number: $n!\,[z^n]\,z/(1 - e^{-z})$	§1.2.11.2
$\det(A)$	determinant of square matrix A	§1.2.3
$\mathrm{sign}(x)$	sign of x: $[x > 0] - [x < 0]$	
$\zeta(x)$	zeta function: $\lim_{n \to \infty} H_n^{(x)}$ (when $x > 1$)	§1.2.7
$\Gamma(x)$	gamma function: $(x - 1)! = \gamma(x, \infty)$	§1.2.5
$\gamma(x, y)$	incomplete gamma function: $\int_0^y e^{-t} t^{x-1}\,dt$	§1.2.11.3
γ	Euler's constant: $-\Gamma'(1) = \lim_{n \to \infty}(H_n - \ln n)$	§1.2.7
e	base of natural logarithms: $\sum_{n \geq 0} 1/n!$	§1.2.2
π	circle ratio: $4\sum_{n \geq 0}(-1)^n/(2n + 1)$	§1.2.2
∞	infinity: larger than any number	
Λ	null link (pointer to no address)	§2.1
$\emptyset$	empty set (set with no elements)	
ϵ	empty string (string of length zero)	
ϵ	unit family: $\{\emptyset\}$	§7.1.4
ϕ	golden ratio: $(1 + \sqrt{5})/2$	§1.2.8
$\varphi(n)$	Euler's totient function: $\sum_{k=0}^{n-1} [k \perp n]$	§1.2.4
$x \approx y$	x is approximately equal to y	§1.2.5
$G \cong H$	G is isomorphic to H	§7
$O(f(n))$	big-oh of $f(n)$, as the variable $n \to \infty$	§1.2.11.1
$O(f(z))$	big-oh of $f(z)$, as the variable $z \to 0$	§1.2.11.1
$\Omega(f(n))$	big-omega of $f(n)$, as the variable $n \to \infty$	§1.2.11.1
$\Theta(f(n))$	big-theta of $f(n)$, as the variable $n \to \infty$	§1.2.11.1

Formal symbolism	Meaning	Where defined
$\overline{G}$	complement of graph (or uniform hypergraph) G	§7
G^T	converse of digraph G (change '$\rightarrow$' to '$\leftarrow$')	§7.2.2.3
$G \mid U$	G restricted to the vertices of set U	§7
$u — v$	u is adjacent to v	§7
$u \not\!\!- v$	u is not adjacent to v	§7
$u \longrightarrow v$	there is an arc from u to v	§7
$u \longrightarrow^* v$	transitive closure: v is reachable from u	§7.1.3
$d(u,v)$	distance from u to v	§7
$G \cup H$	union of G and H	§7
$G \oplus H$	direct sum (juxtaposition) of G and H	§7
$G — H$	join of G and H	§7
$G \longrightarrow H$	directed join of G and H	§7
$G \mathbin{\square} H$	Cartesian product of G and H	§7
$G \otimes H$	direct product (conjunction) of G and H	§7
$G \boxtimes H$	strong product of G and H	§7
$G \mathbin{\triangle} H$	odd product of G and H	§7
$G \circ H$	lexicographic product (composition) of G and H	§7
e_j	elementary family: $\{\{j\}\}$	§7.1.4
$\wp$	universal family: all subsets of a given universe	§7.1.4
$\mathcal{F} \cup \mathcal{G}$	union of families: $\{S \mid S \in \mathcal{F} \text{ or } S \in \mathcal{G}\}$	§7.1.4
$\mathcal{F} \cap \mathcal{G}$	intersection of families: $\{S \mid S \in \mathcal{F} \text{ and } S \in \mathcal{G}\}$	§7.1.4
$\mathcal{F} \setminus \mathcal{G}$	difference of families: $\{S \mid S \in \mathcal{F} \text{ and } S \notin \mathcal{G}\}$	§7.1.4
$\mathcal{F} \oplus \mathcal{G}$	symmetric difference of families: $(\mathcal{F} \setminus \mathcal{G}) \cup (\mathcal{G} \setminus \mathcal{F})$	§7.1.4
$\mathcal{F} \sqcup \mathcal{G}$	join of families: $\{S \cup T \mid S \in \mathcal{F}, T \in \mathcal{G}\}$	§7.1.4
$\mathcal{F} \sqcap \mathcal{G}$	meet of families: $\{S \cap T \mid S \in \mathcal{F}, T \in \mathcal{G}\}$	§7.1.4
$\mathcal{F} \boxplus \mathcal{G}$	delta of families: $\{S \oplus T \mid S \in \mathcal{F}, T \in \mathcal{G}\}$	§7.1.4
$\mathcal{F}/\mathcal{G}$	quotient (cofactor) of families	§7.1.4
$\mathcal{F} \bmod \mathcal{G}$	remainder of families: $\mathcal{F} \setminus (\mathcal{G} \sqcup (\mathcal{F}/\mathcal{G}))$	§7.1.4
$\mathcal{F} \S k$	symmetrized family, if $\mathcal{F} = e_{j_1} \cup e_{j_2} \cup \cdots \cup e_{j_n}$	§7.1.4
$\mathcal{F}^\uparrow$	maximal elements of $\mathcal{F}$: $\{S \in \mathcal{F} \mid T \in \mathcal{F} \text{ and } S \subseteq T \text{ implies } S = T\}$	§7.1.4
$\mathcal{F}^\downarrow$	minimal elements of $\mathcal{F}$: $\{S \in \mathcal{F} \mid T \in \mathcal{F} \text{ and } S \supseteq T \text{ implies } S = T\}$	§7.1.4
$\mathcal{F} \nearrow \mathcal{G}$	nonsubsets: $\{S \in \mathcal{F} \mid T \in \mathcal{G} \text{ implies } S \not\subseteq T\}$	§7.1.4
$\mathcal{F} \searrow \mathcal{G}$	nonsupersets: $\{S \in \mathcal{F} \mid T \in \mathcal{G} \text{ implies } S \not\supseteq T\}$	§7.1.4
$\mathcal{F} \swarrow \mathcal{G}$	subsets: $\{S \in \mathcal{F} \mid T \in \mathcal{G} \text{ implies } S \subseteq T\} = \mathcal{F} \setminus (\mathcal{F} \nearrow \mathcal{G})$	§7.1.4
$\mathcal{F} \nwarrow \mathcal{G}$	supersets: $\{S \in \mathcal{F} \mid T \in \mathcal{G} \text{ implies } S \supseteq T\} = \mathcal{F} \setminus (\mathcal{F} \searrow \mathcal{G})$	§7.1.4

Formal symbolism	Meaning	Where defined
$X \cdot Y$	dot product of vectors: $x_1 y_1 + x_2 y_2 + \cdots + x_n y_n$, if $X = x_1 x_2 \ldots x_n$ and $Y = y_1 y_2 \ldots y_n$	§7
$X \subseteq Y$	containment of vectors: $x_k \leq y_k$ for $1 \leq k \leq n$, if $X = x_1 x_2 \ldots x_n$ and $Y = y_1 y_2 \ldots y_n$	§7.1.3
$\alpha(G)$	independence number of G	§7
$\gamma(G)$	domination number of G	461
$\kappa(G)$	vertex connectivity of G	§7.4.1.3
$\lambda(G)$	edge connectivity of G	§7.4.1.3
$\nu(G)$	matching number of G	§7.5.5
$\chi(G)$	chromatic number of G	§7
$\omega(G)$	clique number of G	§7
$c(G)$	number of spanning trees of G	§7.2.1.6
$C' \diamond C''$	resolvent of clauses C' and C''	336
$\Pr\bigl(S(X)\bigr)$	probability that statement $S(X)$ is true, when X is a random variable	§1.2.10
$\mathrm{E}\,X$	expected value of the random variable X: $\sum_x x \Pr(X = x)$	§1.2.10
$\mathrm{var}\,X$	variance of the random variable X: $\mathrm{E}\bigl((X - \mathrm{E}\,X)^2\bigr)$	2
$\Pr\bigl(A \mid B\bigr)$	conditional probability of A given B: $\Pr(A \text{ and } B)/\Pr(B)$	1
$\mathrm{E}(X \mid Y)$	expected value of X given Y	3
$\blacksquare$	end of algorithm, program, or proof	§1.1

In the end, however, I did put in one equation,
Einstein's famous equation, $E = mc^2$.
I hope that this will not scare off half of my potential readers.
— STEPHEN HAWKING, *A Brief History of Time* (1987)

APPENDIX C

INDEX TO ALGORITHMS AND THEOREMS

There is a curious poetical index to the Iliad in Pope's Homer,
referring to all the places in which similes are used.
— HENRY B. WHEATLEY, *What is an Index?* (1878)

INDEX TO COMBINATORIAL PROBLEMS

The purpose of this appendix is to present concise descriptions of the major problems treated in the present book, and to associate each problem description with the name under which it can be found in the main index. Some of these problems can be solved efficiently, while others appear to be very difficult in general although special cases might be easy. No indication of problem complexity is given here.

Combinatorial problems have a chameleon-like tendency to assume many forms. For example, certain properties of graphs and hypergraphs are equivalent to other properties of 0–1 matrices; and an $m \times n$ matrix of 0s and 1s can itself be regarded as a Boolean function of its index variables (i, j), with 0 representing FALSE and 1 representing TRUE. Each problem also has many flavors: We sometimes ask only whether a solution to certain constraints exists at all; but usually we ask to see at least one explicit solution, or we try to count the number of solutions, or to visit them all. Often we require a solution that is optimum in some sense.

In the following list — which is intended to be helpful but by no means complete — each problem is presented in more-or-less formal terms as the task of "finding" some desired objective. This characterization is then followed by an informal paraphrase (in parentheses and quotation marks), and perhaps also by further comments.

Any problem that is stated in terms of directed graphs is automatically applicable also to undirected graphs, unless the digraph must be acyclic, because an undirected edge $u \longrightarrow v$ is equivalent to the two directed arcs $u \longrightarrow v$ and $v \longrightarrow u$.

- Satisfiability: Given a Boolean function f of n Boolean variables, find Boolean values $x_1, \ldots, x_n$ such that $f(x_1, \ldots, x_n) = 1$. ("If possible, show that f can be true.")

- kSAT: The satisfiability problem when f is the conjunction of clauses, where each clause is a disjunction of at most k literals x_j or $\bar{x}_j$. ("Can all the clauses be true?") The cases 2SAT and 3SAT are most important. Another significant special case arises when f is a conjunction of *Horn clauses*, each having at most one nonnegated literal x_j.

- Boolean chain: Given one or more Boolean functions of n Boolean values $x_1, \ldots, x_n$, find $x_{n+1}, \ldots, x_N$ such that each x_k for $n < k \leq N$ is a Boolean function of x_i and x_j for some $i < k$ and $j < k$, and such that each of the given functions is either constant or equal to x_l for some $l \leq N$. ("Construct a straight-line program to evaluate a given set of functions, sharing intermediate values.") ("Build a circuit to compute a given collection of outputs from the inputs 0, 1, $x_1, \ldots, x_n$, using 2-input Boolean gates with unlimited fanout.") The goal is usually to minimize N.

- Broadword chain: Like a Boolean chain, but using bitwise and/or arithmetic operations on integers modulo 2^d instead of Boolean operations on Boolean values; the given value of d can be arbitrarily large. ("Work on several related problems at once.")

- Boolean programming: Given a Boolean function f of n Boolean variables, together with given weights $w_1, \ldots, w_n$, find Boolean values $x_1, \ldots, x_n$ such that $f(x_1, \ldots, x_n) = 1$ and $w_1 x_1 + \cdots + w_n x_n$ is as large as possible. ("How can f be satisfied with maximum payoff?")

• Matching: Given a graph G, find a set of disjoint edges. ("Pair up the vertices so that each vertex has at most one partner.") The goal is usually to find as many edges as possible; a "perfect matching" includes all the vertices. In a bipartite graph with m vertices in one part and n vertices in the other, matching is equivalent to selecting a set of 1s in an $m \times n$ matrix of 0s and 1s, with at most one selected in each row and at most one selected in each column.

• Assignment problem: A generalization of bipartite matching, with weights associated with each edge; the total weight of the matching should be maximized. ("What assignment of people to jobs is best?") Equivalently, we wish to select elements of an $m \times n$ matrix, at most one per row and at most one per column, so that the sum of selected elements is as large as possible.

• Covering: Given a matrix A_{jk} of 0s and 1s, find a set of rows R such that we have $\sum_{j \in R} A_{jk} > 0$ for all k. ("Mark a 1 in each column and select all rows that have been marked.") Equivalently, find an implicant of a monotone Boolean function, given its clauses. The goal is usually to minimize $|R|$.

• Exact cover: Given a matrix A_{jk} of 0s and 1s, find a set of rows R such that $\sum_{j \in R} A_{jk} = 1$ for all k. ("Cover with mutually orthogonal rows.") The perfect matching problem is equivalent to finding an exact cover of the transposed incidence matrix.

• Independent set: Given a graph or hypergraph G, find a set of vertices U such that the induced graph $G \mid U$ has no edges. ("Choose unrelated vertices.") The goal is usually to maximize $|U|$. Classical special cases include the 8 queens problem, when G is the graph of queen moves on a chessboard, and the no-three-on-a-line problem.

• Clique: Given a graph G, find a set of vertices U such that the induced graph $G \mid U$ is complete. ("Choose mutually adjacent vertices.") Equivalently, find an independent set in $\sim G$. The goal is usually to maximize $|U|$.

• Vertex cover: Given a graph or hypergraph, find a set of vertices U such that every edge includes at least one vertex of U. ("Mark some vertices so that no edge remains unmarked.") Equivalently, find a covering of the transposed incidence matrix. Equivalently, find U such that $V \setminus U$ is independent, where V is the set of all vertices. The goal is usually to minimize $|U|$.

• Dominating set: Given a graph, find a set of vertices U such that every vertex not in U is adjacent to some vertex of U. ("What vertices are within one step of them all?") The classic 5-queens problem is the special case when G is the graph of queen moves on a chessboard.

• Kernel: Given a directed graph, find an independent set of vertices U such that every vertex not in U is the predecessor of some vertex of U. ("In what independent positions of a 2-player game can your opponent force you to remain?") If the graph is undirected, a kernel is equivalent to a maximal independent set, and to a dominating set that is both minimal and independent.

• Coloring: Given a graph, find a way to partition its vertices into k independent sets. ("Color the vertices with k colors, never giving the same color to adjacent points.") The goal is usually to minimize k.

• Shortest path: Given vertices u and v of a directed graph in which weights are associated with every arc, find the smallest total weight of an oriented path from u to v. ("Determine the best route.")

- Longest path: Given vertices u and v of a directed graph in which weights are associated with every arc, find the largest total weight of a simple oriented path from u to v. ("What route meanders the most?")

- Reachability: Given a set of vertices U in a directed graph G, find all vertices v such that $u \longrightarrow^* v$ for some $u \in U$. ("What vertices occur on paths that start in U?")

- Spanning tree: Given a graph G, find a free tree F on the same vertices, such that every edge of F is an edge of G. ("Choose just enough edges to connect up all the vertices.") If weights are associated with each edge, a *minimum spanning tree* is a spanning tree of smallest total weight.

- Hamiltonian path: Given a graph G, find a path P on the same vertices, such that every edge of P is an edge of G. ("Discover a path that encounters every vertex exactly once.") This is the classic knight's tour problem when G is the graph of knight moves on a chessboard. When the vertices of G are combinatorial objects — for example, tuples, permutations, combinations, partitions, or trees — that are adjacent when they are "close" to each other, a Hamiltonian path is often called a Gray code.

- Hamiltonian cycle: Given a graph G, find a cycle C on the same vertices, such that every edge of C is an edge of G. ("Discover a path that encounters every vertex exactly once and returns to the starting point.")

- Traveling Salesrep Problem: Find a Hamiltonian cycle of smallest total weight, when weights are associated with each edge of the given graph. ("What's the cheapest way to visit everything?") If the graph has no Hamiltonian cycle, we extend it to a complete graph by assigning a very large weight W to every nonexistent edge.

- Topological sorting: Given a directed graph, find a way to label each vertex x with a distinct number $l(x)$ in such a way that $x \longrightarrow y$ implies $l(x) < l(y)$. ("Place the vertices in a row, with each vertex to the left of all its successors.") Such a labeling is possible if and only if the given digraph is acyclic.

- Optimum linear arrangement: Given a graph, find a way to label each vertex x with a distinct integer $l(x)$, such that $\sum_{u \longrightarrow v} |l(u) - l(v)|$ is as small as possible. ("Place the vertices in a row, minimizing the sum of the resulting edge lengths.")

- Knapsack problem: Given a sequence of weights $w_1, \ldots, w_n$, a threshold W, and a sequence of values $v_1, \ldots, v_n$, find $K \subseteq \{1, \ldots, n\}$ such that $\sum_{k \in K} w_k \leq W$ and $\sum_{k \in K} v_k$ is maximum. ("How much value can be carried?")

- Orthogonal array: Given positive integers m and n, find an $m \times n^2$ array with entries $A_{jk} \in \{0, 1, \ldots, n-1\}$ and with the property that $j \neq j'$ and $k \neq k'$ implies $(A_{jk}, A_{j'k}) \neq (A_{jk'}, A_{j'k'})$. ("Construct m different $n \times n$ matrices of n-ary digits in such a way that all n^2 possible digit pairs occur when any two of the matrices are superimposed.") The case $m = 3$ corresponds to a latin square, and the case $m > 3$ corresponds to $m - 2$ mutually orthogonal latin squares.

- Nearest common ancestor: Given nodes u and v of a forest, find w such that every inclusive ancestor of u and of v is also an inclusive ancestor of w. ("Where does the shortest path from u to v change direction?")

- Range minimum query: Given a sequence of numbers $a_1, \ldots, a_n$, find the minimum elements of each subinterval $a_i, \ldots, a_j$ for $1 \leq i < j \leq n$. ("Solve all possible queries concerning the minimum value in any given range.") Exercises 150 and 151 of Section 7.1.3 show that this problem is equivalent to finding nearest common ancestors.

• Universal cycle: Given b, k, and N, find a cyclic sequence of elements x_0, x_1, ..., x_{N-1}, x_0, ... of b-ary digits $\{0, 1, \ldots, b-1\}$ with the property that all combinatorial arrangements of a particular kind are given by the consecutive k-tuples $x_0 x_1 \ldots x_{k-1}$, $x_1 x_2 \ldots x_k$, ..., $x_{N-1} x_0 \ldots x_{k-2}$. ("Exhibit all possibilities in a circular fashion.") The result is called a de Bruijn cycle if $N = b^k$ and all possible k-tuples appear; it's a universal cycle of combinations if $N = \binom{b}{k}$ and if all k-combinations of b things appear; and it's a universal cycle of permutations if $N = b!$, $k = b-1$, and if all $(b-1)$-variations appear as k-tuples.

In most cases we have been able to give a set-theoretic definition that describes the problem completely, although the need for conciseness has often led to some obscuring of the intuition behind the problem.

— M. R. GAREY and D. S. JOHNSON, *A List of NP-Complete Problems* (1979)

ANSWERS TO PUZZLES IN THE ANSWERS

All answers here refer to exercises in Section 7.2.2.1.

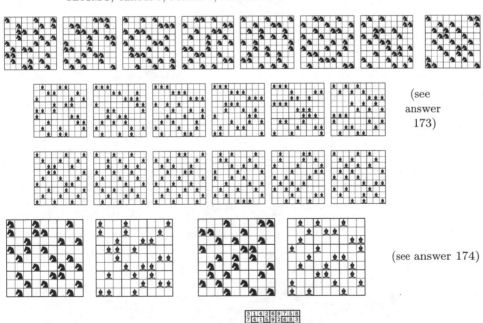

1	2	8	3	7	9	4	6	5
4	6	7	1	5	2	9	8	3
9	3	5	8	6	4	7	2	1
3	9	4	6	2	8	5	1	7
8	7	6	5	9	1	2	3	4
2	5	1	7	4	3	6	9	8
5	4	3	2	1	6	8	7	9
6	1	9	4	8	7	3	5	2
7	8	2	9	3	5	1	4	6

(see answer 52)

8	1	2	3	4	5	6	9	7
3	9	6	1	7	2	4	5	8
5	4	7			6	3	2	1
7	2		4	5		1	6	3
6	3		2	1	7		4	5
4	5	1		6	3		7	2
1	7	4	5			2	3	6
9	6	3	7	2	1	5	8	4
2	8	5	6	3	4	7	1	9

(see answer 58)

```
SEVENTH, FOURTEEN, FIGHTER, REINVENT, VENTURES;
NONE, FORGIVEN, FORGIVES, UNTHRONE;
UNDOERS, FOUNDERS, CONDORS, TRIODES, ROUNDEST,
   SECONDO, CERTIFY, FORTIFY, EXTRUDES.
```

(see answer 112)

(see answer 173)

(see answer 174)

 (see answer 282)

3	1	4	2	6	9	7	5	8
7	4	1	5	9	2	6	8	3
6	9	2	7	8	1	3	4	5
8	3	5	9	2	7	4	6	1
5	8	6	1	3	4	2	7	9
4	6	7	8	1	5	9	3	2
1	5	9	6	4	3	8	2	7
9	2	3	4	7	8	5	1	6
2	7	8	3	5	6	1	9	4

(see answer 302(c))

red bot $= \frac{188}{335}$, mid $= \frac{179}{435}$, top $= \frac{279}{446}$; green bot $= \frac{599}{866}$, mid $= \frac{557}{443}$, top $= \frac{112}{433}$ (see answer 337)

3 1 4 2 5
1 5 2<4 3
5 2 1<3 4   (see answer 395)
2 4>3 5 1
4 3 5 1<2

3 4<5<7<8 1 6<9 2
8 1 2 5<6<7 9 3 4
9 5 4 6<7<8 1<2<3
5<7<8 1 9 2 3<4<6
1<2<3<4 5 6 7<8 9   (see answer 396)
2<3<6<8 1 9 4<5<7
6<8<9 3<4<5 2 7 1
7<9 1 2<3<4 5 6 8
4 6<7<9 2<3 8 1 5

(see answer 403)

23	24	31	32	6	5	14	13
22	30	25	17	7	15	4	12
21	29	18	26	16	8	3	11
20	19	28	27	1	2	9	10

(see answer 407)

1	2	3	4	5	6
28	29	16	17	7	19
27	15	30	8	18	20
14	26	9	31	21	36
13	10	25	22	32	35
11	12	23	24	34	33

;

3	2	7	6	11	10
1	4	5	8	9	12
22	23	18	19	13	15
24	21	20	17	16	14
27	25	31	30	33	36
26	28	29	32	35	34

.   (see answer 408)

60	30	31	32	33	34	35	41	40	39
59	61	29	26	27	54	53	36	42	38
62	58	25	28	55	97	52	93	37	43
63	24	57	56	98	96	94	51	92	44
23	64	84	85	86	99	95	91	50	45
22	21	65	83	100	87	88	90	49	46
19	20	66	67	82	81	80	89	48	47
18	69	68	74	75	1	79	3	5	6
70	17	73	76	14	78	2	4	7	9
71	72	16	15	77	13	12	11	10	8

(see answer 409)

(see answer 411)

(see answer 415)

(see answer 416)

(see answer 418)

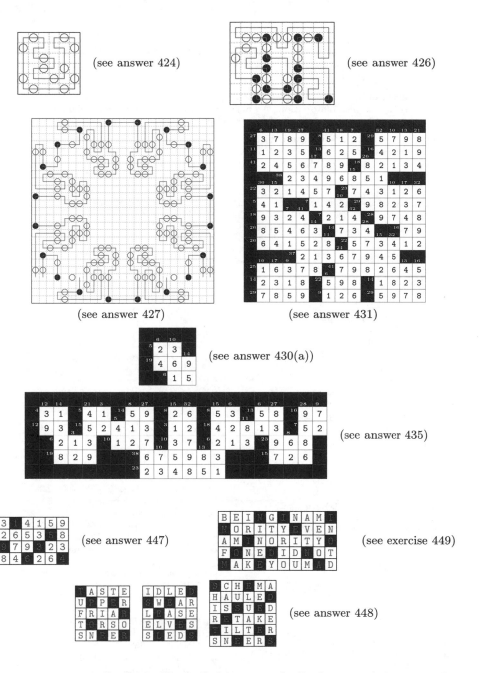

(see answer 424)

(see answer 426)

(see answer 427)

(see answer 431)

(see answer 430(a))

(see answer 435)

(see answer 447)

(see exercise 449)

(see answer 448)

By my troth, we that have good wits, have much to answer for.
— SHAKESPEARE (*As You Like It*, Act V, Scene 1, Line 11)

INDEX AND GLOSSARY

There is an easy index,
so you can find whatever you wish without delay.
— McCall's Cook Book (1963)

When an index entry refers to a page containing a relevant exercise, see also the *answer* to that exercise for further information. An answer page is not indexed here unless it refers to a topic not included in the statement of the exercise.

THIS BOOK was composed on an Dell Precision 3600 with Computer Modern typefaces, using the TEX and METAFONT software as described in the author's books *Computers & Typesetting* (Reading, Mass.: Addison–Wesley, 1986), Volumes A–E. The illustrations were produced with John Hobby's METAPOST system. Some names in the index were typeset with additional fonts developed by Yannis Haralambous (Greek, Hebrew, Arabic), Olga G. Lapko (Cyrillic), Frans J. Velthuis (Devanagari), Masatoshi Watanabe (Japanese), and Linbo Zhang (Chinese).